ISBN 978-1-332-10879-4
PIBN 10285791

1 MONTH OF
FREE
READING

at
www.ForgottenBooks.com

By purchasing this book you are eligible for one month membership to ForgottenBooks.com, giving you unlimited access to our entire collection of over 700,000 titles via our web site and mobile apps.

To claim your free month visit:
www.forgottenbooks.com/free285791

CAMPBELL'S

ABSTRACT

OF

CREEK INDIAN CENSUS CARDS

AND

INDEX

1915

PHOENIX JOB PRINTING COMPANY
MUSKOGEE, OKLAHOMA

PREFACE.

The preparation of this record has been a tedious work. It is believed by the Compiler that its publication will have a decided effect for good on land titles in Eastern Oklahoma. No one thing has been more responsible for the bad titles of Eastern Oklahoma than the lack of knowledge of the facts on the part of the public.

Congress after the making of certain treaties under which citizens of the Creek Nation were enrolled and received their allotments, enacted many laws materially effecting these treaty provisions and as a result the title to land. These laws, of course, were made public, but the facts under which any one of these laws were applicable, in any specific instance, were not given the same publicity. Many facts were purposely suppressed by the Government, and this was done in an effort to protect these allottees from the land shark. Their day, however, is now passed, and Congress, by subsequent laws, has so protected the allottee that the widest publicity of the facts is for the best interest of the allottee, as well as the public generally.

The publication of the Tribal Rolls, in 1907, gave the roll number, name of the allottee, age, sex and blood, and operated to a large extent to inform the public, but this information was not sufficient, in fact, it aided only those who, by reason of their familiarity with the workings and records of the Indian Offices, knew how to secure additional information. I emphasize the words "those who knew how" for this reason: only those who had a working familiarity with the procedure and the records of the Dawes Commission, later the office of the Commissioner to the Five Civilized Tribes, and now the office of the Superintendent of the Five Civilized Tribes, knew what to ask for to advise themselves. An investor from Iowa, Illinois or New York knows nothing of these records. He is shown the roll book, published by the Interior Department, and he takes the information there given as a verity. It did not occur to him to make further investigation, in the office of the Commissioner to the Five Civilized Tribes. If he did think of making further investigation he was given a copy of the census card of the particular allottee in which he was interested. He was told that this was the family card,—he was not told that a member of that same family might be found on 1, 2, 5, 10 or 15 other cards, as the case might be. In fact, no one knew of this in each particular instance. Those familiar with the records knew that members of the same family might appear on different cards, but what cards no one knew.

The records here presented are the first effort at cross-indexing, the purpose being to locate the different members of any particular family. The indexing has been made with great care, and we have not been content with indexing under the name as spelled on the card, but have, in many instances, indexed under two, three and even four different spellings. An examination of the card itself will show the necessity for this. The same names have on these records been spelled many different ways, in fact, in many cases the same name appearing twice on the same card will be spelled differently, and we have sought by this index to cover all such discrepancies, and in cases where

. 3

doubt may exist, we have indexed so as to cover both ends of the doubt.   Where different members of families spell their names differently, we have likewise covered both ways of spelling.

Your index may refer you to a particular card, turning to that card you do not find the name given in the index, if you will look at the card carefully, study it, you will in most instances see the reason for the reference.   In some cases this reason is not apparent from the card, but there is a reason, nevertheless, in each case, and cross references of names found on the card will undoubtedly show the reason.

Many believe that the date of enrollment is the date from which you calculate to determine the age of the allottee.   In a great many instances this is true, but in many cases this is not true.   The law says, that the enrollment record shall govern as to age.   The enrollment record may include the testimony taken at the time of enrollment, affidavits, birth certificates, etc.   Everyone ought before purchasing, or leasing lands, to secure from the Commissioner a certified copy of the enrollment testimony, if there be any question as to age.

More than one-third of the Creek allottees are dead, at this time: the balance must die.   The object of this record is to present to the public a means of determining the heirs.   It is a presentation of the material facts which the public should know in order that they may secure further information from the Superintendent's office.

Thousands and thousands of deeds have been placed of record, one might say at ramdom, because of lack of information on the part of those taking the deeds.   It is believed that the publication of this record will put a stop to such practise.

The enrollment records are the basis of title of these Indian lands.   Judge Sanborn has so declared them to be, and even if he had not so declared, common sense would tell us that they are.   These facts should be given the same publicity as other public records.   The magnitude of the task has prevented this.   The government at some time will make all these records public in some form, but when it does it will be complete, it will not be an abstract such as is given here.   Lack of knowledge of these essential facts is almost universal. An instance possibly will show something of this.   The compiler of this record prepared a brief in a case, pending in the Supreme Court of Oklahoma, and filed this brief with the court.   In this brief was detailed the procedure and manner of work of the Dawes Commission and of its records.   One of the justices wrote the writer that he had read the brief and was amazed at the contents.   He stated that he had no idea that the facts were such as they were shown to be and added that the public generally were not advised of this, and asked permission to file the original brief in the Historical Library of this State.

The need of such a book as this has been so apparent for years that the writer had in course of preparation a copy for his own use.   Other lawyers seeing the work wanted copies, and this was the inspiration for publication. A canvass of the larger cities of the Creek Nation convinced the compiler of the record and index that the public wanted it.   After deciding to publish the work it was necessary that all records be gone over carefully again, and compared with the originals in the office of the Superintendent to the Five Civilized Tribes.   The work was begun under the administration of Mr. J. George Wright, Commissioner, continued under the administration of Mr

4

Dana H. Kelsey, Superintendent, and concluded under the administration of Mr. Gabe E. Parker, Superintendent. The writer wishes to thank these several gentlemen for the uniform courtesy extended to him and to Mr. George Bixby, who compiled the original data. Also do I wish to thank the several heads of the Departments, and clerks in charge, for the courtesies extended to me by them. I trust that in no way have I over-stepped the limitations imposed on me.

There are some items of data which I desired to incorporate in this Abstract, but permission to get this data was denied me. I was informed at the time, the reason for denying me, and while, as it was then suggested to me, I might go over their heads and get the information, I had no thought of doing so. I appreciated the position of the department. If it be possible at any near future date to get the dates of selection of allotment, and copies of the annotated Creek rolls, I will do so and have these published and sell at a nominal price to the subscribers of the present work.

It is hoped that the purchasers of this book will familiarize themselves with the plan of work, by careful study of the instructions, which will be inserted hereafter, throughout the book. Unless this be done they will not get the full benefit of the book, and will not see its full value. It is an Abstract of the Creek Indian cards, giving data tending to show the status of the individual citizens, his father and mother. It is not a copy of the card. The index is arranged so as to show the different cards where the name of the citizen and all others of the same family may be found.

The sale of the book will be, of course, limited to a certain class of business men in the Creek Nation, and as the work of preparation is great, and the printing—by reason of its being all tabulated—very expensive, it will be seen that the price is reasonable.

Those who have aided in the preparation of the book for publication, Mr. George Bixby, Miss Maude Miller, Miss Gladys Fearnside and Miss Ostara Bixby, have been careful and painstaking, and I feel that I have been very happy in my choice of assistants. It is too much to hope that we have made no error. We have checked and rechecked and proof-read twice, but even so, with this great mass of tabulated matter, error in some instances may have crept in. At this date we know of no error. It is to be hoped that there is none. We will say, however, that if there is any error in the Abstract and Index it is a trifling error and will mislead no one.

As I have stated more than one-third of the Creeks have now departed this life. I have not been able to show all of these deaths,—the reason being that there is no record of deaths in hundreds of cases in the office of the Superintendent of the Five Civilized Tribes, and this true, because there is no necessity for such record. In the early days of the Dawes Commission, and after the allotments of land had begun, proofs of death were taken, but later acts of Congress made the taking of these proofs of death unnecessary, as it provided for the issuance of deeds in every case in the name of the original citizen to whom the allotment was made whether he be living or dead. There was no need of further filing of proofs of death until the present making of the equalization payment. As this payment was to be made only to those whose allotments were of value $800.00, or under, it will be seen that a very large percentage of the Indians did not come under this class, and no proofs of death were taken unless they did come under the class where equalization money was

5

due. I will speak of these proofs of death under another heading and so will make no further reference here.

The law of descent and distribution relative to these allotted lands of the Creeks presents possibly the most complicated system of descent and distribution in history. I have thought best to set forth these laws of descent and distribution. I have my own opinion as to the effect of some of these laws, but will make no comment. I realize that descent and distribution is to be the law of the future of this eastern half of the State, and the lawyer who is well equipped to take care of that business will have all that he can do. I have said that our laws of descent and distribution are complicated. Much of this complication arises by reason of the many changes in the law. The law of the date of selection governs, providing the citizen be dead when the land is selected in allotment. In such case the heirs are identified as of the date of the death of the allottee, under the law of the date of selection.

J. B. CAMPBELL,

Muskogee, Oklahoma, April 3, 1915.

EXPLANATORY OF THE ABSTRACT.

Our canvas for the sale of this Abstract and Index showed such woeful lack of information on the part of the public generally, of the records in the office of the Superintendent of the Five Civilized Tribes, at Muskogee, Oklahoma, that when we presented our copy it was as "Greek" to them. This lack of knowledge was not universal, but we were surprised to find to what extent it was true. Therefore, in explaining our record we must go to every detail, and will ask those who read this detailed explanation to open the book at any card they may choose and read this text in connection with that card, in order that they may fully understand it. If they once understand our plan they will have no trouble thereafter.

The first, or title line, to each card shows that it is a Creek Indian, (not freedman) card. The number of this card is given, after which follows the last known post office address of the enrolled citizen. Then follows the date or dates of enrollment. Suppose we had six persons enrolled on any particular card, and the first four of these enrolled citizens were enrolled in the month of August, 1898, the fifth enrolled on the card was enrolled July 1, 1900, and the sixth was enrolled June 24, 1904. Unless it be more specifically noted on the card these entries will be made as follows:

Enrolled August 1898; No. 5 July 1, 1900; No. 6 June 24, 1904.

It will be noted that under the first date we include the enrollment of all these citizens, who are not specifically numbered, such as Nos. 5 and 6 in this particular instance. Note also that the enrollment date is in the "title line" and not at the lower right hand corner of the card as on the original card in the office of the Superintendent.

Now taking up the tabulated matter in detail:

(1) The first column is under the heading "Roll No." This needs no explanation except to say that it is the roll number of the enrolled citizen whose name is found under the heading "name" later, on the same line. This roll number will be the roll number given in the roll book, published by the Department of the Interior.

(2) The next column is under the heading "No." and under this is given the number of those as they appear on the card. It has no other significance. It is used simply for certainty in future reference. Wherever the enrolled citizen whose name follows this number is referred to the number in front of his name is used, and not his name. Brevity was not the only reason for using the numbers, instead of the name. It may be that there will be two enrolled citizens on the same card, having the same name, and if we used the name it would lead to uncertainty. Therefore, we use the numbers. Its use may be explained as follows. Suppose we had three citizens on the card as follows:

No. 1.   Smith, John
No. 2.   Smith, Martha
No. 3.   Smith, John

Suppose that the John Smith first named was the father of the John Smith last named. In the columns under the heading "Name of father" on the same line where the name of the second John Smith appears we write No. 1, thus meaning that John Smith, who appears after No. 1 on this card, is the father of John Smith whose name appears after No. 3 on this card. Again, in the notations at the bottom of the card you will see "No. 1 died January 14, 1913," "No. 3 died August 6, 1904." By using the numbers we make our references certain, and you know at once which John Smith died on January 14, 1913, and which died in August 1904.

(3) Under the heading "Name" we give the name of the enrolled citizen, whose roll number appears in the column under the heading "Roll No."

(4) Next follows the columns under the headings "age" "sex" and "blood," and these we think need no explanation. This refers to the age, sex and blood of the citizen whose name immediately precedes these notations. The ages given are the ages shown by the census cards in the office of the Superintendent—not the ages at the time of the preparation of this Abstract.

(5) Above the next column is the heading "Rel." This abbreviation is for "relationship to No. 1 on the card." The first citizen enrolled on the card is usually the head of the family. There is usually no notation in this column after his name. The names of those enrolled, and which follow his enrollment, and who are on this card are, as a usual thing, related to him in some way, and this relationship is noted in this column. Thus, if "No. 2" on the card be the wife of "No. 1" then in this column will be the abbreviation "Wf," if "No. 3" be the daughter of "No. 1", then the letter "D" will appear in this column, if a son, then the letter "S", and here we use "StS" for step-son, "SD" for step-daughter, "GD" for granddaughter, "GS" for grandson, "Neph" for nephew, and niece, ward, etc. We think with this explanation no one will have trouble in determining the relationship of those on the card, as shown in this column.

(6) Under the heading "Name of Father" is found the name of the father of the enrolled citizen. This enrolled citizen being the one whose name appears on this same line on the card. Remember names of the enrolled citizens appear only in the column under the heading "Name." The father and mother may, or may not, be enrolled citizens. If they are enrolled their names will be found in the column under the heading "Name." What has been said here of the names appearing under the heading "Name of Father" is also true of the names found under the heading "Name of Mother". If the father or mother be enrolled their names may or may not appear on the card, as enrolled citizens, with their child.

(7) After the names of father and mother will be found columns headed "living" and "citizen." We now take up these two headings and ask that you carefully note what they say.

(a) "Living." Under this heading we show whether or not the parent was living at the time his, or her, child, the citizen, was enrolled. If the parent was living at that time the letter "L" will be found under this column heading. If the parent was dead at that time the letter "D", meaning dead, will be found in this column. On the original cards in the office of the Superintendent if the father or mother be living, or if there be any doubt of his or her death, than this column was left blank. We have made no changes in the notations of death as noted on the original cards. We have, however, added the notation as to the living and in doing so have used the knowledge gained by our continued working at the cards and have noted those whom we believe to be dead with a question mark thus (?)

(b) "Citizen." Under this column we note whether or not the particular parent was a member of the Creek Nation of Indians. If the parent was a member of the Creek Nation of Indians then the letters "Cr" is found under this column heading. If, however, the parent was not a member of the Creek Nation of Indians, then in this column will be found such notation as this,— "Non", meaning non-citizen; "Chick," meaning Chickasaw, "Choc," meaning Choctaw, "Cher" meaning Cherokee, "Sem" meaning Seminole, etc. On the original cards no notation was made in this column in a vast proportion of instances. We have studied the cards and the cross references and have given the result of the examination. In doing so we adopted certain rules such as the following:

(1) If the child was of Creek blood greater than a half blood, then of course both parents must have Creek blood.

(2) If one of the parents was enrolled as of a certain quantum of Indian blood and the other parent not enrolled and the child was noted as having Indian blood just half of the amount of the enrolled parent, then we noted the other parent as a non-citizen.

(3) Our acquaintance is large and we knew personally the status of many.

(4) By reference to other cards. There were many of whom we could not be certain and we noted these with a question mark thus (?).

(8) The notations at the bottom of each card need little explanation, when it is remembered that the numbers there used, such as No. 1 and No. 3, etc., mean the enrolled citizens, whose names are found after the numbers 1 and 3, as these numbers are used in the second column of tabulated matter on the card.

(9) The making of the Abstract of the New-Born and Minor Creek cards is somewhat different from that used for the Abstract of the original Creek cards. The cards themselves were different and this necessitated a different Abstract. An explanatory note will precede the New Born and Minor Creek cards.

(10) The Index to follow the record itself will be preceded by an explanatory note thereto. Everyone should carefully read and thoroughly understand the explanatory notes, which appear in this record and index. If they do not fully familiarize themselves with the manner of making this Abstract, and what each notation means much of the value of the book will be lost to them.

In the making of the Abstract and Index we made notes of matters which we believed would aid those in examining the cards in difficult cases. Though many of these "Helps" have been noted in the preface and the explanatory notes, we have made note of the following:

(1) During the year 1914 Congress admitted sixty-two persons to citizenship in the Creek Nation. These have no allotments. In making census cards for these newly admitted citizens, in the office of the Superintendent to the Five Civilized Tribes, they were given roll numbers beginning with the next number after the last originally enrolled Creek. By an error duplication was the result in numbering the cards. You will note by an examination of the Creek Rolls, published by the Department that in the last few numbers the card numbers are not in consecutive order. As a result the last enrollment number 1 0181 is not on the highest numbered census card. In the making

of these new cards for those whom we have designated "Congressional Enrollments" the numbers of the cards from 4015 to 4026 have been duplicated. To avoid uncertainty we have put the letter "CE" in front of the numbers in the Index, when reference is made to one of these Congressional Enrollment Cards.

(2) In searching the Index for any name look under the different spellings of the name, as Deer-Deere, Kernall-Kernal-Kernel, Heneha-Henneha-Hennehah-Henehar-Hinneha, Mahala-Maholey-Mahole-Meholi.

(3) In looking for an Indian name and finding it, then look back for a few names and also forward. The index is so arranged that if the name is misspelled you will often catch it near to where it should be if spelled correctly. Different clerks spelled the names differently in preparing the cards, but even at that the two spellings ought to be close together. Where we have been able to determine that these two spellings refer to one and the same person we have cross indexed, but have not been able in every case to so determine.

(4) The Index may refer you to a card where you do not find the name. If the card itself does not show why the reference was made look up the cross reference to other names on the card and this will make the reference clear.

(5) We have tried to make reference to Freedmen cards, but in all cases, could not do so as we could not get sufficient data.

(6) From our investigation we believe that fully two-fifths of the Creek allottees are dead. We have worked diligently to show the dead. Only a part of this data was on the census cards and the balance scattered throughout the various divisions of the Superintendent's office. We show about 3300. We could not show all, for the reason that the Superintendent has no record of them.

In noting the dead in some cases the dates of death are given and in others they are simply "reported dead." In those cases where the data of death is given, proofs of death are on file in the office of the Superintendent of the Five Civilized Tribes. In some cases where the dates are not given proofs are on file, but the proofs do not show the date of death. For those who are noted "reported dead" we secured our information from the Creek Indian ledger, but this did not give the date of death. In many other instances we knew from our personal knowledge that the allottee was dead and have noted these "reported dead." In many cases several proofs of death of any particular allottee are on file, in the office of the Superintendent, and these show different dates, varying in some instances from one to ten years in the date of death. We have selected only one date, taking the proof which we deemed most trustworthy, but, as a matter of fact these proofs of death are not reliable in arriving at the true date, nor are they reliable in naming the surviving relatives and heirs at law. It is always well to send for a certified copy of one of these proofs of death, if you are interested, but do not rely on it.

(7) The different laws of descent and distribution applicable at any time to these Creek allottees will be inserted in the back of the book as a sort of an appendix. They will be arranged in chronological order, and in connection therewith will be notes explanatory thereof. We have tried, however, to avoid any expression of opinion as to the effect of any or all of these laws.

10

ABSTRACT

OF

CREEK INDIAN CENSUS CARDS

Compiled from the Originals, now in the Office of the
Superintendent of the Union Agency,
Muskogee, Oklahoma

Roll No.	No.	NAME	Age	Sex	Blood	Rel.	NAME OF FATHER	Liv.	Cit.	NAME OF MOTHER	Liv.	Cit.
		Census Card No. 1, P. O. Tulsa, Enrolled March 29, 1899										
	1	Barnett, Sussanne	19	F	¾		Petoche Barnett	D	Cr	Nancy Barnett	D	Cr
		Census Card No. 2, P. O. Muskogee, Enrolled March 29, 1899										
2	1	Meagher, Isabelle	18	F	¼		T. F. Meagher	L	Non	Mary Meagher	D	Cr
3	2	Meagher, Sarah	16	F	¼	Sis	T. F. Meagher	L	Non	Mary Meagher	D	Cr
4	3	Meagher, Edward	14	M	¼	Bro	T. F. Meagher	L	Non	Mary Meagher	D	Cr
5	4	Meagher, Walter	12	M	¼	Bro	T. F. Meagher	L	Non	Mary Meagher	D	Cr
		Census Card No. 3, P. O. Muskogee, Enrolled March 30, 1899										
6	1	Meagher, John S.	24	M	¼		T. F. Meagher	L	Non	Mary Meagher	D	Cr
		Died December 12, 1899										
		Census Card No. 4, P. O. Tuscon, Arizona, Enrolled March 30, 1899										
7	1	Meagher, Thos. F. Jr.,	21	M	¼		T. F. Meagher	L	Non	Mary Meagher	D	Cr
		Census Card No. 5, P. O. Okemah, Enrolled March 30, 1899										
8	1	Dunn, Tupper	26	M	Full		Beaver Dunn	D	Cr	Mannie Dunn	D	Cr
9	2	Dunn, Susie	27	F	Full	Wf	Tom Fox	D	Cr	Lizzie Fox	D	Cr
10	3	Dunn, Harry	5	M	Full	S	No. 1	L	Cr	No. 2	L	Cr
11	4	Dunn, Nannie	3	F	F	D	No. 1	L	Cr	No. 2	L	Cr
12	5	Dunn, Reuben	2mo	M	F	S	No. 1	L	Cr	No. 2	L	Cr
13	6	Sullivan, Hattie	7	F	F	St.	D Jas. Sullivan	D	Cr	No. 2	L	Cr
		No. 5 died May 3, 1899										
		No. 1 died March 9, 1906										
		Census Card No. 6, P. O. Irene, Enrolled March 30, 1899										
14	1	Bunner	40	M	F		Okchema Fixico	D	Cr	Hoe Koh	D	Cr
15	2	Bunner, Losie	30	F	F	Wf	Unknown	D	Cr	Notchee	L	Cr
16	3	Bunner, Martha	17	F	F	D	No. 1	L	Cr	No. 2	L	Cr
17	4	Bunner, Indie	15	F	F	D	No. 1	L	Cr	No. 2	L	Cr
18	5	Bunner, Mosey	14	M	F	S	No. 1	L	Cr	No. 2	L	Cr
19	6	Bunner, Fenie	13	F	F	D	No. 1	L	Cr	No. 2	L	Cr
20	7	Bunner, Miley	12	F	F	D	No. 1	L	Cr	No. 2	L	Cr
21	8	Bunner, Masaner	4	F	F	D	No. 1	L	Cr	No. 2	L	Cr
22	9	Marshall, Lizzie	18	F	F	Niece	Marshall	D	Cr	Arany	L	Cr
23	10	Bunner, Nancy	18	F	F	D	No. 1	L	Cr	No. 2	L	Cr
24	11	Notchee	70	F	F	M-L	Unknown	D	Cr	Unknown	D	Cr
25	12	Bunner, Barney	2	M	F	S	No. 1	L	Cr	No. 2	L	Cr
		No. 2 died April 2, 1902										
		No. 8 died April 16, 1905										
		No. 12 died September 5, 1899										
		Census Card No. 7, P. O. Bearden, Enrolled March 30, 1899										
26	1	Michiley	18	M	F		Artus Henehar	D	Cr	Lucy Alwir	D	Cr
		Census Card No. 8, P. O. Bearden, Enrolled March 30, 1899										
27	1	Cornelius, Elias	45	M	F		Unknown		Cr	Ista Hoey	D	Cr
		Died December 6, 1900										
		Census Card No. 9, P. O. Muskogee, Enrolled March 30, 1899										
28	1	Rulison, Ruth L.	34	F	½		John Meyers	D	Cher	Susan Ann Butler	D	Cr
29	2	Rulison, Edgar R. Jr.,	11	M	¼	S	Edgar R. Rulison	L	Non	No. 1	L	Cr
30	3	Rulison, Irving M.	9	M	¼	S	Edgar R. Rulison	L	Non	No. 1	L	Cr
31	4	Jourdan, Mason F.	11	M	¼	Neph	John C. Jourdan	L	Cher	Arlie Jourdan	D	Cr
		Census Card No. 10, P. O. Bearden, Enrolled March 30, 1899										
32	1	Frank, Barney	24	M	F		Tom Frank	D	Cr	Mesena Frank	D	Cr
33	2	Frank, Liddy	27	F	F	Wf	Ahlepahte Harjo	D	Cr	Mattie	D	Cr
		No. 1 died December 7, 1914										

11

No.	No.	NAME	Age	Sex	Blood	Rel.	NAME OF FATHER	Liv.	Cit.	NAME OF MOTHER	Liv.	Cit.

Census Card No. 11, P. O. Irene, Enrolled March 30, 1899

Roll No.	No.	NAME	Age	Sex	Blood	Rel.	NAME OF FATHER	Liv.	Cit.	NAME OF MOTHER	Liv.	Cit.
34	1	Frank, Tingo	28	M	F		Tom Frank	D	Cr	Marsena Frank	D	Cr
35	2	Frank, Amanda	26	F	F	Wf	No. 1	L	Cr	Lucinda Jones	L	Cr
36	3	Frank, Joseph	4	M	7-8	S	No. 1	L	Cr	No. 2	L	Cr
37	4	Frank, Norah	6da	F	7/8	D	No. 1	L	Cr	No. 2	L	Cr
38	5	Frank, Henry	27	M	1/8	S	No. 1	L	Cr	No. 2	L	Cr

Census Card No. 12, P. O. Wagoner, Enrolled March 30, 1899; No. 3 August 12, 1899

Roll No.	No.	NAME	Age	Sex	Blood	Rel.	NAME OF FATHER	Liv.	Cit.	NAME OF MOTHER	Liv.	Cit.
39	1	Cane, Charlie R.	28	M	1/2		Charlie Cane	D	Non	Priscilla Cane	D	Cr
40	2	Cane, Minnie P.	3	F	1-16 D		No. 1	L	Cr	Mollie B. Cane	L	Non
41	3	Cane, Hattie M.	1.	F	1-16 D		No. 1	L	Cr	Mollie B. Cane	L	Non

Census Card No. 13, P. O. Tulsa, Enrolled March 31, 1899

Roll No.	No.	NAME	Age	Sex	Blood	Rel.	NAME OF FATHER	Liv.	Cit.	NAME OF MOTHER	Liv.	Cit.
42	1	Crowell, Edward	45	M	1/2		Joseph Crowell	L	?	Elizabeth. Porter	D	?
43	2	Crowell, Edward L. Jr	19	M	1/8	S	No. 1	L	Cr.	Martha Crowell	L	Non
44	3	Crowell, Robert A.	17	M	1/8	S	No. 1	L	Cr	Martha Crowell	L	Non

Census Card No. 14, P. O. Eufaula, Enrolled March 31, 1899

Roll No.	No.	NAME	Age	Sex	Blood	Rel.	NAME OF FATHER	Liv.	Cit.	NAME OF MOTHER	Liv.	Cit.
45	1	Atkins, Thomas	37	M	F		Oseabola	D	Cr	Soxlopinkala	L?	Cr
46	2	Atkins, Tommy	6	M	F	S	No. 1	L	Cr	Rina Atkins	L?	Cr

No. 2 died December 18, 1909

Census Card No. 15, Tulsa, Enrolled March 31, 1899

Roll No.	No.	NAME	Age	Sex	Blood	Rel.	NAME OF FATHER	Liv.	Cit.	NAME OF MOTHER	Liv.	Cit.
47	1	Crowell, Benj. F.	22	M	5/8		Edward Crowell	L	Cr	Martha Crowell	L	Non

Census Card No. 16, P. O. Hoffman, Enrolled March 31, 1899

Roll No.	No.	NAME	Age	Sex	Blood	Rel.	NAME OF FATHER	Liv.	Cit.	NAME OF MOTHER	Liv.	Cit.
48	1	Hill, George W.	41	M	1/2		Robert Hill	D	?	Unknown	?	?
49	2	Hill, Lucy	24	F	1/2	Wf	William Grayson	L	Cr	Nancy Grayson	L	Cr
50	3	Hill, Wm. McKinley	1	M	1/2	S	No. 1	L	Cr	No. 2	L	Cr
51	4	Hill, Amanda	14	F	3/4	D	No. 1	L	Cr	Melissa Hill	D	Cr
52	5	Hill, Walter	12	M	3/4	S	No. 1	L	Cr	Melissa Hill	D	Cr
53	6	Hill, Melissa	10	F	3/4	D	No. 1	L	Cr	Melissa Hill	D	Cr

Census Card No. 17, P. O. Coweta, Enrolled March 31, 1899

Roll No.	No.	NAME	Age	Sex	Blood	Rel.	NAME OF FATHER	Liv.	Cit.	NAME OF MOTHER	Liv.	Cit.
54	1	Crowell, Thos. J.	23	M	1/2		Edward Crowell	L	Cr	Martha Crowell	L	Non

Census Card No. 18, P. O. Bixby, Enrolled March 31, 1899; No. 5 June 7, 1899

Roll No.	No.	NAME	Age	Sex	Blood	Rel.	NAME OF FATHER	Liv.	Cit.	NAME OF MOTHER	Liv.	Cit.
55	1	Bruner, John	40	M	F		Lewis Bruner	D	Cr	Nannie Bruner	D	Cr
56	2	Bruner, Pamela	28	F	F	Wf	Jococe	?	Cr	Mollie Bruner	D	Cr
57	3	Bruner, Benjamin	2	M	F	S	No. 1	L	Cr	No. 2	L	Cr
58	4	Coachman, Josephine	9	F		St.D	Wattie Coachman	L	Cr	No. 2	L	Cr
59	5	Bruner, May Bell	2wk	F		D	No. 1	L	Cr	No. 2	L	Cr

No. 2 died July 28, 1914

Census Card No. 19, P. O. Muskogee, Enrolled March 31, 1899

Roll No.	No.	NAME	Age	Sex	Blood	Rel.	NAME OF FATHER	Liv.	Cit.	NAME OF MOTHER	Liv.	Cit.
60	1	Davis, John	51	M	1/8		Job Davis	L	Non	Nancy Davis	D	Cr
61	2	Davis, Benjamin	21	M	1-16 S		No. 1	L	Cr	Arabella Davis	D	Non
62	3	Davis, Rebecca	11	F	1-16 D		No. 1	L	Cr	Mary Childers	D	Non

No. 1 died February 22, 1902

Census Card No. 20, P. O. Dustin, Enrolled April 1, 1899

Roll No.	No.	NAME	Age	Sex	Blood	Rel.	NAME OF FATHER	Liv.	Cit.	NAME OF MOTHER	Liv.	Cit.
63	1	Benson, David M.	62	M	1/2		Jack Benson	D	Cr	Rhoda Benson	D	Cr
64	2	Benson, Lena E.	23	F	1/2	D	No. 1	L	Cr	Louisa Benson	D	Cr
65	3	Benson, William	22	M	1/2	D	No. 1	L	Cr	Louisa Benson	D	Cr
66	4	Benson, Lillie M.	20	F	1/2	D	No. 1	L	Cr	Louisa Benson	D	Cr
67	5	Benson, Hattie	18	F	1/2	D	No. 1	L	Cr	Louisa Benson	D	Cr
68	6	Manley, Siah	15	M	F	Wd	Tarby Manley	D	Cr	Sarah Dier	L	Cr
69	7	Manley, Jonas	17	M	F	Wd	Tarby Manley	D	Cr	Sarah Dier	L	Cr

No. 1 died

Census Card No. 21, P. O. Okmulgee, Enrolled March 31, 1899

Roll No.	No.	NAME	Age	Sex	Blood	Rel.	NAME OF FATHER	Liv.	Cit.	NAME OF MOTHER	Liv.	Cit.
70	1	Larney, Tommy	45	M	F		Chetko Larney	D	Cr	Sometka	D	Cr
71	2	Larney, Lydia	47	F	F	Wf	Woxie Yahola	D	Cr	Mocknarlee	D	Cr
72	3	Larney, David	17	M	F	S	No. 1	L	Cr.	No. 2	L	Cr
73	4	Larney, Harrison	9	M	F	S	No. 1	L	Cr.	No. 2	L	Cr
74	5	Larney, Jackson	7	M	F	S	No. 1	L	Cr.	No. 2	L	Cr
75	6	Larney, Minnie	5	F	F	D	No. 1	L	Cr	No. 2	L	Cr

No. 1 died September 1905
No. 4 died September 17, 1907. No. 3 reported dead.

Census Card No. 22, P. O. Muskogee, Enrolled March 31, 1899; No. 2 May 9, 1900

Roll No.	No.	NAME	Age	Sex	Blood	Rel.	NAME OF FATHER	Liv.	Cit.	NAME OF MOTHER	Liv.	Cit.
76	1	Bailey, Mattie	25	F	7/8		C. W. Murphy	D	Non	Eliza Murphy	L	Cr
77	2	Bailey, Joseph Martin	1.	M	1-16 S		Joe A. Bailey	L	Non	No. 1	L	Cr

Census Card No. 23, P. O. Okmulgee; No. 10 Wetumka, Enrolled March 31, 1899

Roll No.	No.	NAME	Age	Sex	Blood	Rel.	NAME OF FATHER	Liv.	Cit.	NAME OF MOTHER	Liv.	Cit.
78	1	Tiger, Motey	57	M	3/4		Tulsa Fixico	D	Cr	Louisa	D	Cr
79	2	Tiger, Kissie	59	F	1/2	Wf	Louis	D	Cr	Louisa	D	Cr
80	3	Ryan, Eliza	17	F	1/2	Wd	Ryan	D	Cr	Arabella	D	Cr
81	4	Tiger, Amos	16	M	3/4	S	No. 1	L	Cr	Hattie Tiger	D	Cr
82	5	Webster, Edward	14	M	F	Wd	Daniel Webster	D	Cr	Sookey Webster	L	Cr
83	6	Webster, Betsey	10	F	F	Wd	Daniel Webster	D	Cr	Sookey Webster	L	Cr
84	7	Webster, Albert	7	M	F	Wd	Daniel Webster	D	Cr	Sookey Webster	L	Cr
85	8	Berryhill, Joseph	16	M	F.	Wd	John Berryhill	L	Cr	Mille Berryhill	D	Cr
86	9	Sullivan, Annie	17	F	F	Wd	James Sullivan	D	Cr	Louisa Sullivan	D	Cr
87	10	Sullivan, Obey	10	F	F	Wd	James Sullivan	D	Cr	Louisa Sullivan	D	Cr
88	11	Sullivan, Helen	18	F	F	Wd	James Sullivan	D	Cr	Louisa Sullivan	D	Cr

No. 6 died October 10, 1904. Nos. 4, 9 and 11 reported dead.

Census Card No. 24, Checotah, Enrolled March 31, 1899

Roll No.	No.	NAME	Age	Sex	Blood	Rel.	NAME OF FATHER	Liv.	Cit.	NAME OF MOTHER	Liv.	Cit.
89	1	Rogers, Wm. P.	28	M	1/2.		W. B. Rogers	L	Cr	Kate D. Rogers	L	Cr

No. 1 died December 26, 1903

Roll No.	No.	NAME	Age	Sex	Blood	Rel.	NAME OF FATHER	Liv.	Cit.	NAME OF MOTHER	Liv.	Cit.
	Census Card No. 25, P. O. Okmulgee, Enrolled March 31, 1899											
90	1	Davis, Alex	46	M	F		Tom Davis	D	Cr	Hannah Davis	D	Cr
91	2	Davis, Josiah	12	F	F	S	No. 1	L	Cr	Lucy Davis	L	Cr
92	3	Davis, George	6	M	F	S	No. 1	L	Cr	Lucy Davis	L	Cr
93	4	Berryhill, Susie	20	F	F	St.D	Albert Berryhill	D	Cr	Lucy Davis	L	Cr
		No. 4 died August 18, 1900										
		No. 1 died September 7, 1907										
	Census Card No. 26, P. O. Okmulgee, Enrolled March 31, 1899											
94	1	Blue, Sampson	39	M	F		Holotta	D	Cr	Tiger	D	Cr
	Census Card No. 27, P. O. Wagoner, Enrolled March 31, 1899											
95	1	Farrill, Sarah	48	F	½		Wm. McDermite	D	Non	Winnie McDermite	?	Cr
96	2	Farrill, Katie	12	F	¼	D	Stephen W. Farrill	L	Non	No. 1	L	Cr
97	3	Farrill, Henry	10	M	¼	S	Stephen W. Farrill	L	Non	No. 1	L	Cr
98	4	Farrill, May	6	F	¼	D	Stephen W. Farrill	L	Non	No. 1	L	Cr
		No. 1 died April 7, 1901										
	Census Card No. 28, P. O. Okmulgee, Enrolled March 31, 1899											
99	1	Checotah, Martin	40	M	F		Samuel Checotah	D	Cr	Priscella Checotah	D	Cr
100	2	Checotah, Louisiana	28	F	F	Wf	Peter Nelson	D	Cr	Jennetta	D	Cr
	Census Card No. 29, P. O. Kelleyville, Enrolled March 31, 1899											
101	1	Hardridge, Julia	33	F	¾		Alec Belcher	D	Cr	Sila Belcher	D	Cr
102	2	Hardridge, Lon	16	M	¾	S	Shawnee Hardridge	D	Cr	No. 1	L	Cr
		No. 1 and 2 reported dead										
	Census Card No. 30, P. O. Okmiulgee, Enrolled March 31, 1899											
103	1	Berryhill, David L.	51	M	¾		Pleasant Berryhill	D	Cr	Winnie Berryhill	D	Cr
104	2	Berryhill, Peggy	50	F	F	Wf	Henegochee	D	Cr	Unknown	L	Cr
105	3	Berryhill, Newman	12	M	⅞	S	No. 1			No. 2	L	Cr
		No. 2 reported dead										
	Census Card No. 31, P. O. Okmulgee, Enrolled March 31, 1899											
106	1	Gibson, Joseph	44	M	F		Cheparney Gibson	D	Cr	Mary Gibson	D	Cr
107	2	Gibson, Martha	44	F	F	Wf	Sam Checotah	L	Cr	Silla Checotah	D	Cr
108	3	Gibson, Gilbert	12	M	F	S	No. 1	L	Cr	No. 2	L	Cr
		No. 2 died January 5, 1901										
	Census Card No. 32, P. O. Okmulgee, Enrolled March 31, 1899											
109	1	Asbury, Moses	45	M	F		Tommy Yahola	D	Cr	Unknown	D	Cr
110	2	Asbury, Lucy	18	F	F	D	No. 1	L	Cr	Nicey Asbury	D	Cr
111	3	Asbury, Rhoda	16	F	F	D	No. 1	L	Cr	Nicey Asbury	D	Cr
112	4	Asbury, Louina	8	F	F	D	No. 1	L	Cr	Nicey Asbury	D	Cr
		No. 3 died March 10, 1912. Nos. 1 and 3 reported dead.										
	Census Card No. 33, P. O. Wagoner, Enrolled March 31, 1899; No. 3 April 19, 1899											
113	1	Weldon, Mrs. Ruby D.	48	F	⅛		Willison	D	Non	Catherine McIntosh	D	Cr
114	2	Weldon, Viola	17	F	1-16	D	A. E. Weldon	L	Non	No. 1	L	Cr
115	3	Weldon Robert Lee	11	M	1-16	S	A. E. Weldon	L	Non	No. 1	L	Cr
	Census Card No. 34, P. O. Wagoner, Enrolled March 31, 1899											
116	1	West, Arabella W.	27	F	1-16	....	W. R. West	D	Non	Ruby D. Weldon	L	Cr
	Census Card No. 35, P. O. Okmulgee, Enrolled March 31, 1899; Nos. 8 and 9, October 21, 1899											
117	1	Berryhill, Pleasant	43	M	⅛		Jefferson Berryhill	D	Cr	Nancy Berryhill	L	No
118	2	Berryhill, Sarah Lee	30	F	F	Wf	Sam Bradley	D	Cr	Unknown	D	Cr
119	3	Berryhill, Sam	13	M	¼	S	No. 1	L	Cr	No. 2	L	Cr
120	4	Berryhill, Oscar	11	M	¼	S	No. 1	L	Cr	No. 2	L	Cr
121	5	Berryhill, Josephine	9	F	¼	D	No. 1	L	Cr	No. 2	L	Cr
122	6	Berryhill, Clarence	7	M	¼	S	No. 1	L	Cr	No. 2	L	Cr
123	7	Berryhill, Effie L.	5	F	¼	D	No. 1	L	Cr	No. 2	L	Cra
124	8	Pigeon, Lizzie	17	F	½	Orph	Jesse Pigeon	D?	Cr	Sallie Pigeon	D	Cr
125	9	Pigeon, Robert	11	M	½	Orph	Jesse Pigeon	D	Cr	Sallie Pigeon	D ?	Cr
		No. 2 died June 4, 1900. No. 8 died May 23, 1904										
	Census Card No. 36, P. O. Okmulgee, Enrolled March 31, 1899											
126	1	Chully, Taylor	37	M	F		Chully	D	Cr	Siley	D	Cr
127	2	Chully, Millie	19	F	F	Wf	Wesley Sugar	D	Cr	Adeline Sugar	D	Cr
128	3	Chully, Mulsey	15	F	F	Niece	Sika Chully	......	Cr	Nancy Chully	D	Cr
129	4	Chully, Jimboy	9	M	F	S	No. 1	L	Cr	Matilda Tiger	....	Cr
		Nos. 1, 2, 3 and 4 reported dead.										
	Census Card No. 37, P. O. Okmulgee, Enrolled March 31, 1899											
130	1	Berryhill, Alec	27	M	¾		Jefferson Berryhill	D	Cr	Peggy Berryhill	D	Cr
131	2	Berryhill, Annie	20	F	F	Wf	Ahlejetchchee	D	Cr	Lucy	D	Cr
132	3	Perryhill, David L.	1	M	¾	S	No. 1	L	Cr	No. 2	L	Cr
133	4	Milker, Lucy	6	F	F	St.D	John Miller	L	Cr	No. 2	L	Cr.
	Census Card No. 38, P. O. Wagoner, Enrolled March 31, 1899											
134	1	West, Sue Hettie	24	F	1-16		W. R. West	D	Non	Ruby D. Weldon	L	Cr
	Census Card No. 39, P. O. Haskell, Enrolled March 31, 1899											
135	1	Smith, Daniel B.	39	M	¼		Sheldon White	L	Non	Lucinda Smith	L	Cr
136	2	Smith, Mary I.	25	F	¼	Wf	B. F. Berryhill	D	Cr	Unknown	D	Non
137	3	Smith, Pearl	10	F	¼	D	No. 1	L	Cr	No. 2	L	Co
138	4	Smith, Alfred C.	8	M	¼	S	No. 1	L	Cr	No. 2	L	Cr
139	5	Smith, William S.	6	M	¼	S	No. 1	L	Cr	No. 2	L	Cr
140	6	Smith, Albert L.	3	M	¼	S	No. 1	L	Cr	No. 2	L	Cr
141	7	Smith, Franklin M.	5mo	M	¼	S	No. 1	L	Cr	No. 2	L	Cr
		No. 7 died October 9, 1914										

Roll No.	No.	NAME	Age	Sex	Blood	Rel.	NAME OF FATHER	Liv.	Cit.	NAME OF MOTHER	Liv.	Cit.
		Census Card No. 40, P. O. Eufaula, Enrolled March 31, 1899; No. 6 May 16, 1900 No. 2 Hanna.										
142	1	Tiger, George W.	41	M	F		John Tiger	D	Cr	Nancy Tiger	D	Cr
143	2	Tiger, Susan	15	F	½	D	No. 1	L	Cr	Rebecca W. Tiger	L	Non
144	3	Tiger, Adolphus	12	M	½	S	No. 1	L	Cr	Rebecca W. Tiger	L	Non
145	4	Tiger, Luther	10	M	½	S	No. 1	L	Cr	Rebecca W. Tiger	L	Non
146	5	Tiger, Oscar	8	M	½	S	No. 1	L	Cr	Rebecca W. Tiger	L	Non
147	6	Tiger, Minnie	9mo	F	½	D	No. 1	L	Cr	Rebecca W. Tiger	L	Non
		No. 1 reported dead.										
		Census Card No. 41, P. O. Stone Bluff, Enrolled March 31, 1899										
148	1	Rothhammer, Louisa J.	37	F	¼		Sheldon Smith	L	Non	Lucinda Smith	L	Cr
149	2	Rothhammer, WillieA.	11	M	⅛	S	J. H. Rothhammer	L	Non	No. 1	L	Cr
150	3	Rothhammer, Lillie E.	9	F	⅛	D	J. H. Rothhammer	L	Non	No. 1	L	Cr
151	4	Rothhammer, Joseph H. Jr	5	M	⅛	S	J. H. Rothhammer	L	Non	No. 1	L	Cr
		No. 1 died April 14, 1912										
		Census Card No. 42, P. O. Okmulgee, Enrolled March 31, 1899										
152	1	Scott, Thomas	50	M	F		Thomas Scott	D	Cr	Soffike	?	Cr
153	2	Scott, Mulley	45	F	F	Wf	Shumchechoga	D	Cr	Toffeka	?	Cr
154	3	Scott, Sookie	14	F	F	D	No. 1	L	Cr	No. 2	L	Cr
155	4	Scott, Kizzie	12	F	F	D	No. 1	L	Cr	No. 2	L	Cr
156	5	Nelson, Eli	16	M	F	Neph	Nelson	D	Cr	Mitchey	?	Cr
		No. 1 died July 1, 1901. No. 4 Died February, 1908. Nos. 3 and 6 reported dead.										
		Census Card No. 43, P. O. Eufaula, Enrolled March 31, 1899										
157	1	Francis, John	64	M	½		Dorsey Francis	D	....	Annie Francis	L	Cr
158	2	Francis, Millie	51	F	F	Wf	Ahkonah	D	Cr	Nellie Ahkonah	?	Cr
159	3	Francis, Emma	14	F	¾	D	No. 1	L	Cr	No. 2	L	Cr
160	4	Francis, Locha	6	M	¾	S	No. 1	L	Cr	No. 2	L	Cr
161	5	Francis, Martha	16	F	¾	D	No. 1	L	Cr	No. 2	L	Cr
		No. 1 died May 22, 1906. No. 5 died August 12, 1904										
		Census Card No. 44, P. O. Checotah, Enrolled March 31, 1899										
162	1	Davis, Annie C.	31	F	¼		John Scott	D	Non	Martha Scott	D	Cr
		Census Card No. 45, P. O. Okmulgee, Enrolled March 31, 1899 No. 2 June 16, 1899; No. 3 March 23, 1901; No. 4 May 22, 1901										
163	1	Scott, Willie	21	M	F		Thomas Scott	L	Cr	Mulley Scott	L	Cr
164	2	Scott, Betty	21	F	F	Wf	Hillabee Grayson	D	Cr	Aggie Smith	L	Cr
165	3	Wesley, Jimsey	7	M	F	SS	Washington Wesley	L	Cr	No. 2	L	Cr
166	4	Grayson, Sophia	7	F	F	Sis No 2	Hillabee Grayson	D	Cr	Aggie Smith	L	Cr
		Nos. 1, 2, 3 and 4 reported dead.										
		Census Card No. 46, P. O. Naudack, Enrolled March 31, 1899										
167	1	Porter, Susan	16	F	½		Stephen W. Farill	L	Non	Sarah Farill	L	Cr
168	2	Porter, Katie May	2	F	⅛	D	Sam Porter	L	Non	No.	L	Cr
		Census Card No. 47, P. O. Okmulgee, Enrolled March 31, 1899										
169	1	Grisson, Maggie J.	43	F	¾		James M. C. Smith	D	Cr	Peggy Smith	D	Cr
170	2	Grissom, Myrtle M.	16	F	3-8	D	J. E. F. Grissom	L	Non	No. 1	L	Cr
171	3	Grissom, John F.	15	M	3-8	S	J. E. F. Grissom	L	Non	No. 1	L	Cr
172	4	Grissom, James H.	13	M	3-8	S	J. E. F. Grissom	L	Non	No. 1	L	Cr
173	5	Grissom, Joseph M.	10	M	3-8	S	J. E. F. Grissom	L	Non	No. 1	L	Cr
174	6	Grissom, Thomas B.	7	M	3-8	S	J. E. F. Grissom	L	Non	No. 1	L	Cr
175	7	Grissom, Fred M.	6	M	3-8	S	J. E. F. Grissom	L	Non	No. 1	L	Cr
176	8	Grissom, Viola	3	F	3-8	D	J. E. F. Grissom	L	Non	No. 1	L	Cr
		Census Card No. 48, P. O. Okmulgee, Enrolled March 31, 1899; No. 2 October 3, 1899										
177	1	Gaither, Alice M	18	F	⅛		J. E. F. Grissom	L	Non	Maggie J. Grissom	L	Cr
178	2	Gaither, WooleryL.F.	2mo	M	3-16	S	W. J. Gaither	L	Non	No. 1	L	Cr
		Census Card No. 49, P. O. Choska, Enrolled March 31, 1899										
179	1	Brown, William C.	50	M	½		William F. Brown	D	Non	Harriet	?	Cr
		No. 1 died February 2, 1908										
		Census Card No. 50, P. O. Morse, Enrolled March 31, 1899; No. 3 June 25, 1900										
180	1	Martin Anna	18	F	½		Stephen W. Farill	L	Non	Sara Farril	L	Cr
181	2	Martin, James	3	M	⅛	S	Thomas Martin	L	Non	No. 1	L	Cr
182	3	Martin, Etta Elmory	2	F	⅛	D	Thomas Martin	L		No. 1	L	Cr
183	4	Martin, Ida May	4mo	F	½	D	Thomas Martin	L		No. 1	L	Cr
		Census Card No. 51, P. O. Muskogee, Enrolled March 31, 1899										
184	1	Barnett, George	50	M	½		Jackson Barnett	D	?	Seohtanney	D	Cr
185	2	Barnett, Cita	18	F	¾	D	No. 1	L	Cr	Pacananney	D	Cr
186	3	Barnett, Moses	15	M	¾	S	No. 1	L	Cr	Pacananney	D	Cr
187	4	Barnett, Johnson	13	M	¾	S	No. 1	L	Cr	Pacananney	D	Cr
188	5	Barnett, Jeanetta	11	F	¾	D	No. 1	L	Cr	Pacananney	D	Cr
189	6	Barnett, Louisa	8	F	¾	D	No. 1	L	Cr	Pacananney	D	Cr
190	7	Barnett, Melissa	7	F	¾	D	No. 1	L	Cr	Pacananney	D	Cr
		No. 1 died March 17, 1900. No. 2 died February 8, 1900. No. 3 died August 31, 1899.										
		Census Card No. 52, P. O. Haskell, Enrolled March 31, 1899										
191	1	Rolland, Amos	46	M	½		Joe Rowlands	D	?	Muskogee	D	Cr
192	2	Rolland, Jacob	14	M	¼	S	No. 1	L	Cr	Low Rowland	L	Cher
193	3	Rolland, Peter	11	M	¼	S	No. 1	L	Cr	Low Rowland	L	Cher
		No. 1 died September 29, 1909										
		Census Card No. 53, P. O. Checotah, Enrolled April 1, 1899; No. 6 May 16, 1900										
194	1	Turner, Fannie H.	42	F	¼		Jim Scott	L	Non	Lou W. Scott	?	Cr
195	2	Turner, Hattie	13	F	⅛	D	Hammer Turner	L	Non	No. 1	L	Cr
196	3	Turner, Annie	11	F	⅛	D	Hammer Turner	L	Non	No. 1	L	Cr
197	4	Turner, George P. M.	9	M	⅛	S	Hammer Turner	L	Non	No. 1	L	Cr
198	5	Turner, Hamner G. Jr.,	7	M	⅛	S	Hammer Turner	L	Non	No. 1	L	Cr
199	6	Turner, Margurrite Estella	21	F	⅛	D	Hammer Turner	L	Non	No. 1	L	Cr

Roll No.	No.	NAME	Age	Sex	Blood	Rel.	NAME OF FATHER	Liv.	Cit.	NAME OF MOTHER	Liv.	Cit
		Census Card No. 54, P. O. Morris, Enrolled March 31, 1899; No. 9 April 12, 1899										
200	1	Ashley, Isabel Jane	45	F	½		Henry Walker	D	Cr.	Nancy Walker	D	Non
201	2	Ashley, John R.	18	M	¼	S	J. R. Ashley	L	Non	No. 1	L	Cr
202	3	Ashley, Amanda S.	17	F	¼	D	J. R. Ashley	L	Non	No. 1	L	Cr
203	4	Ashley, Hettie E.	15	F	¼	D	J. R. Ashley	L	Non	No. 1	L	Cr
204	5	Ashley, James T.	14	M	¼	S	J. R. Ashley	L	Non	No. 1	L	Cr
205	6	Ashley, Daniel	12	M	¼	S	J. R. Ashley	L	Non	No. 1	L	Cr
206	7	Ashley, Adolphus K.	9	M	¼	S	J. R. Ashley	L	Non	No. 1	L	Cr
207	8	Ashley, George S.	6	M	¼	S	J. R. Ashley	L	Non	No. 1	L	Cr
208	9	Ashley, Emma	2	F	¼	D	J. R. Ashley	L	Non	No. 1	L	Cr
		No. 7 died September 7, 1908										
		Census Card No. 55, P. O. Muskogee, Enrolled March 31, 1899; No. 7 September 6, 1899										
209	1	Minter, Millie	37	F	¼		Jackson Durant	L	Cr	Sarah Durant	L	Non
210	2	Minter, Harry	17	M	⅛	S	Marcus S. Minter	D	Non	No. 1	L	Cr
211	3	Minter, Rupert	14	M	⅛	S	Marcus S. Winter	D	Non	No. 1	L	Cr
212	4	Minter, John	12	M	⅛	S	Marcus S. Minter	D	Non	No. 1	L	Cr
213	5	Minter, Douglas	10	M	⅛	S	Marcus S. Minter	D	Non	No. 1	L	Cr
214	6	Minter, Coachman	7	M	⅛	S	Marcus S. Minter	D	Non	No. 1	L	Cr
215	7	Minter, Mark	20	M	⅛	S	Marcus S. Minter	D	Non	No. 1	L	Cr
		No. 2 reported dead										
		Census Card No. 56, P. O. Checotah, Enrolled April 1, 1899										
216	1	Scott, Lou M.	65	F	½		Benjamin Hawkins	D	?	Rebecca Hawkins	D	?
		Census Card No. 57, P. O. Coweta, Enrolled April 1, 1899; Nos. 2 to 7 April 30, 1901										
217	1	Murphy, Conny	37	M	⅛		Conny Murphy	D	Non	Eliza J. Murphy	L	Cr
218	2	Murphy, Conny Jr.,	16	M	1-16	S	No. 1	L	Cr	Sarah Murphy	L	Cher
219	3	Murphy, Mattie	14	F	1-16	D	No. 1	L	Cr	Sarah Murphy	L	Cher
220	4	Murphy, Robert	12	M	1-16	S	No. 1	L	Cr	Sarah Murphy	L	Cher
221	5	Murphy, Augustus	11	M	1-16	S	No. 1	L	Cr	Sarah Murphy	L	Cher
222	6	Murphy, Sallie	8	F	1-16	D	No. 1	L	Cr	Sarah Murphy	L	Cher
223	7	Murphy, Eliza Jane	6	F	1-16	D	No. 1	L	Cr	Sarah Murphy	L	Cher
		Census Card No. 58, P. O. Wetumka, Enrolled April 1, 1899										
224	1	Tiger, Johnson E.	24	M	¾		Motey Tiger	L	Cr	Hettie Tiger	D	Cr
		Census Card No. 59, P. O. Haskell, Enrolled April 1, 1899										
225	1	Moore, Napoleon B.	71	M	⅛		Wm. Moore	D	Non	Lucy Moore	D	Cr
		No. 1 dead										
		Census Card No. 60, P. O. Okmulgee, Enrolled April 1, 1899										
226	1	Kanard, Thomas Jr.,	26	M	F		Jim Kanard	D	Cr	Simeno Kanard	D	Cr
227	2	Kanard, Eliza	22	F	F	Wf	Josiah Watson	L	Cr	Hannah Watson	?	Cr
228	3	Kanard, Annie	7	F	F	D	No. 1	L	Cr	No. 2	L	Cr
229	4	Kanard, Polly	5	F	F	D	No. 1	L	Cr	No. 2	L	Cr
230	5	Kanard, Louis	3	M	F	S	No. 1	L	Cr	No. 2	L	Cr
231	6	Kanard, Louisa	6mo	F	F	D	No. 1	L	Cr	No. 2	L	Cr
		No. 1 reported dead										
		Census Card No. 61, P. O. Wetumka, Enrolled April 1, 1899										
232	1	Carr, Robert	53	M	F		Thomas	D	Cr	Cosoe	D	Cr
233	2	Carr, Bettie	43	F	F	Wf	Daniel Barnett	D	Cr	Sally Barnett	D	Cr
234	3	Carr, Addie	20	F	F	D	No. 1	L	Cr	No. 2	L	Cr
235	4	Carr, Ida	16	F	F	D	No. 1	L	Cr	No. 2	L	Cr
236	5	Carr, Lulu	14	F	F	D	No. 1	L	Cr	No. 2	L	Cr
237	6	Carr, Annis	8	F	F	D	No. 1	L	Cr	No. 2	L	Cr
		Census Card No. 62, P. O. Coweta, Enrolled April 1, 1899; Nos. 6 and 7 February 27, 1900										
238	1	Apueka, William	46	M	F		Makakpoyah	D	Cr	Lucy	D	Cr
239	2	Apueka, Nancy	36	F	F	Wf	Posuk Harjo	D	Cr	Susie Harjo	D	Cr
240	3	Apueka, Willie	11	M	F	S	No. 1	L	Cr	No. 2	L	Cr
241	4	Apueka, Tooka	6	F	F	D	No. 1	L	Cr	No. 2	L	Cr
242	5	Apueka, Nathaniel	1	M	F	S	No. 1	L	Cr	No. 2	L	Cr
243	6	Apueka, Setty	9	F	F	Niece	Una Arpueka	D	Cr	Louisa Arpueka	D	Cr
244	7	Apueka, Jemima	7	F	F	Niece	Una Arpueka	D	Cr	Louisa Arpueka	D	Cr
		No. 6 died May 21, 1914										
		No. 1 died November 11, 1902										
		No. 2 died October 23, 1900										
		No. 3 died December 3, 1905										
		Census Card No. 63, Okmulgee, Enrolled April 1, 1899										
245	1	Checote, Samuel J.	32	M	½		Jefferson Checote	D	Cr	Eliza J. Checote	L	?
246	2	Checote, Annie	29	F	¾	Wf	George Fisher	D	Cr	Dinah Fisher	L	Cr
247	3	Checote, Martin L.	6	M	5-8	S	No. 1	L	Cr	No. 2	L	Cr
248	4	Checote, Samuel J. Jr.	4	M	5-8	S	No. 1	L	Cr	No. 2	L	Cr
249	5	Checote, George W.	2	M	5-8	S	No. 1	L	Cr	No. 2	L	Cr
		Census Card No. 64, Okmulgee, Enrolled April 1, 1899										
250	1	Grayson, Colbert	28	M	F		Gibson Grayson	D	Cr	Judy Grayson	D	Cr
		No. 1 died August 27, 1899										
		Census Card No. 65, Sharpe, Enrolled April 3, 1899										
251	1	Thompson, Alex	26	M	F		Cheesupka	D	Cr	Nicey	D	Cr
		Census Card No. 66, P. O. Coweta, April 3, 1899; No. 6 February 19, 1900 No. 3, Muskogee										
252	1	Lovett, George	48	M	F		Philie Lovett	D	Cr	Thasahhe	D	Cr
253	2	Lovett, Annie	19	F	¾	Wf	Samuel Checote	D	Cr	Lizzie Checote	D	Cr
254	3	Lovett, Wisey	12	F	F	D	No. 1	L	Cr	Sallie Lovett	D	Cr
255	4	Lovett, Lucy	7	F	F	D	No. 1	L	Cr	Sallie Lovett	D	Cr
256	5	Davis, Noah	18	M	¾	Ward	Major Chupco	L	Cr	No. 2	L	Cr
257	6	Lovett, Lizzie	2mo	F	¾	D	No. 1	L	Cr	No. 2	L	Cr
		No. 1 died June 20, 1901 No. 2 died January ,1903										

Roll No.	No.	NAME	Age	Sex	Blood	Rel.	NAME OF FATHER	Liv.	Cit.	NAME OF MOTHER	Liv.	Cit.
		Census Card No. 67, P. O. Fentress, Enrolled April 3, 1899										
258	1	Thompson, March	45	M	F		Woxie Yahola	D	Cr	Makannocke	D	Cr
		No. 1 died April 10, 1903										
		Census Card No. 68, Okmulgee, Enrolled April 3, 1899; No. 6 June 23, 1899										
259	1	Bird, Moses	31	M	F		Fus Harjo	D	Cr	Kissie Harjo	L	Cr
260	2	Bird, Sallie	31	F	F	Wf	Concharty Yahola	D	Cr	Salizy Yahola	L	Cr
261	3	Bird, Amında	11	F	F	D	No. 1	L	Cr	No. 2	L	Cr
262	4	Bird, Louisa	7	F	F	D	No. 1	L	Cr	No. 2	L	Cr
263	5	Bird, Ellis	4	F	F	D	No. 1	L	Cr	No. 2	L	Cr
264	6	Bird, Nannie	10	F	F	D	No. 1	L	Cr	Nelson	L	Cr
		Census Card No. 69, P. O. Irene, Enrolled April 3, 1899										
265	1	Scott, James	42	M	F		Artus Yahola	D	Cr	Larney Yahola	D	Cr
		Census Card No. 70, P. O. No. 1 Sapulpa; No. 2 Beggs, Enrolled April 3, 1899										
266	1	Simms, Maxey	20	M	F		Mark Simms	L	Cr	Liza Simms	L	Cr
267	2	Simms, Bunner	22	M	F	Bro	Mark Simms	L	Cr	Liza Simms	L	Cr
		Census Card No. 71, Coweta, Enrolled April 3, 1899										
268	1	Lovett, Kizzie	40	F	F		Philie Lovett	D	Cr	Thasahhe	D	Cr
269	2	Cousins, Mattie	13	F	F	Niece	Willie Cousins	?	Cr	Wisey Lovett	L	Cr
270	3	Haynie, Jeff	10	M	F	Nep	Haynie	?	Cr	Wisey Lovett	L	Cr
		Census Card No. 72, P. O. No. 1 Irene; No. 2 Wetumka, Enrolled April 3, 1899										
271	1	Fatt, Dick	24	M	F		Joseph Fatt	D	Cr	Fohlokhe	D	Cr
272	2	Fatt, Hannah	17	F	F		Joseph Fatt	D	Cr	Fohlokhe	D	Cr
		No. 1 reported dead										
		Census Card No. 73, P. O. Holdenville, Enrolled April 3, 1899; No. 7 February 3, 1900										
273	1	Jacobs, Frank D.	59	M	1/8		Eli Jacobs	D	?	Betsey Jacobs	D	?
274	2	Jacobs, Jennie C.	36	F	1/2	Wf	London Coker	L	Cr	Mary Coker	L	?
275	3	Jacobs, Newman F.	14	M	1/2	S	No. 1	L	Cr	No. 2	L	Cr
276	4	Jacobs, Sarah	12	F	1/2	D	No. 1	L	Cr	No. 2	L	Cr
277	5	Jacobs, Josie	8	F	1/2	D	No. 1	L	Cr	No. 2	L	Cr
278	6	Jacobs, Willie	4	F	1/2	D	No. 1	L	Cr	No. 2	L	Cr
279	7	Jacobs, Louis	11mo	M	1/2	S.	No. 1	L	Cr	No. 2	L	Cr
		Census Card No. 74, P. O. Coweta, Enrolled April 3, 1899										
280	1	Adkins, Hattie	24	F	F		Billy Atkins	L	Cr	Kizzie Lovett	L	Cr
		Census Card No. 75, Haskell, Enrolled April 3, 1899										
281	1	Barnett, William	45	M	1/2		Jackson Barnett	D	?	Okautina	?	Cr
282	2	Barnett, Linda	31	F	F	Wf	Iuquena	?	Cr	No. 2	L	Cr
283	3	Barnett, Wm. A. Jr.,	11	M	3/4	S	No. 1	L	Cr	No. 2	L	Cr
284	4	Barnett, Mary	8	F	3/4	D	No. 1	L	Cr	No. 2	L	Cr
285	5	Barnett, Martha	3	F	3/4	D	No. 1	L	Cr	No. 2	L	Cr
286	6	Barnett, Benache	1	M	3/4	S	No. 1	L	Cr	No. 2	L	Cr
		No. 2 died July 16, 1914										
		Census Card No. 76, P. O. Choska, Enrolled April 3, 1899										
287	1	Barnett, Susannah	48	F	1/2		Jackson, Barnett	D	?	Unknown	?	
		No. 1 died February 21, 1901										?
		Census Card No. 77, P. O. Bristow, April 3, 1899; No. 2 May 23, 1901										
288	1	Barnett, Pompey	20	M	F		Kokone	D	Cr	Pocananney	D	Cr
289	2	Barnett, Yahlawe	18	F	F	Wf	Kacoquanney	L	Cr	Minna	D	Cr
		Census Card No. 78, P. O. Coweta, Enrolled April 3, 1899										
290	1	Sarty, Googan	46	M	F		Sardy	D	Cr	Amy Sardy	D	Cr
291	2	Sarty, Susan	40	F	F	Wf	Chisso	D	Cr	Pholothoka	D	Cr
292	3	Sarty, Abbie	11	F	F	D	No. 1	L	Cr	No. 2	L	Cr
293	4	Sarty, Jenette	8	F	F	D	No. 1	L	Cr	No. 2	L	Cr
294	5	Sarty, Pokar	4	F	F	D	No. 1	L	Cr	No. 2	L	Cr
		No. 4 died March 16, 1903										
		Census Card No. 79, Okmulgee, Enrolled April 3, 1899										
295	1	Hughes, Jimmie P.	53	F	1/8		Henry Morris	D	Non	Peggy Morris	D	Cr
		No. 1 died August 5, 1914										
		Census Card No. 80, Okmulgee, Enrolled April 3, 1899										
296	1	Grayson, Ben	25	M	F		Henry Grayson	D	Cr	Mary Jane Grayson	D	Cr
297	2	Grayson, Mary	28	F	1/8	Wf	Henry Coker	D	Cr	Eliza Coker	D	?
298	3	Grayson, Christina	16mo	F	1/2	D	No. 1	L	Cr	No. 2	L	Cr
299	4	Dunn, Thomas	9	M	1-16	St.S	Joseph Dunn	L	Non	No. 2	L	Cr
300	5	Dunn, Beulah	6	F	1-16	St.D	Joseph Dunn	L	Non	No. 2	L	Cr
		Census Card No. 81, P. O. Econtuchka, Enrolled April 3, 1899										
301	1	Stidham, Wilson	48	M	F		Jack Stidham	D	Cr	Sowanhoke	D	Cr
		No. 1 reported dead										
		Census Card No. 82, P. O. Checotah, Enrolled April 3, 1899										
302	1	Foshee, Mary A.	43	F	1/4		Wm. Berryhill	D	Cr	Jane Berryhill	D	Non
303	2	Foshee, Simon Lee	19	M	1/8	S	L. A. Foshee	L	Non	No. 1	L	Cr
304	3	Foshee, Sarah	14	F	1/8	D	L. A. Foshee	L	Non	No. 1	L	Cr
305	4	Foshee, Walter A.	12	M	1/8	S	L. A. Foshee	L	Non	No. 1	L	Cr
306	5	Foshee, AndrewJackson	7	M	1/8	S	L. A. Foshee	L	Non	No. 1	L	Cr
		No. 3 died August 9, 1899										
		Census Card No. 83, P. O. Morris, Enrolled April 3, 1899										
307	1	Berryhill, Susannah C.	17	F	1/8		L. A. Foshee	L	Non	May A. Foshee	L	Cr
308	2	Berryhill, Isabenda	16mo	F	1-16	D	P. D. Berryhill	L	Non	No. 1	L	Cr
		No. 1 died September 7, 1899										
		Census Card No. 84, P. O. Checotah, Enrolled April 3, 1899										
309	1	Foshee, William R.	21	M	1/8		L. A. Foshee	L	Non	Mary A. Foshee	L	Cr

Census Card No. 85, P. O. Fame, Enrolled April 4, 1899; No. 3 March 22, 1901

Roll No.	No.	NAME	Age	Sex	Blood	Rel.	NAME OF FATHER	Liv.	Cit.	NAME OF MOTHER	Liv.	Cit.
310	1	Laslie, John	75	M	F		Joe Laslie	D	Cr	Mollie Laslie	D	Cr
311	2	Laslie, Fannie	30	F	F	Wf	Peester	?	Cr	Makithle	?	Cr
312	3	Laslie, Ella	14	F	F	St.D	John Patarkey	D	Cr	No. 2	L	Cr

Census Card No. 86, P. O. Hitchita, Enrolled April 3, 1899; No. 6 June 21, 1900

Roll No.	No.	NAME	Age	Sex	Blood	Rel.	NAME OF FATHER	Liv.	Cit.	NAME OF MOTHER	Liv.	Cit.
313	1	Morton, Mattie	23	F	1/8		L. A. Foshee	L	Non	Mary A. Foshee	L	Cr
314	2	Morton, William Arthur	6	M	1-16	S	Joseph Morton	L	Non	No. 1	L	Cr
315	3	Morton, Benjamin H.	5	M	1-16	S	Joseph Morton	L	Non	No. 1	L	Cr
316	4	Morton, Joseph L.	3	M	1-16	S	Joseph Morton	L	Non	No. 1	L	Cr
317	5	Morton, Minnie May	1	F	1-16	D	Joseph Morton	L	Non	No. 1	L	Cr
318	6	Morton, Austin A.	3mo	M	1-16	S	Joseph Morton	L	Non	No. 1	L	Cr

Census Card No. 87, P. O. Onapa, Enrolled April 4, 1899

Roll No.	No.	NAME	Age	Sex	Blood	Rel.	NAME OF FATHER	Liv.	Cit.	NAME OF MOTHER	Liv.	Cit.
319	1	July, Louisa	46	F	F		John Laslie	D	Cr	Hojabda	D	Cr
320	2	July, Turner	12	M	F	S	Sam July	D	Cr	No. 1	L	Cr

Census Card No. 88, P. O. Okmulgee, April 4, 1899; No. 4 Sapulpa Enrolled April 4, 1899

No. 4 Sapulpa

Roll No.	No.	NAME	Age	Sex	Blood	Rel.	NAME OF FATHER	Liv.	Cit.	NAME OF MOTHER	Liv.	Cit.
321	1	Gray, Amy	55	F	F		Unknown	?	Cr	Liza	D	Cr
322	2	Gray, Louina	15	F	F	D	Isperney Harjo	D	Cr	No. 1	L	Cr
333	3	Gray, Sandy	14	M	F	S	Isperney Harjo	D	Cr	No. 1	L	Cr
324	4	Barnett, Wesley	9	M	F	Ward	Wesley Barnett	D	Cr	Annie Barnett	D	Cr

No. 1 died January 7, 1909 No. 2 died July 16, 1905 No. 3 reported dead

Census Card No. 89, P. O. Coweta, Enrolled April 4, 1899; No. 6 April 15, 1899

Roll No.	No.	NAME	Age	Sex	Blood	Rel.	NAME OF FATHER	Liv.	Cit.	NAME OF MOTHER	Liv.	Cit.
325	1	Chissoe, Austin	32	M	F		Oldman Choisse	D	Cr	Folothokkoche	L	Cr
326	2	Chissoe, Elnora	32	F	1/2	Wf	John Cruel	D	?	Sally Cruel	D	?
327	3	Chissoe, Sally	9	F	3/4	D	No. 1	L	Cr	No. 2	L	Cr
328	4	Chissoe, Taylor	5	M	3/4	S	No. 1	L	Cr	No. 2	L	Cr
329	5	Fulsom, William	12	M	1/4	St.S	Rufus Folsom	L	Non	No. 2	L	Cr
330	6	Chissoe, Dora	2mo	F	3/4	D	No. 1	L	Cr	No. 2	L	Cr

No. 2 died March 20, 1901

Census Card No. 90, P. O. Council Hill, Enrolled April 4, 1899

Roll No.	No.	NAME	Age	Sex	Blood	Rel.	NAME OF FATHER	Liv.	Cit.	NAME OF MOTHER	Liv.	Cit.
331	1	Kernells, Temiye	70	M	F		Narbuckay Harjo	D	Cr	Winey	D	Cr
332	2	Kernells, Sissie	25	F	F	Wf	Mistabale McGilbra	L	Cr	Unknown	?	Cr
333	3	Kernells, Nettie	5	F	F	D	No. 1	L	Cr	No. 2	L	Cr
334	4	Kernells, Amanda	3	F	F	D	No. 1	L	Cr	No. 2	L	Cr
335	5	Kernells, Annie	1	F	F	D	No. 1	L	Cr	No. 2	L	Cr

No. 1 died September 7, 1908. No. 4 died June 9, 1910

Census Card No. 91, P. O. Tulsa, Enrolled April 4, 1899

Roll No.	No.	NAME	Age	Sex	Blood	Rel.	NAME OF FATHER	Liv.	Cit.	NAME OF MOTHER	Liv.	Cit.
336	1	Chissoe, Taylor	43	M	F		Oldman Chissoe	D	Cr	Folothokkoche		Cr
337	2	Chissoe, William	19	M	F	S	No. 1	L	Cr	Annie B. Chissoe		Cr
338	3	Chissoe, Sadie	17	F	F	D	No. 1	L	Cr	Annie B. Chissoe		Cr
339	4	Chissoe, Newton B.	12	M	F	S	No. 1	L	Cr	Annie B. Chissoe	D	Cr
340	5	Chissoe, Hazel	10	F	F	D	No. 1	L	Cr	Annie B. Chissoe		Cr

No. 1 reported dead

Census Card No. 92, P. O. Okmulgee, Enrolled April 4, 1899

Roll No.	No.	NAME	Age	Sex	Blood	Rel.	NAME OF FATHER	Liv.	Cit.	NAME OF MOTHER	Liv.	Cit.
341	1	Wisner, Annie D.	23	F	1/4		Douglas Wisner	D	?	Sallie Foster	L	?
342	2	Allen, Lular	8	F	1/8	D	Jesse Allen	L	Cr	No. 1	L	Cr

Census Card No. 93, P. O. Coweta, Enrolled April 4, 1899; No. 4 March 31, 1900

Roll No.	No.	NAME	Age	Sex	Blood	Rel.	NAME OF FATHER	Liv.	Cit.	NAME OF MOTHER	Liv.	Cit.
343	1	Haynie, Andy	45	M	F		Haynie	D	Cr	Mofah Haynie	D	Cr
344	2	Haynie, March	16	M	F	S	No. 1	L	Cr	Mariah Haynie	D	Cr
345	3	Haynie, Edward	2	M	1/2	S	No. 1	L	Cr	Fannie Haynie	L	Non
346	4	Haynie, Minnie May	1mo	F	1/2	D	No. 1	L	Cr	Fannie Haynie	L	Non

No. 1 died March 23, 1901
No. 3 died September 24, 1900

Census Card No. 94, P. O. Okmulgee, Enrolled April 4, 1899; Nos. 4, 5, 6, May 23, 1899

Roll No.	No.	NAME	Age	Sex	Blood	Rel.	NAME OF FATHER	Liv.	Cit.	NAME OF MOTHER	Liv.	Cit.
347	1	Alexander, Lity	48	M	F		Alexander	D	Cr	Shoktas Hoge	D	Cr
348	2	Alexander, Mary	37	F	F	Wf	Joastare Harjo	D	Cr	Unknown	D	Cr
349	3	Simmer, Sammy	12	M	F	Ward	Simmer	D	Cr	Loucinda	D	Cr
350	4	Gambler, Miley	14	F	F	Cou	Billie Gambler	D	Cr	Rhoda Gambler	D	Cr
351	5	Gambler, Tommie	12	M	F	Cou	Billie Gambler	D	Cr	Rhoda Gambler	D	Cr
352	6	Gambler, Lizzie	10	F	F	Cou	Billie Gambler	D	Cr	Rhoda Gambler	D	Cr

No. 4 died January 15, 1900, No. 5 died October 9, 1899

Census Card No. 95, P. O. Okmulgee, Enrolled April 4, 1899; No. 3 October 5, 1899

Roll No.	No.	NAME	Age	Sex	Blood	Rel.	NAME OF FATHER	Liv.	Cit.	NAME OF MOTHER	Liv.	Cit.
353	1	Daniel, Unah	27	M	F		Daniel Johnson	L	Cr	Nicey Scott	L	Cr
354	2	Daniel, Mary	27	F	F	Wf	John Randall	L	Cr	Loska Randall	L	Cr
355	3	Daniel, John	1	M	F	S	No. 1	L	Cr	No. 2	L	Cr

No. 1 died July 28, 1909

Census Card No. 96, P. O. Okmulgee; Enrolled April 4, 1899

Roll No.	No.	NAME	Age	Sex	Blood	Rel.	NAME OF FATHER	Liv.	Cit.	NAME OF MOTHER	Liv.	Cit.
356	1	Tarpeliche	50	M	F		Unknown	?	Cr	Unknown	?	Cr

No. 1 (Blind) lives with Lity and Mary Alexander, see Creek Census Card No. 94
No. 1 reported dead

Census Card No. 97, P. O. Okmulgee; Enrolled April 4, 1899, No. 9, Oct. 7, 1899; No. 10, Dec. 7, 1900

Roll No.	No.	NAME	Age	Sex	Blood	Rel.	NAME OF FATHER	Liv.	Cit.	NAME OF MOTHER	Liv.	Cit.
357	1	Alexander, Arty	46	M	F		Alexander	D	Cr	Sarktersboke	D	Cr
358	2	Alexander, Nancy	36	F	F	Wf	Unknown	?	Cr	Unknown	?	Cr
359	3	Alexander, Miley	17	F	F	D	No. 1	L	Cr	No. 2	L	Cr
360	4	Alexander, Reuben	15	M	F	S	No. 1	L	Cr	No. 2	L	Cr
361	5	Alexander, Tecumseh	13	M	F	S	No. 1	L	Cr	No. 2	L	Cr
362	6	Alexander, Liza	7	F	F	D	No. 1	L	Cr	No. 2	L	Cr
363	7	Alexander, Alex	5	M	F	S	No. 1	L	Cr	No. 2	L	Cr
364	8	Alexander, Sealy	3	F	F	D	No. 1	L	Cr	No. 2	L	Cr
365	9	Alexander, George	1	M	F	S	No. 1	L	Cr	No. 2	L	Cr
366	10	Daniel, Annie	10mo	F	F	GrD	Unah Daniel	L	Cr	No. 3	L	Cr

No. 2 died February 28, 1903; Nos. 1, 5 and 9 reported dead; No. 4 died January 17, 1902

Roll No.	No.	NAME	Age	Sex	Blood	Rel.	NAME OF FATHER	Liv.	Cit.	NAME OF MOTHER	Liv.	Cit.

Census Card No. 98, P. O. Okmulgee, Enrolled April 4, 1899

Roll No.	No.	NAME	Age	Sex	Blood	Rel.	NAME OF FATHER	Liv.	Cit.	NAME OF MOTHER	Liv.	Cit.
367	1	King, William	23	M	F		Willie King	D	Cr	Leah Wiley	D	Cr

Census Card No. 99, P. O. Muskogee, Enrolled April 4, 1899

| 368 | 1 | Nero, Mose | 25 | M | F | | Mose Nero | L | Cr | Leah Wiley | D | Cr |

No. 1 died July 30, 1913

Census Card No. 100, P. O. Okmulgee, Enrolled April 4, 1899

| 369 | 1 | Alexander, Roly | 22 | M | F | | Arty Alexander | L | Cr | Nancy Alexander | L | Cr |
| 370 | 2 | Alexander, Tisey | 19 | F | F | Wf | Daniel | D | Cr | Minnechar | L | Cr |

Census Card No. 101, P. O. Okmulgee, Enrolled April 4, 1899

| 371 | 1 | Sneed, Artra | 34 | M | 3-8 | | Charley Sneed | D | ? | Martha Smith | L | ? |

Census Card No. 102, P. O. Oktaha, Enrolled April 4, 1899

| 372 | 1 | Jones, Charlie | 35 | M | F | | Unknown | D | Cr | Mollie | D | Cr |

Census Card No. 103, P. O. Sapulpa, Enrolled April 4, 1899; Nos. 3 and 4, March 4, 1901; No. 5, May 17, 1901

373	1	Partridge, Lucinda	18	F	F		Gibson Partridge	D	Cr	Bessie Partridge	D	Cr
374	2	Bruner, Mamie	1½	F	F	D	Mcculla Bruner	L	Cr	No. 1	L	Cr
375	3	Bruner, Megually	20	M	F	Hus	Eli Bruner	L	Cr	Salina Bruner	D	Cr
376	4	Bruner, Willie	10mo	M	F	S	No. 3	L	Cr	No. 1	L	Cr
377	5	Monnie	65	F	F	Aunt	Unknown	?	Cr	Unknown	D	Cr

No. 5 died September 18, 1899

Census Card No. No. 104, P. O. Wenoka, Enrolled April 4, 1899

| 378 | 1 | Johnson, Colbert | 45 | M | F | | Johnson | D | Cr | Youbocklothoga | D | Cr |

Census Card No. 105, P. O. Summit; No. 3 Dustin, Enrolled April 5, 1899

379	1	Jackson, Chowa	46	M	F		Artus Hopiyee	D	Cr	Conahigee	D	Cr
388	2	Jackson, Susie	24	F	F	Wf	Panoska	D	Cr	Allie Panoska	D	Cr
381	3	Jackson, Susanna	13	F	F	Niece	Chastieskey	D	Cr	Chaluggee	D	Cr
382	4	Simmons, Charley	14	M	F	Bro-L	Simmons	D	Cr	Allie Panoska	D	Cr

No. 1 died February 14, 1901

Census Card No. 106, P. O. Muskogee, Enrolled April 5, 1899

313	1	Washington, Rhoda	40	F	F		Panoska	D	Cr	Allie Panoska	D	Cr
384	2	Washington, Winey	15	F	F	D	Fikhuna	D	Cr	No. 1	L	Cr
385	3	Washington, Casinie	14	M	F	S	Fikhuna	D	Cr	No. 1	L	Cr
386	4	Washington, Peter	10	M	M	S	Fikhuna	D	Cr	No. 1	L	Cr
387	5	Washington, George	8	M	F	S	Peter Washington	L	Cr	No. 1	L	Cr
388	6	Washington, Austin	4	M	F	S	Peter Washington	L	Cr	No. 1	L	Cr
389	7	Washington, Wesley	3	M	F	S	Peter Washington	L	Cr	No. 1	L	Cr
390	8	Washington, Peter	25	M	F	Hus	Unknown	?	Cr	Unknown	?	Cr

No. 1 died September 29, 1901; No. 4 died September 1, 1899

Census Card No. 107, P. O. Wagoner, Enrolled April 6, 1899; No. 12 May 14, 1901

| 391 | 1 | Bowers, Fred | 31 | M | ¼ | | Lewis Bowers | D | ? | Rebecca Bowers | D | ? |
| 392 | 2 | Bowers, Harold | 5 | M | ¼ | S | No. 1 | L | Cr | Ida Bowers | | Cher |

No. 1 reported dead

Census Card No. 108, P. O. No. 1, Morris; No. 2, 4, 5, Fame; No. 3, Oktaha, Enrolled April 5, 1899; No. 6, December 11, 1899

393	1	Fife, Elijah L.	40	M	F		Ben Fife	D	Cr	Iyokhogee	D	Cr
394	2	Fife, Millie	29	F	F	Wf	Sartelo Micco	D	Cr	Losochee	?	Cr
395	3	Fife, Nancy	6	F	F	D	No. 1	L	Cr	No. 2	L	Cr
396	4	Fife, Nellie	5	F	F	D	No. 1	L	Cr	No. 2	L	Cr
397	5	Fife, Lena	2	F	F	D	No. 1	L	Cr	No. 2	L	Cr
398	6	Fife, Sillar	3mo	F	F	D	No. 1	L	Cr	No. 2	L	Cr

No. 6 died October 28, 1901

Census Card No. 109, Eufaula, Enrolled April 5, 1899; No. 6, June 13, 1900

399	1	Francis, Wm.	26	M	F		John Francis	L	Cr	Millie Francis	L	Cr
400	2	Francis, Minkey	24	F	F	Wf	Tussekiah Hutke	L	Cr	Silla	L	Cr
401	3	Francis, Thomas	6	M	F	S	No. 1	L	Cr	No. 2	L	Cr
402	4	Francis, Lena	4	F	F	D	No. 1	L	Cr	No. 2	L	Cr
403	5	Francis, Leah	1	F	F	D	No. 1	L	Cr	No. 2	L	Cr
404	6	Francis, Minnie	1	F	F	D	No. 1	L	Cr	No. 2	L	Cr

No. 2 died February 1, 1907

Census Card No. 110, P. O. Muskogee; No. 2, Sapulpa, Enrolled April 5, 1899; No. 4, July 26, 1900

405	1	McKellop, Albert P.	40	M	½		James M. McKellop	D	?	Annie McKellop	D	Cr
406	2	McKellop, Annie	7	F	¼	Niece	J. M. McKellop	L	?	Alena McKellop	D	Cr
407	3	McKellop, Barney	5	M	¼	Neph	J. M. McKellop	L	?	Alena McKellop	D	Cr
408	4	McKellop, Arthur A.	15	M	¼	S	No. 1	L	Cr	Florence White	?	Cher

No. 2 died December 2, 1905; No. 1 dead

Census Card No. 111, P. O. Sapulpa, Enrolled April 5, 1899

| 409 | 1 | Marshall, Rufus | 24 | M | F | | Wor Marshall | D | Cr | Winey Marshall | D | Cr |

Census Card No. 112, P. O. Wagoner, Enrolled April 5, 1899

| 410 | 1 | Hunter, Ellis | 21 | M | F | | Wilson | D | Cr | Rachel Marshall | ? | Cr |

Census Card No. 113, P. O. Tulsa, Enrolled April 5, 1899

| 411 | 1 | Lindsey, Lila D. | 39 | F | ¼ | | John Denton | D | ? | Susan Denton | D | ? |

Census Card No. 114, P. O. Porter, Enrolled April 5, 1899

412	1	Smith, Mose	31	M	F		Chokussahola	D	Cr	Sindy Sizemore	D	Cr
413	2	Smith, Lizzie	41	F	F	Wf	Jacob	D	Cr	Kochaky	D	Cr
414	3	Smith, Sallie	2	F	F	D	No. 1	L	Cr	No. 2	L	Cr
415	4	Marshall, Lewis	19	M	¾	St.S	Mitchell Marshall	D	Cr	No. 2	L	Cr
416	5	Marshall, Elsie	15	F	¾	St.D	Mitchell Marshall	D	Cr	No. 2	L	Cr
417	6	Porter, Lewis	17	M	¾	Neph	John Porter	D	Cr	Rose Jones	D	Cr

No. 2 died July 25, 1913; No. 6 died November 15, 1909

Roll No.	No.	NAME	Age	Sex	Blood	Rel.	NAME OF FATHER	Liv.	Cit.	NAME FO MOTHER	Liv.	Cit.
	Census Card No. 115, Broken Arrow, Enrolled April 5, 1889											
418	1	McIntosh, Jno.	75	M	F		Rolen McIntosh	D	Cr	Muskogee McIntosh	D	Cr
419	2	McIntosh, Susan	65	F	F	Wf	John Davis	D	Cr	Mariah Davis	D	Cr
420	3	Sunday, Edmund	14	M	F	GGS	Ellis B. Sunday	D	Cr	Miley Sunday	D	Cr
421	4	Brown, Samuel	13	M	F	Ward	John Brown	D	Cr	Lizzie Brown	D	Cr
		Nos. 1, 2, 4 reported dead: Nos. 3 died February 28, 1906										
	Census Card No. 116, P. O. Broken Arrow, Enrolled April 5, 1899											
422	1	McIntosh, Annetta	44	F	F		John McIntosh	L	Cr	Susan McIntosh	L	Cr
423	2	McIntosh, Etta	7	F	F	D	Dawson	D	Cr	No. 1	L	Cr
		No. 1 reported dead										
	Census Card No. 117, P. O. Okmulgee, Enrolled April 5, 1899											
424	1	Sugar, Wesley	44	M	F		Tom Sugar	D	Cr	Nancy Sugar	D	Cr
425	2	Sugar, Togy	40	F	F	Wf	Chitto Carnie	D	Cr	Unknown	D	Cr
426	3	Sugar, Armster	12	M	F	S	No. 1	L	Cr	Adeline Sugar	D	Cr
		No. 2 died September 17, 1899; No. 1 reported dead										
	Census Card No. 118, P. O. Eufaula, Enrolled April 5, 1899											
427	1	Loney, Major	50	M	F		Loney	D	Cr	Mollie Timmunchee	D	Cr
428	2	Loney, Lucy	40	F	F	Wf	Dick Thlocco	L	Cr	Mele	?	Cr
429	3	Turk, George	16	M	F	St.S	Frank Turk	L	Cr	No. 2	L	Cr
430	4	Turk, Nepsey	11	F	F	St.D	Frank Turk	L	Cr	No. 2	L	Cr
		No. 1 died May 3, 1907										
	Census Card No. 119, P. O. Checotah, Enrolled April 5, 1899											
431	1	Aultman, Benjamin	23	M	⅛		Henry Aultman	D	?	Melvina Aultman	D	?
	Census Card No. 120, P. O. Hitchita, Enrolled April 5, 1899											
432	1	Freeman, Jno	53	M	½		Rueben Freeman	D	?	Lucy Freeman	L	?
433	2	Freeman, Louis	19	M	¾	S	No. 1	L	Cr	Liza Freeman	D	?
434	3	Freeman, William	18	M	¾	S	No. 1	L	Cr	Liza Freeman	D	?
435	4	Freeman, John, Jr.	16	M	¾	S	No. 1	L	Cr	Liza Freeman	D	?
		No 2 died March 25, 1902										
		No 3 reported dead										
	Census Card No. 121, P. O. Coweta, Enrolled April 5, 1899											
436	1	Sarty, Ned	22	M	F		Googan Sarty	L	Cr	Susan Sarty	L	Cr
	Census Card No. 122, P. O. Porter; No. 6, Wagoner. Enrolled April 5, 1899											
437	1	Marshall, Thomas	45	M	F		Tom Tulmarsey	D	Cr	Unknown	D	Cr
438	2	Marshall, Rachel	39	F	F	Wf	Chissoe	L	Cr	Folothoka	D	Cr
439	3	Marshall, James	18	M	F	S	No. 1	L	Cr	No. 2	L	Cr
440	4	Marshall, Waitie	13	M	F	S	No. 1	L	Cr	No. 2	L	Cr
441	5	Marshall. Mattie	11	F	F	D	No. 1	L	Cr	No. 2	L	Cr
442	6	Marshall, Ida	9	F	F	D	No. 1	L	Cr	No. 2	L	Cr
		No. 1 died November 5, 1905										
	Census Card No. 123, Eufaula, Enrolled April 6, 1899; No. 6, May 22, 1901											
443	1	Francis, Mitchell	27	M	F		John Francis	L	Cr	Mary Francis	L	Cr
444	2	Francis, Manerva	25	F	F	Wf	Daniel McGillwary	D	Cr	Lizzie McGillwary	L	Cr
445	3	Francis, Mary	2	F	F	D	No. 1	L	Cr	No. 2	L	Cr
446	4	Francis, Lizzie	1	F	F	D	No. 1	L	Cr	No. 2	L	Cr
447	5	Francis,. Hattie	4	F	F	D	No. 1	L	Cr	No. 2	L	Cr
448	6	Francis, Garfield	1	M	F	S	No. 1	L	Cr	No. 2	L	Cr
	Census Card No. 124, P. O. Wagoner, Enrolled April 6, 1899											
449	1	Chissoe, Sam	23	M	⅞		Taylor Chissoe	L	Cr	Annie McIntosh	D	Cr
450	2	Chissoe, Lena E.	18	F	⅞	Wf	W. F. McIntosh	L	Cr	Martha McIntosh	D	Cr
451	3	Chissoe, William	6mo	M	⅞	S	No. 1	L	Cr	No. 2	L	Cr
	Census Card No. 125, P. O. Tullahassee, Enrolled April 6, 1899											
452	1	Francis, Jeff	37	M	¾		John Francis	L	Cr	Louisa Francis	D	?
453	2	Francis, Mack	10	M	½	Cou	William Francis	L	Cr	Silla Francis	D	?
		No. 2 reported dead										
	Census Card No. 126, P. O. Inola, Enrolled April 6, 1899											
454	1	Gregory, James R.	57	M	¼		Edward W. Gregory	D	?	Eliza Gregory	D	?
455	2	Gregory, Annie	54	F	F	Wf	John Ayechiche	D	Cr	Besey	D	Cr
456	3	Gregory, Gilbert R.	26	M	⅝	S	No. 1	L	Cr	No. 2	L	Cr
457	4	Gregory, Albert	24	M	⅝	S	No. 1	L	Cr	No. 2	L	Cr
458	5	Gregory, Archie A.	20	M	⅝	S	No. 1	L	Cr	No. 2	L	Cr
459	6	Gregory, Arthur	14	M	⅝	S	No. 1	L	Cr	No. 2	L	Cr
		No. 1 died September 5, 1912										
		No. 4 died January 13, 1909										
	Census Card No. 127, P. O. Muskogee, Enrolled April 7, 1899											
460	1	Francis, Wm.	47	M	½		Mack Francis	D	?	Annie Francis	D	?
	Census Card No. 128, P. O. Okmulgee, Enrolled April 7, 1899											
461	1	Hardridge, Goldie	20	F	⅛		Josiah Terrell	D	?	Mary E. Terrell	L	?
462	2	Hardridge, Joe	3	M	½		Taylor Hardridge	L	Cr	No. 1	L	Cr
	Census Card No. 129, P. O. Muskogee, Enrolled April 7, 1899											
463	1	Terrell, Mary E.	58	F	¼		Henry Morris	D	?	Peggie Morris	D	?
464	2	Terrell, Henry	18	M	⅛	S	Josiah Terrell	D	?	No. 1	L	?
	Census Card No. 130, P. O. Coweta, Enrolled April 7, 1899											
465	1	Lynch, Joe	60	M	F		Unknown	D	Cr	Little Mary	D	Cr
466	2	Lynch, Yanah	48	F	F	Wf	Woxie Harjo	D	Cr	Mafolika	D	Cr
467	3	Lynch, Isparhecher	4	M	F	S	No. 1	L	Cr	No. 2	L	Cr
468	4	Reddy, Kizziah	14	F	F	St.D	Mededahka Reddy	?	Cr	No. 2	L	Cr
469	5	Reddy, Maggie	10	F	F	St.D	Mededahka Reddy	?	Cr	No. 2	L	Cr
		No. 5 died July 4, 1909										

		Census Card No. 131, P. O. Preston, Enrolled April 8, 1899										
470	1	Stake, Lizzie	60	F	F		Lockta Harjo	D	Cr	Polly Harjo	D	Cr
471	2	Stake, Joseph	19	M	F	S	David Stake	D	Cr	No. 1	L	Cr
472	3	Stake, Salina	16	F	F	D	David Stake	D	Cr	No. 1	L	Cr
473	4	Stake, James	14	M	F	S	David Stake	D	Cr	No. 1	L	Cr
		No. 3 died November 10, 1910										
		Census Card No. 132, P. O. Edna, Enrolled April 8, 1899; No. 6, May 22, 1901										
474	1	Foster, Sandy	45	M	F		Sakowah	D	Cr	Unknown	?	Cr
475	2	Foster, Millie	21	F	F	D	No. 1	L	Cr	Unknown	?	Cr
476	3	Foster, Gabriel	20	M	F	S	No. 1	L	Cr	Jennie Stick	L	Cr
477	4	Foster, Noah	12	M	F	S	No. 1	L	Cr	Jennie Stick	L	Cr
478	5	Foster, Moses	10	M	F	S	No. 1	L	Cr	Jennie Stoick	L	Cr
479	6	Miller, Robert	2	M	F	Gr.S	Johnson Miller	L	Cr	No. 2	L	Cr
		No. 1 died August, 1907										
		No. 3 died February, 1907										
		No. 5 died August 4, 1909										
		No. 6 died 1899										
		No. 4 reported dead										
		Census Card No. 133, P. O. Checotah, Enrolled April 8, 1899; No. 6, April 26, 1900										
480	1	Sevier, Vicey	38	F	F		Sam McNac	D	Cr	Unknown	?	Cr
481	2	Sevier, Kizzie	16	F	½	D	William Sevier	D	?	Ellen McNac	L	?
482	3	Sevier, Lena	12	F	½	D	William Sevier	D	?	No. 1	L	Cr
483	4	Sevier, Emma	8	F	½	D	William Sevier	D	?	No. 1	L	Cr
484	5	Sevier, Fannie	2	F	½	D	William Sevier	D	?	No. 1	L	Cr
485	6	Sevier, Joseph	4mo	M	½	S	Lewis Sevier	L	Non	No. 1	L	Cr
		No. 4 reported dead										
		Census Card No. 134, P. O. Boynton, Enrolled April 8, 1899; No. 3, May 25, 1900										
486	1	Weaver, Emma	22	F	½		Paul Weaver	D	Cr	Mollie Weaver	L	Cr
487	2	Walker, Mary	1	F	¾	D	Eddie Walker	L	Cr	No. 1	L	Cr
488	3	McNac, Julia	4mo	F	¼	D	Robinson McNac	L	Cr	No. 1	L	Cr
		No. 3 died March 31, 1904										
		Census Card No. 135, P. O. Boynton, Enrolled April 8, 1899										
489	1	Weaver, Mary	37	F	F		Hokussey	D	Cr	Nellie Hope	D	Cr
490	2	Weaver, Edward	17	M	½	S	Paul Weaver	D	Non	No. 1	L	Cr
491	3	Weaver, Georgia	6	F	½	D	Paul Weaver	D	Non	No. 1	L	Cr
492	4	Hawkins, Samuel	2mo	M	F	S	Daniel Hawkins	L	Cr	No. 1	L	Cr
		Nos. 2 and 3 died January, 1901										
		No. 4 died January 12, 1901										
		Census Card No. 136, P. O. Pierce, Enrolled April 8, 1899; No. 11, May 17, 1901, No. 12, Oct. 22,1901										
493	1	Greenleaf, Sarah	45	F	F		Company	D	Cr	Nellie Hope	D	Cr
494	2	Greenleaf, Annie	18	F	F	D	Peter Greenleaf	D	Cr	No. 1	L	Cr
495	3	Greenleaf, Ida	15	F	F	D	Peter Greenleaf	D	Cr	No. 1	L	Cr
496	4	Greenleaf, Malissa	13	F	F	D	Peter Greenleaf	D	Cr	No. 1	L	Cr
497	5	Greenleaf, Taylor	10	M	F	S	Peter Greenleaf	D	Cr	No. 1	L	Cr
498	6	Greenleaf, Nellie	8	F	F	D	Peter Greenleaf	D	Cr	No. 1	L	Cr
499	7	King Nancy	17	F	F	Niece	King	L	Cr	Fannie King	L	Cr
500	8	King, Ludie	16	F	F	Niece	King	L	Cr	Fannie King	L	Cr
501	9	King, Hully	12	M	F	Neph	King	L	Cr	Fannie King	L	Cr
502	10	King, Albert	11	M	F	Neph	King	L	Cr	Fannie King	L	Cr
503	11	McNac, Robert	1	M	½	GrS	Fred McNac	L	Cr	No. 2	L	Cr
504	12	Miller, Katie	2	F	½	GrN	Okosko Miller	L	Cr	No. 8	L	Cr
		No. 11 died September 24, 1900										
		No. 12 reported dead										
		Census Card No. 137, P. O. Beggs, Enrolled April 10, 1899										
505	1	Adams, Dicey	42	F	⅝		Jacob Isaac	D	Cr	Tenabe	?	Cr
506	2	Adams, Israel	10	M	5-16	S	Isaac Adams	L	Non	No. 1	L	Cr
507	3	Adams, Delia	8	F	5-16	D	Isaac Adams	L	Non	No. 1	L	Cr
508	4	Adams, Henry	6	M	5-16	S	Isaac Adams	L	Non	No. 1	L	Cr
509	5	Gooden, Toney	17	M	½	Ward	Daniel Gooden	L	Cr	Unknown	D	?
		No. 2 died November 5, 1910										
		No. 3 died November 25, 1909										
		Census Card No. 138, P. O. Salem, Enrolled No. 1, April 10, 1899; No. 2, March 27, 1901										
510	1	Johnson, Fred	32	M	¼		Chas. Johnson	D	?	Dorcas Johnson	D	?
511	2	Johnson, Wisey	28	F	¾	Wf	Henry Hope	L	Cr	Mollie Hope	L	Cr
		Census Card No. 139, P. O. Beggs, Enrolled No. 1, April 10, 1899; No. 2, January 12, 1901										
512	1	Adams, Richard	22	M	½		Thomas Adams	L	Cr	Wabale Adams	L	Cr
513	2	Adams, Garfield	6mo	M	¼	S	No. 1	L	Cr	Falby Adams	?	Non
		No. 1 reported dead										
		Census Card No. 140, P. O. Checotah, Enrolled April 11, 1899										
514	1	West Polly	36	F	½		John Lowe	D	?	Abbie Lowe	L	Cr
515	2	Chapman, Mary Lu	17	F	¼	D	Frank Chapman	D	Non	No. 1	L	Cr
516	3	McIntosh, Jennette	7	F	½	Niece	John McIntosh	L	Cr	Salina McIntosh	D	Cr
		Census Card No. 141, P. O. Brush Hill, Enrolled April 11, 1899										
517	1	Lowe, Abbie	75	F	F		George Goodin	D	Cr	Lizzie Goodin	D	Cr
		No. 1 died May 1, 1913										
		Census Card No. 142, P. O. Morse, Enrolled April 11, 1899										
518	1	Knight, Thomas	48	M	F		Nardowake	D	Cr	Maggie	D	Cr
519	2	Knight, Robert	7	M	F	S	No. 1	L	Cr	Mary Knight	D	Cr
520	3	Knight, Mary	39	F	F	Wf	Isparnee Hopiye	D	Cr	Neehah	D	Cr
		No. 1 died April 6, 1901										
		No. 3 died December 24, 1899										

Roll No.	No.	NAME	Age	Sex	Blood	Rel.	NAME OF FATHER	Liv.	Cit.	NAME OF MOTHER	Liv.	Cit.
		Census Card No. 143, P. O. Checotah, Enrolled April 11, 1899; No. 3, March 7, 1900										
521	1	Howard, Abbie Lee	19	F	¼		Frank Chapman	D	Non	Polly West	L	Cr
522	2	Howard, Benjamin F.	4mo	M	⅛	S	George Howard	L	Non	No. 1	L	Cr
523	3	Howard, Polly Lue	1mo	F	⅛	D	George Howard	L	Non	No. 1	L	Cr
		Census Card No. 144, P. O. Okfuskee, Enrolled April 11, 1899										
524	1	Yahola, Billey	28	M	F		Yaholar Chupco	D	Cr	Artochee	D	Cr
525	2	Yahola, Winey	26	F	F	Wf	George Hicks	L	Cr	Elsie Hicks	L	Cr
526	3	Yahola, Katie	7	F	F	D	No. 1	L	Cr	No. 2	L	Cr
527	4	Yahola, Addie	5	F	F	D	No. 1	L	Cr	No. 2	L	Cr
528	5	Yahola, Molllie	2	F	F	D	No. 1	L	Cr	No. 2	L	Cr
529	6	Yahola, Sadie	4mo	F	F	D	No. 1	L	Cr	No. 2	L	Cr
530	7	Yahola, Mary	17	F	F	Sis	Yaholar Chupco	D	Cr	Sarchekilley	D	Cr
531	8	Yahola, Loper	13	M	F	Bro	Yaholar Chupco	D	Cr	Sarchekilley	D	Cr
		No. 7 died June 27, 1902										
		No. 4 died 1910										
		No. 5 died 1900										
		Census Card No. 145, P. O. Morse, Enrolled April 11, 1899; No. 5, June 19, 1900; No. 6, May 17, 1901										
532	1	Knight, Ramsey	2o	M	F		Thomas Knight	L	Cr	Mary Knight	L	Cr
533	2	Knight, Amy	21	F	F	Wf	Pahos Emarthloge	D	Cr	Upsey	?	Cr
534	3	Johnson, Noah	5	M	F	SS	Moses Johnson	L	Cr	No. 2	L	Cr
535	4	Johnson, Peter	3	M	F	SS	Moses Johnson	L	Cr	No. 2	L	Cr
536	5	Knight, Jacob	1mo	M	F	S	No. 1	L	Cr	No. 2	L	Cr
537	6	Knight, James	1	M	F	S	No. 1	L	Cr	No. 2	L	Cr
		No. 5 died October 12, 1900										
		No. 6 died October 27, 1899										
		No. 2 died 1904										
		Census Card No. 146, P. O. Okfuskee, Enrolled April 11, 1899										
538	1	Knight, London	25	M	F		Thomas Knight	L	Cr	Mary Knight	L	Cr
539	2	Knight, Susan	26	F	F	Wf	Ogeeleesawa	D	Cr	Sosolee	D	Cr
540	3	Knight, Walter	3	M	F	S	No. 1	L	Cr	No. 2	L	Cr
541	4	Knight, Lucy	7mo	F	F	D	No. 1	L	Cr	No. 2	L	Cr
		No. 1 died December 11, 1910										
		No. 4 died 1905 or 1906										
		Census Card No. 147, P. O. Morse, Enrolled April 11, 1899										
542	1	Key, Thomas	48	M	F		Unknown	?	Cr	Unknown	?	Cr
		No. 1 died December 9, 1899										
		Census Card No. 148, P. O. No. 6, Felt, Idaho; Okemah, Enrolled April 11, 1899										
543	1	Coon, Sam	42	M	F		Karpitchar Yarhola	D	Cr	Unknown	D	Cr
544	2	Coon, Munner	26	F	F	Wf	Katcher Fixico	D	Cr	Cheyanny	L	Cr
545	3	Coon, Narlie	3	F	F	D	No. 1	L	Cr	No. 2	L	Cr
546	4	Coon, Simer	1	F	F	D	No. 1	L	Cr	No. 2	L	Cr
547	5	Coon, Lizzie	16	F	F	D	No. 1	L	Cr	Senila	D	Cr
548	6	Coon, Taylor	9	M	F	S	No. 1	L	Cr	Senila	D	Cr
549	7	Coon, Wotka	3mo	M	F	S	No. 1	L	Cr	No. 2	L	Cr
		No. 5 died December 20, 1899										
		No. 4 died July 7, 1912										
		No. 7 died December 28, 1900										
		Census Card No. 149, P. O. Morse, Enrolled April 11, 1899; No. 4 December 22, 1899										
550	1	Fields, Ponsey	22	M	F		Wheeley	D	Cr	Annie	L	Cr
551	2	Fields, Cinda	20	F	F	Wf	Inechuppo Harjo	L	Cr	Polly	D	Cr
552	3	Fields, Lartie	8	M	F	Bro	Pahos Emarthla	D	Cr	Iny	D	Cr
553	4	Fields, Jno	10	mo	M	F	S	No. 1	L	Cr	No. 2	L	Cr
		No. 1 died December 21, 1900. No. 4 died June 20, 1900										
		Census Card No. 150, P. O. Morse, Enrolled April 11, 1899										
554	1	Hennehah, Eli	21	M	F		Hulothinea	D	Cr	Leah	D	Cr
555	2	Hennehah, Lucinda	20	F	F	Wf	Wesley Deer	L	Cr	Witochee	L	Cr
556	3	Stricken from roll										
557	4	Deere, Melanie	3	F	F	Niece	Wesley Deer	L	Cr	Pollie Deer	L	Cr
		Census Card No. 151, P. O. Morse, Enrolled April 11, 1899										
558	1	Fish, Jack	20	M	F		Thlotho Yahola	D	Cr	Hoktelarney	D	Cr
		No. 1 died Aug. 13, 1902										
		Cenuss Card No. 152, P. O. Morse, Enrolled April 11, 1899										
559	1	Beaver, Wilson	40	M	F		Nehei Yahola	D	Cr	Unknown	D	Cr
560	2	Beaver, Emma	9	F	F	D	No. 1	L	Cr	Keatkar	L	Cr
		Census Card No. 153, P. O. Okemah, Enrolled April 11, 1899										
561	1	Harvison, George D.	25	M	1-16		T. C. Harvison	L	?	Sarah Harvison	D	?
562	2	Harvison, Lula E.	23	F	1-16	Wf	George Foster	D	?	Weatherford	D	?
563	3	Harvison, Nellie May	1	F	1-16	D	No. 1	L	Cr	No. 2	L	Cr
		Census Card No. 154, P. O. Muskogee, Enrolled April 11, 1899										
564	1	Is-ka-wa-pee	55	F	F		Hupeeslcy	D	Cr	Tiktinichti	D	Cr
		No. 1 reported dead										
		Census Card No. 155, P. O. Braggs, Enrolled April 11, 1899										
565	1	Harris, Thomas	28	M	F		Cobarse, Marthear	D	Cr	Ewika	D	Cr
		Census Card No. 156, P. O. Checotah, Enrolled April 11, 1899										
566	1	Simmons, Martin	28	M	F		Martin Simmons	D	Cr	Nafey Simmons	D	Cr
		Census Card No. 157, P. O. Okfuskee, Enrolled April 11, 1899; No. 2 April 22, 1901										
567	1	Tiger, Annie	24	F	F		Willie Tiger	D	Cr	Elsie Sarty	L	Cr
568	2	Hencha, Lena	1	F	F	D	Jonas Heneha	L	Cr	No. 1	L	Cr
		Census Card No. 158, P. O. Checotah, Enrolled April 11, 1899										
569	1	Bray, Vicey	40	F	¾		Slafiche	D	Cr	Betsey Marshall	D	?
570	2	Bray, Mary	10	F	⅜	D	William Bray	L	Ncn	No. 1	L	Cr
571	3	Perryman, Ellen	17	F	¾	D	Wright Perryman	L	Cr	No. 1	L	Cr

21

Roll No.	No.	NAME	Age	Sex	Blood	Rel.	NAME OF FATHER	Liv.	Cit.	NAME OF MOTHER	Liv.	Cit.
		Census Card 159, P. O. Oktaha, Enrolled April 11, 1899										
572	1	Harjo, Chenubbe	45	M	F		Nokoseke	L	Cr	Mollie	L	Cr
573	2	Harjo, Sartupe	48	F	F	Wf	Unknown	D	Cr	Sinka	L	Cr
574	3	Harjo, Arley	11	F	F	D	No. 1	L	Cr	No. 2	L	Cr
575	4	Harjo, Mollea	11	F	F	D	No. 1	L	Cr	No. 2	L	Cr
576	5	Harjo, Susan	14	F	F	StD	Ben	D	Cr	No. 2	L	Cr
		No. 1 died Dec. 6, 1909. No. 2 died Nov. 18, 1901. No. 3 died March, 1907.										
		Census Card No. 160, P. O. Onapa, Enrolled April 11, 1899										
577	1	Baker, Annie	55	F	F		Johnnie Katcha	D	Cr	Lothokkee	D	Cr
578	2	Baker, Henry	16	M	F	S	Henry Baker	D	Cr	No. 1	L	Cr
		Census Card No. 161, P. O. Hoffman, Enrolled April 11, 1899										
579	1	Collins, Linda	29	F	F		Unknown	D	Cr	Susie	L	Cr
580	2	Collins, Lila	8	F	F	D	Nokushutche Dick	L	Cr	No. 1	L	Cr
581	3	Collins, Jinnie	2	F	F	D	Sandy Collins	L	Cr	No. 1	L	Cr
		Census Card No. 162, P. O. Sapulpa, Enrolled April 12, 1899										
582	1	Nolan, Sarah Jane	46	F	F		John Minus	D	Cr	Vicey Minus	D	Cr
583	2	Nolan, Thomas Jefferson	17	M	½	S	Henry Nolan	L	Cr	No. 1	L	Cr
584	3	Nolan, Martha Ann Eliz	15	F	½	D	Henry Nolan	L	Cr	No. 1	L	Cr
585	4	Nolan, Isaac	13	M	½	S	Henry Nolan	L	Cr	No. 1	L	Cr
586	5	Nolan, James	7	M	½	S	Henry Nolan	L	Cr	No. 1	L	Cr
		No. 2 died January 19, 1900. No. 3 died October 11, 1899										
		Census Card No. 163, P. O. Oktaha, Enrolled April 12, 1899										
587	1	Walker, Jim	25	M	F		Unknown	D	Cr	Sartupe	L	Cr
588	2	Walker, Lucy	18	F	F	Wf	Henry Baker	D	Cr	Annie Baker	L	Cr
		No. 1 reported dead.										
		Census Card No. 164, P. O. Oktaha, Enrolled April 12, 1899										
589	1	Bullet, James	36	M	F		Takalake Chupco	D	Cr	Wiley Chupco	D	Cr
590	2	Bullet, Lucy	35	F	F	Wf	Unknown	D	Cr	Annie Worker	D	Cr
591	3	Bullet, Arthur	17	M	F	S	No. 1	L	Cr	No. 2	L	Cr
592	4	Bullet, Nellie	15	F	F	D	No. 1	L	Cr	No. 2	L	Cr
593	5	Bullet, Johnnie	13	M	F	S	No. 1	L	Cr	No. 2	L	Cr
594	6	Bullet, Annie	5	F	F	D	No. 1	L	Cr	No. 2	L	Cr
595	7	Bullet, Ben	6 mo	M	F	S	No. 1	L	Cr	No. 2	L	Cr
		No. 7 died Oct. 11, 1899. No. 3 died July 3, 1904. No. 4 died January 7, 1910. No. 5 died May 1909										
		Census Card No. 165, P. O. Checotah, Enrolled April 12, 1899										
596	1	Rogers, Kate D.	52	F	¼		William Drew	D	?	Delilah Drew	D	?
597	2	Rogers, Mary R.	16	F	⅛	D	Woods B. Rogers	L	Non	Kate D. Rogers	L	Cr
		Census Card No. 166, P. O. Checotah, Enrolled April 12, 1899										
598	1	Jones, Pearl D.	22	F	⅛		Woods B. Rogers	L	Non	Kate D. Rogers	L	Cr
		Census Card No. 167, P. O. Cheotah, Enrolled April 12, 1899										
599	1	Rogers, W. B.	26	M	⅛		Woods B. Rogers	L	Non	Kate D. Rogers	L	Cr
		Census Card No. 168, P. O. Summit, Enrolled April 12, 1899										
600	1	West, Thomas	26	M	F		John West	D	Cr	Nafey West	L	Cr
		No. 1 reported dead.										
		Census Card No. 169, P. O. Muskogee, Enrolled April 12, 1899										
601	1	Collins, Ned	19	M	F		Sandy Collins	L	Cr	Dina Collins	L	Cr
		No. 1 reported dead										
		Census Card No. 170, P. O. Weir, Enrolled April 13, 1899										
602	1	Kelley, Annie	43	F	F		Wiley	D	Cr	Peggy	D	Cr
603	2	Kelley, Lucy	13	F	F	D	Joseph Kelly	L	Cr	No. 1	L	Cr
604	3	Kelley, Minnie	11	F	F	D	Joseph Kelly	L	Cr	No. 1	L	Cr
605	4	Kelley, Ida	8	F	F	D	Joseph Kelly	L	Cr	No. 1	L	Cr
606	5	Kelley, Marsey	3	M	F	S	Joseph Kelly	L	Cr	No. 1	L	Cr
		No. 1 died April 19, 1908										
		Census Card No. 171, P. O. Coweta, Enrolled April 13, 1899										
607	1	Childers, Robert	33	M	F		Robert Childers	D	Cr	Rachel Childers	D	Cr
608	2	Childers, Hattie	24	F	F	Wf	Haley Wiley	D	Cr	Lucy Wiley	D	Cr
609	3	Childers, Sam	1	M	F	S	No. 1	L	Cr	No. 2	L	Cr
		No. 2 died Januazy 31, 1911. No. 1 died February 26, 1902. No. 3 reported dead.										
		Census Card No. 172, P. O. Broken Arrow, Enrolled April 13, 1899										
610	1	Wiley, Nettie	22	F	F		Haley Wiley	D	Cr	Lucy Wiley	D	Cr
611	2	Wiley, Angie	16	F	F	Sis	Haley Wiley	D	Cr	Lucy Wiley	D	Cr
612	3	Wiley, Benny	5	M	F	Bro	Haley Wiley	D	Cr	Lucy Wiley	D	Cr
		No. 2 died January, 1900										
		Census Card No. 173, P. O. Coweta, Enrolled April 13, 1899										
613	1	Davis, Kizzie	26	F	F		Spuncher	D	Cr	Susan Atkins	L	Cr
614	2	Haney, William	1	M	F	S	Philip Haney	L	Cr	No. 1	L	Cr
		Census Card No. 174, P. O. Coweta, Enrolled April 13, 1899										
615	1	Atkins, Billy	42	M	F		Wiley Atkins	D	Cr	Missena Atkins	D	Cr
616	2	Atkins, Susan	42	F	F	Wf	Charkoche	D	Cr	Peggy	D	Cr
617	3	Atkins, Mary	20	F	F	D	No. 1	L	Cr	No. 2	L	Cr
618	4	Atkin, Daniel	18	M	F	S	No. 1	L	Cr	No. 2	L	Cr
619	5	Atkins, Annie	15	F	F	D	No. 1	L	Cr	No. 2	L	Cr
620	6	Atkins, Thomas	10	M	F	S	No. 1	L	Cr	No. 2	L	Cr
621	7	Atkins, Janie	8	F	F	D	No. 1	L	Cr	No. 2	L	Cr
622	8	Atkins, Elmira	5	F	F	D	No. 1	L	Cr	No. 2	L	Cr
		No. 5 died August 1901. No. 8 died 1911										

Roll No.	No.	NAME	Age	Sex	Blood	Rel.	NAME OF FATHER	Liv.	Cit.	NAME OF MOTHER	Liv.	Cit.

Census Card No. 175, P. O. Coweta, Enrolled April 13, 1899

Roll No.	No.	NAME	Age	Sex	Blood	Rel.	NAME OF FATHER	Liv.	Cit.	NAME OF MOTHER	Liv.	Cit.
623	1	Bird, Upler	52	M	F		Coahkoche	D	Cr	Nancy	D	Cr
624	2	Bird, Margaret	45	F	F	Wf	Billy	D	Cr	No. 9	L	Cr
625	3	Bird, Eliza	19	F	F	D	No. 1	L	Cr	No. 2	L	Cr
626	4	Bird, Annie	15	F	F	D	No. 1	L	Cr	No. 2	L	Cr
627	5	Bird, Nancy	13	F	F	D	No. 1	L	Cr	No. 2	L	Cr
628	6	Bird, Joanna	9	F	F	D	No. 1	L	Cr	No. 2	L	Cr
629	7	Bird, Charlie	6	M	F	S	No. 1	L	Cr	No. 2	L	Cr
630	8	Bird, Eva	4	F	F	D	No. 1	L	Cr	No. 2	L	Cr
631	9	Snake, Cotahyar	65	F	F	M-L	Louis Webber	D	Cher	Yishohya	D	Cr

No. 1 died October 7, 1899. No. 9 died February 20, 1907.

Census Card No. 176, P. O. Wetumka, Enrolled April 13, 1899

Roll No.	No.	NAME	Age	Sex	Blood	Rel.	NAME OF FATHER	Liv.	Cit.	NAME OF MOTHER	Liv.	Cit.
632	1	Simon, Sam	22	M	F		Joe Simon	L	Cr	Annie	D	Cr

Census Card No. 177, P. O. Wier, Enrolled April 13, 1899

Roll No.	No.	NAME	Age	Sex	Blood	Rel.	NAME OF FATHER	Liv.	Cit.	NAME OF MOTHER	Liv.	Cit.
633	1	Miller, Wilson	66	M	F		Daniel Miller	D	Cr	Unknown	D	Cr

No. 1 died January 9, 1901

Census Card No. 178, P. O. Broken Arrow, Enrolled April 13, 1899

Roll No.	No.	NAME	Age	Sex	Blood	Rel.	NAME OF FATHER	Liv.	Cit.	NAME OF MOTHER	Liv.	Cit.
634	1	McHenry, Lewis	33	M	½		James McHenry	D	Cr	Rachel McHenry	D	Non
635	2	McHenry, Silla	27	F	½	Wf	Thomas Tiger	D	Cr	Bettie Kennard	D	Cr
636	3	McHenry, Lewis, Jr.	7	M	½	S	No. 1	L	Cr	No. 2	L	Cr
637	4	McHenry, Jesse	5	M	½	S	No. 1	L	Cr	No. 2	L	Cr
638	5	McHenry, David	3	M	½	S	No. 1	L	Cr	No. 2	L	Cr
639	6	McHenry, Greely	1	M	½	S	No. 1	L	Cr	No. 2	L	Cr
640	7	Berryhill, Henrietta	28	F	½	Sis	James McHenry	D	Cr	Rachel McHenry	D	Non

No. 2 died December 26, 1900

Census Card No. 179, P. O. Coweta, Enrolled April 13, 1899

Roll No.	No.	NAME	Age	Sex	Blood	Rel.	NAME OF FATHER	Liv.	Cit.	NAME OF MOTHER	Liv.	Cit.
641	1	Chissoe, Willie	24	M	F		Chissoe	D	Cr	Mahaley Chissoe	D	Cr
642	2	Chissoe, Mary	29	F	F	Wf	Cato Vann	D	Cr	Wisey Vann	D	Cr

No. 4 May 22, 1901

Census Card No. 180, P. O. Coweta, Enrolled April 13, 1899

Roll No.	No.	NAME	Age	Sex	Blood	Rel.	NAME OF FATHER	Liv.	Cit.	NAME OF MOTHER	Liv.	Cit.
643	1	Boudinot, Cornelius	27	M	F		Nebey	D	Cr	Ada	D	Cr
644	2	Boudinot, Susanna	19	F	F	Wf	Mitchell Kennard	L	Cr	Parthena	D	Cr
645	3	Boudinot, Jessie	1	F	F	D	No. 1	L	Cr	No. 2	L	Cr
646	4	Boudinot, Belfoure	1	M	F	S	No. 1	L	Cr	No. 2	L	Cr

No. 3 died September 28, 1899. No. 4 died May 5, 1904.

Census Card No. 181, P. O. Porter, Enrolled April 13, 1899

Roll No.	No.	NAME	Age	Sex	Blood	Rel.	NAME OF FATHER	Liv.	Cit.	NAME OF MOTHER	Liv.	Cit.
647	1	Morey, Jacob	55	M	½		Morey	D	?	Sukey	D	?

Census Card No. 182, P. O. Coweta, Enrolled April 13, 1899

Roll No.	No.	NAME	Age	Sex	Blood	Rel.	NAME OF FATHER	Liv.	Cit.	NAME OF MOTHER	Liv.	Cit.
648	1	Cousin, Thompson	50	M	F		Quassate Chupco	D	Cr	Oklarney	D	Cr
649	2	Martin, Johnson	18	M	F	Ward	Jackson Martin	D	Cr	Liley Martin	D	Cr

No. 1 reported dead

Census Card No. 183, P. O. Coweta, Enrolled April 13, 1899

Roll No.	No.	NAME	Age	Sex	Blood	Rel.	NAME OF FATHER	Liv.	Cit.	NAME OF MOTHER	Liv.	Cit.
650	1	Childers, Benjamin	27	M	½		Daniel Childers	D	?	Lyddie Childers	L	?
651	2	Childers, Annie	25	F	F	Wf	Leonard Gibson	L	Cr	Lizzie Gibson	D	?
652	3	Childers, Alice	6	F	¾	D	No. 1	L	Cr	No. 2	L	Cr
653	4	Childers, Red Eagle	4	M	¾	S	No. 1	L	Cr	No. 2	L	Cr
654	5	Childers, Lizzie	6 mo	F	¾	D	No. 1	L	Cr	No. 2	L	Cr

No. 1 died December 17, 1904

Census Card No. 184, P. O. Coweta, Enrolled April 13, 1899

Roll No.	No.	NAME	Age	Sex	Blood	Rel.	NAME OF FATHER	Liv.	Cit.	NAME OF MOTHER	Liv.	Cit.
655	1	Davis, Hilly	35	M	F		Chepon Davis	D	Cr	Loska	D	Cr
656	2	Davis, Martha	25	F	F	Wf	James Berryhill	D	Cr	Lochotkee	D	Cr
657	3	Davis, Cheparnee	8	M	F	S	No. 1	L	Cr	No. 2	L	Cr
658	4	Davis, Annie	4	F	F	D	No. 1	L	Cr	No. 2	L	Cr
659	5	Davis, Lucy	2	F	F	D	No. 1	L	Cr	No. 2	L	Cr

Census Card No. 185, P. O. Coweta, Enrolled April 13, 1899

Roll No.	No.	NAME	Age	Sex	Blood	Rel.	NAME OF FATHER	Liv.	Cit.	NAME OF MOTHER	Liv.	Cit.
660	1	Chenewee, Joe	29	M	F		Chenewee	D	Cr	Mary Rose	D	Cr
661	2	Chenewee, Ella	27	F	F	Wf	Watty Kelly	D	Cr	Susanna Kelly	L	Cr
662	3	Chenewee, Rider	10	M	F	S	No. 1	L	Cr	Sarah Ann	D	Cr

No. 1 died July 17, 1901

Census Card No. 186, P. O. Sapulpa, Enrolled April 13, 1899

Roll No.	No.	NAME	Age	Sex	Blood	Rel.	NAME OF FATHER	Liv.	Cit.	NAME OF MOTHER	Liv.	Cit.
663	1	Tiger, Nellie	27	F	F		Jack Tiger	L	Cr	Minnah Davis	L	Cr
664	2	Sapulpa, Esther	4	F	F	D	John Sapulpa	D	Cr	No. 1	L	Cr
665	3	Helton, Lonie	2 mo	M	½	S	Will Helton	L	Non	No. 1	L	Cr

No. 3 reported dead

Census Card No. 187, P. O. Yahola, Enrolled April 13, 1899

Roll No.	No.	NAME	Age	Sex	Blood	Rel.	NAME OF FATHER	Liv.	Cit.	NAME OF MOTHER	Liv.	Cit.
666	1	McGilbray, Farsey	50	M	F		Wealey	D	Cr	No. 2	L	Cr
667	2	Hoktee	75	F	F	Moth	Monah	D	Cr	Katie	D	Cr
668	3	Harjo, Yahola	72	M	F	Uncle	Monah	D	Cr	Katie	D	Cr

No. 2 died February 1, 1901

Census Card No. 188, P. O. Yahola, Enrolled April 13, 1899

Roll No.	No.	NAME	Age	Sex	Blood	Rel.	NAME OF FATHER	Liv.	Cit.	NAME OF MOTHER	Liv.	Cit.
669	1	McGilbray, Linda	52	F	F		Wealey	D	Cr	Hoktee	L	Cr

Census Card No. 189, P. O. Yahola, Enrolled April 13, 1899

Roll No.	No.	NAME	Age	Sex	Blood	Rel.	NAME OF FATHER	Liv.	Cit.	NAME OF MOTHER	Liv.	Cit.
670	1	McGilbray, Jennie	40	F	F		Wealey	D	Cr	Hoktee	L	Cr

Census Card No. 190, P. O. Stidham, Enrolled April 13, 1899

Roll No.	No.	NAME	Age	Sex	Blood	Rel.	NAME OF FATHER	Liv.	Cit.	NAME OF MOTHER	Liv.	Cit.
671	1	Bean, Rhoda	20	F	F		Jacob Bean	L	Cr	Jennie McGilbray	L	Cr
672	2	Brown, Dewey	2 mo	M	F	S	John Brown	L	Cr	No. 1	L	Cr

Census Card No. 191, P. O. Yahola, Enrolled April 13, 1899

Roll No.	No.	NAME	Age	Sex	Blood	Rel.	NAME OF FATHER	Liv.	Cit.	NAME OF MOTHER	Liv.	Cit.
673	1	McGilbray, Rose	35	F	F		Wealey	D	Cr	Hoktee	L	Cr
674	2	McGilbray, John	10	M	F	S	Illegitimate	?	Cr	No. 1	L	Cr

No. 1 died February 1, 1901

Roll No.	No.	NAME	Age	Sex	Blood	Rel.	NAME OF FATHER	Liv.	Cit.	NAME OF MOTHER	Liv.	Cit.
		Census Card No. 192, P. O. Checotah, Enrolled April 13, 1899										
		No. 2 Onapa										
675	1	Taylor, Melvina L.	48	F	1/4		Winchester Doyle	D	Cr	Nancy Doyle	D	Cr
676	2	Taylor, William	14	M	1/8	S	James Taylor	D	Cr	No. 1	L	Cr
677	3	Taylor, Royal B.	10	M	1/8	S	James Taylor	D	Cr	No. 1	L	Cr
		Census Card No. 193, P. O. Hanna, Enrolled April 14, 1899; No. 2 March 22, 1900										
678	1	Aultman, Frank B.	29	M	1/8		Henry E. Aultman	D	Non	Melvina L. Taylor	L	Cr
679	2	Aultman, Jessie M.	5	F	1-16	D	No. 1	L	Cr	Georgia A. Aultman	L	Non
		Census Card No. 194, P. O. Checotah, Enrolled April 14, 1899										
680	1	Aultman, James	22	M	1/8		Henry E. Aultman	D	Non	Melvina L. Taylor	L	Cr
		Census Card No. 195, P. O. Checotah, Enrolled April 14, 1899										
681	1	Butler, Sam	33	M	F		Jim Butler	D	Cr	Jennie Butler	D	Cr
		No. 1 died January 10, 1900										
		Census Card No. 196, P. O. Checotah, Enrollrd April 14, 1899										
682	1	Doyle, George	29	M	F		David Doyle	D	Cr	Precilla Doyle	D	Cr
		No. 1 died September 10, 1907										
		Census Card No. 197, P. O. Morris, Enrolled April 14, 1899										
683	1	Yardy, Thomas	34	M	1/2		Joseph Yardy	D	Cr	Lizzie Connor	L	Cr
684	2	Yardy, Wisey	45	F	F	Wf	Abarloke Yahola	D	Cr	Unknown	D	Cr
685	3	Yardy, Joseph	14	M	3/4	S	No. 1	L	Cr	No. 2	L	Cr
686	4	Yardy, Thomas, Jr.	10	M	3/4	S	No. 1	L	Cr	No. 2	L	Cr
		No. 2 reported dead										
		Census Card No. 198, P. O. Wildcat, Enrolled April 14, 1899										
687	1	McGilvray, Haley	60	M	F		Emarthloge	D	Cr	Tukwelala	D	Cr
		No. 1 died January 16, 1901										
		Census Card No. 199, P. O. Hitchita, Enrolled April 14, 1899										
688	1	Melton, Edward	22	M	F		Maxey Melton	D	Cr	Micey Melton	D	Cr
		Census Card No. 200, P. O. Okmulgee, Enrolled April 14, 1899										
689	1	Sugar, Thomas	23	M	F		Wesley Sugar	L	Cr	Adaline Sugar	D	Cr
		Census Card No. 201, P. O. Coweta, Enrolled April 15, 1899										
690	1	Tiger, Billy	50	M	1/2		Willie Tiger	D	Cr	Mafolage	L	Cr
691	2	Tiger, Lilah	48	F	F	Wf	Conchartoge	D	Cr	Louisa	L	Cr
692	3	Tiger, Eliza	19	F	3/4	D	No. 1	L	Cr	No. 2	L	Cr
693	4	Tiger, Thomas	17	M	3/4	S	No. 1	L	Cr	No. 2	L	Cr
694	5	Tiger, Lyman	14	M	3/4	S	No. 1	L	Cr	No. 2	L	Cr
		No. 3 died September 7, 1904. No. 5 died January 27, 1900.										
		Census Card No. 202, P. O. Coweta, Enrolled April 15, 1899										
695	1	Kenerd, Martin	23	M	F		Michell, Kenard	D	Cr	Parthena Kenard	D	Cr
		Census Card No. 203, P. O. McAlester, Enrolled April 15, 1899. No. 1 April 18, 1899										
696	1	Haikey, Frank	23	M	F		John Haikey	D	Cr	Sukey Haikey	L	Cr
697	2	Haikey, Nancy	20	F	F	Wf	Thomas Tiger	D	Cr	Bettie Kenard	L	Cr
698	3	Drew, Emmet	3	M	F	StS	Amos Drew	L	Cr	No. 2	L	Cr
		No. 2 died September 2, 1903										
		No. 3 died November 1, 1899										
		Census Card No. 204, P. O. Coweta; Nos. 2, 3, 4, Hitchita, Enrolled April 15, 1899; No. 4. May 22, 1901										
699	1	Chockley, Pusler	56	M	F		Chockley	D	Cr	Inlooker Chockley	D	Cr
700	2	Chockley, Mollie	38	F	F	Wf	Unknown	?	Cr	Unknown	?	Cr
701	3	Chockley, Sebon	1	M	F	S	No. 1	L	Cr	No. 2	L	Cr
702	4	Chockley, Billie	2	M	F	S	No. 1	L	Cr	No. 2	L	Cr
		No. 2 died March 13, 1901										
		No. 4 died April 13, 1899										
		No. 3 died September 12, 1899										
		Census Card No. 205, P. O. Coweta, Enrolled No. 1, April 15, 1899; No. 2, May 14, 1900										
703	1	Lovett, Pilot	21	M	F		George Lovett	L	Cr	Sallie Lovett	D	Cr
704	2	Lovett, Lawrence	1moM	F	S		No. 1	L	Cr	Liza Lovett	L	Cr
		No. 1 died April 8, 1901										
		Census Card No. 206, P. O. Broken Arrow, Enrolled April 15, 1899										
705	1	Pike, Albert	39	M	F		Concharty	D	Cr	Louisa	D	Cr
706	2	Pike, Joseph	17	M	F	S	No. 1	L	Cr	Pamelia Pike	D	Cr
707	3	Pike, George	8	M	F	S	No. 1	L	Cr	Pamelia Pike	D	Cr
		No. 1 died Spring of 1900										
		Census Card No. 207, P. O. Wier, Enrolled April 15, 1899										
708	1	Green, Charley	25	M	F		Waley, Haney	D	Cr	Cissey Fife	L	Cr
		No. 1 died 1906										
		Census Card No. 208, P. O. Broken Arrow, Enrolled April 15, 1899										
		No. 4 Coweta										
709	1	Johnson, Isaac	24	M	1/4		Charlie Johnson	D	?	Nancy Lott	D	?
710	2	Johnson, Nicey	35	F	F	Wf	John Coffee	L	Cr	Ijenny	D	Cr
711	3	Johnson, Annie	2	F	5/8	D	No. 1	L	Cr	No. 2	L	Cr
712	4	McKellop Eliza	15	F	F	StD	Wilson McKellop	D	Cr	No. 2	L	Cr
713	5	Drew, Maggie	8	F	F	StD	Daniel Drew	D	Cr	No. 2	L	Cr
714	6	Drew, Alice	6	F	F	StD	Daniel Drew	D	Cr	No. 2	L	Cr
		Census Card No. 209, P. O. Coweta, Enrolled April 15, 1899										
715	1	Buslar, James	28	M	F		Fusler Chockley	L	Cr	Mary Chockley	L	Cr
		Census Card No. 210, P. O. Broken Arrow, Enrolled April 15, 1899										
716	1	Haikey, Sukey	43	F	F		Robert Childers	D	Cr	Lucy Childers	D	Cr
717	2	Haikey, Eliza	16	F	F	D	John Haikey	L	Cr	No. 1	L	Cr
718	3	Haikey, Susanna	12	F	F	D	John Haikey	L	Cr	No. 1	L	Cr
719	4	Haikey, Ella	1	F	F	D	John Haikey	L	Cr	No. 1	L	Cr
720	5	Childers, Emma	15	F	F	Ward	Henry Childers	L	Cr	Mary Childers	D	Cr

24

Roll No.	No.	NAME	Age	Sex	Blood	Rel.	NAME OF FATHER	Liv.	Cit.	NAME OF MOTHER	Liv.	Cit.
		Census Card No. 211, P. O. Coweta, Enrolled April 15, 1899										
721	1	Gaines, Willie	54	M	½		Gaines	D	Non	Ohme	D	Cr
		No. 1 died June, 1913										
		Census Card No. 212, P. O. Broken Arrow, Enrolled April 15, 1899										
722	1	Johnson, Robert F.	26	M	¼		Charlie Johnson	D	?	Nancy Lott	D	?
723	2	Johnson, Ella	1	F	⅛	D	No. 1	L	Cr	Azalie Johnson	L	Non
		Census Card No. 213, P. O. Broken Arrow, Enrolled April 17, 1899										
724	1	Haynes, Lasley	28	M	F		John Haynes	D	Cr	Munzey	D	Cr
725	2	Lizzie	6	F	F	D	No. 1	L	Cr	Annie Cooper	I.	Cr
		Census Card No. 214, P. O. Coweta, Enrolled April 17, 1899										
726	1	Haynie, Felix	27	M	F		Thomas Haynie	D	Cr	Susanna Haynie	L	Cr
		No. 1 reported dead										
		Census Card No. 215, P. O. Morse, Enrolled April 17, 1899										
727	1	Chupco, Joney	43	M	F		Enath Harjo	D	Cr	Sokenah	L	Cr
728	2	Chupco, Mary	51	F	F	Wf	Arharlox Yahola	D	Cr	Polledagee	L	Cr
729	3	Chupco, Mistaley	17	M	F	S	No. 1	L	Cr	No. 2	L	Cr
730	4	Chupco, Barnocbe	15	M	F	S	No. 1	L	Cr	No. 2	L	Cr
731	5	Tiger, Eliza	8	F	F	Step Grand Niece	Marcy Tiger	L	Cr	Louisa Tiger	L	Cr
732	6	Tiger, Niloge	6	F	F	Step Grand Niece	Marcy Tiger	L	Cr	Louisa Tiger	L	Cr
733	7	Tiger, Selina	4	F	F	Step Grand Niece	Marcy Tiger	L	Cr	Louisa Tiger	L	Cr
		Nos. 1, 2 and 4 reported dead.										
		Census Card No. 216, P. O. Emahaka, Enrolled April 17, 1899										
734	1	Fixico, Yarhar	62	M	F		Kosar Mekko	D	Cr	Unknown	D	Cr
		Census Card No. 217, P. O. Broken Arrow, Enrolled April 17, 1899; No. 4, May 29, 1900										
735	1	Jefferson, Lena	40	F	F		Oche Harjo	D	Cr	Sartharnohkee	D	Cr
736	2	Jefferson, Moses	11	M	F	S	Thomas Jefferson	D	Cr	No. 1	L	Cr
737	3	Jefferson, Thomas	6	M	F	S	Thomas Jefferson	D	Cr	No. 1	L	Cr
738	4	Jefferson, Walter	20	M	F	S	Thomas Jefferson	D	Cr	No. 1	L	Cr
		No. 1 died January 9, 1907. No. 4 reported dead.										
		Census Card No. 218, P. O. Broken Arrow, Enrolled April 17, 1899										
739	1	Beaver, Tiller	46	M	F		Lihtiffee	D	Cr	Lucy	D	Cr
740	2	Beaver, Beckey	40	F	F	Wf	Unknown	?	Cr	Fanny	D	Cr
741	3	Beaver, Harry	14	M	F	S	No. 1	L	Cr	Katie Beaver	L.	Cr
742	4	Moore, Lola	18	M	F	St-S	Noah Moore	L	Cr	No. 2	L	Cr
743	5	Moore, Noah	8	M	F	St-S	Noah Moore	L	Cr	No. 2	L	Cr
		No. 1 died October 14, 1904.										
		Census Card No. 219, P. O. Grayson, Enrolled April 17, 1899										
744	1	Kernells, Martha	25	F	F		Timiye Kernells	L	Cr	Lucy Kernells	D	Cr
		No. 1 reported dead.										
		Census Card No. 220, P. O. Okmulgee, Enrolled April 17, 1899										
		No. 6 October 28, 1899										
745	1	Cumseh, Charley	46	M	F		Tecumseh	D	Cr	Arkahneche	D	Cr
746	2	Cumseh, Sissie	15	F	F	D	No. 1	L	Cr	Lucy Cumseh	D	Cr
747	3	Cumseh, John	13	M	F	S	No. 1	L	Cr	Fannie Cumseh	D	Cr
748	4	Cumseh, Myer	9	M	F	S	No. 1	L	Cr	Fannie Cumseh	D	Cr
749	5	Cumseh, Annie	7	F	F	D	No. 1	L	Cr	Fannie Cumseh	D	Cr
750	6	Cumseh, Thomas	10	M	F	Neph	Moses Cumseh	D	Cr	Loucinda	D	Cr
		No. 5 died June 4, 1907. Nos. 1 and 2 reported dead										
		Census Card No. 221, P. O. Grayson, Enrolled April 18, 1899										
751	1	Seagro, Chepahnoche	23	M	F		Tom Seagro	L	Cr	Annie Seagro	D	Cr
752	2	Seagro, Susan	17	F	F	Sis.	Tom Seagro	L	Cr	Annie Seagro	D	Cr
		No. 1 and 2 reported dead										
		Census Card No. 222, P. O. Brush Hill; No. 3, Okmulgee, Enrolled April 18, 1899; No. 3, January 23, 1900										
753	1	Island, Joe	47	M	F		Easy Island	D	Cr	Abbie Lowe	L	Cr
754	2	Island, Sallie	50	F	F	Wf	Tallarkee	D	Cr	Sehomatigee	D	Cr
755	3	Lowe, Katie	6	F	F	Ward	Motlie	D	Cr	Aggie	D	Cr
		Census Card No. 223, P. O. Okmulgee, Enrolled April 18, 1899										
756	1	Freeman, Mary	21	F	¾		John Freeman	L	Cr	Liza Freeman	D	Cr
757	2	Brown, Nora	5 mo	F	⅞	D	Billy Brown	L	Cr	No. 1	L	Cr
		Census Card No. 224, P. O. Coweta, Enrolled April 18, 1899										
758	1	Flanley, William	26	M	F		Edward Flanley	D	Cr	Cooty	D	Cr
		No. 1 reported dead										
		Census Card No. 225, P. O. Broken Arrow, Enrolled April 18, 1899										
759	1	Davis, Tommie	22	M	F		John Davis	L	Cr	Nellie Davis	D	Cr
		No. 1 died December 1901.										
		Census Card No. 226, P. O. Hitchita, Enrolled April 18, 1899										
760	1	McIntosh, Alex	38	M	½		John McIntosh	L	Cr	Sarah McIntosh	D	Cr
761	2	McIntosh, Martha	33	M	F	Wf	Bony Hawkins	D	Cr	Martha Hawkins	D	Cr
762	3	McIntosh, Solomon	13	M	¾	S	No. 1	L	Cr	No. 2	L	Cr
763	4	McIntosh, Newman	11	M	¾	S	No. 1	L	Cr	No. 2	L	Cr
764	5	McIntosh, Cora	9	F	¾	D	No. 1	L	Cr	No. 2	L	Cr
765	6	McIntosh, Lucy	6	F	¾	D	No. 1	L	Cr	No. 2	L	Cr
766	7	McIntosh, William	4	M	¾	S	No. 1	L	Cr	No. 2	L	Cr
		No. 2 reported dead										

25

Roll No.	No.	NAME	Age	Sex	Blood	Rel.	NAME OF FATHER	Liv.	Cit.	NAME OF MOTHER	Liv.	Cit.
		Census Card No. 227, P. O. Red Fork, Enrolled April 18, 1899										
767	1	Morgan, Chilly W.	49	M	¼		Edwin S. Morgan	D	?	Milly Morgan	D	?
768	2	Morgan, Ranny M.	7	F	⅛	D	No. 1	L	Cr	Lizzie Morgan	L	Non
769	3	Morgan, Edith M.	5	F	⅛	D	No. 1	L	Cr	Lizzie Morgan	L	Non
770	4	Morgan, Florence	3mo	F	⅛	D	No. 1	L	Cr	Lizzie Morgan	L	Non
771	5	Morgan, Lawrence	3mo	M	⅛	S	No. 1	L	Cr	Lizzie Morgan	L	Non
		Nos. 1 and 5 reported dead			W							
		Census Card No. 228, P. O. Henrietta, Enrolled April 18, 1899										
772	1	Lowe, Louie	21	M	F		Innaney	D	Cr	Farnie	L	Cr
		Census Card No. 229, P. O. Porter; No.4 Vinita, Enrolled April 18, 1899; No. 5, March 31, 1900										
773	1	Perryman, Enos	32	M	F		Daniel Perryman	D	Cr	Dicey Gibson	L	Cr
774	2	Perryman, Dora	11	F	½	D	No. 1	L	Cr	Rachel Perryman	D	Cr
775	3	Perryman, Lillian	4	F	½	D	No. 1	L	Cr	Rachel Perryman	D	Cr
776	4	Anderson, Phoebe	16	F	F	Cou	Iamakka	D	Cr	Amy Anderson	L	Cr
777	5	Island, Mamie	3mo	F	F	Cou	Ben Island	L	Cr	No. 4	L	Cr
		Census Card No. 230, P. O. Tulsa, Enrolled April 18, 1899										
778	1	Cox, Lydia	36	F	F		Robert Childers	D	Cr	Lucy Childers	D	Cr
779	2	Madison, John	15	M	½	S	William Madison	L	Non	No. 1	L	Cr
780	3	Madison, Alice	13	F	½	D	William Madison	L	Non	No. 1	L	Cr
781	4	Cox, Isparhecher	7	M	½	S	Burrel Cox	L	Non	No. 1	L	Cr
782	5	Cox, Wm. McKinley	2	M	½	S	Burrel Cox	L	Non	No. 1	L	Cr
		Census Card No. 231, P. O. Tulsa, April 18, 1899; No. 5, April 9, 1900										
783	1	Childers, Chisso	26	M	F		Robert Childers	D	Cr	Rachel Childers	D	Cr
784	2	Childers, Millie	23	F	F	Wf	Sabieche	D	Cr	Lucy	D	Cr
785	3	Childers, Lena	6	F	F	D	No. 1	L	Cr	No. 2	L	Cr
786	4	Childers, Emmet	2	M	F	S	No. 1	L	Cr	No. 2	L	Cr
787	5	Childers, Ida	7mo	F	F	D	No. 1	L	Cr	No. 2	L	Cr
		No. 5 died August 31, 1900										
		Census Card No. 232, P. O. Choska, Enrolled April 18, 1899										
788	1	Barnett, Thomas	48	M	F		Satney Barnett	D	Cr	Sally Barnett	D	Cr
		Census Card No. 233, P. O. No. 2 Leonard; No. 3 Tulsa, Enrolled April 18, 1899										
789	1	Barnett, Jackson	50	M	F		Satney Barnett	D	Cr	Sally Barnett	D	Cr
790	2	Barnett, Malissa	29	F	F	Wf	Kiger Brown	D	Cr	Tahpothanney	D	Cr
791	3	Barnett, Frank	8	M	F	Cou	Squire	D	Cr	Ahquntha	D	Cr
		No. 1 died January 4, 1902										
		Census Card No. 234, P. O. Lenna, Enrolled April 18, 1899										
792	1	Brown, Ella	18	F	F		Kiger Brown	D	Cr	Tahpothanny	D	Cr
		Census Card No. 235, P. O. Coweta, Enrolled April 19, 1899										
793	1	George Long	40	M	F		Conwe	D	Cr	Abandey	D	Cr
794	2	George, Jessie	37	F	F	Wf	Satney Barnett	D	Cr	Sally Barnett	D	Cr
795	3	Jerry, Louis	16	M	F	Neph	Cheparney	D	Cr	Satowey	D	Cr
		No. 3 died February 18, 1900										
		Census Card No. 236, P. O. Choska, Enrolled April 19, 1899										
796	1	Littlehead Cowee	16	M	F		Cotoesee	D	Cr	Poconweny	D	Cr
		No. 1 died March 15, 1902										
		Census Card No. 237, P. O. Coweta, Enrolled April 19, 1899; Nos. 3 and 4, September 15, 1899; No. 5, May 23, 1901										
797	1	Berryhill, Wm.	56	M	F		Jim Berryhill	D	Cr	Lucy Berryhill	D	Cr
798	2	Berryhill, Jennie	48	F	F	Wf	Hillis Yahola	D	Cr	Martha	D	Cr
799	3	Belcher, Simon	20	M	F	Neph	-Illegitimate	?	Cr	Nupsey Fixico	D	Cr
800	4	McKellop, Peter	17	M	F	Neph	Wilson McKellop	D	Cr	Yarnah McKellop	D	Cr
801	5	McKellop, Wilson	43	M	F	Neph	Unknown	?	Cr	Unknown	D	Cr
		No. 5 died October 23, 1899										
		No. 4 reported dead										
		No. 5 Father No. 4										
		Census Card No. 238, P. O. Morse, Enrolled April 19, 1899										
802	1	Watson, Kate	28	F	½		William Harvison	D	Cr	Annie Harvison	D	?
803	2	Watson, Milburn L.	11	M	½	D	Daniel Watson	L	Cr	No. 1	L	Cr
804	3	Watson, Annie L	9	F	½	D	Daniel Watson	L	Cr	No. 1	L	Cr
805	4	Watson, Jane	5	F	½	D	Daniel Watson	L	Cr	No. 1	L	Cr
806	5	Watson, Young	1	M	½	S	Daniel Watson	L	Cr	No. 1	L	Cr
		Census Card No. 239, P. O. Ridge, Enrolled April 19, 1899										
807	1	Manuel, Mary	40	F	¼		Grayson Taylor	D	?	Parthena Bean	D	?
		Census Card No. 240, P. O. Coweta, Enrolled April 20, 1899										
808	1	Sarty, Elsie	47	F	½		Unknown	D	?	Sahkonokke	D	Cr
		Census Card No. 241, P. O. Catoosa, Rolled April 20, 1899										
809	1	Bird, Lewis	29	M	F		Uplee Bird	L	Cr	Yanah Bird	L	Cr
810	2	Bird, Walter	12	M	F	S	No. 1	L	Cr	Sarah Ann Bird	D	Cr
		No. 1 died April 14, 1901										
		No. 2 died June, 1904										
		Census Card No. 242, P. O. Coweta, Enrolled April 20, 1899										
811	1	Childers, Googee	22	M	F		Louis Childers	L	Cr	Susie Childers	D	Cr
		Census Card No. 243, P. O. Coweta, Enrolled April 20, 1899										
812	1	Gulley, Lizzie	28	F	½		George Beaver	D	Cr	Sophie Beaver	D	Cr
813	2	Burgess, Lee	10	M	¼	S	Dick Burgess	D	Cr	No. 1	L	Cr
814	3	Burgess, Cumsch	5	M	¼	S	Dick Burgess	D	Cr	No. 1	L	Cr
		Nos. 1 and 3 reported dead										
		Census Card No. 244, P. O. Muskogee, Enrolled April 20, 1899										
815	1	Carr, Cornelius	33	M	F		Richard Carr	D	Cr	Lucy Carr	D	Cr
		No. 1 died December 22, 1903										

Roll No.	No.	NAME	Age	Sex	Blood	Rel.	NAME OF FATHER	Liv.	Cit.	NAME OF MOTHER	Liv.	Cit.
		Census Card No. 245, P. O. Coweta, Enrolled April 20, 1899										
816	1	Childers, Lewis C.	51	M	½		Bill Childers	D	?	Mariah Childers	D	?
817	2	Childers, Mahaley	29	F	F	Wf	Tolabte	D	Cr	Susanna	L	Cr
818	3	Childers, Amos	5	M	¾	S	No. 1	L	Cr	No. 2	L	Cr
819	4	Childers, Susanna	7mo	F	¾	D	No. 1	L	Cr	No. 2	L	Cr
		No. 1 died January 14, 1902										
		Census Card No. 246, P. O. Coweta, Enrolled April 20, 1899; No. 4, June 23, 1899										
820	1	Tiger, Thomas	27	M	F		Thos. Tiger	D	Cr	Bettie Kennard	D	Cr
821	2	Tiger, Martha	19	F	F	Wf	Matatahke	D	Cr	Yarnah Lynch	L	Cr
822	3	Tiger, Leaster	2	F	F	D	No. 1	L	Cr	No. 2	L	Cr
823	4	Tiger, Ben	5mo	M	F	S	No. 1	L	Cr	No. 2	L	Cr
		No. 1 died July 16, 1899										
		Census Card No. 247, P. O. Wier, Enrolled April 20, 1899										
824	1	Tiger, Jim	48	M	F		Unknown	?	Cr	Lodie Tiger	D	Cr
825	2	Stricken from roll										
		No. 1 reported dead										
		Census Card No. 248, P. O. Coweta, Enrolled April 20, 1899										
826	1	Atkins, Billy	45	M	F		Thomas Atkins	D	Cr	Mowelahke	D	Cr
827	2	Atkins, Salina	33	F	F	Wf	Unknown	D	Cr	Unknown	D	Cr
828	3	Atkins, Anderson	6	M	F	S	No. 1	L	Cr	No. 2	L	Cr
829	4	Brown, Taylor	11	M	F	St.S	Charley Brown	L	Cr	No. 2	L	Cr
		Census Card No. 249, P. O. Coweta, Enrolled April 20, 1899										
830	1	Sarty, Hebert	19	M	F		Sarty	D	Cr	Dena Sarty	D	Cr
		Census Card No. 250, P. O. Coweta, Enrolled April 20, 1899										
831	1	Sarty, Jasper	27	M	F		Sarty	D	Cr	Dena Sarty	D	Cr
832	2	Sarty, Lizzie	16	F	F	Sis	Sarty	D	Cr	Dena Sarty	D	Cr
		Census Card No. 251, P. O. Catoosa, Enrolled April 20, 1899										
833	1	Thompson, Willie	27	M	F		Chisey	D	Cr	Louisa	D	Cr
		No. 1 died June 28, 1903										
		Census Card No. 252, P. O. Coweta, Enrolled April 20, 1899										
834	1	Brown, Younger	50	M	F		Futcbahokke	D	Cr	Sokahoye	D	Cr
835	2	Brown, Martha	33	F	F	Wf	Fabbe	D	Cr	Tahkole	D	Cr
836	3	Brown, Dick	9	M	F	S	No. 1	I.	Cr	No. 2	L	Cr
837	4	Brown, Pilot	18	M	F	S	No. 1	L	Cr	Sealy Brown	D	Cr
		Census Card No. 253, P. O. Coweta, Enrolled April 20, 1899										
838	1	Sarty, Wesley	36	M	F	F	Sarty	D	Cr	Dena Sarty	D	Cr
839	2	Sarty, Hattie	27	F	F	Wf	Willie Tiger	L	Cr	Elsie Tiger	L	Cr
840	3	Sarty, Austin	11	M	F	S	No. 1	L	Cr	No. 2	L	Cr
841	4	Sarty, Thomas	8	M	F	S	No. 1	L	Cr	No. 2	L	Cr
842	5	Sarty, Sarah	1	F	F	D	No. 1	L	Cr	No. 2	L	Cr
843	6	Sarty, Roman	14	M	F	S	No. 1	L	Cr	Elsie Sarty	L	Cr
		No. 1 died March 6, 1903										
		No. 3 reported dead										
		Census Card No. 254, P. O. Broken Arrow, Enrolled April 20, 1899										
844	1	Chisholm, Anderson	26	M	F		Sampson Chisholm	D	Cr	Sally Chisholm	D	Cr
845	2	Chisholm, Rosa	26	F	F	Wf	Futloka	L	Cr	Susie	L	Cr
		Census Card No. 255, P. O. Bixby, Enrolled April 20, 1899										
846	1	Morrison, Jeremiah	43	M	½		A. Morrison	D	Cr	Martha Morrison	D	Cr
847	2	Morrison, Mary	36	F	F	Wf	Louis Swop	D	Cr	Unknown	?	Cr
848	3	Morrison, Henry	10	M	¾	S	No. 1	L	Cr	No. 2	L	Cr
849	4	Morrison, Bessie	6mo	F	¾	D	No. 1	L	Cr	No. 2	L	Cr
850	5	Morrison, Bluford	6	M	¾	S	No. 1	L	Cr	No. 2	L	Cr
		No. 4 died June 23, 1899										
		Census Card No. 256, P. O. Boken Arrow, Enrolled April 20, 1899										
851	1	Loler, Kizzie	37	F	F		Haikey	D	Cr	Martha	D	Cr
852	2	Alexander, Willie	16	M	F	S	Loley Alexander	L	Cr	No. 1	L	Cr
853	3	Burgess, Alice	13	F	F	D	Daniel Burgess	D	Cr	No. 1	L	Cr
854	4	Loler, Maggie	8	F	F	D	Wilson Loler	L	Cr	No. 1	L	Cr
		Census Card No. 257, P. O. Fry, Enrolled April 21, 1899										
855	1	Morrison, Annan'as R.	21	M	½		Henry Morrison	L	?	Sally Morrison	L	?
		No. 1 died December 10, 1899										
		Census Card No. 258, P. O. Broken Arrow, Enrolled April 21, 1899										
856	1	Morrison, Henry	46	M	½		Ennis Morrison	D	?	Martha Morrison	D	?
857	2	Morrison, Sallie	38	F	½	Wf	Wm. Frank	L	Cr	Eliza Frank	D	Cr
858	3	Morrison, Jerry	10	M	½	S	No. 1	L	Cr	No. 2	L	Cr
859	4	Morrison, Duffey	5	M	½	S	No. 1	L	Cr	No. 2	L	Cr
		Census Card No. 259, P. O. Okemah, Enrolled April 21, 1899; No. 6, May 12, 1900										
860	1	Knight, Jacob	50	M	F		Knighty Walker	D	Cr	Wigey	D	Cr
861	2	Knight, Malinda	40	F	F	Wf	Unknown	D	Cr	Unknown	D	Cr
862	3	Long, Yusie	10	F	F	G-N	Micco Chupco	D	Cr	Teyohe	D	Cr
863	4	Long, Israel	6	M	F	G-N	Illigitimate	?	Cr	Teyohe	D	Cr
864	5	McKellop, Minnie	3	F	F	Ward	Joseph McKellop	L	Cr	Alena McKellop	D	Cr
865	6	Micco, Robert	1	M	F	Neph	Peter Micco	L	Cr	Sallie	L	?
		No. 1 reported dead										
		Census Card No. 260, P. O. Boynton, Enrolled April 21, 1899										
866	1	Rentie, Susan	26	F	¼		Chas. Johnson	D	?	Dorcus Johnson	D	?
		Census Card No. 261, P. O. Holdenville, Enrolled April 21, 1899										
867	1	Sartoris, Martha	26	F	⅛		James Edwards	D	Non	Nancy M. Haywood	L	Cr
868	2	Walker, William Walter	9	M	1-16	S	Joll Walker	D	Non	No. 1	L	Cr
869	3	O'Brien, Albert Victor	6	M	1-16	S	Thomas O'Brien	D	Non	No. 1	L	Cr
		Census Card No. 262, P. O. Beggs, Enrolled April 22, 1899										
870	1	Grayson, James L.	30	M	¼		Doc Grayson	D	Cr	Susie Grayson	L	Cr

27

Roll No.	No.	NAME	Age	Sex	Blood	Rel.	NAME OF FATHER	Liv.	Cit.	NAME OF MOTHER	Liv.	Cit.
		Census Card No. 263, P. O. Beggs, Enrolled April 22, 1899										
871	1	Grayson, Ben	38	M	¼		Doc Grayson	D	Cr	Susie Grayson	L	Cr
		No. 1 reported dead										
		Census Card No. 264, P. O. Fry, Enrolled April 22, 1899										
872	1	Thatcher, Nancy	19	F	¼		Wm. Sunday	L	Cher	Malissa Burgess	L	Cr
873	2	Thatcher, Jno. Douglas	5mo	M	⅛	S	Douglas Thatcher	L	Non	No. 1	L	Cr
		Census Card No. 265, P. O. Broken Arrow, Enrolled April 22, 1899										
874	1	Burgess, Malissa	42	F	½		Ananias Morrison	D	Cr	Martha Porter	D	Cr
875	2	Burgess, Hettie	7	F	¼	D	John B. Burgess	L	Cr	No. 1	L	Cr
876	3	Burgess, Mattie	5	F	¼	D	John B. Burgess	L	Cr	No. 1	L	Cr
877	4	Burgess, Sarah	3	F	¼	D	John B. Burgess	L	Cr	No. 1	L	Cr
		Census Card No. 266, P. O. Broken Arrow, Enrolled April 22, 1899										
878	1	Childers, Silas	31	M	¾		Daniel Childers	D	Cr	Lydia Childers	L	Cr
879	2	Childers, Robert	10	M	⅞	S	No. 1	L	Cr	Louina	D	Cr
		Census Card No. 267, P. O. Wagoner, Enroleld April 24, 1899										
880	1	Barber, John C.	46	M	¼		Silas H. Barber	L	Non	Sarah A. Barber	D	Cr
881	2	Barber, Robert T.	13	M	⅛	S	No. 1	L	Cr	Mollie Barber	D	Non
		Census Card No. 268, P. O. Wagoner, Enrolled April 24, 1899										
882	1	Garner, Susan L.	26	M	⅛		John C. Barber	L	Cr	Josephine C. Barber	D	Non
883	2	Garner, John L.	8	M	1-16	S	William Garner	L	Non	No. 1	L	Cr
884	3	Garner, Willie B.	4	M	1-16	S	William Garner	L	Non	No. 1	L	Cr
		Census Card No. 269, P. O. Boynton, Enrolled April 24, 1899; No. 8, May 2, 1899										
885	1	Hutton, Annie	29	F	¼		Wm. Nero	D	Cr	Nancy Nero	L	Cr
886	2	Hutton, Bessie	13	F	⅛	D	Henry Hutton	L	Non	No. 1	L	Cr
887	3	Hutton, Sedalia	12	F	⅛	D	Henry Hutton	L	Non	No. 1	L	Cr
888	4	Hutton, Salina	10	F	⅛	D	Henry Hutton	L	Non	No. 1	L	Cr
889	5	Hutton, Alex	6	M	⅛	S	Henry Hutton	L	Non	No. 1	L	Cr
890	6	Hutton, Robert	4	M	⅛	S	Henry Hutton	L	Non	No. 1	L	Cr
891	7	Hutton, Billy	2	M	⅛	S	Henry Hutton	L	Non	No. 1	L	Cr
892	8	Hutton, Houston	3mo	M	⅛	S	Henry Hutton	L	Non	No. 1	L	Cr
		No. 3 died May, 1907										
		Census Card N9. 270, P. O. Eufaula, Enrolled April 24, 1899										
893	1	Phillips, Tecumseh	64	M	F		Pahos Harjo Phillips	D	Cr	Eliza Phillips	D	Cr
894	2	Phillips, Coosie	48	F	F	Wf	Unknown	D	Cr	Coosie Harjo	D	Cr
895	3	Phillips, Thomas	15	M	F	S	No. 1	L	Cr	No. 2	L	Cr
896	4	Phillips, Sarah	14	F	F	D	No. 1	L	Cr	No. 2	L	Cr
897	5	Phillips, Eliza	13	F	F	D	No. 1	L	Cr	No. 2	L	Cr
898	6	Phillips, Bettie	12	F	F	D	No. 1	L	Cr	No. 2	L	Cr
899	7	Phillips, Jennetta	10	F	F	D	No. 1	L	Cr	No. 2	L	Cr
900	8	Phillips, Hattie	8	F	F	D	No. 1	L	Cr	No. 2	L	Cr
901	9	Phillips, Joe	7	M	F	S	No. 1	L	Cr	No. 2	L	Cr
902	10	Phillips, Walter	3	M	F	S	No. 1	L	Cr	No. 2	L	Cr
903	11	Grayson, Jennie	19	F	F	St-D	Pilot Grayson	D	Cr	No. 2	L	Cr
		Nos. 1 and 11 reported dead										
		Census Card No. 271, P. O. Muskogee, Enrolled April 24, 1899										
904	1	Wiley, Walter	19	M	F		George Wiley	D	Cr	Betsey Wiley	D	Cr
		No. 1 died October 25, 1908										
		Census Card No. 272, P. O. Haskell, Enrolled April 25, 1899										
905	1	Kelly, Ferdinand	29	M	¼		A. B. Kelly	L	Non	Sarah Kelly	D	Cr
		Census Card No. 273, P. O. Big Springs, Texas, Enrolled April 25, 1899										
906	1	Miles, Rosalie	30	F	½		Joshua Ross	L	Cher	Muskogee Ross	L	Cr
907	2	Miles, Louise	8	F	¼	D	W. S. Miles	L	Non	No. 1	L	Cr
		Census Card No. 274, P. O. Checotah, Enrolled April 25, 1899										
908	1	Escoe, Charlie J.	43	M	¼		Thomas Escoe	L	Non	Mary Escoe	L	Cr
909	2	Escoe, Zelmo	18	M	⅛	S	No. 1	L	Cr	Cornelia Escoe	D	Cr
910	3	Escoe, James	16	M	⅛	S	No. 1	L	Cr	Cornelia Escoe	D	Cr
911	4	Escoe, Tommie	13	M	⅛	S	No. 1	L	Cr	Cornelia Escoe	D	Cr
912	5	Escoe, Jean	13	M	⅛	S	No. 1	L	Cr	Cornelia Escoe	D	Cr
913	6	Escoe, Isaiah	9	M	⅛	S	No. 1	L	Cr	Cornelia Escoe	D	Cr
914	7	Escoe, Hattie	7	F	⅛	D	No. 1	L	Cr	Cornelia Escoe	D	Cr
		Census Card No. 275, P. O. Okemah, Enrolled April 26, 1899										
915	1	Phillips, John	26	M	F		Tecumseh Phillips	L	Cr	Wysie Phillips	D	Cr
		Census Card No. 276, P. O. Morse, Enrolled April 26, 1899										
916	1	Fox, Ada	25	F	F		Hokalis Hennehah	D	Cr	Susan Hennehah	D	Cr
		No. 1 died March 24, 1904										
		Census Card No. 277, P. O. Castle, Enrolled April 26, 1899										
917	1	Hicks, George	45	M	F		Emartha Chupco	D	Cr	Unknown	D	Cr
918	2	Hicks, Elsie	45	F	F	Wf	Chelokkee	L	Cr	Kinha	D	Cr
919	3	Hicks, Bunner	14	M	F	S	No. 1	L	Cr	No. 2	L	Cr
920	4	Hicks, Johnson	10	M	F	S	No. 1	L	Cr	No. 2	L	Cr
921	5	Hicks, Robert	7	M	F	S	No. 1	L	Cr	No. 2	L	Cr
922	6	Scott, Lucy	16	F	F	G-N	Jim Scott	D	Cr	Cheniwee	D	Cr
923	7	Sinhoethar	80	F	F	A-L	Unknown	D	Cr	Unknown	D	Cr
		No. 2 died March 16, 1910										
		Census Card No. 278, P. O. Castle, Enrolled April 26, 1899										
924	1	Chupco, Hennehah	24	M	F		Alberta Harjochee	L	Cr	Unknown	D	Cr
		Census Card No. 279, P. O. Coweta, Enrolled April 26, 1899										
925	1	Washington, Willie	21	M	¾		George Washington	D	Cr	Koger Washington	D	Cr

Roll No.	No.	NAME	Age	Sex	Blood	Rel.	NAME OF FATHER	Liv.	Cit.	NAME OF MOTHER	Liv.	Cit.
		Census Card No. 280, P. O. Okmulgee, Enrolled April 26, 1899										
926	1	Haynes, Thomas	38	M	F		Unknown	D	Cr	Nicey Kenard	L	Cr
927	2	Haynes, Tochee	40	F	F	Wf	Pahos Fixico	D	Cr	Unknown	D	Cr
928	3	Haynes, Thomas, Jr.,	6	M	F	S	No. 1	L	Cr	No. 2	L	Cr
929	4	Kenard, Nicey	65	F	F	Mot'h	Unknown	D	Cr	Unknown	D	Cr
930	5	Larney, Jimmy	13	M	F	Neph	Jack Larney	L	Cr	Sissie Larney	D	Cr
		No. 1 died 1900										
		No. 2 died 1902										
		No. 5 died December 10, 1899										
		No. 4 reported dead										
		Census Card No. 281, P. O. Broken Arrow, Enrolled April 26, 1899										
931	1	Cooper, Annie	25	F	F		John Haikey	D	Cr	Sookey Haikey	L	Cr
932	2	Cooper, Emma	4mo	F	½	D	Ezra E. Cooper	L	Non	No. 1	L	Cr
933	3	Haynes, Liddie	5	F	F	D	Lasley Haynes	L	Cr	No. 1	L	Cr
		Census Card N9. 282, P. O. Hitchita; No. 5, Hoffman, Enrolled April 27, 1899; No. 7, May 15, 1900										
934	1	McGilbray Captain	48	M	F		Sawaahola	D	Cr	Sophie	D	Cr
935	2	McGilbray, Lizzie	28	F	F	Wf	Cully Micco	D	Cr	Unknown	D	Cr
936	3	McGilbray, Minnie	2	F	F	D	No. 1	L	Cr	No. 2	L	Cr
937	4	McGilbray, Katie	2	F	F	D	No. 1	L	Cr	No. 2	L	Cr
938	5	Carr, Nancy	13	F	F	St-D	John Carr	L	Cr	No. 2	L	Cr
939	6	Taylor, Teperke	70	F	F	A-L	Unknown	?	Cr	Unknown	?	Cr
940	7	McGilbray, Louisa	14	F	F	D	No. 1	L	Cr	Lucy McGilbray	L	Cr
		No. 2 died May 5, 1901										
		No. 1 reported dead										
		No. 3 died September 15, 1900										
		No. 4 died August 1, 1900										
		Census Card No. 283, P. O. Grayson, Enrolled April 27, 1899										
941	1	Deer, Jonas	55	M	F		Fixico Harjo	D	Cr	Polly	D	Cr
		Census Card No. 284, P. O. Broken Arrow, Enrolled April 27, 1899; No. 5, May 22, 1901										
942	1	Bible, Lewis	23	M	F		Lewis Bible	L	Cher	Tigo Bible	D	Cr
943	2	Bible, Mulsie	24	F	½	Wf	Sampson Chisholm	D	Mex	Tushoge	D	Cr
944	3	Bible, Lewis Jr.,	10mo	M	¾	S	No. 1	L	Cr	No. 2	L	Cr
945	4	Grayson, Sam	3	M	¾	St-S	Peter Grayson	L	Cr	No. 2	L	Cr
946	5	Bible, Emmet	1	M	¾	S	No. 1	L	Cr	No. 2	L	Cr
		Census Card No. 285, P. O. Fry, Enrolled April 27, 1899										
947	1	Haikey, Ben Jr.,	27	M	F		Ben Haikey	D	Cr	Macey Haikey	D	Cr
		Census Card No. 286, P. O. Broken Arrow, Enrolled April 27, 1899										
948	1	Lumkin, Barney	30	M	F		Fort Jim	D	Cr	Hepsey	D	Cr
		No. 1 reported dead										
		Census Card No. 287, P. O. Broken Arrow, Enrolled April 27, 1899										
949	1	Steele, Edward	10	M	F		Wyley Steele	D	Cr	Louisa Steele	D	Cr
		No. 1 died 1906										
		Census Card No. 288, P. O. Broken Arrow, Enrolled April 27, 1899; No. 6, June 7, 1899										
950	1	Haikey, Ben	48	M	F		Haikey	D	Cr	Martha	D	Cr
951	2	Haikey, Jennetta	15	F	F	D	No. 1	L	Cr	Macey Haikey	D	Cr
952	3	Haikey, Dave	14	M	F	S	No. 1	L	Cr	Macey Haikey	D	Cr
953	4	Haikey, Ellis	11	M	F	S	No. 1	L	Cr	Macey Haiskey	D	Cr
954	5	Haikey, John	8	M	F	S	No. 1	L	Cr	Macey Haikey	D	Cr
955	6	Haikey, Edward	6	M	F	S	No. 1	L	Cr	Macey Haikey	D	Cr
		Census Card No. 289, P. O. Broken Arrow, Enrolled April 27, 1899										
956	1	Chisholm, Louisa	23	F	F		Albert Sunny	D	Cr	Katie	D	Cr
		Census Card No. 290, P. O. Braggs, Enrolled April 28, 1899										
957	1	Vann, Jno	28	M	¾		Dave Vann	D	Cr	Judy Vann	D	Cr
958	2	Vann, Dicey	17	F	F	Wf	Nail	D	Cr	Sally Nail	L	Cr
		No. 1 died January 18, 1901										
		No. 2 died August 1907										
		Census Card No. 291, P. O. Coweta, Enrolled April 28, 1899										
959	1	Childers, Sauce	45	M	F		Bob Childers	D	Cr	Eliza Childers	D	Cr
960	2	Childers, Mary	45	F	F	Wf	Tom Atkins	D	Cr	Jane Atkins	L	Cr
961	3	Childers, Bowman	18	M	F	S	No. 1	L	Cr	No. 2	L	Cr
962	5	Childers, John	15	M	F	S	No. 1	L	Cr	No. 2	L	Cr
963	5	Childers, Ellis	11	M	F	S	No. 1	L	Cr	No. 2	L	Cr
964	6	Childers, Edward	8	M	F	S	No. 1	L	Cr	No. 2	L	Cr
965	7	Childers, Tackie	6	M	F	S	No. 1	L	Cr	No. 2	L	Cr
966	8	Atkins, Jane	67	F	F	M-L	Ninnechuppo Harjo	D	Cr	Unknown	D	Cr
		No. 1 died 1907										
		No. 4 died 1903										
		No. 8 died 1906										
		No. 5 reported dead										
		Census Card No. 292, P. O. Porter, Enrolled April 28, 1899										
967	1	Childers, Lewis	21	M	F		Sauce Childers	L	Cr	Mary Childers	L	Cr
968	2	Childers, Sarah	21	F	F	Wf	Mitchell Marshall	D	Cr	Lizzie Smith	L	Cr
969	3	Childers, Sauce No. 2	4	M	F	S	No. 1	L	Cr	No. 2	L	Cr
		No. 1 reported dead										
		Census Card No. 293, P. O. Muskogee, Enrolled April 28, 1899										
970	1	Wineblood, Mary E.	43	F	1-16		Wm. Clark	L	Non	Sarah Clark	D	Cr
971	2	Price, Lelia	19	F	1-32	D	Wm. Price	D	Non	No. 1	L	Cr
972	3	Price, Oscar	17	M	1-32	S	Wm. Price	D	Non	No. 1	L	Cr
973	4	Price, Owen	15	M	1-32	S	Wm. Price	D	Non	No. 1	L	Cr
974	5	Price, Benny	13	M	1-32	S	Wm. Price	D	Non	No. 1	L	Cr
975	6	Wineblood, Laura	7	F	1-32	D	F. A. Wineblood	L	Non	No. 1	L	Cr
976	7	Wineblood, Eva	5	F	1-32	D	F. A. Wineblood	L	Non	No. 1	L	Cr

29

Roll No.	No.	NAME	Age	Sex	Blood	Rel.	NAME OF FATHER	Liv.	Cit.	NAME OF MOTHER	Liv.	Cit.
Census Card No. 294, P. O. Checotah, Enrolled April 28, 1899												
977	1	Johnson, Sophia	22	F	1-16		Wm. Price	D	Non	Mary E. Wineblood	L	Cr
978	2	Johnson, Clay	4	M	1-32	S	W. L. Johnson	L	Non	No. 1	L	Cr
979	3	Johnson, Todd	2	M	1-32	S	W. L. Johnson	L	Non	No. 1	L	Cr
Census Card No. 295, P. O. Okmulgee, Mo. Enrolled May 1, 1899												
980	1	Rowley, Charles	40	M	1/2		Henry Rowley	L	Non	Mrs. T. Rowley	D	Cr
Census Card No. 296, P. O. Mounds; No. 2, Lamar, Enrolled May 1, 1899												
981	1	Montgomery, Bessie	34	F	1/2		Henry Rowley	L	Non	Mrs. T. Rowley	D	Cr
982	2	Montgomery, George	10	M	1/4	S	George Montgomery (Wyandotte, Ind.)	L	Non	No. 1	D	Cr
983	3	Montgomery, Eliza	9	F	1/4	D	George Montgomery	L	Non	No. 1	D	Cr
984	4	Montgomery, Thomson	9	F	1/4	D	George Montgomery	L	Non	No. 1	D	Cr
985	5	Montgomery, Josie Belle	6	F	1/4	D	George Montgomery	L	Non	No. 1	D	Cr
986	6	Montgomery, Hattie	1 1/2	F	1/4	D	George Montgomery	L	Non	No. 1	D	Cr
		No. 1 died March 6, 1913										
Census Card No. 297, P. O. Mounds, Enrolled May 1, 1899												
987	1	Rowley, Josie	30	F	1/4		Henry Rowley	L	Non	Mrs. T. Rowley	D	Cr
Census Card No. 298, P. O. Cathay; No. 2, Hitchita, Enrolled May 1, 1899												
988	1	Doyle, Sam H. Sr.	58	M	1/2		Jackson Doyle	D	Cr	Sarah Doyle	D	?
989	2	Doyle, Seaborn J.	21	M	1/4	S	No. 1	L	Cr	Rachel A. Doyle	L	Non
990	3	Doyle, Pearl	11	F	1/4	D	No. 1	L	Cr	Rachel A. Doyle	L	Non
991	4	Doyle, Mary	9	F	1/4	S	No. 1	L	Cr	Rachel A. Doyle	L	Non
992	5	Doyle, George S.	39	M	1/2	Bro	Jackson Doyle	D	Cr	Sarah Doyle	D	?
Census Card No. 299, P. O. Mounds, Enrolled May 1, 1899												
993	1	Perryman, Nicey	22	F	3/4		Dogwood Sharp	D	Cr	Mary Sharp	L	Cr
994	2	Perryman, Willie	6	M	3/4	S	Philip Perryman	L	Cr	No. 1	L	Cr
		No. 2 died March 20, 1901										
Census Card No. 300, P. O. Broken Arrow, Enrolled May 1, 1899												
995	1	Sunday, Anderson	16	M	F		Wm. Sunday	L	Cher	Kizzie Sunday	D	Cr
996	2	Sunday, Alex	14	M	F	Bro	Wm. Sunday	L	Cher	Kizzie Sunday	D	Cr
997	3	Sunday, Ellen	12	F	F	Sis.	Wm. Sunday	L	Cher	Kizzie Sunday	D	Cr
Census Card No. 301, P. O. Checotah, Enrolled May 2, 1899												
998	1	Fisher, Henry C.	37	M	1/2		Wm. Fisher	L	Cr	Sarah Fisher	L	Non
999	2	Fisher, Lucy B.	38	F	1/4	Wf	James Willison	D	Non	Hettie Willison	D	Cr
1000	3	Fisher, Carrie	16	F	3/8	D	No. 1	L	Cr	No. 2	L	Cr
1001	4	Fisher, Ollie C.	13	F	3/8	D	No. 1	L	Cr	No. 2	L	Cr
1002	5	Fisher, Eloise B.	8	F	3/8	D	No. 1	L	Cr	No. 2	L	Cr
Census Card No. 302, P. O. Coweta, Enrolled May 2, 1899												
1003	1	Childers, James	62	M	F		Wm. Childers	D	Cr	Maria Childers	D	Cr
1004	2	Childers, Garfield	15	M	F	S	No. 1	L	Cr	Matilda Childers	D	Cr
1005	3	Childers, Susie	13	F	F	D	No. 1	L	Cr	Matilda Childers	D	Cr
1006	4	Childers, Pearlie	12	F	F	D	No. 1	L	Cr	Matilda Childers	D	Cr
1007	5	Cloud, Eliza	20	F	F	St-D	Jim Cloud	D	Cr	Matilda Childers	D	Cr
1008	6	Wiley, Lizzie	13	F	F	G-D	Jackson Wiley	D	Cr	Maria Wiley	D	Cr
1009	7	Wiley, Louisa	12	F	F	G-D	Jackson Wiley	D	Cr	Maria Wiley	D	Cr
		No. 6 reported dead										
Census Card No. 303, P. O. Okmulgee, Enrolled May 2, 1899												
1010	1	Marshall, Lafayette	14	M	F		Freeland Marshall	D	Cr	Ellen Marshall	D	Cr
1011	2	Marshall, Mattie	13	F	F	S	Freeland Marshall	D	Cr	Ellen Marshall	D	Cr
1012	3	Hardridge, Ella	11	F	1/4	None	David D. Hardridge	D	Cr	Cordelia Marshall	L	Non
		No. 1 died July 19, 1909										
		No. 2 reported dead										
Census Card No. 304, P. O. Coweta, Enrolled May 3, 1899; No. 3, June 29, 1900												
1013	1	Taylor, Rosa	26	F	F		Henry Grayson	L	Chick	Mary Grayson	L	Cr
1014	2	Taylor, Pearl	4	F	1/2	D	Will Taylor	L	Non	No. 1	L	Cr
1015	3	Taylor, Harry C.	3mo		1/2	S	Will Taylor	L	Non	No. 1	L	Cr
Census Card No. 305, P. O. Hitchita, Enrolled May 2, 1899												
1016	1	McNac, Alex	33	M	1/2		Wallace McNac	D	Cr	Dicey McNac	D	Cr
1017	2	McNac, Mary	26	F	F	Wf	James Gray	D	Cr	Louisa Gray	D	Cr
1018	3	McNac, Alice	6	F	3/4	D	No. 1	L	Cr	No. 2	L	Cr
1019	4	McNac, Myrtie	5	F	3/4	D	No. 1	L	Cr	No. 2	L	Cr
1020	5	McNac, Albert	1 1/2	M	3/4	S	No. 1	L	Cr	No. 2	L	Cr
1021	6	McNac, Mary	3 mo	F	3/4	D	No. 1	L	Cr	No. 2	L	Cr
		No. 2 died Dec. 3, 1899										
		No. 6 died Oct. 19, 1900										
Census Card No. 306, P. O. Checotah, Enrolled May 2, 1899; No. 4 February 27, 1900												
1022	1	Minton, Ida Amelia	23	F	1-16		Wm. Price	D	Non	Mary E. Wineblood	L	Cr
1023	2	Minton, Nona	8	F	1-32	D	Chaney Minton	L	Non	No. 1	L	Cr
1024	3	Minton, Malven	5	M	1-32	S	Chaney Minton	L	Non	No. 1	L	Cr
1025	4	Minton, Jarritt O.	27das	M	1-32	S	Chaney Minton	L	Non	No. 1	L	Cr
		No. 4 died April 25, 1901										
Census Card No. 307, P. O. Okmulgee, Enrolled May 2, 1899; No. 3 March 25, 1901												
1026	1	Sneed, Charley	36	M	5/8		Charley Sneed	D	Non	Martha Smith		Cr
1027	2	Sneed, Peoria	1 1/2	M	3-16	S	No. 1	L	Cr	Panina Sneed		Non
1028	3	Sneed, Almorene	10 mo	M	3-16	S	No. 1	L	Cr	Panina Sneed		Non

No.	NAME	Age	Sex	Blood	Rel.	NAME OF FATHER	Liv.	Cit.	NAME OF MOTHER	Liv.	Cit.

Census Card No. 308, P. O. Coweta, Enrolled May 3, 1899

1	Mantooth, Annie	34	F	F		Little John	D	Cr	Josephine Thompson	L	Cr
2	Walker, Josephine	14	F	F	D	Daniel Walker	D	Cr	No. 1	L	Cr
3	Payne, Charley	9	M	F	S	Richard Payne	D	Cr	No. 1	L	Cr
4	Mantooth, Laura	1	F	½	D	Jim Mantooth	L	Non	No. 1	L	Cr

No. 1 died November 4, 1906.   No. 3 died December 21, 1909

Census Card No. 309, P. O. Okmulgee, Enrolled May 3, 1899

| 1 | Hightower, Lydia A. | 29 | F | ½ | | David Carr | D | ? | Caroline Carr | D | ? |
| 2 | Hightower, William S. | 2 | M | ¼ | S | Tom Hightower | L | Non | No. 1 | L | Cr |

Census Card No. 310, P. O. Coweta, Enrolled May 3, 1899

1	Fulotka	54	M	F		Emarthloge	D	Cr	Sallie	D	Cr
2	Fulotka, Susan	26	F	F	Wf	Tobey Kelley	L	Cr	Tilsie Kelley	D	Cr
3	Fulotka, Oscar	3	M	F	S	No. 1	L	Cr	No. 2	L	Cr
4	Fulotka, Nellie	1	F	F	D	No. 1	L	Cr	No. 2	L	Cr

No. 4 died August 15, 1908

Census Card No. 311, P. O. Coweta, Enrolled May 3, 1899

1	Tiger, Martha	25	F	F		Robert Pinehill	D	Cr	Louisa Tiger	L	Cr
2	Tiger, Sam	4	M	F	S	William Tiger	D	Cr	No. 1	L	Cr
3	Tiger, Lydia	2	F	F	D	William Tiger	D	Cr	No. 1	L	Cr

No. 1 died 1902.   No. 2 died 1901.   No. 3 died 1903

Census Card No. 312, P. O. Coweta, Enrolled May 3, 1899

| 1 | Burgess, Ida | 21 | F | F | | Tillar Beaver | L | Cr | Nancy Fisher | D | Cr |
| 2 | Burgess, Ellen | 10 moF | F | D | | Edmund Burgess | L | Cr | No. 1 | L | Cr |

No. 1 died 1911

Census Card No. 313, P. O. Coweta, Enrolled May 3, 1899

| 1 | Tiger, Louisa | 45 | F | F | | Tulwa Micco | D | Cr | Unknown | ? | Cr |
| 2 | Tiger, Marchie | 12 | M | F | S | William Tiger | D | Cr | No. 1 | L | Cr |

No. 1 died 1903

Census Card No. 314, P. O. Catoosa, Enrolled May 3, 1899

| 1 | Chisholm, Nancy | 26 | F | ½ | | Sampson Chisholm | D | Cr | Sally Chisholm | D | Cr |
| 2 | Partridge, Sam | 11 | M | ¾ | S | Gibson Partridge | D | Cr | No. 1 | ? | Cr |

Census Card No. 315, P. O. Muskogee, Enrolled May 3, 1899

1	Turner, Tookah B.	38	F	¼		Edward Butler	D	Adtd Cher	Elizabeth Butler	L	Non
2	Turner, Tookah K.	13	F	⅛	S	C. W. Turner	L	Non	No. 1	L	Cr
3	Turner, Clarence W.Jr.	10	M	⅛	S	C. W. Turner	L	Non	No. 1	L	Cr
4	Turner, Marion	3	F	⅛	S	C. W. Turner	L	Non	No. 1	L	Cr

Census Card No. 316, P. O. Coweta, Enrolled May 3, 1899; No. 3 June 27, 1900

1	Charles, Ellen	20	F	½		N. B. Childers	L	Cr	Sophia Childers	D	Cr
2	Charles, Gustavus A.	2	M	½	S	Nero Charles	L	Cr	No. 1	L	Cr
3	Charles, Reuben	6 moM	½	S		Nero Charles	L	Cr	No. 1	L	Cr

Census Card No. 317, P. O. Broken Arrow, Enrolled May 3, 1899

1	Childers, William	26	M	F		James Childers	L	Cr	Jennie Childers	D	Cr
2	Childers, Annie	23	F	F	Wf	Jim Cloud	L	Cr	Matilda Childers	D	Cr
3	Childers, Mary	6	F	F	D	No. 1	L	Cr	Jane Childers	D	Cr
4	Childers, Winfield	1	M	F	S	No. 1	L	Cr	No. 2	L	Cr

Census Card No. 318, P. O. Coweta, Enrolled May 3, 1899

1	Kelley, Tobey	65	M	F		Mose Kelley	D	Cr	Misteothle	D	Cr
2	Kelley, Wesley	16	M	F	S	No. 1	L	Cr	Tilsie Kelley	D	Cr
3	Kelley, Eliza	14	F	F	D	No. 1	L	Cr	Tilsie Kelley	D	Cr
4	Kelley, Emma	12	F	F	D	No. 1	L	Cr	Tilsie Kelley	D	Cr
5	Kelley, Sukey	10	F	F	D	No. 1	L	Cr	Tilsie Kelley	D	Cr

No. 5 died January 6, 1901

Census Card No. 319, P. O. Hitchita, Enrolled May 22, 1899

1	Davis, John	57	M	F		Davis	D	Cr	Sally Davis	D	Cr
2	Davis, Celina	35	F	F	Wf	Hobuthke Harjo	L	Cr	Melina Harjo	D	Cr
3	Bradley, Lewis	14	M	F	StS	Sam Bradley	D	Cr	No. 2	L	Cr
4	Bradley, Sam	12	M	F	StS	Sam Bradley	D	Cr	No. 2	L	Cr

No. 4 died June 29, 1899.   No. 1 died 1912.   No. 3 died September 27, 1907.   No. 2 reported dead

Census Card No. 320, P. O. Nowata, Enrolled May 3, 1899

| 1 | Walker, Minnie | 24 | F | F | | Henry Grayson | L | Cr | Mary Grayson | L | Cr |
| 2 | Walker, Nettie | 7 | F | F | D | Billie Walker | D | Cr | No. 1 | L | Cr |

Census Card No. 321, P. O. Okmulgee, Enrolled May 4, 1899

1	Johnson, Daniel	56	M	F		Enoch Johnson	D	Cr	Me'issa Johnson	D	Cr
2	Johnson, Chutkee	45	F	F	Wf	Ninnechuppo Harjo	D	Cr	Unknown	?	Cr
3	Johnson, Wiley	20	M	F	S	No. 1	L	Cr	No. 2	L	Cr

No. 2 died June 6, 1902.   No. 3 died November 25, 1905.   No. 1 reported dead.

Census Card No. 322, P. O. Okfuskee, Enrolled May 4 1899

| 1 | Micco, Parfena | 40 | F | F | | Tulmachuse Micco | D | Cr | Quosoday | D | Cr |

No. 1 died March 12, 1913

Census Card No. 323, P. O. Okmulgee, Enrolled May 4, 1899

1	Perryman, William	45	M	F		Prince Perryman	D	Cr	Sallie Perryman	D	Cr
2	Perryman, Lucy	40	F	F	Wf	Hillis Harjo	D	Cr	Unknown	D	Cr
3	Perryman, Emma	9	F	F	D	No. 1	L	Cr	No. 2	L	Cr
4	Perryman, Eddie	19	M	F	S	No. 1	L	Cr	Liley Perryman	D	Cr

No. 1 died January 12, 1904.   No. 3 died December 12, 1904.   No. 2 died 1899

Census Card No. 324, P. O. Tulsa, Enrolled May 4, 1899

| 1 | Grayson, Pete | 22 | M | ⅜ | | Henry Grayson | L | Cr | Mary Grayson | L | Cr |

No. 1 died March 10, 1912

Census Card No. 325, P. O. Okmulgee, Enrolled May 4, 1899

| 1 | Berryhill, Konsie | 19 | M | F | | John Berryhill | L | Cr | Nicey Berryhill | D | Cr |

No. 1 died March 18, 1910

31

Census Card No. 326, P. O. Catoosa, Enrolled May 5, 1899; No. 4 Coweta; No. 8 October 27, 1899

Roll No.	No.	NAME	Age	Sex	Blood	Rel.	NAME OF FATHER	Liv.	Cit.	NAME OF MOTHER	Liv.
1080	1	Harrison, Eli	35	M	F		Nokoseka	D	Cr	Susana	D
1081	2	Harrison, Ellen	29	F	F	Wf	Timmye Cornell	L	Cr	Lucinda	L
1082	3	Harrison, Jimmy	3	M	F	S	No. 1	L	Cr	No. 2	L
1083	4	Harrison, Lizzie	13	F	F	D	No. 1	L	Cr	Mary Harvison	D
1084	5	Lynch, Wesley R.	10	M	F	StS	Unknown	?	Cr	No. 2	L
1085	6	Harrison, Nero	14	M	F	Neph	Enochie Harvison	D	Cr	Lydia Harvison	D
1086	7	Lynch, Hannah	13	F	F	N-inL	Joe Lynch	L	Cr	Eliza Lynch	D
1087	8	Harrison, Benjamin	4 mo	M	F	S	No. 1	L	Cr	No. 2	L

No. 6 died December 27, 1899.   No. 1 died January 1, 1909
No. 8 died November 10, 1900

Census Card No. 327, P. O. No. 1 and 4 Morris; No. 3 Haskell, Enrolled May 5, 1899

Roll No.	No.	NAME	Age	Sex	Blood	Rel.	NAME OF FATHER	Liv.	Cit.	NAME OF MOTHER	Liv.
1088	1	Moore, William N.	27	M	F		John R. Moore	D	Cr	Martha Moore	D
1089	2	Moore, Lizzie	29	F	F	Sis	John R. Moore	D	Cr	Martha Moore	D
1090	3	Moore, Wright	17	M	F	Bro	John R. Moore	D	Cr	Susan Moore	D
1091	4	Moore, John R.	15	M	F	Bro	John R. Moore	D	Cr	Susan Moore	D

Census Card No. 328, P. O. Okmulgee, Enrolled May 5, 1899

Roll No.	No.	NAME	Age	Sex	Blood	Rel.	NAME OF FATHER	Liv.	Cit.	NAME OF MOTHER	Liv.
1092	1	Micco, Lucy	56	F	F		Aleck	D	Cr	Sarktushogey	D

Census Card No. 329, P. O. Okmulgee, Enrolled May 5, 1899; No. 4 July 20, 1900

Roll No.	No.	NAME	Age	Sex	Blood	Rel.	NAME OF FATHER	Liv.	Cit.	NAME OF MOTHER	Liv.
1093	1	Checotah, Millie	30	F	F		Checotah Yahola	D	Cr	Lucy Micco	L
1094	2	Monday, Jackson Louis	4	M	F	S	March Monday	L	Cr	No. 1	L
1095	3	Monday, McKinley	2	M	F	S	March Monday	L	Cr	No. 1	L
1096	4	Gray, Lizzie	4 mo	F	F	D	Will Gray	L	Cr	No. 1	L

No. 4 died July 27, 1900
No. 3 died June 18, 1912

Census Card No. 330, P. O. Okmulgee, Enrolled May 5, 1899

Roll No.	No.	NAME	Age	Sex	Blood	Rel.	NAME OF FATHER	Liv.	Cit.	NAME OF MOTHER	Liv.
1097	1	Wiley, Malissa	39	F	F		Checotah Yahola	D	Cr	Lucy Micco	L
1098	2	Wiley, Cinda	6	F	F	D	Jersey Wiley	L	Cr	No. 1	L
1099	3	Wiley, Major	4	M	F	GnS	Jersey Wiley	L	Cr	No. 1	L
1100	4	Wiley, Martha	3 mo	F	F	D	Jersey Wiley	L	Cr	No. 1	L
1101	5	Tarpalechee, Miller	9	M	F	S	Tarparlechee	L	Cr	No. 1	L

No. 4 died October 21, 1899.   Nos. 1 reported dead

Census Card No. 331, P. O. Catoosa; No. 3 Coweta, Enrolled May 5, 1899; No. 7 June 13, 1900

Roll No.	No.	NAME	Age	Sex	Blood	Rel.	NAME OF FATHER	Liv.	Cit.	NAME OF MOTHER	Liv.
1102	1	Chalakee, Jimsey	43	M	F		Thomas Chalakee	D	Cr	Mary Gbalake	D
1103	2	Chalakee, Louvina	43	F	F	Wf	Unknown	D	Cr	Unknown	D
1104	3	Chalakee, Nicey	13	F	F	D	No. 1	L	Cr	No. 2	L
1105	4	Chalakee, Thomas	11	M	F	S	No. 1	L	Cr	No. 2	L
1106	5	Chalakee, Jimmy	4	M	F	S	No. 1	L	Cr	No. 2	L
1107	6	Chalakee, Johnny	1	M	F	S	No. 1	L	Cr	No. 2	L
1108	7	Chalakee, Daniel	2 mo	M	F	S	No. 1	L	Cr	No. 2	L

No. 7 died September 1900.   No. 2 July 27, 1900

Census Card No. 332, P. O. Catoosa, Enrolled May 5, 1899

Roll No.	No.	NAME	Age	Sex	Blood	Rel.	NAME OF FATHER	Liv.	Cit.	NAME OF MOTHER	Liv.
1109	1	Burgess, Dave	24	M	F		Daniel Burgess	D	Cr	Ellen Burgess	D

No. 1 died April 10, 1901

Census Card No. 333, P. O. Bixby, Enrolled May 5, 1899

Roll No.	No.	NAME	Age	Sex	Blood	Rel.	NAME OF FATHER	Liv.	Cit.	NAME OF MOTHER	Liv.
1110	1	Crosby, Mary A.	48	F	1/2		Michael McCann	D	Non	Elizabeth McCann	D
1111	2	Hill, Ada	4	F	3/4	GrD	George Hill	L	Cr	Mary E. Brockman	L

No. 2 died August 1, 1904

Census Card No. 334, Okmulgee, Enrolled May 5, 1899; No. 6 Sperry

Roll No.	No.	NAME	Age	Sex	Blood	Rel.	NAME OF FATHER	Liv.	Cit.	NAME OF MOTHER	Liv.
1112	1	Crosby, Charles E.	29	M	1/4		B. M. Crosby	L	Non	Mary A. Crosby	L
1113	2	Crosby, Elizabeth A.	29	F	1/4	Wf	F. B. Berryhill	D	Cr	Rachel Perryman	D
1114	3	Crosby, Mary Elizabeth	4	F	1/8	D	No. 1	L	Cr	No. 2	L
1115	4	Crosby, Ellis Charles	1	M	1/8	S	No. 1	L	Cr	No. 2	L
1116	5	Smith, Nina	11	F	1/4	StD	Samuel Smith	D	Cr	No. 2	L
1117	6	Smith, Daniel B. No. 2	10	M	1/4	StS	Samuel Smith	D	Cr	No. 2	L

No. 1 died August 1903

Census Card No. 335, P. O. Catoosa, Enrolled May 5, 1899

Roll No.	No.	NAME	Age	Sex	Blood	Rel.	NAME OF FATHER	Liv.	Cit.	NAME OF MOTHER	Liv.
1118	1	Tiger, Ben	46	M	F		Cowake Yahola	D	Cr	Unknown	?
1119	2	Tiger, Mary	25	F	F	Wf	Washington, Childers	D	Cr	Mandy Childers	I.
1120	3	Tiger, Mandy	4	F	F	D	No. 1	L	Cr	No. 2	L
1121	4	Tiger, Rosie	10 mo	F	F	D	No. 1	L	Cr	No. 2	I.

No. 2 died March 12, 1910.   No. 4 reported dead.

Census Card No. 336, P. O. Broken Arrow, Enrolled May 5, 1899; No. 6, December 12, 1899

Roll No.	No.	NAME	Age	Sex	Blood	Rel.	NAME OF FATHER	Liv.	Cit.	NAME OF MOTHER	Liv.
1122	1	Tiger, Jim	28	M	F		Billy Tiger	L	Cr	Liley Tiger	L
1123	2	Tiger, Nancy	28	F	F	Wf	Sippey	D	Cr	Amy	D
1124	3	Tiger, Amy	6	F	F	D	No. 1	L	Cr	Sarah Tiger	L
1125	4	Morris, Susan	8	F	F	St-D	Cheparney Morris	D	Cr	No. 2	L
1126	5	Morris, Emma	1	F	F	St-D	Cheparney Morris	D	Cr	No.	L
1127	6	Tiger, Jno	2 mo	M	F	S	No. 1	L	Cr	No. 2	L

No. 4 died September 13, 1914.   No. 5 reported dead.

Census Card No. 337, P. O. Catoosa, Enrolled May 5, 1899

Roll No.	No.	NAME	Age	Sex	Blood	Rel.	NAME OF FATHER	Liv.	Cit.	NAME OF MOTHER	Liv.
1128	1	White, Mose	25	M	F		Unknown	D	Cher	Iyoka	D

Census Card No. 338, P. O. Okmulgee, Enrolled May 6, 1899

Roll No.	No.	NAME	Age	Sex	Blood	Rel.	NAME OF FATHER	Liv.	Cit.	NAME OF MOTHER	Liv.
1129	1	Lee, Barney	23	M	F		Robert Lee	D	Cr	Lucy Lee	D

Census Card No. 339, P. O. Morris, Enrolled May 6, 1899

Roll No.	No.	NAME	Age	Sex	Blood	Rel.	NAME OF FATHER	Liv.	Cit.	NAME OF MOTHER	Liv.
1130	1	Lynch, Sarah	19	F	1/2		Wm. Lynch	D	Non	Lizzie Company	D

Census Card No. 340, P. O. Porter, Enrolled May 6, 1899

Roll No.	No.	NAME	Age	Sex	Blood	Rel.	NAME OF FATHER	Liv.	Cit.	NAME OF MOTHER	Liv.
1131	1	Perryman, Wm.	47	M	1/4		Sam Perrymna	D	Cr	Mary Perryman	D
1132	2	Perryman, Mary	1 mo	F	1/8	D	No. 1	L	Cr	Trona Perryman	L

No. 2 died January 1907

Roll No. | No. | NAME | Age | Sex | Blood | Rel. | NAME OF FATHER | Liv. | Cit. | NAME OF MOTHER | Liv. | Cit.

Census Card No. 341, P. O. Morris, Enrolled May 6, 1899; No. 3 June 29, 1900

Roll No.	No.	NAME	Age	Sex	Blood	Rel.	NAME OF FATHER	Liv.	Cit.	NAME OF MOTHER	Liv.	Cit.
1133	1	Cable, Mary Isabel	23	F	1/8		John R. Ashley	L	Non	Isabel Jane Ashley	L	Cr
1134	2	Cable, John Henry	2	M	1-16		Adam M. Cable	L	Non	No. 1	L	Cr
1135	3	Cable, Cora E.	23d as	F	1-16	D	Adam M. Cable	L	Non	No. 1	L	Cr

Census Card No. 342, P. O. Catoosa, Enrolled May 6, 1899

Roll No.	No.	NAME	Age	Sex	Blood	Rel.	NAME OF FATHER	Liv.	Cit.	NAME OF MOTHER	Liv.	Cit.
1136	1	Tiger, Dave	45	M	F		Cotsar Tiger	D	Cr	Unknown	D	Cr
1137	2	Tiger, Neosho	34	F	1/2	Wf	Moody	D	Non	Yarna	L	Cr
1138	3	Tiger, Willie	2	M	3/4	S	No. 1	L	Cr	No. 2	L	Cr
1139	4	Tiger, Cotsar	3 moM		3/4	S	No. 1	L	Cr	No. 2	L	Cr
1140	5	Perryman, Hattie	4	F	3/4	StD	Sanford Perryman	L	Cr	No. 2	L	Cr
1141	6	Wilson, Jesse	15	M	F	Neph	Taylor Wilson	D	Cr	Lizzie Wilson	D	Cr

No. 6 died 1902

Census Card No. 343, P. O. Catoosa, Enrolled May 6, 1899

Roll No.	No.	NAME	Age	Sex	Blood	Rel.	NAME OF FATHER	Liv.	Cit.	NAME OF MOTHER	Liv.	Cit.
1142	1	Asbury, Francis	44	M	3/4		Daniel Asbury	D	Cr	Katie Asbury	L	Cr
1143	2	Asbury, Jennetta	25	F	F	Wf	Sippy	D	Cr	Amy	L	Cr
1144	3	Asbury, Eliza	16	F	3/8	D	No. 1	L	Cr	Cooty Asbury	L	Cr
1145	4	Scott, Amos	6	M	F	St-D	Thomas Scott	D	Cr	No. 2	L	Cr

No. 3 died October 11, 1900.   No. 4 died October 28, 1905.   No. 2 reported dead.

Census Card No. 344, P. O. Coweta, Enrolled May 6 1899

Roll No.	No.	NAME	Age	Sex	Blood	Rel.	NAME OF FATHER	Liv.	Cit.	NAME OF MOTHER	Liv.	Cit.
1146	1	Pinehill, Sarah	22	F	F		Sapiye	D	Cr	Salina	D	Cr

Census Card No. 345, P. O. Laredo, Texas. Enrolled May 8, 1899
P. O. Box No. 7, So. Laredo

Roll No.	No.	NAME	Age	Sex	Blood	Rel.	NAME OF FATHER	Liv.	Cit.	NAME OF MOTHER	Liv.	Cit.
1147	1	Tarvin, Marion E.	62	M	1/4		Elisha Tarvin	D	Non	Theresa Tarvin	D	Cr
1148	2	Tarvin, Rita	11	F	1-16	GnD	Pleasant F. Tarvin	L	Cr	Patience Tarvin	L	Non

Census Card No. 346, P. O. Tulsa, Enrolled May 12, 1899

Roll No.	No.	NAME	Age	Sex	Blood	Rel.	NAME OF FATHER	Liv.	Cit.	NAME OF MOTHER	Liv.	Cit.
1149	1	Fry, Susie	25	F	F		Oches Harjo	D	Cr	Mary	D	Cr

Census Card No. 347, P. O. Muskogee, Enrolled May 8, 1899

Roll No.	No.	NAME	Age	Sex	Blood	Rel.	NAME OF FATHER	Liv.	Cit.	NAME OF MOTHER	Liv.	Cit.
1150	1	Tarvin, Beauregard C.	38	M	1/8		Marion E. Tarvin	L	Cr	Sophia F. Tarvin	L	Non

Census Card No. 348, P. O. Coweta, Enrolled May 8, 1899

Roll No.	No.	NAME	Age	Sex	Blood	Rel.	NAME OF FATHER	Liv.	Cit.	NAME OF MOTHER	Liv.	Cit.
1151	1	Williams, George	13	M	3/4		Alex Williams	L	Cr	Jane Williams	D	Cr
1152	2	Williams, Daniel	5	M	3/4	Bro	Alex Williams	L	Cr	Jane illiams	D	Cr

Census Card No. 349, P. O. Catoosa, Enrolled May 8, 1899

Roll No.	No.	NAME	Age	Sex	Blood	Rel.	NAME OF FATHER	Liv.	Cit.	NAME OF MOTHER	Liv.	Cit.
1153	1	White, Malissa	17	F	F	Wf	John White	D	Cr	Ada White	D	Cr
1154	2	White, Tellie	25	M	F		Joe Lynch	L	Cr	Lucinda Kernels	L	Cr

No. 1 died August 23, 1902

Census Card No. 350, P. O. Muskogee, Enrolled May 9, 1899

Roll No.	No.	NAME	Age	Sex	Blood	Rel.	NAME OF FATHER	Liv.	Cit.	NAME OF MOTHER	Liv.	Cit.
1155	1	English, Bessie E.	27	F	1/4		Frederick B. Severs	L	AW	Annie A. Severs	L	Cr
1156	2	English, Frederick S.	4	M	1/8	S	Albert Z. English	L	Non	No. 1	L	Cr

Census Card No. 351, P. O. Okmulgee, Enrolled May 8, 1899

Roll No.	No.	NAME	Age	Sex	Blood	Rel.	NAME OF FATHER	Liv.	Cit.	NAME OF MOTHER	Liv.	Cit.
1157	1	Berryhill, Harrison	28	M	F		Robert Berryhill	D	Cr	Elsie Berryhill	D	Cr
1158	2	Berryhill, Bettie	25	F	F	Wf	Unknown	D	Cr	Millie	D	Cr
1159	3	Berryhill, William	8	M	F	S	No. 1	L	Cr	No. 2	L	Cr
1160	4	Berryhill, Elizabeth	3	F	F	D	No. 1	L	Cr	No. 2	L	Cr
1161	5	Berryhill, Lucy	8moF		F	D	No. 1	L	Cr	No. 2	L	Cr

No. 2 died January 17, 1904

Census Card No. 352, P. O. Muskogee, Enrolled May 9, 1899

Roll No.	No.	NAME	Age	Sex	Blood	Rel.	NAME OF FATHER	Liv.	Cit.	NAME OF MOTHER	Liv.	Cit.
1162	1	Severs, Frederick B.	63	M	Ad-W		Chas. J. Severs	D	Non	Vasina T. Severs	D	Non
1163	2	Severs, Anna A.	59	F	1/2	Wf	Geo. Anderson	D	Cr	Nancy Anderson	D	Cr
1164	3	Severs, Annie E.	20	F	1/4	D	No. 1	L	Cr	No. 2	L	Cr

No. 1 died.   No. 2 died.

Census Card No. 353, P. O. Beggs, Enrolled May 9, 1899

Roll No.	No.	NAME	Age	Sex	Blood	Rel.	NAME OF FATHER	Liv.	Cit.	NAME OF MOTHER	Liv.	Cit.
1165	1	Jefferson, Manuel	77	M	1/4		Jeffrey George	D	Col	Bessie	D	Cr
1166	2	Jefferson, Jane	61	F	AC	Wf	Phe Reed	D	?	Mary Reed	D	?

No. 1 died February 1, 1902

Census Card No. 354, P. O. Onapa, Enrolled May 9, 1899

Roll No.	No.	NAME	Age	Sex	Blood	Rel.	NAME OF FATHER	Liv.	Cit.	NAME OF MOTHER	Liv.	Cit.
1167	1	Scott, Bosie	37	M	1/2		James Scott	L	Non	Lou M. Scott	L	Cr
1168	2	Scott, Willie	13	M	1/2	S	No. 1	L	Cr.	Martha Scott	L	Cr
1169	3	Scott, Annie	10	F	1/2	D	No. 1	L	Cr.	Martha Scott	L	Cr
1170	4	Scott, Vollie	6	F	1/2	D	No. 1	L	Cr.	Martha Scott	L	Cr
1171	5	Scott, Fuller	5	M	1/2	S	No. 1	L	Cr.	Martha Scott	L	Cr
1172	6	Scott, Wallace	3	M	1/2	S	No. 1	L	Cr.	Martha Scott	L	Cr

Census Card No. 355, P. O. Muskogee; No. 1 and 7, Hartshorne, Enrolled May 9,1899; No. 7, May 16,1901

Roll No.	No.	NAME	Age	Sex	Blood	Rel.	NAME OF FATHER	Liv.	Cit.	NAME OF MOTHER	Liv.	Cit.
1173	1	Lynch, James H.	39	M	1/2		James Lynch	D	Non	Lucy Lynch	D	Cr
1174	2	Lynch, Dolly	30	F	1/8	Wf	W. B. Self	L	Cr	Mary Self	L	Non
1175	3	Lynch, James H. Jr.	1	M	5-16	S	No. 1	L	Cr	No. 2	L	Cr
1176	4	Lynch, John T.	3moM		5-16	S	No. 1	L	Cr	No. 2	L	Cr
1177	5	Scott, James N.	11	M	1/4	StS	Spire Scott	D	Cr	No. 2	L	Cr
1178	6	Scott, Buck	9	M	1/4	StS	Spire Scott	D	Cr	No. 2	L	Cr
1179	7	Lynch, Bessie	15	F	5-16	D	No. 1	L	Cr	Kate Lynch	L	Cr

Census Card No. 356, Wetumka; No. 5, Wenoka, Enrolled May 9, 1899; No. 8, February 17, 1900

Roll No.	No.	NAME	Age	Sex	Blood	Rel.	NAME OF FATHER	Liv.	Cit.	NAME OF MOTHER	Liv.	Cit.
1180	1	Brown, Julia	27	F	1/4		Caesar Simon	L	Sem	Charity Simon	D	Cr
1181	2	Brown, John	10	M	1/8	S	T. J. Brown	L	Non	No. 1	L	Cr
1182	3	Brown, Charity	8	F	1/8	D	T. J. Brown	L	Non	No. 1	L	Cr
1183	4	Brown, Charles	6	M	1/8	S	T. J. Brown	L	Non	No. 1	L	Cr
1184	5	Brown, Elwood	4	M	1/8	S	T. J. Brown	L	Non	No. 1	L	Cr
1185	6	Brown, Rose	2	F	1/8	D	T. J. Brown	L	Non	No. 1	L	Cr
1186	7	Brown, Madison	1	M	1/8	S	T. J. Brown	L	Non	No. 1	L	Cr
1187	8	Brown, Minnie	6moF		1/8	D	T. J. Brown	L	Non	No. 1	L	Cr

No. 1 died February 10, 1911

Census Card No. 357, P. O. Eufaula, Enrolled May 9, 1899

Roll No.	No.	NAME	Age	Sex	Blood	Rel.	NAME OF FATHER	Liv.	Cit.	NAME OF MOTHER	Liv.	Cit.
1188	1	Simpson, Robert L.	25	M	1-32		John F. Simpson	L	Non	Susan N. Simpson	L	Cr

33

Roll No.	No.	NAME	Age	Sex	Blood	Rel.	Name of Father	Liv.	Cit.	Name of Mother	Liv.	Cit.
Census Card No. 358, P. O. Beggs, Enrolled May 9, 1899												
1189	1	Grayson, Robert	38	M	¼		Doc Grayson	D	Cr	Susan Grayson	L	Cr
Census Card No. 359, P. O. Beggs, Enrolled May 11, 1899												
1190	1	Grayson, Willie	24	M	¼		Doc Grayson	D	Cr	Susan Grayson	L	Cr
Census Card No. 360, P. O. Muskogee, Enrolled May 11, 1899												
1191	1	Stidham, Theodore E.	27	M	¼		G. W. Stidham	D	Cr	Sarah Stidham	D	Non
Census Card No. 361, P. O. Checotah, Enrolled May 11, 1899												
1192	1	Wadsworth, Ben	27	M	⅛		Cad Wadsworth	D	?	Malinda Wadsworth	D	?
		No. 1 died November 3, 1910										
Census Card No. 362, P. O. Tulsa, Enrolled May 12, 1899; No. 2 October 18, 1899												
1193	1	Hodge, Katie	30	F	F		Folotka	L	Cr	Susie	D	Cr
1194	2	Chisholm, Samuel	12	M	F	S	Andrew Chisholm	D	Cr	No. 1	L	Cr
		No. 1 died October 5, 1914										
Census Card No. 363, P. O. No. 2, Fame; No. 3, Eufaula; No. 4, Brush Hill, Enrolled May 12, 1899; No. 6, October 7, 1899												
1195	1	Huckaby, Elsie	27	F	½		Wm. Lynch	D	Non	Fannie Laslie	L	Cr
1196	2	Lowe, Susie	9	F	¾	D	Alex Lowe	D	Cr	No. 1 ⅛	L	Cr
1197	3	Lowe, Nancy	8	F	¾	D	Alex Lowe	D	Cr	No. 1	L	Cr
1198	4	Lowe, Lizzie	5	F	¾	D	Alex Lowe	D	Cr	No. 1	L	Cr
1199	5	Huckaby, William	3	M	¼	S	R. W. Huckaby	L	Non	No. 1	L	Cr
1200	6	Huckaby, Aaron	3mo	M	¼	S	R. W. Huckaby	L	Non	No. 1	L	Cr
Census Card No. 364, P. O. Eufaula, Enrolled May 12, 1899												
1201	1	Whitlow, David	30	M	½		David B. Whitlow	L	Cr	Millie Whitlow	D	Cr
Census Card No. 365, P. O. Muskogee, Enrolled May 13, 1899												
1202	1	Herrick, Mary	27	F	⅛		W. B. Self	L	Cr	Mary E. Self	L	Non
1203	2	Herrick, Leo, Jr.	5	M	1-16	S	Leo Herrick	L	Non	No. 1	L	Cr
1204	3	Herrick, Juanita	3	F	1-16	D	Leo Herrick	L	Non	No. 1	L	Cr
Census Card No. 366, P. O. Muskogee, Enrolled May 15, 1899; No. 5 May 22, 1901												
1205	1	Jobe, Louis N. B.	38	M	¼		L. P. Jobe	D	Cr	Cherokee Jobe	D	Cr
1206	2	Jobe, Cherokee Mary	7	F	⅛	D	No. 1	L	Cr	Mary G. Jobe	L	Non
1207	3	Jobe, Gertrude	4	F	⅛	D	No. 1	L	Cr	Mary G. Jobe	L	Non
1208	4	Jobe, Florence	2	F	⅛	D	No. 1	L	Cr	Mary G. Jobe	L	Non
1209	5	Jobe, Eliza M.	2	F	⅛	D	No. 1	L	Cr	Mary Jobe	L	Non
		No. 2 died June 26, 1910										
Census Card No. 367, P. O. Eufaula, Enrolled May 15, 1899												
1210	1	Chartie, Washington	88	M	F		Unknown	D	Cr	Jennie	D	Cr
		No. 1 died Dec. 7, 1900										
Census Card No. 368, P. O. Mounds, Enrolled May 15, 1899												
1211	1	Self, Mid T.	25	M	⅛		W. R. Self	L	Cr	Mary E. Self	L	Non.
Census Card No. 369, P. O. Mounds, Enrolled May 15, 1899												
1212	1	Self,. W. B.	78	M	¼		W. B. Self	D	Non	Mary E. Self	D	Cr
		No. 1 died June 1904.										
Census Card No. 370, P. O. No. 1 Wainwright; No. 2 Oktaha, Enrolled May 16, 1899; No. 3 March 1, 1901												
1213	1	Durant, Nancy	26	F	½		Stephen Durant	L	Cr	Eliza Coonhead	L	Cr
1214	2	Berryhill, Eliza	2	F	¾	D	David L. Berryhill	L	Cr	No. 1	L	Cr
1215	3	Williams, Eddie	1	M	⅜	S	Elmer Williams	L	Non	No. 1	L	Cr
Census Card No. 371, P. O. Broken Arrow, Enrolled May 16, 1899												
1216	1	Hodge, Elum B.	43	M	⅛		Nathaniel Hodge	D	Non	Nancy Hodge	D	Cr
Census Card No. 372, P. O. Tulsa, Enrolled May 16, 1899												
1217	1	Flippin, Mary Jane	23	F	½		Fain Burgess	D	Cr	Kizzie Milford	D	Cr
1218	2	Flippin. Jerome	2	M	¼	S	Walter Flippin	L	Non	No. 1	L	Cr
Census Card No. 373, P. O. Tulsa, Enrolled May 16, 1899												
1219	1	Burgess, Jane	62	F	F		Mose Perryman	D	Cr	Mollie Perryman	D	Cr
		No. 1 died about January 1, 1901										
Census Card No. 374, P. O. Tulsa, Enrolled May 16, 1899												
1220	1	Burgess, Ben	25	M	½		Fain Burgess	D	Cr	Kizzie Melford	D	Cr
Census Card No. 375, P. O. Red Fork, Enrolled May 18, 1899												
1221	1	Russell, Mary A.	25	F	1-16		Thos. H. Berryhill	L	Cr	Sarah H. Berryhill	L	Non
1222	2	Russell, Earl C.	3	M	1-32	S	James W. Russell	L	Non	No. 1	L	Cr
1223	3	Russell, Estle I.	2	F	1-32	D	James W. Russell	L	Non	No. 1	L	Cr
1224	4	Russell, Leva	6 mo	F	1-32	D	James W. Russell	L	Non	No. 1	L	Cr
Census Card No. 376, P. O. Okmulgee, Enrolled May 19, 1899												
1225	1	Isparhecher	70	M	F		Yaddike Tustannugee	D	Cr	Kecharte	D	Cr
1226	2	IpsarhecherCindochee	34	F	F	Wf	Kussar Nehathlocco	D	Cr	Katy	D	Cr
		No. 1 died December 22, 1902										
Census Card No. 377, P. O. Okmulgee, Enrolled October 12, 1899												
1227	1	Buffalo, George	42	M	F		Oche Yahola	D	Cr	Meley	D	Cr
1228	2	Buffalo, Uana	25	F	F	Wf	Thomas Haynes	D	Cr	Lucy Haynes	D	Cr
		No. 1 reported dead										
Census Card No. 378, P. O. Okmulgee, Enrolled May 20, 1899												
1229	1	Checote, Emma	24	F	F		Samuel Checotah	D	Cr	Lizzie Checotah	D	Cr
Census Card No. 379, P. O. Okmulgee, Enrolled May 20, 1899; No. 4 March 4, 1901												
1230	1	Kanard, James	22	M	F		Major Kenard	D	Cr	Mary Kenard	D	Cr
1231	2	Kanard, Annie	17	F	F	Wf	Peter Buflow	D	Cr	Miley Buflow	L	Cr
1232	3	Kanard, William	5 mo	M	F	S	No. 1	L	Cr	No. 2	L	Cr
1233	4	Kanard, Nellie	22	F	F	Wf	John Davis	L	Cr	Mehaka	L	Cr
		No. 2 died November 18, 1908										
		No. 3 died April 19, 1900										
		No. 4 died December 28, 1905										

Roll No.	No.	NAME	Age	Sex	Blood	Rel.	NAME OF FATHER	Liv.	Cit.	NAME OF MOTHER	Liv.	Cit.
		Census Card No. 380, P. O. Okmulgee, Enrolled May 22, 1899										
1234	1	Johnson, Samuel	22	M	F		Daniel Johnson	L	Cr	Chutkee Johnson	L	Cr
		Census Card No. 381, P. O. Okmulgee, Enrolled May 22, 1899										
1235	1	Davison, David	61	M	F		Fus Emarthla	D	Cr	Saboka	D	Cr
1236	2	Davison, Dicey	55	F	F	Wf	Tommie Harjo	D	Cr	Suffekah	D	Cr
1237	3	Davison, John	10	M	F	S	No. 1	L	Cr	No. 2	L	Cr
1238	4	Scott, Philip	21	M	F	N-I.	Neahlocka Chupco	L	Cr	Lucy Scott	D	Cr
		No. 2 died November 23, 1903. No. 3, 4, reported dead.										
		Census Card No. 382, P. O. Morris, Enrolled May 22, 1899										
1239	1	Scott, James	22	M	F		Neahlocka Chupco	D	Cr	Lucy Scott	D	Cr
		Census Card No. 383, P. O. Okmulgee, Enrolled May 22, 1899										
1240	1	Harjo, Jennetta	30	F	F		Hobuth Harjo	D	Cr	Melina Harjo	D	Cr
		Census Card No. 384, P. O. Okmulgee, Enrolled May 23, 1899										
		Nos. 2 and 3 Coweta										
1241	1	Scott, Nicey	50	F	F		Oche Harjo	D	Cr	Missah	D	Cr
1242	2	Scott, Josephine	17	F	F	StD	Billy Scott	D	Cr	Polly Scott	D	Cr
1243	3	Scott, Sanford	19	M	F	StS	Billy Scott	D	Cr	Polly Scott	D	Cr
1244	4	Willie, Sam	15	M	F	StS	Willie Chupco	D	Cr	Lizzie Chupco	D	Cr
		No. 1 died November 1, 1902										
		Census Card No. 385, P. O. Okmulgee, Enrolled May 22, 1899										
1245	1	Semikee	58	M	F		Artus Honubbe	D	Cr	Sathlahoye	L	Cr
1246	2	Jemima	35	F	F	Wf	Concharty Micco	D	Cr	Sadeloke	L	Cr
1247	3	Josie	3	M	F	D	No. 1	L	Cr	No. 2	L	Cr
		No. 1 died November 1, 1902										
		Census Card No. 386, P. O. Okmulgee, Enrolled May 22, 1899; No. 3, May 31, 1900										
1248	1	Carruth, Lewis	23	M	F		Wildcat	D	Cr	Katie Barnwell	L	Cr
1249	2	Carruth, Dicey	19	F	F	Wf	Bunny Scott	D	Cr	Sallie Solomon	L	Cr
1250	3	Carruth, Katie	9mo	F	F	D	No. 1	L	Cr	No. 2	L	Cr
		Census Card No. 387, P. O. Okmulgee, Enrolled May 23, 1899										
1251	1	Marsey, Dave	23	M	F		Marsey	D	Cr	Nancy Marsey	D	Cr
		No. 1 died December 12, 1908										
		Census Card No. 388, P. O. Henryetta, Enrolled May 23, 1899										
1252	1	Sullivan, Wm.	48	M	½		Sam Sullivan	D	?	Sallie Sullivan	D	?
1253	2	Sullivan, Louina	32	F	F	Wf	Micco Yahola	D	Cr	Millaka	D	Cr
		Census Card No. 389, P. O. Okmulgee, Enrolled May 24, 1899; Nos. 4, 5, 6, October 4, 1899										
1254	1	Snakeya, David	38	M	F		Pinnege	D	Cr	Unknown	D	Cr
1255	2	Snakeya, Molleanna	20	F	F	Wf	Joney	D	Cr	Louisa	L	Cr
1256	3	Snakeya, Mary	4mo	F	F	D	No. 1	L	Cr	No. 2	L	Cr
1257	4	Snakeya, Abram	12	M	F	S	No. 1	L	Cr	Louisa	L	Cr
1258	5	Snakeya, Gabriel	8	M	F	S	No. 1	L	Cr	Louisa	L	Cr
1259	6	Snakeya, Onie	5	F	F	D	No. 1	L	Cr	Louisa	L	Cr
		No. 3 died July 21, 1899. No. 5 reported dead. No. 1 died March 18, 1909.										
		Census Card No. 390, P. O. Eufaula, Enrolled May 25, 1899										
1260	1	Island, Lizzie	40	F	F		Billy Island	D	Cr	Milloche Island	D	Cr
		Census Card No. 391, P. O. Muskogee, Enrolled May 29, 1899										
1261	1	Williams, Thomas	40	M	F		Bill Williams	D	Cr	Louisa Williams	D	Cr
		Census Card No. 392, P. O. McDermott, Enrolled May 29, 1899										
1262	1	Berry, Louisa	38	F	½		Dave McNac	D	Cr	Dicey McNac	L	Cr
1263	2	McDermott, Jesse	18	M	F	Neph	Daniels	L	Cr:	Sally Smith	D	Cr
1264	3	Smith, Marsey	16	F	F	Niece	Lumsey Smith	L	Cr	Sally Smith	D	Cr
1265	4	Smith, Lewis	12	M	F	Neph	Lumsey Smith	L	Cr	Sally Smith	D	Cr
1266	5	Smith, Emma	9	F	F	Niece	Lumsey Smith	L	Cr	Sally Smith	D	Cr
1267	6	Tiger, Lucy	11	F	F	Cous	Jim Tiger	L	Cr	Cinda Tiger	D	Cr
		Census Card No. 393, P. O. Salem, Enrolled May 29, 1899; No. 6, May 15, 1901										
1268	1	McNac, Peter	27	M	F		Dave McNac	D	Cr	Dicey McNac	L	Cr
1269	2	McNac, Lousanna	23	F	F	Wf	Henneha Micco	D	Cr	Polly Thomas	L	Cr
1270	3	McNac, Parney	3	M	F	S	No. 1	L	Cr	No. 2	L	Cr
1271	4	McNac, Tommie	10mo	M	F	S.	No. 1	L	Cr	No. 2	L	Cr
1272	5	Micco, Mannie	7	F	F	StD	John Tyler	L	Cr	No. 2	L	Cr
1273	6	McNac, Martha	1	F	F	D	No. 1	L	Cr	No. 2	L	Cr
		Census Card No. 394, P. O. Mounds, Enrolled May 29, 1899										
1274	1	Gant, Cordelia	48	F	¼		Henry Rowley	L	Non	MrsThompson Rowley	D	Cr
		Census Card No. 395, P. O. Senora, Enrolled May 29, 1899										
		No. 1 Henryetta; No. 4 May 23, 1901										
1275	1	Kelly, Wadly	24	M	F		Ahfolaka	D	Cr	Lownie Kelly	L	Cr
1276	2	Kelly, Mahaley	18	F	F	Wf	Wilson Tiger	L	Cr	Eliza Tiger	L	Cr
1277	3	Kelly, Jackson	1½	M	F	S	No. 1	L	Cr	No. 2	L	Cr
1278	4	Kelly, David	1	M	F	S	No. 1	L	Cr	No. 2	L	Cr
		No. 3 died 1900										
		No. 4 died January 5, 1901										
		No. 2 died January 20, 1915										
		Census Card No. 396, P. O. Oktaha, Enrolled May 29, 1899										
1279	1	Harjo, Willie	25	M	F		Ochess Harjo	D	Cr	Leah Harjo	D	Cr
		Census Card No. 397, P. O. Okemah, Enrolled May 29, 1899										
1280	1	Yahola, Arbeka	31	M	F		Pena Emarthla	D	Cr	Hollea	D	Cr
1281	2	Yahola, Rhoda	21	F	F	Wf	Arholoc Fixico	D	Cr	Mulleana	D	Cr
1282	3	Yahola, Willie	5mo	M	F	S	No. 1	L	Cr	No. 2	L	Cr
		No. 1 died August 1904.										

Roll No.	No.	NAME	Age	Sex	Blood	Rel.	NAME OF FATHER	Liv.	Cit.	NAME OF MOTHER	Liv.	Cit.

Census Card No. 398, P. O. Kellyville, Enrolled May 31, 1899; No. 8, May 23, 1901

1283	1	Tiger, Jack	52	M	F		Tiger, Bone	L	Cr	Yahpónna		
1284	2	Tiger, Jennetta	32	F	F	Wf	Robert McKellop	L	Cr	Sallie Deere	D	Cr
1285	3	Tiger, Lucy	8	F	F	D	No. 1	L	Cr	No. 2	L	Cr
1286	4	Tiger, Walter	4	M	F	S	No. 1	L	Cr	No. 2	L	Cr
1287	5	Tiger. Siller	2	F	F	D	No. 1	L	Cr	No. 2	L	Cr
1288	6	Baily, Moses	10	M	F	StS	Charles Bailey	L	Cr	No. 2	L	Cr
1289	7	Yahponna	100	F	F	Mot	Unknown	?	Cr	Unknown	?	Cr
1290	8	Tiger, Eliza	1	F	F	D	No. 1	L	Cr	No. 2	L	Cr

No. 1 died February 18, 1902. No. 4 died May 15, 1901. No. 7 died May 20, 1900.

Census Card No. 399, P. O. Paden, Enrolled May 31, 1899

1291	1	Harper, Albert	45	M	F		Harper Compeer	D	Cr	Euthlegee	D	Cr
1292	2	Harper, Jennie	42	F	F	Wf	Jesse Chisholm	D	Cr	Sukkahke	D	Cr
1293	3	Harper, Alfred	6	M	F	S	No. 1	L	Cr	No. 2	L	Cr
1294	4	Beaver, Cora	17	F	F	StD	Buck Beaver	D	Cr	No. 2	L	Cr
1295	5	Beaver, Lucy	15	F	F	StD	Buck Beaver	D	Cr	No. 2	L	Cr
1296	6	Beaver, Frank	13	M	F	StS	Buck Beaver	D	Cr	No. 2	L	Cr

No. 1 died October 2, 1901. No. 5 reported dead

Census Card No. 400, P. O. Kellyville, Enrolled May 31, 1899

Nos. 5 and 6 April 25, 1901

1297	1	Crow, Ahlacohonny	39	F	F		Chupkapony	D	Cr	Fannie	D	Cr
1298	2	Crow, Babie	17	F	F	D	Hokoletche	D	Cr	No. 1	L	Cr
1299	3	Crow, Mollie	14	F	F	D	Hokoletche	D	Cr	No. 1	L	Cr
1300	4	Snap, James	15	M	F	Neph	Fahkoweny	D	Cr	Sillubbee	D	Cr
1301	5	Fulsom, George	35	M	F	Hus	Auquanay	D	Cr	Ahkotaney	D	Cr
1302	6	Fish, Wothlarsha	16	M	F	StS	Cocan	D	Cr	Pantoney	D	Cr

No. 5 and 6 reported dead.

Census Card No. 401, P. O. Wagoner; No. 4, Hoffman, Enrolled May 31, 1899

1303	1	Vann, Katie	33	F	½		John Robins	D	Cr	Yartochee	L	Cr
1304	2	Love, Jonas	18	M	¼	S	Rgbert Love	D	Cr	No. 1	L	Cr
1305	3	Love, Willie	16	M	¼	S	Robert Love	D	Cr	No. 1	L	Cr
1306	4	Robinson, George	14	M	¼	S	Robert Robinson	L	Cr	No. 1	L	Cr

Census Card No. 402, P. O. Catoosa, Enrolled May 31, 1899

| 1307 | 1 | Chamberlain, Susie | 20 | F | ¼ | | Hugh Cowans | D | ? | Rose Perryman | D | Cr |
| 1308 | 2 | Chamberlain, Charlie Leroy | 2 | M | ⅛ | S | John C. Chamberlain | L | ? | No. 1 | L | Cr |

Census Card No. 403, P. O. Broken Arrow, Enrolled May 31, 1899

No. 9 August 22, 1899

1309	1	Presley, Mary M.	28	F	¼		Tom Escoe	L	Non	Mary Escoe	L	Cr
1310	2	Presley, Rosetta	12	F	⅛	D	Harrison Presley	L	Non	No. 1	L	Cr
1311	3	Presley, Arthur	11	M	⅛	S	Harrison Presley	L	Non	No. 1	L	Cr
1312	4	Presley, Smith	9	M	⅛	S	Harrison Presley	L	Non	No. 1	L	Cr
1313	5	Presley, Louisa	7	F	⅛	D	Harrison Presley	L	Non	No. 1	L	Cr
1314	6	Presley, Lillie	6	F	⅛	D	Harrison Presley	L	Non	No. 1	L	Cr
1315	7	Presley, Farilla	4	F	⅛	D	Harrison Presley	L	Non	No. 1	L	Cr
1316	8	Presley, Harrison E.	1¾	M	⅛	S	Harrison Presley	L	Non	No. 1	L	Cr
1317	9	Presley, Thomas Jefferson	3 mo	M	⅛	S	Harrison Presley	L	Non	No. 1	L	Cr

No. 5 died December 5, 1902. No. 2 died May 23, 1913
No. 1 died February 27, 1911

Census Card No. 404, P. O. Tulsa, Enrolled May 31, 1899

No. 3 Arkansas City, Kan.

1318	1	Cowans, Thompson	23	M	¼		Hugh Cowans	D	Cr	Rose Perryman	D	Cr
1319	2	Cowans, Austin	14	M	¼	Bro	Hugh Cowans	D	Cr	Rose Perryman	D	Cr
1320	3	Cowans, Katie	12	F	¼	Sis.	Hugh Cowans	D	Cr	Rose Perryman	D	Cr

No. 3 died December 26, 1913

Census Card No. 405, P. O. Tulsa, Enrolled May 31, 1899

| 1321 | 1 | Perryman, Martha | 72 | F | ½ | | Dick Eaton | L | Non | Hepsey Eaton Nee Grayson | D | Cr |

Census Card No. 406, P. O. Coyle, Enrolled June 1, 1899

| 1322 | 1 | Gordon, Vinita | 17 | F | ¼ | | Hugh Cowans | D | ? | Rose Perryman | D | Cr |
| 1323 | 2 | Bird, Hughey Elmer | 1½ | M | ⅝ | S | Sandy Bird | L | Cr | No. 1 | L | Cr |

Census Card No. 407, P. O. Senora, Enrolled June 1, 1899

| 1324 | 1 | Watson, Homer | 22 | M | F | | Joe Watson | L | Cr | Hannah Mitchell | L | Cr |

No. 1 died December 1, 1901

Census Card No. 408, P. O. Broken Arrow, Enrolled June 1, 1899

No. 3 March 26, 1900

1325	1	Chisholm, Mose	23	M	F		Sampson Chisholm	D	Cr	Sallie Chisholm	D	Cr
1326	2	Chisholm, Sophie	4	F	F	D	No. 1	L	Cr	Tilda Chisholm	D	Cr
1327	3	Chisholm, Fannie	21	F	F	Wf	Joseph Mingo	L	Cr	Louisanna Mingo	L	Cr

No. 3 died 1901

Census Card No. 409, P. O. Grayson, Enrolled June 1, 1899; No. 4, June 7, 1899

1328	1	Sampson, Marthon	24	F	F		Sansoche	D	Cr	Vinnie Sampson	D	Cr
1329	2	Sampson, Washington	14	M	F	Bro	Sansoche	D	Cr	Vinnie Sampson	D	Cr
1330	3	Sampson, Thomas	15	M	F	H-Br	Sansoche	D	Cr	Inche	D	Cr
1331	4	McCombs, Mollie	2	F	F	Niece	Marshall. McCombs	D	Cr	Yarna McCombs	D	Cr

No. 2 died October 1908. No. 3 died November 1899. No. 1 reported dead.

Census Card No. 410, P. O. Broken Arrow, Enrolled June 1, 1899

1332	1	Boles, Mattie	29	F	⅛		Benj. Harmon	D	?	Laura Harmon	D	Non
1333	2	Boles, James	2	M	1-16	S	Chas. Boles	L	Non	No. 1	L	Cr
1334	3	Horn, Nellie W.	12	F	1-16	D	John Horn	D	Non	No. 1	L	Cr
1335	4	Horn, Minnie E.	11	F	1-16	D	John Horn	D	Non	No. 1	L	Cr
1336	5	Horn, Mattie E.	9	F	1-16	D	John Horn	D	Non	No. 1	L	Cr

Roll No.	No.	NAME	Age	Sex	Blood	Rel.	NAME OF FATHER	Liv.	Cit.	NAME OF MOTHER	Liv.	Cit.
		Census Card No. 411, P. O. Corinne, Enrolled June 1, 1899										
1337	1	Harmon, Dan. A.	25	M	½		Benj. Harmon	D	Cr	Laura Harmon	D	Non
		Census Card No. 412, P. O. Lenna, Enrolled June 1, 1899										
		No. 6 April 10, 1900										
1338	1	Barnette, Wm.	44	M	F		Yarda Barnette	D	Cr	Judie Barnette	D	Cr
1339	2	Barnette, Lizzie	44	F	F	Wf	Insucka	L	Cr	Boxy Thomas	D	Cr
1340	3	Barnette, Alex	18	M	F	S	No. 1	L	Cr	Tilsey Barnette	D	Cr
1341	4	Barnette, Polly	16	F	F	D	No. 1	L	Cr	Tilsey Barnette	D	Cr
1342	5	Barnette, Susie	14	F	F	D	No. 1	L	Cr	Tilsey Barnette	D	Cr
1343	6	Barnette, Judie	83	F	F	Moth	Unknown	?	Cr	Unknown	?	Cr
		No. 6 stricken from the roll January 26, 1914. See Indian Office letter No. 208-1914										
		No. 5 died October 30, 1908. No. 4 died April 30, 1907. No. 2 died December 27, 1901										
		No. 3 died December 21, 1906.										
		Census Card No. 413, P. O. Fame, Enrolled June 1, 1899; No. 6, April 11, 1900										
1344	1	Barnette, James	52	M	F		Yarda Barnette	D	Cr	Judie Barnette	D	Cr
1345	2	Barnette, Martha	40	F	F	Wf	Insucka	D	Cr	Boxy Thomas	D	Cr
1346	3	Barnette, Wesley	11	M	F	S	No. 1	L	Cr	No. 2	L	Cr
1347	4	Barnette, Benjamin	9	M	F	S	No. 1	L	Cr	No. 2	L	Cr
1348	5	Barnette, John	6	M	F	S	No. 1	L	Cr	No. 2	L	Cr
1349	6	Barnette, Lucy	1	F	F	D	No. 1	L	Cr	No. 2	L	Cr
		No. 2 died June 6, 1907. No. 6 died 1902.										
		Census Card No. 414, P. O. Salem; Nos. 3 and 4, Henryetta, Enrolled June 1, 1899										
1350	1	Turk, Frank	46	M	F		Pena Harjo	D	Cr	Oneka	D	Cr
1351	2	Turk, Peggie	30	F	F	Wf	Sinpuska	D	Cr	Lena Fields	D	Cr
1352	3	Field, Thomas	10	M	F	StS	Watt·Field	D	Cr	No. 2	L	Cr
1353	4	Field, Lunder	19	M	F	B-L	Watt Field	D	Cr	Lena Fields	D	Cr
1354	5	Turk, Lucinda	1	F	F	D	No. 1	L	Cr	No. 2	L	Cr
		No. 5 died July 25, 1899										
		Census Card No. 415, P. O. Burney, Enrolled June 1, 1899										
		No. 6 March 21, 1900										
1355	1	Willingham, Doc	45	M	F		John Willingham	D	Cr	Jane Willingham	D	Cr
1356	2	Willingham, Nisey	40	F	F	Wf	Daniel Roberts	D	Cr	Unknown	D·	Cr
1357	3	Willingham, Mary	10	F	F	D	No. 1	L	Cr	No. 2	L	Cr
1358	4	Willingham, Rachael	14	F	F	D	No. 1	L	Cr	Harriet Willingham	D	Cr
1359	5	Willingham, Lizzie	12	F	F	D	No. 1	L	Cr	Harriet Willingham	D	Cr
1360	6	Willingham, Bettie	1 moF		F	D	No. 1	L	Cr	No. 2	L	Cr
		No. 2 died February 16, 1904. No. 1 died December 4, 1910. No. 5 died June 15, 1914										
		No. 3 died February 1900.										
		Census Card No. 416, P. O. Barney, Enrolled June 1, 1899										
1361	1	Barnett, Joe	27	M	F		James Barnett	L	Cr	Mary Ann Barnett	D	Cr
		No. 1 died July 4, 1901										
		Census Card No. 417, P. O. Choska, Enrolled June 1, 1899										
1362	1	Marshall, Choatkey	80	F	F		Tustanukoche	D	Cr	Ahkate	D	Cr
		Census Card No. 418, P. O. Eufaula, Enrolled June 1, 1899										
1363	1	Derrisaw, Cooper	30	M	F		Chepon Deerisaw	D	Cr	Polly Deerisaw·	L	Cr
		No. 1 died about 1904										
		Census Card No. 419, P. O. Bryant, Enrolled June 1, 1899										
1364	1	Field, David	22	M	F		Unknown	D	Cr	Sewika	L	Cr
		Census Card No. 420, P. O. Lenna, Enrolled June 1, 1899										
1365	1	Collins, Lewis	35	M	F		Austin Collins	D	Cr	Jennie Collins	D	Cr
1366	2	Collins, Sophie	24	F	F	Wf	Barney Riley	L	Cr	Julie Yarker	D	Cr
1367	3	Collins, Jennie	2	F	F	D	No. 1	L	Cr	No. 2	L	Cr
1368	4	Collins, Roman	15	M	F	S	No. 1	L	Cr	Lucy Collins	D	Cr
		No. 3 died August 25, 1899. No. 1 reported dead										
		No. 4 died June 21, 1904										
		Census Card No. 421, P. O. Eufaula; No. 3, Hanna, Enrolled June 2, 1899										
1369	1	Riley, Barney	45	M	F		Buss Riley	D	Cr	Hannah Riley	D	Cr
1370	2	Riley, Nancy	40	F	F	Wf	Emockla	D	Cr	Sindayogee	D	Cr
1371	3	Riley, Thomas	18	M	F	S	No. 1	L	Cr	No. 2	L	Cr
1372	4	Riley, Bunner	16	M	F	S	No. 1	L	Cr	No. 2	L	Cr
1373	5	Riley, Moses	13	M	F	S	No. 1	L	Cr	No. 2	L	Cr
1374	6	Riley, Suter	9	M	F	S.	No. 1	L	Cr	No. 2	L	Cr
1375	7	Riley, Peter	5	M	F	S	No. 1	L	Cr	No. 2	L·	Cr
1376	8	Riley, Easma	4	M	F	S	No. 1	L	Cr	·No. 2	L	Cr
1377	9	Riley, James	5moM	F		S	No. 1	L	Cr	No. 2	L	Cr
		No. 6 died January 25, 1910. No. 7 died February 13, 1911. No. 8 died August 5, 1912.										
		No. 9 died March 17, 1912. No. 2 reportd dead										
		Census Card No. 422, P. O. Henrietta, Enrolled June 2, 1899; Nos. 2, 3 and 4. April 15, 1901										
1378	1	Tiger, Simpson	22	M	F		Thomas Tiger	D	Cr	Luffie	D	Cr
1379	2	Tiger, Jennie	35	F	F	Wf	Unknown	D	Cr	Lieka Hutka	L	Cr
1380	3	Tiger, Sallie	20	F	F	Sis	Thomas Tiger	D	Cr	Luffie	D	Cr
1381	4	Tiger, Lena	16	F	F	Sis	Thomas Tiger	D	Cr	Luffie	D	Cr
1382	5	Tiger, Albert	13	M	F	Bro	Thomas Tiger	D	Cr	Luffie	D	Cr
1383	6	Tiger, Lovey	46	F	F	Mot'h	Tusekiah Micco	D	Cr	Tustonarggie	D	Cr
		No. 2 died September 1903. No. 5 died July 1, 1907. No. 6, died October 15, 1899.										
		Census Card No. 423, P. O. Mellette, Enrolled June 2, 1899; Nos. 2, 3, 4, April 15, 1901										
1384	1	Davis, Sampson	23	M	F		Ben Davis	D	Cr	Mary Jessie	L	Cr
1385	2	Davis, Betty	21	F	F	Wf	Charlie Sullivan	D	Cr	Sahepahke	L	Cr
1386	3	Davis, Yoman	1	M	F	S	No. 1	L	Cr	No. 2	L	Cr
1387	4	Bright, Nannie	2	F	F	St.-D	Watty Bright	D	Cr	No. 2	L	Cr
		No. 4 died April 14, 1900										
		No. 2 died March 30, 1909										

Roll No.	No.	NAME	Age	Sex	Blood	Rel.	NAME OF FATHER	Liv.	Cit.	NAME OF MOTHER	Liv.	Cit.
		Census Card No. 424, P. O. Eufaula, Enrolled June 2, 1899, No. 4 May 3, 1901										
1388	1	King, Johnson	24	M	F		Bill Smith	D	Cr	Lizzie Smith	D	Cr
1389	2	King, Millie	24	F	F	Wf	Geo. Washington	D	Cr	Nancy Washington	D	Cr
1390	3	King, John Emmet	2	M	F	S	No. 1	L	Cr	No. 2	L	Cr
1391	4	King, Lizzie	1	F	F	D	No. 1	L	Cr	No. 2	L	Cr
		No. 1 died July 28, 1914										
		No. 3 died June 2, 1914										
		Census Card No. 425, P. O. Eufaula, Enrolled June 2, 1899										
1392	1	Jessie, Billy	36	M	F		Tusekiah Hutka	D	Cr	Lika Jessie	L	Cr
1393	2	Jessie, Mary	40	F	F	Wf	Tom Sullen	L	Cr	Susie Thlocco	D	Cr
1394	3	Jessie, Emma	17	F	F	D	No. 1	L	Cr	No. 2	L	Cr
1395	4	Jessie, Susan	14	F	F	D	No. 1	L	Cr	No. 2	L	Cr
		Census Card No. 426, P. O. Mellette, Enrolled June 2, 1899										
1396	1	McGilbray, Lizzie	42	F	F		Louie McNac	D	Cr	Hokte	D	Cr
1397	2	McGilbray, Jackson	16	M	F	S	Daniel McGilbray	D	Cr	No. 1	L	Cr
1398	3	McGilbray, Wisey	14	F	F	D	Daniel McGilbray	D	Cr	No. 1	L	Cr
1399	4	McGilbray Hepsey	12	F	F	D	Daniel McGilbray	D	Cr	No. 1	L	Cr
		No. 2 reported dead										
		Census Card No. 427, P. O. Muskogee, Enrolled June 3, 1899; No. 6 August 14, 1900										
1400	1	Ross, Muskogee	52	F	F		Yarger	D	Cr	Jennie Yarger	L	Cr
1401	2	Ross, Susie	28	F	½	D	Joshua Ross	L	Cher	No. 1	L	Cr
1402	3	Ross, J. Ewing	22	M	½	S	Joshua Ross	L	Cher	No. 1	L	Cr
1403	4	Ross, John Y.	20	M	½	S	Joshua Ross	L	Cher	No. 1	L	Cr
1404	5	Ross, Jennie P.	13	F	½	D	Joshua Ross	L	Cher	No. 1	L	Cr
1405	6	Ross, Frank Leslie	25das	M	½	Gr-S	J. Ewing Ross	L	Cr	Nellie Ross	L	Non
		No. 1 died March 14, 1913										
		Census Card No. 428, P. O. Council Hill, Enrolled June 3, 1899										
1406	1	Ansill, Samuel E.	30	M	⅛		Stephen Ansill	D	Cr	Jane Tiger	L	Non
1407	2	Ansill, Daisy	6	F	1-16	D	No. 1	L	Cr	Kate Ansill	L	Non
1408	3	Ansill, Sallie	4	F	1-16	D	No. 1	L	Cr	Kate Ansill	L	Non
1409	4	Ansill, Wm. Oscar	2	M	1-16	S	No. 1	L	Cr	Kate Ansill	L	Non
		No. 4 died November 27, 1899										
		Census Card No. 429, P. O. Hoardsville, Enrolled June 3, 1899										
1410	1	Herrod Samuel	36	M	F		Herrod	D	Cr	Louisa Runner	D	Cr
		Census Card No. 430, P. O. Oktaha, Enrolled June 3, 1899										
1411	1	Herrod, Cilla	45	F	½		Bill Grayson	D	?	Maria Grayson	D	?
1412	2	Herrod, Maria	13	F	¼	D	Cyrus Herrod	L	Non	No. 2	L	Cr
1413	3	Herrod, Mary	10	F	¼	D	Cyrus Herrod	L	Non	No. 2	L	Cr
		Census Card No. 431, P. O. Beggs; No. 4, Bristow, Enrolled June 3, 1899; Nos. 3, 4, 5, June 7, 1899; No. 6, May 22, 1901										
1414	1	Stake, Albert	28	M	F		Jonas Stake	D	Cr	Sallie Barnett	L	Cr
1415	2	Stake, Sallie	24	F	F	Wf	Micco Charlie	D	Cr	Loucinda	D	Cr
1416	3	Stake, Jennie	4	F	F	D	No. 1	L	Cr	No. 2	L	Cr
1417	4	Barnett, Sallie	50	F	F	Mot'h	Alfred Hopwood	D	Cr	Louisa Barnett	D	Cr
1418	5	Stake, Ellen	3mo	F	F	D	No. 1	L	Cr	No. 2	L	Cr
1419	6	Stake, Jeffie	1	M	F	S	No. 1	L	Cr	No. 2	L	Cr
		No. 5 died May 29, 1901										
		No. 2 died November 10, 1910										
		No. 4 died 1908 or 1909										
		No. 6 died May 19, 1899										
		Census Card No. 432, P. O. Porter, Enrolled June 3, 1899; No. 5, May 2, 1901										
1420	1	Carter, Sarah	32	F	F		Daniel Perryman	D	Cr	Lizzie Perryman	D	Cr
1421	2	Scott, Miller	12	M	F	S	Thomas Scott	D	Cr	No. 1	L	Cr
1422	3	Scott, Ella	7	F	F	D	Thomas Scott	D	Cr	No. 1	L	Cr
1423	4	Carter, Rufus M.	1½	M	½	S	Berry Carter	L	Non	No. 1	L	Cr
1424	5	Carter, Jno. Calvin	1	M	½	S	Berry Carter	L	Non	No. 1	L	Cr
		Census Card No. 433, P. O. Muskogee, Enrolled June 5, 1899										
1425	1	Callahan, Jas. O.	38	M	⅞		S. B. Callahan	L	Cr	Sarah E. Callahan	D	Non
1426	2	Callahan, Eula	13	F	1-16	D	No. 1	L	Cr	Josie E. Callahan	D	Non
		No. 1 died August 29, 1913										
		Census Card No. 434, P. O. Broken Arrow, Enrolled June 6, 1899; No. 6, June 12, 1899										
1427	1	Fry, Robert	35	M	½		Muttellokee	D	Cr	Milly Fry	L	?
1428	2	Fry, Dema	24	F	½	Wf	John Craig	D	Non	Phoebe Craig	D	Cr
1429	3	Fry, Lawrence	6	M	½	S	No. 1	L	Cr	No. 2	L	Cr
1430	4	Fry, Leona	4	F	½	D	No. 1	L	Cr	No. 2	L	Cr
1431	5	Fry, Lottie	2	F	½	D	No. 1	L	Cr	No. 2	L	Cr
1432	6	Fry, Milly	60	F	½	Mot'h	Cho Harjo	D	Cr	Unknown	D	Non
		No. 2 died September 6, 1903										
		Census Card No. 435, P. O. Sperry, Enrolled June 6, 1899										
1433	1	Chisholm, Shawnee	42	M	½		Jackson Chisholm	D	Cr	Amy	D	Cr
		Census Card No. 436, P. O. Fry, Enrolled June 6, 1899; No. 2, May 22, 1901										
1434	1	Ayers, Gussie	22	F	½		John Craig	D	Non	Phoebe Craig	D	Cr
1435	2	Ayers, Lester	2	M	¼	S	William Ayers	L	Non	No. 1	L	Cr
		Census Card No. 437, P. O. Lee, Enrolled June 6, 1899										
1436	1	Johnson, Harry	27	M	¼		Charles Johnson	D	Cr	Dorcas Johnson	D	Cr
		No. 1 died March 28, 1905										
		Census Card No. 438, P. O. Choska, Enrolled June 6, 1899										
1437	1	Sharp, Lewis E.	23	M	¾		D. W. Sharp	D	Cr	Mary Owen	L	?
		No. 1 died January 13, 1901										
		Census Card No. 439, P. O. Muskogee, Enrolled June 6, 1899										
1438	1	Davis, Amanda S.	83	F	¼		Nimrod Doyle	D	Non	Mary Doyle	D	Cr
		No. 1 died June 1, 1902										

Census Card No. 440, P. O. Muskogee, Enrolled June 6, 1899

Roll No.	No.	NAME	Age	Sex	Blood	Rel.	NAME OF FATHER	Liv.	Cit.	NAME OF MOTHER	Liv.	Cit.
1439	1	Spaulding, Josephine	39	F	1-32		S. B. Callahan	L	Cr	Sarah Callahan	D	Non
1440	2	Spaulding, Samuel B.	15	M	1-64	S	H. B. Spaulding	L	Non	No. 1	L	Cr
1441	3	Spaulding, Lelia A.	13	F	1-64	D	H. B. Spaulding	L	Non	No. 1	L	Cr
1442	4	Spaulding, Homer O.	11	M	1-64	S	H. B. Spaulding	L	Non	No. 1	L	Cr
1443	5	Spaulding, Gracie B.	8	F	1-64	D	H. B. Spaulding	L	Non	No. 1	L	Cr.
1444	6	Spaulding, Etta	6	F	1-64	D	H. B. Spaulding	L	Non	No. 1	L	Cr
1445	7	Spaulding, Thomas L	3	M	1-64	S	H. B. Spaulding	L	Non	No. 1	L	Cr
1446	8	Spaulding, James S.	2mo	M	1-64	S	H. B. Spaulding	L	Non	No. 1	L	Cr

Census Card No. 441, P. O. Okmulgee, Enrolled June 6, 1899

1447	1	Jefferson, John	52	M	F		Long Sam	D	Cr	Arsluthlecha	D	Cr

No. 1 died June 1, 1900

Census Card No. 442, P. O. Broken Arrow, Enrolled June 7, 1899

1448	1	Litka, Martha	24	F	F		Lola Wilson	D	Cr	Louisa Burgess	D	Cr
1449	2	Litka, Lucy	2	F	F	D	Dick Litka	L	Cr	No. 1	L	Cr

Census Card No. 443, P. O. Broken Arrow, Enrolled June 7, 1899

1450	1	Carr, Alex	50	M	F		John Carr	L	Cr	Annie Caesar	L	Cr
1451	2	Carr, Annie	45	F	F	Wf	Mataloke	D	Cr	Luffey	L	Cr
1452	3	Carr, John	17	M	F	S	No. 1	L	Cr	No. 2	L	Cr
1453	4	Carr, Susanna	14	F	F	D	No. 1	L	Cr	No. 2	L	Cr
1454	5	Carr, Sallie	2	F	F	D	No. 1	L	Cr	No. 2	L	Cr
1455	6	Scott, Ellis	16	M	F	Neph	Thomas Scott	D	Cr	Milley Scott	D	Cr

Census Card No. 444, P. O. Broken Arrow, Enrolled June 7, 1899

1456	1	Coser, Annie	70	F	F		Suthoneche	D	Cr	Wahnahye	D	Cr
1457	2	Coser, Nancy	26	F	F	D	Coser	D	Cr	No. 1	L	Cr
1458	3	Tulsa, Emma	14	F	F	G-D	Joe Tulsa	D	Cr	Mary Tulsa	D	Cr
1459	4	Haikey, Malissa	4	F	F	GG-D	Ben Haikey, Jr.,	L	Cr	Tildy Porter	L	Cr

No. 1 died March 13, 1901

Census Card No. 445, P. O. Preston; No. 3, McAlester, Enrolled July 7, 1899

1460	1	Fife, July	35	M	F		Ben Fife	D	Cr	Hiokfugge	D	Cr
1461	2	Fife, Sissie	35	F	F	Wf	Meliktche	L	Cr	Annie	D	Cr
1462	3	Fife, Samuel	14	M	F	S	No. 1	L	Cr	No. 2	L	Cr
1463	4	Fife, Chapman	10	M	F	S	No. 1	L	Cr	No. 2	L	Cr
1464	5	Fife, Gibson	6	M	F	S	No. 1	L	Cr	No. 2	L	Cr

No. 2 died 1900

Census Card No. 446, P. O. Morris; No. 8, Hoffman, Enrolled June 7, 1899; No. 8, Nov. 27, 1900

1465	1	King, Jackson	30	M	F		Micco Harjo	D	Cr	Louisa Harjo	L	Cr
1466	2	King, Jennie	33	F	F	Wf	Tobe Tiger	L	Cr	Susan Tiger	L	Cr
1467	3	King, Wiley	7	M	F	S	No. 1	L	Cr	No. 2	L	Cr
1468	4	Butler, Jim	3	M	F	St-S	Sam Butler	L	Cr	No. 2	L	Cr
1469	5	King, Louisa	60	F	F	Mot'h	Chisso Harjo	D	Cr	Sofa	D	Cr
1470	6	King, Peter	18	M	F	Bro	Micco Harjo	D	Cr	No. 5	L	Cr
1471	7	King, Cogee	16	F	F	Sis.	Micco Harjo	D	Cr	No. 5	L	Cr
1472	8	Smith, Matilda	13	F	F	Gr-D	Sam Smith	D	Cr	Sarah Smith	D	Cr

Census Card No. 447, P. O. Wagoner, Enrolled June 7, 1899

1473	1	Wiley, Andrew	45	M	F		Wiley	D	Cr	Peggie Wiley	L	Cr
1474	2	Wiley, Annie	16	F	F	D	No. 1	L	Cr	Milley Wiley	L	Cr
1475	3	Wiley, Susie	14	F	F	D	No. 1	L	Cr	Milley Wiley	L	Cr
1476	4	Wiley, Mary	8mo	F	F	D	No. 1	L	Cr	Milley Wiley	L	Cr

No. 4 died September 6, 1899
Nos. 1 and 3 reported dead

Census Card No. 448, P. O. Beggs, Enrolled June 7, 1899

1477	1	Stake, Eliza	26	F	F		Jonas Stake	D	Cr	Sallie Barnett	L	Cr
1478	2	Pidgeon, Jesse	6	M	F	S	Dave Pidgeon	L	Cr	No. 1	L	Cr
1479	3	Asbury, Anderson	1	M	F	S	Thomas Asbury	L	Cr	No. 1	L	Cr

Census Card No. 449, P. O. Bristow; No. 3, Tulsa, Enrolled June 8, 1899

1480	1	Perryman, Noble	40	M	½		Samuel Perryman	D	Cr	Mary Perryman	D	Non
1481	2	Perryman, Susanna	47	F	F	Wf	Kinhesoggee	D	Cr	Lucy	D	Cr
1482	3	Perryman, Hattie	14	F	¾	D	No. 1	L	Cr	No. 2	L	Cr
1483	4	Perryman, Phoebe	12	F	¾	D	No. 1	L	Cr	No. 2	L	Cr
1484	5	Perryman, Enos	9	M	¾	S	No. 1	L	Cr	No. 2	L	Cr
1485	6	Walker, William	35	M	F	B-L	Sahpahieche	D	Cr	Lucy	D	Cr

No. 1 died January 27, 1907
No. 2 died May 22, 1906
No. 6 died December 1905

Census Card No. 450, P. O. Okmulgee, Enrolled June 8, 1899

1486	1	Thompson, Betty	25	F	F		Chesopka	D	Cr	Nicey	D	Cr
1487	2	Moore, Lizzie	2	F	F	D	Mark Moore	L	Non	No. 1	L	Cr

Census Card No. 451, P. O. Okmulgee, Enrolled June 8, 1899

1488	1	Derisaw, Hettie	26	F	F		Sam Checotah	D	Cr	Priscilla Checotah	D	Cr
1489	2	Freeman, Celia	8	F	F	D	John Freeman	L	Cr	No. 1	L	Cr
1490	3	Jones, Napoleon	3	M	F	S	William Jones	D	Cr	No. 1	L	Cr

No. 3 reported dead

Census Card No. 452, P. O. Senora, Enrolled June 8, 1899

1491	1	Fat, John	57	M	F		Tulmas Heneha	D	Cr	Nancy Heneha	D	Cr
1492	2	Fat, Lucinda	50	F	F	Wf	Samuel Hawkins	D	Cr	Clutha Hawkins	D	Cr

No. 1 died December 14, 1899
No. 2 died May 10, 1911

Roll No.	No.	NAME	Age	Sex	Blood	Rel.	NAME OF FATHER	Liv.	Cit.	NAME OF MOTHER	Liv.	Cit.
		Census Card No. 453, P. O. Salem, Enrolled June 8, 1899										
1493	1	Beaver, Rosa	27	F	F		Sandy Beaver	D	Cr	Nicey Carr	L	Cr
1494	2	Carr, Nicey	70	F	F	Mot'h	Unknown	D	Cr	Unknown	D	Cr
1495	3	Carr, Hepsey	6	F	F	D-2?	Unknown	?	Cr	No. 2 ?	?	Cr
		No. 2 died April 28, 1903										
		No. 3 reported dead										
		Census Card No. 454, P. O. Mounds, Enrolled June 9, 1899										
1496	1	Owens, Mary	45	F	½		Wm. Patterson	D	?	Elsie Bosen	D	?
1497	2	Sharp, Johnnie	13	M	¾	S	Dogwood Sharp	L	Cr	No. 1	L	Cr
		No. 1 died January 18, 1901										
		Census Card No. 455, P. O. Broken Arrow, Enrolled June 9, 1899										
1498	1	Perryman, George R.	38	M	½		Riley Perryman	D	Cr	Ruth Perryman	D	Non
1499	2	Johnson, Ruth	18	F	½	D	No. 1	L	Cr	Martha Perryman	D	Non
1500	3	Perryman, Lydia	16	F	½	D	No. 1	L	Cr	Martha Perryman	D	Non
1501	4	Perryman, Annie	14	F	½	D	No. 1	L	Cr	Martha Perryman	D	Non
1502	5	Perryman, Mary	9	F	½	D	No. 1	L	Cr	Martha Perryman	D	Non
1503	6	Hodge, Pearl	2	F	½	Gr-D	David M. Hodge	L	Cr	No. 2	L	Cr
		Census Card No. 456, P. O. Leonard, Enrolled June 9, 1899										
1504	1	Gilcrease, Lizzie	25	F	¼		H. G. Vowell	L	Non	Martha Self Vowell	L	Cr
1505	2	Gilcrease, Thomas	9	M	⅛	S	Wm. 1.. Gilcrease	L	Non	No. 1	L	Cr
1506	3	Gilcrease, Eddie	7	M	⅛	S	Wm. L. Gilcrease	L	Non	No. 1	L	Cr
1507	4	Gilcrease, Ben	5	M	⅛	S	Wm. L. Gilcfrease	L	Non	No. 1	L	Cr
1508	5	Gilcrease, Lena	3	F	⅛	D	Wm. L. Gilcrease	L	Non	No. 1	L	Cr
1509	6	Gilcrease, Florence	1	F	⅛	D	Wm. L. Gilcrease	L	Non	No. 1	L	Cr
		Census Card No. 457, P. O. Mounds, Enrolled June 9, 1899										
1510	1	Vowell, Martha	44	F	½		Samuel Self	D	Cr	Clarinda S. Self	D	Cr
1511	2	Vowell, Tom	17	M	¼	S	Hamp G. Vowell	L	Non	No. 1	L	Cr
1512	3	Vowell, John	13	M	¼	S	Hamp G. Vowell	L	Non	No. 1	L	Cr
1513	4	Vowell, Rena	11	F	¼	D	Hamp G. Vowell	L	Non	No. 1	L	Cr
1514	5	Vowell, Cassie	7	M	¼	S	Hamp G. Vowell	L	Non	No. 1	L	Cr
1515	6	Vowell, Leroy	4	M	¼	S	Hamp G. Vowell	L	Non	No. 1	L	Cr
1516	7	Vowell, Jesse	1	M	¼	S	Hamp G. Vowell	L	Non	No. 1	L	Cr
		No. 2 died February 6, 1912										
		Census Card No. 458, P. O. No. 1, Okema; No. 2, Paden, Enrolled June 9, 1899										
1517	1	Fipps, Alice M.	34	F	⅛		Eli A. Self	D	Cr	Minerva Self	L	Non
1518	2	Fipps, Myrta May	12	F	1-16	D	Samuel Fipps	L	Non	No. 1	L	Cr
1519	3	Fipps, Beulah E.	10	F	1-16	D	Samuel Fipps	L	Non	No. 1	L	Cr
1520	4	Fipps, William B.	8	M	1-16	S	Samuel Fipps	L	Non	No. 1	L	Cr
1521	5	Fipps, Pearl	6	F	1-16	D	Samuel Fipps	L	Non	No. 1	L	Cr
1522	6	Fipps, Gertie E.	3	F	1-16	D	Samuel Fipps	L	Non	No. 1	L	Cr
1523	7	Fipps, Aaron	1	M	1-16	S	Samuel Fipps	L	Non	No. 1	L	Cr
		Census Card No. 459, P. O. Checotah, Enrolled June 12, 1899										
1524	1	McGilbray, George	24	M	¾		Lipscomb, McGilbray	D	Cr	Susie McGilbray	D	Cr
		Census Card No. 460, P. O. Bixby, Enrolled June 12, 1899										
1525	1	Brown, Carrie C.	35	F	½		Henry Rowley	L	Non	MrsThompson Rowley	D	Cr
1526	2	Brown, Tussekiehutkie	5	M	¼	S	James Brown	L	Non	No. 1	L	Cr
		Census Card No. 461, P. O. Muskogee, Enrolled June 12, 1899										
1527	1	Porter, William A.	25	M	½		Pleasant Porter	L	Cr	Mary E. Porter	D	Cher
1528	2	Porter, Pleasant Jr.,	3	M	¼	S	No. 1	L	Cr	Milly M. Porter	L	Non
1529	3	Porter, Will	1	M	¼	S	No. 1	L	Cr	Milly M. Porter	L	Non
1530	4	Porter, Stockton	5mo	M	¼	S	No. 1	L	Cr	Milly M. Porter	L	Non
		Census Card No. 462, P. O. Chicago, Ill.; 2550 Cottage Grove Ave.; Enrolled June 12, 1899										
1531	1	Smith, Hattie	43	F	½		Henry Rowley	L	Non	MrsThompson Rowley	D	Cr
1532	2	Blackwell, Tecumseh	23	M	¼	S	Henry Blackwell	D	Non	No. 1	L	Cr
1533	3	Blackwell, Thomas	18	M	¼	S	Henry Blackwell	D	Non	No. 1	L	Cr
		Census Card No. 463, P. O. Okmulgee, Enrolled June 12, 1899										
1534	1	Moore, Mamie	20	F	¼		Henry Blackwell	D	Non	Hattie Smith	L	Cr
		Census Card No. 464, P. O. Muskogee, Enrolled June 12, 1899										
1535	1	Callahan, Samuel B.	65	M	⅛		James O. Callahan	D	Non	Amanda S. Davis	L	Cr
1536	2	Callahan, Evelyn	34	F	1-16	D	No. 1	L	Cr	Sarah E. Callahan	D	Non
1537	3	Callahan, Gipsie	27	F	1-16	D	No. 1	L	Cr	Sarah E. Callahan	D	Non
		Census Card No. 465, P. O. Owyhe, Nevada, Enrolled June 12, 1899										
1538	1	Callahan, Walter K.	24	M	1-16		S. B. Callahan	L	Cr	Sarah E. Callahan	D	Non
		Census Card No. 466, P. O. Dustin, Enrolled June 13, 1899; No. 6, April 23, 1901										
1539	1	Wills, John J.	36	M	¼		Vardy J. Wills	D	Cr	Georgia Ann Wills	D	Non
1540	2	Wills, Louis Leroy	10	M	⅛	S	No. 1	L	Cr	Polly Ann Wills	L	Non
1541	3	Wills, Mollie L.	7	F	⅛	D	No. 1	L	Cr	Polly Ann Wills	L	Non
1542	4	Wills, Bluford	5	M	⅛	S	No. 1	L	Cr	Polly Ann Wills	L	Non
1543	5	Wills, Buford	5	M	⅛	S	No. 1	L	Cr	Polly Ann Wills	L	Non
1544	6	Wills, Theodore Dewey	2	M	⅛	S	No. 1	L	Cr	Polly Ann Wills	L	Non
		No. 1 died August 15, 1905										
		Census Card No. 467, P. O. Senora, Enrolled June 13, 1899										
1545	1	Berryhill,Zachariah T.	48	M	⅛		Eli Berryhill	D	Cr	Ellander Berryhill	L	Non
1546	2	Berryhill, Ida Belle	4	F	⅜	D	No. 1	L	Cr	Evaline Berryhill	L	Non
		Census Card No. 468, P. O. Wetumka, Enrolled June 13, 1899										
1547	1	Dunson, Thomas	21	M	F		Joseph Dunson	D	Cr	Hokosy Dunson	D	Cr
		Census Card No. 469, P. O. Catoosa, No. 3, Chico, Texas, Enrolled June 13, 1899										
1548	1	Wright, Walter D.	23	M	1-16		E. A. Wright	L	Non	Mary E. Wright	D	Cr
1549	2	Wright, Charles F.	21	M	1-16	Bro.	E. A. Wright	L	Non	Mary E. Wright	D	Cr
1550	3	Wright, Maysie A.	19	F	1-16	Sis.	E. A. Wright	L	Non	Mary E. Wright	D	Cr
1551	4	Wright, Lela S.	16	F	1-16	Sis.	E. A. Wright	L	Non	Mary E. Wright	D	Cr
1552	5	Wright, Annie E.	14	F	1-16	Sis.	E. A. Wright	L	Non	Mary E. Wright	D	Cr

Roll No.	No.	NAME	Age	Sex	Blood	Rel.	NAME OF FATHER	Liv.	Cit.	NAME OF MOTHER	Liv.	Cit
		Census Card No. 470, P. O. Mounds, Enrolled June 13, 1899										
1553	1	Williams, Vina	40	F	1/4		Alex De Priest	L	Non	Patience De Priest	L	Cr
1554	2	Williams, Alex	20	M	1/8	S	W. F. Williams	L	Non	No. 1	L	Cr
1555	3	Williams, Emma	14	F	1/8	D	W. F. Williams	L	Non	No. 1	L	Cr
1556	4	Williams, Naoma	12	F	1/8	D	W. F. Williams	L	Non	No. 1	L	Cr
		Census Card No. 471, P. O. Bixby, Enrolled June 13, 1899										
1557	1	Call, Pearl	21	F	1/8		Tom De Priest	D	Cr	Dolly Bowman	L	Non
1558	2	Call, Gracie	4	F	1-16	D	John Call	L	Non	No. 1	L	Cr
1559	3	Call, Nellie	2	F	1-16	D	John Call	L	Non	No. 1	L	Cr
1560	4	Call, Archibald	4mo	M	1-16	S	John Call	L	Non	No. 1	L	Cr
1561	5	De Priest, Cordie	14	F	1/2	Sis.	Tom De Priest	D	Cr	Dolly Bowman	L	Non
1562	6	De Priest, Nicey	9	F	1/2	Sis.	Tom De Priest	D	Cr	Dolly Bowman	L	Non
		No. 2 died July 25, 1899										
		Census Card No. 472, P. O. Bixby, Enrolled June 13, 1899										
1563	1	De Priest, Jeff	19	M	1/8		Tom De Priest	D	Cr	Dolly Bowman	L	Non
		Census Card No. 473, P. O. Boynton, Enrolled June 13, 1899										
1564	1	Johnson, Peter	21	M	1/4		Charles Johnson	D	?	Dorcas Johnson	D	?
		Census Card No. 474, P. O. Eufaula, Enrolled June 13, 1899; No. 3, May 22, 1901										
1565	1	Boone, Charley	27	M	3/4		Thos. Boone	L	Cr	Priscilla Boone	L	Cr
1566	2	Boone, Zenus	2	M	3/8	S	No. 1	L	Cr	Sallie Boone	L	Non
1567	3	Boone, Ural	2	F	3/8	D	No. 1	L	Cr	Sallie Boone	L	Non
		No. 3 died October 22, 1900										
		No. 1 died March 26, 1904										
		Census Card No. 475, P. O. Red Bird, Enrolled June 13, 1899										
1568	1	Watson, Mahala A.	43	F	1/2		Riley Perryman	D	Cr	Ruth Perryman	D	Non
1569	2	Burke, Maggie J.	16	F	1/4	D	John Burke	D	Non	No. 1	L	Cr
1570	3	Burke, John Thomas	4	M	1/4	S	John Burke	D	Non	No. 1	L	Cr
		No. 1 died December 27, 1901										
		Census Card No. 476, P. O. Muskogee, Enrolled June 13, 1899										
1571	1	Davis, Lewis H.	24	M	1/4		Sam Davis	D	Non	Mahala Watson	L	Cr
1572	2	Davis, Florence M.	1	F	1/8	D	No. 1	L	Cr	Susanna Davis	L	Non
		Census Card No. 477, P. O. Beland, Enrolled June 13, 1899										
1573	1	Johnson, John	29	M	1/2		Jesse Johnson	L	?	Polly Johnson	D	?
		Census Card No. 478, P. O. Lenna, Enrolled June 14, 1899; No. 6, January 3, 1900										
1574	1	Moore, Thomas	30	M	1/4		Moses Moore	D	Cr	Lizzie Moore	D	Non
1575	2	Moore, Mattie	8	F	1/8	D	No. 1	L	Cr	Rosa Moore	L	Non
1576	3	Moore, Linney	4	F	1/8	D	No. 1	L	Cr	Rosa Moore	L	Non
1577	4	Moore, Julie	3	F	1/8	D	No. 1	L	Cr	Rosa Moore	L	Non
1578	5	Moore, Moses	1	M	1/8	S	No. 1	L	Cr	Rosa Moore	L	Non
1579	6	Moore, Limon	2mo	M	1/8	S	No. 1	L	Cr	Rosa Moore	L	Non
		Census Card No. 479, P. O. Checotah, Enrolled June 15, 1899										
1580	1	Horn, Sam	22	M	1/2		Sam Horn	L	Cher	Melvina Hughes	L	Cr
		Census Card No. 480, P. O. Checotah, Enrolled June 15, 1899										
1581	1	Hughes, Robert	23	M	1/8		Wm. Hughes	L	Non	Melvina Hughes	L	Cr
1582	2	Hughes, Willie	1	M	1/8	S	No. 1	L	Cr	Electa Hughes	L	Non
		No. 2 reported dead										
		Census Card No. 481, P. O. Eufaula, Enrolled June 15, 1899										
1583	1	Jones, Thomas	48	M	F		Concharty	D	Cr	Louanna	D	Cr
1584	2	Jones, Lila	45	F	F	Wf	Lochar Yahola	D	Cr	Unknown	D	Cr
1585	3	Jones, Louiney	18	F	F	D	No. 1	L	Cr	Nancy Jones	D	Cr
1586	4	Jones, Martha	12	F	F	D	No. 1	L	Cr	Nancy Jones	D	Cr
		No. 3 died 1900										
		No. 1 died January 6, 1910										
		No. 4 died 1911										
		Census Card No. 482, P. O. McAlester, Enrolled June 15, 1899										
1587	1	LaFavor, Saladen	25	M	1/2		Thos. La Favor	L	Cher	Susan Drake	L	Cr
		Census Card No. 483, P. O. Checotah, Enrolled June 15, 1899										
1588	1	Hughes, Melvina	37	F	1/2		Alex Simmons	D	Cr	Sarah Simmons	D	Non
1589	2	Hughes, Loonie	16	M	1/4	S	Wm. Hughes	L	Non	No. 1	L	Cr
1590	3	Hughes, Amos	14	M	1/4	S	Wm. Hughes	L	Non	No. 1	L	Cr
1591	4	Hughes, John	11	M	1/4	S	Wm. Hughes	L	Non	No. 1	L	Cr
1592	5	Hughes, Lena	9	F	1/4	D	Wm. Hughes	L	Non	No. 1	L	Cr
1593	6	Hughes, James	4	M	1/4	S	Wm. Hughes	L	Non	No. 1	L	Cr
		No. 1 died July 4, 1903										
		No. 2 reported dead										
		No. 6 died September 18, 1904										
		Census Card No. 484, P. O. Okmulgee, Enrolled June 15, 1899										
1594	1	Sutton, Mollie	38	F	1/4		V. J. Wills	D	Cr	Georgia Ann Wills	D	Non
1595	2	Sutton, James D.	10	M	1/8	S	John W. Sutton	L	Non	No. 1	L	Cr
1596	3	Sutton, Samuel Jesse	8	M	1/8	S	John W. Sutton	L	Non	No. 1	L	Cr
1597	4	Sutton, Lorena	4	F	1/8	D	John W. Sutton	L	Non	No. 1	L	Cr
1598	5	Sutton, Loretta	4	F	1/8	D	John W. Sutton	L	Non	No. 1	L	Cr
		Census Card No. 485, P. O. Oktaha, Enrolled June 15, 1899										
1599	1	Blackston, Albert	23	M	1/2		Tom Blackstone	L	Cher	Patsy Blackstone	D	Cr
		Census Card No. 486, P. O. Okemah, Enrolled June 16, 1899										
1600	1	Barnwell, David	56	M	1/2		John Barnwell	L	Non	Vicey Barnwell	D	Cr
1601	2	Barnwell, Katie	45	F	F	Wf	Chokotte Emarthla	D	Cr	Wikke	D	Cr
1602	3	Grace, John	10	M	F	St-S	Peter Grace	D	Cr	No. 2	L	Cr
		No. 2 reported dead										

41

Roll No.	No.	NAME	Age	Sex	Blood	Rel.	NAME OF FATHER	Liv.	Cit.	NAME OF MOTHER	Liv.	Cit.
		Census Card No. 487, P. O. Summit, Enrolled June 17, 1899										
1603	1	Durant, Otho	50	M	1/8		A. J. Durant	L	Cr	Sarah J. Durant	D	Non
1604	2	Durant, Belle	19	F	1-16	D	No. 1	L	Cr	Anna Durant	L	Non
1605	3	Durant, Inez P.	15	F	1-16	D	No. 1	L	Cr	Anna Durant	L	Non
		Census Card No. 488, P. O. Okemah, Enrolled June 17, 1899										
1606	1	Jimboy, Hepsie	25	F	F		Wm. Jimboy	L	Cr	Mahala Jimboy	L	Cr
		Census Card No. 489, P. O. Tullahassee, Enrolled June 17, 1899, No. 4, April 24, 1901										
1607	1	Murrell, Lucy	21	F	F		Wiley Sookey	L	Cr	Dinah Sookey	D	Cr
1608	2	Murrell, Sambo	6	M	1/2	S	Calhoun Merrill	L	Non	No. 1	L	Cr
1609	3	Murrell, Crawford	4	M	1/2	S	Calhoun Merrill	L	Non	No. 1	L	Cr
1610	4	Murrell, Louisa	11mo	F	1/2	D	Calhoun, Merrill	L	Non	No. 1	L	Cr
		Census Card No. 490, P. O. Enterprise; No. 2, Boynton, Enrolled June 17, 1899										
1611	1	Flack, Cornelia	50	F	3/8		Bill Nero	L	Cr	Nancy Nero	L	Cr
1612	2	Flack, Mattie	21	F	3-16	D	Enoch Flack	L	Ch. F.	No. 1	L	Cr
1613	3	Flack, John	23	M	3-16	S	Enoch Flack	L	Ch. F.	No. 1	L	Cr
		Census Card No. 491, P. O. Muskogee, Enrolled June 17, 1899										
1614	1	Lyden, Susanna	45	F	3/4		Billy Carr	D	Cr	Eliza Carr	D	Cr
		No. 1 reported dead										
		Census Card No. 492, P. O. Braggs, Enrolled June 19, 1899										
1615	1	Crosslin, Martha	52	F	1/2		Jim Cuffy	D	?	Vicey Cuffy	D	?
		Census Card No. 493, P. O. Boynton, Enrolled June 19, 1899										
1616	1	Dan, Siah	21	M	1/2		Sandy Dan	D	?	Hobie Dan	D	?
		Census Card No. 494, P. O. Checotah, Enrolled June 20, 1899; No. 3 Setember 4, 1900										
1617	1	Combs, Katie	22	F	1/4		Tom Grayson	D	?	Millie Marshall	D	?
1618	2	Combs, Joseph	1	M	1/8	S	J. W. Combs	L	Non	No. 1	L	Cr
1619	3	Combs, Rena	2mo	F	1/8	D	J. W. Combs	L	Non	No. 1	L	Cr
1620	4	Combs, Birl	8mo	M	1/8	S	J. W. Combs	L	Non	No. 1	L	Cr
		No. 4 died August 6, 1899										
		Census Card No. 495, P. O. Schulter, Enrolled June 20, 1899										
1621	1	Foster, Samuel	46	M	F		Abraham Foster	D	Cr	Lucy Foster	D	Cr
1622	2	Foster, Jennie	16	F	F	D	No. 1	L	Cr	Hettie Foster	D	Cr
		Census Card No. 496, P. O. Mounds, Enrolled June 20, 1899										
1623	1	Phillips, Lewis E.	27	M	F		P. H. Phillips	D	Cr	Eliza Phillips	D	Cr
		No. 1 died August 1909										
		Census Card No. 497, P. O. Mounds, Enrolled June 20, 1899										
1624	1	Tiger, Lydia	87	F	F		Tewahtahliche	D	Cr	Nancy	D	Cr
		Census Card No. 498, P. O. Tulsa, Enrolled June 20, 1899										
1625	1	Bellsted, Tookah	5	F	1-16		Chas. Bellsted	D	Cr	Myrtle Belsted	D	Non
		Census Card No. 499, P. O. Okmulgee, Enrolled June 20, 1899										
1626	1	Morton, Tucker W.	36	M	1/4		Wm. Morton	L	Non	Delilah Morton	L	Cr
1627	2	Morton, Martha L.	30	F	F	Wf	Henry Thompson	D	Cr	Polly Thompson	D	Cr
1628	3	Morton, Richard L.	11	M	3/4	S	No. 1	L	Cr	No. 2	L	Cr
1629	4	Morton, William V.	9	M	3/4	S	No. 1	L	Cr	No. 2	L	Cr
1630	5	Morton, Oscar M.	6	M	3/4	S	No. 1	L	Cr	No. 2	L	Cr
1631	6	Morton, Stanton R.	2	M	3/4	S	No. 1	L	Cr	No. 2	L	Cr
1632	7	Morton, Roy H.	3mo	M	3/4	S	No. 1	L	Cr	No. 2	L	Cr
		No. 2 died July 27, 1901										
		No. 7 died July 3, 1900										
		Census Card No. 500, P. O. Mounds, Enrolled June 20, 1899										
1633	1	Thompson, Robert	37	M	F		Henry Thompson	D	Cr	Mary Thompson	L	Cr
1634	2	Thompson, Hepsey	40	F	F	Wf	McGilbray	L	Cr	Wisey McGilbray	L	Cr
		No. 1 reported dead										
		Census Card No. 501, P. O. Mounds, Enrolled June 20, 1899										
1635	1	Harry, Simon	25	M	3/8		David Harry	L	Cr	Grace Harry	D	Cr
1636	2	Harry, Rebecca	17	F	F	Wf	Fox Missouri	D	Cr	Nellie Fox	L	Cr
		No. 1 died August 14, 1904										
		Census Card No. 502, P. O. Mounds, Enrolled June 20, 1899										
1637	1	Fox, Nellie	46	F	F		Unknown	D	Cr	Unknown	D	Cr
1638	2	Fox, Sutar	10	M	F	S	Fox Missouri	D	Cr	No. 1	L	Cr
1639	3	Fox, Yarner	7	F	F	D	Fox Missouri	D	Cr	No. 1	L	Cr
		No. 1 died January 11, 1907										
		No. 2 died February 27, 1911										
		No. 3 died May 1902										
		Census Card No. 503, P. O. Kelleyville, Enrolled June 20, 1899										
1640	1	Fox, Alice	20	F	F		Fox Missouri	D	Cr	Nellie Fox	L	Cr
1641	2	Brady, Lucinda	3	F	F	D	Albert Brady	L	Cr	No. 1	L	Cr
1642	3	Freeman, Columbus	1	M	F	S	Mitchell Freeman	L	Cr	No. 1	L	Cr
		No. 2 died September 8, 1912										
		Census Card No. 504, P. O. Checotah, Enrolled June 20, 1899										
1643	1	Gentry, R. J.	44	M	1/4		James Gentry	D	Cr	Caroline Gentry	D	Non
1644	2	Gentry, Lizzie	16	F	3/8	D	No. 1	L	Cr	Lizzie Gentry	L	Cr
1645	3	Gentry, Pearl	13	F	1/8	D	No. 1	L	Cr	Etta Gentry	L	Non
1646	4	Gentry, Robert J. Jr.	11	M	1/8	S	No. 1	L	Cr	Etta Gentry	L	Non
		No. 1 died November 11, 1900										
		Census Card No. 505, P. O. Wagoner, Enrolled June 21, 1899										
1647	1	Schrimsher, Edward L.	27	M	1/4		J. N. Schrimsher	L	Cher	Rebecca Schrimsher	D	Cr
1648	2	Schrimsher, Gertrude	2	F	1/8	D	No. 1	L	Cr	Addie Schrimsher	L	Non
		Census Card No. 506, P. O. No. 1, Morris; No. 2, Okmulgee, Enrolled June 21, 1899										
1649	1	Litka, Arma	22	F	F		Joe Litka	D	Cr	Wisey Yardy	L	Cr
1650	2	Yardy, Willie	2	M	3/4	S	Thomas Yardy	L	Cr	No. 1	L	Cr
		Census Card No. 507, P. O. Eufaula, Enrolled June 21, 1899										
1651	1	Lerblance, Alice	18	F	1/2		W. P. Lerblance	D	Cr	Eliza Lerblance	L	Cr

Roll No.	No.	NAME	Age	Sex	Blood	Rel.	Name of Father	Liv.	Cit.	Name of Mother	Liv.	Cit.
		Census Card No. 508, P. O. Muskogee, Enrolled June 21, 1899										
1652	1	Grayson, Isaac	22	M	1/4		Doc Grayson	D	?	Susie Grayson	L	?
		No. 1 died October 6, 1900										
		Census Card No. 509, P. O. Council Hill, Enrolled June 21, 1899										
1653	1	Gentry, William E.	57	M	1/4		James Gentry	D	Cr	Caroline Gentry	D	Non
1654	2	Gentry, Sallie D.	39	F	1/2	Wf	Chipley Carr	D	Cr	Carr	L	Cr
1655	3	Gentry Caroline	17	F	3/8	D	No. 1	L	Cr	No. 2	L	Cr
1656	4	Gentry, Mary E.	15	F	3/8	D	No. 1	L	Cr	No. 2	L	Cr
1657	5	Gentry, Sallie P.	13	F	3/8	D	No. 1	L	Cr	No. 2	L	Cr
1658	6	Gentry, Robert L.	11	M	3/8	S	No. 1	L	Cr	No. 2	L	Cr
1659	7	Gentry, Bluford M.	9	M	3/8	S	No. 1	L	Cr	No. 2	L	Cr
1660	8	Gentry, Rachael J.	7	F	3/8	D	No. 1	L	Cr	No. 2	L	Cr
1661	9	Gentry, Boyd E.	5	M	3/8	S	No. 1	L	Cr	No. 2	L	Cr
		Census Card No. 510, P. O. Brush Hill, Enrolled June 22, 1899; No. 2, May 18, 1901										
1662	1	Green, Martha	17	F	F		King	D	Cr	Fannie King	D	Cr
1663	2	Green, Stepney	3	M	1/2	S	Davis Green	L	Non	No. 1	L	Cr
		No. 1 died July 1, 1901										
		Census Card No. 511, P. O. Brush Hill; No. 4, Pierce; No. 5, Checotah, Enrolled June 22, 1899										
1664	1	Dan, Amy	35	F	1/4		Brister	D	?	Kate	L	Cr
1665	2	Dan, Tena	11	F	1/8	D	Sampson Dan	L	Non	No. 1	L	Cr
1666	3	Dan, Billy	8	M	1/8	S	Sampson Dan	L	Non	No. 1	L	Cr
1667	4	Dan, Benjamin	5	M	1/8	S	Sampson Dan	L	Non	No. 1	L	Cr
1668	5	Sizemore, Stephen	19	M	5/8	St-S	Cumseh Sizemore	L	Cr	No. 1	L	Cr
		No. 4 died November 17, 1914										
		No. 5 died July 27, 1908										
		Census Card No. 512, P. O. Pierce, Enrolled June 22, 1899										
1669	1	Bristor, Sudom	39	M	1/4		Bristor	D	?	Kate Thlocco	D	?
		Census Card No. 513, P. O. Checotah, Enrolled June 22, 1899; No. 4, May 24, 1901										
1670	1	Wilson, John Emmet	19	M	3/8		John W. Wilson	L	Non	Louisa Wilson	D	Cr
1671	2	Wilson, Hattie L.	16	F	3/8	Sis	John W. Wilson	L	Non	Louisa Wilson	D	Cr
1672	3	Wilson, Margaret A.	13	F	3/8	Sis	John W. Wilson	L	Non	Louisa Wilson	D	Cr
1673	4	Wilson, Earnest C.	1	M	3-16	S	No. 1	L	Cr	Cora D. Wilson	L	Non
		Census Card No. 514, P. O. Brush Hill, Enrolled June 22, 1899										
1674	1	Grayson, Josephine	22	F	1/2		Wm. Lynch	D	Non	Lizzie Company	D	Cr
		Census Card No. 515, P. O. Brush Hill, Enrolled June 22, 1899										
1675	1	McIntosh, Thomas	22	M	3/8		Morey McIntosh	L	?	Rose Thompson	L	?
		No. 1 died December 2, 1899										
		Census Card No. 516, P. O. Broken Arrow, Enrolled June 22, 1899										
1676	1	Hickory, Joe	30	M	F		Oches Harjo	D	Cr	Mary	D	Cr
		Census Card No. 517, P. O. Eufaula, Enrolled June 22, 1899										
1677	1	Whitlow, David B.	75	M	AW		Joseph Whitlow	D	Non	Elizabeth Whitlow	D	Non
1678	2	Whitlow, Cleveland	13	M	1/2	S	No. 1	L	Cr	Mary Whitlow	D	Cr
		No. 1 died February 2, 1902										
		Census Card No. 518, P. O. Broken Arrow, Enrolled June 22, 1899										
1679	1	Drew, Ella	15	F	1/2		Daniel Drew	D	Cher	Maggie Drew	D	Cr
		Census Card No. 519, P. O. Wildcat, Enrolled June 22, 1899										
1680	1	Tiger, John	19	M	F		Major Chupco	D	Cr	Jennie King	L	Cr
		No. 1 reported dead										
		Census Card No. 520, P. O. Bryant; No. 3, 4, 6, 7, Henryetta, Enrolled June 22, 1899; No. 5, December 8, 1899; Nos. 6 and 7, January 19, 1900										
1681	1	Looney, Josiah	48	M	F		Looney	D	Cr	Semeherke	D	Cr
1682	2	Looney, Fannie	26	F	F	Wf	George Sullivan	D	Cr	Becky Sullivan	D	Cr
1683	3	Looney, Geo. Barney	6	M	F	S	No. 1	L	Cr	Rany Looney	D	Cr
1684	4	Looney, Chas. William	4	M	F	S	No. 1	L	Cr	Rany Looney	D	Cr
1685	5	Sullivan, Ellen	22	F	F	S-L	George Sullivan	D	Cr	Peggy Sullivan	D	Cr
1686	6	West, Lizzie	3	F	F	Niece	Lumsey West	L	Cr	No. 5	L	Cr
1687	7	West, Rosie	1	F	F	Niece	Lumsey West	L	Cr	No. 5	L	Cr
		Nos. 1 and 2 reported dead										
		Census Card No. 521, P. O. Westumka, Enrolled June 22, 1899										
1688	1	Sullivan, Wm.	22	M	F		Sunday Sullivan	D	Cr	Addie Sullivan	D	Cr
1689	2	Sullivan, Kizzie	21	F	F	Wf	Geo. W. Walker	L	Cr	Mollie Walker	L	Cr
		Census Card No. 522, P. O. Okmulgee, Enrolled June 22, 1899										
1690	1	Sapulpa, Elizabeth	31	F	F		Billy Hardridge	D	Cr	Miley Starr	L	Cr
1691	2	Starr, Miley	73	F	F	Moth	Komp Harjo	D	Cr	Unknown	D	Cr
		No. 2 Died January 9, 1910										
		Census Card No. 523, P. O. Senora, Enrolled June 23, 1899										
1692	1	Tiner, Tecumseh	60	M	F		Unknown	D	Cr	Lucinda	D	Cr
1693	2	Tiner, Katie	50	F	1/2	Wf	Ben Broadnax	D	Non	Mary Barnett	L	Cr
1694	3	Tiner, John	16	M	3/4	S	No. 1	L	Cr	No. 2	L	Cr
		No. 1 Died Dec. 26, 1901. No. 2 Died Oct. 1911										
		Census Card No. 524, P. O. Sapulpa, Enrolled June 23, 1899										
1695	1	Land, Joseph Henry	40	M	1/2		J. A. Land	L	Non	Wisey Land	D	Cr
1696	2	Land, Salina	28	F	F	Wf	Watt Grayson	D	Cr	Lucy Grayson	D	Cr
1697	3	Land, Paul	12	M	3/4	S	No. 1	L	Cr	No. 2	L	Cr
1698	4	Land, Job A.	8	M	3/4	S	No. 1	L	Cr	No. 2	L	Cr
1699	5	Land, Alvin G.	4mo	M	3/4	S	No. 1	L	Cr	No. 2	L	Cr
1700	6	Land, Willie	1	M	3/4	S	No. 1	L	Cr	No. 2	L	Cr
		No. 6 died April 10, 1899										

Roll No.	No.	NAME	Age	Sex	Blood	Rel.	Name of Father	Liv.	Cit.	Name of Mother	Liv.	Cit.
	Census Card No. 525, P. O. Sapulpa, Enrolled June 23, 1899; No. 6 March 27, 1901; No. 7 May 23, 1901											
1701	1	Lee, Gano	30	M	F		Timmy Lee	D	Cr	Sally Lee	D	Cr
1702	2	Lee, Cinda	30	F	F	Wf	Jim Grayson	D	Cr	Lousally	D	Cr
1703	3	Lee, Albert	8	M	F	S	No. 1	L	Cr	No. 2	L	Cr
1704	4	Lee, Sallie	7	F	F	D	No. 1	L	Cr	No. 2	L	Cr
1705	5	Lee, Willie	2	M	F	S	No. 1	L	Cr	No. 2	L	Cr
1706	6	Lee, Lucy	1	F	F	D	No. 1	L	Cr	No. 2	L	Cr
1707	7	Stricken from roll										
		No. 2 died August 1901.										
	Census Card No. 526, P. O. Okmulgee, Enrolled June 23, 1899; No. 4 March 26, 1901											
1708	1	Roberts, Wm. J.	32	M	¼		Church Roberts	D	Non	N. E. Throckmorton	L	Cr
1709	2	Roberts, Maud	6	F	⅛	D	No. 1	L	Cr	Annie Roberts	L	Non
1710	3	Roberts, Ethel	2	F	⅛	D	No. 1	L	Cr	Annie Roberts	L	Cr
1711	4	Roberts, Edward L.	1	M	⅛	S	No. 1	L	Cr	Annie Roberts	L	Non
	Census Card No. 527, P. O. Okemah, Enrolled June 23, 1899											
1712	1	Jimboy, Wm.	47	M	F		Tustenugge Emarthla	D	Cr	Isnahaley	D	Cr
1713	2	Jimboy, Mahala	42	F	F	Wf	Lochar Harjo	D	Cr	Sakhatup Hokey	D	Cr
1714	3	Jimboy, Wiley	20	M	F	S	No. 1	L	Cr	No. 2	L	Cr
1715	4	Jimboy, Lucy	18	F	F	D	No. 1	L	Cr	No. 2	L	Cr
1716	5	Jimboy, Willie	16	M	F	S	No. 1	L	Cr	No. 2	L	Cr
1717	6	Jimboy, Reuben	14	M	F	S	No. 1	L	Cr	No. 2	L	Cr
1718	7	Jimboy, Newton	11	M	F	S	No. 1	L	Cr	No. 2	L	Cr
1719	8	Jimboy, Fannie	9	F	F	D	No. 1	L	Cr	No. 2	L	Cr
1720	9	Jimboy, Amos	7	M	F	S	No. 1	L	Cr	No. 2	L	Cr
1721	10	Jimboy, Lizzie	5	F	F	D	No. 1	L	Cr	No. 2	L	Cr
1722	11	Jimboy, Alex	4	M	F	S	No. 1	L	Cr	No. 2	L	Cr
1723	12	Jimboy, J. S. Lamar	2	M	F	S	No. 1	L	Cr	No. 2	L	Cr
1724	13	Jimboy, Amanda	2 mo	F	F	D	No. 1	L	Cr	No. 2	L	Cr
		No. 4 died February 11, 1902. No. 5 died February 22, 1901. No. 12 died February 13, 1901. Nos. 1, 3, 8 and 9 reported dead.										
	Census Card No. 528, P. O. Wetumka, Enrolled June 23, 1899											
1725	1	Grayson, Jimson	60	M	F		Okfuska Harjo	D	Cr	Unknown	D	Cr
		No. 1 died February 13, 1903										
	Census Card No. 529, P. O. Bryant, Enrolled June 23, 1899											
1726	1	Fisher, Joe	25	M	F		Dave Fisher	D	Cr	Larney Fisher	D	Cr
1727	2	Fisher, Nancy	18	F	¾	Wf	Tecumseh Tiner	L	Cr	Katie Tiner	L	Cr
1728	3	Fisher, Alice	1	F	7-8	D	No. 1	L	Cr	No. 2	L	Cr
1729	4	Fisher, Yarner	1mo	F	7-8	D	No. 1	L	Cr	No. 2	L	Cr
		No 3 died June 6, 1900. No. 1 died Feby. 2, 1910										
	Census Card No. 530, P. O. Muskogee, Enrolled June 23, 1899											
1730	1	Drew, Charley	17	M	½		Daniel Drew	D	?	Maggie Drew	D	?
	Cencus Card No. 531, P. O. Okmulgee, Enrolled June 23, 1899											
1731	1	Larney, Thompson	23	M	F		Tommy Harjo	D	Cr	Hokte Larney	L	Cr
1732	2	Larney, Betsy	21	F	F	Wf	Chok Charty	D	Cr	Koska	D	Cr
1733	3	Larney, Mitchell	1	M	F	S	No. 1	L	Cr	No. 2	L	Cr
	Census Card No. 532, P. O. Bixby, Enrolled June 23, 1899											
1734	1	Berryhill, Andrew J.	43	M	⅛		A. J. Berryhill	D	Cr	Maria Berryhill	D	Non
1735	2	Berryhill, Buford O.	12	M	1-16	S	No. 1	L	Cr	Lula Berryhill	L	Non
1736	3	Berryhill, Altie May	4	F	1-16	D	No. 1	L	Cr	Lula Berryhill	L	Non
1737	4	Berryhill, Walter Ray	2	M	1-16	S	No. 1	L	Cr	Lula Berryhill	L	Non
	Census Card No. 533, P. O. Okmulgee, Enrolled June 23, 1899											
1738	1	Miller, Seborn	31	M	Full		Sam Miller	D	Cr	Polly Miller	D	Cr
1738	2	Miller, Effa	23	F	3-4	Wf	Jefferson Berryhill	D	Cr	Peggy Berryhill	L	Cr
1740	3	Miller, Tobias	8mo	M	7-8	S	No. 1	L	Cr	No. 2	L	Cr
	Ceusus Card No. 534, P. O. Tulsa, Enrolled June 24, 1899											
1741	1	Morton, Osborna	28	M	1-4		Wm. Morton	L	Non	Delilah Marton	L	Cr
	Census Card No. 535, P. O. Wagoner, Enrolled June 24, 1899											
1742	1	Posey, Walter	39	M	¼		Thos. B. Posey	D	Cr	Hulda E. Posey	L	Non
1743	2	Posey, Laura S.	7	F	⅛	D	No. 1	L	Cr	Dora M. Posey	D	Non
1744	3	Posey, Ola B.	2	F	⅛	D	No. 1	L	Cr	Mary L. Posey	L	Non
1745	4	Stricken from roll										
	Census Card No. 536, P. O. Morse, Enrolled June 24, 1899; No. 4 June 16, 1900											
1746	1	Callahan, Benton	32	M	1-16		Sam'l B. Callahan	L	Cr	Sarah E. Callahan	D	Non
1747	2	Callahan, James W.	8	M	1-32	S	No. 1	L	Cr	Celia M. Callahan	L	Non
1748	3	Callahan, Muskogee J.	2	F	1-32	D	No. 1	L	Cr	Celia M. Callahan	L	Non
1749	4	Callahan, Homer Bryan	28ds	M	1-32	S	No. 1	L	Cr	Celia M. Callahan	L	Non
	Census Card No. 537, P. O. Preston, Enrolled June 24, 1899											
1750	1	Beaver, Martha	27	F	⅛		Robert Berryhill	D	?	Elsie Berryhill	D	?
1751	2	Beaver, Daniel	2	M	¾	S	Martin Beaver	D	Cr	No. 1	L	Cr
	Census Card No. 538, P. O. Red Fork, Enrolled June 27, 1899											
1752	1	Covey, Mary J.	30	F	¼		Joe Allen	L	Non	Eliza H. Allen	L	Cr
1753	2	Covey, John	12	M	⅛	S	Byron Covey	L	Non	No. 1	L	Cr
1754	3	Covey, Marcus William	8	M	⅛	S	Byron Covey	L	Non	No. 1	L	Cr
1755	4	Covey, Byron L.	8mo	M	⅛	S	Byron Covey	L	Non	No. 1	L	Cr
	Census Card No. 539, P. O. Bixby, Enrolled June 27, 1899											
1756	1	Baysinger, Eliza	39	F	¼		Joe Allen	L	Non	Eliza H. Allen	L	Cr
1757	2	Baysinger, Columbus	9	M	⅛	S	Columbus Baysinger	D	Non	No. 1	L	Cr
1758	3	Baysinger, Nellie	5	F	⅛	D	Perry Baysinger	D	Non	No 1	L	Cr
1759	4	Baysinger, William	2	M	⅛	S	Perry Baysinger	D	Non	No. 1	L	Cr

Census Card No. 540, P. O. Bixby, Enrolled June 27, 1899; No. 3 November 29, 1899

Roll No.	No.	NAME	Age	Sex	Blood	Rel.	NAME OF FATHER	Liv.	Cit.	NAME OF MOTHER	Liv.	Cit.
1760	1	Allen, John W.	26	M	$\frac{1}{4}$		Joe Allen	L	Non	Eliza H. Allen	L	Cr
1761	2	Allen, Suey M.	1	F	$\frac{1}{8}$	D	No. 1	L	Cr	Cora Allen	L	Non
1762	3	Allen, Joseph W.	9 ds	M	$\frac{1}{8}$	S	No. 1	L	Cr	Cora Allen	L	Non

Census Card No. 541, P. O. Mounds, Enrolled June 27, 1899

| 1763 | 1 | Allen, Benjamin T. | 25 | M | $\frac{1}{4}$ | | Joe Allen | L | Non | Eliza H. Allen | L | Cr |

Census Card No. 542, P. O. Bixby, Enrolled June 27, 1899

| 1764 | 1 | Sherrill, Mattie M. | 23 | F | $\frac{1}{4}$ | | Joe Allen | L | Non | Eliza H. Allen | L | Cr |

Census Card No. 543, P. O. Eufaula, Enrolled June 27, 1899

| 1765 | 1 | Watson, Fanny Anna | 7 | F | $\frac{5}{8}$ | | Robert Watson | L | Cr | Docia Lovell | ? | Non |

Census Card No. 544, P. O. Checotah, Enrolled June 27, 1899

1766	1	McIntosh, Roley C.	40	M	$\frac{1}{8}$		D. M. McIntosh	D	Cr	Jane McIntosh	D	Non
1767	2	McIntosh, Fannie	32	F	1-16	Wf	Unknown	?	?	Unknown	?	?
1768	3	McIntosh, Roley C. Jr.	13	M	3-32	S	No. 1	L	Cr	No. 2	L	Cr
1769	4	McIntosh, Hector	7	M	3-32	S	No. 1	L	Cr	No. 2	L	Cr
1770	5	McIntosh, Mamie	4	F	3-32	D	No. 1	L	Cr	No. 2	L	Cr

Census Card No. 545, P. O. Ridge, Enrolled June 27, 1899

| 1771 | 1 | Taylor, Solomon | 42 | M | $\frac{5}{8}$ | | Grandison Taylor | D | Non | Parthenia Taylor | D | Cr |
| 1772 | 2 | Taylor, Fred | 19 | M | 1-16 | S | No. 1 | L | Cr | Nellie Taylor | D | Cr |

No. 1 died April 12, 1909

Census Card No. 546, P. O. Bristow, Enrolled June 27, 1899

| 1773 | 1 | Carnard, Samuel | 59 | M | F | | Harry Carnard | D | Cr | Annie Garnard | D | Cr |

No. 1 died October 20, 1906

Census Card No. 547, P. O. Fame; No. 3, Eufaula, Enrolled June 27, 1899

1774	1	McIntosh, Monodese	18	M	$\frac{1}{8}$		Daniel McIntosh	D	Cr	Emma B. McIntosh	L	Non
1775	2	McIntosh, Lula N.	15	F	$\frac{1}{8}$	Sis	Daniel McIntosh	D	Cr	Emma B. McIntosh	L	Non
1776	3	McIntosh, Wm. Yancey	9M	$\frac{1}{8}$		Bro	Daniel McIntosh	D	Cr	Emma B. McIntsh	L	Non
1777	4	McIntosh, Zolena Kaniah	6	F	$\frac{1}{8}$	Sis	Daniel McIntosh	D	Cr	Emma B. McIntosh	L	Noh

Census Card No. 548, P. O. Fame, Enrolled June 27, 1899

| 1778 | 1 | McIntosh, Xenophon | 21 | M | $\frac{1}{8}$ | | Daniel M. McIntosh | D | Cr | Emma B. McIntosh | ? | Non |

Census Card No. 549, P. O. Eufaula, Enrolled June 27, 1899

1779	1	Scott, Samuel	39	M	F·		Samuel Scott	D	Cr	Polly Scott	D	Cr
1780	2	Scott, Nancy	35	F	F	Wf	Silitka McIntosh	D	Cr	Hepsey Scott	L	Cr
1781	3	Scott, Daniel	9	M	F	S	No. 1	L	Cr	No. 2	L	Cr
1782	4	Scott, John	8	M	F	S	No. 1	L	Cr	No. 2	L	Cr
1783	5	Scott, Bennie	2	M	F	S	No. 1	L	Cr	No. 2	L	Cr

Census Card No. 550, P. O. Catoosa, Enrolled June 27, 1899

1784	1	Woodward, Pollie	27	F	$\frac{1}{4}$		Chas. Johnson	D	Non	Darcus Johnson	D	Cr
1785	2	Woodward, Clarence	2	M	$\frac{1}{8}$	S	Henry Woodward	L	Non	No. 1	L	Cr
1786	3	Johnson, Ida	17	F	$\frac{1}{4}$	Sis	Chas. Johnson	D	Non	Darcus Johnson	D	Cr

No. 3 died July 8, 1909. No. 1 reported dead

Census Card No. 551, P. O. Wagoner, Enrolled June 27, 1899

| 1787 | 1 | Skeen, Julia | 51 | F | $\frac{1}{2}$ | | George Carter | D | Non· | Annie Carter | D | Cr |

Census Card No. 552, P. O. Wagoner, Enrolled June 27, 1899; No. 3, March 7, 1900

1788	1	Turnham, Curley	19	F	$\frac{1}{4}$		James R. Skeen	L	Non	Julia Skeen	L	Cr
1789	2	Turnham, William R.	1	M	$\frac{1}{8}$	S	Joe Turnham	L	Non	No. 1	L	Cr
1790	3	Turnham, Violet	2mo	F	$\frac{1}{8}$	D	Joe Turnham	L	Non	No. 1	L	Cr

No. 3 died November 12, 1900

Census Card No. 553, P. O. Wagoner, Enrolled June 27, 1899; No. 3 May 24, 1901

1791	1	Ware, Lula	22	F	$\frac{1}{4}$		James R. Skeens	L	Non	Julia Skeen	L	Cr
1792	2	Ware, Oren	1	M	$\frac{1}{8}$	S	Henderson Ware	L	Non	No. 1	L	Cr
1793	3	Ware, Ivy	1	F	$\frac{1}{8}$	D	Henderson Ware	L	Non	No. 1	L	Cr

Census Card No. 554, P. O. Wagoner, Enrolled June 27, 1899

| 1794 | 1 | Holman, Dora | 31 | F | $\frac{1}{4}$ | | John Walters | L | Non | Julia Skeen | L | Cr |

Census Card No. 555, P. O. Okmulgee, Enrolled June 28, 1899

1795	1	Harjo, Henry M.	37	M	F		Marsey Harjo	D	Cr	Unknown	D	Cr
1796	2	Harjo, Katie	24	F	F	Wf	David Monnawee	D	Cr	Hoye	D	Cr
1797	3	Harjo, Naomi	3	F	F	D	No. 1	L	Cr	No. 2	L	Cr
1798	4	Harjo, Lillie May	9mo	F	F	D	No. 1	L	Cr	No. 2	L	Cr

No. 4 died January 1, 1900

Census Card No. 556, P. O. Sapulpa, Enrolled June 28, 1899

1799	1	Pickett, Daniel	42	M	F		Shahkey	D	Cr	Mary	D	Cr
1800	2	Pickett, Malinda	35	F	F	Wf	Billy Barrett	D	Cr	Mabaley Barnett	D	Cr
1801	3	Pickett, Jennie:	15	F	F	D	No. 1	L	Cr	No. 2	L	Cr
1802	4	Pickett, Jennetta	13	F	F	D	No. 1	L	Cr	No. 2	L	Cr
1803	5	Pickett, Louisa	10	F	F	D	No. 1	L	Cr	No. 2	L	Cr
1804	6	Pickett, Ella	8	F	F	D	No. 1	L	Cr	No. 2	L	Cr
1805	7	Pickett, Lucy	6	F	F	D	No. 1	L	Cr	No. 2	L	Cr
1806	8	Pickett, Ada	3	F	F	D	No. 1	L	Cr	No. 2	L	Ct

No. 1 died December 29, 1911. No. 2 died May 1910. No. 3 died July 27, 1913.

Census Card No. 557, P. O. Sapulpa, Enrolled June 28, 1899

| 1807 | 1 | Bigpond, Susanna | 21 | F | F | | Charles Bigpond | L | Cr | Malinda Pickett | L | Cr |

Census Card No. 558, P. O. Coweta, Enrolled June 28, 1899

1808	1	Orcutt, Adaline	30	F	$\frac{1}{4}$		Alvin Hodge	D	?	Mary Hodge	D	?
1809	2	Orcutt, Annie	11	F	$\frac{1}{8}$	D	Dolph Orcutt	L	Non	No. 1	L	Cr
1810	3	Orcutt, Alvin	9	M	$\frac{1}{8}$	S	Dolph Orcutt	L	Non	No. 1	L	Cr
1811	4	Orcutt, Elam	7	M	$\frac{1}{8}$	S	Dolph Orcutt	L	Non	No. 1	L	Cr
1812	5	Orcutt, David	4	M	$\frac{1}{8}$	S	Dolph Orcutt	L	Non	No. 1	L	Cr
1813	6	Orcutt, Ollie	2	F	$\frac{1}{8}$	D	Dolph Orcutt	L	Non	No. 1	L	Cr
1814	7	Orcutt, Christina	7 mo	F	$\frac{1}{8}$	D	Dolph Orcutt	L	Non	No. 1	L	Cr

No. 4 reported dead.

45

Census Card No. 559, P. O. Stone Bluff, Enrolled June 28, 1899

Roll No.	No.	NAME	Age	Sex	Blood	Rel.	NAME OF FATHER	Liv.	Cit.	NAME OF MOTHER	Liv.	Cit.
1815	1	Brown, Th3mas	19	M	F		George Brown	L	Cr	Lizzie Brown	D	Cr

Census Card No. 560, P. O. Bixbp, Enrolled June 28, 1899

Roll No.	No.	NAME	Age	Sex	Blood	Rel.	NAME OF FATHER	Liv.	Cit.	NAME OF MOTHER	Liv.	Cit.
1816	1	Fox, Luke	26	M	F		Carthonnay	L	Cr	Tarsillee	L	Cr
1817	2	Fox, Maggie	24	F	F	Wf	Robert Brown	L	Cr	Katie Brown	L	Cr
1818	3	Fox, Mary	5	F	F	D	No. 1	L	Cr	No. 2	L	Cr
1819	4	Fox, Henry	2	M	F	S	No. 1	L	Cr	No. 2	L	Cr

No. 2 died October 30, 1903

Census Card No. 561, P. O. Wealaka, Enrolled June 28, 1899

Roll No.	No.	NAME	Age	Sex	Blood	Rel.	NAME OF FATHER	Liv.	Cit.	NAME OF MOTHER	Liv.	Cit.
1820	1	Fixico, Cholar	78	M	F		Tahconthla	D	Cr	Chapana	D	Cr

Census Card No. 562, P. O. Wealaka Okla, Enrolled June 28, 1899

Roll No.	No.	NAME	Age	Sex	Blood	Rel.	NAME OF FATHER	Liv.	Cit.	NAME OF MOTHER	Liv.	Cit.
1821	1	Fox, Charlie	40	M	F		Cholar Fixico	L	Cr	Embehe	D	Cr
1822	2	Fox, Andewe	42	F	F	Wf	Addenna	D	Cr	Cotahsowena	D	Cr
1823	3	Fox, Sakena	18	F	F	Niece in Law	Daycha	D	Cr	Yacopahnay	D	Cr

No. 2 and 3 reported dead

Census Card No. 563, P. O. Wealaka, Enrolled June 28, 1899

Roll No.	No.	NAME	Age	Sex	Blood	Rel.	NAME OF FATHER	Liv.	Cit.	NAME OF MOTHER	Liv.	Cit.
1824	1	Grant, U. S.	48	M	F		Thlaconshona	D	Cr	Ahkona	D	Cr
1825	2	Grant, Assie	35	F	F	Wf	Kogeefa	D	Cr	Akuonko	D	Cr
1826	3	Grant, Sam Miller	16	M	F	S	No. 1	L	Cr	No. 2	L	Cr
1827	4	Grant, Timmie	12	M	F	S	No. 1	L	Cr	No. 2	L	Cr
1828	5	Grant, Lucy	10	F	F	D	No. 1	L	Cr	No. 2	L	Cr
1829	6	Grant, Frank	4	M	F	S	No. 1	L	Cr	No. 2	L	Cr

No. 6 died February 28, 1909. No. 1 died April 1911. No. 2 died March 1911.
Nos. 1 and 3 reported dead.

Census Card No. 564, P. O. Mounds, Enrolled June 28, 1899

Roll No.	No.	NAME	Age	Sex	Blood	Rel.	NAME OF FATHER	Liv.	Cit.	NAME OF MOTHER	Liv.	Cit.
1830	1	Frank, Short	55	M	F		Unknown	D	Cr	Unknown	D	Cr
1831	2	Frank, Bettie	20	F	F	Wf	Goulay Mingo	D	Cr	Guseanna	D	Cr
1832	3	Frank, Josie	3	M	F	S	No. 1	L	Cr	No. 2	L	Cr

No. 1 reported dead

Census Card No. 565, P. O. Sapulpa, Enrolled June 28, 1899

Roll No.	No.	NAME	Age	Sex	Blood	Rel.	NAME OF FATHER	Liv.	Cit.	NAME OF MOTHER	Liv.	Cit.
1833	1	Pitman, Lucinda	26	F	F		John Hunt	D	Cr	Annie	D	Cr
1834	2	Pitman, Rowie Elizabeth	7	F	$\frac{1}{2}$	D	Bob Pitman	L	Non	No. 1	L	Cr

No. 2 reported dead

Census Card No. 566, P. O. Bixby, Enrolled June 28, 1899

Roll No.	No.	NAME	Age	Sex	Blood	Rel.	NAME OF FATHER	Liv.	Cit.	NAME OF MOTHER	Liv.	Cit.
1835	1	Johnson, Andrew	48	M	F		Hulbutta Micco	D	Cr	Sasena Micco	D	Cr
1836	2	Johnson, Eliza	40	F	F	Wf	Thlakunchana	D	Cr	Ahlikouncona	D	Cr
1837	3	Johnson, Anderson	14	M	F	S	No. 1	L	Cr	No. 2	L	Cr

No. 3 died 1903

Census Card No. 567, P. O. Mounds, Enrolled June 28, 1899

Roll No.	No.	NAME	Age	Sex	Blood	Rel.	NAME OF FATHER	Liv.	Cit.	NAME OF MOTHER	Liv.	Cit.
1838	1	Bigpond, Daniel	30	M	F		John Bigpond	D	Cr	Ajubee	D	Cr
1839	2	Bigpond, Nancy	25	F	F	f	Robert Brown	D	Cr	Katie Brown	D	Cr
1840	3	Bigpond, Shackleford	10	M	F	S	No. 1	L	Cr	No. 2	L	Cr
1841	4	Bigpond, Joseph	2	M	F	S	No. 1	L	Cr	No. 2	L	Cr

Census Card No. 568, P. O. Sapulpa, Enrolled June 28, 1899

Roll No.	No.	NAME	Age	Sex	Blood	Rel.	NAME OF FATHER	Liv.	Cit.	NAME OF MOTHER	Liv.	Cit.
1842	1	Edwards, Sarah C.	32	F	$\frac{1}{8}$		Wm. Clarke	D	Non	Rebecca Clark	D	Cr

Census Card No. 569, P. O. Wealaka, Enrolled June 28, 1899

Roll No.	No.	NAME	Age	Sex	Blood	Rel.	NAME OF FATHER	Liv.	Cit.	NAME OF MOTHER	Liv.	Cit.
1843	1	Soffie, John	50	M	F		Aknutana	D	Cr	Kaalay	D	Cr

Census Card No. 570, P. O. Eufaula, Enrolled June 28, 1899

Roll No.	No.	NAME	Age	Sex	Blood	Rel.	NAME OF FATHER	Liv.	Cit.	NAME OF MOTHER	Liv.	Cit.
1844	1	Self, James B.	41	M	$\frac{1}{4}$		Sam Self	D	Cr	Safrona Self	D	Cr
1845	2	Self, James H.	16	M	$\frac{1}{8}$	S	No. 1	L	Cr	Martha Self	L	Non
1846	3	Self, Della	14	F	$\frac{1}{8}$	D	No. 1	L	Cr	Martha Self	L	Non
1847	4	Self, Sam	11	M	$\frac{1}{8}$	S	No. 1	L	Cr	Martha Self	L	Cr
1848	5	Self, Ruben	9	M	$\frac{1}{8}$	S	No. 1	L	Cr	Martha Self	L	Cr
1849	6	Self, Lelah	7	F	$\frac{1}{8}$	D	No. 1	L	Cr	Martha Self	L	Non
1850	7	Self, Millie	5	F	$\frac{1}{8}$	D	No. 1	L	Cr	Martha Self	L	Non

Census Card No. 571, P. O. Wealaka, Enrolled June 28, 1899

Roll No.	No.	NAME	Age	Sex	Blood	Rel.	NAME OF FATHER	Liv.	Cit.	NAME OF MOTHER	Liv.	Cit.
1851	1	Carthlony	48	M	F		Calachoney	L	Cr	Embethlena	D	Cr
1852	2	Carthlony, Tahsalay	50	F	F	Wf	Thlaconshony	D	Cr	Alacuuncona	D	Cr

Census Card No. 572, P. O. Choska, Enrolled June 29, 1899

Roll No.	No.	NAME	Age	Sex	Blood	Rel.	NAME OF FATHER	Liv.	Cit.	NAME OF MOTHER	Liv.	Cit.
1853	1	Gentry, Scott	52	M	$\frac{1}{4}$		James Gentry	D	Cr	Caroline Gentry	D	Non
1854	2	Gentry, Abbie	52	F	$\frac{3}{4}$	Wf	Atoney Rogers	D	Cr	Louvina Rogers	D	Cr

No. 2 died July 1, 1902. No. 1 reported dead.

Census Card No. 573, P. O. Mounds, Enrolled June 29, 1899

Roll No.	No.	NAME	Age	Sex	Blood	Rel.	NAME OF FATHER	Liv.	Cit.	NAME OF MOTHER	Liv.	Cit.
1855	1	Big Head, Stanwaitie	50	M	F		Hetakowe	D	Cr	Unknown	D	Cr
1856	2	Big Head, Millie	35	F	F	Wf	Tabshawe	D	Cr	Dochee	D	Cr
1857	3	Big Head, Sallie	7	F	F	D	No. 1	L	Cr	No. 2	L	Cr
1858	4	Big Head, Konzie	6	M	F	S	No. 1	L	Cr	No. 2	L	Cr
1859	5	Big Head, Addie	3	F	F	D	No. 1	L	Cr	No. 2	L	Cr
1860	6	Big Head, Nancy	3 mo	F	F	D	No. 1	L	Cr	No. 2	L	Cr

No. 5 died February 1900. No. 1 reported dead

Census Card No. 574, P. O. Boynton, Enrolled June 29, 1899

Roll No.	No.	NAME	Age	Sex	Blood	Rel.	NAME OF FATHER	Liv.	Cit.	NAME OF MOTHER	Liv.	Cit.
1861	1	Johnson, Miley	20	F	$\frac{1}{4}$		Charles Johnson	D	Non	Dorcas Johnson	D	Cr
1862	2	Deer, Elizabeth	4	F	$\frac{3}{8}$	D	August Deere	L	Non	No. 1	L	Cr
1863	3	Deer, Charles	2	M	$\frac{1}{8}$	S	August Deere	L	Non	No. 1	L	Cr

No. 3 reported dead

Census Card No. 575, P. O. Eufaula, Enrolled June 29, 1899; No. 3, October 13, 1899

Roll No.	No.	NAME	Age	Sex	Blood	Rel.	NAME OF FATHER	Liv.	Cit.	NAME OF MOTHER	Liv.	Cit.
1864	1	Timmunichee, Taylor	25	M	F		Timmunichee	D	Cr	Lucy Loney	L	Cr
1865	2	Timmunichee, Mollie	30	F	F	Wf	Loney	L	Cr	Ahboga	D	Cr
1866	3	Timmunichee, Mary	1	F	F	D	No. 1	L	Cr	No. 2	L	Cr

No. 2 died about 1908. Nos. 1 and 3 reported dead.

Roll No.	No.	NAME	Age	Sex	Blood	Rel.	NAME OF FATHER	Liv.	Cit.	NAME OF MOTHER	Liv.	Cit.
		Census Card No. 576, P. O. Stidham, Enrolled June 29, 1899										
1867	1	Moore, Albert	27	M	½		Jim Moore	L	Cr	Susan Moore	L	Non
1868	2	Frank, Leah	15	F	½	StD	Wilson Frank	D	Cr	Carrie Moore	L	Non
		Census Card No. 577, P. O. Eufaula, Enrolled June 29, 1899										
1869	1	Wadsworth, Mattie	23	F	¾		Wash Collins	L	Cr	Nicey Collins	L	Cr
1870	2	Wadsworth, Irene	6	F	¾	D	Pude J. Wadsworth	L	Sem	No. 1	L	Cr
1871	3	Wadsworth, John	5	M	¾	S	Pude J. Wadsworth	L	Sem	No. 1	L	Cr
1872	4	Wadsworth, William	3	M	¾	S	Pude J. Wadsworth	L	Sem	No. 1	L	Cr
1873	5	Wadsworth, Newman	1	M	¾	S	Pude J. Wadsworth	L	Sem	No. 1	L	Cr
		No. 5 died September 1899. No. 1 died April 23, 1901										
		Census Card No. 578, P. O. Bixby, Enrolled June 29, 1899										
1874	1	Clinton, Sallie	27	F	F		Marshie Pickett	D	Cr	Cahlowee	D	Cr
		Census Card No. 579, P. O. Checotah, Enrolled June 29, 1899; No. 9, September 28, 1900										
1875	1	McNulty, Cherokee	33	F	½		Thos. Watts	L	Cher	Mary Watts	L	Cr
1876	2	McNulty, Lena	16	F	¼	D	Jeff McNulty	L	Cher	No. 1	L	Cr
1877	3	McNulty, George W.	15	M	¼	S	Jeff McNulty	L	Cher	No. 1	L	Cr
1878	4	McNulty, Maude M.	13	F	¼	D	Jeff McNulty	L	Cher	No. 1	L	Cr
1879	5	McNulty, Annie	10	F	¼	D	Jeff McNulty	L	Cher	No. 1	L	Cr
1880	6	McNulty, Beulah	8	F	¼	D	Jeff McNulty	L	Cher	No. 1	L	Cr
1881	7	McNulty, Thomas J.	5	M	¼	S	Jeff McNulty	L	Cher	No. 1	L	Cr
1882	8	McNulty, Wanney	3	F	¼	D	Jeff McNulty	L	Cher	No. 1	L	Cr
1883	9	McNulty, John	2	M	¼	S	Jeff McNulty	L	Cher	No. 1	L	Cr
		Census Card No. 580, P. O. Gibson Station, Enrolled June 29, 1899										
1884	1	Barbee, Sarah M.	52	F	⅛		James D. Willison	D	Non	Hettie Willison	D	Cr
		Census Card No. 581, P. O. Muskogee, Enrolled June 29, 1899										
1885	1	Farmer, Liza	30	F	½		George Anderson	D	?	Nancy Anderson	D	?
1886	2	Farmer, Nellie W.	4	F	¼	D	N. K. Farmer	L	Non	No. 1	L	Cr
		Census Card No. 582, P. O. Bixby, Enrolled June 29, 1899										
1887	1	Fox, William	30	M	F		Carthlony	L	Cr	Tabsalay	L	Cr
1888	2	Fox, Sukey	20	F	F	Wf	Sankothla	D	Cr	Fahquay	D	Cr
1889	3	Fox, William Jr.	6	M	F	S	No. 1	L	Cr	Sukey Fox	D	Cr
		Census Card No. 583, P. O. Coweta, Enrolled June 29, 1899										
1890	1	Grayson, Jim	18	M	⅜		Henry Grayson	L	F-Chic	Mary Grayson	L	Cr
		Census Card No. 584, P. O. Wealaka, Enrolled June 29, 1899										
1891	1	Buck, John	64	M	½		Buck	D	Non	Uwakalee	D	Cr
1892	2	Buck, Rosa	50	F	½	Wf	Hotka	L	Cr	Unknown	D	?
1893	3	Buck, Reuben	7	M	½	S	No. 1	L	Cr	No. 2	L	Cr
1894	4	Buck, Sillibee	17	F	¾	GrD	Warrior Buck	D	Cr	Marsa Buck	D	Cr
		No. 4 died August 1901. No. 2 died April 28, 1911. No. 3 died March 1900.										
		Census Card No. 585, P. O. Coweta, Enrolled June 29, 1899										
1895	1	Holden, Thomas	50	M	⅜		Holden	D	Non	Beckey Holden	D	Cr
1896	2	Holden, Kate	40	F	½	Wf	Thos. Atkin	D	Non	Mollie Tiger	D	Cr
		No. 2 died January 9, 1909										
		Census Card No. 586, P. O. Bixby, Enrolled June 29, 1899										
1897	1	Rolland, Master	42	M	F		Joseph Roland	D	Cr	Caahthlenna	D	Cr
1898	2	Rolland, Annie	29	F	F	Wf	John Buck	L	Cr	Rosa Buck	L	Cr
1899	3	Rolland, Susie	5	F	F	D	No. 1	L	Cr	No. 2	L	Cr
1900	4	Rolland, Wilson	13	M	F	S	No. 1	L	Cr	Honnie Rolland	D	Cr
1901	5	Rolland, Temarye	10	M	F	S	No. 1	L	Cr	Honnie Rolland	D	Cr
1902	6	Stewart, Jno.	9	M	F	StS	Robert Stewart	L	Cr	No. 2	L	Cr
1903	7	Harrison, Mamie	6	F	F	StD	Wilson Harrison	D	Cr	No. 2	L	Cr
		No. 1 died February 21, 1902. No. 6 died June 15, 1900. No. 2 died December 14, 1907										
		Census Card No. 587, P. O. Bristow, Enrolled June 29, 1899										
1904	1	Big Mosquito	50	M	F		Caponey	D	Cr	Shaknutaney	D	Cr
1905	2	Big Mosquito, Jensey	26	F	F	Wf	Sakuntaney	L	Cr	Teshanquaney	D	Cr
1906	3	Big Mosquito, Albert	18	M	F	S	No. 1	L	Cr	Lizzie Big Mosquito	D	Cr
1907	4	Big Mosquito, Tacoconwee	10	M	F	S	No. 1	L	Cr	Lizzie Big Mosquito	D	Cr
1908	5	Big Mosquito, Coyonfolany	8	M	F	S	No. 1	L	Cr	Lizzie Big Mosquito	D	Cr
		No. 2 reported dead										
		Census Card No. 588, P. O. Mounds, Enrolled June 29, 1899										
1909	1	Staley, John	30	M	F		Chatete	D	Cr	Shatohe	D	Cr
1910	2	Staley, Sakcota	27	F	F	Wf	Wootsha	L	Cr	Aconconey	D	Cr
1911	3	Staley, Euconcocon- thla	8	M	F	S	No. 1	L	Cr	No. 2	L	Cr
1912	4	Staley, Tarsacoconthla	8	M	F	Neph	Shockcothla	D	Cr	Lena	D	Cr
		Census Card No. 589, P. O. Bixby, Enrolled June 29, 1899; No. 2 May 22, 1901										
1913	1	Daniels, Saloma	20	F	F		John Buck	L	Cr	Rosa Buck	L	Cr
1914	2	Daniels, Jasper	5	M	F	S	Bob Daniels	L	Cr	No. 1	L	Cr
		No. 2 died 1900										
		Census Card No. 590, P. O. Bixby, Enrolled June 29, 1899										
1915	1	Buck, Annie	21	F	F		James Larney	D	Cr	Susanna	D	Cr
1916	2	Buck, Perryman	3	M	F	D	Rufus Buck	L	Cr	No. 1	L	Cr
		Census Card No. 591, P. O. Bixby, Enrolled June 29, 1899										
1917	1	Agent, Jim	27	M	F		Yahtalevy	D	Cr	Tekoma	L	Cr
1918	2	Agent, Lizzie	19	F	F	Wf	John Buck	L	Cr	Rosa Buck	L	Cr
1919	3	Agent, Bruce	6moM		F	S	No. 1	L	Cr	No. 2	L	Cr
1920	4	Bruner, Jensey	3	F	F	StD	Freeland Bruner	L	Cr	No. 2	L	Cr
		No. 1 died February 1902. No. 2 died May 12, 1911.										

47

Roll No.	No.	NAME	Age	Sex	Blood	Rel.	NAME OF FATHER	Liv.	Cit.	NAME OF MOTHER	Liv.	Cit.
		Census Card No. 592, P. O. Inola, Enrolled June 29, 1899; No. 3, July 25, 1900										
1921	1	Thomas, Mack	25	M	½		Wm. R. Thomas	D	Non	Emma Thomas	L	Cr
1922	2	Thomas, Sarah	22	F	¾	Wf	Wiley Tiger	D	Cr	Katie Tiger	D	Cr
1923	3	Thomas, Philip	3moM	¾	S		No. 1	L	Cr	No. 2	L	Cr
		No. 3 died August 27; 1901										
		Census Card No. 593, P. O. Coweta, Enrolled June 29, 1899										
1924	1	Thomas, Sam	22	M	½		Wm. R. Thomas	D	Non	Emma Thomas	L	Cr
1925	2	Thomas, Sophia	18	F	¾	Wf	Wesley Tiger	L	Cr	Katie Tiger	D	Cr
		Census Card No. 594, P. O. Coweta, Enrolled June 29, 1899										
1926	1	Thomas, Emma	48	F	F		Thompson Perryman	D	Cr	Cinda Perryman	L	Cr
1927	2	Thomas, William	14	M	½	S	Wm. R. Thomas	D	Non	No. 1	L	Cr
1928	3	Thomas, Johnson	9	M	½	S	Wm. R. Thomas	D	Non	No. 1	L	Cr
		Census Card No. 595, P. O. Mounds, Enrolled June 29, 1899										
1929	1	Allen, Eliza H.	50	F	½		Benj. Posey	D	Cr	Eliza Posey	D	Cr
		Census Card No. 596, P. O. Bixby, Enrolled June 29, 1899										
1930	1	Squire, John	23	M	F		Cocathlaney	D	Cr	Kittie	D	Cr
1931	2	Squire, Alashoocon-conay	1	F	F	D	No. 1	L	Cr	Sukey Squire	D	Cr
		Census Card No. 597, P. O. Wagoner, Enrolled June 29, 1899										
1932	1	Ahrens, Kate E.	35	F	¼		Wm. Shaw	D	Non	Kissie Tiger	L	Cr
1933	2	Ahrens, Juliette	4	F	⅛	D	A. J. W. Ahrens	L	Non	No. 1	L	Cr
1934	3	Ahrens, Henry Shaw	1	M	⅛	S	A. J. W. Ahrens	L	Non	No. 1	L	Cr
		Census Card No. 598, P. O. Mounds, Enrolled June 29, 1899										
1935	1	Tiger, Stanwaitie	26	M	F		Chatotey	D	Cr	Shatohe	D	Cr
1936	2	Tiger, Jessie	5	M	F	S	No. 1	L	Cr	Sacopocheney	D	Cr
1937	3	Tiger, Minnie	3	F	F	D	No. 1	L	Cr	Sacopocheney	D	Cr
1938	4	Thomas, Lizzie	19	F	F	StD	Marsie Short	D	Cr	Sacopocheney	D	Cr
1939	5	Parkinson, Jim	11	M	F	StS	Marsie Short	D	Cr	Sacopocheney	D	Cr
1940	6	Tiger, Lodie	10	F	F	Niece	Shakothla	D	Cr	Lena	D	Cr
1941	7	Tiger, Dollie	4 moF	F	D		No. 1	L	Cr	Sacopocheney	L	Cr
		No. 7 died September 10, 1899										
		Census Card No. 599, P. O. Muskogee, Enrolled June 30, 1899										
1942	1	Marshall, Benjamin	33	M	⅝		George Marshall	D	Cr	Eliabeth Marshall	D	Cr
1943	2	Marshall, Beauregarde	5	M	5-16	S	No. 1	L	Cr	Lizzie B. Marshall	L	Non
1944	3	Matrshall, Anne E.	3	F	5-16	D	No. 1	L	Cr	Lizzie B. Marshall	L	Non
1945	4	Marshall, Alva Ruth	1	F	5-16	D	No. 1	L	Cr	Lizzie B. Marshall	L	Non
1946	5	Marshall, Gertrude Belle	10moF		5-16	D	No. 1	L	Cr	Lizzie B. Marshall	L	Non
		Census Card No. 600, P. O. Bristow, Enrolled June 30, 1899										
1947	1	Brown, Timmie	15	M	F		Catah	D	Cr	Betsey	D	Cr
		Census Card No. 601, P. O. Wealaka, Enrolled June 30, 1899										
1948	1	Pumpkin, Deconthla	62	F	F		Tacathley	D	Cr	Dasacowee	D	Cr
1949	2	Cahwee, Peter	10	M	F	Neph	Cahwee	D	Cr	Betsey Cahwee	D	Cr
		No. 1 died November 10, 1904. No. 2 reported dead.										
		Census Card No. 602, P. O. Bixby, Enrolled June 30, 1899										
1950	1	Littlehead, Nancy	26	F	F		Yahtalonwe	D	Cr	Deconthla	L	Cr
1951	2	Littlehead, Wesley	4	M	F	S	Jim Littlehead	D	Cr	No. 1	L	Cr
1952	3	Littlehead, Tom	1	M	F	S	Jim Littlehead	D	Cr	No. 1	L	Cr
		No. 1 died March 2, 1910. Nos. 2 and 3 reported dead										
		Census Card No. 603, P. O. Bixby, Enrolled June 30, 1899										
1953	1	Cooper, Albert	38	M	F		Cooper	D	Cr	Tasathla	D	Cr
1954	2	Cooper, John	18	M	F	Bro	Cooper	D	Cr	Tasathla	D	Cr
1955	3	Cooper, Sam	16	M	F	Bro	Cooper	D	Cr	Tasathla	D	Cr
		No. 1 reported dead										
		Census Card No. 604, P. O. Mounds; No. 6, Bixby, Enrolled June 30, 1899										
1956	1	Squire, Candy	32	M	F		Cocathlanay	D	Cr	Kittie	D	Cr
1957	2	Squire, Beckie	23	F	F	Wf	Tasheteapathla	D	Cr	Pollie	D	Cr
1958	3	Squire, John	7	M	F	S	No. 1	L	Cr	No. 2	L	Cr
1959	4	Squire, Hannah	3	F	F	D	No. 1	L	Cr	No. 2	L	Cr
1960	5	Squire, Noah	6moM	F	S		No. 1	L	Cr	No. 2	L	Cr
1961	6	Squire, Tekecoconoy	10	M	F	Bro	Cocathlanay	D	Cr	Ahochtey	D	Cr
1962	7	Squire, Delia	6	F	F	Niece	Tom Squire	D	Cr	Hepsey Squire	D	Cr
		No. 1 died December 25, 1901. Nos. 2, 3, 4, 5, reported dead.										
		Census Card No. 605, P. O. Kelleyville, Enrolled June 30, 1899										
1963	1	Brown, Jake	25	M	F		Catah	D	Cr	Betsey	D	Cr
1964	2	Brown, Sallie	21	F	F	Wf	Cuthenay	D	Cr	Parkany	D	Cr
1965	3	Brown, Jennette	6 moF	F	D		No. 1	L	Cr	No. 2	L	Cr
		No. 2 died April 4, 1907. No. 1 died April 1905										
		Census Card No. 606, P. O. Wealaka, Enrolled June 30, 1899										
1966	1	Bear, Walter	23	M	F		Okpethlonay	D	Cr	Tekeufah	D	Cr
1967	2	Bear, Polly	18	F	F	Wf	Robert Brown	D	Cr	Katie Brown	D	Cr
		No. 1 died March 15, 1900										
		Census Card No. 607, P. O. Braggs, Enrolled June 30, 1899										
1968	1	Dansby, Vicy	32	F	¼		Sunny Grayson	L	?	Martha Chisholm	L	?
1969	2	Dansby, Ella	7	F	⅛	D	Walter Dansby	L	Non	No. 1	L	Cr
1970	3	Dansby, Martha	5	F	⅛	D	Walter Dansby	L	Non	No. 1	L	Cr
1971	4	Dansby, Andy	2	M	⅛	S	Walter Dansby	L	Non	No. 1	L	Cr
1972	5	Dansby, Bertha	1moF	⅛	D		Walter Dansby	L	Non	No. 1	L	Cr
		No. 1 died 1908										

48

Roll No.	No.	NAME	Age	Sex	Blood	Rel.	NAME OF FATHER	Liv.	Cit.	NAME OF MOTHER	Liv.	Cit.
		Census Card No. 608, P. O. Porter, Enrolled June 30, 1899										
1973	1	Daniels, Mollie	39	F	¼		Saucer Brady	D	?	Amy Grayson	L	?
1974	2	Daniels, Sanford	18	M	¼	S	Bob Daniels	L	Cr	No. 1	L	Cr
1975	3	Daniels, Lemus	10	M	¼	S	Bob Daniels	L	Cr	No. 1	L	Cr
		No. 2 died May 1, 1905										
		Census Card No. 609, P. O. Wealaka, Enrolled June 30, 1899										
1976	1	Wolf, John	26	M	F		Heatchonay	D	Cr	Sekanay	D	Cr
1977	2	Wolf, Lucy	22	F	F	Wf	Yatalowe	D	Cr	Teconthla	L	Cr
		No. 1 reported dead. No. 2 reported dead										
		Census Card No. 610, P. O. Bristow, Enrolled June 30, 1899										
1978	1	Jo-be-la-fah-ny	36	M	F		Sakquenay	D	Cr	Hacoco	D	Cr
1979	2	Jo-be-la-fah-ny, Mary	26	F	F	Wf	John Davis	L	Cr	Unknown	D	Cr
1980	3	Jo-be-la-fah-ny, Sarah	10	F	F	D	No. 1	L	Cr	No. 2	L	Cr
1981	4	Jo-be-la-fah-ny, Wesley	5	M	F	S	No. 1	L	Cr	No. 2	L	Cr
		Census Card No. 611, P. O. Bixby, Enrolled June 30, 1899										
1982	1	McCoy, Henry	22	M	F		McCoy	D	Cr	Liza McCoy	L	Cr
		No. 1 died September 1908.										
		Census Card No. 612, P. O. Olive, Enrolled June 30, 1899										
1983	1	Brown, Larry	29	M	F		Robert Brown	D	Cr	Katie Brown	D	Cr
1984	2	Brown, Hardin	27	M	F	Wf	Catah	D	Cr	Betsey	D	Cr
1985	3	Brown, Buster	7	M	F	S	No. 1	L	Cr	No. 2	L	Cr
1986	4	Brown, Robert	4	M	F	S	No. 1	L	Cr	No. 2	L	Cr
1987	5	Brown, Bessie	1	F	F	D	No. 1	L	Cr	No. 2	L	Cr
		No. 3 died December 25, 1900										
		Census Card No. 613, P. O. Dustin, Enrolled June 30, 1899										
1988	1	Smith, John F.	46	M	¾		John G. Smith	D	Cr	Lucinda Smith	D	Cr
1989	2	Smith, Rannie	33	F	⅞	Wf	Vard Wills	D	Cr	Georgiana Wills	D	Cr
1990	3	Smith, Lewis	16	M	⅞	S	No. 1	L	Cr	No. 2	L	Cr
1991	4	Smith, Ella	14	F	⅞	D	No. 1	L	Cr	No. 2	L	Cr
1992	5	Smith, Edna	12	F	⅞	D	No. 1	L	Cr	No. 2	L	Cr
1993	6	Smith, Lawrence	10	M	⅞	S	No. 1	L	Cr	No. 2	L	Cr
1994	7	Smith, Guy	8	M	⅞	S	No. 1	L	Cr	No. 2	L	Cr
1995	8	Smith, Pearl	4	F	⅞	D	No. 1	L	Cr	No. 2	L	Cr
1996	9	Smith, Willis	9 mo	M	⅞	S	No. 1	L	Cr	No. 2	L	Cr
		No. 1 died November 22, 1906										
		Census Card No. 614, P. O. Mounds, Enrolled June 30, 1899; No. 3 Kiefer										
1997	1	Leath, Louisa	43	F	1-16		W. B. Self	L	Cr	Mary Self	L	Non
1998	2	Leath, John Henry	21	M	1-32	S	T. M. Leath	L	Non	No. 1	L	Cr
1999	3	Leath, Thomas J.	19	M	1-32	S	T. M. Leath	L	Non	No. 1	L	Cr
2000	4	Leath, Wm. Bogle	15	M	1-32	S	T. M. Leath	L	Non	No. 1	L	Cr
		Census Card No. 615, P. O. Coweta, Enrolled August 1, 1899										
2001	1	Dryden, Mattie B.	17	F	⅛		Henry R. Dryden	L	Non	Mary E. Dryden	D	Cr
2002	2	Dryden, Lucy	16	F	⅛	Sis	Henry R. Dryden	L	Non	Mary E. Dryden	D	Cr
2003	3	Dryden, Leona	14	F	⅛	Sis	Henry R. Dryden	L	Non	Mary E Dryden	D	Cr
2004	4	Dryden, Rosella	11	F	⅛	Sis	Henry R. Dryden	L	Non	Mary E. Dryden	D	Cr
2005	5	Dryden, William	10	M	⅛	Bro	Henry R. Dryden	L	Non	Mary E. Dryden	D	Cr
		Census Card No. 616, P. O. Wagoner, Enrolled August 1, 1899										
2006	1	Childers, Robert Jr.	9	M	⅓		Robert Childers	L	Cr	Hattie Underwood	L	Non
		Census Card No. 617, P. O. Tuskegee, Enrolled August 1, 1899; Nos. 3 and 4 Edna										
2007	1	Bruner, Richard R.	67	M	½		Jacob Bruner	D	Cr	Eliza Brown	D	Cr
2008	2	Bruner, Harriet	53	F	½	Wf	Joe Bones	D	Cr	Eliza Bones	D	Cr
2009	3	Bruner, Pinky	18	M	½	S	No. 1	L	Cr	No. 2	L	Cr
2010	4	Bruner, Eliza Jane	16	F	½	D	No. 1	L	Cr	No. 2	L	Cr
2011	5	Steele, Tula	27	F	½	StD	Dave Steele	D	Cr	No. 2	L	Cr
2012	6	Sharp, Noah	7	M	¼	StGrS	Sharp	L	Non	No. 5	L	Cr
2013	7	Bruner, Henry	19	M	½	S	No. 1	L	Cr	No. 2	L	Cr
		No. 5 died October 10, 1903. No. 7 died May 26, 1912										
		Census Card No. 618, P. O. Fry, Enrolled August 1, 1899; No. 2 November 1, 1899										
2014	1	McKim, William A.	21	M	⅛		W. A. McKim	D	Non	Texanna Brumett	L	Cr
2015	2	McKim, Hattie	4ds	F	1-16	D	No. 1	L	Cr	Maggie McKim	L	Non
		Census Card No. 619, P. O. Stidham; No. 2, Checotah, Enrolled August 1, 1899										
2016	1	Pemberton, Charity R.	45	F	¼		W. Lafayette	D	Cr	Willie Lafayette	D	Non
2017	2	Pemberton, William T	19	M	⅛	S	Wm. J. Pemberton	L	Non	No. 1	L	Cr
2018	3	Pemberton, John C.	17	M	⅛	S	Wm. J. Pemberton	L	Non	No. 1	L	Cr
2019	4	Pemberton, James A.	14	M	⅛	S	Wm. J. Pemberton	L	Non	No. 1	L	Cr
2020	5	Pemberton, Washington L.	12	M	⅛	S	Wm. J. Pemberton	L	Non	No. 1	L	Cr
2021	6	Pemberton, Viola C.	10	F	⅛	D	Wm. J. Pemberton	L	Non	No. 1	L	Cr
2022	7	Pemberton, Wilton	8	M	⅛	S	Wm. J. Pemberton	L	Non	No. 1	L	Cr
2023	8	Pemberton, Ida L.	6	F	⅛	D	Wm. J. Pemberton	L	Non	No. 1	L	Cr
		No. 1 died March 10, 1911. No. 2 died February 13, 1911. No. 4 died April 1, 1908.										
		Census Card No. 620, P. O. Wagoner; No. 2, Bucknum, Wyo., Enrolled August 1, 1899										
2024	1	Posey, George A.	35	M	¼		Uriah, Posey	D	Cr	Mary E. Hicks	L	Non
2025	2	Posey, Edward U.	11	M	⅛	S	No. 1	L	Cr	Mary V. Posey	L	Non
		Census Card No. 621, P. O. Bristow, Enrolled August 1, 1899										
2026	1	Beaver, Wattie	26	M	F		Iksossoche	D	Cr	Pitchee	D	Cr
		Census Card No. 622, P. O. Okemah, Enrolled August 2, 1899										
2027	1	Dunson, Andy	27	M	F		Arbeka Harjo	D	Cr	Hokosy Berryhill	L	Cr
2028	2	Dunson, Hokty	39	F	F	Wf	Mittewaky	D	Cr	Ishulka	L	Cr
2029	3	Dunson, Edmond	3	M	F	S	No. 1	L	Cr	No. 2	L	Cr
2030	4	Harjo, Bennie	9	M	F	StS	Arharlok Harjo	D	Cr	No. 2	L	Cr
		No. 1 died April 2, 1903										

Roll No.	No.	NAME	Age	Sex	Blood	Rel.	NAME OF FATHER	Liv.	Cit.	NAME OF MOTHER	Liv.	Cit.
		Census Card No. 623, P. O. Wetumka, Enrolled August 2, 1899										
2031	1	Berryhill, Jno	41	M	F		Simon Berryhill	D	Cr	Martha Berryhill	D	Cr
2032	2	Berryhill, Hokosy	41	F	F	Wf	Chelokee Harjo	D	Cr	Unknown	D	Cr
2033	3	Berryhill, Houston	17	M	F	S	No. 1	L	Cr	Fickhumker Berryhill	D	Cr
2034	4	Berryhill, Lucinda	15	F	F	D	No. 1	L	Cr	Fickhumker Berryhill	D	Cr
2035	5	Berryhill, Martha	12	F	F	D	No. 1	L	Cr	Fickhumker Berryhill	D	Cr
2036	6	Dunson, Luna E.	18	M	F	StS	Arbeka Harjo	D	Cr	No. 2	L	Cr
2037	7	Dunson, Lewis	17	M	F	StS	Joseph Dunson	L	Cr	No. 2	L	Cr
2038	8	Dunson, Lucy	15	F	F	StD	Joseph Dunson	L	Cr	No. 2	L	Cr
2039	9	Dunson, Jemima	12	F	F	StD	Joseph Dunson	L	Cr	No. 2	L	Cr
2040	10	Dunson, Mattie	9	F	F	StD	Joseph Dunson	L	Cr	No. 2	L	Cr
2041	11	Dunson, Alice	6	F	F	StD	Joseph Dunson	L	Cr	No. 2	L	Cr
		No. 11 died April 9, 1900. No. 9 died 1906. No. 8 died October 1909.										
		Census Card No. 624, P. O. Arthur City Texas, Enrolled August 2, 1899; No. 6, May 22, 1901										
2042	1	Scott, Daniel N.	46	M	1/8		Thos. H. Scott	D	Non	Kianitia Scott	D	Cr
2043	2	Scott, Emma	36	F	3/8	Wf	Wm. Fisher	L	Cr	Sarah Fisher	L	Non
2044	3	Scott, Kiamish	13	F	1/4	D	No. 1	L	Cr	No. 2	L	Cr
2045	4	Scott, Gertude	7	F	1/4	D	No. 1	·L	Cr	No. 2	L	Cr
2046	5	Scott, Roy Edward	5	M	1/4	S	No. 1	L	Cr	No. 2	L	Cr
2047	6	Scott, Thomas H.	2	M	1/4	S	No. 1	L	Cr	No. 2	L	Cr
		No. 6 died June 25, 1899										
		Census Card No. 625, P. O. Checotah, Enrolled August 2, 1899										
2048	1	Scott, Jim Ben	39	M	1/4		James Scott	L	Non	Lou Scott Nee Hawkins	L	Cr
		Census Card No. 626, P. O. No. 1 Dustin; No. 2 Salem, Enrolled August 2,1899; No. 4, Henryetta										
2049	1	Artusse, Annie	28	F	F		Nocos Harjo	D	Cr	Lydia Harjo	D	Cr
2050	2	Harjo, Mattie	18	F	F	Sis	Nocos Harjo	D	Cr	Lydia Harjo	D	Cr
2051	3	Harjo, Minda	16	F	F	Sis	Nocos Harjo	D	Cr	Lydia Harjo	D	Cr
2052	4	Harjo, Tommy	13	F	F	Bro	Nocos Harjo	D	Cr	Lydia Harjo	D	Cr
		No. 2 died December 5, 1899										
		Census Card No. 627, P. O. Okmulgee, Enrolled August 2, 1899										
2053	1	Brown, Eliza	27	F	3/4		George Bell	D	Cr	Georgiana Bell	D	Cr
2054	2	Brown, Oliver	10	M	3/8	S	Robert S. Brown	L	Non	No. 1	L	Cr
2055	3	Brown, Myrtle	7	F	3/8	D	Robert S. Brown	L	Non	No. 1	L	Cr
2056	4	Brown, Ralph	5	M	3/8	S	Robert S. Brwon	L	Non	No. 1	L	Cr
2057	5	Brown, Flora	4	F	3/8	D	Robert S. Brown	L	Non	No. 1	L	Cr
2058	6	Brown, George A.	2	M	3/8	S	Robert S. Brown	L	Non	No. 1	L.	Cr
		No. 3 died May 15, 1910. No. 6 died April 4, 1909.										
		Census Card No. 628, P. O. Natura, Enrolled August 2, 1899										
2059	1	Throckmorton, James W.	23	M	1/4		Wm.E.Throckmorton	L	Non	N.E.Throckmorton	L	Cr
2060	2	Throckmorton Ida	22	F	1/2	Wf	David Cummings	L	?	Mildred Cummings	D	?
		Census Card No. 629, P. O. Bristow, Enrolled August 2, 1899										
2061	1	Hawkins, Sunday	50	M	F		Kinne Hawke	D	Cr	Wethla	D	Cr
2062	2	Hawkins, Sarah	30	F	F	Wf	Taylor	D	Cr	Unknown	?	Cr
2063	3	Hawkins, Fannie	14	F	F	D	No. 1	L	Cr	No. 2	L	Cr
2064	4	Hawkins, Lucy	8	F	F	D	No. 1	L	Cr	No. 2	L	Cr
2065	5	Hawkins, Winey	3	F	F	D	No. 1	L	Cr	No. 2	L	Cr
		No. 1 died August 1901. No. 4 died December 1909										
		Census Card No. 630, P. O. Okmulgee, Enrolled August 2, 1899										
2066	1	Throckmorton,Natura E.	54	F	1/2		Algee Newman	D	Non	Elizabeth Newman	D	Cr
		No. 1 died October 26, 1906										
		Census Card No. 631, P. O. Creek; Nos. 3 and 5, Welty, Enrolled August 2, 1899										
2067	1	Vanderslice, Roxan	32	F	1-16		Isaac Hosey	L	Non	Harriet Hosey	L	Cr
2068	2	Vanderslice, Isaac	11	M	1-32	S	J. R. Vanderslice	L	Non	No. 1	L	Cr
2069	3	Vanderslice, Harvey L	8	M	1-32	S	J. R. Vanderslice	L	Non	No. 1	L	Cr
2070	4	Vanderslice, Harriet	5	F	1-32	D	J. R. Vanderslice	L	Non	No. 1	L	Cr
2071	5	Vanderslice, Ida Jane	3	F	1-32	D	J. R. Vanderslice	L	Non	No. 1	L	Cr
		No. 1 died September 11, 1907										
		Census Card No. 632, P. O. Mounds, Enrolled August 2, 1899										
2072	1	Curtain, Richard	29	M	1/4		Richard Curtain	D	Non	Rebecca Curtain	D	Cr
		No. 1 reported dead										
		Census Card No. 633, P. O. Wealaka, Enrolled August 2, 1899										
2073	1	Tiger, Isaac	43	M	F		Cotser Emarthla	D	Cr	Unknown	D	Cr
2074	2	Tiger, Mary	45	F	1/2	Wf	William Clinton	D	Non	Winnie Clinton	D	Cr
2075	3	Clinton, Rosa	15	F	3/4	StD	Tom Hulbulta	L	Cr	No. 2	L	Cr
2076	4	Coonhead, Hannah	10	F	F	StCou	Wm. Coonhead	D	Cr	Eliza Coonhead	D	Cr
2077	5	Coonhead, Nicey	6	F	F	StCou	Wm. Coonhead	D	Cr	Eliza Coonhead	·D	Cr
		No. 1 died October 14, 1901. No. 2 reported dead										
		Census Card No. 634, P. O. Coweta, Enrolled August 3, 1899; No. 3 Broken Arrow										
2078	1	Simon, Joe	47	M	F		Tulwa Micco	D	Cr	Unknown	D	Cr
2079	2	Simon, Sophie	47	F	F	Wf	Unknown	D	Cr	Thahaygee	L	Cr
2080	3	Simon, Caesar	14	M	F	S	No. 1	L	Cr	No. 2	L	Cr
2081	4	Simon, Mandy	12	F	F	D	No. 1	L	Cr	No. 2	L	Cr
2082	5	Simon, George	10	M	F	S	No. 1	L	Cr	No. 2	L	Cr
2083	6	Simon, Peter	7	M	F	S	No. 1	L	Cr	No. 2	L	Cr
2084	7	Simon, Ida	4	F	F	D	No. 1	L	Cr	No. 2	L	Cr
2085	8	Reed, Jim	16	M	3/4	StS	Robert Reed	D	Cr	No. 2	L	Cr
		No. 2 died March 18, 1907. No. 6 reported dead.										

Roll No.	No.	NAME	Age	Sex	Blood	Rel.	NAME OF FATHER	Liv.	Cit.	NAME OF MOTHER	Liv.	Cit.
		Census Card No. 635, P. O. Haskell, Enrolled August 3, 1899										
2086	1	Bruner, Billy	47	M	½		Loney Bruner	D	?	Nancy Bruner	D	?
2087	2	Bruner, Adaline	31	F	F	Wf	Edward Flanders	D	Cr	Coody Asbury	D	Cr
2088	3	Bruner, Iona	13	F	¾	D	No. 1	L	Cr	No.	L	Cr
2089	4	Bruner, Bessie	11	F	¾	D	No. 1	L	Cr	No.	L	Cr
2090	5	Bruner, Lilly	9	F	¾	D	No. 1	L	Cr	No.	L	Cr
2091	6	Bruner, Loney	6	M	¾	S	No. 1	L	Cr	No. 2	L	Cr
2092	7	Bruner, Nellie	4	F	¾	D	No. 1	L	Cr	No.	L	Cr
2093	8	Bruner, William	2	M	¾	S	No. 1	L	Cr	No.	L	Cr
2094	9	Bruner, Lyman	2moM		¾	S	No. 1	L	Cr	No.	L	Cr
		No. 1 died November 9, 1910										
		Census Card No. 636, P. O. Senora; Nos. 2, 4, 5, 6, Edna, Enrolled August 3, 1899										
2095	1	Hardridge, Adam	41	M	¼		Moche Hardridge	D	?	Nancy Hardridge	D	?
2096	2	Hardridge, Lizzie	47	F	F	Wf	Jacob	D	Cr	Scahdache	D	Cr
2097	3	Grayson, Robert	16	M	¾	StS	Austin Grayson	D	Cr	No. 2	L	Cr
2098	4	Grayson, James	14	M	¾	StS	Austin Grayson	D	Cr	No. 2	L	Cr
2099	5	Grayson, David	12	M	¾	StS	Austin Grayson	D	Cr	No. 2	L	Cr
2100	6	Grayson, Emma	10	F	¾	StD	Austin Grayson	D	Cr	No. 2	L	Cr
		No. 2 died December 1899. No. 6 died November 12, 1900.										
		No. 5 died October 11, 1903. No. 1 died 1904.										
		Census Card No. 637, P. O. Stone Bluff, Enrolled August 3, 1899; No. 9 May 22, 1901										
2101	1	Berryhill, Columbus	33	M	⅛		Geo. W. Berryhill	D	Cr	Hare Berryhill	L	Non
2102	2	Berryhill, Emma	32	F	⅛	Wf	Shelton Smith	L	Non	Lucinda Smith	L	Cr
2103	3	Berryhill, John H.	9	M	⅛	S	No. 1	L	Cr	No.	L	Cr
2104	4	Berryhill, David	8	M	⅛	S	No. 1	L	Cr	No.	L	Cr
2105	5	Berryhill, William	6	M	⅛	S	No. 1	L	Cr	No.	L	Cr
2106	6	Berryhill, Abert	5	M	⅛	S	No. 1	L	Cr	No. 2	L	Cr
2107	7	Berryhill, Daniel B.	3	M	⅛	S	No. 1	L	Cr	No. 2	L	Cr
2108	8	Berryhill, Columbus D.	1	M	⅛	S	No. 1	L	Cr	No.	L	Cr
2109	9	Berryhill, Ara Ann	1	F	⅛	D	No. 1	L	Cr	No.	L	Cr
		Census Card No. 638, P. O. Sapulpa, Enrolled August 3, 1899										
2110	1	Tah-co-we-nay	50	M	F		Cayponney	D	Cr	Louisa Tahcowenay	D	Cr
2111	2	Tah-co-we-nay, Jennetta	24	F	F	D	No. 1	L	Cr	Louisa Tahcowenay	L	Cr
2112	3	Pickett, Albert	22	M	F	S	No. 1	L	Cr	Louisa Tahcowenay	L	Cr
		No. 1 died October or November 1899. No. 3 March 1900										
		Census Card No. 639, P. O. Mannford, Enrolled August 4, 1899										
2113	1	Mann, Sarah E.	31	F	⅛		J. E. Crowell	L	Cr	Martha Crowell	L	Non
2114	2	Mann, Addie B.	12	F	1-16	D	Wm. J. Mann	L	Non	No. 1	L	Cr
2115	3	Mann, Thomas E.	9	M	1-16	S	Wm. J. Mann	L	Non	No. 1	L	Cr
2116	4	Mann, Hazel	7	F	1-16	D	Wm. J. Mann	L	Non	No. 1	L	Cr
2117	5	Mann, William	5	M	1-16	S	Wm. J. Mann	L	Non	No. 1	L	Cr
2118	6	Mann, Manila	1	F	1-16	D	Wm. J. Mann	L	Non	No. 1	L	Cr
		Census Card No. 640, P. O. Okmulgee, Enrolled August 4, 1899										
2119	1	Miller, Bluford	51	M	¼		Jacob Miller	D	Non	Sarah Field Miller	L	Ad Cr
2120	2	Miller, Lizzie A.	42	F	¾	Wf	George Anderson	D	Cr	Nannie Anderson	L	Cr
2121	3	Miller, Florence A.	18	F	½	D	No. 1	L	Cr	No. 2	L	Cr
2122	4	Miller, Ida T.	17	F	½	D	No. 1	L	Cr	No. 2	L	Cr
2123	5	Miller, Mary M.	12	F	½	D	No. 1	L	Cr	No. 2	L	Cr
2124	6	Miller, Bluford W.	10	M	½	S	No. 1	L	Cr	No. 2	L	Cr
		No. 1 reported dead										
		Census Card No. 641, P. O. Coweta, Enrolled August 5, 1899										
2125	1	Davis, Nancy W.	26	F	F		John W. Perryman	L	Cr	Nettie Perryman	D	Cr
2126	2	Davis, Amos	5	M	½	S	John Davis	L	Non	No. 1	L	Cr
2127	3	Davis, Lena	2	F	½	D	John Davis	L	Non	No. 1	L	Cr
		Census Card No. 642, P. O. Stone Bluff, Enrolled August 5, 1899; No. 3 November 13, 1899										
2128	1	Barnett, Daniel	25	M	F		Dave Barnett	D	Cr	Mary Barnett	L	Cr
2129	2	Barnett, Samara	20	F	F	Wf	Wotke Harjo	D	Cr	Louina Wotkee	L	Cr
2130	3	Barnett, Sarah	7mo	F	F	D	No. 1	L	Cr	No. 2	L	Cr
		Census Card No. 643, P. O. Checotah, Enrolled August 5, 1899										
2131	1	Bard, Daniel N.	29	M	¼		Richard Bard	D	Non	Lucy Bard	D	Cr
2132	2	Bard, William J. B.	1	M	⅛	S	No. 1	L	Cr	Emma Bard	L	Non
		No. 1 died March 14, 1909										
		Census Card No. 644, P. O. Haynes, Enrolled August 5, 1899										
2133	1	Sookey, Wiley	72	M	F		Charley Sookey	D	Cr	Sookey	D	Cr
2134	2	Sookey, Boney	19	M	F	S	No. 1	L	Cr	Dinah Sookey	D	Cr
2135	3	Sookey, Martha	27	F	F	D	No. 1	L	Cr	Dinah Sookey	D	Cr
2136	4	Marshall, Dinah	3	F	F	GrD	Willie Marshall	L	Cr	No. 3	L	Cr
		No. 2 died May 29, 1905. No. 4 illigitimate daughter No. 3.										
		Census Card No. 645, P. O. Okmulgee, Enrolled August 7, 1899										
2137	1	Herrod, Mary L.	65	F	½		John E. Lewis	D	Non	Louisa Lewis	D	Cr
		Census Card No. 646, P. O. Lyons, Enrolled August 7, 1899										
2138	1	Grayson, Dick	28	M	F		Jim Grayson	L	Cr	Chotie Gooden	L	Cr
		No. 1 reported dead										
		Census Card No. 647, P. O. Checotah, Enrolled August 7, 1899										
2139	1	Rucker, Mary M.	34	F	1-16		John M. Hampton	D	Non	Amanda Hampton	D	Cr
		Census Card No. 648, P. O. Eufaula, Enrolled August 7, 1899										
2140	1	Ansiel, James F.	28	M	⅛		Stephen Ansil	D	Cr	Jane Tiger	L	Non
		Census Card No. 649, P. O. Eufaula, Enrolled August 8, 1899										
2141	1	Whitlow, William	38	M	½		D. B. Whitlow	L	Non	Millie Whitlow	D	Cr
2142	2	Whitlow, Leo	7	M	¼	S	No. 1	L	Cr	Rosa Whitlow	L	Non
2143	3	Whitlow, Ralph	4	M	¼	S	No. 1	L	Cr	Rosa Whitlow	L	Non
		No. 1 reported dead										

51

Roll No.	No.	NAME	Age	Sex	Blood	Rel.	NAME OF FATHER	Liv.	Cit.	NAME OF MOTHER	Liv.	Cit.
		Census Card No. 650, P. O. Fry, Enrolled August 8, 1899										
2144	1	Richard, Mary	18	F	1/8		W. A. McKim	L	Non	Texanna Brumett	L	Cr
		Census Card No. 651, P. O. Okmulgee, Enrolled August 8, 1899; No. 5, June 7, 1900										
2145	1	Adams, Thomas J.	57	M	F		Adams	D	Cr	Hepsey Adams	L	Cr
2146	2	Adams, Mahala	55	F	F	Wf	Unknown	D	Cr	Betsey Grayson	L	Cr
2147	3	Adams, Martha	15	F	F	D	No. 1	L	Cr	No. 2	L	Cr
2148	4	Adams, Mary	12	F	F	D	No. 1	L	Cr	No. 2	L	Cr
2149	5	Washington, Wm.	2mo	M	F	GrS	Dixon Washington	L	Cr	No 3	L	Cr
		No. 5 died March 16, 1901. Nos. 2, 4, reported dead.										
		Census Card No. 652, P. O. Okmulgee, Enrolled August 9, 1899										
2150	1	Kelly, Newman	28	M	F		Marshall Kelly	D	Cr	Jurie Kelly	D	Cr
		No. 1 reported dead										
		Census Card No. 653, No. 1 West Palm Beach, Fla.; No. 2 Arthur City, Texas, Enrolled August 9, 1899										
2151	1	Fisher, William	74	M	3/4		Samuel Fisher	D	Cr	Sally Fisher	D	Cr
2152	2	Fisher, Sarah	63	F	Adpd	Wf	John Lambkin	D	Non	Mary Lambkin	D	Non
		No. 1 died May 1, 1902. No. 2 died July 15, 1905										
		Census Card No. 654, P. O. Oktaha, Enrolled August 9, 1899										
2153	1	Grayson, Jenetta	39	F	3/4		Jack Gobler	D	Cr	Emma Gobler	L	Cr
		Census Card No. 655, P. O. Haskell, Enrolled Aug. 9, 1899; No. 6, May 4, 1900; No. 7, May 7, 1901										
2154	1	Bruner, Miller	47	M	F		Luney Bruner	D	Cr	Nicey Bruner	D	Cr
2155	2	Bruner, Lucy	29	F	F	Wf	George Carter	D	Cr	Arlie Bruner	D	Cr
2156	3	Bruner, Fannie	9	F	F	D	No. 1	L	Cr	No 2	L	Cr
2157	4	Bruner, Edward	6	M	F	S	No. 1	L	Cr	No. 2	L	Cr
2158	5	Bruner, Lee	17	M	F	S	No. 1	L	Cr	Arlie Bruner	D	Cr
2159	6	Bruner, Emma	6mo	F	F	D	No. 1	L	Cr	No. 2	L	Cr
2160	7	Bruner, Chas. Eberle	2	M	F	S	No. 1	L	Cr	No. 2	L	Cr
		No. 5 died November 25, 1904 No. 2 died April 10, 1912. No. 7 died August or September 1899										
		Census Card No. 656, P. O. Beggs, Enrolled August 9, 1899										
2161	1	Harjo, Littiff	41	M	F		Unknown	D	Cr	Machekeliyee	D	Cr
2162	2	Harjo, Mary	35	F	F	Wf	Unknown	D	Cr	Hepsey Perryman	D	Cr
2163	3	Harjo, Ben	14	M	F	S	No. 1	L	Cr	No. 2	L	Cr
2164	4	Harjo, Salina	12	F	F	D	No. 1	L	Cr	No. 2	L	Cr
2165	5	Harjo, Cinda	9	F	F	D	No. 1	L	Cr	No. 2	L	Cr
2166	6	Harjo, Buzzie	7	M	F	S	No. 1	L	Cr	No. 2	L	Cr
2167	7	Harjo, Sarah	5	F	F	D	No. 1	L	Cr	No. 2	L	Cr
		No. 1 died April 30, 1900. No. 2 died August 4, 1904.										
		Census Card No. 657, P. O. Okmulgee, Enrolled August 9, 1899										
2168	1	Sugar, James	43	M	F		Thomas Sugar	D	Cr	Nancy Sugar	D	Cr
2169	2	Sugar, Helen	41	F	F	Wf	Jim Hanson	D	Cr	Dollie Hanson	D	Cr
2170	3	Sugar, Kizzie	8	F	F	D	No. 1	L	Cr	No. 2	L	Cr
2171	4	Sugar, Yarner	4	M	F	D	No. 1	L	Cr	No. 2	L	Cr
2172	5	Sugar, Pilot	6 mo	M	F	S	No. 1	L	Cr	No. 2	L	Cr
		No. 2 died April 25, 1901. No. 5 reported dead										
		*No. 4 sex changed from M to F, see Indian Office letter No. 4092-1914										
		Census Card No. 658, P. O. Tulsa; No. 3 Muskogee, Enrolled No. 1 August 9, 1899; No. 2 May 22, 1901; No. 3 May 8, 1901										
2173	1	Drew, Emma	23	F	1/2		George Perryman	D	Cr	Rachel Perryman	L	Cr
2174	2	Drew, Rachel F.	1	F	1/4	D	Clifton Drew	L	Non	No. 1	L	Cr
2175	3	Drew, Dave	20	M	1/2	NoKin	Daniel Drew	L	Cr	Maggie Drew	D	Cr
		No. 2 died May 1, 1899										
		Census Card No. 659, P. O. Okmulgee, Enrolled August 9, 1899										
2176	1	Sampson, Lucy	40	F	F		Isparne Emarthla	D	Cr	Sowwnihe	D	Cr
2177	2	Sampson, Rhoda	20	F	F	D	Daniel Gooden	L	Cr	No. 1	L	Cr
2178	3	Sampson, Walter	7	M	F	S	Sampson	L	Sem	No. 1	L	Cr
2179	4	Sampson, John	2	M	F	S	Sampson	L	Sem	No. 1	L	Cr
		Census Card No. 660, P. O. Muskogee, Enrolled August 10, 1899										
2180	1	Harris, Cheasquah	26	M	1/8		Bird Harris	L	Cher	Ellen Harris	L	Cr
2181	2	Harris, Buena Vista	4	F	1-16	D	No. 1	L	Cr	Nellie Harris	L	Non
2182	3	Harris, Mabel Anna	2	F	1-16	D	No. 1	L	Cr	Nellie Harris	L	Non
		Census Card No. 661, P. O. Nos. 1 and 2 Checotah; No. 3 Fame; No. 4 Council Hill; Enrolled August 10, 1899; No. 5 October 10, 1899										
2183	1	McIntosh, Amos	43	M	1/2		John McIntosh	L	Cr	Sarah McIntosh	D	Cr
2184	2	McIntosh, Louina	28	F	F	Wf	Peter Kanard	D	Cr	Sarah McIntosh	D	Cr
2185	3	McIntosh, Walley	11	F	3/4	D	No. 1	L	Cr	Hannie McIntosh	D	Cr
2186	4	McIntosh, John	6	M	3/4	S	No. 1	L	Cr	Mary Colbert	D	Cr
2187	5	McIntosh, Tayola	2	M	3/4	S	No. 1	L	Cr	No. 2	L	Cr
		No. 2 died July 24, 1914. No. 1 died February 20, 1907										
		Census Card No. 662, P. O. Muskogee, Enrolled August 10, 1899; No. 2 March 11, 1901										
2188	1	Lieber, Dora	24	F	1/8		James M. Scott	D	Non	Martha Scott	D	Cr
2189	2	Lieber, James Howard	8 mo	M	1-16	S	John G. Lieber	L	Non	No. 1	L	Cr
		Census Card No. 663, P. O. Mounds, Enrolled August 11, 1899										
2190	1	Criswell, Mary J.	56	F	1/4		Wm. Wills	D	Cr	Mary Wills	D	Non
		No. 1 reported dead										
		Census Card No. 664, P. O. Mounds, Enrolled August 11, 1899										
2191	1	Wills, Henry F.	27	M	1/8		Wm. H Wills	L	Cr	N. J. Wills	D	Non
2192	2	Wills, Lottie Ruth	1	F	1-16	D	No. 1	L	Cr	Mary A. Wills	D	Non

Roll No.	No.	NAME	Age	Sex	Blood	Rel.	NAME OF FATHER	Liv.	Cit.	NAME OF MOTHER	Liv.	Cit.

Census Card No. 665, P. O. No. 1, Stone Bluff; Nos. 3 and 4, Bixby, Enrolled August 11, 1899; Nos. 1 and 4, October 18, 1899

2193	1	Wilson, Thomas	32	M	F		Tunupsee	D	Cr	Cynda	D	Cr
2194	2	Wilson, Manana	45	F	F	Wf	Abner Pinehill	D	Cr	Unknown	D	Cr
2195	3	Green, John	12	M	F	St-S	Jim Green	D	Cr	No. 2	L	Cr
2196	4	Bruner, Grace	22	F	F	St-D	Daniel Bruner	L	Cr	No. 2	L	Cr

No. 4 died 1907. No. 2 died 1906.

Census Card No. 666, P. O. Broken Arrow, Enrolled August 11, 1899

| 2197 | 1 | Molone, Louisa | 19 | F | F | | Wattie Molone | D | Cr | Sissie Molone | D | Cr |
| 2198 | 2 | Molone, Billy | 13 | M | F | Bro. | Wattie Molone | D | Cr | Sissie Molone | D | Cr |

Census Card No. 667, P. O. Coweta, Enrolled August 11, 1899; No. 3, August 13, 1899

2199	1	Posey, Frank	22	M	¼		L. Hena Posey	L	Cr	Nancy Posey	L	Cr
2200	2	Posey, Emma	19	F	F	Wf	Joe Mingo	L	Cr	Lousanna Mingo	L	Cr
2201	3	Posey, Gertrude	4mo	F	⅝	D	No. 1	L	Cr	No. 2	L	Cr

Census Card No. 668, P. O. Oktaha, Enrolled August 11, 1899

2202	1	Grayson, Eli	36	M	¾		Jack Gobler	D	Cr	Emma Gobler	L	Cr
2203	2	Grayson, Katie	26	F	F	Wf	Sampson	L	Cr	Lucy Sampson	D	Cr
2204	3	Grayson, Edmond	8	M	⅞	S	No. 1	L	Cr	No. 2	L	Cr
2205	4	Grayson, Henry	6	M	⅞	S	No. 1	L	Cr	No. 2	L	Cr

Census Card No. 669, P. O. Summit, Enrolled August 11, 1899

| 2206 | 1 | Finniegan, Onie | 21 | M | ½ | | Phil Finnegan | D | Non | Jennetta Grayson | L | Cr |

Census Card No. 670, P. O. Choska, Enrolled August 11, 1899

| 2207 | 1 | Deer, Silas | 28 | M | F | | Barney Deer | D | Cr | Dicey Deer | D | Cr |

No. 1 died Setember 1, 1901

Census Card No. 671, P. O. Choska, Enrolled August 12, 1899

| 2208 | 1 | Deer, Wesley | 24 | M | F | | Barney Deer | D | Cr | Dicey Deer | D | Cr |

No. 1 died September 1, 1901

Census Card No. 672, P. O. Oktaha, Enrolled August 12, 1899

| 2209 | 1 | Sampson | 50 | M | F | | Tuwase Emarthla | D | Cr | Polly | D | Cr |

No. 1 died October 1909

Census Card No. 673, P. O. Summit, Enrolled August 12, 1899

2210	1	Casey, Julia	43	F	½		Wm. McIntosh	D	Cr	Katie McIntosh	D	Cr
2211	2	Casey, Nellie	22	F	¼	D	John Casey	L	Non	No. 1	L	Cr
2212	3	Casey, John Jr.	19	M	¼	S	John Casey	L	Non	No. 1	L	Cr

Census Card No. 674, P. O. Tulsa, Enrolled August 12, 1899; Nos. 3 and 4, April 7, 1900

2213	1	Woodward, Nellie E.	24	F	½		Dave Riley	D	?	Tulsa Riley	L	Cr
2214	2	Woodward, Helen M.	3	F	¼	D	H. E. Woodward	L	Non	No. 1	L	Cr
2215	3	Woodward, Hazel D.	1	F	¼	D	H. E. Woodward	L	Non	No. 1	L	Cr
2216	4	Woodward, Grace E.	1mo	F	¼	D	H. E. Woodward	L	Non	No. 1	L	Cr

Census Card No. 675, P. O. Broken Arrow, Enrolled August 12, 1899

| 2217 | 1 | Escoe, John C. | 25 | M | ¼ | | Tom Escoe | L | Non | Mary Escoe | L | Cr |

Census Card No. 676, P. O. Muskogee, Enrolled August 12, 1899

| 2218 | 1 | Escoe, Mary | 65 | F | ½ | | Unip Barbeche | L | Cr | Mary Steel | D | Non |

Census Card No. 677, P. O. Broken Arrow; No. 3, Boley, Enrolled August 12, 1899

2219	1	Perryman, Clarissa	26	F	½		Alvin Hodge	L	Cr	Mary Hodge	L	Cr
2220	2	Perryman, Nathaniel	11	M	½	S	Louis Perryman	D	Cr	No. 1	L	Cr
2221	3	Perryman, Addie	8	F	½	D	Louis Perryman	D	Cr	No. 1	L	Cr
2222	4	Perryman, Mary	6	F	½	D	Louis Perryman	D	Cr	No. 1	L	Cr
2223	5	Perryman, Flossie	3	F	½	D	Louis Perryman	D	Cr	No. 1	L	Cr
2224	6	Perryman, John W.	3mo	M	½	S	Louis Perryman	D	Cr	No. 1	L	Cr

Census Card No. 678, P. O. Coweta, Enrolled August 12, 1899

2225	1	Hodge, Alvin T.	54	M	½		Nathaniel Hodge	D	Non	Nancy Hodge	D	Cr
2226	2	Hodge, Mary Jane	47	M	½	Wf	John Burgess	L	Cr	Sarah Burgess	L	Non
2227	3	Hodge, Mary Jane	14	F	½	D	No. 1	L	Cr	No. 2	L	Cr
2228	4	Hodge, David Mc	11	M	½	S	No. 1	L	Cr	No. 2	L	Cr
2229	5	Hodge, May	4	F	½	D	No. 1	L	Cr	No. 2	L	Cr

Census Card No. 679, P. O. Beggs, Enrolled August 12, 1899

| 2230 | 1 | Bruner, Thomas | 22 | M | ½ | | Richard R. Bruner | L | Cr | Harriet Bruner | L | Cr |

Census Card No. 680, P. O. Tuskegee; Nos. 1, 2, 3, 5, 6, Beggs, Enrolled August 12, 1899; No. 4, October 12, 1899; No. 6, May 8, 1901

2231	1	Postoak, Rachael	30	F	¼		Joseph Hawkins	L	Non	Nancy Bruner	D	Cr
2232	2	Fish, Joseph	11	M	¾	S	Fish	D	Cr	No. 1	L	Cr
2233	3	Postoak, Bettie	2	F	⅛	D	Charley Postoak	L	Non	No. 1	L	Cr
2234	4	Williams, Nora	15	F	⅛	D	Ben Williams	L	Non	No. 1	L	Cr
2235	5	Fish, Nancy	8	F	¾	D	Sotka Fish	D	Cr	No. 1	L	Cr
2236	6	Postoak, George	1	M	⅛	S	Charley Postoak	L	Non	No. 1	L	Cr

No. 6 died August 1910

Census Card No. 681, P. O. Dustin; No. 3, Lane, Enrolled August 14, 1899; Nos. 2, 3, 4, 5, 6, October 19, 1899; No. 7, May 11, 1901

2237	1	Morey, Calley D.	50	F	¼		Wash Perryman	D	Cr	Willie Perryman	D	Non
2238	2	Morey, Samuel	15	M	⅛	S	Wm. Morey	L	Non	No. 1	L	Cr
2239	3	Morey, Tally D.	11	F	⅛	D	Wm. Morey	L	Non	No. 1	L	Cr
2240	4	Morey, George W.	8	M	⅛	S	Wm. Morey	L	Non	No. 1	L	Cr
2241	5	Perryman, John T.	10	M	⅛	Neph	Wm. Perryman	D	Cr	Sally Perryman	D	Non
2242	6	Perryman, Washington L.	8	M	⅛	Neph	Wm. Perryman	D	Cr	Sally Perryman	D	Non
2243	7	Morey, Anson	22	M	⅛	S	Wm. Morey	L	Non	No. 1	L	Cr

No. 1 died February 11, 1902

Census Card No. 682, P. O. Red Fork, Enrolled August 14, 1899

| 2244 | 1 | Brown, Nathaniel | 19 | M | ⅛ | | W. F. Brown | D | Non | Elizabeth Jack | D | Cr |

No. 1 reported dead

53

Roll No.	No.	NAME	Age	Sex	Blood	Rel.	NAME OF FATHER	Liv.	Cit.	NAME OF MOTHER	Liv.	Cit.
		Census Card No. 683, P. O. Red Fork, Enrolled August 14, 1899										
2245	1	Perryman, Cornelius	B48	M	1/2		Samuel Perryman	D	Cr	Betsy Porter	D	Cr
		Census Card No. 684, P. O. Haskell, Enrolled August 14, 1899										
2246	1	Smith, Stephen	30	M	1/4		Shelton Smith	L	Non	Lucinda Smith	L	Cr
2247	2	Smith, Arthur Ray	7	M	1/8	S	No. 1	L	Cr	Emma Smith	L	Non
2248	3	Smith, Anna A.	1	F	1/8	D	No. 1	L	Cr	Emma Smith	L	Non
		Census Card No. 685, P. O. Checotah; Nos. 1, 3, 6, Crowell, Texas, Enrolled August 15, 1899										
2249	1	Watson, Ellen	39	F	1/2		Frank Pettit	L	Cher	Nellie Fife	D	Cr
2250	2	Watson, Robert	19	M	1/4	S	Thos. Watson	L	Non	No. 1	L	Cr
2251	3	Watson, George	16	M	1/4	S	Thos. Watson	L	Non	No. 1	L	Cr
2252	4	Watson, John	15	M	1/4	S	Thos. Watson	L	Non	No. 1	L	Cr
2253	5	Watson, Nellie	13	F	1/4	D	Thos. Watson	L	Non	No. 1	L	Cr
2254	6	Watson, Louisa	10	F	1/4	D	Thos. Watson	L	Non	No. 1	L	Cr
2255	7	Watson, Annie	9	F	1/4	D	Thos. Watson	L	Non	No. 1	L	Cr
		No. 1 died January 10, 1904										
		Census Card No. 686, P. O. Mounds, Enrolled August 15, 1899										
2256	1	Harwell, Mary L.	40	F	1/8		John B. Self	L	Cr	Elizabeth Self	L	Non
		Census Card No. 687, P. O. Checotah, Enrolled August 15, 1899										
2257	1	Depriest, Thompson	24	M	1/8		John Depriest	D	Cr	Eliz. Depriest	D	Non
		No. 1 died August 25, 1905										
		Census Card No. 688, P. O. Broken Arrow, Enrolled August 15, 1899										
2258	1	Perryman, Sanford	27	M	F		John W. Perryman	L	Cr	Nettie Perryman	D	Cr
		Census Card No. 689, P. O. Council Hill; No. 3, El Reno, Enrolled August 15, 1899										
2259	1	Stidham, Geo. W. Sr.	40	M	1/4		Geo. W. Stidham	D	Cr	Sarah Stidham	D	Non
2260	2	Stidham, Ottie	12	F	1/8	D	No. 1	L	Cr	Hallie Chastine	L	Non
2261	3	Stidham, Lela	10	F	1/8	D	No. 1	L	Cr	Hallie Chastine	L	Non
2262	4	Stidham, Kittie	8	F	1/8	D	No. 1	L	Cr	Hallie Chastine	L	Non
2263	5	Stidham, Geo. W. Jr.	4	M	1/8	S	No. 1	L	Cr	Jennie Stidham	L	Non
2264	6	Stidham, Albert L.	3	M	1/8	S	No. 1	L	Cr	Jennie Stidham	L	Non
2265	7	Stidham, Marie Oleta	8mo	F	1/8	D	No. 1	L	Cr	Jennie Stidham	L	Non
		Census Card No. 690, P. O. Fry, Enrolled August 15, 1899										
2266	1	Loler, Lewis	30	M	F		Eb. Loler	D	Cr	Mary Kelly	L	Cr
		Census Card No. 691, P. O. Okmulgee, Enrolled August 15, 1899										
2267	1	Hodge, Lula M.	21	F	1/4		Johnson Hodge	D	Cr	Margaret Hodge	D	Non
		No. 1 died December 15, 1903										
		Census Card No. 692, P. O. Wetumka, Enrolled August 15, 1899; No. 4, August 17, 1899										
2268	1	Robison, William	66	M	1/4		Alex Robison	D	Non	Elizabeth Robison	D	Cr
2269	2	Robison, Cherokee	57	F	1/2	Wf	Davis	D	Non	Nancy Davis	D	Cr
2270	3	Austin, Daniel	18	M	F	Cous	Daniel Austin	D	Cr	Susan Austin	D	Cr
2271	4	Robison, Elizabeth	12	F	3-16	Gr-D	Geo. Frazir Robison	L	Cr	Jane Robison	D	Cr
		Nos. 1, 2 and 3 reported dead										
		Census Card No. 693, P. O. Grayson, Enrolled August 16, 1899										
2272	1	Downing, Watley	57	M	F		Holata Fixico	D	Cr	Mary Fixico	D	Cr
2273	2	Downing, Toche	45	F	F	Wf	Tom Yahola	D	Cr	Sowa	D	Cr
2274	3	Downing, Sanford	15	M	F	S	No. 1	L	Cr	No. 2	L	Cr
2275	4	Downing, Nannie	12	F	F	D	No. 1	L	Cr	No. 2	L	Cr
2276	5	Downing, Bessie	9	F	F	D	No. 1	L	Cr	No. 2	L	Cr
		No. 1 died October 22, 1905. No. 4 died June 2, 1906. No. 2 died November 6, 1910. No. 3 died October 29, 1908										
		Census Card No. 694, P. O. Wildcat, Enrolled August 16, 1899										
2277	1	McMinn, Annie	23	F	F		Watley Downing	L	Cr	Toche Downing	L	Cr
		No. 1 died March 1903										
		Census Card No. 695, P. O. Wagoner, Enrolled August 16, 1899; No. 4, May 23, 1901										
2278	1	Pitts, Emma	24	F	1/8		Stephen W. Farill	L	Non	Sarah Farill	L	Cr
2279	2	Pitts, Pearlie	4	F	1-16	D	Frank Pitts	L	Non	No. 1	L	Cr
2280	3	Pitts, David Franklin	2-3	M	1-16	S	Frank Pitts	L	Non	No. 1	L	Cr
2281	4	Pitts, William R.	2	M	1-16	S	Frank Pitts	L	Non	No. 1	L	Cr
		No. 4 died April 6, 1899										
		Census Card No. 696, P. O. Okemah; No. 2, Yeager, Enrolled August 16, 1899										
2282	1	Cook, Zachariah	53	M	1/4		Rueben Cook	D	Non	Hannah Cook	D	Cr
2283	2	Cook, Daniel	22	M	1/2	S	No. 1	L	Cr	Chily Cook	D	Cr
2284	3	Cook, Wallace	18	M	1/2	S	No. 1	L	Cr	Chily Cook	L	Cr
2285	4	Cook, Joseph	16	M	1/2	S	No. 1	L	Cr	Gbily Cook	L	Cr
2286	5	Cook, Reuben	13	M	1/2	S	No. 1	L	Cr	Ghily Cook	L	Cr
2287	6	Cook, Louisa	11	F	1/2	D	No. 1	L	Cr	Gbily Cook	L	Cr
2288	7	Cook, Jesse	9	M	1/2	S	No. 1	L	Cr	Ghily Cook	L	Cr
		Census Card No. 697, P. O. Wetumka, Enrolled August 16, 1899; Nos. 2 and 3, March 27, 1901										
2289	1	Carter, Millie C.	8	F	1/4		John W. Carter	L	Non	Annie Carter	D	Cr
2290	2	Carter, Sally	6	F	1/4	Sis.	John W. Carter	L	Non	Annie Carter	D	Cr
2291	3	Carter, Rosa	5	F	1/4	Sis.	John W. Carter	L	Non	Annie Carter	D	Cr
		No. 2 died April 7, 1899 No. 3 died April 8, 1899										
		Census Card No. 698, P. O. Morris, Enrolled August 16, 1899										
2292	1	Foster, Abe W.	37	M	7/8		Major Taylor	D	Cr	Sallie Foster	L	Cr
2293	2	Foster, Sallie	59	F	3/4	Mot'h	Abraham Foster	D	Cr	Bessie Foster	D	Cr
		No. 1 reported dead										
		Census Card No. 699, P. O. Okmulgee, Enrolled August 16, 1899										
2294	1	Wisener, Ben J.	26	M	3/4		Douglas Wisener	L	Cr	Sallie Foster	L	Cr
		Census Card No. 700, P. O. Wetumka, Enrolled August 16, 1899										
2295	1	Smith, Geo. W.	69	M	1/8		Sam Smith	D	Cr	Eliza Smith	D	Non
		No. 1 died April 23, 1909										

Roll No.	No.	NAME	Age	Sex	Blood	Rel.	NAME OF FATHER	Liv.	Cit.	NAME OF MOTHER	Liv.	Cit.
		Census Card No. 701, P. O. Yeager, Enrolled August 16, 1899; No. 4, September 12, 1900; No. 5, May 7, 1901										
2296	1	Tuttle, Mary Ann	28	F	⅛		Geo. W. Smith	L	Cr	Jemima Smith	D	Non
2297	2	Tuttle, Lura Lee	9	F	1-16 D		Frank Tuttle	D	Non	No. 1	L	Cr
2298	3	Tuttle, Lilly May	7	F	1-16 D		Frank Tuttle	D	Non	No. 1	L	Cr
2299	4	Wesley, John Lowe	2mo M	M	½	S	Roley Wesley	L	Cr	No. 1	L	Cr
2300	5	Wesley, Bettie May	3mo F	F	½	D	Roley Wesley	L	Cr	No. 1	L	Cr
		No. 5 died July 6, 1899										
		Census Card No. 702, P. O. Yeager, Enrolled August 16, 1899										
2301	1	Wesley, Roley	25	M	F		Nutta Wesley	D	Cr	Louisa Wesley	L	Cr
		Census Card No. 703, P. O. Coweta; No. 1, Mounds, Enrolled August 16, 1899										
2302	1	Marshall, David	27	M	F		Warrior Marshall	D	Cr	Winey Marshall	D	Cr
2303	2	Marshall, Hildred	4	F	½	D	No. 1	L	Cr	Laura Marshall	L	Non
		Census Card No. 704, P. O. Keokuk Falls, Enrolled August 16, 1899										
2304	1	Chisholm, Mary	32	F	F		Jess Chisholm	L	Cher	Sukkahke	D	Cr
2305	2	Cochran, Rockey F.	2	M	F	S	Jesse Cochran	L	Cher	No. 1	L	Cr
		No. 1 reported dead										
		Census Card No. 705, P. O. Wetumka, Enrolled August 16, 1899										
2306	1	Laport, Jennie	40	F	⅛		Wm. J. Mastin	D	Non	Mary S. Marston	D	Cr
2307	2	Laport, William J.	3	M	1-16 S		John C. Laport	L	Non	No. 1	L	Cr
2308	3	Marston, Nannie	13	F	1-16 D		Thos. W. Marston	D	Non	No. 1	L	Cr
2309	4	Marston, May Malinda	10	F	1-16 D		Thos. W. Marston	D	Non	No. 1	L	Cr
2310	5	Marston, John	7	M	1-16 S		Thos. W. Marston	D	Non	No. 1	L	Cr
		No. 4 died October 1909										
		Census Card No. 706, Leonard; No. 5 Coweta, Enrolled August 17, 1899; No. 5, March 1, 1901										
2311	1	Bell, Eli	47	M	F		Cosar Custanugge	D	Cr	Unknown	D	Cr
2312	2	Bell, Silby	32	F	F	Wf	Senutbey	D	Cr	Unknown	D	Cr
2313	3	Bell, Silla	10	F	F	D	No. 1	L	Cr	No. 2	L	Cr
2314	4	Bell, Cornelius	2	M	F	S	No. 1	L	Cr	No. 2	L	Cr
2315	5	Bell, Willie	7	M	F	Neph	Losmar Bell	L	Cr	Martha Bell	D	Cr
		No. 3 died February 10, 1910										
		Census Card No. 707, P. O. Columbus, Ohio, Enrolled August 17, 1899										
2316	1	Freeman, Major	25	M	F		Tutcheto	D	Cr	Nupsey Fixico	D	Cr
2317	2	Stricken from roll										
		Census Card No. 708, Void										
		Census Card No. 709, P. O. Mounds, Enrolled August 17, 1899; No. 6, October 9, 1899										
2318	1	Whetstone, James	30	M	⅛		Anderson Whetstone	D	Non	Nancy C. Whetstone	L	Cr
2319	2	Whetstone, Edward	9	M	1-16 S		No. 1	L	Cr	Dorcia Whetstone	L	Non
2320	3	Whetstone, Carrie	7	F	1-16 D		No. 1	L	Cr	Dorcia Whetstone	L	Non
2321	4	Whetstone, Charlie	4	M	1-16 S		No. 1	L	Cr	Dorcia Whetstone	L	Non
2322	5	Whetstone, Alvin	2	M	1-16 S		No. 1	L	Cr	Dorcia Whetstone	L	Non
2323	6	Whetstone, Mary Ella	8mo F	F	1-16 D		No. 1	L	Cr	Dorcia Whetstone	L	Non
		No. 2 reported dead No. 4 reported dead										
		Census Card No. 710, P. O. Red Fork; No. 7, Jenks, Enrolled August 17, 1899										
2324	1	Postoak, Lincoln	30	M	F		Taylor, Postoak	D	Cr	Maria Fife	L	Cr
2325	2	Postoak, Lilly	28	F	F	Wf	John Buster	L	Cber	Betsey Buster	D	Cr
2326	3	Postoak, Tecumseh	8	M	F	S	No. 1	L	Cr	No. 2	L	Cr
2327	4	Postoak, Gracie	3	F	F	D	No. 1	L	Cr	No. 2	L	Cr
2328	5	Postoak, Nannie	2	F	F	D	No. 1	L	Cr	No. 2	L	Cr
2329	6	Bruner, Arlinger	14	M	F	Neph	Eli Bruner	D	Cr	Salina Bruner	D	Cr
2330	7	Bruner, Patty	12	F	F	Niece	Eli Bruner	D	Cr	Salina Bruner	D	Cr
		No. 3 died May 2, 1900										
		Census Card No. 711, P. O. Wagoner, Enrolled August 18, 1899										
2331	1	Price, Sallie	23	F	⅛		Charlie Cane	D	Non	Priscilla Price	D	Cr
2332	2	Price, James Lawrence	4	M	1-16 S		Mose B. Price	L	Non	No. 1	L	Cr
		Census Card No. 712, P. O. Jenks, Enrolled August 18, 1899										
2333	1	Gregory, Noah	43	M	½		Joe Gregory	D	Non	Lucinda Gregory	D	Cr
2334	2	Gregory, Carrie E.	31	F	½	Wf	W. G. Norman	L	Non	Novella Norman	D	Cr
2335	3	Gregory, Ara N.	8	F	½	D	No. 1	L	Cr	No. 2	L	Cr
2336	4	Gregory, Jesse L.	5	M	½	S	No. 1	L	Cr	No. 2	L	Cr
2337	5	Gregory, Asa B.	2	F	½	D	No. 1	L	Cr	No. 2	L	Cr
2338	6	Gregory, Foster L.	9	M	F	A-D	Tahqueaney	L	Cr	Louisa	D	Cr
		Census Card No. 713, P. O. Spencer, Enrolled August 18, 1899										
2339	1	Dunson, David	22	M	F		Arbeka Harjo	D	Cr	Sinna Harjo	D	Cr
		No. 1 died September 19, 1904										
		Census Card No. 714, P. O. Red Fork, Enrolled August 18, 1899										
2340	1	Vance, Mary E.	35	F	¼		Eli Posey	D	Cr	Mary E. Posey	D	Non
2341	2	Vance, Joseph	18	M	⅛	S	William Vance	L	Non	No. 1	L	Cr
2342	3	Vance, George William	4	M	⅛	S	William Vance	L	Non	No. 1	L	Cr
2343	4	Vance, Samuel E.	11	M	⅛	S	William Vance	L	Non	No. 1	L	Cr
2344	5	Vance, Florence A.	6	F	⅛	D	William Vance	L	Non	No. 1	L	Cr
2345	6	Vance, Benjamin	8	M	⅛	S	William Vance	L	Non	No. 1	L	Cr
2346	7	Vance, Ollie May	2	F	⅛	D	William Vance	L	Non	No. 1	L	Cr
		Census aCrd No. 715, P. O. Okmulgee, Enrolled August 19, 1899										
2347	1	Garrett, Mary	33	F	¼		George Sharp	D	Non	Cinda Walker	D	Cr
2348	2	Lowe, Missouri	16	F	⅜	D	Peter Lowe	D	Cr	No. 1	L	Cr
2349	3	Lowe, Gertude	11	F	⅜	D	Peter Lowe	D	Cr	No. 1	L	Cr
2350	4	Whitten, Willie	3	M	⅛	S	John Whitten	D	Non	No. 1	L	Cr

Roll No.	No.	NAME	Age	Sex	Blood	Rel.	NAME OF FATHER	Liv.	Cit.	NAME OF MOTHER	Liv.	Cit.
	Census Card No. 716, P. O. Haynes, Enrolled August 19, 1899											
2351	1	Marshall, Sallie	21	F	F		Wiley Sookey	L	Cr	Dinah Sookey	D	Cr
	Census Card No. 717, P. O. Oktaha, Enrolled August 19, 1899											
2352	1	Weatherspoon, Vicey	57	F	F		Wm. Grayson	D	Cr	Judy Grayson	D	Cr
	Census Card No. 718, P. O. Checotah, Enrolled August 21, 1899; No. 4, February 10, 1900											
2353	1	Storm, Lou	22	F	¼		Frank Wells	L	Non	Lydia Wells	L	Cr
2354	2	Storm, Annie	6	F	⅛	D	John Storm	L	Non	No. 1	L	Cr
2355	3	Storm, Eliza	3	F	⅛	D	John Storm	L	Non	No. 1	L	Cr
2356	4	Storm, Porelee	8mo	F	⅛	D	John Storm	L	Non	No. 1	L	Cr
	Census Card No. 719, P. O. Muskogee; No. 1125 S. 2nd Street, Enrolled August 21, 1899; No. 6, May 1, 1900											
2357	1	Hood, Sarah	25	F	¼		James Hughes	D	Non	Lydia Wells	L	Cr
2358	2	Hood, Henry	8	M	⅛	S	Sterling Hood	L	Non	No. 1	L	Cr
2359	3	Hood, Jackson	5	M	⅛	S	Sterling Hood	L	Non	No. 1	L	Cr
2360	4	Hood, William	3	M	⅛	S	Sterling Hood	L	Non	No. 1	L	Cr
2361	5	Hood, John	1	M	⅛	S	Sterling Hood	L	Non	No. 1	L	Cr
2362	6	Hood, James	3mo	M	⅛	S	Sterling Hood	L	Non	No. 1	L	Cr
	Census Card No. 720, P. O. Checotah, Enrolled August 21, 1899											
2363	1	Wells, Lydia	45	F	½		Bill Dvvis	D	Cr	Sarah Davis	D	Non
2364	2	Wells, Ellen	20	F	¼	D	Frank Wells	L	Non	No. 1	L	Cr
2365	3	Wells, Martha	18	F	¼	D	Frank Wells	L	Non	No. 1	L	Cr
2366	4	Wells, Joseph	16	M	¼	S	Frank Wells	L	Non	No. 1	L	Cr
2367	5	Wells, Lizzie	14	F	¼	D	Frank Wells	L	Non	No. 1	L	Cr
2368	6	Wells, Loyal	12	M	¼	S	Frank Wells	L	Non	No. 1	L	Cr
2369	7	Wells, Watie	9	M	¼	S	FrankWells	L	Non	No. 1	L	Cr
2370	8	Wells, Walter	6	M	¼	S	Frank Wells	L	Non	No. 1	L	Cr
2371	9	Wells, Lee	3	M	¼	S	Frank Wells	L	Non	No. 1	L	Cr
2372	10	Wells, Viola	1	F	¼	D	Frank Wells	L	Non	No. 1	L	Cr
	Census Card No. 721, P. O. Checotah, Enrolled August 21, 1899; No. 4, September 6, 1899											
2373	1	Coon, Sallie	24	F	⅛		Albert Carr	L	?	Sallie Carr	L	Non
2374	2	Coon, Roy	5	M	1-16	S	Fred Coon	L	Non	No. 1	L	Cr
2375	3	Coon, Charles	3	M	1-16	S	Fred Coon	L	Non	No. 1	L	Cr
2376	4	Coon, Freedie Carr	6mo	M	1-16	S	Fred Coon	L	Non	No. 1	L	Cr
		No. 1 died May 30, 1913										
	Census Card No. 722, P. O. Checotah, Enrolled August 21, 1899											
2377	1	Carr, Albert	52	M	⅛		Paddy Carr	L	?	Nancy Carr	D	?
2378	2	Carr, Thomas	19	M	¼	S	No. 1	L	Cr	Sallie Carr	L	Non
2379	3	Carr, Severs	16	M	¼	S	No. 1	L	Cr	Sallie Carr	L	Non
2380	4	Carr, Frank	12	M	¼	S	No. 1	L	Cr	Sallie Carr	L	Non
		No. 3 died November 29, 1911										
	Census Card No. 723, P. O. Eufaula, Enrolled August 21, 1899											
2381	1	Collins, Jno	30	M	¾		Shawnee Collins	D	Cr	Linda Collins	D	Cr
2382	2	Collins, Arcelia	19	F	¾	Wf	A. J. Murray	L	Non	Martha Murray	L	Cr
		No. 1 died February 1, 1903										
	Census Card No. 724, P. O. Tulsa, Enrolled August 21, 1899											
2383	1	Thomas, Melesse	45	F	¾		Shawnee Collins	D	Cr	Linda Collins	D	Cr
2384	2	Crabtree, Gertie	15	F	⅝	D	Jas. H. Crabtree	L	Cr	No. 1	L	Cr
	Census Card No. 725, P. O. Bristow, Enrolled August 22, 1899											
2385	1	Bruner, Richmnond	60	M	½		Paro Bruner	D	Cr	Eliza Bruner	D	Cr
2386	2	Bruner, Bettie	56	F	½	Wf	Dick McNac	D	Cr	Mollie McNac	D	Cr
		No. 2 died January 1910										
	Census Card No. 726, P. O. Hoffman, Enrolled August 22, 1899; No. 4, November 21, 1899											
2387	1	Gray, Louis	29	M	¾		James Gray	D	Cr	Louisa Gray	L	Cr
2388	2	Gray, Nancy	9	F	⅞	D	No. 1	L	Cr	Lizzie Gray	D	Cr
2389	3	Gray, Miley	6	F	⅞	D	No. 1	L	Cr	Lizzie Gray	D	Cr
2390	4	Gray, Louisa	20	F	F	Wf	Cha Yahola	D	Cr	Unknown	?	Cr
		No. 3 died December 7, 1907 No. 1 reported dead No. 4 died October 2, 1902										
	Census Card No. 727, P. O. Checotah, Enrolled August 22, 1899											
2391	1	Sampson, Mary	32	F	¼		Alex Depriest	L	Non	Patience Depriest	L	Cr
2392	2	Sampson, Ophelia	10	F	⅛	D	Pat Sampson	L	Non	No. 1	L	Cr
2393	3	Sampson, Joseph	8	M	⅛	S	Pat Sampson	L	Non	No. 1	L	Cr
2394	4	Sampson, Bonnie A.	6	M	⅛	S	Pat Sampson	L	Non	No. 1	L	Cr
2395	5	Sampson, Lee	3	M	⅛	S	Pat Sampson	L	Non	No. 1	L	Cr
2396	6	Sampson, George	1	M	⅛	S	Pat Sampson	L	Non	No. 1	L	Cr
	Census Card No. 728, P. O. Tulsa, Enrolled August 23, 1899											
2397	1	Vannest, Grace O.	10	F	⅜		P. H. Vannest	L	Non	Ellen Vannest	D	Cr
2398	2	Vannest, Annie M.	8	F	⅜	Sis.	P. H. Vannest	L	Non	Ellen Vannest	D	Cr
2399	3	Vannest, Harry L.	5	M	⅜	Bro	P. H. Vannest	L	Non	Ellen Vannest	D	Cr
2400	4	Vannest, Ada E.	3	F	⅜	Sis.	P. H. Vannest	L	Non	Ellen Vannest	D	Cr
2401	5	Nail, James	16	M	¾	H-Bro	Nail	D	Cr	Ellen Vannest	D	Cr
	Census Card No. 729, P. O. Muskogee; No. 6, Rosedale, Kans. Enrolled August 23, 1899											
2402	1	Sanders, Sarah E.	40	F	⅛		Edward Butler	D	Non	Elizabeth Butler	D	Cr
2403	2	Sanders, Edna	13	F	1-16	D	John W. Sanders	L	Non	No. 1	L	Cr
2404	3	Sanders, Elizabeth	10	F	1-16	D	John W. Sanders	L	Non	No. 1	L	Cr
2405	4	Sanders, Maud	6	F	1-16	D	John W. Sanders	L	Non	No. 1	L	Cr
2406	5	Sanders, Millard	4	M	1-16	S	John W. Sanders	L	Non	No. 1	L	Cr
2407	6	Porter, Edward B.	18	M	⅛	S	Ben E. Porter	D	Cr	No. 1	L	Cr
2408	7	Porter, Ben E.	15	M	⅛	S	Ben E. Porter	D	Cr	No. 1	L	Cr
		No. 1 died April 28, 1900										

Roll No.	No.	NAME	Age	Sex	Blood	Rel.	NAME OF FATHER	Liv.	Cit.	NAME OF MOTHER	Liv.	Cit.
Census Card No. 730, P. O. Inola, Enrolled August 23, 1899												
2409	1	Simmons, Esther	45	F	F		Peter, Collins	D	Cr	Annie Collins	D	Cr
2410	2	Wiley, James	17	M	F	S	Cheparney Wilson	D	Cr	No. 1	L	Cr
No. 1 died January 31, 1910												
Census Card No. 731, P. O. Milton, Enrolled August 23, 1899												
2411	1	Collins, Jacob M.	22	M	¼		John Collins	L	Non	Mary Erwin	L	Cr
Census Card No. 732, P. O. Talihina, Enrolled August 23, 1899												
2412	1	Erwin, Mary	45	F	½		Wm. Fisher	L	Cr	Becky Fisher	D	Cr
Census Card No. 733, P. O. Okmulgee; No. 2, Hoffman, Enrolled August 23, 1899												
2413	1	Harjo, Wilyarmy	55	M	F		Cussetah Harjo	D	Cr	Lodie Harjo	D	Cr
2414	2	Harjo, Susie	53	F	F	Wf	Tockeley Chupco	D	Cr	Mollie	L	Cr
2415	3	Yahola, Charfukner	18	M	F	St-S	Ahharlox Yahola	D	Cr	No. 2	L	Cr
2416	4	Yahola, Wattey	16	M*	F	St-D	Ahharlox Yahola	D	Cr	No. 2	L	Cr
2417	5	Yahola, Nancy	12	F	F	St-D	Ahharlox Yahola	D	Cr	No. 2	L	Cr
No. 1 died April 23, 1902 *No. 4 sex xhanged "M" to "F" Indian Office letter No. 1226-1911												
Census Card No. 734, P. O. Haskell, Enrolled August 23, 1899												
2418	1	Davis, Ellen	38	F	F		Louis Bruner	D	Cr	Nancy Bruner	D	Cr
2419	2	Isaac, Louis	14	M	F	S	Richard Isaac	D	Cr	No. 1	L	Cr
2420	3	Isaac, Lena	12	F	F	D	Richard Isaac	D	Cr	No. 1	L	Cr
2421	4	Isaac, Lydia	9	F	F	D	Richard Isaac	D	Cr	No. 1	L	Cr
No. 1 died October 11, 1907 No. 3 died December 2, 1911												
Census Card No. 735, P. O. Eufaula, Enrolled August 24, 1899												
2422	1	Coodey, William S.	26	M	⅛		Joseph Coodey	D	Cger	Mary Whitlow	D	Cr
2423	2	Coodey, Minnie	20	F	⅛	Sis.	Joseph Coodey	D	Cher	Mary Whitlow	D	Cr
2424	3	Coodey, Amanda	18	F	⅛	Sis.	Joseph Coodey	D	Cher	Mary Whitlow	D	Cr
Census Card No. 736, P. O. Redfork; Nos. 1, 2, 3 Sapulpa, Enrolled August 24, 1899												
2425	1	Posey, Robert A.	27	M	¼		William Posey	D	Cr	Bettie Posey	D	Non
2426	2	Posey, Lee A.	6	M	⅛	S	No. 1	L	Cr	Flora Posey	L	Non
2427	3	Posey, Mary E.	4	F	⅛	D	No. 1	L	Cr	Flora Posey	L	Non
2428	4	Posey, William A.	2	M	⅛	S	No. 1	L	Cr	Flora Posey	L	Non
No. 1 died February 1901												
Census Card No. 737, P. O. Checotah, Enrolled August 24, 1899												
2429	1	Audd, Flora R.	30	F	⅛		Joseph Coodey	L	Cher	Mary Whitlow	D	Cr
2430	2	Audd, Coodey L.	12	M	1-16	S	R. Y. Audd	L	Non	No. 1	L	Cr
2431	3	Audd, Clarence Y.	10	M	1-16	S	R. Y. Audd	L	Non	No. 1	L	Cr
2432	4	Audd, Oma M.	7	M	1-16	S	R. Y. Audd	L	Non	No. 1	L	Cr
2433	5	Audd, Clyde B.	5	M	1-16	S	R. Y. Audd	L	Non	No. 1	L	Cr
2434	6	Audd, Ellen M.	3	F	1-16	D	R. Y. Audd	L	Non	No. 1	L	Cr
2435	7	Audd, Leonard G.	1	M	1-16	S	R. Y. Audd	L	Non	No. 1	L	Cr
Census Card No. 738, P. O.No. 1 Warner; No. 2, Jenks, Enrolled August 24, 1899												
2436	1	Oswalt, Marion W.	42	M	⅛		C. D. Oswalt.	L	Non	Nancy Oswalt	D	Cr
2437	2	Oswalt, William M.	15	M	1-16	S	No. 1	L	Cr	Mary E. Oswalt	L	Non
Census Card No. 739, P. O. Sapulpa; No. 2, Jenks, Enrolled Aug. 24, 1899; Nos. 2 and 3, Dec. 4, 1899												
2438	1	Ricketts, Robert J.	18	M	⅛		Thos Ricketts	D	Non	Sarah C. Ricketts	D	Cr
2439	2	Ricketts, Malinda Ann	20	F	⅛	Sis.	Thos Ricketts	D	Non	Sarah C. Ricketts	D	Cr
2440	3	Ricketts, Margaret	11	F	⅛	Sis.	Thos Ricketts	D	Non	Sarah C. Ricketts	D	Cr
No. 2 died September 17, 1902												
Census Card No. 740, P. O. Wagoner, Enrolled August 24, 1899; No. 2, August 28, 1899												
2441	1	Childers, Hattie	22	F	½		J. C. Barr	L	Non	Matilda Jackson	L	Cr
2442	2	Childers, Effie	4mo	F	¾	D	Samuel Childers	L	Cr	No. 1	L	Cr
Census Card No. 741, P. O. Wagoner, No. 2, Coweta, Enrolled August 24, 1899												
2443	1	Jackson, Matilda	42	F	F		Root	D	Cr	Alice Oatkey	D	Cr
2444	2	Barr, Emma	19	F	½	D	J. C. Barr	L	Non	No. 1	L	Cr
2445	3	Barr, Laura	14	F	½	D	J. C. Barr	L	Non	No. 1	L	Cr
Census Card No. 742, P. O. Mounds, Enrolled August 25 1899												
2446	1	Self, William Buck	7	M	1-16		Benj. Self	D	Cr	Florence Walker	L	Non
Census Card No. 743, P. O. Holdenville, Enrolled August 25, 1899												
2447	1	Foster, Ira P.	24	M	¼		George Foster	D	Non	Rosa Foster	D	Cr
2448	2	Foster, Mattie L.	19	F	½	Wf	Frank D. Jacobs	L	Cr	Jennie C. Jacobs	L	Cr
Census Card No. 744, P. O. Cathy, Enrolled August 25, 1899; No. 2, February 14, 1900												
2449	1	Fisher, Sam	26	M	½		Wm. Fisher	L	Cr	Sarah Fisher	L	Non
2450	2	Fisher, Louis Henry	1	M	¼	S	No. 1	L	Cr	Lena Fisher	L	Non
2451	3	Fisher, Freida Chenena	4mo	F	¼	D	No. 1	L	Cr	Lena Fisher	L	Non
Census Card No. 745, P. O. Eufaula, Enrolled August 25, 1899												
2452	1	Depriest, James	22	M	⅛		John Depriest	D	Cr	Eliza Depriest	D	Non
2453	2	Depriest, Emily	22	F	F	Wf	Daniel Chisholm	D	Cr	Betty Chisholm	D	Cr
2454	3	Depriest, Bettie	4	F	½	D	No. 1	L	Cr	No. 2	L	Cr
2455	4	Depriest, Rufert	2	M	½	S	No. 1	L	Cr	No. 2	L	Cr
No. 1 died September 9, 1908												
Census Card No. 746, P. O. Fry, Enrolled August 26, 1899												
2456	1	Simmons, Clara	33	F	⅛		Jacob Bittle	D	Non	Mary M. Bittle	L	Cr
Census Card No. 747, P. O. Sapulpa, Enrolled August 28, 1899												
2457	1	Biggs, Susanna	30	F	F		Pompey, Biggs	D	Cr	Yarmah Biggs	D	Cr
Census Card No. 748, P. O. Stone Bluff, Enrolled August 28, 1899; No. 2, May 17, 1901												
2458	1	Smith, Lucinda A.	67	F	½		Samuel Hopper	D	Non	Sarah Hopper	D	Cr
2459	2	Smith, Shelton	63	M	Adpd	Hus.	Stephen Smith	D	Non	Catherine Parker	D	Non
Census Card No. 749, P. O. Muskogee, Enrolled August 28, 1899												
2460	1	Murphy, Eliza J.	56	F	⅛		Leroy Jobe	D	Non	Cherokee Jobe	D	Cr
2461	2	Murphy, Wm. S.	17	M	1-16	S	C. M. Murphy	D	Non	No. 1	L	Cr

Roll No.	No.	NAME	Age	Sex	Blood	Rel.	Name of Father	Liv.	Cit.	Name of Mother	Liv.	Cit.
Census Card No. 750, P. O. Haskell, Enrolled August 28, 1899												
2462	1	Bruner, Daniel	51	M	F		Louis Bruner	D	Cr	Nancy Bruner	D	Cr
2463	2	Bruner, Bettie	27	F	F	Wf	Watko Harjo	D	Cr	Aley Bruner	D	Cr
2464	3	Bruner, Mattie	8	F	F	D	No. 1	L	Cr	No. 2	L	Cr
2465	4	Bruner, Mahala	6	F	F	D	No. 1	L	Cr	No. 2	L	Cr
2466	5	Bruner, Overton	3	M	F	S	No. 1	L	Cr	No. 2	L	Cr
2467	6	Bruner, Link	4mo	M	F	S	No. 1	L	Cr	No. 2	L	Cr
Census Card No. 751, P. O. Haskell, Enrolled August 28, 1899; No. 3, May 24, 1901												
2468	1	Tecumseh, Tecumseh	27	M	F		Alec Tecumseh	L	Cr	Nicey Tecumseh	L	Cr
2469	2	Tecumseh, Ellis	4	M	F	S	No. 1	L	Cr	Eliza Tecumseh	D	Cr
2470	3	Tecumseh, Eliza	24	F	F	Wf	Big Sam	D	Cr	Mullie	D	Cr
No. 1 died June 17, 1900 No. 3 died July 30, 1899												
Census Card No. 752, P. O. Haskell, Enrolled August 28, 1899												
2471	1	Tecumseh, Alec	48	M	F		Tecumseh	D	Cr	Unknown	D	Cr
2472	2	Tecumseh, Nicey	40	F	F	Wf	Hodulge	D	Cr	Unknown	D	Cr
2473	3	Tecumseh, Austin	21	M	F	S	No. 1	L	Cr	No. 2	L	Cr
2474	4	Tecumseh, Nero	14	M	F	S	No. 1	L	Cr	No. 2	L	Cr
2475	5	Tecumseh, Willie	11	M	F	S	No. 1	L	Cr	No. 2	L	Cr
2476	6	Tecumseh, Eddie	9	M	F	S	No. 1	L	Cr	No. 2	L	Cr
Census Card No. 753, P. O. Mannford, Enrolled August 28, 1899; No. 3, September 5, 1899												
2477	1	Nave, Alice	18	F	½		J. C. Barr	L	Non	Matilda Jackson	L	Cr
2478	2	Nave, Ethel	3	F	¼	D	John Nave	L	Non	No. 1	L	Cr
2479	3	Nave, Eva	1	F	¼	D	John Nave	L	Non	No. 1	L	Cr
Census Card No. 754, P. O. Eufaula, Enrolled August 29, 1899; No. 3, May 24, 1901												
2480	1	Houston, Eva C.	20	F	¼		A. J. McDuff	L	Non	Sally McDuff	D	Cr
2481	2	Houston, Carrie	2	F	⅛	D	George Houston	L	Non	No. 1	L	Cr
2482	3	Houston, Lucien A.	1	M	⅛	S	George Houston	L	Non	No. 1	L	Cr
Census Card No. 755, P. O. Arlington, Enrolled August 29, 1899												
2483	1	Berryhill, Wm. F.	25	M	⅜		Z. T. Berryhill	L	Cr	Martha Berryhill	D	Cr
Census Card No. 756, P. O. Okmulgee, Enrolled August 29, 1899												
2484	1	Malone, Hepsey	50	F	F		Eufaula	D	Cr	Homoletke	D	Cr
No. 1 died January 1906												
Census Card No. 757, P. O. Okmulgee, Enrolled August 2199												
2485	1	Wicey	75	F	F		Talledga	D	Cr	Sinnedinihoye	D	Cr
No. 1 died November 23, 1902												
Census Card No. 758, P. O. Leonard, Enrolled August 29, 1899												
2486	1	Lewis, Thomas	30	M	F		Efi Emarthla	D	Cr	Susanna	D	Cr
2487	2	Brown, Sparhechar	14	M	F	Neph	Kinney	D	Cr	Cinda	D	Cr
Census Card No. 759, P. O. Okmulgee, Enrolled August 29, 1899												
2488	1	Brown, Sinnie	21	M	F		Kinney	D	Cr	Cinda	D	Cr
No. 1 died December 1903												
Census Card No. 760, P. O. Okmulgee, Enrolled August 29, 1899												
2489	1	Grayson, Charley	47	M	¾		Elijah Grayson	D	Cr	Louisa Grayson	D	Cr
2490	2	Grayson, Agnes P.	10	F	⅜	D	No. 1	L	Cr	Josie Grayson	L	Non
No. 1 died December 1899 No. 2 died January 15, 1900												
Census Card No. 761, P. O. Checotah, Enrolled August 29, 1899												
2491	1	Scott, George W.	38	M	⅛		James N. Scott	D	Non	Martha Scott	D	Cr
2492	2	Scott, James G.	7	M	1-16	S	No. 1	L	Cr	Cora Scott	L	Non
2493	3	Scott, Fred T.	5	M	1-16	S	No. 1	L	Cr	Cora Scott	L	Non
Census Card No. 762, P. O. Holdenville, Enrolled August 29, 1899												
2494	1	Posey, Henry	22	M	⅛		Bill Posey	D	Cr	Susan Posey	D	Non
No. 1 died June 10, 1904												
Census Card No. 763, P. O. Broken Arrow; R. F. D. No. 2, Enrolled August 29, 1899												
2495	1	Drew Amos	23	M	½		Daniel Drew	D	Cher	Maggie Drew	D	Cr
2496	2	Drew, Nettie	20	F	½	Wf	John Hagen	L	?	Sukey Hagen	L	?
2497	3	Drew, Daniel	3	M	½	S	No. 1	L	Cr	No. 2	L	Cr
Census Card No. 764, P. O. Coweta, Enrolled August 30' 1890												
2498	1	Harman, Ben T.	30	M	⅛		Benj. Harmon	D	Cr	Laura Harmon	D	Non
2499	2	Harmon, Will S.	27	M	⅛	Bro	Benj. Harmon	D	Cr	Laura Harmon	D	Non
No. 2 died March 1, 1900												
Census Card No. 765, P. O. Muskogee, Enroled August 30, 1899												
2500	1	Berryhill, Jake (A.J.)	42	M	1-16		Jeff Berryhill	D	Cr	Nancy Berryhill	L	Non
2501	2	Berryhill, James	18	M	1-32	S	No. 1	L	Cr	Jane Berryhill	L	Non
2502	3	Berryhill, Rachel	16	F	1-32	D	No. 1	L	Cr	Jane Berryhill	L	Non
2503	4	Berryhill, Gertrude	12	F	1-32	D	No. 1	L	Cr	Jane Berryhill	L	Non
2504	5	Berryhill, Bessie	7	F	1-32	D	No. 1	L	Cr	Jane Berryhill	L	Non
2505	6	Berryhill, Lee	3	F	1-32	D	No. 1	L	Cr	Jane Berryhill	L	Non
Census Card No. 766, P. O. Checotah, Enrolled August 30, 1899												
2506	1	Keys, Edward	29	M	1-16		Sam Keys	L	Cher	Sarah Keys	L	Cr
Census Card No. 767, P. O. Checotah, Enrolled August 30, 1899												
2507	1	Keys, James	24	M	1-16		Sam Keys	L	Cher	Sarah Keys	L	Cr
Census Card No. 768, P. O. Checotah, Enrolled August 30, 1899												
2508	1	Grayson, Van	23	M	½		Wm. Grayson	L	Cr	Nancy Grayson	L	Cr
Census Card No. 769, Pl O. Checotah, Enrolled August 30, 1899												
2509	1	McDermit, Henry	46	M	¼		William McDermit	D	Non	Leona McDermit	D	Cr
2510	2	McDermit, Ella Grace	2	F	⅛	D	No. 1	L	Cr	Ella May McDermit	L	Non
Census Card No. 770, P. O. Mounds, Enrolled August 31, 1899; No. 3, July 12, 1900												
2511	1	Berryhill, William	27	M	⅛		Geo. W. Berryhill	D	Cr	Hare Berryhill	L	Non
2512	2	Berryhill, Joseph F.	1	M	1-16	S	No. 1	L	Cr	Alice Berryhill	L	Non
2513	3	Berryhill, Nevada	5mo	F	1-16	D	No. 1	L	Cr	Alice Berryhill	L	Non
No. 1 died February 15, 1912												

Roll No.	No.	NAME	Age	Sex	Blood	Rel.	NAME OF FATHER	Liv.	Cit.	NAME OF MOTHER	Liv.	Cit.
Census Card No. 771, P. O. Kiefer, Enrolled August 31, 1899												
2514	1	Kiefer, Martha Lee	36	F	⅛		Geo. W. Berryhill	D	Cr	Arie A. Berryhill	L	Non
2515	2	Kiefer, Annie E.	7	F	1-16	D	Smith H. Kiefer	L	Non	No. 1	L	Cr
2516	3	Kiefer, Leroy R.	4	M	1-16	S	Smith H. Kiefer	L	Non	No. 1	L	Cr
2517	4	Kiefer, John D.	2	M	1-16	S	Smith H. Kiefer	L	Non	No. 1	L	Cr
2518	5	Kiefer, George D.	1	M	1-16	S	Smith H. Kiefer	L	Non	No. 1	L	Cr
Census Card No. 772, P. O. Mounds, Enrolled August 31, 1899												
2519	1	Berryhill, Theodore	24	M	⅛		Geo. W. Berrhyill	D	Cr	Arie A. Berryhill	L	Non
2520	2	Berryhill, Lony Love	3	F	1-16	D	No. 1	L	Cr	Rilla Berryhill	L	Non
2521	3	Berryhill, Jackson G.	2	M	1-16	S	No. 1	L	Cr	Rilla Berryhill	L	Non
2522	4	Berryhill, Ollie	2wks	F	1-16	D	No. 1	L	Cr	Rilla Berryhill	L	Non
		No. 4 died February 21, 1901										
Census Card No. 773, P. O. Muskogee, Enrolled August 31, 1899												
2523	1	Hodge, Horace	24	M	⅛		Johnson Hodge	D	Cr	Margaret Hodge	D	Non
Census Card No. 774, P. O. Hosey, Enrolled August 31, 1899; No. 2, October 4, 1899												
2524	1	Hosey, Harriet	52	F	⅛		Alex Depriest	L	Non	Patience Depriest	L	Cr
2525	2	Hosey, Lee	14	M	1-16	G-S	Bob Huckaby	L	Non	Roxan Vanderslice	L	Cr
		No. 2 died November 30, 1899										
Census Card No. 775, P. O. Checotah, Enrolled August 31, 1899												
2526	1	Depriest, Franklin	19	M	⅛		John Depriest	D	Cr	Eliza Depriest	D	Non
Census Card No. 776, P. O. Hosey, Enrolled August 31, 1899												
2527	1	Hosey, John B.	28	M	⅛		Isaac Hosey	L	Non	Harriet Hosey	L	Cr
2528	2	Hosey, Orlando	5	M	1-32	S	No. 1	L	Cr	Maggie Hosey	L	Non
2529	3	Hosey, Isaac	3	M	1-32	S	No. 1	L	Cr	Maggie Hosey	L	Non
Census Card No. 777, P. O. Mounds; No. 2, Sapulpa, Enrolled September 2, 1899												
2530	1	Huffstetler, Mary L.	40	F	⅛		Thos. Summers	D	Non	Nancy C. Whetstone	L	Cr
2531	2	Burrow, Thomas R.	19	M	1-16	S	Wiley Burrow	D	Non	No. 1	L	Cr
2532	3	Burrow, John D.	13	M	1-16	S	Wiley Burrow	D	Non	No. 1	L	Cr
Census Card No. 778, P. O. Summit, Enrolled Sept. 2, 1899												
2533	1	McQueen, James	44	M	F		Dave McQueen	D	Cr	No. 2	L	Cr
2534	2	McQueen, Sarah	80	F	F	Moth	Mechusco Harjo	D	Cr	Mariah	D	Cr
		No. 2 died Jan. 10, 1901										
Census Card No. 779, P. O. Wagoner, Enrolled September 2, 1899												
2535	1	Childers Cooie	28	M	¾		N. B. Childers	L	Cr	Sophie Childers	D	Cr
2536	2	Childers, Hubert	4	M	⅝	S	No. 1	L	Cr	Emma Childers	D	Cr
Census Card No. 780, P. O. Bixby, Enrolled September 5, 1899												
2537	1	Bailey, Charles	35	M	½		Charles Bailey	D	Non	Elizabeth Bailey	D	Cr
Census Card No. 781, P. O. Senora, Enrolled September 5, 1899												
2538	1	Withers, Maggie	16	F	¼		Hamp G. Vowell	L	Non	Martha Vowell	L	Cr
Census Card No. 782, P. O. Checotah; No. 3 Cathay; Enrolled September 5, 1899												
2539	1	Murray, Martha	46	F	⅛		Eli A. Self	D	Cr	Minerva Self	D	Non
2540	2	Murray, Jesse	13	M	1-16	S	A. J. Murray	L	Non	No. 1	L	Cr
2541	3	Murray, Ada	11	F	1-16	D	A. J. Murray	L	Non	No. 1	L	Cr
2542	4	Murray, Clarence Lee	8	M	1-16	S	A. J. Murray	L	Non	No. 1	L	Cr
Census Card No. 783, P. O. Checotah, Enrolled September 7, 1899												
2543	1	Graves, Leona	23	F	⅛		Henry E. Aultman	D	Non	Melvina L. Taylor	L	Cr
2544	2	Graves Bonnie Gertrude	4	F	1-16	D	George Grace	L	Non	No. 1	L	Cr
Census Card No. 784, P. O. Sapulpa, Enrolled September 7 1899												
2545	1	Sanger, Clemmie H.	27	F	⅛		Wesley G. Norman	D	Non	Navelle Norman	D	Cr
2546	2	Sanger, George N.	9	F	1-16	S	George P. Sanger	L	Non	No. 1	L	Cr
Census Card No. 785, P. O. Broken Arrow, R. F. D. No. 2, Enrolled September 7, 1899												
2547	1	McIntosh, Commodore	43	M	F		John McIntosh	L	Cr	Susan McIntosh	L	Cr
2548	2	McIntosh, Arsyno	17	F	½	D	No. 1	L	Cr	Jemima McIntosh	L	Non
2549	3	McIntosh, Maggie	15	F	½	D	No. 1	L	Cr	Jemima McIntosh	L	Non
2550	4	McIntosh, Lizzie	10	F	½	D	No. 1	L	Cr	Jemima McIntosh	L	Non
2551	5	McIntosh, Edna	7	F	½	D	No. 1	L	Cr	Jemima McIntosh	L	Non
2552	6	McIntosh, Iona	5	F	½	D	No. 1	L	Cr	Jemima McIntosh	L	Non
2553	7	McIntosh, Della	1	F	½	D	No. 1	L	Cr	Jemima McIntosh	L	Non
Census Card No. 786, P. O. Drumright, Enrolled Sept. 7, 1899												
2554	1	McIntosh, Wm. R.	40	M	¾		Wm. R. McIntosh	D	Cr	Annie McIntosh	D	Cr
2555	2	McIntosh, Annie	7	F	⅜	D	No. 1	L	Cr	Theodocia McIntosh	L	Non
2556	3	McIntosh, Sarah	5	F	⅜	D	No. 1	L	Cr	Theodocia McIntosh	L	Non
2557	4	McIntosh, Viola	3	F	⅜	D	No. 1	L	Cr	Theodocia McIntosh	L	Non
Census Card No. 787, P. O. Jenks, Enrolled September 8, 1899												
2558	1	Ishmael, James M.	18	M	⅛		Ben R. Ishmael	L	Non	Maggie Ishmael	D	Cr
Census Card No. 788, P. O. Bristow, Enrolled September 8 1899												
2559	1	Montgall, Lizzie E.	49	F	¼		Jacob Miller	D	Non	Sarah Field Miller	D	A-Chr
Census Card No. 789, P. O. Red Fork, Enrolled September 8, 1899												
2560	1	Smith, Janie	20	F	⅛		Ben R. Ishmael	L	Non	Maggie Ishmael	D	Cr
Census Card No. 790, P. O. Tulsa, Enrolled September 8, 1899												
2561	1	Wray, Claud	7	M	⅛		George T. Wray	L	Non	Sarah E. Wray	D	Cr
2562	2	Wray, Benjamin	6	M	⅛	Bro	George T. Wray	L	Non	Sarah E. Wray	D	Cr
2563	3	Wray, Lillie	3	F	⅛	Sis	George T. Wray	L	Non	Sarah E. Wray	D	Cr
2564	4	Wray, Lee	3	M	⅛	Bro	George T. Wray	L	Non	Sarah E. Wray	D	Cr
Census Card No. 791, P. O. Porter, Enrolled September 8, 1899												
2565	1	Harrington, Amanda	15	F	½		Isaac Harrington	L	Non	Allie Harrington	D	Cr
2566	2	Harrington, Lucy	10	F	½	Sis	Isaac Harrington	L	Non	Allie Harrington	D	Cr

Roll No.	No.	NAME	Age	Sex	Blood	Rel.	NAME OF FATHER	Liv.	Cit.	NAME OF MOTHER	Liv.	Cit.
		Census Card No. 792, P. O. Red Fork, Enrolled September 11, 1899; No. 5 October 9, 1899										
2567	1	Perryman, Robert L.	28	M	F		Jos. M. Perryman	D	Cr	Eliza Perryman	L	Cr
2568	2	Perryman, Lucy	27	F	1/2	Wf	Crawford Thomas	D	?	Melissi Thomas	L	?
2569	3	Perryman, Joseph	6	M	3/4	S	No. 1	L	Cr	No. 2	L	Cr
2570	4	Perryman, Ralph	4	M	3/4	S	No. 1	L	Cr	No. 2	L	Cr
2571	5	Perryman, Eliza	67	F	F	Moth	Unknown	D	Cr	No. 2	L	Cr
		No. 5 died February 9, 1901. No. 2 died February 19, 1909										
		Census Card No. 793, P. O. Oktaha, Enrolled September 11, 1899										
2572	1	Newton, Sarah Eliza-beth	25	F	1-16		Otho Durant	L	Cr	Anna Durant	L	Non
2573	2	Newton, Valley Ruth	2	F	1-32	D	E. G. Newton	L	Non	No. 1	L	Cr
2574	3	Newton, Ruby E.	3 mo	F	1-32	D	E. G. Newton	L	Non	No. 1	L	Cr
		Census Card No. 794, P. O. Okmulgee, Enrolled September 11, 1899										
2575	1	Proctor, Toney E.	32	M	F		Emarthla Harjo	D	Cr	Louisa	D	Cr
2576	2	Proctor, Susan	22	F	1/2	Wf	Dr. Tennant	L	Non	Amanda Sanger	L	Cr
2577	3	Procter, Mabel	5 mo	F	3/4	D	No. 1	L	Cr	No. 2	L	Cr
		Census Card No. 795, P. O. Brush Hill, Enrolled September 12, 1899										
2578	1	Brown, Joseph Wm.	11	M	3-16		J. W. Brown	L	Non	Nancy Brown	D	Cr
2579	2	Brown, Elmer Wesley	9	M	3-16	Bro	J. W. Brown	L	Non	Nancy Brown	D	Cr
2580	3	Brown, Geraldine	7	F	3-16	Sis	J. W. Brown	L	Non	Nancy Brown	D	Cr
		Census Card No. 796, P. O. Red Fork, Enrolled September 12, 1899										
2581	1	Mullen, Celestie	37	F	F		Tom Deer	D	Cr	Louisa Deer	D	Cr
		No. 1 died October 7, 1901										
		Census Card No. 797, P. O. Red Fork, Enrolled September 12, 1899										
2582	1	Berryhill, Thomas H.	56	M	1/8		John Berryhill	D	Cr	America Berryhill	D	Non
2583	2	Berryhill, Theodore F.	23	M	1-16	S	No. 1	L	Cr	Sarah Berryhill	L	Non
2584	3	Berryhill, John P.	20	M	1-16	S	No. 1	L	Cr	Sarah Berryhill	L	Non
2585	4	Berryhill, Cora F.	15	F	1-16	D	No. 1	L	Cr	Sarah Berryhill	L	Non
2586	5	Berryhill, William T.	11	M	1-16		No. 1	L	Cr	Sarah Berryhill	L	Non
2587	6	Berryhill, Della I.	7	F	1-16	D	No. 1	L	Cr	Sarah Berryhill	L	Non
		Census Card No. 798, P. O. Mounds, Enrolled September 12, 1899										
2588	1	Vowell, Sam	22	M	1/4		Hamp G. Vowell	L	Non	Martha Vowell	L	Cr
2589	2	Vowell, Floyd	1	M	1/8	S	No. 1	L	Cr	Rosa Vowell	L	Non
		Census Card No. 799, P. O. Sapulpa, Enrolled September 12, 1899										
2590	1	Maxwell, John C.	36	M	1/8		Thomas Maxwell	D	Non	Sarophy Maxwell	D	Cr
2591	2	Maxwell, Jessie L.	9	F	1-16	D	No. 1	L	Cr	Laura J. Maxwell	L	Non
2592	3	Maxwell, Laura E.	7	F	1-16	D	No. 1	L	Cr	Laura J. Maxwell	L	Non
2593	4	Maxwell, Maude P.	6	F	1-16	D	No. 1	L	Cr	Laura J. Maxwell	L	Non
2594	5	Maxwell, John B.	4	M	1-16	S	No. 1	L	Cr	Laura J. Maxwell	L	Non
2595	6	Maxwell, Colbert J.	3	M	1-16	S	No. 1	L	Cr	Laura J. Maxwell	L	Non
2596	7	Maxwell, Rollie C.	1	M	1-16	S	No. 1	L	Cr	Laura J. Maxwell	L	Non
2597	8	Maxwell, Leona V.	1 mo	F	1-16	D	No. 1	L	Cr	Laura J. Maxwell	L	Non
		Census Card No. 800, P. O. Mounds; No. 1 Dustin; Enrolled September 13, 1899										
2598	1	Wills, William H.	53	M	1/4		Wm. Wills	D	Cr	Mary E. Wills	D	Non
2599	2	Wills, Albert G.	16	M	1/8	S	No. 1	L	Cr	N. J. Wills	L	Non
2600	3	Wills, Bonnie	13	F	1/8	D	No. 1	L	Cr	N. J. Wills	L	Non
2601	4	Wills, Joe B.	11	M	1/8	S	No. 1	L	Cr	N. J. Wills	L	Non
		No. 1 died February 1901										
		Census Card No. 801, P. O. Mounds, Enrolled September 13, 1899										
2602	1	Withers, Lydia	20	F	1/4		Hamp G. Vowell	L	Non	Martha Vowell	L	Cr
2603	2	Withers, Loney Ethel	1	F	1/8	D	Roberts Withers	L	Non	No. 1	L	Cr
		Census Card No. 802, P. O. Stone Bluff, Enrollrf September 13, 1899										
2604	1	Kelly, Mary	47	F	F		Gristie Perryman	D	Cr	Sallie Perryman	D	Cr
2605	2	Kelly, Louina	18	F	F	D	James Kelly	D	Cr	No. 1	L	Cr
2606	3	Kelly, Rueben	14	M	F	S	James Kelly	D	Cr	No. 1	L	Cr
2607	4	Kelly, Mary	10	F	F	D	James Kelly	D	Cr	No. 1	L	Cr
2608	5	Kelly, Thomas	7	M	F	S	James Kelly	D	Cr	No. 1	L	Cr
		No. 4 died May 9, 1903										
		Census Card No. 803, P. O. Checotah, Enrolled September 13, 1899										
2609	1	Arnett, Maggie	22	F	1/2		Jim Smith	D	Cr	Delphine Marshall	L	Non
2610	2	Arnett, Iona	3	F	1/4	D	Albert W. Arnett	L	Non	No. 1	L	Cr
2611	3	Arnett, Fred	1	M	1/4	S	Albert W. Arnett	L	Non	No. 1	L	Cr
		No. 3 died February 22, 1900.										
		Census Card No. 804, P. O. Broken Arrow, Enrolled September 13, 1899										
2612	1	Childers, Lydia	48	F	3/4		Thompson Perryman	D	Cr	Hannah Perryman	D	Cr
2613	2	Childers, James	24	M	3/4	S	Daniel Childers	D	Cr	No. 1	L	Cr
2614	3	Childers, Joe	22	M	3/4	S	Daniel Childers	D	Cr	No. 1	L	Cr
2615	4	Childers, Pratt	17	M	3/4	S	Daniel Childers	D	Cr	No. 1	L	Cr
2616	5	Childers, Paul	15	M	3/4	S	Daniel Childers	D	Cr	No. 1	L	Cr
		No. 4 died July 19, 1902. No. 3 died December 21, 1909. No. 5 reported dead										
		Census Card No. 805, P. O. Oktaha, Enrolled September 14, 1899										
2617	1	Grayson, Nannie	40	F	1/2		Jim McIntosh	D	?	Vicey McIntosh	D	?
2618	2	Hamilton, Pearly	8	F	1/4	D	Price Hamilton	L	Non	No. 1	L	Cr
2619	3	Chambers, Lewis	5	M	1/4	S	Dick Chambers	L	h - Ebcer Freed	No. 1	L	Cr
		Census Card No. 806, P. O. Checotah, Enrolled September 14, 1899										
2620	1	Murray, Charles E.	24	M	1-16		A. J. Murray	L	Non	Martha Murray	L	Cr
2621	2	Murray, William A.	3	M	1-32	S	No. 1	L	Cr	Delphine Murray	L	Non
2622	3	Murray, Gertie May	8 mo	F	1-32	D	No. 1	L	Cr	Delphine Murray	L	Non

Roll No.	No.	NAME	Age	Sex	Blood	Rel.	NAME OF FATHER	Liv.	Cit.	NAME OF MOTHER	Liv.	Cit.
		Census Card No. 807, P. O. Checotah, Enrolled September 14, 1899										
2623	1	Ansiel, Arnecie	22	F	1-16		A. J. Murray	L	Non	Martha Murray	L	Cr
2624	2	Ansiel, Charley D.	5	M	1-32	S	Will Ansil	D	Non	No. 1	L	Cr
2625	3	Carr, Wm. H.	3	M	1-32	S	Will Carr	L	Non	No. 1	L	Cr
		Census Card No. 808, P. O. Tulsa, Enrolled September 14, 1899; No. 6 May 15, 1901										
2626	1	Perryman, Rachel	47	F	F		Alexander	D	Cr	Hannah	D	Cr
2627	2	Perryman, Ab	21	M	¾	S	Geo. B. Perryman	D	Cr	No. 1	L	Cr
2628	3	Perryman, Mamie	19	F	¾	D	Geo. B. Perryman	D	Cr	No. 1	L	Cr
2629	4	Perryman, George B.	15	M	¾	S	Geo. B. Perryman	D	Cr	No. 1	L	Cr
2630	5	Davis, Oliver	8	M	¾	Ward	Sam Davis	L	Cr	Louisa Partridge	D	Cr
2631	6	Perryman, George B.	45	M	½	Hus	Lewis Perryman	D	Cr	Hellen Perryman	D	Cr
		No. 6 died April 21, 1899										
		Census Card No. 809, P. O. Tulsa, Enrolled September 14, 1899										
2632	1	Beaver, David	21	M	F		Milton Beaver	D	Cr	Lydia Beaver	D	Cr
		Census Card No. 810, P. O. Tulsa, Enrolled September 14, 1899										
2633	1	Harner, Ella	25	F	¾		Geo. B. Perryman	D	Cr	Rachel Perryman	L	Cr
2634	2	Harner, Leo George	1	M	⅜	S	W. M. Harner	L	Non	No. 1	L	Cr
		Census Card No. 811, P. O. Tulsa, Enrolled September 14, 1899										
2635	1	Thurman, Alice	19	F	½		Wm. Thurman	L	Non	China Thurman	D	Cr
		Census Card No. 812, P. O. Tulsa, Enrolled September 14, 1899										
2636	1	Perryman, Moses	29	M	¾		Geo. B. Perryman	D	Cr	Rachel Perryman	L	Cr
2637	2	Perryman, Rachel H.	4	F	⅜	D	No. 1	L	Cr	Lula Perryman	L	Non
2638	3	Perryman, Cosetta	2	F	⅜	D	No. 1	L	Cr	Lula Perryman	L	Non
		No. 1 died February 8, 1901										
		Census Card No. 813, P. O. Wagoner, Enrolled September 14, 1899; No. 6, November 16, 1899										
2639	1	Posey, John M.	37	M	¼		Thos. B. Posey	D	Cr	Hurley E. Posey	L	Non
2640	2	Posey, Annie L.	13	F	⅛	D	No. 1	L	Cr	Laura E. Posey	L	Non
2641	3	Posey, John W.	10	M	⅛	S	No. 1	L	Cr	Laura E. Posey	L	Non
2642	4	Posey, Jim H.	8	M	⅛	S	No. 1	L	Cr	Laura E. Posey	L	Non
2643	5	Posey, Walter A.	5	M	⅛	S	No. 1	L	Cr	Laura E. Posey	L	Non
2644	6	Posey, Ruby	1mo	F	⅛	D	No. 1	L	Cr	Laura E. Posey	L	Non
		Census Card No. 814, P. O. Eufaula, Enrolled September 14, 1899										
2645	1	Bailey, George Ella	38	F	¼		Geo. W. Stidham	D	Cr	Sarah C. Stidham	D	Non
2646	2	Bailey, Georgie Ella	15	F	⅛	D	W. H. Bailey	L	Non	No. 1	L	Cr
2647	3	Bailey, Howard L.	12	M	⅛	S	W. H. Bailey	L	Non	No. 1	L	Cr
2648	4	Bailey, Lonie Lee	3	F	⅛	D	W. H. Bailey	L	Non	No. 1	L	Cr
		No. 4 died October 7, 1899. No. 3 died June 18, 1907.										
		Census Card No. 815, P. O. Lenna, Enrolled September 14, 1899										
2649	1	Morrison, John Sr.	63	M	½		John Morrison	D	Non	Nicotia Morrison	D	Cr
2650	2	Morrison, Louisa	57	F	¾	Wf	Wm. Marshall	D	Cr	Polly Marshall	D	Cr
2651	3	Morrison, Manny	20	M	⅝	S	No. 1	L	Cr	No. 2	L	Cr
2652	4	Morrison, Mary	17	F	⅝	D	No. 1	L	Cr	No. 2	L	Cr
2653	5	Morrison, Major	15	M	⅝	S	No. 1	L	Cr	No. 2	L	Cr
2654	6	Morrison, John Jr.	13	M	⅝	S	No. 1	L	Cr	No. 2	L	Cr
		Census Card No. 816, P. O. Lenna, Enrolled September 14, 1899										
2655	1	Leverett, Kogee	25	F	⅝		John Morrison, Sr.	L	Cr	Louisa Morrison	L	Cr
		Census Card No. 817, P. O. Eufaula; No. 3, Dustin, Enrolled September 14, 1899										
2656	1	Wilson, Hettie	28	F	¾		John Morrison, Sr.	L	Cr	Louisa Morrison	L	Cr
2657	2	Wilson, Verbena	9mo	F	⅜	D	R. B. Wilson	L	Non	No. 1	L	Cr
2658	3	Kanard, Washington	10	M	¾	S	Roman Kanard	D	Cr	No. 1	L	Cr
		Census Card No. 818, P. O. Okemah; No. 2, Salem; Enrolled Sept. 14, 1899; Nos. 3, 4, 5, May 22, 1901										
2659	1	McNac, Dicey	75	F	F		Echu Yahola	D	Cr	Polly	D	Cr
2660	2	McGilbray, Polly	14	F	F	Niece	Johny McGilbra	D	Cr	Winey McGilbra	D	Cr
2661	3	Tiger, Johnson	18	M	F	G-N	Heneha Micco	D	Cr	Cinda Micco	D	Cr
2662	4	Hill, Lucy	26	F	F	G-N	Tommy	L	Cr	Cinda Micco	D	Cr
2663	5	McGilbray, Walter	11	M	F	Neph	John McGilbra	D	Cr	Winey McGilbra	D	Cr
		No. 3 died February 7, 1901. No. 1 died August 4, 1901. No. 4 died July 1899.										
		No. 5 died August 23, 1899										
		Census Card No. 819, P. O. Council Hill, Enrolled September 14, 1899										
2664	1	Wolf, Geroge	30	M	F		William Wolf	L	Cr	Mary	L	Cr
2665	2	Wolf, Nannie	27	F	F	Wf	Sam Richard	L	Cr	Kizzie Richard	D	Cr
2666	3	Wolf, Kizzie	8	F	F	D	No. 1	L	Cr	No. 2	L	Cr
2667	4	Wolf, Josie	6	F	F	D	No. 1	L	Cr	No. 2	L	Cr
2668	5	Wolf, Linda	6	F	F	D	No. 1	L	Cr	No. 2	L	Cr
2669	6	Wolf, Mattie	1	F	F	D	No. 1	L	Cr	No. 2	L	Cr
2670	7	Wolf, Buck	1	M	F	S	No. 1	L	Cr	No. 2	L	Cr
		No. 7 died September 28, 1899										
		Census Card No. 820, P. O. Checotah, Enrolled September 14, 1899										
2671	1	Richard, Jasper	29	M	F		Sam Richard	L	Cr	Kizzie Richard	D	Cr
2672	2	Richard, Minnie	19	F	F	Wf	Sam July	D	Cr	Louisa July	L	Cr
		No. 1 died December 20, 1905										
		Census Card No. 821, P. O. Henryetta, Enrolled September 15, 1899										
2673	1	Whetstone, Presley	21	M	⅛		Anderson Whetstone	D	Non	Nancy Whetstone	L	Cr
		Census Card No. 822, P. O. Wetumka, Enrolled September 16, 1899; No. 4, October 11, 1899										
2674	1	Gray, Louisa	45	F	F		Daniel Barnett	D	Cr	Sallie Barnett	D	Cr
2675	2	Wesley, Bella	18	F	F	D	Nutka Wesley	D	Cr	No. 1	L	Cr
2676	3	Wesley, Daniel	16	M	F	S	Nutka Wesley	D	Cr	No. 1	L	Cr
2677	4	Wallow, Lucy	16	F	F	Ward	Wilson Wallow	D	Cr	Lizzie Wallow	D	Cr
		No. 2 died December 30, 1899										

Roll No.	No.	NAME	Age	Sex	Blood	Rel.	NAME OF FATHER	Liv.	Cit.	NAME OF MOTHER	Liv.	Cit.
		Census Card No. 823, P. O. Brush Hill, Enrolled September 16, 1899										
2678	1	Jackson, Lou	34	F	1/4		Sunny Grayson	L	Cr	Kate Thlocco	D	Cr
2679	2	Jackson, Ella	14	F	1/8	D	Stephney Jackson	L	Non	No. 1	L	Cr
2680	3	Jackson, Thomas	12	M	1/8	S	Stephney, Jackson	L	Non	No. 1	L	Cr
2681	4	Jackson, William	10	M	1/8	S	Stephney Jackson	L	Non	No. 1	L	Cr
2682	5	Jackson, James	8	M	1/8	S	Stephney Jackson	L	Non	No. 1	L	Cr
2683	6	Jackson, Henry	6	M	1/8	S	Stephney Jackson	L	Non	No. 1	L	Cr
2684	7	Jackson, Susie	3	F	1/8	D	Stephney Jackson	L	Non	No. 1	L	Cr
		Census Card No. 824, P. O. Bixby, Enrolled September 18, 1899										
2685	1	Bunger, William	1	M	F		John Bungee	L	Cr	Annie Bungee	D	Cr
		Census Card No. 825, P. O. Checotah, Enrolled September 18, 1899										
2686	1	Carr, William	27	M	1/4		Albert Carr	L	Cr	Susan E. Carr	D	Non
		Census Card No. 826, P. O. Phoenix, Arizona; 110 No. 10th Ave., Enrolled September 18, 1899										
2687	1	White, Tennessee	21	F	1/2		Wm. H. Wills	L	Cr	Norcissa Wills	L	Non
2688	2	White, Everett B.	2	M	1-16	S	W. E. White	L	Non	No. 1	L	Cr
		Census Card No. 827, P. O. Muskogee, Enrolled September 18, 1899										
2689	1	Owen, Mary Severs	25	F	1/4		F. B. Severs	L	A-W	Annie A. Severs	L	Cr
		Census Card No. 828, P. O. Lee; No. 2 and 3, Okmulgee, Enrolled September 19, 1899										
2690	1	Flint, Lizzie	25	F	1/4		Ad. Taylor	D	?	Peggy Taylor	D	?
2691	2	Flint, Brown.	3	M	1/8	S	Thomas Flint	L	Non	No. 1	L	Cr
2692	3	Flint, Morris	2	M	1/8	S	Thomas Flint	L	Non	No. 1	L	Cr
		Census Card No. 829, P. O. Eufaula, Enrolled September 19, 1899										
2693	1	Jones, Taylor	26	M	F		Rabbit Jones	D	Cr	Milea Jones	D	Cr
2694	2	Jones, Betsey	31	F	F	Wf	Blackbird	D	Cr	Unknown	?	Cr
2695	3	Deere, Isaac	13	M	St-S		Isaac Deer	D	Cr	No. 2	L	Cr
		No. 1 died January 15, 1900. No. 2 died September 1900. No. 3 died October 1900.										
		Census Card No. 830, P. O. Eufaula, Enrolled September 20, 1899										
2696	1	Smith, Joseph	26	M	1/4		Jim Smith	D	?	Mary Smith	D	?
		No. 1 died June 1, 1901										
		Census Card No. 831, P. O. Catoosa, Enrolled September 20, 1899										
2697	1	Rogers, Caesar	71	M	F		Escheeye	D	Cr	Heehhoya	D	Cr
2698	2	Rogers, Mollie	56	F	F	Wf	Noble Perryman	D	Cr	Lucy Larney	D	Cr
		No. 1 reported dead										
		Census Card No. 832, P. O. Muskogee, Enrolled September 21, 1899										
2699	1	Mingo, Joseph	51	M	F		Mingo	D	Cr	Bettie Mingo	D	Cr
2700	2	Mingo, Louisana	46	F	F	Wf	Phillip Lovett	D	Cr	Therserye	D	Cr
2701	3	Mingo, Carrie	14	F	F	D	No. 1	L	Cr	No. 2	L	Cr
2702	4	Mingo, Louella	12	F	F	D	No. 1	L	Cr	No. 2	L	Cr
2703	5	Mingo, Warnie	7	F	F	D	No. 1	L	Cr	No. 2	L	Cr
		No. 1 died January 25, 1900. No. 2 died 1907. No. 5 died August 1900.										
		Census Card No. 833, P. O. Haskell, Enrolled September 21, 1899; No. 3, May 22, 1901										
2704	1	Mingo, Robert J.	21	M	F		Josehp Mingo	L	Cr	Lousana Mingo	L	Cr
2705	2	Mingo, Irene	21	F	1/2	Wf	David Cummings	L	Cr	Millie Cummings	L	Cr
2706	3	Mingo, Youpehake	1	F	3/4	S	R. J. Mingo	L	Cr	Irene Mingo	L	Cr
		No. 2 died July 27, 1904. No. 1 died July 27, 1904. No. 3 died September 12, 1900										
		Census Card No. 834, P. O. South Canadian, Enrolled September 21, 1899										
2707	1	McDuff, Rachel	40	F	Ad		James Gentry	D	Non	Caroline Gentry	D	Non
		Census Card No. 835, P. O. Broken Arrow, Enrolled September 21, 1899; No. 3, February 12, 1900										
2708	1	Childers, Daniel	19	M	3/4		Daniel Childers	D	Cr	Lydia Childers	L	Cr
2709	2	Childers, Mildred	30	F	F	Wf	Roley McIntosh	L	Cr	Bessie McIntosh	L	Cr
2710	3	Childers, Clarence Wm.	1moM	7/8	S		No. 1	L	Cr	No. 2	L	Cr
		Census Card No. 836, P. O. Checotah, Enrolled September 22, 1899										
2711	1	McIntosh, D. N. Jr.	37	M	1/4		D. N. McIntosh	D	Cr	Jane E. McIntosh	D	Non
2712	2	McIntosh, Hannah Vera	4	F	1/8	D	No. 1	L	Cr	Alice McIntosh	L	Non
2713	3	McIntosh, Virgie May	1	F	1/8	D	No. 1	L	Cr	Alice McIntosh	L	Non
		Census Card No. 837, P. O. Oktaha; Nos. 1 and 2, Muskogee, Enrolled September 22, 1899; No. 5, April 28, 1900										
2714	1	Newberry, Jeannetta	26	F	1/2		David Sizemore	D	?	Ellen Sizemore	D	?
2715	2	Newberry, Lulu	7	F	1/4	D	John Newberry	L	Non	No. 1	L	Cr
2716	3	Newberry, Maud A.	6	F	1/4	D	John Newberry	L	Non	No. 1	L	Cr
2717	4	Newberry, Millard F.	2	M	1/4	S	John Newberry	L	Non	No. 1	L	Cr
2718	5	Newberry, Carl	1moM	1/4	S		John Newberry	L	Non	No. 1	L	Cr
		Census Card No. 838, P. O. Oktaha, Enrolled September 22, 1899										
2719	1	Hosmer, Susie	52	F	3/4		Sam Sizemore	D	Cr	Parsey Collins	L	Cr
2720	2	Hosmer, Frank	15	M	3/8	S	Solomon Hosmer	L	Cher	No. 1	L	Cr
2721	3	Gibson, Josephine	18	F	7/8	Niece	Sampson Fish	L	Cr	Salina Fish	L	Cr
2722	4	Hosmer, Fannie	4	F	3/8	S	Solomon Hosmer	L	Cher	No. 1	L	Cr
		Census Card No. 839, P. O. Wagoner, Enrolled September 22, 1899; No. 1, October 25, 1900										
2723	1	Kennard, George	47	M	F		Johnson Kennard	D	Cr	Fannie Kennard	D	Cr
2724	2	Kennard, William	4moM	1/2	S		No. 1	L	Cr	Mary Kennard	L	Non
		No. 1 died December 15, 1901. No. 2 died June 25, 1901.										
		Census Card No. 840, P. O. Hosey, Enrolled September 23, 1899; No. 4, October 4, 1899										
2725	1	Vanderslice, Patience	25	F	1/8		Isaac Hosea	L	Non	Harriet Hosea	L	Cr
2726	2	Vanderslice, Thomas J. Jr.	7	M	1-16	S	Thomas Vanderslice	L	Non	No. 1	L	Cr
2727	3	Vanderslice, Bertha May	4	F	1-16	D	Thomas Vanderslice	L	Non	No. 1	L	Cr
2728	4	Vanderslice, Annie Maud	6moF	1-16	D		Thomas Vanderslice	L	Non	No. 1	L	Cr

62

Census Card No. 841, P. O. Wier, Enrolled September 23, 1899

Roll No.	No.	NAME	Age	Sex	Blood	Rel.	NAME OF FATHER	Liv.	Cit.	NAME OF MOTHER	Liv.	Cit
2729	1	Cox, John	21	M	1/2		Lewis Cox	L	Sem	Cooty Cox	D	Cr
2730	2	Cox, Daniel	18	M	1/2	Bro.	Lewis Cox	L	Sem	Cooty Cox	D	Cr

Census Card No. 842, P. O. Bristow, Enrolled September 23, 1899

Roll No.	No.	NAME	Age	Sex	Blood	Rel.	NAME OF FATHER	Liv.	Cit.	NAME OF MOTHER	Liv.	Cit
2731	1	Knoll, Sally	40	F	5-16		Peter Scott	D	Cr	Mary Scott	D	Cr
2732	2	Knoll, Dora	5	F	5-32	D	Frank Knoll	L	Non	No. 1	L	Cr
2733	3	Jack, Eddie	10	M	21-32	S	Caesar Jack	L	Cr	No. 1	L	Cr

Census Card No. 843, P. O. Eufaula, Enrolled September 23, 1899

Roll No.	No.	NAME	Age	Sex	Blood	Rel.	NAME OF FATHER	Liv.	Cit.	NAME OF MOTHER	Liv.	Cit
2734	1	Perry, Maud	21	F	1/8		H. E. Aultman	L	Non	Melvina Aultman	L	Cr
2735	2	Perry, Charles Owen	2	M	1-16	S	Ed. Perry	L	Non	No. 1	L	Cr

Census Card No. 844, P. O. Mounds, Enrolled September 25, 1899

Roll No.	No.	NAME	Age	Sex	Blood	Rel.	NAME OF FATHER	Liv.	Cit.	NAME OF MOTHER	Liv.	Cit
2736	1	Berryhill, Stanford	43	M	1/8		G. W. Berryhill	D	Cr	Ara Ann Berryhill	L	Non
2737	2	Berryhill, Jessie L.	14	F	1-16	D	No. 1	L	Cr	Nancy Berryhill	L	Non
2738	3	Berryhill, Bluford W.	11	M	1-16	S	No. 1	L	Cr	Nancy Berryhill	L	Non
2739	4	Berryhill, George F.	8	M	1-16	S	No. 1	L	Cr	Nancy Berryhill	L	Non
2740	5	Berryhill, Carl C.	5	M	1-16	S	No. 1	L	Cr	Nancy Berryhill	L	Non
2741	6	Berryhill, Charles Lawson	2moM		1-16	S	No. 1	L	Cr	Nancy Berryhill	L	Non

Census Card No. 845, P. O. McDermott, Enrolled September 25, 1899

Roll No.	No.	NAME	Age	Sex	Blood	Rel.	NAME OF FATHER	Liv.	Cit.	NAME OF MOTHER	Liv.	Cit
2742	1	Tucker, Hettie	36	F	1/2		Sampson Bruner	D	Non	Amanda Gouge	D	Cr

Census Card No. 846, P. O. Checotah; No. 2, Dustin, Enrolled September 25, 1899

Roll No.	No.	NAME	Age	Sex	Blood	Rel.	NAME OF FATHER	Liv.	Cit.	NAME OF MOTHER	Liv.	Cit
2743	1	Howell, Lee	19	M	1/2		Scott Howell	D	Non	Selina McIntosh	D	Cr
2744	2	Howell, Annie	18	F	1/2	S	Scott Howell	D	Non	Selina McIntosh	D	Cr

Census Card No. 847, P. O. Redden, Enrolled September 25, 1899; No. 3, May 22, 1901

Roll No.	No.	NAME	Age	Sex	Blood	Rel.	NAME OF FATHER	Liv.	Cit.	NAME OF MOTHER	Liv.	Cit
2745	1	Emery, Melissa B.	24	F	1/2		L. H. Posey	L	?	Nancy Posey	L	?
2746	2	Emery, Byron Posey	1 1/2	M	1/4	S	John E. Emery	L	Non	No. 1	L	Cr
2747	3	Emery, Jones Gladstone	1	M	1/4	S	John E. Emery	L	Non	No. 1	L	Cr

Census Card No. 848, P. O. Bristow, Enrolled September 25, 1899

Roll No.	No.	NAME	Age	Sex	Blood	Rel.	NAME OF FATHER	Liv.	Cit.	NAME OF MOTHER	Liv.	Cit
2748	1	Hamilton, Peter	26	M	5/8		Alec Hamilton	D	Cr	Sallie Hamilton	L	Cr
2749	2	Hamilton, Rose	8	F	9-16	D	No. 1	L	Cr	Annie Wisener	L	Cr

Census Card No. 849, P. O. Fame; No. 1, Pierce, Enrolled September 25, 1899

Roll No.	No.	NAME	Age	Sex	Blood	Rel.	NAME OF FATHER	Liv.	Cit.	NAME OF MOTHER	Liv.	Cit
2750	1	Gray, Isaac	35	M	F		George Monk	D	Cr	Nancy Monk	D	Cr
2751	2	Gray, Susan	40	F	F	Wf	Lonie Fife	D	Cr	Unknown	D	Cr
2752	3	Reynolds, Auty	12	M	F	St-S	G. W. Reynolds	D	Cr	No. 2	L	Cr
2753	4	Reynolds, Ellis	11	M	F	St-S	G. W. Reynolds	D	Cr	No. 2	L	Cr
2734	5	Reynolds, Leona	10	F	F	St-D	G. W. Reynolds	D	Cr	No. 2	L	Cr

No. 2 died August 10, 1910

Census Card No. 850, P. O. Eufaula, Enrolled September 25, 1899

Roll No.	No.	NAME	Age	Sex	Blood	Rel.	NAME OF FATHER	Liv.	Cit.	NAME OF MOTHER	Liv.	Cit
2755	1	Post, Thomas	29	M	1/8		John Post	D	?	Adaline Young	L	?
2756	2	Post, John	4	M	1-16	S	No. 1	L	Cr	Laura Post	L	Non
2757	2	Post, Cornelius	2	M	1-16	S	No. 1	L	Cr	Laura Post	L	Non

Census Card No. 851, P. O. Eufaula, Enrolled September 26, 1899

Roll No.	No.	NAME	Age	Sex	Blood	Rel.	NAME OF FATHER	Liv.	Cit.	NAME OF MOTHER	Liv.	Cit
2758	1	Marshall, Tip	50	M	1/4		John Marshall	D	?	Arie Ann Marshall	D	?
2759	2	Marshall, Arthur	17	M	1/4	S	No. 1	L	Cr	Unknown	?	Non
2760	3	Marshall, Nettie	13	F	1/4	D	No. 1	L	Cr	Unknown	?	Non
2761	4	Marshall, Nora	11	F	1/4	D	No. 1	L	Cr	Unknown	?	Non

Census Card No. 852, P. O. Wagoner, Enrolled September 26, 1899

Roll No.	No.	NAME	Age	Sex	Blood	Rel.	NAME OF FATHER	Liv.	Cit.	NAME OF MOTHER	Liv.	Cit
2762	1	Harvison, Thomas C.	55	M	1/4		John Harvison	D	Cr	Muscogee Harvison	D	Cr

Census Card No. 853, P. O. Muskogee; Nos. 2 and 3, Okmulgee, Enrolled September 26, 1899; Nos. 2 and 3, April 8, 1901

Roll No.	No.	NAME	Age	Sex	Blood	Rel.	NAME OF FATHER	Liv.	Cit.	NAME OF MOTHER	Liv.	Cit
2763	1	Ward, Effie	37	F	1/2		Johnson, Hodge	L	Cr	Margaret Hodge	D	Non
2764	2	Hodge, Green	16	M	1/2	Bro	Johnson Hodge	L	Cr	Margaret Hodge	D	Non
2765	3	Ward, Charlie	17	M	1/4	S	Ed. Ward	L	Non	No. 1	L	Cr

Census Card No. 854, P. O. Bixby, Enrolled September 26, 1899

Roll No.	No.	NAME	Age	Sex	Blood	Rel.	NAME OF FATHER	Liv.	Cit.	NAME OF MOTHER	Liv.	Cit
2766	1	Berryhill, Oliver P.	51	M	1/8		A. J. Berryhill	D	Cr	Mariah Beckett	D	Non

No. 1 died April 20, 1910

Census Card No. 855, P. O. Stone Bluff, Enrolled September 26, 1899; No. 2, March 23, 1900

Roll No.	No.	NAME	Age	Sex	Blood	Rel.	NAME OF FATHER	Liv.	Cit.	NAME OF MOTHER	Liv.	Cit
2767	1	Brown, Joanna	22	F	F		James Kelly	D	Cr	Mary Kelly	L	Cr
2768	2	Brown, Willie	1	M	3/4	S	John Brown	L	Cr	No. 1	L	Cr

Census Card No. 856, P. O. Tulsa, Enrolled September 26, 1899

Roll No.	No.	NAME	Age	Sex	Blood	Rel.	NAME OF FATHER	Liv.	Cit.	NAME OF MOTHER	Liv.	Cit
2769	1	Davis, Samuel C.	27	M	1/2		W. T. Davis	D	Non	Arlie Davis	D	Cr
2770	2	Davis, Ethel Irene	7	F	1/4	D	No. 1	L	Cr	Carrie Ethel Davis	L	Non

Census Card No. 857, P. O. Eufaula, Enrolled September 26, 1899

Roll No.	No.	NAME	Age	Sex	Blood	Rel.	NAME OF FATHER	Liv.	Cit.	NAME OF MOTHER	Liv.	Cit
2771	1	McGee, John W.	21	M	1-64		R. C. McGee	L	Non	Elizabeth McGee	D	Cr
2772	2	McGee, Tamar Belle	18	F	1-64	S	R. C. McGee	L	Non	Elizabeth McGee	D	Cr

Census Card No. 858, P. O. Kellyville, Enrolled September 27, 1899; No. 2, March 23, 1901

Roll No.	No.	NAME	Age	Sex	Blood	Rel.	NAME OF FATHER	Liv.	Cit.	NAME OF MOTHER	Liv.	Cit
2773	1	Penaka	45	M	F		Chato Micco	D	Cr	Hiyeepuchee	D	Cr
2774	2	Muskogee	9	M	F	Sis	No. 1	L	Cr	Wity	L	Cr

No. 1 died March 1907

Census Card No. 859, P. O. Wagoner, Enrolled September 27, 1899

Roll No.	No.	NAME	Age	Sex	Blood	Rel.	NAME OF FATHER	Liv.	Cit.	NAME OF MOTHER	Liv.	Cit
2775	1	Williams, Sarah E.	17	F	1/4		Walter Posey	L	Cr	Johann Posey	D	Non
2776	2	Williams, Sadie May	1	F	1-16	D	John Williams	L	Non	No. 1	L	Cr

Census Card No. 860, Ft. Gibson; No. 1, Muskogee, Enrolled September 27, 1899; No. 4, April 17, 1901

Roll No.	No.	NAME	Age	Sex	Blood	Rel.	NAME OF FATHER	Liv.	Cit.	NAME OF MOTHER	Liv.	Cit
2777	1	Fox, Sarah	56	F	1/4		Earl Cordy	D	Cher	Charlotte Cordry	D	Cr
2778	2	Fox, Eliza	25	F	1/4		Trig Jim Fox	D	Cher	No. 1	L	Cr
2779	3	Miller, Jennie	26	F	1/2	D	Trig Jim Fox	D	Cher	No. 1	L	Cr
2780	4	Miller, Zela	3	F	1/4	Gr-D	Robert Miller	D	Cher	No. 3	L	Cr

N o. 2 died March 28, 1906

Roll No.	No.	NAME	Age	Sex	Blood	Rel.	NAME OF FATHER	Liv.	Cit.	NAME OF MOTHER	Liv.	Cit.
		Census Card No. 861, P. O. Checotah, Enrolled September 27, 1899										
2781	1	Bertholf, Amanda J.	43	F	1/4		James McLemore	D	?	Charlotte McLemore	D	?
2782	2	Bartholf, Alice K.	23	F	1/8	D	W. H. Bertholf	L	Non	No. 1	L	Cr
2783	3	Bertholf, Emma H.	21	F	1/8	D	W. H. Bertholf	L	Non	No. 1	L	Cr
2784	4	Bertholf, Myrtle M.	16	F	1/8	D	W. H. Bertholf	L	Non	No. 1	L	Cr
2785	5	Bertholf, Dewitt T.	9	M	1/8	S	W. H. Bertholf	L	Non	No. 1	L	Cr
2786	6	Bertholf, Bettie L.	6	F	1/8	D	W. H. Bertholf	L	Non	No. 1	L	Cr
2787	7	Bertholf, Rubie Cherokee	2	F	1/8	D	W. H. Bertholf	L	Non	No. 1	L	Cr
		No. 2 died June 20, 1914.										
		Census Card No. 862, P. O. Red Fork; No. 1, Tulsa, Enrolled Sept. 28, 1899; No. 3, Feb. 20, 1900										
2788	1	Jack, Alice	20	F	1/4		G. W. Yeager	D	Cr	Amanda Yeager	D	Non
2789	2	Yargee, Elizabeth	16	F	1/4	Sis	G. W. Yeager	D	Cr	Amanda Yeager	D	Non
2790	3	Jack, Alice Luvina	18da	F	1/8	D	John Jack	L	Non	No. 1	L	Cr
		Census Card No. 863, P. O. Wagoner, Enrolled September 28, 1899										
2791	1	Childers, N. B.	55	M	1/2		Wm. Childers	D	Cr	Maria Childers	D	Cr
2792	2	Childers, Susan K.	46	F	F	Wf	Coweta Micco	D	Cr	Lydia Micco	D	Cr
		Census Card No. 864, P. O. Wagoner, Enrolled September 28, 1899; No. 3, May 1, 1901										
2793	1	Perryman, Sam	22	M	F		Isaac Perryman	D	Cr	Annie Perryman	D	Cr
2794	2	Perryman, Mollie	26	F	F	Wf	Joseph Lynch	L	Cr	Mallie Lynch	D	Cr
2795	3	Perryman, Mamie	5mo	F	F	D	No. 1	L	Cr	No. 2	L	Cr
		No. 2 died December 7, 1907										
		Census Card No. 865, P. O. Eufaula, Enrolled September 29, 1899										
2796	1	Lewis, Lizzie	41	F	1/2		Samuel Fisher	D	Cr	Mary Fisher	D	Non
2797	2	Lewis, Ruth Oneita	1	F	1/4	D	Wm. Lewis	D	Non	No. 1	L	Cr
2798	3	Akans, Noah	14	M	1/4	S	James Akans	D	Non	No. 1	L	Cr
		No. 3 died August 1905										
		Census Card No. 866, P. O. Oktaha; No. 2, Tulsa; No. 4, Checotah; No. 7, Mellette, Enrolled September 30, 1899										
2799	1	Holt, Abbie	36	F	1/4		William Nero	D	Cr	Nancy Nero	L	Cr
2800	2	Woodard, Mollie	17	F	1/8	D	Charlie Woodward	L	Choc	No. 1	L	Cr
2801	3	Holt, Henry	13	M	1/8	S	Littleton Holt	L	Choc	No. 1	L	Cr
2802	4	Holt, Emanuel	11	M	1/8	S	Littleton Holt	L	Choc	No. 1	L	Cr
2803	5	Holt, Sarah Jane	9	F	1/8	D	Littleton Holt	L	Choc	No. 1	L	Cr
2804	6	Holt, Mattie	3	F	1/8	D	Littleton Holt	L	Choc	No. 1	L	Cr
2805	7	Crabtree, George	21	M	1/4	S	James Crabtree	D	Cr	No. 1	L	Cr
		No. 2 died November 8, 1907										
		Census Card No. 867, P. O. Checotah, Enrolled September 30, 1899										
2806	1	Thompson, Jackson	27	M	F		Marsh Thompson	L	Cr	Silby Thompson	L	Cr
		Census Card No. 868, P. O. Muskogee, Enrolled September 30, 1899										
2807	1	Crabtree, William F. Sr.	53	M	1-16		Wm. B. Crabtree	L	Non	Priscilla Crabtree	D	Cr
2808	2	Crabtree, Elizabeth	21	F	1-32	D	No. 1	L	Cr	Hattie Crabtree	L	Non
2809	3	Crabtree, Hattie H.	15	F	1-32	D	No. 1	L	Cr	Hattie Crabtree	L	Non
2810	4	Crabtree, William F. Jr.	12	M	1-32	S	No. 1	L	Cr	Hattie Crabtree	L	Non
2811	5	Crabtree, Sue Anna	10	F	1-32	D	No. 1	L	Cr	Hattie Crabtree	L	Non
		No. 1 died March 27, 1900. No. 2 died December 13, 1900.										
		Census Card No. 869, P. O. Sapulpa; R. F. D. No. 3, Enrolled October 3, 1899										
2812	1	Maloney, Annie C.	23	F	1/8		Geo. W. Turvin	D	Cr	Mary B. Turvin	L	Non
2813	2	Maloney, Ruby	2	F	1-16	D	Dave Maloney	L	Non	No. 1	L	Cr
		Census Card No. 870, P. O. Wetumka, Enrolled October 3, 1899										
2814	1	Gotts, Lucy R.	21	F	F		Tulwa Harjo	D	Cr	Tiah Harjo	D	Cr
2815	2	Gotts, Harry	2	M	1/2	S	Henry Gatts	L	Non	No. 1	L	Cr
		Census Card No. 871, P. O. Sapulpa, Enrolled October 3, 1899; No. 5, October 5, 1899										
2816	1	Anderson, William	40	M	3/4		George Anderson	D	Cr	Liza Anderson	D	Cr
2817	2	Anderson, Cilla	29	F	3/4	Wf	William Frank	D	Cr	Liza Frank	D	Cr
2818	3	Anderson, Walter	7	M	3/4	S	No. 1	L	Cr	No. 2	L	Cr
2819	4	Anderson, Andrew	3	M	3/4	S	No. 1	L	Cr	No. 2	L	Cr
2820	5	Thompson, Mary	16	F	3/4	Cou	Olmstead Thompson	D	Cr	Betsy Thompson	D	Cr
		No. 5 died January 1900										
		Census Card No. 872, P. O. Edna, Enrolled October 3, 1899										
2821	1	Bruner, Freeland	25	M	1/2		Richard R. Bruner	L	Cr	Harriet Bruner	L	Cr
2822	2	Bruner, Rhoda	23	F	1/2	Wf	Sam Gooden	D	Cr	Sina Kay	L	Cr
2823	3	Bruner, Mitchell	1	M	1/2	S	No. 1	L	Cr	No. 2	L	Cr
2824	4	Fisher, Sam	3	M	1/2	St-S	Joe Fisher	L	Cr	No. 2	L	Cr
		No. 4 reported dead										
		Census Card No. 873, P. O. Beggs, Enrolled October 3, 1899; Nos. 9 and 10, November 26, 1900										
2825	1	McIntosh, Ben	38	M	3/4		Del McIntosh	D	Cr	Winnie McIntosh	L	Cr
2826	2	McIntosh, Lizzie	38	F	3/4	Wf	Jacobs	D	Cr	Tena	D	Cr
2827	3	McIntosh, Mattie	10	F	3/4	D	No. 1	L	Cr	No. 2	L	Cr
2828	4	McIntosh, David H.	8	M	3/4	S	No. 1	L	Cr	No. 2	L	Cr
2829	5	McIntosh, John D.	6	M	3/4	S	No. 1	L	Cr	No. 2	L	Cr
2830	6	McIntosh, Sadie	4	F	3/4	D	No. 1	L	Cr	No. 2	L	Cr
2831	7	McIntosh, Grace	3	F	3/4	D	No. 1	L	Cr	No. 2	L	Cr
2832	8	McIntosh, William C.	1	M	3/4	S	No. 1	L	Cr	No. 2	L	Cr
2833	9	McIntosh, Bertha	12	F	3/4	D	No. 1	L	Cr	Malissa McIntosh	L	Non
2834	10	McIntosh, Ben R.	10	M	3/4	S	No. 1	L	Cr	No. 2	L	Non
		No. 1 reported dead										

Roll No.	No.	NAME	Age	Sex	Blood	Rel.	NAME OF FATHER	Liv.	Cit.	NAME OF MOTHER	Liv.	Cit.
		Census Card No. 874, P. O. Beggs, Enrolled October 3, 1899; No. 3, October 23, 1899										
2835	1	Hance, Jennie	21	F	3/4		Ben Jacobs	D	Cr	Bessie Jacobs	D	Cr
2836	2	Hance, Elzonie	3	F	3/8	D	John Hance	L	Non	No. 1	L	Cr
2837	3	Hance, William W.	6mo	M	3/8	S	John Hance	L	Non	No. 1	L	Cr
		No. 1 died June 8, 1903. No. 2 reported dead										
		Census Card No. 875, P. O. Welty, Enrolled October 3, 1899										
2838	1	Summers, Clinton P.	42	M	1/8		Thomas Summers	D	Non	N. C. Whetstone	L	Cr
2839	2	Summers, Thomas	19	M	1-16	S	No. 1	L	Cr	M. J. Summers	L	Non
2840	3	Summers, James	18	M	1-16	S	No. 1	L	Cr	M. J. Summers	L	Non
2841	4	Summers, Dee	14	M	1-16	S	No. 1	L	Cr	M. J. Summers	L	Non
2842	5	Summers, Ada	11	F	1-16	D	No. 1	L	Cr	M. J. Summers	L	Non
2843	6	Summers, Frank	9	M	1-16	S	No. 1	L	Cr	M. J. Summers	L	Cr
2844	7	Summers, Cordia	5	F	1-16	D	No. 1	L	Cr	M. J. Summers	L	Non
2845	8	Summers, Mary	3	F	1-16	D	No. 1	L	Cr	M. J. Summers	L	Non
2846	9	Summers, Pet	7mo	F	1-16	D	No. 1	L	Cr	M. J Summers	L	Non
		No. 4 died January 20, 1907										
		Census Card No. 876, P. O. Okmulgee, Enrolled October 3, 1899										
2847	1	Holleyman, Maggie G.	29	F	1/4		Johnson Hodge	D	Cr	Margaret Hodge	D	Non
2848	2	Holleyman, Delila	8	F	1/8	D	T. E. Holleyman	L	Non	No. 1	L	Cr
2849	3	Holleyman, Myrtle V.	6	F	1/8	D	T. E. Holleyman	L	Non	No. 1	L	Cr
2850	4	Holleyman, Herman O.	4	M	1/8	S	T. E. Holleyman	L	Non	No. 1	L	Cr
2851	5	Holleyman, Homer A.	2	M	1/8	S	T. E. Holleyman	L	Non	No. 1	L	Cr
		Census Card No. 877, P. O. Red Fork, Enrolled October 3, 1899										
2852	1	Vore, Lizzie	23	F	1/4		W. McIntosh	L	Non	Winnie McIntosh	L	Cr
2853	2	Vore, Fred	4	M	5/8	S	Charles Vore	D	Cr	No. 1	L	Cr
		Census Card No. 878, P. O. Eufaula, Enrolled October 3, 1899; No. 4, July 25, 1900										
2854	1	Price, Susan	33	F	F		Amos Fields	D	Cr	Lucy Fields	L	Cr
2855	2	Price, Lucy	5	F	1/2	D	James Price	L	Non	No. 1	L	Cr
2856	3	Price, James Jr.	3	M	1/2	S	James Price	L	Non	No. 1	L	Cr
2857	4	Price, Pleasant Porter	1mo	M	1/2	S	James Price	L	Non	No. 1	L	Cr
		Census Card No. 879, P. O. Okfuskee, Enrolled October 3, 1899; No. 4, March 23, 1901										
2858	1	Stoddard, William	27	M	F		Fushutche Mekko	D	Cr	Sadie	D	Cr
2859	2	Stoddard, Lousana	22	F	F	Wf	George Hicks	L	Cr	Elsie Hicks	L	Cr
2860	3	Stoddard, Mamie	3	F	F	D	No. 1	L	Cr	No. 2	L	Cr
2861	4	Stoddard, Jesse	1	M	F	S	No. 1	L	Cr	No. 2	L	Cr
		No. 4 died September 3, 1901										
		Census Card No. 880, P. O. Hanna, Enrolled October 4, 1899										
2862	1	Stratton, Louisa	33	F	F		Chepon Sulphur	D	Cr	Unknown	D	Cr
		Census Card No. 881, P. O. Eufaula, Enrolled October 4, 1899; No. 5. August 7, 1900										
2863	1	Sulphur, James	24	M	F		Chepon Sulphur	D	Cr	Kizzie Sulphur	L	Cr
2864	2	Sulphur, Kizzie	19	F	F	Wf	Pin Scott	D	Cr	Litka Scott	L	Cr
2865	3	Sulphur, Edmond	1	M	F	S	No. 1	L	Cr	No. 2	L	Cr
2866	4	Sulphur, Kizzie	60	F	F	Moth	Okkumo	D	Cr	Unknown	D	Cr
2867	5	Sulphur, George	4mo	M	F	S	No. 1	L	Cr	No. 2	L	Cr
		No. 2 died August 31, 1902. No. 3 died November 7, 1900. No. 5, died June 3, 1901										
		Census Card No. 882, P. O. Bixby, Enrolled October 4. 1899										
2868	1	Brown, James	22	M	F		Kichee Brown	D	Cr	Thathlapthlanna	D	Cr
2869	2	Brown, Conthlany	20	F	F	Wf	Behen	D	Cr	Judy Behen	L	Cr
		No. 1 died November 16 1901										
		Census Card No. 883, P. O. Okra, No. 4, Gonzales, Texas, Enrolled Oct. 4, 1899; No. 4, Oct. 7, 1899										
2870	1	Grayson, Ellen	27	F	1/4		Wiley Scott	L	Cr	Dicey Adams	L	Cr
2871	2	Grayson, Eli	6	M	1/8	S	Warrior Grayson	L	Non	No. 1	L	Cr
2872	3	Grayson, Cora	4	F	1/8	D	Warrior Grayson	L	Non	No. 1	L	Cr
2873	4	Grayson, Parthena	1	F	1/8	D	Warrior Grayson	L	Non	No. 1	L	Cr
		Census Card No. 884, P. O. Okmulgee, Enrolled October 4, 1899; No. 3, February 23, 1900										
2874	1	Monday, March	24	M	F		Monday	D	Cr	Millie Annie	D	Cr
2875	2	Monday, Jennetta	21	F	F	Wf	Nocha Jack	D	Cr	Fannie Jack	L	Cr
2876	3	Monday, Martin	18da	M	F	S	No. 1	L	Cr	No. 2	L	Cr
		Census Card No. 885, P. O. Checotah, Enrolled October 4, 1899										
2877	1	McIntosh, Freeland B.	47	M	1/8		D. M. McIntosh	D	Cr	Jane McIntosh	D	Non
2878	2	McIntosh, Eulala	13	F	1/8	D	No. 1.	L	Cr	Annie McIntosh	D	Cr
2879	3	McIntosh, Rufus C.	1	M	1-16	S	No. 1	L	Cr	Kate McIntosh	L	Non
		Census Card No. 886, P. O. Okmulgee, Enrolled October 4, 1899										
2880	1	Gray, Amos	40	M	F		John Steinmachee	D	Cr	Pingolichchee	D	Cr
2881	2	Gray, Louina	25	F	F	Wf	Lumsey	L	Sem	Toger Thlocco	L	Cr
		No. 1 died March 17, 1906										
		Census Card No. 887, P. O. Okmulgee, Enrolled October 4, 1899										
2882	1	Brockman, Mary E.	24	F	1/4		B. M. Crosby	L	Non	Mary A. Crosby	L	Cr
		No. 1 died February 4, 1914										
		Census Card No. 888, P. O. Keystone, Enrolled October 4, 1899; No. 4, October 9, 1899										
2883	1	Harry, John	29	M	1/2		Henry Harry	D	Cr	Jane Dasher	D	Cr
2884	2	Harry, Mary	24	F	1/2	Wf	John Bruner	D	Cr	Tilda Cat	L	Cr
2885	3	Bruner, Joe	5	M	1/4	St-S	Unknown	?	?	No. 2	L	Cr
2886	4	Harry, Willie	1	M	1/2	S	No. 1	L	Cr	No. 2	L	Cr
		No. 4 died February 22, 1910										

65

Roll No.	No.	NAME	Age	Sex	Blood	Rel.	NAME OF FATHER	Liv.	Cit.	NAME OF MOTHER	Liv.	Cit.
		Census Card No. 889, P. O. Okmulgee, Enrolled October 4, 1899										
2887	1	Town, James	49	M	F		Tolaf Harjo	D	Cr	Liney Harjo	D	Cr
2888	2	Town, Sallie	40	F	F	Wf	Siah Hardridge	D	Cr	Betsy	D	Cr
2889	3	Town, James Jr.	21	M	F	S	No. 1	L	Cr	Lebana	D	Cr
2890	4	Town, Emma	10	F	F	D	No. 1	L	Cr	Annie Bear	D	Cr
2891	5	Hannah	25	F	F	Niece	Woxoche	L	Cr	Salle	L	Cr
2892	6	Tiger, Amanda	10	F	F	Niece	Timmie Tiger	D	Cr	Millie Tiger	D	Cr
2893	7	Tiger, John	9	M	F	Neph	Timmie Tiger	D	Cr	Millie Tiger	D	Cr
		No. 4 died October 6, 1899. Nos. 1, 2, 3, reported dead. No. 5, died May 1899. No. 6 died April 1, 1901. No. 7 died March 8, 1900.										
		Census Card No. 890, P. O. Okmulgee, Enrolled October 5, 1899										
2894	1	Bell, James	28	M	¾		George Bell	D	Cr	Yarnah Bell	D	Cr
		No. 1 reported dead										
		Census Card No. 891, P. O. Kellyville, Enrolled October 5, 1899										
2895	1	Ralston, Electa J.	52	F	¼		Nathaniel Hodge	D	Non	Nancy Hodge	D	Cr
		Census Card No. 892, P. O. Mounds; No. 6, Tulsa, Enrolled October 5, 1899										
2896	1	Posey, Lewis H.	56	M	1-16		William Posey	D	Cr	Harriet Posey	D	Non
2897	2	Posey, Nancy	42	F	F	Wf	Parhos Harjo	L	Cr	Unknown	D	Cr
2898	3	Posey, John	20	M	½	S	No. 1	L	Cr	No. 2	L	Cr
2899	4	Posey, Mattie	18	F	½	D	No. 1	L	Cr	No. 2	L	Cr
2900	5	Posey, Conny	15	M	½	S	No. 1	L	Cr	No. 2	L	Cr
2901	6	Posey, Horace	10	M	½	S	No. 1	L	Cr	No. 2	L	Cr
2902	7	Posey, Darwin	8	M	½	S	No. 1	L	Cr	No. 2	L	Cr
2903	8	Posey, Ella	6	F	½	D	No. 1	L	Cr	No. 2	L	Cr
2904	9	Posey, Mendum	3	M	½	S	No. 1	L	Cr	No. 2	L	Cr
		No. 1 died January 17, 1900										
		Census Card No. 893, P. O. Okmulgee, Enrolled October 5, 1899										
2905	1	Hardridge, Taylor	38	M	F		Billy Hardridge	D	Cr	Miley Starr	L	Cr
		Census Card No. 894, P O. Wealaka, Enrolled October 5, 1899										
2906	1	McCoy, Mary	25	F	F		McCoy	D	Cr	Eliza Johnson	L	Cr
		No 1 died August 16, 1900										
		Census Card No. 895, P. O. Bristow, Enrolled October 5, 1899										
2907	1	Pinehill, Lasley	47	M	F		Wm Pinehill	D	Cr	Unknown	D	Cr
2908	2	Pinehill, Sally	36	F	F	Wf	Toladey	D	Cr	Susie Perryman	L	Cr
2909	3	Pinehill, Leo	4	M	F	S	No. 1	L	Cr	No. 2	L	Cr
		No. 1 died October 7, 1913										
		Census Card No. 896, P. O. Eufaula, Enrolled October 5, 1899										
2910	1	Posey, William	23	M	½		Lewis H. Posey	L	Cr	Nancy Posey	L	Cr
		Census Card No. 897, P. O. Okmulgee, Enrolled October 5, 1899										
2911	1	Williams, Eli	45	M	F		William Sell	D	Cr	Jennie Sugar	D	Cr
		Census Card No. 898, P. O. Tulsa, Enrolled October 5, 1899										
2912	1	Beef, Jim	23	M	F		John Beef	D	Cr	Fanny Beef	D	Cr
2913	2	Beef, Kizzie	19	F	F	Wf	Emarthla	L	Cr	Jane Loker	L	Cr
		No. 1 died March 15, 1905. No. 2 reported dead										
		Census Card No. 899, P O. Sapulpa, Enrolled October 5, 1899; Nos. 6, 7, May 31, 1900										
2914	1	Tahladege, Chepan	45	M	F		Tahledege	D	Cr	Sarah	D	Cr
2915	2	Tahladege, Mary	44	F	F	Wf	Unknown	D	Cr	Unknown	D	Cr
2916	3	Tahladege, Millie	11	F	F	D	No. 1	L	Cr	No. 2	L	Cr
2917	4	Tahladege, Wattie	6	M	F	S	No. 1	L	Cr	No. 2	L	Cr
2918	5	Tahladege, Cable	1	M	F	S	No. 1	L	Cr	No. 2	L	Cr
2919	6	Bruner, Dave	2	M	F	Gr-S	Eli Bruner	D	Cr	Sarah Bruner	D	Cr
2920	7	Bruner, Josie	11mo	M	F	Gr-S	Eli Bruner	D	Cr	Sarah Bruner	D	Cr
		No. 7 died July 2, 1900. No. 1 reported dead.										
		Census Card No. 900, P. O. Bristow, Enrolled October 5, 1899										
2921	1	Fish, Tom	22	M	F		Long Fish	D	Cr	Totothlike	D	Cr
		Census Card No. 901, P. O. Wetumka, Enrolled October 6, 1899										
2922	1	Winters, Nelson	46	M	½		Henry Winters	D	Non	Matilda Winters	D	Cr
2923	2	Winters, Ed	18	M	¼	S	No. 1	L	Cr	Ada Winters	L	Non
2924	3	Winters, Rosa	13	F	¼	D	No. 1	L	Cr	Ada Winters	L	Non
2925	4	Winters, Mary	6	F	¼	D	No. 1	L	Cr	Ada Winters	L	Non
2926	5	Winters, William	5	M	¼	S	No. 1	L	Cr	Ada Winters	L	Non
		No. 2 died July 28, 1911. No. 5 reported dead										
		Census Card No. 902, P. O. Bixby, Enrolled October 6, 1899										
2927	1	Simmons, Emma	36	F	¼		Alex Depriest	L	Non	Patience Depriest	L	Cr
2928	2	Simmons, Ella	11	F	⅜	D	Jeff Simmons	D	Cr	No. 1	L	Cr
2929	3	Simmons, Viola	9	F	⅜	D	Jeff Simmons	D	Cr	No. 1	L	Cr
		No. 1 died September 9, 1909										
		Census Card No. 903, P. O. Coweta, Enrolled May 14, 1900										
2930	1	Lovett, Austin	14	M	F		George Lovett	L	Cr	Sallie Lovett	D	Cr
		Census Card No. 904, P. O. Okmulgee, Enrolled May 22, 1901										
2931	1	Sugar, Joseph	2	M	F		James Sugar	L	Cr	Helen Sugar	L	Cr
		No. 1 died June 11, 1901										
		Census Card No. 905, P. O. Okmulgee, Enrolled October 6, 1899										
2932	1	Leader, John	45	M	F		Sahobiye	D	Cr	Nancy	D	Cr
2933	2	Leader, Sussie	45	F	F	Wf	Joe Derisaw	D	Cr	Lizzie	D	Cr
2934	3	Leader, Joshua	17	M	F	S	No. 1	L	Cr	Katie Phillips	D	Cr
2935	4	Leader, Eliza	11	F	F	D	No. 1	L	Cr	No. 2	L	Cr
2936	5	Leader, Sam	9	M	F	S	No. 1	L	Cr	No. 2	L	Cr
		No. 5 died April 11, 1913. Nos. 1, 4 reported dead. No. 3 died October 1907.										
		Census Card No. 906, P. O. Checotah, Enrolled October 6, 1899										
2937	1	Depriest, Patience	73	F	½		Sam Strickland	D	Cr	Jennie Strickland	D	Cr
		No. 1 reported dead										

Roll No.	No.	NAME	Age	Sex	Blood	Rel.	NAME OF FATHER	Liv.	Cit.	NAME OF MOTHER	Liv.	Cit.
	Census Card No. 907, P. O. Beggs, Enrolled October 6, 1899											
2938	1	Peters, Simon	23	M	F		Peters	D	Cr	Winey	D	Cr
	Census Card No. 908, P. O. Beggs; No. 3, Sapulpa, Enrolled October 6, 1899											
2939	1	Grayson, Annie	24	F	¾		Lynchie	L	Sem	Kizzie Bruner	D	Cr
2940	2	Grayson, Robert	8	M	⅜	S	George Grayson	L	Non	No. 1	L	Cr
2941	3	Grayson, Ben	6	M	⅜	S	George Grayson	L	Non	No. 1	L	Cr
	Census Card No. 909, P. O. Hoffman, Enrolled October 6, 1899											
2942	1	Wilson, Martha	22	F	F		James Butler	D	Cr	Dinah Butler	D	Cr
	Census Card No. 910 P. O. Tulsa; No. 3, Colorado Springs, Col.; Enrolled October 7, 1899											
2943	1	Perryman, Legus C.	61	M	F		Lewis Perryman	D	Cr	Ellen Perryman	D	Cr
2944	2	Perryman, Arparye	51	F	F	Wf	Miller	L	Cr	Sathanaka	D	Cr
2945	3	Perryman, Henry W.	23	M	F	S	No. 1	L	Cr	No. 2	L	Cr
2946	4	Perryman, Homer	6	M	F	Gr-S	Andrew Perryman	L	Cr	Kazzie Partridge	D	Cr
2947	5	Thurman, Silas	16	M	½	Neph	Wm. Thurman	L	Non	China Thurman	D	Cr
	Census Card No. 911, P. O. Okmulgee, Enrolled October 7, 1899											
2948	1	Brinton, Samuel	35	M	F		Thompson	D	Cr	Lizzie	D	Cr
2949	2	Brinton, Sussie	28	F	F	Wf	Keyulta Harrison	L	Cr	Adaline Harrison	D	Cr
2950	3	Brinton, Carrie	9	F	F	D	No. 1	L	Cr	No. 2	L	Cr
2951	4	Brinton, Samey	5	M	F	S	No. 1	L	Cr	No. 2	L	Cr
2952	5	Brinton, Edith	1	F	F	D	No. 1	L	Cr	No. 2	L	Cr
		No. 1 died 1904. No. 2 died 1907.										
	Census Card No. 912, P. O. Grayson, Enrolled October 7, 1899											
2953	1	Smith, James Ross	33	M	⅛		George W. Smith	L	Cr	Martha Smith	D	Non
	Census Card No. 913, P. O. Sapulpa, Okla.; No. 2, Neodosha, Mo., Enrolled October 7, 1899											
2954	1	Warner, Rosa L.	37	F	¼		John Yarger	D	Cr	Susan Yargee	D	Cr
2955	2	Carvy, Lewis	8	M	⅛	S	John Carvy	D	Non	No. 1	L	Cr
	Census Card No. 914, P. O. Wagoner, Enrolled October 7, 1899											
2956	1	Root, Jennie	5	F	¼		Thomas Root	D	Cr	Ida Hill	L	Non
2957	2	Root, Martha May	2	F	¼	Sis	Thomas Root	D	Cr	Ida Hill	L	Non
	Census Card No. 915, P. O. Jenks, Enrolled October 9, 1899; Nos. 2, 3, 4, 8, 9, 10, October 27, 1899											
2958	1	Brown, Samuel W.	56	M	½		Samuel Williams	D	Non	Polly Williams	D	Cr
2959	2	Brown, Jennie E.	40	F	¼	Wf	John Yargee	D	Cr	Susan Yargee	D	Cr
2960	3	Brown, Bessie	9	F	⅜	D	No. 1	L	Cr	No. 2	L	Cr
2961	4	Brown, Alice	4	F	⅜	D	No. 1	L	Cr	No. 2	L	Cr
2962	5	Brown, Susan	1	F	⅜	D	No. 1	L	Cr	No. 2	L	Cr
2963	6	Brown, Samuel W. Jr.	19	M	½	S	No. 1	L	Cr	Neosho Brown	D	Cr
2964	7	Brown, Neosho P.	16	F	½	D	No. 1	L	Cr	Neosho Brown	D	Cr
2965	8	Steele, Samuel Edward	9	M	½	Gr-S	Alex W. Steele	D	Cr	Rachel Steele	D	Cr
2966	9	Steele, Lena N.	4	F	½	Gr-D	Alex W. Steele	D	Cr	Rachel Steele	D	Cr
2967	10	Brown, Jennie	12	F	½	D	No. 1	L	Cr	No. 2	L	Cr
		No. 10 died July 7, 1899. No. 5 died December 1901. No. 5 reported dead										
	Census Card No. 916, P. O. Mounds, Enrolled October 9, 1899											
2968	1	Glenn, Ida E.	19	F	⅛		B. F. Berryhill	D	Cr	Zena Berryhill	D	Non
2969	2	Glenn, Mabel C.	3	F	1-16	D	Robert J. Glenn	L	Non	No. 1	L	Cr
2970	3	Glenn, Gracie	8mo	F	1-16	D	Robert J. Glenn	L	Non	No 1	L	Cr
2971	4	Berryhill, Roby B.	5	F	⅛	Sis	B. F. Berryhill	D	Cr	Alice Berryhill	D	Non
	Census Card No. 917, P. O. Sapulpa; No. 4, Haskell, Enrollled October 9, 1899											
2972	1	Fife, Soda	22	M	F		Benie Fife	D	Cr	Nellie Fife	D	Cr
2973	2	Fife, Molea	52	F	F	Wf	Timmy Fisher	D	Cr	Hepsey Fisher	D	Cr
2974	3	Fife, Amy	8	F	F	D	No. 1	L	Cr	Kiamitia Fife	D	Cr
2975	4	Fife, Bessie	6	F	F	D	No. 1	L	Cr	Kiamitia Fife	D	Cr
		No. 1 and 2 reported dead										
	Census Card No. 918, P. O. Welty, Enrolled October 9, 1899											
2976	1	Rhodes, Martha Ella	29	F	⅛		Anderson Whetstone	D	Non	N. C. Whetstone	L	Cr
2977	2	Rhodes, Leona Dee	11	F	1-16	D	Taylor Rhodes	L	Non	No. 1	L	Cr
2978	3	Rhodes, Annie May	7	F	1-16	D	Taylor Rhodes	L	Non	No. 1	L	Cr
2979	4	Rhodes, John P.	4	M	1-16	S	Taylor Rhodes	L	Non	No. 1	L	Cr
	Census Card No. 919, P. O. Bixby, Enrolled October 9, 1899											
2980	1	Techarna, Jackson	32	M	F		Techarna	D	Cr	Susie	D	Cr
2981	2	Techarna, Eliza	36	F	F	Wf	Ahbeunga	D	Cr	Koga Fanna	D	Cr
2982	3	Techarna, Lochar	11	F	F	D	No. 1	L	Cr	No. 2	L	Cr
2983	4	Techarna, Louisa	7	F	F	D	No. 1	L	Cr	No. 2	L	Cr
2984	5	Techarna, Malissa	3	F	F	D	No. 1	L	Cr	No. 2	L	Cr
2985	6	Carr, Willie	14	M	F	St-S	Siah Carr	D	Cr	No. 2	L	Cr
		No. 5 died March 1900										
	Census Card No. 920, P. O. Wealaka, Enrolled October 9, 1899											
2986	1	Mingo, Narhe	33	M	F		Mingo	D	Cr	Koseanna	D	Cr
	Census Card No. 921, P. O. Okfuskee, Enrolled October 9, 1899											
2987	1	Manwarring, Melita	29	F	¼		Edward Kellam	D	Cr	Melita Kellam	D	Non
2988	2	Manwarring, Silver	3	F	⅛	D	T. A. Manwarring	L	Non	No. 1	L	Cr
2989	3	Manwarring, Melita Grace	1	F	⅛	D	T. A. Manwarring	L	Non	No. 1	L	Cr
	Census Card No. 922, P. O. Sapulpa, Enrolled October 9, 1899											
2990	1	Bruner, Archie	45	M	½		Lewis Bruner	D	Cr	Nan Bruner	D	Cr
2991	2	Bruner, Mary	14	F	¾	D	No. 1	L	Cr	Cessie Bruner	D	Cr
2992	3	Bruner, Maggie	12	F	¾	D	No. 1	L	Cr	Rhoda Bruner	D	Cr
	Census Card No. 923, P. O. Sapulpa, Enrolled October 9, 1899											
2993	1	Bruner, Annie	40	F	F		Cosar Harjo	D	Cr	Lodie Harjo	D	Cr
2994	2	Partridge, Jemima	18	F	F	D	Noah Partridge	D	Cr	No. 1	L	Cr
		No. 2 died May 1908										

Roll No.	No.	NAME	Age	Sex	Blood	Rel.	NAME OF FATHER	Liv.	Cit.	NAME OF MOTHER	Liv.	Cit.
		Census Card No. 924, P. O. Okmulgee, Enrolled October 9, 1899										
2995	1	Myers, Betsey	24	F	½		Jefferson Berryhill	D	Cr	Peggy Berryhill	L	Cr
2996	2	Myers, Minnie L.	3	F	¼	D	William F. Myers	L	Non	No. 1	L	Cr
2997	3	Myers, Jefferson M.	9moM	¼	S		William F. Myers	L	Non	No. 1	L	Cr
		Census Card No. 925, P. O. Beggs, Enrolled October 9, 1899										
2998	1	Adams, Thomas Jr.	29	M	½		Thomas Adams	L	Cr	Mahaley Adams	L	Cr
		Census Card No. 926, P. O. Checotah, Enrolled October 9, 1899										
2999	1	McCaughan, L. Elizabeth	40	F	⅛		Ellis Bridges	D	Non	Elizabeth Bridges	D	Cr
3000	2	McCaughan, Thomas	13	M	1-16	S	John McCaughan	L	Non	No. 1	L	Cr
3001	3	McCaughan, Nellie	10	F	1-16	D	John McCaughan	L	Non	No. 1	L	Cr
3002	4	McCaughan, Ninon	1	F	1-16	D	John McCaughan	L	Non	No. 1	L	Cr
		Census Card No. 927, P. O. Okmulgee; No. 4, Cushing, Enrolled October 10, 1899; No. 6, March 27, 1901										
3003	1	Adams, Bettie	35	F	F		Thomas J. Adams	L	Cr	Mahala Adams	L	Cr
3004	2	Adams, Julia	12	F	F	D	Abraham Foster	L	Cr	No. 1	L	Cr
3005	3	Adams, Dicey	9	F	½	D	George Grayson	L	Cr	No. 1	L	Cr
3006	4	Adams, Ellen	9	F	½	D	George Grayson	L	Cr	No. 1	L	Cr
3007	5	Adams, Hattie	3	F	½	D	George Grayson	L	Cr	No. 1	L	Cr
3008	6	Grayson, Mahala	1	F	½	D	George Grayson	L	Cr	No. 1	L	Cr
		No. 6 died August 28, 1901. No. 4 died July 23, 1910										
		Census Card No. 928, P. O. Clearview, Enrolled October 10, 1899; No. 2, May 13, 1901										
3009	1	McCoy, Delphic	20	F	½		Jim Chief	L	Chic-F	Celia Chief	L	Cr
3010	2	McCoy, Lemuel	1	M	¼	S	Tecumseh McCoy	L	Choc-F	No. 1	L	Cr
		No. 2 died October 1898										
		Census Card No. 929, P. O. Checotah, Enrolled October 10, 1899										
3011	1	Campbell, Susan	19	F	1-16		David T. McCoy	D	Non	Lucy Nolen	L	Cr
3012	2	Campbell, William	2	M	1-32	S	Albert Campbell	L	Non	No. 1	L	Cr
3013	3	Campbell, Fannie	1	F	1-32	D	Albert Campbell	L	Non	No. 1	L	Cr
		Census Card No. 930, P. O. Eufaula, Enrolled October 10, 1899										
3014	1	McGee, Mary	40	F	¼		William Nero	L	Cr	Nancy Nero	L	Cr
3015	2	McGee, Walter	20	M	⅛	S	Richmond McGee	L	Choc-F	No. 1	L	Cr
3016	3	McGee, Nancy	18	F	⅛	D	Richmond McGee	L	Choc-F	No. 1	L	Cr
3017	4	McGee, Clarence	16	M	⅛	S	Richmond McGee	L	Choc-F	No. 1	L	Cr
3018	5	McGee, Sudie	13	F	⅛	D	Richmond McGee	L	Choc-F	No. 1	L	Cr
3019	6	McGee, Frank	10	M	⅛	S	Richmond McGee	L	Choc-F	No. 1	L	Cr
3020	7	McGee, Cornelia	7	F	⅛	D	Richmond McGee	L	Choc-F	No. 1	L	Cr
		Census Card No. 931, P. O. Gowan, Enrolled October 10, 1899										
3021	1	Gregory, Emma A.	31	F	⅛		E. A. Self	D	Cr	Martha A. Self	L	Non
3022	2	Gregory, Andie Lee	6	M	1-16	S	C. C. Gregory	L	Non	No. 1	L	Cr
		No. 1 died 1912										
		Census Card No. 932, P. O. Kellyville, Enrolled October 10, 1899; No. 5, January 20, 1900										
3023	1	Self, James A.	28	M	⅛		E. A. Self	D	Cr	Martha A. Self	L	Non
3024	2	Self, Henry A.	9	M	1-16	S	No. 1	L	Cr	Mollie Self	L	Non
3025	3	Self, Louvina L.	7	F	1-16	D	No. 1	L	Cr	Mollie Self	L	Non
3026	4	Self, Ethel Lee	3	F	1-16	D	No. 1	L	Cr	Mattie Self	L	Non
3027	5	Self, Bertha May	1	F	1-16	D	No. 1	L	Cr	Mattie Self	L	Non
		No. 3 died June 22, 1910										
		Census Card No. 933, P. O. Kellyville, Enrolled October 10, 1899										
3028	1	Livingston, Lillious	22	F	⅛		E. A. Self	D	Cr	Martha A. Self	L	Non
		Census Card No. 934, P. O. Kellyville, Enrolled October 10, 1899										
3029	1	Self, Lula T.	19	F	⅛		E. A. Self	D	Cr	Martha A. Self	L	Non
3030	2	Self, Blanche C.	17	F	⅛	Sis	E. A. Self	D	Cr	Martha A. Self	L	Non
3031	3	Self, Cordelia A.	14	F	⅛	Sis	E. A. Self	D	Cr	Martha A. Self	L	Non
		Census Card No. 935, P. O. Kellyville, Enrolled October 10, 1899										
3032	1	Self, John H.	26	M	⅛		E. A. Self	D	Cr	Martha A. Self	L	Non
3033	2	Self, Plezzie Lee	6moF	1-16	D		No. 1	L	Cr	Dolley Self	L	Non
		Census Card No. 936, P. O. Nuyaka, Enrolled October 10, 1899										
3034	1	Jordan, Emma	19	F	½		Hosa Castile	L	Mex	Lizzie Castile	D	Cr
3035	2	McIntosh, Sanubure	3	M	½	S	August McIntosh	L	?	No. 1	L	Cr
		No. 2 died November 14. 1903. No. 1 died May 8, 1914.										
		Census Card No. 937, P. O. Sapulpa; No. 1, Muskogee; No. 3, Mounds, Enrolled October 10, 1899; No. 5, May 17, 1900										
3036	1	Behen	45	M	F		Kasagotin	D	Cr	Abbeloka	D	Cr
3037	2	Behen, Micco	20	M	F	S	No. 1	L	Cr	July Behen	D	Cr
3038	3	Behen, Chetargee	18	F	F	D	No. 1	L	Cr	July Behen	D	Cr
3039	4	Behen, Walie	10	F	F	D	No. 1	L	Cr	July Behen	D	Cr
3040	5	Behen, Helay	28	F	F	D	No. 1	L	Cr	July Behen	D	Cr
		No. 3 died December 7. 1908. No. 1 died June 5, 1909. No. 5 reported dead.										
		Census Card No. 938, P. O. Okfuskee, Enrolled October 11, 1899										
3041	1	Larney, Jack	29	M	F		Parnosky	D	Cr	Togy Sugar	D	Cr
3042	2	Larney, Cilla	30	F	F	Wf	Holome	D	Cr	Hoye	L	Cr
		No. 1 reported dead										
		Census Card No. 939, P. O. Sapulpa, Enrolled October 11, 1899										
3043	1	Pickett, Johnson	38	M	F		Shahkey	D	Cr	Mary	D	Cr
3044	2	Pickett, Arlaquinny	50	F	F	Sis	Wahouto	D	Cr	Yahtahwe	D	Cr
		Census Card No. 940, P. O. Sapulpa, Enrolled October 11, 1899; No. 2, November 12, 1901										
3045	1	Jones, Kawee	18	M	F		Cahkokethlon	D	Cr	Canpethlela	D	Cr
3046	2	Cahkokethlon, Agie	8	F	F	Sis	Cahkokethlon	D	Cr	Canpethlela	D	Cr
		No. 2 died January 25, 1900										
		Census Card No. 941, P. O. Wetumka, Enrolled October 11, 1899										
3047	1	Smith, Allen	26	M	⅛		Geo. W Smith	L	Cr	Jemima Smith	L	Non

Roll No.	No.	NAME	Age	Sex	Blood	Rel.	NAME OF FATHER	Liv.	Cit.	NAME OF MOTHER	Liv.	Cit.
	Census Card No. 942, P. O. Fame, Enrolled October 11, 1899											
3048	1	Franklin, Lena	26	F	½		Henry Island	D	?	Susan Island	D	Cr
3049	2	Franklin, James E.	8	M	¼	S	William Franklin	L	Non	No. 1	L	Cr
3050	3	Franklin, Samuel B.	4	M	¼	S	William Franklin	L	Non	No. 1	L	Cr
3051	4	Franklin, Ethel May	1	F	⅛	D	William Franklin	L	Non	No. 1	L	Cr
	No. 1 died July 16, 1901. No. 4 died February 10, 1907.											
	Census Card No. 943, P. O. Okmulgee; No. 3, Checotah, Enrolled October 11, 1899; No. 7, March 5, 1900; No. 8, March 30, 1900											
3052	1	Doyle, Winrod	51	M	¼		Winchester, Doyle	L	Cr	Nancy Doyle	D	Non
3053	2	Doyle, Albert	19	M	⅛	S	No. 1	L	Cr	Fannie Doyle	D	Non
3054	3	Doyle, Arthur	19	M	⅛	S	No. 1	L	Cr	Fannie Doyle	D	Non
3055	4	Doyle, Burris	17	M	⅛	S	No. 1	L	Cr	Fannie Doyle	D	Non
3056	5	Doyle, William	8	M	⅛	S	No. 1	L	Cr	Lydia Doyle	L	Non
3057	6	Doyle, Roy	3	M	⅛	S	No. 1	L	Cr	Lydia Doyle	L	on
3058	7	Doyle, Myrtle	10da	F	⅛	D	No. 1	L	Cr	Lydia Doyle	L	Non
3059	8	Doyle, Lee	12	M	⅛	S	No. 1	L	Cr	Eliza Doyle	L	Non
	No. 6 died January 15, 1900											
	Census Card No. 944, P. O. Sapulpa, Enrolled October 11, 1899; No. 2, May 4, 1901											
3060	1	McKim, Robert A.	24	M	⅛		W. A. McKim	D	Non	Texanna Brunell	L	Cr
3061	2	McKim, Robert M.	5	M	1-16	S	No. 1	L	Cr	Hattie Davis	L	Non
	Census Card No. 945, P. O. Okmulgee, Enrolled October 11, 1899											
3062	1	Bell, Jasper	23	M	¾		George Bell	D	Cr	Yarnah Bell	D	Cr
	Census Card No. 946, P. O. Sapulpa, Enrolled October 11, 1899											
3063	1	Davis, Martin	33	M	F		Tom Davis	D	Cr	Hannah Davis	D	Cr
3064	2	Davis, Minnah	45	F	F	Wf	Crow	D	Cr	Unknown	D	Cr
3065	3	Davis, Joseph	8	M	F	S	No. 1	L	Cr	No. 2	L	Cr
3066	4	Cahwee, Ekalamey	13	M	F	Neph	Cahwee	D	Cr	Betsey Cahwee	D	Cr
3067	5	Riley, Alice	7	F	½	GrD	Henry Riley	L	Non	Nancy Riley	D	Cr
	No. 1 died April 26, 1900											
	Census Card No. 947, P. O. Lenna, Enrolled October 1 , 1899											
3068	1	Morrison, Hence	22	M	½		John Morrison	L	Cr	Louisa Morrison	L	Cr
3069	2	Morrison, Luke	1	M	½	S	No. 1	L	Cr	Nancy Morrison	L	Non
	Census Card No. 948, P. O. Wetumka, Enrolled October 11, 1899											
3070	1	Thomas, Mollie E.	42	F	⅛		George W. Turvin	D	Cr	Mary B. Turvin	L	Non
3071	2	Thomas, George W.	13	M	1-16	S	John Thomas	L	Non	No. 1	L	Cr
3072	3	Thomas, Mary Ellen	9	F	1-16	D	John Thomas	L	Non	No. 1	L	Cr
3073	4	Thomas, Douglass	4	M	1-16	S	John Thomas	L	Non	No. 1	L	Cr
	Census Card No. 949, P. O. Irene, Enrolled October 11, 1899											
3074	1	Pierce, Jacob	42	M	F		Okolabisha Harjo	D	Cr	Unknown	D	Cr
3075	2	Pierce, Sallie	42	F	F	Wf	Tommy Harjo	D	Cr	Unknown	D	Cr
3076	3	Pierce, Jennetta	11	F	F	D	No. 1	L	Cr	No. 2	L	Cr
3077	4	Pierce, Silla	8	F	F	D	No. 1	L	Cr	No. 2	L	Cr
	No. 3 reported dead											
	Census Card No. 950, P. O. Red Fork, Enrolled October 11, 1899											
3078	1	Burgess, Lee	25	M	½		Caesar Burgess	D	Cr	Elizabeth Jack	D	Cr
	No. 1 died June 30, 1900											
	Census Card No. 951, P. O. Stone Bluff, Enrolled October 12, 1899											
3079	1	Warlecy	40	M	F		Unknown	D	Cr	Tewahhohye	D	Cr
3080	2	Warlecy, Nancy	16	F	F	D	No. 1	L	Cr	Jennetta Warlecy	D	Cr
3081	3	Warlecy, James	10	M	F	S	No. 1	L	Cr	Jennetta Warlecy	D	Cr
	Census Card No. 952, P. O. Tulsa, Enrolled October 12, 1899											
3082	1	Clinton, Louise	43	F	¼		James Atkins	L	Non	Mary Jane Atkins	D	Cr
3083	2	Clinton, Vera	20	F	⅛	D	Charles Clinton	D	Non	No. 1	L	Cr
3084	3	Clinton, Paul	16	M	⅛	S	Charles Clinton	D	Non	No. 1	L	Cr
	Census Card No. 953, P. O. Tulsa, Enrolled October 12, 1899; No. 3, December 7, 1899											
3085	1	Clinton, Lee	22	M	⅛		Charles Clinton	D	Non	Louise Clinton	L	Cr
3086	2	Clinton, Walton S.	2	M	1-16	S	No. 1	L	Cr	Susie M. Clinton	L	Non
3087	3	Clinton, Celia	11da	F	1-16	D	No. 1	L	Cr	Susie M. Clinton	L	Non
	No 3 died February 2, 1904.											
	Census Card No. 954, P. O. Wetumka; No. 2, Yeager, Enrolled October 12, 1899											
3088	1	Riley, Micco	46	M	½		David Riley	D	Cr	Eliza Riley	D	Cr
3089	2	Riley, Annie E.	21	F	¼	D	No. 1	L	Cr	Mary Riley	L	Non
3090	3	Riley, Horace R.	14	M	¼	S	No. 1	L	Cr	Mary Riley	L	Non
3091	4	Riley, Mary Elizabeth	11	F	¼	D	No. 1	L	Cr	Mary Riley	L	Non
3092	5	Riley, Isaih	9	M	¼	S	No. 1	L	Cr	Mary Riley	L	Non
3093	6	Riley, Marzell	7	F	¼	D	No. 1	L	Cr	Mary Riley	L	Non
3094	7	Riley, Francis	5	M	¼	S	No. 1	L	Cr	Mary Riley	L	Non
	No. 6 died February 17, 1901											
	Census Card No. 955, P. O. Wetumks, Enrolled October 12, 1899											
3095	1	Adkins, Martha J.	23	F	¼		Micco Riley	L	Cr	Mary Riley	L	Non
3096	2	Adkins, Otheola	6	F	⅛	D	W. B. Adkins	L	Non	No. 1	L	Non
3097	3	Adkins, Louise	3	F	⅛	D	W. B. Adkins	L	Non	No. 1	L	Non
3098	4	Adkins, Ira	4mo	M	⅛	S	W. B. Adkins	L	Non	No. 1	L	Non
	No. 2 died October 21. 1900											
	Census Card No. 956, P. O. Wetumka, Enrolled October 12, 1899											
3099	1	Bennett, Lou Ellen	18	F	¼		Micco Riley	L	Cr	Mary Riley	L	Non
	Census Card No. 957, P. O. Sapulpa, Enrolled October 12, 1899											
3100	1	Tiger, Conzie	27	M	F		Chartla	D	Cr	Parthla	D	Cr
3101	2	Tiger, Fancy	20	F	F	Wf	Farconee	D	Cr	Arlaquianny	L	Cr
	Census Card No. 958, P. O. Sapulpa, Enrolled October 12, 1899											
3102	1	Tiger, Aney	47	M	F		Hekaconthla	D	Cr	Unka	D	Cr
3103	2	Tiger, Betsey	37	F	F	Wf	Unkah	D	Cr	Hekawahthlaney	L	Cr

Roll No.	No.	NAME	Age	Sex	Blood	Rel.	NAME OF FATHER	Liv.	Cit.	NAME OF MOTHER	Liv.	Cit.

Census Card No. 959, P. O. Grayson, Enrolled October 12, 1899; No. 4, April 19, 1901

3104	1	Smith, Thomas M.	27	M	¼		Jim Smith	D	?	Mary Smith	D	?
3105	2	Smith, Martin W.	2	M	⅛	S	No. 1	L	Cr	Adeline Smith	L	Non
3106	3	Smith, Samuel C.	9	M	¼	StS	Sam Smith	D	Cr	Adeline Smith	L	Non
3107	4	Smith, Phatimma	1	F	⅛	D	No. 1	L	Cr	Adeline Smith	L	Non

No. 2 died January 31, 1912

Census Card No. 960, P. O. Okmulgee, Enrolled October 12, 1899; No. 3, April 25, 1900

3108	1	Anderson, Susan	22	F	F		Unknown	D	Cr	Sallie Tiger	D	Cr
3109	2	Kelley, Edna	3	F	F	D	Newman Kelley	L	Cr	No. 1	L	Cr
3110	3	Bell, George	2mo	M	F	S	Jim Bell	L	Cr	No. 1	L	Cr

No. 1 died August 27, 1905

Census Card No. 961, P. O. Okmulgee; No. 3, Natura, Enrolled October 12, 1899

3111	1	Anderson, Austin	56	M	½		George Anderson	D	Cr	Nancy Anderson	D	Cr
3112	2	Anderson, Lucy	43	F	½	Wf	Taylor Dick	D	Cr	Julia Dick	D	Cr
3113	3	Anderson, Ruth	17	F	½	D	No. 1	L	Cr	No. 2	L	Cr

No. 1 died October 3, 1904. No. 2 died February 19, 1906.

Census Card No. 962, P. O. Eufaula; No. 2, Raiford, Enrolled October 13, 1899

3114	1	Wallace, Ella	23	F	¼		Unknown	?	?	Mary Grayson	D	?
3115	2	Wallace, Tula	3	F	⅛	D	Wm. A. Wallace	L	Non	No. 1	L	Cr
3116	3	Wallace, Albert	1mo	M	⅛	S	Wm. A. Wallace	L	Non	No. 1	L	Cr

Census Card No. 963, P. O. Okmulgee, Enrolled October 13, 1899

| 3117 | 1 | Harrison, Keltie | 52 | M | F | | Peter Harrison | D | Cr | Hepsey Harrison | D | Cr |

Census Card No. 964, P. O. Sapulpa; No. 2, Mannford; No. 3, Wekiwa, Enrolled October 13, 1899; Nos. 2 and 3, March 20, 1901

3118	1	Rogers, Chepon	37	M	F		Chepan Azulie	D	Cr	Louina	D	Cr
3119	2	Rogers, Johnnie	17	M	F	S	No. 1	L	Cr	Sarney Rogers	D	Cr
3120	3	Rogers, Robert	12	M	F	S	No. 1	L	Cr	Sarney Rogers	D	Cr

No. 1 died April 1, 1910

Census Card No. 965, P. O. Tuskegee, Enrolled October 13, 1899

| 3121 | 1 | Willis, Kogee | 33 | F | F | | Mark Sims | D | Cr | Eliza Sims | D | Cr |
| 3122 | 2 | Willis, Wesley | 13 | M | F | S | Daniel Willis | D | Cr | No. 1 | L | Cr |

No. 1 died May 7, 1902. No. 2 died 1908.

Census Card No. 966, P. O. Weleetka, Enrolled October 14, 1899

3123	1	Barnett, Elizabeth	55	F	½		Scipio Barnett	D	Cr	Annie Barnett	D	Cr
3124	2	Barnett, Scipio	26	M	¼	S	Dick Barnett	L	CrF	No. 1	L	Cr
3125	3	Barnett, Austin	24	M	¼	S	Dick Barnett	L	CrF	No. 1	L	Cr
3126	4	Barnett, Dock	20	M	¼	S	Dick Barnett	L	CrF	No. 1	L	Cr
3127	5	Barnett, Pollie	18	F	¼	D	Dick Barnett	L	CrF	No. 1	L	Cr
3128	6	Barnett, Sandy	16	M	¼	S	Dick Barnett	L	CrF	No. 1	L	Cr
3129	7	Barnett, Chillie	15	M	¼	S	Dick Barnett	L	CrF	No. 1	L	Cr
3130	8	Loney, Annie	31	F	¾	StD	Conger Looney	D	Cr	No. 1	L	Cr

Census Card No. 967, P. O. Tulsa, Enrolled October 13, 1899

3131	1	Tiger, Tecumseh	43	M	F		Nehathlocco	D	Cr	Lucy	D	Cr
3132	2	Tiger, Judy	38	F	F	Wf	Semeyardee	D	Cr	Mehale	D	Cr
3133	3	Gooden, John	17	M	F	StS	Charley Gooden	D	Cr	No. 2	L	Cr
3134	4	Gooden, Sagone	11	M	F	StS	Charley Gooden	D	Cr	No. 2	L	Cr

No. 1 died February 6, 1900

Census Card No. 968, P. O. Tulsa, Enrolled October 12, 1899

| 3135 | 1 | Fife, Robert | 21 | M | F | | Timmie Fife | L | Cr | Judy Tiger | L | Cr |

Census Card No. 969, P. O. Beggs, Enrolled October 14, 1899

3136	1	Tiger, John	36	M	F		Farney Tiger	D	Cr	Wisey Tiger	D	Cr
3137	2	Tiger, Winey	42	F	F	Wf	Joe Marshall	D	Cr	Polly	D	Cr
3138	3	Tiger, Jacob	17	M	F	S	No. 1	L	Cr	No. 2	L	Cr
3139	4	Tiger, Samuel	12	M	F	S	No. 1	L	Cr	No. 2	L	Cr
3140	5	Scott, Peggy	5	F	F	GrD	Alex Scott	L	Cr	Tochee Scott	D	Cr
3141	6	Miller, Nancy	5	F	F	Niece	Johnson Miller	L	Cr	Mary Lewis	L	Cr

No. 3 died April 1903. No. 1 reported dead. No. 2 reported dead. No. 4 reported dead. No. 5 reported dead.

Census Card No. 970, P. O. Sapulpa, Enrolled October 14, 1899

| 3142 | 1 | Bruner, Joseph | 27 | M | F | | John Bruner | D | Cr | Lucy Bruner | L | Cr |
| 3143 | 2 | Bruner, Lucy | 60 | F | F | Mo | Unknown | D | Cr | Unknown | D | Cr |

No. 2 died June 12, 1901

Census Card No. 971, P. O. Catoosa, Enrolled October 14, 1899

| 3144 | 1 | Haynes, Laslie | 35 | M | F | | Unknown | D | Cr | Chimka | D | Cr |

Census Card No. 972, P. O. Bristow, Enrolled October 16, 1899

| 3145 | 1 | Fair, Hannah | 18 | F | F | | John Davis | L | Cr | Mehaka Davis | D | Cr |

Census Card No. 973, P. O. Mounds, Enrolled October 16, 1899

| 3146 | 1 | Bittle, Jacob | 39 | M | ⅛ | | Jacob Bittle | D | Non | Mary M. Bittle | L | Cr |

Census Card No. 974, P. O. Wildcat, Enrolled October 16, 1899

| 3147 | 1 | Spaulding, Sophia | 45 | F | AW | | Isaac Riley | D | Non | Nancy Riley | D | Non |

Census Card No. 975, P. O. Henryetta, Enrolled October 16, 1899

3148	1	Brown, Rosannah	26	F	F		Yahola Fixico	D	Cr	Liza Fixico	D	Cr
3149	2	Nail, Cornelius	7	M	F	S	Adam Nail	D	Cr	No. 1	L	Cr
3150	3	Brown, Echaluste	5mo	M	F	S	Jimsey Brown	L	Sem	No. 1	L	Cr

Census Card No. 976, P. O. Haskell, Enrolled October 16, 1899

3151	1	Anderson, Solomon	30	M	½		David Anderson	L	Cr	Betsey Anderson	D	Cr
3152	2	Anderson, Emma	26	F	½	Wf	David Carr	D	Cr	Caroline Carr	D	Cr
3153	3	Anderson, Emmett A.	7	M	½	S	No. 1	L	Cr	No. 2	L	Cr
3154	4	Anderson, Beatrice	5	F	½	D	No. 1	L	Cr	No. 2	L	Cr
3155	5	Anderson, Sam Clarence	2	M	½	S	No. 1	L	Cr	No. 2	L	Cr
3156	6	Anderson, Earnest	5mo	M	½	S	No. 1	L	Cr	No. 2	L	Cr

Roll No.	No.	NAME	Age	Sex	Blood	Rel.	NAME OF FATHER	Liv.	Cit.	NAME OF MOTHER	Liv.	Cit.
		Census Card No. 977, P. O. Sapulpa; No. 2, Fisher, Enrolled October 16, 1899; No. 4, June 6, 1900										
3157	1	Island, George	26	M	F		John Island	D	Cr	Wisey Harjo	L	Cr
3158	2	Island, Callie	19	F	F	Wf	Amos Fisher	L	Cr	Aggie Fisher	L	Cr
3159	3	Island, Eliza	2	F	F	D	No. 1	L	Cr	No. 2	L	Cr
3160	4	Island, Jim	10moM	F	S		No. 1	L	Cr	No. 2	L	Cr
3161	5	Samuel, Abraham Pin	12	M	F		Ward Ben Samuel	L	Cr	Wisey Harjo	D	Cr
		No. 3 died August 20, 1906. No. 4 died 1907.										
		Census Card No. 978, P. O. Yeager, Enrolled October 16, 1899										
3162	1	Hallford, Emaline	26	F	⅛		Geo. W. Smith	L	Cr	Jemima Smith	D	Non
3163	2	Posey, Edith	7	F	1-16	D	Will Posey	L	Non	No. 1	L	Cr
3164	3	Hallford, Ross	4	M	1-16	S	M. A. Hallford	L	Non	No. 1	L	Cr
3165	4	Hallford, Annie Bell	2	F	1-16	D	M. A. Hallford	L	Non	No. 1	L	Cr
3166	5	Hallford, Anoma	1-16moF		D		M. A. Hallford	L	Non	No. 1	L	Cr
		No. 5 died May 11, 1899										
		Census Card No. 979, P. O. Mounds, Enrolled October 16, 1899										
3167	1	Cumsey, Lewis	23	M	F		Charley Cumsey	L	Cr	Marcey	D	Cr
3168	2	Cumsey, Emma	2	F	F	D	No. 1	L	Cr	Helay	D	Cr
		Census Card No. 980, P. O. Weleetka, Enrolled October 17, 1899; No. 5, May 10, 1901										
3169	1	Nelson, Amos	42	M	F		Smudayee	D	Cr	Nicey	D	Cr
3170	2	Nelson, Sallie	32	F	F	Wf	Oldman Rabbit	L	Cr	Lund	D	Cr
3171	3	Nelson, Mahala	14	F	F	StD	George Bighead	L	Cr	No. 2	L	Cr
3172	4	Nelson, Nora	4	F	F	D	No. 1	L	Cr	No. 2	L	Cr
3173	5	Nelson, John	2	M	F	S	No. 1	L	Cr	No. 2	L	Cr
		No. 5 died September 1899. No. 1 died June 5, 1912. No. 2 died December 25, 1905.										
		Census Card No. 981, P. O. Hoffman, Enrolled October 17, 1899										
3174	1	Kelley, Robert	45	M	½		Tecumseh Kelly	D	Cr	Lucinda Kelley	D	Cr
		Census Card No. 982, P. O. Okemah, Enrolled October 17, 1899										
3175	1	Foster, Lonie	21	F	½		John Berryhill	L	Cr	Melinda Knight	L	Cr
3176	2	Foster, William	3	M	¼	S	G. C. Foster	L	Non	No. 1	L	Cr
3177	3	Foster, Cora	1	F	¼	D	G. C. Foster	L	Non	No. 1	L	Cr
		No. 2 died November 25, 1914										
		Census Card No. 983, P. O. McDermott, Enrolled October 17, 1899										
3178	1	Hopwood, George W.	33	M	1-32		Leonard Hopwood	D	Cr	Mary E. Hopwood	D	Non
3179	2	Hopwwod, Mary L.	7moF		1-64	D	No. 1	L	Cr	Jennie Hopwood	L	Non
		No. 1 died April 14, 1903										
		Census Card No. 984, P. O. Okmulgee, Enrolled October 17, 1899										
3180	1	Derisaw, David	43	M	F		Joe Derisaw	D	Cr	Eliza Derisaw	D	Cr
3181	2	Derisaw, Sarah	1	F	F	D	No. 1	L	Cr	Maggie Derisaw	L	Cr
		No. 2 died March 11, 1900										
		Census Card No. 985, P. O. Morse, Enrolled October 18, 1899										
3182	1	Hopwwod, Kellem F.	27	M	1-16		Len Hopwood	D	Cr	Elizabeth Hopwood	D	Non
3183	2	Hopwood, John L.	3	M	1-32	S	No. 1	L	Cr	Mollie Hopwood	L	Non
3184	3	Hopwood, Edgar Denton	1	M	1-32	S	No. 1	L	Cr	Mollie Hopwood	L	Non
		Census Card No. 986, P. O. Okmulgee, Enrolled October 18, 1899										
3185	1	Bruner, Nathan	25	M	½		Daniel Bruner	L	Cr	Minnie Wilson	L	?
		Census Card No. 987, P. O. Cushing, Enrolled October 18, 1899										
3186	1	Miller, Charles H.	54	M	¼		Jacob Miller	L	Non	Sarah Fields	D	Non
3187	2	Miller, Ambrose	23	M	⅛	S	No. 1	L	Cr	Civilla Miller	D	Non
		Census Card No. 988, P. O. Yale, Enrolled October 18, 1899; No. 2, May 19, 1900										
3188	1	Walker, Izora E.	21	F	⅛		Chas. H. Miller	L	Cr	Civilla Miller	D	Non
3189	2	Way, Vida M.	3	F	1-16	D	Thos. Way	L	Non	No. 1	L	Cr
		Census Card No. 989, P. O. Red Fork, Enrolled October 18, 1899										
3190	1	Bruner, Rider F.	27	M	½		Lewis Bruner	D	Cr	Jane Bruner	D	A-W
3191	2	Bruner, Katie	5	F	¼	D	No. 1	L	Cr	Jane Bruner	L	Non
3192	3	Bruner, Amanda	3	F	¼	D	No. 1	L	Cr	Jane Bruner	L	Non
		Census Card No. 990, P. O. Checotah, Enrolled October 18, 1899; No. 6, April 30, 1900; No. 7, May 14, 1901										
3193	1	McIntosh, Kate	23	F	½		John Casey	L	Non	Julia Casey	L	Cr
3194	2	McIntosh, John	6	M	¼	S	Thos. McIntosh	L	Cher	No. 1	L	Cr
3195	3	McIntosh, Julia	5	F	¼	D	Thos. McIntosh	L	Cher	No. 1	L	Cr
3196	4	McIntosh, Bettie	3	F	¼	D	Thos. McIntosh	L	Cher	No. 1	L	Cr
3197	5	McIntosh, Jewel	1	F	¼	D	Thos. McIntosh	L	Cher	No. 1	L	Cr
3198	6	McIntosh, Roy	1moM		¼	S	Thos. McIntosh	L	Cher	No. 1	L	Cr
3199	7	McIntosh, Thomas	33	M	½	Hus	Wm. F. McIntosh	D	Cr	Bettie McIntosh	D	Cher
		No. 6 died May 1, 1901										
		Census Card No. 991, P. O. Coweta, Enrolled October 18, 1899										
3200	1	Vann, Watlie	18	M	F		Habey Vann	D	Cr	Mulcie Vann	D	Cr
		Census Card No. 992 P. O. Wetumka, Enrolled October 18, 1899										
3201	1	Dunzy, Jackson	33	M	½		Henry Dunzy	L	Non	Kogee Dunzy	D	Cr
3202	2	Dunzy, Lucinda	29	F	F	Wf	George Long	L	D	Tilda Long	D	Cr
3203	3	Dunzy, Louis	12	M	¾	S	No. 1	L	Cr	No. 2	L	Cr
3204	4	Dunzy, Dallas	9	F	¾	D	No. 1	L	Cr	No. 2	L	Cr
3205	5	Dunzy, Nathan	6	M	¾	S	No. 1	L	Cr	No. 2	L	Cr
3206	6	Dunzy, Joseph	2	M	¾	S	No. 1	L	Cr	No. 2	L	Cr
		Census Card No. 993 P O. Yeager, Enrolled October 18, 1899										
3207	1	Burt, Eliza	28	F	F		Lawa Smith	D	Cr	Louina Smith	D	Cr

Roll No.	No.	NAME	Age	Sex	Blood	Rel.	NAME OF FATHER	Liv.	Cit.	NAME OF MOTHER	Liv.	Cit.
		Census Card No. 994 P. O. Fame, Enrolled October 18 1899										
3208	1	Ireland, Susan	.50	F	½		Hotachee Herrod	D	?	Mary Herrod	D	?
3209	2	Ireland, Mildred	20	F	½	D	Henry Island	D	?	No. 1	L	Cr
3210	3	Ireland, Susan	16	F	½	D	Henry Island	D	?	No. I	L	Cr
3211	4	Ireland, John	15	M	½	S	Henry Island	D	?	No. 1	L	Cr
		No. 2 died October 14, 1904. No. 4 reported dead.										
		Census Card No. 995, P. O Clearfield; No. 6, Coweta, Enrolled Oct. 18, 1899; No. 5, Feb. 24, 1900										
3212	1	Simmer, John	36	M	F		Hillis Yahola	D	Cr	Martha	D	Cr
3213	2	Simmer, Lena	27	F	F	Wf	Timchehe	D	Cr	Matalukke	D	Cr
3214	3	Simmer, Hattie	5	F	F	D	No. 1	L	Cr	No. 2	L	Cr
3215	4	Simmer, Alex	3	M	F	S	No. 1	L	Cr	No. 2	L	Cr
3216	5	Simmer, Lucinda	2mo	F	F	D	No. 1	L	Cr	No. 2	L	Cr
3217	6	Fixico, John	12	M	F	Ward	Pahose Fixico	D	Cr	Kisse	L	Cr
		Census Card No. 996, P. O. Eufaula, Enrolled October 18, 1899										
3218	1	Ewing, Peter R.	37	M	F		Daniel Roberts	D	Cr	Lydia Roberts	D	Cr
3219	2	Ewing, Susan A.	29	F	¼	Wf	Wm. McCombs	L	Cr	Sallie McCombs	L	Cr
3220	3	Ewing, Arthur E.	7	M	⅝	S	No. 1	L	Cr	No. 2	L	Cr
3221	4	Ewing, Orie	3	F	⅝	D	No. 1	L	Cr	No. 2	L	Cr
		No. 3 died February 15, 1907										
		Census Card No. 997, P. O. Mounds Enrolled October 18, 1899										
3222	1	Missouri, Davis	19	M	F		Fox Missouri	D	Cr	Nellie Missouri	L	Cr
		No. 1 died December 13, 1904										
		Census Card No. 998, P. O. Okmulgee, Enrolled October 18, 1899										
3223	1	Roberts, George	51	M	F		Hosey,Chupka	D	Cr	Soheparke	D	Cr
		No. 1 reported dead.										
		Census Card No. 999, P. O. Kellyville, Enrolled October 18, 1899										
3224	1	Tiger, John	23	M	F		Marshe	D	Cr	Lucy	D	Cr
3225	2	Tiger, Millie	20	F	F	Wf	Coneah Bigpond	L	Cr	Ninnee	D	Cr
3226	3	Tiger, Casey	18	F	F	Sis	Marshe Tiger	D	Cr	Lucy	D	Cr
		No. 2 died October 16, 1906. No. 3 died April 12, 1912.										
		Census Card No. 1000, P. O. Sapulpa, Enrolled October 18, 1899										
3227	1	Harkawathlany	59	F	F		Ahkacofah	D	Cr	Unknown	D	Cr
3228	2	Robinson, Addie	19	F	F	GrD	Robinson	D	Cr	Lena	D	Cr
3229	3	Marshall, Charles	18	M	F	S	Labindabe	D	Choc	No. 1	L	Cr
		No. 2 reported dead. No. 3 died July 28, 1912.										
		Census Card No. 1001, P. O. Brush Hill, Enrolled October 18, 1899										
3230	1	Thompson, Simmer	45	M	F		Tecumseh	D	Cr	Bettie	D	Cr
3231	2	Thompson, Misey	40	F	F	Wf	Ensache Harjo	D	Cr	Louisa Harjo	D	Cr
3232	3	Thompson, Phoebe	12	F	F	D	No. 1	L	Cr	No. 2	L	Cr
		Census Card No. 1002, P. O. Coweta; No. 3, Broken Arrow, Enrolled Oct. 18, 1899; No. 5, May 21, 1901										
3233	1	Peters, Betsy	39	F	F		Unknown	D	Cr	Tilsey	D'	Cr
3234	2	Peters, Ellen	15	F	F	D	Sampson Peters	D	Cr	No. 1	L	Cr
3235	3	Peters, Ben	11	M	F	S	Sampson Peters	D	Cr	No. 1	L	Cr
3236	4	Peters, Kizzie	9	F	F	D	Sampson Peters	D	Cr	No. 1	L	Cr
3237	5	Peters, Cilla	2	F	F	D	Sampson Peters	D	Cr	No. 1	L	Cr
		No. 5 died October 7, 1899. No. 4 died July 10, 1910. No. 2 died July 2, 1903.										
		Census Card No. 1003, P. O. Nerotown, Enrolled October 18, 1899										
3238	1	Herrod, Sophia	60	F	F		Cheponaka	D	Cr	Simmahta	D	Cr ·
3239	2	Tiger, George	16	M	F	GrS	Thomas Tiger	D	Cr	Annie Tiger	D	Cr
3240	3	Tiger, Willie	14	M	F	GrS	Thomas Tiger	D	Cr	Annie Tiger	D	Cr
3241	4	Tiger, Lucy	7	F	F	GrD	Thomas Tiger	D	Cr	Annie Tiger	D	Cr
		No. 4 died February 15, 1903										
		Caensus Card No. 1004, P. O. Salem, Enrolled October 19, 1899										
3242	1	Hicks, George	65	M	F		Unknown	D	Cr	Unknown	D	Cr
3243	2	Hicks, Dicey	55	F	F	Wf	Unknown	D	Cr	Abwe	D	Cr
3244	3	Hicks, Bunny	13	M	F	S	No. 1	L	Cr	No. 2	L	Cr
		No. 1 died January 1904										
		Census Card No. 1005, P. O. Lenna, Enrolled October 19, 1899										
3245	1	Hicks, Henry	35	M	F		George Hicks	L	Cr	Dicey Hicks	L	Cr
3246	2	Hicks, Louana	30	F	F	Wf	Catche Emartha	D	Cr	Sinechetche	D	Cr
3247	3	Hicks, Joe	1½	M	F	S	No. 1	L	Cr	No. 2	L	Cr
		No. 2 died June 1903										
		Census Card No. 1006, P. O. Senora, Enrolled October 19, 1899										
3248	1	Harjo, Jackson	35	M	F		Harjo	D	Cr	Abwe	D	Cr
		No. 1 died December 27, 1910										
		Census Card No. 1007, P. O. Eufaula, Enrolled October 19, 1899; No. 5, February 7, 1900										
3249	1	Deere, Louis	29	M	¾		Echo Emarthla	D	Cr	Jennie Deere	D	Cr
3250	2	Deere, Jennie	27	F	¾	Wf	Lusta Williams	L	Cr	Sallie Williams	L	Cr
3251	3	Deere Thomas	14	M	¾	Bro	Echo Emarthla	L	Cr	Jennie Deere	D	Cr
3252	4	Deere, Albert	12	M	¾	Bro	Echo Emarthla	L	Cr	Jennie Deere	D	Cr
3253	5	Deere, Hannah	15	F	¾	Sis	Echo Emarthla	L	Cr	Jennie Deere	D	Cr
		No. 5 died September 1905										
		Census Card No. 1008, P. O. Kellyville, Enrolled October 19, 1899										
3254	1	Bigpond, Johnson	22	M	F		Goneh Bigpond	L	Cr	Ninnee	D	Cr
3255	2	Bigpond, Lucy	24	F	F	Wf	Taikany	L	Cr	Tahpanfah	L	Cr
3256	3	Stricken from roll.										
		Census Card No. 1009, P. O. Hitchita, Enrolled October 19, 1899; No. 3, March 27, 1901										
3257	1	Thompson, Haga	24	M	F		Marsh Thompson	L	Cr	Silby Thompson	L	Cr
3258	2	Thompson, Tauchie	20	F	F	Wf	George Hicks	L	Cr	Dicey Hicks	L	Cr
3259	3	Thompson, Newman	1	M	F	S	No. 1	L	Cr	No. 2	L	Cr
		Census Card No. 1010, P. O. Sapulpa, Enrolled October 19, 1899										
3260	1	Hagie, Ben	21	M	F		Coconnee	D	Cr	Pathla	D	Cr

Roll No.	No.	NAME	Age	Sex	Blood	Rel.	NAME OF FATHER	Liv.	Cit.	NAME OF MOTHER	Liv.	Cit.
Census Card No. 1011, P. O. Stidham, Enrolled October 19, 1899												
3261	1	Stover, Daniel	40	M	F		Sarhowithle	D	Cr	Letkah	D	Cr
3262	2	Stover, Lavina	30	F	F	Wf	Monkey	D	Cr	Unknown	D	Cr
3263	3	Stover, Lillie	10	F	F	D	No. 1	L	Cr	No. 2	L	Cr
3264	4	Stover, Eli	7	M	F	S	No. 1	L	Cr	No. 2	L	Cr
3265	5	Stover, Wasa	3	M	F	S	No. 1	L	Cr	No. 2	L	Cr
3266	6	Stover, Willie	1	M	F	S	No. 1	L	Cr	No. 2	L	Cr
Census Card No. 1012, P. O. Bixby, Enrolled October 19, 1899												
3267	1	Barnett, Joe	23	M	F		Timshonney	D	Cr	Lucinney	D	Cr
3268	2	Barnett, Wanney	18	F	F	Wf	Coconwee	L	Cr	Pothla	D	Cr
3269	3	Barnett, Annie	2wk	F	F	D	No. 1	L	Cr	No. 2	L	Cr
		No. 3 died November 14, 1904										
Census Card No. 1013, P. O. Wildcat, Enrolled October 19, 1899												
3270	1	Smith, Martha	52	F	3/4		Peter Harrison	D	Cr	Hannah Harrison	D	Cr
3271	2	Sneed, Frank	17	M	3/8	S	Charley Sneed	D	Non	No. 1	L	Cr
		No. 1 died October 12, 1901										
Census Card No. 1014, P. O. Kellyville; No. 3, Sapulpa, Enrolled Oct. 19, 1899; No. 5, Feb. 7, 1900												
3272	1	Yellowhead, Folsom	34	M	F		Unknown	D	Cr	Unknown	D	Cr
3273	2	Yellowhead, Tahcowee	29	F	F	Wf	Chotlar	D	Cr	Cotesa	L	Cr
3274	3	Yellowhead, Lucinda	6	F	F	D	No. 1	L	Cr	No. 2	L	Cr
3275	4	Yellowhead, Kelley	3	M	F	S	No. 1	L	Cr	No. 2	L	Cr
3276	5	Yellowhead, Jonah	1mo	M	F	S	No. 1	L	Cr	No. 2	L	Cr
		No. 5 died January 23, 1904										
Census Card No. 1015, P. O. Pierce; Nos. 2 and 3, Lenna, Enrolled October 19, 1899												
3277	1	Thompson, March	54	M	F		Manuel Thompson	D	Cr	Nannie Thompson	D	Cr
3278	2	Thompson, Silby	52	F	F	Wf	Nocus Harjo	L	Cr	Unknown	D	Cr
3279	3	Thompson, Manuel	20	M	F	S	No. 1	L	Cr	No. 2	L	Cr
3280	4	Thompson, George	18	M	F	S	No. 1	L	Cr	No. 2	L	Cr
		No. 2 died September 1908. No. 3 died 1905.										
Census Card No. 1016, P. O. Sapulpa, Enrolled October 19, 1899; No. 4, March 26, 1901												
3281	1	Sapulpa, William A.	38	M	F		Sapulpa	D	Cr	Mary	L	Cr
3282	2	Sapulpa, Harrison	10	M	F	S	No. 1	L	Cr	Elizabeth Harrison	L	Cr
3283	3	Sapulpa, George A.	1	M	F	S.	No. 1	L	Cr	Phoebe Sapulpa	D	Cr
3284	4	Sapulpa, Phoebe	27	F	F	Wf	J. M. Perryman	D	Cr	Eliza Perryman	D	Cr
		No. 4 died May 23, 1899										
Census Card No. 1017, P. O. Coweta, Enrolled October 19, 1899												
3285	1	Sarty, Rollie	24	M	F		Sarty	D	Cr	Dena Sarty	D	Cr
Census Card No. 1018, P. O. Dustin, Enrolled October 19, 1899												
3286	1	Gamble, Willie. S.	18	F	1/4		Wm. Morey	L	Non	Calley D. Morey	L	Cr
3287	2	Gamble, Robert Lee	1	M	1/8	S	Howard Lee Gamble	L	Non	No. 1	L	Cr
Census Card No. 1019, P. O. Okmulgee, Enrolled October 19, 1899												
3288	1	Meyers, Martha	24	F	1/2		Jonathan Barkinson	D	Non	Jennie Parkinson	D	Cr
3289	2	Meyers, Mabel	5	F	1/4	D	Charles Meyers	L	Non	No. 1	L	Cr
3290	3	Meyers, Joseph	3	M	1/4	S	Charles Meyers	L	Non	No. 1	L	Cr
Census Card No. 1020, P. O. Checotah, Enrolled October 20, 1899												
3291	1	Nolen, Lucy	38	F	1/8		Ellison Bridges	D	Non	Elizabeth Bridges	D	Cr
3292	2	Nolen, Jesse	10	M	1-16	S	Lee Nolen	D	Non	No. 1	L	Cr
3293	3	Nolen, Samuel	5	M	1-16	S	Lee Nolen	D	Non	No. 1	L	Cr
3294	4	Nolen, William	5	M	1-16	S	Lee Nolen	D	Non	No. 1	L	Cr
3295	5	Nolen, Lee	2	M	1-16	S	Lee Nolen	D	Non	No. 1	L	Cr
3296	6	McCoy, Robert	17	M	1-16	S	Joe McCoy	D	Non	No. 1	L	Cr
Census Card No. 1021, P. O. Beggs, Enrolled October 20, 1899												
3297	1	Foster, Mary E.	23	F	1/8		Wm. Morey	L	Non	Calley D. Morey	L	Cr
3298	2	Foster, Edna Earle	1	M	1-16	S	Geo. W. Foster	L	Non	No. 1	L	Cr
Census Card No. 1022, P. O. Okmulgee, Enrolled October 20, 1899												
3299	1	McIntosh, Martha	24	F	3/8		Charley Sneed	D	Non	Martha Smith	L	Cr
Census Card No. 1023, P. O. Lenna, Enrolled October 20, 1899												
3300	1	Derrisaw, Polly	65	F	F		Charley Marshall	D	Cr	Lizzie Marshall	D	Cr
3301	2	Derrisaw, Sissy	35	F	F	D	Chepon Derisaw	D	Cr	No. 1	L	Cr
3302	3	Derrisaw, Millie	20	F	F	D	Chepon Derisaw	D	Cr	No. 1	L	Cr
		No. 3 died August 15, 1903. No. 1 died June 1904.										
Census Card No. 1024, P. O. Okmulgee, Enrolled October 20, 1899												
3303	1	Harjo, Aharlok	52	M	F		Chogottey	D	Cr	Wigget	D	Cr
3304	2	Harjo, Jockey	12	M	F	S	No. 1	L	Cr	Jannetta Harjo	L	Cr
		No. 1 reported dead										
Census Card No. 1025, P. O. Beggs, Enrolled October 20, 1899												
3305	1	Adams, Hepsey	31	F	F		Thomas J. Adams	L	Cr	Mehala Adams	L	Cr
3306	2	Adams, Annie	13	F	1/2	D	David Lee	D	Non	No. 1	L	Cr
3307	3	Adams, Daniel	11	M	1/2	S	David Lee	D	Non	No. 1	L	Cr
3308	4	Adams, Aggie	9	F	1/2	D	David Lee	D	Non	No. 1	L	Cr
3309	5	Adams, Emma	6	F	1/2	D	David Lee	D	Non	No. 1	L	Cr
		No. 4 reported dead										
Census Card No. 1026, P. O. Stidham, Enrolled October 20, 1899; No. 6, May 22, 1901												
3310	1	Estes, Kizzie	37	F	1/4		Sam Hawkins	D	Cr	Lucinda Hawkins	L	Non
3311	2	Estes, Ollie Caroline	11	F	1/8	D	Osier Estes	L	Non	No. 1	L	Cr
3312	3	Estes, Joseph Elmer	8	M	1/8	S	Osier Estes	L	Non	No. 1	L	Cr
3313	4	Estes, Julius Benny	4	M	1/8	S	Osier Estes	L	Non	No. 1	L	Cr
3314	5	Estes, William D.	2	M	1/8	S	Osier Estes	L	Non	No. 1	L	Cr
3315	6	Estes, Clarence Davis	1	M	1/8	S	Osier Estes	L	Non	No. 1	L	Cr
		No. 3 died April 6, 1904. No. 4 died March 12, 1902. No. 6 died March 2, 1905.										
Census Card No. 1027, P. O. Tulsa, Enrolled October 20, 1899												
3316	1	Sevier, Martha	62	F	F		Jim Sevier	D	Cr	Aggie Sevier	D	Cr

Roll No.	No.	NAME	Age	Sex	Blood	Rel.	NAME OF FATHER	Liv.	Cit.	NAME OF MOTHER	Liv.	Cit.
		Census Card No. 1028, P. O. Stidham, Enrolled October 20, 1899; No. 5, May 22, 1901										
3317	1	Rumsey, Louisa	27	F	¾		Samuel Hawkins	D	Cr	Cynthia Hawkins	L	Cr
3318	2	Rumsey, Mitchell	6	M	⅜	S	Elisha P. Rumsey	L	Non	No. 1	L	Cr
3319	3	Rumsey, Jennie	4	F	⅜	D	Elisha P. Rumsey	L	Non	No. 1	L	Cr
3320	4	Rumsey, Napoleon	2	M	⅜	S	Elisha P. Rumsey	L	Non	No. 1	L	Cr
3321	5	Rumsey, Pink	1	M	⅜	S	Elisha P. Rumsey	L	Non	No. 1	L	Cr
		No. 1 died December 13, 1902										
		Census Card No. 1029, P. O. Newby; No. 1, Sapulpa, Enrolled October 21, 1899										
3322	1	Mayes, Martha	23	F	F		Monte Beaver	D	Cr	Jennie Beaver	L	Cr
3323	2	Mayes, Thomas	1	M	½	S	W. A. Mayes	L	Non	No. 1	L	Cr
		Census Card No. 1030, P. O. Sapulpa, Enrolled October 21, 1899; Nos. 2, 3, 4, October 25, 1899										
3324	1	Stevens, Idella M.	25	F	⅛		Harvis Berryhill	D	Cr	Huelda Berryhill	L	Non
3325	2	Stevens, Myrtle M.	7	F	1-16	D	Cicero Stevens	L	Non	No. 1	L	Cr
3326	3	Stevens, Stella I.	5	F	1-16	D	Cicero Stevens	L	Non	No. 1	L	Cr
3327	4	Stevens, Pearl V.	1	F	1-16	D	Cicero Stevens	L	Non	No. 1	L	Cr
		Census Card No. 1031, P. O. Tuskegee, Enrolled October 21, 1899										
3328	1	Taylor, Frank	42	M	⅛		Ab Taylor	D	Non	Peggy Taylor	D	Cr
		Census Card No. 1032, P. O. Mounds, Enrolled October 1899										
3329	1	Berryhill, Thomas J.	23	M	⅛		Harris Berryhill	D	Cr	Hulda Berryhill	L	Non
		Census Card No. 1033, P. O. Okmulgee, Enrolled October 23, 1899										
3330	1	Manuel, Lucy	25	F	¼		Charles Sneed	D	Non	Martha Sneed	L	Cr
		Census Card No. 1034, P. O. Bristow, Enrolled October 23, 1899										
3331	1	Harry, Edmond	55	M	½		Harry Harry	D	Cr	Caroline Harry	D	Cr
3332	2	Harry, Sartarpeka	42	F	F	Wf	Jack	L	Cr	Lizzie Jack	D	Cr
3333	3	Harry, Ella	14	F	¾	D	No. 1	L	Cr	No. 2	L	Cr
3334	4	Harry, Shawnee	9	M	¾	S	No. 1	L	Cr	No. 2	L	Cr
3335	5	Harry, Willie	6	M	¾	S	No. 1	L	Cr	No. 2	L	Cr
		No. 4 died July 2, 1903										
		Census Card No. 1035, P. O. Edna; No. 4, Kellyville, Enrolled October 23, 1899										
3336	1	Kay Thomas	46	M	F		Chak Charty	D	Cr	Unknown	D	Cr
3337	2	Kay, Sina	40	F	¼	Wf	Harry	D	Cr	Caroline Harry	D	Cr
3338	3	Kay, John	17	M	⅝	S	No. 1	L	Cr	No. 2	L	Cr
3339	4	Kay, Betsy	15	F	⅝	D	No. 1	L	Cr	No. 2	L	Cr
3340	5	Kay, James	10	M	⅝	S	No. 1	L	Cr	No. 2	L	Cr
3341	6	Kay, Eli	8	M	⅝	S	No. 1	L	Cr	No. 2	L	Cr
3342	7	Kay, Willie	6	M	⅝	S	No. 1	L	Cr	No. 2	L	Cr
3343	8	Kay, Chisso	4	M	⅝	S	No. 1	L	Cr	No. 2	L	Cr
3344	9	Kay, Lucy	1	F	⅝	D	No. 1	L	Cr	No. 2	L	Cr
3345	10	Gooden, Henderson	19	M	½	StS	Sam Gooden	D	Cr	No. 2	L	Cr
		No. 1 died December 12, 1910. No. 2 died March 6, 1912. No. 10 died December 7, 1914.										
		Census Card No. 1036, P. O. Stidham, Enrolled October 23, 1899; No. 5, May 22, 1901										
3346	1	Rumsey, Della	24	F	¾		Samuel Hawkins	D	Cr	Cynthia Hawkins	L	Cr
3347	2	Rumsey, Sam J.	6	M	⅜	S	Frank M. Bumsey	L	Non	No. 1	L	Cr
3348	3	Rumsey, Alonzo	3	M	⅜	S	Frank M. Rumsey	L	Non	No. 1	L	Cr
3349	4	Rumsey, Edmond	1	M	⅜	S	Frank M. Rumsey	L	Non	No. 1	L	Cr
3350	5	Rumsey, Daniel	1	M	⅜	S	Frank M. Rumsey	L	Non	No. 1	L	Cr
		No. 1 died 1901										
		Census Card No. 1037, P. O. Wetumka; No. 3, Hanna, Enrolled October 23, 1899										
3351	1	Coachman, Peter	55	M	F		Watt Coachman	L	Cr	Lizzie Coachman	D	Cr
3352	2	Coachman, Nancy	45	F	F	Wf	Tulsa Yahola	D	Cr	Unknown	D	Cr
3353	3	Scott, Bennie	14	M	F	Neph	Pigeon Scott	L	Cr	Wisey Scott	D	Cr
3354	4	Chupko, Sarkarye	10	M	F	Neph	Micco Chupco	L	Cr	Katy Chupco	L	Cr
		No. 1 died March 26, 1900										
		Census Car No. 1038, P. O. Eufaula, Enrolled October 23, 1899										
3355	1	Boone, Thomas	65	M	⅛		Dock Boone	D	Non	Millie Boone	D	Cr
3356	2	Boone, Imy	22	F	¼	S	No. 1	L	Cr	Cilla Brown	D	Non
3357	3	Boone, Newman	19	M	¼	S	No. 1	L	Cr	Cilla Brown	D	Non
3358	4	Boone, Josephine	17	F	¼	D	No. 1	L	Cr	Cilla Brown	D	Non
3359	5	Boone, Daniel	10	M	¼	S	No. 1	L	Cr	Cilla Brown	D	Non
		Census Card No. 1039, P. O. Okmulgee, Enrolled October 23, 1899										
3360	1	Smith, Maria E.	45	F	¼		Michael McCann	D	Non	Elizabeth McCann	D	Cr
		Census Card No. 1040, P. O. Sapulpa, Enrolled October 23, 1899										
3361	1	Butler, Mollie	37	F	½		Henderson Butler	D	Cr	Bessie Harry	D	Cr
3362	2	Jacobs, Della	17	F	½	D	Eli Jacobs	D	Cr	No. 1	L	Cr
		No. 2 died March 16, 1905. No. 1 died May 16 1914.										
		Census Card No 1041, P. O. Edna, Enrolled October 23, 1899										
3363	1	Harjo, Woxey	57	M	F		Fus Harjo	D	Sem	Muscogee	D	Cr
3364	2	Harjo, Hepsey	47	F	F	Wf	Wekus Harjo	D	Cr	Nitketa	D	Cr
3365	3	Harjo, Peter	20	M	F	S	No. 1	L	Cr	No. 2	L	Cr
3366	4	Harjo, Rosanna	17	F	F	D	No. 1	L	Cr	No. 2	L	Cr
3367	5	Harjo, Nathan	13	M	F	S	No. 1	L	Cr	No. 2	L	Cr
3368	6	Harjo, Obie	11	M	F	S	No. 1	L	Cr	No. 2	L	Cr
3369	7	Harjo, Joe	8	M	F	S	No. 1	L	Cr	No. 2	L	Cr
3370	8	Harjo, Louvina	6	F	F	D	No. 1	L	Cr	No. 2	L	Cr
		No. 1 died December 1901. No. 7 died May 21, 1909. No. 5 died December 5, 1914. Nos. 3 and 6 reported dead.										
		Census Card No. 1042, P. O. Okfuskee; No. 2, Beggs, Enrolled October 23, 1899										
3371	1	Bighead, Sampsey	30	M	F		Gambler	D	Cr	Unknown	D	Cr
3372	2	Bighead, Salina	20	F	F	Wf	Fulsome	L	Cr	Nagee	L	Cr
3373	3	Bighead, John	6mo	M	F	S	No. 1	L	Cr	No. 2	L	Cr
		No. 1 died December 28, 1902. No. 2 died January 19, 1906. No. 3 died February 4, 1901.										

Roll No.	No.	NAME	Age	Sex	Blood	Rel.	NAME OF FATHER	Liv.	Cit.	NAME OF MOTHER	Liv.	Cit.
		Census Card No. 1043, P. O. Bearden, Enrolled Nos. 1 and 2, October 24, 1899; No. 3, May 24 1901; No. 4, March 26, 1901.										
3374	1	Simon, Joe	23	M	¼		Caesa Simon	L	Sem	Charity Simon	D	Cr
3375	2	Simon, Frank	2	M	⅛	S	No. 1	L	Cr	Emma Simon	L	Non
3376	3	Simon, Rater	1	M	⅛	S	No. 1	L	Cr	Emma Simon	L	Non
3377	4	Simon, Simon	21	M	¼	Bro	Caesar Simon	L	Sem	Charity Simon	D	Cr
		Census Card No. 1044, P. O. Broken Arrow, Enrolled October 24, 1899										
3378	1	Hodge, David M.	58	M	¼		Nathaniel Hodge	D	Non	Nancy Hodge	D	Cr
3379	2	Hodge, Susan	53	F	½	Wf	J. Yeager (Yargee)	L	Cr	Susan Yarger	D	Cr
		Census Card No. 1045, P. O. Wetumka, Enrolled October 24, 1899										
3380	1	Chisholm, George	60	M	AMex		Unknown	?	?	Unknown	?	?
3381	2	Chisholm, Lucy	33	F	F	Wf	Haney Scott	D	Cr	Tewahke	D	Cr
3382	3	Yahola, Sallie	19	F	F	½S-2	Thos. Yahola	L	Cr	Mitiague	D	Cr
		No. 2 died March 1907										
		Census Card No. 1046, P. O. Beggs, Enrolled October 24, 1899										
3383	1	Lunsford, John C.	36	M	¼		Lunsford	L	Non	Winnie McIntosh	L	Cr
3384	2	Lunsford, Martha	27	F	½	Wf	William Gooden	D	Cr	Louisa Gooden	D	Cr
3385	3	Lunsford, Thomas	10	M	⅜	S	No. 1	L	Cr	No. 2	L	Cr
3386	4	Lunsford, William	8	M	⅜	S	No. 1	L	Cr	No. 2	L	Cr
3387	5	Lunsford, Lula	6	F	⅜	D	No. 1	L	Cr	No. 2	L	Cr
3388	6	Lunsford, John	5	M	⅜	S	No. 1	L	Cr	No. 1	L	Cr
3389	7	Lunsford, Paul	3	M	⅜	S	No. 1	L	Cr	No. 2	L	Cr
3390	8	Lunsford, Ben	1	M	⅜	S	No. 1	L	Cr	No. 2	L	Cr
		Census Card No. 1047, P. O. Okmulgee, Enrolled October 24, 1899										
3391	1	Sanger, Stephen	23	M	¼		Ed. E. Sanger	L	Non	Amanda Sanger	L	Cr
		Census Card No. 1048, P. O. Krebs, Enrolled October 24, 1899										
3392	1	Brown, Frances	46	F	¼		Isaac Riley	D	Non	Sophie Riley	D	Cr
3393	2	Brown, Peter	20	M	⅛	S	Elijah Brown	L	Non	No. 1	L	Cr
3394	3	Brown, Joe	8	M	⅛	S	Elijah Brown	L	Non	No. 1	L	Cr
3395	4	Brown, Lucinda	8	F	⅛	D	Elijah Brown	L	Non	No. 1	L	Cr
3396	5	Brown, Charlie	2	M	⅛	S	Elijah Brown	L	Non	No. 1	L	Cr
		No. 3 died February 24, 1906										
		Census Card No. 1049, P. O. Bristow, Enrolled October 24, 1899										
3397	1	Stevens, Mary	24	F	⅛		Elijah Brown	L	Non	Francis Brown	L	Cr
3398	2	Stevens, Bryan	1	M	1-16	S	William Stevens	L	Non	No. 1	L	Cr
		Census Card No. 1050, P. O. Krebs, Enrolled October 24, 1899										
3399	1	Hendrickson, Eliza	22	F	⅛		Elijah Brown	L	Non	Francis Brown	L	Cr
3400	2	Hendrickson, Frank	2	M	1-16	S	Jim Hendrickson	L	Non	No. 1	L	Cr
		Census Card No. 1051, P. O. Okmulgee, Enrolled October 24, 1899; No. 4, May 14, 1901										
3401	1	Nukmellee, Meshaney	32	F	F		Taletsa Jarney	D	Cr	Lucy Perryman	D	Cr
3402	2	Nukmellee, Willie	12	M	F	S	Nukmellee	D	Cr	No. 1	L	Cr
3403	3	Nukmellee, Rosa	4	F	F	D	Nukmellee	D	Cr	No. 1	L	Cr
3404	4	Nukmellee	48	M	F	Hus	Lula Kogee	D	Cr	Unknown	?	Cr
		No. 1 died May 10, 1901. No. 4 reported dead. No. 2 died January 1900.										
		Census Card No. 1052, P. O. Mounds; No. 1, Heyburn, Enrolled Oct 24, 1899; No. 2, April 13, 1901										
3405	1	Self, John R.	44	M	¼		John Clark Self	D	?	Sofronia Self	D	?
3406	2	Self, John C.	1	M	⅛	S	No. 1	L	Cr	Sarah E. Self	L	Non
		Census Card No. 1053, P. O. Stidham, Enrolled October 24, 1899										
3407	1	Walker, Edward H.	37	M	½		Geo. W. Walker	D	?	Susan Ireland	L	?
3408	2	Walker, Eula	25	F	¼	Wf	Joseph Coodey	D	Cher	Mary Coodey	D	Cr
3409	3	Walker, Mary	7mo	F	⅜	D	No. 1	L	Cr	No. 2	L	Cr
		No. 2 died February 15, 1911										
		Census Card No. 1054, P. O. Brush Hill, Enrolled October 24, 1899										
3410	1	Logan, Samuel	44	M	F		Logan	D	Cr	Sally Logan	L	Cr
3411	2	Logan, Mary	33	F	½	Wf	Geo. W. Walker	D	?	Susan Ireland	L	?
3412	3	Logan, Bessie	12	F	¾	D	No. 1	L	Cr	Eliza Logan	D	Cr
		Census Card No. 1055, P. O. Mounds Enrolled October 24, 1899; No. 8, November 15, 1899										
3413	1	Barber, Robert T.	52	M	¼		Silas H. Barber	L	Non	Sarah Ann Barber	D	Cr
3414	2	Barber, John W.	16	M	⅛	S	No. 1	L	Cr	Alice Ann Barber	L	Non
3415	3	Barber, Lula F.	14	F	⅛	D	No. 1	L	Cr	Alice Ann Barber	L	Non
3416	4	Barber, Minnie P.	12	F	⅛	D	No. 1	L	Cr	Alice Ann Barber	L	Non
3417	5	Barber, Walter C.	10	M	⅛	S	No. 1	L	Cr	Alice Ann Barber	L	Non
3418	6	Barber, Dovie E.	6	F	⅛	D	No. 1	L	Cr	Alice Ann Barber	L	Non
3419	7	Barber, Shellie L.	4	F	⅛	D	No. 1	L	Cr	Alice Ann Barber	L	Non
3420	8	Garner, Robert T.	9	M	1-16	GrS	Gus Garner	L	Non	Virginia A. Garner	L	Non
		Census Card No. 1056, P. O. Bristow, Enrolled October 25, 1899										
3421	1	Barnett, Sallie	57	F	F		Barnett	D	Cr	Hannah Barnett	D	Cr
		No. 1 died December 30, 1902										
		Census Card No. 1057, P. O. Bristow, Enrolled October 25, 1899										
3422	1	Clinton, Billie	37	M	F		Ahtata	D	Cr	Unknown	D	Cr
3423	2	Clinton, Willie	13	M	F	S	No. 1	L	Cr	Tarsharheantay	D	Cr
3424	3	Clinton, Elsie	9	F	F	D	No. 1	L	Cr	Tarsharheantay	D	Cr
3425	4	Clinton, Wilson	7	M	F	S	No. 1	L	Cr	Tarsharheantay	C	Cr
		No. 1 died April 4, 1903. No. 3 reported dead.										
		Census Card No. 1058, P. O. Pierce, Enrolled October 25, 1899; No. 2, May 17. 1901										
3426	1	Broadnax, Nannie	22	F	F		John Porter	D	Cr	Meley Buffalo	D	Cr
3427	2	King, Robert	2½	M	F	S	Willie King	L	Cr	No. 1	L	Cr

Roll No.	No.	NAME	Age	Sex	Blood	Rel.	NAME OF FATHER	Liv.	Cit.	NAME OF MOTHER	Liv.	Cit.
		Census Card No. 1059, P. O. Bristow, Enrolled October 28, 1889; No. 5, March 18, 1901										
3428	1	Cloud. Nancy	27	F	F		Jim Anderson	D	Cr	Susan Anderson	D	Cr
3429	2	Cloud, David	2	M	F	S	Stephen Cloud	L	Cr	No. 1	L	Cr
3430	3	Wisener, Joe	8	M	F	S	Ben Wisener	L	Cr	No. 1	L	Cr
3431	4	Wisener, Katie	5	F	F	D	Ben Wisener	L	Cr	No. 1	L	Cr
3432	5	Bigpond, John	21	M	F	Hus	Billy Bigpond	D	Cr	Kissie Bigpond	D	Cr
		No. 4 reported dead											
		Census Card No. 1060, P. O. Kellyville, Enrolled October 25, 1899										
3433	1	Daniel Lusanna	32	F	F		Daniel	D	Cr	Jude Coweny	D	Cr
3434	2	Jack, Wallace	9	M	F	S	Colonel Jack	L	Cr	No. 1	L	Cr
3435	3	Perryman, Katie	5	F	F	D	Noble Perryman	L	Cr	No. 1	L	Cr
		No. 2 reported dead											
		Census Card No. 1061, P. O. Okmulgee, Enrolled October 25, 1899										
3436	1	Asbury, Thomas	24	M	F		Moses Asbury	L	Cr	Nicey Asbury	L	Cr
		No. 1 died August 26, 1903											
		Census Card No. 1062, P. O. Bristow, Enrolled October 25, 1899										
3437	1	Allen, Jesse	47	M	¼		Bill Allen	L	Non	Lucinda Allen	D	Cr
3438	2	Allen, Lizzie	31	F	F	Wf	James Anderson	D	Cr	Susie Anderson	L	Cr
3439	3	Allen, Ada	15	F	⅝	D	No. 1	L	Cr	Louisa Allen	L	Cr
3440	4	Allen, Abraham	13	M	⅝	S	No. 1	L	Cr	No. 2	L	Cr
3441	5	Allen, Joseph	11	M	⅝	S	No. 1	L	Cr	No. 2	L	Cr
3442	6	Allen, Roy	10	M	⅝	S	No. 1	L	Cr	Hannah Anderson	D	Cr
3443	7	Allen, Ella	8	F	⅝	D	No. 1	L	Cr	No. 2	L	Cr
3444	8	Allen, James	7	M	⅝	S	No. 1	L	Cr	Hannah Anderson	D	Cr
3445	9	Allen, Lucinda	5	F	⅝	D	No. 1	L	Cr	No. 2	L	Cr
3446	10	Allen, Annie	3	F	⅝	D	No. 1	L	Cr	No. 2	L	Cr
		Census Card No. 1063, P. O. Okemah, Enrolled October 25, 1899										
3447	1	Hill, David	43	M	F		Jackson Hill	D	Cr	Kizzie Hill	D	Cr
3448	2	Hill, Jennie	30	F	F	Wf	Yahola Harjo	D	Cr	Huelmshoey	D	Cr
3449	3	Hill, John	10	M	F	S	No. 1	L	Cr	No. 2	L	Cr
3450	4	Hill, Lilly	7	F	F	D	No. 1	L	Cr	No. 2	L	Cr
3451	5	Hill, Jackson	5	M	F	S	No. 1	L	Cr	No. 2	L	Cr
		No. 2 died March 5, 1900. No .1 died April 11, 1904. No. 3 died November 19, 1904.											
		No. 4 died September 3, 1904.											
		Census Card No. 1064, P. O. Weleetka, Enrolled October 25, 1899; No. 2, May 14, 1901.										
3452	1	Bruner, Thompson	48	M	F		Chowastiye	D	Cr	Saidahkahke	D	Cr
3453	2	Topartheche	18	F	F	Sis	Chowastiye	D	Cr	Saidahkahke	D	Cr
		No. 2 died August 1899											
		Census Card No. 1065, P. O. Olive, Enrolled October 26, 1899; No. 2 June 18, 1900										
3454	1	Raabe, Ida May	17	F	¼		Thos. Carlile	L	Non	Sylvia Carlile	D	Cr
3455	2	Raabe, Rosa Pearl	2moF		⅛	D	Chris Raabe	L	Non	No. 1	L	Cr
		Census Card No. 1066, P. O. Bristow, Enrolled October 26, 1899										
3456	1	Carlile, Bessie	12	F	¼		Thos. Carlile	L	Non	Sylvia Carlile	D	Cr
3457	2	Carlile Ora	10	F	¼	Sis	Thos. Carlile	L	Non	Sylvia Carlile	D	Cr
		Census Card No. 1067, P. O. Eufaula, Enroooled Octber 26, 1899; No. 4, May 21, 1901										
3458	1	Kelley, Wilson	30	M	F		Hulley Kelley	D	Cr	Kelley	D	Cr
3459	2	Kelley, Mary	30	F	F	Wf	Tom Chenupy	D	Cr	Jennie Chenupy	D	Cr
3460	3	Bruner, Charley	11	M	F	StS	Rider Bruner	L	Cr	No. 2	L	Cr
3461	4	Kelley, Lonie	1	M	F	S	No. 1	L	Cr	No. 2	L	Cr
		No. 2 died September 26, 1900. No. 4 died April 15, 1902.											
		Census Card No. 1068, P. O. Catoosa, Enrolled October 26, 1899										
3462	1	Harrison, William	30	M	F		Nokoseka	D	Cr	Susana	D	Cr
		No. 1 died March 3, 1901											
		Census Card No. 1069, P. O. Creek, Enrolled October 26, 1899										
3463	1	Davis, John	50	M	F		Arholox Fixico	D	Cr	Hannah Davis	L	Cr
		Cenuss Card No. 1070, P. O. Stone Bluff, Enrolled October 26, 1899										
3464	1	Colbert, Louvina	46	F	F		Folischa	D	Cr	Linda	D	Cr
3465	2	Colbert, Ella	16	F	F	D	George Colbert	D	Cr	No. 1	L	Cr
3466	3	Colbert, George	12	M	F	S	George Colbert	D	Cr	No. 1	L	Cr
3467	4	Colbert, Benjamin	7	M	F	S	George Colbert	D	Cr	No. 1	L	Cr
		No. 1 died May 26, 1914											
		Census Card No. 1071, P. O. Okmulgee, Enrolled October 26, 1899										
3468	1	Sone, Dickey	39	M	F		Kassoney	D	Cr	Soapey	D	Cr
3469	2	Sone, Sallie	30	F	F	Wf	Sekiega	D	Cr	Unknown	D	Cr
		Census Card No. 1072, P. O. Okmulgee, Enrolled October 26, 1899										
3470	1	McIntosh, Charles	28	M	¾		D. N. McIntosh	D	Cr	Winnie McIntosh	L	Cr
3471	2	McIntosh, Katie	8	F	⅝	D	No. 1	L	Cr	Lila Taylor	L	Cr
3472	3	McIntosh, Ben Dave	6	M	⅝	S	No. 1	L	Cr	Lila Taylor	L	Cr
3473	4	McIntosh, Charles Lee	3	M	⅝	S	No. 1	L	Cr	Lila Taylor	L	Cr
		No. 1 died September 12, 1902											
		Census Card No. 1073, P. O. Carroll, Enrolled October 26, 1899										
3474	1	King, Sylvia	57	F	¼		Hope	D	?	Fanny Hope	D	?
		No. 1 died March 30, 1906											

Roll No.	No.	NAME	Age	Sex	Blood	Rel.	NAME OF FATHER	Liv.	Cit.	NAME OF MOTHER	Liv.	Cit.

Census Card No. 1074, P. O. Eufaula, Enrolled October·26, 1899; No. 10, June 28, 1900

3475	1	Hutton, Louisa	46	F	¼		Mitchell Beams	D	Choc-F	Tooka Beams	D	Cr
3476	2	Hutton, Tooka	23	F	⅛	D	Joe Hutton, Jr.	L	Cr	No. 1	L	Cr
3477	3	Hutton, Rebella	19	F	⅛	D	Joe Hutton, Jr.	L	Cr	No. 1	L	Cr
3478	4	Hutton, Sarah	14	F	⅛	D	Joe Hutton, Jr.	L	Cr	No. 1	L	Cr
3479	5	Hutton, Lizzie	12	F	⅛	D	Joe Hutton, Jr.	L	Cr	No. 1	L	Cr
3480	6	Hutton, Jeff	10	M	⅛	S	Joe Hutton, Jr.	L	Cr	No. 1	L	Cr
3481	7	Hutton, Lucy	8	F	⅛	D	Joe Hutton, Jr.	L	Cr	No. 1	L	Cr
3482	8	Hutton, Fannie	6	F	⅛	D	Joe Hutton, Jr.	L	Cr	No. 1	L	Cr
3483	9	Hutton, Ben	3	M	⅛	S	Joe Hutton, Jr.	L	Cr	No. 1	L	Cr
3484	10	Crabtree, Dollie	1	F	⅛	GrD	George Crabtree	L	Cr	No. 2	L	Cr

No. 2 died March 31, 1907. No. 4 reported dead.

Census Card No. 1075, P. O. Eufaula, Enrolled October 26, 1899

3485	1	Wilson, Emily	25	F	⅛		Joe Hutton, Jr.	L	Cr	Louisa Hutton	L	Cr
3486	2	Wilson, Kate	5	F	1-16	D	Frank Wilson	L	Non	No. 1	I.	Cr
3487	3	Wilson, Lillie	4	F	1-16	D	Frank Wilson	L	Non	No. 1	L	Cr
3488	4	Wilson, Harvey	3	M	1-16	S	Frank Wilson	L	Non	No. 1	L	Cr
3489	5	Wilson, William	1	M	1-16	S	Frank Wilson	L	Non	No. 1	L	Cr

Nos. 1 and 2 reported dead

Census Card No. 1076, P. O. Holdenville, Enrolled October 26, 1899; No. 3, December 20, 1899; No. 4, May 3, 1900.

3490	1	Sawyer, Alice	29	F	½		Wm. Stewart	D	?	Jane Harjo	L	Cr
3491	2	Narcome, Lizzie	7	F	½	D	Charley Narcome	D	Cr	No. 1	L	Cr
3492	3	Narcome, Sunday	12	M	¾	S	Charley Narcome	D	Cr	No. 1	L	Cr
3493	4	Carbage, Monky	2	M	½	S	John Carbage	L	Non	No. 1	L	Cr

No. 1 died March 1910. No. 2 reported dead.

Census Card No. 1077, P. O. Allen, Enrolled October 27, 1899

3494	1	McLish, Sallie	74	F	F		Wm. McIntosh	D	Cr	Louisa McIntosh	D	Cr

Census Card No. 1078, P. O. Okmulgee, Enrolled October 27, 1899

3495	1	Grayson, Sam	21	M	F		Simpson Grayson	D	Cr	Annie Grayson	D	Cr

No. 1 died April 28, 1900

Census Card No. 1079, P. O. Beggs, Enrolled October 27, 1899

3496	1	Grayson, Joe	22	M	F		Simpson Grayson	D	Cr	Annie Grayson	D	Cr
3497	2	Grayson, Dave	16	M	F	Neph	Stephen Grayson	D	Cr	Sallie Grayson	D	Cr

Census Card No. 1080, P. O. Sharp, Enrolled October 27, 1899

3498	1	Bird, Susie	19	F	F		Chockcharty	D	Cr	Koska	D	Cr

Census Card No. 1081, P. O. Okmulgee, Enrolled October 27, 1899; No. 5, March 13, 1901; No. 6, May 20, 1901

3499	1	Marshall, Philip	62	M	F		Hillabechee	D	Cr	Lucy	D	Cr
3500	2	Marshall, David	11	M	F	S	No. 1	L	Cr	Yarner	D	Cr
3501	3	Harjo, Lizzie	7	F	F	Niece	Koncharty Harjo	D	Cr	Jennie Fox	D	Cr
3502	4	Harjo, Johnson	3	M	F	Neph	Koncharty Harjo	D	Cr	Jennie Fox	D	Cr
3503	5	Marshall, Eliza	20	F	F	Wf	Cusseta Fixeco	D	Cr	Warney	D	Cr
3504	6	Marshall, Timmie	3	M	F	S	No. 1	L	Cr	Yarner Marshall	D	Cr
3505	7	Fox, Jennie	28	F	F	Niece	Tom Fox	L	Cr	Lissie Fox	D	Cr

No. 5 died November 5, 1904. No. 6 died April 30, 1899. No. 7 died September 1899.

Census Card No. 1082, P. O. Jenks, Enrolled October 27, 1899

3506	1	Harvison, Reese	30	M	½		Thos. Harvison	L	Cr	Millie Yarger	D	Cr

Census Card No. 1083, P. O. Okmulgee, Enrolled October 27, 1899

3507	1	Hardridge, Eli E.	41	M	F		Young Hardridge	D	Cr	Lucy Hardridge	L	Cr
3508	2	Hardridge, Millie	33	F	F	Wf	Monday Chupco	D	Cr	Mary Ann Chupco	D	Cr
3509	3	Martin, Evaline	8	F	F	StD	Henry Martin	L	Sem	No. 2	L	Cr

No. 2 died January 3, 1902

Census Card No. 1084, P. O. Catoosa, Enrolled October 27, 1899

3510	1	Kernell, Lucinda	60	F	F		Nero Charty	D	Cr	Unknown	D	Non

No. 1 died April 6, 1906

Census Card No. 1085, P. O. Okmulgee, Enrolled October 28, 1899

3511	1	Belcher, Christopher	69	M	A.W.		Geo. W. Belcher	D	Non	Eliza Belcher	D	Non
3512	2	Byrd, Annie C.	21	F	¾	StGN	Wm. Byrd	D	Cr	Betsey Byrd	D	Cr

No. 2 reported dead

Census Card No. 1086, P. O. Okataha, Enrolled October 28, 1899

3513	1	Marcum, Rose	18	F	⅛		Doc Marcum	D	Non	Patty Thompson	D	Cr
3514	2	Marcum, Sarah	18	F	⅛	Sis	Doc Marcum	D	Non	Patty Thompson	D	Cr

Census Card No. 1087, P. O. Holdenville, Enrolled October 28, 1899; No. 6, November 1, 1900

3515	1	McCaslin, Jennie	31	F	½		Chester Tuttle	D	Non	Betsey Tuttle	D	Cr
3516	2	McCaslin, May	12	F	¼	D	John McCaslin	D	Non	No. 1	L	Cr
3517	3	McCaslin, Nettie	10	F	¼	D	John McCaslin	D	Non	No. 1	L	Cr
3518	4	McCaslin, Myrtle	8	F	¼	D	John McCaslin	D	Non	No. 1	L	Cr
3519	5	McCaslin, Jessie	6	F	¼	D	John McCaslin	D	Non	No. 1	L	Cr
3520	6	McRay, Bellzora	5moF	¼	D		Frank McRay	L	Non	No. 1	L	Cr

Census Card No. 1088, P. O. Okmulgee, Enrolled October 28, 1899

3521	1	Hardridge, Lucy	59	F	F		Unknown	D	Cr	Unknown	D	Cr

No. 1 died November 27, 1901

Census Card No. 1089, P. O. enryetta, Enrolled October 28, 1899

3522	1	Furr, Jude	36	F	⅛		Anderson Whetstone	L	Non	Nancy C. Whetstone	L	Cr
3523	2	Furr, William G.	19	M	1-16	S	Arthur Furr	D	Non	No. 1	L	Cr
3524	3	Furr, Benjamin C.	16	M	1-16	S	Arthur Furr	D	Non	No. 1	L	Cr
3525	4	Furr, Samuel	11	M	1-16	S	Arthur Furr	D	Non	No. 1	L	Cr
3526	5	Furr, Perry	8	F	1-16	S	Arthur Furr	M	Non	No. 1	L	Cr
3527	6	Furr, Mamie	6	F	1-16	D	Arthur Furr	D	Non	No. 1	L	Cr
3528	7	Furr, Arthur B.	3	M	1-16	S	Arthur Furr	D	Non	No. 1	L	Cr
3529	8	Furr, Archie D.	10moM	1-16	S		Arthur Furr	D	Non	No. 1	J.	Cr

77

Roll No.	No.	NAME	Age	Sex	Blood	Rel.	NAME OF FATHER	Liv.	Cit.	NAME OF MOTHER	Liv.	Cit.
		Census Card No. 1090, P. O. Fame, Enrolled October 28, 1899										
3530	1	Lasley, Jim	30	M	F		Sam Lasley	D	Cr	Unknown	D	Cr
3531	2	Lasley, Lizzie	34	F	F	Wf	Tommy	D	Cr	Martha	D	Cr
3532	3	Lasley, Bob	9	M	F	S	No. 1	L	Cr	No. 2	L	Cr
3533	4	Lasley, Minnie	6	F	F	S	No. 1	L	Cr	No. 2	L	Cr
3534	5	Lasley, Sam	7mo	M	F	S	No. 1	L	Cr	No. 2	L	Cr
		No. 5 died May 13, 1900. No. 1 died October 31, 1905.										
		Census Card No. 1091, P. O. Eufaula, Enrolled November 1, 1899; No. 4, May 17, 1900										
3535	1	Boulton, Etta C.	22	F	⅛		D. N. McIntosh	D	Cr	E. B. McIntosh	L	Non
3536	2	Boulton, Howard H.	4	M	1-16	S	Geo. H. Boulton	L	Non	No. 1	L	Cr
3537	3	Boulton, Etta Marie	2	F	1-16	D	Geo. H. Boulton	L	Non	No. 1	L	Cr
3538	4	Boulton, Noco C.	1mo	M	F	D	Geo. H. Boulton	L	Non	No. 1	L	Cr
		Census Card No. 1092, P. O. Muskogee; Nos. 2 and 3, Beggs, Enrolled Nov. 1, 1899										
3539	1	Sango, Millie	43	F	½		Sam Callahan	L	Cr	Sarah Muckey	L	Non
3540	2	Brown, Willie	17	M	¼	S	Simon Brown	D	Cr-F	Millie Sango	L	Cr
3541	3	Brown, Julia	15	F	¼	D	Simon Brown	D	Cr-F	Millie Sango	L	Cr
3542	4	Manuel, Sam	10	M	¼	S	Tom Manuel	L	Cr-F	Millie Sango	L	Cr
3543	5	Sango, Edward	8	M	¼	S	Morris Sango	L	Cr-F	Millie Sango	L	Cr
3544	6	Sango, Bertha	7	F	¼	D	Morris Sango	L	Cr-F	Millie Sango	L	Cr
		No. 3 died April 29, 1909. No. 6 died July 20, 1899.										
		Census Card No. 1093, P. O. Dustin, Enrolled Nov. 2, 1899; No. 3 April 4, 1900										
3545	1	Henry, Lucy	20	F	⅛		James B. Self	L	Cr	Martha Self	L	Non
3546	2	Henry ,Estella May	3	F	1-16	D	James S. Henry	L	Non	No. 1	L	Cr
3547	3	Henry, Louise	3mo	F	1-16	D	James S. Henry	L	Non	No. 1	L	Cr
		Nos. 2 and 3 reported dead.										
		Census Card No. 1094, P. O. Dustin, Enrolled November 2, 1‡99										
3548	1	Henry, Lula	18	F	⅛		James B. Self	L	Cr	Martha Self	L	Cr
3549	2	Henry, Beulah	3	F	1-16	D	Willie A. Henry	L	Non	No. 1	L	Cr
3550	3	Henry, Jessie	8mo	M	1-16	S	Willie A. Henry	L	Non	No. 1	L	Cr
		Census Card No. 1095, P. O. Sapulpa, Enrolled November 3, 1899; No. 2 May 2, 1900										
3551	1	Beaver, Samuel	25	M	F		Milton Beaver	D	Cr	Lydia Beaver	D	Cr
3552	2	Beaver, Viola	1mo	F	½	D	N.o 1	L	Cr	Ollie Beaver	L	Non
		Census Card No. 1096, P. O. Eufaula, Enrolled November 1899										
3553	1	Crabtree, Leotia	16	F	1-32		James H. Crabtree	D	Cr	Amelia Crabtree	L	Non
3554	2	Crabtree, James Walrond	4	M	1-32	Bro	James H. Crabtree	D	Cr	Amelia Crabtree	L	Non
		Census Card No. 1097, P. O. Coweta, Enrolled Nov. 6, 1899										
3555	1	McIntosh, George	19	M	F		Sam McIntosh	D	Cr	Lizzie Lasley	L	Cr
		Census Card No. 1098, P. O. Fame, Enrolled November 6, 1899										
3556	1	Reynolds, Silas	22	M	F		G. W. Reynolds	L	Cr	Susan Gray	L	Cr
3557	2	Reynolds, Lucy	35	F	F	Wf	Tulmuchesse	D	Cr	Martha Tulmuchesse	D	Cr
3558	3	Reynolds, Elsey	70	F	F	GrMo	Unknown	D	Cr	Unknown	D	Cr
		No. 1 died April 25, 1901. No. 2 died December 25, 1901. No. 3 died November 21, 1906.										
		Census Card No. 1099, P. O. Red Fork, Enrolled November 7, 1899										
3559	1	Bland. Sue A.	31	F	½		W. T. Davis	D	?	Arlie Davis	D	?
3560	2	Bland, Vera	10	F	¼	D	J. C. W. Bland	L	Non	No. 1	L	Cr
3561	3	Bland, Era	·8	F	¼	D	J. C. W. Bland	L	Non	No. 1	L	Cr
3562	4	Bland, Owen W.	5	M	¼	S	J. C. W. Bland	L	Non	No. 1	L	Cr
3563	5	Bland Hazel M.	2	F	¼	D	J. C. W. Bland	L	Non	No. 1	L	Cr
3564	6	Bland, John C.	8mo	M	¼	S	J. C. W. Bland	L	Non	No. 1	L	Cr
		Census Card No. 1100, P. O. Tulsa, Enrolled November 8, 1899										
3565	1	Clinton. Fred S.	25	M	⅛		Charles Clihnton	D	Non	Louise Clinton	L	Cr
		Census Card No. 1101, P. O. Red Fork, Enrolled November 8, 1899; No. 4 March 25, 1901										
3566	1	Atkins, Alice	24	F	¾		Beaver	D	Cr	Lydia Beaver	D	Cr
3567	2	Atkins, Charles	2	M	⅛	S	Robert D. Atkins	L	Cr	No. 1	L	Cr
3568	3	Atkins, Hellen C.	2mo	F	½	D	Robert D. Atkins	L	Cr	No. 1	L	Cr
3569	4	Atkins, Robert D.	31	M	¼	Hus	James Atkins	L	Non	May Atkins	D	Cr
		No. 2 died February 20, 1901. No. 3 died March 9, 1901.										
		Census Card No. 1102, P. O. Stone Bluff, No. 2 Haskell, Enrolled November 8, 1899										
3570	1	Gibson, Jerusha	47	F	⅛		William Berryhill	D	Cr	Jane Berryhill	L	Non
3571	2	Gibson, William S.	18	M	1-16	S	Joseph Gibson	L	Non	No. 1	L	Cr
3572	3	Gibson, John E.	16	M	1-16	S	Joseph Gibson	L	Non	No. 1	L	Cr
3573	4	Gibson, Joseph A.	15	M	1-16	S	Joseph Gibson	L	Non	No. 1	L	Cr
3574	5	Gibson, James T.	12	M	1-16	S	Joseph Gibson	L	Non	No. 1	L	Cr
3575	6	Gibson, Silas B.	9	M	1-16	S	Joseph Gibson	L	Non	No. 1	L	Cr
3576	7	Gibson, Mary E.·	7	F	1-16	D	Joseph Gibson	L	Non	No. 1	L	Cr
		No. 4 died January 23, 1901. No. 1 died December 18, 1912.										
		Census Card No. 1103, P. O. Stidham, Enrolled November 8, 1899										
3577	1	Doyle, Sarah A.	55	F	F		Moses Perryman	D	Cr	Elsie Perryman	D	Cr
3578	2	Doyle, Thomas E.	20	M	¾	S	Archibald Doyle	D	Cr	No. 1	L	Cr
		Census Card No. 1104, Morse, Enrolled November 8, 1899										
3579	1	Self, William J.	39	M	¼		John C. Self	D	Cr	Sophronia Self	D	Non
3580	2	Self, Vessie E.	7	F	⅛	D	No. 1	L	Cr	Delilah Self	L	Non
3581	3	Self, William L.	5	M	⅛	S	No. 1	L	Cr	Delilah Self	L	Non
		Census Card No. 1105, P. O. Okmulgee, Enrolled November 8, 1899										
3582	1	Carter, Annie	16	F	⅛		Wm. J. Self	L	Cr	Lou Katey Self	D	Non
3583	2	Carter, Ethel Lee	6mo	F	1-16	D	Joseph Carter	L	Non	No. 1	L	Cr
		No. 2 died August 10, 1900										

Roll No.	No.	NAME	Age	Sex	Blood	Rel.	NAME OF FATHER	Liv.	Cit.	NAME OF MOTHER	Liv.	Cit.
		Census Card No. 1106, P. O. Mounds, Enrolled November 8, 1899										
3584	1	Self, Samuel C.	25	M	1/8		John C. Self	D	Cr	Sophronia Self	D	Non
		Census Card No. 1107, P. O. Kellyville, Enrolled November 8 1899										
3585	1	Provence, Mary	41	F	1/8		John C. Self	D	Cr	Sophronia Self	D	Non
3586	2	Provence, Bertie	17	M	1-16	S	W. H. Provence	L	Non	No. 1	L	Cr
3587	3	Provence, Mathew	9	M	1-16	S	W. H. Provence	L	Non	No. 1	L	Cr
3588	4	Provence, Ruth	7	F	1-16	D	W. H. Provence	L	Non	No. 1	L	Cr
		No. 2 died November 31, 1903.										
		Census Card No. 1108, P. O. Mounds, Enrolled November 8, 1899										
3589	1	Stewart, America	35	F	1/4		John C. Self	D	Cr	Sophronia Self	D	Non
3590	2	Stewart, Ammie	6	F	1/8	D	Wm. H. Stewart	L	Non	No. 1	L	Cr
3591	3	Stewart, Effie	4	F	1/8	D	Wm. H. Stewart	L	Non	No. 1	L	Cr
3592	4	Stewart, Alice	3	F	1/8	D	Wm. H. Stewart	L	Non	No. 1	L	Cr
3593	5	Stewart, Ruthie Pearl	1	F	1/8	D	Wm. H. Stewart	L	Non	No. 1	L	Cr
3594	6	Self, Mattie	37	F	1/4	Sis	John C. Self	D	Cr	Sophronia Self	D	Non
		Census Card No. 1109, P. O. Okmulgee, Enrolled November 9, 1899										
3595	1	Taylor, Nancy	26	F	F		Taylor Dick	D	Cr	Ellen Taylor	D	Cr
3596	2	Taylor, Barney	3	M	F	S	Mose Moulton	L	Cr	No. 1	L	Cr
		No. 1 died February 17, 1905										
		Census Card No. 1110, P. O. Wealaka, Enrolled November 9, 1899										
3597	1	England, Susannah	24	F	F		Tom Hulpata	L	Cr	Mary Tiger	L	Cr
		No. 1 died April 26, 1910										
		Census Card No. 1111, P. O. Haskell, Enrolled November 9, 1899										
3598	1	Deere, Tecumseh	40	M	F		Cho Harjo	D	Cr	Sanogay	D	Cr
3599	2	Deere, Nancy	21	F	3/4	Wf	Tom Hulberter	L	Cr	Mary Tiger	L	Cr
3600	3	Deere, Noah	4	M	7/8	S	No. 1	L	Cr	No. 2	L	Cr
		No. 1 died April 9, 1990										
		Census Card No. 1112, P. O. Checotah; No. 4, Henryetta, Enrolled November 10, 1899										
3601	1	Woods, Eliza	28	F	1/4		Russell McKinney	D	Ck	Susan McKinney	D	Cr
3602	2	Woods, Claude	9	M	1/8	S	Will Wingo	L	Non	No. 1	L	Cr
3603	3	Woods, Florence Lillian	5	F	1/8	D	John W. Woods	L	Non	No. 1	L	Cr
3604	4	Woods, John R.	3	M	1/8	S	John W. Woods	L	Non	No. 1	L	Cr
		Census Card No. 1113, P. O. Henryetta, Enrolled November 10, 1899										
3605	1	Adams, Lizzie	18	F	1/4		Wiley Adams	L	Non	Susan Adams	D	Cr
		No. 1 died February 12, 1902										
		Census Card No. 1114, P. O. Paden; No. 3, Schulter, Enrolled November 10, 1899										
3606	1	Yarbrough, John	48	M	F		Heneha Micco	D	Cr	Cowasta	D	Cr
3607	2	Yarbrough, Betsey	18	F	F	D	No. 1	L	Cr	Tasehoke	D	Cr
3608	3	Yarbrough, Thomas	9	M	F	S	No. 1	L	Cr	Wattie	D	Cr
		Census Card No. 1115, P. O. Checotah, Enrolled November 10, 1899										
3609	1	Doyle, John N.	29	M	1/8		Nimrod P. Doyle	L	Cr	Fannie Doyle	D	Non
		No. 1 died March 23, 1904										
		Census Card No. 1116, P. O. Coweta, Enrolled November 10, 1899										
3610	1	Gibson, Montie	19	M	1/2		Walter Gibson	D	Cr	Rose Gibson	D	Non
		Census Card No. 1117, P. O. Oktaha, Enrolled November 11, 1899										
3611	1	Evans, Laura	30	F	1/4		Thos. Escoe	L	Non	Mary Escoe	L	Cr
3612	2	Evans, Florence	14	F	1/8	D	Alexander Evans	L	Non	No. 1	L	Cr
3613	3	Evans, Mary	13	F	1/8	D	Alexander Evans	L	Non	No. 1	L	Cr
3614	4	Evans, Minnie	11	F	1/8	D	Alexander Evans	L	Non	No. 1	L	Cr
3615	5	Evans, Alexander	9	M	1/8	S	Alexander Evans	L	Non	No. 1	L	Cr
3616	6	Evans, Thomas	7	M	1/8	S	Alexander Evans	L	Non	No. 1	L	Cr
3617	7	Evans, Cora	5	F	1/8	D	Alexander Evans	L	Non	No. 1	L	Cr
3618	8	Evans, Ida	3	F	1/8	D	Alexander Evans	L	Non	No. 1	L	Cr
3619	9	Evans, Arch N.	8moM		1/8	S	Alexander Evans	L	Non	No. 1	L	Cr
		No. 9 died September 22, 1899										
		Census Card No. 1118, P. O. Oktaha, Enrolled November 11, 1899										
3620	1	Hall, James	22	M	1/2		Joseph Hall	L	Non	Wynie Hall	D	Cr
3621	2	Hall, Sandy	15	M	1/2	Bro	Joseph Hall	L	Non	Wynie Hall	D	Cr
3622	3	Hall, David	14	M	1/2	Bro	Joseph Hall	L	Non	Wynie Hall	D	Cr
3623	4	Hall, George	10	M	1/2	Bro	Joseph Hall	L	Non	Wynie Hall	D	Cr
		No. 1 died July 26, 1900. No. 2 reported dead.										
		Census Card No. 1119, P. O. Oktaha; No. 1, Salina, Kas.; No. 8, Morris, Enrolled November 11, 1899										
3624	1	Evans, Lettie	40	F	1/4		Thos. Escoe	L	Non	Mary Escoe	L	Cr
3625	2	Evans, Wiley	19	M	1/8	S	Wiley Evans	L	Non	No. 1	L	Cr
3626	3	Evans, James	17	M	1/8	S	Wiley Evans	L	Non	No. 1	L	Cr
3627	4	Evans, Richard	15	M	1/8	S	Wiley Evans	L	Non	No. 1	L	Cr
3628	5	Evans, Charlie	13	M	1/8	S	Wiley Evans	L	Non	No. 1	L	Cr
3629	6	Evans, Savanah	13	F	1/8	D	Wiley Evans	L	Non	No. 1	L	Cr
3630	7	Evans, Dora	11	F	1/8	D	Wiley Evans	L	Non	No. 1	L	Cr
3631	8	Evans, Clarence	9	M	1/8	S	Wiley Evans	L	Non	No. 1	L	Cr
3632	9	Evans, Alta	7	F	1/8	D	Wiley Evans	L	Non	No. 1	L	Cr
3633	10	Evans, Clemm	5	M	1/8	S	Wiley Evans	L	Non	No. 1	L	Cr
3634	11	Evans, Lee	3	M	1/8	S	Wiley Evans	L	Non	No. 1	L	1/4 Cr
3635	12	Evans, Rex Dewey	6moM		1/8	S	Wiley Evans	L	Non	No. 1	L	Cr
		No. 1 reported dead										
		Census Card No. 1120, P. O. Jennings, Enrolled November 11, 1899										
3636	1	Harris, Walter	21	M	1/4		D. W. Harris	L	Non	Ellen Harris	D	Cr

Roll No.	No.	NAME	Age	Sex	Blood	Rel.	NAME OF FATHER	Liv.	Cit.	NAME OF MOTHER	Liv.	Cit.
		Census Card No. 1121, P. O. Red Fork, Enrolled November 13, 1899; No. 4, November 17, 1899										
3637	1	Inscho, Hattie	23	F	1/8		William McKim	D	Non	Annie Brummett	L	Cr
3638	2	Inscho, Ruth	4	F	1-16	D	Charles Inscho	L	Non	No. 1	L	Cr
3639	3	Inscho, Willie	2	M	1-16	S	Charles Inscho	L	Non	No. 1 .	L	Cr
3640	4	Inscho, Claburn	1mo	M	1-16	S	Charles Inscho	L	Non	No. 1	L	Cr
		Census Card No. 1122, P. O. Henryetta, Enrolled November 13, 1899										
3641	1	Henry, Hugh	52	M	1/4		Wood Henry	D	Non	Vicey Henry	D	Cr
3642	2	Henry, Luella	17	F	1/8	D	No. 1	L	Cr	Mintie Henry	L	Non
3643	3	Henry, Patrick	13	M	1/8	S	No. 1	L	Cr	Mintie Henry	L	Non
3644	4	Henry, Mack	10	M	1/8	S	No. 1	L	Cr	Mintie Henry	L	Non
3645	5	Henry, Annie May	6	F	1/8	D	No. 1	L	Cr	Mintie Henry	L	Non
3646	6	Henry, Woodson	5	M	1/8	S	No. 1	L	Cr	Mintie Henry	L	Non
3647	7	Henry, Hettie	2	F	1/8	D	No. 1	L	Cr	Mintie Henry	L	Non
3648	8	Henry, Hugh Jr.	3mo	M	1/8	S	No. 1	L	Cr	Mintie Henry	L	Non
		Census Card No. 1123, P. O. Muskogee, Enrolled November 13, 1899										
3649	1	Grayson, Emma	72	F	1/2		William Grayson	D	Cr	Judy Grayson	D	Cr
		No. 1 died March 3, 1907										
		Census Card No. 1124, P. O. Oktaha, Enrolled November 13, 1899										
3650	1	Carter, Henry	50	M	1/2		Fred Carter	D	?	Rachel Carter	D	?
3651	2	Carter, Annie	21	F	F	Wf	Lewis	D	Cr	Arkie	D	Cr
3652	3	Carter, Fred	1	M	3/8	S	No. 1	L	Cr	No. 2	L	Cr
		No. 1 reported dead										
		Census Card No. 1125, P. O. Oktaha, Enrolled November 13, 1899										
3653	1	Lucy	60	F	F		Gotso Fixico	D	Cr	Linda Fixico	D	Cr
3654	2	Coffee, Willie	28	M	F	S	Cabeche Harjo	D	Cr	No. 1	L	Cr
3655	3	Lewis, Holly	18	M	F	S	Lewis	D	Cr	No. 1	L	Cr
3656	4	Coffee, Effie	10	F	F	StD	Cabeche Harjo	D	Cr	Susan Harjo	D	Cr
		Census Card No. 1126, P. O. Oktaha, Enrolled November 13, 1899										
3657	1	Coffee, Micco	25	M	F		Kabiche Harjo	D	Cr	Lucy	L	Cr
3658	2	Coffee, Polly	20	F	F	Wf	Nocus Harjo	L	Cr	Cinda	D	Cr
		Census Card No. 1127, P. O. Wetumka, Enrolled November 14, 1899										
3659	1	Riley, Cleveland	15	M	1/4		Dave Riley	D	Cr	Mary Homer	L	Cher
3660	2	Homer, Henry	11	M	1/2	H-B	Alex Homer	L	Cr	Mary Homer	L	Cher
		Census Card No. 1128, P. O. Oktaha, Enrolled November 14, 1899										
3661	1	Whitfield, Millie	24	F	1/2		Joseph Hall	L	Non	Wynie Hall	D	Cr
3662	2	Whitfield, Rachel	3	F	1/4	D	Wm. Whitfield	L	Cher	No. 1	L	Cr
		No. 2 died July 14, 1900										
		Census Card No. 1129, P. O. Bald Hill, Enrolled November 14, 1899										
3663	1	Morton, Joan	29	F	1/2		G. W. Berryhill	L	Cr	Airy Ann Berryhill	L	Non
3664	2	Morton, George F.	6	M	1-16	S	Thomas Morton	L	Non	No. 1 .	L	Cr
3665	3	Morton, Airy Ethel	3	F	1-16	S	Thomas Morton	L	Non	No. 1	L	Cr
		Census Card No. 1130, P. O. Oktaha, Enrolled November 14, 1899										
3666	1	Coffee, Jimmy	21	M	F		Habeche Harjo	D	Cr	Susan Harjo	D	Cr
		Census Card No. 1131, P. O. Eufaula, Enrolled November 14, 1899; Nos. 3 and 4, April 4, 1901										
3667	1	Rhyne, Elizabeth	34	F	F		John G. Smith	D	?	Lucinda Smith	D	?
3668	2	Rhyne, Altus	4	F	1/4	D	J. S. Rhyne	L	Non	No. 1	L	Cr
3669	3	Doughty, Gertrude	15	F	1/4	D	James Daughty	L	Non	No. 1	L	Cr
3670	4	Doughty, Daisy	12	F	1/4	D	James Daughty	L	Non	No. 1	L	Cr
		Census Card No. 1132, P. O. Eufaula, Enrolled November 14, 1899; No. 3, December 8, 1899										
3671	1	Posey, Alexander L.	26	M	1/4		Lewis H. Posey	L	Cr	Nancy Posey	L	Cr
3672	2	Posey, Irving	2	M	1/4	S	No. 1	L	Cr	Minnie Posey	L	Non
3673	3	Posey, Kipling	9mo	M	1/4	S	No. 1	L	Cr	Minnie Posey	L	Non
		No. 1 died April 28, 1908. No. 3 died June 17, 1900.										
		Census Card No. 1133, P. O. Eufaula, Enrolled November 15, 1899; No..3. November 1, 1900										
3674	1	White, Phenia	19	F	1/2		Eli Jacob	D	Cr	Millie Jacob	D	Cr
3675	2	White, Maud Annie	2	F	1/4	D	Mack White	L	Non	No. 1	L	Cr
3676	3	White, Rosella	1	F	1/4	D	Mack White	L	Non	No. 1	L	Cr
		No. 3 died January 15, 1903										
		Census Card No. 1134, P. O. Sapulpa, Enrolled November 15, 1899										
3677	1	Brummet, Anna	40	F	-16		James Atkins	L	Non	Mary Atkins	D	Cr
		Census Card No. 1135, P. O. Sasakwa, Enrolled November 15, 1899										
3678	1	Johnson, Lorena	18	F	1/4		James A. Kane	D	Non	Lizzie Lewis	L	Cr
		No. died December 11, 1905										
		Census Card No. 1136, P. O. Eufaula, Enrolled November 15, 1899										
3679	1	Young, Adeline	48	F	1/2		Bill Nero	D	?	Nancy Nero	L	Cr
3680	2	Young, Harry	15	M	1/4	S	Joseph Young	L	Non	No. 1	L	Cr
3681	3	Young, Polly	13	F	1/4	D	Joseph Young	L	Non	No. 1	L	Cr
3682	4	Young, Katie	11	F	1/4	D	Joseph Young	L	Non	No. 1	L	Cr
3683	5	Young, Mary Ella	8	F	1/4	D	Joseph Young	L	Non	No. 1	L	Cr
3684	6	Young, Fay	7	F	1/4	D	Joseph Young	L	Non	No. 1	L	Cr
		No. 1 died July 26, 1907. No. 2 died May 1909. No. 4 died June 4, 1905.										
		Census Card No. 1137, P. O. Sapulpa, Enrolled November 15, 1899										
3685	1	Coser, Nuttetsa	3	M	F		Cosar Harjo	D	Cr	Rhoda	D	Cr
3686	2	Coser, Lizzie	27	F	F	Wf	Nocose Martbla	D	Cr	U known	D	Cr
3687	3	Coser, Nancy	4mo	F	D		No. 1	L	Cr	No. 2	L	Cr
		No. 1 died April 4, 1904. No. 2 died May 1909. No. 4 died June 4, 1905.										
		Cens s Card No. 1138, P. O. Sand Springs, Enrolled November 15, 1899										
3688	1	Holahta, Cheparn	25	M	F		Holotachee	D	Cr	Winey	D	Cr
3689	2	Holahta, Lucy	22	F	F	Wf	Ispokogee	D	Cr	Winnie	D	Cr
		No. 1 died August 1907										

Roll No.	No.	NAME	Age	Sex	Blood	Rel.	Name of Father	Liv.	Cit.	Name of Mother	Liv.	Cit.
	Census Card No. 1139, P. O. Okmulgee, Enrolled November 16, 1899											
3690	1	Marshall, John	28	M	F		Jeff Marshall	D	Cr	Angeline Marshall	D	Cr
		No. 1 died March 1909										
	Census Card No. 1140, P. O. Edna, Enrolled November 16, 1899											
3691	1	West, Louisa	50	F	F		Mack Bruner	D	Cr	Mary Bruner	D	Cr
3692	2	Gooden, Mary	17	F	¾	D	Jim Gooden	L	Cr	No. 1	L	Cr
3693	3	West, Cogee	11	F	F	D	George West	L	Cr	No. 1	L	Cr
	Census Card No. 1141, P. O. Tuskegee, Enrolled November 16, 1899											
3694	1	Jefferson, Silas	65	M	½		Jeffrey Manac	D	Cr	Betsey Manae	D	Cr
		No. 1 reported dead										
	Census Card No. 1142, P. O. Bristow, Enrolled November 16, 1899											
3695	1	Bruner, Sam	55	M	F		Mack Bruner	D	Cr	Mary Bruner	D	Cr
3696	2	Bruner, Sindoche	55	F	F	Wf	Sullivan	D	Cr	Unknown	D	Cr
		No. 1 died March 1900										
	Census Card No. 1143, P. O. Tuskegee, Enrolled November 16, 1899											
3697	1	Casteel, Sammie	18	M	¼		Hose Casteel	L	Non	Lizzie Casteel	D	Cr
	Census Card No. 1144, P. O. Edna, Enrolled November 16, 1899											
3698	1	Yargee, James	45	M	F		Micco Charty	D	Cr	Unknown	D	Cr
3699	2	Yargee, Mandy	45	F	F	Wf	Cochar Tiger	D	Cr	Wisey	L	Cr
3700	3	Yargee, Rhody	18	F	F	D	No. 1	L	Cr	No. 2	L	Cr
3701	4	Yargee, Lizzie	14	F	F	D	No. 1	L	Cr	No. 2	L	Cr
3701	5	Yargee, John	12	M	F	S	No. 1	L	Cr	No. 2	L	Cr
3703	6	Yargee, Walter	8	M	F	S	No. 1	L	Cr	No. 2	L	Cr
3704	7	Yargee, Cordelia	4	F	F	D	No. 1	L	Cr	No. 2	L	Cr
3705	8	Stricken from the roll. No. 1 died September 5, 1908. No. 3 died January 23, 1911.										
	Census Card No. 1145, P. O. Checotah, Enrolled November 16, 1899											
3706	1	Williams, Elizabeth	43	F	¾		Henderson Grayson	D	Cr	Abbey Grayson	D	Cr
		No. 1 died about 1909										
	Census Card No. 1146, P. O. Beggs, Enrolled November 16, 1899											
3707	1	Grayson, Joe	36	M	¼		Doc Grayson	D	?	Susan Grayson	L	?
		No. 1 died November 16, 1908										
	Census Card No. 1147, P. O. Okmulgee, Enrolled November 16, 1899											
3708	1	Taylor, Abraham	22	M	F		Taylor	D	Cr	Leah Bartley	D	Cr
3709	2	Taylor, Lilia	25	F	¼	Wf	Hosey Casteel	L	Non	Lizzie Casteel	D	Cr
3710	3	Taylor, Sammy	2mo	M	⅝	S	No. 1	L	Cr	No. 2	L	Cr
		No. 1 died June 1901										
	Census Card No. 1148, P. O. Hanna, Enrolled May 22, 1901											
3711	1	Proctor, Lewis	50	M	F		Osache Harjo	D	Cr	Temorthle	D	Cr
3712	2	Proctor, Sehokah	60	F	F	Wf	Etho Fixico Chupco	D	Cr	Unknown	D	Cr
3713	3	Proctor, Ellen	30	F	F	StD	David Chupco	L	Cr	No. 2	L	Cr
3714	4	Proctor, Nancy	15	F	F	D	No. 1	L	Cr	No. 2	L	Cr
3715	5	Proctor, Susie	14	F	F	D	No. 1	L	Cr	No. 2	L	Cr
3716	6	Proctor, Johnson	12	M	F	S	No. 1	L	Cr	No. 2	L	Cr
3717	7	Proctor, Billie	11	M	F	S	No. 1	L	Cr	No. 2	L	Cr
		No. 2 died 1907. No. 3 died October 7, 1908.										
	Census Card No. 1149, P. O. Okmulgee, Enrolled November 16, 1899; No. 4, March 22, 1900											
3718	1	Sarwarhie	30	M	F		Isparcher	L	Cr	Lucy	D	Cr
3719	2	Jennetta	22	F	F	Wf	Micco Nubba	D	Cr	Silpee	L	Cr
3720	3	Sarwarhie, Isparhecher	1	M	F	S	No. 1	L	Cr	No. 2	L	Cr
3721	4	Silpee	50	F	F	M-L	Unknown	D	Cr	Unknown	D	Cr
		No. 2 died January 1902. No. 1 died July 10, 1910. No. 3 died March 13, 1900. No. 4 died January 8, 1901.										
	Census Card No. 1150, P. O. Beggs, Enrolled November 16, 1899											
3722	1	Taylor, Turner F.	29	M	F		Billy James	D	Cr	Sophia James	D	Cr
3723	2	Taylor, Sissie	41	F	F	Wf	Joe Derisaw	D	Cr	Lizzie Derisaw	D	Cr
3724	3	Pinky, Willie	18	M	F	StS	Pinky	L	Cr	No. 2	L	Cr
		No. 1 died March 25, 1910. No. 3 died March 30, 1905										
	Census Card No. 1151, P. O. Okemah, Enrolled November 17, 1899											
3725	1	Harjo, Liza	22	F	F		Nocus Harjo	D	Cr	Leader Harjo	D	Cr
3726	2	Harjo, Oscar	2	M	F	S	Sommy	L	Cr	No. 1	L	Cr
	Census Card No. 1152, P. O. Muskogee, Enrolled November 16, 1899											
3727	1	Escoe, Edward	21	M	⅛		Wiley T. Escoe	L	Cr	Josphine Escoe	L	Non
	Census Card No. 1153, P. O. Oklahoma City; 1717 W. 18 St., Enrolled November 17, 1899											
3728	1	Marts, Daisy	20	F	⅛		Enoch Pendleton	L	Non	Martha Owens	L	Cr
	Census Card No. 1154, P. O. Stidham; No. 1, Eufaula; Nos. 3 and 5, Checotah, Enrolled Nov. 17, 1899											
3729	1	Pitman, Rosanna	34	F	¼		Robert White	D	Non	Louvina Price	L	Cr
3730	2	Pitman, Lewis	18	M	⅛	S	John W. Pitman	L	Non	No. 1	L	Cr
3731	3	Pitman, Edward	16	M	⅛	S	John W. Pitman	L	Non	No. 1	L	Cr
3732	4	Pitman, Laurel	14	M	⅛	S	John W. Pitman	L	Non	No. 1	L	Cr
3733	5	Pitman, Homer	12	M	⅛	S	John W. Pitman	L	Non	No. 1	L	Cr
3734	6	Pitman, Walter	10	M	⅛	S	John W. Pitman	L	Non	No. 1	L	Cr
3735	7	Pitman, Rosella	8	F	⅛	D	John W. Pitman	L	Non	No. 1	L	Cr
3736	8	Pitman, Mary	6	F	⅛	D	John W. Pitman	L	Non	No. 1	L	Cr
3737	9	Pitman, Arthur	4	M	⅛	S	John W. Pitman	L	Non	No. 1	L	Cr
3738	10	Pitman, Sammie	2	F	⅛	D	John W. Pitman	L	Non	No. 1	L	Cr
		No. 1 died April 4, 1906										
	Census Card No. 1155, P. O. Eufaula, Enrolled November 17, 1899; No. 2, May 22, 1901											
3739	1	Artusse, John	27	M	F		Artus Henneha	L	Cr	Chulokee	D	Cr
3740	2	Walker, Dick	16	M	F	Bro	Yucuppa	D	Cr	Chieka	D	Cr

Roll No.	No.	NAME	Age	Sex	Blood	Rel.	NAME OF FATHER	Liv.	Cit.	NAME OF MOTHER	Liv.	Cit.
		Census Card No. 1156, P. O. Broken Arrow, Enrolled November 18, 1899										
3741	1	Childers, Ellis B.	34	M	¾		N. B. Childers	L	Cr	Sophia Childers	D	Cr
3742	2	Childers, Walter A.	11	M	¾	S	No. 1	L	Cr	Fannie Childers	D	Cr
3743	3	Childers, Irene	9	F	¾	D	No. 1	L	Cr	Fannie Childers	D	Cr
		Census Card No. 1157 P. O. Beggs, Enrolled November 20, 1899										
3744	1	Gooden, Nancy	32	F	¾		Jim Gooden	L	Cr	Louisa West	L	Cr
3745	2	West, Sally	8	F	⅝	D	George West	L	Cr	No. 1	L	Cr
3746	3	West, Eliza	7	F	⅝	D	George West	L	Cr	No. 1	L	Cr
3747	4	West, Kizzie	5	F	⅝	D	George West	L	Cr	No. 1	L	Cr
3748	5	West, George	2	M	⅝	S	George West	L	Cr	No. 1	L	Cr
		No. 1 died April 16, 1901										
		Census Card No. 1158, P. O. Tuskegee, Enrolled November 20 1899										
3749	1	Gooden, Bessie	26	F	¾		Jim Gooden	D	Cr	Louisa West	L	Cr
3750	2	West, Thomas	8	M	⅝	S	George West	D	Cr	No. 1	L	Cr
3751	3	West, Lucy	4	F	⅝	D	George West	D	Cr	No. 1	L	Cr
		No. 2 died April 1, 1912										
		Census Card No. 1159, P. O. Beggs Enrolled November 20, 1899										
3752	1	Marshall, Jim	38	M	F		Jeff Marshall	D	Cr	Angeline Marshall	D	Cr
3753	2	Marshall, Liley	35	F	F	Wf	Marcy	D	Cr	Beaty	L	Cr
3754	3	Marshall, Aggie	15	F	F	D	No. 1	L	Cr	No. 2	L	Cr
3755	4	Marshall, Billie	13	M	F	S	No. 1	L	Cr	No. 2	L	Cr
3756	5	Marshall, Judy	6	F	F	D	No. 1	L	Cr	No. 2	L	Cr
3757	6	Marshall, Londo	4	M	F	S	No. 1	L	Cr	No. 2	L	Cr
		Nos. 2, 3, 4, 5, 6, reported dead.										
		Census Card No. 1160, P. O. Okmulgee, Enrolled November 20, 1899										
3758	1	Grayson, Robert	45	M	¾		Sandy Grayson	D	Cr	Ten Tiger	D	Cr
3759	2	Grayson, Annie	24	F	F	Wf	Cowe Harjo	D	Cr	Hagee Harjo	D	Cr
3760	3	Grayson, Lena	1	F	⅞	D	No. 1	D	Cr	No. 2	L	Cr
		No. 2 died November 25, 1904. No. 1 died February 14, 1909. No. 3 reported dead.										
		Census Card No. 1161, P. O. Okfuskee, Enrolled November 20, 1899										
3761	1	Sarsar	21	M	F		Taskeeg Harjo	D	Cr	Safix Chumba	L	Cr
		No. 1 died March 25, 1903										
		Census Card No. 1162, P. O. Okmulgee, Enrolled November 20, 1899										
3762	1	Marweoly	50	M	F		Hotulchoche	D	Cr	Speeny	D	Cr
		No. 1 reported dead										
		Census Card No. 1163, P. O. Beggs, Enrolled November 20, 1899										
3763	1	Tiger, John	50	M	F		Hotulge	D	Cr	Unknown	D	Cr
		Census Card No. 1164, P. O. Okfuskee, Enrolled November 20, 1899										
3764	1	Scott, Pigeon	46	M	F		Charles Harjo	D	Cr	Hannah Scott	D	Cr
		No. 1 died June 1904										
		Census Card No. 1165, P. O. Okfuskee, Enrolled November 20, 1899										
3765	1	Scott, Hannah	19	F	F		Pigeon Scott	L	Cr	Nochumba Scott	D	Cr
3766	2	Deer, Lizzie	3wksF	F	D		Wash Deer	L	Cr	No. 1	L	Cr
		No. 2 died August 21, 1900. No. 1 died May 20, 1906.										
		Census Card No. 1166, P. O. Okfuskee, Enrolled November 20, 1899										
3767	1	Davis Joe	40	M	F		Tulmochus Micco	D	Cr	Nochumba Scott	D	Cr
3768	2	Davis, Kogee	22	F	F	Wf	Pigeon Scott	L	Cr	Nochumba Scott	D	Cr
3769	3	Davis, William	19	M	F	S	No. 1	L	Cr	Cinda Davis	D	Cr
3770	4	Dav s Sartie	12	M	F	S	No. 1	L	Cr	Cinda Davis	D	Cr
3771	5	Davis, Munna	9	F	F	D	No. 1	L	Cr	Cinda Davis	D	Cr
3772	6	Davis, March	5	M	F	S	No. 1	L	Cr	Cinda Davis	D	Cr
		Nos. 1, 3, 4, 5, reported dead										
		Census Card No. 1167, P. O. Eufaula, Enrolled November 20, 1899										
3773	1	Taylor, Cub	30	M	F		Billy James	D	Cr	Sophia James	D	Cr
		Census Card No. 1168, P. O. Broken Arrow, Enrolled November 20, 1899										
3774	1	Marshall, Mary	52	F	½		Cho Harjo	D	Cr	Unknown	D	?
3775	2	Grayson, Henry	16	M	¼	S	Henry Grayson	L	Non	No. 1	L	Cr
3776	3	Grayson, Lilly	12	F	¼	D	Henry Grayson	L	Non	No. 1	L	Cr
		Census Card No. 1169, P. O. Tulsa, Enrolled November 23, 1899										
3777	1	Partridge, Reuben L.	31	M	¾		Sarnokitchee	D	Cr	China Thurman	D	Cr
3778	2	Partridge, Leonard C.	5	M	⅜	S	No. 1	L	Cr	Clara Partridge	L	Non
3779	3	Partridge, Ruby M.	4moF		⅜	D	No. 1	L	Cr	Clara Partridge	L	Non
		Census Card No. 1170, P. O. Beggs, Enrolled November 23, 1899; No. 6, September 6, 1900; No. 7, May 22, 1901.										
3780	1	Adams, George W.	36	M	½		Thomas Adams	L	Cr	Mahala Adams	L	Cr
3781	2	Adams, Sarah	28	F	½	Wf	Hosey Casteel	L	Non	Millie Sango	L	Cr
3782	3	Adams, Benjamin	6	M	½	S	No. 1	L	Cr	No. 2	L	Cr
3783	4	Adams, John	4	M	½	S	No. 1	L	Cr	No. 2	L	Cr
3784	5	Manuel, Robert	10	M	¼	StS	Thomas Manuel	L	Non	No. 2	L	Cr
3785	6	Adams, Willie	6moM	½	S		No. 1	L	Cr	No. 2	L	Cr
3786	7	Adams, Fred	1	M	½	S	No. 1	L	Cr	No. 2	L	Cr
		No. 7 died August 10, 1899										
		Census Card No. 1171, P. O. Okmulgee, Enrolled November 23, 1899; No. 3, June 7, 1900										
3787	1	Harjo, Moser	26	M	F		Conchart Harjo	D	Cr	Lucinda Harjo	D	Cr
3788	2	Harjo, Mahaley	20	F	F	Wf	James Sugar	L	Cr	Ellen Sugar	L	Cr
3789	3	Kelly, John	4	M	F	StS	Newman Kelly	L	Cr	No. 2	L	Cr
		No. 2 died March 7, 1901										

Roll No.	No.	NAME	Age	Sex	Blood	Rel.	NAME OF FATHER	Liv.	Cit.	NAME OF MOTHER	Liv.	Cit.
		Census Card No. 1172, P. O. Beggs, Enrolled November 23, 1899										
3790	1	Adams, Lewis	27	M	½		Thomas Adams	L	Cr	Mahala Adams	L	Cr
3791	2	Adams, Washington	3	M	¼	S	No. 1	L	Cr	Annie Adams	L	Non
3792	3	Adams, Leo	2	M	¼	S	No. 1	L	Cr	Annie Adams	L	Non
3793	4	Adams, Hepsa	8moF	¼	D		No. 1	L	Cr	Annie Adams	L	Non
		Nos. 3 and 4 reported dead										
		Census Card No. 1173, P. O. Sapulpa, Enrolled November 23, 1899										
3794	1	Tiger, John	9	M	F		Tiger	D	Cr	Unknown	D	Cr
		Census Card No. 1174, P. O. Okmulgee, Enrolled November 23, 1899										
3795	1	Nail, Joe	20	M	F		Archopa	D	Cr	Marleah	D	Cr
		Census Card No. 1175, P. O. Beggs, Enrolled November 23, 1899										
3796	1	Adams, Lee	25	M	½		Thomas Adams	L	Cr	Mahala Adams	L	Cr
		Census Card No. 1176, P. O. Tuskegee, Enrolled November 23, 1899										
3797	1	Beaver, Fred	25	M	¾		John Beaver	L	Cr	Sina Kay	L	Cr
		No. 1 died January 1, 1903										
		Census Card No. 1177, P. O. Taber, Enrolled November 23, 1899										
3798	1	McNack, Berry	25	M	¾		Aleck McNack	L	Cr	Caroline McNack	L	Cr
		Census Card No. 1178, P. O. Edna, Enrolled Nov. 23, 1899										
3799	1	McNack, Alex	60	M	¾		Dick McNack	D	Cr	Mollie McNack	D	Cr
3800	2	McNack, Caroline	48	F	¾	Wf	Joe Hulinger	D	Cr	Hannah Roberson	D	Cr
3801	3	McNack, Charley	18	M	¾	S	No. 1	L	Cr	No. 2	L	Cr
3802	4	McNack, Rosana	16	F	¾	D	No. 1	L	Cr	No. 2	L	Cr
3803	5	McNack, Shawnee	10	M	¾	S	No. 1	L	Cr	No. 2	L	Cr
3804	6	McNack, Stella	8	F	¾	D	No. 1	L	Cr	No. 2	L	Cr
3805	7	Mukes, Maggie	7moF	¾	GrD	Tom Mukes		L	Non	No. 4	L	Cr
		No. 2 reported dead										
		Census Card No. 1179, P. O. Depew; No. 2, Edna, Enrolled November 23, 1899										
3806	1	Mukes, Alice	22	F	¾		Alex McNack	L	Cr	Caroline McNack	L	Cr
3807	2	Robin, Lulu	3	F	⅜	D	Charley Robin	L	Frd	No. 1	L	Cr
3808	3	Mukes, Alex	2moM	⅜	S	Thomas Mukes		L	Non	No. 1	L	Cr
		No. 1 died July 9, 1914										
		Census Card No. 1180, P. O. Kellyville, Enrolled November 23, 1899										
3809	1	Sewel, Parney	41	M	F		Ben Sewel	D	Cr	Sallie Moonie	L	Cr
3810	2	Sewel, Sinda	48	F	F	Wf	Thlejummy Harjo	D	Cr	Winey Harjo	D	Cr
3811	3	Sewel, Ben	28	M	F	S	No. 1	L	Cr	No. 2	L	Cr
3812	4	Sewel, Thomas	25	M	F	S	No. 1	L	Cr	No. 2	L	Cr
3813	5	Sewel, Waddie	14	M	F	S	No. 1	L	Cr	No. 2	L	Cr
3814	6	Sewel, Laslie	11	M	F	S	No. 1	L	Cr	No. 2	L	Cr
3815	7	Sewel, Liza	9	F	F	D	No. 1	L	Cr	No. 2	L	Cr
3816	8	Sewel, Loney	7	M	F	S	No. 1	L	Cr	No. 2	L	Cr
3817	9	Sewel, Noah	5	M	F	S	No. 1	L	Cr	No. 2	L	Cr
		No. 2 reported dead										
		Census Card No. 1181, P. O. No. 1, Eufaula; No. 2, Clearview, Enrolled November 23, 1899										
3818	1	Harry, Robert	23	M	½		David Harry	L	Cr	Grace Harry	D	Cr
3819	2	Harry, Sally	26	F	¾	Wf	John Tiger	D	Cr	Lucinda Tiger	D	Cr
		Census Card No. 1182, P. O. No. 1, Gonzales, Texas, Enrolled November 23, 1899										
3820	1	Scott, Charles	22	M	¼		Wiley Scott	L	?	Dicey Adams	L	?
3821	2	Scott, Julia	20	F	¼	Sis	Wiley Scott	L	?	Dicey Adams	L	?
		Census Card No. 1183, P. O. Edna, Enrolled November 1899										
3822	1	McNack, Aaron	33	M	¾		Alex McNack	L	Cr	Caroline McNack	L	Cr
		Census Card No. 1184, P. O. Beggs, Enrolled November 23, 1899										
3823	1	Brown, George	42	M	F		Yahwe ho	D	Cr	Seofanny	D	Cr
3824	2	Brown, Legus	11	M	F	S	No. 1	L	Cr	Lizzie Brown	D	Cr
		Census Card No. 1185, P. O. Tuskegee, Enrolled November 1899										
3825	1	Marshall, Susanab	56	F	F		Wilsey	D	Cr	Fanny	D	Cr
3826	2	Davis, Sallie	20	F	F	Niece	Sahconcahny	L	Cr	Desanconny	D	Cr
		No. 1 died February 6, 1906.										
		Census Card No. 1186, P. O. Bristow, Enrolled November 23, 1899										
3827	1	Moonie, Sallie	75	F	F		Micco	D	Cr	Katie	D	Cr
		Census Card No. 1187, P. O. Muskogee, Enrolled November 23, 1899										
3828	1	Bigpond, Albert	13	M	F		Joe Bigpond	D	Cr	Kalakony Bigpond	L	Cr
		Census Card No. 1188, P. O. Tuskogee, Enrolled November 23, 1899										
3829	1	Cotanny	35	M	F		Kelay	D	Cr	Sahconthlanny	D	Cr
		No. 1 reported dead										
		Census Card No. 1189, P. O. Edna, Enrolled November 23, 1899										
3830	1	Harry, Albert	40	M	½		Harry Harry	D	?	Caroline Harry	D	?
3831	2	Harry, Dick	17	M	¼	S	No. 1	L	Cr	Bess Harry	D	?
		Census Card No. 1190, P. O. Bristow, Enrolled November 23, 1899										
3832	1	Harry, Cornelius	22	M	¼		Albert Harry	L	?	Eliza Harry	D	?
		Census Card No. 1191, P. O. Broken Arrow, Enrolled April 15, 1899										
3833	1	Childers, Rachel	13	F	F		Henry Childers	D	Cr	Mary Childers	D	Cr
3834	2	Childers, Maggie	8	F	F	Sis	Henry Childers	D	Cr	Mary Childers	D	Cr
		No. 2 died March 12, 1902										
		Census Card No. 1192, P. O. Beggs, Enrolled November 24, 1899										
3735	1	Shepherd, Annie	22	F	¼		Simon Brown	D	?	Millie Sango	L	?
3836	2	Shepherd, Hannah	1	F	⅛	D	Geo. Shepard	L	Non	No. 1	L	Cr

Roll No.	No.	NAME	Age	Sex	Blood	Rel.	NAME OF FATHER	Liv.	Cit.	NAME OF MOTHER	Liv.	Cit.

Census Card No. 1193, P. O. Fentress; No. 2 Okemah, Enrolled November 24, 1899; No. 4 March 6, 1901

3837	1	Berryhill, Sam	37	M	¾		Simon Berryhill	D	Cr	Unknown	D	Cr
3838	2	Berryhill, Sophie	21	F	F	Wf	Joslin Davis	L	Cr	Jenny Davis	D	Cr
3839	3	Berryhill, Maudie	6	F	⅞	D	No. 1	L	Cr	Sally Berryhill	D	Cr
3840	4	Berryhill, Louisa	1	F	⅞	D	No. 1	L	Cr	Sophia Berryhill	L	Cr

No. 1 died August 5, 1904. No. 4 died October 10, 1901

Census Card No. 1194, P. O. Stidham, Enrolled November 27, 1899

| 3841 | 1 | Hawkins, Daniel | 30 | M | ½ | | Samuel Hawkins | D | Cr | Cynthia Hawkins | L | Non |

Census Card No. 1195, P. O. Burney, Enrolled November 27, 1899

| 3842 | 1 | Fields, Lucy | 42 | F | F | | Nehahajo | D | Cr | Sounah | D | Cr |
| 3843 | 2 | Fields, Legus | 27 | M | F | S | • Amos Fields | D | Cr | No. 1 | L | Cr |

No. 2 died February 22, 1901

Census Card No. 1196, P. O. Henryetta, Enrolled November 27, 1899

| 3844 | 1 | Grayson, Alice | 20 | F | ⅜ | | Tip Marshall | L | Cr | Delaphine Marshall | L | Non |
| 3845 | 2 | Grayson, Vinnie Ree | 2 | F | 3-16 | D | Joseph Grayson | L | Non | No. 1 | L | Cr |

Census Card No. 1197, P. O. Sapulpa, Enrolled November 27, 1899

3846	1	Offutt, Minnie	30	F	½		W. T. Davis	D	Non	Arlie Davis	D	Cr
3847	2	Ground, Willie	11	M	¼	S	Al. Ground	L	Non	No. 1	L	Cr
3848	3	Offutt, Bessie	8	F	¼	D	J. W. Offutt	L	Non	No. 1	L	Cr
3849	4	Offutt, Raymond	6	M	¼	S	J. W. Offutt	L	Non	No. 1	L	Cr

Census Card No. 1198, P. O. Eufaula, Enrolled November 27, 1899; No. 2 January 28, 1901

| 3850 | 1 | Day, Vinita | 21 | F | ¼ | | John Matoy | D | ? | Martha Matoy | L | ? |
| 3851 | 2 | Day, Roy L. | 1 | M | ⅛ | D | R. L. Day | L | Non | Vinita Day | L | Cr |

No. 1 died March 10, 1912

Census Card No. 1199, P. O. Beggs, Enrolled November 27, 1899

3852	1	Grayson, Lyna	45	F	¾		Jacob	D	Cr	Tena	D	Cr
3853	2	Gooden, Edward	27	M	⅝	S	Wm. Gooden	D	Cr	No. 1	L	Cr
3854	3	Gooden, Susan	20	F	⅝	D	Wm. Gooden	D	Cr	No. 1	L	Cr
3855	4	Durant, Dicey	17	F	⅜	D	Frank Durant	D	Cr	No. 1	L	Cr
3856	5	Durant, Robert	17	M	⅜	S	Frank Durant	D	Cr	No. 1	L	Cr

Census Card No. 1200, P. O. Edna; No. 6 Bristow, Enrolled November 27, 1899

3857	1	Harry, David	48	M	¼		Harry	D	?	Caroline Harry	D	?
3858	2	Harry, Martha	38	F	¼	Wf	Dock Grayson	L	?	Susan Grayson	L	?
3859	3	Harry, Nora	14	F	¼	D	No. 1	L	Cr	No. 2	L	Cr
3860	4	Harry, Luke	13	M	¼	S	No. 1	L	Cr	No. 2	L	Cr
3861	5	Harry, Legus	11	M	¼	S	No. 1	L	Cr	No. 2	L	Cr
3862	6	Harry, Peggie	16	F	⅜	D	No. 1	L	Cr	Grace Harry	L	Cr
3863	7	Nero, Zedrick	17	M	¼	StS	Joe Nero	L	Cr	No. 2	L	Cr

No. 3 died May 1911

Census Card No. 1201, P. O. Edna; No. 6 Bristow, Enrolled November 27, 1899

3864	. 1	Harry, Henry	55	M	⅛		Harry Harry	D	?	Caroline Harry	D	?
3865	2	Harry, Micey	50	F	⅝	Wf	Jocktybohee	D	Cr	Lizzie Jack	D	Cr
3866	3	Harry, Aggie	23	F	⅜	D	No. 1	L	Cr	No. 2	L	Cr
3867	4	Harry, Jackson	22	M	⅜	S	No. 1	L	Cr	No. 2	L	Cr
3868	5	Harry, August	20	M	⅜	S	No. 1	L	Cr	No. 2	L	Cr
3869	6	Harry, Tony	19	M	⅜	S	No. 1	L	Cr	No. 2	L	Cr
3870	7	Harry, Nellie	15	F	⅜	D	No. 1	L	Cr	No. 2	L	Cr
3871	8	Harry, Eddie	3	M	⅜	S	No. 1	L	Cr	No. 2	L	Cr
3872	9	Harry, Robert	8 mo	M	⅜	S	No. 1	L	Cr	No. 2	L	Cr
3873	10	Robins, Johnson	1	M: 1-16		GnS	Will Robin	L	CrFr	No. 3	L	Cr
3874	11	Harry, Rufus	5	M	½	S	No. 1	L	Cr	Lucy Fisher	D	Cr

No. 1 died April 1910. No. 6 died December 24, 1907

Census Card No. 1202, P. O. Okmulgee, Enrolled November 27, 1899

3875	1	Tiger, Pufney	45	M	F		Cotchar Tiger	D	Cr	Wicey Tiger	D	Cr
3876	2	Tiger, Winey	40	F	F	Wf	Haton Harjo	D	Cr	Lizzie Tiger	D	Cr
3877	3	Tiger, Mary	13	F	F	D	No. 1	L	Cr	No. 2	L	Cr
3878	4	Tiger, Susie	10	F	F	D	No. 1	L	Cr	No. 2	L	Cr
3879	5	Tiger, Roman	7	M	F	S	No. 1	L	Cr	No. 2	L	Cr
3880	6	Tiger, Daniel	6	M	F	S	No. 1	L	Cr	No. 2	L	Cr
3881	7	Tiger, Malinda	4	F	F	D	No. 1	L	Cr	No. 2	L	Cr

No. 1 died July 31, 1900. No. 6 died May 18, 1904. No. 2 died January 5, 1902. No. 3 died July 26, 1908

Census Card No. 1203, P. O. Okfuskee, Enrolled November 27, 1899

| 3882 | 1 | Scott, Alick | 35 | M | F | | Tullemarsee Scott | L | Cr | Unknown | D | Cr |

No. 1 died May 18, 1901

Census Card No. 1204, P. O. Durango, Mex., care American Consul, Enrolled November 27, 1899

| 3883 | 1 | Henry, Frank | 35 | M | ½ | | Sulpee Henry | L | Non | Bessie Harry | D | Cr |

Census Card No. 1205, P. O. Muskogee, Enrolled November 27, 1899

| 3884 | 1 | Durant, Thos. J. | 26 | M | 1-16 | | Otho Durant | L | Cr | Anna Durant | L | Non |

Census Card No. 1206, P. O. Depew, Enrolled November 28, 1899

3885	1	Bigpond, John	50	M	F		John Bigpond	D	Cr	Hecahlothany	D	Cr
3886	2	Bigpond, Rachel	21	F	F	Wf	Sakcofahny Bighead	L	Cr	Louisa	D	Cr
3887	3	Bigpond, Sam	13	M	F	S	No. 1	L	Cr	Polly	D	Cr
3888	4	Bigpond, Lallo	11	F	F	S	No. 1	L	Cr	Polly	D	Cr
3889	5	Bigpond, Lallie	7	F	F	D	No. 1	L	Cr	Polly	D	Cr
3890	6	Bigpond, Jackson	5	M	F	S	No. 1	L	Cr	Polly	D	Cr

No. 3 died March 1, 1900. No. 6 died April 22, 1904

Roll No.	No.	NAME	Age	Sex	Blood	Rel.	NAME OF FATHER	Liv.	Cit.	NAME OF MOTHER	Liv.	Cit.
	Census Card No. 1207, P. O. Eufaula, Enrolled November 28, 1899; No. 3 May 22, 1900											
3891	1	Kite, Jemima	24	F	3/4		Loster Williams	L	Cr	Sally Ann Williams	L	Cr
3892	2	Kite, William Foley	4	M	7/8	S	A. L. Kite	L	Non	No. 1	L	Cr
3893	3	Kite, Abe L., Jr.	2 mo	M	7/8	S	A. L. Kite	L	Non	No. 1	L	Cr
		No. 3 died June 22, 1901										
	Census Card No. 1208, P. O. Sapulpa, Enrolled November 28, 1899											
3894	1	Wiley, Dickson	21	M	F		Algogehney	D	Cr	Pothla	D	Cr
		No. 1 died April 4, 1903										
	Census Card No. 1209, P. O. Bristow, Enrolled December 1, 1899											
3895	1	Sorrell, Dorothy	18	F	1/4		Frank Dasher	L	Non	Jane Dasher	D	Cr
3896	2	Sorrell, Julia	1	F	1/8	D	William Sorrell	L	Non	No. 1	L	Cr
	Census Card No. 1210, P. O. Tuskegee, Enrolled December 2, 1899											
3897	1	Miller, Taylor	24	M	F		Jim Miller	L	Cr	Susan Miller	D	Cr
3898	2	Miller, Betty	19	F	F	Wf	Keeper Johnson	L	Cr	Chocfolecha	D	Cr
		No. 1 died October 1902										
	Census Card No. 1211, P. O. Tuskegee, Enrolled December 2, 1899											
3899	1	Scott, Tullemarsey	55	M	F		Charlo Harjo	D	Cr	Hannah Scott	D	Cr
		No. 1 died January 7, 1912										
	Census Card No. 1212, P. O. Edna, Enrolled December 2, 1899											
3900	1	Harjo, Sulphur	32	M	F		Concharty Harjo	D	Cr	Unknown	D	Cr
3901	2	Harjo, Lizzie	30	F	F	Wf	Osab Fixico	D	Cr	Narheathowee	D	Cr
3902	3	Harjo, Loesta	5 mo	F	F	D	No. 1	L	Cr	No. 2	L	Cr
3903	4	Harjo, Louisa	6	F	F	D	No. 1	L	Cr	Betsey Coachman	D	Cr
3904	5	Davis, Jesse	6	M	F	StS	Pose Larney	D	Cr	No. 2	L	Cr
3905	6	Harjo, Kogee	12	F	F	1/2 Sis	Concharty Harjo	D	Cr	Lucy Harjo	D	Cr
		No. 3 died November 1, 1901. No. 1 reported dead										
	Census Card No. 1213, P. O. Edna, Enrolled December 2, 1899; No. 4 May 7, 1900											
3906	1	Johnson, Keeper	45	M	F		Conchart Emarthla	D	Cr	Unknown	D	Cr
3907	2	Johnson, Jennette	30	F	F	Wf	Pigeon Scott	L	Cr	Tilda Scott	L	Cr
3908	3	Johnson, Susie	6	F	F	D	No. 1	L	Cr	No. 2	L	Cr
3909	4	Johnson, Harber	1 mo	M	F	S	No. 1	L	Cr	No. 2	L	Cr
		No. 1 died September 1902										
	Census Card No. 1214, P. O. Bristow, Enrolled December 2, 1899											
3910	1	Williams, Rena	21	F	1/2		Choty Fish	D	Cr	Jane Dasher	D	?
3911	2	Grayson, Samuel	2	M	1/4	S	Thomas Grayson	L	Cr	No. 1	L	Cr
	Census Card No. 1215, P. O. Bristow; No. 4 Ft. Lapwia, Idaho; Enrolled December 2, 1899											
3912	1	Yahola, Conip	45	M	F		Chola Yahola	D	Cr	Mahta	D	Cr
3913	2	Yahola, Cinda	40	F	F	Wf	Artusse Micco	D	Cr	Polly	D	Cr
3914	3	Wolf, Isla	11	M	F	GrNe	George Wolf	L	Cr	Sissie Wolf	D	Cr
3915	4	Wolf, Ebia	8	M	F	GrNe	George Wolf	L	Cr	Sissie Wolf	D	Cr
		No. 1 died August 1904. No. 2 reported dead										
	Census Card No. 1216, P. O. Okfuskee, Enrolled December 2, 1899											
3916	1	Folsom, Thomas	55	M	F		Tom	D	Cr	Unknown	D	Cr
3917	2	Folsom, Louisa	40	F	F	Wf	Kowakoche	D	Cr	Koktee	L	Sem
		No. 1 died May 17, 1904. No. 2 died 1905										
	Census Card No. 1217, P. O. Edna, Enrolled December 2, 1899; No. 5 May 7, 1900											
3918	1	Scott, Samuel	30	M	F		Tullemarsey Scott	L	Cr	Hatapulfkee	D	Cr
3919	2	Scott, Nancy	26	F	F	Wf	Cholar Fixico	D	Cr	Fologa Fixico	D	Cr
3920	3	Scott, Wicey	6	F	F	D	No. 1	L	Cr	No. 2	L	Cr
3921	4	Jacob, Pilot	12	M	F	Cousin	Unknown	L	Cr	Nancy Martin	D	Cr
3922	5	Scott, James	1 mo	M	F	S	No. 1	L	Cr	No. 2	L	Cr
		No. 1 died February 1910										
	Census Card No. 1218, P. O. Tuskegee; No. 2 Newby, Enrolled December 2, 1899; No. 5 February 20, 1900											
3923	1	Bear, Katie	50	F	F		Micco Poeca	D	Cr	Ficconihe	D	Cr
3924	2	Bear, Marche	18	M	F	S	Nocus Fixico	D	Cr	No. 1	L	Cr
3925	3	Bear, Juda	17	F	F	D	Nocus Fixico	D	Cr	No. 1	L	Cr
3926	4	Bear, Hannah	16	F	F	D	Nocus Fixico	D	Cr	No. 1	L	Cr
3927	5	Bear, Paro	22	M	F	S	Nocus Fixico	D	Cr	No. 1	L	Cr
		No. 3 died September 1902. No. 4 died January 1, 1911. No. 5 died April 1905										
	Census Card No. 1219, P. O. Okmulgee, Enrolled December 2, 1899											
3928	1	Morton, William P.	2	M	1/4		William Morton	L	Non	Delilah Morton	L	Cr
	Census Card No. 1220, P. O. Okfuskee, Enrolled December 2, 1899											
3929	1	Mitchell, Levi	45	M	F		Inneha Micco	D	Cr	Tiedochkee	D	Cr
3930		Mitchell, Sally	13	F	F	D	No 1	L	Cr	Melesie Mitchell	D	Cr
3931	3	Mitchell, Albert	6	M	F	S	No. 1	L	Cr	Melesie Mitchell	D	Cr
		No. 2 died September 26, 1903. No. 3 died December 2, 1910. No. 1 reported dead										
	Census Card No. 1221, P. O. Muskogee, Enrolled December 2, 1899											
3932	1	Bemo, Myrtle L.	10	F	3/8		John Bemore	L	Cr	Alice Bemore	D	Non
	Census Card No. 1222, P. O. Ridge, Enrolled December 2, 1899											
3933	1	Beams, Mitchell	14	M	1/2		Jake Beams	L	Cr	Jane Henry	L	Cr
		No. 1 died November 6, 1904										
	Census Card No. 1223, P. O. Okfuskee, Enrolled December 2, 1899											
3934	1	Fixico, Wegus	60	M	F		Hotulka Fixico	D	Cr	Unknown	D	Cr
		No. 1 died 1900										

Roll No.	No.	NAME	Age	Sex	Blood	Rel.	NAME OF FATHER	Liv.	Cit.	NAME OF MOTHER	Liv.	Cit.
		Census Card No. 1224, P. O. Bristow, Enrolled December 2, 1899; Nos. 6 and 7 May 23, 1901										
3935	1	Tiger, Daniel	45	M	F		Parbeche	D	Cr	Hoyebar	L	Cr
3936	2	Tiger, Sarah	18	F	F	Wf	Charley Brown	D	Cr	Annie Dickson	D	Cr
3937	3	Tiger, Palmer	19	M	F	S	No. 1	L	Cr	Senna Tiger	D	Cr
3938	4	Tiger, David	11	M	F	S	No. 1	L	Cr	Senna Tiger	D	Cr
3939	5	Tiger, Medelia	8	F	F	D	No. 1	L	Cr	Senna Tiger	D	Cr
3940	6	Tiger, Lonie	20	F	F	DinL	Copathanney	L	Cr	Conseney	L	Cr
3941	7	Tiger, Bessie	1	F	F	GrD	No. 3	L	Cr	No. 6	L	Cr
		No. 2 died December 17, 1902. No. 4 died December 30, 1900. No. 5 died June 4, 1901. No. 6 died November 19, 1899. No. 7 died March 4, 1900										
		Census Card No. 1225, P. O. Haskell, Enrolled December 4, 1899										
3942	1	Anderson, David V.	55	M	½		George Anderson	D	Cr	Nancy Anderson	D	Cr
3943	2	Anderson, Lizzie M.	24	F	¾	D	No. 1	L	Cr	Betsey Anderson	D	Cr
3944	3	Anderson, Robert	21	M	¾	S	No. 1	L	Cr	Betsey Anderson	D	Cr
3945	4	Anderson, George W.	11	M	¾	S	No. 1	L	Cr	Nellie Anderson	D	Cr
		No. 1 died April 13, 1910										
		Census Card No. 1226, P. O. Hitchita, Enrolled December 4, 1899; Nos. 4 and 5 May 18, 1901										
3946	1	Barnwell, John	45	M	½		John Barnwell	D	Non	Wisey Barnwell	D	Cr
3947	2	Barnwell, Jane	48	F	⅝	Wf	Sam Berryhill	D	Cr	Fannie Berryhill	D	Cr
3948	3	Runner, Susan	18	F	F	Ward	Dave Runner	D	Cr	Louisa Runner	D	Cr
3949	4	Runner, Bunnie	11	M	F	Ward	Dave Runner	D	Cr	Louisa Runner	D	Cr
3950	5	Logan, Stella	6	F	F	Ward	Lincoln Logan	D	Cr	Louisa Logan	D	Cr
		No. 3 died April 22, 1903. No. 4 reported dead										
		Census Card No. 1227, P. O. Mounds, Enrolled December 5, 1899										
3951	1	Wills, John S.	29	M	⅛		William H. Wills	L	Cr	M. J. Wills	L	Non
		Census Card No. 1228, P. O. Muskogee, Enrolled December 5, 1899										
3952	1	Escoe, Wiley T.	45	M	¼		Thomas Escoe	L	Non	Mary Escoe	L	Cr
3953	2	Escoe, Walter J.	20	M	⅛	S	No. 1	L	Cr	Josephene Escoe	L	Non
3954	3	Escoe, Charlie J.	18	M	⅛	S	No. 1	L	Cr	Josephene Escoe	L	Non
3955	4	Escoe, John H.	17	M	⅛	S	No. 1	L	Cr	Josephene Escoe	L	Cr
3956	5	Escoe, Ida Maude	12	F	⅛	D	No. 1	L	Cr	Josephene Escoe	L	Non
3957	6	Excoe, Ethel May	10	F	⅛	D	No. 1	L	Cr	Josephene Escoe	L	Non
3958	7	Escoe, Lenora Francis	7	F	⅛	D	No. 1	L	Cr	Josephene Escoe	L	Non
3959	8	Escoe, Earnest B.	5	M	⅛	S	No. 1	L	Cr	Josephene Escoe	L	Non
3960	9	Escoe, Ella Mabel	3	F	⅛	D	No. 1	L	Cr	Josephene Escoe	L	Non
		Census Card No. 1229, P. O. Coweta, Enrolled December 5, 1899										
3961	1	Chisholm, March	28	M	½		Sampson Chisholm	D	Cr	Sally Chisholm	D	Cr
		No. 1 died August 5, 1901										
		Census Card No. 1230, P. O. Bristow, Enrolled December 5, 1899										
3962	1	Seber, Sampson	23	M	F		Seber	L	Cr	Sumhobka	D	Cr
		Census Card No. 1231, P. O. Tulsa, Enrolled December 5, 1899; Nos. 2 and 3 February 23, 1900										
3963	1	Hickory, Thomas	27	M	F		Joe Chisholm	D	Cr	Lucy	D	Cr
3964	2	Hickory, Jennie	26	F	F	Wf	Mose Kunke	L	Cr	Sally Kunke	D	Cr
3965	3	Hickory, Lucinda	8 mo	F	F	D	No. 1	L	Cr	No. 2	L	Cr
		Census Card No. 1232, P. O. Tulsa, Enrolled December 5, 1899										
3966	1	Scott, Andy	23	M	F		Skull	D	Cr	Narchey Seper	L	Cr
3967	2	Scott, Nora	18	F	¾	Wf	J. W. Perryman	L	Cr	Unknown	D	Cr
3968	3	Scott, Lou	1	F	⅞	D	No. 1	L	Cr	No. 2	L	Cr
		No. 1 died January 2, 1903. No. 3 died May 9, 1900										
		Census Card No. 1233, P. O. Broken Arrow, Enrolled December 5, 1899										
3969	1	Grayson, Watty	20	M	F		Stephen Grayson	D	Cr	Lucy Grayson	D	Cr
		Census Card No. 1234, P. O. Wagoner, Enrolled December 6, 1899										
3970	1	Childers, Anderson	30	M	¾		N. B. Childers	L	Cr	Sophie Childers	D	Cr
3971	2	Childers, Lydia	21	F	F	Wf	Henry Washington	D	Cr	Unknown	D	Cr
		No. 2 reported dead										
		Census Card No. 1235, P. O. Bixby, Enrolled December 6, 1899										
3972	1	Bunger, John	32	M	½		Bunger	D	Non	Beckie Bunger	D	Cr
3973	2	Bunger, Enoch	8	M	½	S	No. 1	L	Cr	Annie Bunger	D	Cr
		Census Card No. 1236, P. O. Sapulpa, Enrolled December 6, 1899										
3974	1	Brown, Lalley	22	F	F		Nuttecha Kosa	L	Cr	Sukey Kosa	D	Cr
3975	2	Brown, Lucy	3	F	F	D	Charley Brown	L	Cr	No. 1	L	Cr
3976	3	Brown, Nellie	1	F	F	D	Charley Brown	L	Cr	No. 1	L	Cr
		Census Card No. 1237, P. O. Hitchita, Enrolled December 7, 1899										
3977	1	Wadsworth, Caddo	62	M	¼		Joshua Wadsworth	D	Non	Louvina Allen	L	Cr
		No. 1 reported dead										
		Census Card No. 1238, P. O. Tulsa, Enrolled December 7, 1899										
3978	1	Perryman, Ben	26	M	½		Benj. Perryman	D	Cr	Martha Perryman	L	Cr
3979	2	Perryman, Martha	2	F	¼	D	No. 1	L	Cr	Sophia Perryman	L	Non
3980	3	Perryman, Frances E.	3mo	F	¼	D	No. 1	L	Cr	Sophia Perryman	L	Non
		No. 1 died March 24, 1900										
		Census Card No. 1239, P. O. Checotah, Enrolled December 7, 1899										
3981	1	Dyer, Eliza	27	F	1-16		Sam Keys	L	Cher	Sarah Keys	L	Cr
3982	2	Dyer, Sarah	7	F	1-32	D	Fred S. Dyer	L	Non	No. 1	L	Cr
3983	3	Dyer, Amanda	5	F	1-32	D	Fred S. Dyer	L	Non	No. 1	L	Cr
3984	4	Dyer, Abbie	3	F	1 32	D	Fred S. Dyer	L	Non	No. 1	L	Cr
3985	5	Dyer, Rebecca	2	F	1-32	D	Fred S. Dyer	L	Non	No. 1	L	Cr
3986	6	Dyer, Francis	6 mo	F	1-32	D	Fred S. Dyer	L	Non	No. 1	L	Cr
		No. 5 died October 10, 1900										
		Census Card No. 1240, P. O. Okmulgee; Nos. 2 ad 3 Sharp, Enrolled December 7, 1899										
3987	1	Sunny, Walter	30	M	F		Sunny	L	Sem	Peggie Sunny	L	Cr
3988	2	Sunny, Mary	37	F	½	Wf	Charnochee	L	Sem	Josephine Thompson	L	Cr
3989	3	Barnett, Ellen	5	F	¾	D	Barnett	D	Cr	No. 2	L	Cr

Roll No.	No.	NAME	Age	Sex	Blood	Rel.	NAME OF FATHER	Liv.	Cit.	NAME OF MOTHER	Liv.	Cit.
		Census Card No. 1241, P. O. Catoosa, Enrolled December 8, 1899; No. 3 December 20, 1899										
3990	1	Hooks, Alice	29	F	½		Heaster Payne	D	Cr	Patsy Rollins	D	Cher
3991	2	Hooks, Ruby Mildred	4	F	¼	D	L. P. Hooks	L	Non	No. 1	L	Cr
3992	3	Hooks, Ruth	1	F	¼	D	L. P. Hooks	L	Non	No. 1	L	Cr
		Census Card No. 1242, P. O. Weleetka, Enrolled December 8, 1899										
3993	1	Deer, Thomas	52	M	F		Dick Riley	D	Cr	Sumihahye	D	Cr
3994	2	Deer, Mary	32	F	F	Wf	George Sullivan	D	Cr	Eliza Sullivan	D	Cr
3995	3	Deer, Bettie	9	F	F	D	No. 1	L	Cr	No.	L	Cr
3996	4	Deer, George	6	M	F	S	No. 1	L	Cr	No.	L	Cr
3997	5	Deer, Louis	5	M	F	S	No. 1	L	Cr	No. 2	L	Cr
3998	6	Deer, Huldy	3	F	F	D	No. 1	L	Cr	No.	L	Cr
3999	7	Deer, Daniel	1	M	F	S	No. 1	L	Cr	No.	L	Cr
4000	8	Sullivan, Mary Ann	14	F	F	SinL	George Sullivan	D	Cr	Peggy Sullivan	L	Cr
		No. 1 died February 27, 1900. No. 2 died January 1, 1899. No. 8 reported dead										
		Census Card No. 1243, P. O. Tuskegee, Enrolled December 8, 1899										
4001	1	Marshall, Nitty	18	F	F		Okfuskee Micco	L	Cr	Hoye Micco	L	Cr
4002	2	Marshall, Hepsey	2 mo	F	F	D	Farney Marshall	L	Cr	No. 1	L	Cr
		No. 2 died September 1901										
		Census Card No. 1244, Okfuskee; No. 2 Edna, Enrolled December 8, 1899										
4003	1	Fixico, Lettif	45	M	F		Unknown	D	Cr	Unknown	D	Cr
4004	2	Fixico, Hinny	19	F	F	Wf	Okfuskee Micco	L	Cr	Hoye Micco	L	Cr
		No. 1 reported dead										
		Census Card No. 1245, P. O. Okfuskee, Enrolled December 8, 1899										
4005	1	Fish, Josiah	16	M	F		Thorthlo Fixico	D	Cr	Nanny Fixico	L	Cr
		No. 1 died February 1910										
		Census Card No. 1246, P. O. Bristow, Enrolled December 8, 1899										
4006	1	Sutor, Robert	45	M	F		Maneeche	D	Cr	Sindiega	D	Cr
		Census Card No. 1247, P. O. Okfuskee, Enrolled December 8, 1899										
4007	1	Annie	50	F	F		Lahtahoma	D	Cr	Lasochee	D	Cr
		No. 1 died April 2, 1901										
		Census Card No. 1248, P. O. Okfuskee, Enrolled December 8, 1899										
4008	1	Yahola, Woxie	40	M	F		Ocer Yahola	D	Cr	Nachakee	D	Cr
		No. 1 reported dead										
		Census Card No. 1249, P. O. Mason, Enrolled December 8, 1899										
4009	1	Micco, Okfusky	45	M	F		Nagusche Fixico	D	Cr	Arsamarhe	D	Cr
4010	2	Micco, Hoye	40	F	F	Wf	Nehathloccoche	D	Cr	Suwagee	D	Cr
4011	3	Micco, Henry	20	M	F	S	No. 1	L	Cr	No. 2	L	Cr
4012	4	Micco, Thompson	12	M	F	S	No. 1	L	Cr	No. 2	L	Cr
		No. 1 died July 13, 1907. No. 2 died March 30, 1903										
		Census Card No. 1250, P. O. Bristow, Enrolled December 8, 1899										
4013	1	Marpiyecher	44	M	F		Allicky	D	Cr	Thlesemothoke	D	Cr
		No. 1 died July 25, 1900										
		Census Card No. 1251, P. O. Leonard, Enrolled December 9, 1899										
4014	1	Lewis, Jack	28	M	F		Eli Emarthla	D	Cr	Susanna	D	Cr
4015	2	Lewis, Delilah	28	F	F	Wf	Tecumseh Uni	D	Cr	Jane	D	Cr
4016	3	Lewis, John	1½	M	F	S	Tecumseh Uni	D	Cr	No. 2	L	Cr
		No. 3 died July 24, 1900										
		Census Card No. 1252, P. O. Eufaula, Enrolled December 11, 1899										
4017	1	"Lucy"	60	F	F		Unknown	D	Cr	Unknown	D	Cr
		No. 1 died August 26, 1914										
		Census Card No. 1253, P. O. Okfuskee, Enrolled December 12, 1899										
4018	1	Scott, Louis	23	M	F		Tulmarcy Scott	L	Cr	Scott	D	Cr
4019	2	Scott, Nicey	29	F	F	Wf	Mekko Harjo Mikko	D	Cr	Sarhosekar	L	Cr
		Census Card No. 1254, P. O. Wetumka, Enrolled December 12, 1899										
4020	1	Scott, Sampson	27	M	F		Tulmarcy Scott	L	Cr	Scott	D	Cr
4021	2	Scott, Peer	21	F	F	Wf	Sunderler Fixico	D	Cr	Polly Fixico	L	Cr
		Census Card No. 1255, P. O. Checotah, Enrolled December 12, 1899										
4022	1	Keys, Lee	19	M	1-16		Sam Keys	L	Cher	Sarah Keys	L	Cr
		Census Card No. 1256, P. O. Brush Hill, Enrolled December 12, 1899										
4023	1	Grayson, Robert	40	M	¾		Bill Grayson	D	Cr	Mariah Grayson	L	Cr
4024	2	Grayson, Louisa	35	F	½	Wf	Unknown	?	?	Libbie	D	?
4025	3	Grayson, Robert, Jr.	10	M	⅝	S	No. 1	L	Cr	No. 2	L	Cr
4026	4	Grayson, Emma	5	F	⅝	D	No. 1	L	Cr	No. 2	L	Cr
4027	5	Grayson, Billy	3	M	⅝	S	No. 1	L	Cr	No. 2	L	Cr
		Census Card No. 1257, P. O. Okfuskee; No. 3 Bryqnt, Enrolled December 14, 1899										
4028	1	Johnson, Jacob	55	M	F		Artusse Micco	L	Cr	Iege Micco	D	Cr
4029	2	Johnson, Nannie	45	F	F	Wf	Talmatustanugga	D	Cr	Unknown	D	Cr
4030	3	Johnson, Yarner	12	F	F	D	No. 1	L	Cr	Lowina Bear	D	Cr
		No. 2 died April 28, 1901. No. 1 died May 9, 1902										
		Census Card No. 1258, P. O. Okemah, Enrolled December 14, 1899										
4031	1	Johnson, Colberson	W22	M	F		Jacob Johnson	L	Cr	Lowina Bear	D	Cr
4032	2	Johnson, Millie	22	F	F	Wf	John Smith	L	Cr	Mary Smith	L	Cr
		No. 1 died August 12, 1902										
		Census Card No. 1259, P. O. Okfuskee, Enrolled December 14, 1899										
4033	1	Johnson, Joseph	20	M	F		Jacob Johnson	L	Cr	Lowina Bear	D	Cr

Roll No.	No.	NAME	Age	Sex	Blood	Rel.	NAME OF FATHER	Liv.	Cit.	NAME OF MOTHER	Liv.
		Census Card No. 1260, P. O. Morse, Enrolled December 14, 1899									
4034	1	Ahfonoke	48	M	F		Chola Yahola	D	Cr	Absechage	D
4035	2	Ahfonoke, Hoktoche	47	F	F	Wf	Nokosche	D	Cr	Unknown	D
4036	3	Ahfonoke, Parnoskey	25	M	F	S	. No. 1	L	Cr	No. 2	L
4037	4	Ahfonoke, Nicey	16	F	F	D	No. 1	L	Cr	No. 2	L
4038	5	Ahfonoke, Simmer	14	M	F	S	No. 1	L	Cr	No. 2	L
4039	6	Ahfonoke, Sayochee	12	M	F	S	No. 1	L	Cr	No. 2	L
4040	7	Ahfonoke, Cheparney	10	M	F	S	No. 1	L	Cr	No. 2	L
4041	8	Ahfonoke, Malley	3moF	F	F	D	No. 1	L	Cr	No. 2	L
		No. 3 died June 12, 1901. No. 5 died January 7, 1907. No. 1 died 1900.									
		Census Card No. 1261, P. O. Morse, Enrolled December 14, 1899									
4042	1	Deer, Joe	49	M	F		Aktiarchee Micco	D	Cr	Wichie	D
4043	2	Deer, Yarnar	20	F	F	Wf	Nokas Harjo	D	Cr	Wiley Harjo	D
4044	3	Deer, Lucy	12	F	F	D	No. 1	L	Cr	Chalega	D
4045	4	Deer, Daniel	14	M	F	S	No. 1	L	Cr	Chalega	D
		No. 4 died September 3, 1900. No. 3 reported dead.									
		Census Card No. 1262, P. O. Morse, Enrolled December 14, 1899; No. 3, May 22, 1901									
4046	1	Keys, Charley	46	M	F		Ahala Emarthla	D	Cr	Nuchaka	D
4047	2	Keys, Semarhetchkar	28	F	F	Wf	Joe Deer	L	Cr	Chalega	D
4048	3	Keys, Lesta	2	F	F	D	No. 1	L	Cr	No. 2	L
		No. 1 died June 7, 1902. No. 2 reported dead.									
		Census Card No. 1263, P. O. Okfuskee, Enrolled December 14, 1899									
4049	1	Harjochee, Isparney	28	M	F		Chula Harjo	D	Cr	Iyan	D
4050	2	Harjochee, Amanda	25	F	F	Wf	Joe Deer	L	Cr	Chalega	D
4051	3	Harjochee, Amos	2	M	F	S	No. 1	L	Cr	No. 2	L
		No. 3 died March 18, 1913.									
		Census Card No. 1264, P. O. Morse, Enrolled December 14, 1899									
4052	1	Marshall, Barney	25	M	F		Conup Harjochee	D	Cr	Wiley Harjochee	D
		No. 1 died April 5, 1903									
		Census Card No. 1265, P. O. Morse; Nos. 1 and 3, Okemah, Enrolled December 14, 1899									
4053	1	Harjo, Melinhoda	25	F	F		Billy Tiger	D	Cr	Sothar	D
4054	2	Harjo, Millyanna	4	F	F	D	Toney Harjo	D	Cr	No. 1	L
4055	3	Harjo, Thaneda	2	F	F	D	Toney Harjo	D	Cr	No. 1	L
		No. 1 died February 7, 1908. No. 3 died January 1900.									
		Census Card No. 1266, P. O. Okemah, Enrolled December 14, 1899									
4056	1	Harjo, Hutchenubbe	75	M	F		Tulwa Harjo	D	Cr	Yukse	D
4057	2	Harjo, Silbie	33	F	F	D	No. 1	L	Cr	Tahwiheche	D
4058	3	Harjo, Oklossie	16	F	F	D	No. 1	L	Cr	Sothar	D
4059	4	Harjo, Samson	11	M	F	S	No. 1	L	Cr	Sothar	D
4060	5	Harjo, Nancy	10	F	F	D	No. 1	L	Cr	Sothar	D
4061	6	Harjo, Nekie	9	F	F	D	No. 1	L	Cr	Sothar	D
4062	7	Harjo, Mulley	6	F	F	D	No. 1	L	Cr	Sothar	D
		No. 2 died April 15, 1907. No. 4 died 1903. No. 5 died February 14, 1908. No. 6 died Jan 31, 1913. No. 7 died February 1909. No. 3 reported dead.									
		Census Card No. 1267, P. O. Okemah, Enrolled December 14, 1899									
4063	1	Coon, William	33	M	F		Watkoche	D	Cr	Unknown	D
4064	2	Coon, Sealey	33	F	F	Wf	Tulwa Fixico	D	Cr	Betsie Fixico	L
4065	3	Coon, Kaney	15	M	F	S	No. 1	L	Cr	No. 2	L
4066	4	Coon, Cumpsy	11	M	F	S	No. 1	L	Cr	No. 2	L
4067	5	Coon, Tobler	9	M	F	S	No. 1	L	Cr	No. 2	L
		No. 4 died November 28, 1908. No. 3 died June 16, 1906. No. 1 died June 19, 1912.									
		Census Card No. 1268, P. O. Morse, Enrolled December 14, 1899									
4068	1	Ablow, Nicey	27	F	F		Abloe	D	Cr	Lizzie	D
		Census Card No. 1269, P. O. Morse, Enrolled December 14, 1899									
4069	1	Yahola, Wotko	69	M	F		Okchiye Fixico	D	Cr	Ardodey	D
		No. 1 died February 1902									
		Census Card No. 1270, P. O. Castle, Enrolled December 14, 1899									
4070	1	Yahola, Kowockkochi	45	M	F		Narbutche Harjo	D	Cr	Tharsamaye	D
4071	2	Yahola, Nelly	30	F	F	Wf	Wotka Yahola	L	Cr	Somecha	D
4072	3	Yahola, Sunday	7	M	F	S	No. 1	L	Cr	No. 2	L
4073	4	Yahola, Linda	5	F	F	D	No. 1	L	Cr	No. 2	L
4074	5	Yahola, Wanchee	19	M	F	S	No. 1	L	Cr	Ayah	D
		Census Card No. 1271, P. O. Welty; Nos. 2 and 3, Morse, Enrolled December 14,1899; No. 4, May 16,									
4075	1	Fish, Janie	24	F	F		John Porter	D	Cr	Topsy Porter	D
4076	2	Porter, Misey	16	F	F	Sis	John Porter	D	Cr	Topsy Porter	D
4077	3	Porter, Sallie	80	F	F	GrM	Oktayarchee Harjo	D	Cr	Wattie	D
4078	4	Fish, Willie	4	M	F	S	Dick Richard	D	Cr	No. 1	L
		No. 4 died May 18, 1899. No. 2 and 3 reported dead.									
		Census Card No. 1272, P. O. Creek, Enrolled December 14, 1899									
4079	1	Porter, Ochee	26	F	F		Tustoguthkee	L	Cr	Topsy Porter	D
		No. 1 died August 20, 1909									
		Census Card No. 1273, P. O. Morse, Enrolled December 14, 1899									
4080	1	Heneha, Eannah	18	F	F		Hobe Henneha	D	Cr	Leah	D
		Census Card No. 1274, P. O. Checotah, Enrolled December 14, 1899; No. 4, March 30, 1900									
4081	1	Wright, Jane P.	23	F	⅛		Isaac Hosey	L	Non	Harriet Hosey	L
4082	2	Wright, Annie F.	7	F	1-16	D	C. J. Wright	L	Non	No. 1	L
4083	3	Wright, Cora Adeline	2	F	1-16	D	C. J. Wright	L	Non	No. 1	L
4084	4	Wright, Judge William	4	M	1-16	S	C. J. Wright	L	Non	No. 1	L
		Census Card No. 1275, P. O. Wealaka, Enrolled December 15, 1899									
4085	1	Clinton, Willis	28	M	F		Cahtutah	D	Cr	Mary Beartail	L

88

Roll No.	No.	NAME	Age	Sex	Blood	Rel.	NAME OF FATHER	Liv.	Cit.	NAME OF MOTHER	Liv.	Cit.
		Census Card No. 1276, P. O. Wagoner, Enrolled December 15, 1899										
4086	1	Marlow, Ellen	31	F	¼		Charles Cane	D	Non	Priscilla Kane	D	Cr
4087	2	Marlow, Ruth	7	F	⅛	D	James P. Marlow	L	Non	No. 1	L	Cr
		Census Card No. 1277, P. O. Wealaka; No. 3, Sapulpa, Enrolled December 16, 1899										
4088	1	Brown, Madison H.	30	M	½		S. W. Brown	L	Cr	Neosho P. Brown	D	Cr
4089	2	Brown, Cilla	28	F	F	Wf	McCoy	D	Cr	Liza Brown	L	Cr
4090	3	Brown, Esther M.	11	F	¾	D	No. 1	L	Cr	No. 2	L	Cr
4091	4	Brown, Sammie	7	M	¾	S	No. 1	L	Cr	No. 2	L	Cr
4092	5	Brown, Nettie	9moF		¾	D	No. 1	L	Cr	No. 2	L	Cr
		No. 1 died September 1911. No. 4 died August 18, 1902. No. 5 died August 4, 1910.										
		Census Card No. 1278, P. O. Castle; No. 4, Hanna, Enrolled December 18, 1899										
4093	1	Johnson, Miller	50	M	F		Unknown	D	Cr	Unknown	D	Cr
4094	2	Johnson, Halley	18	F	F	D	No. 1	L	Cr	Tarwoligee	D	Cr
4095	3	Johnson, Maggie	12	F	F	D	No. 1	L	Cr	Tarwoligee	D	Cr
4096	4	Johnson, Willie	9	M	F	S	No. 1	L	Cr	Tarlowgee	D	Cr
4097	5	Johnson, Chenowee	6	M	F	S	No. 1	L	Cr	Tarwoligee	D	Cr
		No. 1 died May 5, 1902										
		Census Card No. 1279, P. O. Okemah; No. 6, Mason, Enrolled December 19, 1899										
4098	1	Johnson, Cullie	25	M	F		Miller Johnson	L	Cr	Lowiney	D	Cr
4099	2	Johnson, Mahaley	24	F	F	Wf	Sebor	D	Cr	Rosana	D	Cr
4100	3	Johnson, Lena	1wkF		D		No. 1	L	Cr	No. 2	L	Cr
4101	4	Johnson, Sunny	6	M	F	S	No. 1	L	Cr	Tenner Johnson	D	Cr
4102	5	Johnson, Missaley	4	F	F	D	No. 1	L	Cr	Tenner Johnson	D	Cr
4103	6	Harjo, Annie	15	F	F	Sis	Abhorlock Harjo	L	Cr	Lowiney	D	Cr
		No. 4 died May 5, 1910										
		Census Card No. 1280, P. O. Morse, Enrolled December 19, 1899										
4104	1	Parhosey, Jemima	35	F	F		Halahockey	D	Cr	Unknown	D	Cr
4105	2	Davis, Allie	15	M	F	S	Parhosey	D	Cr	No. 1	L	Cr
4106	3	Harjo, Missey	13	M	F	S	Hutchenubbe Harjo	L	Cr	No. 1	L	Cr
4107	4	Fields, Filda	4	F	F	D	Ponsey Fields	L	Cr	No. 1	L	Cr
		No. 3 reported dead										
		Census Card No. 1281, P. O. No. 1, Weir; No. 2, Jennings, Enrolled December 19, 1899										
4108	1	McElroy, Jennie H.	11	F	¼		W. A. McElroy	L	Non	Hattie McElroy	D	Cr
4109	2	McElroy, Oma G.	9	F	¼	Sis	W. A. McElroy	L	Non	Hattie McElroy	D	Cr
		No. 2 died December 19, 1911										
		Census Card No. 1282, P. O. Morse, Enrolled December 19, 1899										
4110	1	Key, Ety	33	F	F		Parhos Emarthlochee	D	Cr	Hebsey Fixico	L	Cr
4111	2	Keeny, Joe	16	M	F	S	Watko Homarte	D	Cr	No. 1	L	Cr
		Census Card No. 1283, P. O. Okemah; No. 3, Waldron, Ark., Enrolled December 19, 1899										
4112	1	Hall, Hannah E.	27	F	¾		David Doyle	D	Cr	Precilla Doyle	D	Cr
4113	2	Hall, Alvie	4	M	⅜	S	Samuel Hall	L	Non	No. 1	L	Cr
4114	3	Hall, Melburn	1	M	⅜	S	Samuel Hall	L	Non	No. 1	L	Cr
		No. 3 died October 2, 1907										
		Census Card No. 1284, P. O. Mason, Enrolled December 19, 1899										
4115	1	West, George	55	M	F		Eufaula Harjo	D	Cr	Unknown	D	Cr
4116	2	West, Siker	17	M	F	S	No. 1	L	Cr	Nancy	D	Cr
4117	3	West, Ledie	9	F	F	D	No. 1	L	Cr	Nancy	D	Cr
		No. 2 died March 9, 1914										
		Census Card No. 1285, P. O. Morse, Enrolled December 19, 1899										
4118	1	Hicks, Wesley	25	M	F		George Hicks	L	Cr	Lisochee	D	Cr
		No. 1 reported dead										
		Census Card No. 1286, P. O. Okemah, Enrolled December 19, 1899										
4119	1	Simmons, Peggie	43	F	F		Tum Emarthla	D	Cr	Gagee	D	Cr
4120	2	Simmons, Mary	10	F	F	D	Oktaryarchee Harjochee	D	Cr	No. 1	L	Cr
4121	3	Simmons, Bettie	8	F	F	D	Oktaryarchee Harjochee	L	Cr	No. 1	L	Cr
4122	4	Simmons, Scott	4moM	F	S		Oktaryarchee Harjochee	D	Cr	No. 1	L	Cr
		No. 1 died 1906										
		Census Card No. 1287, P. O. Okemah, Enrolled December 19, 1899										
4123	1	Fixico, Pefeny	25	F	F		Katcher Fixico	D	Cr	Peggy Simmons	L	Cr
4124	2	Simmons, Benhakka	5	M	F	S	O. Harjochee	D	Cr	No. 1	L	Cr
4125	3	Simmons, Fannie	3	F	F	D	O. Harjochee	D	Cr	No. 1	L	Cr
		No. 3 died September 30, 1899. No. 1 died January 1912.										
		Census Card No. 1288, P. O. Edna, Enrolled December 19, 1899										
4126	1	Harjo, Nannie	35	F	F		Unknown	D	Cr	Unknown	D	Cr
4127	2	Harjo, Willie	5	M	F	S	Nokus Harjo	D	Cr	No. 1	L	Cr
4128	3	Micco, Sarkinnarne	12	M	F	Neph	Lahtar Micco	D	Cr	Mary Yarticka	D	Cr
4129	4	Micco, Kate	7	F	F	Niece	Lahtar Micco	D	Cr	Mary Yarticka	D	Cr
4130	5	Micco, Charley	3	M	F	Neph	Lahtar Micco	D	Cr	Mary Yarticka	D	Cr
		No. 3 reported dead										
		Census Card No. 1289, P. O. Holdenville; No. 3, Okema, Enrolled December 20, 1899; No. 3, May 4, 1900										
4131	1	Harjo, Johnson	54	M	¾		Lumsey Harjo	D	Cr	Munna Sewell	D	Cr
4132	2	Harjo, June	54	F	½	Wf	Samuel Berryhill	D	Cr	Berryhill	D	?
4133	3	Harjo, Louvina	13	F	F	Ward	Sam Scott	L	Cr	Soma	D	Cr
		No. 1 died January 22, 1902										
		Census Card No. 1290, P. O. Bristow, Enrolled December 20, 1899										
4134	1	Johnson, Samuel	45	M	F		Chlechuchee	D	Cr	Unknown	D	Cr

Census Card No. 1291, P. O. Holdenville, Enrolled December 20, 1899

Roll No.	No.	NAME	Age	Sex	Blood	Rel.	NAME OF FATHER	Liv.	Cit.	NAME OF MOTHER	Liv.	Cit.
4135	1	Fixico, Locher	40	M	F		Cahshe Emarwe	D	Cr	Unknown	D	Cr

No. 1 reported dead

Census Card No. 1292, P. O. Edna, Enrolled December 20, 1899

Roll No.	No.	NAME	Age	Sex	Blood	Rel.	NAME OF FATHER	Liv.	Cit.	NAME OF MOTHER	Liv.	Cit.
4136	1	Knight, David	21	M	F		Tehitke Larney	D	Cr	Maryticka	D	Cr

Census Card No. 1293, P. O. Bristow, Enrolled December 20, 1899

Roll No.	No.	NAME	Age	Sex	Blood	Rel.	NAME OF FATHER	Liv.	Cit.	NAME OF MOTHER	Liv.	Cit.
4137	1	West, Waddie	30	M	F		George West	L	Cr	Polly	D	Cr
4138	2	West, Sissy	30	F	F	Wf	Conip Harjochee	L	Cr	Waley	D	Cr
4139	3	West, Williamsee	6	M	F	S	No. 1	L	Cr	Unknown	?	Cr
4140	4	West, Milochee	.5	F	F	D	No. 1	L	Cr	Unknown	?	Cr

No. 3 died October 1901

Census Card No. 1294, P. O. Eufaula, Enrolled December 20, 1899

Roll No.	No.	NAME	Age	Sex	Blood	Rel.	NAME OF FATHER	Liv.	Cit.	NAME OF MOTHER	Liv.	Cit.
4141	1	Simpson, Susan A.	58	F	1-16		W. D. Crabtree	D	Non	Precilla Crabtree	D	Cr
4142	2	Simpson, James H.	16	M	1-32	S	John F. Simpson	D	Non	No. 1	L	Cr

Census Card No. 1295, P. O. Morse; No. 3, Bristow, Enrolled December 20, 1899

Roll No.	No.	NAME	Age	Sex	Blood	Rel.	NAME OF FATHER	Liv.	Cit.	NAME OF MOTHER	Liv.	Cit.
4143	1	Fixico, Hotulke	45	M	F		Yaha Fixico	D	Cr	Firlina	D	Cr
4144	2	Fixico, Hebsey	45	F	F	Wf	Neha Yarhola	D	Cr	Unknown	D	Cr
4145	3	Hinneha, Eny	15	F	F	Niece	Artus Hinneha	D	Cr	Ieka	D	Cr

Census Card No. 1296, P. O. Morse, Enrolled December 20, 1899; No. 3, June 19, 1900

Roll No.	No.	NAME	Age	Sex	Blood	Rel.	NAME OF FATHER	Liv.	Cit.	NAME OF MOTHER	Liv.	Cit.
4146	1	Beaver, Joe	21	M	F		Wilson Beaver	L	Cr	Fanny	D	Cr
4147	2	Beaver, Lela	27	F	F	Wf	Clothlo Harjochee	L	Cr	Leah	D	Cr
4148	3	Beaver, John	6moM	F	S		No. 1	L	Cr	No. 2	L	Cr

No. 1 reported dead

Census Card No. 1297, P. O. Okfuskee, Enrolled December 20, 1899

Roll No.	No.	NAME	Age	Sex	Blood	Rel.	NAME OF FATHER	Liv.	Cit.	NAME OF MOTHER	Liv.	Cit.
4149	1	Teke	22	M	F		Tuskegee Harjo	D	Cr	Sinegesta	D	Cr
4150	2	Scott, Hunter	16	F	F	Wf	Tulmars Scott	L	Cr	Kochetly	L	Cr

No. 1 died January 27, 1912

Census Card No. 1298, P. O. Morse; No. 3, Bristow, Enrolled December 20, 1899

Roll No.	No.	NAME	Age	Sex	Blood	Rel.	NAME OF FATHER	Liv.	Cit.	NAME OF MOTHER	Liv.	Cit.
4151	1	Mikey, Silwar	50	F	F		Yaha Fixico	D	Cr	Faulena	D	Cr
4152	2	Mikey, Amy	20	F	F	D	Mikey	D	Cr	No. 1	L	Cr
4153	3	Mikey, Lizzie	16	F	F	D	Mikey	D	Cr	No. 1	L	Cr

No. 2 died 1911

Census Card No. 1299, P., O. Morse, Enrolled December 20, 1899

Roll No.	No.	NAME	Age	Sex	Blood	Rel.	NAME OF FATHER	Liv.	Cit.	NAME OF MOTHER	Liv.	Cit.
4154	1	Kizzie	50	F	F		Yaha Fixico	D	Cr	Faulena	D	Cr
4155	2	Bear, Munnie	6	F	F	Niece	Nobos Emarthla	L	Cr	Loparklarthchchee	D	Cr

Census Card No. 1300, P. O. Okmulgee, Enrolled December 21, 1899

Roll No.	No.	NAME	Age	Sex	Blood	Rel.	NAME OF FATHER	Liv.	Cit.	NAME OF MOTHER	Liv.	Cit.
4156	1	Marsey, Sam	28	M	F		Marsey	D	Cr	Nancy Marsey	L	Cr
4157	2	Marsey, Louisa	26	F	F	Wf	John Micco	L	Cr	Marsey Micco	L	Cr
4158	3	Marsey, Sam Jr.	3	M	F	S	No. 1	L	Cr	No. 2	L	Cr
4159	4	Marsey, Katie	10	F	F	Sis	Marsey	D	Cr	Jennie	L	Cr
4160	5	Daniel, Sallie	7	F	F	StD	Kano Daniel	D	Cr	No. 2	L	Cr

No. 1 died February 13, 1901

Census Card No. 1301, P. O. Checotah, Enrolled December 21, 1899; No. 4, April 29, 1901

Roll No.	No.	NAME	Age	Sex	Blood	Rel.	NAME OF FATHER	Liv.	Cit.	NAME OF MOTHER	Liv.	Cit.
4161	1	Bruner, Sulda	36	M	F		Unknown	?	Cr	Ogee	D	Cr
4162	2	Bruner, Lucy	32	F	F	Wf	John Goodey	?	Cr	Jadie Goodey	?	Cr
4163	3	Mitchell, Severs	14	M	F	StS	Lrwis Mitchell	D	Cr	No. 2	L	Cr
4164	4	Bruner, Emma	5	F	F	D	No. 1	L	Cr	No. 2	L	Cr

No. 2 died October 15, 1909. No. 1 died March 1, 1908. No. 3 reported dead.

Census Card No. 1302, P. O. Sapulpa, Enrolled December 21, 1899

Roll No.	No.	NAME	Age	Sex	Blood	Rel.	NAME OF FATHER	Liv.	Cit.	NAME OF MOTHER	Liv.	Cit.
4165	1	McKellop, Almarine E.	39	M	3/4		James McKellop	D	Cr	Annie McKellop	D	Cr
4166	2	McKellop, Ruth A.	7	F	3/8	D	No. 1	L	Cr	Hattie S. McKellop	L	Non
4167	3	McKellop, James E.	4	M	3/8	S	No. 1	L	Cr	Hattie S. McKellop	L	Non
4168	4	McKellop, Grace	2	F	3/8	D	No. 1	L	Cr	Hattie S. McKellop	L	Non

Census Card No. 1303, P. O. Eufaula, Enrolled December 21, 1899

Roll No.	No.	NAME	Age	Sex	Blood	Rel.	NAME OF FATHER	Liv.	Cit.	NAME OF MOTHER	Liv.	Cit.
4169	1	Beshers, Mary	33	F	1/4		Moses Moore	D	Cr	Lizzie Moore	D	Non

Census Card No. 1304, P. O. Sapulpa, Enrolled December 21, 1899; No. 4, May 24, 1901

Roll No.	No.	NAME	Age	Sex	Blood	Rel.	NAME OF FATHER	Liv.	Cit.	NAME OF MOTHER	Liv.	Cit.
4170	1	Aubrey, Millie	31	F	1/2		Samuel W. Brown	L	Cr	Elizabeth Brown	D	Cr
4171	2	Wilson, Della	11	F	3/4	D	Geo. H. Wilson	D	Non	No. 1	L	Cr
4172	3	Watkins, U. S. Grant	8	M	1/4	S	U. S. Watkins	D	Non	No. 1	L	Cr
4173	4	Aubrey, Olla	13moF	3/8		D	C. B. Aubrey	L	Non	No. 1	L	Cr

No. 4 died October 26, 1899

Census Card No. 1305, P. O. Tulsa, Enrolled December 22, 1899

Roll No.	No.	NAME	Age	Sex	Blood	Rel.	NAME OF FATHER	Liv.	Cit.	NAME OF MOTHER	Liv.	Cit.
4174	1	Orcutt, Annie B.	26	F	1/4		Alvin Hodge	L	Cr	Mary Hodge	L	Cr
4175	2	Orcutt, William A.	8	M	1/4	S	S. A. Orcutt	L	Non	No.	L	Cr
4176	3	Orcutt, Homer A.	6	M	1/8	S	S. A. Orcutt	L	Non	No. 1	L	Cr
4177	4	Orcutt, Pleasant E.	2	M	1/8	S	S. A. Orcutt	L	Non	No.	L	C
4178	5	Orcutt, Archibold M.	8moM	1/8	S		S. A. Orcutt	L	Non	No. 1	L	Cr

No. 5 reported dead

Census Card No. 1306, P. O. Morse, Enrolled December 22, 89

Roll No.	No.	NAME	Age	Sex	Blood	Rel.	NAME OF FATHER	Liv.	Cit.	NAME OF MOTHER	Liv.	Cit.
4179	1	Richmond	17	M	F		Henehar Rochokne	D	C	Mieler	D	Cr
4180	2	Chenosky	14	M	F	Bro	Henehar Rochokne	D	Cr	Mieler	D	Cr

No. 1 died fall of 1899

Census Card No. 1307, P. O. Morse, Enrolled December 22, 1899

Roll No.	No.	NAME	Age	Sex	Blood	Rel.	NAME OF FATHER	Liv.	Cit.	NAME OF MOTHER	Liv.	Cit.
4181	1	Harjo, Chofolop	43	M	F		Parskover	D	Cr	Thlahomerhety	D	Cr
4182	2	Harjo, Lucy	3	F	F	D	No. 1	L	Cr	Lucinda	D	Cr
4183	3	Harjo, Lody	1	F	F	D	No. 1	L	C	Lucinda	D	Cr

Roll
No.   No.   NAME   Age Sex Blood Rel. NAME OF FATHER Liv. Cit. NAME OF MOTHER Liv. Cit.

Roll No.	No.	NAME	Age	Sex	Blood	Rel.	NAME OF FATHER	Liv.	Cit.	NAME OF MOTHER	Liv.	Cit.
		Census Card No. 1308, P. O Morse, Enrolled December 22, 189										
4184	1	Scott, Tulmars	45	M	F		Jenny Chupco	D	Cr	Lodey Chupco	D	C
4185	2	Scott, Koch tty	42	F	F	Wf	Unknown	D	Cr	Synkoky	D	Cr
4186	3	Harjo, Annoche	14	F	F	GrS	Tarmoche	D	Cr	Lucinda	D	Cr
4187	4	Mikey, Simon	16	M	F	Neph	Mikey	D	Cr	Marme	D	Cr
		No. 4 reported dead										
		Census Card No. 1309 P. O. Morse, Enrolled December 22, 1899										
4188	1	Taryole	18	M	F		Quakus Henehutche	D	Cr	Mollier	D	C:
4189	2	Mikey Marfy	18	F	F	W	Mikey	D	Cr	Silwar Mikey	L	Cr
		Census Card No. 1310, P. O. Okfuskee. Enrolled December 22 18 9										
4190	1	Scott Thomas	45	M	F		Tecumseh	D	Cr	Unknown	D	Cr
4191	2	Scott, Louisa	47	F	F	Wf	Tulmochus Micco	D	Cr	Wosode	D	Cr
4192	3	Harjochee, Joseph	17	M	F	Ward	Conchart Harjochee	D	C	Lucy	D	Cr
		No. 1 reported dead. No. 3 died May 13, 1 03.										
		Census Card No. 1311, P. O. Okfuskee, Enrolled December 22, 1899										
4193	1	Porter, James	23	M	F		Jack Porter	D	Cr	Sarlso Summer	D	Cr
4194	2	Porter, Nancy	23	F	F	Wf	Jacob Marshall	D	Cr	Puddie	D	Cr
		Census Card No. 1312, P. O. Okfuskee, Enrolled December 22, 1899										
4195	1	Deere, Mose	32	M	F		Chofolup Yahola	D	Cr	Unknown	D	Cr
4196	2	Deere, Eliza	37	F	F	Wf	Tecumseh	D	Cr	Lizzie	D	Cr
4197	3	Hinneha, Daniel	17	M	F	StS	Johnnie Moon	D	Cr	No. 2	L	Cr
4198	4	Hinneha, Noah	14	M	F	StS	Johnnie Noon	D	Cr	No. 2	L	Cr
4199	5	Hinneha, Peter	12	M	F	StS	Johnnie Moon	D	Cr	No. 2	L	Cr
4200	6	Deere, Hulíie	12	M	F	S	No. 1	L	Cr	Pittie Yahola	D	Cr
		No. 4 died April 6 1901. No. 1, 2 3, 5 reported dead.										
		Census Card No. 1313. P. O. Coweta. Enrolled December 22, 1899										
4201	1	Hinneha, Jonas	19	M	F		Johnnie Moon	D	Cr	Eliza Deere	L	Cr
		Census Card No. 1314, P. O. Okfuskee, Enrolled December 22, 1899										
4202	1	Pussey, Sarah	58	F	F		Tommy Harjo	D	Cr	Nosey	D	Cr
		Census Card No. 1315, P. O. Morse; No. 8 Weleetka. Enrolled December 22, 1899										
4203	1	Yarhola, Osuchee	59	M	F		Kartschnomartee	D	Cr	Parney	D	Cr
4204	2	Yarhola, Arsfolechar	45	F	F	Wf	Unknown	D	Cr	Temonchelechee	D	Cr
4205	3	Roberts, Weleyar	23	M	F	S	No. 1	L	Cr	Abbey	D	C
4206	4	Roberts, Warley	22	F	F	D	No. 1	L	C	No. 2	L	Cr
4207	5	Roberts, Mitchell	20	M	F	S	No. 1	L	Cr	No. 2	L	Cr
4208	6	Roberts, Wisey	16	F	F	D	No. 1	L	Cr	No. 2	L	Cr
4209	7	Roberts, Joe	14	M	F	S	No. 1	L	Cr	No. 2	L	Cr
4210	8	Roberts, Cholichar	11	M	F	S	No. 1	L	Cr	No. 2	L	Cr
4211	9	Roberts, Arnie	10	F	F	D	No. 1	L	Cr	No. 2	L	Cr
4212	10	Roberts, Louisa	6	F	F	D	No. 1	L	Cr	No. 2	L	Cr
		No. 1 died January 30, 1910. No. 7 died April 15, 1910. No 2 died December 28 1905. No. 6 died January 28, 1908.										
		Census Card No. 1316, P. O. Okfuskee, Enrolled December 22, 1899										
4213	1	Yarhola, Nokos	25	M	F		Cona Yarhola	D	Cr	Millie	D	Cr
4214	2	Yarhola, Judy	8	F	F	Sis	Cona Yarhola	D	Cr	Millie	D	Cr
		No. 2 reported dead										
		Census Card No. 1317, P. O. Morse, Enrolled December 22, 1899										
4215	1	Hennehughee, Watley	18	M	F		Henechochee	D	Cr	Kihetar	D	Cr
4216	2	Hennehughee, Hene	12	M	F	Bro	Henechochee	D	Cr	Kihetar	D	Cr
4217	3	Hennehughee, Roney	10	M	F	Bro	Henechochee	D	Cr	Kihetar	D	Cr
		No. 1 reported dead. Nos. 2 and 3 reported dead.										
		Census Card No. 1318, P. O. Okemah; No. 2, Castle. Enrolled December 22, 1899										
4218	1	Sampson, Elsie	55	F	F		Arche Yarhola	D	Cr	Ahmana	D	Cr
4219	2	Sampson, Johnson	16	M	F	S	Sampson	L	Cr	No. 1	L	Cr
4220	3	Harjochee, Losana	32	F	F	Niece	John	L	Cr	Cona Histcha	D	Cr
4221	4	Harjochee, Jimmie	5	M	F	GrNe	Yahtika Harjochee	L	Cr	No. 3	L	Cr
4222	5	Harjochee, Harper	3	M	F	GrNe	Yahtika Harjochee	L	Cr	No. 3	L	Cr
		No. 3 died February 12, 1900. No. 2 reported dead. No. 3 died June 1, 1912.										
		Census Card No. 1319, P. O. Okfuskee, Enrolled December 22, 1899										
4223	1	Johnson, Miley	21	F	F		Nokus Fixico	L	Cr	Lowina Bear	L	Cr
4224	2	Johnson, Adam	1	M	F	S	Jonas Hinneha	L	Cr	No. 1	L	Cr
4225	3	Yarhola, Aaron	20	M	F	Hus	Cona Yarhola	D	Cr	Millie	D	Cr
		No. 2 died January 29, 1900										
		Census Card No. 1320, P. O. Broken Arrow, Enrolled December 23, 1899										
4226	1	Burgess, Tyler	21	M	F		Daniel Burgess	D	Cr	Lowisa Burgess	D	Cr
		Census Card No. 1321, P. O. Okfuskee, Enrolled December 22, 1899										
4227	1	Davis, Karneyoh	30	F	F		Holleputa Harjo	D	Cr	Linda	D	Cr
4228	2	Yarhola, Lucy	12	F	F	D	Yaha Yarhola	L	Cr	No. 1	L	Cr
4229	3	Tamochee, Patsy	3	F	F	D	Tamochee	D	Cr	No. 1	L	Cr
		No. 1 died February 1903. No. 3 reported dead.										
		Census Card No. 1322, P. O. Okfuskee, Enrolled December 22, 1899										
4230	1	Fixico, Hulberta	30	M	F		Osoch Yarhola	L	Cr	Abolin	D	Cr
4231	2	Fixico, Loisoche	28	F	F	Wf	Tulmarsey Emarthla	L	Cr	Kise Larney	D	Cr
		No. 2 died November 5, 1906. No. 1 died January 3, 1906.										
		Census Card No. 1323, P. O. Morse, Enrolled December 22, 1899										
4232	1	Harjo, Holtuke	60	M	F		Neha Harjo	D	Cr	Lucinda	D	Cr
4233	2	Harjo, Hannah	25	F	F	Wf	Hoputh Harjo	D	Cr	Keatka	D	Cr
4234	3	Simmer, John	18	M	F	S	No. 1	L	Cr	Sarls Simmer	D	Cr
4235	4	Fixico, Angie	20	F	F	Niece	Oktaiche Fixico	D	Cr	Wisely	D	Cr
		No. 4 died December 21, 1903. No. 1 died February 3, 1906. Nos. 2 and 3 reported dead.										

Roll No.	No.	NAME	Age	Sex	Blood	Rel.	NAME OF FATHER	Liv.	Cit.	NAME OF MOTHER	Liv.	Cit.

Census Card No. 1324, P. O. Okfuskee, Enro led December 22, 1899
| 4236 | 1 | Davis, Phoebe | 18 | F | F | | Davey | D | Cr | Sarnoschsye | D | Cr |

Census Card No. 1325, P. O. Wetumka, Enrolled December 22, 1899
| 4237 | 1 | Sulka | 65 | F | F | | Emartha Thlocco | D | Cr | Unknown | D | Cr |

Census Card No. 1326, P. O. Coweta, Enrolled December 23, 1899
| 4238 | 1 | Taylor, Tom | 20 | M | F | | Mitchell Taylor | D | Cr | Susana Taylor | D | Cr |
No. 1 reported dead

Census Card No. 1327, P. O. Stidham, Enrolled December 29, 1899; No. 7, May 10, 1901
4239	1	Moore, Robert	52	M	¼		Moses Moore	D	Cr	Lizzie Moore	D	Non
4240	2	Moore, Robert Lee	10	M	⅛	S	No. 1	L	Cr	Winnie Moore	D	Non
4241	3	Moore, Ada V.	9	F	⅛	D	No. 1	L	Cr	Winnie Moore	D	Non
4242	4	Moore, Georgiana	7	F	⅛	D	No. 1	L	Cr	Winnie Moore	D	Non
4243	5	Moore, Oliver Lee	3	M	⅛	S	No. 1	L	Cr	Winnie Moore	D	Non
4244	6	Moore, Verna Ellen	2	F	⅛	D	No. 1	L	Cr	Winnie Moore	D	Non
4245	7	Moore, Thomas J.	18	M	⅛	S	No. 1	L	Cr	Winnie Moore	D	Non

Census Card No. 1328, P. O. Okmulgee; No. 5, Eufaula, Enrolled Jan. 3, 1900; No. 8, May 22, 1901
4246	1	Thomas, John	32	M	F		Tomosey	D	Cr	Chatma	D	Cr
4247	2	Thomas, Bettie	30	F	F	Wf	Lasttah	D	Cr	Anneha	D	Cr
4248	3	Sumehcha	16	M	F	StS	Nokose	D	Cr	No. 2	L	Cr
4249	4	Micco, Johnson	14	M	F	StS	Lahta Micco	D	Cr	No. 2	L	Cr
4250	5	Lewis, Lucy	12	F	F	StD	Mose Lewis	D	Cr	No. 2	L	Cr
4251	6	Thomas, Parnosky	7	M	F	S	No. 1	L	Cr	No. 2	L	Cr
4252	7	Thomas, Adam	5	M	F	S	No. 1	L	Cr	No. 2	L	Cr
4253	8	Thomas, Kaley	3	M	F	S	No. 1	L	Cr	No. 2	L	Cr
No. 3 reported dead

Census Card No. 1329, P. O. Hoffman; No. 4, Morris, Enrolled January 3, 1900
4254	1	West, Robert	29	M	F		Tulmochus Harjo	D	Cr	Chemonah	D	Cr
4255	2	West, Sarnie	24	F	F	Wf	Tuskeek Harjo	D	Cr	Sarfixsomgah	D	Cr
4256	3	West, Katie	4	F	F	D	No. 1	L	Cr	No. 2	L	Cr
4257	4	West, Ella	13	F	F	Sis	Tumlochus Harjo	D	Cr	Chemonah	D	Cr
4258	5	Harjo, Tulmochus	47	M	F	Fath	Nehemarthochee	D	Cr	Marbeah	D	Cr
4259	6	Harjo, Chemona	46	F	F	Moth	Tustarna Emarthla	D	Cr	Unknown	D	Cr
4260	7	Marhoyee	65	F	F	GrAunt	Nehemarthochee	D	Cr	Marbeah	D	Cr
No. 5 died May 1, 1899. No. 2 died July 21, 1903. No. 6 died May 15, 1899. No. 7 died April 7, 1899.

Census Card No. 1330, P. O. Okemah, Enrolled January 3, 1900
| 4261 | 1 | Morton, Mossie | 27 | M | ¼ | | Wm. Morton | L | Non | Delilah Morton | L | Cr |

Census Card No. 1331, P. O. Checotah; No. 2, San Francisco, Cal., Guard Panama Exposition, Enrolled December 4, 1899
4262	1	Whaley, Fannie	15	F	⅛		Rufus M.Whaley,Sr.	L	Non	Rebecca Whaley	D	Cr
4263	2	Whaley, Rufus M. Jr.	13	M	⅛	Bro	Rufus M.Whaley,Sr.	L	Non	Rebecca Whaley	D	Cr
4264	3	Whaley, Elizabeth D.	11	F	⅛	Sis	Rufus M.Whaley,Sr.	L	Non	Rebecca Whaley	D	Cr

Census Card No. 1332, P. O. Brush Hill; No. 2, Checotah, Enrolled January 4, 1900; Nos. 3, 4, 5, January 22, 1900; No. 6, May 8, 1901.
4265	1	Fox, John	30	M	F		Chula Harjo	D	Cr	Nancy Harjo	D	Cr
4266	2	Fox, Lena	28	F	F	Wf	Togo Laslie	D	Cr	Laslie	D	Cr
4267	3	Fox, Cumsey	6	M	F	S	No. 1	L	Cr	No. 2	L	Cr
4268	4	Fox, Katy	4	F	F	D	No. 1	L	Cr	No. 2	L	Cr
4269	5	Fox, William	2	M	F	S	No. 1	L	Cr	No. 2	L	Cr
4270	6	Fox, Lucy	1	F	F	D	No. 1	L	Cr	No. 2	L	Cr
No. 5 died August 22, 1900

Census Card No. 1333, P. O. Bristow, Enrolled January 5, 1900; Nos. 4 and 5, March 13, 1901
4271	1	Cat, Matilda	42	F	½		Silas Jefferson	L	Cr	Mollie Jefferson	D	?
4272	2	Snapp, Amanda	21	F	¼	D	Dick Snapp	D	Non	No. 1	L	Cr
4273	3	Cat, Annie	12	F	¼	D	Monday Cat	L	Non	No. 1	L	Cr
4274	4	Cat, John	10	M	¼	GrS	Monday Cat	L	Non	Mary Harry	L	
4275	5	Cat, Lou	11	F	¼	D	Monday Cat	L	Non	No. 1	L	
No. 2 died September 1901. No. 3 died February 1901.

Census Card No. 1334, P. O. Sapulpa, Enrolled January 5, 1900
| 4276 | 1 | Campbell, Willie | 19 | M | F | | Cahwee | D | Cr | Betsey Cahwee | D | Cr |
No. 1 reported dead

Census Card No. 1335, P. O. Eufaula, Enrolled January 8, 1900
| 4277 | 1 | Ansiel, John G. | 23 | M | ⅛ | | Wm. Stephen Ansill | D | Cr | Mrs. John Tiger | L. | Non |

Census Card No. 1336, P. O. Stroud, Enrolled January 9, 1900
4278	1	Ellis, Hannah	29	F	⅝		Alex Hamilton	D	Cr	Sally Knoll	L	Cr
4279	2	Ellis, Emma C.	14	F	5-16	D	James Ellis	L	Non	No. 1	L	Cr
4280	3	Ellis, Hattie B.	10	F	5-16	D	James Ellis	L	Non	No. 1	L	Cr
4281	4	Ellis, Maud	7	F	5-16	D	James Ellis	L	Non	No. 1	L	Cr
No. 3 died March 22, 1907. No. 4 reported dead.

Census Card No. 1337, P. O. Lamar, Enrolled January 10, 1900
4282	1	Kernal, Louis	45	M	F		Osagee Yarholar	D	Cr	Silda	D	Cr
4283	2	Kernal, Aggie	43	F	F	Wf	Uknown	D	Cr	Millie	D	Cr
4284	3	Kernal, Charlie	20	M	F	S	No. 1	L	Cr	No. 2	L	Cr
4285	4	Kernal, Isaac	18	M	F	S	No. 1	L	Cr	No. 2	L	Cr
4286	5	Kernal, Amey	10	F	F	D	No. 1	L	Cr	No. 2	L	Cr
4287	6	Kernal, Sam	6	M	F	S	No. 1	L	Cr	No. 2	L	Cr
4288	7	Kernal, Johnson	3	M	F	S	No. 1	L	Cr	No. 2	L	Cr
No. 1 died April 1900. Nos. 2 and 6 reported dead.

Census Card No. 1338, P O. Checotah, Enrolled January 10, 1900; No. 3, February 18 1900
4289	1	Asbell, Emma	31	F	¼		David Yargee	D	Cr	Sarah Asbell	L	Cr
4290	2	Asbell, Glen	6	M	⅛	S	Art Asbell	L	Non	No. 1	L	Cr
4291	3	Asbell, Wallace	9da	M	⅛	S	Art Asbell	L	Non	No. 1	L	Cr

Roll No.	No.	NAME	Age	Sex	Blood	Rel.	NAME OF FATHER	Liv.	Cit.	NAME OF MOTHER	Liv.	Cit.
		Census Card No. 1339, P. O. Yeager, Enrolled January 10 1910										
4292	1	Noon, Jim	30	M	F		Billy Noon	D	Cr	Annie Noon	D	Cr
4293	2	Noon, Sophie	23	F	F	Wf	Unknown	D	Cr	Fikhumba	D	Cr
4294	3	Noon, Nathan	1	M	F	S	No. 1	L	Cr	No. 2	L	Cr
		No. 1 died December 1899. No. 2 died December 1899. No. 3 died.										
		Census Card No. 1340, P. O. Okfuskee Enrolled January 10 1900										
4295	1	Roberts, Kenda	27	M	F		Osoch Yarholar	L	Cr	Eblie	D	Cr
4296	2	Roberts, Mary	23	F	F	Wf	Tulmochus Harjo	D	Cr	Chemonah	D	Cr
4297	3	Roberts, Johnson	1mo	M	F	S	No. 1	L	Cr	No. 2	L	Cr
		Census Card No. 1341, P. O. Morse, Enrolled January 10, 1900										
4298	1	Fixico, Cheyamy	50	F	F		Oktiyche Marthla	D	Cr	Mahahchee	D	Cr
		No. 1 died June 19, 1901										
		Census Card No. 1342, P. O. Morse, Enrolled January 10, 1900										
4299	1	Jonasee, Parcilla	24	F	F		Pahos Emarthlochee	D	Cr	Tilsie	D	Cr
		No 1 died May 15, 1900										
		Census Card No. 1343, P. O. Castle, Enrolled January 10, 1900										
4300	1	Taylor, Sunda	18	M	F		Sam Taylor	D	Cr	Silmy	D	Cr
		Census Card No. 1344, P. O. Okfuskee, Enrolled January 10, 1900										
4301	1	Harchoche, Tulwar	30	M	F		Hulleputa Harjo	D	Cr	Sally	D	Cr
4302	2	Harchoche, Finar	30	F	F	Wf	Tulmarsy Emarthlar	L	Cr	Kise Larney	D	Cr
4303	3	Harchoche Lydia	8	F	F	D	No. 1	L	Cr	No. 2	L	Cr
4304	4	Harchoche, Dicey	7	F	F	D	No. 1	L	Cr	No. 2	L	Cr
		No. 2 died March 13, 1902. No. 1 died May 15, 1903.										
		Census Card No. 1345, P O. Eufaula, Enrolled January 11, 1900										
4305	1	Emarthla, Tulmarsy	55	M	F		Halatahee	D	Cr	Unknown	D	Cr
4306	2	Emarthla, Milly	45	F	F	Wf	Wizo Fixico	D	Cr	Hoyecha	D	Cr
4307	3	Leecher, Mutter	20	F	F	StD	Samochee	L	Cr	No 2	L	Cr
		No. 1 reported dead No 3 died September 2, 1908.										
		Census Card No. 1346, P. O Eufaula, Enrolled January 11, 1900										
4308	1	Nelson, Mary S.	22	F	1/8		Wm. J. Pemberton	L	Non	Charity R. Pemberton	L	Cr
4309	2	Nelson, Eula May	1	F	1-16	D	Wm. Nelson	L	Non	No. 1	L	Cr
		Census Card No. 1347, P. O. Okfuskee, Enrolled January 11, 1900										
4310	1	Harjo, Ochees	50	M	F		Okcha Emarthlar	D	Cr	Elee:hka	D	Cr
4311	2	Harjo, Mitchie	14	F	F	D	No. 1	L	Cr	Taloomga	D	Cr
		No. 2 died July 1899. No. 1 reported dead.										
		Census Card No. 1348, P. O. Castle, Enrolled January 11, 1900										
4312	1	Butcher, Norfer	27	M	F		Butcher	D	Cr	Hoktochee Ahfonoke	L	Cr
4313	2	Butcher, Mussy	25	F	F	Wf	Albert Scott	D	Cr	Nannie	L	Cr
		No. 2 died January 1909.										
		Census Card No. 1349, P. O. Morse, Enrolled January 1 , 1900										
4314	1	Henehochee, Miny	32	F	F		Concharty Micco	L	Cr	Kintar Micco	L	Cr
4315	2	Henehochee, Beenie	10	M	F	S	Tamochee	D	Cr	No. 1	L	Cr
4316	3	Henehochee, Engie	7	F	F	D	Tamochee	D	Cr	No 1	L	Cr
4317	4	Henehochee, Lena	4	F	F	D	Will Henehochee	L	Cr	No. 1	L	Cr
		Census Card No. 1350, P. O. Morse, Enrollled January 11, 190										
4318	1	Micco, Concharty	62	M	F		Aktaryarche Marthla	D	Cr	Unknown	D	Cr
4319	2	Micco, Kintar	65	F	F	Wf	Unknown	D	Cr	Unknown	D	Cr
		No. 1 died August 1904. No. 2 died January 27, 1904.										
		Census Card No. 1351 P. O. Henryetta, Enrolled January 11, 1900										
4 20	1	Randall, Bony	55	M	F		Matulka Randall	D	Cr	Sallie Randall	L	Cr
4321	2	Randall, Timmie	25	M	F	S	No. 1	L	Cr	Jemima Randall	L	Cr
4322	3	Randall, Lizzie	8	F	F	D	No. 1	L	Cr	Jemima Randall	L	Cr
		Census Card No. 1352 P. O. Burney, Enrolled January 11, 1900										
4323	1	Hope, Sharper	60	M	1/4		Hope Grayson	D	Cr	Fannie Hope	D	Cr
		Census Card No. 1353 P. O. Eufaula, Enrolled January 11, 1900										
4324	1	Morrison, Waitie	30	M	5/8		John Morrison	L	Cr	Louisa Morrison	L	Cr
4325	2	Morrison, Eliza	19	F	5/8	Wf	Little Watt Grayson	D	Cr	Lucy Grayson	D	Cr
4326	3	Morrison, Ellen	1	F	5/8	D	No. 1	L	Cr	No 2	L	Cr
		No. 1 reported dead										
		Census Card No 1354 P. O. Morse, Enrolled January 11, 190)										
4327	1	Bear, Cinda	45	F	F		Lumsey	D	Cr	Kintar Micco	L	Cr
		Census Card No. 1355, P. O. Okfuskee, Enrolled January 11, 1900										
4328	1	Deere, Wesley	52	M	F		Choyarholar	D	Cr	Arnicha	D	Cr
		No. 1 died January 8, 1899										
		Census Card No. 1356, P. O. Okfuskee, Enrolled January 11, 1900										
4329	1	Bear, Little	45	M	F		Uknnown	D	Cr	Kintar	L	Cr
4330	2	Bear, Sarley	42	F	F	Wf	Martrup Yarholar	D	Cr	Unknown	D	Cr
4331	3	Bear, Senie	20	F	F	D	No. 1	L	Cr	No 2	L	Cr
4332	4	Bear, Pinar	18	F	F	D	No. 1	L	Cr	No. 2	L	Cr
4333	5	Bear, Sampson	15	M	F	S	No. 1	L	Cr	No. 2	L	Cr
4334	6	Bear, Johnson	12	M	F	S	No. 1	L	Cr	No 2	L	Cr
4335	7	Bear, Sammie	8	M	F	S	No. 1	L	Cr	No. 2	L	Cr
4336	8	Bear, Lonie	2	M	F	S	No. 1	L	Cr	No. 2	L	Cr
		No. 1 died February 15, 1900. No. 6 died Febuary 25, 1905. No. 5 died August 2, 1908. No. 4 died June 22, 1902. No. 3 reported dead										
		Census Card No. 1357, P. O. Holdenville, Enrolled January 11, 1900										
4337	1	Sealie	90	F	F		Tustenuck Harjo	D	Cr	Tinfolagee	D	Cr
4338	2	Eagle, Ullie	8	F	F	GGD	David Eagle	D	Cr	Tochee Eagle	D	Cr
		No. 1 died October 2, 1900. No. 2 died 1912.										

Roll No.	No.	NAME	Age	Sex	Blood	Rel.	NAME OF FATHER	Liv.	Cit.	NAME OF MOTHER	Liv.	Cit.
		Census Card No. 1358, P. O. Okfuskee, Enrolled January 11 1900										
4339	1	Fixico, Sinhejeschee	38	F	F		Taskeek Harjo	D	Cr	Sofix Sunga	D	Cr
4340	2	Harjo, Wattie	13	M	F	S	Kokus Harjo	D	Cr	No. 1	L	Cr
4341	3	Fixico, Benjamin	11	M	F	S	Wotka Fixico	D	Cr	No. 1	L	Cr
4342	4	Fixico, Cheparney	8	M	F	S	Wotka Fixico	D	Cr	No. 1	L	Cr
		No. 2 died September 3, 1912. Nos 3 and 4 reported dead.										
		Census Card No. 1359, P. O. Mason; Nos. 2 3, 6, Welty, Enrolled January 11, 1900										
4343	1	Harjoche, Yarteka	40	M	F		Osiah Yarholar	D	Cr	Monochagee	D	Cr
4344	2	Harjoche, Charfeny	40	F	F	Wf	Nokus Hutchee	D	Cr	Unknown	D	Cr
4345	3	Jims, Holee	18	M	F	StS	Okchunobiyee	D	Cr	No. 2	L	Cr
4346	4	Harjoche, Nity	15	F	F	D	No. 1	L	Cr	Lisochee	L	Cr
4347	5	Harjoche, Keseathor	12	F	F	D	No. 1	L	Cr	Lisochee	L	Cr
4348	6	Mikey, Ollie	3	F	F	StD	Loley Mikey	D	Cr	No. 2	L	Cr
4349	7	Chemarye	70	F	F	S-L	Unknown	D	Cr	Unknown	D	Cr
		No. 4 reported dead										
		Census Card No. 1360, P. O. Okmulgee, Enrolled January 11, 1900										
4350	1	Carr, Leaster	29	F	3/4		John James	D	Cr	Sally Berryhill	D	Cr
4351	2	James, Edward	20	M	3/4	1/2Bro	Little Dear Berryhill	D	Cr	Sally Berryhill	D	Cr
4352	3	Berryhill, Anderson	17	M	3/4	1/2Bro	Unknown	D	Cr	Sally Berryhill	D	Cr
4353	4	White, Susie	19	F	3/4	Ward	George Hutka	L	Cr	Nancy White	L	Cr
		No. 1 reported dead										
		Census Card No. 1361, P. O. Stidham, Enrolled January 11, 1900										
4354	1	Nubbie, George W.	20	M	F		Cossa Harjo	D	Cr	Lossie Harjo	D	Cr
		No. 1 reported dead										
		Census Card No. 1362, P. O. Okmulgee, Enrolled January 12, 1900										
4355	1	Chupco, Spatker	60	M	F		Tunnie Harjo	D	Cr	Nosey	D	Cr
		No. 1 died December, 1904.										
		Census Card No. 1363, P. O. Okmulgee, Enrolled January 12, 1900										
4356	1	Sunny, Peggie	60	M	F		Unknown	D	Cr	Hartegee	D	Cr
		Census Card No 1364, P. O. Eufaula, Enrolled January 12 1900										
4357	1	Crabtree, Braxton B.	34	M	1-32		Gabriel M. Crabtree	D	Cr	Sallie Crabtree	?	Non
4358	2	Crabtree Malinda	22	F	F	Wf	Tecumseh Phillips	L	Cr	Wicey Phillips	D	Cr
4359	3	Crabtree, Bessie	5	F	1/2	D	No. 1	L	Cr	No. 2	L	Cr
4360	4	Crabtree, Gabriel B.	3	M	1/2	S	No. 1	L	Cr	No. 2	L	Cr
4361	5	Crabtree, William B.	1	M	1/2	S	No. 1	L	Cr	No 2	L	Cr
4362	6	Crabtree, Lynn	1	F	1/2	D	No. 1	L	Cr	No. 2	L	Cr
		Census Card No. 1365, P. O. Red Fork, Enrolled Jan. 12, 1900; No. 6 April 22, 1901										
4363	1	Naharkey, Moses	41	M	F		Naharkey	D	Cr	Wahhiley	D	Cr
4364	2	Naharkey, Millie	38	F	F	Wf	Sheley	L	Cr	Unknown	D	Cr
4365	3	Naharkey, Sammie	15	M	F	S	No. 1	L	Cr	No 2	L	Cr
4366	4	Naharkey Wehiley	78	F	F	Moth	Unknown	D	Cr	Unknown	D	Cr
		No. 2 died February 2, 1901. No. 4 died September 26, 1899.										
		Census Card No. 1366, P. O. Henryetta, Enrolled January 12, 1900										
4367	1	Johnson, Sango	45	M	F		Artus Fixico	D	Cr	Cossunger	D	Cr
4368	2	Johnson, Linar	40	F	1/2	Wf	Taylor	D	Non	Betsey	D	Cr
4369	3	Derisaw, John	10	M	F	Neph	Ben Derisaw	D	Cr	Nellie	D	Cr
4370	4	Derisaw, Liza	15	F	F	Niece	Ben Derisaw	D	Cr	Nellie	D	Cr
		Census Card No. 1367, P. O. Muskogee, Enrolled January 12, 1900; No. 3, October 8, 1900										
4371	1	Linton, Pauline B.	26	F	1/4		George Shannon	L	Non	Mary B. Shannon	D	Cr
4372	2	Linton, Shannon R.	4	M	1/8	S	Wm E. Linton	L	Non	No. 1	L	Cr
4373	3	Linton, Pauline E.	2mo	F	1/8	D	Wm. E. Linton	L	Non	No. 1	L	Cr
		Census Card No. 1368, P O. Keokuk Falls, Enrolled January 12, 1900										
4374	1	Kernall, Mose	33	M	F		Temahue Kernells	L	Cr	Lucy Kernells	D	C
4375	2	Kernall, Sallie	16	F	F	A-D	Nokaf Harjo	L	Cr	Losogegee	L	Cr
4376	3	Kernall, Cheparney	4	M	F	S	No. 1	L	Cr	Sophia Kernall	L	Cr
		No. 2 died December 1901.										
		Census Card No. 1369, P. O. Morse, Enrolled January 12, 1900										
4377	1	Fixico, Chular	56	M	F		Woatko Yahola	D	Cr	Unknown	D	Cr
4378	2	Fixico, Sallie	0	F	F	Wf	Cussehta Yahola	D	Cr	Warkcke	D	Cr
		No 1 died September 21 1900. No 2 died July 21, 1904.										
		Census Card No. 1370 P. O Henryetta, Enrolled January 3, 1900										
4379	1	Mitchell, Enock	18	M	F		Sam Mitchell	D	Cr	Hannah Mitchell	L	Cr
		No. 1 died 1905										
		Census Card No. 1371, P. O. Okmulgee, Enrolled January 13, 1900										
4380	1	Fixico, Sewika	59	F	F		Lahta Yahola	D	Cr	Unknown	D	Cr
4381	2	Fixico, Liddie	30	F	F	D	Thlotho Fixico	D	C	No. 1	L	Cr
4382	3	Fixico, Thomas	20	M	F	S	Thlotho Fixico	D	Cr	No. 1	L	Cr
		No. 1 reported dead										
		Census Card No. 1372, P. O. Okmulgee; Nos. 2 and 5 Wetumka, Enrolled January 13, 1900										
4383	1	Kannard, Joseph	37	M	F		Smith Kennard	L	Cr	Lizzie Kennard	D	Cr
4384	2	Kannard, Onida	45	F	F	Wf	Tumme Harjo	L	Cr	Nosey	D	Cr
4385	3	Kannard, Joanna	8	F	F	D	No. 1	L	Cr	Louisa Kennard	D	Cr
4386	4	King, Annie	14	F	F	Niece	Miccoche	L	Cr	Sisey Kennard	D	Cr
4387	5	Mason, Polly	12	F	F	Niece	Mason	L	Cr	Sisey Kennard	D	Cr
		No. 1 died April 4, 1094. No. 2 reported dead										
		Census Card No. 1373, P. O. Okemah, Enrolled January 13, 190)										
4388	1	Kannard, Martin	27	M	F		James Kennard	D	Cr	Pitchee Kennard	D	Sem
		Census Card No. 1374, P. O. Welty, Enrolled January 13 190										
4389	1	Porter, Hager	20	F	F		John Porter	L	Cr	Tobce	L	Cr
4390	2	Porter, March	3	M	F	S	Unknown	L	Cr	No. 1	L	Cr
		No. 2 reported dead. No. 1 reported dead										

Roll No.	No.	NAME	Age	Sex	Blood	Rel.	NAME OF FATHER	Liv.	Cit.	NAME OF MOTHER	Liv.	Cit.
		Census Card No. 1375, P. O. Okfuskee, Enrolled January 13, 1900										
4391	1	Emarthlochee Yarhar	30	M	F		Nokus Miccochee	D	Cr	Sally Tarney	L	Cr
4392	2	Emarthlochee, Numsy	26	F	F	Wf	Tulmarsey Emarthla	L	Cr	Ayah	D	Cr
4393	3	Emarthlochee, Maudie	1	F	F	D	No. 1	L	Cr	No. 2	L	Cr
		Census Card No. 1376, P. O. Morse, Enrolled January 13, 1900										
4394	1	Butcher, Edmond	19	M	F		Butcher	D	Cr	Hoktoche Ahfonoke	L	Cr
		No. 1 died March 15, 1904										
		Census Card No. 1377, P. O. Okmulgee, Enrolled January 13, 1900										
4395	1	Morton, Delilah	60	F	¾		Tom Johnson	D	Cr	Hannah Harger	D	Cr
4396	2	Morton, Ellis	18	M	⅜	S	William Morton	L	Non	No. 1	L	Cr
4397	3	Morton, Clarence	16	M	⅜	S	William Morton	L	Non	No. 1	L	Cr
		Nos. 1 and 2 reported dead										
		Census Card No. 1378, P. O. Okmulgee, Enrolled January 13, 1900										
4398	1	Morton, Lelora	23	F	⅜		William Morton	L	Non	Delilah Morton	L	Cr
		Census Card No. 1379, P. O. Okmulgee, Enrolled January 13, 1900										
4399	1	Morton, Walter W.	24	M	⅜		William Morton	L	Non	Delilah Morton	L	Cr
		Census Card No. 1380, P. O. Okmulgee, Enrolled January 13, 1900										
4400	1	Gray, Mary	37	F	F		Phillips Marshall	L	Cr	Sally Marshall	D	Cr
		Census Card No. 1381, P. O. Okmulgee, Enrolled January 13, 1900										
4401	1	Kemarye	23	F	F		Oktiarchee Fixico	D	Cr	Wisely	D	Cr
4402	2	Sarwarhie, Willie	5 mo	M	F	S	Sarwarhie	L	Cr	No. 1	L	Cr
		No. 1 died December 30, 1907. No 2 died 1904										
		Census Card No. 1382, P. O. Sharp, Enrolled January 13, 1900										
4403	1	Brown, Roland	83	M	F		Carbiekcha Harjo	D	Cr	Patcheshe	D	Cr
4404	2	Brown, Lizzie	55	F	F	Wf	Matulka Randall	D	Cr	Sally Randall	D	Cr
		No. 1 reported dead										
		Census Card No. 1383 P. O. Okmulgee, Enrolled January 13, 1900										
4405	1	Halley, Hosa	21	M	F		Joe Haley	D	Cr	Nancy Haley	D	Cr
		Census Card No 1384, P. O. Boley, Enrolled January 13, 1900										
4406	1	Jameson, Hepsey	41	F	½		Andrew Marshall	D	Col'd	Ahweththla	D	Cr
		Census Card No. 1385, P. O. Boley, Enrolled January 15, 1900										
4407	1	Mitchell, Addie	28	F	F		Barney Riley	L	Cr	Tocha Derisaw	L	Cr
4408	2	Mitchell, Monroe	2	M	½	S	Mack Mitchell	L	Non	No. 1	L	Cr
		Census Card No. 1386, P. O. Checotah; No. 4 Oktaha Enrolled January 16, 1900										
4409	1	Collins, Aurora	42	F	⅛		Thomas Scott	D	Non	Kiamisha Scott	D	Cr
4410	2	Collins, Wynema	19	F	1-16	D	Henry Collins	L	Non	No. 1	L	Cr
4411	3	Collins, Shannon R.	13	M	1-16	S	Henry Collins	L	Non	No 1	L	Cr
4412	4	Collins, Orvid L.	11	M	1-16	S	Henry Collins	L	Non	No. 1	L	Cr
4413	5	Collins, Emma L.	9	F	1-16	D	Henry Collins	L	Non	No. 1	L	Cr
4414	6	Collins, Howard R.	5	M	1-16	S	Henry Collins	L	Non	No. 1	L	Cr
4415	7	Collins, Bryan S.	2	M	1-16	S	Henry Collins	L	Non	No. 1	L	Cr
4416	8	Collins, Norma	1	F	1-16	D	Henry Collins	L	Non	No. 1	L	Cr
4417	9	Collins, Cora L.	6	F	1-16	D	Henry Collins	L	Non	No 1	L	Cr
		No. 8 died September 9, 1899. No. 9 died August 14 1899										
		Census Card No. 1387, P. O Bryant, Enrolled January 17, 1900										
4418	1	Barnett James	48	M	⅝		Thomas Barnett	D	Cr	Hannah Barnett	D	Cr
4419	2	Barnett, Mebote	45	F	F	Wf	Concharty	D	Cr	Unknown	D	Cr
		No. 1 died May 10, 1901										
		Census Card No. 1388, P. O. Bryant Enrolled January 17, 1900										
4420	1	Barnett, Winey	25	F	¾		James Barnett	L	Cr	Mebote Barnett	L	Cr
		Census Card No. 1389, P. O. Senora, Enrolled January 17, 1900										
4421	1	Sevier, Mary	23	F	F		Willie Sevier	D	Cr	Katy Tiner	L	Cr
4422	2	Fisher, Albert	3	M	F	S	Joe Fisher	L	Cr	No. 1	L	Cr
4423	3	Fisher, Amos	3 mo	M	F	S	Joe Fisher	L	Cr	No. 1	L	Cr
		Nos. 1 and 3 reported dead										
		Census Card No. 1390, P. O. Okmulgee, Enrolled January 17, 1900										
4424	1	McClosky, Mamie M.	23	F	½		Fosh Harjo	D	Sem	Eliza Fosh Harjo	D	Cr
		No. 1 reported dead										
		Census Card No. 1391, P. O. Holdenville Enrolled January 18, 1900; No. 5 March 26 1901										
4425	1	Brown, Julia	28	F	⅛		Chester Tuttle	D	Non	Betsey Tuttle	D	Cr
4426	2	Brown, Melia	10	F	¼	D	S. E. Brown	L	Sem	No. 1	L	Cr
4427	3	Brown, Bertha	6	F	¼	D	S. E. Brown	L	Sem	No. 1	L	Cr
4428	4	Brown James C.	3	M	¼	S	S. E. Brown	L	Sem	No. 1	L	Cr
4429	5	Brown, Francis	10 mo	M	¼	S	S. E. Brown	L	Sem	No. 1	L	Cr
		Census Card No. 1392, P. O. Henryetta, Enrolled January 18 1900										
4430	1	Henry, James	24	M	⅛		Hugh Henry	L	Cr	Ann Henry	D	Non
		Census Card No. 1393, P. O. Muskogee, Enrolled January 18, 1900										
4431	1	Hammonds, Jennie	8	F	½		John Hammond	D	Non	Betsey Hammond	D	Cr
4432	2	Hammonds, Embry	7	M	½	Bro	John Hammond	D	Non	Betsey Hammond	D	Cr
		No. 2 died 1906										
		Census Card No. 1394, P. O. Muskogee; No. 2 Haskell, Enrolled January 18, 1900										
4433	1	Harris, Ellen	60	F	¼		Robert Rogers	D	Cr	Mary Ann Rogers	D	Cr
4434	2	Harris, Charles	35	M	⅛	S	R. B. Harris	D	Cher	No 1	L	Cr
		Census Card No. 1395, P. O. Eufaula; No. 3 Checotah, Enrolled January 18, 1900										
4435	1	McCalvey Margaret	51	F	¼		James Lynch	D	Non	Lucy Lynch	D	Cr
4436	2	McCalvey, Edward	25	M	⅛	S	Joseph McCalvey	L	Non	No. 1	L	Cr
4437	3	McCalvey, Everett	23	M	⅛	S	Joseph McCalvey	L	Non	No. 1	L	Cr
4438	4	McCalvey, Joseph	19	M	⅛	S	Joseph McCalvey	L	Non	No. 1	L	Cr
4439	5	McCalvey, Lucy	17	F	⅛	D	Joseph McCalvey	L	Non	No. 1	L	Cr
4440	6	McCalvey, Cornelius	10	M	⅛	S	Joseph McCalvey	L	Non	No. 1	L	Cr
		No. 1 died December 9, 1901. No. 4 died March 15, 1903										

Roll No.	No.	NAME	Age	Sex	Blood	Rel.	NAME OF FATHER	Liv.	Cit.	NAME OF MOTHER	Liv.	Cit.
		Censu Card No. 1396, P. O. Muskogee, Enrolled January 19, 1900										
4441	1	Cummings, Lonie	18	F	⅛		David Cummings	L	Cr	Mildred Cummings	L	Cr
		Census Card No. 1397, P. O. Bryant; No. 3 Okmulgee, Enrolled January 19, 1900										
4442	1	Asbury, Joshua	44	M	½		Josiah Asbury	D	Cr	Lizzie Asbury	D	Cr
4443	2	Asbury, Miley	39	F	F	Wf	Aharloc Yahola	D	Cr	Chemehaka	D	Cr
4444	3	Asbury, Rosie	22	F	¾	D	No. 1	L	Cr	Mary Asbury	L	Cr
4445	4	Asbury George T.	19	M	¾	S	No. 1	L	Cr	Mary Asbury	L	Cr
4446	5	Asbury, Josephine	17	F	¾	D	No. 1	L	Cr	Mary Asbury	L	Cr
4447	7	Aabury, James	14	M	¾	S	No. 1	L	Cr	Mary Asbury	L	Cr
4448	7	Asbury, Siah E.	11	M	¾	S	No. 1	L	Cr	Mary Asbury	L	Cr
4449	8	Grayson, Nancy	21	F	F	StD	Sosa Grayson	L	Cr	No. 2	L	Cr
4450	9	Barnett, Kogee	4 mo	F	⅞	StGrD	Jackson Barnett	L	Cr	No. 8	L	Cr
		No. 1 died October 5, 1903. No. 7 reported dead. No. 3 died December 9, 1900. No. 8 reported to be duplicate of No 8092 this roll										
		Census Card No. 1398, P. O. Muskogee, Enrolled January 19, 1900										
4451	1	Mickens, Margie	9	F	¼		G. W. Mickens	L	Non	Nettie Mickens	D	Cr
4452	2	Mickens, Oscar	7	M	¼	Bro	G. W. Mickens	L	Non	Nettie Mickens	D	Cr
4453	3	Mickens, Walter	5	M	¼	Bro	G. W. Mickens	L	Non	Nettie Mickens	D	Cr
		Census Card No. 1399, P. O. Lee, Enrolled January 19, 1900										
4454	1	Bellstedt Lula	36	F	¼		George Bellstedt	D	Non	Catharine Bellstedt	D	Cr
4455	2	Steele, Catherine C.	55	F	½	Moth	Jefferson Davis	D	Non	Polly Davis	D	?
		No. 2 stricken from roll. See U. S. Indian Commissioner' Letter No. 1545, 1909										
		Census Card No. 1400, P. O. Tulsa, Enrolled January 20, 1900; No. 2 March 26, 1901										
4456	1	Dunn, Jennie	60	F	½		Adam Perryman	D	Cr	Simbok	D	Cr
4457	2	Jefferson, Manuel	27	M	⅛	S	Silas Jefferson	L	Cr	No. 1	L	Cr
		Census Card No. 1401, P. O. Eufaula, Enrolled January 22, 1900; No. 7 February 13, 1900										
4458	1	Smith, Charles S.	50	M	⅝		John G. Smith	D	Cr	Lucinda Smith	D	Cr
4459	2	Smith, Louisa B.	46	F	⅝	Wf	James Grayson	D	Cr	Jennie Grayson	D	Cr
4460	3	Smith, Jay G.	19	M	⅝	S	No. 1	L	Cr	No. 2	L	Cr
4461	4	Smith, Horace Greeley	17	M	⅝	S	No. 1	L	Cr	No. 2	L	Cr
4462	5	Smith, Walter C.	8	M	⅝	S	No. 1	L	Cr	No. 2	L	C
4463	6	Smith, Lucile	5	F	⅝	D	No. 1	L	Cr	No. 2	L	Cr
4464	7	Day, Lena	17	F	F	Ward	Wm. Day	D	Cr	Millie Day	D	Cr
		Census Card No. 1402, P. O. Raiford; No. 2 Vivian Enrolled January 23, 1900										
4465	1	Smith, Louis N.	36	M	⅝		John G. Smith	D	Cr	Lucinda Smith	D	Cr
4466	2	Smith, Rashie C.	9	M	½	S	No. 1	L	Cr	Jennie Grayson	L	Cr
4467	3	Smith, Zular M.	7	F	½	D	No. 1	L	Cr	Nannie Lou Smith	L	Non
		Census Card No. 1403, P. O. Yeager Enrolled January 23, 1900										
4468	1	Deer, Lawyer	43	M	F		Jo Harjo	D	Cr	Linda Harjo	D	Cr
4469	2	Deer, Hepsey	42	F	F	Wf	Kenehahhopayh	D	Cr	Unknown	D	Cr
4470	3	Deer, Willie	20	M	F	S	No. 1	L	Cr	Anna	L	Cr
4471	4	Deer William	19	M	F	StS	Billy Noon	D	Cr	No 2	L	Cr
4472	5	Deer, Walter	18	M	F	S	No. 1	L	Cr	Anna	L	Cr
4473	6	Deer, Amos	8	M	F	S	No. 1	L	Cr	No. 2	L	Cr
4474	7	Deer, Butler	6	M	F	S	No. 1	L	Cr	No. 2	L	Cr
		No. 3 died April 29, 1906. No. 1 died May 26, 1910										
		Census Card No. 1404, P. O. Holdenville; No. 3 McAlester, Enrolled January 23, 1900										
4475	1	Stewart, Robert W.	32	M	½		Robert W. Stewart	D	Adop	Sophia McQueen	D	Cr
4476	2	Stewart, Lucy	27	F	F	Wf	Nocus Yahola	D	Cr	Litka Scott	L	Cr
4477	3	Narcomey, Daniel	9	M	F	Neph	Cogegee	D	Cr	Lizzie Chupco	D	Cr
4478	4	Stewart, Noah	7	M	F	Neph	Barney Toney	D	Cr	Lizzie Chupco	D	Cr
4479	5	Bruner, Charley	3	M	F	Neph	Wm. Bruner	L	Cr	Leah Reed	D	Cr
		No. 1 died July 12, 1901. No. 2 reported dead.										
		Census Card No. 1405, P. O. Muskogee, Enrolled January 24, 1900; No. 6 May 21, 1900										
4480	1	Harris, William R.	37	M	⅛		R. B. Harris	L	Cher	Ellen Harris	L	Cr
4481	2	Harris, Johnson E.	9	M	1-16	S	No. 1	L	Cr	Lela Harris	L	Non
4482	3	Harris, Ella	7	F	1-16	D	No. 1	L	Cr	Lela Harris	L	Non
4483	4	Harris, Bird	5	F	1-16	D	No. 1	L	Cr	Lela Harris	L	Non
4484	5	Harris, Su Anna	2	F	1-16	D	No. 1	L	Cr	Lela Harris	L	Non
4485	6	Harris, Isparhecher	2 mo	M	1-16	S	No. 1	L	Cr	Lela Harris	L	Non
		Census Card No. 1406, P. O. Oktaha, Enrolled January 24, 1900										
4486	1	Simmons, Joe	21	M	F		Charley Simmer	L	Cr	Jennie Simmer	L	Cr
		Census Card No. 1407, P. O. Henryetta, Enrolled January 24, 1900										
4487	1	Barnett, Nancy	33	F	F		Parney	D	Cr	Jennie Sarls	L	Cr
4488	2	Barnett, Losana	15	F	F	D	Jimsey Brown	L	Sem	No. 1	L	Cr
4489	3	Barnett, Joseph	11	M	F	S	Jimsey Brown	L	Sem	No. 1	L	Cr
4490	4	Barnett, George	8	M	F	S	Jimsey Brown	L	Sem	No. 1	L	Cr
4491	5	Barnett, Helie	6	F	F	D	Jimsey Brown	L	Sem	No. 1	L	Cr
		No. 4 died July 4, 1910										
		Census Card No. 1408, P. O. Henryetta, Enrolled January 24, 1900										
4492	1	Sarls, Jennie	60	F	F		Okchun Harjo	D	Cr	Pefatka	D	C
4493	2	Hen, Betsey	19	F	F	D	Eblow Hen	D	Cr	No. 1	L	Cr
		No. 2 died August 1, 1905. No. 1 reported dead.										
		Census Card No. 1409, P.O. North Fork, Enrolled January 24, 1900										
4494	1	Barnett, Mollie	24	F	F		Micco Apueka	D	Cr	Jennie Sarls	L	Cr
		Census Card No. 1410, P. O. Dustin, Enrolled January 24, 1900										
4495	1	Wesley, Charley	21	F	F		Wesley Chuppa	L	Cr	Jennie Sarls	L	Cr

Roll No.	No.	NAME	Age	Sex	Blood	Rel.	NAME OF FATHER	Liv.	Cit.	NAME OF MOTHER	Liv.	Cit.
		Census Card No. 1411, P. O. Bryant; No. 1 Tulsa, Enrolled January 24, 1900										
4496	1	Barnett, Nancy	21	M	F		Ward	D	Cr	Patty Barnett	L	Cr
4497	2	Barnett, Jimmy	10	M	F	S	David Barnett	L	Cr	No. 1	L	Cr
4498	3	Barnett, Nellie	8	F	F	D	David Barnett	L	Cr	No. 1	L	Cr
4499	4	Barnett, Robert	7	M	F	S	David Barnett	L	Cr	No. 1	L	Cr
4500	5	Barnett, George	4	M	F	S	David Barnett	L	Cr	No. 1	L	Cr
4501	6	Barnett, Ida	1	F	F	D	David Barnett	L	Cr	No. 1	L	Cr
		Census Card No. 1412, P. O. Henryetta, Enrolled January 24, 1900										
4502	1	Barnett, Tom	22	M	¾		David Barnett	L	Cr	Patty Barnett	L	Cr
4503	2	Barnett, Himer	6 moM	⅞	S	No. 1	L	Cr	Lucy Fisher	D	Cr
		No. 2 died May 9, 1900										
		Census Card No. 1413, P. O. Bryant; No. 2 Henryetta, Enrolled January 24, 1900										
4504	1	Beams, Annie	24	F	F		David Barnett	L	Cr	Patty Barnett	L	C
4505	2	Beams, Isom	1	M	F	S	Charley Beams	L	Non	No. 1	L	Cr
		Census Card No. 1414, P. O. Senora; No. 1 Bryant, Enrolled January 24, 1900										
4506	1	Barnett, Mary	70	F	F		Gideon Bean	D	Non	Nancy	D	Cr
4507	2	Davis, Benjamin	15	M	F	GrS	John Davis	D	Cr	Sissy Davis	D	Cr
4508	3	West, Pompey	10	M	F	GrS	Billy West	L	Cr	Sissy Davis	D	Cr
4509	4	Walker, George	12	M	F	GrS	John Walker	D	Cr	Ellen Seaborn	L	Cr
4510	5	Seaborn, Joe	10	M	F	GrS	Seaborn	D	Cr	Ellen Seaborn	L	Cr
4511	6	Seaborn, Stella	6	F	F	GrD	Seaborn	D	Cr	Ellen Seaborn	L	Cr
		No. 2 died June 1900. No. 4 died October 7, 1911. No. 5 died April 7, 1913. No. 6 died 1899.										
		No. 3 reported dead										
		Census Card No. 1415, P. O. Bryant, Enrolled January 24, 1900										
4512	1	Fisher, James	50	M	F		Timmy Fisher	D	Cr	Hepsey	D	Cr
4513	2	Fisher, Hannah	40	F	F	Wf	Siah Barnett	D	Cr	Mary Barnett	L	Cr
4514	3	Fisher, William	15	M	F	S	No. 1	L	Cr	No. 2	L	Cr
4515	4	Fisher, Mariah	12	F	F	D	No. 1	L	Cr	No. 2	L	Cr
4516	5	Fisher, Lewis	3	M	F	S	No. 1	L	Cr	No. 2	L	Cr
		No. 2 died February 17, 1901										
		Census Card No. 1416, P. O. Bryant, Enrolled January 24, 1900										
4517	1	Fisher, Seaborn	21	M	F		James Fisher	L	Cr	Hannah Fisher	L	Cr
		Census Card No. 1417, P. O. Henryetta, Enrolled January 24, 1900; No. 4 May 24, 1901										
4518	1	Watson, Katie	29	F	F		Josiah Watson	L	Cr	Hannah Mitchell	L	Cr
4519	2	Watson, Bessie	10	F	F	D	Sam Mitchell	D	Cr	No. 1	L	Cr
4520	3	Watson, George	7	M	F	S	Sam Mitchell	D	Cr	No. 1	L	Cr
4521	4	Carr, Eunice	1	F	½	D	Willie Carr	L	Non	No. 1	L	Cr
		No. 2 died March 25, 1901. Nos. 1 and 3 and 4 reported dead										
		Census Card No. 1418, P. O. Henryetta, Enrolled January 24, 1900										
4522	1	Francis, Jackson	43	M	F		John Fronges	D	Cr	Yomhochee	D	Cr
4523	2	Francis, Sukey	45	F	F	Wf	Dickey Partaka	D	Cr	Liza	D	Cr
		No. 1 died August 23, 1907										
		Census Card No. 1419, P. O. Bryant, Enrolled January 24, 1900										
4524	1	Barnett, Jackson	48	M	F		Siah Barnett	D	Cr	Tblesothle	D	Cr
		Census Card No. 1420, P. O. Bryant, Enrolled January 24, 1900										
4525	1	West, Billy	38	M	F		Thlegummie Harjo	D	Cr	Somechichee	D	Cr
4526	2	West, Louisa	25	F	F	Wf	George Sullivan	D	Cr	Eliza Fisher	D	Cr
4527	3	West, Daniel	2	M	F	S	No. 1	L	Cr	No. 2	L	Cr
4528	4	West, Louisa	6 moF	F	D	No. 1	L	Cr	No. 2	L	Cr
4529	5	West, Susan	17	F	F	StD	No. 1	L	Cr	Sarchoke	D	Cr
		No. 4 died February 3, 1901. No. 5 died June 6, 1908										
		Census Card No. 1421, P. O. Henryetta, Enrolled January 24, 1900										
4530	1	Mitchell, Hannah	55	F	F		John Francis	D	Cr	Yomhoke	L	Cr
4531	2	Mitchell, Rachel	12	F	F	D	Sam Mitchel!	D	Cr	No. 1	L	Cr
4532	3	Mitchell, Mintie	8	F	F	D	Sam Mitchell	D	Cr	No. 1	L	Cr
		No. 3 reported dead										
		Census Card No. 1422, P. O. Hanna, Enrolled January 24, 1900										
4533	1	West, Thomas	25	M	F		Thlechumme Harjo	D	Cr	Somechechee	D	Cr
		Census Card No. 1423, P. O. Henryetta, Enrolled January 24, 1900										
4534	1	Barnett, Jimsey	24	M	F		Micco Apueka	D	Cr	Jennie Sarls	L	Cr
4535	2	Barnett, Katie	24	F	F	Wf	Big Ben	L	Cr	Mary Ben	L	Cr
		Census Card No. 1424, P. O. Dustin; No. 4 Henryetta, Enrolled January 24, 1900										
4536	1	Riley, Cheesie	25	M	F		Joe Riley	D	Cr	Wata	D	Cr
4537	2	Riley, Maley	23	F	F	Wf	Jim Benson	L	Cr	Lizzie	L	Cr
4538	3	Benson, Haney	21	F	F	SinL	Jim Benson	L	Cr	Lizzie	L	Cr
4539	4	Watson, Daniel	15	M	F	BinL	Daniel Watson	D	Cr	Lizzie	L	Cr
4540	5	Goober, Nicey	6	F	F	SinL	John Goober	D	Cr	Lizzie	L	Cr
		No. 3 died September 2, 1907. No. 1 died 1910. No. 5 reported dead										
		Census Card No. 1425, P. O. Henryetta, Enrolled January 24, 1900										
4541	1	Chupko, John	32	M	F		Micco Apueka	D	Cr	Jennie Sarls	L	Cr
4542	2	Chupko, Rosanna	26	F	F	Wf	Big Ben	L	Cr	Mary Ben	L	Cr
4543	3	Riley, Wannie	5	F	F	StD	Wilyunka Riley	L	Sem	No. 2	L	Cr
		Census Card No. 1426, P. O. Senora, Enrolled January 25, 1900										
4544	1	Bruner, Jesse	60	M	½		Jim Sampson	D	Cr	Lucinda Bruner	D	Cr
		Census Card No. 1427, P. O. Brush Hill, Enrolled January 25, 1900										
4545	1	Logan, Sallie	85	F	F		Tobe	D	Cr	Unknown	D	Cr
		No. 1 reported dead										
		Census Card No. 1428, P. O. Dustin, Enrolled January 25, 1900										
4546	1	Riley, Washington	58	M	F		John Riley	D	Cr	Chakic	D	Cr

97

Roll No.	No.	NAME	Age	Sex	Blood	Rel.	NAME OF FATHER	Liv.	Cit.	NAME OF MOTHER	Liv.	Cit.
Census Card No. 1429 P. O. Dustin, Enrolled January 25, 1900												
4547	1	Riley, Annie	25	F	F		Woxie Harjo	D	Cr	Sally	D	Cr
4548	2	Riley, Amosee	3	M	F	S	Wilyunka	L	Sem	No. 1	L	Cr
No. 1 died December 30, 1904												
Census Card No. 1430, P. O. Salem, Enrolled January 25, 1900												
4549	1	Kelly, Sam	35	M	F		Ahfoloka	D	Cr	Lowina Killer	L	Cr
No. 1 reported dead												
Census Card No. 1431, P. O. Eufaula, Enrolled January 25, 1900												
4550	1	Simpson, John C.	23	M	1-32		John F. Simpson	L	Non	Susan N. Simpson	L	Cr
4551	2	Simpson, John Francis	2mo	M	1-64	S	No. 1	L	Cr	Alice Simpson	L	Cr
Census Card No. 1432, P. O. Clearview, Enrolled January 25, 1900												
4552	1	Barnett, Soocer	45	M	1/2		Scipio Barnett	D	Non	Annie Moore	L	Cr
Census Card No. 1433, P. O. Newby, Enrolled January 25, 1900												
4553	1	Davis, Milley	29	F	3/4		Austin Barnett	D	Cr	Lizzie Barnett	L	Cr
4554	2	Barnett, Aldine	12	F	5/8	D	Daniel Barnett	L	Cr	No. 1	L	Cr
4555	3	Hardridge, Edmond	9	M	1/2	S	Adam Hardridge	L	Cr	No. 1	L	Cr
4556	4	Robison, Thomas	7	M	1/2	S	David Robison	L	Cr	No. 1	L	Cr
No. 1 died March 19, 1908												
Census Card No. 1434, P. O. North Fork, Enrolled January 25, 1900												
4557	1	Watson, Josiah	50	M	3/8		Daniel G. Watson	D	Non	Fannie Watson	D	Cr
4558	2	Watson, Yarner	33	F	3/4	Wf	Alex McGirt	D	Cr	Sodes McGirt	D	Cr
4559	3	Watson, Hettie	13	F	3/4	D	No. 1	L	Cr	Nellie Watson	D	Cr
4560	4	Watson, Webster	11	M	5/8	S	No. 1	L	Cr	No. 2	L	Cr
4561	5	Watson, Fannie	7	F	5/8	D	No. 1	L	Cr	No. 2	L	Cr
4562	6	Watson, Jane	4	F	5/8	D	No. 1	L	Cr	No. 2	L	Cr
Nos. 2 and 3 reported dead												
Census Card No. 1435, P. O. Senora, Enrolled January 25, 1900												
4563	1	Field, Lucy	28	F	F		Big Ben	L	Cr	Mary Ben	L	Cr
4564	2	Field, Punskee	3	M	F	S	Stepney Field	D	Cr	No. 1	L	Cr
No. 1 died August 1900												
Census Card No. 1436, P. O. Wetumka; No. 7, Dustin, Enrolled January 25, 1900												
4565	1	Ben, Big	50	M	F		Neha Harjo	D	Cr	Sookie	D	Cr
4566	2	Ben, Martha	24	F	F	Wf	Artus Micco	D	Cr	Unknown	D	Cr
4567	3	Ben, John	18	M	F	S	No. 1	L	Cr	Mary Ben	D	Cr
4568	4	Ben, Willie	15	M	F	S	No. 1	L	Cr	Mary Ben	D	Cr
4569	5	Ben, Wicey	10	F	F	D	No. 1	L	Cr	Mary Ben	D	Cr
4570	6	Hen, Willie	8	M	F	StS	Thomas Hen	D	Cr	No. 2	L	Cr
4571	7	Lowe, Eliza	18	F	F	Ward	Louis Lowe	D	Cr	Chuddy	D	Cr
Nos. 1 and 4 reported dead. No. 2 died February 7, 1901. No. 7 died February 21, 1911.												
Census Card No. 1437, P. O. Dustin, Enrolled January 25, 1900												
4572	1	Canard, Sallie	48	F	F		Neha Harjo	D	Cr	Sookie	L	Cr
4573	2	Canard, David	19	M	F	S	Hulley Canard	D	Cr	No. 1	L	Cr
4574	3	Canard, Hannah	17	F	F	D	Hulley Canard	D	Cr	No. 1	L	Cr
No. 2 died November 5, 1900												
Census Card No. 1438, P. O. Dustin, Enrolled January 25, 1900												
4575	1	Larney, William	27	M	F		Micco Charty	D	Cr	Sallie Canard	L	Cr
4576	2	Larney, Maner	18	F	3/4	Wf	Lambert Scott	L	Cr	Wicey Scott	L	Cr
No. 2 died February 16, 1912.												
Census Card No. 1439, P. O. Clearview, Enrolled January 25, 1900												
4577	1	Deer, Isaac	50	M	F		Joilly Harjo	D	Cr	Satim Hokar	D	Cr
4578	2	Deer, Sarforcher	45	F	F	Wf	Ohlepasa	D	Cr	Tiboka	D	Cr
4579	3	Fixico, Bastie	20	M	F	StS	Tharlip Harjo	L	Cr	No. 2	L	Cr
4580	4	Fixico, Sunny	18	M	F	StS	Tharlip Harjo	L	Cr	No. 2	L	Cr
4581	5	Fixico, Tagie	11	M	F	S	No. 1	L	Cr	No. 2	L	Cr
No. 1 died June 30, 1900												
Census Card No. 1440, P. O. Okemah, Enrolled January 25, 1900												
4582	1	Foster, Mary	28	F	F		Parhose	D	Cr	Montarly	D	Cr
4583	2	Foster, Chotka	28	M	F	Bro	Parhose	L	Cr	Montarly	D	Cr
4584	3	Jones, Benjamin	34	M	F	Hus	William Jones	D	Cr	Unknown	D	Cr
No. 3 reported dead												
Census Card No. 1441, P. O. Clearview, Enrolled January 25, 1900												
4585	1	Jacob, Charles	30	M	F		Parhose	D	Cr	Jennie	D	Cr
4586	2	Jacob, Nancy	28	F	F	Wf	Yarhola Harjo	D	Cr	Homahhoey	D	Cr
4587	3	Jacob, Hully	2	M	F	S	No. 1	L	Cr	No. 2	L	Cr
4588	4	Jacob, Sam	8	M	F	StS	John Davis	L	Cr	No. 2	L	Cr
No. 3 died March 15, 1900												
Census Card No. 1442, P. O. Morse; No. 2, Okmulgee, Enrolled January 25, 1900												
4589	1	West, Parsinder	28	F	F		Locher Fixico	D	Cr	Noscy	D	Cr
4590	2	Hailey, Melissa	9	F	F	D	John Hailey	D	Cr	No. 1	L	Cr
4591	3	Hailey, Lony	7	F	F	D	John Hailey	L	Cr	No. 1	L	Cr
4592	4	West, Ferry	4mo	F	F	D	Robert West	L	Cr	No. 1	L	Cr
No. 4 died June 1900												
Census Card No. 1443, P. O. Okemah or Weleetka, Enrolled January 25, 1900												
4593	1	Barnett, Daniel	32	M	F		John Barnett	D	Cr	Tochee Barnet	L	Cr
4594	2	Barnett, Eliza	28	F	F	Wf	Hinneha	D	Cr	Hettie Danley	L	Cr
4595	3	Berryhill Albert	7	M	F	StS	Sam Berryhill	L	Cr	No. 2	L	Cr
No. 2 died January 1901												

Roll No.	No.	NAME	Age	Sex	Blood	Rel.	NAME OF FATHER	Liv.	Cit.	NAME OF MOTHER	Liv.	Cit.
		Census Card No. 1444, P. O. Weleetka, Enrolled January 25, 1900										
4596	1	Fixico Oscoce	35	M	F		Yarhola Wike	D	Cr	Mansy	L	Cr
4597	2	Fixico, Semarhichkar	35	F	F	Wf	Henneha	D	Cr	Hettie Danley	L	Cr
4598	3	Fixico, Willie	11	M	F	S	No. 1	L	Cr	No. 2	L	Cr
4599	4	Fixico, Ilbo	7	M	F	S	No. 1	L	Cr	No. 2	L	Cr
4600	5	Lucy	17	F	F	StD	Barnogee	D	Cr	No. 2	L	Cr
		No. 3 reported dead										
		Census Card No. 1445, P. O. Clearview, Enrolled January 25, 1900										
4601	1	Barnett, Tochee	55	F	F		Dick Barnett	D	Cr	Susan Rawson	L	Cr
4602	2	Barnett, Palmer	14	M	F	S	Henry Martin	L	Cr	No. 1	L	Cr
4603	3	Barnett, Sampson	12	M	F	S	Elijah Fisher	D	Cr	No. 1	L	Cr
		No. 2 reported dead										
		Census Card No. 1446, P. O. Weleetka; No. 4, Carson, Enrolled January 25, 1900										
4604	1	Scott, Lambert	62	M	½		Lambert Scott	L	Non	Hultcher Scott	D	Cr
4605	2	Scott, Lucy	42	F	F	Wf	William Robison	L	D	Hannah Robison	D	Cr
4606	3	Brown, Willie	20	M	F	StS	Alex Brown	D	Sem	No. 2	L	Cr
4607	4	Brown, Melinda	18	F	F	StD	Alex Brown	D	Sem	No. 2	L	Cr
4608	5	Scott, Frazier	13	M	¾	S	No. 1	L	Cr	No. 2	L	Cr
4609	6	Scott, Martha	11	F	¾	D	No 1	L	Cr	No. 2	L	Cr
4610	7	Scott, Jane	7	F	¾	D	No 1	L	Cr	No 2	L	Cr
4611	8	Scott, Pearlie	3	F	¾	D	No. 1	L	Cr	No. 2	L	Cr
		No. 1 died November 4, 1907. Nos. 5 and 7 reported dead.										
		Census Card No. 1447, P. O. Weleetka, Enrolled January 25, 1900										
4612	1	Robison, Louisa	30	F	¾		Lambert Scott	L	Non	Wicey Scott	D	Cr
4613	2	Robison, Benjamin	10	M	¾	S	Amos Robison	L	Cr	No. 1	L	Cr
4614	3	Robison, Holmes	7	M	¾	S	Amos Robison	L	Cr	No. 1	L	Cr
4615	4	Robison, Josephus	4	M	¾	S	Amos Robison	L	Cr	No. 1	L	Cr
4616	5	Robison, Eddie A.	2	M	¾	S	Amos Robison	L	Cr	No. 1	L	Cr
		Census Card No. 1448, P. O. Bryant; No. 2, Okemah, Enrolled January 25, 1900										
4617	1	Barnett, Jackson	22	M	¾		James Barnett	L	Cr	Mehote Barnett	L	Cr
4618	2	Barnett, Phoebe	28	F	¾	Wf	Lambert Scott	L	Cr	Wicey Scott	L	Cr
4619	3	Fields, Simon	7	M	⅝	StS	Fecunner	D	Cr	No. 2	L	Cr
		Census Card No. 1449, P. O. Henryetta, Enrolled January 25, 1900										
4620	1	King, Herlesthoye	27	F	F		Okchun Yarhola	D	Cr	Smoermeryeche	D	Cr
4621	2	West Losanna	5	F	F	D	Thomas West	D	Cr	No. 1	L	Cr
4622	3	King, John	3mo	M	¾	S	John King	L	Cr	No. 1	L	Cr
		No. 3 died August 1900. Nos. 1 and 2 reported dead.										
		Census Card No. 1450, P. O. Weleetka, Enrolled January 25, 1900										
4623	1	Birdcreek, Jesse	40	M	F		Foashutchee Chupko	D	Cr	Losochee	D	Cr
4624	2	Birdcreek, Mandy	39	F	F	Wf	Josiah Asbury	D	Cr	Lizzie Barnett	D	Cr
4625	3	Birdcreek, Peggie	13	F	F	D	No. 1	L	Cr	No. 2	L	Cr
4626	4	Birdcreek, Moses	11	M	F	S	No. 1	L	Cr	No. 2	L	Cr
4627	5	Birdcreek, Timmie	7	M	F	S	No. 1	L	Cr	No. 2	L	Cr
4628	6	Birdcreek, Stanley	5	M	F	S	No. 1	L	Cr	No. 2	L	Cr
4629	7	Birdcreek, Belcher	3	M	F	S	No. 1	L	Cr	No. 2	L	Cr
		Census Card No. 1451, P. O. Checotah; No. 2, Hitchita, Enrolled January 25, 1900; No. 4, May 24, 1901										
4630	1	McNally, Cassie	11	F	1-16		N. N. McNally	D	Cr	Belle McNally	L	Non
4631	2	McNally, Samuel	7	M	1-16	Bro	N. N. McNally	D	Cr	Belle McNally	L	Non
4632	3	McNally, Susan	4	F	1-16	Sis	N. N. McNally	D	Cr	Belle McNally	L	Non
4633	4	McNally, Mack	1	M	1-16	Bro	N. N. McNally	D	Cr	Belle McNally	L	Non
		No. 4 died June 17, 1899										
		Census Card No. 1452, P. O. Salem, Enrolled January 25, 1900										
4634	1	Lena, Hettie	30	F	½		Lena	D	Sem	Loskochee	L	Cr
4635	2	Long, Jacob	11	M	¼	S	Mose Larney	L	?	No. 1	L	Cr
4636	3	McKellop, Lucinda	8	F	¼	D	McKellop	L	Cr	No. 1	L	Cr
4637	4	Sumka, Willie	5	M	¼	S	Sumka	L	Cr	No. 1	L	Cr
4638	5	Soweka, Lewis	2	M	¼	S	Soweka	L	Cr	No. 1	L	Cr
		No. 2 reported dead										
		Census Card No. 1453, P. O. Holdenville; No. 6, Salem, Enrolled January 27, 1900										
4639	1	Sewell, Washington	42	M	½		Ben Sewell	D	Cr	Munna Sewell	D	Cr
4640	2	Sewell, Sophia	37	F	½	Wf	David Tina	D	Non	Tina	D	Cr
4641	3	Sewell, Ben	19	M	½	S	David Tina	D	Non	No. 2	L	Cr
4642	4	Sewell, George	17	M	½	S	David Tina	D	Non	No. 2	L	Cr
4643	5	Sewell, Anna	10	F	½	D	David Tina	D	Non	Jennetta	L	Cr
4644	6	Sewell, Amanda	8	F	½	D	David Tina	D	Non	No. 2	L	Cr
4645	7	Sewell, Edmond	6	M	½	S	David Tina	D	Non	Jennetta	L	Cr
		Nos. 3, 4 and 7 reported dead										
		Census Card No. 1454, P. O. Holdenville, Enrolled January 27, 1900										
4646	1	Bruner, Jennetta	37	F	F		Unknown	D	Cr	Sowarley	D	Cr
4647	2	Bruner, John	2	M	F	S	Siah Bruner	D	Cr	No. 1	L	Cr
		Census Card No. 1455, P. O. Wewoka, Enrolled January 27, 1900										
4648	1	McNevins, Lee	32	M	¼		McNevins	D	Non	Mary Compier	D	Cr
4649	2	McNevins, Nancy	21	F	F	Wf	Nocus Yahola	D	Cr	Litka Scott	L	Cr
4650	3	McNevins, Andrew S.	2	M	⅝	S	No. 1	L	Cr	No. 2	L	Cr
4651	4	McNevins, George Dewey	10mo	M	⅝	S	No. 1	L	Cr	No. 2	L	Cr
		Census Card No. 1456, P. O. Sapulpa, Enrolled January 27, 1900										
4652	1	Thompson, Ella	18	F	F		Olmstead Thompson	D	Cr	Betsey Thompson	D	Cr

Census Card No. 1457, P. O. Sapulpa, Enrolled January 27, 1900; No. 5, May 23, 1901

Roll No.	No.	NAME	Age	Sex	Blood	Rel.	NAME OF FATHER	Liv.	Cit.	NAME OF MOTHER	Liv.	Cit.
4653	1	Fife, Timmie	39	M	F		Ben Fife	D	Cr	Liza Frank	D	Cr
4654	2	Fife, Sarah	37	F	F	Wf	Sapulpa	D	Cr	Liza Sapulpa	D	Cr
4655	3	Hays, Henry	5	M	F	StS	Shawnee Hayes	D	Cr	No. 2	L	Cr
4656	4	Bosen, Sam	12	M	F	Cou	John Bosen	D	Cr	Unknown	D	Cr
4657	5	Fife, Jessie	10moF	F	D		No. 1	L	Cr	No. 2	L	Cr

No. 5 died July 1, 1899

Census Card No. 1458, P. O. EWetumka, Enrolled January 29, 1900

4658	1	Fife, Susan	70	F	½		Miste Stalla	D	Non	Miss Reed	D	Cr

Census Card No. 1459, P. O. Weleetka, Enrolled January 29, 1900

4659	1	Hill, Cilla	28	F	¾		Jackson Hill	D	Cr	Lizzie Hill	D	Cr
4660	2	Robison, Lizzie	10	F	¾	D	Amos R. Robison	L	Cr	No. 1	L	Cr
4661	3	Robison, Mariah	7	F	¾	D	Amos R. Robison	L	Cr	No. 1	L	Cr
4662	4	Robison, Arline	2	F	¾	D	Amos R. Robison	L	Cr	No. 1	L	Cr

Census Card No. 1460, P. O. Weleetka, Enrolled January 29, 1900

4663	1	Hill, Charley	21	M	¾		Jackson Hill	D	Cr	Lizzie Hill	D	Cr

No. 1 reported dead

Census Card No. 1461, P. O. Weleetka, Enrolled January 29, 1900

4664	1	Hill, James H.	21	M	¾		Jackson Hill	D	C	Lizzie Hill	D	Cr

No. 1 reported dead

Census Card No. 1462, P. O. Weleetka, Enrolled January 29 1900

4665	1	Robison, Amos R.	30	M	¾		William R. Robison	D	Cr	Anteline	D	Cr

Census Card No. 1463, P. O. Weleetka, Enrolled January 29, 1900

4666	1	Fife, Jennie	60	F	F		Unknown	D	Cr	Suffochechee	D	Cr
4667	2	Dixon, Lela	4	F	F	Niece	Pin Harjo	D	Cr	Suckbecha	D	Cr

Census Card No. 1464, P. O. Wetumka, Enrolled January 29, 1900; Nos. 4 and 5, March 19, 1901

4668	1	Canard, Samuel	30	M	F		Tom Canard	D	Cr	Maggie Canard	D	Cr
4669	2	Canard, Judy	7	F	F	D	No. 1	L	Cr	Nancy Canard	D	Cr
4670	3	Canard, Sophia	2	F	F	D	No. 1	L	Cr	Nancy Canard	D	Cr
4671	4	Canard, Nancy	24	F	F	Wf	Haney Scott	L	Cr	Mollie Scott	D	Cr
4672	5	Dunzy, Philip	3	M	F	StS	Jack on Dunzy	L	Cr	No. 1	L	Cr

No. 3 reported dead

Census Card No. 1465, P. O. Okemah, Enrolled January 29, 1900

4673	1	Danly, Hittie	54	F	F		Osegee Emarthla	D	Cr	Martha	D	Cr

No 1 reported dead

Census Card No. 1466, P. O. Clea view, Enrolled January 29, 1900

4674	1	Martin, Henry	60	M	F		Unknown	D	Cr	Unknown	D	C
4675	2	Martin, Betsy	24	F	F	Wf	Elijah Fisher	L	Cr	Tochee Barnett	L	Cr
4676	3	Deer, Willie	2	M	F	StS	Ben Deer	L	Cr	No. 2	L	Cr

No. 1 reported dead

Census Card No. 1467, P. O. Clearview, Enrolled January 29, 1900

4677	1	Fixico, Linda	23	F	F		Tharlip Harjo	D	Cr	Sarfarchar Fixico	L	Cr
4678	2	Scott, Winchley	8moM	F	S		Sampson Scott	L	Cr	No. 1	L	C

Census Card No. 1468, P. O. Okemah, Enrolled January 29, 1900

4679	1	Jefley, Thomas	40	M	F		Oklabesar	L	Cr	Tobosky	D	Cr
4680	2	Jefley, Cogee	18	F	F	D	No. 1	L	Cr	Satie	D	Cr
4681	3	Jefley, Willie	14	M	F	S	No. 1	L	Cr	Satie	D	Cr
4682	4	Jefley, John	10	M	F	S	No. 1	L	Cr	Satie	D	Cr
4683	5	Jefley, Tewee	6	M	F	S	No. 1	L	Cr	Satie	D	Cr

Nos. 1, 3 and 4 repo ted dead

Census Card No. 1469, P. O. Weleetka, Enrolled January 29, 1900

4684	1	Anderson, Tifney	25	M	F		Osiah Yarhola	D	Cr	Peggy	D	Cr
4685	2	Anderson, Narto	20	F	F	Wf	Thomas Jefley	L	Cr	Satie	D	Cr
4686	3	Anderson, Simon	8	M	F	S	No. 1	L	Cr	Annie	D	Cr
4687	4	Anderson, Amos	6	M	F	S	No. 1	L	Cr	Annie	D	Cr

No. 2 died March 1900

Census Card No. 1470, P. O. McDermott, Enrolled January 29, 1900; No. 3, February 7, 1900

4688	1	Webster, Jefferson	26	M	F		Daniel Webster	D	Cr	Winey	D	Cr
4689	2	Webster, Mattie	20	F	F	Wf	John Yarholar	D	Cr	Chahoya	D	Cr
4690	3	Jones, Jemima	14	F	F	Ward	Washington Jones	D	Cr	Sallie Jones	D	Cr

No. 1 died January 21, 1908. No. 2 reported dead.

Census Card No. 1471, P. O. Okemah, Enrolled January 29, 1900

4691	2	Rawson, Susan	75	F	F		Stephen Sullivan	D	Cr	Jinney	D	Cr

No. 1 died March 9, 1903

Census Card No. 1472, P. O. Checotah, Enrolled January 29, 1900; No. 2, March 14 1901

4692	1	Walker, Mary	25	F	F		Geo. H. Walker	L	Cr	Mollie Walker	D	Cr
4693	2	Walker, Eddie	11	M	F	Bro	Geo. H. Walker	L	Cr	Mollie Walker	D	Cr

Census Card No. 1473, P. O. Wetumka, Enrolled January 29, 1900

4694	1	Walker, George W.	44	M	F		William Walker	D	Cr	Susan Walker	D	Cr
4695	2	Walker, Ellen	18	F	F	D	No. 1	L	Cr	Mottie Walker	D	Cr
4696	3	Walker, William	11	M	F	S	No. 1	L	Cr	Mottie Walker	D	Cr
4697	4	Walker, Susan	9	F	F	D	No. 1	L	Cr	Mottie Walker	D	Cr

No 1 died January 7, 1900. Nos. 2 and 3 reported dead.

Census Card No. 1474, P. O. Okemah, Enrolled January 29, 1900

4698	1	Harjo, Joseph	22	M	F		Tuhnar Harjo	D	Cr	Farye	D	Cr

Roll No.	No.	NAME	Age	Sex	Blood	Rel.	NAME OF FATHER	Liv.	Cit.	NAME OF MOTHER	Liv.	Cit.
		Census Card No. 1475, P. O. Weleetka, Enrolled January 29, 1900										
4699	1	Fife, Nixey	43	M	F		Tully Fife	D	Cr	Unknown	D	Cr
4700	2	Fife, Jacob	17	M	F	S	No. 1	L	Cr	Jane Fife	D	Cr
4701	3	Fife, Nellie	15	F	F	D	No. 1	L	Cr	Jane Fife	D	Cr
4702	4	Fife, Sukey	13	F	F	D	No. 1	L	Cr	Jane Fife	D	Cr
4703	5	Fife, Betsy	9	F	F	D	No. 1	L	Cr	Jane Fife	D	Cr
4704	6	Fife, Robert	7	M	F	S	No. 1	L	Cr	Jane Fife	D	Cr
		Nos 1 and 6 reported dead										
		Census Card No. 1476, P. O. Wetumka, Enrolled January 29, 1900										
4705	1	Fife, Liza	22	F	F		Nixey, Fife	L	Cr	Jane Fife	D	Cr
		No. 1 died January 20, 1905										
		Census Card No. 1477, P. O. Wetumka, Enrolled January 29, 1900										
4706	1	Fixico, Pahose	50	M	F		Joilly Harjo	D	Cr	Satumhoker	D	Cr
4707	2	Fixico, Edward	17	M	F	S	No. 1	L	Cr	Kisse	D	Cr
		No. 1 died February 24, 1901. No. 2 reported dead.										
		Census Card No. 1478, P. O. Weleetka, Enrolled January 29, 1900										
4708	1	Buckley, Polly	22	F	F		Sam Buckley	L	Cr	Liza Buckley	L	Cr
		Census Card No. 1479, P. O. Weleetka, Enrolled January 29, 1900										
4709	1	Buckley, Sam	55	M	F		Tewee	D	Cr	Tharyahkah	D	Cr
4710	2	Buckley, Liza	50	F	F	Wf	Harthun Harjo	D	Cr	Cyntoxgee	D	Cr
4711	3	Buckley, Henry	20	M	F	S	No. 1	L	Cr	No. 2	L	Cr
4712	4	Buckley, Sallie	18	F	F	S	No. 1	L	Cr	No. 2	L	Cr
4713	5	Buckley, Solomon	15	M	F	S	No. 1	L	Cr	No. 2	L	Cr
4714	6	Buckley, James	13	M	F	S	No. 1	L	Cr	No. 2	L	Cr
4715	7	Buckley, George	11	M	F	S	No. 1	L	Cr	No. 2	L	Cr
4716	8	Buckley, Lucinda	6	F	F	D	No. 1	L	Cr	No. 2	L	Cr
4717	9	Buckley, Rufus	3	M	F	S	No. 1	L	Cr	No. 2	L	Cr
		Nos. 1 and 6 reported dead										
		Census Card No. 1480, P. O. Dustin, Enrolled January 29, 1900										
4718	1	Wynn, Lizzie	40	F	3/4		Josiah Daniels	D	Cr	Sallie Watson	L	Cr
4719	2	Fish, Elmer	13	M	3/4	S	George Fish	D	Cr	No. 1	L	Cr
4720	3	Wynn, Pearl L.	6	F	3/8	D	Earl Wynn	L	Non	No. 1	L	Cr
4721	4	Fields, Nellie	5	F	3/4	Cou	Abraham Field	L	Cr	Ayamka	D	Cr
		Census Card No. 1481, P. O. Weleetka, Enrolled January 29, 1900										
4722	1	Scott, Turner	25	M	F		Lambert Scott	L	Cr	Wisey Scott	D	Cr
4723	2	Scott, Lucinda	24	F	F	Wf	Dick	D	Cr	Lucinda	D	Cr
4724	3	Scott, Lucy	7mo	F	5/8	D	No. 1	L	Cr	No. 2	L	Cr
		No. 3 died July 1900										
		Census Card No. 1482, P. O. Price, Enrolled January 29, 1900										
4725	1	Tiger, Lietka	26	M	F		Henneha Chupko	D	Cr	Pootka	D	Cr
4726	2	Tiger, Jinalee	30	F	F	Wf	Thortho Fixico	D	Cr	Sewikee	L	Cr
4727	3	Field, Eblo	11	M	F	StS	Chenashe	D	Cr	No. 2	L	Cr
4728	4	Field, Jesse	10	M	F	StS	Chenashe	D	Cr	No. 2	L	Cr
4729	5	Tiger, Mattie	2	F	F	D	No. 1	L	Cr	No. 2	L	Cr
		No. 2 died June 8, 11912										
		Census Card No. 1483, P. O. Dustin, Enrolled January 29, 1900										
4730	1	Wildcat, Willie	24	M	F		Sandy Wildcat	L	Cr	Sochalagee	D	Cr
		No. 1 died April 12, 1904										
		Census Card No. 1484, P. O. Henryetta, Enrolled January 29, 1900; No. 2, May 23, 1901										
4731	1	Hill, Emma	21	F	F		Sandy Wildcat	L	Cr	Sochalagee	D	Cr
4732	2	Hill, Belcher	20	M	F	Hus	Upuly Hill	D	Cr	Linda	D	Cr
		No. 2 died February 20, 1900										
		Census Card No. 1485, P. O. Okemah, Enrolled January 29, 1900										
4733	1	Hotulkoce	54	M	F		Yahar Tblocco	D	Cr	Leacher	D	Cr
4734	2	Wind, Fanny	53	F	F	Wf	Lola	D	Cr	Yoparhecher	L	Cr
4735	3	Wind, David	18	M	F	S	No. 1	L	Cr	No. 2	L	Cr
4736	4	Wind, James	12	M	F	S	No. 1	L	Cr	No. 2	L	Cr
4737	5	Severs, Shawnee	14	M	F	Ward	Sever	D	Cr	Folotker	L	Cr
4738	6	Severs, William	11	M	F	Ward	Server	D	Cr	Folotker	L	Cr
		Census Card No. 1486, P. O. Weleetka, Enrolled January 29, 1900										
4739	1	Simmer, John	29	M	F		Sam Simmer	D	Cr	Annie Simmer	D	Cr
4740	2	Simmer, Selie	28	F	F	Wf	Thortho Fixico	L	Cr	Sewikey	L	Cr
4741	3	Simmer, Kogee	5	F	F	D	No. 1	L	Cr	No. 2	L	Cr
		No. 1 died January 1903										
		Census Card No. 1487, P. O. Henryetta, Enrolled January 29, 1900; No. 5, May 22, 1901										
4742	1	Randall, Sam	28	M	F		Boney Randall	L	Cr	Mamie	D	Cr
4743	2	Randall, Dicy	20	F	F	Wf	Thortho Fixico	D	Cr	Sewikey	L	Cr
4744	3	Randall, Emma	5	F	F	D	No. 1	L	Cr	- No. 2	L	Cr
4745	4	Randall, Ida	4	F	F	D	No. 1	L	Cr	No. 2	L	Cr
4746	5	Randall, Amy	1	F	F	D	No. 1	L	Cr	No. 2	L	Cr
		No. 2 died August 3, 1913										
		Census Card No. 1488, P. O. Henryetta, Enrolled January 29, 1900; No. 8, April 26, 1901										
4747	1	Fish, Little	40	M	F		Joe	D	Cr	Malarher	D	Cr
4748	2	Fish, Winey	12	F	F	D	No. 1	L	Cr	Eliza Fish	D	Cr
4749	3	Fish, Mehaley	10	F	F	D	No. 1	L	Cr	Eliza Fish	D	Cr
4750	4	Fish, Katie	8	F	F	D	No. 1	L	Cr	Eliza Fish	D	Cr
4751	5	Fish, Frazier	6	M	F	S	No. 1	L	Cr	Eliza Fish	D	Cr
4752	6	Fish, Milley	2	F	F	D	No. 1	L	Cr	Eliza Fish	D	Cr
4753	7	Fish, Billy	1moM	F	S		No. 1	L	Cr	Eliza Fish	D	Cr
4754	8	Fish, Eliza	25	F	F	Wf	Siah Barnett	D	Cr	Mary Barnett	L	Cr
		No. 7 died October or September 1900. No. 8 died January 7, 1900										

Roll No.	No.	NAME	Age	Sex	Blood	Rel.	NAME OF FATHER	Liv.	Cit.	NAME OF MOTHER	Liv.
		Census Card No. 1489, P. O. Senora, Enrolled January 29, 1900									
4755	1	Harjo, Waxie	55	M	F		Woxie Holatte	D	Cr	Semistone	D
4756	2	Harjo, Suwerneryeche	50	F	F	Wf	Pin Emathler	L	Cr	Semowickke	D
4757	3	Harjo, Ceasar	17	M	F	StS	Tony	L	Cr	No. 2	L
		No. 2 died October 14, 1905. No. 1 reported dead.									
		Census Card No. 1490, P. O. Senora, Enrolled January 29, 1900									
4758	1	Yarhola, Magie	26	M	F		Okchun Yarhola	D	Cr	Suwerneryeche	L
		No. 1 died 1908									
		Census Card No. 1491, P. O. Senora, Enrolled January 29, 1900									
4759	1	Harjo, Abbie	23	M	F		Woxie Harjo	L	Cr	Yopacholadee	D
		No. 1 reported dead									
		Census Card No. 1492, P. O. Sallisaw, Enrolled January 29, 1900									
4760	1	Scott, Henry	24	M	F		Yarhola Warga	D	Cr	Mosey	D
4761	2	Perryman, Millie	18	F	F	Wf	Robert Starr	L	Cr	Sarner	D
		No. 2 died April 24, 1907									
		Census Card No. 1493, P. O. Henryetta, Enrolled January 29, 1900									
4762	1	Lewis, John	30	M	F		Kerseta Harjo	D	Cr	Fola	L
4763	2	Lewis, Manna	26	F	F	Wf	Hopiyee	D	Cr	Lasley Fields	L
4764	3	Lewis, Edmond	5	M	F	S	No. 1	L	Cr	No. 2	L
4765	4	Lewis, Fannie	2	F	F	D	No. 1	L	Cr	No. 2	L
4766	5	Harjo, Chapley	8	M	F	Bro	Kerseta Harjo	D	Cr	Fola	L
		No. 4 reported dead									
		Census Card No. 1494, P. O. Weleetka, Enrolled January 29, 1900									
4767	1	Fields, Mitchell	21	M	F		Hulley	D	Cr	Sokinnogee	D
		Census Card No. 1495, P. O. Okemah, Enrolled January 29, 1900									
4768	1	Wind, George	21	M	F		Hotelkochee Harjo	L	Cr	Fanny Wind	L
4769	2	Wind, Milly	20	F	½	Wf	Isaac Burrows	L	Cr	Malinda Knight	L
4770	3	Wind, Susie	1	F	¾	D	No. 1	L	Cr	No. 2	L
		Census Card No. 1496, P. O. Wetumka, Enrolled January 29, 1900									
4771	2	Robertson, Myer	20	M	F		York Robison	D	Cr	Soma	D
		Census Card No. 1497, P. O. Okemah, Enrolled January 29, 1900									
4772	1	Yargee, Jennie	24	F	F		Jeff Yargee	D	Cr	Martha	D
		Census Card No. 1498, P. O. Eufaula, Enrolled January 31, 1900									
4773	1	Grayson, Walter C.	24	M	¼		G. W. Grayson	L	Cr	Annie Grayson	L
4774	2	Grayson, Lenore	2	F	⅛	D	No. 1	L	Cr	Sallie Grayson	L
		Census Card No. 1499, P. O. Sapulpa, Enrolled January 31, 1900; No. 3, May 22, 1901									
4775	1	Berryhill, Louisa	25	F	F		George Bruner	D	Cr	Anna Bruner	L
4776	2	Berryhill, Charlie	4	M	F	S	Samuel Berryhill	D	Cr	No. 1	L
4777	3	Berryhill, Susanna	2	F	F	D	Samuel Berryhill	D	Cr	No. 1	L
		No. 3 died July 26, 1899									
		Census Card No. 1500, P. O. Holdenville, Enrolled February 1, 1900									
4778	1	Breeding, Eliza	37	F	½		London Koker	L	Cr	Mary Washburn	D
4779	2	Brown, Flora A.	16	F	¼	D	Robert Brown	D	Non	No. 1	L
4780	3	Brown, Lilly	14	F	¼	D	Robert Brown	D	Non	No. 1	L
4781	4	Miller, Emma	7	F	¼	D	Samuel Miller	L	Non	No. 1	L
4782	5	Breeding, Dick Bland	4	M	¼	S	Henry Breeding	L	Non	No. 1	L
		No. 1 reported dead									
		Census Card No. 1501, P. O. Holdenville, Enrolled February 1, 1900									
4783	1	Coker, Lewis	27	M	½		London Coker	L	Cr	Mary Washburn	D
		No. 1 died November 16, 1905									
		Census Card No. 1502, P. O. Keokuk Falls, Enrolled February 1, 1900									
4784	1	Sharp, Frances	28	F	½		Jim Chief	L	Chich	Celia Chief	D
4785	2	Sharp, Culberson	10	M	¼	S	No. 1	L	Cr	John Fenley	L
		No. 1 died August 1905. NOTE—Parents of No. 2 probably reversed.									
		Census Card No. 1503, P. O. Yeager, Enrolled February 1, 1900; No. 9, November 4, 1901									
4786	1	Culler, Thomas	45	M	F		Conip Harjo	D	Cr	Nancy	D
4787	2	Culler, Mary	30	F	F	Wf	Daniel McGirt	D	Cr	Susie	D
4788	3	Culler, Major	19	M	F	S	No. 1	L	Cr	No. 2	L
4789	4	Culler, Jimmie	17	M	F	S	No. 1	L	Cr	Winnie	D
4790	5	Culler, David	11	M	F	S	No. 1	L	Cr	Winnie	L
4791	6	Culler, Johnny	9	M	F	S	No. 1	L	Cr	Winnie	L
4792	7	Culler, Anniey	6	F	F	D	No. 1	L	Cr	No. 2	L
4793	8	Culler, Yarner	4	F	F	D	No. 1	L	Cr	No. 2	L
4794	9	Culler, Susie	18	F	F	StD	Arber	D	Cr	No. 2	L
		No. 4 died December 22, 1909. No. 6 died January 1, 1913. No. 9, died November 15,									
		Nos. 2, 3, 5 and 7 reported dead									
		Census Card No. 1504, P. O. Yeager, Enrolled February 1, 1900; No. 7, February 13, 1900									
4795	1	Marshall, Philip	27	M	F		Osagee Harjo	D	Cr	Nogaska	D
4796	2	Marshall, Aggie	30	F	F	Wf	Nehar Yaholar	L	Cr	Sallie	D
4797	3	Marshall, Molsie	7	F	F	D	No. 1	L	Cr	No. 2	L
4798	4	Marshall, Susie	4	F	F	D	No. 1	L	Cr	No. 2	L
4799	5	Marshall, Watie	3	M	F	S	No. 1	L	Cr	Millie	D
4800	6	Marshall, Johnny	1	M	F	S	No. 1	L	Cr	No. 2	L
4801	7	Lowe, Comma	15	M	F	StS	Ispahoke Harjo	D	Cr	No. 2	L
		No. 3 reported dead									

Roll No.	No.	NAME	Age	Sex	Blood	Rel.	NAME OF FATHER	Liv.	Cit.	NAME OF MOTHER	Liv.	Cit.

Census Card No. 1505, P. O. Yeager, Enrolled February 1, 1900

4802	1	Harjo, Wacus	63	M	F		Ocbee Harjo	D	Cr	Unknown	?	Cr
4803	2	Harjo, Millie	52	F	F	Wf	Osage Harjo	D	Cr	Yokchee	?	Cr
4804	3	Harjo, Nancy	15	F	F	D	Jogarty Y. Micco	D	C	Rhoda	?	Cr
4805	4	Harjo, Addie	13	F	F	D	No. 1	L	Cr	No. 2	L	Cr
4806	5	Harjo, Lillie	9	F	F	D	No. 1	L	Cr	No. 2	L	Cr
4807	6	Harjo, Bunny	7	M	F	S	No. 1	L	Cr	No. 2	L	Cr
4808	7	Harjo, Lucy	3	F	F	D	No. 1	L	Cr	No. 2	L	Cr
4809	8	Coachman, Mattie	18	F	F	StD	Peter Cochman	L	Cr	No. 2	L	Cr

No. 1 died May 6, 1903

Census Card No. 1506, P. O. Okmulgee, Enrolled February 1, 1900

4810	1	Davis, Nocos	45	M	F		Wocus Harjo	L	Cr	Sarlarhakky	D	Cr
4811	2	Davis, Polly	22	F	F	Wf	Peter Coachman	L	Cr	Millie Harjo	L	Cr
4812	3	Davis, John	17	M	F	S	No. 1	L	Cr	Katie Davis	D	Cr
4813	4	Davis, George	7	M	F	S	No. 1	L	Cr	Katie Davis	D	Cr
4814	5	Davis, Sissie	5	F	F	D	No. 1	L	Cr	Lena	L	Cr

Nos. 1 and 2 reported dead

Census Card No. 1507, P. O. Yeager, Enrolled February 1, 1900

4815	1	Davis, John	28	M	F		Cosar Fixico	L	Cr	Wisey Fixico	D	Cr
4816	2	Davis, Polly	23	F	F	Wf	Wegus Harjo	L	Cr	Sarlarhakky	D	Cr
4817	3	Davis, Turner	8	M	F	S	No. 1	L	Cr	No. 2	L	Cr
4818	4	Davis, Jack	6	M	F	S	No. 1	L	Cr	No. 2	L	Cr
4819	5	Davis, Peggie	3	F	F	D	No. 1	L	Cr	No. 2	L	Cr

No. 3 died June 6, 1900

Census Card No. 1508, P. O. Weleetka, Enrolled February 2, 1900

4820	1	Berryhill, Joseph	36	M	F		Simon Berryhill	D	Cr	Martha Berryhill	D	Cr
4821	2	Berryhill, Sallie	28	F	F	Wf	Hencha	D	Cr	Hettie Danley	D	Cr
4822	3	Berryhill, Annie	10	F	F	D	No. 1	L	Cr	No. 2	L	Cr
4823	4	Berryhill, Emma	6	F	F	D	No. 1	L	Cr	No. 2	L	Cr
4824	5	Berryhill, John	4	M	F	S	No. 1	L	Cr	No. 2	L	Cr
4825	6	Berryhill, Anderson	2	M	F	S	No. 1	L	Cr	No. 2	L	Cr
4826	7	Berryhill, Louisa	16	F	F	D	No. 1	L	Cr	Martha Berryhill	L	Cr

No. 2 died December 8, 1902

Census Card No. 1509, P. O. Yeager, Enrolled February 2, 1900

4827	1	Harjo, Lumka	25	M	F		Wecus Harjo	L	Cr	Sarlarhakky	D	Cr
4828	2	Harjo, Kissie	23	F	F	Wf	Warcheeman	L	Sem	Suche	?	Cr
4829	3	Harjo, Wargie	8	F	F	D	No. 1	L	Cr	No. 2	L	Cr
4830	4	Harjo, Annie	4	F	F	D	No. 1	L	Cr	No. 2	L	Cr
4831	5	Harjo, Seyada	15day	F	F	D	No. 1	L	Crr	No. 2	L	Cr

No. 5 died February 4, 1900

Census Card No. 1510, P. O. Tulsa, Enrolled February 2, 1900; No. 4, May 14, 1901

4832	1	Coney, Moses	46	M	F		Charley Gunke	D	Cr	Sahahgee	D	Cr
4833	2	Coney, Liza	35	F	F	Wf	Mistohale Magilbe	L	Cr	Unknown	D	Cr
4834	3	Coney, Tom	10	M	F	S	No. 1	L	Cr	Sally Kunke	D	Cr
4835	4	Jackson, Lilly	3½	F	F	StD	Jackson King	L	Cr	No. 2	L	Cr

No. 1 died June 1900. No. 2 died August 9, 1900.

Census Card No. 1511, P. O. Weleetka, Enrolled February 2, 1900

4836	1	Sawyer, Wesley	28	M	F		Moses Sawyer	L	Cr	Linda Sawyer	D	Cr
4837	2	Sawyer, Ellen	19	F	F	Wf	Sunday Tiger	D	Cr	Piner Tiger	L	Cr

No. 2 died October 1900

Census Card No. 1512, P. O. Wetumka, Enrolled February 2, 1900; No. 4, May 15, 1901

4838	1	Hale, Sumner	28	M	F		Woxey Holohta	L	Cr	Yubukta	L	Cr
4839	2	Hale, Lucy	24	F	F	Wf	Thomas Canard	D	Cr	Yarner Canard	D	Cr
4840	3	Hale, Mabel	2	F	F	D	No. 1	L	Cr	No. 2	L	Cr
4841	4	Youbartka	63	F	F	M	Unknown	?	Cr	Unknown	?	Cr

No. 4 died November 10, 1900. No. 1 reported dead.

Census Card No. 1513, P. O. Wetumka, Enrolled February 2, 1900

4842	1	Canard, Felix	21	M	F		Thomas Canard	D	Cr	Yarner Canard	D	Cr

Census Card No. 1514, P. O. Wetumka, Enrolled February 2, 1900; No. 8, May 18, 1901

4843	1	Canard, Jeff	28	M	F		Thomas Canard	D	Cr	Yarner Canard	D	Cr
4844	2	Canard, Summer	21	F	F	Wf	Daniel McGirt	D	Cr	Wisey McGirt	D	Cr
4845	3	Canard, Rachel	2	F	F	D	No. 1	L	Cr	No. 2	L	Cr
4846	4	Canard, Roly	15	M	F	Bro	Thomas Canard	D	Cr	Yarner Canard	D	Cr
4847	5	Tiplow, John	18	M	F	Neph	Saw Tiplow	L	Cr	Lizzie Tiplow	D	Cr
4848	6	Tiplow, Susan	15	F	F	Niece	Saw Tiplow	L	Cr	Lizzie Tiplow	D	Cr
4849	7	Henshaw, Thomas	3	M	F	Neph	Lou Henshaw	L	Non	Malinda Henshaw	D	Cr
4850	8	Sammy, Lucinda	11	F	F	Niece	Jim Sammy	D	Cr	Lizzie	D	Cr

No. 3 died December 5, 1901. No. 5 died June 30, 1905. No. 6 died August 14, 1900. No. 8 died April 12, 1899.

Census Card No. 1515, P. O. Wetumka, Enrolled February 2, 1900; No. 9, March 18, 1901

4851	1	Yarholar, Chapley	39	M	F		Yarholer Harjo	D	Cr	Homarhoywee	D	Cr
4852	2	Yarholar, Wisey	35	F	F	Wf	Thomas Canard	D	Cr	Nekeye	D	Cr
4853	3	Yarholar, Lizzie	2	F	F	D	No. 1	L	Cr	No. 2	L	Cr
4854	4	Scott, Annie	17	F	F	StD	James Scott	D	Cr	No. 2	L	Cr
4855	5	Scott, Roman	15	M	F	StS	James Scott	D	Cr	No. 2	L	Cr
4856	6	Scott, Silas	12	M	F	StS	James Scott	D	Cr	No. 2	L	Cr
4857	7	Scott, Nancy	10	F	F	StD	James Scott	D	Cr	No. 2	L	Cr
4858	8	Harjo, Mehaley	13	F	F	Ward	Temarheseh	D	Cr	Lucy Harjo	D	Cr
4859	9	Yarholar, Stella	9moF		?	D	No. 1	L	Cr	No. 2	L	Cr

Nos. 2 and 5 reported dead

Rol No.	No.	NAME	Age	Sex	Blood	Re.	NAME OF FATHER	Liv.	Cit.	NAME OF MOTHER	Liv.	Cit.

Census Card No. 1516, P. O. Holdenville, Enrolled February 2, 1900; Nos. 4 and 5, April 12, 1900; No. 6, May 20, 1900

	1	Scott, Litka	50	F	F		Tamarthlee Micco	D	Cr	Sehethika	D	Cr
4860	1	Scott, Litka	50	F	F		Tamarthlee Micco	D	Cr	Sehethika	D	Cr
4861	2	Colonel, Agnes	7	F	F	GrD	George Colonel	D	Cr	Fannie Tiger	D	Cr
4862	3	Deer, Mabel	4	F	F	GrD	Louis Deer	L	Cr	Emma Scott	L	Cr
4863	4	Cornells, Emma	18	F	F	D	Noens Yahola	D	Cr	No. 1	L	Cr
4864	5	Scott, James	15	M	F	Ward	Ben Scott	D	Cr	Louiska Scott	D	Cr
4865	6	Cornells, Melissey	2	F	½	GrD	Robt. Cornell	L	Sem	No. 4	L	Cr

No. 1 died December 28, 1902. No. 3 Illigitimate. No. 4 died April 26, 1902. No. 6 died September 1899.

Census Card No. 1517, P. O. Red Fork, Enrolled February 2, 1900

4866	1	Yargee, John I.	42	M	¾		Peter Yargee	D	Cr	Mary Cloud	L	Cr
4867	2	Yargee, Nancy	48	F	½	Wf	Ben Porter	D	Non	Phoebe Porter	D	Cr
4868	3	Yargee, Nathaniel V.	18	M	½	S	No. 1	L	Cr	No. 2	L	Cr
4869	4	Yargee, Pleasant	14	M	½	S	No. 1	L	Cr	No. 2	L	Cr
4870	5	Yargee, Hattie L.	12	F	½	D	No. 1	L	Cr	No. 2	L	Cr
4871	6	Yargee, Charley	6	M	½	S	No. 1	L	Cr	No. 2	L	Cr
4872	7	Cloud, Mary P.	63	F	½	M	Penn	D	Non	McGirt	D	Cr
4873	8	Sanger, Lena	18	F	¼	Niece	F. M. Sawyer	D	Non	Hannah Sanger	D	Cr

Census Card No. 1518, P. O. Holdenville, Enrolled February 3, 1900

4874	1	Kernal, Chotka	40	F	F		Tahnarthe Micco	D	Cr	Sagetha	D	Cr
4875	2	Kernal, Winey	21	F	F	D	David Kernal	D	Cr	No. 2	L	Cr
4876	3	Kernal, Mary	17	F	F	D	David Kernal	D	Cr	No. 2	L	Cr
4877	4	Kernal, Louis	16	M	F	S	David Kernal	D	Cr	No. 2	L	Cr
4878	5	Kernal, Nellie	13	F	F	D	David Kernal	D	Cr	No. 2	L	Cr
4879	6	Kernal, Louisa	8	F	F	D	David Kernal	D	Cr	No. 2	L	Cr

No. 3 died September 1901. No. 2 died May 7, 1902. Nos. 4 and 5 reported dead.

Census Card No. 1519, P. O. Yeager, Enrolled February 3, 1900

4880	1	Long, Thomas	46	M	F		Tulmarthla Micco	D	Cr	Segethlar	D	Cr
4881	2	Long, Sindy	40	F	F	Wf	Argee Yahola	D	Cr	Tilda	D	Cr
4882	3	Long, Noah	22	M	F	S	No. 1	L	Cr	No. 2	L	Cr
4883	4	Long, Tusie	15	F	F	D	No. 1	L	Cr	No. 2	L	Cr
4884	5	Long, Betsy	13	F	F	D	No. 1	L	Cr	No. 2	L	Cr
4885	6	Long, Taylor	9	M	F	S	No. 1	L	Cr	No. 2	L	Cr
4886	7	Long, David	2moM	F	S		No. 1	L	Cr	No. 2	L	Cr
4887	8	Long, Thomas	7	M	F	S	No. 1	L	Cr	No. 2	L	Cr
4888	9	McGertt, John	14	M	F	Neph	Daniel Deer	D	Cr	Wisey Deer	D	Cr

Nos. 6 and 7 reported dead.

Census Card No. 1520, P. O. Wetumka, Enrolled February 3, 1900; No. 3, March 22, 1901

4889	1	McGertt, Linda	17	F	F		Daniel McGirt	D	Cr	Wisey Deer	D	Cr
4890	2	Canard, Pusley	10moM	F	S		Felix Canard	D	Cr	No. 1	L	Cr
4891	3	Cowe, Sarty	40	M	F	Hus	Conup Yaholar	D	Cr	Sinlatka	D	Cr
4892	4	Deere, Wisey	52	F	F	M	Tomathle Maco	D	Cr	Sinny hethla	D	Cr

No. 2 died October 10, 1900. No. 1 reported dead. No. 4 died October 29, 1899.

Census Card No. 1521, P. O. Holdenville, Enrolled February 2, 1900

4893	1	Bruner, Miller	22	M	F		Jarey Bruner	D	Cr	Sophia Robertson	L	Cr
4894	2	Bruner, Liza	18	F	F	Wf	Long George	D	Cr	Annie Long	L	Cr

No. 1 reported dead

Census Card No. 1522, P. O. Holdenville. Enrolled February 3, 1900

4895	1	Thomas, Amos	20	M	F		Thomas	D	Cr	Bepsey Thomas	L	Cr

No. 1 reported dead

Census Card No. 1523, P. O. Holdenville; No. 4, Okmulgee, Enrolled February 3, 1900

4896	1	Thomas, Bepsey	40	F	F		John Reed	L	Cr	Lecha	L	Cr
4897	2	Sullivan, Minnie	28	F	F	D	Thomas	D	Cr	No. 1	L	Cr
4898	3	Thomas, Milly	11	F	F	D	Thomas	D	Cr	No. 1	L	Cr
4899	4	Thomas, Emma	7	F	F	D	Thomas	D	Cr	No. 1	L	Cr
4900	5	Thomas, Bettie	3	F	F	D	Thomas	D	Cr	No. 1	L	Cr
4901	6	Sullivan, Jimmie	4	M	F	GrS	Jim Sullivan	D	Cr	No. 2	L	Cr

No. 1 reported dead

Census Card No. 1524, P. O. Yeager, Enrolled February 3, 1900

4902	1	Lowe, Canuky	25	M	F		Oclayache	D	Cr	Aggie	L	Cr
4903	2	Lowe, Toche	20	F	F	Wf	Misseh	D	Cr	Sukey	L	Cr

Census Card No. 1525, P. O. Wewoka, Enrolled February 3, 1900

4904	1	Buck, Joe	30	M	½		Josa Buck	D	Cr	Hepsey	L	Cr

Census Card No. 1526, P. O. Wewoka, Enrolled February 3, 1900

4905	1	Lindsey, Amos	20	M	½		Lindsey	L	Sem	Hepsey	L	Cr

No. 1 reported dead

Census Card No. 1527, P. O. Yeager, Enrolled February 3, 1900

4906	1	Harjo, Lindo	47	F	F		Neha Yaholar	D	Cr	Sallie	D	Cr
4907	2	Harjo, Sunday	17	M	F	S	Ispohoke Harjo	D	Cr	No. 1	L	Cr
4908	3	Harjo, Jenna	15	F	F	D	Ispohoke Harjo	D	Cr	No. 1	L	Cr
4909	4	Harjo, Cheparney	12	M	F	S	Ispohoke Harjo	D	Cr	No. 1	L	Cr
4910	5	Harjo, Thompson	10	M	F	S	Ispohoke, Harjo	D	Cr	No. 1	L	Cr
4911	6	Edmund	8	M	F	S	Ispohoke Harjo	D	Cr	No. 1	L	Cr
4912	7	Harjo, Marsey	4	M	F	S	Ispohoke Harjo	D	Cr	No. 1	L	Cr

Harjo No. 7 died in fall of 1899

Census Card No. 1528, P. O. Yeager, Enrolled February 3, 1900

4913	1	Harjo, Cho-co-te	30	M	F		Woddie	L	Cr	Mullie	D	Cr
4914	2	Harjo, Annie	45	F	F	Wf	Cheparney Chupco	D	Cr	Betty Chupco	L	Cr
4915	3	Long, Susanna	13	F	F	StD	George Long	L	Cr	No. 2	L	Cr
4916	4	Long, Bunny	9	M	F	StS	George Long	L	Cr	No. 2	L	Cr

Roll No.	No.	NAME	Age	Sex	Blood	Rel.	NAME OF FATHER	Liv.	Cit.	NAME OF MOTHER	Liv.	Cit.
		Census Card No. 1529, P. O. Holdenville; No. 6 Wewoka, Enrolled February 3, 1900										
4917	1	Chupco, Katie	45	F	F		Tulsa Yahola	D	Cr	Unknown	?	Cr
4918	2	Chupco, Toney	24	M	F	S	Micco Chupco	D	Cr	No. 1	L	Cr
4919	3	Chupco, James	16	M	F	S	Micco Chupco	D	Cr	No. 1	L	Cr
4920	4	Chupco, Amos	12	M	F	S	Micco Chupco	D	Cr	No. 1	L	Cr
4921	5	Chupco, Moses	4	M	F	S	Micco Chupco	D	Cr	No. 1	L	Cr
4922	6	Chupco, Joseph	18	M	F	S	Micco Chupco	D	Cr	No. 1	L	Cr
4923	7	Chupco, Tomy	9	M	F	S	Micco Chupco	D	Cr	No. 1	L	Cr

No. 1 died April 26, 1900. No. 4 died September 15, 1907

		Census Card No. 1530, P. O. Okemah, Enrolled February 3, 1900										
4924	1	Sawyer, Moses A.	53	M	F		Andrew Sawyer	D	Cr	Hannah Sawyer	D	Cr
4925	2	Sawyer, Polly	26	F	F	Wf	Arbeka Harjo	D	Cr	Cinna	L	Cr
4926	3	Sawyer, Amanda	7	F	F	D	No. 1	L	Cr	No. 2	L	Cr
4927	4	Sawyer, Yokum	1 mo	M	F	D	No. 1	L	Cr	No. 2	L	Cr
4928	5	Sand, Hully	11	M	F	StS	Isaac Sand	L	Cr	No. 2	L	Cr
4929	6	Sawyer, Minda	1	F	F	D	No. 1	L	Cr	No. 2	L	Cr

No. 1 died April 1, 1901. No. 4 died December 16, 1901. No. 5 died February 23, 1901. No. 6 died August 18, 1899

		Census Card No. 1531, P. O. Okemah, Enrolled February 3, 1900; No. 4 March 13, 1900										
4930	1	McKellop, Joseph M.	40	M	F		James McKellop	D	Cr	Annie McKellop	D	Cr
4931	2	McKellop, Sallie	19	F	F	Wf	Jacob Knight	L	Cr	Martha Knight	D	Cr
4932	3	McKellop, Cherokee	11	F	F	D	No. 1	L	Cr	Alena McKellop	D	Cr
4933	4	McKellop, Effie	1 mo	F	F	D	No. 1	L	Cr	No. 2	L	Cr
4934	5	McKellop, Thomas	19	M	F	S	No. 1	L	Cr	Alena McKellop	D	Cr

No. 1 reported dead

		Census Card No. 1532, P. O. Okemah, Enrolled February 3, 1900										
4935	1	White, James	20	M	F		John White	D	Cr	Eliza Davis	L	Cr

		Census Card No. 1533, P. O. Okemah, Enrolled February 3, 1900; No. 3 May 17, 1901										
4936	1	Davis, John	24	M	F		Joslin Davis	L	Cr	Jenny Davis	D	Cr
4937	2	Davis, Susan	22	F	F	Wf	Colte Harjo	D	Cr	Lucy White	D	Cr
4938	3	Davis, Annie	10 mo	F	F	D	No. 1	L	Cr	No. 2	L	Cr

No. 3 died January 13,1901. No. 1 died February 22, 1904

		Census Card No. 1534, P. O. Fentress, Enrolled February 3, 1900										
4939	1	Deer, Ben	27	M	F		Tulmochus Harjo	D	Cr	Molitche	D	Cr

No. 1 died April 10, 1902

		Census Card No. 1535, P. O. Senora, Enrolled February 3, 1900										
4940	1	Fields, Artus	50	M	F		David Fields	D	Cr	Unknown	D	Cr
4941	2	Fields, Waitie	35	F	F	Wf	Thlechumme Harjo	D	Cr	Sumeyischee	D	Cr

No. 1 reported dead

		Census Card No. 1536, P. O. Dustin, Enrolled February 3, 1900										
4942	1	Sarhilla	24	M	F		Muckner	D	Cr	Fola	D	Cr
4943	2	Annie	18	F	F	Wf	Harry Fields	D	Cr	Sokinnogee	D	Cr

No. 2 died February 20, 1910

		Census Card No. 1537, P. O. Henryetta, Enrolled February 3, 1900										
4944	1	West, Lumsey	22	M	F		Thlechunme Harjo	D	Cr	Sumeyischee	D	Cr

		Census Card No. 1538, P. O. Henryetta, Enrolled February 3, 1900										
4945	1	Fields, Lasley	60	F	F		David Fields	D	Cr	Unknown	D	Cr

		Census Card No. 1539, P. O. Senora; No. 2 Henryetta, Enrolled February 3, 1900										
4946	1	Starr, Moses	35	M	F		Robert Star	L	Cr	Sina	D	Cr
4947	2	Starr, Susie	35	F	F	Wf	Ochun Harjo	D	Cr	Pefotka	D	Cr
4948	3	Starr, Hebsey	9	F	F	D	No. 1	L	Cr	No. 2	L	Cr
4949	4	Starr, Minnie	7	F	F	D	No. 1	L	Cr	No. 2	L	Cr
4950	5	Starr, Nina	2	F	F	D	No. 1	L	Cr	No. 2	L	Cr

No. 1 died March 13, 1901. Nos. 3 and 4 reported dead. No. 2 died December 15, 1902

		Census Card No. 1540, P. O. Bryant, Enrolled February 3, 1900										
4951	1	Barnett, David	45	M	F		Siah Barnett	D	Cr	Mary Barnett	L	Cr
4952	2	Barnert, Patty	45	F	F	Wf	Hillabee Harjo	D	Cr	Unknown	?	Cr
4953	3	Barnett, Melviney	19	F	F	D	No. 1	L	Cr	No. 2	L	Cr
4954	4	Barnett, Hettie	15	F	F	D	No. 1	L	Cr	No. 2	L	Cr
4955	5	Barnett, Wesley	10	M	F	S	No. 1	L	Cr	No. 2	L	Cr
4956	6	Barnett, Amosy	2	M	F	S	No. 1	L	Cr	No. 2	L	Cr

Nos. 2 and 6 reported dead

		Census Card No. 1541, P. O. Okemah, Enrolled February 3, 1900; No. 4 May 17, 1901										
4957	1	Davis, Joslin	40	M	F		Aharle Emarthla	D	Cr	Nekrahah	D	Cr
4958	2	Davis, Eliza	45	F	F	Wf	Tomechichee	D	Cr	Wisey	D	Cr
4959	3	Davis, James	8	M	F	S	No. 1	L	Cr	Jenny Davis	D	Cr
4960	4	Davis, Esther	14	F	F	D	No. 1	L	Cr	Jenny Davis	D	Cr

No. 4 died April 13, 1899. No. 1 died May 25, 1909

		Census Card No. 1542, P. O. Weleetka, Enrolled February 3, 1900										
4961	1	Lowe, William	60	M	F		Intermish Harjo	D	Cr	Parsachkee	D	Cr
4962	2	Lowe, Sally	52	F	F	Wf	Osotock Harjo	D	Cr	Milley Chupko	D	Cr
4963	3	Lowe, Tutler	6	M	F	GrNep	Fosbutcke Harjo	L	Cr	Eliza Listka	L	Cr

No. 3 reported dead

		Census Card No. 1543, P. O. Weleetka, Enrolled February 3, 1900; No. 6 May 17, 1901										
4964	1	Canard, Billy	45	M	F		Arharlok Yarhola	D	Cr	Tilda	L	Cr
4965	2	Canard, Katie	18	F	F	D	No. 1	L	Cr	Lusaryar Canard	D	Cr
4966	3	Canard, Lucy	13	F	F	D	No. 1	L	Cr	Lusaryar Sanard	D	Cr
4967	4	Canard, Joseph	11	M	F	S	No. 1	L	Cr	Lusaryar Canard	D	Cr
4968	5	Canard, Narburg	5	M	F	S	No. 1	L	Cr	Lusaryar Canard	D	Cr
4969	6	Canard, Rosanna	30	F	F	Wf	William Lowe	L	Cr	Katie	D	Cr

No. 6 died November 26, 1809. No. 2 reported dead

Roll No.	No.	NAME	Age	Sex	Blood	Rel.	NAME OF FATHER	Liv.	Cit.	NAME OF MOTHER	Liv.	Cit.
		Census Card No. 1544, P. O. Weleetka, Enrolled February 3, 1900										
4970	1	Yarhola, Cussehta	40	M	F		Joker	D	Cr	Sokheyathka	D	Cr
4971	2	Yarhola, Linda	30	F	F	Wf	Mack Marsey	L	Cr	Nancy	L	Cr
4972	3	Yarhola, Maley	16	F	F	D	No. 1	L	Cr	Ohcunda	L	Cr
4973	4	Yarhola, Nancy	8	F	F	D	No. 1	L	Cr	No. 2	L	Cr
4974	5	Yarhola, Billy	5	M	F	S	No. 1	L	Cr	No. 2	L	Cr
4975	6	Yarhola, Lessey	3	F	F	D	No. 1	L	Cr	No. 2	L	Cr
		No. 5 died Februaru 8, 1902										
		Census Card No. 1545, P. O. Weleetka, Enrolled February 3, 1900										
4976	1	Lowe, Alex	21	M	¾		William Lowe	I	Cr	Sally	D	Cr
4977	2	Lowe, Martha	28	F	F	Wf	Cowe, Harjo	L	Cr	Jennie	D	Cr
4978	3	Lowe, Sally	6 mo	F	⅞	D	No. 1	L	Cr	No. 2	L	Cr
		Census Card No. 1546, P. O. Weleetka, Enrolled February 3, 1900										
4979	1	Barnett, Tucker	46	M	¾		Tony Barnett	D	Cr	Eliza Gooden	D	Cr
4980	2	Barnett, Cilla	21	F	F	Wf	Mike Marsey	L	Cr	Nancy	D	Cr
4981	3	Barnett, Hannah	12	F	⅝	D	No. 1	L	Cr	Milley	D	Cr
4982	4	Barnett, Winey	10	F	⅝	D	No. 1	L	Cr	Milley	D	Cr
		No. 2 died September 18, 1900										
		Census Card No. 1547, P. O. Weleetka, Enrolled February 3, 1900										
4983	1	Robinson, Maggie	22	F	F		Daniel Barnett	L	Cr	Sarah	D	Cr
		Census Card No. 1548, P. O. Weleetka, Enrolled February 3, 1900										
4984	1	Marsey, Mike	55	M	F		Unknown	D	Cr	Unknown	D	Cr
4985	2	Marsey, Lumsey	16	M	F	S	No. 1	L	Cr	Mabala	D	Cr
4986	3	Marsey, Katie	14	F	F	D	No. 1	L	Cr	Mabala	D	Cr
4987	4	Marsey, Wisey	12	F	F	D	No. 1	L	Cr	Mabala	D	Cr
4988	5	Marsey, Intey	10	F	F	D	No. 1	L	Cr	Mabala	D	Cr
		No. 5 died November 26, 1907. No. 1 reported dead										
		Census Card No. 1549, P. O. Weleetka, Enrolled February 3, 1900										
4989	1	Cubbie, Jacob, Jacob	45	M	½		Unknown	?	Cr	Chofochaye	D	Cr
4990	2	Cubbie, Rhoda	24	F	F	Wf	Mike Marsey	L	Cr	Nancy	D	Cr
4991	3	Cubbie, John J.	1	M	¾	S	No. 1	L	Cr	No. 2	L	Cr
		Census Card No. 1550, P. O. Weleetka, Enrolled February 3, 1900										
4992	1	Reed, Stephen	25	M	F		Jimson Reed	D	Cr	Arstohartar	D	Cr
		No. 1 died November 7, 1901										
		Census Card No. 1551, P. O. Weleetka, Enrolled February 3, 1900										
4993	1	Yarhola, Fushutche	48	M	F		Ospatock Harjo	D	Cr	Milley Chupco	D	Cr
4994	2	Yarhola, Mary	40	F	F	Wf	Ose Yarhola	D	Cr	Simmabihye	D	Cr
4995	3	Yarhola, Willie	16	M	F	S	No. 1	L	Cr	No. 2	L	Cr
4996	4	Yarhola, Malinda	8	F	F	D	No. 1	L	Cr	No. 2	L	Cr
		No. 3 reported dead										
		Census Card No. 1552, P. O. Weleetka, Enrolled February 3, 1900										
4997	1	Yarhola, Kizzie	21	F	F		Fushutche Yarhola	L	Cr	Mary Yarhola	L	Cr
		Census Card No. 1553, P. O. Weleetka, Enrolled February 3, 1900										
4998	1	Bird, Jimmie	24	M	F		Fushutche Yarhola	L	Cr	Mary Yarhola	L	Cr
4999	2	Bird, Annie	24	F	F	Wf	Tucker Barnett	L	Cr	Sarah	D	Cr
		No. 2 reported dead.										
		Census Card No. 1554, P. O. Weleetka, Enrolled February 3, 1900; No. 7 April 26, 1901										
5000	1	Harjo, Fushutche	40	M	F		Ospotoch Harjo	D	Cr	Millie Chupko	D	Cr
5001	2	Harjo, Eliza	38	F	F	Wf	Samsochee	L	Cr	Sochker	D	Cr
5002	3	Harjo, Sunday	13	F	F	D	No. 1	L	Cr	No.	L	Cr
5003	4	Harjo, Sampson	8	M	F	S	No. 1	L	Cr	No.	L	Cr
5004	5	Harjo, James	3	M	F	S	No. 1	L	Cr	No. 2	L	Cr
5005	6	Harjo, Joseph	3	M	F	S	No. 1	L	Cr	No.	L	Cr
5006	7	Harjo, Jonas	1	M	F	S	No. 1	L	Cr	No.	L	Cr
		No. 1 died March 1901. Nos. 3 and 5 reported dead										
		Census Card No. 1555, P. O. Weleetka, Enrolled February 3, 1900; Nos. 2 and 3 March 6, 1901; No. 4 May 31, 1901										
5007	1	Deer, Moses	50	M	F		Pahose Harjo	D	Cr	Mutalocha	D	Cr
5008	2	Deer, Ellen	28	F	F	Wf	Sam Long	L	Cr	Hannah	L	Cr
5009	3	Deer, Enos	9	M	½	StS	Unknown	?	Non	No. 2	L	Cr
5010	4	Yargee, Dave	3	M	F	StS	Alex Yargee	D	Cr	No. 2	L	Cr
		No. 1 died October 27, 1905. No. 3 reported dead										
		Census Card No. 1556, P. O. Wallace, Enrolled February 3, 1900										
5011	1	Hully, Tom	40	M	F		Tulmochus Harjo	D	Cr	Mothlachee	L	Cr
5012		Hully, Betsy	30	F	F	Wf	Osachee Emarthla	L	Cr	Martha	L	Cr
5013		Hully, Wisey	16	F	F	D	No. 1	L	Cr	No. 2	L	Cr
5014		Hully, Betty	12	F	F	D	No. 1	L	Cr	No. 2	L	Cr
5015		Hully, Kogee	7	F	F	D	No. 1	L	Cr	No. 2	L	Cr
5016	8	Hully, Emma	5	F	F	D	No. 1	L	Cr	No. 2	L	Cr
		Nos. 1, 3 and 4 reported dead.										
		Census Card No. 1557, P. O. Wetumka, Enrolled February 5, 1900										
5017	1	Dacon, Sardy	45	M	F		Chowastieyee	D	Cr	Sinda	D	Cr
5018	2	Dacon, Harney	40	F	F	Wf	Thomas Yaholar	L	Cr	Millie Yaholar	L	Cr
5019	3	Dacon, Lina	10	F	F	D	No. 1	L	Cr	No. 2	L	Cr
5020	4	Dacon, Chilly	4	M	F	S	No. 1	L	Cr	No. 2	L	Cr
5021	5	Dacon, Sandy	2	M	F	S	No. 1	L	Cr	No. 2	L	Cr
		No. 3 died September 1912										

Roll No.	No.	NAME	Age	Sex	Blood	Rel.	NAME OF FATHER	Liv.	Cit.	NAME OF MOTHER	Liv.	Cit.
		Census Card No. 1558, P. O. Weleetka, Enrolled February 5, 1900										
5022	1	Baker, John	48	M	F		Pofner	D	Cr	Sartaloyah	D	Cr
5023	2	Baker, Mentie	46	F	F	Wf	Osce Yarholar	D	Cr	Simneparyee	D	Cr
5024	3	Baker, Tarsey	19	M	F	StS	Esparne Harjo	D	Cr	No. 2	L	Cr
5025	4	Baker, Wiley	16	M	F	StS	Esparne Harjo	D	Cr	No. 2	L	Cr
5026	5	Harjo, Melosia	5	F	F	Niece	Tom Sochee	L	Cr	Nancy	D	Cr
		No. 4 died April 7, 1906. No. 3 reported dead										
		Census Card No. 1559, P. O. Wetumka, Enrolled February 3, 1900; No. 8 May 24, 1901										
5027	1	Hill, William	30	M	F		Jackson Hill	D	Cr	Lizzie Hill	D	Cr
5028	2	Hill, Lena	24	F	F	Wf	Totulkah	D	Cr	Homat Tiger	D	Cr
5029	3	Hill, Jesse	4	M	F	S	No. 1	L	Cr	Hannah Hill	D	Cr
5030	4	Hill, Tony	3	M	F	S	No. 1	L	Cr	No. 2	L	Cr
5031	5	Hill, Johnston	2	M	F	S	No. 1	L	Cr	Hannah Hill	D	Cr
5032	6	Tiger, Billy	11	M	F	StS	Jacob Tiger	D	Cr	Hannah Hill	D	Cr
5033	7	Hill, Sunday	10	M	F	S	No. 1	L	Cr	Lena Hill	D	Cr
5034	8	Hill, Hannah	35	F	F	Wf	Tulsa Fixico	D	Cr	Wincy Tiger	D	Cr
		No. 3 died April 25, 1900. Nos. 6 and 8 reported dead. No. 5 died May 25, 1900. No. 7 died 1898										
		Census Card No. 1560, P. O. Fentress, Enrolled February 3, 1900										
5035	1	Tiger, Lumyer	40	M	F		Tulsa Fixico	D	Cr	Chormiller	D	Cr
5036	2	Chamela	80	F	F	Aunt	Unknown	D	Cr	Unknown	D	Cr
		No. 1 died March 4, 1901. No. 2 died September 24, 1899										
		Census Card No. 1561, P. O. Holdenville, Enrolled February 3, 1900; No. 3 May 23, 1901										
5037	1	Marks, Martha	24	F	F		Jackson Lewis	L	Cr	Nancy Lewis	L	Cr
5038	2	Marks, Thomas J.	3	M	F	S	J. N. Marks	L	Non	No. 1	L	Cr
5039	3	Marks, Samuel	1	M	F	S	J. N. Marks	L	Non	No. 1	L	Cr
		No. 3 died September 16, 1899										
		Census Card 1562, P. O. Holdenville, Enrolled February 3, 1900										
5040	1	Miller, Louis	38	M	5/8		Daniel Miller	D	Cr	Sophia Miller	D	Cr
5041	2	Miller, Lillie	22	F	F	Wf	Thomas	L	Cr	Polly	L	Cr
5042	3	Miller, Lizzie	4	F	7/16	S	No. 1	L	Cr	No. 2	L	Cr
5043	4	Miller, Otto	10 mo	M	7/8	S	No. 1	L	Cr	No. 2	L	Cr
		Census Card No. 1563, P. O. Holdenville, Enrolled February 3, 1900										
5044	1	Curtain, Lewis	26	M	1/2		Dick Curtain	D	Cr	Becky Curtain	D	Cr
		Census Card No. 1564, P. O. Holdenville, Enrolled February 3, 1900										
5045	1	McGirtt, Billy	30	M	F		Alex McGirt	D	Cr	Sedeah	D	Cr
5046	2	McGirtt, Dora	26	F	F	Wf	Daniel Miller	D	Cr	Sophia Miller	D	Cr
5047	3	McGirtt, Sophia	2	F	F	D	No. 1	L	Cr	No. 2	L	Cr
		Nos. 1 and 3 reported dead										
		Census Card No. 1565, P. O. Yeager, Enrolled February 3, 1900										
5048	1	Reed, Porter	20	M	F		Toney	D	Cr	Lister Reed	L	Cr
5049	2	Reed, Jennie	21	F	F	Wf	Renty	D	Cr	Unknown	?	Cr
5050	3	Reed, Ella	2 mo	F	F	D	No. 1	L	Cr	No. 2	L	Cr
5051	4	Reed Leister	40	F	F	Moth	John Reed	L	Cr	Rachel Reed	L	Cr
		No. 1 died October 1, 1904. No. 2 died June 15, 1910. No. 3 died September 22, 1905										
		Census Card No. 1566, P. O. Wetumka, Enrolled February 5, 1900; No. 3 May 14, 1901										
5052	1	Jennie	22	F	F		Daniel Barnett	D	Cr	Minnechar	L	Cr
5053	2	Barnett, Samochee	6	M	F	S	Legus	L	Cr	No. 1	L	Cr
5054	3	Bruner. Abney	22	M	F	Hus	Johnche	D	Cr	Salina	D	Cr
		No. 3 reported dead										
		Census Card No. 1567, P. O. Wetumka, Enrolled February 5, 1900										
5055	1	Billy, Billiy	22	M	F		William Billy	L	Cr	Sunday	D	Cr
		Census Card No. 1568, P. O. Wetumka, Enrolled February 5, 1900; No. 6 February 24, 1900										
5056	1	Billy, William	45	M	F		Billy	L	Cr	Mollie	D	Cr
5057	2	Billy, Minnechar	50	F	F	Wf	Albutter Harjo	D	Cr	Yarhogee	D	Cr
5058	3	Billy, Hannah	17	F	F	D	No. 1	L	Cr	Sunday	D	Cr
5059	4	Billy, Millisey	15	F	F	D	No. 1	L	Cr	Sunday	D	Cr
5060	5	Lasley, Roman	6	M	F	StS	Sam Lasley	D	Cr	No. 2	L	Cr
5061	6	Billy, Sinnie	16	F	F	D	No. 1	L	Cr	Esther	L	Cr
		No. 2 died January 4, 1910. No. 3 reported dead										
		Census Card No. 1569, P. O. Okemah, Enrolled February 5, 1900										
5062	1	Sawyer, Solomon	29	M	F		Mose Sawyer	L	Cr	Arsebme	D	Cr
5063	2	Sawyer, Sukey	42	F	F	Wf	Karbytehchar	D	Cr	Somarley	D	Cr
		No. 1 died May 24, 1905. No. 2 reported dead										
		Census Card 1570, P. O. Weleetka, Enrolled February 5, 1900										
5064	1	Baker, Sunday	28	M	F		John Baker	L	Cr	Emma	D	Cr
5065	2	Baker, Lasley	20	M	F	Bro	John Baker	L	Cr	Emma	D	Cr
		No. 1 died April 1903										
		Census Card No. 1571, P. O. Henryetta, Enrolled February 5, 1900										
5066	1	Tiger, Catchochee	45	M	F		Hutchcutte Fixico	D	Cr	Hatopka	D	Cr
5067	2	Tiger, Lucinda	35	F	F	Wf	Yahola Fixico	L	Cr	Lizzie Betsy	D	Cr
5068	3	Tiger, Jesse	11	M	F	S	No. 1	L	Cr	No. 2	L	Cr
5069	4	Tiger, Jeanetta	8	F	F	D	No. 1	L	Cr	No. 2	L	Cr
5070	5	Tiger, Miller	4	F	F	D	No. 1	L	Cr	No. 2	L	Cr
5071	6	Tiger, Hettie	1	F	F	D	No. 1	L	Cr	No. 2	L	Cr
		No. 1 died September 1911. No. 2 died August 1907										

Roll No.	No.	NAME	Age	Sex	Blood	Rel.	NAME OF FATHER	Liv.	Cit.	NAME OF MOTHER	Liv.	Cit.
		Census Card No. 1572, P. O. Dustin, Enrolled February 5, 1900										
5072	1	Wildcat, Sandy	48	M	F		Hutchecutte Fixico	D	Cr	Hatopka	D	Cr
5073	2	Wildcat, Losanna	30	F	F	Wf	Pin Harjo	D	Cr	Nancy	L	Cr
5074	3	Wildcat, Aleck	18	M	F	S	No. 1	L	Cr	Sochalagee	D	Cr
5075	4	Wildcat, Annie	10	F	F	D	No. 1	L	Cr	Sochalagee	D	Cr
5076	5	"Yarner"	12	F	F	StD	Labus	D	Cr	No. 2	L	Cr
5077	6	Wildcat, George	6	M	F	S	No. 1	L	Cr	No. 2	L	Cr
		No. 4 duplicate No. 8033. Nos. 1, 3 and 6 reported dead										
		Census Card No. 1573, P. O. Bryant, Enrolled February 5, 1900										
5078	1	Barnett, Ellie	21	F	F		Archola	D	Cr	Sukey	D	Cr
		Census Card No. 1574, P. O. Senora, Enrolled February 5, 1900										
5079	1	Fixico, Fushutche	80	M	F		Fustinnokochee	D	Cr	Unknown	D	Cr
		No. 1 reported dead										
		Census Card No. 1575, P. O. Senora, Enrolled February 5, 1900										
5080	1	Byrd, Leah	28	F	F		Ossetame	L	Cr	Judy	D	Cr
5081	2	Barnett, William	7	M	F	S	Thomas Barnett	L	Cr	No. 1	L	Cr
5082	3	Watson, Ida	2	F	F	D	Joe Watson	D	Cr	No. 1	L	Cr
		No. 1 reported dead										
		Census Card No. 1576, P. O. Dustin, Enrolled February 5, 1900										
5083	1	Byrd, Louisa	18	F	F		Seborn Byrd	L	Cr	Judy	L	Cr
5084	2	Watson, Louisa	1	F	F	D	Homer Watson	L	Cr	No. 1	L	Cr
		Census Card No. 1577, P. O. Senora, Enrolled February 5, 1900										
5085	1	Beaver, Jimsey	50	M	F		Pickcarty Fixico	D	Cr	Hotopka	D	Cr
5086	2	Beaver, Tiner	50	F	F	Wf	Thlokchat Henneha	D	Cr	Cochart Howie	D	Cr
5087	3	Beaver, Riley	13	M	F	S	No. 1	L	Cr	Sarhoyethkee	D	Cr
5088	4	Beaver, Thomas	11	M	F	S	No. 1	L	Cr	Sarhoyethkee	D	Cr
		No. 1 died February 1901. No. 2 died 1911										
		Census Card No. 1578, P. O. Wenoka, Enrolled February 6, 1900										
5089	1	Reed, John	54	M	F		Charley Reed	D	Cr	Bety	D	Cr
5090	2	Reed, Rachel	60	F	F	Wf	Billy McGirt	L	Cr	Unknown	?	Cr
5091	3	Reed, Judie	37	F	F	D	No. 1	L	Cr	No. 2	L	Cr
		No. 1 died May 12, 1901. No. 3 reported dead. No. 2 died June 4, 1904										
		Census Card No. 1579, P. O. Holdenville, Enrolled February 6, 1900										
5092	1	Yargee, George	21	M	¾		Unknown	D	Cr	Annie Yargee	L	Cr
		Census Card No. 1580, P. O. Holdenville, Enrolled February 6, 1900; Nos. 2 and 3 March 26, 1900										
5093	1	Jacobs, John A.	28	M	½		Frank Jacobs	L	Cr	Rebecca Jacobs	D	Cr
5094	2	Jacobs, Frank	5	M	¾	S	No. 1	L	Cr	Mary Jacobs	L	Non
5095	3	Jacobs, Lizzie	8 mo	F	¾	D	No. 1	L	Cr	Mary Jacobs	L	Non
		Census Card No. 1581, P. O. Mekesukey, Enrolled February 6, 1900										
5096	1	Coker, David	35	M	½		London Coker	L	Cr	Mary	D	Cr
		Census Card No. 1582, P. O. Muskogee, Enrolled February 6, 1900										
5097	1	Garland, Tookah	44	F	¼		John Nevins	D	?	Delilah Nevins	D	?
5098	2	Garland, Louis	23	M	⅛	S	S. F. Garland	L	Choc	No. 1	L	Cr
5099	3	Garland, Libbie M.	17	F	⅛	D	S. F. Garland	L	Choc	No. 1	L	Cr
5100	4	Garland, David M.	10	M	⅛	S	S. F. Garland	L	Choc	No. 1	L	Cr
5101	5	Garland, Floyd H.	3	M	⅛	S	S. F. Garland	L	Choc	No. 1	L	Cr
		Census Card No. 1583, P. O. Clarksville, Enrolled February 6, 1900										
5102	1	Perryman, Benjamin	21	M	F		Daniel Perryman	D	Cr	Dicey Perryman	L	Cr
		Census Card No. 1584, P. O. Weleetka, Enrolled February 6, 1900										
5103	1	Stephenson, Polly	22	F	F		Big Ben	L	Cr	Mary Ben	L	Cr
5104	2	Stephenson, Augusta	4 mo	F	½	D	A. P. Stephenson	L	Non	No. 1	L	Cr
		No. 2 died November 10, 1905										
		Census Card No. 1585, P. O. Henryetta, Enrolled February 6, 1900										
5105	1	Scott, Sukey	26	F	F		Jimsey Beaver	L	Cr	Hotopka	D	Cr
5106	2	Scott, Sally	5	F	⅝	D	Turner Scott	L	Cr	No. 1	L	Cr
5107	3	Watson, Eddie	6 mo	M	F	S	Homer Watson	L	Cr	No. 1	L	Cr
		No. 1 reported dead										
		Census Card No. 1586, P. O. Senora, Enrolled February 6, 1900										
5108	1	Beaver, Sam	25	M	F		Jimsey Beaver	L	Cr	Sarhoyethkee	D	Cr
		No. 1 reported dead										
		Census Card No. 1587, P. O. Wetumka, Enrolled February 6, 1900										
5109	1	Coachman, Ward	75	M	F		Seco Pitcher	D	Cr	Polly	D	Cr
5110	2	Coachman, George	20	M	F	S	No. 1	L	Cr	No. 3	L	Cr
5111	3	Coachman, Lizzie	41	F	F	Wf	Ahtushahola	D	Cr	Unknown	D	Cr
		No. 1 died March 1900. No. 2 died May 6, 1904. No. 3 died April 10, 1899										
		Census Card No. 1588, P. O. Weleetka, Enrolled February 6, 1900										
5112	1	Buckley, Ceasar	28	M	F		Sam Buckley	L	Cr	Eliza Buckley	L	Cr
5113	2	Buckley, Betsey	23	F	F	Wf	Tuscona	D	Cr	Nancy	D	Cr
5114	3	Amos	16	M	F	Ward	Tuscona	D	Cr	Nancy	D	Cr
		Census Card No. 1589, P. O. Weleetka, Enrolled February 6, 1900										
5115	1	Harjo, Connuggy	30	M	F		Yarhola Harjo	D	Cr	Upsey	L	Cr
5116	2	Harjo, Polly	26	F	F	Wf	Nechthlocco Harjo	D	Cr	Uparharka	L	Cr
5117	3	Harjo, Minar	7	F	F	D	No. 1	L	Cr	No. 2	L	Cr
5118	4	Harjo, Mussey	6	F	F	D	No. 1	L	Cr	No. 2	L	Cr
5119	5	Harjo, Joseph	1	M	F	S	No. 1	L	Cr	No. 2	L	Cr
		Nos. 3, 4 and 5 reported dead										

No.	NAME	Age	Sex	Blood	Rel.	NAME OF FATHER	Liv.	Cit.	NAME OF MOTHER	Liv.	Cit.
Census Card No. 1590, P. O. Weleetka, Enrolled February 6, 1900											
1	Yaholar, Josey	42	M	F		Yartika	L	Cr	Thiescher	D	Cr
2	Yaholar, Betsey	38	F	F	Wf	Yaholar	L	Cr	Uparharka	L	Cr
3	Yaholar, Lucy	2	F	F	D	No. 1	L	Cr	Betty	D	Cr
4	Byrd, Lucinda	7	F	F	StD	James Byrd	L	Cr	No. 2	L	Cr
5	Byrd, Chiskā	5	M	F	StS	James Byrd	L	Cr	No. 2	L	Cr
	No. 3 reported dead										
Census Card No. 1591, P. O. Weleetka, Enrolled February 6, 1900											
1	Sandy, Jacob	28	M	F		Sandy	L	Cr	Lida Sandy	L	Cr
2	Sandy, Sophia	25	F	F	Wf	Solomon Sand	L	Cr	Wisey	L	Cr
3	Sandy, Malinda	3	F	F	D	No. 1	L	Cr	No. 2	L	Cr
Census Card No. 1592, P. O. Weleetka, Enrolled February 6, 1900											
1	U-par-har-ha	65	F	F		Tuska Harjo	D	Cr	Arwolichee	D	Cr
2	Harjo, Johnson	19	M	F	S	Neckthlocco Harjo	D	Cr	No. 1	L	Cr
Census Card No. 1593, P. O. Wetumka, Enrolled February 6, 1900											
1	Fish, Jonas	28	M	F		Tharthlo Harjo	L	Cr	Marhechar	D	Cr
2	Fish, Morleyar	36	F	F	Wf	Benny	D	Cr	Saryes	D	Cr
3	Holmes, Hully	9	M	F	Ward	Lolie Homer	D	Cr	Hokte Thlocco	D	Cr
	Nos. 1 and 3 reported dead										
Census Card No. 1594, P. O. Weleetka, Enrolled February 6, 1900											
1	Lasley, Colbert	25	M	F		Sam Lasley	D	Cr	Sollie Lasley	D	Cr
2	Lasley, Winey	20	F	F	Wf	Daniel Barnett	D	Cr	Minnechar	L	Cr
Census Card No. 1595, P. O. Weleetka, Enrolled February 6, 1900											
1	Yarhola, George	25	M	F		Conchart Yahola	D	Cr	Timohbusche	D	Cr
Census Card No. 1596, P. O. Weleetka, Enrolled February 6, 1900											
1	Marsey, Thomas	25	M	F		Mike Marsey	L	Cr	Nancy	D	Cr
2	Marsey, Winey	23	F	F	Wf	Peter Coachman	L	Cr	Fobitscoyee	L	Cr
3	Larney, Thompsey	8	M	F	StS	James Larney	D	Cr	No. 2	L	Cr
4	Larney, Fannie	6	F	F	StD	Wattie Harjo	D	Cr	No. 2	L	Cr
	Nos. 2 and 4 reported dead										
Census Card No. 1597, P. O. Wetumka, Enrolled February 6, 1900											
1	Yarhola, Tuskehewneha	55	M	F		Okchun Yarhola	D	Cr	Tyhesttee	D	Cr
2	Yarhola, Polhoya	50	F	F	Wf	Neha Yarhola	L	Cr	Unknown	?	Cr
3	Yarhola, Simochee	14	M	F	S	No. 1	L	Cr	No. 2	L	Cr
	No. 1 reported dead										
Census Card No. 1598, P. O. Weleetka, Enrolled February 6, 1900											
1	Fier, Dick	26	M	F		Totkie Harjo	L	Cr	Mothoye	L	Cr
2	Fier, Elizabeth	45	F	F	Wf	Timmie Fisher	D	Cr	Ipsey	L	Cr
3	Fier, Emma	5	F	F	D	No. 1	L	Cr	No. 2	L	Cr
4	McKinney, Hepsey	20	F	F	StD	Sam McKinney	D	Cr	No. 2	L	Cr
5	McKinney, Roley	17	M	F	StS	Sam McKinney	D	Cr	No. 2	L	Cr
6	McKinney, Susie	12	F	F	StD	Sam McKinney	D	Cr	No. 2	L	Cr
Census Card No. 1599, P. O. Weleetka, Enrolled February 6, 1900											
1	McKinney, Unah	22	M	F		Sam McKinney	D	Cr	Elizabeth Fier	L	Cr
Census Card No. 1600, P. O. Kellyville, Enrolled February 7, 1900											
1	Tiger, Dave	23	M	F		Jim Tiger	D	Cr	Consanna Tiger	L	Cr
	No. 1 died July 31, 1905										
Census Card No. 1601, P. O. Okmulgee, Enrolled February 8, 1900											
1	Morton, Perry K.	34	M	3/8		William Morton	L	Non	Delilah Morton	L	Cr
2	Morton, Annie	23	F	3/4	Wf	Jackson Bruner	L	Cr	Annie Bruner	L	Cr
3	Morton, Irene	1	F	9-16	D	No. 1	L	Cr	No. 2	L	Cr
	No. 3 reported dead										
Census Card No. 1602, P. O. Wetumka; No. 4 Hanna; No. 5 Wewoka, Enrolled February 9, 1900; No. 8 May 23, 1901											
1	Alexander, George A.	58	M	1/4		James Alexander	D	Non	Elizabeth Fife	D	Cr
2	Alexander, Nancy	54	F	3/4	Wf	John Chisholm	D	Cher	Polly Chisholm	L	Cr
3	Fox, Willie	18	M	F	Ward	Chular Harjochee	D	Cr	Sofa Fox	L	Cr
4	Fox, Wash	10	M	F	Ward	Chular Harjochee	D	Cr	Sofa Fox	L	Cr
5	Fox, Harney	8	M	F	Ward	Chular Harjochee	D	Cr	Sofa Fox	L	Cr
6	Atkins, Mary	6	F	3/4	Ward	Lee Atkins	D	Cr	Katie Atkins	L	Cr
7	McCosar, Katie	12	F	F	Ward	Bunny McCosar	L	Cr	Bettie McCosar	L	Cr
8	Alexander, Lewis	27	M	1/2	S	No. 1	L	Cr	No. 2	L	Cr
	No. 5 died August 28, 1900. No. 8 died										
Census Card No. 1603, P. O. Holdenville; No. 6 Coweta, Enrolled February 9, 1900											
1	Brooks, George	44	M	1/2		Brooks	L	Non	Betsey Tuttle	D	Cr
2	Brooks, Widey	40	F	1/2	Wf	Unknown	D	Cr	Unknown	?	Cr
3	Brooks, Lucinda	13	F	1/2	D	No. 1	L	Cr	No. 2	L	Cr
4	Brooks, Eddie	12	M	1/2	S	No. 1	L	Cr	No. 2	L	Cr
5	Brooks, Mona	5	F	1/2	D	No. 1	L	Cr	No. 2	L	Cr
6	Long, Ben	17	M	F	Neph	Sampson Chupco	D	Cr	Lizzie Chupco	D	Cr
	Nos. 5 and 6 reported dead										
Census Card No. 1604, P. O. Holdenville, Enrolled February 9, 1900											
1	Hardage, Lewis	38	M	1/2		Unknown	D	?	Amy Lott	D	?
2	Hardage, Rebecca	39	F	1/2	Wf	Jackson Doyle	L	Cr	Sarah Doyle	L	Cr
3	Hardage, Ruth	17	F	1/2	D	No. 1	L	Cr	No. 2	L	Cr
4	Hardage, Joseph H.	15	M	1/2	S	No. 1	L	Cr	No. 2	L	Cr
5	Hardage, Hannah	13	F	1/2	D	No. 1	L	Cr	No. 2	L	Cr
6	Hardage, May	11	F	1/2	D	No. 1	L	Cr	No. 2	L	Cr
	Nos. 1, 2 and 5 reported dead										

Roll No.	No.	NAME	Age	Sex	Blood	Rel.	NAME OF FATHER	Liv.	Cit.	NAME OF MOTHER	Liv.	Cit
Census Card No. 1605, P. O. Wewoka, Enrolled Nos. 1, 2 and 3 February 9, 1900; No. 4 May 21, 1901												
5174	1	Palmer, Watty A.	37	M	F		Palmer	D	Cr	Lucy Palmer	D	Cr
5175	2	Harjo, Edmond	8	M	½	Neph	Tustanuk Harjo	L	Sem	Leah Reed	D	Cr
5176	3	Harjo, Newman	6	M	½	Neph	Tusica	L	Sem	Leah Reed	D	Cr
5177	4	Reed, Martha	6	F	F	Niece	Jim Factor	L	Sem	Leah Reed	D	Cr
Census Card No. 1606, P. O. Dustin, Enrolled February 9, 1900												
5178	1	Tilly, Christie	42	F	½		Robert Grayson	D	Cr	Martha Grayson	D	Cr
5179	2	Tilly, Myrtle	4	F	¼	D	J. S. Tilly	L	Non	No. 1	L	Cr
5180	3	Tilly, Nannie E.	2	F	¼	D	J. S. Tilly	L	Non	No. 1	L	Cr
5181	4	Tilly, Anna	1	F	¼	D	J. S. Tilly	L	Non	No. 1	L	Cr
5182	5	Tilly, Ina	8 da	F	¼	D	J. S. Tilly	L	Non	No. 1	L	Cr
Census Card No. 1607, P. O. Wetumka, Enrolled February 9, 1900; Nos. 5 and 6 May 13, 1901												
5183	1	Tiger, Barney	40	M	¾		Two Wagie	D	Cr	Kissie Miller	D	Cr
5184	2	Tiger, Katie	20	F	F	Wf	Jack Robinson	D	Cr	Lucy	L	Cr
5185	3	Tiger, George	12	M	⅞	S	No. 1	L	Cr	Lucy Bear	D	Cr
5186	4	Tiger, Charley	4	M	⅞	S	No. 1	L	Cr	Lucy Bear	D	Cr
5187	5	Tiger, Leona	2	F	⅞	D	No. 1	L	Cr	Fannie Tiger	D	Cr
5188	6	Tiger, Fannie	30	F	F	Wf	Nocus Yahola	D	Cr	Litka Scott	L	Cr
		No. 4 died October 1900. Nos. 2, 4, 5 and 6 reported dead										
Census Card No. 1608, P. O. Eufaula, Enrolled February 9, 1900; Nos. 2-3-4-5, February 10, 1900.												
5189	1	Grayson, George W.	57	M	½		James Grayson	D	Cr	Jennie Grayson	D	Cr
5190	2	Grayson, Annie	49	F	½	Wf	G. W. Stidham	D	Cr	Ariada Stidham	D	Cr
5191	3	Grayson, Washington	17	M	½	S	No. 1	L	Cr	No. 2	L	Cr
5192	4	Grayson, Tsianina	13	F	½	D	No. 1	L	Cr	No. 2	L	Cr
5193	5	Sanger, alias Tiger Stella	18	F	¾	Ward	John Tiger	D	Cr	Fannie Tiger	D	Cr
		No. 5 died March 14, 1905										
Census Card No. 1609, P. O. Wewoka, Enrolled February 12, 1900; No. 6 May 2, 1900												
5194	1	Benden, Louis	25	M	F		Thomas Benden	D	Cr	Kogee	L	Cr
5195	2	Benden, Dicey	30	F	F	Wf	George Sullivan	D	Cr	Hepsey	L	Cr
5196	3	Brown, Bernard	11	M	F	StS	Lisha Brown	D	Sem	No. 2	L	Cr
5197	4	Benden, Anna	8	F	F	D	No. 1	L	Cr	No. 2	L	Cr
5198	5	Benden, Jeff	3	M	F	S	No. 1	L	Cr	No. 2	L	Cr
5199	6	Benden, George	2 mo	M	F	S	No. 1	L	Cr	No. 2	L	Cr
		No. 3 reported dead										
Census Card No. 1610, P. O. Holdenville, Enrolled February 12, 1900												
5200	1	Bruner, Berry	56	M	½		Joe Bruner	D	Cr	Lucinda Bruner	L	Cr
5201	2	Bruner, Polly	45	F	½	Wf	Dave Tyner	D	Cr	Katy Tyner	L	Cr
5202	3	Bruner, Eddie	15	M	½	S	No. 1	L	Cr	No. 2	L	Cr
5203	4	Bruner, Mattie L.	13	F	½	D	No. 1	L	Cr	No. 2	L	Cr
5204	5	Bruner, Mindie H.	9	F	½	D	No. 1	L	Cr	No. 2	L	Cr
		No. 4 died September 14, 1913										
Census Card No. 1611, P. O. Holdenville, Enrolled February 12, 1900												
5205	1	Bruner, Dave	22	M	½		Berry Bruner	L	?	Polly Bruner	L	?
Census Card No. 1612, P. O. Holdenville, Enrolled February 12, 1900												
5206	1	Todd, Katie	20	F	½		Berry Bruner	L	?	Polly Bruner	L	?
5207	2	Todd, Jesse J.	4	M	¼	S	J. W. Todd	L	Non	No. 1	L	Cr
5208	3	Todd, Lela E.	2	F	¼	D	J. W. Todd	L	Non	No. 1	L	Cr
Census Card No. 1613, P. O. Henryetta, Enrolled February 12, 1900												
5209	1	Freeman, John	20	M	F		Peter Freeman	D	Cr	Lucinda Fat	L	Cr
		No. 1 reported dead										
Census Card No. 1614, P. O. Sapulpa, Enrolled February 12, 1900												
5210	1	Cosar, Tom	45	M	F		Cosar Harjo	D	Cr	Loda	D	Cr
5211	2	Cosar, Jennie	23	F	F	Wf	So-kah-chee	D	Cr	Tafne	L	Cr
5212	3	Martin, Dave	6	M	F	StS	Tab-ley	L	Cr	No. 2	L	Cr
5213	4	Cosar, Beeker	3	F	F	D	No. 1	L	Cr	No. 2	L	Cr
5214	5	Cosar, Lydia	1	F	F	D	No. 1	L	Cr	No. 2	L	Cr
		No. 2 reported dead										
Census Card No. 1615, P. O. Stroud, Enrolled February 13,1900												
5215	1	Foster, Edward	20	M	⅛		George Foster	D	Non	Rosa Foster	D	Cr
Census Card No. 1616, P. O. Holdenville, Enrolled February 13,1900												
5216	1	Fixico, Cosar	70	M	F		Cheyo Harjo	D	Cr	Tiger	D	Cr
5217	2	Fixico, Maley	30	F	F	Wf	Neha Yaholar	D	Cr	Sallie	D	Cr
5218	3	Fixico, Emma	16	F	F	D	No. 1	L	Cr	Paygee	L	Cr
5219	4	Fixico, Nupsey	3	F	F	D	No. 1	L	Cr	No. 2	L	Cr
		No. 1 reported dead. No. 3 should be Amon. "M.", this change authorized by Department authority May 10, 1913										
Census Card No. 1617, P. O. Holdenville, Enrolled February 13, 1900												
5220	1	Noon, Palmer	27	M	F		Billy Noon	D	Cr	Annie Noon	D	Cr
5221	2	Noon, Martha	25	F	F	Wf	Mageeley	D	Cr	Harney	L	Cr
5222	3	Noon, Fisher	8	M	F	S	No. 1	L	Cr	No. 2	L	Cr
		No. 1 reported dead										
Census Card No. 1618, P. O. Holdenville, Enrolled February 13, 1900												
5223	1	Fixico, Mapetta	70	F	F		Tuckabatchee Micco	D	Cr	Unknown	D	Cr
5224	2	Larney, Mary	15	F	F	GrD	Louis Larney	D	Cr	Liddy Larney	D	Cr
5225	3	Larney, Annie	10	F	F	GrD	Louis Larney	D	Cr	Liddy Larney	D	Cr
5226	4	Larney, Moses	2	M	F	GrS	Louis Larney	D	Cr	Liddy Larney	D	Cr
		No. 1 died March 15, 1904. No. 4 reported dead										
Census Card No. 1619, P. O. Holdenville, Enrolled February 13, 1900												
5227	1	Deere, Wysie	40	F	F		Redmouth	D	Cr	Unknown	D	Cr

Roll No.	No.	NAME	Age	Sex	Blood	Rel.	NAME OF FATHER	Liv.	Cit.	NAME OF MOTHER	Liv.	Cit.
		Census Card No. 1620, P. O. Red Fork, Enrolled February 13, 1900										
5228	1	McIntosh, Winnie	60	F	¼		Unknown	D	?	Tampa Canard	D	?
		Census Card No. 1621, P. O. Coweta, Enrolled February 13, 1900; No. 3 April 12, 1901										
5229	1	Byrd, Mary	24	F	F		Kissoe	D	Cr	Mahaley	L	Cr
5230	2	Byrd, Melissee	5	F	F	D	Lewis Bird	L	Cr	No. 1	L	Cr
5231	3	Geneva, Sallie	2	F	F	D	Joe Geneva	L	Cr	No. 1	L	Cr
		Nos. 2 and 3 reported dead										
		Census Card No. 1622, P. O. Eufaula, Enrolled February 13, 1900										
5232	1	Brown, Ada J.	21	F	⅝		Chas. S. Smith	L	Cr	Louisa B. Smith	L	Cr
5233	2	Brown, Athalene	1	F	5-16	D	A. W. Brown	L	Non	No. 1	L	Cr
5234	3	Brown, Claud W.	24 da	M	5-16	S	A. W. Brown	L	Non	No. 1	L	Cr
		Census Card No. 1623, P. O. Eufaula, Enrolled February 13, 1900										
5235	1	Grayson, William	58	M	¾		Sandy Grayson	D	Cr	Lucy Grayson	D	Cr
5236	2	Grayson, Nancy	42	F	¾	Wf	Finney Chism	D	Cher	Kate Chism	D	Cr
5237	3	Grayson, John	26	M	¾	S	No. 1	L	Cr	No. 2	L	Cr
		Census Card No. 1624, P. O. Yeager, Enrolled February 14, 1900										
5238	1	McKan, John	27	M	¾		James McKan	D	Cr	Sukey	D	Cr
5239	2	McKan, Hepsey	19	F	F	Wf	Tusmock Chupco	D	Cr	Semelacher	D	Cr
5240	3	Compier, Mitchell	19	M	F	Neph	Albert Harper	L	Cr	Anna Mitchell	D	Cr
		No. 1 died August 1905. No. 2 reported dead										
		Census Card No. 1625, P. O. Wetumka, Enrolled February 14, 1900										
5241	1	Harjo, Nancy	24	F	½		Warcheenar	D	Sem	Sukey	D	Cr
5242	2	Long, Bessie	10	F	¾	D	Wash Long	L	Cr	No. 1	L	Cr
5243	3	Long, Carcharty	2	M	¾	S	Ispokok Yaholar	D	Cr	No. 1	L	Cr
5244	4	Harjo, Bennie	48	M	F	Hus	Nocus Harjo	L	Cr	Sanlanhohkey	D	Cr
		Nos. 2, 3 and 4 reported dead										
		Census Card No. 1626, P. O. Holdenville, Enrolled February 14, 1900										
5245	1	Coker, William	24	M	½		London Coker	L	Cr	Mary	D	Cr
		Census Card No. 1627, P. O. Sapulpa, Enrolled February 14, 1900; No. 7 May 21, 1901										
5246	1	Wilson, Mahala	34	F	F		Katcha Fixico	D	Cr	Tewohley Vore	L	Cr
5247	2	Wilson, Noonley	7	M	F	S	Solomon Wilson	D	Cr	No. 1	L	Cr
5248	3	Wilson, Simon J.	4	M	F	S	Solomon Wilson	D	Cr	No. 1	L	Cr
5249	4	Wilson, Abbey	2	F	F	D	Solomon Wilson	D	Cr	No. 1	L	Cr
5250	5	Biggs, William	14	M	F	S	George Biggs	D	Cr	No. 1	L	Cr
5251	6	Vore, Tewohley	70	F	F	Moth	Tulwa Harjo	D	Cr	Unknown	D	Cr
5252	7	Wilson, Solomon	40	M	F	Hus	Soklutke	D	Cr	Somolake	D	Cr
		No. 7 died September 23, 1899. No. 2 reported dead										
		Census Card No. 1628, P. O. Eufaula, Enrolled February 14, 1900										
5253	1	Sanger, George H.	10	M	¼		Ward W. Sanger	L	Non	Lena Sanger	D	Cr
5254	2	Sanger, Mabel M.	8	F	¼	Sis	Ward W. Sanger	L	Non	Lena Sanger	D	Cr
		Census Card No. 1629, P. O. Holdenville, Enrolled February 14, 1900										
5255	1	Tate, Mary	27	F	½		London Coker	L	Cr	Mary	D	Cr
		Census Card No. 1630, P. O. Carson, Enrolled February 14, 1900; No. 6 May 22, 1901										
5256	1	Robison, Barney C.	25	M	½		William Robison	D	Cr	Cherokee Robison	D	Cr
5257	2	Robison, Ida B.	20	F	½	Wf	G. A. Alexander	L	Cr	Nancy Alexander	L	Cr
5258	3	Robison, George E.	2	M	½	S	No. 1	L	Cr	No. 2	L	Cr
5259	4	Robison, Fannie	8	F	½	Niece	Frazier Robison	L	Cr	Jane Robison	D	Cr
5260	5	Bruner, Louisa	10	F	¾	Ward	Wiley	L	Cr	Healey	D	Cr
5261	6	Robison, Alexander W.	2½	M	½	S	No. 1	L	Cr	No. 2	L	Cr
		No. 6 died January 4, 1900										
		Census Card No. 1631, P. O. Holdenville, Enrolled February 15, 1900										
5262	1	Jimboy, Fuller	28	M	F		Bruner, Jimboy	D	Cr	Nimhoktee	D	Cr
5263	2	Jimboy, Mollie	25	F	F	Wf	Tulmochus Fixico	D	Cr	Adaline	D	Cr
5264	3	Jimboy, Addie	1 mo	F	F	D	No. 1	L	Cr	No. 2	L	Cr
		No. 1 died November 4, 1907										
		Census Card No. 1632, P. O. Boley, Enrolled February 15, 1900										
5265	1	Johnson, Hannah	28	F	¼		Tecumseh Bruner	D	Cr	Tena Bruner	D	Cr
5266	2	Johnson, Polly	6	F	⅛	D	Paro Johnson	L	CrFd	No. 1	L	Cr
5267	3	Johnson, Emmett	4	M	⅛	S	Paro Johnson	L	CrFd	No. 1	L	Cr
5268	4	Johnson, Ada	2	F	⅛	D	Paro Johnson	L	CrFd	No. 1	L	Cr
5269	5	Johnson, Nathan	2 mo	M	⅛	S	Paro Johnson	L	CrFd	No. 1	L	Cr
		No. 1 died January 3, 1908										
		Census Card No. 1633, P. O. Wetumka, Enrolled February 15, 1900										
5270	1	Tiger, Louis	60	M	F		Nuscup Micco	D	Cr	Lydia	L	Cr
5271	2	Tiger, Joseph	14	M	F	S	No. 1	L	Cr	Sarah Tiger	L	Cr
5272	3	Tiger, Nettie	11	F	F	D	No. 1	L	Cr	Rhoda Tiger	L	Cr
		No. 1 reported dead										
		Census Card No. 1634, P. O. Fentress, Enrolled February 15, 1900										
5273	1	Robison, Leah	26	F	½		Zacariah Cook	L	CrFd	Chilly Harjo	?	Cr
5274	2	Robison, Clem	4	M	¼	S	Eddie Robison	L	CrFd	No. 1	L	Cr
5275	3	Robison, Susie	2	F	¼	D	Eddie Robison	L	CrFd	No. 1	L	Cr
		No. 1 died January 26, 1902										
		Census Card No. 1635, P. O. Wetumka, Enrolled February 15, 1900										
5276	1	Harjo, Willie	25	M	F		Megillus Harjo	D	Cr	Laskey Harjo	D	Cr
5277	2	Harjo, Tilda	26	F	F	Wf	Caney	L	Cr	Hepsey	L	Cr
5278	3	Harjo, Hagie	2	M	F	S	No. 1	L	Cr	No. 2	L	Cr
		No. 3 died June 16, 1900. No. 1 died April 26, 1911. No. 2 reported dead										

Roll No.	No.	NAME	Age	Sex	Blood	Rel.	NAME OF FATHER	Liv.	Cit.	NAME OF MOTHER	Liv.	Cit.
		Census Card No. 1636, P. O. Wetumka, Enrolled February 16, 1900										
5279	1	King, Saline	55	F	F		Miargee	D	Cr	Unknown	D	Cr
5280	2	King, Peter	18	M	F	S	Micco Emarthlar	D	Cr	No. 1	L	Cr
		No. 1 reported dead										
		Census Card No. 1637, P. O. Fentress, Enrolled February 16, 1900										
5281	1	Micco, Katie	21	F	F		Somika	D	Cr	Marhosena	D	Cr
		No. 1 reported dead										
		Census Card No. 1638, P. O. Wetumka; No. 1 Wewoka, Enrolled February 16, 1900										
5282	1	Noon, Wiley	30	M	F		Billy Noon	D	Cr	Rosanna	L	Cr
5283	2	Long, Selver	15	M	F	Bro	George Long	L	Cr	Rosanna	L	Cr
5284	3	Deer, Jimsey	13	M	F	Bro	Lawyer Deere	L	Cr	Rosanna	L	Cr
		Nos. 1 and 3 reported dead										
		Census Card No. 1639, P. O. Fentress, Enrolled February 15, 1900										
5285	1	Foster, Eliza	36	F	1/2		David Bruner	D	Cr	Lucinda Bruner	D	Cr
5286	2	Foster, William C.	19	M	1/4	S	John J. Foster	L	Non	No. 1	L	Cr
5287	3	Foster, Ida M.	17	F	1/4	D	John J. Foster	L	Non	No. 1	L	Cr
5288	4	Foster, Claude C.	14	M	1/4	S	John J. Foster	L	Non	No. 1	L	Cr
5289	5	Foster, Walter S.	12	M	1/4	S	John J. Foster	L	Non	No. 1	L	Cr
5290	6	Foster, Robert H.	10	M	1/4	S	John J. Foster	L	Non	No. 1	L	Cr
5291	7	Foster, Charles E.	7	M	1/4	S	John J. Foster	L	Non	No. 1	L	Cr
		No. 3 died October 29, 1900										
		Census Card No. 1640, P. O. Eufaula, Enrolled February 16, 1900										
5292	1	Burdett, Sudie M.	28	F	1-32		G. N. Crabtree	D	Cr	Sarah Crabtree	L	Non
		Census Card No. 1641, P. O. Yeager, Enrolled February 17, 1900										
5293	1	Yahola, Jackson	30	M	F		Yarharlargee	D	Cr	Hannah	L	Cr
5294	2	Yahola, Celia	28	F	F	Wf	Johnogee	L	Cr	Wisey	L	Cr
5295	3	Yahola, Parnogee	1 mo	M	F	S	No. 1	L	Cr	No. 2	L	Cr
		Census Card No. 1642, P. O. Yeager, Enrolled February 17, 1900										
5296	1	Yargee, Hannah	53	F	F		Conup Yahola	D	Cr	Hodesee	D	Cr
		Census Card No. 1643, P. O. Yeager, Enrolled February 17, 1900										
5297	1	Brown, Banner	40	F	F		Yarholargee	L	Cr	Hannah	L	Cr
5298	2	Anderson, Leah	14	F	F	D	Wiley Anderson	D	Cr	No. 1	L	Cr
5299	3	Brown, Mollie	8	F	F	D	Jerry Brown	D	Cr	No. 1	L	Cr
		Census Card No. 1644, P. O. Holdenville, Enrolled February 17, 1900										
5300	1	For-leeyer	42	M	F		Chulchart Fixico	D	Cr	Timarlarchy	D	Cr
		Census Card No. 1645, P. O. Holdenville, Enrolled February 17, 1900										
5301	1	Harjo, Sunduller	56	M	F		Fokcohesty Harjo	D	Cr	Secthlogee	D	Cr
5302	2	Harjo, Susie	35	F	F	Wf	Neho Thloccogee	D	Cr	Sofa	L	Cr
5303	3	Harjo, Peter	20	M	F	S	No. 1	L	Cr	No. 2	L	Cr
		No. 1 died July 7, 1906. No. 3 died 1904										
		Census Card No. 1646, P. O. Yeager, Enrolled February 17, 1900										
5304	1	Sipley, Jim	28	M	F		Cheparney Chupco	D	Cr	Betty Chupco	D	Cr
5305	2	Sipley, Co-cha-gee	40	F	F	Wf	Abaluke	D	Cr	Mayatka	D	Cr
5306	3	Sipley, Timmy	12	M	F	S	No. 1	L	Cr	No. 2	L	Cr
5307	4	Sipley, William	10	M	F	S	No. 1	L	Cr	No. 2	L	Cr
5308	5	Sipley, Emma	5	F	F	D	No. 1	L	Cr	No. 2	L	Cr
5309	6	McGirt, Jackson	14	M	F	Neph	Big John	D	Cr	Lusana McGirt	D	Cr
		Nos. 1, 2, 3, 4 and 6 reported dead										
		Census Card No. 1647, P. O. Yeager, Enrolled February 17, 1900										
5310	1	McGirt, Lincoln	50	M	F		Alex McGirt	D	Cr	Scipio	D	Cr
		Census Card No. 1648, P. O. Wewoka, Enrolled February 17, 1900										
5311	1	Simon, Robert	25	M	1/4		Ceasar Simon	L	Sem	Tena McQueen	D	Cr
5312	2	Simon, Lena	3	F	1/8	D	No. 1	L	Cr	Mariah Simon	L	Non
5313	3	Simon, Granville	7 mo	M	1/8	S	No. 1	L	Cr	Mariah Simon	L	Non
5314	4	Simon, Jennie	7	F	1/8	D	No. 1	L	Cr	Mariah Simon	L	Non
		Census Card No. 1649, P. O. Morris, Enrolled February 17, 1900										
5315	1	Tiger, Tobe	60	M	F		Thaxwah Harjo Chupco	D	Cr	Josie Tiger	D	Cr
5316	2	Stricken from roll										
5317	3	Tiger, Susan	40	F	F	Wf	Unknown	?	Cr	Unknown	D	Cr
		No. 3 died January 3, 1900. No. 1 reported dead										
		Census Card No. 1650, P. O. Yeager, Enrolled Fenruary 18, 1900										
5318	1	Long, Henry	45	M	F		Fushutche Yahola	D	Cr	Lucy Chupco	D	Cr
5319	2	Long, Martha	38	F	F	Wf	D. B. Whitlow	L	Non	Sawarehche	D	Cr
5320	3	Long, Milton	18	M	F	S	No. 1	L	Cr	Adeline	D	Cr
5321	4	Long, Jesse	15	M	F	S	No. 1	L	Cr	Adeline	D	Cr
5322	5	Long, Annie	9	F	F	D	No. 1	L	Cr	Adeline	D	Cr
5323	6	Yahola, Henry	10	M	F	StS	Efer Yahola	D	Cr	No. 2	L	Cr
5324	7	Stricken from roll										
		Nos. 1 and 2 reported dead										
		Census Card No. 1651, P. O. Holdenville, Enrolled February 18, 1900										
5325	1	McGirt, Buckner	27	M	F		Alex McGirt	D	Cr	Suttoah	D	Cr
5326	2	McGirt, Linda	21	F	F	Wf	Char Fixico	D	Cr	Wysa	D	Cr
5327	3	McGirt, Robert	2 mo	M	F	S	No. 1	L	Cr	No. 2	L	Cr
5328	4	McGirt, Alex	1	M	F	S	No. 1	L	Cr	No. 2	L	Cr
		Nos. 3 and 4 reported dead										
		Census Card No. 1652, P. O. Henryetta, Enrolled February 19, 1900										
5329	1	Warden, Coy	7	M	1-16		C. W. Warden	L	Non	Levicey Warden	D	Cr
5330	2	Warden, Hugh	8 mo	M	1-16	Bro	C. W. Warden	L	Non	Levicey Warden	D	Cr
		No. 2 died November 1899										

Roll No.	No.	NAME	Age	Sex	Blood	Rel.	NAME OF FATHER	Liv.	Cit.	NAME OF MOTHER	Liv.	Cit.
		Census Card No. 1653, P. O. Henryetta, Enrolled February 19, 1900; No. 5 March 15, 1901										
5331	1	Perryman, John	50	M	F		Tolwa Harjo	D	Cr	Hannah	D	Cr
5332	2	Perryman, Silla	45	F	F	Wf	Ceasar Burgess	D	Cr	Simen Chat Key	D	Cr
5333	3	Perryman, William	19	M	F	S	No. 1	L	Cr	No. 2	L	Cr
5334	4	Perryman, Martha	12	F	F	D	No. 1	L	Cr	No. 2	L	Cr
5335	5	Secrow, Bettie	15	F	F	Niece	Tom Secrow	D	Cr	Sarah Secrow	D	Cr
		No. 3 died May 10, 1908. No. 5 reported dead										
		Census Card No. 1654, P. O. Holdenville, Enrolled February 19, 1900; No. 2 May 23, 1901										
5336	1	Myers, Caroline	18	F	½		Austin Barnett	D	Cr	Lizzie Hardridge	D	?
5337	2	Myers, Lizzie	1	F	¼	D	Dave Myers	L	Non	No. 1	L	Cr
		No. 2 reported dead										
		Census Card No. 1655, P. O. No. 1 Wagoner; No. 2 Tulsa, Enrolled February 19, 1900										
5338	1	Harrison, Charles	9	M	¼		Harris	D	Non	Minnie Harris	L	Cr
5339	2	Harrison, Harvey	7	M	¼	Bro	Harris	D	Non	Minnie Harris	L	Cr
		Census Card No. 1656, P. O. Holdenville, Enrolled February 20, 1900										
5340	1	Long, Washington	28	M	F		George Long	D	Cr	Matilda Long	D	Cr
5341	2	Long, Martha	23	F	F	Wf	Billy Noon	D	Cr	Hepsey Noon	L	Cr
5342	3	Long, George	3	M	F	S	No. 1	L	Cr	No. 2	L	Cr
		No. 2 died February 12, 1906										
		Census Card No. 1657, P. O. Hoffman, Enrolled February 20, 1900										
5343	1	Lowe, John	25	M	½		A. D. Lowe	D	Non	Malissa Hill	D	Cr
		Census Card No. 1658, P. O. Tulsa, No. 4 Wetumka, Enrolled February 20, 1900										
5344	1	Pigeon, Dave	39	M	F		Joe Pigeon	D	Cr	Unknown	?	Cr
5345	2	Pigeon, Nancy	20	F	F	Wf	Stephen Fife	D	Cr	Ellen Fife	L	Cr
5346	3	Pigeon, Tiger	15	M	F	S	No. 1	L	Cr	Leacha	L	Cr
5347	4	Pigeon, Peggy	10	F	F	D	No. 1	L	Cr	Leacha	L	Cr
		No. 1 died March 9, 1901. No. 2 reported dead										
		Census Card No. 1659, P. O. Hitchita, Enrolled February 21, 1900										
5318	1	Watts, Anna H.	25	F	½		John Heber	L	Non	Unknown	D	Cr
5349	2	Watts, Mary Etta	8 mo	F	½	D	William T. Watts	L	Non	No. 1	L	Cr
5350	3	Watts, Robert L.	3	M	½	S	William T. Watts	L	Non	No. 1	L	Cr
		No. 1 died December 13, 1902. No. 3 reported dead										
		Census Card No. 1660, P. O. Keokuk Falls, Enrolled February 21, 1900										
5351	1	Chisholm, Sallie	24	F	½		Jackson Chisholm	L	Non	Shokahky	D	Cr
		Census Card No. 1661, P. O. Sperry, Enrolled February 21, 1900										
5352	1	Chisholm, William	26	M	½		Jackson Chisholm	L	Non	Shokahky	D	Cr
		Census Card No. 1662, P. O. Checotah, Enrolled February 22, 1900										
5353	1	Noble, Annie V.	24	F	½		William Fisher	L	Cr	Sarah Fisher	L	Cr
5354	2	Noble, Lucile	4	F	¼	D	J. H. Noble	L	Non	No. 2	L	Cr
5355	3	Noble, Myrtle	2	F	¼	D	J. H. Noble	L	Non	No. 2	L	Cr
		Census Card No. 1663, P. O. Coweta, Enrolled February 22, 1900										
5356	1	McGilbray, Rosanna	19	F	F		Hailey McGilbra	L	Cr	Miley McGilbra	D	Cr
		Census Card No. 1664, P. O. Hitchia; No. 3 Sharp, Enrolled February 23, 1900										
5357	1	Gray, Louisa	57	F	½		Manuel Thompson	D	?	Nannie Brown	D	?
5358	2	Gray, Jackson	27	M	¾	S	James Gray	D	Cr	No. 1	L	Cr
5359	3	Gray, Lee	14	M	¾	S	James Gray	D	Cr	No. 1	L	Cr
		No. 1 reported dead										
		Census Card No. 1665, P. O. Holdenville, Enrolled February 23, 1900										
5360	1	Stubblefield, Lousanna	20	F	⅛		John Hulsey	L	Non	Eliza Hulsey	D	Cr
		Census Card No. 1666, P. O. Okmulgee, Enrolled February 23, 1900										
5361	1	Dice, Dove	21	F	⅛		John Hulsey	L	Non	Eliza Hulsey	D	Cr
5362	2	McCray, Otto	8 mo	M	1-16	S	Tommy McCray	L	?	No. 1	L	Cr
		Census Card No. 1667, P. O. Wetumka, Enrolled February 24, 1900										
5363	1	Yarhola, Joe	30	M	F		Thomas Yarhola	L	Cr	Mollie Yarhola	D	Cr
5364	2	Yarhola, Yarner	28	F	F	Wf	Quesko Harjo	L	Cr	Sylahoke	D	Cr
		Census Card No. 1668, P. O. Wetumka, Enrolled February 24, 1900; No. 7 April 17, 1900										
5365	1	Coachman, Charles	45	M	F		Ward Coachman	L	Cr	Lizzie Coachman	D	Cr
5366	2	Coachman, Anna	25	F	F	Wf	Neha Yarhola	D	Cr	Nettie	D	Cr
5367	3	Coachman, Gussie	7	F	F	D	No. 1	L	Cr	No. 2	L	Cr
5368	4	Coachman, Guy	6	M	F	S	No. 1	L	Cr	No. 2	L	Cr
5369	5	Coachman, Aggie	4	F	F	D	No. 1	L	Cr	No. 2	L	Cr
5370	6	Coachman, C. Hobson	2	M	F	S	No. 1	L	Cr	No. 2	L	Cr
5371	7	Coachman, J. Bryan	9 da	M	F	S	No. 1	L	Cr	No. 2	L	Cr
		No. 7 died August 20, 1900										
		Census Card No. 1669, P. O. Okmulgee, Enrolled February 24, 1900										
5372	1	Johnson, Little Tom	32	M	F		Hulbutta Fixico	D	Cr	Tenohehokee	D	Cr
5373	2	Johnson, Ellie	20	F	F	Wf	Hulleputta Harjo	D	Cr	Sallie	D	Cr
5374	3	Johnson, Albert	1	M	F	S	No. 1	L	Cr	No. 2	L	Cr
		No. 1 reported dead										
		Census Card No. 1670, P. O. Morse, Enrilled February 24, 1900										
5375	1	Albert	35	M	F		Artus Yaholar	D	Cr	Kintar Micco	L	Cr
5376	2	Cumseh	15	M	F	S	No. 1	L	Cr	Narchichar	D	Cr
5377	3	Nancy	8	F	F	D	No. 1	L	Cr	Narchichar	D	Cr
		No. 1 reported dead										
		Census Card No. 1671, P. O. Morse, Enrolled February 24, 1900										
5378	1	Elissy	70	F	F		Unknown	?	Cr	Unknown	?	Cr
		No. 1 reported dead										
		Census Card No. 1672, P. O. Morse, Enrolled February 24, 1900										
5379	1	Semarte	45	F	F		Neha Yarhola	D	Cr	Elessy	L	Cr
		No. 1 died April 4, 1901										

Roll No.	No.	NAME	Age	Sex	Blood	Rel.	NAME OF FATHER	Liv.	Cit.	NAME OF MOTHER	Liv.	Cit.
		Census Card No. 1673, P. O. Morse, Enrolled February 24, 1900										
5380	1	Tarkey	60	F	F		No data given; would not talk					
		No. 1 reported dead										
		Census Card No. 1674, P. O. Morse, Enrolled February 24, 1900										
5381	1	Winey	25	F	F		Ahfonoke	L	Cr	Hoktoche Ahfonoke	L	Cr
5382	2	Arlie	3	F	F	D	Cully Johnson	L	Cr	No. 1	L	Cr
5383	3	Parlie	6 mo	F	F	D	Albert Bear	D	Cr	No. 1	L	Cr
		No. 2 died June 20, 1911										
		Census Card No. 1675, P. O. Red Fork, Enrolled February 24, 1900										
5384	1	"Standwaitie"	50	M	F		Unknown	D	Cr	Simetah	D	Cr
5385	2	"Standwaitie" Foady	57	F	F	Wf	Joseph	D	Non	A-tar-thle	D	Cr
5386	3	"Standwaitie", Joseph	18	M	F	S	No. 1	L	Cr	No. 2	L	Cr
5387	4	"Standwaitie",Wilson	19	M	F	S	No. 1	L	Cr	No. 2	L	Cr
		Nos. 3 and 4 reported dead										
		Census Card No. 1676, P. O. Sapulpa, Enrolled February 24, 1900										
5388	1	Samuel Ben	40	M	F		Dickey	L	Cr	Lucinda	D	Cr
5389	2	Bigpond, Sissie	20	F	F	D	No. 1	L	Cr	Yata	D	Cr
5390	3	Bigpond, Ella	7 mo	F	F	GdD	John Bigpond	L	Cr	No. 2	L	Cr
		No. 3 died July 11, 1900. No. 1 and 3 reported dead										
		Census Card No. 1677, P. O. Wetumka, Enrolled February 26, 1900										
5391	1	Cheek, Levia	28	F	⅛		Vard Wills	D	Cr	Georgiannia Wills	D	Non
		Census Card No. 1678, P. O. Yeager, Enrolled February 27, 1900										
5392	1	Yargee, Annie	45	F	½		Ad Taylor	D	Non	Sarwannechee	D	Cr
5393	2	Yargee, Wynie	16	F	¾	D	Carcho Harjo	D	Cr	No. 1	L	Cr
5394	3	Yargee, Culley	14	M	¾	S	Tarmochee	D	Cr	No. 1	L	Cr
		Census Card No. 1679, P. O. Eufaula, Enrolled February 27, 1900										
5395	1	Smith, Martha	26	F	⅛		Joe Hutton	L	Non	Lou Hutton	L	Cr
5396	2	Smith, Annie Belle	4	F	1-16	D	Wade Smith	L	Non	No. 1	L	Cr
5397	3	Smith, Louisa	11 mo	F	1-16	D	Wade Smith	L	Cr	No. 1	L	Cr
		Census Card No. 1680, P. O. Eufaula, Enrolled February 27, 1900										
5398	1	McGilbra, Lewis	39	M	F		Pothka	D	Cr	Amy McGilbra	L	Cr
5399	2	McGilbra, Ciuda	26	F	F	Wf	Tuskegee Micco	D	Cr	Lizzie Micco	L	Cr
5400	3	McGilbra, Joseph	5	M	F	S	No. 1	L	Cr	No. 2	L	Cr
5401	4	McGilbra, Solomon	3	M	F	S	No. 1	L	Cr	Nol 1	L	Cr
		No. 2 died September 17, 1900. No. 3 died August 24, 1914										
		Census Card No. 1681, P. O. Holdenville, Enrolled February 28, 1900										
5402	1	Harnogee	51	F	F		Thlechimy Fixico	D	Cr	Yasee	D	Cr
5403	2	McGeely, Timmie	17	M	F	S	McGeeley	D	Cr	No. 1	L	Cr
		No. 1 died January 19, 1903										
		Census Card No. 1682, P. O. Wewoka, Enrolled February 28, 1900										
5404	1	Ahaisse, Sissie	41	F	F		Hillis Fixico	D	Cr	Mabeta	L	Cr
5405	2	Abaisse, Allie	15	F	½	D	Abaisse	L	Cr	No. 1	L	Cr
5406	3	Ahaisse, Joseph	12	M	½	S	Abaisse	L	Cr	No. 1	L	Cr
5407	4	Abaisse, Winey	9	F	½	D	Abaisse	L	Cr	No. 1	L	Cr
5408	5	Abaisse, David	8	M	½	S	Ahaisse	L	Cr	No. 1	L	Cr
5409	6	Abaisse, Addie	5	F	½	D	Abaisse	L	Cr	No. 1	L	Cr
5410	7	Ahaisse, Sebert	3	M	½	S	Abaisse	L	Cr	No. 1	L	Cr
5411	8	Abaisse, Minnie	11 mo	F	½	D	Ahaisse	L	Cr	No. 1	L	Cr
		Nos. 4 and 8 reported dead										
		Census Card No. 1683, P. O. Wewoka, Enrolled February 28, 1900										
5412	1	Factor, Nancy	24	F	F		Thos. Benton	D	Cr	Cokey	L	Cr
5413	2	Factor, Sarah	6	F	½	D	Wm. Factor	L	Sem	No. 1	L	Cr
5414	3	Factor, Harry	2	M	½	S	Wm. Factor	L	Sem	No. 1	L	Cr
		Census Card No. 1684, P. O. Broken Arrow, Enrolled February 28, 1900										
5415	1	Mathewson, Phoebe	17	F	½		F. M. Mathewson	L	Non	Hettie Ann Mathewson	D	Cr
		Census Card No. 1685, P. O. Wewoka, Enrolled February 28, 1900										
5416	1	Benton, Louisa	20	F	F		Thos. Benton	L	Cr	Cokey	L	Cr
5417	2	Cloud, Barney	6	M	½	S	George Cloud	L	Sem	No. 1	L	Cr
		Census Card No. 1686, P. O. Grayson, Enrolled February 28, 1900										
5418	1	Brown, Chailey	41	M	F		Hardy Brown	D	Cr	Simpsey Brown	D	Cr
		No. 1 died March 18, 1901										
		Census Card No. 1687, P. O. McAlester, Enrolled February 28, 1900										
5419	1	Owen, Samuel	26	M	⅛		C. A. Owens	L	Non	Jane Wolf	L	Cr
5420	2	Owen, Pearl	6	F	1-16	D	No. 1	L	Cr	Mary Owen	L	Non
5421	3	Owen, Myrtle	4	F	1-16	D	No. 1	L	Cr	Mary Owen	L	Non
		Census Card No. 1688, P. O. Holdenville, Enrolled February 28, 1900										
5422	1	Tea, Thomas	40	M	F		Ussy Yaholar	D	Cr	Martha Yaholar	D	Cr
5423	2	Tea, Judy	35	F	F	Wf	Tommy Harjo	D	Cr	Taryoboska	D	Cr
5424	3	Tea, Anna	19	F	F	D	No. 1	L	Cr	No. 2	L	Cr
5425	4	Tea, Lucy	17	F	F	D	No. 1	L	Cr	No. 2	L	Cr
5426	5	Tea, Nancy	14	F	F	D	No. 1	L	Cr	No. 2	L	Cr
5427	6	Tea, Amos	10	M	F	S	No. 1	L	Cr	No. 1	L	Cr
5428	7	Tea, Ellen	8	F	F	D	No. 1	L	Cr	No. 2	L	Cr
5429	8	Tea, Emma	6	F	F	D	No. 1	L	Cr	No. 2	L	Cr
		No. 6 died February 24, 1911. No. 8 reported dead										
		Census Card No. 1689, P. O. Oktaha, Enrolled February 28, 1900										
5430	1	Thompson, Alice	12	F	½		John Thompson	L	Non	Patsy Johnson	D	Cr
5431	2	Thompson, Ellen	9	F	½	Sis	John Thompson	L	Non	Patsy Johnson	D	Cr
5432	3	Thompson, Victoria	7	F	½	Sis	John Thompson	L	Non	Patsy Johnson	D	Cr

Roll No.	No.	NAME	Age	Sex	Blood	Rel.	NAME OF FATHER	Liv.	Cit.	NAME OF MOTHER	Liv.	Cit.
		Census Card No. 1690, P. O. Eufaula, Enrolled March 1, 1900										
5433	1	Grayson, Della E.	18	F	⅛		Sam Grayson	L	Cr	Kate Grayson	D	Cr
		No. 1 died March 8, 1900										
		Census Card No. 1691, P. O. Holdenville, Enrolled March 2, 1900										
5434	1	Stewart, Albert P.	34	M	½		Robert W. Stewart	L	Non	Sophia Stewart	D	Cr
5435	2	Stewart, Louisa	22	F	F	Wf	Spoka	D	Cr	Sukey	L	Cr
5436	3	Stewart, Clyde	2	M	¾	S	No. 1	L	Cr	No. 2	L	Cr
		No. 2 died August 26, 1904. No. 3 died March 22, 1914										
		Census Card No. 1692, P. O. Holdenville, Enrolled March 2, 1900										
5437	1	Stewart, Annie	45	F	F		Absalom Cornells	D	Cr	Lucy	D	Cr
5438	2	Hummecher, Joseph	22	M	F	S	Hummicher	D	Cr	No. 1	L	Cr
5439	3	Hummecher, Wynie	20	F	F	D	Hummicher	D	Cr	No. 1	L	Cr
5440	4	Stewart, Thomas A.	42	M	½	Hus	R. W. Stewart	L	Non	Sophia Stewart	D	Cr
		No. 4 died November 1, 1899. No. 3 died March 21, 1908										
		Census Card No. 1693, P. O. Wetumka, Enrolled March 2, 1900										
5441	1	Robinson, Sophia	42	F	F		John Reed	L	Cr	Rachel Reed	L	Cr
5442	2	Robinson, Monkey	16	M	F	S	Jack Robinson	D	Cr	No. 1	L	Cr
5443	3	Robinson, Hilley	14	F	F	D	Jack Robinson	D	Cr	No. 1	L	Cr
5444	4	Robinson, Annie	10	F	F	D	Jack Robinson	D	Cr	No. 1	L	Cr
5445	5	Robinson, Daniel	8	M	F	S	Jack Robinson	D	Cr	No. 1	L	Cr
5446	6	Robinson, Lona	6	F	F	D	Jack Robinson	D	Cr	No. 1	L	Cr
5447	7	Robinson, Celia	4	F	F	D	Jack Robinson	D	Cr	No. 1	L	Cr
		No. 1 died January 22, 1904. No. 6 died April 5, 1906. No. 2 reported dead										
		Census Card No. 1694, P. O. Holdenville, Enrolled March 2, 1900; No. 3 May 22, 1901										
5448	1	Bruner, Eddie	21	M	F		Jerry Bruner	D	Cr	Lena Bruner	D	Cr
5449	2	Bruner, Lizzie	18	F	F	Sis	Jerry Bruner	D	Cr	Lena Bruner	D	Cr
5450	3	Proctor, Alex	1	M	F	Neph	Timothy Proctor	L	Cr	Lizzie Bruner	L	Cr
		Nos. 1 and 2 reported dead										
		Census Card No. 1695, P. O. Holdenville, Enrolled March 2, 1900										
5451	1	Beaver, Peter	28	M	F		Itchar Fixico	D	Cr	Wisey	D	Cr
5452	2	Beaver, Babie	30	F	F	Wf	Nehar Thlocochee	D	Cr	Sofa	L	Cr
5453	3	Beaver, Simmer	4	F	F	D	No. 1	L	Cr	No. 2	L	Cr
		Nos. 1 and 2 reported dead										
		Census Card No. 1696, Holdenville, Enrolled March 2, 1900										
5454	1	Cornell, Willie	26	M	¾		David Cornell	D	Cr	Emily Cornell	D	Cr
5455	2	Cornell, Manie	17	F	F	Wf	Anochee	D	Cr	Siller	D	Cr
5456	3	Cornell, Benjamin	4	M	⅞	S	No. 1	L	Cr	Cinda Cornell	D	Cr
5457	4	Cornell, Annie	1	F	⅞	D	No. 1	L	Cr	Cinda Cornell	D	Cr
		No. 4 died July 14, 1901										
		Census Card No. 1697, P. O. Holdenville, Enrolled March 2, 1900										
5458	1	Grayson, Charles L.	25	M	¾		Colbert Grayson	D	Cr	Elizabeth Grayson	D	Cr
5459	2	Grayson, Cleveland	8	M	½	Bro	Colbert Grayson	D	Cr	Susan Grayson	D	Cr
		No. 1 reported dead										
		Census Card No. 1698, P. O. Eufaula, Enrolled March 3, 1900										
5460	1	Burton, Robert O.	24	M	⅛		Robert P. Burton	D	Non	Eliza N. Burton	D	Cr
5461	2	Burton, Samuel	16	M	⅛	Bro	Robert P. Burton	D	Non	Eliza N. Burton	D	Cr
5462	3	Burton, Abie L.	14	F	⅛	Sis	Robert P. Burton	D	Non	Eliza N. Burton	D	Cr
5463	4	Burton, Minnie Ola	12	F	⅛	Sis	Robert P. Burton	D	Non	Eliza N. Burton	D	Cr
5464	5	Burton, Mary E.	10	F	⅛	Sis	Robert P. Burton	D	Non	Eliza N. Burton	D	Cr
		Census Card No. 1699, P. O. Sasakwa, Enrolled March 2, 1900										
5465	1	Williams, Charles	48	M	½		Sol Williams	D	Non	Kissie Williams	L	Cr
5466	2	Williams, Emma	34	F	F	Wf	Temish Coronel	L	Cr	Jane Frank	L	Cr
5467	3	Herrod, Andy	15	M	F	StS	Dave Herrod	L	Cr	No. 2	L	Cr
5468	4	Williams, Abbie	14	F	¾	D	No. 1	L	Cr	No. 2	L	Cr
5469	5	Williams, Rose Ann	10	F	¾	D	No. 1	L	Cr	No. 2	L	Cr
5470	6	Williams, Mary Ann	5	F	¾	D	No. 1	L	Cr	No. 2	L	Cr
5471	7	Williams, Clara May	1	F	¾	D	No. 1	L	Cr	No. 2	L	Cr
		No. 1 died October 1904. No. 2 died April 1, 1906.										
		Census Card No. 1700, P. O. Eufaula, Enrolled March 5, 1900										
5472	1	Sorbe, Susan	54	F	½		John Lewis	D	Non	Louis Lewis	D	Cr
5473	2	Sorbe, Mary E.	16	F	¼	D	Wm. Sorbe	L	Non	No. 1	L	Non
5474	3	Sorbe, Anna Belle	12	F	⅛	D	Wm. Sorbe	L	Non	No. 1	L	Non
		No. 1 died November 27, 1900										
		Census Card No. 1701, P. O. Bristow, Enrolled March 6, 1900										
5475	1	Brady, Albert	24	M	F		Jackson Barnett	D	Cr	Sinda Sewell	L	Cr
5476	2	Brady, Dora	4mo	F	½	D	No. 1	L	Cr	Mary Brady	L	Non
		Census Card No. 1702, P. O. Holdenville, Enrolled March 6, 1900										
5477	1	Goat, John R.	57	M	F		Chuahdulga	D	Cr	Hulwichchee	D	Cr
5478	2	Goat, Angeline	56	F	F	Wf	Peter Harrison	D	Cr	Malinda Harrison	D	Cr
5479	3	Goat, Roman	22	M	F	S	No. 1	L	Cr	No. 2	L	Cr
5480	4	Goat, Martin	16	M	F	S	No. 1	L	Cr	No. 2	L	Cr
5481	5	Goat, Peggy	14	F	F	D	No. 1	L	Cr	No. 2	L	Cr
5482	6	Goat, Katie	12	F	F	D	No. 1	L	Cr	No. 2	L	Cr
		Census Card No. 1703, P. O. Holdenville, Enrolled March 6, 1900										
5483	1	Goat, Wardley	29	M	F		John R. Goat	L	Cr	Angeline Goat	L	Cr
5484	2	Goat, Susie	28	F	F	Wf	Wiley Hawkins	L	Cr	Chowey	D	Cr
5485	3	Goat, Wisey	4	F	F	D	No. 1	L	Cr	No. 2	L	Cr
5486	4	Stricken from roll.										
		No. 2 died October 31, 1900. No. 1 reported dead.										

Roll No.	No.	NAME	Age	Sex	Blood	Rel.	NAME OF FATHER	Liv.	Cit.	NAME OF MOTHER	Liv.
		Census Card No. 1704, P. O. Holdenville, Enrolled March 6, 1900									
5487	1	Goat, Alfred	26	M	F		John R. Goat	L	Cr	Angeline Goat	L
5488	2	Goat, Rachael	30	F	F	Wf	Samuel Checotah	D	Cr	Cilla Checotah	L
5489	3	Monahwee, Minnie	6	F	F	StS	John Manahwee	L	Cr	No. 2	L
		Census Card No. 1705, P. O. Holdenville, Enrolled March 7, 1900									
5490	1	Cosar, Mack	30	M	F		Caeser Fixico	D	Cr	Katy	D
5491	2	Cosar, Sissie	30	F	F	Wf	Thomas Anderson	D	Cr	Selay	D
5492	3	Cosar, Lillie	2	F	F	D	No. 1	L	Cr	No. 2	L
5493	4	Washington, Willie	14	M	F	StS	George Washington	L	Sem	No. 2	L
5494	5	Washington, Waitie	12	M	F	StS	George Washington	L	Sem	No. 2	L
5495	6	Lowe, Lizzie	18	F	F	SinL	Dobe Lewis	L	Cr	Selay	L
5496	7	Anderson, Minnie	8	F	F L	Ward	Tom Anderson	D	Cr	Haley Anderson	D
		No. 4 died April 8, 1901. Nos. 4 and 7 reported dead.									
		Census Card No. 1706, P. O. Holdenville, Enrolled March 7, 1900									
5497	1	Harrison, Napoleon	39	M	F		Peter Harrison	D	Cr	Malinda Harrison	D
5498	2	Harrison, Susan	37	F	F	Wf	Unknown	D	Cr	Fannie Manley	L
5499	3	Harrison, Peter	17	M	F	S	No. 1	L	Cr	No. 2	L
5500	4	Harrison, Lena	12	F	F	D	No. 1	L	Cr	No. 2	L
5501	5	Harrison, Lucy	8	F	F	D	No. 1	L	Cr	No. 2	L
5502	6	Harrison, John	2	M	F	S	No. 1	L	Cr	No. 2	L
		No. 6 died April 11, 1914. Nos. 1 and 6 reported dead.									
		Census Card No. 1707, P. O. Haskell, Enrolled March 7, 1900									
5503	1	Peters, Isom	31	M	F		Jesse Peters	D	Cr	Unknown	D
5504	2	Peters, Louisa	39	F	F	Wf	Cotchute	D	Cr	Tewoley Vore (Nore)	L
5505	3	Peters, Lula	6	F	F	D	No. 1	L	Cr	No. 2	L
		No. 2 reported dead.									
		Census Card No. 1708, P. O. Lima, Enrolled March 8, 1900; No. 3, May 18, 1901									
5506	1	Narcome, Johnson	38	M	F		Peter Narcome	D	Cr	Teakah Monday	D
5507	2	Lowe, Mack	6	M	F	Neph	Tom Lowe	L	Sem	Lizzie Lowe	L
5508	3	Lowe, Lizzie	19	F	F	Sis	Monday	L	Cr	Teakah Monday	D
		No. 1 died April 19, 1900. No. 3 died April 21, 1899.									
		Census Card No. 1709, P. O. Holdenville, Enrolled March 8, 1900									
5509	1	Long Sam	53	M	F		Tulmarthla Mikko	D	Cr	Mabala Long	D
5510	2	Long, Kizzie	44	F	F	Wf	Tokkilheste	D	Cr	Soska	D
5511	3	Long, Joshway	23	M	F	S	No. 1	L	Cr	No. 2	L
5512	4	Long, Loday	19	F	F	D	No. 1	L	Cr	No. 2	L
5513	5	Long, Hannah	17	F	F	D	No. 1	L	Cr	No. 2	L
5514	6	Long, Thomas	11	M	F	S	No. 1	L	Cr	No. 2	L
5515	7	Long, Coley	9	F	F	D	No. 1	L	Cr	No. 2	L
		No. 3 died March, 1903. No. 5 died March 27, 1908. No. 6 died August 3, 1909. No. 7 rep dead. No. 1 died June 3, 1902.									
		Census Card No. 1710, P. O. Dustin, Enrolled March 8, 1900; No. 2, March 27, 1901									
5516	1	Sleep, Tom	23	M	F		Solomon Sand	D	Cr	Wisey	D
5517	2	Sleep, Saheche	28	F	F	Wf	Nocus Fixico	L	Cr	Unknown	D
		Census Card No. 1711, P. O. Checotah, Enrolled March 9, 1900									
5518	1	McKinney, Albert	25	M	¼		Russell McKinney	D	Chick	Susan McKinney	D
		Census Card No. 1712, P. O. Checotah, Enrolled March 9, 1900									
5519	1	McKinney, John A.	33	M	¼		Russell McKinney	D	Chick	Susan McKinney	D
5520	2	McKinney, Sadie C.	4	F	⅛	D	No. 1	L	Cr	Anna B. McKinney	D
		Census Card No. 1713, P. O. Eufaula, Enrolled March 10, 1900									
5521	1	Walker, Martha Jane	50	F	½		John Gibson	D	Non	Polly Leacher	D
		Census Card No. 1714, P. O. Eufaula, Enrolled March 10, 1900									
5522	1	Jones, Goliah	42	M	F		Jones	D	Cr	Unknown	D
		Census Card No. 1715, P. O. Wetumka, Enrolled March 10, 1900									
5523	1	Jones, Mikey	38	M	F		Arkleyarchee Fixico	D	Cr	Unknown	D
5524	2	Jones, Lucy	30	F	F	Wf	Kousa Harjo	L	Cr	Solkar	L
5525	3	Jones, William	6	M	F	S	No. 1	L	Cr	No. 2	L
5526	4	Harjo, Bunny	16	M	F	Neph	Bahos Harjo	D	Cr	Munna	D
		No. 2 died October 21, 1907									
		Census Card No. 1716, P. O. Wetumka, Enrolled March 10, 1900									
5527	1	Anderson, Sampson	23	M	F		Sam Anderson	D	Cr	Chokfalitchee	D
5528	2	Anderson, Tyler	18	F	F	Wf	Neha Yahola	D	Cr	Sokwa Negee	D
		No. 1 died January 23, 1905. No. 2 died May 17, 1900.									
		Census Card No. 1717, P. O. Wetumka, Enrolled March 10, 1900									
5529	1	Anderson, Willie	27	M	F		Sam Anderson	D	Cr	Chokfalitchee	D
		No. 1 died April 4, 1899									
		Census Card No. 1718, P. O. Wetumka, Enrolled March 10, 1900									
5530	1	Harjo, Toney	22	M	F		Babos Harjo	D	Cr	Munna	D
		No. 1 reported dead									
		Census Card No. 1719, P. O. Wewoka, Enrolled March 10, 1900; Nos. 5 and 6, May 15, 1901									
5531	1	Hully, Baby	39	F	F		Isparney Harjo	L	Cr	Unknown	D
5532	2	Hully, Annie	12	F	½	D	John Hully	L	Sem	No. 1	L
5533	3	Hully, Wesley	8	M	½	S	John Hully	L	Sem	No. 1	L
5534	4	Hully, Arnie	6	F	½	D	John Hully	L	Sem	No. 1	L
5535	5	Hully, Ida	3	F	½	D	John Hully	L	Sem	No. 1	L
5536	6	Hully, Lucy	18moF	½		D	John Hully	L	Sem	No. 1	L
		No. 2 died December 1913									

116

Census Card No. 1720, P. O. Wetumka, Enrolled March 10, 1900

Roll No.	No.	NAME	Age	Sex	Blood	Rel.	NAME OF FATHER	Liv.	Cit.	NAME OF MOTHER	Liv.	Cit.
5537	1	Tiger, Jeff	24	M	F		Candy Tiger	D	Cr	Louisa	D	Cr
5538	2	Tiger, Kogee	37	F	F	Wf	Daniel Barnett	L	Cr	Sally Barnett	D	Cr
5539	3	Yargee, Hattie	9	F	F	D	Alex Yargee	D	Cr	No. 1	L	Cr
5540	4	Yargee, Alvey	6	F	F	D	Alex Yargee	D	Cr	No. 1	L	Cr

Census Card No. 1721, P. O. Wetumka, Enrolled March 12, 1900

5541	1	Tiger, Dave	33	M	F		Candy Tiger	D	Cr	Louisa	D	Cr
5542	2	Tiger, Coge	40	F	F	Wf	Cotcherthlepaya	D	Cr	Lewestey	D	Cr
5543	3	Benden, Joseph	13	M	F	S	Thos. Benden	D	Cr	No. 2	L	Cr
5544	4	Benden, Jonas	10	M	F	S	Thos. Benden	D	Cr	No. 2	L	Cr

Nos. 1 and 2 reported dead

Census Card No. 1722, P. O. Lamar, Enrolled March 12, 1900

5545	1	Lowe, Tobler	40	M	F		Unknown	D	Cr	Unknown	D	Cr
5546	2	Lowe, Sallie	37	F	F	Wf	Candy Tiger	D	Cr	Louisa Tiger	D	Cr
5547	3	McGirt, Morgy	16	M	F	StS	Unknown	?	Cr	No. 2	L	Cr
5548	4	McGirt, John	14	M	F	StS	Unknown	?	Cr	No. 2	L	Cr

No. 1 died May 3, 1914. No. 2 died July 25, 1905. No. 3 reported dead.

Census Card No. 1723, P. O. Wetumka, Enrolled March 12, 1900

5549	1	Tiger, Chapley	26	M	F		Candy Tiger	D	Cr	Louisa Tiger	D	Cr
5550	2	Tiger, Nancy	20	F	F	Sis	Candy Tiger	D	Cr	Louisa Tiger	D	Cr

No. 1 reported dead

Census Card No. 1724, P. O. Wewoka, Enrolled March 12, 1900; No. 2, May 16, 1901

5551	1	Panter, Jemima	20	F	F		Thos. Benden	D	Cr	Kogee	?	Cr
5552	2	Lindsey, Samantha	4	F	F	D	Walter Lindsey	L	Cr	No. 1	L	Cr

Nos. 1 and 2 reported dead.

Census Card No. 1725, P. O. Wetumka, Enrolled March 12, 1900

5553	1	Harjo, Jimsey	21	M	F		Marge Harjo	D	Cr	Sulka	L	Cr

Census Card No. 1726, P. O. Wetumka, Enrolled March 12, 1900

5554	1	Harjo, Sulka	45	F	F		Holote Emarthler	D	Cr	Unknown	?	Cr
5555	2	Harjo, Joshua	15	M	F	S	Marchie Harjo	D	Cr	No. 1	L	Cr
5556	3	Tiger, Mickey	15	F	F	Ward	Hotala	D	Cr	Wisey	L	Cr

Nos. 2 and 3 reported dead.

Census Card No. 1727, P. O. Wetumka, Enrolled March 12, 1900

5557	1	Harjo, Jack	24	M	F		Pahos Harjo	D	Cr	Munna	L	Cr
5558	2	Harjo, Katie	19	F	F	Wf	Moty Beaver	D	Cr	Mollie Beaver	L	Cr
5559	3	Harjo, Mollie	4mo	F	F	D	No. 1	L	Cr	No. 2	L	Cr

No. 1 died March 6, 1904. No. 2 died May 12, 1902.

Census Card No. 1728, P. O. Morris, Enrolled March 12, 1900

5560	1	Milam, Laura R.	27	F	¼		Samuel Doyle	L	Cr	Alva Doyle	L	Non
5561	2	Milam, Kate W	5	F	⅛	D	A. M. Milam	L	Non	No. 1	L	Cr
5562	3	Milam, Charles A.	4	M	⅛	S	A. M. Milam	L	Non	No. 1	L	Cr
5563	4	Milam, Arthelus M.	1	M	⅛	S	A. M. Milam	L	Non	No. 1	L	Cr

Census Card No. 1729, P. O. Broken Arrow, Enrolled March 12, 1900

5564	1	Simmons, Charley	33	M	F		Simmissee	D	Cr	Susie	D	Cr

Census Card No. 1730, P. O. Stidham, Enrolled March 14, 1900

5565	1	Island, Boney	23	M	½		Henry Island	D	Cr	Susan Island	L	Cr
5566	2	Island, Bessie M.	1mo	F	¼	D	No. 1	L	Cr	Maggie Island	L	Non

No. 1 died April 24, 1906. No. 2 died October 12, 1900.

Census Card No. 1731, P. O. Hoffman, Enrolled March 15, 1900

5567	1	Patton, Emma	20	F	F		James Butler	D	Cr	Dinah Butler	D	Cr

Census Card No. 1732, P. O. Henryetta, Enrolled March 16, 1900

5568	1	Adams, Frank	21	M	¼		Wiley Adams	L	Cr	Susan Adams	D	Cr

Census Card No. 1733, P. O. Okmulgee, Enrolled March 16, 1900

5569	1	Hodge, Johnson F.	18	M	¼		Johnson Hodge	D	Cr	Margaret Hodge	D	Non
5570	2	Hodge, Mary	12	F	¼	Sis	Johnson Hodge	D	Cr	Margaret Hodge	D	Non

Census Card No. 1734, P. O. Coweta, Enrolled March 17, 1900

5571	1	Bruner, Richard	34	M	F		Luna Bruner	D	Cr	Rachel Bruner	D	Cr
5572	2	Bruner, Sarah	20	F	F	Wf	Goga Sarty	L	Cr	Susan Sarty	L	Cr
5573	3	Bruner, Drefus	6moM	F	S		No. 1	L	Cr	No. 2	L	Cr
5574	4	Sugar, Sam	18	M	F	Ward	James Sugar	L	Cr	Helen Sugar	L	Cr
5575	5	Sugar, Eddie	8	M	F	Ward	James Sugar	L	Cr	Helen Sugar	L	Cr
5576	6	Bruner, Winfield	2	M	F	S	No. 1	L	Cr	No. 2	L	Cr

No. 6 died December 5, 1899

Census Card No. 1735, P. O. Hoffman, Enrolled March 21, 1900

5577	1	Smith, Martin	74	M	½		Sam Smith	D	Cr	Liza Smith	D	Non

Census Card No. 1736, P. O. Hoffman, Enrolled March 21, 1900

5578	1	Smith, Isaac	40	M	½		Martin Smith	L	Cr	Millie Smith	D	Cr
5579	2	Smith, Mollie	12	F	¼	D	No. 1	L	Cr	Neeley Smith	D	Non
5580	3	Smith, Ida	6	F	¼	D	No. 1	L	Cr	Susan Smith	D	Non

Census Card No. 1737, P. O. Hitchita, Enrolled March 21, 1900

5581	1	Barnwell, Joe	24	M	¾		Robinson Barnwell	D	Cr	Sissy	D	Cr

Census Card No. 1738, P. O. Beggs, Enrolled March 21, 1900

5582	1	Friday, Jennie	19	F	½		Eli Jacobs	D	Cr	Kissie Bruner	D	Cr

Census Card No. 1739, P. O. Wetumka, Enrolled March 22, 1900

5583	1	Porter, Ben	20	M	¾		John S. Porter	D	Cr	Mary Porter	D	Cr
5584	2	Porter, Lena	20	F	F	Wf	Thomas Canard	D	Cr	Wannie Scott	L	Cr

No. 1 died November 23, 1906

Census Card No. 1740, P. O. Sasakwa, Enrolled March 22, 1900; No. 2, May 18, 1901

5585	1	Miller, Samuel H.	31	M	¾		Samuel Miller	D	Cr	Sophia Miller	D	Cr
5586	2	Miller, Mollie	15	F	F	Ward	Farcosa Harjo	L	Cr	Lizzie	D	Cr

Roll No.	No.	NAME	Age	Sex	Blood	Rel.	NAME OF FATHER	Liv.	Cit.	NAME OF MOTHER	Liv.	Cit.
		Census Card No. 1741, P. O. Okmulgee, Enrolled March 23, 1900										
5587	1	Tiger, Alberd	19	M	F		Sampson Tiger	L	Cr	Sallie Tiger	D	Cr
		Census Card No. **1742, P. O. Okemah, Enrolled March 23, 1900**										
5588	1	Harjo, Maggie	50	F	F		Tustinock Harjo	D	Cr	Manhosena	D	Cr
5589	2	Harjo, Emarthla	80	M	F	Hus	Unknown	D	Cr	Unknown	D	Cr
		No. 2 died February 1900										
		Census Card No. **1743, P. O. Okemah, Enrolled March 23, 1900**										
5590	1	Micco, Mary	23	F	F		Sumaga	D	Cr	Marhosena	D	Cr
5591	2	Tiger, George	3mo	M	F	S	Lewis Tiger	L	Cr	No. 1	L	Cr
		No. 2 died 1902										
		Census Card No. 1744, P. O. Grayson, Enrolled March 26, 1900										
5592	1	Sampson, John	18	M	F		Samsoche	D	Cr	Inchie	D	Cr
		Census Card No. 1745, P. O. Olive, Enrolled March 26, 1900										
5593	1	Codenny	28	M	F		Cotah	D	Cr	Betsey	D	Cr
5594	2	Youconcoconthlanay	23	F	F	Wf	Thomas Barnett	L	Cr	Shagoney	D	Cr
		Nos. 1 and 2 reported dead										
		Census Card No. 1746, P. O. Choska, Enrolled March 26, 1900										
5595	1	Island, Ben	40	M	F		Madison Island	D	Cr	Nancy Marshall	D	Cr
		Census Card No. 1747, P. O. Hanna, Enrolled March 26, 1900; No. 6, April 6, 1900; No. 7, April 20, 1900										
5596	1	Starr, Robert	40	M	F		Tusekiga	D	Cr	Unknown	D	Cr
5597	2	Starr, Lillie	25	F	1/2	Wf	Tom Frazier	D	Chick	Margaret Frazier	D	Cr
5598	3	Starr, Ella	8	F	3/4	D	No. 1	L	Cr	No. 2	L	Cr
5599	4	Starr, Thomas	6	M	3/4	S	No. 1	L	Cr	No. 2	L	Cr
5600	5	Starr, Lydia	2	F	3/4	D	No. 1	L	Cr	No. 2	L	Cr
5601	6	Starr, Lena	20	F	F	D	No. 1	L	Cr	Sarna	D	Cr
5602	7	Starr, Lona	12	M	F	S	No. 1	L	Cr	Sarna	D	Cr
		No. 1 died October 27, 1908										
		Census Card No. 1748, P. O. Checotah, Enrolled March 29, 1900										
5603	1	Asbill, Sarah A.	58	F	1/8		Rueben Cook	D	Non	Hannah L. Cook	D	Cr
5604	2	Asbill, Edna	18	F	1-16	D	Samuel Asbill	L	Non	No. 1	L	Cr
5605	3	Asbill, Brina	15	F	1-16	D	Samuel Asbill	L	Non	No. 1	L	Cr
		Census Card No. 1749, P. O. Okmulgee, Enrolled March 27, 1900										
5606	1	Yargee, William	26	M	1/4		David Yargee	D	Cr	Sarah Asbill	L	Cr
		Census Card No. 1750, P. O. Eufaula, Enrolled March 28, 1900										
5607	1	Riddle, Tokie	35	F	1/4		Bill Nero	D	Cr	Nancy Nero	D	Cr
5608	2	Riddle, Sam	14	M	1/8	S	Stuart Riddle	L	Choc	No. 1	L	Cr
5609	3	Riddle, Fibbie	10	F	1/8	D	Stuart Riddle	L	Choc	No. 1	L	Cr
5610	4	Riddle, Rafert	8	M	1/8	S	Stuart Riddle	L	Choc	No. 1	L	Cr
5611	5	Riddle, Cub	6	M	1/8	S	Stuart Riddle	L	Choc	No. 1	L	Cr
5612	6	Riddle, William	5	M	1/8	S	Sturat Riddle	L	Choc	No. 1	L	Cr
5613	7	Riddle, Gertie	2	F	1/8	D	Stuart Riddle	L	Choc	No. 1	L	Cr
5614	8	Vandivew, James	17	M	1/8	S	Doc Vandervere	L	Non	No. 1	L	Cr
		Census Card No. 1751, P. O. Paden, Enrolled March 28, 1900										
5615	1	Sumka	27	M	F		Cabecha	D	Cr	Nannie	D	Cr
		Census Card No. 1752, P. O. Vivian, Enrolled March 29, 1900										
5616	1	Colbert, Lizzie	35	F	3/4		Wm. McCombs	L	Cr	Sally McCombs	L	Cr
5617	2	Colbert, Robert	11	M	7/8	S	James Colbert	D	Cr	No. 1	L	Cr
5618	3	Colbert, Joe	9	M	7/8	S	James Colbert	D	Cr	No. 1	L	Cr
5619	4	Colbert, Mary	7	F	7/8	D	James Colbert	D	Cr	No. 1	L	Cr
5620	5	Colbert, Willie	3	M	7/8	S	James Colbert	D	Cr	No. 1	L	Cr
		No. 1 died October 15, 1905. No. 5 died October 13, 1899.										
		Census Card No. 1753, P. O. Vivian, Enrolled March 29, 1900										
5621	1	Freeman, Sudie	30	F	3/4		Wm. McCombs	L	Cr	Sally McCombs	L	Cr
		Census Card No. 1754, P. O. Vivian; No. 4, Lenna, Enrolled March 29, 1900										
5622	1	McCombs, David	52	M	1/4		Sam'l McCombs	D	Non	Susan McCombs	D	Cr
5623	1	McCombs, Millie	45	F	7/8	Wf	Jacob	L	Cr	Lucy Jacobs	D	Cr
5624	3	McCombs, Tom	25	M	3/4	S	No. 1	L	Cr	No. 2	L	Cr
5625	4	McCombs, Lena	19	F	3/4	D	No. 1	L	Cr	No. 2	L	Cr
5626	5	McCombs, Pollie	15	F	3/4	D	No. 1	L	Cr	No. 2	L	Cr
5627	6	McCombs, Leah	13	F	3/4	D	No. 1	L	Cr	No. 2	L	Cr
5628	7	McCombs, Bessie	8	F	3/4	D	No. 1	L	Cr	No. 2	L	Cr
		No. 1 died October 2, 1913										
		Census Card No. 1755, P. O. Eufaula; No. 4, Muskogee, Enrolled March 29, 1900										
5629	1	McCombs, William	56	M	1/4		Sam'l McCombs	D	Non	Susie McCombs	L	Cr
5630	2	McCombs, Sallie	56	F	7/8	Wf	Jacob	L	Cr	Lucy Jacobs	L	Cr
5631	3	McCombs, Porter	18	F	3/4	D	No. 1	L	Cr	No. 2	L	Cr
5632	4	McCombs, Bettie	15	F	3/4	D	No. 1	L	Cr	No. 2	L	Cr
5633	5	McCombs, George W.	13	M	3/4	S	No. 1	L	Cr	No. 2	L	Cr
		No. 2 died March 21, 1901										
		Census Card No. 1756, P. O. Eufaula, Enrolled March 29, 1900										
5634	1	McCombs, William P.	25	M	3/4		Wm. McCombs	L	Cr	Sallie McCombs	L	Cr
		Census Card No. 1757, P. O. Vivian, Enrolled March 29, 1900										
5635	1	Washington, Isaac	20	M	1/2		George Washington	D	Cr	Sarah Washington	D	?
		Census Card No. 1758, P. O. Vivian, Enrolled March 29, 1900										
5636	1	McCombs, Joseph	45	M	1/4		Samuel McCombs	D	Non	Susan McCombs	D	Cr
		Census Card No. 1759, P. O. Vivian, Enrolled March 29, 1900										
5637	1	McCombs, James	32	M	3/4		David McCombs	L	Cr	Millie McCombs	L	Cr

No.	NAME	Age	Sex	Blood	Rel.	NAME OF FATHER	Liv.	Cit.	NAME OF MOTHER	Liv.	Cit.

Census Card No. 1760, P. O. Schulter, Enrolled March 29, 1900

1	Burgess, James	38	M	½		Dave Burgess	D	Cher	Tina Burgess	D	Cr
2	Burgess, Susanna	20	F	F	Wf	Noksa Randall	D	Cr	Ulsa Randall	L	Cr
3	Burgess, Senora	9	M	⅞	S	No. 1	L	Cr	Anna Randall	D	Cr
4	Burgess, Ellis	6	M	⅞	S	No. 1	L	Cr	Anna Randall	D	Cr
5	Burgess, Emma	4	F	⅞	D	No. 1	L	Cr	Anna Randall	D	Cr

No. 5 died February 10, 1906

Census Card No. 1761, P. O. Schulter, Enrolled March 29, 1900; No. 6, May 20, 1901

1	Burgess, Albert	47	M	½		Dave Burgess	D	Cher	Tina Burgess	D	Cr
2	Burgess, Yarna	28	F	F	Wf	Harvey Hawkins	D	Cr	Mary Hawkins	D	Cr
3	Burgess, Edward	9	M	¾	S	No. 1	L	Cr	No. 2	L	Cr
4	Burgess, Riley	7	M	¾	S	No. 1	L	Cr	No. 2	L	Cr
5	Burgess, Mary E.	3	F	¾	D	No. 1	L	Cr	No. 2	L	Cr
6	Burgess, Barney	1	M	¾	S	No. 1	L	Cr	No. 2	L	Cr

No. 1 and 6 died August 27, 1899. No. 5 died June 22, 1901.

Census Card No. 1762, P. O. Pierce, Enrollde March 29, 1900

| 1 | Yargee, Mitchell | 50 | M | ¾ | | Capt. Yargee | D | Cr | Nancy Yargee | D | Cr |
| 2 | Yargee, Mariah | 52 | F | F | Wf | Manuel Thompson | D | Cr | Nannie Thompson | D | Cr |

No. 1 died February 19, 1905

Census Card No. 1763, P. O. Okmulgee, Enrolled March 29, 1900

| 1 | Randall, Thomas | 53 | M | F | | James Randall | D | Cr | Tecoweka | D | Cr |

No. 1 died March 2, 1903

Census Card No. 1764, P. O. Eufaula, Enrolled March 29, 1900

1	Stidham, Leonidas G.	44	M	½		G. W. Stidham	D	Cr	Ara A. Stidham	D	Cr
2	Stidham, Leola May	14	F	¼	D	No. 1	L	Cr	Lura M. Stidham	L	Non
3	Stidham, Georgiana	11	F	¼	D	No. 1	L	Cr	Lura M. Stidham	L	Non
4	Stidham, Eloita	2	F	¼	D	No. 1	L	Cr	Lura M. Stidham	L	Non

Census Card No. 1765, P. O. Okmulgee, Enrolled March 29, 1900

| 1 | Blend, Roley | 25 | M | F | | Joe Blend | D | Cr | Lucy Blend | L | Cr |

No. 1 died April 7, 1901

Census Card No. 1766, P. O. Okemah, Enrolled March 29, 1900

1	Knight, Jackson	45	M	F		Natowaga	D	Cr	Iogee	D	Cr
2	Knight, Mollie A.	17	F	F	D	No. 1	L	Cr	Diarah Jackson	D	Cr
3	Knight, Peter	13	M	F	S	No. 1	L	Cr	Diarah Jackson	D	Cr
4	Knight, Lena	8	F	F	D	No. 1	L	Cr	Diarah Jackson	D	Cr

Census Card No. 1767, P. O. Paden, Enrolled March 29, 1900; No. 4, March 26, 1901

1	Grant, Niffey	21	M	F		Billy Grant	D	Cr	Nannochee	D	Cr
2	Grant, Meley	20	F	F	Wf	Lotto Harjo Sand	L	Cr	Dinah	D	Cr
3	Grant, Billiey	3	M	F	S	No. 1	L	Cr	No. 2	L	Cr
4	Grant, Minnie	2	F	F	D	No. 1	L	Cr	No. 2	L	Cr

No. 2 died December 8, 1904

Census Card No. 1768, P. O. Welty, Enrolled March 30, 1900

| 1 | London, Betsy | 42 | F | F | | Unknown | D | Cr | Thlemey | D | Cr |
| 2 | Proctor, Sallie | 9 | F | F | D | Kailey Proctor | L | Cr | No. 1 | L | Cr |

Census Card No. 1769, P. O. Baron, Enrolled March 30, 1900

| 1 | Jones, Willie | 27 | M | F | | Nero Jones | D | Cr | Eliza Jones | D | Cr |

Census Card No. 1770, P. O. Bixby, Enrolled March 30, 1900

| 1 | Burgess, Edmond | 18 | M | ½ | | Sampson Burgess | D | Cr | Katie Burgess | D | Cr |

Census Card No. 1771, P. O. Eufaula, Enrolled March 31, 1900

| 1 | Allen, Lovina | 82 | F | ½ | | Canard | D | Cr | Canard | D | Cr |

No. 1 reported dead

Census Card No. 1772, P. O. Hitchita, Enrolled March 31, 1900

| 1 | Berryhill, Richard | 50 | M | ⅝ | | Sam Berryhill | D | Cr | Nawkee | D | Cr |
| 2 | Berryhill, Josephine | 55 | F | ¼ | Wf | Wadsworth | D | Non | Louina Allen | L | Cr |

Census Card No. 1773, P. O. Henryetta, Enrolled April 2, 1900

| 1 | Starr, Daniel | 35 | M | F | | Tusekiah Hotke | D | Cr | Hotke | D | Cr |
| 2 | Starr, Louisa | 20 | F | F | Wf | Simmer Thompson | L | Cr | Sophia Thompson | D | Cr |

Census Card No. 1774, P. O. Salem, Enrolled April 2, 1900; No. 3, March 19, 1901

1	Sands, Phillip	26	M	F		Titanecha	D	Cr	Lucinda	D	Cr
2	Sands, Martha	16	F	F	Wf	Wady Fields	D	Cr	Lena Fields	D	Cr
3	Sands, Stella	1	F	F	D	No. 1	L	Cr	No. 2	L	Cr

No. 1 died May 8, 1905. No. 3 reported dead.

Census Card No. 1775, P. O. Salem, Enrolled April 2, 1900

| 1 | Thompson, Thomas | 23 | M | F | | Fa Emarthla | D | Cr | Youthega | D | Cr |
| 2 | Thompson, Rose | 25 | F | F | Wf | Titanecha | D | Cr | Lucinda | D | Cr |

Census Card No. 1776, P. O. Weleetka, Enrolled April 2, 1900

1	Likowski, Sarah A.	22	F	¾		David C. Ingram	L	Cr	Mary Ingram	L	Cr
2	Likowski, Herman A.	2	M	⅜	S	John W. Likowski	L	Non	No. 1	L	Cr
3	Likowski, William H.	1moM		⅜	S	John W. Likowski	L	Non	No. 1	L	Cr

No. 1 died January 25, 1904. No. 3 died June 23, 1908.

Census Card No. 1777, P. O. Senora, Enrolled April 2, 1900

| 1 | Fisher, Sarah A. | 60 | F | ⅛ | | Wiley Ingram | D | Cr | Louisa Ingram | D | Cr |

No. 1 died April 9, 1900

Census Card No. 1778, P. O. Okmulgee, Enrolled April 2, 1900

1	Haynes, Samuel J.	40	M	F		John Haynes	D	Cr	Lucy Nelson	D	Cr
2	Haynes, Sarah	39	F	¾	Wf	E. H. LeBlance	L	Cr	Miley LeBlance	D	Cr
3	Haynes, Stella J.	11	F	⅞	D	No. 1	L	Cr	No. 2	L	Cr
4	Haynes, John	6	M	⅞	S	No. 1	L	Cr	No. 2	L	Cr
5	Haynes, Elijah	1	M	⅞	S	No. 1	L	Cr	No. 2	L	Cr
6	Thorpe, Fannie	19	F	¼	StD	No. 1	L	Cr	No. 2	L	Cr

119

Roll No.	No.	NAME	Age	Sex	Blood	Rel.	NAME OF FATHER	Liv.	Cit.	NAME OF MOTHER	Liv.
		Census Card No. 1779, P. O. Checotah, Enrolled April 3, 1900									
5689	1	Sevier, Louis	23	M	F		Willie Sevier	D	Cr	Louiney Sekinna	D
		No. 1 reported dead									
		Census Card No. 1780, P. O. Holdenville, Enrolled April 4, 1900									
5690	1	Buck, Simpson	25	M	¼		Walter Buck	L	Sem	Sarah Parnosky	D
		Census Card No. 1781, P. O. Eufaula, Enrolled April 4, 1900									
5691	1	Raiford, Arthur E.	21	M	¼		Philip Raiford	D	Cr	Jennetta Raiford	L
		Census Card No. 1782, P. O. Eufaula, Enrolled April 4, 1900									
5692	1	Raiford, Jennetta	56	F	½		John Thomas	D	Non	Metayaha	D
5693	2	Raiford, Ferdinand	27	M	¼	S	Phillip Raiford	D	Non	No. 1	L
		No. 1 died November 20, 1903									
		Census Card No. 1783, P. O. Eufaula, Enrolled April 4, 1900									
5694	1	Coon, Suckie	40	F	F		Watka Harjo	D	Cr	Salihohkee	D
5695	2	Gouge, Daisy	15	F	F	D	Dave Gouge	D	Cr	No. 1	L
		No. 1 died August 20, 1902. No. 2 died February 11, 1905.									
		Census Card No. 1784, P. O. Eufaula, Enrolled April 4, 1900									
5696	1	Raiford, Ossie	25	M	¼		Phillip Raiford	D	Non	Jennetta Raiford	L
		Census Card No. 1785, P. O. Muskogee, Enrolled April 6, 1900									
5697	1	Smith, Grace	21	F	⅛		John T. Smith	D	Non	Rachel Smith	D
		Census Card No. 1786, P. O. Schulter, Enrolled April 6, 1900									
5698	1	Randall, Elsie	40	F	F		Chockota Yahola	D	Cr	Sukey	D
		No. 1 reported dead									
		Census Card No. 1787, P. O. Okmulgee, Enrolled April 6, 1900; No. 2, May 20, 1901									
5699	1	Randall, Mollie	43	F	F		Jim Randall	D	Cr	Kinba	D
5700	2	Randall, Peter	40	M	F	Bro	Jim Randall	D	Cr	Tecoake	D
		No. 2 died March 3, 1900									
		Census Card No. 1788, P. O. Schulter, Enrolled April 6, 1900									
5701	1	Pakoska, Lucy	42	F	F		Jim Randall	D	Cr	Tekoge	D
5702	2	Pakoska, Lewis	17	M	F	S	Joe Pokoska	D	Cr	No. 1	L
5703	3	Pakoska, Noah	14	M	F	S	Joe Pokoska	D	Cr	No. 1	L
5704	4	Pakoska, Liza	11	F	F	D	Joe Pokoska	D	Cr	No. 1	L
		Census Card No. 1789, P. O. Schulter, Enrolled April 6, 1900; No. 4, May 20, 1901									
5705	1	Toskey, Ned	23	M	F		Toskey	D	Cr	Annie Toskey	D
5706	2	Toskey, Cinda	20	F	F	Niece	Siah Canard	D	Cr	Lucy Toskey	D
5707	3	Toskey, Susana	16	F	F	Niece	Topley Carr	D	Cr	Lucy Toskey	D
5708	4	Toskey, Lucy	48	F	F	Aunt	Cho Emarthla	D	Cr	Lucy Toskey	D
		Nos. 1 and 4 reported dead									
		Census Card No. 1790, P. O. Schulter, Enrolled April 6, 1900									
5709	1	Toskey, Eli	20	M	F		Toskey	D	Cr	Annie Toskey	D
		Census Card No. 1791, P. O. Schulter, Enrolled April 6, 1900									
5710	1	Hawkins, Jammie	26	M	F		Parney Hawkins	D	Cr	Mary Hawkins	D
		Census Card No. 1792, P. O. Schulter, Enrolled April 6, 1900; Nos. 2 and 3, July 2, 1900									
5711	1	Simer, Moonie	30	M	F		Samochee	D	Cr	Amochee	D
5712	2	Simer, Millie	35	F	F	Wf	John Micco	D	Cr	Marsey Micco	D
5713	3	Stake, Winey	12	F	F	StD	Jonas Stake	D	Cr	No. 2	L
		Census Card No. 1793, P. O. Springfield, Mo.; 1726 Miner Street, Enrolled April 7, 1900									
5714	1	Grayson, John	29	M	¼		Doc Grayson	D	Cr	Susan Grayson	L
		Census Card No. 1794, P. O. Okmulgee, Enrolled April 9, 1900									
5715	1	Haynes, Joseph	40	M	F		John Haynes	D	Cr	Lossie Nelson	D
5716	2	Haynes, Dicey	50	F	F	Wf	Unknown	D	Cr	Malinda	D
		No. 1 died January 1905. No. 2 died October or November 1906.									
		Census Card No. 1795, P. O. Wetumka, Enrolled April 9, 1900; No. 3, May 4, 1900									
5717	1	Mingo, Joseph	26	M	F		Billy Mingo	D	Cr	Homa Hoey	D
5718	2	Mingo, Aggie	17	F	F	Wf	Thos. Yahola	L	Cr	Mitiagne	D
5719	3	Mingo, Monroe	4mo	M	F	S	No. 1	L	Cr	No. 2	L
		Census Card No. 1796, P. O. Muskogee, Enrolled April 9, 1900									
5720	1	Farrell, Fred	15	M	1-16		John Farrell	L	Non	Adda Farrell	D
		Census Card No. 1797, P. O. Bearden, Enrolled April 9, 1900									
5721	1	Anderson, Millie	22	F	½		Jim Chief	L	Chick Freed	Celia Chief	D
5722	2	Anderson, Phoebe	1	F	¾	D	Tom Anderson	D	Cr	No. 1	L
		No. 2 died December 15, 1901									
		Census Card No. 1798, P. O. Fame, Enrolled April 11, 1900									
5723	1	Barnett, Jonas	22	M	F		Yarda Barnett	D	Cr	Judie Barnett	D
		No. 1 died June 1, 1912									
		Census Card No. 1799, P. O. Eufaula, Enrolled April 11, 1900									
5724	1	Barnett, Louisa	27	F	F		Yarda Barnett	D	Cr	Judie Barnett	D
		No. 1 died 1905									
		Census Card No. 1800, P. O. Fame, Enrolled April 11, 1900									
5725	1	Barnett, Harley	20	F	F		James Barnett	L	Cr	Mollie Anna	D
		Census Card No. 1801, P. O. Wetumka, Enrolled April 11, 1900									
5726	1	Cain, Daniel	30	M	F		Nokos Yahola	D	Cr	Sissy Yahola	D
5727	2	Cain, Nisey	30	F	F	Wf	Magillis Harjo	L	Cr	Losky Harjo	L
5728	3	Cain, Roman	7mo	M	F	S	No. 1	L	Cr	No. 2	L
5729	4	Cain, Allie	7	F	F	D	No. 1	L	Cr	No. 2	L
5730	5	Cain, Polly	6	F	F	D	No. 1	L	Cr	No. 2	L

No.	NAME	Age	Sex	Blood	Rel.	NAME OF FATHER	Liv.	Cit.	NAME OF MOTHER	Liv.	Cit.
Census Card No. 1802, P. O. Coweta, Enrolled April 12, 1900											
1	Bruner, Mary	25	F	F		Wm. Berryhill	L	Cr	Rachel Berryhill	D	Cr
2	Bruner, Emmett	5	M	F	S	Richard Bruner	L	Cr	No. 1	L	Cr
3	Bruner, George E.	5moM	F		S	Richard Bruner	L	Cr	No. 1	L	Cr
4	Bruner, Georgia	10moF	F	D		Richard Bruner	L	Cr	No. 1	L	Cr
	No. 4 died 1900										
Census Card No. 1803, P. O. Wewoka, Enrolled April 12, 1900											
1	Long, Daniel A.	25	M	¾		Jacob Long	L	Sem	Lucy Long	L	Cr
Census Card No. 1804, P. O. Wewoka, Enrolled April 12, 1900											
1	Long, Lucy B.	40	F	½		Robert Stewart	L	Non	Sofa Stewart	D	Cr
Census Card No. 1805, P. O. Okemah, Enrolled April 12, 1900											
1	Beddoe, Virona	12	F	¼		Louzo Beddoe	L	Non	Martha R. Beddoe	D	Cr
2	Beddoe, Morrellis R.	10	M	¼	Bro	Louzo Beddoe	L	Non	Martha R. Beddoe	D	Cr
3	Beddoe, Hettie R.	8	F	¼	Sis	Lonzo Beddoe	L	Non	Nartha R. Beddoe	D	Cr
4	Beddoe, Lonzo A.	6	M	¼	Bro	Lonzo Beddoe	L	Non	Martha R. Beddoe	D	Cr
5	Beddoe, Malvina P.	4	F	¼	Sis	Louzo Beddoe	L	Non	Martha R. Beddoe	D	Cr
	No. 3 died July 12, 1907.										
Census Card No. 1806, P. O. Lee, Enrolled April 13, 1900											
1	McNack, Wallace C.	63	M	¾		Elic McNac	D	Cr	Vicey McNac	D	Cr
	No. 1 reported dead										
Census Card No. 1807, P. O. Eufaula, Enrolled April 13, 1900											
1	McIntosh, Luke G.	49	M	½		Chillie McIntosh	D	Cr	Leah McIntosh	D	Cr
2	McIntosh, Leona	35	F	½	Wf	P. H. Raiford	L	Cr	Jennetta Raiford	L	Cr
3	McIntosh, Lucius	14	M	½	S	No. 1	L	Cr	No. 2	L	Cr
4	McIntosh, Jennetta	8	F	½	D	No. 1	L	Cr	No. 2	L	Cr
5	McIntosh, Minnie	6	F	½	D	No. 1	L	Cr	No. 2	L	Cr
6	McIntosh, Dessie Lee	1	F	½	D	No. 1	L	Cr	No. 2	L	Cr
	No. 1 died December 1, 1912. Nos. 2, 5 and 6 reported dead.										
Census Card No. 1808, P. O. Vivian, Enrolled April 13, 1900											
1	Barnett, Jonas	16	M	F		Thomas Barnett	D	Cr	Millie Barnett	D	Cr
2	Barnett, Morris	14	M	F	Bro	Thomas Barnett	D	Cr	Millie Barnett	D	Cr
3	Barnett, Lillie	11	F	F	Sis	Thomas Barnett	D	Cr	Millie Barnett	D	Cr
4	Barnett, Hannah	9	F	F	Sis	Thomas Barnett	D	Cr	Millie Barnett	D	Cr
	No. 1 died July 27, 1911. No. 4 died March 4, 1908.										
Census Card No. 1809, P. O. Coweta, Enrolled April 14, 1900											
1	Gibson, Leonard	50	M	F		Wilson Tiger	D	Cr	Tumfumahke	D	Cr
2	Gibson, Dicey	45	F	F	Wf	Mittilahke	D	Cr	Unknown	D	Cr
3	Island, Haymen	15	M	F	StS	Ben Island	L	Cr	No. 2	L	Cr
4	Island, Hettie	12	F	F	StD	Ben Island	L	Cr	No. 2	L	Cr
	No. 1 died January 28, 1905. No. 2 died September 3, 1904. No. 3 died November 14, 1902. No. 4 died May 12, 1903.										
Census Card No. 1810, P. O. Porter, Enrolled April 14, 1900											
1	Marshall, George	30	M	¼		George Marshall	D	C	Elizabeth Marshall	D	Cr
2	Marshall, Violet	7	F	⅛	D	No. 1	L	Cr	Nettie Marshall	L	Non
	No. 1 died Summer 1906										
Census Card No. 1811, P. O. Eufaula, Enrolled April 16, 1900											
1	Self, Mary J.	48	F	⅛		E. A. Self	D	Cr	Minerva Self	D	Non
2	Self, Callie M.	17	F	3-16	D	Thomas J. Self	D	Cr	No. 1	L	Cr
3	Self, Homer J.	13	M	3-16	S	Thomas J. Self	D	Cr	No. 1	L	Cr
4	Self, Roxy Anna	12	F	3-16	D	Thomas J. Self	D	Cr	No. 1	L	Cr
5	Self, Katie	9	F	3-16	D	Thomas J. Self	D	Cr	No. 1	L	Cr
6	Self, Grover	7	M	3-16	S	Thomas J. Self	D	Cr	No. 1	L	Cr
Census Card No. 1812, P. O. Vivian, Enrolled April 16, 1900.											
1	Barnett, Charles	42	M	F		Hosiah Hola	D	Cr	Sofoala Dogee	D	Cr
2	Barnett, Jennie	32	F	F	Wf	Wash Canard	D	Cr	Jennie Canard	D	Cr
3	Barnett, Samuel	8	M	F	S	No. 1	L	Cr	No. 2	L	Cr
4	Barnett, George	7	M	F	S	No. 1	L	Cr	No. 2	L	Cr
5	Barnett, Leah	4	F	F	D	No. 1	L	Cr	No. 2	L	Cr
6	Barnett, Roman	2	M	F	D	No. 1	L	Cr	No. 2	L	Cr
7	Barnett, Ella	1	F	F	D	No. 1	L	Cr	No. 2	L	Cr
8	Hardridge, Solomon	10	M	F	St-S	Taylor Hardridge	L	Cr	No. 2	L	Cr
	No. 8 reported dead.										
Census Card No. 1813, P. O. Gibson Station, Enrolled April 16, 1900.											
1	Shannon, Floyd	21	M	⅛		George Shannon	L	Non	Mary B. Shannon	D	Cr
Census Card No. 1814, P. O. Gib on Station, Enrolled April 16, 1900.											
1	Shannon, Daisy	25	F	⅛		George Shannon	L	Non	Mary D. Shannon	D	Cr
Census Card No. 1815, P. O. Muskogee, Enrolled April 16, 1900.											
1	Shannon, Lucy H.	23	F	⅛		George Shannon	L	Non	Mary D. Shannon	D	Cr
Census Card No. 1816, P. O. Wetumka, Enrolled April 17, 1900.											
1	"Lucy"	27	F	F		Nocus Harjo	D	Cr	Tothohyee	L	Cr
2	"Lucinda"	7	F	F	D	Charles Coachman	L	Cr	No. 1	L	Cr
3	"Porter"	6	M	F	S	Charles Coachman	L	Cr	No. 1	L	Cr
4	"Culbert"	5	M	F	S	Charles Coachman	L	Cr	No. 1	L	Cr
	No. 4 died April, 1903. No. 2 reported dead.										
Census Card No. 1817, P. O. Wetumka, Enrolled April 16, 1900.											
1	Buck Joseph	28	M	F		Daniel Buck	L	Cr	Mary Buck	L	Cr
2	Buck, Annie	26	M	F	Wf	Artus Hobie	L	Cr	Losana	L	Cr
3	Buck, Roman	2	M	F	S	No. 1	L	Cr	No. 2	L	Cr
	No. 1 died February 16, 1904.										

Roll No.	No.	NAME	Age	Sex	Blood	Rel.	NAME OF FATHER	Liv.	Cit.	NAME OF MOTHER	Liv.	Cit.
	Census Card No. 1818, P. O. Eufaula, Enrolled April 16, 1900. No.. 2, May 24, 1901.											
5783	1	McWilliams, Thomas	56	M	½		Unknown	D	Non	Sukey Fox	D	Cr
5784	2	McWilliams, Miley	66	F	F	Wf	Unknown	D	Cr	Mary Monack	D	Cr
		No. 2 d ed May 3, 1899.										
	Census Card No. 1819, P. O. Hoffman, Enrolled April 17, 1900.											
5785	1	Larney, Jennie	61	F	F		Nehah, Thlocco	D	Cr	Unknown	D	Cr
	Census Card No. 1820, P. O. Senora, Enrolled April 17, 1900; No. 2 May 7, 1900; No. 3, June 6, 1900.											
5786	1	"Sumsey"	45	M	F		Nehah Thlocco	D	Cr	Lucy	D	Cr
5787	2	"Sumsey", Lissie	40	F	F	Wf	Allummee	D	Cr	Itcolachee	D	Cr
5788	3	Hawkins, Millie	18	F	½	StD.	Tom Hawkins	D	Sem	No. 2	L	Cr
		No. 1 died Jan. 12, 1903. No. 2 died Dec., 1901. No. 3 died Dec., 1901.										
	Census Card No. 1821, P. O. Yeager, Enrolled April 17, 1900.											
5789	1	Hill, Mitchell	18	M	F		George Hill	L	Cr	Annie Harjo	L	Cr
	Census Card No. 1822, P. O. Brush Hill, Enrolled April 18, 1900.											
5790	1	Thompson, Rose	41	F	¼		Bristow	D	Cr	Kate Thlocco	D	Cr
	Census Card No. 1823, P. O. Checotah, Enrolled April 18, 1900.											
5791	1	Keys, Sam R.	30	M	1-16		Sam Keys	L	Chee	Sarah Keys	L	Cr
5792	2	Keys, Jesse	9	m	1-32	S	No. 1	L	Cr	Martha Keys	L	Non
5793	3	Keys, Pearl	2	F	1-32	D	No. 1	L	Cr	Martha Keys	L	Non
	Census Card No. 1824, P. O. Wetumka, Enrolled April 18, 1900.											
5794	1	Bird, Charlie	37	M	F		Fos Harjo	D	Cr	Kissie Harjo	D	Cr
5795	2	Bird, Katie	28	F	F	Wf	Osche Harjo	D	Cr	Louiney Lowe	L	Cr
5796	3	Bird, Hullie	10	M	F	S	No. 1	L	Cr	No. 2	L	Cr
5797	4	Bird, Willie	8	M	F	S	No. 1	L	Cr	No. 2	L	Cr
5798	5	Bird, Edmund	6	M	F	S	No. 1	L	Cr	No. 2	L	Cr
5799	6	Bird, Albert	2	M	F	S	No. 1	L	Cr	No. 2	L	Cr
		No. 2 died Sept. 25, 1900. No. 3 died April 9, 1906. No. 5 died July 12, 1902.										
	Census Card No. 1825, P. O. Wetumka, Enrolled April 18, 1900											
5800	1	Lowe, Jackson	26	M	F		Osche Harjo	D	Cr	Louiney Lowe	L	Cr
5801	2	Lowe, Lena	22	F	F	Wf	Succharty Thlocco	D	Cr	Kissie Harjo	D	Cr
5802	3	Lowe, Joanna	2	F	F	D	No. 1	L	Cr	No. 2	L	Cr
	Census Card No. 1826, P. O. Holdenville, Enrolled April 18, 1900; No. 2, March 28, 1901											
5803	1	Smith, Seper	21	M	F		Aharlok, Yahola	D	Cr	Unknown	D	Cr
5804	2	Smith, Napka	16	M	F	Bro	Aharlok Yahola	D	Cr	Unknown	D	Cr
	Census Card No. 1827, P. O. Eufaula, Enrolled April 20, 1900											
5805	1	Jessie, Lillie	70	F	F		Unknown	D	Cr	Pinyer	D	Cr
	Census Card No. 1828, P. O. Eufaula, Enrolled April 20, 1900											
5806	1	Crabtree, James C.	32	M	1-32		Gabriel M. Crabtree	D	Cr	Sallie Crabtree	L	Non
5807	2	Crabtree, Shelton B.	4	M	1-64	S	No. 1	L	Cr	Janie Crabtree	L	Non
5808	3	Crabtree, Lurline R.	3mo	F	1-64	D	No. 1	L	Cr	Janie Crabtree	L	Non
	Census Card No. 1829, P. O. Muskogee, Enrolled April 20, 1900											
5809	1	McNac, Lena	8	F	F		Cully McNac	D	Cr	Leah McNac	D	Cr
	Census Card No. 1830, P. O. Muskogee, Enrolled April 21, 1900											
5810	1	Higgins, Josephine	42	F	½		John C. Nevins	D	Cher	Delilah Nevins	D	Cr
5811	2	Nivens, Willie	19	M	¼	S	William Jones	L	Non	No. 1	L	Cr
5812	3	Nivens, Jessie	14	F	¼	D	William Jones	L	Non	No. 1	L	Cr
	Census Card No. 1831, P. O. Tulsa, Enrolled April 23, 1900; No. 4 May 22, 1901											
5813	1	Bruner, William G.	28	M	F		George Bruner	D	Cr	Anna Partridge	L	Cr
5814	2	Bruner, Jennie	22	F	F	Wf	Albert Sunny	D	Cr	Katie	L	Cr
5815	3	Bruner, Emanuel	10 mo	M	F	S	No. 1	L	Cr	No. 2	L	Cr
5816	4	Bruner, Lewis	3	M	F	S	No. 1	L	Cr	Bettie Vore	D	Cr
		No. 3 died September 30, 1900. No. 4 died May 25, 1899										
	Census Card No. 1832, P. O. Wetumka, Enrolled April 23, 1900; No. 3 May 3, 1901											
5817	1	Dawson, Willie	27	M	F		Lawrence	D	Cr	Unknown	D	Cr
5818	2	Dawson, Alice	3	F	F	D	No. 1	L	Cr	Martha Dawson	L	Cr
5819	3	Dawson, Martha	19	F	F	Wf	Sampson Scott	L	Cr	Sarah Scott	L	Cr
		Nos. 1 and 3 reported dead										
	Census Card No. 1833, P. O. Keokuk Falls, Enrolled April 23, 1900											
5820	1	Yahola, Barney	51	M	F		Nocha Yahola	D	Cr	Nothohye	D	Cr
5821	2	Yahola, Kizzie	51	F	F	Wf	Unknown	D	Cr	Unknown	D	Cr
5822	3	Harjo, Beasley	17	F	F	Ward	Fushutche Mekko	D	Cr	Sadie	D	Cr
		No. 3 died March 10, 1904. No. 1 died February 25, 1905										
	Census Card No. 1834, P. O. Eufaula, Enrolled April 23, 1900											
5823	1	Marshall, Walter	22	M	F		Phillip Marshall	D	Cr	Unknown	D	Cr
	Census Card No. 1835, P. O. Bryant, Enrolled April 23, 1900; No. 2 April 24, 1900											
5824	1	Smith, Charity	20	F	½		James Grayson	D	Cr	Ellen Grayson	D	Cr
5825	2	Smith, Willie G.	1	M	½	S	Lee Anderson Smith	L	Cr	No. 1	L	Cr
		No. 1 died August 2, 1902. No. 2 died 1900										
	Census Card No. 1836, P. O. Eufaula, Enrolled April 23, 1900											
5826	1	Carr, Limbo	43	M	F		Folwatustanoga	D	Cr	Mahala	D	Cr
5827	2	Carr, Millie	35	F	F	Wf	Hunter	L	Cr	Lizzie	D	Cr
5828	3	Carr, Bessie	8	F	F	D	No. 1	L	Cr	No. 2	L	Cr
5829	4	Carr, Salina	3	F	F	D	No. 1	L	Cr	No. 2	L	Cr
5830	5	Carr, Ellen	1	F	F	D	No. 1	L	Cr	No. 2	L	Cr
		No. 1 died March 14, 1908										
	Census Card No. 1837, P. O. Calvin, Enrolled April 24, 1900											
5831	1	Alexander, James	38	M	F		Alex Alexander	D	Cr	Sally Alexander	D	Cr
5832	2	Alexander, Nancy	24	F	F	Wf	Barefoot	L	Cr	Ulsar	L	Cr

Roll No.	No.	NAME	Age	Sex	Blood	Rel.	NAME OF FATHER	Liv.	Cit.	NAME OF MOTHER	Liv.	Cit.
		Census Card No. 1838, P. O. Irene, Enrolled April 25, 1900										
5833	1	Baker, Rebecca J.	29	F	F		Barney Yahola	L	Cr	Hannah Wolf	L	Cr
5834	2	Baker, Eldo	7	M	F	S	Kinkehe N. Baker	L	Sem	No. 1	L	Cr
5835	3	Baker, Butler	6	M	F	S	Kinkehe N. Baker	L	Sem	No. 1	L	Cr
5836	4	Baker, Maud Anna	4	F	F	D	Kinkehe N. Baker	L	Sem	No. 1	L	Cr
5837	5	Baker, Clara Belle	2	F	F	D	Kinkehe N. Baker	L	Sem	No. 1	L	Cr
5838	6	Baker, Benjamin W.	8 mo	M	F	S	Kinkehe N. Baker	L	Sem	No. 1	L	Cr
		No. 5 died February 24, 1900. No. 2 died March 29, 1905										
		Census Card No. 1839, P. O. Schoolton, Enrolled April 25, 1900; No. 7 March 27, 1901; No. 8 May 8, 1901										
5839	1	Knight, Wilson	46	M	F		Knightley Walker	D	Cr	Iyogee	D	Cr
5840	2	Knight, Haney	34	F	F	Wf	Emarthley Harjo	D	Cr	Conarhohay	D	Cr
5841	3	Knight, Tochee	18	F	F	D	No. 1	L	Cr	No. 2	L	Cr
5842	4	Knight, Mary	16	F	F	D	No. 1	L	Cr	No. 2	L	Cr
5843	5	Knight, Misley	8 mo	M	F		No. 1	L	Cr	No. 2	L	Cr
5844	6	Sands, Roley	7	M	F	Ward	Daniel Sands	L	Cr	Miley Sands	D	Cr
5845	7	Harjo, Lumsey	15	M	F	Ward	Marthanockee	L	Cr	Millie Cornelius	L	Cr
5846	8	Knight, Georgie	3	M	F	S	No. 1	L	Cr	No. 2	L	Cr
		No. 8 died November 9, 1901. Nos. 1 and 4 reported dead										
		Census Card No. 1840, P. O. Arbeka, Enrolled April 25, 1900; No. 3 May 8, 1901										
5847	1	Sands, Daniel	45	M	F		Old Sands	D	Cr	Unknown	D	Cr
5848	2	Sands, Robert	12	M	F	S	No. 1	L	Cr	No. 3	L	Cr
5849	3	Sands, Miley	22	F	F	Wf	Jackson	D	Cr	Okowelahgee	D	Cr
		No. 2 died October 1904. No. 3 died April 26, 1900										
		Census Card No. 1841, P. O. Arbeka, Enrolled April 25, 1900										
5850	1	Yarbrough, James	42	M	F		Henneha Micco	D	Cr	Coashta	D	Cr
		Census Card No. 1842, P. O. Schoolton, Enrolled April 25, 1900										
5851	1	Cornelius, George	47	M	F		Unknown	D	Cr	Ishogoye	D	Cr
5852	2	Cornelius, Millie	54	F	F	Wf	Lemahte Harjo	D	Cr	Konahoke	D	Cr
		No. 2 died May 1, 1914. No. 1 reported dead										
		Census Card No. 1843, P. O. Arbeka, Enrolled April 25, 1900										
5853	1	Jackson, Saber	28	M	F		Jackson	D	Cr	Charlage	D	Cr
5854	2	Jackson, Nancy	2 mo	F	F	D	No. 1	L	Cr	Lucy Jackson	L	Cr
		No. 2 died May 10, 1901										
		Census Card No. 1844, P. O. Coweta, Enrolled April 25, 1900										
5855	1	Marshall, Thomas J.	2	M	5/8		George Marshall	D	Cr	Elizabeth Marshall	D	Cr
		No. 1 died February 4, 1905										
		Census Card No. 1845, P. O. Arbeka, Enrolled April 25, 1900										
5856	1	Chupko, Misley	46	M	F		Ema Harjo	D	Cr	Unknown	D	Cr
5857	2	Chupko, Martha	40	F	F	Wf	Nahkup Micco	D	Cr	Lydey	D	Cr
		No. 1 died May 15, 1911. No. 2 reported dead										
		Census Card No. 1846, P. O. Arbeka, Enrolled April 25, 1900										
5858	1	Sands, Moley	30	M	F		Okdasus Harjo	D	Cr	Louisa Sands	D	Cr
5859	2	Sands, Emma	20	F	F	Wf	Hodalga Harjo	D	Cr	Millie Cornelius	L	Cr
5860	3	Sands, John	4	M	F	S	No. 1	L	Cr	No. 2	L	Cr
5861	4	Sands, Amous	5 mo	M	F	S	No. 1	L	Cr	No. 2	L	Cr
		No. 1 died January 1903. No. 4 died January 1, 1904										
		Census Card No. 1847, P. O. Wetumka, Enrolled April 25, 1900										
5862	1	Knight, David	28	M	F		Wm. Knight	D	Cr	Louviney	D	Cr
5863	2	Knight, Nicey	22	F	F	Wf	Unknown	D	Cr	Miley	L	Cr
		No. 1 reported dead										
		Census Card No. 1848, P. O. Paden, Enrolled April 25, 1900										
5864	1	Sands, Taylor	21	M	F		Carlano Sand	D	Cr	Dannar	D	Cr
5865	2	Sands, Annie	17	F	F	Wf	Jackson Knight	L	Cr	Halloga	D	Cr
5866	3	Sands, Ella	1	F	F	D	No. 1	L	Cr	No. 2	L	Cr
		No. 3 died June 3, 1902. No. 1 reported dead										
		Census Card No. 1849, P. O. Schoolton, Enrolled April 26, 1900; Nos. 6, 7 and 8 March 19, 1901										
5867	1	Jones, Lucinda	42	F	1/2		D. C. Cox	L	Non	Lucy Cox	D	Cr
5868	2	Jones, Emma	20	F	3/4	D	N. B. Jones	D	Cr	No. 1	L	Cr
5869	3	Jones, John	16	M	3/4	D	N. B. Jones	D	Cr	No. 1	L	Cr
5870	4	Jones, Lillie	8	F	3/4	D	N. B. Jones	D	Cr	No. 1	L	Cr
5871	5	Lena, Peter	8	M	1/2	Ward	Willie Lena	L	Sem	Loda Lena	L	Cr
5872	6	Lena, Bessie	13	F	1/2	Ward	Willie Lena	L	Sem	Loda Lena	L	Cr
5873	7	Lena, John	10	M	1/2	Ward	Willie Lena	L	Sem	Loda Lena	L	Cr
5874	8	Lena, Betsey	7	F	1/2	Ward	Willie Lena	L	Sem	Loda Lena	L	Cr
		Nos. 6 and 7 reported dead										
		Census Card No. 1850, P. O. Schoolton, Enrolled April 26, 1900										
5875	1	Davis, Ella	19	F	3/4		N. B. Jones	D	Cr	Lucy Cox	D	Cr
5876	2	Davis, Willie	1 mo	M	7/8	S	Jessie Davis	L	Sem	No. 1	L	Cr
		Census Card No. 1851, P. O. Tulsa, Enrolled April 26, 1900										
5877	1	Smith, Frank	14	M	1-16		David C. Barnett	D	Cr	Louisa Smith	D	Non
		Census Card No. 1852, P. O. Wagoner, Enrolled April 26, 1900; No. 2 June 7, 1900; No. 3 May 22, 1901										
5878	1	Renfro, Bettie	20	F	1/4		Dick Sutherland	L	Non	Adelaid Sutherland	D	Cr
5879	2	Renfro, Willie	4 mo	M	1/8	S	William Renfro	L	Non	No. 1	L	Cr
5880	3	Renfro, Roy Tillman	2 1/2	M	1/8	S	William Renfro	L	Non	No. 1	L	Cr
		No. 3 died September 14, 1899										

Roll No.	No.	NAME	Age	Sex	Blood	Rel.	NAME OF FATHER	Liv.	Cit.	NAME OF MOTHER	Liv.	Cit.
		Census Card No. 1853, P. O. Lenna, Enrolled April 26, 1900										
5881	1	Evans, Vina	38	F	½		Tiger Phillip	D	Cr	Jane Phillip	D	Cr
5882	2	Evans, Mary A.	12	F	¼	D	R. W. Evans	L	Non	No. 1	L	Cr
5883	3	Evans, Minnie	10	F	¼	D	R. W. Evans	L	Non	No. 1	L	Cr
5884	4	Evans, Newton	8	M	¼	S	R. W. Evans	L	Non	No. 1	L	Cr
5885	5	Evans, Lona	6	F	¼	D	R. W. Evans	L	Non	No. 1	L	Cr
5886	6	Evans, Harrison	4	M	¼	S	R. W. Evans	L	Non	No. 1	L	Cr
5887	7	Evans, Lena	2	F	¼	D	R. W. Evans	L	Non	No. 1	L	Cr
		Census Card No. 1854, P. O. Senora, Enrolled April 26, 1900										
5888	1	Crawford, Henry	24	M	¼		Virgil Crawford	?	Non	Victoria Crawford	D	Cr
		Census Card No. 1855, P. O. Eufaula, Enrolled April 26, 1900										
5889	1	Matoy, Charles	24	M	⅛		John Matoy	D	Cher	Martha J. Walker	L	Cr
		Census Card No. 1856, P. O. Council Hill, Enrolled April 30, 1900										
5890	1	Post, Homer	22	M	¼		John Post	D	Cher	Adeline Young	L	Cr
		Census Card No. 1857, P. O. Wewoka, Enrolled May 1, 1900										
5891	1	Larney, Lucinda	25	F	F		John Chupco	D	Cr	Katie Chupco	L	Cr
5892	2	Larney, Pollie	15	F	F	D	Micco Larney	D	Cr	No. 1	L	Cr
5893	3	Larney, Eddie	8	M	F	S	Micco Larney	D	Cr	No. 1	L	Cr
5894	4	Larney, Dick	5	M	F	S	Micco Larney	D	Cr	No. 1	L	Cr
5895	5	Larney, Sarkerparcher	13	M	F	S	Micco Larney	D	Cr	No. 1	L	Cr
		No. 1 died January 1902. No. 5 died 1904										
		Census Card No. 1858, P. O. Pierce, Enrolled May 1, 1900										
5896	1	Lerblance, Jennie	37	F	½		Wm. Grimes	D	Cr	Wotka	D	Cr
5897	2	Lerblance, Ellen	11	F	½	D	W. P. Lerblance	D	Cr	No. 1	L	Cr
5898	3	Lerblance, Jeanetta	8	F	½	D	W. P. Lerblance	D	Cr	No. 1	L	Cr
5899	4	Lerblance, Harriet	5	F	½	D	W. P. Lerblance	D	Cr	No. 1	L	Cr
		Census Card No. 1859, P. O. Wetumka, Enrolled May 1, 1900										
5900	1	Hopiye, Isparney	36	M	F		Tulsa Yahola	D	Cr	Salothoga	D	Cr
5901	2	Hopiye, Jennie	29	F	F	Wf	Kanip Fixico	D	Cr	Marpeater	L	Cr
5902	3	Hopiye, Edmond	8	M	F	S	No. 1	L	Cr	No. 2	L	Cr
		No. 1 died January 30, 1907										
		Census Card No. 1860, P. O. Eufaula, Enrolled May 1, 1900										
5903	1	Glass, Neller	19	F	¼		John Post	D	Cr	Adeline Young	L	Cr
		Census Card No. 1861, P. O. Broken Arrow, Enrolled May 2, 1900										
5904	1	Perryman, Edmond	22	M	F		John W. Perryman	L	Cr	Nettie Perryman	D	Cr
		Census Card No. 1862, P. O. Schulter, Enrolled May 2, 1900										
5905	1	Henry, Thomas	50	M	F		Sicogee	D	Cr	Mahonihche	D	Cr
5906	2	Henry, Mary	50	F	F	Wf	Parhos Fixico	D	Cr	Lydia	D	Cr
5907	3	Henry, Francis	20	M	F	S	No. 1	L	Cr	Louisa	D	Cr
5908	4	Henry, Walter	16	M	F	S	No. 1	L	Cr	Louisa	D	Cr
		No. 1 died October 29, 1913. No. 2 reported dead										
		Census Card No. 1863, P. O. Senora, Enrolled May 2, 1900; No. 3 May 23, 1901										
5909	1	Lewis, Mary	30	F	F		Hichete Frank	L	Cr	Nancy	D	Cr
5910	2	Proctor, Nicey	4	F	F	D	Louis Proctor	L	Cr	No. 1	L	Cr
5911	3	Frank, Hitchete	70	M	F	Fath	Unknown	D	Cr	Unknown	D	Cr
		No. 3 died June 2, 1899										
		Census Card No. 1864, P. O. Holdneville, Enrolled May 2, 1900										
5912	1	Manley, Joseph	36	M	F		Fus Keneha	D	Cr	Unknown	D	Cr
5913	2	Manley, Sunny	30	F	F	Wf	Micco Charte	D	Cr	Lucinda	D	Cr
5914	3	Manley, Samuel	13	M	F	S	No. 1	L	Cr	No. 2	L	Cr
5915	4	Manley, Sarah	9	F	F	D	No. 1	L	Cr	No. 2	L	Cr
		No. 2 died May 3, 1900. No. 3 died December 1905										
		Census Card No. 1865, P. O. Mounds, Enrolled May 2, 1900										
5916	1	Boling, Martha	27	F	⅛		J. B. Self	L	Cr	Bettie Self	L	Non
5917	2	Boling, Sophia O.	3	F	1-16	D	W. F. Boling	L	Non	No. 1	L	Cr
		Census Card No. 1866, P. O. Yeager, Enrolled May 3, 1900										
5918	1	Harjo, Lilla	20	M	F		Neha Yaholar	D	Cr	Sallie	D	Cr
5919	2	Harjo, Rhoda	20	F	F	Wf	Yahologee	D	Cr	Louisa	D	Cr
		No. 2 died January 1907										
		Census Card No. 1867, P. O. Yeager, Enrolled May 3, 1900										
5920	1	Reed, Johnson	37	M	F		Peter	D	Cr	Louisa	D	Cr
5921	2	Lewis, Kizey	15	F	F	Niece	Lewis	D	Cr	Nancy	D	Cr
		Census Card No. 1868, P. O. Fentress, Enrolled May 4, 1900										
5922	1	Wesley, Joe	19	M	F		Muska	D	Cr	Soma	D	Cr
		Census Card No. 1869, P. O. Weleetka, Enrolled May 4, 1900										
5923	1	Wesley, Kentucky	28	M	F		Hulka Wesley	D	Cr	Lucinda Fat	L	Cr
		Census Card No. 1870, P. O. Bristow, Enrolled May 4, 1900										
5924	1	Beaver, John	40	M	F		Beaver	D	Cr	Unknown	D	Cr
		Census Card No. 1871, P. O. Fame, Enrolled May 4, 1900										
5925	1	Haynes, James	44	M	F		John Haynes	D	Cr	Sinta Haynes	D	Cr
5926	2	Haynes, Martha	23	F	F	Wf	Billy Tiger	D	Cr	Nancy Thompson	D	Cr
		No. 2 died April 16, 1909. No. 1 reported dead										
		Census Card No. 1872, P. O. Porter, Enrolled May 5, 1900										
5927	1	Thompson, Tom	23	M	F		March Thompson	L	Cr	Nicey Thompson	L	Cr
		Census Card No. 1873, P. O. Hitchita, Enrolled May 5, 1900										
5928	1	Thompson, Nicey	43	F	F		Hotulkey Tustarnug-gee	D	Cr	Esuthlka	D	Cr
5929	2	Thompson, Captain	19	M	F	S	March Thompson	L	Cr	No. 1	L	Cr
5930	3	Thompson, Rosa	16	F	F	D	March Thompson	L	Cr	No. 1	L	Cr
5931	4	Thompson, Sonny	14	M	F	S	March Thompson	L	Cr	No. 1	L	Cr
		No. 1 died July 27, 1901. No. 2 reported dead										

Roll No.	No.	NAME	Age	Sex	Blood	Rel.	NAME OF FATHER	Liv.	Cit.	NAME OF MOTHER	Liv.	Cit.
	Census Card No. 1874, P. O. Checotah, Enrolled May 5, 1900											
5932	1	Thompson, Sam	23	M	F		March Thompson	L	Cr	Nicey Thompson	L	Cr
	Census Card No. 1875, P. O. Burney Enrolled May 5, 1900											
5933	1	Thompson, Hully	25	M	F		Sola Thompson	D	Cr	Loska	D	Cr
	Census Card No. 1876, P. O. Pierce, Enrolled May 5, 1900											
5934	1	Thompson, Sarah	26	F	F		March Thompson	L	Cr	Nicey Thompson	L	Cr
5935	2	Morrison, Addie	1	F	F	D	Watie Morrison	L	Cr	No. 1	L	Cr
	Census Card No. 1877, P. O. Gibson Station, Enrolleed May 5, 1900											
5936	1	Grayson, Rose	38	F	¾		Charley Grayson	D	Cr	Chloe Grayson	D	Cr
5937	2	Andy, Cornelius	14	M	½	S	Lee Andy	L	Non	No. 1	L	Cr
5938	3	Brown, Nannie	12	F	½	D	John Brown	L	Cr	No. 1	L	Cr
5939	4	Brewer, Jessie	8	F	½	D	Nick Brewer	L	Cr	No. 1	L	Cr
5940	5	Tell, Amos	3	M	¼	GrS	Andy Tell	L	Non	Addie Tell	D	Cr
	Census Card No. 1878, P. O. Sapulpa, Enrolled May 5, 1900; Nos. 4, 5 and 6 May 16, 1901											
5941	1	Samuel, Jennie	45	F	F		Emarthloche	D	Cr	Nokehche	D	Cr
5942	2	Fulton, Friday	17	F	F	D	Fulton	L	Cr	No. 1	L	Cr
5943	3	Sarkache, Feney	15	F	F	D	Sarkahche	D	Cr	No. 1	L	Cr
5944	4	Billie, Emma	12	F	F	GrD	Billie Bigpond	L	Cr	Sophie Bigpond	L	Cr
5945	5	Billie, Jonas	10	M	F	GrS	Billie Bigpond	L	Cr	Sophie Bigpond	L	Cr
5946	6	Billie, Lena	8	F	F	GrD	Billie Bigpond	⅓L	Cr	Sophie Bigpond	L	Cr
		Nol 2 died January 8, 1902. No. 5 died January 15, 1903. No. 3 died January 16, 1903										
	Census Card No. 1879, P. O. Gibson Station, Enrolled May 5, 1900											
5947	1	Rogers, Melvina	19	F	½		Ollie Davis	L	Cr	Rose Grayson	L	Cr
5948	2	Rogers, Viola	1	F	¼	D	John Rogers	L	Non	No. 1	L	Cr
	Census Card No. 1880, P. O. Wetumka, Enrolled May 7, 1900											
5949	1	Hickman, Jack	50	M	½		Unknown	D	Non	Nellie Hickman	D	Cr
5950	2	Hickman, Eliza	50	F	F	Wf	Unknown	D	Cr	Unknown	D	Cr
		No. 1 reported dead										
	Census Card No. 1881, P. O. Wetumka, Enrolled May 7, 1900											
5951	1	Buck, Daniel	53	M	F		Cono Harjo	D	Cr	Harjo	D	Cr
5952	2	Buck, Mary	50	F	F	Wf	Woxie Fixico	D	Cr	Fixico	D	Cr
5953	3	Buck, Toney	7	M	F	S	No. 1	L	Cr	No. 2	L	Cr
5954	4	Buck, Roley	5	M	F	S	No. 1	L	Cr	No. 2	L	Cr
		No. 2 reported dead										
	Census Card No. 1882, P. O. Wetumka, Enrolled May 7, 1900											
5955	1	Piegon, Leetchee	37	F	F		Woxie Fixico	D	Cr	Fixico	D	Cr
	Census Card No. 1883, P. O. Wetumka, Enrolled May 7, 1900											
5956	1	Buck, William	22	M	F		Daniel Buck	L	Cr	Mary Buck	L	Cr
	Census Card No. 1884, P. O. Edna, Enrolled May 7, 1900											
5957	1	Osab, Solomon	21	M	F		Osah Fixico	D	Cr	Narheathowee	D	Cr
		No. 1 reported dead										
	Census Card No. 1885, P. O. Sasakwa, Enrolled May 7, 1900											
5958	1	Childers, Joe	21	M	F		Louis Childers	L	Cr	Susie Childers	D	Cr
	Census Card No. 1886, P. O. Wetumka, Enrolled May 7, 1900; No. 7 March 20, 1901											
5959	1	Scott, Winey	47	F	F		Conup Fixico	D	Cr	Chuthole	D	Cr
5960	2	Scott, Alec	16	M	F	S	Sampson Scott	D	Cr	No. 1	L	Cr
5961	3	Scott, Lucinda	10	F	F	D	Sampson Scott	D	Cr	No. 1	L	Cr
5962	4	Scott, Marcy	5	M	F	S	Sampson Scott	D	Cr	No. 1	L	Cr
5963	5	Scott, Harper	19	M	F	Neph	Margee Scott	D	Cr	Nazy Scott	D	Cr
5964	6	Tiger, Louisa	16	F	F	Niece	Lewis Scott	D	Cr	Nazy Scott	D	Cr
5965	7	Scott, Sampson	40	M	F	Hus	Huthlan Harjo	D	Cr	Unknown	D	Cr
		No. 7 died August 19, 1906										
	Census Card No. 1887, P. O. Tulsa, Enrolled May 8, 1900											
5966	1	Broyles, Ida B.	23	F	¼		Thomas W. Perry-man	L	Cr	Ella B. Perryman	L	Non
	Census Card No. 1888, P. O. Checotah; No. 4 Wagoner, Enrolled May 8, 1900											
5967	1	Lerblance, Frank H.	20	M	F		E. H. Lerblance	D	Cr	Nettie Lerblance	D	Cr
5968	2	Lerblance, Addie L.	17	F	F	Sis	E. H. Lerblance	D	Cr	Nettie Lerblance	D	Cr
5969	3	Lerblance, Howard P.	14	M	F	Bro	E. H. Lerblance	D	Cr	Nettie Lerblance	D	Cr
5970	4	Lerblance, Lizzie	12	F	F	Sis	E. H. Lerblance	D	Cr	Nettie Lerblance	D	Cr
	Census Card No. 1889, P. O. Hitchita, Enrolled May 9, 1900											
5971	1	Doyle, Wallace	24	M	¾		Dave Doyle	D	Cr	Scilla Doyle	D	Cr
		No. 1 died July 7, 1907										
	Census Card No. 1890, P. O. Wagoner, Enrolled May 10, 1900											
5972	1	Berry, Louise A.	39	F	⅛		Sam McFarland	D	Non	Anna Hawkins	D	Cr
5973	2	Berry, Anna Marie	17	F	1-16	D	W. D. Berry	L	Non	No. 1	L	Cr
	Census Card No. 1891, P. O. Morse, Enrolled May 10, 1900											
5974	1	King, Robert	21	M	F		Micco Chupco	D	Cr	Teyohe	D	Cr
		No. 1 died May 18, 1903										
	Census Card No. 1892, P. O. Castle, Enrolled May 10, 1900											
5975	1	Foster, Henry	32	M	F		Unknown	D	Cr	Betsey	D	Cr
5976	2	Foster, Janie	19	F	F	Wf	Micco Chupco	L	Cr	Teyohe	D	Cr
5977	3	Foster, Robinson	2	M	F	S	No. 1	L	Cr	Mylie	D	Cr
		No. 1 died October 1904. No. 3 died May 18, 1912										
	Census Card No. 1893, P. O. Rulsa, Enrolled May 10, 1900; No. 3 June 22, 1900											
5978	1	Hodge, John M.	25	M	½		Alvin T. Hodge	L	Cr	Mary Jane Hodge	L	Cr
5979	2	Hodge, Ethel	4	F	¼	D	No. 1	L	Cr	Minnie L. Hodge	L	Non
5980	3	Hodge, Oma M.	1	F	¼	D	No. 1	L	Cr	Minnie L. Hodge	L	Non
		No. 2 died May 18, 1912										

Census Card No. 1894, P. O. Arbeka, Enrolled May 11, 1900; Nos. 2 and 3 May 8, 1901

Roll No.	No.	NAME	Age	Sex	Blood	Rel.	NAME OF FATHER	Liv.	Cit.	NAME OF MOTHER	Liv.	Cit.
5981	1	Nevey, Annie	20	F	F		Lumhihche	D	Cr	Sohuleche	D	Cr
5982	2	Nevey, John	21	M	F	Hus	Hillubbe Emarthla	D	Cr	Linda	L	Cr
5983	3	Nevey, Johnie	3	M	F	S	No. 2	D	Cr	No. 1	L	Cr

No. 1 died July 7, 1904.   No. 2 died May 3, 1899.   No. 3 died April 7, 1900

Census Card No. 1895, P. O. Castle, Enrolled May 11, 1900

Roll No.	No.	NAME	Age	Sex	Blood	Rel.	NAME OF FATHER	Liv.	Cit.	NAME OF MOTHER	Liv.	Cit.
5984	1	Miller, Sam	57	M	F		Archie Yahola	D	Cr	Millie	D	Cr
5985	2	Miller, Lizzie	45	F	F	Wf	Carna	D	Cr	Mehakey	D	Cr
5986	3	Miller, Louisa	15	F	F	D	No. 1	L	Cr	No. 2	L	Cr
5987	4	Miller, Jennie	12	F	F	D	No. 1	L	Cr	No. 2	L	Cr
5988	5	Miller, Joney	10	M	F	S	No. 1	L	Cr	No. 2	L	Cr
5989	6	Miller, Nessey	6	F	F	D	No. 1	L	Cr	No. 2	L	Cr

No. 4 died December 27, 1909

Census Card No. 1896, P. O. Salem, Enrolled May 11, 1900

Roll No.	No.	NAME	Age	Sex	Blood	Rel.	NAME OF FATHER	Liv.	Cit.	NAME OF MOTHER	Liv.	Cit.
5990	1	Smith, John	29	M	$\frac{5}{8}$		John F. Smith	L	Cr	Louisa Smith	D	Cr

Census Card No. 1897, P. O. Arbeka, Enrolled May 11, 1900

Roll No.	No.	NAME	Age	Sex	Blood	Rel.	NAME OF FATHER	Liv.	Cit.	NAME OF MOTHER	Liv.	Cit.
5991	1	Knight, Fuller	24	M	F		Peter Knight	D	Cr	Labaney	D	Cr

No. 1 reported dead

Census Card No. 1898, P. O. Kellyville, Enrolled May 12, 1900

Roll No.	No.	NAME	Age	Sex	Blood	Rel.	NAME OF FATHER	Liv.	Cit.	NAME OF MOTHER	Liv.	Cit.
5992	1	John, McCully	20	M	F		Ahgogethlon	D	Cr	Majole	D	Cr

Census Card No. 1899, P. O. Kellyville, Enrolled May 12, 1900

Roll No.	No.	NAME	Age	Sex	Blood	Rel.	NAME OF FATHER	Liv.	Cit.	NAME OF MOTHER	Liv.	Cit.
5993	1	Harris, Mahele	22	M	F		Ahtah	D	Cr	Betsie	D	Cr
5994	2	Harris, Willie	1	M	$\frac{1}{2}$	S	Henry Harris	L	Non	No. 1	L	Cr

No. 1 died 1906 or 1907

Census Card No. 1900, P. O. No. 1, Holdenville, No. 3, Keokuk Falls, Enrolled May 12, 1901; No. 3, May 3, 1901

Roll No.	No.	NAME	Age	Sex	Blood	Rel.	NAME OF FATHER	Liv.	Cit.	NAME OF MOTHER	Liv.	Cit.
5995	1	Kernell, Dixon	32	M	F		Joe Kernell	D	Cr	Jane Harjo	L	Cr
5996	2	Kernell, Ida	12	F	$\frac{3}{4}$	D	No. 1	L	Cr	Lucy Kernell	D	Cr
5997	3	Davis, Selina	9	F	F	StD	Sam Davis	L	Cr	Lucy Toney	D	Cr

No. 3 died November 15, 1899

Census Card No. 1901, P. O. Pierce, Enrolled May 14, 1900

Roll No.	No.	NAME	Age	Sex	Blood	Rel.	NAME OF FATHER	Liv.	Cit.	NAME OF MOTHER	Liv.	Cit.
5998	1	King, Elizabeth	14	F	F		John McIntosh	L	Cr	Salina McIntosh	L	Cr

Census Card No. 1902, P. O. Wetumka, Enrolled May 14, 1900; No. 4, May 23, 1901

Roll No.	No.	NAME	Age	Sex	Blood	Rel.	NAME OF FATHER	Liv.	Cit.	NAME OF MOTHER	Liv.	Cit.
5999	1	Alexander, John L.	23	M	$\frac{3}{8}$		Geo. A. Alexander	L	Cr	Nancy Alexander	L	Cr
6000	2	Alexander, Hettie	24	F	F	Wf	Joseph Dunison	D	Cr	Unknown	D	Cr
6001	3	Alexander, Mattie G.	4moF		$\frac{7}{8}$	D	No. 1	L	Cr	No. 2	L	Cr
6002	4	Alexander, Nathan	16moM		$\frac{7}{8}$	S	No. 1	L	Cr	No. 2	L	Cr

No. 4 died August 14, 1899

Census Card No. 1903, P. O. Wetumka, Enrolled May 14, 1900; No. 6, March 20, 1901; No. 7, May 23, 1901.

Roll No.	No.	NAME	Age	Sex	Blood	Rel.	NAME OF FATHER	Liv.	Cit.	NAME OF MOTHER	Liv.	Cit.
6003	1	Robison, Mattie	25	F	$\frac{1}{2}$		Geo. A. Alexander	L	Cr	Nancy Alexander	L	Cr
6004	2	Robison, William R.	13	M	$\frac{1}{4}$	S	Joe S. Robison	L	Cr	Lizzie Robison	L	Cr
6005	3	Robison, George H.	11	M	$\frac{1}{4}$	S	Joe S. Robison	L	Cr	Lizzie Robison	L	Cr
6006	4	Robison, Rufus M.	10	M	$\frac{1}{4}$	S	Joe Robison	L	Cr	Lizzie Robison	L	Cr
6007	5	McGirth, Houston	16	M	F	Ward	John McGirth	D	Cr	Pollie McGirth	D	Cr
6008	6	Robison, Joe S.	44	M	$\frac{1}{4}$	Hus	William Robison	D	Cr	Adeline Robison	D	Chick
6009	7	Robison, Lizzie	4	F	$\frac{3}{8}$	D	No. 6	L	Cr	No. 1	L	Cr

No. 4 died November 18, 1901.   No. 1 died July 5, 1906.   No. 7 died October 1899.

Census Card No. 1904, P. O. Wetumka, Enrolled May 14, 1900

Roll No.	No.	NAME	Age	Sex	Blood	Rel.	NAME OF FATHER	Liv.	Cit.	NAME OF MOTHER	Liv.	Cit.
6010	1	Alexander, Robert L.	26	M	$\frac{1}{2}$		Geo. A. Alexander	L	Cr	Nancy Alexander	L	Cr

Census Card No. 1905, P. O. Wetumka, Enrolled May 14, 1900

Roll No.	No.	NAME	Age	Sex	Blood	Rel.	NAME OF FATHER	Liv.	Cit.	NAME OF MOTHER	Liv.	Cit.
6011	1	Lumkin, Homer	30	M	F		Billy Lumpkin	D	Cr	Polly	D	

No. 1 died October 6, 1902

Census Card No. 1906, P. O. Holdenville, Enrolled May 14, 1900; No. 2, March 25, 1901

Roll No.	No.	NAME	Age	Sex	Blood	Rel.	NAME OF FATHER	Liv.	Cit.	NAME OF MOTHER	Liv.	Cit.
6012	1	Tiger, Louisa	37	F	$\frac{3}{4}$		Furvaga	D	Cr	Lizzie Narcome	L	Cr
6013	2	Brown, Bettie	20	F	$\frac{3}{8}$	D	A. J. Brown	L	Sem	No. 1	L	Cr

No. 2 died January 1901

Census Card No. 1907, P. O. Holdenville, Enrolled May 14, 1900; No. 2, May 16, 1901

Roll No.	No.	NAME	Age	Sex	Blood	Rel.	NAME OF FATHER	Liv.	Cit.	NAME OF MOTHER	Liv.	Cit.
6014	1	Taylor, Frank	27	M	$\frac{3}{4}$		Frank Taylor	D	Cr	Maria Taylor	D	Cr
6015	2	Taylor, Maria	52	F	$\frac{3}{4}$	Moth	George Brinton	D	Cr	Unknown	D	Cr

No. 1 died November 27, 1904.   No. 2 died September or December 1899.

Census Card No. 1908, P. O. Holdenville, Enrolled May 14, 1900

Roll No.	No.	NAME	Age	Sex	Blood	Rel.	NAME OF FATHER	Liv.	Cit.	NAME OF MOTHER	Liv.	Cit.
6016	1	Taylor, Lewis	22	M	$\frac{7}{8}$		Taylor	D	Cr	Maria Taylor	D	Cr

No. 1 reported dead

Census Card No. 1909, P. O. Holdenville, Enrolled May 14, 1900

Roll No.	No.	NAME	Age	Sex	Blood	Rel.	NAME OF FATHER	Liv.	Cit.	NAME OF MOTHER	Liv.	Cit.
6017	1	Taylor, Emma	18	F	$\frac{7}{8}$		Taylor	D	Cr	Maria Taylor	D	Cr
6018	2	Taylor, Kizzie	19	F	$\frac{7}{8}$	Sis	Taylor	D	Cr	Maria Taylor	D	Cr

Census Card No. 1910, P. O. Holdenville, Enrolled May 14, 1900

Roll No.	No.	NAME	Age	Sex	Blood	Rel.	NAME OF FATHER	Liv.	Cit.	NAME OF MOTHER	Liv.	Cit.
6019	1	Narcome, Simpson	43	M	F		Narcome	D	Cr	Eliza Narcome	D	Cr
6020	2	Narcome, Lizzie	52	F	$\frac{1}{2}$	Wf	Nick Miller	D	Non	Betsey Miller	D	Cr

No. 1 died November 24, 1910.   No. 2 reported dead.

Census Card No. 1911, P. O. Wetumka, Enrolled May 14, 1900

Roll No.	No.	NAME	Age	Sex	Blood	Rel.	NAME OF FATHER	Liv.	Cit.	NAME OF MOTHER	Liv.	Cit.
6021	1	Chisholm, Polly	80	F	F		Emarthler Harjo	D	Cr	Welorkee	D	Cr

No. 1 died November 7, 1900

Roll No.	No.	NAME	Age	Sex	Blood	Rel.	NAME OF FATHER	Liv.	Cit.	NAME OF MOTHER	Liv.	Cit.
		Census Card No. 1912, P. O. Weleetka, Enrolled May 15, 1900										
6022	1	Chisholm, James	45	M	½		John Chisholm	D	Cher	Polly Chisholm	L	Cr
6023	2	Chisholm, Mary	45	F	½	Wf	Lewis Martin	D	Choc	Polly Martin	D	Cr
6024	3	Chisholm, Polly	18	F	½	D	No. 1	L	Cr	No. 2	L	Cr
6025	4	Chisholm, Lizzie	17	F	½	D	No. 1	L	Cr	No. 2	L	Cr
6026	5	Chisholm, Henry S.	9	M	½	S	No. 1	L	Cr	No. 2	L	Cr
6027	6	Chisholm, Grover C.	5	M	½	S	No. 1	L	Cr	No. 2	L	Cr
6028	7	Chisholm, William	3	M	½	S	No. 1	L	Cr	No. 2	L	Cr
6029	8	Chisholm, Ida	22	F	½	D	No. 1	L	Cr	No. 2	L	Cr
		No. 1 died February 14, 1902. No. 3 died November 4, 1901.										
		Census Card No. 1913, P. O. Wetumka, Enrolled May 15, 1900										
6030	1	Lewis, Jane	48	F	½		John Chisholm	D	Cher	Polly Chisholm	L	Cr
6031	2	Lewis, Francis	9	F	¾	D	Babe Lewis	D	Cr	No. 1	L	Cr
		No. 1 died October 19, 1913. No. 2 died April 14, 1906.										
		Census Card No. 1914, P. O. Council Hill, Enrolled May 15, 1900										
6032	1	Carr, Nellie	21	F	¾		Thomas Carr	D	Cr	Rachel Carr	D	Cr
		Census Card No. 1915, P. O. Sapulpa, Enrolled May 16, 1900										
6033	1	Bittle, William	18	M	⅛		George Bittle	D	Cr	Lizzie Thomas		Non
		Census Card No. 1916, P. O. Sharpe, Enrolled May 16, 1900										
6034	1	Tiger, George W.	34	M	¾		Motey Tiger	L	Cr	Hettie Tiger	L	Non
6035	2	Tiger, Susan H.	28	F	½	Wf	John Hampton	L	Non	Hampton	L	Cr
6036	3	Tiger, Ada M.	10	F	⅞	D	No. 1	L	Cr	Rose Tiger	D	Cr
6037	4	Tiger, Ida R.	8	F	⅞	D	No. 1	L	Cr	Rose Tiger	D	Cr
6038	5	Tiger, Eugene M.	6	M	⅝	S	No. 1	L	Cr	No. 2	L	Cr
6039	6	Tiger, Dewitt, F.	3	M	⅝	S	No. 1	L	Cr	No. 2	L	Cr
		No. 5 died December 27, 1912. No. 1 reported dead.										
		Census Card No. 1917, P. O. Muskogee, Enrolled May 16, 1900										
6040	1	Wilcox, Ella	24	F	1-16		William Harvison	D	?	Anna Harvison	D	?
		Census Card No. 1918, P. O. Hanna; No. 6, Dustin, Enrolled May 16, 1900; No. 5, March 21, 1901										
6041	1	Smith, Joe	28	M	¾		Wiley Smith	L	Cr	Tilda Smith	D	Cr
6042	2	Smith, Rose	27	F	½	Wf	George Smith	L	Cr	Matilda Smith	L	Cr
6043	3	Smith, Kogee	5	F	⅝	D	No. 1	L	Cr	No. 2	L	Cr
6044	4	Smith, Annie	3	F	⅝	D	No. 1	L	Cr	No. 2	L	Cr
6045	5	Smith, Tilda	12	F	½	Ward	Ellis Sunday	D	Cr	Mollie Sunday	D	Cr
6046	6	Smith, Katie	13	F	½	StD	Unknown	L	Cr	No. 2	L	Cr
		Census Card No. 1919, P. O. Tulsa, Enrolled May 16, 1900										
6047	1	Woods, Cora	17	F	¼		Wiley Adams	L	Non	Susan Adams	D	Cr
		No. 1 died October 12, 1905										
		Census Card No. 1920, P. O. Eufaula, Enrolled May 21, 1900										
6048	1	Grayson, Sam	52	M	½		James Grayson	D	Cr	Jane Grayson	D	Cr
6049	2	Grayson, Claude R.	15	M	½	S	No. 1	L	Cr	Katherine Grayson	D	Cr
6050	3	Grayson, Jennie May	12	F	½	D	No. 1	L	Cr	Katherine Grayson	D	Cr
6051	4	Grayson, Vinnie	10	F	½	D	No. 1	L	Cr	Katherine Grayson	D	Cr
6052	5	Grayson, Kate M.	6	F	½	D	No. 1	L	Cr	Katherine Grayson	D	Cr
		No. 2 died March 8, 1908										
		Census Card No. 1921, P. O. Holdenville, Enrolled May 24, 1900										
6053	1	Proctor, Timmie H.	22	M	F		Tulsa Proctor	L	Cr	Mandy Proctor	L	Cr
6054	2	Proctor, Nellie	19	F	F	Wf	Toney Reed	L	Cr	Liester Reed	L	Cr
6055	3	Proctor, Monroe	5moM	F	S		No. 1	L	Cr	No. 2	L	Cr
		Census Card No. 1922, P. O. Gibson Station, Enrolled May 24, 1900										
6056	1	Davis, Eli	21	M	½		Ollie Davis	L	Cr	Rose Grayson	L	Cr
		Census Card No. 1923, P. O. Wetumka, Enrolled May 25, 1900										
6057	1	McGirt, Isaac	20	M	F		Daniel McGirt	D	Cr	Jennie McGirt	D	Cr
		Census Card No. 1924, P. O. Tulsa, Enrolled May 26, 1900										
6058	1	Grayson, Sunday	15	M	F		Stephen Grayson	D	Cr	Lucy Grayson	D	Cr
		Census Card No. 1925, P. O. Eufaula, Enrolled May 25, 1900										
6059	1	Canard, Cogee	51	F	F		Daniel Roberts	D	Cr	Lydia Roberts	D	Cr
		No. 1 died January 15, 1902										
		Census Card No. 1926, P. O. Eufaula, Enrolled May 29, 1900										
6060	1	Green, Leah	26	F	F		Harris Canard	D	Cr	Cogee Canard	L	Cr
6061	2	Walker, Benjamin	9	M	⅞	S	Eddie Walker	L	Cr	No. 1	L	Cr
6062	3	Green, James	4	M	F	S	Barney Green	L	Cr	No. 1	L	Cr
		No. 2 reported dead										
		Census Card No. 1927, P. O. Okmulgee, Enrolled May 29, 1900										
6063	1	Nero, Jack	45	M	F		Apallo Harjo	D	Cr	Molloche	D	Cr
6064	2	Nero, Louisa	50	F	F	Wf	Thomas Sugar	D	Cr	Nancy Sugar	D	Cr
		No. 2 died September 26, 1908. No. 1 reported dead.										
		Census Card No. 1928, P. O. Eufaula, Enrolled May 29, 1900										
6065	1	Barnett, Toney	18	M	F		Wm. Barnett	L	Cr	Nicey Willingham	L	Cr
		Census Card No. 1929, P. O. Wetumka, Enrolled May 29, 1900										
6066	1	Barnett, Dave	44	M	F		Timothy Barnett	D	Cr	Mary Barnett	L	Cr
6067	2	Barnett, Polly	41	F	¾	Wf	Ben Fife	L	Cr	Mary Lewis	L	Cr
6068	3	Barnett, Mary Alice	16	F	⅞	D	No. 1	L	Cr	No. 2	L	Cr
6069	4	Barnett, Daniel W.	10	M	⅞	S	No. 1	L	Cr	No. 2	L	Cr
		No. 4 died July 17, 1909										
		Census Card No. 1930, P. O. Wetumka, Enrolled May 29, 1900; No. 3, May 13, 1901										
6070	1	Frank, John	29	M	¾		David Frank	D	Cr	Jennie Frank	L	Cr
6071	2	Frank, Sallie	21	F	⅞	Wf	Dave Barnett	L	Cr	Katie Barnett	D	Cr
6072	3	Frank, Katie	4	F	13-16	D	No. 1	L	Cr	No. 2	L	Cr
		No. 1 died September 18, 1901. No. 3 died November 1899.										

Roll No.	No.	NAME	Age	Sex	Blood	Rel.	NAME OF FATHER	Liv.	Cit.	NAME OF MOTHER	Liv.	Cit.
		Census Card No. 1931, P. O. Wetumka, Enrolled May 29, 1900										
6073	1	Barnett, Mary	68	F	F		Jack Benson	D	Cr	Lydia Benson	D	Cr
6074	2	Manly, Levi	13	M	F	Ward	Tobe Manly	D	Cr	Sina Manly	L	Cr
		Census Card No. 1932, P. O. Wetumka, Enrolled May 29, 1900										
6075	1	Barnett, Tim	30	M	⅞		Timothy Barnett	D	Cr	Mary Barnett	D	Cr
6076	2	Barnett, Tarhinner	41	F	F	Wf	Tommy Harjo	D	Cr	Nosey	D	Cr
		Census Card No. 1933, P. O. Wetumka, Enrolled May 29, 1900										
6077	1	Barnett, Wash	29	M	F		Billy Noon	D	Cr	Peggy Barnett	D	Cr
6078	2	Barnett, Thomas	17	M	F	Bro	Jerry Bruner	D	Cr	Peggy Barnett	D	Cr
6079	3	Barnett, Louisa	13	F	F	Sis	George Scott	D	Cr	Peggy Barnett	D	Cr
6080	4	Barnett, Albert	11	M	F	Bro	George Scott	D	Cr	Peggy Barnett	D	Cr
6081	5	Barnett, Bennie	10	M	F	Bro	George Scott	D	Cr	Peggy Barnett	D	Cr
6082	6	Barnett, Dennis	6	M	F	Bro	George Scott	D	Cr	Peggy Barnett	D	Cr
		Nos. 3 and 6 reported dead.										
		Census Card No. 1934, P. O. Nos. 1 and 2, Council Hill; No. 3, Eufaula, Enrolled May 29, 1900										
6083	1	Lerblance, Andrew	12	M	½		W. P. Lerblance	D	Cr	Eliza Lerblance	D	Cr
6084	2	Lerblance, Willie	11	M	½	Bro	W. P. Lerblance	D	Cr	Eliza Lerblance	D	Cr
6085	3	Lerblance, Nora	7	F	½	Sis	W. P. Lerblance	D	Cr	Eliza Lerblance	D	Cr
		Census Card No. 1935, P. O. Mounds, Enrolled June 1, 1900										
6086	1	Ahgokela, Waittie	10	F	F		Ahgokela	D	Cr	Conpethlela	D	Cr
		Census Card No. 1936, P. O. Holdenville, Enrolled June 2, 1900										
6087	1	Jackson, Sallie	20	F	F		Ithus Harjo	D	Cr	Jutkie	D	Cr
		Census Card No. 1937, P. O. Eufaula, Enrolled June 2, 1900										
6088	1	Richard, Sam	50	M	F		Tom Richard	D	Cr	Polly Richard	D	Cr
6089	2	Richard, Wesley	13	M	F	S	No. 1	L	Cr	Wisey Richard	D	Cr
		Census Card No. 1938, P. O. Grayson, Enrolled June 2, 1900										
6090	1	Downing, Miley	19	F	F		Watley Downing	L	Cr	Toche Downing	L	Cr
		No. 1 reported dead										
		Census Card No. 1939, P. O. Salem; No. 3, Okmulgee, Enrolled June 6, 1900										
6091	1	Davis, Jesse	57	M	F		Efer Harjo	D	Cr	Pote Thlucco	D	Cr
6092	2	Davis, Wisey	42	F	F	Wf	Jacobs	D	Cr	Lossie	D	Cr
6093	3	Stidham, Leah	8	F	F	Ward	John Stidham	D	Cr	Millie Stidham	D	Cr
6094	4	Davis, Cokey	6moF	F	D		No. 1	L	Cr	No. 2	L	Cr
		No. 2 reported dead										
		Census Card No. 1940, P. O. Sapulpa, Enrol.ed June 8, 1900										
6095	1	Grayson, Willie	22	M	⅝		Henry Grayson	L	Chich	Mary Grayson	L	Cr
		Census Card No. 1941, P. O. Wetumka, Enrolled June 8, 1900										
6096	1	Proctor, Washington	28	M	F		Emarthla Harjo	D	Cr	Louisa	D	Cr
		Census Card No. 1942, P. O. Coweta, Enrolled June 9, 1900										
6097	1	Frank, Thomas	40	M	½		Seminole Chupco	D	Sem	Semeto	D	Cr
		Census Card No. 1943, P. O. Okmulgee, Enrolled June 11, 1900										
6098	1	Grayson, Addie	23	F	⅜		Tom Grayson	D	Cr	Martha Brown	D	Cr
		No. 1 reported dead										
		Census Card No. 1944, P. O. Okmulgee, Enrolled June 11, 1900										
6099	1	Tiger, Matilda	40	F	F		Simmesee	D	Cr	Losutchey	D	Cr
		No. 1 died February 19, 1912										
		Census Card No. 1945, P. O. Sapulpa, Enrolled June 11, 1900										
6100	1	Bosen, George	21	M	F		John Bosen	D	Cr	Lousanna Bosen	D	Cr
		Census Card No. 1946, P. O. Wewoka, Enrolled June 11, 1900; No. 2, March 27, 1901										
6101	1	Alex, F. G.	27	M	F		H. Alex	L	Cr	Susan Alex	D	Cr
6102	2	Alex, Elizabeth	28	F	½	Wf	Frank D. Jacobs	L	Cr	Rebecca Jacobs	D	Cr
		Census Card No. 1947, P. O. Kellyville, Enrolled June 12, 1900										
6103	1	Tiger, Consanna	50	F	F		Unknown	D	Cr	Unknown	D	Cr
6104	2	Tiger, Timmie	17	M	F	S	James Tiger	D	Cr	No. 1	L	Cr
6105	3	Tiger, Salina	15	F	D		James Tiger	D	Cr	No. 1	L	Cr
6106	4	Tiger, Noah	13	M	F	S	James Tiger	D	Cr	No. 1	L	Cr
6107	5	Tiger, Saloma	13	F	F	D	James Tiger	D	Cr	No. 1	L	Cr
6108	6	Tiger, Lucy	10	F	F	D	James Tiger	D	Cr	No. 1	L	Cr
		No. 6 reported dead										
		Census Card No. 1948, P. O. Sapulpa, Enrolled June 12, 1900										
6109	1	Snow, Martha	21	F	F		James Tiger	D	Cr	Consana Tiger	L	Cr
6110	2	Snow, Jessie	6moM	F	S		Teciumseh Snow	D	Cr	No. 1	L	Cr
		No. 2 reported dead										
		Census Card No. 1949, P. O. Mounds, Enrolled June 13, 1900										
6111	1	Skeeter, Willie	20	M	F		Big Mosquito	L	Cr	Lizzie Big Mosquito	D	Cr
		No. 1 died July 9, 1905										
		Census Card No. 1950, P. O. Holdenville, Enrolled June 14, 1900										
6112	1	Tiner, Martha	50	F	½		Dave Tiner	D	Non	Katy Tiner	D	Cr
		No. 1 reported dead										
		Census Card No. 1951, P. O. Holdenville, Enrolled June 14, 1900; No. 7, May 18, 1901										
6113	1	Foley, William	42	M	F		Unknown	D	Cr	Toyoposka	D	Cr
6114	2	Foley, Amey	35	F	F	Wf	Ahalak Hopie	D	Cr	Binney	D	Cr
6115	3	Yahola, Rhoda	12	F	F	StD	Efar Yahola	L	Cr	No. 2	L	Cr
6116	4	Foley, John	11	M	F	S	No. 1	L	Cr	No. 2	L	Cr
6117	5	Foley, Kissie	8	F	F	D	No. 1	L	Cr	No. 2	L	Cr
6118	6	Foley, Lonie	2	F	F	D	No. 1	L	Cr	No. 2	L	Cr
6119	7	Foley, Minnie	18moF	F	D		No. 1	L	Cr	No. 2	L	Cr
		No. 7 died November 10, 1900. No. 2 died January 20, 1902. No. 1 died December 28, 1908.										
		No. 3 reported dead. No. 6 died July 3, 1913										

Roll No.	No.	NAME	Age	Sex	Blood	Rel.	NAME OF FATHER	Liv.	Cit.	NAME OF MOTHER	Liv.	Cit.
		Census Card No. 1952, P. O. Jennings, Enrolled June 16, 1900										
6120	1	McElroy, Joanna	39	F	1/8		Nathaniel Hodge	D	Non	Nancy Hodge	D	Cr
6121	2	McElroy, Clarence	15	M	1-16	S	Geo. H. McElroy	L	Non	No. 1	L	Cr
6122	3	McElroy, Emmett	13	M	1-16	S	Geo. H. McElroy	L	Non	No. 1	L	Cr
		Census Card No. 1953, P. O. Muskogee, Enrolled June 19, 1900										
6123	1	Marshall, Louisa	21	F	F		Wor Marshall	D	Cr	Winey Marshall	D	Cr
		Census Card No. 1954, P. O. Eufaula, Enrolled June 19, 1900										
6124	1	Marshall, Elvina	19	F	F		Wor Marshall	D	Cr	Winey Marshall	D	Cr
		Census Card No. 1955, P. O. Weleetka, Enrolled June 19, 1900										
6125	1	Robinson, Annie	23	F	3/8		David Harry	L	Cr	Grace Henry	D	Cr
6126	2	Robinson, George	2	M	3-16	S	Dave Robinson	L	Non	No. 1	L	Cr
6127	3	Robinson, Henry	1	M	3-16	S	Dave Robinson	L	Non	No. 1	L	Cr
		No. 3 died May 1901										
		Census Card No. 1956, P. O. Tuskegee, Enrolled June 20, 1900										
6128	1	Bruner, Tom	65	M	1/2		Paro Bruner	D	Cr	Eliza Bruner	D	Cr
		No. 1 died 1904 or 1905										
		Census Card No. 1957, P. O. Stone Bluff, Enrolled June 23, 1900; No. 3, April 25, 1901										
6129	1	Barnett, George	23	M	1/2		George Sofley	D	Non	Tabbieundeney	D	Cr
6130	2	Barnett, Columbus R.	2	F	1/4	S	No. 1	L	Cr	Hattie Barnett	L	Non
6131	3	Barnett, Ada P.	1	F	1/4	D	No. 1	L	Cr	Hattie Barnett	L	Non
		Census Card No. 1958, P. O. Dustin, Enrolled June 23, 1900										
6132	1	Thomas, Aggie	26	F	F		Cubbie, Yahola	D	Cr	Mary Yahola	D	Cr
6133	2	Thomas, James C.	4	M	1/2	S	James A. Thomas	L	Non	No. 1	L	Cr
6134	3	Thomas, Lizzie Lou	10mo	F	1/2	D	James A. Thomas	L	Non	No. 1	L	Cr
6135	4	Scott, Louisa	15	F	F	Sis	Cubbie Yahola	D	Non	Mary Yahola	D	Cr
		No. 4 died June 4, 1900										
		Census Card No. 1959, P. O. Muskogee, Enrolled June 25, 1900										
6136	1	Murphy, N. P.	34	F	1/8		C. M. Murphy	D	Non	Eliza Murphy	L	Cr
		No. 1 reported dead										
		Census Card No. 1960, P. O. Eufaula, Enrolled June 26, 1900										
6137	1	Smock, Eloise Grayson	18	F	1/2		Geo. W. Grayson	L	Cr	Annie Grayson	L	Cr
		Census Card No. 1961, P. O. Okemah, Enrolled June 26, 1900										
6138	1	Brock, Jennetta A.	26	F	1/2		Tom Harvison	L	Cr	Amy McGilbray	L	Cr
6139	2	Brock, Jennetta L.	3	F	1/4	D	J. H. Brook	L	Non	No. 1	L	Cr
6140	3	Brock, Lillie	4mo	F	1/4	D	J. H. Brook	L	Non	No. 1	L	Cr
6141	4	Brock, John	4mo	M	1/4	S	J. H. Brook	L	Non	No. 1	L	Cr
6142	5	Brock, Lucile E.	13mo	F	1/4	D	J. H. Brook	L	Non	No. 1	L	Cr
		No. 3 died July 20, 1900. No. 4 died September 20, 1900. No. 5 died October 6, 1899.										
		Census Card No. 1962, P. O. Wetumka, Enrolled June 27, 1900										
6143	1	Socer	55	M	F		Carbecher Yahola	D	Cr	Mothliche	D	Cr
		Census Card No. 1963, P. O. Hanna, Enrolled June 27, 1900; No. 5, April 4, 1901										
6144	1	Chisholm, Mattie	37	F	F		John Lowe	D	Cr	Abbie Lowe	L	Cr
6145	2	Chisholm, George	19	M	3/4	S	Tom Chisholm	D	Cher	No. 1	L	Cr
6146	3	Chisholm, Bettie	18	F	3/4	D	Tom Chisholm	D	Cher	No. 1	L	Cr
6147	4	Chisholm, Jackson	16	M	3/4	S	Tom Chisholm	D	Cher	No. 1	L	Cr
6148	5	Chisholm, Lena	9	F	3/4	D	Tom Chisholm	D	Cher	No. 1	L	Cr
		No. 1 died March 23, 1911. No. 5 died March 18, 1912.										
		Census Card No. 1964, P. O. Sapulpa, Enrolled June 28, 1900										
6149	1	Ispocogee, Belcher	23	M	F		Topley Ispocogee	L	Cr	Yadie Ispocogee	D	Cr
6150	2	Ispocogee, Jennie	19	F	F	Wf	Joe Kernell	D	Cr	Polly Ispocogee	L	Cr
		No. 1 reported dead										
		Census Card No. 1965, P. O. Mellette, Enrolled July 5, 1900										
6151	1	Scott, Albert	45	M	F		Samuel Scott	D	Cr	Polly Scott	D	Cr
6152	2	Scott, Bettie	30	F	F	Wf	Chaleka	D	Cr	Hepsey McIntosh	L	Cr
6153	3	Scott, Bessie	8	F	F	D	No. 1	L	Cr	No. 2	L	Cr
6154	4	Scott, Ether	6	F	F	D	No. 1	L	Cr	No. 2	L	Cr
6155	5	Scott, Peter	5	M	F	S	No. 1	L	Cr	No. 2	L	Cr
		No. 1 died 1900										
		Census Card No. 1966, P. O. Okmulgee, Enrolled Junly 7, 1900										
6156	1	Hodges, Green F.	65	M	3/4		Tom Johnson	D	Cr	Hannah Hodge	D	Cr
		Census Card No. 1967, P. O. Eufaula, Enrolled July 10, 1900										
6157	1	Hardage, Lucy	82	F	F		David Hardage	D	Cr	Sahtehikee	D	Cr
		No. 1 died November 30, 1900										
		Census Card No. 1968, P. O. Eufaula, Enrolled July 18, 1900										
6158	1	Post, William	27	M	1/8		John Post	D	Cr	Adeline Young	L	Non
		No. 1 died February 21, 1903										
		Census Card No. 1969, P. O. Bearden, Enrolled July 21, 1900										
6159	1	Simmer	35	M	F		Unknown	D	Cr	Semehoke	D	Cr
6160	2	Simmer, Arch	2	M	F	S	No. 1	L	Cr	Sallie Simmer	D	Cr
6161	3	Simmer, Sallie	34	F	F	Wf	Saryee	D	Cr	Unknown	D	Cr
		No. 3 died April 1, 1900										

Roll No.	No.	NAME	Age	Sex	Blood	Rel.	NAME OF FATHER	Liv.	Cit.	NAME OF MOTHER	Liv.	Cit.
		Census Card No. 1970, P. O. Okemah, Enrolled July 21, 1900										
6162	1	Arhalokoche,	50	M	F		Woxie Emarthar Harjo	D	Cr	Tharwitche	D	Cr
6163	2	Arhalokoche, Sofa	45	F	F	Wf	Joilly Ocbee	D	Cr	Siah	D	Cr
6164	3	Arhalokoche, Winey	20	F	F	D	No. 1	L	Cr	No. 2	L	Cr
6165	4	Arhalokoche, George	17	M	F	S	No. 1	L	Cr	No. 2	L	Cr
6166	5	Arhalokoche, Maggie	15	F	F	D	No. 1	L	Cr	No. 2	L	Cr
6167	6	Arhalokoche, Lewis	13	M	F	S	No. 1	L	Cr	No. 2	L	Cr
6168	7	Arhalokoche, Maxey	12	M	F	S	No. 1	L	Cr	No. 2	L	Cr
6169	8	Arhalokoche, Rosanna	9	F	F	D	No. 1	L	Cr	No. 2	L	Cr
		No. 7 died May 17, 1900.. No. 2 died August 18, 1914.										
		Census Card No. 1971, P. O. Bearden, Enrolled July 21, 1900										
6170	1	King, Jack	27	M	F		Sunnikkeya	D	Cr	Susanna	D	Cr
6171	2	King, Annie	6	F	F	D	No. 1	L	Cr	Chotkey King	D	Cr
6172	3	King, Wilson	3	M	F	S	No. 1	L	Cr	Chotkey King	D	Cr
6173	4	King, Sarah	15	F	F	Sis	Sunnikkeya	D	Cr	Susanna	D	Cr
6174	5	King, Joseph	12	M	F	Bro	Sunnikkeya	D	Cr	Susanna	D	Cr
6175	6	King, Hepsey	10	F	F	Sis	Sunnikkeya	D	Cr	Susanna	D	Cr
6176	7	King, Chotkey	22	F	F	Wf	Sehoatka	D	Cr	Louisa Harjo	L	Cr
6177	8	King, Louisa	15	F	F	Sis	Sunnikkeya	D	Cr	Susanna King	D	Cr
		No. 4 died 1901. No. 1 died March 9, 1902. Nos. 2 and 7 reported dead. No. 5 died October 8, 1903. No. 8 died December 1901.										
		Census Card No. 1972, P. O. Bearden, Enrolled July 21, 1900										
6178	1	Deer, Pinky	21	M	F		Cho Harjoge	D	Cr	Silby	D	Cr
		Census Card No. 1973, P. O. No. 1, Muskogee; No. 2, Wetumka, Enrolled July 23, 1900										
6179	1	Robison, William R.	35	M	1-16		William Robison	D	Cr	Adeline Robison	D	Chick
6180	2	Robison, Augusta	10	F	3-16	Niece	Geo. Frazier	D	Cr	Jane Robison	D	Cr
		Census Card No. 1974, P. O. Broken Arrow, Enrolled July 23, 1900										
6181	1	Brown, Lou	19	F	5/8		John Brown	D	Cr	Elizabeth Brown	D	Cr
		Census Card No. 1975, P. O. Wagoner, Enrolled July 24, 1900										
6182	1	Childers, James E.	25	M	F		N. B. Childers	L	Cr	Sophia Childers	D	Cr
6183	2	Childers, Susie May C.	3	F	1/2	D	No. 1	L	Cr	Mattie Childers	L	Non
		Census Card No. 1976, P. O. Eufaula, Enrolled July 25, 1900										
6184	1	Ingram, John F.	63	M	1/2		Willy Ingram	D	Non	Louisa Ingram	D	Cr
		Census Card No. 1977, P. O. Eufaula, Enrolled July 25, 1900										
6185	1	Ingram, David C.	61	M	1/2		Wiley Ingram	D	Non	Louisa Ingram	D	Cr
6186	2	Ingram, Mary A.	54	F	F	Wf	Cocheryah	D	Cr	Lucy Cocheryah	D	Cr
		No. 1 died April 1903. No. 2 died May 1902.										
		Census Card No. 1978, P. O. Fame, Enrolled July 25, 1900										
6187	1	Ingram, Thomas J.	33	M	3/4		David C. Ingram	L	Cr	Mary A. Ingram	L	Cr
6188	2	Ingram, Janetta	23	F	F	Wf	Unknown	D	Cr	Nancy Reilly	L	Cr
6189	3	Ingram, David P.	6	M	7/8	S	No. 1	L	Cr	No. 2	L	Cr
6190	4	Ingram, Eliza J.	3	F	7/8	D	No. 1	L	Cr	No. 2	L	Cr
6191	5	Ingram, Mary Ella	2	F	7/8	D	No. 1	L	Cr	No. 2	L	Cr
6192	6	Ingram, Lotta E.	3mo	F	7/8	D	No. 1	L	Cr	No. 2	L	Cr
		No. 1 died May 27, 1910										
		Census Card No. 1979, P. O. Okemah, Enrolled July 28, 1900										
6193	1	Sarhoseker	45	F	F		Unknown	D	Cr	Hoyoker	D	Cr
		Census Card No. 1980, P. O. Eufaula, Enrolled July 28, 1900										
6194	1	Miller, Reuben J.	39	M	1/4		David Miller	D	Cr	Catherine Miller	D	Non
		No. 1 died September 15, 1912										
		Census Card No. 1981, P. O. Coweta, Enrolled July 28, 1900										
6195	1	Wadsworth, Mitchell	33	M	1/2		Mitchell Wadsworth	D	Cr	Kate Holden	L	Cr
		Census Card No. 1982, P. O. Coweta, Enrolled July 30, 1900										
6196	1	Noble, Minnie	25	F	F		Chissoe	D	Cr	Mahaley Chissoe	D	Cr
6197	2	Chisholm, John	8	M	F	S	Mack Chisholm	L	Cr	No. 1	L	Cr
		Census Card No. 1983, P. O. Wetumka, Enrolled July 31, 1900										
6198	1	Bruner, Wash	23	M	F		Jerry Bruner	D	Cr	Hannah Bruner	D	Cr
		Census Card No. 1984, P. O. Eufaula, Enrolled August 2, 1900										
6199	1	Morgan, Leona P.	24	F	1/2		John F. Ingram	L	Cr	Elizabeth Ingram	L	Cr
6200	2	Morgan, Fannie	9mo	F	1/4	D	Frank Morgan	L	Non	No. 1	L	Cr
6201	3	Morgan, Luther F.	1	M	1/4	S	Frank Morgan	L	Non	No. 1	L	Cr
		No. 3 died June 8, 1899										
		Census Card No. 1985, P. O. Eufaula, Enrolled August 3, 1900										
6202	1	Francis, Robert	24	M	F		John Francis	L	Cr	Millie Francis	L	Cr
6203	2	Francis, Millie	22	F	F	Wf	Thomas Polk	L	Cr	Lucinda Polk	L	Cr
		No. 2 died June 8, 1908										
		Census Card No. 1986, P. O. Checotah; No. 2, Porter, Enrolled August 7, 1900										
6204	1	Keys, Sarah	50	F	1/8		Wm. F. McIntosh	D	Cr	Eliza Island	D	Cr
6205	2	Keys, Ella	16	F	1-16	D	Sam Keys	L	Non	No. 2	L	Cr
6206	3	Keys, Ada	13	F	1-16	D	Sam Keys	L	Non	No. 2	L	Cr
		No. 1 died October 10, 1906										
		Census Card No. 1987, P. O. Eufaula, Enrolled August 8, 1900; No. 3, April 26, 1901										
6207	1	Asbury, Jim	45	M	F		Jack Asbury	D	Cr	Polly Asbury	D	Cr
6208	2	Asbury, Wisey	32	F	F	Wf	Wilson Tiger	L	Cr	Tiger	D	Cr
6209	3	Turkey, Colbert	8	M	F	StD	Frank Turkey	L	Cr	No. 2	L	Cr
		No. 2 died February 22, 1908										

Roll No.	No.	NAME	Age	Sex	Blood	Rel.	NAME OF FATHER	Liv.	Cit.	NAME OF MOTHER	Liv.	Cit.
	Census Card No. 1988, P. O. Creek; No. 5, Peru, Indiana, Enrolled August 13, 1900; Nos. 4 and 5, May 20, 1901											
6210	1	Fine, Charity	27	F	½		Jesse Gooch	L	Ncn	Toebie Fish	D	Cr
6211	2	Fine, Edna Albert	4	M	¼	S	Chas. P. Fine	L	Non	No. 1	L	Cr
6212	3	Fine, Gertie Elbertha	1	F	¼	D	Chas. P. Fine	L	Non	No. 1	L	Cr
6213	4	Gooch, Henry	15	M	½	Ward	Jesse Gooch	L	Non	Tochey Gooch	L	Cr
6214	5	Gooch, George	13	M	½	Ward	Jesse Gooch	L	Cr	Tochey Gooch	L	Cr
	Census Card No. 1989, P. O. Muskogee, Enrolled August 14, 1900											
6215	1	Butler, Manny G.	40	M	¼		Edward Butler	D	Cr	Elizabeth Butler	D	Non
6216	2	Butler, Elizabeth	17	F	⅛	D	No. 1	L	Cr	Anna Butler	L	Non
6217	3	Butler, Fount G.	14	M	⅛	S	No. 1	L	Cr	Anna Butler	L	Non
6218	4	Butler, Sammie	3	F	⅛	D	No. 1	L	Cr	Anna Butler	L	Non
	Census Card No. 1990, P. O. Eufaula, Enrolled August 14, 1900											
6219	1	Per yman, Ellen	39	F	¾		Nicholson, Marshall	D	Cr	Eliza Marshall	D	Cr
	Census Card No. 1991, P. O. Muskogee, Enrolled August 14, 1900											
6220	1	Porter, Pleasant	59	M	½		Benjamin E. Porter	D	Cr	Phoebe Porter	D	Cr
6221	2	Porter, Annetta Mary	16	F	½	D.	No. 1	L	Cr	Mary Ellen Porter	D	Cher
6222	3	Porter, Leonora E.	11	F	¼	D	No. 1	L	Cr	Mattie L. Porter	D	Cher
		No. 1 died										
	Census Card No. 1992, P. O. Lamar, Enrolled September 4, 1900											
6223	1	James, Morris	30	F	F		Arbeka Jim	D	Cr	Melar Scott	L	Cr
	Census Card No. 1993, P. O. Wetumka, Enrolled September 5, 1900											
6224	1	Wesley, John	27	M	F		Joilla	D	Cr	Rosanna Harjo	L	Cr
	Census Card No. 1994, P. O. Holdenville, Enrolled September 8, 1900; No. 5, May 23, 1901											
6225	1	Harjo, Lizzie	30	F	F		Micco Hutke	L	Cr	Jennie Hutke	D	Cr
6226	2	Bruner, Judy	14	F	F	D	Robert Bruner	D	Cr	No. 1	L	Cr
6227	3	Bruner, Suther	10	M	F	S	Jesse Bruner	L	Cr	No. 1	L	Cr
6228	4	Harjo, Lucinda	9	F	F	D	Cheparnoche Harjo	L	Cr	No. 1	L	Cr
6229	5	Harjo, Anna	2	F	F	D	Cheparnoche Harjo	L	Cr	No. 1	L	Cr
6230	6	Harjo, Betty	13	F	F	D	Cheparnoche, Harjo	L	Cr	No. 1	L	Cr
		No. 6 died May 17, 1899. Nos. 1 and 2 reported dead.										
	Census Card No. 1995, P. O. Okmulgee, Enrolled September 10, 1900											
6231	1	Roberson, Mary	28	F	F		John Perryman	L	Cr	Louisa	L	Cr
6232	2	Roberson, Amos	2	M	¾	S	Philip Roberson	L	Cr	No. 1	L	Cr
	Census Card No. 1996, P. O. Wewoka, Enrolled September 12, 1900											
6233	1	Tikoche	53	F	F		Kosar Harjo	D	Cr	Istahiye	D	Cr
		No. 1 died June 26, 1908										
	Census Card No. 1997, P. O. Wewoka, Enrolled September 13, 1900											
6234	1	Wolf, Nancy	25	F	F		Mehie	D	Cr	Tikoche	L	Cr
6235	2	Wolf, Ella	5	F	½	D	Wallace Wolf	L	Sem	No. 1	L	Cr
6236	3	Wolf, Freeland	9	M	½	S	Wallace Wolf	L	Sem	No. 1	L	Cr
6237	4	Wolf, Motey	1	M	½	S	Wallace Wolf	L	Sem	No. 1	L	Cr
	Census Card No. 1998, P. O. Beggs, Enrolled September 13, 1900											
6238	1	Foster, Lucy	25	F	⅞		Jim Bruner	D	Cr	Susy Bruner	D	Cr
		No. 1 died June 22, 1913										
	Census Card No. 1999, P. O. Bearden, Enrolled September 14, 1900											
6239	1	Harjo, Wotko	54	M	F		Chuchee Harjo	D	Cr	Fullhoogee	D	Cr
6240	2	Harjo, Millie	32	F	F	Wf	Woxie Holotka	D	Cr	Yuputka	L	Cr
6241	3	Davis, Emma	8	F	F	Niece	Jim Davis	L	Cr	Tuckabatchee	L	Cr
		No. 2 died										
	Census Card No. 2000, P. O. Castle, Enrolled September 14, 1900; No. 3, March 21, 1901											
6242	1	Hill, David	26	M	F		Woxie Holotka	D	Cr	Youbutka	L	Cr
6243	2	Hill, Millie	26	F	F	Wf	Lubby Sam	D	Cr	Lizzie	L	Cr
6244	3	Hill, Minnie	1	F	F	D	No. 1	L	Cr	No 2	L	Cr
		No. 1 died January 4, 1908										
	Census Card No. 2001, P. O. Wetumka; No. 2, Yeager, Enrolled September 14, 1900											
6245	1	King, Dick	30	M	F		Mickie Emarthla	?	Cr	Nellie Emarthla	D	Cr
6246	2	King, Emina	34	F	F	Wf	Osoch Harjo	D	Cr	Eliza Harjo	D	Cr
		No. 1 died December 25, 1901.										
	Census Card No. 2002, P. O. Holdenville, Enrolled September 21, 1900											
6247	1	Shawnego, Stella	12	F	¾		Shawnego	D	Cr	Tilda Shawnego	D	Cr
6248	2	Shawnego, John	9	M	¾	Bro	Shawnego	D	Cr	Tilda Shawnego	D	Cr
	Census Card No. 2003, P. O. Broken Arrow, Enrolled September 25, 1900											
6249	1	Wallace, Janison	25	M	F		Warlese	D	Cr	Unknown	D	Cr
	Census Card No. 2004, P. O. Holdenville, Enrolled October 1, 1900											
6250	1	Monahwee, Ella	11	F	F		David Monahwee	D	Cr	Miley Monahwee	D	Cr
	Census Card No. 2005, P. O. Muskogee, Enrolled October 9, 1900											
6251	1	Escoe, Anna	23	F	¼		Thomas Escoe	L	Non	Mary Escoe	L	Cr
		No. 1 died June 2, 1902										
	Census Card No. 2006, P. O. Muskogee, Enrolled October 10, 91900											
6252	1	Minugh, Alice V.	25	F	⅛		John T. Smith	D	Non	Rachel Smith	D	Cr
6253	2	Minugh, Daisy Lee	2	F	1-16	D	Clarence E. Minugh	L	Non	No. 1	L	Cr
	Census Card No. 2007, P. O. Brush Hill, Enrolled October 19, 1900											
6254	1	Price, Louvina	47	F	½		Hotochee Herrod	D	Cr	Mary Herrod	D	Cr
	Census Card No. 2008, P. O. Bixby, Enrolled October 31, 1900											
6255	1	Green, Taylor	14	M	F		Jimmie Larney	D	Cr	Sukey Kelly	D	Cr
		No. 1 died July 24, 1904										

Roll No.	No.	NAME	Age	Sex	Blood	Rel.	NAME OF FATHER	Liv.	Cit.	NAME OF MOTHER	Liv.	Cit.
	Census Card No. 2009, P. O. Bearden, Enrolled November 5, 1900											
6256	1	Knight, Boston	23	M	F		William Knight	D	Cr	Lowiney Knight	D	Cr
6257	2	Knight, Dochee	21	F	F	Wf	Martain Beaver	D	Cr	Jennie Beaver	L	Cr
	No. 1 died June 1901. No. 2 died April 5, 1905.											
	Census Card No. 2010, P. O. Eufaula, Enrolled November 14, 1900											
6258	1	McIntosh, Bunnie	36	M	F		Roley McIntosh	L	Cr	Bessie McIntosh	D	Cr
6259	2	McIntosh, Leah	29	F	½	Wf	Frank Jacobs	L	Cr	Rebecca Jacobs	D	Cr
6260	3	McIntosh, May	8	F	¾	D	No. 1	L	Cr	No. 2	L	Cr
6261	4	McIntosh, Roley	4	M	¾	S	No. 1	L	Cr	No. 2	L	Cr
6262	5	McIntosh, Mildred	2	F	¾	D	No. 1	L	Cr	No. 2	L	Cr
	Census Card No. 2011, P. O. Sasakwa, Enrolled November 27, 1900; No. 7, May 23, 1901											
6263	1	Brown, Elizabeth A.	38	F	½		Geo. A. Alexander	L	Cr	Nancy Alexander	L	Cr
6264	2	Brown, Alice	17	F	¼	D	J. F. Brown	L	Sem	No. 1	L	Cr
6265	3	Brown, Josephine	13	F	¼	D	J. F. Brown	L		No. 1	L	Cr
6266	4	Brown, Jackson	11	M	¼	S	J. F. Brown	L		No. 1	L	Cr
6267	5	Brown, Louis	6	M	¼	S	J. F. Brown	L		No. 1	L	Cr
6268	6	Brown, Zora	1	F	¼	D	J. F. Brown	L		No. 1	L	Cr
6269	7	Brown, James	3	M	¼	S	J. F. Brown	L		No. 1	L	Cr
	No. 1 died May 29, 1900. No. 6 died June 1903. No. 7 died May 29, 1900.											
	Census Card No. 2012, P. O. Wetumka, Enrolled November 27, 1900											
6270	1	Alexander, Leah	32	F	F		Toley Bruner	D	Cr	Sorbsey Bruner	D	Cr
6271	2	Alexander, Cora	10	F	¾	D	Louis Alexander	D	Cr	No. 1	L	Cr
6272	3	Alexander, Lucy	7	F	¾	D	Louis Alexander	D	Cr	No. 1	L	Cr
6273	4	Hawkins, Simpson	22	M	F	Neph	Harris Hawkins	D	Cr	Sallie Hawkins	D	Cr
	No. 1 died January 28, 1913. No. 4 reported dead.											
	Census Card No. 2013, P. O. Holdenville, Enrolled November 30, 1900											
6274	1	Brown, Jennie	40	F	½		George Chisholm	L	Cr	Nancy Chisholm	L	Cr
6275	2	Brown, Nancy	2	F	¼	D	Nick Brown	L	Non	No. 1	L	Cr
	No. 2 died April 2, 1902											
	Census Card No. 2014, P. O. Stone Bluff; No. 5 Coweta, Enrolled December 1, 1900											
6276	1	Colbert, Joe	40	M	F		Wotko Harjo	D	Cr	Unknown	D	Cr
6277	2	Colbert, Semondy	30	F	F	Wf	Matiyecher	D	Cr	Nancy White	D	Cr
6278	3	Colbert, Jackson	17	M	F	S	No. 1	L	Cr	Sarah Colbert	L	Cr
6279	4	Colbert, Charley	15	M	F	S	No. 1	L	Cr	Sarah Colbert	L	Cr
6280	5	White, Ben	14	M	F	Ward	George White	D	Cr	Nancy White	D	Cr
	No. 4 died November 29, 1909											
	Census Card No. 2015, P. O. Brush Hill, Enrolled December 1, 1900											
6281	1	Lewallen, Louisa	22	F	¼		Thomas Grayson	D	Cr	Winey Grayson	L	Cr
6282	2	Deer, Nora	3	F	¼	D	Jonas Deer	D	Cr	No. 1	L	Cr
	Census Card No. 2016, P. O. Brush Hill, Enrolled December 1, 1900											
6283	1	Grayson, Winey	45	F	F		Ben Fife	L	Cr	Mrs. Fife	D	Cr
6284	2	Grayson, Mollie	3	F	¾	D	Jonas Deer	L	Cr	No. 1	L	Cr
	No. 2 reported dead											
	Census Card No. 2017, P. O. Jenks, Enrolled December 4, 1900											
6285	1	Crow, James	42	M	F		Crow	D	Cr	Kowarkana	D	Cr
	Census Card No. 2018, P. O. Krebs, Enrolled December 6, 1900											
6286	1	Brown, Jackson	27	M	¼		Elijah Brown	L	Non	Frances Brown	L	Cr
	Census Card No. 2019, P. O. Brush Hill, Enrolled December 8, 1900; No. 3 April 11, 1901											
6287	1	Thompson, Legus	31	M	F		Parhos Harjo	L	Cr	Sofa Harjo	D	Cr
6288	2	Thompson, Lena	29	F	F	Wf	Tuskegee Micco	D	Cr	Micco	L	Cr
6289	3	Thompson, Legus, Jr.	1	M	F	S	No. 1	L	Cr	No. 2	L	Cr
	No. 3 reported dead											
	Census Card No. 2020, P. O. Wewoka, Enrolled December 8, 1900											
6290	1	Noble, Mariah	82	F	¼		Jeffry George	D	Non	Bessie George	D	Cr
	Census Card No. 2021, P. O. Eufaula, Enrolled December 11, 1900											
6291	1	McGilbra, Amie	75	F	F		Unknown	D	Cr	Betsy	D	Cr
	No. 1 died November 1902											
	Census Card No. 2022, P. O. Coodys Bluff, Enrolled December 21, 1900											
6292	1	Atkins, Nancy	27	F	F		Thomas Atkins	L	Cr	Mary Jane Atkins	D	Cr
	Census Card No. 2023, P. O. Coweta, Enrolled December 26, 1900											
6293	1	Flowers, John	53	M	½		Joe Flowers	L	Non	Sukey Fox	D	Cr
6294	2	Flowers, Susan	10	F	¼	D	No. 1	L	Cr	Arminta Flowers	D	Cher
6295	3	Flowers, Mattie	7	F	¼	D	No. 1	L	Cr	Arminta Flowers	D	Cher
	Census Card No. 2024, P. O. Coweta, Enrolled December 26, 1900											
6296	1	Flowers, Joseph	21	M	¼		John Flowers	L	Cr	Ariminta Flowers	D	Cher
	Census Card No. 2025, P. O. Porter, Enrolled December 31, 1900											
6297	1	Marshall, Nora	22	F	⅝		George Marshall	D	Cr	Elizabeth Marshall	D	Cr
	Census Card No. 2026, P. O. Holdenville, Enrolled January 11, 1901; No. 2 May 24, 1901											
6298	1	Washington, Catherine	22	F	1-32		J. F. Simpson	L	Non	Susan A. Simpson	L	Cr
6299	2	Washington, Marion M.	1	F	1-64	D	E. M. Washington	L	Non	No. 1	L	Cr
	Census Card No. 2027, P. O. Eufaula, Enrolled January 16, 1901											
6300	1	McIntosh, John	67	M	¼		Chilly McIntosh	L	Cr	Polly McIntosh	D	Cr
6301	2	McIntosh, Mary	29	F	F	Wf	Cubbitcha	D	Cr	Lucy	L	Cr
6302	3	McIntosh, Minerola	5	F	⅝	D	No. 1	L	Cr	No. 2	L	Cr
6303	4	McIntosh, Job	13	M	¼	S	No. 1	L	Cr	Salina McIntosh	L	Cr
	No. 1 died December 1906											

Roll No.	No.	NAME	Age	Sex	Blood	Rel.	NAME OF FATHER	Liv.	Cit.	NAME OF MOTHER	Liv.	Cit.
Census Card No. 2028, P. O. Eufaula, Enrolled January 21, 1901; Nos. 5 and 6 March 27, 1901												
6304	1	Phillips, Johnson	34	M	F		B. H. Phillips	D	Cr	Eliza Phillips	D	Cr
6305	2	Phillips, Hettie	21	F	F	Wf	Barney Riley	L	Cr	Nancy Riley	L	Cr
6306	3	Phillips, Ben	10	M	F	S	No. 1	L	Cr	Hannah Phillips	D	Cr
6307	4	Phillips, Betsie	8	F	F	D	No. 1	L	Cr	Hannah Phillips	D	Cr
6308	5	Phillips, Wallace	3½	M	F	S	No. 1	L	Cr	No. 2	L	Cr
6309	6	Phillips, Daniel	1	M	F	S	No. 1	L	Cr	No. 2	L	Cr
No. 1 died December 21, 1914. No. 2 died September 23, 1914. No. 3 died February 27, 1914												
Census Card No. 2029, P. O. Eufaula, Enrolled January 23, 1901												
6310	1	Polk, Thomas K.	50	M	F		Thomas K. Polk	D	Cr	Sarshoye	D	Cr
6311	2	Polk, Lucinda	45	F	F	Wf	Unknown	D	Cr	Polly	L	Cr
6312	3	Polk, Sarshoye	9	F	F	D	No. 1	L	Cr	No. 2	L	Cr
No. 1 reported dead												
Census Card No. 2030, P. O. Eufaula, Enrolled January 24, 1901												
6313	1	Simpson, Mary U.	20	F	1-32		John F. Simpson	D	Non	Susan A. Simpson	L	Cr
Census Card No. 2031, P. O. Hanna, Enrolled January 30, 1901												
6314	1	Moore, Heney	23	F	F		Nocos Fixecoche	D	Cr	Tohkullikee	D	Cr
6315	2	Moore, Bessie	8	F	½	D	John W. Moore	L	Mex	No. 1	L	Cr
6316	3	Moore, Phillip	2	M	½	S	John W. Moore	L	Mex	No. 1	L	Cr
Census Card No. 2032, P. O. Hanna, Enrolled January 30, 1901												
6317	1	Smith, Wesley	65	M	F		Henehe Emarthoge	D	Cr	Totee	D	Cr
6318	2	Smith, Louina	42	F	¾	Wf	Sam Simmons	D	Cr	Chowestas Simmons	D	Cher
6319	3	Smith, Anna Eliza	12	F	⅞	D	No. 1	L	Cr	No. 2	L	Cr
No. 1 died February 17, 1901. No. 2 reported dead												
Census Card No. 2033, P. O. Eufaula, Enrolled No. 1 January 30, 1901; Nos. 2 and 3 March 8, 1901. No. 4 May 24, 1901												
6320	1	Tiger, William	45	M	F		Archie Tiger	L	Cr	Louina	D	Cr
6321	2	Tiger, Nancy	25	F	F	Wf	Sunda Foster	L	Cr	Lizzie McGilbra	L	Cr
6322	3	Jessie Katie	8	F	F	StD	Sampson Jessie	D	Cr	No. 2	L	Cr
6323	4	Francis, Martha	3	F	F	StD	Mitchell Francis	L	Cr	No. 2	L	Cr
No. 1 reported dead												
Census Card No. 2034, P. O. Bixby, Enrolled February 1, 1901												
6324	1	Yargee, John	23	M	F		Bunny Yargee	D	Cr	Louisa Peters	L	Cr
Census Card No. 2035, P. O. Hollow, Enrolled February 4, 1901												
6325	1	Merrell, Josie C.	23	F	1-16		John C. Barber	L	Cr	Annie M. Tovey	L	Cher
Census Card No. 2036, P. O. Mounds, Enrolled February 7, 1901												
6326	1	Miller, Thomas	18	M	F		Jim Miller	L	Cr	Susan Miller	D	Cr
Census Card No. 2037, P. O. Sapulpa, Enrolled February 8, 1901												
6327	1	Burgess, Benjamin E.	26	M	¾		Bean Burgess	L	Cher	Martha Byrgess	D	Cr
6328	2	Burgess, May	23	F	¼	Wf	F. M. Sanger	D	Non	Hannah Sanger	D	Cr
6329	3	Burgess, Walter	5	M	½	S	No. 1	L	Cr	No. 2	L	Cr
6330	4	Burgess, Ethel	1	F	½	D	No. 1	L	Cr	No. 2	L	Cr
Census Card No. 2038, P. O. Fry, Enrolled February 15, 1901												
6331	1	Burgess, Gussie	19	M	F		Daniel Burgess	D	Cr	Lowisa Burgess	D	Cr
No. 1 reported dead												
Census Card No. 2039, P. O. Paden, Enrolled February 15, 1901												
6332	1	Chisholm, Jesse	11	M	F		Frank Chisholm	D	Cr	Lucy Chisholm	L	Cr
6333	2	Chisholm, Nellie	5	F	F	Sis	Frank Chisholm	D	Cr	Lucy Chisholm	L	Cr
6334	3	Chisholm, Lucy	35	F	F	Moth	Little Bear	D	Shaw	Unknown	D	Cr
No. 2 died February 15, 1904. No. 3 died December 1900												
Census Card No. 2040, P. O. Eufaula; No. 2 Wetumka, Enrolled February 18, 1901; No. 2 May 17, 1901												
6335	1	Ansiel, Robert L.	27	M	1-16		William Ansiel	D	Cr	Jane Tiger	L	Non
6336	2	Ansiei, William W.	2	M	1-32	S	No. 1	L	Cr	Sadie A. Ansiel	L	Non
No. 1 died February 8, 1904												
Census Card No. 2041, P. O. Eufaula, Enrolled February 28, 1901												
6337	1	Ansiel, Charles A.	20	M	1-16		William Ansiel	D	Cr	Jane Tiger	L	Non
Census Card No. 2042, P. O. Beggs, Enrolled February 18, 1901; No. 4 March 27, 1901; Nos. 5 and 6 March 27, 1901												
6338	1	Franklin, Frank	16	M	⅛		Rentie Franklin	L	Non	Polly Franklin	L	Cr
6339	2	Franklin, Dave	14	M	⅛	Bro	Rentie Franklin	L	Non	Polly Franklin	L	Cr
6340	3	Franklin, Harriett	12	F	⅛	Sis	Rentie Franklin	L	Non	Polly Franklin	L	Cr
6341	4	Franklin, Polly	35	F	¼	Moth	Cumsey Bruner	D	Cr	Keno McQueen	D	Cr
6342	5	Franklin, Judy	8	F	⅛	Sis	Rentie Franklin	L	Non	Polly Franklin	L	Cr
6343	6	Franklin, Billie	4	M	⅛	Bro	Rentie Franklin	L	Non	Polly Franklin	L	Cr
No. 4 died 1900. No. 2 died February 1903												
Census Card No. 2043, P. O. Vivian, Enrolled February 18, 1901												
6344	1	Hart, Lucy	50	F	½		Toney	D	Cr	Polly Gamble	D	Cr
6345	2	Foster, Caroline	2	F	F	Ward	Mitchell Francis	L	Cr	Nancy Tiger	L	Cr
Census Card No. 2044, P. O. Checotah, Enrolled February 19, 1901												
6346	1	Carr, Addie	27	F	F		John Laslie	D	Cr	Charity Laslie	D	Cr
Census Card No. 2045, P. O. Eufaula, Enrolled February 19, 1901												
6347	1	Manley, Tom	21	M	F		Moses Manley	D	Cr	Disey Bullette	D	Cr
Census Card No. 2046, P. O. Paden, Enrolled February 21, 1901												
6348	1	Long, Mesulta	18	F	F		Sammie Chupko	D	Sem	Hokte Lokko	L	Cr
Census Card No. 2047, P. O. Eufaula, Enrolled February 25, 1901; No. 3 May 23, 1901; No. 4 May 24, 1901												
6349	1	Washington, Watson	30	M	½		George Washington	D	Cr	Kogee Washington	D	Cr
6350	2	Washington, Lucy	25	F	F	Wf	Cabecha	D	Cr	Nannie	D	Cr
6351	3	Washington, Ida	3	F	¾	D	No. 1	L	Cr	No. 2	L	Cr
6352	4	Washington, Minnie	1	F	¾	D	No. 1	L	Cr	No. 2	L	Cr
No. 2 died July 9, 1906. No. 4 died July 1912												

Roll No.	No.	NAME	Age	Sex	Blood	Rel.	NAME OF FATHER	Liv.	Cit.	NAME OF MOTHER	Liv.	Cit.
		Census Card No. 2048, P. O. Eufaula, Enrolled February 25, 1901										
6353	1	Riley, Moese	23	M	F		Joe Riley	D	Cr	Chinna	D	Cr
		No. 1 died January 14, 1911										
		Census Card No. 2049, P. O. Vivian, Enrolled February 25, 1901										
6354	1	Jackson, George	26	M	F		Simmon Jackson	L	Cr	Unknown	D	Cr
		Census Card No. 2050, P. O. Eufaula, Enrolled February 26, 1901; No. 3 March 2, 1901; No. 4 April 23, 1901; No. 5 May 22, 1901										
6355	1	Polk, Benjamin	6	M	¼		Walter R. Polk	L	Non	No. 4	L	Cr
6356	2	Polk, Comfort	4	F	¼	Sis	Walter R. Polk	L	Non	No. 4	L	Cr
6357	3	Polk, Delilah	3	F	¼	Sis	Walter R. Polk	L	Non	No. 4	L	Cr
6358	4	Polk, Delilah	32	F	½	Moth	Johnson Hodge	D	Cr	Margaret Hodge	L	Non
6359	5	Polk, Walter	6 mo	M	¼	Bro	Walter R. Polk	L	Cr	No. 4	L	Cr
		No. 4 died April 21, 1900. No. 5 died October 1900										
		Census Card No. 2051, P. O. Muskogee, Enrolled February 26, 1901										
6360	1	Hodge, Lela	18	F	½		Johnson Hodge	D	Cr	Margaret Hodge	L	Non
		No. 1 reported dead										
		Census Card No. 2052, P. O. Tulsa, Enrolled March 1, 1901; No. 2 May 23, 1901; No. 3 May 24, 1901										
6361	1	Starr, Chesley	28	M	F		Chowastia	D	Cr	Unknown	D	Cr
6362	2	Starr, Katie	30	F	F	Wf	Unknown	D	Cr	Unknown	D	Cr
6363	3	Starr, Martha	6	F	F	D	No. 1	L	Cr	No. 2	L	Cr
		No. 2 died April 14, 1900. No. 3 died 1900										
		Census Card No. 2053, P. O. Hanna, Enrolled March 4, 1901; No. 2 March 15, 1901										
6364	1	Washington, Moses	24	M	¾		George Washington	D	Cr	Kogee Washington	D	Cr
6365	2	Washington, Linda	30	F	F	Wf	Pin Emarthla	D	Cr	Lizzie	D	Cr
		No. 2 died February 17, 1906										
		Census Card No. 2054, P. O. Bristow, Enrolled March 4, 1901										
6366	1	Cates, Joseph	50	M	F		Jeff Cates	D	Cr	Harriet Cates	D	Cr
		Census Card No. 2055, P. O. Checotah, Enrolled March 4, 1901										
6367	1	Spaulding, Edith	20	F	1-16		S. C. Asbell	D	Non	Sarah Asbell	L	Cr
		Census Card No. 2056, P. O. Fentress, Enrolled March 6, 1901										
6368	1	Yaholar, Thomas	65	M	F		Tulmars Fixico	D	Cr	Unknown	D	Cr
6369	2	Yaholar, Mary	60	F	F	Wf	Parhos Harjo	D	Cr	Matalokee	D	Cr
6370	3	Yaholar, Roman	15	M	F	S	No. 1	L	Cr	No. 2	L	Cr
		No. 1 died July 13, 1912. No. 2 died July 9, 1910										
		Census Card No. 2057, P. O. Fentress, Enrolled March 6, 1901										
6371	1	Cook, Leah	19	F	F		Thomas Yaholar	L	Cr	Mary Yaholar	L	Cr
		No. 1 reported dead										
		Census Card No. 2058, P. O. Fentress, Enrolled March 6, 1901										
6372	1	Yaholar, Louis	35	M	F		Thomas Yaholar	L	Cr	Mary Yaholar	L	Cr
		No. 1 reported dead										
		Census Card No. 2059, P. O. Hanna, Enrolled March 6, 1901										
6373	1	Hill, James	40	M	F		Hilly	D	Cr	Allyah	D	Cr
6374	2	Hill, Polly	23	F	F	Wf	Chewey Motley	D	Cr	Mary Deer	D	Cr
6375	3	Hill, Luetta	14	F	F	D	No. 1	L	Cr	Louisa Hill	D	Cr
6376	4	Hill, Kate	12	F	F	D	No. 1	L	Cr	Louisa Hill	D	Cr
6377	5	Hill, Leah	7	F	F	D	No. 1	L	Cr	Louisa Hill	D.	Cr
6378	6	Hill, Fanny	3	F	F	D	No. 1	L	Cr	No. 2	L	Cr
		No. 4 died May 1. 1910. No. 3 died March 13, 1902										
		Census Card No. 2060, P. O. Okmulgee, Enrolled March 8, 1901										
6379	1	Blackwell, Lucy	21	F	¾		Henry Thompson	L	Cr	Josephene Thompson	L	Cr
		Census Card No. 2061, P. O. Hanna; No. 3 Dustin, Enrolled March 9, 1901										
6380	1	Byrd, James	50	M	F		Thomas Bird	D	Cr	Nancy Bird	D	Cr
6381	2	Byrd, Judy	40	F	F	Wf	Osuch Fixico	D	Cr	Behaye	L	Cr
6382	3	Byrd, Jennetta	19	F	F	D	No. 1	L	Cr	No. 2	L	Cr
		No. 1 died January 13, 1905. No. 3 died April 6, 1912										
		Census Card No. 2062, P. O. Onapa, Enrolled March 9, 1901										
6383	1	Richard Kogee	30	F	F		Samuel Richard	L	Cr	Kizzie Richard	D	Cr
		Census Card No. 2063, P. O. Okmulgee, Enrolled March 9, 1901										
6384	1	Beaver, Halleyamson	27	M	F		Echas Yahola	D	Cr	Unknown	D	Cr
		Census Card No. 2064, P. O. Beggs, Enrolled March 11, 1901										
6385	1	Washington, Dixon	22	M	F		George Washington	D	Cr	Martha Sevier	L	Cr
		Census Card No. 2065, P. O. Okmulgee, Enrolled March 11, 1901										
6386	1	Micco, Hully	50	M	F		Iyechache	D	Cr	Unknown	D	Cr
		No. 1 reported dead										
		Census Card No. 2066, P. O. Wetumka, Enrolled March 11, 1901										
6387	1	Scott, William	23	M	F		George Scott	D	Cr	Jennie Scott	D	Cr
6388	2	Scott, Mahoye	25	F	F	Wf	Tabus Harjo	L	Cr	Luffie	L	Cr
6389	3	Butler, Pusler	10	M	F	StS	John Butler	D	Cr	No. 2	L	Cr
		No. 1 died October 1, 1905										
		Census Card No. 2067, P. O. Okmulgee, Enrolled March 11, 1901										
6390	1	Thompson, Josephene	67	F	½		Wm. Childers	D	Non	Mariah Childers	D	Cr
6391	2	Thompson, Henry	13	M	¼	GrS	Samuel Thompson	D	Cr	Cora Thompson	D	Non
6392	3	Thompson, Riley	14	M	¼	GrS	Samuel Thompson	D	Cr	Cora Thompson	D	Cr
		Census Card No. 2068, P. O. Checotah, Enrolled March 12, 1901										
6393	1	Collins, Wash	50	M	F		Shawnee Collins	D	Cr	Linda Collins	D	Cr
6394	2	Collins, Jennie	30	F	F	Wf	Jim Grayson	D	Cr	Louisa Grayson	D	Cr
6395	3	Collins, Willie	18	M	F	S	No. 1	L	Cr	Nicey Collins	D	Cr
6396	4	Collins, Addie	15	F	F	D	No. 1	L	Cr	Nicey Collins	D	Cr
6397	5	Collins, Wash, Jr.	13	M	F	S	No. 1	L	Cr	Nicey Collins	D	Cr
		No. 2 died 1905. No. 5 died October 11, 1909. No. 1 died July 15, 1909										

Roll No.	No.	NAME	Age	Sex	Blood	Rel.	NAME OF FATHER	Liv.	Cit.	NAME OF MOTHER	Liv.	Cit.
		Census Card No. 2069, P. O. Bearden, Enrolled March 13, 1901; Nos. 2 and 3 March 25, 1901										
6398	1	Harjo, Shanco	27	M	F		Oche Harjo	D	Cr	Minte Harjo	L	Cr
6399	2	Harjo, Maudie	50	F	F	Moth	Carpitcha Fixico	D	Cr	Hokte	L	Cr
6400	3	Harjo, Sandy	10	M	F	Bro	Oche Harjo	D	Cr	No. 2	L	Cr
		Census Card No. 2070, P. O. Wetumka, Enrolled March 13, 1901										
6401	1	Marshall, Leonidas	43	M	F		Concharte Micco	L	Cr	Sadeloke	D	Cr
		Census Card No. 2071, P. O. Wetumka, Enrolled March 13, 1901										
6402	1	Yargee, Sam	19	M	F		Alex Yargee	D	Cr	Leasker	L	Cr
		Census Card No. 2072, P. O. Bristow, Enrolled March 14, 1901										
6403	1	Dasher, Louisa	16	F	½		Frank Dasher	D	Non	Jane Dasher	D	Cr
6404	2	Dasher, Annie Zora	12	F	½	Sis	Frank Dasher	D	Non	Jane Dasher	D	Cr
6405	3	Dasher, Ida Belle	8	F	½	Sis	Frank Dasher	D	Non	Jane Dasher	D	Cr
		Census Card No. 2073, P. O. Wetumka, Enrolled March 14, 1901										
6406	1	Scott, Billie	45	M	F		Hathlen Harjo	D	Cr	Mollie Harjo	D	Cr
6407	2	Scott, Losanna	42	F	F	Wf	Csoche Emarthla	D	Cr	Martha Emarthla	D	Cr
6408	3	Harjo, Willie	11	M	F	StS	Tulwa Harjo	D	Cr	No. 2	L	Cr
6409	4	Harjo, Charley	6	M	F	StS	Tulwa Harjo	D	Cr	No. 2	L	Cr
6410	5	Scott, Sowitee	35	F	F	Wf	Unknown	D	Cr	Tachka	D	Cr
6411	6	Scott, Kissie	18	F	F	D	No. 1	L	Cr	No. 5	L	Cr
6412	7	Scott, Annie	5	F	F	D	No. 1	L	Cr	No. 5	L	Cr
		No. 5 died July 1900. No. 1 reported dead. No. 6 died August 22, 1900. No. 7 died June 1900										
		Census Card No. 2074, P. O. Wetumka, Enrolled March 14, 1901										
6413	1	Tiger, Thloppie	21	M	F		Jacob Tiger	D	Cr	Hannah Hill	D	Cr
		Census Card No. 2075, P. O. Wetumka, Enrolled March 14, 1901										
6414	1	Gray, Walter	30	M	F		Elijah Gray	D	Cr	Choctiger	D	Cr
6415	2	Gray, Annie	25	F	F	Wf	Nutta Wesley	D	Cr	Louisa Gray	L	Cr
		No. 1 died November 17, 1902. No. 2 died October 20, 1906										
		Census Card No. 2076, P. O. Sapulpa, Enrolled March 15, 1901; No. 6 May 24, 1901										
6416	1	Partridge, Toby	24	M	F		Thahepne Partridge	D	Cr	Beeker Partridge	D	Cr
6417	2	Partridge, Mary	27	F	F	Wf	George Bruner	D	Cr	Anna Bruner	L	Cr
6418	3	Berryhill, Willie	8	M	F	StS	Sam Berryhill	D	Cr	No. 2	L	Cr
6419	4	Partridge, Amos	13	M	F	StS	Noah Partridge	D	Cr	No. 2	L	Cr
6420	5	Partridge, Ollie	1	F	F	D	No. 1	L	Cr	No. 2	L	Cr
6421	6	Partridge, Alice	2	F	F	D	No. 1	L	Cr	No. 2	L	Cr
		No. 1 died December 1899. No. 6 reported dead										
		Census Card No. 2077, P. O. Checotah, Enrolled March 15, 1901										
6422	1	McIntosh, Morie	49	M	¼		Cuffey McIntosh	D	Cr	Wisey McIntosh	D	Cr
		No. 1 died March 10, 1904										
		Census Card No. 2078, P. O. Sasakwa, Enrolled March 15, 1901										
6423	1	McGirt, William	54	M	F		Daniel McGirt	D	Cr	Susie McGirt	D	Cr
		Census Card No. 2079, P. O. Broken Arrow, Enrolled March 15, 1901										
6424	1	Lee, Nicey	13	F	F		Apaula Harjo	D	Cr	Lucy Lee	D	Cr
		Census Card No. 2080, P. O. Hanna, Enrolled March 15, 1901										
6425	1	Green, Tecumseh	34	M	F		Coweta	D	Cr	Lechakueche	D	Cr
6426	2	Green, Jimmy	14	M	F	S	No. 1	L	Cr	Absey	L	Cr
6427	3	Green, Nicey	11	F	F	D	No. 1	L	Cr	Absey	L	Cr
		No. 3 died August 7, 1911										
		Census Card No. 2081, P. O. Salem, Enrolled March 18, 1901										
6428	1	Homer, Alex	46	M	F		Capecha Fixico	D	Cr	Polly White	D	Cr
		Census Card No. 2082, P. O. Salem, Enrolled March 18, 1901										
6429	1	Hall, Lena	18	F	F		Alex Homer	L	Cr	Chowanie	D	Cr
		Census Card No. 2083, P. O. Hitchita, Enrolled March 18, 1901										
6430	1	Bosen, Mary	43	F	F		Amos Bosen	D	Cr	Peggy Bosen	D	Cr
6431	2	Gray, Annie	11	F	F	D	Lewis Gray	L	Cr	No. 1	L	Cr
		Census Card No. 2084, P. O. Sapulpa, Enrolled March 18, 1901										
6432	1	Tom, Euchee	22	M	F		Warnarkee	D	Cr	Yanfohcoconthla	D	Cr
6433	2	Warnarkee, Silla	15	F	F	Sis	Warnarkee	D	Cr	Yanfohcoconthla	D	Cr
6434	3	Warnarkee, Wicey	10	F	F	Sis	Warnarkee	D	Cr	Yanfohcoconthla	D	Cr
		Census Card No. 2085, P. O. Wewoka, Enrolled March 18, 1901										
6435	1	Johnson, Lydia	14	F	½		Peter Johnson	D	Cr	Ella Johnson	D	Non
6436	2	Johnson, Mahala	8	F	½	Sis	Peter Johnson	D	Cr	Ella Johnson	D	Non
		No. 2 died July 17, 1907										
		Census Card No. 2086, P. O. Salem, Enrolled March 18, 1901; No. 2 and 3 May 20, 1901										
6437	1	Fife, Jimmie	27	M	F		Tulwa Fixico	D	Cr	Millie Fife	D	Cr
6438	2	Fife, Lucinda	19	F	F	Wf	Katchoche	D	Cr	Meleah	L	Cr
6439	3	Fife, Timmie	18	moM	F	S	No. 1	L	Cr	No. 2	L	Cr
		No. 3 reported dead										
		Census Card No. 2087, P. O. Arbeka, Enrolled March 19, 1901; No. 2 May 22, 1901										
6440	1	Harjo, Cowe	49	M	F		Tarcos Yahola	D	Cr	Katie	D	Cr
6441	2	Harjo, Peggy	48	F	F	Wf	Parhos Mekko	D	Cr	Magethhoye	D	Cr
		Nos. 1 and 2 reported dead										
		Census Card No. 2088, P. O. Sapulpa, Enrolled March 19, 1901; No. 4 March 26, 1901										
6442	1	Sapulpa, James	40	M	F		Sapulpa	D	Cr	Eliza	D	Cr
6443	2	Sapulpa, Lizzie B.	23	F	F	Wf	Peter Barnett	D	Cr	Nancy Barnett	D	Cr
6444	3	McComb, Joseph	7	M	F	Ward	Marcellus McCombs	D	Cr	Yarner McCombs	D	Cr
6445	4	Sapulpa, Rosa	14	F	F	D	No. 1	L	Cr	Totba Sapulpa	D	Cr
		No. 4 died February 15, 1900										
		Census Card No. 2089, P. O. Arbeka, Enrolled March 19, 1901; No. 2 May 22, 1901										
6446	1	Hill, Arney	29	F	F		Ahlipahte Harjo	D	Cr	Mattie	D	Cr
6447	2	Hill, Ida	8	F	F	D	Amos Hill	D	Cr	No. 1	L	Cr
		No. 1 died August 28, 1908. No. 2 died May 15, 1900										

135

Census Card No. 2090, P. O. Wetumka, Enrolled March 19, 1901; No. 2 May 22, 1901

Roll No.	No.	NAME	Age	Sex	Blood	Rel.	Name of Father	Liv.	Cit.	Name of Mother	Liv.	Cit.
6448	1	Wesley, Polly	28	F	F		Billie Scott	L	Cr	Sowite	D	Cr
6449	2	Solomon, Lahtah	4	F	F	D	Charny Solomon	D	Cr	No. 1	L	Cr
6450	3	Solomon, Celey	2	F	F	D	Charny Solomon	D	Cr	No. 1	L	Cr

No. 2 died May 1900. No. 3 died February 10, 1900

Census Card No. 2091, P. O. Wewoka, Enrolled March 19, 1901

6451	1	Brown, Clarence W.	21	M	½		A. J. Brown	L	Sem	Lou Brown	L	Cr

Census Card No. 2092, P. O. Wetumka, Enrolled March 19, 1901; No. 2 May 22, 1901

6452	1	Tiller, John	50	M	F		Unknown	D	Cr	Simma	D	Cr
6453	2	Tiller, Loodie	29	F	F	Wf	Fushutche Harjo	D	Cr	Liddie	D	Cr

No. 2 died July 13, 1906

Census Card No. 2093, P. O. Wetumka, Enrolled March 19, 1901; No. 5 May 22, 1901

6454	1	Scott, Wiley	31	M	F		Tigochie	D	Cr	Mitiague	D	Cr
6455	2	Scott, Rosanna	23	F	F	Wf	Fushutch Emarthla	D	Cr	Melissa	L	Cr
6456	3	Scott, Sukey	10	F	F	D	No. 1	L	Cr	Betsy Scott	L	Cr
6457	4	Scott, Mary	7	F	F	D	No. 1	L	Cr	Betsy Scott	L	Cr
6458	5	Scott, Daniel	1	M	F	S	No. 1	L	Cr	No. 2	L	Cr
6459	6	Scott, Betsey	28	F	F	Wf	Woxie Harjo	D	Cr	Peggy Scott	L	Cr

No. 6 died April 28, 1899. No. 5 died February 6, 1907·

Census Card No. 2094, P. O. Holdenville, Enrolled March 19, 1901

6460	1	Lindsey, Walter	25	M	F		Lindsey	L	Sem	Hepsey	L	Cr

Census Card No. 2095, P. O. Wetumka, Enrolled March 19, 1901

6461	1	Penn, William	40	M	F		Tuckabatchee Yahola	D	Cr	Unknown	D	Cr
6462	2	Penn, Miley	32	F	F	Wf	Fushutchee Emarthla	D	Cr	Melissa Emarthla	L	Cr
6463	3	Penn, Annie	12	F	F	D	No. 1	L	Cr	No. 2	L	Cr
6464	4	Penn, Sharpsey	2	M	F	S	No. 1	L	Cr	No. 2	L	Cr

No. 4 died December 28, 1899. No. 1 reported dead

Census Card No. 2096, P. O. Wewoka; No. 2 and 3 Holdenville, Enrolled March 20, 1901; No. 3 May 8, 1901

6465	1	McGirt, Hepsie	57	F	F		Daniel McGirt	D	Cr	Wisey McGirt	D	Cr
6466	2	Lindsey, Mulka	13	M	F	S	Lindsey	L	Sem	No. 1	L	Cr
6467	3	Lindsey, Minnie	16	F	F	D	Lindsey	L	Sem	No. 1	L	Cr

No. 3 died February 8, 1901. No. 2 reported dead

Census Card No. 2097, P. O. Holdenville, Enrolled March 20, 1901

6468	1	Hopaye, Ahalek	80	M	F			D	Cr	Unknown	D	Cr

No. 1 reported dead. John Foley Holdenville, Okla., is a grand son of No. 1

Census Card No. 2098, P. O. Okemah, Enrolled March 20, 1901; No. 3 May 26, 1901

6469	1	Harjo, Alex	27	M	F		Catchar Harjo	D	Sem	Lucy Conner	D	Cr
6470	2	Harjo, Nancy	22	F	F	Wf	Parhose Harjo	D	Cr	Cinda Harjo	D	Cr
6471	3	Frank, Ella	2	F	F	StD	Barney Frank	L	Cr	No. 2	L	Cr

Census Card No. 2099, P. O. Okemah, Enrolled March 20, 1901

6472	1	Harjo, Albert	21	M	F		Catchar Harjo	D	Sem	Lucy Conner	D	Cr
6473	2	Harjo, Martha	18	F	F	Sis	Catchar Harjo	D	Sem	Lucy Conner	D	Cr

Census Card No. 2100, P. O. Wetumka, Enrolled March 20, 1901

6474	1	Bird, James	25	M	F		Fushutcha Emarthla	D	Cr	Melissie	L	Cr
6475	2	Bird, Nelsie	24	F	F	Wf	Sunjony	D	Cr	Sulka	L	Cr
6476	3	Bird, Willie	7	M	F	S	No. 1	L	Cr	No. 2	L	Cr
6477	4	Bird, Malinda	1	F	F	D	No. 1	L	Cr	No. 2	L	Cr

No. 2 died August 6, 1901. No. 4 died February 13, 1912

Census Card No. 2101, P. O. Wetumka, Enrolled March 20, 1901

6478	1	Frazier, Nettie	25	F	⅞		Robert Carr	L	Cr	Bettie Carr	L	Cr

Census Card No. 2102, P. O. Wetumka, Enrolled March 20, 1901

6479	1	King, Amos	31	M	F		Kochus Micco	D	Cr	Unknown	D	Cr
6480	2	King, Simondy	24	F	F	Wf	Haney Scott	D	Cr	Unknown	D	Cr
6481	3	King, Louis	9	M	F	S	No. 1	L	Cr	No. 2	L	Cr
6482	4	King, Harney	3	M	F	S	No. 1	L	Cr	No. 2	L	Cr

No. 4 died September 1900

Census Card No. 2103, P. O. Depew, Enrolled March 21, 1901

6483	1	Conpethloney	35	M	F		John Bigpond	D	?	Yaconney	D	Cr
6484	2	Pelah	17	F	F	D	No. 1	L	?	Lucy	D	Cr
6485	3	Hetawcoweney	15	M	F	S	No. 1	L	?	Lucy	D	Cr
6486	4	Wattie	13	F	F	D	No. 1	L	?	Lucy	D	Cr
6487	5	Cotetan	11	M	F	S	No. 1	L	?	Lucy	D	Cr

No. 3 died in fall of 1904. No. 2 died.

Census:Card No. 2104, P. O. Depew, Enrolled March 21, 1901

6488	1	Bigpond, James	38	M	F		Jack	D	Cr	Unknown	D	Cr
6489	2	Bigpond, Gosse	35	F	F	Wf	John Bigpond	D	Cr	Yaconney	D	Cr
6490	3	Bigpond, Odie	15	M	F	S	No. 1	L	Cr	No. 2	L	Cr
6491	4	Bigpond, William	13	M	F	S	No. 1	L	Cr	No. 2	L	Cr
6492	5	Bigpond, James, Jr.	11	M	F	S	No. 1	L	Cr	No. 2	L	Cr
6493	6	Bigpond, Uconthla	6	M	F	S	No. 1	L	Cr	No. 2	L	Cr

No. 3 died July 25, 1911

Census Card No. 2105, P. O. Holdenville, Enrolled March 21, 1901

6494	1	Ellis, Amos	18	M	½		Edwin Ellis	L	Shaw	Lucy Shawnego	L	Cr

Census Card No. 2106, P. O. Fentress, Enrolled March 21, 1901

6495	1	Tiger, Pinar	35	F	F		Unknown	D	Cr	Roseanna	L	Cr
6496	2	Tiger, Turner	18	M	F	S	Sandy Tiger	D	Cr	No. 1	L	Cr
6497	3	Tiger, Sissy	15	F	F	D	Sandy Tiger	D	Cr	No. 1	L	Cr
6498	4	Tiger, George	12	M	F	S	Sandy Tiger	D	Cr	No. 1	L	Cr

Roll No.	No.	NAME	Age	Sex	Blood	Rel.	NAME OF FATHER	Liv.	Cit.	NAME OF MOTHER	Liv.	Cit.

Census Card No. 2107, P. O. Bristow, Enrolled March 21, 1901

Roll No.	No.	NAME	Age	Sex	Blood	Rel.	NAME OF FATHER	Liv.	Cit.	NAME OF MOTHER	Liv.	Cit.
6499	1	Tiger, Philip	23	M	F		Tiger Jack	L	Cr	Gosse Bigpond	L	Cr
6500	2	Tiger, Lodie	20	F	F	Wf	Sahtah	D	Cr	Sibbie	L	Cr
6501	3	Tiger, Tasharlacocon-thla	5	M	F	S	No. 1	L	Cr	No. 2	L	Cr

No. 1 died December 30, 1902. No. 2 died December 13, 1902

Census Card No. 2108, P. O. Wewoka, Enrolled March 21, 1901

6502	1	Harjo, Aharluck	65	M	F		Unknown	D	Cr	Monadezie	D	Cr
6503	2	Harjo, Tommie	17	M	F	S	No. 1	L	Cr	Janoleezie	D	Cr

No. 1 died April 7, 1908

Census Card No. 2109, P. O. Hitchita, Enrolled March 21, 1901

6504	1	Doyle, Tyler	22	M	¾		Dave Doyle	D	Cr	Scilla Doyle	D	Cr

Census Card No. 2110, P. O. Council Hill, Enrolled March 21, 1901

6505	1	Likowski, Senora E.	29	F	¼		John McIntosh	L	Cr	Lydia	D	Cr
6506	2	Likowski, Joseph	9	M	⅛	S	Frank Likowski	L	Non	No. 1	L	Cr
6507	3	Likowski, Lydia Lucile	6	F	⅛	D	Frank Likowski	L	Non	No. 1	L	Cr
6508	4	Likowski, James B.	4	M	⅛	S	Frank Likowski	L	Non	No. 1	L	Cr
6509	5	Likowski, Frank Jr.,	1	M	⅛	S	Frank Likowski	L	Non	No. 1	L	Cr

Census Card No. 2111, P. O. Carson, Enrolled March 21, 1901

6510	1	Bruner, Thomas	45	M	F		Cotcha Micco	D	Cr	Tutchepe	D	Cr
6511	2	Bruner, Mekey	40	F	F	Wf	Parbose Yahola	D	Cr	Peggy	D	Cr
6512	3	Bruner, Losanna	12	F	F	StD	Cowe Harjo	D	Cr	No. 2	L	Cr

No. 2 died March 7, 1902. No. 3 died March 3, 1902.

Census Card No. 2112, P. O. Pierce, Enrolled March 21, 1901

6513	1	Tiger, Joseph	53	M	F		Cotsar Tustenuggy	D	Cr	Lucy Charlie	D	Cr
6514	2	Tiger, Dosie	50	F	F	Wf	Sardy	D	Cr	Katie	D	Cr
6515	3	Tiger, Lillie	13	F	F	D	No. 1	L	Cr	No. 2	L	Cr
6516	4	Tiger, Katie	12	F	F	D	No. 1	L	Cr	No. 2	L	Cr

No. 2 died July 11, 1907. No. 1 died March 10, 1908.

Census Card No. 2113, P. O. Schulter, Enrolled March 21, 1901

6517	1	Kernell, Sam	37	M	F		Poppy Kernell	D	Cr	Nancy Kernell	D	Cr

Census Card No. 2114, P. O. Holdenville, Enrolled March 21, 1901

6518	1	Stubblefield, Ida	20	F	⅛		John Hulsey	L	Non	Eliza Hulsey	D	Cr
6519	2	Stubblefield, Ella M.	1	F	1-16 D		J. M. Stubblefield	L	Non	No. 1	L	Cr

Census Card No. 2115, P. O. Holdenville, Enrolled March 22, 1901; No. 4, May 22, 1901

6520	1	Anderson, Martha	23	F	F		Tom Anderson	D	Cr	Geley	D	Cr
6521	2	Anderson, Annie	8	F	F	D	John Brown	D	Sem	No. 1	L	Cr
6522	3	Anderson, Alma	2	M	F	S	John Brown	D	Sem	No. 1	L	Cr
6523	4	Charley, Stella	1	F	F	D	Thomas Charley	L	Cr	No. 1	L	Cr

No. 3 died January 6, 1900. No. 4 died December 8, 1900.

Census Card No. 2116, P. O. Okemah, Enrolled March 22, 1901

6524	1	Hill, Elmer	19	M	F		Upney Hill	D	Cr	Lucinda Hill	D	Cr

Census Card No. 2117, P. O. Schulter, Enrolled March 22, 1901; No. 4, April 26, 1901

6525	1	Kanard, Washington	34	M	F		Peter Kanard	D	Cr	Puttie	D	Cr
6526	2	Kanard, Fannie	23	F	F	Wf	Joe Watson	L	Cr	Hannah Mitchell	L	Cr
6527	3	Watson, Amos	7	M	F	StD	Unknown	D	Cr	No. 2	L	Cr
6528	4	Kanard, Bettie	2	F	F	D	No. 1	L	Cr	No. 2	L	Cr

No. 1 died October 8, 1900. No. 2 died December 30, 1910.

Census Card No. 2118, P. O. Grayson, Enrolled March 22, 1901

6529	1	Segro, Tom	46	M	F		Unknown	D	Cr	Unknown	D	Cr

No. 1 died January 9, 1900

Census Card No. 2119, P. O. Fame, Enrolled March 22, 1901; Nos. 8 and 9, April 16, 1901

6530	1	Gray, Siah	37	M	F		Tuswa Harjo	D	Cr	Lucinda Harjo	D	Cr
6531	2	Gray, Mary	32	F	F	Wf	Simmer Thompson	D	Cr	Sophia	D	Cr
6532	3	Gray, Thomas	16	M	F	S	No. 1	L	Cr	No. 2	L	Cr
6533	4	Gray, Emma	14	F	F	S	No. 1	L	Cr	No. 2	L	Cr
6534	5	Gray, Edmond	12	M	F	D	No. 1	L	Cr	No. 2	L	Cr
6535	6	Gray, Jobie	8	M	F	S	No. 1	L	Cr	No. 2	L	Cr
6536	7	Gray, Lucinda	6	F	F	D	No. 1	L	Cr	No. 2	L	Cr
6537	8	Gray, Nancy	4	F	F	D	No. 1	L	Cr	No. 2	L	Cr
6538	9	Gray, Nettie	2	F	F	D	No. 1	L	Cr	No. 1	L	Cr

No. 9 died March 24, 1899. No. 2 died October 9, 1906.

Census Card No. 2120, P. O. Wetumka, Enrolled March 22, 1901

6539	1	Tiger, Annie	21	F	F		Louis Tiger	D	Cr	Aga Tiger	D	Cr
6540	2	Bird, Stella	1	F	F	D	Felix Bird	D	Cr	No. 1	L	Cr

Census Card No. 2121, P. O. Hanna, Enrolled March 22, 1901

6541	1	Thompson, Susanna	20	F	F		Dick Isaac	D	Cr	Nancy Thompson	D	Cr

Census Card No. 2122, P. O. Salem, Enrolled March 23, 1901

6542	1	Ryal, Annie	36	F	F		Jim Gray	D	Cr	Louisa Gray	D	Cr
6543	2	Ryal, Emma	14	F	½	D	L. B. Ryal	L	Non	No. 1	L	Cr
6544	3	Ryal, John B.	10	M	½	S	L. B. Ryal	L	Non	No. 1	L	Cr
6545	4	Ryal, Grover	8	M	½	S	L. B. Ryal	L	Non	No. 1	L	Cr
6546	5	Ryal, Hallie	5	F	½	D	L. B. Ryal	L	Non	No. 1	L	Cr
6547	6	Ryal, Lewis J.	1	M	½	S	L. B. Ryal	L	Non	No. 1	L	Cr

Census Card No. 2123, P. O. Broken Arrow, Enrolled March 23, 1901

6548	1	Drew, Legus C.	13	M	½		Daniel Drew	D	Cr	Maggie Drew	D	Cr

No. 1 reported dead

Census Card No. 2124, P. O. Lenna, Enrolled March 23, 1901

6549	1	Thompson, Roman.	20	M	F		Sota Thompson	D	Cr	Loska	D	Cr

Roll No.	No.	NAME	Age	Sex	Blood	Rel.	NAME OF FATHER	Liv.	Cit.	NAME OF MOTHER	Liv.	Cit.
	Census Card No. 2125, P. O. Lenora, Enrolled March 25, 1901											
6550	1	Arpinculikee	43	F	F		Tallemarsey	D	Cr	Elizabeth	D	Cr
6551	2	Starr, Chipley	23	M	F	S	Martin Starr	L	Cr	No. 1	L	Cr
6552	3	Starr, Nancy	15	F	F	D	Martin Starr	L	Cr	No. 1	L	Cr
6553	4	Starr, Reuben	12	M	F	S	Martin Starr	L	Cr	No. 1	L	Cr
		No. 2 died in fall of 1902. Nos. 3 and 4 reported dead.										
	Census Card No. 2126, P. O. Wetumka; No. 3, Wewoka, Enrolled March 25, 1901											
6554	1	Harjo, Eufala	48	M	F		Haba	D	Cr	Sutanage	D	Cr
6555	2	Harjo, Sulsey	40	F	F	Wf	Pahos Harjo	D	Cr	Cinda	D	Cr
6556	3	Harjo, Nancy	12	F	F	D	No. 1	L	Cr	No. 2	L	Cr
6557	4	Harjo, Lewey	7	M	F	S	No. 1	L	Cr	No. 2	L	Cr
6558	5	Harjo, Isaac	4	M	F	S	No. 1	L	Cr	No. 2	L	Cr
6559	6	Harjo, Henry	1	M	F	S	No. 1	L	Cr	No. 2	L	Cr
		No. 1 died July 5, 1903										
	Census Card No. 2127, P. O. Indianola, Enrolled March 25, 1901; No. 4, April 9, 1901; No. 6, April 19, 1901											
6560	1	Bright, John	40	M	F		Mechiska Harjo	D	Cr	Mockta	D	Cr
6561	2	Marshall, Tucker	16	M	F	Neph	Tulmarsey	D	Cr	Bettie Tulmarsey	D	Cr
6562	3	Yonder, Polly	18	F	F	Niece	George Fish	D	Cr	Bettie Tulmarsey	D	Cr
6563	4	Peter, Lizzie	17	F	F	Cou	Simon Peter	D	Cr	Nicey Peter	L	Cr
6564	5	Bright, Rhoda	20	F	F	Wf	Lofa Manley	L	Cr	Lizzie Manley	L	Cr
		No. 4 died April 16, 1905. No. 1 died November 18, 1910.										
	Census Card No. 2128, P. O. Bearden, Enrolled March 25, 1901											
6565	1	King, Haney	26	M	F		Hotulke Micco	D	Cr	Susanna	D	Cr
		No. 1 reported dead										
	Census Card No. 2129, P. O. Wetumka, Enrolled March 25, 1901											
6566	1	Bird, Melissa	60	F	F		Unknown	D	Cr	Hannah	D	Cr
		No. 1 reported dead										
	Census Card No. 2130, P. O. Wetumka, Enrolled March 25, 1901; No. 3, May 13, 1901											
6567	1	Lucas, Sallie	23	F	F		Tupios (?) Harjo	L	Cr	Dinah Harjo	D	Cr
6568	2	Lucas, Bettie	5	F	½	D	John Lucas	L	Non	No. 1	L	Cr
6569	3	Lucas, Amos	1	M	½	S	John Lucas	L	Non	No. 1	L	Cr
		No. 2 reported dead										
	Census Card No. 2131, P. O. Okemah, Enrolled March 25, 1901											
6570	1	Comie, Thomas	21	M	F		Euchee Micco	D	Cr	Lucy	D	Cr
		No. 1 reported dead										
	Census Card No. 2132, P. O. Wetumka, Enrolled March 25, 1901											
6571	1	Harjo, Turpus	45	M	F		Neha Yaholar	D	Cr	Unknown	D	Cr
6572	2	Harjo, Sarwakhoche	43	F	F	Wf	Sodedon Emartha	D	Cr	- Welakakochee	D	Cr
6573	3	Harjo, Lucy	18	F	F	D	No. 1	L	Cr	No.	L	Cr
6574	4	Harjo, William	12	M	F	F S	No. 1	L	Cr	No.	L	Cr
6575	5	Harjo, Annie	10	F	F	D	No. 1	L	Cr	No. 2	L	Cr
6576	6	Harjo, James	6	M	F	F S	No. 1	L	Cr	No.	L	Cr
6577	7	Harjo, Belle	4	F	F	D	No. 1	L	Cr	No.	L	Cr
		No. 1 died July 21, 1911										
	Census Card No. 2133, P. O. Wetumka, Enrolled March 25, 1901											
6578	1	Lucas, Susan	21	F	F		Turpus (Turpios) Harjo	L	Cr	Sarwokhobkee	L	Cr
		No. 1 died March 21, 1902										
	Census Card No. 2134, P. O. Wetumka, Enrolled March 25, 1901											
6579	1	Harjo, Marsey	37	M	F		Tommy Harjo	D	Cr	Lizzie	D	Cr
6580	2	Harjo, Folohkee	60	F	F	Wf	Unknown	D	Cr	Unknown	D	Cr
		No. 2 died April 18, 1903										
	Census Card No. 2135, P. O. Holdenville, Enrolled March 25, 1901											
6581	1	Narcomay, Thomas	22	M	F		Simpson Narcomay	L	Cr	Lizzie Narcomay	L	Cr
	Census Card No. 2136, P. O. Carson, Enrolled March 25, 1901; No. 2, May 13, 1901											
6582	1	Lucas, Mary	20	F	F		Jimson Grayson	L	Cr	Milley	D	Cr
6583	2	Lucas, Famous	1	M	½	S	Thomas Lucas	L	Non	No. 1	L	Cr
	Census Card No. 2137, P. O. Holdenville, Enrolled March 25, 1901											
6584	1	Marks, Annie	14	F	¼		John N. Marks	L	Non	Lucy Marks	D	Cr
6585	2	Marks, Lizzie	12	F	¼	Sis	John N. Marks	L	Non	Lucy Marks	D	Cr
6586	3	Marks, Charles B.	10	M	¼	Bro	John N. Marks	L	Non	Lucy Marks	D	Cr
	Census Card No. 2138, P. O. Okemah, Enrolled March 25, 1901											
6587	1	Pittman, Jennie	31	F	¾		David Doyle	D	Cr	Priscilla Doyle	D	Cr
6588	2	Pittman, Celia	9	F	⅜	D	Edwin Pittman	L	Non	No. 1	L	Cr
	Census Card No. 2139, P. O. Yeager, Enrolled March 25, 1901											
6589	1	Harjo, Willie	27	M	F		Wacus Harjo	L	Cr	Sarlarhahkey	D	Cr
6590	2	Harjo, Lowiney	24	F	F	Wf	John Pigeon	L	Cr	Mahtee	L	Cr
		No. 2 died March 3, 1906										
	Census Card No. 2140, P. O. Wetumka, Enrolled March 25, 1901											
6591	1	Tiger, Roley	21	M	F		Catchoche	D	Cr	Millie	D	C

No.	NAME	Age	Sex	Blood	Rel.	NAME OF FATHER	Liv.	Cit.	NAME OF MOTHER	Liv.	Cit.

Census Card No. 2141, P. O. Holdenville; No. 2, Paden; No. 3 and 4, Tecumseh; Enrolled March 25, 1901

No.	NAME	Age	Sex	Blood	Rel.	NAME OF FATHER	Liv.	Cit.	NAME OF MOTHER	Liv.	Cit.
1	Shawnego. Lucy	43	F	F		Jackson Chisholm	D	Cr	Amey Chisholm	D	Cr
2	Ellis, Lizzie	15	F	F	D	Edwin Ellis	L	Shaw	No. 1	L	Cr
3	Ellis, Nellie	13	F	F	D	Edwin Ellis	L	Shaw	No. 1	L	Cr
4	Ellis, Minnie	11	F	F	D	Edwin Ellis	L	Shaw	No. 1	L	Cr
5	Shawnego, Henry	5	M	F	S	Shawnego	L	Shaw	No. 1	L	Cr
6	Shawnego, Sisie	2	F	F	D	Shawnego	L	Shaw	No. 1	L	Cr

No. 6 reported dead

Census Card No. 2142, P. O. Yeager, Enrolled March 25, 1901

No.	NAME	Age	Sex	Blood	Rel.	NAME OF FATHER	Liv.	Cit.	NAME OF MOTHER	Liv.	Cit.
1	Thlocco, Toche	55	F	F		Tustenuck Chupco	D	Cr	Temahlaker	D	Cr
2	Williams, Nellie	15	F	F	D	Choka	D	Cr	No. 1	L	Cr

Census Card No. 2143, P. O. Holdenville, Enrolled March 25, 1901

No.	NAME	Age	Sex	Blood	Rel.	NAME OF FATHER	Liv.	Cit.	NAME OF MOTHER	Liv.	Cit.
1	Lowe, Washington	36	M	F		Oche Harjo	D	Cr	Lowinay Lowe	D	Cr
2	Lowe, Liza	38	F	F	Wf	Unknown	D	Cr	Unknown	D	Cr
3	Lowe, Amos	9	M	F	S	No. 1	L	Cr	No. 2	L	Cr
4	Lowe, Nicey	7	F	F	D	No. 1	L	Cr	No. 2	L	Cr
5	Lowe, Josie	4	M	F	S	No: 1	L	Cr	No. 2	L	Cr

Nos. 1, 2 and 5 reported dead

Census Card No. 2144, P. O. Henryetta, Enrolled March 25, 1901

No.	NAME	Age	Sex	Blood	Rel.	NAME OF FATHER	Liv.	Cit.	NAME OF MOTHER	Liv.	Cit.
1	Grimes, Willie	25	M	F		Willie Grimes	D	Cr	Josie Tiger	L	Cr

Census Card No. 2145, P. O. Wetumka, Enrolled March 25, 1901

No.	NAME	Age	Sex	Blood	Rel.	NAME OF FATHER	Liv.	Cit.	NAME OF MOTHER	Liv.	Cit.
1	Harjo, Billy	27	M	F		Sosar	D	Cr	Mary Harjo	L	Cr
2	Harjo, Kizzie	27	F	F	Wf	Mingo	D	Cr	Linda	D	
3	Scott, Lillie	7	F	F	StD	Sampsey Scott	L	Cr	No. 2	L	Cr
4	Harjo, Mary	47	F	F	Moth	Tuckabatchee Harjo	D	Cr	Chacogee	D	Cr
5	Yargee, Cullie	17	M	F	Bro	Alex Yargee	D	Cr	No. 4	L	Cr

No. 5 died January 19, 1909. No. 3 died November 1909.

Census Card No. 2146, P. O. Holdenville, Enrolled March 25, 1901

No.	NAME	Age	Sex	Blood	Rel.	NAME OF FATHER	Liv.	Cit.	NAME OF MOTHER	Liv.	Cit.
1	Charlochee	21	M	F		Aktayihchugahola	L	Cr	Liza Lowe	L	Cr

No. 1 reported dead

Census Card No. 2147, P. O. Tulsa, Enrolled March 25, 1901

No.	NAME	Age	Sex	Blood	Rel.	NAME OF FATHER	Liv.	Cit.	NAME OF MOTHER	Liv.	Cit.
1	Perryman, John W.	60	M	½		Louis Perryman	D	Cr	Hettie Perryman	D	Cr
2	Perryman, Tecumseh	17	M	¾	S	No. 1	L	Cr	Nitey Perryman	L	Cr

Census Card No. 2148, P. O. Holdenville, Enrolled March 26, 1901

No.	NAME	Age	Sex	Blood	Rel.	NAME OF FATHER	Liv.	Cit.	NAME OF MOTHER	Liv.	Cit.
1	Hulsey, George	17	M	⅛		John Hulsey	L	Non	Eliza Hulsey	D	Cr
2	Hulsey, Mack	13	M	⅛	Bro	John Hulsey	L	Non	Eliza Hulsey	D	Cr
3	Hulsey, Sophia	12	F	⅛	Sis	John Hulsey	L	Non	Eliza Hulsey	D	Cr
4	Hulsey, Lizzie	6	F	⅛	Sis	John Hulsey	L	Non	Eliza Hulsey	D	Cr

Census Card No. 2149, P. O. Holdenville, Enrolled March 26, 1901

No.	NAME	Age	Sex	Blood	Rel.	NAME OF FATHER	Liv.	Cit.	NAME OF MOTHER	Liv.	Cit.
1	Anderson, Ella	26	F	F		Taylor Austin	L	Cr	Hannah Austin	D	Cr
2	Anderson, Emma	8	F	F	D	William Anderson	D	Cr	No. 1	L	Cr
3	Anderson, Richmond	6	M	F	S	William Anderson	D	Cr	No. 1	L	Cr

No. 1 died October 1905. No. 2 reported dead.

Census Card No. 2150, P. O. Sapulpa, Enrolled March 26, 1901

No.	NAME	Age	Sex	Blood	Rel.	NAME OF FATHER	Liv.	Cit.	NAME OF MOTHER	Liv.	Cit.
1	Hutke, Mary	70	F	F		Unknown	D	Cr	Unknown	D	Cr

Census Card No. 2151, P. O. Wetumka, Enrolled March 26, 1901

No.	NAME	Age	Sex	Blood	Rel.	NAME OF FATHER	Liv.	Cit.	NAME OF MOTHER	Liv.	Cit.
1	Tiller, Noah	26	M	F		George	D	Cr	Toyeh	D	Cr
2	William, Doctor	21	M	F	½Bro	Unknown	D	Cr	Toyeh	D	Cr

No. 2 died October 4, 1903

Census Card No. 2152, P. O. Arbeka, Enrolled March 26, 1901; No. 4, May 7, 1901

No.	NAME	Age	Sex	Blood	Rel.	NAME OF FATHER	Liv.	Cit.	NAME OF MOTHER	Liv.	Cit.
1	Narcome, Eliza	30	F	F		Alptta Harjo	D	Cr	Mutta	D	Cr
2	Stircken from roll.										
3	Narcome, Sunday	6	M	F	S	James Narcome	L	Cr	No. 1	L	Cr
4	Narcome, John	12	M	F	S	James Narcome	L	Cr	No. 1	L	Cr

No. 2 died 1900. No. 3 died September 1, 1899. No. 4 died February 28, 1900.

Census Card No. 2153, P. O. Yeager, Enrolled March 26, 1901

No.	NAME	Age	Sex	Blood	Rel.	NAME OF FATHER	Liv.	Cit.	NAME OF MOTHER	Liv.	Cit.
1	Kalarney,	28	M	F		Sammie Hobiah	D	Cr	Peggy	L	Cr
2	Kalarney, Lydia	22	F	F	Wf	John Pigeon	L	Cr	Mahtee	D	Cr
3	Kalarney, Isom	5	M	F	S	No. 1	L	Cr	No. 2	L	Cr
4	Kalarney, Alex	3	M	F	S	No. 1	L	Cr	No. 2	L	Cr

No. 2 died March 1, 1902

Census Card No. 2154, P. O. Okemah, Enrolled March 26, 1901

No.	NAME	Age	Sex	Blood	Rel.	NAME OF FATHER	Liv.	Cit.	NAME OF MOTHER	Liv.	Cit.
1	Hill, Dave	25	M	F		Parhose Harjo	D	Cr	Cynda	D	Cr
2	Hill, Sallie	30	F	F	Wf	Nocos Ellis	L	Cr	Unknown	D	Cr
3	Pigeon, Lesbee	7	F	F	StD	Jimmy Pigeon	L	Cr	No. 2	L	Cr

Census Card No. 2155, P. O. Wetumka, Enrolled March 26, 1901; No. 2, May 2, 1901

No.	NAME	Age	Sex	Blood	Rel.	NAME OF FATHER	Liv.	Cit.	NAME OF MOTHER	Liv.	Cit.
1	Harjo, Amos	24	M	F		Peney Harjo	D	Cr	May Fox	L	Cr
2	Fox, Martha	23	F	F	Wf	Chular Harjogee	D	Cr	Sophia Harjogee	D	Cr

No. 2 died February 22, 1900

Census Card No. 2156, P. O. Faden, Enrolled March 26, 1901

No.	NAME	Age	Sex	Blood	Rel.	NAME OF FATHER	Liv.	Cit.	NAME OF MOTHER	Liv.	Cit.
1	Foster, David	27	M	F		George Foster	L	Sem	Petsy London	L	Cr
2	Foster, Meleny	26	F	F	Wf	March Thompson	L	Cr	Nunochee	D	Cr

No. 1 died November 22, 1904

Census Card No. 2157, P. O. Arbeka; No. 2, Bearden, Enrolled March 26, 1901

No.	NAME	Age	Sex	Blood	Rel.	NAME OF FATHER	Liv.	Cit.	NAME OF MOTHER	Liv.	Cit.
1	Williams, Nathan	26	M	F		Thomas McWilliams	L	Cr	Hannah McWilliams	L	Cr
2	Williams, Lillie D.	20	F	F	Wf	Thomas Williams	L	Cr	Kepsey Williams	L	Cr

139

Roll No.	No.	NAME	Age	Sex	Blood	Rel.	NAME OF FATHER	Liv.	Cit.	NAME OF MOTHER	Liv.	Cit.
		Census Card No. 2158, P. O. Wewoka, Enrolled March 26, 1901										
6641	1	Williams, Hannah	50	F	F		Neddie	D	Cr	Bettie	D	Cr
6642	2	Williams, Susie	24	F	F	D	Jimmy Toney	D	Cr	No. 1	L	Cr
6643	3	Williams, Jennie	7	F	½	GrD	K. N. Baker	L	Sem	No. 2	L	Cr
6644	4	Williams, Martha	1	F	½	GrD	Hully	L	Sem	No. 2	L	Cr
		No. 4 died April 20, 1899. No. 2 died May 24, 1908. No. 1 died 1910. No. 3 died December 24, 1909.										
		Census Card No. 2159, P. O. Senora, Enrolled March 26, 1901										
6615	1	Stidham, Rose	50	F	½		Joe McFields	D	Cher	Ellen Winters	D	Cr
		No. 1 died August 6, 1901										
		Census Card No. 2160, P. O. Holdenville, Enrolled March 26, 1901										
6646	1	McCoy, Barney	24	M	F		McCoy	D	Sem	Solthie	D	Cr
6647	2	McCoy, Susan	20	F	F	Wf	Katcha Homathe	D	Cr	Leah Tiger	L	Cr
		Nos. 1 and 2 reported dead										
		Census Card No. 2161, P. O. Kellyville, Enrolled March 26, 1901; No. 6, March 27, 1901										
6648	1	Snow, Capahny	55	M	F		Unknown	D	Cr	Keahteny	D	Cr
6649	2	Snow, Yarlacoweny	50	F	F	Wf	Ahequany	D	Cr	Ahgothany	D	Cr
6650	3	Snow, Louisa	17	F	F	D	No. 1	L	Cr	No. 2	L	Cr
6651	4	Snow, Wesley	15	M	F	S	No. 1	L	Cr	No. 2	L	Cr
6652	5	Snow, Harthlie	12	F	F	D	No. 1	L	Cr	No. 2	L	Cr
6653	6	Snow, Tecumseh	18	M	F	S	No. 1	L	Cr	No. 2	L	Cr
		No. 6 died July 24, 1899. No. 2 died November 1902. No. 3 reported dead.										
		Census Card No. 2162, P. O. Bristow, Enrolled March 26, 1901										
6654	1	Goodman, Sahcon-cohny	55	M	F		Tesontahny	D	Cr	Confahny	D	Cr
6655	2	Goodman, Ahhaco-nanny	60	F	F	Wf	Hakepahny	D	Cr	Sahcontany	D	Cr
6656	3	Goodman, Tatahla-coconthla	12	F	F	D	No. 1	L	Cr	Desawconny	L	Cr
		No. 2 reported dead										
		Census Card No. 2163, P. O. Okmulgee, Enrolled March 28, 1901										
6657	1	Canard, Susan	28	F	½		James Canard	D	Cr	Pitchie Canard	D	Cr
6658	2	Canard, Malinda	7	F	¼	D	John Porter	D	Non	No. 1	L	Cr
6659	3	Tiger, Coody	2	M	¾	S	Motey Tiger	D	Cr	No. 1	L	Cr
		Census Card No. 2164, P. O. Paden, Enrolled March 26, 1901										
6660	1	Tommie, Hulpata	46	M	F		Conner	D	Cr	Temoche	D	Cr
		Census Card No. 2165, P. O. Sapulpa, Enrolled March 26, 1901										
6661	1	Hayes, Marchie	42	M	F		Carpetha Hays	D	Cr	Unknown	D	Cr
6662	2	Hayes, Parbie	19	M	F	S	No. 1	L	Cr	Martha Hays	D	Cr
		Census Card No. 2166, P. O. Bristow, Enrolled March 26, 1901										
6663	1	Tiger, Jumbo	28	M	F		Jim Tiger	D	Cr	Conthenny	D	Cr
6664	2	Tiger, Kakaney	30	F	F	Wf	Sakashtheny	D	Cr	Sarah	L	Cr
6665	3	Tiger, John	7	M	F	S	No. 1	L	Cr	No. 2	L	Cr
6666	4	Tiger, Willie	6	M	F	S	No. 1	L	Cr	No. 2	L	Cr
6667	5	Tiger, Jim	18	M	F	S	No. 1	L	Cr	No. 2	L	Cr
		No. 2 died June 4, 1904. No. 3 died February 22, 1900. No. 4 died February 11, 1900. No. 5 died March 14, 1900.										
		Census Card No. 2167, P. O. Castle, Enrolled March 27, 1901; No. 5, April 5, 1901										
6668	1	Wesley, Victor	25	M	F		John Wesley	L	Cr	Linda Wesley	D	Cr
6669	2	Wesley, Elsie	24	F	F	Wf	Holuk Yahola	D	Cr	Emmie Yahola	L	Cr
6670	3	Wesley, Louis	4	M	F	S	No. 1	L	Cr	No. 2	L	Cr
6671	4	Wesley, John	50	M	F	Fath	Unknown	D	Cr	Litkeba	D	Cr
6672	5	Wesley, Bessie	1	F	F	D	No. 1	L	Cr	No. 2	L	Cr
		No. 1 died January 1, 1903. No. 4 died January 21, 1901. No. 5 died May 1901.										
		Census Card No. 2168, P. O. Okemah; No. 3, Hoffman, Enrolled March 27, 1901										
6673	1	Wesley, Thomas	22	M	F		John Wesley	L	Cr	Linda Wesley	D	Cr
6674	2	Wesley, Rhoda	20	F	F	Sis	John Wesley	L	Cr	Linda Wesley	D	Cr
6675	3	Wesley, Lizzie	14	F	F	Sis	John Wesley	L	Cr	Linda Wesley	D	Cr
		Census Card No. 2169, P. O. Okemah, Enrolled March 27, 1901										
6676	1	Smith, William	26	M	F		Hodulga, Fixico	D	Cr	Mary Smith	L	Cr
6677	2	Smith, Winey	24	F	F	Wf	Baby Harjo	D	Cr	Karishlarney	D	Cr
6678	3	Smith, Orrey	5	F	F	D	No. 1	L	Cr	No. 2	L	Cr
6679	4	Smith, Ella	2½	F	F	D	No. 1	L	Cr	No. 2	L	Cr
		No. 2 died May 31, 1905										
		Census Card No. 2170, P. O. Wetumka, Enrolled March 27, 1901										
6680	1	Warlesee	46	F	F		Thlewatley Emathla	D	Cr	Unknown	D	Cr
6681	2	Suder, Lobla	8	F	F	S	Robert Sooder	L	Cr	No. 1	D	Cr
6682	3	Suder, Bunny	9	F	F	S	Robert Sooder	L	Cr	No. 1	L	Cr
		No. 2 died October 1902. No. 1 reported dead. No. 3 died June 1902.										
		Census Card No. 2171, P. O. Welty, Enrolled March 27, 1901										
6683	1	Foster, Meseley	44	F	F		Capitcha Harjo	D	Cr	Eschemky	D	Cr
6684	2	Thompson, Melisa	7	F	F	D	Hege Thompson	L	Cr	No. 1	L	Cr
6685	3	Foster, Kinder	7	M	F	StD	George Foster	L	Sem	Annie Foster	L	Cr
		No. 3 died July 14, 1905. No. 1 reported dead.										
		Census Card No. 2172, P. O. Wetumka, Enrolled March 27, 1901										
6686	1	King, Millie	18	F	F		Micke Emarthar	D	Cr	Nellie Emarthar	D	Cr
		No. 1 died March 15, 1900										
		Census Card No. 2173, P. O. Sapulpa, Enrolled March 27, 1901										
6687	1	Fixico, Neha	47	M	F		Abalok Yahola	D	Cr	Unknown	D	Cr
		No. 1 reported died in 1902										

140

Roll No.	No.	NAME	Age	Sex	Blood	Rel.	NAME OF FATHER	Liv.	Cit.	NAME OF MOTHER	Liv.	Cit.
		Census Card No. 2174, P. O. Okemah, Enrolled March 27, 1901										
6688	1	Knight, Katie	25	F	F		Mulkersy	D	Cr	Linda	D	Cr
6689	2	Davis, John	3	M	½	S	George Davis	L	Sem	No. 1	L	Cr
6690	3	Tiger, Sam	12	M	½	Neph	Tommy Tiger	L	Sem	Eliza Tiger	L	Cr
		Census Card No. 2175, P. O. Okmulgee, Enrolled March 27, 1901										
6691	1	Cumsey, Vinita	12	F	F		Jake Bearhead	D	Cr	Matilda	D	Cr
		Census Card No. 2176, P. O. Castle, Enrolled March 27, 1901										
6692	1	Fixico, Tulmochuss	42	M	F		Ishpokyahola	D	Cr	Mecus Uphoye	D	Cr
6693	2	Fixico, Sallie	32	F	F	Wf	Hullok Yahola	L	Cr	Suequegah	D	Cr
6694	3	Fixico, Barney	14	M	F	S	No. 1	L	Cr	No. 2	L	Cr
6695	4	Fixicco, Daley	13	F	F	D	No. 1	L	Cr	No. 2	L	Cr
6696	5	Fixico, Martha	11	F	F	D	No. 1	L	Cr	No. 2	L	Cr
6697	6	Fixico, Minta	5	F	F	D	No. 1	L	Cr	No. 2	L	Cr
6698	7	Fixico, Roman	1	M	F	S	No. 1	L	Cr	No. 2	L	Cr
		No. 1 died May 16, 1914. No. 4 died December 23, 1909. No. 6 died September 22, 1911.										
		Census Card No. 2177, P. O. Kellyville, Enrolled March 27, 1901										
6699	1	Dickson, Chicken	46	M	F		Coquay	D	Cr	Unknown	D	Cr
6700	2	Dickson, Nancy	17	F	F	D	No. 1	L	Cr	Annie Dickson	D	Cr
6701	3	Dickson, Linda	14	F	F	D	No. 1	L	Cr	Annie Dickson	D	Cr
6702	4	Dickson, Wilson	11	M	F	S	No. 1	L	Cr	Annie Dickson	D	Cr
		No. 3 died October 1902. No. 4 died July 1, 1902.										
		Census Card No. 2178, P. O. Watsonville, Enrolled March 27, 1901										
6703	1	Guinn, William Ivory	3	M	⅛		Wm. F. Guinn	L	Non	Clara Self Guinn	D	Cr
		Census Card No. 2179, P. O. Okmulgee, Enrolled March 27, 1901										
6704	1	Narcome, Dinah	42	F	F		Whooping John	D	Cr	Unknown	D	Cr
		Census Card No. 2180, P. O. Bristow, Enrolled March 27, 1901										
6705	1	Soconthlaney	27	F	F		Fahkoweny	D	Cr	Sillibbee	D	Cr
6706	1	Cahtahwon, Willie	6	M	F	S	Cahtahwon	L	Cr	No. 1	L	Cr
6707	3	Cahtahwon, Minnie	4	F	F	S	Cahtahwon	L	Cr	No. 1	L	Cr
6708	4	Cahtahwon, Maggie	3	F	F	D	Chatahwon	L	Cr	No. 1	L	Cr
		No. 4 died September 1899. No. 3 reported dead.										
		Census Card No. 2181, P. O. Okemah, Enrolled March 27, 1901										
6709	1	Field, William	25	M	F		Parhose	D	Cr	Motable	D	Cr
		Census Card No. 2182, P. O. Sapulpa, Enrolled March 27, 1901										
6710	1	Eufaula, Eliza	75	F	F		Unknown	D	Cr	Unknown	D	Cr
		Census Card No. 2183, P. O. Eufaula, Enrolled March 27, 1901										
6711	1	McIntosh, Louis	27	M	F		Tibadahkey	D	Cr	Betsey Phillips	L	Cr
6712	2	McIntosh, Leah	24	F	F	Wf	Chatman Smith	D	Cr	Nellie Smith	D	Cr
		Census Card No. 2184, P. O. Eufaula, Enrolled March 27, 1901										
6713	1	Phillips, Betsey	48	F	F		Buss Riley	D	Cr	Hannah Riley	D	Cr
6714	2	Phillips, Louisa	17	F	F	D	Parhose Harjo Phillips	D	Cr	No. 1	L	Cr
6715	3	Phillips, Taylor	15	M	F	S	Parhose Harjo Phillips	D	Cr	No. 1	L	Cr
6716	4	Phillips, Abbie	12	F	F	D	Parhose Harjo Phillips	D	Cr	No. 1	L	Cr
		No. 2 died February 1904. No. 3 died 1904. No. 4 died 1908.										
		Census Card No. 2185, P. O. Castle, Enrolled March 27, 1901										
6717	1	Harjo, Amos	18	M	F		Odache	D	Cr	Millie Harjo	D	Cr
		Census Card No. 2186, P. O. Morse, Enrolled March 28, 1901; No. 2, April 5, 1901										
6718	1	Smith, John	60	M	F		Mik Emarthar	D	Cr	Litkeber	D	Cr
6719	2	Smith, Mary	53	F	F	Wf	Catus Fixico	D	Cr	Mary Susey	D	Cr
		No. 1 died October 2, 1900. No. 2 died October 31, 1911.										
		Census Card No. 2187, P. O. Castle, Enrolled March 29, 1901										
6720	1	Harjo, Tulsa	40	M	F		Narbuckchee Harjo	D	Cr	Polly	D	Cr
6721	2	Harjo, Ebner	14	M	F	S	No. 1	L	Cr	Eliza Harjo	D	Cr
6722	3	Harjo, Josiah	12	M	F	S	No. 1	L	Cr	Eliza Harjo	D	Cr
		Census Card No. 2188, P. O. Wealaka, Enrolled March 29, 1901										
6723	1	Littlehead, William	24	M	F		Cotoesee	D	Cr	Poconweny	D	Cr
		No. 1 died 1904										
		Census Card No. 2189, P. O. Holdenville, Enrolled March 29, 1901										
6724	1	Sewell, Willie	21	M	F		Frank Sewell	D	Cr	Sarah Sewell	D	Cr
6725	2	Sewell, Nancy	24	F	¾	Wf	David Reed	D	Cr	Youlheluche	D	Cr
6726	3	Harper, Ida	5	F	⅞	StD	Albert Harper	D	Cr	No. 2	L	Cr
		No. 2 reported dead										
		Census Card No. 2190, P. O. Carroll, Enrolled March 29, 1901										
6727	1	Chiye	40	F	F		Taho Fixico	D	Cr	Lydia	D	Cr
6728	2	Hope, Robert	16	M	F	S	Henry Hope	L	Cr	No. 1	L	Cr
		Census Card No. 2191, P. O. Carroll, Enrolled March 29, 1901										
6729	1	Hope, Henry	60	M	⅓		Hope	D	Cr	Fannie Hope	D	Cr
6730	2	Hope, Millie	50	F	F	Wf	Tusekia Harjo	D	Cr	Iyoke	D	Cr
		Census Card No. 2192, P. O. Pierce, Enrolled March 29, 1901										
6731	1	Thompson, Nancy	54	F	F		Nokos Harjo	D	Cr	Unknown	D	Cr
6732	2	Thompson, Charlie	14	M	F	S	Sota Thompson	D	Cr	No. 1	L	Cr
6733	3	Thompson, Robert	12	M	F	S	Sota Thompson	D	Cr	No. 1	L	Cr
		No. 2 died October 1901. No. 1 died 1901.										
		Census Card No. 2193, P. O. Hitchita, Enrolled March 29, 1901; No. 2, May 22, 1901										
6734	1	Thompson, Amanda	20	F	F		Soto Thompson	D	Cr	Nancy Thompson	L	Cr
6735	2	Thompson, Lucy	1	F	F	D	Unknown	L	Cr	No. 1	L	Cr
		No. 2 died March 22, 1901										

Roll No.	No.	NAME	Age	Sex	Blood	Rel.	NAME OF FATHER	Liv.	Cit.	NAME OF MOTHER	Liv.	Cit.
		Census Card No. 2194, P. O. Lenna, Enrolled March 29, 1901; No. 6, May 15, 1901										
6736	1	Monahwee, John	29	M	¾		David Monahwee	L	Cr	Millie Monahwee	L	Cr
6737	2	Monhawee, Cynda	34	F	F	Wf	March Thompson	L	Cr	Susan Thompson	L	Cr
6738	3	Daniel, Lizzie	18	F	⅞	StD	Wm. Daniel	L	Cr	No. 2	L	Cr
6739	4	Daniel, Martin	13	M	⅞	StS	Wm. Martin	L	Cr	No. 2	L	Cr
6740	5	Monahwee, David	3	M	⅞	S	No. 1	L	Cr	No. 2	L	Cr
6741	6	Monahwee, Sambo	1	M	⅞	S	No. 1	L	Cr	No. 2	L	Cr
		No. 5 died June 30, 1899. No. 3 died September 29, 1902. No. 2 reported dead.										
		Census Card No. 2195, P. O. Lenna, Enrolled March 29, 1901										
6742	1	Canard, Katie	35	F	F		Concharty	D	Cr	Mulley	D	Cr
6743	2	Canard, Susanna	7	F	F	D	Jim Canard	L	Cr	No. 1	L	Cr
		Census Card No. 2196, P. O. Checotah, Enrolled April 2, 1901										
6744	1	McIntosh, Kogee	20	F	½		John McIntosh	L	Cr	Lydia McIntosh	D	Cr
		Census Card No. 2197, P. O. Calvin, Enrolled April 2, 1901										
6745	1	Island, Mary	10	M	¼		William Island	D	Cr	Rosa Honley	L	Non
		No. 1 died 1906										
		Census Card No. 2198, P. O. Mounds, Enrolled April 3, 1901; No. 2, April 12, 1901; No. 3, May 23, 1901										
6746	1	Colmon, Nettie G.	19	F	⅛		Robert T. Barber	L	Cr	Alice A. Barber	L	Non
6747	2	Colmon, Dollie C.	3	F	1-16	D	William E. Colmon	L	Non	No. 1	L	Cr
6748	3	Colmon, William E.	1	M	1-16	S	William E. Colmon	L	Non	No. 1	L	Cr
		No. 3 died February 8, 1901										
		Census Card No. 2199, P. O. Tulsa, Enrolled April 3, 1901										
6749	1	Perryman, Thomas W.	61	M	½		Louis Perryman	D	Cr	Hattie W. Perryman	D	Cr
6750	2	Perryman, Thomas L.	20	M	¼	S	No. 1	L	Cr	Ella Perryman	L	Non
6751	3	Perryman, Aurthur R.	20	M	¼	S	No. 1	L	Cr	Ella Perryman	L	Non
6752	4	Perryman, Walter L.	16	M	¼	S	No. 1	L	Cr	Ella Perryman	L	Non
		No. 1 reported dead										
		Census Card No. 2200, P. O. Muskogee, Enrolled April 4, 1901										
6753	1	Dubois, B. R.	30	M	1-16		Barney Dubois	D	Cr	Lizzie Dubois	D	Non
		Census Card No. 2201, P. O. Hanna, Enrolled April 5, 1901; No. 4, April 25, 1901										
6754	1	Gaino, Yabe	60	M	F		Wegus Yahola	D	Cr	Lucy Yahola	D	Cr
6755	2	Gaino, Sallie	14	F	F	D	No. 1	L	Cr	Harriet Gaino	D	Cr
6756	3	Gaino, Aggie	12	F	F	D	No. 1	L	Cr	Harriet Gaino	D	Cr
6757	4	Gaino, Amanda	18	F	F	Wf	Stephen Barnett	D	Cr	Susie Barnett	D	Cr
		Census Card No. 2202, P. O. Okemah, Enrolled April 5, 1901										
6758	1	Harjoche, Nokos	30	M	F		Nokus Holahta	L	Cr	Allinda	D	Cr
6759	2	Harjoche, Melosey	24	F	F	Wf	Henneha	D	Cr	Marwakike	D	Cr
6760	3	Harjoche, Lizzie	7	F	F	D	No. 1	L	Cr	Munihoche	D	Cr
		No. 3 died November 1910										
		Census Card No. 2203, P. O. Okemah, Enrolled April 5, 1901										
6761	1	Mulgussie, Lucy	18	F	F		Mulgussie	D	Cr	Cinda Mulgussie	D	Cr
		No. 1 reported dead										
		Census Card No. 2204, P. O. Okema, Enrolled April 5, 1901										
6762	1	Smith, Belcher	24	M	F		John Smith	L	Cr	Mary Smith	L	Cr
6763	2	Smith, Sarah	19	F	F	Wf	Pin Fixico	L	Cr	Leah	D	Cr
		No. 1 reported dead										
		Census Card No. 2205, P. O. Okemah, Enrolled April 5, 1901										
6764	1	Panoske, Daniel	33	M	F		Panoske	D	Cr	Wagey	D	Cr
6765	2	Panoske, Meisey	24	F	F	Wf	Heluck Yahola	D	Cr	Amey	L	Cr
6766	3	Panoske, Susan	6	F	F	D	No. 1	L	Cr	No. 2	L	Cr
6767	4	Panoske, Andy	3	M	F	S	No. 1	L	Cr	No. 2	L	Cr
		Census Card No. 2206, P. O. Hanna, Enrolled April 5, 1901										
6768	1	Taylor, Monny	29	F	F		Holuck Yahola	D	Cr	Amy	L	Cr
6769	2	Taylor, Mollie	5	F	F	D	Jonas Taylor	L	Cr	No. 1	L	Cr
6770	3	Tayor, Silla	3	F	F	D	Jonas Taylor	L	Cr	No. 1	L	Cr
6771	4	Taylor, Jonas	32	M	F	Hus	Sam Taylor	L	Cr	Silwey Taylor	D	Cr
		No. 3 died July 1910. No. 4 died October 1901.										
		Census Card No. 2207, P. O. Castle, Enrolled April 5, 1901										
6772	1	Ekar, Echo	45	M	F		Oches Harjo	D	Cr	Sukanatah	D	Cr
6773	2	Ekar, Amey	40	F	F	Wf	Tuskek Harjo	D	Cr	Sokugker Yahola	D	Cr
6774	3	Ekar, Dickey	12	M	F	S	No. 1	L	Cr	Sarpefortke	D	Cr
		No. 3 died 1904										
		Census Card No. 2208, P. O. Castle, Enrolled April 5, 1901										
6775	1	Sohkuekar	73	F	F		Chowastie	D	Cr	Sahyekehe	D	Cr
		Census Card No. 2209, P. O. Calvin, Enrolled April 6, 1901										
6776	1	Hawkins, Wizey	20	F	F		Wiley Hawkins	D	Cr	Hethlucky	D	Cr
		No. 1 reported dead										
		Census Card No. 2210, P. O. Hanna, Enrolled April 8, 1901										
6777	1	Colbert, William	60	M	F		Cotcha Yahola	D	Cr	Unknown	D	Cr
6778	2	Colbert, Mahala	30	F	F	Wf	Ussee Yahola	D	Cr	Mollie Tea	D	Cr
6779	3	Bearhead, Robison	13	M	F	Neph	Cooper Bearhead	D	Cr	Lucinda Bearhead	D	Cr
6780	4	Bearhead, Louisa	7	F	F	Niece	Cooper Bearhead	D	Cr	Lucinda Bearhead	D	Cr
		No. 4 died February 17, 1910. No. 1 reported dead.										
		Census Card No. 2211, P. O. Fame, Enrolled April 8, 1901; Nos. 3 and 4, May 11, 1901										
6781	1	Jacobs, Joseph	21	M	F		Stephen Jacobs	D	Cr	Lizzie Lasley	L	Cr
6782	2	Jacobs, Stephen	55	M	F	Father	Unknown	D	Cr	Unknown	D	Cr
6783	3	Jacobs, Jennie	70	F	F	Step-Mother	Unknown	D	Cr	Unknown	D	Cr
		No. 2 died October 15, 1900. No. 3 died August 16, 1900.										

Roll No.	No.	NAME	Age	Sex	Blood	Rel.	NAME OF FATHER	Liv.	Cit.	NAME OF MOTHER	Liv.	Cit.
	Census Card No. 2212, P. O. Eufaula, Enrolled April 8, 1901											
6784	1	Doyle, Sam H. Jr.	25	M	1/4		Sam H. Doyle Sr.	L	Cr	Rachel Doyle	L	Non
	Census Card No. 2213, P. O. McAlester, Enrolled April 8, 1901											
6785	1	Killer, Caesar	22	M	F		Adam Killer	D	Cr	Sunthlupehcher	D	Cr
	Census Card No. 2214, P. O. Hanna, Enrolled April 8, 1901											
6786	1	Foster, Wolley	47	F	F		Iskochuckney	D	Cr	Wisey	D	Cr
6787	2	Foster, Turner	11	M	F	S	Foster	D	Cr	No. 1	L	Cr
		No. 1 died 1904										
	Census Card No. 2215, P. O. Vivian, Enrolled April 8, 1901											
6788	1	McNac, Susie	9	F	F		Cully McNac	D	Cr	Leah McNac	D	Cr
	Census Card No. 2216, P. O. Eufaula, Enrolled April 8, 1901											
6789	1	Sartolumka	100	F	F		Unknown	D	Cr	Unknown	D	Cr
		No. 1 died January 11, 1900										
	Census Card No. 2217, P. O. Okemah, Enrolled April 9, 1901											
6790	1	Reynolds, Lewis	15	M	3/8		Richard Reynolds	L	Non	Eliza Reynolds	L	Cr
6791	2	Reynolds, Dave	9	M	3/8	Bro	Richard Reynolds	L	Non	Eliza Reynolds	L	Cr
6792	3	Reynolds, Jerry	7	M	3/8	Bro	Richard Reynolds	L	Non	Eliza Reynolds	L	Cr
6793	4	Reynolds, Eliza	33	F	3/4	Moth	Unknown	D	Non	Unknown	D	Cr
6794	5	Reynolds, Susie	4	F	3/8	Sis	Richard Reynolds	L	Non	Eliza Reynolds	L	Cr
		No. 4 reported dead										
	Census Card No. 2218, P. O. Indianola, Enrolled April 9, 1901											
6795	1	Green, Jessie	57	M	F		Echo Harjo	D	Cr	Mahtar	D	Cr
6796	2	Green, Louisanna	40	F	F	Wf	Nocus Fixico	L	Cr	Kerwarphoka	D	Cr
		No. 2 died July 23, 1900. No. 1 died May 18, 1905.										
	Census Card No. 2219, P. O. Mellette, Enrolled April 9, 1901											
6797	1	Givens, Choctaw	51	M	F		Lawyer Givens	D	Cr	Sahecher	D	Cr
6798	2	Givens, Kizzie	30	F	F	Wf	Fisher	D	Cr	Folothokee	D	Cr
6799	3	Givens, Robert	17	M	F	S	No. 1	L	Cr	Silla Givens	D	Cr
6800	4	Givens, Sam	2	M	F	S	No. 1	L	Cr	No. 2	L	Cr
		No. 2 died September 28, 1911. No. 1 reported dead.										
	Census Card No. 2220, P. O. Wagoner, Enrolled April 9, 1901											
6801	1	Shannon, Sally H.	17	F	1/8		George Shannon	L	Non	Mary B. Shannon	D	Cr
	Census Card No. 2221, P. O. Calvin, Enrolled April 11, 1901											
6802	1	Leader, Barney	28	M	1/8		Edward Leader	L	Choc	Annie Leader	D	Cr
6803	2	Leader, Tilda	29	F	F	Wf	Echo Emarthla	D	Cr	Cinda Deer	D	Cr
		No. 2 died November 5, 1907										
	Census Card No. 2222, P. O. Lee, Enrolled April 11, 1901											
6804	1	Johnson, Robert	17	M	1/4		Charles Johnson	D	Cr	Dorcas Johnson	D	Cr
	Census Card No. 2223, P. O. Morris, Enrolled April 13, 1901											
6805	1	Johnson, Alex	24	M	3/8		Charles Johnson	D	Cr	Dorcas Johnson	D	Cr
	Census Card No. 2224, P. O. Wagoner, Enrolled April 13, 1901											
6806	1	Posey, M. A.	33	M	1/4		W. A. Posey	D	Cr	Elizabeth Posey	D	Non
	Census Card No. 2225, P. O. Mellette, Enrolled April 15, 1901.											
6807	1	Brown, Wilson	28	M	F		Sam Brown	D	Cr	Lucy Brown (Nee Sullivan)	D	Cr
	Census Card No. 2226, P. O. Muskogee, Enrolled April 15, 1901											
6808	1	Tiger, Robert	19	M	1/8		Willie Tiger	D	Cr	Lucy Lynch	L	Cher
	Census Card No. 2227, P. O. Muskogee, Enrolled April 15, 1901											
6809	1	Burton, Mary	18	F	1/8		Willie Tiger	D	Cr	Lucy Lynch	L	Cher
	Census Card No. 2228, P. O. Checotah, Enrolled April 15, 1901											
6810	1	Shepherd, Addie M.	21	F	1/8		V. N. McNally	D	Cr	Susan McNally	D	Chic
6811	2	Shepherd, Maud	2	F	1-16	D	K. H Shepherd	L	Non	No. 1	L	Cr
6812	3	Shepherd, Oscar Lee	1	M	1-16	S	K. H. Shepherd	L	Non	No. 1	L	Cr
		No. 3 died September 5, 1900										
	Census Card No. 2229, P. O. Wagoner, Enrolled April 15, 1901											
6813	1	Posey, Albert W.	32	M	1/4		W. A. Posey	D	Cr	Elizabeth Posey	D	Non
6814	2	Posey, Leonard Earle	4	M	1/8	S	No. 1	L	Cr	Mary Ann Posey	L	Non
6815	3	Posey, Elmer Carl	1	M	1/8	S	No. 1	L	Cr	Mary Ann Posey	L	Non
	Census Card No. 2230, P. O. Eufaula, Enrolled April 15, 1901											
6816	1	Fisher, Barney	35	M	F		George Fisher	D	Cr	Folothokee	D	Cr
		No. 1 died April 20, 1900										
	Census Card No. 2231, P. O. Eufaula, Enrolled April 15, 1901											
6817	1	Fisher, George	52	M	F		Chowastasye	D	Cr	Sotanhley	D	Cr
		No. 1 died April 25, 1899										
	Census Card No. 2232, P. O. Eufaula, Enrolled April 16, 1901; No. 7, May 15, 1901											
6818	1	Cummings, David	58	M	1/2		Unknoen	D	Non	Sinhotosey	D	Cr
6819	2	Cummings, Louisa	38	F	1/2	Wf	Thomas Grayson	D	Cr	Susan Grayson	L	Cr
6820	3	Cummings, Benjamin	12	M	1/2	S	No. 1	L	Cr	No. 2	L	Cr
6821	4	Cummings, Rufus	11	M	1/2	S	No. 1	L	Cr	No. 2	L	Cr
6822	5	Cummings, Thomas R.	8	M	1/2	S	No. 1	L	Cr	No. 2	L	Cr
6823	6	Cummings, Howard	3	M	1/2	S	No. 1	L	Cr	No. 2	L	Cr
6824	7	Cummings, Boyd	1	M	1/2	S	No. 1	L	Cr	No. 2	L	Cr
		No. 2 died May 27, 1914										
	Census Card No. 2233, P. O. Hanna, Enrolled April 16, 1901											
6825	1	Barnett, William	45	M	F		Barney	D	Cr	Meteholke	D	Cr
6826	2	Barnett, Lucy	39	F	F	Wf	John Tiger	D	Cr	Nicey Tiger	L	Cr
6827	3	Artussee	13	F	F	Ward	Artus Honabe	D	Cr	Eliza Fooey	D	Cr
		No. 3 died October 25, 1903. No. 1 reported dead.										

Roll No.	No.	NAME	Age	Sex	Blood	Rel.	NAME OF FATHER	Liv.	Cit.	NAME OF MOTHER	Liv.	Cit.
		Census Card No. 2234, P. O. Senora, Enrolled April 16, 1901										
6828	1	Yetekahajo, Wisey	30	F	F		Joe Tiger	L	Cr	Unknown	D	Cr
6829	2	Tyler, Joe	5	M	F	S	Billie Tyler	D	Cr	No. 1	L	Cr
		No. 2 reported dead										
		Census Card No. 2235, P. O. Calvin, Enrolled April 17, 1901										
6830	1	Bruner, John	22	M	F		Takosa Harjo	D	Cr	Ogeisie	D	Cr
6831	2	Bruner, Nicey	20	F	F	Wf	Nocus Ille	L	Cr	Margaret Bruner	L	Cr
6832	3	Tiger, George	18	M	F	Ward	Cotsey Harjo	D	Cr	Unknown	D	Cr
		No. 3 died February 17, 1910										
		Census Card No. 2236, P. O. Checotah, Enrolled April 17, 1901										
6833	1	Boatmun, Laura	18	F	¼		Jeff Simmons	D	Cr	Lizzie Simmons	D	Non
		Census Card No. 2237, P. O. Calvin, Enrolled April 17, 1901; No. 2, May 22, 1901										
6834	1	Alexander, David	40	F	M		Alex Alexander	D	Cr	Sallie Alexander	D	Cr
6835	2	Alexander, Martha	2	F	F	D	No. 1	L	Cr	Lizzie Alexander	L	Cr
		No. 1 reported dead										
		Census Card No. 2238, P. O. Eufaula, Enrolled April 17, 1901										
6836	1	Lotka	100	M	F		Alpatochee	D	Cr	Thlarsarpaken	D	Cr
6837	2	Lotka, Supsie	85	F	F	Wf	Heneha Fixico	D	Cr	Thloskogee	D	Cr
		Nos. 1 and 2 reported dead										
		Census Card No. 2239, P. O. Eufaula, Enrolled April 18, 1901										
6838	1	Simpson, Hattie M.	28	F	1-32		John F. Simpson	D	Non	Susan A. Simpson	L	Cr
		Census Card No. 2240, P. O. Kellyville, Enrolled April 19, 1901										
6839	1	Tiger, John	21	M	F		Cotimmy	D	Cr	Lucy	D	Cr
6840	2	Tiger, David	23	M	F	Bro	Cotimmy	D	Cr	Lucy	D	Cr
		No. 2 died October 1, 1903. No. 1 died January 8, 1908.										
		Census Card No. 2241, P. O. Holdenville, Enrolled April 19, 1901										
6841	1	Alexander, James H.	30	M	½		George A. Alexander	L	Cr	Nancy Alexander	L	Cr
6842	2	Alexander, Hannah	M 26	F	F	Wf	David Monahwee	D	Cr	Miley Monahwee	D	Cr
		Census Card No. 2242, P. O. Eufaula, Enrolled April 19, 1901										
6843	1	Manley, Lofa	50	M	F		Tuske Heneha	D	Cr	Linda Manley	D	Cr
6844	2	Manley, Lizzie	56	F	F	Wf	Sparney Fixeco	D	Cr	Unknown	D	Cr
6845	3	Manley, Hallie	7	F	F	D	No. 1	L	Cr	No. 2	L	Cr
		No. 1 died April 29, 1905. No. 2 died January 31, 1901.										
		Census Card No. 2243, P. O. Eufaula, Enrolled April 19, 1901										
6846	1	Polk, Daniel W.	26	M	F		Thomas H. Polk	L	Cr	Cinda Polk	L	Cr
6847	2	Polk, Katie	18	F	½	Wf	Cubbitcha	D	Cr	Lucy Deere	L	Cr
		Census Card No. 2244, P. O. Jenny Lund, Arkansas, Enrolled April 19, 1901										
6648	1	Moore, Sallie	21	F	⅛		William Ancil	D	Cr	Jane Tiger	L	Non
		Census Card No. 2245, P. O. Stidham, Enrolled April 23, 1901										
6849	1	Washington, Dav	21	M	F		George Washington	D	Cr	Sallie Washington	D	Cr
		Census Card No. 2246, P. O. Eufaula, Enrolled April 23, 1901										
6850	1	Tiger, John	45	M	F		John Tiger	D	Cr	Nicey Tiger	D	Cr
		Census Card No. 2247, P. O. Calvin, Enrolled April 24, 1901										
6851	1	Hawkins, Eliza	35	F	F		Washington Smith	D	Cr	Lydia Smith	D	Cr
6852	2	Hawkins, Katie	13	F	F	D	Wiley Hawkins	L	Cr	No. 1	L	Cr
6853	3	Hawkins, Amanda	12	F	F	D	Wiley Hawkins	L	Cr	No. 1	L	Cr
6854	4	Hawkins, Jonas	10	M	F	S	Wiley Hawkins	L	Cr	No. 1	L	Cr
6855	5	Hawkins, Wiley	52	M	F	Hus	Unknown	D	Cr	Unknown	D	Cr
		No. 5 died February 23, 1901. No. 3 reported dead										
		Census Card No. 2248, P. O. Calvin, Enrolled April 24, 1901										
6856	1	Bruner, Maggie	35	F	F		Washington Smith	D	Cr	Lydia Smith	D	Cr
6857	2	Bear, Sarah	17	F	F	D	Nocus Ille Harjo	L	Cr	No. 1	L	Cr
6858	3	Johnson, Louis	15	M	F	S	Ben Fixeco	D	Cr	No. 1	L	Cr
6859	5	Wolf, George	9	M	F	S	Sarnie	D	Cr	No. 1	L	Cr
		Census Card No. 2249, P. O. Calvin, Enrolled April 24, 1901										
6860	1	Hawkins, Okla Hosta	13	M	F		Wiley Hawkins	D	Cr	Huthlucky	D	Cr
		No. 1 died April 20, 1900										
		Census Card No. 2250, P. O. Hanna, Enrolled April 25, 1901										
6861	1	Smith, Wiley	57	M	F		Cosar Yoholar	D	Cr	Temardy	D	Cr
6862	2	Smith, Rhoda	32	F	F	Wf	Foster Grayson	L	Cr	Toche Grayson	D	Cr
6863	3	Smith, Lena	13	F	F	D	No. 1	L	Cr	No. 2	L	Cr
6864	4	Smith, Jim	11	M	F	S	No. 1	L	Cr	No. 2	L	Cr
6865	5	Smith, Lizzie	9	F	F	D	No. 1	L	Cr	No. 2	L	Cr
6866	6	Smith, Sallie	5	F	F	D	No. 1	L	Cr	No. 2	L	Cr
		No. 1 died 1905										
		Census Card No. 2251, P. O. Brush Hill, Enrolled April 25, 1901										
6867	1	Washington, Walter	21	M	F		George Washington	D	Cr	Martha Washington	D	Cr
		Census Card No. 2252, P. O. Depew, Enrolled April 25, 1901										
6868	1	Ekoconney	36	F	F		Unknown	D	Cr	Unknown	D	Cr
6869	2	Polakaconthla	13	M	F	S	Harkaconthlaney	D	Cr	No. 1	L	Cr
6870	3	Ahla-quan	10	F	F	D	Harkaconthlaney	D	Cr	No. 1	L	Cr
6871	4	Harlarchar	7	M	F	S	Harkaconthlaney	D	Cr	No. 1	L	Cr
		No. 1 died July 7, 1905. No. 2 died September 1912										
		Census Card No. 2253, P. O. Tulsa, Enrolled April 26, 1901										
6872	1	Scott, Sunday	25	M	F		Skull Scott	D	Cr	Narchie Scott	L	Cr
6873	2	Scott, Narchie	48	F	F	Moth	Unknown	D	Cr	Unknown	D	Cr
		No. 2 died September 29, 1899										

Roll No.	No.	NAME	Age	Sex	Blood	Rel.	NAME OF FATHER	Liv.	Cit.	NAME OF MOTHER	Liv.	Cit.
		Census Card No. 2254, P. O. Tulsa, Enrolled April 26, 1901										
6874	1	"Emartbla"	44	M	F		Ewiheche	D	Cr	Unknown	D	Cr
6875	2	"Emartbla" Jimhoker	46	F	F	Wf	Tulmarsey	D	Cr	Susanna	L	Cr
6876	3	"Emartbla", Hattie	20	F	F	D	No. 1	L	Cr	No. 2	L	Cr
6877	4	"Emartbla", Gabriel	16	M	F	S	No. 1	L	Cr	No. 2	L	Cr
		No. 2 died May 16, 1899. Nos. 1 and 4 reported dead. No. 3 died September 20, 1899										
		Census Card No. 2255, P. O. Tulsa, Enrolled April 26, 1901										
6878	1	Cedar, Susan	24	F	⅛		Robert Childers	D	Cr	Rachel Childers	D	Cr
		No. 1 died September 15, 1899										
		Census Card No. 2256, P. O. Eufaula, Enrolled April 26, 1901										
6879	1	Roberts, Annie	22	F	F		Simon Peter	D	Cr	Nicey Peter	D	Cr
		No. 1 died August 22, 1902										
		Census Card No. 2257, P. O. Kellyville, Enrolled April 27, 1901										
6880	1	Peeper, Mary	29	F	F		Capahny Snow	L	Cr	Yarlacoweny	D	Cr
6881	2	Peeper, Everett	2	M	½	S	Frank Peeper	L	Non	No. 1	L	Cr
		No. 1 died April 1902										
		Census Card No. 2258, P. O. Sapulpa, Enrolled April 29, 1901										
6882	1	Brown, Joseph	23	M	F		Charles Brown	D	Cr	Annie Brown	D	Cr
		Census Card No. 2259, P. O. Kellyville, Enrolled April 29, 1901										
6883	1	Painkiller, Peter	20	M	F		Watashe	L	Cr	Tetakanay	L	Cr
		Census Card No. 2260, P. O. Sapulpa, Enrolled April 30, 1901; Nos. 5, 6, 7 May 10, 1901										
6884	1	Watashe	40	M	F		Cotoney	D	Cr	Unknown	D	Cr
6885	2	Watashe, Rosa	30	F	F	Wf	Holder	L	Cr	Unknown	D	Cr
6886	3	Watashe, Celia	12	F	F	D	No. 1	L	Cr	No. 2	L	Cr
6887	4	Watashe, Barney	11 mo	M	F	S	No. 1	L	Cr	No. 2	L	Cr
6888	5	Watashe, Wiley	11	M	F	S	No. 1	L	Cr	No. 2	L	Cr
6889	6	Watashe, Eliza	5	F	F	D	No. 1	L	Cr	No. 2	L	Cr
6890	7	Watashe, Lofahye	3	M	F	S	No. 1	L	Cr	No. 2	L	Cr
		No. 3 reported dead										
		Census Card No. 2261, P. O. Kellyville, Enrolled April 30, 1901										
6891	1	Charcotetenna	65	M	F		Unknown	D	Cr	Unknown	D	Cr
6892	2	Charcotetenna, Polly	40	F	F	Wf	Paconthla	D	Cr	Unknown	D	Cr
6893	3	Charcotetenna, Katie	16	F	F	D	No. 1	L	Cr	No. 2	L	Cr
6894	4	Charcotetenna, Elder	6	M	F	S	No. 1	L	Cr	No. 2	L	Cr
		No. 1 died February 3, 1902. No. 3 died September 5, 1906										
		Census Card No. 2262, P. O. Kellyville, Enrolled Apeil 30, 1901										
6895	1	Hay, John	22	M	F		Charcotetenna	L	Cr	Polly Charcotetenna	L	Cr
6896	2	Hay, Egie	20	F	F	Wf	Manka	L	Cr	Pantany	L	Cr
6897	3	Hay, Deshalecoweney	3	M	F	S	No. 1	L	Cr	No. 2	L	Cr
		Census Card No. 2263, P. O. Sasakwa, Enrolled May 7, 1901										
6898	1	Palmer, Mary	17	F	½		Dave Frank	D	Cr	Jane Frank	L	Cr
6899	2	Palmer, Jennie	2	F	¼	D	Tom Palmer	L	Sem	No. 1	L	Cr
		Census Card No. 2264, P. O. Coweta, Enrolled April 30, 1901										
6900	1	Flowers, Lewis	24	M	¼		John Flowers	L	Cr	Ariminta Flowers	D	Cher
		Census Card No. 2265, P. O. Wagoner, Enrolled May 1, 1901										
6901	1	Damet, Eliza	17	F	¼		Fall M. Brady	L	Cr	Martha Brady	L	Cr
		Census Card No. 2266, P. O. Eufaula, Enrolled May 1, 1901										
6902	1	Gibson, Charles	55	M	½		John C. Gibson	L	Non	Polly Gibson	D	Cr
		Census Card No. 2267, P. O. Sapulpa, Enrolled May 1, 1901										
6903	1	Jack, Phillip	41	M	F		Warren Jack	D	Cr	Unknown	D	Cr
6904	2	Jack, Sam	20	M	F	S	No. 1	L	Cr	Katie Jack	D	Cr
6905	3	Jack, Jennie	15	F	F	D	No. 1	L	Cr	Katie Jack	D	Cr
		No. 2 died May 7, 1901. No. 3 died April 10, 1901										
		Census Card No. 2268, P. O. Sapulpa, Enrolled May 1, 1901										
6906	1	Sak-ka-senny	75	M	F		Unknown	D	Cr	Unknown	D	Cr
		No. 1 died September 7, 1899										
		Census Card No. 2269, P. O. Tulsa, Enrolled May 1, 1901										
6907	1	Smiley, Lottie	10	F	⅛		T. E. Smiley	L	Non	Nora Smiley	D	Cr
6908	2	Smiley, Earnest	8	M	⅛	Bro	T. E. Smiley	L	Non	Nora Smiley	D	Cr
6909	3	Smiley, Allen	4	M	⅛	Bro	T. E. Smiley	L	Non	Nora Smiley	D	Cr
		Census Card No. 2270, P. O. Coweta, Enrolled May 3, 1901										
6910	1	House, Lottie	18	F	1-16		Conny Murphy	L	Cr	Sarah Murpby	L	Non
		Census Card No. 2271, P. O. Eufaula, Enrolled May 3, 1901										
6911	1	Sanger, Amanda	51	F	¼		London Coker	L	Cr	Kogie Coker	D	Cr
6912	2	Sanger, Joseph	20	M	⅛	S	E. E. Sanger	L	Non	No. 1	L	Cr
6913	3	Sanger, Fannie E.	18	F	⅛	D	E. E. Sanger	L	Non	No. 1	L	Cr
6914	4	Sanger, Walter G.	15	M	⅛	S	E. E. Sanger	L	Non	No. 1	L	Cr
		Census Card No. 2272, P. O. Checotah, Enrolled May 3, 1901; No. 4 May 16, 1901										
6915	1	McNac, Nulsey	45	F	F		John Patake	D	Cr	Unknown	D	Cr
6916	2	Holahta, Hettie	18	F	F	D	Seborn Holahta	D	Cr	No. 1	L	Cr
6917	3	McNac, Peter	65	M	F	Hus	Unknown	D	Cr	Unknown	D	Cr
6918	4	Cross, Moses	19	M	F	S	Sammy Cross	D	Cr	No. 1	L	Cr
		No. 3 reported dead										
		Census Card No. 2273, P. O. Okemah, Enrolled May 7, 1901										
6919	1	Yahola, Parhose	60	M	F		Mecheska Harjo	D	Cr	Tuparliche	D	Cr
6920	2	Yahola, Mawokike	70	F	F	Wf	Cundarlee	D	Cr	Semicb Hoye	D	Cr
6921	3	Buck, Lottie	20	F	F	D	No. 1	L	Cr	No. 2	L	Cr
6922	4	Yahola, Lila	15	F	F	D	No. 1	L	Cr	No. 2	L	Cr
6923	5	Yahola, Lowe	8	M	F	S	No. 1	L	Cr	No. 2	L	Cr
		No. 4 died June 1899. No. 1 died November 16, 1909. No. 3 died 1909										

Roll No.	No.	NAME	Age	Sex	Blood	Rel.	Name of Father	Liv.	Cit.	Name of Mother	Liv.	Cit.
		Census Card No. 2274, P. O. Okemah, Enrolled May 7, 1901										
6924	1	Yahola, Lizzie	30	F	F		Hencha Fixico	D	Cr	Mawokike	D	Cr
6925	2	Yahola, Nellie	12	F	F	D	Parhose Yahola	L	Cr	No. 1	L	Cr
6926	3	Yahola, Rhoda	7	F	F	D	Parhose Yahola	L	Cr	No. 1	L	Cr
		No. 1 reported dead										
		Census Card No. 2275, P. O. Bearden, Enrolled May 7, 1901										
6927	1	Little, Thomas	33	M	F		Heneha Chupco	D	Cr	Hokte	D	Cr
6928	2	Little, Sallie	33	F	F	Wf	Sokikee	L	Cr	Kerselahne	D	Cr
6929	3	Little, Sam	13	M	F	S	No. 1	L	Cr	No. 2	L	Cr
6930	4	Little, Standon	8	M	F	S	No. 1	L	Cr	No. 2	L	Cr
6931	5	Little, Susanna	3	F	F	D	No. 1	L	Cr	No. 2	L	Cr
		No. 1 died in 1900. No. 2 reported dead										
		Census Card No. 2276, P. O. Coweta, Enrolled May 7, 1901										
6932	1	Miller, John	21	M	F		Jim Miller	L	Cr	Susan Miller	D	Cr
6933	2	Miller, Jim	51	M	F	Fath	Miller	D	Cr	Nadahee	D	Cr
		Census Card No. 2277, P. O. Okemah, Enrolled May 7, 1901										
6934	1	Fixico, Nocus	55	M	F		Youlke Harjo	D	Cr	Linda	D	Cr
6935	2	Stricken from roll										
6936	3	Stricken from roll										
6937	4	Stricken from roll										
6938	5	Stricken from roll										
6939	6	Bear, Rhina	7	F	F	D	No. 1	L	Cr	Lowakoche	D	Cr
6940	7	Stricken from roll										
		Census Card No. 2278, P. O. Arbeka, Enrolled May 7, 1901										
6941	1	Fixeco, Anderson	23	M	F		Nocus Fixico	L	Cr	Seluskey Bear	L	Cr
		No. 1 dead										
		Census Card No. 2279, P. O. Arbeka, Enrolled May 7, 1901										
6942	1	Mahola	50	F	F		Yulke Horche	D	Cr	Kenda	D	Cr
6943	2	Jennie	18	F	F	D	Harjo	L	Cr	No. 1	L	Cr
6944	3	Hillie	12	F	F	D	Arharlock Fixico	L	Cr	No. 1	L	Cr
6945	4	Stricken from roll										
6946	5	Stricken from roll										
6947	6	Stricken from roll										
6948	7	Stricken from roll										
		Original enrollment on Census Cards No. 2280 and 2281 stricken from roll										
		Census Card No. 2282, P. O. Calvin, Enrolled May 8, 1901										
6949	1	Leader, Emma	21	F	F		Edward Leader	L	Choc	Annie Leader	D	Cr
		Census Card No. 2283, P. O. Barnard, Enrolled May 8, 1901										
6950	1	Leader, Nancy	24	F	F		Edward Leader	L	Choc	Annie Leader	D	Cr
		No. 1 died March 2, 1903										
		Census Card No. 2284, P. O. Arbeka, Enrolled May 8, 1901										
6951	1	Jackson, Lucy	20	F	½		Woxie Yahola	D	Sem	Coasta	D	Cr
6952	2	Jackson, Ceasar	6	M	¾	S	Saber Jackson	L	Cr	No. 1	L	Cr
6953	3	Jackson, Wiley	2	M	¾	S	Saber Jackson	L	Cr	No. 1	L	Cr
		No. 1 died April 10, 1900. No. 2 died April 4, 1899. No. 3 died May 25, 1899										
		Census Card No. 2285, P. O. Tulsa, Enrolled May 8, 1901										
6954	1	Harjo, Nocus	67	M	F		Niggie	D	Cr	Unknown	D	Cr
6955	2	Harjo, Moleyar	45	F	F	Wf	Nehathloccogee	D	Cr	Hocoletchee	D	Cr
6956	3	Harjo, Selina	12	F	F	D	No. 1	L	Cr	No. 2	L	Cr
6957	4	Adams, Samuel	19	M	F	StS	Lieutenant Adams	D	Cr	No. 2	L	Cr
6958	5	Adams, Thomas	16	M	F	StS	Lieutenant Adams	D	Cr	No. 2	L	Cr
		No. 5 died March 1901. No. 4 died February 13, 1911. Nos. 1 and 4 reported dead										
		Census Card No. 2286, P. O. Boley, Enrolled May 8, 1901										
6959	1	Deere, Peter	45	M	F		Unknown	D	Cr	Unknown	D	Cr
6960	2	Deere, Betty	46	F	F	Wf	Dello Harjo	D	Cr	Ailsey Harjo	D	Cr
6961	3	Willior, Peggy	19	F	½	StD	Willior	D	Cr	No. 2	L	Cr
6962	4	Willior, Lena	16	F	½	StD	Willior	D	Cr	No. 2	L	Cr
		No. 1 died October 1900. No. 4 died April 16, 1900										
		Census Card No. 2287, P. O. Arbeka, Enrolled May 8, 1901										
6963	1	Willior, Seper	20	M	½		Willior	D	Cr	Betty Deere	L	Cr
		Census Card No. 2288, P. O. Holdenville, Enrolled May 8, 1901										
6964	1	Davis, Selina	63	F	F		Unknown	D	Cr	Unknown	D	Cr
		No. 1 died May 1907										
		Census Card No. 2289, P. O. Holdenville, Enrolled May 8, 1901										
6965	1	Davis, James	28	M	F		George Davis	D	Cr	Selina Davis	L	Cr
6966	2	Davis, Millie	24	F	F	Wf	Waddie	D	Cr	Onuffer	D	Cr
6967	3	Davis, Katie	3	F	F	D	No. 1	L	Cr	No. 2	L	Cr
		No. 2 died October 4, 1899. No. 3 died December 18, 1899										
		Census Card No. 2290, P. O. Jenks, Enrolled May 8, 1901										
6968	1	Doyle, Cora	5	F	1-16		N. C. Doyle	L	Cr	Annie Doyle	L	Non
		Census Card No. 2291, P. O. Earlsboro, Enrolled May 8, 1901										
6969	1	Taylor, Lucy	20	F	F		Tarkosar Harjo	L	Cr	Lizzie Harjo	D	Cr
		Census Card No. 2292, P. O. Coweta, Enrolled May 8, 1901										
6970	1	Miller, Lizzie M.	35	F	½		Charley Stinson	L	Cr	Augusta Rogers	D	Cher
6971	2	Beck, Odus	14	M	¼	S	Leonard Beck	L	Non	No. 1	L	Cr
6972	3	Beck, Gerty	10	F	¼	D	Leonard Beck	L	Non	No. 1	L	Cr
6973	4	Beck, Otto	8	M	¼	S	Leonard Beck	L	Non	No. 1	L	Cr
6974	5	Beck, Fannie	6	F	¼	D	Leonard Beck	L	Non	No. 1	L	Cr
		Census Card No. 2293, P. O. Hanna, Enrolled May 8, 1901										
6975	1	Bruner, Jackson	18	M	¾		Willie Bruner	D	Cr	Sallie Bruner	D	Cr
		No. I supposed to be duplicate of enrollment opposite No. 8509, this roll										

Census Card No. 2294, P. O. Sapulpa, Enrolled May 8, 1901

Roll No.	No.	NAME	Age	Sex	Blood	Rel.	NAME OF FATHER	Liv.	Cit.	NAME OF MOTHER	Liv.	Cit.
6976	1	Bear, Hilly	55	F	F		Unknown	D	Cr	Coweny	D	Cr

Census Card No. 2295, P. O. Stedham; No. 5 Sapulpa, care Wm. Sapulpa, Enrolled May 8, 1901

Roll No.	No.	NAME	Age	Sex	Blood	Rel.	NAME OF FATHER	Liv.	Cit.	NAME OF MOTHER	Liv.	Cit.
6977	1	McIntosh, Roley	60	M	F		Sachpa	D	Cr	Katie	D	Cr
6978	2	McIntosh, Ellen	47	F	F	Wf	J. M. Perryman	D	Cr	Unknown	D	Cr
6979	3	McIntosh, Thomas	19	M	F	S	No. 1	L	Cr	Lucinda	D	Cr
6980	4	Thompson, James	11	M	F	Ward	Hardy Thompson	D	Cr	Lena Thompson	D	Cr
6981	5	Green, Fred	5	M	F	Ward	Barney Green	L	Cr	Phoeba Sapulpa	D	Cr

No. 1 died November 30, 1908

Census Card No. 2296, P. O. Fame, Enrolled May 8, 1901

Roll No.	No.	NAME	Age	Sex	Blood	Rel.	NAME OF FATHER	Liv.	Cit.	NAME OF MOTHER	Liv.	Cit.
6982	1	McIntosh, John	21	M	F		Roley McIntosh	L	Cr	Lucinda	D	Cr

Census Card No. 2297, P. O. Tulsa, Enrolled May 9, 1901

Roll No.	No.	NAME	Age	Sex	Blood	Rel.	NAME OF FATHER	Liv.	Cit.	NAME OF MOTHER	Liv.	Cit.
6983	1	Drake, Benjamin H.	11	M	¾		Richard Drake	L	Non	Nancy Drake	D	Cr

No. 1 died August 12, 1899

Census Card No. 2298, P. O. Tulsa, Enrolled May 9, 1901

Roll No.	No.	NAME	Age	Sex	Blood	Rel.	NAME OF FATHER	Liv.	Cit.	NAME OF MOTHER	Liv.	Cit.
6984	1	Childers, William	25	M	½		Robert Childers	D	Cr	Rachael Childers	D	Cr

No. 1 died May 13, 1902

Census Card No. 2299, P. O. Okemah, Enrolled May 9, 1901

Roll No.	No.	NAME	Age	Sex	Blood	Rel.	NAME OF FATHER	Liv.	Cit.	NAME OF MOTHER	Liv.	Cit.
6985	1	Soloman, Wisey	43	F	F		Parhos Emarthla	D	Cr	Magethloke	D	Cr
6986	2	Soloman, Susie	9	F	F	D	Sam Soloman	L	Cr	No. 1	L	Cr
6987	3	Soloman, Johnson	8	M	F	S	Sam Soloman	L	Cr	No. 1	L	Cr
6988	4	Soloman, Sam	47	M	F	Hus	Hinehochee	D	Cr	Unknown	D	Cr

No. 3 died June 3, 1905.   No. 4 died March 13, 1900.

Census Card No. 2300, P. O. Eufaula, Enrolled May 9, 1901

Roll No.	No.	NAME	Age	Sex	Blood	Rel.	NAME OF FATHER	Liv.	Cit.	NAME OF MOTHER	Liv.	Cit.
6989	1	Manawa, Bunnie	20	M	F		Bunnie Manawa	D	Cr	Leah Manawa	D	Cr
6990	2	Manawa, Lydia	15	F	F	Sis	Bunnie Manawa	D	Cr	Leah Manawa	D	Cr
6991	3	Manawa, George	10	M	F	Bro	Bunnie Manawa	D	Cr	Lezh Manawa	D	Cr

No. 2 died September 4, 1906

Census Card No. 2301, P. O. Tuskegee, Enrolled May 9, 1901

Roll No.	No.	NAME	Age	Sex	Blood	Rel.	NAME OF FATHER	Liv.	Cit.	NAME OF MOTHER	Liv.	Cit.
6992	1	Gooden, Jacob	22	M	¼		Charley Gooden	D	Cr	Leah Gooden	D	Cr
6993	2	Goodey, Louisa	20	F	½	Wf	Sol Taylor	L	Cr	Nellie Taylor	D	Cr
6994	3	Gooden, Mollie	1	F	⅜	D	No. 1	L	Cr	No. 2	L	Cr

No. 2 died April 5, 1908

Census Card No. 2302, P. O. Checotah, Enrolled May 9, 1901

Roll No.	No.	NAME	Age	Sex	Blood	Rel.	NAME OF FATHER	Liv.	Cit.	NAME OF MOTHER	Liv.	Cit.
6995	1	Grimes, Susannah	28	F	F		Willie Grimes	L	Cr	Josie Tiger	L	Cr

Census Card No. 2303, P. O. Arbeka, Enrolled May 9, 1901

Roll No.	No.	NAME	Age	Sex	Blood	Rel.	NAME OF FATHER	Liv.	Cit.	NAME OF MOTHER	Liv.	Cit.
6996	1	Wisey	45	F	F		Atsolugge Espoke	D	Cr	Sarsoho	D	Cr

No. 1 reported dead

Census Card No. 2304, P. O. Holdenville, Enrolled May 9, 1901

Roll No.	No.	NAME	Age	Sex	Blood	Rel.	NAME OF FATHER	Liv.	Cit.	NAME OF MOTHER	Liv.	Cit.
6997	1	Tiger, Polly	26	F	F		John Tiger	L	Cr	Hokte Pocco	D	Cr

Census Card No. 2305, P. O. Bristow, Enrolled May 9, 1901

Roll No.	No.	NAME	Age	Sex	Blood	Rel.	NAME OF FATHER	Liv.	Cit.	NAME OF MOTHER	Liv.	Cit.
6998	1	Harry, Wheaton	25	M	¼		Albert Harry	L	Cr	Liza Harry	D	Cr

Census Card No. 2306, P. O. Edna, Enrolled May 9, 1901

Roll No.	No.	NAME	Age	Sex	Blood	Rel.	NAME OF FATHER	Liv.	Cit.	NAME OF MOTHER	Liv.	Cit.
6999	1	Gooden, Tontah	16	F	F		Mutle Loke	D	Cr	Shequany	D	Cr

Census Card No. 2307, P. O. Depew, Enrolled May 9, 1901

Roll No.	No.	NAME	Age	Sex	Blood	Rel.	NAME OF FATHER	Liv.	Cit.	NAME OF MOTHER	Liv.	Cit.
7000	1	Faconey	35	F	F		Capeconey	D	Cr	Abbelogah	D	Cr
7001	2	Euchee, Billy	52	M	F	Hus	Unknown	D	Cr	Unknown	D	Cr

No. 2 died August 17, 1899

Census Card No. 2308, P. O. Kellyville, Enrolled May 9, 1901

Roll No.	No.	NAME	Age	Sex	Blood	Rel.	NAME OF FATHER	Liv.	Cit.	NAME OF MOTHER	Liv.	Cit.
7002	1	George, John	32	M	F		Billy Euchee	D	Cr	Hannah Sofallah	D	Cr
7003	2	Pahcoquah	38	F	F	Wf	Yulahcocontahney	L	Cr	Salegee	L	Cr
7004	3	George, Willie	11	M	F	S	No. 1	L	Cr	Selegee	L	Cr
7005	4	George, Lizzie	9	F	F	D	No. 1	L	Cr	Selegee	L	Cr
7006	5	George, Alexander	7	M	F	S	No. 1	L	Cr	Selegee	L	Cr
7007	6	Cocotahloney	4	M	F	StS	Tahconthlaney	L	Cr	Selegee	L	Cr

No. 4 reported dead

Census Card No. 2309, P. O. Tulsa, Enrolled May 9, 1901

Roll No.	No.	NAME	Age	Sex	Blood	Rel.	NAME OF FATHER	Liv.	Cit.	NAME OF MOTHER	Liv.	Cit.
7008	1	Perryman, Hamor C.	14	M	¼		J. C. Perryman	D	Cr	Mattie Poquin	L	Non

Census Card No. 2310, P. O. Sapulpa, Enrolled May 9, 1901

Roll No.	No.	NAME	Age	Sex	Blood	Rel.	NAME OF FATHER	Liv.	Cit.	NAME OF MOTHER	Liv.	Cit.
7009	1	Holder, John	50	M	F		Tommy Martyr	D	Cr	Egohney	D	Cr

No. 1 reported dead

Census Card No. 2311, P. O. Depew, Enrolled May 10, 1901

Roll No.	No.	NAME	Age	Sex	Blood	Rel.	NAME OF FATHER	Liv.	Cit.	NAME OF MOTHER	Liv.	Cit.
7010	1	Clinton, George	35	M	F		Unknown	D	Cr	Unknown	D	Cr
7011	2	Clinton, Sallie	29	F	F	Wf	Unknown	D	Cr	Louisa Southlope	D	Cr
7012	3	Clinton, Motey	10	F	F	S	No. 1	L	Cr	No. 2	L	Cr
7013	4	Clinton, Lee	8	M	F	S	No. 1	L	Cr	No. 2	L	Cr
7014	5	Clinton, Lynch	2	M	F	S	No. 1	L	Cr	No. 2	L	Cr
7015	6	Mutte, Loke Willie	10	M	F	Ward	Mutte Loke	D	Cr	Shequany	D	Cr

No. 5 died August 24, 1907

Census Card No. 2312, P. O. Bristow, Enrolled May 10, 1901; No. 2, May 24, 1901

Roll No.	No.	NAME	Age	Sex	Blood	Rel.	NAME OF FATHER	Liv.	Cit.	NAME OF MOTHER	Liv.	Cit.
7016	1	Bigpond, James	18	M	F		Billy Pig Pond	D	Cr	Kissie Big Pond	D	Cr
7017	2	Bigpond, Sarah	15	F	F	Wf	Eehoney	D	Cr	Ahcoconney	L	Cr

No. 2 died March 24, 1902

Census Card No. 2313, P. O. Bristow, Enrolled May 10, 1901

Roll No.	No.	NAME	Age	Sex	Blood	Rel.	NAME OF FATHER	Liv.	Cit.	NAME OF MOTHER	Liv.	Cit.
7018	1	Pigpond, Charley	52	M	F		Takowena	D	Cr	Wyyahka	D	Cr
7019	2	Bigpond, Louisa	50	F	F	Wf	Jacob Barnett	L	Cr	Hothlochee Barnett	D	Cr

No. 1 died January 24, 1905.   No. 2 died February 18, 1907.

Census Card No. 2314, P. O. Eufaula, Enrolled May 10, 1901

Roll No.	No.	NAME	Age	Sex	Blood	Rel.	NAME OF FATHER	Liv.	Cit.	NAME OF MOTHER	Liv.	Cit.
7020	1	Nero, Joseph	40	M	1-16		William Nero	D	Non	Nancy Nero	L	Cr

Roll No.	No.	NAME	Age	Sex	Blood	Rel.	NAME OF FATHER	Liv.	Cit.	NAME OF MOTHER	Liv.	Cit.
		Census Card No. 2315, P. O. Pierce, Enrolled May 10, 1901; No. 3, May 23, 1901										
7021	1	James, Chotkey	40	M	F		D. E. Jamon	D	Cr	Hollie	D	Cr
7022	2	James, Millie	42	F	F	Wf	Fiddler John	D	Cr	Jennie	L	Cr
7023	3	James, Nancy	14	F	F	D	No. 1	L	Cr	Betsey James	D	Cr
		Census Card No. 2316, P. O. Hoffman, Enrolled May 10, 1901										
7024	1	Frank, William	18	M	F		Hitchete Frank	D	Cr	Nancy Frank	D	Cr
		Census Card No. 2317, P. O. Eufaula, Enrolled May 10, 1901										
7025	1	Nero, Nancy	70	F	⅛		Joe Gooden	D	Cr	Elsie Gooden	D	Cr
7026	2	Nero, Governor	25	F	1-16	S	William Nero	D	Non	No. 1	L	Cr
		Census Card No. 2318, P. O. Eufaula, Enrolled May 10, 1901										
7027	1	Nero, William	20	M	½		Mose Nero	D	Cr	Jennie Nero	D	Cr
		No. 1 reported dead										
		Census Card No. 2319, P. O. Hoffman, Enrolled May 10, 1901										
7028	1	Tiger, Sukey	45	F	F		Mikko Harjo	D	Cr	Louisa King	L	Cr
7029	2	Butler, Legus	18	M	F	S	James Butler	D	Cr	No. 1	L	Cr
7030	3	Tiger, Sophia	13	F	F	D	Sandy Tiger	D	Cr	No. 1	L	Cr
7031	4	Tiger, Hapsey	11	F	F	D	Sandy Tiger	D	Cr	No. 1	L	Cr
7032	5	Tiger, Tommie	9	M	F	S	Sandy Tiger	D	Cr	No. 1	L	Cr
7033	6	Tiger, Taylor	7	M	F	S	Sandy Tiger	D	Cr	No. 1	L	Cr
7034	7	Tiger, Annie	2	F	F	D	Sandy Tiger	D	Cr	No. 1	L	Cr
		No. 5 died November 2, 1909. Nos. 1 and 7 reported dead.										
		Census Card No. 2320, P. O. Eufaula, Enrolled May 10, 1901										
7035	1	Scott, Noble	45	M	F		Yulga Harjo	D	Cr	Janie	D	Cr
7036	2	Scott, Judy	35	F	F	Wf	Tusekiyerhutke	D	Cr	Judy	D	Cr
7037	3	Scott, Ella	16	F	F	D	No. 1	L	Cr	No. 2	L	Cr
7038	4	Scott, Jackson	6	M	F	S	No. 1	L	Cr	No. 2	L	Cr
7039	5	Scott, Sallie	4	F	F	D	No. 1	L	Cr	No. 2	L	Cr
7040	6	Scott, Polly	13	F	F	D	No. 1	L	Cr	No. 2	L	Cr
7041	7	Scott, Lona	12	M	F	S	No. 1	L	Cr	No. 2	L	Cr
		No. 1 died February 27, 1902. No. 2 died March 13, 1913. No. 6 died September 10, 1900. No. 5 died 1907. No. 7 died July 28, 1901.										
		Census Card No. 2321, P. O. Hoffman, Enrolled May 10, 1901; No. 2, May 22, 1901										
7042	1	Jenkins, Henrietta	25	F	¼		Thomas Watts	L	Cher	Mary Watts	L	Cr
7043	2	Jenkins, Thomas DeWitt	3	M	¼	S	Gibson R. Jenkins	D	Cr	No. 1	L	Cr
		Census Card No. 2322, P. O. Eufaula, Enrolled May 11, 1901										
7044	1	Emarthloche, Henehe	42	M	F		Fitteda Harjo	D	Cr	Saliaa	D	Cr
7045	2	Emarthloche, Hepsey	35	F	F	Wf	Forsut Semartoge	D	Cr	Tallosaka	D	Cr
7046	3	Emarthloche, Osina	18	F	F	D	No. 1	L	Cr	No. 2	L	Cr
		No. 1 died March 12, 1903. No. 2 died. No. 3 died November 27, 1911.										
		Census Card No. 2323, P. O. Eufaula, Enrolled May 10, 1901										
7047	1	Kelly, Albert	21	M	F		Wiley Kelly	D	Cr	Jennie Thompson	D	Cr
		No. 1 died Summer of 1902										
		Census Card No. 2324, P. O. Eufaula, Enrolled May 10, 1901										
7048	1	Kelly, John	17	M	F		Wiley Kelly	D	Cr	Jennie Thompson	D	Cr
		No. 1 died January 17, 1904										
		Census Card No. 2325, P. O. Boley, Enrolled May 23, 1901										
7049	1	Harjo, Chelokke	45	M	F		Tulmarsse Heneha	D	Cr	Sabse Ohme	D	Cr
7050	2	Iswihhohke	40	F	F	Sis	Tulmarsse Hencha	D	Cr	Sabse Ohme	D	Cr
7051	3	Hokte	15	F	F	Niece	Artus Hencha	L	Cr	No. 2	L	Cr
		Census Card No. 2326, P. O. Eufaula, Enrolled May 10, 1901										
7052	1	Kelley, Wiley	52	M	F		Tecumseh Kelly	D	Cr	Lucinda	D	Cr
		No. 1 died January 12, 1904										
		Census Card No. 2327, P. O. Okmulgee, Enrolled May 10, 1901										
7053	1	McNack, Charley	60	M	F		Sandy McNac	D	Cr	Saktolumba	D	Cr
		No. 1 reported dead										
		Census Card No. 2328, P. O. Hanna, Enrolled May 10, 1901										
7054	1	Byrd, Lucy Ann	19	F	F		William Byrd	D	Cr	Eda Byrd	D	Cr
		Census Card No. 2329, P. O. Calvin, Enrolled May 10, 1901										
7055	1	Brunner, Barey	32	M	F		Toley Bruner	D	Cr	Sorbse Bruner	D	Cr
7056	2	Hawkins, Bunny	17	M	F	Neph	Harris Hawkins	D	Cr	Sallie Hawkins	D	Cr
7057	3	Hickory, Addie	9	F	F	Niece	Amos Hickory	L	Cr	Sallie Hickory	D	Cr
7058	4	Hickory, Amos	35	M	F	Bro-L	Dick Hickory	D	Cr	Katousey	D	Cr
		No. 4 died December 14, 1900. No. 2 reported dead.										
		Census Card No. 2330, P. O. Sasakwa, Enrolled May 10, 1901										
7059	1	Charlesey, Ellen	23	F	F		Thomas West	L	Sem	Bessie	D	Cr
		Census Card No. 2331, P. O. Calvin, Enrolled May 10, 1901; No. 5, May 16, 1901										
7060	1	Deer, James	49	M	F		Unknown	D	Cr	Eliza Washington	L	Cr
7061	2	Deer, Lucy	47	F	F	Wf	Unknown	D	Cher	Unknown	D	Cr
7062	3	Deer, Edmond	20	M	F	S	No. 1	L	Cr	No. 2	L	Cr
7063	4	Deer, Mary A.	14	F	F	D	No. 1	L	Cr	No. 2	L	Cr
7064	5	Deer, Nellie	6	F	F	GrN	Jonas Deer	D	Cr	Jennie McGilbra	L	Cr
		No. 1 died November 19, 1904. No. 2 died March 23, 1913. No. 7064 possible duplicate of No. 7408 and 7907.										
		Census Card No. 2332, P. O. Tulsa, Enrolled May 10, 1901; No. 2, May 14, 1901										
7065	1	Solander, Minnie	19	F	½		T. M. Mathewson	L	Non	H. A. Mathewson	L	Non
7066	2	Solander, Hettie L.	4moF	¼	D		G. A. Solander	L	Non	No. 1	D	Cr
		No. 1 died October 8, 1899. No. 2 reported dead.										

Roll No.	No.	NAME	Age	Sex	Blood	Rel.	NAME OF FATHER	Liv.	Cit.	NAME OF MOTHER	Liv.	Cit.
		Census Card No. 233, P. O. Dustin, Enrolled May 10, 1901										
7067	1	Field, Harper	40	M	F		Hezekiah Harjo	D	Cr	Olageskee	D	Cr
7068	2	Field, Mahala	40	F	F	Wf	Kenas Harjo	D	Cr	Sokena	D	Cr
7069	3	Field, Lucy	17	F	F	D	No. 1	L	Cr	No. 2	L	Cr
7070	4	Field, Millie	15	F	F	D	No. 1	L	Cr	No. 2	L	Cr.
7071	5	Field, Kogee	13	M	F	S	No. 1	L	Cr	No. 2	L	Cr
7072	6	Field, Isom	12	M	F	S	No. 1	L	Cr	No. 2	L	Cr
7073	7	Field, Frank	7	M	F	S	No. 1	L	Cr	No. 2	I.	Cr
		No. 1 died 1910. No. 4 Jancuary 1901.										
		Census Card No. 2334, P. O. Eufaula, Enrolled May 10, 1901										
7074	1	Manley, Pompey	43	M	F		Tuskogee Neha	D	Cr	Linda Neha	D	Cr
7075	2	Manley, Martha	33	F	F	Wf	Daniel Robert	D	Cr	Osliddy Robert	D	Cr
7076	3	Manley, Linda	12	F	F	D	No. 1	L	Cr	No. 2	L	Cr
7077	4	Manley, Lena	10	F	F	D	No. 1	L	Cr	No. 2	L	Cr
		No. 1 died February 19, 1902. No. 3 died January 1914.										
		Census Card No. 2335, P. O. Muskogee, Enrolled May 10, 1901										
7078	1	Brown, Albert	11	M	F		Charley Brown	L	Cr	Louisa Brown	D	Cr
		Census Card No. 2336, P. O. Arbeka, Enrolled May 24, 1901										
7079	1	King, Billy	21	M	F		Sampson	D	Cr	Larney	D	Cr
7080	2	King, Sam	21	M	F	Bro	Sampson	D	Cr	Larney	D	Cr
		No. 1 died January 25, 1900. No. 2 died September 19, 1906.										
		Census Card No. 2337, P. O. Salem, Enrolled May 11, 1901										
7081	1	Farnie	40	F	F		Tulsa Harjo	D	Cr	Artusbahe	D	Cr
		Census Card No. 2338, P. O. Hanna, Enrolled May 11, 1901										
7082	1	Harjo, Kapetcha	53	M	F		Cona Yahola	D	Cr	Unknown	D	Cr
7083	2	Harjo, Nellie	53	F	F	Wf	Unknown	D	Cr	Unknown	D	Cr
7084	3	Arsoyalee, Lovina	18	F	F	D	No. 1	L	Cr	Hettie	D	Cr
		No. 1 died March 10, 1901. No. 2 died March 1901.										
		Census Card No. 2339, P. O. Hanna, Enrolled May 11, 1901										
7085	1	Hawkins, Sepile	28	F	F		Kapetcha Harjo	L	Cr	Nellie	D	Cr
7086	2	Francis, Mack	5	M	F	S	Robert Francis	L	Cr	No. 1	L	Cr
		Census Card No. 2340, P. O. Hanna, Enrolled May 11, 1901										
7087	1	Dorsey, Alice	25	F	F		Wash Canard	D	Cr	Lizzie Canard	I.	Cr
7088	2	Dorsey, Katie	11	F	F	D	Joe Dorsey	D	Cr	No. 1	L	Cr
7089	3	Dorsey, Joseph	6	M	F	S	Joe Dorsey	D	Cr	No. 1	L	Cr
		No. 1 died November 17, 1900										
		Census Card No. 2341, P. O. Hanna, Enrolled May 11, 1901										
7090	1	Kanard, Lizzie	39	F	F		Nehemikkoge	D	Cr	Soma	D	Cr
		No. 1 died January 1901										
		Census Card No. 2342, P. O. Hanna, Enrolled May 11, 1901										
7091	1	Micco, Okchiye	35	M	F		Okfuska Yahola	D	Cr	Otokka	D	Cr
		No. 1 died March 1901										
		Census Card No. 2343, P. O. Hanna, Enrolled May 11, 1901										
7092	1	Marseya	30	F	F		Potolige	D	Cr	Unknown	D	Cr
		No. 1 died 1900										
		Census Card No. 2344, P. O. Hanna, Enrolled May 11, 1901										
7093	1	Smith, Matilda	35	F	F		Chuyemarla	D	Cr	Semarhoge	D	Cr
		No. 1 died April 6, 1901										
		Census Card No. 2345, P. O. Red Fork, Enrolled May 13, 1901										
7094	1	Templin, Benjamin A.	7	M	F		Lewis Bible	L	Cr	Martha Leetka	I.	Cr
		Census Card No. 2346, P. O. Tulsa, Enrolled May 13, 1901										
7095	1	Tuckabatchee, Ned	22	M	F		Tuckabatchee	L	Cr	Unknown	D	Cr
		No. 1 died dead										
		Census Card No. 2347, P. O. Onapa, Enrolled May 13, 1901										
7096	1	Major, Loby	40	M	F		Major	D	Cr	Maley	D	Cr
7097	2	Major, Sallie	40	F	F	Wf	Colaka Harjo	D	Cr	Supefatka	D	Cr
7098	3	Major, Ida	11	F	F	D	No. 1	L	Cr	No. 2	I.	Cr
7099	4	Johnson, Walter	6	M	F	GrS	John Johnson	L	Non	Nellie Major	D	Cr
		No. 1 died August 22, 1910. No. 2 died September 30, 1909. No. 3 died September 20, 1912.										
		No. 4 died July 25, 1904.										
		Census Card No. 2348, P. O. Wetumka, Enrolled May 13, 1901										
7100	1	Bruner, Jackson	75	M	F		Unknown	D	Cr	Unknown	D	Cr
		No. 1 died January 16, 1901										
		Census Card No. 2349, P. O. Mellette, Enrolled May 13, 1901										
7101	1	Bright, Lumber	30	M	F		Macheska Harjo	D	Cr	Martha Harjo	D	Cr
		Census Card No. 2350, P. O. Indianola, Enrolled May 13, 1901										
7102	1	Green, Alexander	25	M	F		Jesse Green	D	Cr	Rosanna Green	D	Cr
7103	2	Green, Nancy	22	F	F	Wf	Motey Gray	D	Cr	Winey	D	Cr
		No. 2 died May 3, 1903. No. 1 reported dead.										
		Census Card No. 2351, P. O. Tulsa, Enrolled May 13, 1901										
7104	1	Siah	45	M	F		Emarthoge	D	Cr	Ahseke	D	Cr
7105	2	Sallie	45	F	F	Wf	Osoche Yahola	D	Cr	Nancy	D	Cr
7106	3	Louiney	13	F	F	D	No. 1	L	Cr	No. 2	L	Cr
7107	4	Jimmie	12	M	F	S	No. 1	L	Cr	No. 2	L	Cr
7108	5	Hully	20	M	F	Bro	Emarthoge	D	Cr	Ahseke	D	Cr

Roll No.	No.	NAME	Age	Sex	Blood	Rel.	NAME OF FATHER	Liv.	Cit.	NAME OF MOTHER	Liv.	Cit.
		Census Card No. 2352, P. O. Wekiwa, Enrolled May 13, 1901										
7109	1	Gooden, William	50	M	F		Gooden	D	Cr	Mary Grayson	L	Cr
7110	2	Gooden, Sordie	50	F	F	Wf	George Dye	D	Cr	Unknown	D	Cr
7111	3	Gooden, Lizzie	19	F	F	D	No. 1	L	Cr	No. 2	L	Cr
7112	4	Gooden, Daniel	16	M	F	S	No. 1	L	Cr	No. 2	L	Cr
7113	5	Gooden, Annie	14	F	F	D	No. 1	L	Cr	No. 2	L	Cr
7114	6	Grayson, Mary	85	F	F	Moth	Unknown	D	Cr	Unknown	D	Cr
		No. 1 died August 17, 1903. No. 8 died Summer 1900.										
		Census Card No. 2353, P. O. Holdenville, Enrolled May 13, 1901										
7115	1	McCosar, Bunnie	39	M	F		Cosa Fixico	D	Cr	Katie Fixico	D	Cr
7116	2	McCosar, Elliott	13	M	F	S	No. 1	L	Cr	Bettie McCosar	L	Cr
7117	3	McCosar, Eliza	11	F	F	D	No. 1	L	Cr	Bettie McCosar	L	Cr
7118	4	McCosar, Ida	9	F	F	D	No. 1	L	Cr	Bettie McCosar	L	Cr
7119	5	McCosar, Bettie	24	F	F	Wf	Watty	D	Cr	Unknown	D	Cr
7120	6	McCosar, Bessie	3	F	F	D	No. 1	L	Cr	No. 5	L	Cr
		No. 3 died December 10, 1899. No. 4 died July 16, 1900. No. 5 died December 9, 1900.										
		Census Card No. 2354, P. O. Henryetta, Enrolled May 13, 1901										
7121	1	Mitchell, Sissie	8	M	F		Dan Mitchell	D	Cr	Nancy Mitchell	L	Cr
		Census Card No. 2355, P. O. Fentress, Enrolled May 13, 1901										
7122	1	Austin, Taylor	45	M	F		Oldman Austin	D	Sem	Temaypatcha	D	Cr
		No. 1 died February 3, 1906										
		Census Card No. 2356, P. O. Salem, Enrolled May 13, 1901										
7123	1	McNac, Phillip	21	M	½		Unknown	L	Non	Nancy	D	Cr
7124	2	McNac, Nannie	19	F	F	Wf	Taskegee	D	Cr	Annie	D	Cr
7125	3	McNac, Johnny	3	M	¾	S	No. 1	L	Cr	No. 2	L	Cr
		No. 2 died October 1905.										
		Census Card No. 2357, P. O. Wetumka, Enrolled May 13, 1901										
7126	1	Jackey	45	M	F		Tulmarsey Yahola	D	Cr	Lizzie	D	Cr
7127	2	Toskey	45	F	F	Wf	Micco Nupper	D	Cr	Millie	D	Cr
		No. 1 died 1900										
		Census Card No. 2358, P. O. Wetumka, Enrolled May 13, 1901										
7128	1	Barnett, Wesley	22	M	F		Quasarty	D	Cr	Nannie	D	Cr
7129	2	Jack, Chapley	18	M	F	Bro	Nero Jack	L	Cr	Nannie	D	Cr
7130	3	Jack, Lena	15	F	F	Sis	Nero Jack	L	Cr	Nannie	D	Cr
		No. 1 died December 18, 1902										
		Census Card No. 2359, P. O. Eufaula, Enriolled May 13, 1901										
7131	1	Lewis, Jackson	65	M	F		Tommy Harjo	D	Cr	Suchemerica	D	Cr
7132	2	Lewis, Nancy	50	F	F	Wf	Hotulke Yahola	D	Cr	Unknown	D	Cr
		No. 2 died October 10, 1907. No. 1 died December 21, 1910.										
		Census Card No. 2360, P. O. Sasakwa, Enrolled May 13, 1901										
7133	1	Frank, Jane	60	F	F		Unknown	D	Cr	Unknown	D	Cr
7134	2	Frank, Jimmie	18	M	F	GrS	Major Frank	D	Cr	Jennetta Frank	D	Cr
		No. 1 died January 11, 1911										
		Census Card No. 2361, P. O. Sasakwa, Enrolled May 13, 1901										
7135	1	Frank, Dave	29	M	F		Dave Frank	D	Cr	Jane Frank	L	Cr
7136	2	Frank, Sammie	21	M	F	Bro	Dave Frank	D	Cr	Jane Frank	L	Cr
		Census Card No. 2362, P. O. Wetumka, Enrolled May 13, 1901										
7137	1	Thomas, Waetie	22	M	F		Thomas Lakey	D	Cr	Cinda Lakey	D	Cr
7138	2	Thomas, John	.7	M	F	Bro	Thomas Lakey	D	Cr	Cinda Lakey	D	Cr
7139	3	Lakey, Thomas	42	M	F	Fath	Parhose Harjogee	D	Cr	Unknown	D	Cr
		No. 3 died March 3, 1901										
		Census Card No. 2363, P. O. Sapulpa, Enrolled May 13, 1901										
7140	1	Grayson, James	48	M	F		Jeff Grayson	D	Cr	Unknown	D	Cr
7141	2	Grayson, Wiley	12	M	F	S	No. 1	L	Cr	Mollie Grayson	D	Cr
		No. 2 died January 1911. No. 1 reported dead.										
		Census Card No. 2364, P. O. Wetumka, Enrolled May 13, 1901										
7142	1	Perryman, Philip	29	M	¾		Wright Perryman	D	Cr	Celie (or Sarah)	D	Cr
		No. 1 reported dead										
		Census Card No. 2365, P. O. Mellette, Enrolled May 13, 1901										
7143	1	Perryman, Leah	22	F	¾		L. C. Perryman	L	Cr	Lucinda Starr	D	Cr
		Census Card No. 2366, P. O. Hitchita, Enrolled May 13, 1901										
7144	1	Grayson, Jeannetta	25	F	F		Gibson Grayson	D	Cr	Juda Grayson	D	Cr
		Census Card No. 2367, P. O. Tulsa; No. 2, Lyons, Enrolled May 14, 1901										
7145	1	Grayson, Buck	24	M	F		Stephen Grayson	D	Cr	Lucy Grayson	D	Cr
7146	2	Grayson, Dickie	18	M	F	Bro	Stephen Grayson	D	Cr	Lucy Grayson	D	Cr
7147	3	Grayson, Janie	16	F	F	Sis	Stephen Grayson	D	Cr	Lucy Grayson	D	Cr
		Census Card No. 2368, P. O. Okemah, Enrolled May 14, 1901										
7148	1	Tiger, Famer	28	M	F		Marsey Tiger	D	Cr	Arnie	D	Cr
7149	2	Tiger, Mesaley	27	F	F	Wf	Porchee	D	Cr	Marfay	D	Cr
7150	3	Harjo, Jimsey	6	M	F	StS	Jim Harjo	D	Cr	No. 2	L	Cr
7151	4	Harjo, Daniel	4	M	F	StS	Jim Harjo	D	Cr	No. 2	L	Cr
		Census Card No. 2369, P. O. Preston, Enrolled May 14, 1901										
7152	1	Harjo, Susie	30	F	F		Stephen Grayson	D	Cr	Lucy Grayson	D	Cr
		Census Card No. 2379, P. O. Checotah, Enrolled May 14, 1901										
7153	1	Carr, George	25	M	¾		Tom Carr	D	Cr	Rachael	D	Cr
		Census Card No. 2371, P. O. Eufaula, Enrolled May 14, 1901										
7154	1	Coodey, Sarah J.	42	F	1-16		Joseph M. Coody	D	Cr	Thornberry Coody	D	Non
		Census Card No. 2372, P. O. Coweta, Enrolled May 14, 1901										
7155	1	Frank, Austin	22	M	F		Thomas Frank	L	Cr	Lizzie Frank	D	Cr
7156	2	Frank, Lucy	19	F	F	Wf	George Canard	L	Cr	Martha Canard	D	Cr
		No. 2 died November 1899										

Roll No.	No.	NAME	Age	Sex	Blood	Rel.	NAME OF FATHER	Liv.	Cit.	NAME OF MOTHER	Liv.	Cit.
		Census Card No. 2373, P. O. Paden, Enrolled May 14, 1901										
7157	1	Chisholm, James	21	M	¾		George Chisholm	L	Cr	Nancy Chisholm	D	Cr
		No. 1 reported dead										
		Census Card No. 2374, P. O. Stone Bluff, Enrolled May 14, 1901										
7158	1	Peters, Ellen	60	F	F		Luny Bruner	D	Cr	Nancy Bruner	D	Cr.
		No. 1 died July 11, 1899										
		Census Card No. 2375, P. O. Brush Hill, Enrolled May 14, 1901										
7159	1	Maloney, Annie	19	F	¼		Walter Pitman	L	Non	Louina Price	L	Cr
		No. 1 died Summer 1907										
		Census Card No. 2376, P. O. Okemah, Enrolled May 14, 1901; No. 4, May 22, 1901										
7160	1	Albert, Prince	38	M	F		Alec Brom	D	Cr	Hesahar Albert	D	Cr
7161	2	Albert, Jackson	11	M	F	S	Alec Brown	D	Cr	Sallie Albert	D	Cr
7162	3	Albert, Watty	6	M	F	S	Alec Brown	D	Cr	Sallie Albert	D	Cr
7163	4	Albert, David	13	M	F	S	Alec Brown	D	Cr	Sallie Albert	D	Cr
		Census Card No. 2377, P. O. Wetumka, Enrolled May 14, 1901										
7164	1	Siah, Mary	21	F	F		Temarschar	D	Cr	Loschokee	D	Cr
		No. 1 reported dead										
		Census Card No. 2378, P. O. Hanna, Enrolled May 14, 1901										
7165	1	Hill, Tobe	54	M	F		Arbeka Fixico	D	Cr	Katie Fixico	D	Cr
7166	2	Hill, Nigee	45	F	F	Wf	Hotulge NeharthloccoD	D	Cr	Halob Hoyee	D	Cr
7167	3	Hill, Mollie	19	F	F	D	No. 1	L	Cr	Mothyoyetchee	D	Cr
7168	4	Hill, Lizzie	17	F	F	D	No. 1	L	Cr	Mothyoyetchee	D	Cr
7169	5	Hill, Willie	13	M	F	S	No. 1	L	Cr	Mothyoyetchee	D	Cr
7170	6	Hill, Annie	19	F	F	StD	Arlinger Hill	D	Cr	No. 2	L	Cr
7171	7	Hill, Tiller	13	M	F	StS	Arlinger Hill	D	Cr	No. 2	L	Cr
7172	8	Hill, Munna	3	F	F	D	No. 1	L	Cr	No. 2	L	Cr
		Nos. 1 and 4 reported dead.　No. 5 died December 12, 1903.　No. 6 died November 10, 1903.										
		Census Card No. 2379, P. O. Muskogee, Enrolled May 7, 1901										
7173	1	DuBois, Mildred	29	F	1-16		Barney DuBois	D	Cr	Lizzie DuBois	D	Non
		Census Card No. 2380, P. O. Wetumka, Enrolled May 14, 1901										
7174	1	Beaver, Jennie	30	F	F		Bigwood	D	Cr	Linda	D	Cr
7175	2	Beaver, Alex	25	M	½	Bro	Unknown	D	Non	Martha	D	Cr
7176	3	Beaver, Marty	8	M	F	S	Beaver	D	Cr	No. 1	L	Cr
7177	4	Beaver, Lizzie	6	F	F	D	Beaver	D	Cr	No. 1	L	Cr
7178	5	Beaver, Lou Ella	4	F	F	D	Beaver	D	Cr	No. 1	L	Cr
7179	6	Harjo, Itshas	45	M	F	Hus	Unknown	D	Cr	Winie	D	Cr
		No. 1 died January 23, 1902.　No. 4 died April 29, 1908.　No. 6 died September 15, 1899.										
		Census Card No. 2381, P. O. Okemah, Enrolled May 14, 1901										
7180	1	Smith, Rosa	23	F	F		Americus Logan	D	Cr	Nancy Logan	D	Cr
		No. 1 died April 1, 1902										
		Census Card No. 2382, P. O. Wetumka, Enrolled May 14, 1901										
7181	1	Hill, Wunche	21	F	F		Arlinger Hill	D	Cr	Nigee Hill	L	Cr
		Census Card No. 2383, P. O. Lamar, Enrolled May 14, 1901										
7182	1	Bruner, Robert	30	M	F		Siah Bruner	L	Cr	Mary Bruner	D	Cr
		Census Card No. 2384, P. O. Holdenville, Enrolled May 14, 1901										
7183	1	Fish, Annie	23	F	F		Toley Bruner	D	Cr	Sopsey	D	Cr
7184	2	Fish, Bessie	4	F	F	D	Watty Fish	L	Cr	No. 1	L	Cr
		Census Card No. 2385, P. O. Carson, Enrolled May 14, 1901										
7185	1	Bruner, David	28	M	F		Siah Bruner	L	Cr	Mary Bruner	D	Cr
7186	2	Bruner, Ilsey	25	F	F	Wf	Caseka Ya Mikko	D	Sem	Cogee	D	Cr
7187	3	Bruner, Lillie	1	F	F	D	No. 1	L	Cr	No. 2	L	Cr
7388	4	Bruner, Jemime	3	F	F	D	No. 1	L	Cr	No. 2	L	Cr
		No. 3 died November 14, 1901.　No. 2 died December 4 1907.　No. 4 died 1900.										
		Census Card No. 2386, P. O. Dustin, Enrolled May 14, 1901										
7189	1	John, Short	60	M	½		Kata	D	Non	Kimohiwa	D	Cr
7190	2	John, Winey	28	F	F	Wf	Chenoska	D	Cr	Kelaza	D	Cr
7191	3	John, Johny	8	M	¾	S	No. 1	L	Cr	No. 2	L	Cr
7192	4	John, Louisa	4	F	¾	D	No. 1	L	Cr	No. 2	L	Cr
7193	5	John, Katie	2	F	¾	D	No. 1	L	Cr	No. 2	L	Cr
		No. 1 died 1906 or 1907										
		Census Card No. 2387, P. O. Holdenville, Enrolled May 14, 1901										
7194	1	Bird, Nellie	23	F	F		Wiley Hawkins	L	Cr	Louisa Hawkins	D	Cr
		Census Card No. 2388, P. O. Bearden, Enrolled May 14, 1901										
7195	1	Bear, Nocos Elle	38	M	F		Okchon Fixico	D	Cr	Hoake	D	Cr
7196	2	Bear, Ulsar	35	F	F	Wf	Arbeka Fixico	D	Cr	Sohulkie	D	Cr
7197	3	Bear, Joseph	23	M	F	S	No. 1	L	Cr	No. 2	L	Cr
7198	4	Bear, Samuel	20	M	F	S	No. 1	L	Cr	No. 2	L	Cr
7199	5	Bear, Bennie	17	M	F	S	No. 1	L	Cr	No. 2	L	Cr
7200	6	Bear, Lucinda	12	F	F	D	No. 1	L	Cr	No. 2	L	Cr
7201	7	Bear, Alexander	8	M	F	S	No. 1	L	Cr	No. 2	L	Cr
		Census Card No. 2389, P. O. Holdenville, Enrolled May 14, 1901										
7202	1	Reed, Andrew	22	M	½		Tustanuk Harjo	L	Sem	Leah Reed	D	Cr
7203	2	Reed, Walton	18	M	½	Bro	Tustanuk Harjo	L	Sem	Leah Reed	D	Cr
7204	3	Reed, Leah	42	F	F	Moth	John Reed	D	Cr	Martha Reed	D	Cr
		No. 2 died October 1904.　No. 3 died November 13, 1899.										
		Census Card No. 2390, P. O. Holdenville, Enrolled May 14, 1901										
7205	1	Bruner, Hyman	26	M	F		Siah Bruner	L	Cr	Mary Bruner	D	Cr
		No. 1 died February 28, 1901										
		Census Card No. 2391, P. O. Wetumka, Enrolled May 14, 1901										
7206	1	Watson, Fannie	58	F	F		Unknown	D	Cr	Unknown	D	Cr

Roll No.	No.	NAME	Age	Sex	Blood	Rel.	NAME OF FATHER	Liv.	Cit.	NAME OF MOTHER	Liv.	Cit.
		Census Card No. 2392, P. O. Wewoka, Enrolled May 14, 1901										
7207	1	Walker, Bettie	22	F	F		Siah Bruner	L	Cr	Mary Bruner	D	Cr
7208	2	Walker, Louis	6	M	F	S	Hardy Walker	L	Sem	No. 1	L	Cr
7209	3	Walker, Wisey	3	F	F	D	Hardy Walker	L	Sem	No. 1	L	Cr
7210	4	Walker, Isaac	1	M	F	S	Hardy Walker	L	Sem	No. 1	L	Cr
		No. 2 died April 14, 1899										
		Census Card No. 2393, P. O. Hoffman, Enrolled May 14, 1901										
7211	1	Polk, Mose	16	M	F		Billy Polk	D	Cr	Martha	L	Cr
		No. 1 died June 26, 1914										
		Census Card No. 2394, P. O. Dustin, Enrolled May 14, 1901										
7212	1	Kanard, George	38	M	F		Arharlock Yahola	D	Cr	Tilda	L	Cr
7213	2	Kanard, Rosana	33	F	F	Wf	Dave McQueen	D	Cr	Harnie	D	Cr
7214	3	Kanard, Lumber	15	M	F	S	No. 1	L	Cr	No. 2	L	Cr
7215	4	Kanard, Annie	12	F	F	D	No. 1	L	Cr	No. 2	L	Cr
7216	5	Kanard, Susan	9	F	F	D	No. 1	L	Cr	No. 2	L	Cr
7217	6	Kanard, Tilda	70	F	F	Moth	Unknown	D	Cr	Unknown	D	Cr
		No. 2 died April 1904. No. 3 died June 30, 1910. No. 5 died November 12, 1912. No. 6 died May 3, 1901. No. 4 died December 9, 1911.										
		Census Card No. 2395, P. O. Calvin, Enrolled May 14, 1901										
7218	1	Powell, Carline	38	M	½		John Powell	L	Non	Tuthoye	D	Cr
		Census Card No. 2396, P. O. Wetumka, Enrolled May 14, 1901										
7219	1	Bird, Polly	43	F	F		Unknown	D	Cr	Unknown	D	Cr
		No. 1 died April 1899										
		Census Card No. 2397, P. O. Okemah, Enrolled May 14, 1901										
7220	1	Harjo, Pin	43	M	F		Nehalakka	D	Cr	Annie	D	Cr
7221	2	Harjo, Miloche	39	F	F	Wf	Mejeska Harjo	D	Cr	Tapaleche	D	Cr
7222	3	Harjo, Alec Little	10	M	F	S	No. 1	L	Cr	No. 2	L	Cr
7223	4	Harjo, Polly	7	F	F	D	No. 1	L	Cr	No. 2	L	Cr
7224	5	Harjo, Peter	5	M	F	S	No. 1	L	Cr	No. 2	L	Cr
		Census Card No. 2398, P. O. Senora, Enrolled May 14, 1901										
7225	1	Gray, Willie	29	M	¾		Espana Fixico	D	Cr	Amy Gray	L	Cr
		No. 1 reported dead										
		Census Card No. 2399, P. O. Wetumka, Enrolled May 14, 1901										
7226	1	Harjo, John	33	M	F		Okchun Harjo	D	Cr	Silla Harjo	D	Cr
7227	2	Harjo, Jennie	38	F	F	Wf	Osage Harjo	D	Cr	Unknown	D	Cr
7228	3	Harjo, Noah	7	M	F	S	No. 1	L	Cr	No. 2	L	Cr
7229	4	Harjo, Addie	5	F	F	D	No. 1	L	Cr	No. 2	L	Cr
7230	5	Harjo, Leah	20	F	F	Wf	Chake Pahose	L	Sem	Armarner	D	Cr
		No. 2 died April 4, 1899. No. 3 died December 9, 1904.										
		Census Card No. 2400, P. O. Wetumka, Enrolled May 14, 1901										
7231	1	Deere, Albert	16	M	F		John Deere	D	Cr	Nellie Deere	D	Cr
		No. 1 reported dead										
		Census Card No. 2401, P. O. Wetumka, Enrolled May 14, 1901										
7232	1	Hill, Louisa	24	F	F		Quasada Fixico	D	Cr	Lindy Fixico	D	Cr
7233	2	Tiger, Lizzie	18	F	F	None	Fus Harjo	D	Cr	Chutty	D	Cr
		No. 1 died March 10, 1904										
		Census Card No. 2402, P. O. Okemah, Enrolled May 14, 1901										
7234	1	Fixico, Cotcha	31	M	F		Qussarte	D	Cr	Chotka	D	Cr
7235	2	Fixico, Samson	10	M	F	S	No. 1	L	Cr	Cinda Fixico	D	Cr
		Census Card No. 2403, P. O. Salem, Enrolled May 14, 1901										
7236	1	Homahte, Cotche	52	M	F		Unknown	D	Cr	Miska	D	Cr
7237	2	Homahte, Harnoche	47	F	F	Wf	Unknown	D	Cr	Wasse	D	Cr
7238	3	Tiger, Willie	22	M	F	S	No. 1	L	Cr	No. 2	L	Cr
7239	4	Tiger, George	17	M	F	S	No. 1	L	Cr	No. 2	L	Cr
7240	5	Tiger, Eliza	20	F	F	Niece	John Long	D	Cr	Lukey Long	D	Cr
		No. 1 died May 9, 1902										
		Census Card No. 2404, P. O. Wetumka, Enrolled May 14, 1901										
7241	1	Watson, Parnoska	23	M	F		Heneha Fixico	D	Cr	Fannie Watson	L	Cr
		No. 1 died March 19, 1911										
		Census Card No. 2405, P. O. Wetumka, Enrolled May 14, 1901										
7242	1	Watson, Chammy	30	M	F		Hencha Fixico	D	Cr	Fannie Watson	L	Cr
		No. 1 reported dead										
		Census Card No. 2406, P. O. Lenna; No. 3, Eufaula, Enrolled May 15, 1901										
7243	1	Derrisaw, Barney	48	M	F		Derrisaw	D	Cr	Polly Deerisaw	L	Cr
7244	2	Derrisaw, Toche	44	F	F	Wf	Unknown	D	Cr	Unknown	D	Cr
7245	3	Derrisaw, William	20	M	F	S	No. 1	L	Cr	Louis Derrisaw	D	Cr
7246	4	Derrisaw, Emma	18	F	F	D	No. 1	L	Cr	Louis Derrisaw	D	Cr
7247	5	Derrisaw, Susie	18	F	F	StS	Blackgrass	D	Cr	No. 2	L	Cr
7248	6	Derrisaw, Polly	9	F	F	D	No. 1	L	Cr	No. 2	L	Cr
7249	7	Derrisaw, Mattie	6	F	F	D	No. 1	L	Cr	No. 2	L	Cr
7250	8	Derrisaw, Oscar	4	M	F	S	No. 1	L	Cr	No. 2	L	Cr
		No. 5 died August 10, 1899. No. 2 died 1904. No. 8 died February 27, 1913. No. 4 died November 8, 1908.										
		Census Card No. 2407, P. O. Senora, Enrolled May 15, 1901										
7251	1	Canard, Louisa	40	F	F		Pink Hawkins	D	Cr	Lydia	D	Cr
		No. 1 died January 20, 1911										
		Census Card No. 2408, P. O. Hoardsville, Enrolled May 14, 1901										
7252	1	Herrod, Rosanna	42	F	F		Pink Hawkins	D	Cr	Lydia	D	Cr

152

Roll
No.   No.   NAME   Age Sex Blood Rel.   NAME OF FATHER   Liv. Cit.   NAME OF MOTHER   Liv. Cit.

Census Card No. 2409, P. O. Hoardsville, Enrolled May 15, 1901

Roll No.	No.	NAME	Age	Sex	Blood	Rel.	NAME OF FATHER	Liv.	Cit.	NAME OF MOTHER	Liv.	Cit.
7253	1	McIntosh, Greely	19	M	F		Al McIntosh	L	Cr	Rosanna Herrod	L	Cr

Census Card No. 2410, P. O. Holdenville, Enrolled May 15, 1901

Roll No.	No.	NAME	Age	Sex	Blood	Rel.	NAME OF FATHER	Liv.	Cit.	NAME OF MOTHER	Liv.	Cit.
7254	1	Sewell, Frank	45	M	½		Ben Sewell	D	Mex	Munna Sewell	D	Cr
7255	2	Sewell, Angeline	35	F	F	Wf	Unknown	D	Cr	Unknown	D	Cr
7256	3	Sewell, Anderson	20	M	¾	S	No. 1	L	Cr	No. 2	L	Cr
7257	4	Sewell, Sophia	18	F	¾	D	No. 1	L	Cr	No. 2	L	Cr
7258	5	Sewell, Nellie	16	F	¾	D	No. 1	L	Cr	No. 2	L	Cr
7259	6	Sewell. Lizzie	11	F	¾	D	No. 1	L	Cr	No. 2	L	Cr

No. 1 died August 16, 1899.   No. 2 died January 3, 1900.

Census Card No. 2411, P. O. Dustin, Enrolled May 15, 1901

Roll No.	No.	NAME	Age	Sex	Blood	Rel.	NAME OF FATHER	Liv.	Cit.	NAME OF MOTHER	Liv.	Cit.
7260	1	Pigeon, Mate	44	F	F		Tonoke	D	Cr	Hiyetka	D	Cr
7261	2	Pigeon, Jonas	19	M	F	S	John Pigeon	L	Cr	No. 1	L	Cr
7262	3	Pigeon, Lena	13	F	F	D	John Pigeon	L	Cr	No. 1	L	Cr
7263	4	Pigeon, Joseph	6	M	F	S	John Pigeon	L	Cr	No. 1	L	Cr
7264	5	Pigeon, Jakeman	3	M	F	S	John Pigeon	L	Cr	No. 1	L	Cr
7265	6	Pigeon, John	40	M	F	Hus	Joe Pigeon	D	Cr	Unknown	D	Cr

No. 2 died October 15, 1906

Census Card No. 2412, P. O. Lenna, Enrolled May 15, 1901

Roll No.	No.	NAME	Age	Sex	Blood	Rel.	NAME OF FATHER	Liv.	Cit.	NAME OF MOTHER	Liv.	Cit.
7266	1	Derrisaw, Sarah	29	F	F		Blackgrass	D	Cr	Toche Derrisaw	L	Cr
7267	2	Derrisaw, Fannie	8	F	F	D	Barney Derrisaw	L	Cr	No. 1	L	Cr
7268	3	Derrisaw, Beeley	5	M	F	S	Barney Derrisaw	L	Cr	No. 1	L	Cr

No. 1 died 1905.   No. 2 died 1905.

Census Card No. 2413, P. O. Wewoka, Enrolled May 15, 1901

Roll No.	No.	NAME	Age	Sex	Blood	Rel.	NAME OF FATHER	Liv.	Cit.	NAME OF MOTHER	Liv.	Cit.
7269	1	Bruner, Jesse	25	M	F		Robert Bruner	D	Cr	Ledeger	D	Cr

Census Card No. 2414, P. O. Bearden, Enrolled May 15, 1901

Roll No.	No.	NAME	Age	Sex	Blood	Rel.	NAME OF FATHER	Liv.	Cit.	NAME OF MOTHER	Liv.	Cit.
7270	1	Harjo, Kepsy	49	F	F		Unknown	D	Cr	Locher	D	Cr

Census Card No. 2415, P. O. Wetumka, Enrolled May 15, 1901

Roll No.	No.	NAME	Age	Sex	Blood	Rel.	NAME OF FATHER	Liv.	Cit.	NAME OF MOTHER	Liv.	Cit.
7271	1	Jesse, Eliza	30	F	F		Parhos Fixico	D	Cr	Marfolochee	D	Cr
7272	2	Jesse ,Massie	10	F	F	D	Timmie Jesse	L	Cr	No. 1	L	Cr
7273	3	Jesse, Bunnie	8	M	F	S	Timmie Jesse	L	Cr	No. 1	L	Cr
7274	4	Jesse, Jennetta	4	F	F	D	Timmie Jesse	L	Cr	No. 1	L	Cr
7275	5	Jesse, Willie	2	M	F	S	Timmie Jesse	L	Cr	No. 1	L	Cr
7276	6	Jesse, Timmie	40	M	F	Hus	Sunduller Fixico	D	Cr	Lizzie	D	Cr

No. 6 died August 1900.   No. 4 died November 23, 1912.   No. 2 died December 26, 1910.

Census Card No. 2416, P. O. Kellyville, Enrolled May 15, 1901

Roll No.	No.	NAME	Age	Sex	Blood	Rel.	NAME OF FATHER	Liv.	Cit.	NAME OF MOTHER	Liv.	Cit.
7277	1	Fulsom, Thomas	50	M	F		Inkaney	D	Cr	Akotaney	D	Cr
7278	2	Fulsom, Millie	26	F	F	Wf	Maka	D	Cr	Pántany	D	Cr
7279	3	Fulsom, Joe	4	M	F	S	No. 1	L	Cr	No. 2	L	Cr

Census Card No. 2417, P. O. Hanna, Enrolled May 15, 1901

Roll No.	No.	NAME	Age	Sex	Blood	Rel.	NAME OF FATHER	Liv.	Cit.	NAME OF MOTHER	Liv.	Cit.
7280	1	Hawkins, John	65	M	F		Pink Hawkins	L	Cr	Littie	D	Cr

No. 1 died February 14, 1901

Census Card No. 2418, P. O. Senora, Enrolled May 15, 1901

Roll No.	No.	NAME	Age	Sex	Blood	Rel.	NAME OF FATHER	Liv.	Cit.	NAME OF MOTHER	Liv.	Cit.
7281	1	Hawkins, Pink	92	M	F		Sam Hawkins	D	Cr	Abkohkee	D	Cr

No. 1 died January 11, 1901

Census Card No. 2419, P. O. Lamar, Enrolled May 15, 1901

Roll No.	No.	NAME	Age	Sex	Blood	Rel.	NAME OF FATHER	Liv.	Cit.	NAME OF MOTHER	Liv.	Cit.
7282	1	McGirt, Soloman	30	M	F		Micco Nuppa	D	Cr	Unknown	D	Cr
7283	2	McGirt, Hattie	36	F	F	Wf	Chowastye Fixico	D	Cr	Fulhoge	D	Cr
7284	3	McGirt, Lonie	16	F	F	S	No. 1	L	Cr	No. 2	L	Cr
7285	4	McGirt, Jimmie	4	M	F	S	No. 1	L	Cr	No. 2	L	Cr

Census Card No. 2420, P. O. Kellyville, Enrolled May 15, 1901

Roll No.	No.	NAME	Age	Sex	Blood	Rel.	NAME OF FATHER	Liv.	Cit.	NAME OF MOTHER	Liv.	Cit.
7286	1	Fulsom, Robert	18	M	F		Thomas Fulson	L	Cr	Kosa	D	Cr

Census Card No. 2421, P. O. Kellyville, Enrolled May 15, 1901

Roll No.	No.	NAME	Age	Sex	Blood	Rel.	NAME OF FATHER	Liv.	Cit.	NAME OF MOTHER	Liv.	Cit.
7287	1	Fulsom, Willie	28	M	F		Thomas Fulsom	L	Cr	Kosa	D	Cr
7288	2	Fulsom, Sarah	26	F	F	Wf	Pachaney	D	Cr	Kosahoney	D	Cr
7289	3	Fulsom, Sam	9	M	F	S	No. 1	L	Cr	No. 2	L	Cr
7290	4	Fulsom, Salo	2	F	F	D	No. 1	L	Cr	No. 2	L	Cr

No. 2 died May 1904

Census Card No. 2422, P. O. Holdenville, Enrolled May 15, 1901

Roll No.	No.	NAME	Age	Sex	Blood	Rel.	NAME OF FATHER	Liv.	Cit.	NAME OF MOTHER	Liv.	Cit.
7291	1	Washington, Sukey	36	F	F		Jowastagee Fixico	D	Cr	Eliza Washington	L	Cr
7292	2	Washington, Colbert	20	M	F	S	James Washington	D	Cr	No. 1	L	Cr
7293	3	Washington, Emma	9	F	F	D	James Washington	D	Cr	No. 1	L	Cr

No. 1 died September 1908.   No. 2 died April 28, 1903.   No. 3 died July 15, 1901.

Census Card No. 2423, P. O. Eufaula, Enrolled May 15, 1901

Roll No.	No.	NAME	Age	Sex	Blood	Rel.	NAME OF FATHER	Liv.	Cit.	NAME OF MOTHER	Liv.	Cit.
7294	1	Belcher, Tobe	35	M	½		John Belcher	D	Non	Amy McGilbra	L	Cr
7295	2	Belcher, Martha	25	F	F	Wf	Tom Williams	L	Cr	Annie Williams	D	Cr
7296	3	Belcher, Bessie	9	F	¾	D	No. 1	L	Cr	No. 2	L	Cr
7297	4	Belcher, Emma	7	F	¾	D	No. 1	L	Cr	Mollie Harjo	D	Cr
7298	5	Belcher, Sunny	2	M	¾	S	No. 1	L	Cr	No. 2	L	Cr

Census Card No. 2424, P. O. Lamar, Enrolled May 15, 1901

Roll No.	No.	NAME	Age	Sex	Blood	Rel.	NAME OF FATHER	Liv.	Cit.	NAME OF MOTHER	Liv.	Cit.
7299	1	Fish, Peter	30	M	F		Thlethlo Fixeco	D	Cr	Takoloche	D	Cr
7300	2	Fish, Lucinda	25	M	F	Wf	Cowesee	D	Cr	Losey	D	Cr

Census Card No. 2425, P. O. Broken Arrow, Enrolled May 15, 1901

Roll No.	No.	NAME	Age	Sex	Blood	Rel.	NAME OF FATHER	Liv.	Cit.	NAME OF MOTHER	Liv.	Cit.
7301	1	Grayson, Menene	25	F	F		Frank	D	Cr	Nancy	D	Cr
7302	2	Gray, Silánie	2	F	F	D	Louie Gray	L	Cr	No. 1	L	Cr

No. 2 died March 1900.   No. 1 died October 24, 1911.

Census Card No. 2426, P. O. Wetumka, Enrolled May 15, 1901

Roll No.	No.	NAME	Age	Sex	Blood	Rel.	NAME OF FATHER	Liv.	Cit.	NAME OF MOTHER	Liv.	Cit.
7303	1	Jim, Sissy	20	F	F		Musker	D	Sem	Melar (Scott)	L	Cr
7304	2	Deer, Isreal	3	M	¾	D	Wash Deer	L	Cr	No. 1	L	Cr

Nos. 1 and 2 reported dead

153

Roll No.	No.	NAME	Age	Sex	Blood	Rel.	NAME OF FATHER	Liv.	Cit.	NAME OF MOTHER	Liv.	Cit.
		Census Card No. 2427, P. O. Eufaula, Enrolled May 15, 1901										
7305	1	Williams, Annie	50	F	F		Carpeche Yahola	D	Cr	Polly Hutke	D	Cr
		No. 1 reported dead										
		Census Card No. 2428, P. O. Kellyville, Enrolled May 15, 1901										
7306	1	Taylor,	40	M	F		Aquanay	D	Cr	Lucy	D	Cr
7307	2	Taylor, Jololonfah	44	F	F	Wf	Apecorney	D	Cr	Unknown	D	Cr
7308	3	Taylor, Timmie	8	M	F	S	No. 1	L	Cr	No. 2	L	Cr
7309	4	Taylor, Eliza	6	F	F	D	No. 1	L	Cr	No. 2	L	Cr
7310	5	Taylor, Ada	2	F	F	D	No. 1	L	Cr	No. 2	L	Cr
		No. 2 died February 10, 1900. No. 1 died March 1912.										
		Census Card No. 2429, P. O. Mellette, Enrolled May 15, 1901										
7311	1	Yarhola, Sampson	28	M	F		Cona Yarhola	D	Cr	Nannie Yarhola	D	Cr
7312	2	Yarhola, Sarah	25	F	F	Wf	Sillier Givens	D	Cr	Choctaw Givens	L	Cr
7313	3	Yarhola, Jemima	1	F	F	D	No. 1	L	Cr	No. 2	L	Cr
		No. 1 died January 18, 1903. No. 2 reported dead.										
		Census Card No. 2430, P. O. Wetumka, Enrolled May 15, 1901										
7314	1	Melar	55	F	F		Siah Bemar	L	Cr	Lizzie	L	Cr
7315	2	Yarmer, Kizzie	18	F	F	D	Yarmer	D	Cr	No. 1	L	Cr
7316	3	Yarmer, Mitchie	16	F	F	D	Yarmer	D	Cr	No. 1	L	Cr
7317	4	Frank, Addie	3	F	F	GrD	Dave Frank	L	Cr	No. 2	L	Cr
		No. 3 died September 26, 1907. Nos. 1, 2 and 4 reported dead.										
		Census Card No. 2431, P. O. Grayson, Enrolled May 15, 1901										
7318	1	Thompson, Susan	30	F	F		William Frank	D	Cr	Eliza Frank	D	Cr
		No. 1 died October 14, 1899.										
		Census Card No. 2432, P. O. Holdenville, Enrolled May 15, 1901										
7319	1	Hawkins, Jackson	26	M	F		Wiley, Hawkins	D	Cr	Chawee	D	Cr
		uensus Card No. 2433, P. O. Dustin, Enrolled May 15, 1901										
7320	1	McFarland, Sarah	35	F	⅝		David C. Watson	D	Cr	Aggie Watson	D	Cr
7321	2	McFarland, David	13	M	¼	S	James McFarland	L	Non	No. 1	L	Cr
7322	3	McFarland, Lilly	10	F	¼	D	James McFarland	L	Non	No. 1	L	Cr
7323	4	McFarland, Lena	6	F	¼	D	James McFarland	L	Non	No. 1	L	Cr
7324	5	McFarland, James	3	M	¼	S	James McFarland	L	Non	No. 1	L	Cr
		No. 2 reported dead										
		Census Card No. 2434, P. O. Holdenville, Enrolled May 15, 1901										
7325	1	Harjo, Nocus	35	M	F		Neha Harjo	D	Cr	Kinha	D	Cr
		Census Card No. 2435, P. O. Okmulgee, Enrolled May 15, 1901										
7326	1	Benjamin, Timmie	19	M	F		Fun Gathlocco	D	Cr	Mulsey Benjamin	D	Cr
		No. 1 died December 11, 1904										
		Census Card No. 2436, P. O. Holdenville, Enrolled May 15, 1901										
7327	1	White, Barney	29	M	F		Tullabasse	D	Cr	Millie	D	Cr
7328	2	White, Peter	16	M	F	Bro	Tullabasse	D	Cr	Judy	D	Cr
7329	3	Micco, Yarkinha	80	M	F	Uncle	Esparney Harjo	D	Cr	Unknown	D	Cr
		No. 3 died October 1899										
		Census Card No. 2437, P. O. Calvin, Enrolled May 15, 1901										
7330	1	Factor, Jakey	30	M	F		Karpitcher Yahola	L	Cr	Loda (Rhoda Factor)	L	Cr
		Census Card No. 2438, P. O. Lamar, Enrolled May 15, 1901										
7331	1	Factor, Liza	29	F	F		Karpitcher Yahola	L	Cr	Loda (Rhoda Factor)	L	Cr
		Census Card No. 2439, P. O. Calvin, Enrolled May 15, 1901										
7332	1	Factor, Peggy	27	F	F		Karpitcher Yarbola	L	Cr	Loda (Rhoda Factor)	L	Cr
		Census Card No. 2440, P. O. Calvin, Enrolled May 15, 1901										
7333	1	Factor, Herbert	28	M	F		Karpitcher Yahola	L	Cr	Loda (Rhoda Factor)	L	Cr
		Census Card No. 2441, P. O. Lamar, Enrolled May 15, 1901										
7334	1	Yahola, Karpitcher	75	M	F		Artus Fixeco	D	Cr	Sumka	D	Cr
7335	2	Yahola, Loda	45	F	F	Wf	Margie Factor	D	Sem	Millie Factor	D	Cr
7336	3	Yahola, Elder	13	M	F	S	No. 1	L	Cr	No. 2	L	Cr
7337	4	Yahola, Katie	16	F	F	D	No. 1	L	Cr	No. 2	L	Cr
7338	5	Yahola, Ida	8	F	F	D	No. 1	L	Cr	No. 2	L	Cr
7339	6	Yahola, Mannie	6	F	F	D	No. 1	L	Cr	No. 2	L	Cr
		No. 4 died April 16, 1908. No. 6 died October 8, 1906										
		Census Card No. 2442, P. O. Lamar, Enrolled May 15, 1901										
7340	1	Johnson, Ceasar	25	M	F		Pin Fixico	D	Cr	Siney	D	Cr
7341	2	Johnson, Eliza	26	F	F	Wf	Cotcher	D	Cr	Leah Tiger	L	Cr
7342	3	Johnson, Wesley	1	M	F	S	No. 1	L	Cr	No. 2	L	Cr
		Census Card No. 2443, P. O. Lamar, Enrolled May 15, 1901										
7343	1	Spaniard, James	42	M	F		Isponny Harjo	D	Cr	Millie	D	Cr
7344	2	Spaniard, Malinda	33	F	F	Wf	Itsbars Harjo	L	Cr	Unknown	D	Cr
7345	3	Spaniard, Alice	14	F	F	D	No. 1	L	Cr	No. 2	L	Cr
7346	4	Spaniard, Misselda	13	F	F	D	No. 1	L	Cr	No. 2	L	Cr
7347	5	Spaniard, Jemima	12	F	F	D	No. 1	L	Cr	No. 2	L	Cr
7348	6	Spaniard, Joe	11	M	F	S	No. 1	L	Cr	No. 2	L	Cr
7349	7	Spaniard, Simon	10	M	F	S	No. 1	L	Cr	No. 2	L	Cr
7350	8	Spaniard, Annie	6	F	F	D	No. 1	L	Cr	No. 2	L	Cr
		No. 2 died July 1899. No. 4 reported dead										
		Census Card No. 2444, P. O. Checotah, Enrolled May 15, 1901										
7351	1	Hawkins, Nicey	48	F	¼		Unknown	D	Cr	Unknown	D	Cr
		Census Card No. 2445, P. O Carson, Enrolled May 16, 1901										
7352	1	Stidham, Timmie	35	M	Full		Johnson Stidham	D	Cr	Harney	D	Cr
7353	2	Stidham, Eliza	28	F	F	Wf	Jimkee	D	Cr	Nettie	D	Cr
7354	3	Stidham, Polly	8	F	F	D	No. 1	L	Cr	No. 2	L	Cr
7355	4	Stidham, George	4	M	F	S	No. 1	L	Cr	No. 2	L	Cr
7356	5	Stidham, Edward	1	M	F	S	No. 1	L	Cr	No. 2	L	Cr

Roll No.	No.	NAME	Age	Sex	Blood	Rel.	NAME OF FATHER	Liv.	Cit.	NAME OF MOTHER	Liv.	Cit.
		Census Card No. 2446, P. O. Wetumka, Enrolled May 16, 1901										
7357	1	Stidham, John	24	M	F		Johnson Stidham	D	Cr	Harney	D	Cr
		No. 1 reported dead										
		Census Card No. 2447, P. O. Wetumka, Enrolled May 16, 1901										
7358	1	Deer, Joe	28	M	F		Hully	D	Cr	Salker	D	Cr
7359	2	Deer, Mary	29	F	F	Wf	Woxseholatla	D	Cr	Kogee King	L	Cr
7360	3	Deer, Challie	4	M	F	S	No. 1	L	Cr	No. 2	L	Cr
		Census Card No. 2448, P. O. Sasakwa, Enrolled May 16, 1901										
7361	1	Harjo, Muska	20	M	F		Hobiyah	D	Cr	Hannah	D	Cr
		Census Card No. 2449, P. O. Raiford, Enrolled May 16, 1901										
7362	1	Cosar, Willie	27	M	F		Cosar Harjo	D	Cr	Tina	D	Cr
		Census Card No. 2450, P. O. Salem, Enrolled May 16, 1901										
7363	1	Scott, Jennie	60	F	F		Unknown	D	Cr	Unknown	D	Cr
7364	2	Scott, Boya	6	M	F	S	George Scott	L	Cr	No. 1	L	Cr
7365	3	Scott, Mesale	8	F	F	D	George Scott	L	Cr	No. 1	L	Cr
		No. 1 died March 1913. No. 2 died August 1904. No. 3 died 1907.										
		Census Card No. 2451, P. O. Wetumka, Enrolled May 16, 1901										
7366	1	Bruner, Rentie	50	F	M		Unknown	D	Cr	Sallie	D	Cr
7367	2	Bruner, Susie	50	F	F	Wf	Fittadega	D	Cr	Selina	L	Cr
		Census Card No. 2452, P. O. Dustin, Enrolled May 16, 1901										
7368	1	Smith, James	60	M	½		Hodge Smith	L	Non	Susie	D	Cr
7369	2	Smith, Mollie	45	F	F	Wf	Chowastahye	D	Cr	Hulleche	D	Cr
7370	3	Roberts, James	12	M	F	GrS	Labotchee	D	Cr	Lizzie Smith	D	Cr
		No. 2 reported dead										
		Census Card No. 2453, P. O. Carson, Enrolled May 16, 1901										
7371	1	Bruner, Robertson	32	M	F		Linda Bruner	L	Cr	Senie	D	Cr
7372	2	Bruner, Millie	40	F	F	Wf	Unknown	D	Cr	Hulleche	D	Cr
7373	3	Bruner, Minnie	13	F	F	D	No. 1	L	Cr	Loucinda Bruner	D	Cr
7374	4	Bruner, Nola	6	F	F	D	No. 1	L	Cr	Loucinda Bruner	D	Cr
7375	5	Bruner, Roman	3	M	F	S	No. 1	L	Cr	Loucinda Bruner	D	Cr
7376	6	Yahola, Tommy	16	M	F	StS	Tulsa Yarhola	D	Cr	No. 2	L	Cr
7377	7	Watson, Bella	7	F	F	StS	John Watson	D	Cr	No. 2	L	Cr
		No. 2 died November 18, 1903. No. 3 died October 1912.										
		Census Card No. 2454, P. O. Calvin, Enrolled May 16, 1901										
7378	1	Barnett, Tom	28	M	F		James Spaniard	L	Cr	Kesselia Wilson	D	Cr
		No. 1 reported dead										
		Census Card No. 2455, P. O. Calvin, Enrolled May 16, 1901										
7379	1	Lott, Thomas	46	M	F		William Lott	D	Cr	Nannie	D	Cr
7380	2	Lott, Lena	38	F	F	Wf	Karpitcher Yarhola	L	Cr	Loda	L	Cr
7381	3	Lott, Nancy	9	F	F	D	No. 1	L	Cr	No. 2	L	Cr
7382	4	Lott, Annie	3½	F	F	D	No. 1	L	Cr	No. 2	L	Cr
7383	5	Lott, Millie	9	F	F	D	No. 1	L	Cr	No. 2	L	Cr
7384	6	Lott, Willie	7	M	F	S	No. 1	L	Cr	No. 2	L	Cr
		No. 3 died June 3, 1900										
		Census Card No. 2456, P. O. Carson, Enrolled May 16, 1901										
7385	1	Casey, Sallie	20	F	F		Sarney	D	Cr	Martha	D	Cr
		Census Card No. 2457, P. O. Calvin, Enrolled May 16, 1901										
7386	1	Barnett, Louisiana	21	F	F		James Spaniard	L	Cr	Kessella Wilson	D	Cr
		No. 1 died June 1900										
		Census Card No. 2458, P. O. Calvin, Enrolled May 16, 1901										
7387	1	Harjo, Yartebka	90	M	½		Peck	D	Non	E-Lowatahge	D	Cr
7388	2	Francis, Christie	60	F	F	Wf	Dorsey	D	Cr	Harney	D	Cr
7389	3	Hawkins, Bunnie	15	M	F	Neph	Boney Hawkins	D	Cr	Tophosie	D	Cr
		No. 3 died 1902. No. 1 reported dead.										
		Census Card No. 2459, P. O. Carson, Enrolled May 16, 1901										
7390	1	Sukey	55	F	F		Artus Sobige	D	Cr	Simmoyhe	D	Cr
7391	2	Jennetta	21	F	F	D	Parcheneya	D	Cr	No. 1	L	Cr
		No. 1 reported dead										
		Census Card No. 2460, P. O. Senora, Enrolled May 16, 1901										
7392	1	Heneha, Artussee	76	M	F		Billie	D	Cr	Unknown	D	Cr
		No. 1 died 1901										
		Census Card No. 2461, P. O. Wetumka, Enrolled May 16, 1901										
7393	1	Bear, Polar	39	M	F		Nokosela Harjo	D	Cr	Unknown	D	Cr
7394	2	Bear, Mannie	26	F	F	Wf	Hully Thlocco	D	Cr	Conhegee	D	Cr
		No. 2 died August 16, 1900										
		Census Card No. 2462, P. O. Wetumka, Enrolled May 16, 1901										
7395	1	Beaver, Mollie	40	F	F		Hillabee Emarthla	D	Cr	Unknown	D	Cr
7396	2	Beaver, Oklow	10	M	F	S	Motey Beaver	D	Cr	No. 1	L	Cr
		Census Card No. 2463, P. O. Calvin, Enrolled May 16, 1901										
7397	1	Leader, Hepsie	20	F	½		Ed Leader	L	Chic	Eliza Smith	L	Cr
7398	2	Conley, William	1	M	¼	S	Oscar Conley	L	Non	No. 1	L	Cr
		Census Card No. 2464, P. O. Eufaula, Enrolled May 16, 1901; No. 4, May 24, 1901										
7399	1	Pahoseyahola, Josie	27	M	F		Aholoe Yahola	D	Cr	Ocloosie	D	Cr
7400	2	Pahoseyahola, Soatka	26	F	F	Wf	Holloddey	D	Cr	Kizzie	D	Cr
7401	3	Pahoseyholaa, Lodie	40	F	F	D	No. 1	L	Cr	No. 2	L	Cr
7402	4	Pahoseyahola, John	1	M	F	S	No. 1	L	Cr	No. 2	L	Cr
		Census Card No. 2465, P. O. Hanna, Enrolled May 16, 1901										
7403	1	Bruner, John	29	M	F		Rentie Bruner	L	Cr	Ollie Seja	L	Cr
7404	2	Bruner, Sallie	25	F	F	Wf	Sulma	D	Cr	Hannah	L	Cr
7405	3	Bruner, Lizzie	2	F	F	D	No. 1	L	Cr	No. 2	L	Cr
		No. 1 died January 8, 1910. No. 3 reported dead.										

Roll No.	No.	NAME	Age	Sex	Blood	Rel.	NAME OF FATHER	Liv.	Cit.	NAME OF MOTHER	Liv.	Cit.
		Census Card No. 2466, P. O. Eufaula, Enrolled May 16, 1901										
7406	1	Harley, Samson	25	M	F		Hallada	D	Cr	Kizzie	D	Cr
7407	2	Harley, Jennie	42	F	F	Wf	Daniel McGilbray	D	Cr	Lizzie McGilbra	L	Cr
7408	3	Porter, Nellie	5	F	F	StD	Pen Porter	L	Cr	No. 2	L	Cr
		No. 1 died March 27, 1906. No. 3 possible duplicate of No. 7064 and 7907.										
		Census Card No. 2467, P. O. Eufaula, Enrolled May 16, 1901										
7409	1	Yahola, Neha	68	M	F		Okchiye Fixeco	D	Cr	Unknown	D	Cr
		No. 1 reported dead										
		Census Card No. 2468, P. O. Council Hill, Enrolled May 16, 1901										
7410	1	Wolf, William	60	M	F		Unknown	D	Cr	Amy	D	Cr
7411	2	Wolf, Bettie	40	F	F	Wf	Tulmochusse	D	Cr	Martha	D	Cr
7412	3	Wolf, Enoch	13	M	F	S	No. 1	L	Cr	No. 2	L	Cr
7413	4	Wolf, Martha	11	F	F	D	No. 1	L	Cr	No. 2	L	Cr
7414	5	Wolf, John	6	M	F	S	No. 1	L	Cr	No. 2	L	Cr
		No. 2 died June 4, 1900. No. 3 reported dead.										
		Census Card No. 2469, P. O. Wetumka, Enrolled May 16, 1901										
7415	1	Culley, Albert	20	M	F		Culley	D	Cr	Lucy	D	Cr
		Census Card No. 2470, P. O. Okfusky, Enrolled May 16, 1901										
7416	1	Arpoika, George	30	M	F		Meka Arpoika	D	Cr	Unknown	D	Cr
7417	2	Arpoika, Sissie	24	F	F	Wf	Muska	D	Cr	Muteloka	D	Cr
		No. 1 died July 1906. No. 2 died March 12, 1904.										
		Census Card No. 2471, P. O. Holdenville, Enrolled May 16, 1901										
7418	1	Sarterpeye	50	F	F		Nocoseloche	D	Cr	Unknown	D	Cr
7419	2	Charlochee	12	M	½	S	Birdhead	L	Sem	No. 1	L	Cr
7420	3	Thomasoche	12	M	½	S	Birdhead	L	Sem	No. 1	L	Cr
7421	4	Birdhead, Lucy	18	F	½	D	Birdhead	L	Sem	No. 1	L	Cr
		No. 4 died February 26, 1900										
		Census Card No. 2472, P. O. Spaulding, Enrolled May 16, 1901										
7422	1	Tiger, Kizzie	18	F	F		Birdhead	L	Sem	Mollie	D	Cr
7423	2	Tiger, Benny	3	M	F	S	Kaley	L	Sem	No. 1	L	Cr
7424	3	Tiger, Annie	1	F	F	D	Bernose Tiger	L	Sem	No. 1	L	Cr
		Census Card No. 2473, P. O. Wetumka, Enrolled May 16, 1901; No. 5, May 24, 1901										
7425	1	Beaver, Wilson	27	M	F		Itseharse Yahola	D	Cr	Unknown	D	Cr
7426	2	Beaver, Levina	26	F	F	Wf	Suntilla Harjo	D	Cr	Unknown	D	Cr
7427	3	Beaver, Nausoche	7	F	F	D	No. 1	L	Cr	No. 2	L	Cr
7428	4	Beaver, Williamsee	6	M	F	S	No. 1	L	Cr	No. 2	L	Cr
7429	5	Beaver, Daniel	1	M	F	S	No. 1	L	Cr	No. 2	L	Cr
		No. 1 reported dead										
		Census Card No. 2474, P. O. Spaulding, Enrolled May 16, 1901										
7430	1	Birdhead, Sinda	27	F	F		Daniel	D	Cr	Mollie	L	Cr
7431	2	Birdhead, Meloche	8	F	F	D	Birdhead	L	Sem	No. 1	L	Cr
7432	3	Birdhead, Robison	6	M	F	S	Birdhead	L	Sem	No. 1	L	Cr
7433	4	Birdhead, Willochee	1	M	F	S	Birdhead	L	Sem	No. 1	L	Cr
		No. 3 reported dead										
		Census Card No. 2475, P. O. Eufaula, Enrolled May 16, 1901										
7434	1	Williams, Luster	64	M	¼		Sol Williams	D	Non	Lucy Williams	D	Cr
7435	2	Williams, Sally	40	F	F	Wf	Capitcher	D	Cr	Sally White	D	Cr
7436	3	Williams, Richard	16	M	¾	S	No. 1	L	Cr	No. 2	L	Cr
		No. 3 reported dead										
		Census Card No. 2476, P. O. Wetumka, Enrolled May 16, 1901										
7437	1	Lowe, Levina	65	F	F		Unknown	D	Cr	Unknown	D	Cr
		No. 1 died November 25, 1900										
		Census Card No. 2477, P. O. Sasakwa, Enrolled May 16, 1901										
7438	1	Karselarney	50	F	F		Tarcosa Tustunnugge	D	Cr	Linda	D	Cr
7439	2	Green, Wesley	19	F	F	S	Lahta Yahola	D	Sem	No. 1	L	Cr
7440	3	Green, John	16	F	F	S	Lahta Yahola	D	Sem	No. 1	L	Cr
		No. 2 reported dead										
		Census Card No. 2478, P. O. Wetumka, Enrolled May 16, 1901										
7441	1	Lowe, Columbus	24	M	F		Ochee Harjo	D	Cr	Levina Lowe	D	Cr
7442	2	Lowe, Mary	35	F	F	Wf	Nocossille Harjo	D	Cr	Unknown	D	Cr
		Census Card No. 2479, P. O. Sasakwa, Enrolled October 24, 1901										
7443	1	Green, Kizzie	30	F	F		Latah Yahola	D	Sem	Karselarney	L	Cr
7444	2	Green, Ena	5	M	F	S	Chebe	L	Sem	No. 1	L	Cr
7445	3	Bruner, Dewey	1	M	F	S	Jesse Bruner	L	Cr	No. 1	L	Cr
		Census Card No. 2480, P. O. Castle, Enrolled May 16, 1901										
7446	1	Hill, Lucy	33	F	F		Hiepa	D	Cr	Sochonagee	D	Cr
7447	2	Hill, Jesse	44	M	F	Hus	Conip Fixico	D	Cr	Harney Fixico	D	Cr
7448	3	Hill, Hettie	11	F	F	D	No. 2	L	Cr	No. 1	L	Cr
7449	4	Hill, Lizzie	9	F	F	D	No. 2	L	Cr	No. 1	L	Cr
7450	5	Hill, Houston	7	M	F	S	No. 2	L	Cr	No. 1	L	Cr
7451	6	Hill, Sampson	5	M	F	S	No. 2	L	Cr	No. 1	L	Cr
		No. 2 died March 4, 1901. No. 4 died June 1899. No. 6 died October 1899.										
		Census Card No. 2481, P. O. Sasakwa, Enrolled May 16, 1901										
7452	1	Greenleaf, Hullyanda	27	M	F		Lata Yahola	D	Sem	Karselarney	L	Cr
		No. 1 reported dead										
		Census Card No. 2482, P. O. Holdenville, Enrolled May 16, 1901										
7453	1	Cain, Ottawa	37	M	F		Canie	D	Cr	Prisa	D	Cr
7454	2	Cain, Mary J.	28	F	F	Wf	Panoskey	L	Cr	Lydia	D	Cr
7455	3	Reed, Benjamin J.	13	M	⅝	StS	Robert Reed	D	Cr	No. 2	L	Cr
7456	4	Cain, Sildy	1	F	F	D	No. 1	L	Cr	No. 2	L	Cr
		No. 4 died October 1899										

156

Roll No.	No.	NAME	Age	Sex	Blood	Rel.	NAME OF FATHER	Liv.	Cit.	NAME OF MOTHER	Liv.	Cit.
	Census Card No. 2483, P. O. Hanna, Enrolled May 16, 1901											
7457	1	Rabbit, Amos	19	M	F		James Rabbit	L	Cr	Unknown	D	Cr
7458	2	Rabbit, James	43	M	F	Fath	Rabbit	D	Cr	Lundey	D	Cr
7459	3	Rabbit, Sakoyike	40	F	F	StMo	Talup Harjo	D	Cr	Unknown	D	Cr
7460	4	Rabbit, Edmond	10	M	F	Bro	No. 2	L	Cr	No. 3	L	Cr
	No. 3 reported dead											
	Census Card No. 2484, P. O. Hanna, Enrolled May 16, 1901											
7461	1	Reynolds, Ariadne	24	F	½		Lee Stidham	D	Cr	Harriet	?	Cr
7462	2	Reynolds, Aunie	7	F	¼	D	J. R. Reynolds	L	Non	No. 1	L	Cr
7463	3	Reynolds, Laura	5	F	¼	D	J. R. Reynolds	L	Non	No. 1	L	Cr
7464	4	Reynolds, William E.	3	M	¼	S	J. R. Reynolds	L	Non	No. 1	L	Cr
	Census Card No. 2485, P. O. Checotah, Enrolled May 17, 1901											
7465	1	Friday, Lewis	20	F	F		Friday	D	Cr	Sookey	D	Cr
	No. 1 died June 3, 1903											
	Census Card No. 2486, P. O. Seminole, Enrolled May 17, 1901											
7466	1	Bowlegs, Lulu	28	F	¾		Dickson Snap	D	Cr	Mary Snap	D	Cr
7467	2	Bowlegs, Florence	5	F	⅜	D	Robert Bowlegs	L	Sem	No. 1	L	Cr
7468	3	Bowlegs, Ethel	1	F	⅜	D	Robert Bowlegs	L	Sem	No. 1	L	Cr
7469	4	Bowlegs, Lulu Winnie	7	F	⅞	D	Unknown	L	Cr	No. 1	L	Cr
	Nos. 2 and 4 reported dead											
	Census Card No. 2487, P. O. Barnard, Enrolled May 17, 1901											
7470	1	Leader, David	24	M	F		Jim Leader	D	Cr	Wiley	D	Cr
	Census Card No. 2488, P. O. Holdenville, Enrolled May 17, 1901; No. 3, May 21, 1901											
7471	1	Anderson, Mose	42	M	F		Iokee	D	Cr	Mary	D	Cr
7472	2	Anderson, Lucy	38	F	F	Wf	David Gooden	L	Cr	Unknown	D	Cr
7473	3	Gooden, George	19	M	F	Bro-L	David Gooden	L	Cr	Susanna	D	Cr
7474	4	Gooden, David	64	M	F	Fat-L	Ahse Yahola	D	Cr	Wynne	D	Cr
	No. 4 died March 4, 1901. No. 1 reported dead.											
	Census Card No. 2489, P. O. Calvin, Enrolled May 17, 1901; No. 3, May 21, 1901											
7475	1	Bruner, James	21	M	F		Taylor Bruner	D	Cr	Lucy Bruner	L	Cr
7476	2	Bruner, Togy	20	F	F	Wf	Robert Reno	D	Cr	Eliza Smith	L	Cr
7477	3	Bruner, Arthur	3	M	F	S	No. 1	L	Cr	No. 2	L	Cr
	No. 2 reported dead											
	Census Card No. 2490, P. O. Eufaula, Enrolled May 17, 1901											
7478	1	McNac, John	42	M	¼		Sam McNac	D	Cr	Jennie Ross	L	Non
	No. 1 reported dead											
	Census Card No. 2491, P. O. Wetumka, Enrolled May 17, 1901											
7479	1	Parnosky, Willie	28	M	F		Parnosky	L	Cr	Unknown	D	Cr
7480	2	Parnosky, Salina	25	F	F	Wf	Coches Harjo	D	Cr	Unknown	D	Cr
7481	3	Parnosky, Noah	7	M	F	S	No. 1	L	Cr	Rosanna Parnosk	D	Cr
7482	4	Parnosky, Minnie	11	F	F	D	No. 1	L	Cr	Rosanna Parnosk	D	Cr
	No. 4 died August 1900											
	Census Card No. 2492, P. O. Holdenville, Enrolled May 17, 1901											
7483	1	Parnosky	50	M	F		Unknown	D	Cr	Fulley	D	Cr
	No. 1 died October 1902											
	Census Card No. 2493, P. O. Fame, Enrolled May 17, 1901											
7484	1	Fife, Parsutta	70	M	F		Unknown	D	Cr	Unknown	D	Cr
7485	2	Fife, Lizzie	60	F	F	Wf	Unknown	D	Cr	Lucinda	D	Cr
	No. 1 died July 1902. No. 2 died March 18, 1903.											
	Census Card No. 2494, P. O. Vivian, Enrolled May 17, 1901											
7486	1	Wolfe, Ellen	33	F	F		Wakige	D	Cr	Unknown	D	Cr
7487	2	Washington, Marchie	15	M	F	S	Johnson	L	Non	No. 1	L	Cr
7488	3	Washington, Waitie	12	M	F	S	Moore	D	Cr	No. 1	L	Cr
	No. 2 died August 19, 1899. No. 3 died May 1900.											
	Census Card No. 2495, P. O. Holdenville, Enrolled May 17, 1901											
7489	1	McPerryman	39	M	F		Lewis Perryman	D	Cr	Annie	D	Cr
7490	2	McPerryman, Celia	30	F	F	Wf	David Gooden	D	Cr	Susanna	D	Cr
	No. 2 died February 28, 1900											
	Census Card No. 2496, P. O. Bristow, Enrolled May 17, 1901											
7491	1	Durant, Adam	66	M	¼		Monday Durant	D	Cr	Cressie Durant	D	Cr
	Census Card No. 2497, P. O. Carson, Enrolled May 17, 1901											
7492	1	Spaniard, Henry	31	M	F		Nocus Yahola	D	Cr	Fiecha(or) Fayecha	D	Cr
7493	2	Spaniard, Louiisa	32	F	F	Wf	Pakalee Harjo	D	Cr	Subbioye	D	Cr
7494	3	Spaniard, Chiler	12	F	F	D	No. 1	L	Cr	No. 2	L	Cr
7495	4	Spaniard, Chotie	10	M	F	S	No. 1	L	Cr	No. 2	L	Cr
7496	5	Spaniard, Martha	4	F	F	D	No. 1	L	Cr	No. 2	L	Cr
	No. 4 died November 18, 1899. No. 1 reported dead. No. 5 died October 15, 1899.											
	Census Card No. 2498, P. O. Holdenville, Enrolled March 17, 1901											
7497	1	Gray, Eliza	47	F	F		Jimka	D	Cr	Monie	D	Cr
7498	2	Deere, Bessie	3	F	F	GrD	John Deere	L	Cr	Katie Deere	L	Cr
7499	3	Deere, Katie	20	F	F	D	Barney Chotke	D	Cr	No. 1	L	Cr
	No. 3 died November 1899											
	Census Card No. 2499, P. O. Hanna, Enrolled May 17, 1901											
7500	1	Lewis, Jackson	20	M	F		Tusko Yanba	D	Cr	Louisa	D	Cr
	Census Card No. 2500, P. O. Holdenville, Enrolled May 17, 1901											
7501	1	Harjo, Talof	21	M	½		Birdhead	L	Sem	Mollie Potato	D	Cr
	Census Card No. 2501, P. O. Hanna, Enrolled May 17, 1901											
7502	1	Green, Barney	40	M	F		Dave Green	D	Cr	Sallie	D	Cr
7503	2	Green, Celia	32	F	F	Wf	Lawyer Manley	D	Cr	Lydia Manly	D	Cr

Roll No.	No.	NAME	Age	Sex	Blood	Rel.	NAME OF FATHER	Liv.	Cit.	NAME OF MOTHER	Liv.	Cit.

Census Card No. 2502, P. O. Bristow, Enrolled May 17, 1901

Roll No.	No.	NAME	Age	Sex	Blood	Rel.	NAME OF FATHER	Liv.	Cit.	NAME OF MOTHER	Liv.	Cit.
7504	1	Long, Tom	29	M	F		Unknown	D	Cr	Unknown	D	Cr
7505	2	Long, Judy	40	F	F	Wf	Jacob Barnett	D	Cr	Wealche Barnett	D	Cr

No. 1 died March 13, 1902

Census Card No. 2503, P. O. Hanna, Enrolled May 17, 1901

Roll No.	No.	NAME	Age	Sex	Blood	Rel.	NAME OF FATHER	Liv.	Cit.	NAME OF MOTHER	Liv.	Cit.
7506	1	Green, Cinda	30	F	F		Lawyer Manley	D	Cr	Lydia Manly	D	Cr
7507	2	Green, David	14	M	F	S	Willie Green	D	Cr	No. 1	L	Cr

No. 1 died September 21, 1899

Census Card No. 2504, P. O. Holdenville, Enrolled May 17, 1901

Roll No.	No.	NAME	Age	Sex	Blood	Rel.	NAME OF FATHER	Liv.	Cit.	NAME OF MOTHER	Liv.	Cit.
7508	1	Ellis, Jack	38	M	F		Yardowa Harjo	D	Cr	Sophie	D	Cr
7509	2	Harjo, Sophia	80	F	F	Moth	Cotcha Yahola	D	Cr	Oklosey Chupco	D	Cr
7510	3	Gray, Neterhe	3	M	F	Neph	Daniel Gray	D	Cr	Dorsey Gray	L	Cr
7511	4	Gray, Dosey	28	F	F	Sis	Yardowa Harjo	D	Cr	Sophie	L	Cr
7512	5	Gray, Cemme	18	F	F	Sis	Yardowa Harjo	D	Cr	Sophie	L	Cr
7513	6	Coon, Lader	1	F	½	Niece	Jackson Coon	L	Sem	No. 5	L	Cr

No. 2 died Winter 1904. No. 4 died January 1901. No. 5 died January 1901. No. 6 died December 1899.

Census Card No. 2505, P. O. Holdenville, Enrolled May 17, 1901

Roll No.	No.	NAME	Age	Sex	Blood	Rel.	NAME OF FATHER	Liv.	Cit.	NAME OF MOTHER	Liv.	Cit.
7514	1	Peter, Jennie	33	F	F		Little Peter	L	Cr	Linda	D	Cr
7515	2	Peter, Louisa	19	F	F	Sis	Little Peter	L	Cr	Linda	D	Cr
7516	3	Binton, Tilda	13	F	F	D	Samuel Brinton	L	Cr	No. 1	L	Cr
7517	4	Martin, Samuel	10	M	½	S	Marty	L	Sem	No. 1	L	Cr
7518	5	Marks, John	8	M	½	S	John Marks	L	Non	No. 1	L	Cr
7519	6	Bighead, Lizzie	5	F	½	D	George Bighead	L	Sem	No. 1	L	Cr
7520	7	Bighead, Lottie	1	F	½	D	George Bighead	L	Sem	No. 1	L	Cr
7521	8	Bighead, Jimmie	1	M	½	S	George Bighead	L	Non	No. 1	L	Cr
7522	9	Bighead, Nancy	1	F	½	D	George Bighead	L	Sem	No. 1	L	Cr

No. 7 died April 1899. No. 8 died September 17, 1914. No. 9 died December 25, 1900.

Census Card No. 2506, P. O. Hanna, Enrolled May 17, 1901

Roll No.	No.	NAME	Age	Sex	Blood	Rel.	NAME OF FATHER	Liv.	Cit.	NAME OF MOTHER	Liv.	Cit.
7523	1	Smith, Aggie	22	M	F		Sam Simmons	D	Cr	Annie Simmons	D	Cr

No. 1 died May 10, 1901

Census Card No. 2507, P. O. Holdenville, Enrolled April 29, 1901

Roll No.	No.	NAME	Age	Sex	Blood	Rel.	NAME OF FATHER	Liv.	Cit.	NAME OF MOTHER	Liv.	Cit.
7524	1	Peter, Little	83	M	F		Watup Yahola	D	Cr	Unknown	D	Cr
7525	2	Peter, Millie	17	F	F	D	No. 1	L	Cr	Linda	D	Cr

No. 1 died 1900

Census Card No. 2508, P. O. Hanna, Enrolled May 17, 1901

Roll No.	No.	NAME	Age	Sex	Blood	Rel.	NAME OF FATHER	Liv.	Cit.	NAME OF MOTHER	Liv.	Cit.
7526	1	Smith, Micky	28	M	F		Chella Smith	D	Cr	Fulga	D	Cr
7527	2	Smith, Lydia	3	F	F	D	No. 1	L	Cr	Cinda Green (Smith)	D	Cr

Census Card No. 2509, P. O. Sasakwa, Enrolled Mau 17, 1901

Roll No.	No.	NAME	Age	Sex	Blood	Rel.	NAME OF FATHER	Liv.	Cit.	NAME OF MOTHER	Liv.	Cit.
7528	1	Peter, Sallie	21	F	F		Little Peter	L	Cr	Linda	D	Cr
7529	2	Davis, Jimmie	3mo	M	½	S	Cally Davis	L	Sem	No. 1	L	Cr

No. 2 died July 15, 1903

Census Card No. 2510, P. O. Holdenville, Enrolled May 17, 1901

Roll No.	No.	NAME	Age	Sex	Blood	Rel.	NAME OF FATHER	Liv.	Cit.	NAME OF MOTHER	Liv.	Cit.
7530	1	Bruner, William	40	M	F		Toley Bruner	D	Cr	Sopsey	D	Cr
7531	2	Bruner, Ida	30	F	F	Wf	Charlochie	D	Sem	Louisaunah	D	Cr

Census Card No. 2511, P. O. Raiford, Enrolled May 17, 1901

Roll No.	No.	NAME	Age	Sex	Blood	Rel.	NAME OF FATHER	Liv.	Cit.	NAME OF MOTHER	Liv.	Cit.
7532	1	Selumber, Robert	36	M	F		Selumber	D	Cr	Connahcha	D	Cr
7533	2	Selumber, Winey	28	F	F	Wf	Casar Harjo	D	Cr	Tina	D	Cr

No. 1 died October 1906

Census Card No. 2512, P. O. Holdenville, Enrolled May 17, 1901

Roll No.	No.	NAME	Age	Sex	Blood	Rel.	NAME OF FATHER	Liv.	Cit.	NAME OF MOTHER	Liv.	Cit.
7534	1	Jones, Louisa	15	F	F		Charlie Jones	D	Cr	Chowa	D	Cr

Census Card No. 2513, P. O. Pierce, Enrolled May 17, 1901

Roll No.	No.	NAME	Age	Sex	Blood	Rel.	NAME OF FATHER	Liv.	Cit.	NAME OF MOTHER	Liv.	Cit.
7535	1	Fish, Robert	30	M	F		William Fish	D	Cr	Mandy	D	Cr
7536	2	Fish, Arnikee	30	F	F	Wf	Unknown	D	Cr	Unknown	D	Cr

No. 2 reported dead

Census Card No. 2514, P. O. Holdenville, Enrolled May 17, 1901

Roll No.	No.	NAME	Age	Sex	Blood	Rel.	NAME OF FATHER	Liv.	Cit.	NAME OF MOTHER	Liv.	Cit.
7537	1	Deere, Annie	80	F	F		Tulwar Harjo	D	Cr	Unknown	D	Cr

Census Crad No. 2515, P. O. Holdenville, Enrolled May 18, 1901

Roll No.	No.	NAME	Age	Sex	Blood	Rel.	NAME OF FATHER	Liv.	Cit.	NAME OF MOTHER	Liv.	Cit.
7538	1	Beaver, Party	20	M	F		Yahola Micco	L	Cr	Tyhoke	D	Cr
7539	2	Beaver, Lucy	28	F	F	Wf	Tom Leader	D	Choc	Aggie Kernal	L	Cr

Census Card No. 2516, P. O. Holdenville, Enrolled May 18, 1901

Roll No.	No.	NAME	Age	Sex	Blood	Rel.	NAME OF FATHER	Liv.	Cit.	NAME OF MOTHER	Liv.	Cit.
7540	1	Tyhoka	70	F	F		Cotcha Yahola	D	Cr	Oklosa Chupco	D	Cr
7541	2	Beaver, Nicey	16	F	F	D	Yahola Micco	L	Cr	No. 1	L	Cr

No. 2 died January 1, 1912

Census Card No. 2517, P. O. Holdenville, Enrolled May 18, 1901

Roll No.	No.	NAME	Age	Sex	Blood	Rel.	NAME OF FATHER	Liv.	Cit.	NAME OF MOTHER	Liv.	Cit.
7542	1	Bruner, Wego	26	M	F		Wilson Bruner	D	Cr	Rhoda Stewart·	D	Cr

Census Card No. 2518, P. O. Holdenville, Enrolled May 18, 1901

Roll No.	No.	NAME	Age	Sex	Blood	Rel.	NAME OF FATHER	Liv.	Cit.	NAME OF MOTHER	Liv.	Cit.
7543	1	Micco, Cosar	48	M	F		Tummie Fixico	D	Cr	Sakkoyege	D	Cr
7544	2	Micco, Lucy	35	F	F	Wf	Aharlock Hobie	L	Cr	Susie	D	Cr
7545	3	Micco, Chona	6	M	F	S	No. 1	L	Cr	No. 2	L	Cr

Census Card No. 2519, P. O. Holdenville, Enrolled May 18, 1901

Roll No.	No.	NAME	Age	Sex	Blood	Rel.	NAME OF FATHER	Liv.	Cit.	NAME OF MOTHER	Liv.	Cit.
7546	1	Deere, John	23	M	F		Cosar Micco	L	Cr	Ithlococeha	D	Cr

Census Card No. 2520, P. O. Tuskegee, Enrolled May 18, 1901

Roll No.	No.	NAME	Age	Sex	Blood	Rel.	NAME OF FATHER	Liv.	Cit.	NAME OF MOTHER	Liv.	Cit.
7547	1	Yargee, Millie	22	F	F		James Yargee	L	Cr	Mauda	D	Cr

No. 1 died March 20, 1900

Roll No.	No.	NAME	Age	Sex	Blood	Rel.	NAME OF FATHER	Liv.	Cit.	NAME OF MOTHER	Liv.	Cit.
		Census Card No. 2521, P. O. Lamar, Enrolled May 18, 1901										
7548	1	Jones, Martin	38	M	F		Jacob Deere	D	Cr	Cinda	L	Cr
7549	2	Jones, Hannah	45	F	F	Wf	Unknown	D	Cr	Millie	L	Cr
7550	3	Jones, Sallie	20	F	F	D	No. 1	L	Cr	No. 2	L	Cr
7551	4	Jones, Pollie	17	F	F	D	No. 1	L	Cr	No. 2	L	Cr
7552	5	Wilson, George	9	M	F	GrS	Thomas Wilson	L	Cr	Bettie Wilson	L	Cr
7553	6	Jones, Hattie	18mo	F	F	GrD	Unknown	L	Cr	No. 3	L	Cr

No. 1 died April 3, 1902. No. 3 died November 27, 1900. No. 4 died 1903.

Roll No.	No.	NAME	Age	Sex	Blood	Rel.	NAME OF FATHER	Liv.	Cit.	NAME OF MOTHER	Liv.	Cit.
		Census Card No. 2522, P. O. Calvin, Enrolled May 18, 1901										
7554	1	Mannie	16	F	F		Takey Coody	D	Cr	Margeda	D	Cr

No. 1 reported dead

Roll No.	No.	NAME	Age	Sex	Blood	Rel.	NAME OF FATHER	Liv.	Cit.	NAME OF MOTHER	Liv.	Cit.
		Census Card No. 2523, P. O. Coweta, Enrolled May 18, 1901										
7555	1	Cox, Annie	40	F	F		Joe Kernal	D	Cr	Nancy Kernal	D	Cr
7556	2	Cox, Maggie	20	F	½	D	Louis Cox	L	Sem	No. 1	L	Cr
7557	3	Cox, Nancy	17	F	½	D	Louis Cox	L	Sem	No. 1	L	Cr

Roll No.	No.	NAME	Age	Sex	Blood	Rel.	NAME OF FATHER	Liv.	Cit.	NAME OF MOTHER	Liv.	Cit.
		Census Card No. 2524, P. O. Hanna, Enrolled May 18, 1901										
7558	1	Emarthla, Okchum	46	M	F		Cotcha Harjo	D	Cr	Ishodoche	D	Cr
7559	2	Emarthla, Selina	45	F	F	Wf	Nocus Fixico	L	Cr	Unknown	D	Cr

No. 2 died November 26, 1901. No. 1 died October 17, 1902.

Roll No.	No.	NAME	Age	Sex	Blood	Rel.	NAME OF FATHER	Liv.	Cit.	NAME OF MOTHER	Liv.	Cit.
		Census Card No. 2525, P. O. Okemah, Enrolled May 18, 1901										
7560	1	Grammar, Charles	30	M	F		Ingersoka	D	Cr	Manwokigee	D	Cr

Roll No.	No.	NAME	Age	Sex	Blood	Rel.	NAME OF FATHER	Liv.	Cit.	NAME OF MOTHER	Liv.	Cit.
		Census Card No. 2526, P. O. Wewoka, Enrolled May 18, 1901										
7561	1	Monday, Haga	22	F	F		Monday	D	Cr	Tookah Monday	D	Cr

No. 1 died April 14, 1899

Roll No.	No.	NAME	Age	Sex	Blood	Rel.	NAME OF FATHER	Liv.	Cit.	NAME OF MOTHER	Liv.	Cit.
		Census Card No. 2527, P. O. Carson, Enrolled May 18, 1901										
7562	1	Smith, George	33	M	F		James Smith	L	Cr	Siejasce	D	Cr
7563	2	Smith, Fildy	35	F	F	Wf	Itshar Fixico	D	Cr	Sussie	D	Cr
7564	3	Smith, Dinah	10	F	F	D	No. 1	L	Cr	No. 2	L	Cr
7565	4	Smith, Joe	7	M	F	S	No. 1	L	Cr	No. 2	L	Cr
7566	5	Smith, William	3	M	F	S	No. 1	L	Cr	No. 2	L	Cr

No. 3 died May 1, 1910

Roll No.	No.	NAME	Age	Sex	Blood	Rel.	NAME OF FATHER	Liv.	Cit.	NAME OF MOTHER	Liv.	Cit.
		Census Card No. 2528, P. O. Wewoka, Enrolled May 18, 1901										
7567	1	Harjo, Alex	7	M	½		Neha Harjo	L	Sem	Nicey Harjo	D	Cr

Roll No.	No.	NAME	Age	Sex	Blood	Rel.	NAME OF FATHER	Liv.	Cit.	NAME OF MOTHER	Liv.	Cit.
		Census Card No. 2529 P. O. None, Enrolled May 18, 1901										
7568	1	Porter, Tobie	40	F	F		Aharlok Yahola	D	Cr	Chokiapy	D	Cr

Died April 1899

Roll No.	No.	NAME	Age	Sex	Blood	Rel.	NAME OF FATHER	Liv.	Cit.	NAME OF MOTHER	Liv.	Cit.
		Census Card No. 2530, P. O. Sapulpa, Enrolled May 18, 1901										
7569	1	Poloke, Sam	40	F	M		Sapaxta	D	Cr	Losay	D	Cr
7570	2	Poloke, Lucy	40	F	F	Wf	Sophoyee	D	Cr	Sofficka	D	Cr
7571	3	Sarte, Luma	15	F	F	StD	Sarte	D	Cr	No. 2	L	Cr

Roll No.	No.	NAME	Age	Sex	Blood	Rel.	NAME OF FATHER	Liv.	Cit.	NAME OF MOTHER	Liv.	Cit.
		Census Card No. 2531, P. O. Sapulpa, Enrolled May 18, 1901										
7572	1	Sarkahche, Fuchie	16	F	F		Sarkahchie	D	Cr	Dufney	D	Cr

No. 1 died July 13, 1907

Roll No.	No.	NAME	Age	Sex	Blood	Rel.	NAME OF FATHER	Liv.	Cit.	NAME OF MOTHER	Liv.	Cit.
		Census Card No. 2532, P. O. Sapulpa, Enrolled May 18, 1901										
7573	1	Tarpley, Jacob	7	M	F		Tarpley	D	Cr	Polly	?	Cr

Roll No.	No.	NAME	Age	Sex	Blood	Rel.	NAME OF FATHER	Liv.	Cit.	NAME OF MOTHER	Liv.	Cit.
		Census Card No. 2533, P. O. Sapulpa, Enrolled May 18, 1901										
7574	1	Ispocogee, Topley	45	F	F		Ispocogee	D	Cr	Sofficy	D	Cr

No. 1 died February 14, 1901

Roll No.	No.	NAME	Age	Sex	Blood	Rel.	NAME OF FATHER	Liv.	Cit.	NAME OF MOTHER	Liv.	Cit.
		Census Card No. 2534, P. O. Okemah, Enrolled May 18, 1901										
7575	1	Soldier, Robert	24	M	F		John Soldier	D	Cr	Caddie	D	Cr

No. 1 reported dead

Roll No.	No.	NAME	Age	Sex	Blood	Rel.	NAME OF FATHER	Liv.	Cit.	NAME OF MOTHER	Liv.	Cit.
		Census Card No. 2535, P. O. Sapulpa, Enrolled May 18, 1901										
7676	1	Tiger, Minerva	15	F	F		Topley Ispogoche	D	Cr	Linda (or Tiger)	D	Cr

No. 1 died June 15, 1900

Roll No.	No.	NAME	Age	Sex	Blood	Rel.	NAME OF FATHER	Liv.	Cit.	NAME OF MOTHER	Liv.	Cit.
		Census Card No. 2536, P. O. Okemah, Enrolled May 16, 1901										
7577	1	Miller, Johnson	28	M	F		Sam Miller	D	Cr	Polly Miller	D	Cr

No. 1 died February 27, 1901

Roll No.	No.	NAME	Age	Sex	Blood	Rel.	NAME OF FATHER	Liv.	Cit.	NAME OF MOTHER	Liv.	Cit.
		Census Card No. 2537, P. O. Wewoka, Enrolled May 18, 1901										
7578	1	Brown, Lou	40	F	¾		Frank Jacobs	L	Cr	Lucinda	L	Cr
7579	2	Fox, Winey	12	F	F		Cholar Harjoche	L	Cr	Sophia Fox	L	Cr

No. 1 reported dead

Roll No.	No.	NAME	Age	Sex	Blood	Rel.	NAME OF FATHER	Liv.	Cit.	NAME OF MOTHER	Liv.	Cit.
		Census Card No. 2538, P. O. Holdenville, Enrolled May 18, 1901										
7580	1	Tiger, Leah	50	F	F		Cowe Harjo	D	Cr	Unknown	D	
7581	2	Tiger, Louis	16	M	F	S	Cotcha Homarta	D	Cr	No. 1	L	Cr

No. 1 died November 29, 1908. No. 2 died February 22, 1908.

Roll No.	No.	NAME	Age	Sex	Blood	Rel.	NAME OF FATHER	Liv.	Cit.	NAME OF MOTHER	Liv.	Cit.
		Census Card No. 2539, P. O. Wetumka, Enrolled May 18, 1901										
7582	1	Litka, Charley	15	M	F		*George Brammir	D	Non	*Susie Litka	D	Cr

Reported duplicate of Enrollment No. 7782 on Census Card No. 2640.
*Note spelling on Census Card No. 2640.

Roll No.	No.	NAME	Age	Sex	Blood	Rel.	NAME OF FATHER	Liv.	Cit.	NAME OF MOTHER	Liv.	Cit.
		Census Card No. 2540, P. O. Salem, Enrolled May 18, 1901										
7583	1	Taylor, Milea	25	F	F		Somdaya	D	Cr	Jinnie	L	Cr
7584	2	Taylor, Isaac	8	M	F	S	Taylor Taylor	D	Cr	No. 1	L	Cr
7585	3	Taylor, Lucinda	7	F	F	D	Taylor Taylor	D	Cr	No. 1	L	Cr
7586	4	Taylor, Emma	1	F	F	D	Bundy	L	Cr	No. 1	L	Cr

No. 4 died July 5, 1900

Roll No.	No.	NAME	Age	Sex	Blood	Rel.	NAME OF FATHER	Liv.	Cit.	NAME OF MOTHER	Liv.	Cit.
		Census Card No. 2541, P. O. Salem, Enrolled May 18, 1901										
7587	1	Thomas, Katie	30	F	F		Charley Taylor	D	Cr	Harday	L	Cr
7588	2	Thomas, Linda	12	F	F	D	Thomasey	D	Cr	No. 1	L	Cr
7589	3	Thomas, Louisa	10	F	F	D	Thomasey	D	Cr	No. 1	L	Cr
7590	4	Thomas, Millie	8	F	F	D	Thomasey	D	Cr	No. 1	L	Cr

No. 2 died March 14, 1911

Roll No.	No.	NAME	Age	Sex	Blood	Rel.	NAME OF FATHER	Liv.	Cit.	NAME OF MOTHER	Liv.	Cit.
		Census Card No. 2542, P. O. Salem, Enrolled May 18, 1901										
7591	1	Scott, Ben	35	M	F		Yahola Fixico	D	Cr	Lizzie Betsey	D	Cr
7592	2	Scott, Kizzie	25	F	F	Wf	Charley Taylor	D	Cr	Hardy Taylor	L	Cr
7593	3	Scott, Sallie	5	F	F	D	Ben Scott	D	Cr	No. 2	L	Cr
7594	4	Scott, Wisey	4	F	F	D	No. 1	L	Cr	No. 2	L	Cr
7595	5	Scott, Emma	1	F	F	D	No. 1	L	Cr	No. 2	L	Cr
		No. 1 died October 17, 1900. No. 5 died 1904.										
		Census Card No. 2543, P. O. Salem, Enrolled May 18, 1901										
7596	1	Taylor, Hardy	65	F	F		Unknown	D	Cr	Mollie	D	Cr
7597	2	Taylor, Sarpsey	17	M	F	S	Charley Taylor	D	Cr	Hardy Taylor	L	Cr
7598	3	Taylor, Jemima	16	F	F	D	Charley Taylor	D	Cr	Hardy Taylor	L	Cr
7599	4	Taylor, Susie	20	F	F	D	Charley Taylor	D	Cr	No. 1	L	Cr
7600	5	Taylor, Eliza	18	F	F	D	Charley Taylor	D	Cr	No. 1	L	Cr
7601	6	Taylor, Jacob	7	M	F	S	Charley Taylor	D	Cr	No. 1	L	Cr
		No. 5 died June 1901. No. 6 died June 1901.										
		Census Card No. 2544, P. O. Eufaula, Enrolled May 20, 1901										
7602	1	Asbury, Mary	19	F	F		Jim Asbury	L	Cr	Vicey Asbury	L	Cr
		Census Card No. 2545, P. O. Senora, Enrolled May 18, 1901										
7603	1	York, James	26	M	F		Yarkibe Harjo	L	Cr	Julie	D	Cr
		No. 1 died February 1, 1901										
		Census Card No. 2546, P. O. Eufaula, Enrolled May 20, 1901										
7604	1	Asbury, John	23	M	F		Jim Asbury	L	Cr	Mary Asbury	D	Cr
		No. 1 died										
		Census Card No. 2547, P. O. Eufaula, Enrolled May 20, 1901										
7605	1	Asbury, Thomas	21	M	F		Jim Asbury	L	Cr	Nancy Asbury	D	Cr
		Census Card No. 2548, P. O. Salem, Enrolled May 20, 1901										
7606	1	Taylor, Taylor	22	M	F		Charles Taylor	D	Cr	Hardy Taylor	L	Cr
7607	2	Taylor, Lizzie	22	F	F	Wf	Norcus Harjo	D	Cr	Lydia	D	Cr
7608	3	Taylor, Marchie	7	M	F	S	No. 1	L	Cr	No. 2	L	Cr
7609	4	Taylor, Dumsey	3	M	F	S	No. 1	L	Cr	No. 2	L	Cr
		No. 4 died February 1901										
		Census Card No. 2549, P. O. Morse, Enrolled May 20, 1901										
7610	1	Hencha, Janie	45	F	F		Hopoethla Heneha	D	Cr	Wallie	D	Cr
		Census Card No. 2550, P. O. Morse, Enrolled May 20, 1901										
7611	1	Harjo, Nancy	23	F	F		Nocus Harjo	D	Cr	Waley	D	Cr
		No. 1 reported dead										
		Census Card No. 2551, P. O. Okemah, Enrolled May 20, 1901										
7612	1	Harjo, Yarner	21	M	F		Nocus Harjo	D	Cr	Waley	D	Cr
		Census Card No. 2552, P. O. Morse, Enrolled May 20, 1901										
7613	1	Lissar	64	F	F		Unknown	D	Cr	Unknown	D	Cr
		No. 1 died November 7, 1909										
		Census Card No. 2553, P. O. Nerotown, Enrolled May 20, 1901										
7614	1	Herrod, Rosanna	29	F	F		John Herrod	D	Cr	Sophia	L	Cr
7615	2	McIntosh, John	3	M	F	S	Dick McIntosh	L	Cr	No. 1	L	Cr
7616	3	McIntosh, Lydia	1	F	F	D	Dick McIntosh	L	Cr	No. 1	L	Cr
		Census Card No. 2554, P. O. Eufaula, Enrolled May 20, 1901										
7617	1	McIntosh, Hepsey	52	F	F		Chebonagie	D	Cr	Hatogee	D	Cr
7618	2	McIntosh, Lizzie	20	F	F	D	Sulletka McIntosh	D	Cr	No. 1	L	Cr
7619	3	McIntosh, Leah	14	F	F	D	Sulletka McIntosh	D	Cr	No. 1	L	Cr
7620	4	McIntosh, David	12	M	F	S	Sulletka McIntosh	D	Cr	No. 1	L	Cr
7621	5	McIntosh, Henry	17	M	F	S	Sulletka McIntosh	D	Cr	No. 1	L	Cr
		No. 2 identified as Jennie Greenwood, mother of N. B. 739.										
		Census Card No. 2555, P. O. Eufaula, Enrolled May 20, 1901										
7622	1	Sullivan, William	40	M	F		Ceyado	D	Cr	Sallie Sullivan	D	Cr
		Census Card No. 2556, P. O. Okmulgee, Enrolled May 20, 1901										
7623	1	Sharlin, Katie	17	F	F		Tom Sharlin	D	Cr	Martha Sharlin	D	Cr
		Census Card No. 2557, P. O. Muskogee, Enrolled May 20, 1901										
7624	1	Rogers, Susan M.	56	F	⅜		Wm. Drew	D	Cr	Delilah Drew	D	Cr
7625	2	Carey, Jessie	17	F	¼	Ward	Tuxie Carey	D	Cr	Jessie Carey	D	Cr
		Census Card No. 2558, P. O. Henryetta, Enrolled May 20, 1901										
7626	1	Deere, Thompson	30	M	F		Ben Derre	L	Cr	Orey (Derre)	D	Cr
		Census Card No. 2559, P. O. Eufaula, Enrolled May 20, 1901										
7627	1	Deere, Sarah	25	F	F		Ben Derre	L	Cr	Orey Deere	D	Cr
7628	2	Deere, Newman	3	M	F	S	Unknown	L	Cr	No. 1	L	Cr
		No. 1 died June 10, 1912										
		Census Card No. 2560, P. O. Coweta, Enrolled May 20, 1901										
7629	1	Deere, Joseph	22	M	F		Ben Deere	L	Cr	Orey Deere	D	Cr
7630	2	Deere, Lewis	18	M	F	Nro	Ben Deere	L	Cr	Orey Deere	D	Cr
7631	3	Deere, Henry	15	M	F	Bro	Ben Deere	L	Cr	Orey Derre	D	Cr
		Census Card No. 2561, P. O. Checotah, Enrolled May 20, 1901										
7632	1	Carr, Willie	25	M	F		Timbo Carr	L	Cr	Sallie Carr	L	Cr
		Census Card No. 2562, P. O. Drumright, Enrolled May 20, 1901										
7633	1	London, Ellen	13	F	½		Cusseta Micco	D	Cr	Dosha London	L	Non
7634	2	London, Ollie	11	F	½	Sis	Cusseta Micco	D	Cr	Dosha London	L	Non
		Census Card No. 2563, P. O. Onapa, Enrolled May 20, 1901										
7635	1	London, Lewis	20	M	F		Washington, Benton	D	Cr	Sally Major	L	Cr
		Census Card No. 2564, P. O. Tulsa, Enrolled May 20, 1901										
7636	1	Jones, Nancy	18	F	F		David Jones	D	Cr	Susie Eufaula	D	Cr
		Census Card No. 2565, P. O. Wenoka, Enrolled May 20, 1901										
7637	1	Joseph, Kittie	35	F	F		Echo Emarthla	L	Cr	Lidda	D	Cr
7638	2	Sam, Kizzie	14	F	F	D	Sammoche	L	Sem	No. 1	L	Cr

160

Roll No.	No.	NAME	Age	Sex	Blood	Rel.	NAME OF FATHER	Liv.	Cit.	NAME OF MOTHER	Liv.	Cit.
		Census Card No. 2566, P. O. Brush Hill, Enrolled May 20, 1901										
7639	1	Wistochee	70	F	F		Pascover	D	Cr	Unknown	D	Cr
		No. 1 died January 1, 1904										
		ensus Card No. 2567, P. O. Lamar, Enrolled May 20, 1901										
7640	1	Bruner, Taylor	26	M	F		Siah Bruner	L	Cr	Kogee	L	Cr
7641	2	Bruner, Nancy	28	F	F	Wf	Ogee Harjo	D	Cr	Louina	D	Cr
7642	3	Cowe, Annie	15	F	F	StS	Major Cowe	D	Cr	No. 2	L	Cr
7643	4	Cowe, Samuel	10	M	F	StS	Major Cowe	D	Cr	No. 2	L	Cr
7644	5	Bruner, Joe	4	M	F	S	No. 1	L	Cr	No. 2	L	Cr
7645	6	Bruner, nnie	1	F	F	D	No. 1	L	Cr	No. 2	L	Cr
		NoA5 died September 23, 1902. No. 4 died February 20, 1910. No. 1 died October 19, 1914.										
		Census Card No. 2568, P. O. Wetumka, Enrolled May 20, 1901										
7646	1	King, Kogee	65	F	F		Cowetochee	D	Cr	Arshotopehe	D	Cr
		No. 1 died February 6, 1910										
		Census Card No. 2569, P. O. Wetumka, Enrolled May 20, 1901										
7647	1	Washington, Liza	75	F	F		Unknown	D	Cr	Unknown	D	Cr
		No. 1 died December 22, 1905										
		Census Card No. 2570, P. O. Sasakwa, Enrolled May 21, 1901										
7648	1	Shicar	15	M	F		Carchee Emarthla	L	Sem	Yarna	D	Cr
7649	2	William	13	M	F	Bro	Carchee Emarthla	L	Sem	Yarna	D	Cr
		Census Card No. 2571, P. O. Salem, Enrolled May 21, 1901										
7650	1	Harjo, Hillis	30	M	F		Artus Yahola	D	Cr	Halthmia	D	Cr
7651	2	Harjo, Mary	30	F	F	Wf	Emarthla	D	Cr	Sinkiyah	D	Cr
7652	3	Harjo, George	6	M	F	S	No. 1	L	Cr	Seyokee	L	Cr
7653	4	Harjo, Willie	17	M	F	S	No. 1	L	Cr	Seyokee	L	Cr
7654	5	Harjo, Louisa	14	F	F	D	No. 1	L	Cr	Seyokee	L	Cr
7655	6	Harjo, Poley	10	F	F	D	No. 1	L	Cr	Seyokee	L	Cr
7656	7	Harjo, Malinda	7	F	F	D	No. 1	L	Cr	Seyokee	L	Cr
7657	8	Tiger, Albert	9	M	F	SS	Cartogee Tiger	D	Cr	No. 2	L	Cr
		No. 1 died April 1909. No. 8 died November 7, 1910. No. 4 died 1910. No. 6 died 1913. No. 3 died April 27, 1900										
		Census Card No. 2572, P. O. Weleetka, Enrolled May 21, 1901										
7658	1	Marye. Hothle	70	F	F		Unknown	D	Cr	Unknown	D	Cr
		No. 1 died May 1910										
		Census Card No. 2573, P. O. Dustin, Enrolled May 21, 1901										
7659	1	Watson, Santy	25	F	3/8		David C. Watson	D	Cr	Sallie Watson	L	Cr
		Census Card No. 2574, P. O. Dustin, Enrolled May 21, 1901										
7660	1	Watson, Sallie	63	F	1/2		Green Anderson	D	Non	Eliza Anderson	D	Cr
7661	2	Scott, Matilda	8	F	1/8	Ward	Turner Scott	L	Cr	Emma Scott	L	Cr
7662	3	Scott, Minnie	6	F	1/8	Ward	Turner Scott	L	Cr	Emma Scott	L	Cr
7663	4	Watson, David C.	57	M	1/2	Hus	Daniel G. Watson	D	Non	Fannie Watson	D	Cr
		No. 4 died March 6, 1900										
		Census Card No. 2575, P. O. Pierce, Enrolled May 21, 1901										
7664	1	Richard, Eastman	37	M	F		Sam Richard	L	Cr	Rina McIntosh	D	Cr
7665	2	Richard, Yarna	25	F	F	Wf	Timothy	D	Cr	Wistocho	L	Cr
7666	3	Richard, Jennetta	8	F	F	D	No. 1	L	Cr	No. 2	L	Cr
7667	4	Richard, Jemima	6	F	F	D	No. 1	L	Cr	No. 2	L	Cr
7668	5	Richard, Samuel	3	M	F	S	No. 1	L	Cr	No. 2	L	Cr
		No. 2 died September 1, 1910. No. 4 died September 26, 1910.										
		Census Card No. 2576, P. O. Wetumka, Enrolled May 21, 1901										
7669	1	Se-yo-ke	35	F	F		Hene Hoge	D	Cr	Hettie	L	Cr
		No. 1 died April 29, 1900										
		Census Card No. 2577, P. O. Dustin, Enrolled May 21, 1901										
7670	1	Benson, James	44	M	1/8		Josiah Benson	D	Cr	Sallie Watson	L	Cr
7671	2	Benson, Silpie	28	F	F	Wf	Parbose Harjo	D	Cr	Sarwalagee	D	Cr
7672	3	Benson, Annie	15	F	5/8	D	No. 1	L	Cr	No. 2	L	Cr
7673	4	Benson, Waley	13	M	5/8	S	No. 1	L	Cr	No. 2	L	Cr
7674	5	Benson, Sallie	7	F	5/8	D	No. 1	L	Cr	No. 2	L	Cr
7675	6	Benson, Katie	5	F	5/8	D	No. 1	L	Cr	No. 2	L	Cr
		No. 1 died September 14, 1904. No. 4 died December 1909. No. 2 died January 30, 1907										
		Census Card No. 2578, P. O. Senora, Enrolled May 21, 1901										
7676	1	Sin-ki-ye	55	F	F		Aholle Emarthla	D	Cr	Unknown	D	Cr
		No. 1 died August 29, 1899										
		Census Card No. 2579, P. O. Hanna, Enrolled May 21, 1901										
7677	1	Hawkins, Turner	21	M	7/8		Ben Hawkins	D	Cr	Jennie Hawkins	D	Cr
		Census Card No. 2580, P. O. Hanna, Enrolled May 21, 1901										
7678	1	Hawkins, Mack	14	M	F		Ben Hawkins	D	Cr	Teehchee	D	Cr
		Census Card No. 2581, P. O. Pierce, Enrolled May 21, 1901										
7679	1	Matoy, Lydia	65	F	F		Pascover	D	Cr	Unknown	D	Cr
		Census Card No. 2582, P. O. Dustin, Enrolled May 21, 1901										
7680	1	Brown, Josiah	23	M	1/4		Alex Brown	D	Sem	Annie Brown	D	Cr
7681	2	Brown, Lizzie	19	F	3/4	Wf	William Charles	D	Cr	Polly Watson	D	Cr
7682	3	Brown, Katie	1	F	1/2	S	No. 1	L	Cr	No. 2	L	Cr
7683	4	Wiley, Moses	15	M	3/4	B-L	Willie Cuntullie	D	Cr	Polly Watson	D	Cr
		No. 2 died March 17, 1912										
		Census Card No. 2583, P. O. Stidham, Enrolled May 21, 1901										
7684	1	Timothy, Taylor	23	M	F		Timothy	D	Cr	Wistoche	L	Cr

161

Roll No.	No.	NAME	Age	Sex	Blood	Rel.	NAME OF FATHER	Liv.	Cit.	NAME OF MOTHER	Liv.	Cit.
		Census Card No. 2584, P. O. Pierce, Enrolled May 21 1901										
7685	1	Timothy, John	40	M	F		Timothy	D	Cr	Wistoche	L	Cr
7686	2	Timothy, Ella	28	F	F	Wf	Heneha Micco	D	Cr	Cinda Micco	D	Cr
7687	3	Timothy, Turner	12	M	F	S	No. 1	L	Cr	Mollie Timothy	D	Cr
7688	4	Timothy, Warsey	11	M	F	S	No. 1	L	Cr	Mollie Timothy	D	Cr
		No. 3 died February 1900. No. 4 died September 1904										
		Census Card No. 2585, P. O. Dustin, Enrolled May 21, 1901										
7689	1	Field, Ablow		M	F		Tusekiah Harjo	D	Cr	Oyekitche	D	Cr
7690	2	Field, Lydia	17	F	F	D	No. 1	L	Cr	Ayumker	D	Cr
7691	3	Field, Walter	15	M	F	S	No. 1	L	Cr	Ayumker	D	Cr
7692	4	Field, John	11	M	F	S	No. 1	L	Cr	Ayumker	D	Cr
		No. 1 reported dead										
		Census Card No. 2586—(Void)—										
7693	1	Stricken from roll										
		Census Card No. 2587, P. O. Hanna, May 21, 1901										
7694	1	Green, Absey	35	F	Full		Tusekiah Harjo	D	Cr	Oyekitche	D	Cr
7695	2	Stephenson, Nancy	20	F	F	D	Buzzard	D	Cr	No. 1	L	Cr
		No. 1 died February 1906										
		Census Card No. 2588, P. O. Tullahassee, Enrolled May 21, 1901										
7696	1	Myers, Sallie	23	F	½		Joe Bruner	L	Cr	Hebsey Jamison	L	Cr
		Census Card No. 2589, P. O. Stone Bluff, Enrolled May 21, 1901										
7697	1	Schrimsher, Geo.	60	M	F		Unknown	D	Cr	Unknown	D	Cr
		No. 1 died 1901										
		Census Card No. 2590, P. O. Stone Bluff, Enrolled May 21, 1901										
7698	1	Hulputta, Thomas	50	M	F		Hulpatta Micco	D	Cr	Unknown	D	Cr
		No. 1 died December 21, 1908										
		Census Card No. 2591, P. O. Holdenville, Enrolled May 21, 1901										
7699	1	Wallow, Sallie	48	F	F		Mekko Hutka	D	Cr	Kanpehoke	D	Cr
7700	2	Wallow, Nellie	19	F	F	D	Wiley Wallow	D	Cr	No. 1	L	Cr
7701	3	Wallow, Simmer	15	M	F	S	Wiley Wallow	D	Cr	No. 1	L	Cr
7702	4	Wallow, Peter	17	M	F	S	Wiley Wallow	D	Cr	No. 1	L	Cr
7703	5	Anderson, Timmie	3	M	F	GrS	Wm. Anderson	L	Cr	No. 2	L	Cr
		No. 1 died February 6, 1907. No. 3 died March 8, 1909										
		Census Card No. 2592, P. O. Holdenville, Enrolled May 21, 1901										
7704	1	Bruner, Hannah	18	F	F		Robert Bruner	D	Cr	Mary Bruner	D	Cr
7705	2	Bruner, Louis	12	M	F	Bro	Robert Bruner	D	Cr	Mary Bruner	D	Cr
7706	3	Bruner, Mary	1	F	½	D	Scipio	L	Sem	No. 1	L	Cr
		Census Card No. 2593, P. O. Sasakwa; No. 4 Holdenville, Enrolled May 21, 1901										
7707	1	Factor, Youthlechee	53	F	F		Tommy Harjo	D	Cr	Unknown	D	Cr
7708	2	Factor, Sissie	19	F	F	D	Joe Factor	D	Sem	No. 1	L	Cr
7709	3	Factor, John	17	M	F	S	Joe Factor	D	Sem	No. 1	L	Cr
7710	4	Factor, Lillie	13	F	F	D	Joe Factor	D	Sem	No. 1	L	Cr
		No. 1 died March 27, 1900. No. 2 died May 17, 1909										
		Census Card No. 2594, P. O. Holdenville, Enrolled May 21, 1901										
7711	1	Tiger, Cinda	28	F	½		Joe Factor	D	Sem	Yonthligee Factor	L	Cr
7712	2	Tiger, Louis	4	M	¼	D	John Tiger	L	Cr	No. 1	L	Cr
		No. 2 died September 12, 1900										
		Census Card No. 2595, P. O. Sasakwa, Enrolled May 21, 1901										
7713	1	Factor, Fannie	23	F	F		Joe Factor	D	Sem	Yarthleche Factor	L	Cr
7714	2	Chupko, Major	1	M	¼	S	Watty Chupko	L	Sem	No. 1	L	Cr
		Census Card No. 2596, P. O. Okmulgee, Enrolled May 21, 1901										
7715	1	White, George	60	M	F		Unknown	D	Cr	Unknown	D	Cr
		No. 1 died January 7, 1900										
		Census Card No. 2597, P. O. Sasakwa, Enrolled May 21, 1901										
7716	1	Factor, Billy	21	M	½		Joe Factor	D	Sem	Yartheche Factor	L	Cr
		No. 1 died May 12, 1901										
		Census Card No. 2598, P. O. Holdenville; No. 2 Boley, Enrolled May 21, 1901										
7717	1	Perryman, Legus	21	M	F		Anoche	D	Cr	Nannie Rabbit	D	Cr
7718	2	Caesar, Sissie	13	F	F	Sis	Ceasar	D	Cr	Nannie Rabbit	D	Cr
		No. 1 died January 22, 1912. No. 2 probably duplicate of Enrollment No. 8895 this roll										
		Census Card No. 2599, P. O. Salem, Enrolled May 21, 1901										
7719	1	Jones, Lizzie	38	F	F		Arbarlock Harjo	L	Cr	Fannie	?	Cr
7720	2	Bear, Lewis	15	M	F	Neph	Nocosse	D	Cr	Parcinda	D	Cr
		No. 1 died 1905										
		Census Card No. 2600, P. O. Pierce, Enrolled May 21, 1901										
7721	1	Jones, Mollie	45	F	F		Arharlock Harjo	L	Cr	Fannie	D	Cr
		Census Card No. 2601, P. O. Wewoka, Enrolled May 21, 1901										
7722	1	Palmer, Malinda	55	F	F		Palmer	D	Cr	Lucy Palmer	D	Cr
		No. 1 died March 29, 1910										
		Census Card No. 2602, P. O. Pierce, Enrolled May 22, 1901										
7723	1	Thompson, Lizzie	20	F	F		DeSota Thompson	D	Cr	Nancy Thompson	D.	Cr
7724	2	McIntosh, Tokka	2	F	F	D	John McIntosh	L	Cr	No. 1	D	Cr
		No. 1 died March 16, 1907										
		Census Card No. 2603, P. O. Wetumka, Enrolled May 23, 1901										
7725	1	Ahulec	55	M	F		Tasekia Micco	D	Cr	Tharstanna	D	Cr
		No. 1 died August 1900										
		Census Card No. 2604, P. O. Dustin, Enrolled May 22, 1901										
7726	1	Kinha, Chotkey	18	F	F		Willie Kinha	D	Cr	Cinda Kinha	D	Cr
		Census Card No. 2605, P. O. Wetumka, Enrolled May 22, 1901										
7727	1	Green, Hagie	24	M	F		Tuskona	D	Cr	Lundgee	D	Cr

162

Roll No.	No.	NAME	Age	Sex	Blood	Rel.	NAME OF FATHER	Liv.	Cit.	NAME OF MOTHER	Liv.	Cit
		Census Card No. 2606, P. O. Pierce, Enrolled May 22, 1901										
7728	1	Thompson, Caesar	25	M	F		DeSota Thompson	D	Cr	Nancy Thompson	D	Cr
7729	2	Thompson, Melinda	25	F	F	Wf	Willie Kinher	D	Cr	Losie	D	Cr
7730	3	Thompson, Leah	9	F	F	D	No. 1	L	Cr	No. 2	L	Cr
		No. 1 died February 17, 1901										
		Census Card No. 2607, P. O. Eufaula; No. 4 Wetumka, Enrolled May 22, 1901										
7731	1	"War-co-che"	60	M	F		Semetee	D	Cr	Tema Walufhogee	D	Cr
7732	2	Temahee	50	F	F	Wf	Unknown	D	Cr	Unknown	D	Cr
7733	3	Sucky	18	F	F	D	No. 1	L	Cr	Eliza	D	Cr
7734	4	Hettie	23	F	F	D	No. 1	L	Cr	Eliza	D	Cr
		No. 1 died October 1905										
		Census Card No. 2608, P. O. Pierce, Enrolled May 22, 1901										
7735	1	Blackgrass, Wisey	27	F	F		Willie Kinher	D	Cr	Losie	D	Cr
		No. 1 died March 11, 1901										
		Census Card No. 2609, P. O. Wetumka, Enrolled May 22, 1901										
7736	1	Lakey, Mollie	18	F	F		Alec Bruner	D	Cr	Silla	D	Cr
		No. 1 died October 1900										
		Census Card No. 2610, P. O. Wetumka, Enrolled May 22, 1901										
7737	1	Harjo, Kussie	22	M	F		Thlocco Harjo	?	Cr	Tibbie	D	Cr
		Census Card No. 2611, P. O. Okemah, Enrolled May 22, 1901										
7738	1	Yahola, Mollie	25	F	F		Tulla	D	Cr	Unknown	D	Cr
7739	2	Fat, Bettie	3	F	F	D	Sam Mitchell	L	Cr	No. 1	L	Cr
		No. 1 died 1910										
		Census Card No. 2612, P. O. Wetumka, Enrolled May 22, 1901										
7740	1	Harjo, Lucy	17	F	F		Thlocco Harjo	?	Cr	Liddy	D	Cr
		No. 1 died 1904										
		Census Card No. 2613, P. O. Carson, Enrolled May 22, 1901										
7741	1	Mitchell, Sam	40	M	F		Sowanoke Harjo	D	Cr	Cathumka	D	Cr
		Census Card No. 2614, P. O. Wetumka, Enrolled May 22, 1901										
7742	1	Fish, Weleya	29	M	F		Thlocco Harjo	?	Cr	Mihege	D	Cr
7743	2	Fish, Nellie	28	F	F	Wf	Suatala	D	Cr	Tiddy	D	Cr
7744	3	Fish, Willie	10	M	F	S	No. 1	L	Cr	No. 2	L	Cr
7745	4	Fish, Daniel	6	M	F	S	No. 1	L	Cr	No. 2	L	Cr
7746	5	Fish, Jackson	2	M	F	S	No. 1	L	Cr	No. 2	L	Cr
		Census Card No. 2615, P. O. Wetumka, Enrolled May 22 1901										
7747	1	Fixeco, Betsey	60	F	F		Unknown	D	Cr	Cathumka	D	Cr
7748	2	Emarthla, Tom	43	M	F	S	Pin Harjo	D	Cr	No. 1	L	Cr
		No. 2 died August 13, 1900. No. 1 died March 15, 1909										
		Census Card No. 2616, P. O. Hanna, Enrolled May 22, 1901										
7749	1	Solomon, Roley	17	M	F		Solomon	D	Cr	Missie Harjo	D	Cr
		Census Card No. 2617, P. O. Okemah, Enrolled May 22, 1901										
7750	1	Te-yo-bee	50	F	F		Unknown	D	Cr	Unknown	D	Cr
		No. 1 died April 1, 1899										
		Census Card No. 2618, P. O. Weleetka, Enrolled May 22, 1901										
7751	1	Yahola, Lena	14	F	F		Soda	D	Cr	Pidgie	D	Cr
		Census Card No. 2619, P. O. Raiford, Enrolled May 22, 1901										
7752	1	Roberts, Mahola	23	F	F		Cooweescoowee Emoutla	D	Cr	Sussanah	D	Cr
		Census Card No. 2620, P. O. Mellette, Enrolled May 22, 1901										
7753	1	Roberts, Noah	28	M	F		Cooweescoowee Emarthla	D	Cr	Susannah	D	Cr
7754	2	Roberts, Hannah Tyler	20	F	F	D	Abjola	D	Cr	Unknown	D	Cr
		Census Card No. 2621, P. O. Indianola, Enrolled May 22, 1901										
7755	1	Fish, Okchie	60	M	F		Thotho Harjoche	D	Cr	Itchke	D	Cr
		No. 1 died February 5, 1902										
		Census Card No. 2622—(Void)										
7756	1	Stricken from roll										
		Census Card No. 2623, P. O. Coweta, Enrolled May 22, 1901										
7757	1	McKellop, Betsey	25	F	F		Emarthlogee	D	Cr	Jennie Berryhill	L	Cr
7758	2	Scott, Alex	6	M	F	S	George Scott	L	Cr	No. 1	L	Cr
		Census Card No. 2624, P. O. Indianola, Enrolled May 23, 1901										
7759	1	Sa-he-pah-ke	60	F	F		Unknown	D	Cr	Unknown	D	Cr
		Census Card No. 2625, P. O. Indianola, Enrolled May 22, 1901										
7760	1	Emarthla, Micco	45	M	F		Unknown	D	Cr	Slunche	D	Cr
7761	2	Emarthla, Sallie	24	F	F	Wf	Charlie Sullivan	D	Cr	Sahepahke	L	Cr
		Census Card No. 2626, P. O. Bristow, Enrolled May 26, 1901										
7762	1	Cah-tah-won	30	M	F		Sahconcahny	D	Cr	Tesaugauny	D	Cr
		Census Card No. 2627, P. O. Burney, Enrolled May 23, 1901										
7763	1	Coffee, John	40	M	F		Falloppo Harjo	D	Cr	Aggie	D	Cr
		No. 1 died December 1900										
		Census Card No. 2628, P. O. McAlester, Enrolled May 22, 1901										
7764	1	Wadsworth, Lussie	25	F	F		Hallok, Harjoche	D	Cr	Sunthlupehcher	D	Cr
		No. 1 died December 24, 1910										
		Census Card No. 2629, P. O. Indianola, Enrolled May 22, 1901										
7765	1	Tiger, Hannah	28	F	F		Thomas Tiger	D	Cr	Sinlatka	D	Cr
		Census Card No. 2630, P. O. Senora, Enrolled May 23, 1901										
7766	1	Starr, Sallie	22	F	F		Martin Starr	D	Cr	Arpincinlike	L	Cr
		No. 1 died January 31, 1904										
		Census Card No. 2631, P. O. Calvin, Enrolled May 23, 1901										
7767	1	Herrod, Liza	32	F	F		Tulwa Harjo	D	Sem	Unknown	D	Cr
7768	2	Herrod, Nettie	11	F	F	D	David Herrod	L	Cr	No. 1	L	Cr
7769	3	Herrod, Lena	10	F	F	D	David Herrod	L	Cr	No. 1	L	Cr

Roll No.	No.	NAME	Age	Sex	Blood	Rel.	NAME OF FATHER	Liv.	Cit.	NAME OF MOTHER	Liv.	Cit.
		Census Card No. 2632, P. O. Wetumka, Enrolled May 22, 1901										
7770	1	Brooks, Joe	28	M	F		George Brooks	L	Cr	Sine Bear	L	Cr
7771	2	Brooks, Annie	29	F	F	Wf	Neha Yahola	D	Cr	Nettie	L	Cr
7772	3	Brooks, Emma	10	F	F	D	No. 1	L	Cr	Louisa Brooks	D	Cr
		No. 3 died November 1899										
		Census Card No. 2633, P. O. Choska, Enrolled May 22, 1901										
7773	1	Gooch, Ed	23	M	½		Jesse Gooch	L	Non	Toebie Gooch	D	Cr
7774	2	Gooch, Dollie	2	F	¼	D	No. 1	L	Cr	Adella Gooch	D	Cr
		No. 2 died November 6, 1900										
		Census Card No. 2634. P. O. Creek, Enrolled May 22, 1901										
7775	1	Gooch, Arthur	21	M	½		Jesse Gooch	L	Non	Toebie Gooch	D	Cr
		Census Card No. 2635, P. O. Eufaula, Enrolled May 22, 1901										
7776	1	Washington, Kogee	10	F	F		George Washington	L	Cr	Roda	D	Cr
7777	2	Washington, Minnie	8	F	F	Sis	George Washington	L	Cr	Roda	D	Cr
		No. 2 reported dead										
		Census Card No. 2636, P. O. Wetumka, Enrolled May 22, 1901										
7778	1	Lucinda	30	F	F		Tustenugge	D	Cr	Monecha	D	Cr
		Census Card No. 2637, P. O. Wetumka, Enrolled May 22, 1901										
7779	1	Jack, Nero	50	M	F		Apallo Harjo	D	Cr	Molloche	D	Cr
		Census Card No. 2638, P. O. Weleetka, Enrolled May 22, 1901										
7780	1	Fife, Narhela	40	F	F		Unknown	D	Cr	Tebiye	D	Cr
		Census Card No. 2639, P. O. Dustin, Enrolled May 22, 1901										
7781	1	McQueen, Willie	25	M	F		David McQueen	D	Cr	Unknown	D	Cr
		Census Card No. 2640, P. O. Wetumka, Enrolled May 22, 1901										
7782	1	Brimer, Wilbert	12	M	F		George Brimer	D	Cr	Susan Litker	D	Cr
		Reported duplicate of Enrollment No. 7582 on Census Card No. 2539										
		Census Card No. 2641, P. O. Holdenville, Enrolled May 22, 1901										
7783	1	Davis, Dochee	28	F	F		Unknown	D	Cr	Unknown	D	Cr
		No. 1 died January 14, 1901										
		Census Card No. 2642, P. O. Arbeka, Enrolled May 22, 1901										
7784	1	Selina	25	F	F		Nocus Holotka	L	Cr	Arlinda	D	Cr
		No. 1 Died April 1899										
		Census Card No. 2643, P. O. Okemah, Enrolled May 22, 1901; No. 2 May 23, 1901										
7785	1	Conner, Adam	35	M	F		Conner	D	Cr	Mehoka	D	Cr
7786	2	Conner, Lucy	45	F	F	Wf	Unknown	D	Cr	Cinda	L	Cr
		No. 1 died January 9, 1900. No. 2 died June 27, 1900										
		Census Card No. 2644, P. O. Arbeka, Enrolled May 22, 1901										
7787	1	Larney, Martha	50	F	F		Unknown	D	Cr	Unknown	D	Cr
		No. 1 died about 1899										
		Census Card No. 2645, P. O. Senora, Enrolled May 23, 1901										
7788	1	Tyler, Cinda	70	F	F		Katch Yahola	D	Cr	Luddy Jache	D	Cr
7789	2	Tyler, Lucy	20	F	F	D	John Tyler	L	Cr	No. 1	L	Cr
		No. 1 died 1903. No. 2 died April 29, 1912										
		Census Card No. 2646, P. O. Bryant, Enrolled May 22, 1901										
7790	1	Yahola, Tulmas	60	M	F		Hotulke Fixico	D	Cr	Unknown	D	Cr
		Census Card No. 2647, P. O. Oktaha, Enrolled May 22, 1901										
7791	1	Simmons, Charley	45	M	F		Simmer	D	Cr	Simhoye	D	Cr
7792	2	Simmons, Jennie	43	F	F	Wf	Huethihche	D	Cr	Lizzie	D	Cr
7793	3	Simmons, Annie	14	F	F	D	No. 1	L	Cr	No. 2	L	Cr
7794	4	Simmons, Lona	25	M	F	S	No. 1	L	Cr	No. 2	L	Cr
		No. 2 died January 19, 1901. No. 4 died April 11, 1901. Nos. 1 and 3 probably duplicates of Nos.										
		20835 and 20836 Cherokee Indian Roll										
		Census Card No. 2648, P. O. Hanna, Enrolled May 22, 1901										
7795	1	"Wilumpka"	50	M	F		Madowa Harjo	D	Cr	Mowelagee	D	Cr
7796	2	Williams, Sinthe	30	F	F	Wf	Effie Harjo	L	Cr	Tuckharkee	D	Cr
7797	3	Williams, Lucy	14	F	F	D	No. 1	L	Cr	No. 2	L	Cr
7798	4	Williams, Taner	6	F	F	D	No. 1	L	Cr	No. 2	L	Cr
		No. 1 reported dead										
		Census Card No. 2649, P. O. Holdenville, Enrolled May 22, 1901										
7799	1	Fish, Wattie	30	M	F		Eli Fish	D	Cr	Follker	D	Cr
		No. 1 died June 14, 1907										
		Census Card No. 2650, P. O. Senora, Enrolled May 23, 1901										
7800	1	Tyler, Kate	25	F	F		Tyler	D	Cr	Yonkogee	D	Cr
		No. 1 died November 12, 1903										
		Census Card No. 2651, P. O. Oktaha, Enrolled May 22, 1901										
7801	1	Hopsey	25	F	F		Charmosey	D	Cr	Nellie Gooden	D	Cr
		Census Card No. 2652, P. O. Wetumka, Enrolled May 23, 1901										
7802	1	Harjo, Cono	30	M	F		Simbalily	D	Cr	Janie	D	Cr
		No. 1 died February 28, 1906										
		Census Card No. 2653, P. O. Wetumka, Enrolled May 23, 1901										
7803	1	Harjo, Yahola	25	M	F		Simbalily	D	Cr	Janie	D	Cr
7804	2	Harjo, Lucy	25	F	F	Wf	Hulberta Harjo	D	Cr	Susie	L	Cr
7805	3	Harjo, James Larney	3	M	F	S	No. 1	L	Cr	No. 2	L	Cr
		No. 3 died August 22, 1899. No. 2 died November 22, 1910										
		Census Card No. 2654, P. O. Senora, Enrolled May 23, 1901										
7806	1	Micco, Yahola	50	M	F		Unknown	D	Cr	Unknown	D	Cr
		No. 1 died January 4, 1904										
		Census Card No. 2655, P. O. Salem, Enrolled May 26, q90q										
7807	1	Thomas, Bettie	30	F	F		Tullamassie	?	Cr	Fokolodaga	D	Cr
7808	2	Green, Simpson	11	M	F	S	Unknown	L	Cr	No. 1	L	Cr
		No. 2 died March 1911										

164

Roll No.	No.	NAME	Age	Sex	Blood	Rel.	Name of Father	Liv.	Cit.	Name of Mother	Liv.	Cit.
		Census Card No. 2656, P. O. Salem, Enrolled May 23, 1901										
7809	1	Green, Caesar	23	M	F		Osee Yahola	D	Cr	Nellie	D	Cr
7810	2	Green, Mary	24	F	F	Wf	Tullamassie	?	Cr	Foklodaga	D	Cr
		No. 2 died November 22, 1903										
		Census Card No. 2657, P. O. Preston, Enrolled May 23, 1901										
7811	1	Talomase, Dickey	20	M	F		Tullamassie	?	Cr	Foklodaga	D	Cr
7812	2	Talomase, Eliza	24	F	F	Wf	Osee Yahola	D	Cr	Nellie	D	Cr
		No. 2 died March 1907										
		Census Card No. 2658, P. O. Henryetta, Enrolled May 23, 1901										
7813	1	Louisiana	26	F	F		Peter Chupco	L	Sem	Watsey	D	Cr
		Census Card No. 2659, P. O. Wewoka, Enrolled May 23, 1901										
7814	1	Lydia	18	F	F		Peter Chupco	L	Sem	Watsey	D	Cr
		No. 1 died March 24, 1904										
		Census Card No. 2660, P. O. Indianola, Enrolled May 22, 1901										
7815	1	Proctor, Kelly	45	M	F		Osoch Harjo	D	Cr	Temohtber	D	Cr
		Census Card No. 2661, P. O. Hanna, Enrolled May 22, 1901										
7816	1	Harjo, Okfuske	45	M	F		Artaryochee Yarhola	D	Cr	Potogigee	D	Cr
		Census Card No. 2662, P. O. Hanna, Enrolled May 23, 1901										
7817	1	Sunday, Mattie	11	F	½		Ellis Sunday	D	Cr	Mollie Sunday	D	Cr
		Census Card No. 2663, P. O. Lenna, Enrolled May 22, 1901										
7818	1	Jones, Levina	40	F	F		Talop Harjo	D	Cr	Narne	D	Cr
7819	2	Jones, Sulloly	25	M	F	S	Hogie Jones	L	Cr	No. 1	L	Cr
7820	3	Jones, Annie	20	F	F	D	Hogie Jones	L	Cr	No. 1	L	Cr
7821	4	Jones, George	15	M	F	S	Hogie Jones	L	Cr	No. 1	L	Cr
7822	5	Jones, William	12	M	F	S	Hogie Jones	L	Cr	No. 1	L	Cr
7823	6	Jones, Nellie	10	F	F	D	Hogie Jones	L	Cr	No. 1	L	Cr
		No. 1 died Spring time 1901. No. 3 died March 30, 1908. No. 6 died October 22, 1912.										
		Census Card No. 2664, P. O. Muskogee, Enrolled May 22, 1901										
7824	1	Sar-ye-che	27	F	½		Dan Keller	D	Cr	Jane Lewis	D	Cr
		No. 1 died May 6 1899										
		Census Card No. 2665, P. O. Hanna, Enrolled May 22, 1901										
7825	1	Beaver, Barney	25	M	F		Itshas Harjo	L	Cr	Houston	D	Cr
		Census Card No. 2666, P. O. Hanna, Enrolled May 22. 1901										
7826	1	Bruner, John	45	M	F		Biker Bruner	D	Cr	Lowina Bruner	D	Cr
7827	2	Bruner, Sallie	31	F	F	Wf	Tom Carr	D	Cr	Masehya	D	Cr
		No. 1 died January 8, 1910										
		Census Card No. 2667, P. O. Hanna, Enrolled May 22, 1901										
7828	1	Proctor, Harry	28	M	F		Louis Proctor	D	Cr	Annie	D	Cr
		Census Card No. 2668, P. O. Hanna, Enrolled May 22, 1901										
7829	1	Simmons, Charley	28	M	F		Unknown	D	Cr	Houston	D	Cr
7830	2	Simmons, Dochee	22	F	F	Wf	Wm. Lasley	L	Cr	Keselar	D	Cr
		No. 2 died July 29, 1912										
		Census Card No. 2669, P. O. Hanna, Enrolled May 22, 1901										
7831	1	Lasley, Dickey	25	M	F		Wm. Lasley	L	Cr	Keselar	D	Cr
7832	2	Lasley, Thompson	19	M	F	Bro	Wm. Lasley	L	Cr	Keselar	D	Cr
7833	3	Lasley, Sukey	15	F	F	Sis	Wm. Lasley	L	Cr	Keselar	D	Cr
		No. 2 died July 1907										
		Census Card No. 2670, P. O. Hanna, Enrolled May 22, 1901										
7834	1	Foley, Eliza	40	F	F		Unknown	D	Cr	Unknown	D	Cr
7835	2	Foley, Kizzie	18	F	F	D	Idas Hounbee	D	Cr	No. 1	L	Cr
7836	3	Foley, Taylor	17	M	F	S	Idas Hounbee	D	Cr	No. 1	L	Cr
		No. 1 died January 1900										
		Census Card No. 2671, P. O. Senora, Enrolled May 22, 1901										
7837	1	Polk, Silla	25	F	F		Osar Harjo	D	Cr	Lunchey	D	Cr
		No. 1 died February 1901										
		Census Card No. 2672, P. O. Hanna, Enrolled May 22, 1901										
7838	1	Byrd, Nellie	25	F	F		Jim Bird	D	Cr	Dudie Bird	D	Cr
		Census Card No. 2673, P. O. Hanna, Enrolled May 22, 1901										
7839	1	Hutkey, Missie	60	F	F		Ruth Yahola	D	Cr	Unknown	D	Cr
		No. 1 died December 31, 1903										
		Census Card No. 2674, P. O. Dustin, Enrolled May 22, 1901										
7840	1	Fixeco, Katcha	35	M	F		Hillabee Harjo	D	Cr	Missie Hutkey	L	Cr
		No. 1 died November 14, 1908										
		Census Card No. 2675, P. O. Hanna, Enrolled May 24, 1901										
7841	1	Proctor, David	26	M	F		Tulsa Harjo	L	Cr	No. 2	L	Cr
7842	2	Proctor, Manda	45	F	F	Moth	Unknown	D	Cr	Louisa	D	Cr
		No. 2 died February 15, 1906										
		Census Card No. 2676, P. O. Henryetta, Enrolled May 23, 1901										
7843	1	Colbert, Daniel	23	M	F		Dick Colbert	D	Cr	Unknown	D	Cr
7844	2	Colbert, Lucy	23	F	F	Wf	Peter Chupco	L	Sem	Watsey	D	Cr
		Census Card No. 2677, P. O. Henryetta, Enrolled May 23, 1901										
7845	1	Chupco, Dinah	6	F	F		Peter Chupco	L	Sem	Watsey	D	Cr
		No. 1 died November 7, 1901										
		Census Card No. 2678, P. O. Indianola, Enrolled May 23, 1901										
7846	1	Yargee, Monday	20	F	F		Stephen	D	Cr	Susie Yargee	D	Cr
		No. 1 died 1904										

Census Card No. 2679, P. O. Wetumka, Enrolled May 22, 1901

Roll No.	No.	NAME	Age	Sex	Blood	Rel.	NAME OF FATHER	Liv.	Cit.	NAME OF MOTHER	Liv.	Cit.
7847	1	Yahola, Wiley	30	M	F		Neha Yahola	L	Cr	Sacohokey	D	Cr
7848	2	Yahola, Addie	17	F	F	Wf	Samoche	D	Cr	Saney Harjo	D	Cr

No. 2 died April 4, 1909.

Census Card No. 2680, P. O. Kellyville, Enrolled May 22, 1901

7849	1	Tahkaney	43	M	F		Danbow	D	Cr	Unknown	D	Cr
7850	2	Tahkaney-Tahpanfah	38	F	F	Wf	Youontah	D	Cr	Unknown	D	Cr
7851	3	Tahkaney Marsie	19	F	F	D	No. 1	L	Cr	No. 2	L	Cr
7852	4	Tahkaney, Dillie	15	F	F	D	No. 1	L	Cr	No. 2	L	Cr
7853	5	Tahkaney, Connee	11	M	F	S	No. 1	L	Cr	No. 2	L	Cr

No. 1 died November 1902. No. 5 died December 27, 1911. No. 2 reported dead.

Census Card No. 2681, P. O. Burney, Enrolled May 22, 1901

7854	1	Cuffee, Bunnie	18	M	F		John Coffee	D	Cr	Susie	D	Cr

No. 1 died 1906

Census Card No. 2682, P. O. Paden, May 22, 1901

7855	1	Davis, Sam B.	30	M	F		Unknown	D	Cr	Unknown	D	Cr

Census Card No. 2683, P. O. Holdenville, Enrolled May 22, 1901

7856	1	Gooden, Chauker	35	F	F		David Goodin	D	Cr	Hokte Larney	D	Cr

No. 1 died March 1899

Census Card No. 2684, P. O. Burney, Enrolled May 22, 1901

7857	1	Paine, Eliza	22	F	F		Tecumseh	D	Cr	Lucy	D	Cr

No. 1 died 1908

Census Card No. 2685, P. O. Okmulgee, Enrolled May 23, 1901

7858	1	Barnett, Sukey	20	F	F		Sam Lowe	L	Cr	Mahala	L	Cr

Census Card No. 2686, P. O. Wagoner, Enrolled May 22, 1901

7859	1	Grayson, Ellis	21	M	F		Elliott Grayson	D	Cr	Mary Ann Grayson	D	Cr

No. 1 died February 25, 1900

Census Card No. 2687, P. O. Kellyville, Enrolled May 22, 1901

7860	1	Bucktrot	53	M	F		Unknown	D	Cr	Unknown	D	Cr
7861	2	Bucktrot, Madie (Wydie)	27	F	F	Wf	Unknown	D	Cr	Unknown	D	Cr
7862	3	Bucktrot, Lucy	10	F	F	D	No. 1	L	Cr	Sallie Clinton	L	Cr
7863	4	Bucktrot, Wysena	8	F	F	D	No. 1	L	Cr	No. 2	L	Cr
7864	5	Bucktrot, Sam Green	6	M	F	S	No. 1	L	Cr	No. 2	L	Cr
7865	6	Bucktrot, Conzey	4	F	F	D	No. 1	L	Cr	No. 2	L	Cr
7866	7	Bucktrot, Angee	1	F	F	D	No. 1	L	Cr	No. 2	L	Cr

No. 1 reported dead

Census Card No. 2688, P. O. Hanna, Enrolled May 22, 1901

7867	1	Proctor, Tom	40	M	F		Tulsa Fixico	D	Cr	Arnakke	D	Cr
7868	2	Proctor, Chaeller	38	M	F	Bro	Tulsa Fixico	D	Cr	Arnakke	D	Cr

No. 1 died January 29, 1910

Census Card No. 2689, P. O. Hanna, Enrolled May 22, 1901

7869	1	Manly, Fannie	65	F	F		Funnaske	D	Cr	Unknown	D	Cr
7870	2	Tiger, Nicey	20	F	F	D	Unknown	?	Cr	Fannie	L	Cr

No. 1 died March 1901. No. 2 died April 10, 1900

Census Card No. 2690, P. O. Thurman, Enrolled May 22, 1901

7871	1	Simmons, Moses	45	M	F		Sam Simmer	D	Cr	Unknown	D	Cr
7872	2	Simmons, Lucy	50	F	F	Wf	Fuskatcha Fixico	D	Cr	Hoyoper	D	Cr
7873	3	Simmons, Walter	16	M	F	S	No. 1	L	Cr	No. 2	L	Cr
7874	4	Simmons, Dorsey	14	M	F	S	No. 1	L	Cr	No. 2	L	Cr
7875	5	Simmons, Louisa	12	F	F	D	No. 1	L	Cr	No. 2	L	Cr

No. 1 died February 20, 1901. No. 2 died November 9, 1902. No. 4 died February 25, 1909.
No. 5 died October 3, 1901.

Census Card No. 2691, P. O. Hanna, Enrolled May 22, 1901

7876	1	Byrd, Thomas	27	M	F		Billie Bird	D	Cr	Ada Byrd (or Bird)	D	Cr
7877	2	Byrd, Felix	23	M	F	Bro	Billie Bird	D	Cr	Ada Byrd	D	Cr
7878	3	Byrd, Dudie	25	F	F	Wf	Katcha Micco	L	Cr	Fannie Manley	D	Cr
7879	4	Byrd, Coleman	6	M	F	S	No. 1	L	Cr	No. 3	L	Cr

No. 4 died October 15, 1904. No. 1 reported dead.

Census Card No. 2692, P. O. Dustin, Enrolled May 22, 1901

7880	1	Bruner, Yoapka	59	F	F		Oktootche	D	Cr	Pothoigee	D	Cr
7881	2	Foluthoker	22	F	F	D	Chochat Heneha	L	Cr	No. 1	L	Cr
7882	3	Mesala	8	F	F	GrD	Yahola Fixico	L	Cr	No. 2	L	Cr

No. 1 died February 22, 1908. No. 2 died January 26, 1909.

Census Card No. 2693, P. O. Okemah, Enrolled May 22, 1901

7883	1	Leetcher	40	F	F		Oche Yahola	D	Cr	Sallie Yahola	D	Cr
7884	2	Lucas, Mollie	22	F	F	D	Fushutche Kochukne	D	Cr	No. 1	L	Cr
7885	3	Lucas, Sam	10	M	F	GrS	Tom Lucas	D	Cr	No. 2	L	Cr

No. 1 died February 1901. No. 3 died October 5, 1902.

Census Card No. 2694, P. O. Castle, Enrolled May 22, 1901

7886	1	Anderson, Charles	40	M	F		Unknown	D	Cr	Unknown	D	Cr
7887	2	Tokhahke	45	F	F	Wf	Kartcher Harjo	D	Cr	Simer Hahkee	D	Cr
7888	3	Barnett, William	25	M	F	StS	Wewoka Yohola	D	Cr	No. 2	L	Cr

No. 1 died June 25, 1901. No. 2 died March 25, 1901. No. 3 died July 1904.

Census Card No. 2695, P. O. Hanna, Enrolled May 22, 1901

7889	1	Harjo, Chocka	30	M	F		Pahos Emarthla	D	Cr	Ohhaboye	D	Cr
7890	2	Yunhoye	75	F	F	GrM	Hillis Fixico	D	Cr	Unknown	D	Cr

No. 2 died October 1904

Census Card No. 2696, P. O. Dustin, Enrolled May 22, 1901

7891	1	Amy	20	F	F		Okchun Emarthla	L	Cr	Hoyihche	D	Cr

Roll No.	No.	NAME	Age	Sex	Blood	Rel.	NAME OF FATHER	Liv.	Cit.	NAME OF MOTHER	Liv.	Cit.

Census Card No. 2697, P. O. Dustin, Enrolle May 22, 1901

7892	1	Temunthlahpe, George	40	M	F		Fushatchi Harjo	D	Cr	Unknown	D	Cr
7893	2	Temunthlahpe, Nellie	30	F	F	Wf	Ahaloc Yahola	D	Cr	Ocloosie	D	Cr
7894	3	Temunthlahpe, Tina	9	F	F	D	No. 1	L	Cr	No. 2	D	Cr

No. 3 died May 3, 1906

Census Card No. 2698, P. O. Hanna, Enrolled May 22, 1901

| 7895 | 1 | Smith, George | 70 | M | F | | Arlapatar Harjo | D | Cr | Siwoke | D | Cr |

No. 1 died September 29, 1901

Census Card No. 2699, P. O. Holdenville, Enrolled May 22, 1901

| 7896 | 1 | James, George | 35 | M | F | | Unknown | D | Cr | Lucinda Underwood | D | Cr |
| 7897 | 2 | Buckner, Samuel | 21 | M | F | None | Wiley Buckner | D | Cr | Susan Harrison | L | Cr |

No. 1 died August 1905

Census Card No. 2700, P. O. Hanna, Enrolled May 22, 1901

| 7898 | 1 | Fixeco, Arhaloc | 65 | M | F | | Pulth Yahola | D | Cr | Unknown | D | Cr |

No. 1 died August 10, 1904

Census Card No. 2701, P. O. Hanna, Enrolled May 22, 1901

7899	1	Hopiyoche	50	M	F		Parthos Emarthla	D	Cr	Unknown	D	Cr
7900	2	Slumker	40	F	F	Wf	Noxie Holatochee	D	Cr	Foluttike	D	Cr
7901	3	Proctor, Caesar	19	M	F	S	No. 1	L	Cr	No. 2	L	Cr
7902	4	Proctor, Huethlego	22	M	F	S	No. 1	L	Cr	No. 2	L	Cr

No. 3 died December 7, 1903

Census Card No. 2702, P. O. Holdenville, Enrolled May 22, 1901

| 7903 | 1 | Deer, Wash | 40 | M | F | | Cowetachee | D | Cr | Ashutebgee | D | Cr |

No. 1 died December 7, 1904

Census Card No. 2703, P. O. Lamar, Enrolled May 22, 1901

7904	1	Wilson, Bettie	30	F	F		Kiamiame	D	Cr	Hannah Jones	L	Cr
7905	2	Wilson, Jasper	8	M	F	S	Thomas Wilson	L	Cr	No. 1	L	Cr
7906	3	Wilson, Toney	7	M	F	S	Thomas Wilson	L	Cr	No. 1	L	Cr

No. 2 died 1906

Census Card No. 2704, P. O. Mellette, Enrolled May 22, 1901

| 7907 | 1 | McGilbra, Lettie | 6 | F | F | | Jonas Deer | D | Cr | Jennie McGilbra | L | Cr |
| 7908 | 2 | McGilbra, Annie | 20 | F | F | Aunt | Daniel McGilbra | D | Cr | Lizzie McGilbra | L | Cr |

No. 1 possible duplicate of No. 7408 and 7064.

Census Card No. 2705, P. O. Kellyville, Enrolled May 22, 1901

7909	1	Deconsac	24	M	F		Salconcahney	D	Cr	Tasonkaynay	D	Cr
7910	2	Jatahkoconcahney	25	F	F	Wf	Ahlacontay	D	Cr	Pokoconweney	D	Cr
7911	3	Nicey	3	F	F	D	No. 1	L	Cr	No. 2	D	Cr

No. 3 died October 1904. No. 2 died July 1906.

Census Card No. 2706, P. O. Stone Bluff, Enrolled May 23, 1901

| 7912 | 1 | Berryhill, Geo. Franklin | 23 | M | 1-32 | | Geo. W. Berryhill | D | Cr | Ary Ann | L | Non |

Census Card No. 2707, P. O. Muskogee, Enrolled May 23, 1901

| 7913 | 1 | Atkins, Thomas | 10 | M | ½ | | Whiteman | L | Non | Minnie Atkins | L | Cr |

Census Card No. 2708, P. O. Bristow, Enrolled May 22, 1901

| 7914 | 1 | Ahlaahcotaney | 40 | F | F | | Tahcowenay | D | Cr | Winoyahcah | D | Cr |

No. 1 died January 31, 1905

Census Card No. 2709, P. O. Depew, Enrolled May 22, 1901

| 7915 | 1 | Coah | 35 | F | F | | Tacowenay | D | Cr | Winoyahcah | D | Cr |

Census Card No. 2710, P. O. Bristow, Enrolled May 22, 1901

| 7916 | 1 | Yarstarcoconthlaney | 52 | F | F | | Hissola | D | Cr | Thlssacoweney | D | Cr |

Census Card No. 2711, P. O. Eufaula, Enrolled May 23, 1901

| 7917 | 1 | Nettie | 22 | F | F | | Sonnahgay | D | Cr | Unknown | D | Cr |

No. 1 duplicate of enrollment as Lydia Johnson, No. 8725 this roll. October 6, 1914. The lands allotted to Lydia Johnson No. 8725 reconveyed to Creek Nation. Enrollment and allotment deeds as Nettie (see above) declared effective.

Census Card No. 2712, (Void)

| 7918 | 1 | Stricken from roll. | | | | | | | | | | |

Census Card No. 2713, P. O. Shawnee, Enrolled May 22, 1901

| 7919 | 1 | Cahcoketblon | 20 | M | F | | Wolf English | D | Cr | Tapaconthle | D | Cr |
| 7920 | 2 | Artarkinnay | 75 | M | F | Fath | Unknown | D | Cr | Unknown | D | Cr |

No. 2 died November 25, 1900

Census Card No. 2714, P. O. Muskogee, Enrolled May 23, 1901

7921	1	Bennett, Gertrude	15	F	1-16		Leo E. Bennett	L	Non	Lonie	D	Cr
7922	2	Bennett, Lonie	14	F	1-16	Sis	Leo E. Bennett	L	Non	Lonie	D	Cr
7923	3	Bennett, Leo E.	10	M	1-16	Bro	Leo E. Bennett	L	Non	Lonie	D	Cr

Census Card No. 2715, P. O. Muskogee, Enrolled May 23, 1901

| 7924 | 1 | Stidham, Clifford | 9 | M | ⅛ | | Albert P. Stidham | D | Cr | Anna C. Bennett | L | Cher |
| 7925 | 2 | Stidham, Albert P. | 40 | M | ⅛ | Fath | Geo. W. Stidham | D | Cr | Sarah | D | Cher |

Census Card No. 2716, P. O. Depew, Enrolled May 23, 1901

7926	1	Coyarkah	35	M	F		Cotahganey	D	Cr	Hocatahyeh	D	Cr
7927	2	Nellie	10	F	F	D	No. 1	L	Cr	Chequawa	L	Cr
7928	3	Larwesaw	6	F	F	D	No. 1	L	Cr	Chequawa	L	Cr
7929	4	Sannorka	21	M	F	StS	Sammy	D	Cr	Chequawa	L	Cr

No. 4 died June 14, 1911

Census Card No. 2717, P. O. Bristow, Enrolled May 23, 1901

7930	1	Bonbee	30	M	F		Ahtaqueney	D	Cr	Hoksetahaque	D	Cr
7931	2	Shequabee	24	F	F	Wf	Unknown	D	Cr	Unknown	D	Cr
7932	3	Commesee	12	F	F	D	Unknown	D	Cr	No. 2	L	Cr
7933	4	Sharshontey	6	M	F	S	No. 1	L	Cr	No. 2	L	Cr

No. 1 died March 15, 1901. No. 2 died February 15, 1901.

167

Roll No.	No.	NAME	Age	Sex	Blood	Rel.	NAME OF FATHER	Liv.	Cit.	NAME OF MOTHER	Liv.	Cit.

Census Card No. 2718, P. O. Brush Hill, Enrolled May 23, 1901

| 7934 | 1 | Harjo, Chitto | 55 | F | F | | Aharlock Harjo | D | Cr | Unknown | D | Cr |

No. 1 died about 1912

Census Card No. 2719, P. O. Castle, Enrolled May 22, 1901

| 7935 | 1 | Unussee Barnosee | 21 | M | F | | Unussee | D | Cr | Harney | D | Cr |

Census Card No. 2720, P. O. Salem, Enrolled May 23, 1901

7936	1	Starr, James	45	M	F		Taskia Harjo	D	Cr	Unknown	D	Cr
7937	2	Starr, Pulhokey	35	F	F	Wf	Unknown	D	Cr	Sosaye	D	Cr
7938	3	Starr, Edward	19	M	F	StS	Petochey	D	Cr	No. 2	L	Cr
7939	4	Starr, Lewis	13	M	F	S	No. 1	L	Cr	No. 2	L	Cr
7940	5	Starr, Nellie	11	F	F	D	No. 1	L	Cr	No. 2	L	Cr
7941	6	Starr, Annie	9	F	F	D	No. 1	L	Cr	No. 2	L	Cr
7942	7	Starr, Lizzie	7	F	F	D	No. 1	L	Cr	No. 2	L	Cr
7943	8	Starr, Melissa	5	F	F	D	No. 1	L	Cr	No. 2	L	Cr

No. 2 died October 2, 1912. No. 6 died August 20, 1904.

Census Card No. 2721, P. O. Hanna, Enrolled May 22, 1901

7944	1	Tiger, Lilly	40	F	F		Albata Harjo	D	Cr	Sothee Harjo	D	Cr
7945	2	Tiger, Amos	28	M	F	S	Karsha Chupco (or Fixico)	L	Cr	No. 1	L	Cr
7946	3	Tiger, Salina	20	F	F	D	Karsha Chupco (or Fixico)	L	Cr	No. 1	L	Cr
7947	4	Tiger, Jeannetta	8	F	F	D	Karsha Chupco (or Fixico)	L	Cr	No. 1	L	Cr

No. 4 died November 28, 1904. No. 1 died March 14, 1905. No. 2 reported dead.

Census Card No. 2722, P. O. Holdenville, Enrolled May 22, 1901

| 7948 | 1 | Tiger, Tom | 25 | M | F | | Conip Harjo | D | Cr | Martha Salumba | D | Cr |

Census Card No. 2723 (Void)

Census Card No. 2724, P. O. Muskogee, Enrolled May 22, 1901

| 7949 | 1 | Stricken from roll. | | | | | | | | | | |
| 7950 | 2 | Petelle | 45 | M | F | | Unknown | D | Cr | Unknown | D | Cr |

No. 2 reported dead

Census Card No. 2725, P. O. Eufaula, Enrolled May 22, 1901

| 7951 | 1 | Tiger, George | 9 | M | F | | Tarloshow | L | Cr | Louisa Salumba | D | Cr |

Census Card No. 2726, P. O. Eufaula, Enrolled May 22, 1901

| 7952 | 1 | Tarloshaw | 40 | M | F | | Cosar Harjo | D | Cr | Chocawaptah | D | Cr |

Census Card No. 2727, P. O. Stidham, Enrolled May 22, 1901

| 7953 | 1 | Taylor, Mary | 4 | F | F | | Taylor Postoak | D | Cr | Mollie | L | Cr |

No. 1 died October 1899

Census Card No. 2728, P. O. Eufaula, Enrolled May 22, 1901

| 7954 | 1 | Leider | 43 | F | F | | Fixico Emarthla | D | Cr | Harpogee | D | Cr |

No. 1 died December 28, 1899

Census Card No. 2729, P. O. Kellyville, Enrolled May 22, 1901

7955	1	Joconfah	28	M	F		Sangana	D	Cr	Esongana	D	Cr
7956	2	Joconfah, Poconweney	25	F	F	Wf	Cocose	D	Cr	Pocofah	D	Cr
7957	3	Joconfah, Melissa	10	F	F	D	No. 1	L	Cr	No. 2	L	Cr

No. 1 died June 2, 1912. No. 2 died July 17, 1909. No. 3 reported dead.

Census Card No. 2730, P. O. Sapulpa, Enrolled May 22, 1901

7958	1	Littlehead, Willie	31	M	F		Cocose	D	Cr	Pogofah	D	Cr
7959	2	Littlehead, Nannie	21	F	F	Wf	Bucktrot	L	Cr	Cahlowe	D	Cr
7960	3	Littlehead, Sarah	2	F	F	D	No. 1	L	Cr	No. 2	L	Cr

No. 3 died July 15, 1900. No. 1 reported dead.

Census Card No. 2731, P. O. Bristow, Enrolled May 22, 1901

| 7961 | 1 | Littlehead, Whiteman | 22 | M | F | | Cotoesee | D | Cr | Poconweny | D | Cr |

Census Card No. 2732, P. O. Salem, Enrolled May 23, 1901

7962	1	Tiger, Wilson	50	M	F		Nocus Emarthla	D	Cr	Lizzie Emarthla	D	Cr
7963	2	Tiger, Eliza	45	F	F	Wf	Heneha Maeche	D	Cr	Unknown	D	Cr
7964	3	Tiger, Addie	17	F	F	D	No. 1	L	Cr	No. 2	L	Cr
7965	4	Tiger, Wesley	15	M	F	S	No. 1	L	Cr	No. 2	L	Cr
7966	5	Tiger, Nancy	15	F	F	D	No. 1	L	Cr	No. 2	L	Cr

No. 2 died March 25, 1901. No. 3 died April 30, 1903. No. 1 died January 25, 1902.

Census Card No. 2733, P. O. Pierce; No. 3, Hanna, Enrolled May 23, 1901

7967	1	Elle Nocus	50	M	F		Unknown	D	Cr	Mollie Dixon	D	Cr
7968	2	Tiger, Jacob	45	M	F	½Bro	Tiger	D	Cr	Mollie Dixon	D	Cr
7969	3	Steele, Manie	43	F	F	½Sis	Tiger	D	Cr	Mollie Dixon	D	Cr
7970	4	Steele, Susan	24	F	F	Wf	Simon Steele	D	Cr	No. 3	L	Cr

No. 3 died January 6, 1902. No. 1 died January 29, 1910. No. 4 died September 6, 1901.

Census Card No. 2734, P. O. Dustin, Enrolled May 23, 1901

7971	1	Fife, Sandy	28	M	F		Artus Harjo	D	Cr	Eucharne	D	Cr
7972	2	Bunny, George	18	M	F	Cou	Ahchulah	D	Cr	Levina Deere	D	Cr
7973	3	Bunny, Jeannetta	12	F	F	Cou	Ahchulah	D	Cr	Levina Deere	D	Cr

Census Card No. 2735, P. O. Henryetta, Enrolled May 23, 1901

| 7974 | 1 | Kelly, Levina | 55 | F | F | | Heles Fixico | D | Cr | Unknown | D | Cr |

No. 1 died November 30, 1907

Census Card No. 2736, P. O. Senora, Enrolled May 23, 1901

7975	1	Micco, Polly	50	F	F		Heles Fixico	D	Cr	Unknown	D	Cr
7976	2	Micco, Billie	25	M	F	S	Tom Moka	D	Cr	No. 1	L	Cr
7977	3	Micco, David	20	M	F	S	Tom Moka	D	Cr	No. 1	L	Cr

No. 2 died March 24, 1902. No. 1 died February 1910. No. 3 died October 30, 1902.

Roll No.	No.	NAME	Age	Sex	Blood	Rel.	NAME OF FATHER	Liv.	Cit.	NAME OF MOTHER	Liv.	Cit.
		Census Card No. 2737, P. O. Salem, Enrolled May 23, 1901										
7978	1	King, Annie	48	F	F		Helus Fixico	D	Cr	Unknown	D	Cr
7979	2	King, Peter	27	M	F	S	Yahola Micco	D	Cr	No. 1	L	Cr
7980	3	King, Lily	15	F	F	D	Yahola Micco	D	Cr	No. 1	L	Cr
7981	4	King, Edmond	10	M	F	S	Yahola Micco	D	Cr	No. 1	L	Cr
		Census Card No. 2738, P. O. Pierce, Enrolled May 23, 1901										
7982	1	Jacobs, Sampson	30	M	F		Wotka Micco	D	Cr	Sallie Jacobs	D	Cr
		Census Card No. 2739, P. O. Hanna, Enrolled May 23, 1901										
7983	1	Milker	35	M	F		Pologe	D	Cr	Unknown	D	Cr
7984	2	Mitchell, Mandy	30	F	F	Sis-L	Coonehead	D	Cr	Unknown	D	Cr
7985	3	Coonhead, Willie	18	M	F	Bro-L	Coonehead	D	Cr	Unknown	D	Cr
7986	4	Coonhead, Nessie	20	F	F	Sis-L	Coonhead	D	Cr	Unknown	D	Cr
7987	5	Mitchell, Selina	10	F	F	Niece	Wattie Mitchell	L	Sem	No. 2	L	Cr
7988	6	Mitchell, Emma	8	F	F	Niece	Wattie Mitchel	L	Sem	No. 2	L	Cr
		No. 1 died January 15, 1901. No. 2 reported dead. No. 4 died August 4, 1900.										
		Census Card No. 2740, P. O. Salem, Enrolled May 23, 1901										
7989	1	Meliah	42	F	F		Unknown	D	Cr	Tathlatakee	D	Cr
7990	2	Conner, Amey	24	F	F	Niece	Wattiw Grayson	D	Cr	Tullega	D	Cr
7991	3	Grayson, Jennie	22	F	F	Niece	Wattie Grayson	D	Cr	Tullega	D	Cr
7992	4	Grayson, Chimker	12	F	F	S	Nocus Harjo	?	Cr	No. 1	L	Cr
		No. 1 reported dead No. 3 died 1902										
		Census Card No. 2741, P. O. Dustin, Enrolled May 23, 1901										
7993	1	Sallie	25	F	F		Laslie	D	Cr	No. 2	L	Cr
7994	2	Martha	50	F	F	Moth	Unknown	D	Cr	Unknown	D	Cr
7995	3	Wiggie	27	F	F	Sis	Unknown	D	Cr	No. 2	L	Cr
		No. 3 died February 7, 1902										
		Census Card No. 2742, P. O. Hanna, Enrolled May 23, 1901										
7996	1	Bearhead, Barney	27	M	F		Nocus Echo	L	Cr	Soharhoye	L	Cr
7997	2	Soharhoye	60	F	F	Moth	Konis Harjo	D	Cr	Honyjagee	D	Cr
7998	3	Bearhead, Betsey	30	F	F	Sis	Nocus Echo	L	Cr	Soharhoye	L	Cr
7999	4	Bearhead, Polly	26	F	F	Sis	Nocus Echo	L	Cr	Soharhoye	L	Cr
8000	5	Gano, Winnie	55	F	F	Aunt	Konis Harjo	D	Cr	Honyjagee	D	Cr
8001	6	Deere, Hunter	50	M	F	Uncle	Konis Harjo	D	Cr	Unknown	D	Cr
8002	7	Nocuseka	60	M	F	Fath	Arbehuk Harjo	D	Cr	Unknown	D	Cr
		No. 5 died February 25, 1901. No. 6 died April 15, 1911. No. 7 died November 7, 1907. No. 4 reported dead.										
		Census Card No. 2743, P. O. Dustin, Enrolled May 23, 1901										
8003	1	Chupko, Katcha	58	M	F		Unknown	D	Cr	Thlesawa	D	Cr
8004	2	Long, Jessie	56	M	F	Bro	Unknown	D	Cr	Thlesawa	D	Cr
8005	3	Long, John	48	M	F	Bro	Unknown	D	Cr	Thlesawa	D	Cr
8006	4	Long, Kizzie	60	F	F	Sis	Unknown	D	Cr	Thlesawa	D	Cr
8007	5	Long, Lucy	44	F	F	Sis	Unknown	D	Cr	Thlesawa	D	Cr
8008	6	Lasley, Tobey	24	M	F	Neph	Colbert Sasley	D	Cr	No. 4	L	Cr
8009	7	Lasley, Yunah	22	M	F	Neph	Colbert Lasley	D	Cr	No. 4	L	Cr
		No. 4 died March 1901. No. 6 died 1900. No. 5 died August 1901. No. 7 died December 19, 1909										
		Census Card No. 2744, P. O. Senora, Enrolled May 23, 1901										
8010	1	Tyler, John	60	M	F		Heneha Emarthochee	D	Cr	Nocihe	D	Cr
8011	2	Powell, Pesaka	55	F	F		Nokus Harjo	D	Cr	Unknown	D	Cr
8012	3	Powell, Elizabeth	4	F	½	D-L	John Powell	L	Non	No. 2	L	Cr
		No. 1 died 1900. No. 2 died 1911. No. 3 died June 1910.										
		Census Card No. 2745, P. O. Dustin, Enrolled May 23, 1901										
8013	1	Fixoco, Cho	38	M	F		Tulwa Yahola	D	Cr	Suckie	D	Cr
8014	2	Sim hoye	29	F	F	Sis	Tulwa Yahola	D	Cr	Suckie	D	Cr
8015	3	Nancy	20	F	F	Sis	Tulwa Yahola	D	Cr	Suckie	D	Cr
8016	4	Whitlow, Edmond	9	M	F	Neph	Whitlow	L	Sem	No. 2	L	Cr
		No. 2 reported dead										
		Census Card No. 2746, P. O. Okfuskee, Enrolled May 23, 1901										
8017	1	Jacobs, Thomas	65	M	F		Unknown	L	Cr	Unknown	L	Cr
		No. 1 died 1911										
		Census Card No. 2747, P. O. Coweta, Enrolled May 23, 1901										
8018	1	Alexander, Lizzie	29	F	F		Lotka	D	Cr	Mulga	D	Cr
8019	2	McGilbra Hepsey	20	F	F	None	Capt. McGilbra	L	Cr	Pikey Freeman	D	Cr
		Census Card No. 2748, P. O. Calvin, Enrolled May 23, 1901										
8020	1	Harrod, Sarah	37	F	F		Arche Yahola	D	Cr	Yahola	D	Cr
		No. 1 died January 30, 1902										
		Census Card No. 2749, P. O. Lima, Enrolled May 23, 1901										
8021	1	Sango, Thomas	24	M	½		Morris Sango	L	?	Silbey	D	Cr
		Census Card No. 2750, P. O. Hoffman, Enrolled May 23, 1901										
8022	1	Harjo, Wotko	45	M	F		Unknown	D	Cr	Unknown	D	Cr
8023	2	Jones, Albert	26	M	F	Neph	Stepney	D	Cr	Hobie	D	Cr
		No. 1 died August 20, 1904										
		Census Card No. 2751, P. O. Pierce, Enrolled May 23, 1901										
8024	1	Jones, Legus	24	M	F		Chitto Harjo	L	Cr	Margey	D	Cr
8025	2	Jones, Salina	22	F	F	Sis	Chitto Harjo	L	Cr	Margey	D	Cr
		Census Card No. 2752, P. O. Hanna, Enrolled May 23, 1901										
8026	1	Jones, Thomas	24	M	F		Halok Haye	D	Cr	Hotkle Haye	D	Cr
8027	2	Jones, Maxey	20	M	F	Bro	Halok Haye	D	Cr	Hotkle Haye	D	Cr
		Census Card No. 2753, P. O. Dustin, Enrolled May 23, 1901										
8028	1	Laslie	45	M	F		Unknown	D	Cr	Tabalecha	D	Cr
		No. 1 died August 14, 1900										

Roll No.	No.	NAME	Age	Sex	Blood	Rel.	NAME OF FATHER	Liv.	Cit.	NAME OF MOTHER	Liv.	Cit.
		Census Card No. 2754, P. O. Dustin, Enrolled May 23, 1901										
8029	1	Benson, Matilda	22	F	F		Jim Benson	L	Cr	Mary Benson	D	Cr
8030	2	Benson, Kokey	16	F	F	Sis	Jim Benson	L	Cr	Mary Benson	D	Cr
		No. 1 reported dead										
		Census Card No. 2755, P. O. Dustin, Enrolled May 23, 1901										
8031	1	Low, Louisa	23	F	F		Canuka Low	L	Cr	Lena Low	L	Cr
8032	2	Low, Taylor	8	M	F	S	Sandy Fife	L	Cr	No. 1	L	Cr
8033	3	Low, Annie	13	F	F	Cou	Kawakagee	D	Cr	Sakhalegee	D	Cr
		Census Card No. 2756, P. O. Pierce, Enrolled May 23, 1901										
8034	1	Hope, Rebecca	55	F	½		Hope	D	Cr	Fannie Hope	D	Cr
8035	2	Smith, Eliza	24	F	½	GrD	Sam Smith	D	Cr	Adaline Bradley	D	Cr
8036	3	Thompson, Henry	8	M	½	SNo. 2	Caesar Thompson	D	Cr	No. 2	L	Cr
		No. 1 died May 4, 1914										
		Census Card No. 2757, P. O. Boynton, Enrolled May 23, 1901										
8037	1	Company, Daniel	29	M	¾		Hoscussee	D	Cr	Nellie Hope	D	Cr
8038	2	Company, Garrett	15	M	⅛	S	No. 1	L	Cr	Sissie Doyle	D	Cr
8039	3	Company, Sam	11	M	⅛	S	No. 1	L	Cr	Sissie Doyle	D	Cr
		No. 3 died June 6, 1908										
		Census Card No. 2758, P. O. Amabala, Enrolled May 23, 1901										
8040	1	Fife, Allie Ola	20	F	F		Archola	D	Cr	Sukey	D	Cr
8041	2	Fife, Melinda	35	F	F	Sis	Archola	D	Cr	Sukey	D	Cr
		No. 1 reported dead										
		Census Card No. 2759, P. O. Wewoka, Enrolled May 23, 1901										
8042	1	Deer, Sparny	26	M	F		Pahos Fixico	D	Cr	Sarwaliche	L	Cr
8043	2	Deer, Sophia	25	F	F	Wf	Amos Hill	D	Cr	Yarner	D	Cr
8044	3	Deer, Alfred	3	M	F	S	No. 1	L	Cr	No. 2	L	Cr
8045	4	Deer, Ella	1	F	F	D	No. 1	L	Cr.	No. 2	L	Cr
		No. 2 died September 1908. No. 4 died 1900'										
		Census Card No. 2760, P. O. Bearden, Enrolled May 23, 1901										
8046	1	Hale, Ollie	18	F	F		Amos Hill	D	Cr	Yarner	D	Cr
		Census Card No. 2761, P. O. Okmulgee, Enrolled April 26, 1901										
8047	1	Barnett, Edmond	22	M	¼		Charlie Barnett	D	Cr	Lucinda Barnett	D	Cr
8048	2	Barnett, Samuel	20	M	¼	Bro	Charlie Barnett	D	Cr	Lucinda Barnett	D	Cr
8049	3	Barnett, Thomas	18	M	¼	Bro	Charlie Barnett	D	Cr	Lucinda Barnett	D	Cr
		Census Card No. 2762, P. O. Holdenville, Enrolled May 23, 1901										
8050	1	Mickey	65	F	F		Lata Yohola	D	Cr	Unknown	D	Cr
		No. 1 died May 29, 1909										
		Census Card No. 2763, P. O. Wewoka, Enrolled May 23, 1901										
8051	1	Kochokney, Henchar	60	M	F		Mechussey	D	Cr	Unknown	D	Cr
		No. 1 died March 1, 1903										
		Census Card No. 2764, P. O. Mounds, Enrolled May 23, 1901										
8052	1	Harjo, Tarkosar	40	M	F		Kotsar Homota	D	Cr	Unknown	D	Cr
8053	2	Tiger, John	12	M	F	S	No. 1	L	Cr	Lizzie Harjo	D	Cr
		No. 2 died June 24, 1913										
		Census Card No. 2765, P. O. Wetumka, Enrolled May 23, 1901										
8054	1	Fixeco, Karwassat	35	M	F		Managee	D	Cr	Sintigah	D	Cr
		No. 1 probably duplicate enrollment, Robert Sutor No. 4006 this roll.										
		Census Card No. 2766, P. O. Mellette, Enrolled May 23, 1901										
8055	1	Givens, William	22	M	F		Charte Givens	L	Cr	Silla	D	Cr
8056	2	Givens, Eddie	20	M	F	Bro	Charte Givens	L	Cr	Silla	D	Cr
		No. 2 died April 1900										
		Census Card No. 2767, P. O. Eufaula, Enrolled May 23, 1901										
8057	1	Hawkins, Lucinda	29	F	F		Choeta Givens	L	Cr	Silla	D	Cr
		Census Card No. 2768, P. O. No. 1, Hanna; No. 2, Yeager; Nos. 3 and 4, Holdenville; No. 5, Eufaula, Enrolled May 23, 1901										
8058	1	Lindsey, Phillip	50	M	F		Spoko Fixico	D	Cr	Unknown	D	Cr
8059	2	Lindsey, Freeland	20	M	F	S	No. 1	L	Cr	Nancy Lindsey	D	Cr
8060	3	Lindsey, Lydia	18	F	F	D	No. 1	L	Cr	Nancy Lindsey	D	Cr
8061	4	Lindsey, Kizzie	16	F	F	D	No. 1	L	Cr	Nancy Lindsey	D	Cr
8062	5	Lindsey, Lewis	10	M	F	S	No. 1	L	Cr	Nancy Lindsey	D	Cr
		No. 4 reported dead										
		Census Card No. 2769, P. O. Eufaula, Enrolled May 23, 1901										
8063	1	Jackson, Barney	42	M	F		Mosey Jackson	D	Cr	Kunohanyo	D	Cr
8064	2	Jackson, Eliza	40	F	F	Wf	Spogeyhala	D	Cr	pAtige	D	Cr
8065	3	Jackson, Johnson	14	M	F	S	No. 1	L	Cr	No. 2	L	Cr
8066	4	Jackson, Malinda	9	F	F	D	No. 1	L	Cr	No. 2	L	Cr
8067	5	Jackson, Bunnie	6	M	F	S	No. 1	L	Cr	No. 2	L	Cr
8068	6	Jackson, Johnnie	5	M	F	S	No. 1	L	Cr	No. 2	L	Cr
		No. 1 died January 10, 1902. No. 2 died October 26, 1908. No. 3 died January 1, 1910. No. 4 died January 1910. No. 5 died October 1, 1911.										
		Census Card No. 2770, P. O. Eufaula, Enrolled May 23, 1901										
8069	1	Betsey	65	F	F		Chokate Yahola	D	Cr	Unknown	D	Cr
		Census Card No. 2771, P. O. Eufaula, Enrolled May 23, 1901										
8070	1	Benton, Robert	35	M	F		Sosah	D	Cr	Nannie	D	Cr
		No. 1 reported dead										

Census Card No. 2772, P. O. Hanna; No. 3, Mellette, Enrolled May 23, 1901

Roll No.	No.	NAME	Age	Sex	Blood	Rel.	NAME OF FATHER	Liv.	Cit.	NAME OF MOTHER	Liv.	Cit.
8071	1	Holuby, Cooper	20	M	F		George Holuby	L	Cr	Hattie Holuby	D	Cr
8072	2	Holuby, Nettie	19	F	F	Sis	George Holuby	L	Cr	Hattie Holuby	D	Cr
8073	3	Holuby, Turner	18	M	F	Bro	George Holuby	L	Cr	Hattie Holuby	D	Cr
8074	4	Holuby, Sally	16	F	F	Sis	George Holuby	L	Cr	Hattie Holuby	D	Cr
8075	5	Holuby, Nora	15	F	F	Sis	George Holuby	L	Cr	Hattie Holuby	D	Cr
8076	6	Holuby, Mollie	12	F	F	Sis	George Holuby	L	Cr	Hattie Holuby	D	Cr

No. 2 died 1900.   No. 5 reported dead.   No. 4 died July 11, 1904.

Census Card No. 2773, P. O. Hanna, Enrolled May 23, 1901

8077	1	Long, Sallie	40	F	F		Hillabee	D	Cr	Socyouthlikee	D	Cr

No. 1 died 1906

Census Card No. 2774, P. O. Eufaula; No. 2, Mellette, Enrolled May 23, 1901

8078	1	Cox, Sarah	30	F	F		Choctaw Givens	L	Cr	Mehakee	D	Cr
8079	2	Brown, Lydia	11	F	F	D	Wilson Brown	L	Cr	No. 1	L	Cr
8080	3	Cox, Cheparnie	4	M	F	S	Culla Cox	L	Cr	No. 1	L	Cr
8081	4	Cox, Kullar	31	M	F	Hus	Coxie Hill	D	Cr	Suma Hill	L	Cr

No. 4 died December 1907

Census Card No. 2775, P. O. Eufaula, Enrolled May 23, 1901

8082	1	McCombs, Sarah	41	F	F		Elijah Scott	D	Cr	Kizzie Scott		
8083	2	Phillips, Mattie	17	F	F	D	Ben Phillips	D	Cr	No. 1	L	Cr
8084	3	Phillips, Billy	12	M	F	S	Ben Phillips	D	Cr	No. 1	L	Cr
8085	4	Phillips, Jennie	9	F	F	D	Ben Phillips	D	Cr	No. 1	L	Cr

No. 1 died May 10, 1911

Census Card No. 2776, P. O. Eufaula, Enrolled May 23, 1901

8086	1	Smith, Emma	25	F	¾		John Smith	L	Cr	Louisa Smith	D	Cr

Census Card No. 2777, P. O. Eufaula, Enrolled May 23, 1901

8087	1	Micco, Seber	60	M	F		Unknown	D	Cr	Unknown	D	Cr

No. 1 died December 22, 1903

Census Card No. 2778, P. O. Okemah, Enrolled May 23, 1901

8088	1	Harjoge, Hulputta	35	M	F		Nocus Fixico	L	Cr	Abbeah	D	Cr
8089	2	Harjoge, Marfey	28	F	F	Wf	Fuchus Harjo	D	Cr	Arbifhoge	D	Cr
8090	3	Harjoge, Frank	10	M	F	Ward	Lawoney	D	Cr	Siotka	D	Cr
8091	4	Harjoge, Chagee	8	M	F	Ward	Lawoney	D	Cr	Siotka	D	Cr

Census Card No. 2779, P. O. Weleetka, Enrolled May 23, 1901

8092	1	Kolvin Lete	21	F	F		Sosa Grayson	D	Cr	Miley	D	Cr

No. 1 died February 1, 1899

Census Card No. 2780, P. O. Wetumka, Enrolled May 23, 1901

8093	1	Harjo, Jeannetta	27	F	F		Ben Hawkins	D	Cr	Jennie	L	Cr
8094	2	Harjo, Willie	7	M	F	S	Barney Deer	L	Cr	No. 1	L	Cr
8095	3	Harjo, Buddie	3	M	F	S	Barney Deer	L	Cr	No. 1	L	Cr
8096	4	Harjo, Jennie	10	F	F	D	Barney Deer	L	Cr	No. 1	L	Cr

No. 1 died 1901.   No. 4 died April 17, 1900

Census Card No. 2781, P. O. Wetumka, Enrolled May 23, 1901

8097	1	Jonasie	21	M	F		Wilyumka	L	Cr	Sylla	L	Cr

No. 1 died about 1903

Census Card No. 2782, P. O. Dustin, Enrolled May 23, 1901

8098	1	Wesley, Keeper	29	M	F		Wesley Chupco	D	Cr	Louisa	?	Cr
8099	2	Wesley, Leah	25	F	F	Wf	Upney Hill	D	Cr	Linda	?	Cr
8100	3	Wesley, Louisa	6	F	F	D	No. 1	L	Cr	No. 2	L	Cr
8101	4	Wesley, Eddie	3	M	F	S	No. 1	L	Cr	No. 2	L	Cr

No. 1 died August 24, 1901.   No. 2 reported dead.

Census Card No. 2783, P. O. Kellyville, Enrolled May 23, 1901

8102	1	Wildcat, Jim	25	M	F		Unknown	D	Cr	Paquain	D	Cr
8103	2	Forlocoweney	22	F	F	Wf	Teshonney	D	Cr	Unknown	D	Cr
8104	3	Coahlalotuney	8	M	F	S	No. 1	L	Cr	No. 2	L	Cr
8105	4	Yarcharney	6	M	F	S	No. 1	L	Cr	No. 2	L	Cr

No. 1 died July 4, 1902

Census Card No. 2784, P. O. Bristow, Enrolled May 23, 1901

8106	1	Long, Henry	21	M	F		Long Jim	D	Cr	Annie	D	Cr
8107	2	Long, Lizzie	19	F	F	Wf	Pacoweney	D	Cr	Selibbee	D	Cr
8108	3	Long, Bob	1	M	F	S	No. 1	L	Cr	No. 2	L	Cr

No. 2 died July 29, 1903

Census Card No. 2785, P. O. Newby, Enrolled May 23, 1901

8109	1	Long, Lewis	29	M	F		Long Jim	D	Cr	Lucy	D	Cr
8110	2	Long, Lannie	24	F	F	Wf	Conpesinney Brown	L	Cr	Polly	D	Cr
8111	3	Long, Harry	10	M	F	S	No. 1	L	Cr	Sagodaney	D	Cr
8112	4	Long, Sawena	3	F	F	D	No. 1	L	Cr	No. 2	L	Cr
8113	5	Long, Jimmie	1	M	F	S	No. 1	L	Cr	No. 2	L	Cr

Census Card No. 2786, P. O. Bristow, Enrolled May 23, 1901

8114	1	Kacoquanney	50	M	F		Hissalla	D	Cr	Saysaneh	D	Cr
8115	2	Stricken from the roll.										
8116	3	Sohcahjahthla	11	M	F	S	No. 1	L	Cr	Minna	D	Cr

No. 3 reported dead

Census Card No. 2787, P. O. Cheyarha, Enrolled May 23, 1901

8117	1	Bear, Yarner	7	F	½		Okaska Miller	?	Sem	Rhoda Chisse	D	Cr

No. 1 possible duplicate of No. 10142.

Census Card No. 2788, P. O. Arbeka, Enrolled May 23, 1901

8118	1	Lizzie	70	F	F		Unknown	D	Cr	Unknown	D	Cr
8119	2	Marwole	48	F	F	D	Cocha Micco	D	Cr	No. 1	L	Cr

No. 1 died August 1899

171

Roll No.	No.	NAME	Age	Sex	Blood	Rel.	NAME OF FATHER	Liv.	Cit.	NAME OF MOTHER	Liv.	Cit.
		Census Card No. 2789, P. O. Wekiwa, Enrolled May 23, 1901										
8120	1	Johnson, Sandy	30	M	F		Johnson	D	Cr	Linda	D	Cr
8121	2	Johnson, Jinnie	17	F	F	Wf	Charlie Gooden	D	Cr	Sukey	D	Cr
		No. 2 died										
		Census Card No. 2790, P. O. Dustin, Enrolled May 23, 1901										
8122	1	Jimsey, Jeannetta	20	F	F		Culla Jimsey	D	Cr	Soshaye Jimsey	D	Cr
		No. 1 died February 12, 1904										
		Census Card No. 2791, P. O. Wetumka, Enrolled May 23, 1901										
8123	1	Bird, Sissie	20	F	F		Chuckhart Thlocco	D	Cr	Kizzie	D	Cr
		Possibly a duplicate of enrollment of roll No. 3498.										
		Census Card No. 2792, P. O. Dustin, Enrolled May 23, 1901										
8124	1	Moffer, Waitie	28	M	F		Tulwa Harjo	D	Cr	Nannie Harjo	D	Cr
		Census Card No. 2793, P. O. Wetumka, Enrolled May 23, 1901										
8125	1	Sakyothlike	70	F	F		Unknown	D	Cr	Techer	D	Cr
		No. 1 died December 24, 1901										
		Census Card No. 2794, P. O. Hanna, Enrolled May 23, 1901										
8126	1	Fixeco, Katcha	70	M	F		Unknown	D	Cr	Unknwon	D	Cr
8127	2	Fixeco, Salina	45	F	F	Wf	Unknown	D	Cr	Unknown	D	Cr
		No. 1 died March 22, 1900										
		Census Card No. 2795, P. O. Wetumka, Enrolled May 23, 1901										
8128	1	Millie	35	F	F		Micco Nuba	D	Cr	Sahalhoga	D	Cr
		Census Card No. 2796, P. O. Hanna, Enrolled May 23, 1901										
8129	1	Harper, Marfe	40	F	F		Fushutch Emarthle	D	Cr	Oklossie	D	Cr
8130	2	Harper, Peggie	20	F	F	D	Harper Field	L	Cr	No. 1	L	Cr
8131	3	Harper, Pettie	11	F	F	D	Harper Field	L	Cr	No. 1	L	Cr
		No. 2 died December 16, 1910. No. 1 died August 31, 1908.										
		Census Card No. 2797, P. O. Dustin; No. 6, Holdenville, Enrolled May 23, 1901										
8132	1	Yahola, Emarthla	65	M	F		Artus Hobie	D	Cr	Simone	D	Cr
8133	2	Fayeche	60	F	F	Wf	Unknown	D	Cr	Sahwahoke	D	Cr
8134	3	Harper, Jim	21	M	F	S	No. 1	L	Cr	No. 2	L	Cr
8135	4	Harper, Koke	18	F	F	D	No. 1	L	Cr	No. 2	L	Cr
8136	5	Harper, Peggie	16	F	F	D	No. 1	L	Cr	No. 2	L	Cr
8137	6	Harper, Somaye	22	F		Dr-L	Cho Emarthla Fixico	D	Cr	Mahte	L	Cr
		No. 6 died January 15, 1903. No. 1 reported dead.										
		Census Card No. 2798, P. O. Red Fork, Enrolled May 23, 1901										
8138	1	Red, Martha	25	F	½		Americus Riley	L	Non	Unknown	D	Cr
8139	2	Red, Foxie	7	M	¾	S	Thomas Red	L	Cr	No. 1	L	Cr
		Census Card No. 2799, P. O. Eufaula, Enrolled May 23, 1901										
8140	1	Sullivan, Willie	50	M	F		Seadah (or Cayado)	D	Cr	Sallie Sullivan	D	Cr
8141	2	Sullivan, Thomas	40	M	F	Bro	Seadah (or Cayado)	D	Cr	Sallie Sullivan	D	Cr
		No. 1 died February 11, 1902										
		Census Card No. 2800, P. O. Hanna, Enrolled May 24, 1901										
8142	1	Grayson, Foster	30	M	F		Tahlutkee	D	Cr	Unknown	D	Cr
8143	2	Grayson, Martha	25	F	F	Wf	Tewalische	D	Cr	Ahpoke	D	Cr
8144	3	Boney, James	10	M	F	StS	Boney	D	Cr	No. 2	L	Cr
		No. 1 died December 20, 1907. No. 2 died February 29, 1912.										
		Census Card No. 2801, P. O. Hanna, Enrolled May 23, 1901										
8145	1	Wikey	42	F	F		Hillabee	D	Cr	Socyouthlikee	D	Cr
		No. 1 reported dead										
		Census Card No. 2802, P. O. Hanna, Enrolled May 23, 1901										
8146	1	Narchubby, Sallie	30	F	F		Unknown	D	Cr	Unknown	D	Cr
8147	2	Narchubby, Ellis	15	M	F	D	Ahlin Chubby	L	Choc	No. 1	D	Cr
8148	3	Narchubby, Sissy	14	F	F	D	Ahlin Chubby	L	Choc	No. 1	L	Cr
		No. 1 reported dead										
		Census Card No. 2803, P. O. Salem, Enrolled May 23, 1901										
8149	1	Jacob, Sam	20	M	F		Jacobs	D	Cr	Unknown	D	Cr
		Census Card No. 2804, P. O. Fishertown, Enrolled May 23, 1901										
8150	1	Thomas, Willie	20	M	F		Jesse Thompson	D	Cr	Unknown	D	Cr
		No. 1 possible duplicate of No. 833. No. 1 in U. S. Penitentiary at Columbus, Ohio, life term.										
		Census Card No. 2805, P. O. Eufaula, Enrolled May 23, 1901										
8151	1	Washington, Thomas	35	M	F		Spokoke Yahola	D	Cr	Lottie	D	Cr
		Census Card No. 2806, P. O. Wetumka, Enrolled May 23, 1901										
8152	1	Crowels, Annie	35	F	F		George Crow	L	Sem	Cilla Crowels	D	Cr
8153	2	Crowels, Jonah	14	M	F	S	Melecher	L	Cr	No. 1	L	Cr
8154	3	Crowels, Freeman	10	M	F	S	Melecher	L	Cr	No. 1	L	Cr
8155	4	Crowels, Katie	6	F	F	D	Melecher	L	Cr	No. 1	L	Cr
8156	5	Milloche	28	M	F	Hus	Okchum Fixico	D	Cr	Yoafker	D	Cr
		No. 5 died July 10, 1910										
		Census Card No. 2807, P. O. Blocker, Enrolled May 23, 1901										
8157	1	Gibson, John	55	M	F		John C. Gibson	D	Non	Unknown	D	Cr
		Census Card No. 2808, P. O. Henryetta, Enrolled May 23, 1901										
8158	1	Scott, Haney	35	M	F		Unknown	D	Cr	Unknown	D	Cr
		Census Card No. 2809, P. O. Henryetta, Enrolled May 23, 1901										
8159	1	Fisher, Daniel	35	M	F		Fushutche Chupco	D	Cr	Hannah Fisher	L	Cr
		Census Card No. 2810, P. O. Indianola, Enrolled May 23, 1901										
8160	1	Emmy	21	M	F		Hobithla	D	Cr	Margaret	D	Cr
		Census Card No. 2811, P. O. Dustin, Enrolled May 23, 1901										
8161	1	Thomas, Dick	20	M	F		Medutwikey	D	Cr	Unknown	D	Cr

Roll No.   No.   NAME   Age Sex Blood Rel.   NAME OF FATHER   Liv.   Cit.   NAME OF MOTHER   Liv.   Cit.

Census Card No. 2812, P. O. Holdenville, Enrolled May 23, 1901

Roll No.	No.	NAME	Age	Sex	Blood	Rel.	NAME OF FATHER	Liv.	Cit.	NAME OF MOTHER	Liv.	Cit.
8162	1	Mitchelly	22	M	F		Albert Compier	D	Cr	Arne Hotke	D	Cr

No. 1 possible duplicate of 5240.

Census Card No. 2813, (Void)

| 8163 | 1 | Stricken from roll. | | | | | | | | | | |

Census Card No. 2814, P. O. Sasakwa, Enrolled May 23, 1901

| 8164 | 1 | Martie | 50 | M | F | | Fushutja Harjo | D | Cr | Peccher | D | Cr |

Census Card No. 2815, P. O. Okmulgee, Enrolled May 23, 1901

| 8165 | 1 | Hemer, Louie | 9 | M | F | | Thomas Haynes | D | Cr | Toche | D | Cr |

No. 1 died 1900

Census Card No. 2816, P. O. Hanna, Enrolled May 23, 1901

| 8166 | 1 | Harjo, Tuckabatchee | 50 | M | F | | Arthun Harjo | D | Cr | Finchee | D | Cr |

No. 1 died November 6, 1912

Census Card No. 2817, P. O. Hanna, Enrolled May 23, 1901

| 8167 | 1 | Homahite | 90 | F | F | | Unknown | D | Cr | Unknown | D | Cr |
| 8168 | 2 | Konabe | 62 | F | F | Niece | Konip Emarthla | D | Cr | Unknown | D | Cr |

No. 2 died October 1900

Census Card No. 2818, P. O. Hanna, Enrolled May 23, 1901; No. 4, May 24, 1901

8169	1	Tuffer	35	M	F		Conchart Fixico	D	Cr	Unknown	D	Cr
8170	2	Tuffer, Sene	30	F	F	Wf	Tommie Fixico	D	Cr	Wisey	D	Cr
8171	3	Tuffer, Mary	12	F	F	D	No. 1	L	Cr	No. 2	L	Cr
8172	4	Tuffer, Lizzie	6	F	F	D	No. 1	L	Cr	No. 2	L	Cr

No. 1 died February 1910. No. 2 died July 7, 1909. No. 3 reported dead.

Census Card No. 2819, P. O. Hanna, Enrolled May 23, 1901

| 8173 | 1 | Cho, Hachoche | 40 | M | F | | Kapecha Harjo | D | Cr | Unknown | D | Cr |

Census Card No. 2820, P. O. Hanna, Enrolled May 23, 1901

| 8174 | 1 | Simmons, Sandy | 25 | M | F | | Sam Simmons | D | Cr | Annie Simmons | D | Cr |

Census Card No. 2821, P. O. Holdenville, Enrolled May 23, 1901

| 8175 | 1 | Proctor, Leber | 26 | M | F | | Wotko Homatie | D | Cr | Tokothee | D | Cr |

Census Card No. 2822, P. O. Dustin, Enrolled May 23, 1901

| 8176 | 1 | Wattie, Parnie | 33 | M | F | | Pen Harjo | D | Cr | Chogee | D | Cr |
| 8177 | 2 | Wattie, Thomas | 30 | M | F | Bro | Pen Harjo | D | Cr | Chogee | D | Cr |

No. 1 died December 20, 1902. No. 2 died July 20, 1906

Census Card No. 2823, P. O. Hanna, Enrolled May 24, 1901

| 8178 | 1 | Wotkoche | 25 | M | F | | Watka Fixico | D | Cr | Unknown | D | Cr |
| 8179 | 2 | Yupahake | 26 | F | F | Sis | Lahta Harjo | D | Cr | Carhokee | D | Cr |

Census Card No. 2824, P. O. Hasson, Enrolled May 23, 1901

8180	1	Harjo, Woxie	50	M	F		Unknown	D	Cr	Unknown	D	Cr
8181	2	Harjo, Estonahe	45	F	F	Wf	Albutta	D	Cr	Sawake	D	Cr
8182	3	Harjo, Jonas	25	M	F	S	No. 1	L	Cr	No. 2	L	Cr
8183	4	Harjo, Tarsee	20	M	F	S	No. 1	L	Cr	No. 2	L	Cr

No. 1 died February 24, 1908. No. 2 died September 1907

Census Card No. 2825, P. O. Hanna, Enrolled May 23, 1901

| 8184 | 1 | Choelle | 30 | M | F | | Tum Emathla | L | Cr | Petha | D | Cr |

No. 1 possible duplicate of 8164.

Census Card No. 2826, P. O. Hanna, Enrolled May 23, 1901

8185	1	Homahta, Hane	45	F	F		Conchart Harjo	D	Cr	Folecheche	D	Cr
8186	2	Homahta, Thomas	28	M	F	S	Wahnahuche	D	Cr	No. 1	L	Cr
8187	3	Stricken from roll										
8188	4	Homahta Mesela	18	F	F	D	Katcher Hermahte	L	Cr	No. 1	L	Cr
8189	5	Stricken from roll										

No. 4 died March 19, 1902

Census Card No. 2827, P. O. Wetumka, Enrolled May 23, 1901

8190	1	Harjo, Sawanoke	45	M	F		Osach Fixico	D	Cr	Pehoye	D	Cr
8191	2	Harjo, Mary	35	F	F	Wf	Watko Harjo	D	Cr	Mchite	D	Cr
8192	3	Harjo, Milley	14	F	F	D	No. 1	L	Cr	No. 2	L	Cr

No. 3 died 1904

Census Card No. 2828, P. O. Wetumka, Enrolled May 23, 1901

8193	1	Harjo, Hotulke	45	M	F		Thlewarthle Emarthle	D	Cr	Sahlahoga	D	Cr
8194	2	Fixeco, Yabola	40	M	F	Cou	Unknown	D	Cr	Nafage	D	Cr
8195	3	Deer, Jim	1	M	F	S	No. 1	L	Cr	Sinah Deer	L	Cr

No. 2 died November 1899. No. 1 died September 16, 1908. No. 3 died April 1899

Census Card No. 2829, P. O. Wetumka, Enrolled May 23, 1901

8196	1	Homahte, Watko	50	M	F		Osoche Fixico	D	Cr	Pehoye	D	Cr
8197	2	Homahte, Nochiheche	40	F	F	Wf	Thlemathle Emarthla	D	Cr	Sahlahoga	D	Cr
8198	3	Homahte, Lena	14	F	F	D	No. 1	L	Cr	No. 2	L	Cr
8199	4	Katie	21	F	F	StD	Waitte	L	Cr	No. 2	L	Cr
8200	5	Pehoye	72	F	F	Moth	Unknown	D	Cr	Unknown	D	Cr

No. 5 died September 1904. No. 2 died 1907. No. 1 reported dead

Census Card No. 2830, P. O. Hanna, Enrolled October 23, 1901

8201	1	Deo, Nasa	40	F	F		Hutche Nubbe	D	Cr	Unknown	D	Cr
8202	2	Deo, Thomas	27	M	F	S	Tulmarsey Yabola	D	Cr	No. 1	L	Cr
8203	3	Deo, Sakiye	16	M	F	S	Tulmarsey Yabola	D	Cr	No. 1	L	Cr
8204	4	Deo, Jennie	15	F	F	D	Tulmarsey Yabola	D	Cr	No. 1	L	Cr
8205	5	Deo, John	18	M	F	S	Tulmarsey Yabola	D	Cr	No. 1	L	Cr
8206	6	Deo, Thompson	50	M	F	Hus	Suffanefka	D	Cr	Yahofke	D	Cr

No. 1 died November 5, 1905. No. 5 died January 4, 1913. No. 6 died April 5, 1901

173

Roll No.	No.	NAME	Age	Sex	Blood	Rel.	NAME OF FATHER	Liv.	Cit.	NAME OF MOTHER	Liv.	Cit.
		Census Card No. 2831, P. O. Hanna, Enrolled May 23, 1901										
8207	1	Heneha, Chukchat	40	M	F		Mechiskoche	D	Cr	Sicklen	D	Cr
8208	2	Gibson, Wilson	21	M	F	Neph	John Gibson	D	Cr	Toge	D	Cr
		No. 1 died January 1901										
		Census Card No. 2832, P. O. Carson, Enrolled May 23, 1901										
8209	1	Fixeco, Yarhola	30	M	F		Matup Hencha	L	Cr	Temelecer	D	Cr
8210	2	Melinda	18	F	F	Sis	Matup Heneha	L	Cr	Temelecer	D	Cr
8211	3	Heneha, Matup	48	M	F	Fath	Yaha Fixico	D	Cr	Unknown	D	Cr
		No. 3 died 1910										
		Census Card No. 2833, P. O. Dustin, care Archie Simpson, Enrolled May 23, 1901										
8212	1	Estepe	32	M	F		Fus Harjo	D	Cr	Jimalee	D	Cr
8213	2	Sena	21	F	½	Sis	George Osawah	?	?	Jimalee	D	Cr
		Census Card No. 2834, P. O. Hanna, Enrolled May 23, 1901										
8214	1	Melia, (Nellie)	65	F	F		Unknown	D	Cr	Unknown	D	Cr
8215	2	Fixeco, Hencha	40	M	F	S	Metesha Yahola	D	Cr	No. 1	L	Cr
		No. 1 died in fall of 1900										
		Census Card No. 2835, P. O. Eufaula, Enrolled May 23, 1901										
8216	1	Deer, Daniel	33	M	F		Eco Emarthlogee	D	Cr	Semoga	D	?
8217	2	Deer, Lucy	38	F	F	Wf	Dave Proctor	D	Cr	Sikey Wesley	D	?
8218	3	Deer, Lydia	5	F	F	D	No. 1	L	Cr	No. 2	L	?
8219	4	Deer, Jackson	4	M	F	S	No. 1	L	Cr	No. 2	L	?
		No. 1 died January 12, 1901										
		Census Card No. 2836, P. O. Hanna, Enrolled May 23, 1901										
8220	1	Jones, Loney	11	F	F		Charlie Jones	D	Cr	Mollie Jones	D	Cr
		No. 1 died August 1899										
		Census Card No. 2837, P. O. Hanna, Enrolled May 23, 1901										
8221	1	Lasley, Sam	38	M	F		Jack Lasley	D	Cr	Eliza Lasley	D	Cr
8222	2	Lasley, Wisey	40	F	F	Wf	Unknown	D	Cr	Unknown	D	Cr
8223	3	Lasley, Liza	14	F	F	D	No. 1	L	Cr	No. 2	L	Cr
8224	4	Lasley, Alec	12	M	F	S	No. 1	L	Cr	No. 2	L	Cr
8225	5	Lasley, Moses	10	M	F	S	No. 1	L	Cr	No. 2	L	Cr
		No. 4 reported dead										
		Census Card No. 2838, P. O. Castle, Enrolled May 23, 1901										
8226	1	Fixeco, Fushutche	22	M	F		Wotka Yaholo	L	Cr	Somie	D	Cr
		Census Card No. 2839, P. O. Dustin, Enrolled May 23, 1901										
8227	1	Fisher, Lucy	37	F	F		Captain Billy	D	Cr	Sophia Billy	D	Cr
8228	2	Fisher, Billie	7	M	⅞	S	Willie Fisher	L	Cr	No. 1	L	Cr
8229	3	Dorsey, Emma	17	F	F	D	Joe Dorsey	D	Cr	No. 1	L	Cr
		No. 3 died January 25, 1905										
		Census Card No. 2840, P. O. Carrol, Enrolled May 23, 1901										
8230	1	Hope, Sanford	46	M	½		Sunnyboy Hope	L	?	Mollie Hope	D	Cr
8231	2	Hope, Willie	21	M	½	Bro	Sunnyboy Hope	L	?	Mollie Hope	D	Cr
		Census Card No. 2841, P. O. Castle, Enrolled May 23, 1901										
8232	1	Yahola, Nocus	34	M	F		Chohoba	D	Cr	Mehotka	D	Cr
8233	2	Bear, Tinor	19	F	F	D	No. 1	L	Cr	Hoko	D	Cr
8234	3	Yabola, Hardy	13	M	F	S	No. 1	L	Cr	Wisey	D	Cr
8235	4	Bear, Susanna	6	M	F	GrD	Lumpka Harjo	L	Cr	No. 2	L	Cr
		No. 3 said to be duplicate of Roll No. 8394. No. 1 died September 22, 1914. No. 2 died May 9, 1914. No. 4 died November 28, 1911.										
		Census Card No. 2842, P. O. Morse, Enrolled May 23, 1901										
8236	1	Lizzie-pe	7	F	F		Wadey	D	Cr	Monnetta	D	Cr
		Census Card No. 2843, P. O. Pierce, Enrolled May 23, 1901										
8237	1	Berryhill, Peter	35	M	F		Tobe Berryhill	L	Cr	Minda	L	Cr
8238	2	Berryhill, Emma	19	F	F	Sis	Tobe Berryhill	L	Cr	Minda	L	Cr
8239	3	Berryhill, Lizzie	23	F	F	Sis	Tobe Berryhill	L	Cr	Minda	L	Cr
8240	4	Berryhill, Hepsey	7	F	½	Niece	John Starfey	L	Non	No. 3	L	Cr
8241	5	Edmond, Ben	11	M	F	Neph	Wilson Bear	L	Cr	Unknown	D	Cr
		No. 2 died December 22, 1900. No. 4 died January 15, 1904. No. 3 died January 15, 1910. No. 5 died 1911.										
		Census Card No. 2844, P. O. Okfuskee, Enrolled May 23, 1901										
8242	1	Holen, David	17	M	⅓		Holen	L	Choc	Unknown	D	Cr
		No. 1 died August 10, 1900										
		Census Card No. 2845, P. O. Hanna, Enrolled May 23, 1901										
8243	1	Elle, Nocus	28	M	F		Josiah Gray	D	Cr	Okunda	D	Cr
		Census Card No. 2846, P. O. Burney, Enrolled May 23, 1901										
8244	1	Nokeche	50	F	F		Unknown	D	Cr	Unknown	D	Cr
8245	2	Phelama	11	M	F	S	Chitto Harjo	L	Cr	No. 1	L	Cr
		No. 2 died January 12, 1910										
		Census Card No. 2847, P. O. Hanna, Enrolled May 23, 1901										
8246	1	Wicey	35	F	F		George Tiger	D	Cr	Sulkoyeste	D	Cr
8247	2	Kinney, George	18	M	F	S	Sarde Cowe	L	Cr	No. 1	L	Cr
8248	3	Smith, Emily	12	F	F	Ward	Lumsey Smith	D	Cr	Lina	D	Cr
		No. 1 died Feburay 1901. No. 2 died February 1901										
		Census Card No. 2848, P. O. Ridge, Enrolled May 23, 1901										
8249	1	Lowe, Willie	26	M	⅝		Washington Lowe	D	Cr	Mary Manuel	L	Cr
		Census Card No. 2849, P. O. No. 1, Eufaula, No. 2, Wetumka, Enrolled May 23, 1901										
8250	1	Bean, Monday	23	M	F		John Bean	D	Cr	Sarthoyachee	D	Cr
8251	2	Kinney, Chowey	16	M	F		Sarte Cowe	L	Cr	Wisey	D	Cr
		Census Card No. 2850, P. O. Arbeka, Enrolled May 23, 1901										
8252	1	Fixico, Sparney	40	M	F		Unknown	D	Cr	Unknown	D	Cr
		Census Card No. 2851, P. O. Raiford, Enrolled May 23, 1901										
8253	1	Clinton, George	25	M	F		Quassarty	D	Cr	Unknown	D	Cr

Census Card No. 2852, P. O. Henryetta, Enrolled May 10, 1901

| 8254 | 1 | Harjo, Lewis | 24 | M | F | | Yardeka Harjo | L | Cr | Nancy Harjo | L | Cr |

Census Card No. 2853, P. O. Eufaula, Enrolled No. 1, May 23, 1901; No. 2, May 18, 1901

| 8255 | 1 | Noble, Wesley | 37 | M | F | | Wotko Harjo | D | Cr | Salarhogee | D | Cr |
| 8256 | 2 | Noble, Susan | 40 | F | F | Wf | Esoraka | D | Cr | Leah | D | Cr |

No. 2 reported dead

Census Card No. 2854, P. O. Hanna, Enrolled May 23, 1901

| 8257 | 1 | Roberts, Josie | 35 | M | F | | Quechus Henehochee | D | Cr | Fihogee | D | Cr |

Census Card No. 2855, P. O. Senora, Enrolled May 23, 1901

| 8258 | 1 | Harjo, Eufaula | 45 | M | F | | Ahate Harjo | D | Cr | Unknown | D | Cr |
| 8259 | 2 | Stricken from roll |

No. 1 died March 9, 1903

Census Card No. 2856, P. O. Braggs, Enrolled May 23, 1901

8260	1	Sallie	40	F	F		Unknown	D	Cr	Unknown	D	Cr
8261	2	John	20	M	F	S	Creek Sahni	?	Cr	No. 1	L	Cr
8262	3	Millie	18	F	F	D	Creek Sahni,	?	Cr	No. 1	L	Cr
8263	4	Jimsey	13	M	F	S	Creek Sahni	?	Cr	No. 1	L	Cr

No. 3 reported dead. No. 3 known as "Hannah." No. 4 known as "George."

Census Card No. 2857, P. O. Paden, Enrolled May 23, 1901

8264	1	Harjo, Hillis	45	M	F		Nocus Talega	D	Cr	Unknown	D	Cr
8265	2	Nidy	40	F	F	Wf	Chelaha	D	Cr	Folothoge	D	Cr
8266	3	Tustunukoche	20	M	F	S	No. 1	L	Cr	No. 2	L	Cr
8267	4	Kalaney	17	M	F	S	No. 1	L	Cr	No. 2	L	Cr
8268	5	Dolly	15	F	F	D	No. 1	L	Cr	No. 2	L	Cr

No. 2 died December 21, 1913

Census Card No. 2858, (Void)

| 8269 | 1 | Stricken from roll |

Census Card No. 2859, P. O. Weleetka, Enrolled May 23, 1901

| 8270 | 1 | Field, Taylor | 28 | M | F | | Tulma Yahola | D | Cr | Sudeka | D | Cr |

Census Card No. 2860, P. O. Dustin, Enrolled May 23, 1901

| 8271 | 1 | Harjo, Cinda | 30 | F | F | | Ithas Harjochee | D | Cr | Sarhoyagee | D | Cr |
| 8272 | 2 | Harjo, Joker | 33 | M | F | Hus | Yarteker Harjo | D | Cr | Tina | D | Cr |

No. 1 died September 10, 1911

Census Card No. 2861, P. O. Hanna, Enrolled May 23, 1901

8273	1	Hawkins, Susan	65	F	F		Unknown	D	Cr	Unknown	D	Cr
8274	2	Hawkins. Corner	21	M	F	S	Pink Hawkins	D	Cr	No. 1	L	Cr
8275	3	Hawkins, Billy	60	M	F	StS?	Pink Hawkins?	D	Cr	Lydia	D	Cr

No. 3 reported dead

Census Card No. 2862, P. O. Hanna, Enrolled May 23, 1901

| 8276 | 1 | Moses, Willie | 36 | M | F | | Hillis Harjo | D | Cr | Slabuggay | D | Cr |

No. 1 reported dead

Census Card No. 2863, P. O. Weleetka, Enrolled May 23, 1901

| 8277 | 1 | Barnett, Lucy | 28 | F | F | | Dave Barnett | L | Cr | Parte Barnett | D | Cr |

Census Card No. 2864, P. O. Hanna, Enrolled May 23, 1901

8278	1	Kano, Marker	45	F	F		Hillis Harjo	D	Cr	Sterbargee	D	Cr
8279	2	Gray, Ben	21	M	F	S	Marte	D	Cr	No. 1	L	Cr
8280	3	Coon, Lumsey	19	M	F	S	Wood Kudzie	D	Cr	No. 1	L	Cr
8281	4	Kano, Jonas	7	M	F	S	Kano	L	Cr	No. 1	L	Cr
8282	5	Mechiskoche	40	M	F	Hus	Okoche Harjo	D	Cr	Unknown	D	Cr

No. 1 died February 5, 1902. No. 3 died March 9, 1902. No. 5 died Otcober 15, 1901. No. 2 died 1903

Census Card No. 2865, P. O. Eufaula, Enrolled May 23, 1901

8283	1	Mitchell, Nancy	40	F	F		Unknown	D	Cr	Unknown	D	Cr
8284	2	Mitchell, Bunnie	13	M	F	S	Ben Mitchell	D	Cr	No. 1	L	Cr
8285	3	Mitchell, Louvina	10	F	F	D	Ben Mitchell	D	Cr	No. 1	L	Cr

No. 3 died January 27, 1909. No. 1 died July 29, 1906. No. 2 reported dead.

Census Card No. 2866, P. O. Hanna, Enrolled May 23, 1901

8286	1	Harjo, Kutchussee	55	M	F		Unknown	D	Cr	Mollie	D	Cr
8287	2	Harjo, Whynie	50	F	F	Wf	Unknown	D	Cr	Unknown	D	Cr
8288	3	Harjo, Haleya	20	F	F	D	No. 1	L	Cr	No. 2	L	Cr
8289	4	Harjo, Charley	17	M	F	S	No. 1	L	Cr	No. 2	L	Cr
8290	5	Harjo, Noah	14	M	F	S	No. 1	L	Cr	No. 2	L	Cr

No. 3 died about 1899

Census Card No. 2867, P. O. Hanna, Enrolled May 23, 1901

8291	1	Big, Jack	50	M	F		Unknown	D	Cr	Unknown	D	Cr
8292	2	Bettie	40	F	F	Wf	Unknown	D	Cr	Uknnown	D	Cr
8293	3	Nicey	23	F	F	D	No. 1	L	Cr	No. 2	L	Cr
8294	4	Lucinda	21	F	F	D	No. 1	L	Cr	No. 2	L	Cr
8295	5	Tecumsey	17	M	F	S	No. 1	L	Cr	No. 2	L	Cr
8296	6	Kizzie	13	F	F	D	No. 1	L	Cr	No. 2	L	Cr

No. 6 died 1910

Census Card No. 2868, P. O. Bristow, Enrolled May 23, 1901

| 8297 | 1 | Tiger, Thomas | 24 | M | F | | Daniel Tiger | L | Cr | Semima | D | Cr |
| 8298 | 2 | Tiger, Wattie | 1 | M | F | S | No. 1 | L | Cr | Emma Tiger | D | Cr |

No. 2 died August 28, 1900

Census Card No. 2869, P. O. Tulsa, Enrolled May 23, 1901

| 8299 | 1 | Smith, Sarney | 40 | F | F | | Semeyardee | D | Cr | Lucy | D | Cr |

No. 1 died February 6, 1901

Census Card No. 2870, P. O. Tulsa, Enrolled May 23, 1901

| 8300 | 1 | Tuckabache | 85 | M | F | | Unknown | D | Cr | Unknown | D | Cr |

Roll No.	No.	NAME	Age	Sex	Blood	Rel.	NAME OF FATHER	Liv.	Cit.	NAME OF MOTHER	Liv.	Cit.
		Census Card No. 2871, P. O. Eufaula, Enrolled May 23, 1901										
8301	1	Hayne, Annie	14	F	F		Unknown	D	Cr	No. 2	L	Cr
8302	2	Hayne, Mollie	29	F	F	Moth	Unknown	D	Cr	Chimka	L	Cr
8303	3	Stricken from roll										
		No. 1 reported dead										
		Census Card No. 2872, P. O. Milfay, Enrolled May 23, 1901										
8304	1	Francis, Annie	20	F	F		Tokus Harjo	D	Cr	Cella White	D	Cr
		Census Card No. 2873, P. O. Morris, Enrolled May 23, 1901										
8305	1	Scott, Alec	30	M	F		Peter Larney	D	Cr	Millie Thlocco	D	Cr
		Census Card No. 2874, P. O. Hulbert, Enrolled May 23, 1901										
8306	1	"Nancy"	75	F	F		Unknown	D	Cr	Unknown	D	Cr
8307	2	"Cinda"	50	F	F	D	Unknown	D	Cr	No. 1	L	Cr
8308	3	"Lucy"	22	F	½	GrD	Money Bean	L	Cher	No. 2	L	Cr
8309	4	"Alecher"	18	F	½	GrS	Jess Hair.	D	Cher	No. 2	L	Cr
		No. 1 died April 9. 1910										
		Census Card No. 2875, P. O. Bristow, Enrolled May 23, 1901										
8310	1	Scott, Wiley	45	M	F		Peter Scott	D	Cr	Mary Scott	D	Cr
		Census Card No. 2876, P. O. Hanna, Enrolled May 23, 1901										
8311	1	Benson, Johnson	35	M	F		Samogee	D	Cr	Tina	D	Cr
		Census Card No. 2877, P. O. Dustin, Enrolled May 23, 1901										
8312	1	Fish, Wisey	23	F	F		Ahobulch Bunney	D	Cr	Martha Bunney	D	Cr
		Census Card No. 2878, P. O. Dustin, Enrolled May 23, 1901										
8313	1	Harjo, Yarkinha	50	M	F		Thomas Anderson	D	Non	Liza Anderson	D	Cr
8314	2	Brown, Cosaye	9	M	F	Neph	Jimsey Brown	L	Sem	Unknown	L	Cr
		No. 2 possible duplicate of No. 7680. No. 1 died February 7, 1900										
		Census Card No. 2879, P. O. Quinton, Enrolled May 23, 1901										
8315	1	Karny, Lizzie	50	F	½		John Morrison	D	Non	Niccatiya	D	Cr
8316	2	Watson, Daniel	33	M	¾	S	Lewe Hawkins	D	Cr	No. 1	L	Cr
8317	3	Carney, Fulsom	23	M	¼	S	Robert Carney	D	Choc	No. 1	L	Cr
		Census Card No. 2880, P. O. Hanna, Enrolled 23, 1901										
8318	1	Hill, Soma	60	F	F		Unknown	D	Cr	Unknown	D	Cr
8319	2	Hill, John	60	M	F	Hus	Unknown	D	Cr	Unknown	D	Cr
8320	3	Barnett, Austin	35	M	F	S	No. 2	L	Cr	No. 1	L	Cr
8321	4	Amster, Susana	30	F	F	D	No. 2	L	Cr	No. 1	L	Cr
		No. 1 died November 1903. No. 3 reported dead.										
		Census Card No. 2881, P. O. Eufaula, Enrolled May 23, 1901										
8322	1	Harjo, Woxie Emarthla	40	M	F		Sowanoke Harjo	D	Cr	Millie Harjo	D	Cr
8323	2	Harjo, Millie	10	F	F	D	No. 1	L	Cr	Alleah Harjo	D	Cr
8324	3	Harjo, Simon	9	M	F	S	No. 1	L	Cr	Alleah Harjo	D	Cr
		No. 1 died March 15, 1906										
		Census Card No. 2882, P. O. Wagoner, Enrolled May 23, 1901										
8325	1	Fish, Elson	45	F	F		Thlotka Yohola	D	Cr	Naguftache	D	Cr
		No. 1 reported dead										
		Census Card No. 2883, P. O. Bearden, Enrolled May 23, 1901										
8326	1	Hellet, Sam	20	M	F		David Herrod	L	Cr	Widey	D	Cr
		Census Card No. 2884, P. O. Wagoner, Enrolled May 23, 1901										
8327	1	Lucy	45	F	F		Westerna	D	Cr	Ottawa	D	Cr
		Notation on card. No. 1 probably died before Apttril 1, 1899										
		Census Card No. 2885, P. O. Hanna, Enrolled May 23, 1901										
8328	1	Sooktey	60	F	F		Unknown	D	Cr	Unknown	D	Cr
8329	2	Stepney, Sissie	33	F	F	D	Unknown	D	Cr	No. 1	L	Cr
8330	3	Stepney, Liley	10	F	F	GrD	Stepney	D	Cr	No. 2	L	Cr
8331	4	Stepney, Thompson	15	M	F	GrS	Stepney	D	Cr	No. 2	L	Cr
		No. 1 died October 3, 1904										
		Census Card No. 2886, P. O. Sasakwa, Enrolled May 23, 1901										
8332	1	Harjo, Shawnee	27	M	F		Unknown	D	Cr	Sukey	D	Cr
8333	2	Harjo, Contah	18	M	F	½Bro	Ussan Harjo	D	Cr	Sukey	D	Cr
		No. 1 reported dead										
		Census Card No. 2887, P. O. Burney, Enrolled May 23, 1901										
8334	1	Fixeco, Nocus	48	M	F		Sunny	D	Cr	Charta	D	Cr
		No. 1 died 1900										
		Census Card No. 2888, P. O. Okmulgee, Enrolled May 23, 1901										
8335	1	Laslie, Lewis	11	M	F		Colbert Laslie	D	Cr	Lucy Laslie	D	Cr
		No. 1 July 25, 1899										
		Census Card No. 2889, P. O. Hanna, Enrolled May 23, 1901										
8336	1	Fish, Rose	21	F	F		Eli Fish	D	Cr	Lizzie Buckner	L	Cr
		Census Card No. 2890, P. O. Hanna, Enrolled May 23, 1901										
8337	1	Fish, Lewis	27	M	F		Eli Fish	D	Cr	Lizzie Buckner	L	Cr
		Census Card No. 2891, P. O. Hanna, Enrolled May 23, 1901										
8338	1	Buckner, Lizzie	55	F	F		Takacho	D	Cr	Liza	D	Cr
		No. 1 reported dead										
		Census Card No. 2892, P. O. Hanna, Enrolled May 23, 1901										
8339	1	Arssee, Albert	18	M	F		Arssee	D	Cr	Sallie Semulge	D	Cr
		Census Card No. 2893, P. O. Hanna, Enrolled May 24, 1901										
8340	1	Simmons, George	33	M	F		Tom Simmons	D	Cr	Delilah McIntosh	D	Cr
8341	2	Simmons, Martha	22	F	F	Wf	Big William	D	Cr	Selina	D	Cr
8342	3	Simmons, Samuel	3	M	F	S	No. 1	L	Cr	No. 2	L	Cr

Roll No.	No.	NAME	Age	Sex	Blood	Rel.	NAME OF FATHER	Liv.	Cit.	NAME OF MOTHER	Liv.	Cit.
		Census Card No. 2894, P. O. Schulter, Enrolled May 23, 1901										
8343	1	Lowe, Samuel	42	M	F		Gaber	D	Cr	Houeel	D	Cr
8344	2	Lowe, Mahaley	30	F	F	Wf	Gibson	D	Cr	Mulsey	D	Cr
8345	3	Lowe, Johnson	12	M	F	S	No. 1	L	Cr	No. 2	L	Cr
8346	4	Lowe, John	10	M	F	S	No. 1	L	Cr	No. 2	L	Cr
8347	5	Lowe, Nancy	8	F	F	D	No. 1	L	Cr	No. 2	L	Cr
8348	6	Lowe, Jennie	7	F	F	D	No. 1	L	Cr	No. 2	L	Cr
8349	7	Lowe, Lena	2	F	F	D	No. 1	L	Cr	No. 2	L	Cr
		No. 1 died May 27, 1910. No. 3 died 1910.										
		Census Card No. 2895, P. O. Eufaula, Enrolled May 23, 1901										
8350	1	Harjo. Itshas	50	M	F		Jacob Hale	D	Cr	Fahishkakee	D	Cr
		No. 1 died August 13, 1908										
		Census Card No. 2896, P. O. Hanna, Enrolled May 23, 1901										
8351	1	Kano, Thomas	24	M	F		Woxie Harjo	L	Cr	Mary Kano	D	Cr
8352	2	Smith, Annie	21	F	F	Cou	Tuskegie Chupco	D	Cr	Harriet Kano	D	Cr
		No. 1 died November 30, 1911										
		Census Card No. 2897, P. O. Indianola, Enrolled May 23, 1901										
8353	1	Washington, George	38	M	F		Tulmochus Harjo	D	Cr	Taye	L	Cr
8354	2	Taye	100	F	F	Moth	Unknown	D	Cr	Unknown	D	Cr
8355	3	Lowe, Leona	25	F	F	Niece	Jim Lowe	D	Cr	Lowina	D	Cr
8356	4	Lowe, Liza	22	F	F	Niece	Jim Lowe	D	Cr	Lowina	D	Cr
		No. 3 died September 1902. No. 4 died July 1902. No. 2 reported dead.										
		Census Card No. 2898, P. O. Hanna, Enrolled May 23, 1901										
8357	1	Bear, Fannie	40	F	F		Nocus Harjo	D	Cr	Marsey	D	Cr
8358	2	Low, Susie	19	F	F	Niece	Jim Low	D	Cr	Lowina	D	Cr
		Census Card No. 2899, P. O. Hanna, Enrolled May 23, 1901										
8359	1	White, George	25	M	F		Charley Hutka	D	Cr	Sally Hutka	D	Cr
		Census Card No. 2900, P. O. Holdenville, Enrolled May 23, 1901										
8360	1	Kano, Missie	50	M	F		Unknown	D	Cr	Lucy Kano	D	Cr
		Census Card No. 2901, P. O. Hanna, Enrolled May 23, 1901										
8361	1	Green, Lucy	18	F	F		Bennie Green	L	Cr	Sally Green	D	Cr
		Census Card No. 2902, P. O. Checotah, Enrolled May 23, 1901										
8362	1	Wolf, Lucy	24	F	½		William Wolf	L	Cr	Mary Wolf	L	Cr
8363	2	Wolf, Janie	21	F	½	Sis	William Wolf	L	Cr	Mary Wolf	L	Cr
8364	3	Wolf, Susie	7	F	¼	D	Walter McIntosh	D	Cr	No. 1	L	Cr
8365	4	Wolf, Mary	60	F	½	Moth	Unknown	D	Cr	Unknown	D	Cr
8366	5	Wolf, Francis	6	F	¼	D	Mose McIntosh	L	Non	No. 1	L	Cr
		No. 5 died August 5, 1899. No. 4 died June 9, 1902.										
		Census Card No. 2903, P. O. Mellette, Enrolled May 23, 1901										
8367	1	Benton, Jennie	40	F	½		Unknown		Cr	Unknown	D	Cr
8368	2	Benton, Mary	11	F	¾	D	Bob Benton	L	Cr	No. 1	L	Cr
8369	3	Hall, Nora	18	F	¾	D	Joe Hall	D	Cr	No. 1	L	Cr
		No. 2 died November 9, 1908										
		Census Card No. 2904, P. O. Mellette, Enrolled May 23, 1901										
8370	1	Holupe, George	55	M	F		Fushutche Micco	D	Cr	Unknown	D	Cr
		Census Card No. 2905, P. O. Eufaula, Enrolled May 23, 1901										
8371	1	Atkins, John	12	M	F		Hotka (or Thomas Atkins)	L	Cr	Rina Atkins	L	Cr
		No. 1 died 1901										
		Census Card No. 2906, P. O. Indianola, Enrolled May 23, 1901										
8372	1	Harjo, Tiger	60	M	F		Unknown	D	Cr	Unknown	D	Cr
		No. 1 died February 20, 1905										
		Census Card No. 2907, P. O. Hanna, Enrolled May 23, 1901										
8373	1	Gray, James L.	45	M	F		Sparney Fixeco	D	Cr	Polly	D	Cr
8374	2	Gray, Belle	18	F	F	D	No. 1	L	Cr	Maria Gray	D	Cr
8375	3	Gray, Mildred	16	F	F	D	No. 1	L	Cr	Maria Gray	D	Cr
		No. 1 reported dead										
		Census Card No. 2908, P. O. Hanna, Enrolled May 23, 1901										
8376	1	Mehate	65	F	F		Lasley	D	Cr	Unknown	D	Cr
8377	2	Susanna	20	F	F	D	Unknown	D	Cr	No. 1	L	Cr
		No. 1 reported dead										
		Census Card No. 2909, P. O. North Fork, Enrolled May 23, 1901										
8378	1	Simapoka	29	F	F		Sam Laslie	D	Cr	Unknown	D	Cr
		Census Card No. 2910, P. O. Eufaula, Enrolled May 23, 1901										
8379	1	Bellen, Nellie	23	F	F		Chehegee	D	Cr	Mehoda	D	Cr
		Census Card No. 2911, P. O. Amabala, Enrolled May 23, 1901										
8380	1	Chofoloche	45	M	F		Chula Fixeco	D	Cr	Unknown	D	Cr
8381	2	Fixico, Choela	45	M	F		Nokin Cho Harjo	D	Cr	Unknown	D	Cr
		No. 2 possible duplicate of No. 4984. No. 1 died January 1, 1900. No. 2 died May 1, 1900.										
		Census Card No. 2912, P. O. Hanna, Enrolled May 23, 1901										
8382	1	Smith, Segomaha	16	M	F		Sarty Smith	L	Cr	Betsy Smith	D	Cr
8383	2	Smith, Ella	12	F	F	Sis	Sarty Smith	L	Cr	Betsy Smith	D	Cr
8384	3	Smith, Sarty	47	M	F	Fath	Cosar Yahola	D	Cr	Kownpka	D	Cr
		No. 3 died February 20, 1901										
		Census Card No. 2913, P. O. Hanna, Enrolled May 23, 1901										
8385	1	Lasley, William	40	M	F		Lasley	D	Cr	Unknown	D	Cr
		No. 1 died 1904										
		Census Card No. 2914, P. O. Hanna, Enrolled May 23, 1901										
8386	1	Lindsey, Silla	40	F	F		Unknown	D	Cr	Suhkcne	D	Cr
8387	2	Lindsey, Roley	17	M	F	S	George Hohke	D	Cr	No. 1	L	Cr
8388	3	Lindsey, Dorsey	14	M	F	S	George Hohke	D	Cr	No. 1	L	Cr

Roll No.	No.	NAME	Age	Sex	Blood	Rel.	NAME OF FATHER	Liv.	Cit.	NAME OF MOTHER	Liv.	Cit.
		Census Card No. 2915, P. O. Hanna, Enrolled May 24, 1901										
8389	1	Kano, Bird Creek	30	M	F		Taskegee	D	Cr	Wicey	D	Cr
8390	2	Kano, John	24	M	F	Bro	Taskegee	D	Cr	Wicey	D	Cr
8391	3	Kano, Louisa	27	F	F	Wf	Haney Bear	D	Cr	Mahala	D	Cr
8392	4	Kano, Jannie	10	F	F	StD	Oscar Gano	D	Cr	No. 3	L	Cr
8393	5	Kano, Barney	5	M	F	S	No. 1	L	Cr	No. 3	L	Cr
8394	6	Bear, Harty	15	M	F	Bro-L	Haney Bear	L	Cr	Mahala	D	Cr
8395	7	Bear, Bamma	13	M	F	Bro-L	Haney Bear	D	Cr	Mahala	D	Cr
8396	8	Stricken from roll.										

No. 2 died October 23, 1901. No. 4 reported dead. No. 5 died January 15, 1900. No. 6 possible duplicate of Enrollment No. 8234.

		Census Card No. 2916, P. O. Lenna, Enrolled May 23, 1901										
8397	1	Jones, Haikey	50	M	F		Unknown	D	Cr	Unknown	D	Cr
		Census Card No. 2917, [Void]										
8398	1	Sricken from roll.										
		Census Card No. 2918, P. O. Salem, Enrolled May 23, 1901										
8399	1	Widy	42	F	F		Unknown	D	Cr	Unknown	D	Cr
8400	2	Cheparney	16	M	F	S	Fus Yahola	D	Cr	No. 1	L	Cr
8401	3	Wisey	11	F	F	D	Fus Yahola	D	Cr	No. 1	L	Cr
8402	4	Willie	8	M	F	S	Fus Yahola	D	Cr	No. 1	L	Cr

No. 2 died about 1910

		Census Card No. 2919, P. O. Choska, Enrolled May 23, 1901										
8403	1	Jackson, Will	35	M	F		Nape Jackson	D	Cr	Ada Jackson	D	Cr

No. 1 died 1900

		Census Card No. 2920, P. O. Brush Hill, Enrolled May 23, 1901										
8404	1	Stand, Phillip	28	M	F		Hoethle	D	Cr	Martha	D	Cr

No. 1 died January 19, 1901

		Census Card No. 2921, P. O. Sasakwa, Enrolled May 23, 1901										
8405	1	Barnett, Mahala	21	F	F		Jicoche	D	Cr	Mulleanna	D	Cr
8406	2	Barnett, Louis	6	M	F	S	Tomsey	L	Sem	No. 1	L	Cr

No. 2 died August 5, 1899

		Census Card No. 2922, P. O. Oktaha, Enrolled May 23, 1901										
8407	1	Wiker, Yarhola	50	M	F		Harjo	D	Cr	Annie Wiker	D	Cr
8408	2	Wiker, Morley	7	M	F	D	No. 1	L	Cr	Susanna	D	Cr
8409	3	Wiker, Belloche	17	M	F		Ward Jonutua	D	Cr	Muchie Gilboa	D	Cr

No. 1 died April 12, 1899

		Census Card No. 2923, P. O. Eufaula, Enrolled May 23, 1901										
8410	1	Warrior, Lydia	60	F	F		Unknown	D	Cr	Unknown	D	Cr
8411	2	Warrior, Dave	22	M	F	S	Tuskenup Chupco	D	Cr	No. 1	L	Cr
8412	3	Warrior, John	18	M	F	S	Tuskenup Chupco	D	Cr	No. 1	L	Cr

No. 2 died 1906. No. 3 died 1906. No. 1 reported dead.

		Census Card No. 2924, P. O. Dustin, Enrolled May 23, 1901										
8413	1	Harper, Shawnee	28	M	F		Emala Yahola	D	Cr	Betsey Harper	D	Cr
8414	2	Harper, Mary	30	F	F	Sis	E,mala Yahola	D	Cr	Betsey Harper	D	Cr
		Census Card No. 2925, P. O. Checotah, Enrolled May 23, 1901										
8415	1	Bear, Lottie	30	F	F		John Goodee	D	Cr	Charity Goodee	D	Cr
		Census Card No. 2926, P. O. Oktaha, Enrolled May 23, 1901										
8416	1	Dick, Timmie	35	M	F		Dick	D	Cr	Mollesy	D	Cr
		Census Card No. 2927, [Void]										
8417	1	Stricken from roll										
		Census Card No. 2928, P. O. Eufaula, Enrolled May 23, 1901										
8418	1	Shelly, Tom	68	M	F		Unknown	D	Cr	Unknown	D	Cr

No. 1 died October 20, 1906

		Census Card No. 2929, P. O. Onapa, Enrolled May 23, 1901										
8419	1	Bear, Ryder	33	M	F		Nokosee	D	Cr	Nancy Bear	D	Cr
		Census Card No. 2930, P. O. Eufaula, Enrolled May 23, 1901										
8420	1	Bear, Hepsey	43	F	F		Nokosee	D	Cr	Nancy Bear	D	Cr
8421	2	Sawyer, Minnie	18	F	F	D	Tom Sawyer	D	Cr	No. 1	L	Cr
8422	3	Lewis, Thomas	19	M	F	S	Daniel Lewis	L	Cr	No. 1	L	Cr
8423	4	Johnson, Susan	10	F	F	D	Jim Johnson	D	Cr	No. 1	L	Cr

No. 2 reported dead

		Census Card No. 2931, P. O. Eufaula, Enrolled May 23, 1901										
8424	1	Bush, Hattie	21	F	F		Jonas Bush	D	Cr	Hepsey Bear	L	Cr
8425	2	Bush, Jessie	3	F	F	D	Unknown	L	Cr	No. 1	L	Cr

No. 2 died November 11, 1900

		Census Card No. 2932, P. O. Morse, Enrolled May 23, 1901										
8426	1	Fields, Mitchell	23	M	F		Watt Field	D	Cr	Lena Fields	D	Cr
		Census Card No. 2933, P. O. Holdenville, Enrolled May 23, 1901										
8427	1	Beaver, Lousanna	18	F	F		Itsus Fixico	D	Cr	Wisey Fixico	D	Cr
		Census Card No. 2934, P. O. Muskogee, Enrolled May 23, 1901										
8428	1	Grayson, Susan	68	F	F		Unknown	D	Cr	Unknown	D	Cr

No. 1 died October 23, 1900

		Census Card No. 2935, P. O. Hanna, Enrolled May 23, 1901										
8429	1	Big ,William Hannah	20	F	F		Big William	D	Cr	Salina	D	Cr
		Census Card No. 2936										
8430	1	Fife, Nixie	45	M	F							

No.,1 duplicate of enrollment opposite No. 4699, this enrollment cancelled by order of Secretary of Interior, see department letter dated August 6, 1909.
No. 1 died March 7, 1909

Roll No.	No.	NAME	Age	Sex	Blood	Rel.	NAME OF FATHER	Liv.	Cit.	NAME OF MOTHER	Liv.	Cit.
		Census Card No. 2937, P. O. Coweta, Enrolled May 23, 1901										
8431	1	Wiley, Jennie	15	F	F		Jackson Wiley	D	Cr	Maria Wiley	D	Cr
		No. 1 died April 15, 1901										
		Census Card No. 2938, P. O. Hanna, Enrolled May 23, 1901										
8432	1	Bruner, David	18	M	F		Lente Bruner	D	Cr	Ulseger	D	Cr
		No. 1 died May 6, 1899										
		Census Card No. 2939, P. O. Calvin, Enrolled May 23, 1901										
8433	1	Hammer, Louis	32	M	F		Cotcha Homarta	D	Cr	Leah Tiger	L	Cr
		No. 1 died February 20, 1901										
		Census Card No. 2940, P. O. Senora, Enrolled May 23, 1901										
8434	1	Chotkey, Nancy	45	F	F		Unknown	D	Cr	Unknown	D	Cr
8435	2	Toney, Rogers	25	M	F	S	Jim Toney	D	Cr	No. 1	L	Cr
8436	3	Chotkey, Addie	14	F	F	D	Fus Yahola	D	Cr	No. 1	L	Cr
8437	4	Chotkey, Mahala	12	F	F	D	Fus Yahola	D	Cr	No. 1	L	Cr
		No. 1 died 1900. No. 2 died April 16, 1903. No. 3 died July 17, 1907.										
		Census Card No. 2941, P. O. Eufaula; No. 3, Porter, Enrolled May 23, 1901										
8438	1	Smith, Chatman	48	M	F		George Smith	D	Cr	Lizzie	D	Cr
8439	2	Smith, Martin	14	M	F	S	No. 1	L	Cr	Nellie Smith	D	Cr
8440	3	Lewis, Ellis J.	11	M	F	GrS	Daniel Lewis	L	Cr	Sarah Lewis	?	Cr
8441	4	Lewis, Frazier	9	M	F	GrS	Daniel Lewis	L	Cr	Sarah Lewis	?	Cr
		No. 1 died 1899. No. 2 reported dead										
		Census Card No. 2942, P. O. Salem, Enrolled May 23, 1901										
8442	1	Taylor, Leechie	20	F	F		Charley Ta lor	D	Cr	Hardy Taylor	L	Cr
		Census Card No. 2943, P. O. Holdenville, Enrolled Mayy23, 1901										
8443	1	Thomas, Albert	22	M	F		Enledego	D	Cr	Unknown	D	Cr
		No. 1 died April 1901										
		Census Card No. 2944, P. O. Eufaula, Enrolled May 23, 1901										
8444	1	Tiger, Archie	80	M	F		Unknown	D	Cr	Godeny	D	Cr
8445	2	Tiger, James	23	M	F	GrS	Roley Tiger	D	Cr	Bessie Tiger	D	Cr
8446	3	Tiger, Silvia	16	F	F	GrS	Roley Tiger	D	Cr	Bessie Tiger	D	Cr
		No. 1 died January 27, 1907										
		Census Card No. 2945, P. O. Salem, Enrolled May 23, 1901										
8447	1	Colbert, Dick	50	M	F		Thlechuma Harjo	D	Cr	Unknown	D	Cr
		Census Card No. 2946, P. O. Earlsboro, Enrolled May 23, 1901										
8448	1	Scott, Louisa	25	F	F		Thompson	D	Cr.	Susan Thompson	D	Cr
		No. 1 reported dead										
		Census Card No. 2947, P. O. Salem, Enrolled May 23, 1901										
8449	1	Semi-hoye	60	F	F		Unknown	D	Cr	Unknown	D	Cr
8450	2	Jeannetta	32	F	F	D	Mickogee	D	Cr	No. 1	L	Cr
8451	3	Annie	29	F	F	D	Mickogee	D	Cr	No. 1	L	Cr
8452	4	Toot-chee	25	F	F	D	Mickogee	D	Cr	No. 1	L	Cr
8453	5	Sukey	22	F	F	D	Mickogee	D	Cr	No. 1	L	Cr
8454	6	Cheparney	15	F	F	D	Mickogee	D	Cr	No. 1	L	Cr
8455	7	Arlike	10	M	F	S	Mickogee	D	Cr	No. 1	L	Cr
		No. 6 died October 13, 1914. Nos. 1 and 7 reported dead										
		Census Card No. 2948, P. O. Henryetta, Enrolled May 23, 1901										
8456	1	Haney, Narchker	40	F	F		Yahola Fixico	D	Cr	Elizabeth Fixico	D	Cr
8457	2	Haney, Lena	14	F	F	D	Haney	L	Cr	No. 1	L	Cr
8458	3	Haney, Leah	12	F	F	D	Haney	L	Cr	No. 1	L	Cr
8459	4	Taylor, Eliza	7	F	F	GrD	Taylor	L	Cr	Silla McGilbra	D	Cr
8460	5	Scott, Lizzie	6	F	F	D	Haney Scott	L	Cr	No. 1	L	Cr
		No. 2 died December 1909. No. 5 died 1900.										
		Census Card No. 2949, P. O. Eufaula, Enrolled May 23, 1901										
8461	1	Harper, John	16	M	F			D	Cr	Fannie Harper	D	Cr
		Census Card No. 2950, P. O. Senora, Enrolled May 23, 1901										
8462	1	Arbuckle, Betsey	35	F	F		Mickogee	D	Cr	Semihoyee	L	Cr
8463	2	Arbuckle, Napsey	9	F	F	D	Arbuckle	D	Cr	No. 1	L	Cr
8464	3	Arbuckle, Battle	8	M	F	S	Arbuckle	D	Cr	No. 1	L	Cr
8465	4	Arbuckle, Fanny	7	F	F	D	Arbuckle	D	Cr	No. 1	L	Cr
8466	5	Arbuckle, Louisa	5	F	F	D	Arbuckle	D	Cr	No. 1	L	Cr
8467	6	Arbuckle, Millie	4	F	F	D	Arbuckle	D	Cr	No. 1	L	Cr
8468	7	Arbuckle, Tommy	3	M	F	S	Arbuckle	D	Cr	No. 1	L	Cr
		No. 1 died December 8, 1908. No. 3 died January 28, 1915. Nos. 2 and 5 reported dead										
		Census Card No. 2951, P. O. Henryetta, Enrolled May 23, 1901										
8469	1	McGilbra, Barney	20	M	F		Tulwa Micco	D	Cr	Unknown	D	Cr
		Census Card No. 2952, P. O. Dustin, Enrolled May 23, 1901										
8470	1	Coker, Wisey	25	F	F		London Coker	L	Cr	Annie Coker	D	Cr
		Census Card No. 2953, P. O. Salem, Enrolled May 23, 1901										
8471	1	Scott, Annie	35	F	F		Cono Yahola	D	Cr	Jinnie Thlocco	D	Cr
8472	2	Scott, George	36	M	F	Bro	Cono Yahola	D	Cr	Jinnie Thlocco	D	Cr
		Census Card No. 2954, P. O. Eufaula, Enrolled May 23, 1901										
8473	1	Riley, Tiger	25	M	F		Joe Riley	D	Cr	Riley	D	Cr
		No. 1 died 1902										
		Census Card No. 2955, P. O. Eufaula, Enrolled May 23, 1901										
8474	1	Siver, George	9	M	F		Unknown	D	Cr	Kizzie	D	Cr·
		Census Card No. 2956, P. O. Eufaula, Enrolled May 23, 1901										
8475	1	Charles, Sukey	46	F	F		Nocus Yahola	D	Cr	Unknown	D	Cr·
8476	2	Charles, James	19	M	F	S	Sammie Charles	D	Cr	No. 1	L	Cr·
8477	3	Charles, Ellen	15	F	F	D	Sammie Charles	D	Cr	No. 1	L	Cr·

179

Roll No.	No.	NAME	Age	Sex	Blood	Rel.	NAME OF FATHER	Liv.	Cit.	NAME OF MOTHER	Liv.	Cit.
		Census Card No. 2957, P. O. Calvin, Enrolled May 23, 1901										
8478	1	Wilson, Thomas	32	M	F		John Wilson	D	Choc	Kessella	D	Cr
8479	2	Wilson, Charley	28	M	F	Bro	John Wilson	D	Choc	Kessella	D	Cr
		No. 1 reported dead										
		Census Card No. 2958, P. O. McAlester, Enrolled May 23, 1901										
8480	1	Wesley, Major	25	M	F		Kapecha Fixico	D	Cr	Lucy Deor	L	Cr
		No. 1 in State Penitentiary										
		Census Card No. 2959, P. O. Eufaula, Enrolled May 23, 1901										
8481	1	Mitchell, Lewis	30	M	F		Yohola Fixico	D	Cr	Lizzie Betsey	D	Cr
8482	2	Mitchell, Billie	28	F	F	Wf	George Carr	L	Cr	Annie Scott	L	Cr
8483	3	Mitchell, Moses	8	M	F	S	No. 1	L	Cr	No. 2	L	Cr
8484	4	Mitchell, Soloman	6	M	F	S	No. 1	L	Cr	No. 2	L	Cr
		No. 3 died July 27, 1912										
		Census Card No. 2960, P. O. Eufaula, Enrolled May 23, 1901										
8485	1	Lewis, Daniel	34	M	F		Jackson Lewis	L	Cr	Hannah Lewis	D	Cr
8486	2	Lewis, Polly	22	F	F	Wf	Max Thompson	D	Cr	Hulda Thompson	D	Cr
8487	3	Lewis, Benjamin	6	M	F	S	No. 1	L	Cr	No. 2	L	Cr
		Census Card No. 2961, P. O. Salem, Enrolled May 23, 1901										
8488	1	Fry, Sam	22	M	F		Emarthla	D	Cr	Sinkiyah	D	Cr
		Census Card No. 2962, P. O. Eufaula, Enrolled May 23, 1901										
8489	1	Thompson, Ben	45	M	F		Maxey	D	Cr	Hutkey	D	Cr
8490	2	Thompson, Jeannetta	30	F	F	Sis	Maxey	D	Cr	Fannie	D	Cr
		Census Card No. 2963, P. O. Senora, Enrolled May 23, 1901										
8491	1	Carr, Archie	50	M	F		Tom Carr	D	Cr	Unknown	D	Cr
8492	2	Carr, Sallie	50	F	F	Wf	Yartekah Harjo	L	Cr	Unknown	D	Cr
		No. 1 died August 12, 1912. No. 2 died 1906										
		Census Card No. 2964, P. O. Eufaula, Enrolled May 23, 1901										
8493	1	Greenwood, Hannah	35	F	F		John Greenwood	D	Cr	Unknown	D	
		No. 1 possible duplicate of enrollment opposite No. 8837, this roll										
		Census Card No. 2965, P. O. Holdenville, Enrolled May 23, 1901										
8494	1	Coser, Annie	21	F	F		Nocus Harjo	?	Cr	Katie	D	Cr
8495	2	Coser, Mattie	20	F	F	Cou	Coser Fixeco	D	Cr	Fannie	D	Cr
		No. 1 died 1902. No. 2 reported dead.										
		Census Card No. 2966, P. O. Hanna, Enrolled May 23, 1901										
8496	1	Red, Thomas	40	M	F		Wash Red	D	Cr	Unknown	D	Cr
8497	2	Gouge, Earnest	26	M	F	Neph	Dave George	D	Cr	Unknown	D	Cr
8498	3	Gouge, Jack	23	M	F	Neph	Dave George	D	Cr	Unknown	D	Cr
		Census Card No. 2967, P. O. Hanna, Enrolled May 23, 1901										
8499	1	James, Martha	30	F	F		Inledegho	D	Cr	Tokogee	D	Cr
8500	2	James, Billie	9	M	F	S	James	D	Cr	No. 1	L	Cr
8501	3	Hawkins, Susie	15	F	F	Sis	Bonnie Hawkins	D	Cr	Tokogee	D	Cr
8502	4	James, Gibson	32	M	F	Hus	Katcha Micco	D	Cr	Fannie Manley	D	Cr
		No. 1 died 1902. No. 3 stricken from roll, see department letter dated Setember 21, 1909										
		Census Card No. 2968, P. O. Holdenville, Enrolled May 23, 1901										
8503	1	Mollie	29	F	F		Micco Harjo	D	Cr	Nancy	D	Cr
		Census Card No. 2969, P. O. Wagoner, Enrolled May 23, 1901; Nos. 2, 3, 4, 5, January 15, 1901										
8504	1	Harvison, Dollie	37	F	1-16		William Mackey	D	Cher	Nancy Drew	D	Cher
8505	2	Harvison, Floyd	14	M	1-16	S	William Harvison	D	Cr	No. 1	L	Cr
8506	3	Harvison, Irene	12	F	1-16	D	William Harvison	D	Cr	No. 1	L	Cr
8507	4	Harvison, Clifford	9	M	1-16	S	William Harvison	D	Cr	No. 1	L	Cr
8508	5	Harvison, Marie	6	F	1-16	D	William Harvison	D	Cr	No. 1	L	Cr
		Census Card No. 2970, P. O. Eufaula, Enrolled May 23, 1901										
8509	1	Bruner, Jackson	18	M	F		Wiley Bruner	D	Cr	Haley (Bruner)	D	Cr
		No. 1 duplicate of enrollment opposite No. 6975, this roll										
		Census Card No. 2971, P. O. Eufaula, Enrolled May 23, 1901										
8510	1	Jim, Tom	10	M	F		Yoloha	D	Cr	Katie	D	Cr
8511	2	Jim, Louisianna	11	F	F	½Sis	Yoharjo	D	Cr	Katie	D	Cr
		No. 1 died 1901. No. 2 died 1900.										
		Census Card No. 2972, P. O. Bristow, Enrolled May 23, 1901										
8512	1	Davy, Wantay	8	F	F		Davy	?	?	Unknown	D	?
		No. 1 has an allotment in Shawnee Country, for further information see Department Letter No. 56880, 1914. Identification erroneous										
		Census Card No. 2973, P. O. Sapulpa, Enrolled May 23, 1901										
8513	1	Eufaula, William	90	M	F		Unknown	D	Cr	Unknown	D	Cr
		No. 1 died December 17, 1899										
		Census Card No. 2974, P. O. Salem, Enrolled May 23, 1901										
8514	1	Coker, Emma	30	F	F		Unknown	D	Sem	Loskey		Cr
		Proably duplicate of Enrollment No. 4634										
		Census Card No. 2975, P. O. Eufaula, Enrolled May 23, 1901										
8515	1	Fisher, Mikey	20	F	F		George Fisher	D	Cr	Folothoke Fisher	D	Cr
		No. 1 died March 26, 1904										
		Census Card No. 2976, P. O. Keokuk Falls, Enrolled May 23, 1901										
8516	1	Jefferson, Prince	48	M	F		Espotoke Harjo	D	Cr	Lucy Partarke	D	Cr
		No. 1 died January 24, 1901										
		Census Card No. 2977, P. O. Tulsa, Enrolled May 23, 1901										
8517	1	Childers, Samuel	32	M	¾		Robert Childers	D	Cr	Rachael Childers	D	Cr
		No. 1 died February 25, 1901										
		Census Card No. 2978, P. O. Fentress, Enrolled May 23, 1901.										
8518	1	McHenry, James	10	M	F		Temarseha	D	Cr	Sena	D	Cr
		No. 1 died October 15, 1900										

Roll No.	No.	NAME	Age	Sex	Blood	Rel.	NAME OF FATHER	Liv.	Cit.	NAME OF MOTHER	Liv.	Cit
		Census Card No. 2979, P. O. McDermott, Enrolled May 23, 1901										
8519	1	Cinda	78	F	F		Tommy Harjo	D	Cr	Unknown	D	Cr
		No. 1 died October 14, 1899										
		Census Card No. 2980, P. O. Kellyville, Enrolled May 24, 1901										
8520	1	Cloud, Sophia	28	F	⅛		Laslie Cloud	L	Cr	Eliza Harry	D	Cr
8521	2	Cloud, Dora	11	F	¼	D	John Whistler	L	Non	No. 1	L	Cr
		No. 1 died December 12, 1911										
		Census Card No. 2981, P. O. Kellyville, Enrolled May 24, 1901										
8522	1	Long, Sakquanny	54	M	F		Jim Long	D	Cr	Unknown	D	Cr
8523	2	Tiger, Mollie	22	F	F	D	No. 1	L	Cr	Losenney	D	Cr
8524	3	Tiger, Malinda	20	F	F	D	No. 1	L	Cr	Losenney	D	Cr
		No. 3 died September 1904. No. 2 died February 27, 1904.										
		Census Card No. 2982, P. O. Bristow, Enrolled May 24, 1901										
8525	1	Copahtanney	35	M	F		Tocokqney	D	Cr	Ahlaconthlancy	L	Cr
8526	2	Coneisenney	45	F	F	Wf	Sofalley	D	Cr	Longtahney	D	Cr
8527	3	Faheoconweney	9	M	F	StS	Ocolekcke	D	Cr	No. 2	L	Cr
8528	4	Martha	15	F	F	StD	Coneyoh	D	Cr	No. 2	L	Cr
		No. 4 died March 14, 1906. No. 1 reported dead.										
		Census Card No. 2983, P. O. Bristow, Enrolled May 24, 1901										
8529	1	Ahcoconney	50	F	F		Charley Brown	D	Cr	Unknown	D	Cr
8530	2	Yargee, John	20	M	F	S	Echonney	D	Cr	No. 1	L	Cr
8531	3	Tarchom	18	M	F	S	Echonney	D	Cr	No. 1	L	Cr
		No. 2 died December 26, 1901. No. 3 died August 1904										
		Census Card No. 2984, P. O. Depew, Enrolled May 24, 1901										
8532	1	Ahsey	20	F	F		Echonney	D	Cr	Ahcoconney	L	Cr
8533	2	Partahkazolee	8	F	F	D	Norbe	L	Cr	No. 1	L	Cr
		Census Card No. 2985, P. O. Kellyville, Enrolled May 24, 1901										
8534	1	Pahcahney	60	F	F		Dimbo	D	Cr	Unknown	D	Cr
		No. 1 reported dead										
		Census Card No. 2986, P. O. Eufaula, Enrolled May 2, 1901										
8535	1	Scott, Edward	38	M	F		Yulka Harjo	D	Cr	Jennie Harjo	D	Cr
8536	2	Scott, Tena	38	F	F	Wf	Okfuskochee	D	Cr	Unknown	D	Cr
8537	3	Scott, Katie	11	F	F	D	No. 1	L	Cr	No. 2	L	Cr
8538	4	Scott, Lizzie	8	F	F	D	No. 1	L	Cr	No. 2	L	Cr
8539	5	Scott, Cheparney	3	M	F	S	No. 1	L	Cr	No. 2	L	Cr
		No. 5 reported dead										
		Census Card No. 2987, P. O. Holdenville, Enrolled May 24, 1901										
8540	1	Toney, Lizzie	45	F	F		Chocla Fixico	D	Cr	Temo Hutkoye	D	Cr
		No. 1 died October 1899										
		Census Card No. 2988, P. O. Hanna, Enrolled May 24, 1901										
8541	1	Buckner, Wiley	35	M	F		Edward Bullett	D	Cr	Potoka	D	Cr
8542	2	Buckner, Susie	25	F	F	Wf	Unknown	D	Cr	Lizzie	L	Cr
8543	3	Buckner, Scott	11	M	F	S	No. 1	L	Cr	Lizzie	L	Cr
8544	4	Buckner, Nancy	3	F	F	D	No. 1	L	Cr	No. 2	L	Cr
		Nol 2 died December 15, 1908. No. 3 reported dead.										
		Census Card No. 2989 [Void]										
8545	1	Stricken from roll.										
		Census Card No. 2990, P. O. Vivian, Enrolled May 24, 1901										
8546	1	Colbert, Thompson	35	M	F		Catcha Yahola	D	Cr	Unknown	D	Cr
8547	2	Colbert, Ellen	31	F	F	Wf	Thomas Sigolo	D	Cr	Mahale Colbert	D	Cr
		Census Card No. 2991, P. O. Eufaula, Enrolled May 24, 1901										
8548	1	Seper, Joseph	20	M	F		Seper	?	Cr	Lucinda Bearhead	D	Cr
		Census Card No. 2992, P. O. Rex, Enrolled May 24, 1901										
8549	1	Sutherland, Lol	16	M	⅛		Dick Sutherland	L	Non	Adalaide Sutherland	D	Cr
8550	2	Sutherland, Earnest	14	M	⅛	Bro	Dick Sutherland	L	Non	Adalaide Sutherland	D	Cr
		No. 1 duplication of Cherokee Enrollment No. 5342. No. 2 possibly enrolled as Cherokee citizen										
		Census Card No. 2993, P. O. Holdenville, Enrolled May 24, 1901										
8551	1	Scott, Agnes	6	F	F		Robert Scott	D	Cr	Louisa Scott	D	Cr
		No. 1 reported dead										
		Census Card No. 2994, P. O. Senora, Enrolled May 24, 1901										
8552	1	Thompson, Minnie	7	F	F		Hardy Thompson	D	Cr	Mary Ann Thompson	L	Cr
		No. 1 died February 14, 1911										
		Census Card No. 2995, P. O. Eufaula, Enrolled May 24, 1901										
8553	1	Deere, Noah	33	M	F		Joe Deere	D	Cr	Mahala Deere	D	Cr
8554	2	Deere, Mary	23	F	F	Wf	Yahola Wika	D	Cr	Mosey	D	Cr
8555	3	Deere, Millie	7	F	F	D	No. 1	L	Cr	No. 2	L	Cr
8556	4	Deere, Hence	6	M	F	S	No. 1	L	Cr	No. 2	L	Cr
8557	5	Bear, Louis	17	M	F	½-Br	Haney Bear	D	Cr	Mahala Deere	D	Cr
		Nos. 1, 2 and 3 reported dead										
		Census Card No. 2996, P. O. Nerotown; No. 2 Pierce, Enrolled May 24, 1901										
8558	1	Tobler, Maria	25	F	F		Jack Tobler	D	Cr	Adeline Tobler	D	Cr
8559	2	Tobler, Paulina	18	F	F	Sis	Jack Tobler	D	Cr	Adeline Tobler	D	Cr
8560	3	Tobler, Alvan	15	M	F	Bro	Jack Tobler	D	Cr	Adeline Tobler	D	Cr
		No. 3 died October 1904										
		Census Card No. 2997, P. O. Muskogee, Enrolled June 11, 1901										
8561	1	Haines, David W.	35	M	½		Newton Haines	D	Non	Keziah Haines	D	Cr
		Census Card No. 2998, P. O. Sapulpa, Enrolled May 24, 1901										
8562	1	Frank, Harry	6	M	F		Noah Frank	L	Cr	Frank	D	Non
		Census Card No. 2999, P. O. Eufaula, Enrolled May 23, 1901										
8563	1	Colbert, Sam	40	M	F		Neha Micco	D	Cr	Soma	D	Cr

Roll No.	No.	NAME	Age	Sex	Blood	Rel.	NAME OF FATHER	Liv.	Cit.	NAME OF MOTHER	Liv.	Cit.
		Census Card No. 3000, P. O. Lenna, Enrolled May 24, 1901										
8564	1	Loney, Sam	28	M	F		Loney		D	Cr	Appogey	D	Cr
		Census Card No. 3001, P. O. Dustin, Enrolled May 23, 1901										
8565	1	Wiley, Adam	20	M	F		Willie Moses	L	Cr	Polly Watson	D	Cr
		Census Card No. 3002, P. O. Bristow, Enrolled May 24, 1901										
8566	1	Tulsa, Joe	29	M	F		Tulsa Fixeco	D	Cr	Sinduche	L	Cr
		Census Card No. 3003, P. O. Hanna, Enrolled May 24, 1901										
8567	1	Green, Sarlarka	4	M	F		Cumsey Gray	?	Cr	Absey		Cr
		No. 1 died June 1899										
		Census Card No. 3004, P. O. Mounds, Enrolled May 17, 1901										
8568	1	Bittle, Muskogee Essie	13	F	F		George Bittle	D	Cr	Martha Meeks	D	Cr
		Census Card No. 3005, P. O. Muskogee, Enrolled May 24, 1901										
8569	1	Brook, Nina	20	F	¼		Ben E. Porter	D	?	Sarah Porter	D	?
8570	2	Brook, Nina T.	6 mo	F	⅛	D	Eck E. Brook	L	Non	No. 1	L	Cr
		No. 1 died May 29, 1899. No. 2 died July 3, 1899										
		Census Card No. 3006, P. O. Braggs, Enrolled May 24, 1901										
8571	1	Scott, Liza	48	F	F		Billie Scott	D	Cr	Cinnie Scott	D	Cr
		No. 1 died February 15, 1907										
		Census Card No. 3007, P. O. Sand Springs, Enrolled May 24, 1901										
8572	1	Salmer	50	F	F		Unknown	D	Cr	Unknown	D	Cr
8573	2	Fuswa, Mary	16	F	F	D	Fus Thlocco	D	Cr	No. 1	L	Cr
8574	3	Harjo	12	M	F	S	Fus Thlocco	D	Cr	No. 1	L	Cr
		No. 1 died June 18, 1899. No. 3 died May 24, 1899										
		Census Card No. 3008, P. O. Okmulgee, Enrolled May 24, 1901										
8575	1	Deer, Alice	6	F	F		Wesley Deer	D	Cr	Lucy Deer (Lizzie Deer)	D	Cr
		Census Card No. 3009, P. O. Holdenville, Enrolled May 24, 1901										
8576	1	Mickey, Palmer	29	M	F		Lahta Fixico	D	Cr	Mickey	?	Cr
8577	2	Mickey, Mollie	30	F	F	Wf	Sandy White	D	Cr	Salla Wallow	D	Cr
8578	3	Mickey, Sandy	9	M	F	S	No. 1	L	Cr	No. 2	L	Cr
		Census Card No. 3010, P. O. Holdenville, Enrolled May 24, 1901										
8579	1	McGirt, Aaron	18	M	F		John McGirt	D	Cr	Louzanna	D	Cr
8580	2	Stricken from roll										
		No. 1 died 1900										
		Census Card No. 3011, Holdenville, Enrolled May 24, 1901										
8581	1	Grayson, Roley	25	M	F		Nehethloccoche	?	Cr	Sophia		Cr
		No. 1 died March 29, 1900										
		Census Card No. 3012, P. O. Yeager, Enrolled May 24, 1901										
8582	1	Grayson, Katie	22	F	F		Marchie Grayson	D	Cr	Toge Thlocco	L	Cr
		Census Card No. 3013, P. O. Okmulgee, Enrolled May 24, 1901										
8583	1	Harjo, Keper	20	M	F		Osoche Harjo	D	Cr	Nocoska	D	Cr
		No. 1 died March 31, 1912										
		Census Card No. 3014, P. O. Yeager, Enrolled May 24, 1901										
8584	1	Smith, Jeffrey	21	M	F		Meseh	D	Cr	Sukey	D	Cr
8585	2	Smith, Miley	20	F	F	Sis	Meseh	D	Cr	Sukey	D	Cr
		Census Card No. 3015, P. O. Bearden, Enrolled May 24, 1901										
8586	1	McGirt, Dick	27	M	¾		Daniel McGirt	D	Cr	Jennie McGirt	D	Cr
		Census Card No. 3016, P. O. Yeager, Enrolled May 24, 1901										
8587	1	Fixeco, Willie	18	M	F		Tommy Leagie	D	Cr	Sana	D	Cr
		Census Card No. 3017, P. O. Wewoka, Enrolled May 24, 1901										
8588	1	Walker, Mabel	20	F	½		Lindsey Lursha	?	Sem	Hepsey McGirt	L	Cr
		Census Card No. 3018, P. O. Holdenville, Enrolled May 24, 1901										
8589	1	Harjo, Sophia	53	F	F		Tulwomicco	D	Cr	Timochocte	D	Cr
		No. 1 died May 1904										
		Census Card No. 3019, P. O. Wetumka, Enrolled May 24, 1901										
8590	1	Dunzy, Sahweheche	18	M	F		Goliah	D	Cr	Loedie	D	Cr
		Census Card No. 3020, P. O. Wetumka, Enrolled May 24, 1901										
8591	1	Harjo, Tulmochus	40	M	F		Spanney Harjo	D	Cr	Marfos Yarhogee	D	Cr
		No. 1 died March 15, 1904										
		Census Card No. 3021, [Void]										
8592	1	Stricken from roll										
		Census Card No. 3022, P. O. Eufaula, Enrolled May 24, 1901										
8593	1	Conner, Thomas	50	M	F		Tuskeego Micco	D	Cr	Unknown	D	Cr
		No. 1 died December 12, 1901										
		Census Card No. 3023, P. O. Eufaula, Enrolled May 24, 1901										
8594	1	Gambler, Wallace	20	M	F		Billy Gambler	D	Cr	Sukey Gambler	D	Cr
8595	2	Gambler, John	14	M	F	Bro	Billy Gambler	D	Cr	Sukey Gambler	D	Cr
		No. 1 died March 13, 1905										
		Census Card No. 3024, P. O. Mellette, Enrolled May 24, 1901										
8596	1	Burton, Mack	23	M	¼		Robert Burton	L	Non	Lucinda	D	Cr
8597	2	Burton, Lydia	18	F	¼	Sis	Robert Burton	L	Non	Lucinda	D	Cr
		Census Card No. 3025, P. O. Konowa, Enrolled May 24, 1901										
8598	1	Mullie	40	F	F		Dunnase	D	Cr	Unknown	D	Cr
8599	2	Mullie, Sam	17	M	F	S	Echoille Chupso	L	Sem	No. 1	L	Cr
8600	3	Mullie, Siah	13	F	F	D	Echoille Chupso	L	Sem	No. 1	L	Cr
8601	4	Mullie, Sallie	10	F	F	D	Echoille Chupso	L	Sem	No. 1	L	Cr
8602	5	Mullie, Phenie	9	F	F	D	Echoille Chupso	L	Sem	No. 1	L	Cr
8603	6	Mullie, Willie	4	M	F	S	Echoille Chupso	L	Sem	No. 1	L	Cr
8604	7	Yargee, Willie	20	M	F	StS	Unknown	D	Cr	Unknown	D	Cr
		No. 3 died 1908										

Roll No.	No.	NAME	Age	Sex	Blood	Rel.	NAME OF FATHER	Liv.	Cit.	NAME OF MOTHER	Liv.	Cit.
		Census Card No. 3026, P. O. Eufaula, Enrolled Jay 24, 1901										
8605	1	Colbert, Matilda	75	F	F		Unknown	D	Cr	Unknown	D	Cr
		No. 1 died October 1899										
		Census Card No. 3027, P. O. Eufaula, Enrolled May 24, 1901										
8606	1	Colbert, Louis	20	M	F		Sam Colbert	L	Cr	Peggy Colbert	D	Cr
8607	2	Colbert, Walter	18	M	F	Bro	Sam Colbert	L	Cr	Peggy Colbert	D	Cr
		No. 1 died March 4, 1915										
		Census Card No. 3028, P. O. Paden, Enrolled May 21, 1901										
8608	1	Nichols, Emma	22	F	1-16		Burns	L	Non	Eveline Berryhill	L	Cr
8609	2	Nichols, William B.	2	M	1-16	S	S. F. Field	L	Non	No. 1	L	Cr
		Census Card No. 3029, P. O. Catoosa, Enrolled May 4, 1901										
8610	1	Tiger, Wesley	14	M	F		Wesley Tiger	D	Cr	Katie Tiger	D	Cr
		Census Card No. 3030, P. O. Tulsa, Enrolled April 19, 1901										
8611	1	Boone, Belle	20	F	3/8		Berry Hogan	?	Non	Malissa Hogan	?	Cr
8612	2	Boone, Blanche	3	F	3-16		Otto Boone	L	Non	No. 1	L	Cr
		Census Card No. 3031, P. O. Phillipsburg, Enrolled April 24, 1901										
8613	1	Bigpond, Sophia	28	F	F		Samuel Ben	?	Cr	Jennie Samuel	L	Cr
8614	2	Bigpond, Martha	4	F	F	D	Billie Bigpond	?	Cr	No. 1	L	Cr
		No. 1 died April 26, 1899. No. 2 died September 1900										
		Census Card No. 3032, P. O. Kellyville, Enrolled April 24, 1901										
8615	1	Po-char-ney	63	M	F		Unknown	D	Cr	Unknown	D	Cr
		No. 1 died May 18, 1912										
		Census Card No. 3033, P. O. Micawber, Enrolled April 25, 1901										
8616	1	Tiger, Jim	28	M	F		Tiger, Jack	?	Cr	Jennie Tiger	D	Cr
8617	2	Tiger, Co-ke-thar-ney	11	M	F	S	No. 1	L	Cr	Zasakcoconcharney	D	Cr
8618	3	Tiger, Char-ke-char-ney	9	M	F	S	No. 1	L	Cr	Zasakcoconcharney	D	Cr
		No. 3 died August 15, 1901										
		Census Card No. 3034, P. O. Kellyville, Enrolled April 25, 1901										
8619	1	Tiger, Pa-sak-ta	19	F	F		Goody Tiger	D	Cr	Abcoconnay	D	Cr
8620	2	Tiger, Ke-e-co-ka-ney	17	F	F	Sis	Goody Tiger	D	Cr	Abcoconnay	D	Cr
		No. 1 died February 1900. No. 2 died September 1900										
		Census Card No. 3035, P. O. Eufaula; No. 2 Morris, Enrolled April 20, 1901										
8621	1	Smith, Mary	51	F	1/2		Bolling	D	Non	Unknown	D	Cr
8622	2	Gray, James	22	M	3/4	S	Dickson Gray	D	Cr	No. 1	L	Cr
8623	3	Gray, Walter	20	M	3/4	S	Dickson Gray	D	Cr	No. 1	L	Cr
8624	4	Gray, Louisa	16	F	3/4	S	Dickson Gray	D	Cr	No. 1	L	Cr
8625	5	Gray, Barney	14	M	3/4	S	Dickson Gray	D	Cr	No. 1	L	Cr
8626	6	Gray, Lena	7	F	1/4	D	Dave Goodman	L	Non	No. 1	L	Cr
		No. 3 died December 4, 1904. No. 1 reported dead. No. 6 illegitimate										
		Census Card No. 3036, P. O. Okmulgee, Enrolled April 30, 1901										
8627	1	Simmons, Jeff	7	M	F		Jeff Simmons	D	Cr	Mary Grayson	D	Cr
		Census Card No. 3037, P. O. Checotah, Enrolled April 19, 1901; No. 4 May 23, 1901										
8628	1	Wadsworth, Eliza	26	F	F		Daniel Chisholm	D	Cr	Bettie Chisholm	D	Cr
8629	2	Wadsworth, Annie	6	F	7/8	D	John Wadsworth	L	Sem	No. 1	L	Cr
8630	3	Wadsworth, Richard	3	M	7/8	S	John Wadsworth	L	Sem	No. 1	L	Cr
8631	4	Wadsworth, Daniel	2	M	7/8	S	John Wadsworth	L	Sem	No. 1	L	Cr
		No. 2 died. No. 3 reported dead.										
		Census Card No. 3038, P. O. Wewoka, Enrolled April 20, 1901										
8632	1	Bemo, Alexander	47	M	1/2		John Bemo	?	Sem	Harriet Lewis	D	Cr
		Census Card No. 3039, P. O. Eufaula, Enrolled April 26, 1901										
8633	1	Henry, Peggy	23	F	F		Joe Henry	D	Cr	Massey Henry	D	Cr
		No. 1 died March 1908										
		Census Card No. 3040, P. O. Eufaula, Enrolled April 26, 1901										
8634	1	Greenwood, Lewis	27	M	F		Dick Greenwood	?	Cr	Numpsey	D	Cr
		No. 1 died April 2, 1912										
		Census Card No. 3041, P. O. Bearden, Enrolled April 25, 1901										
8635	1	Hale, Jasper	19	M	F		Woxie Holatka	D	Cr	Gopoatker Hale	?	Cr
		Census Card No. 3042, P. O. Bearden; No. 2 Wewoka, Enrolled April 25, 1901										
8636	1	Yahola, Thomas	48	M	F		Sarnipka	D	Cr	Sema Hoyka	D	Cr
8637	2	Yahola, Lizzie	46	F	F	Wf	Joilla	D	Cr	Siah	?	Cr
8638	3	Yahola, James	13	M	F	S	No. 1	L	Cr	No. 2	L	Cr
8639	4	Yahola, Bessey	8	F	F	D	No. 1	L	Cr	No. 2	L	Cr
		No. 1 died August 4, 1905. No. 4 died April 23, 1914										
		Census Card No. 3043, P. O. Bearden, Enrolled April 25, 1901										
8640	1	Yahola, Lucinda	23	F	F		Thomas Yahola	L	Cr	Lizzie Yahola	L	Cr
		No. 1 died 1906										
		Census Card No. 3044, P. O. Wewoka, Enrolled April 25, 1901										
8641	1	Yahola, Willie	21	M	F		Thomas Yahola	L	Cr	Lizzie Yahola	L	Cr
		Census Card No. 3045, P. O. Pierce, Enrolled April 27, 1901										
8642	1	Thompson, Otie	3	F	F		Unknown	D	Cr	Leah Thompson	D	Cr
		No. 1 died July 10, 1899										
		Census Card No. 3046, P. O. Arbeka, Enrolled April 25, 1901										
8643	1	Lucinda	48	F	F		Katchomarte	D	Cr	Emwihoke	D	Cr
8644	2	Siah	15	M	F	S	Chawazte	D	Cr	No. 1	L	Cr
8645	3	Millie	8	F	F	D	Chawazte	D	Cr	No. 1	L	Cr
		No. 3 died										
		Census Card No. 3047, P. O. Morse, Enrolled April 19, 1901										
8646	1	Key, Naggy	7	F	F		Charley Key	?	Cr	Simma Hitchka Key	?	Cr
8647	2	Key, Katy	4	F	F	Sis	Charley Key	?	Cr	Simma Hitchka Key	?	Cr
		No. 1 died September 4, 1899 No. 2 died September 9, 1899										

Roll No.	No.	NAME	Age	Sex	Blood	Rel.	NAME OF FATHER	Liv.	Cit.	NAME OF MOTHER	Liv.	Cit.
		Census Card No. 3048, P. O. Morse, Enrolled May 1, 1901										
8648	1	Harge, George	34	M	F		Harge	D	Cr	Selane	D	Cr
		Census Card No. 3049, P. O. Morse, Enrolled May 1, 1901										
8649	1	Harjoche, Hulbutta	46	M	F		Chowastie	D	Cr	Sinthlochulo	D	Cr
8650	2	Harjoche, Mabwe	46	F	F	Wf	Unknown	D	Cr	Unknown	D	Cr
		No. 1 died March 30, 1900. No. 2 reported dead										
		Census Card No. 3050, P. O. Arbeka, Enrolled April 26, 1901										
8651	1	Mulkusee, Sente	45	F	F		Cochnekney	?	Cr	Litkaba	D	Cr
		No. 1 died June 2, 1900										
		Census Card No. 3051, P. O. Creek, Enrolled April 25, 1901										
8652	1	Harjo, Jennie	28	F	F		Watkogee	D	Cr	Tewahoye	?	Cr
8653	2	Harjo, Chinee	6	F	F	D	Martin Harjo	?	Cr	No. 1	L	Cr
8654	3	Harjo, Polly	4	F	F	D	Martin Harjo	?	Cr	No. 1	L	Cr
8655	4	Harjo, Taylor	10	M	F	S	Martin Harjo	?	Cr	No. 1	L	Cr
		No. 4 died August 16, 1902										
		Census Card No. 3052, P. O. Okfuskee, Enrolled May 1, 1901										
8656	1	Nevy, Moseley	21	F	F		Sipley	D	Cr	Nicey	D	Cr
8657	2	Parnoskie, Barnoge	6	M	F	S	Tom Panoskey	?	Cr	No. 1	L	Cr
		No. 1 died 1899										
		Census Card No. 3053, P. O. Okemah; Nos. 2 and 6 Hanna, Enrolled April 19, 1901										
8658	1	Bullett, Millie	33	F	F		Ninna Chubba Harjo	?	Cr	Polly	D	Cr
8659	2	Scott, Sammie	12	M	F	S	Nocus Fixico	D	Cr	No. 1	L	Cr
8660	3	Scott, Hattie	10	F	F	D	Nocus Fixico	D	Cr	No. 1	L	Cr
8661	4	Scott, Frank	7	M	F	S	Nocus Fixico	D	Cr	No. 1	L	Cr
8662	5	Scott, Martha	4	F	F	D	Nocus Fixico	D	Cr	No. 1	L	Cr
8663	6	Bullett, Solomon	22	M	F	Hus	Bill Bullett	D	Cr	Harriet Kano	D	Cr
		Census Card No. 3054, P. O. Morse, Enrolled April 19, 1901										
8664	1	Annie	42	F	F		Joe Yahola	D	Cr	Unknown	D	Cr
		No. 1 died October 9, 1900										
		Census Card No. 3055, P. O. Red Fork, Enrolled April 26, 1901										
8665	1	Riley, Boone P.	25	M	½		Americus Riley	?	?	Sookey	D	Cr
		Census Card No. 3056, P. O. Oktaha, Enrolled April 26, 1901										
8666	1	Wolf, Annie	40	F	F		Fres Harjo	D	Cr	Unknown	D	Cr
		No. 1 died October 13, 1912										
		Census Card No. 3057, P. O. Okemah, Enrolled May 1, 1901										
8667	1	Mikey, Louie	25	F	F		Mikey Grayson	D	Cr	Silvah Mikay	L	Cr
8668	2	Mikey, Bessie	3	F	F	D	John Simpson	L	Cr	No. 1	L	Cr
		Census Card No. 3058, Eufaula, Enrolled April 20, 1901										
8669	1	Grayson, Cecil W.	17	M	½		Pilot Grayson	D	Cr	Mattie Grayson	D	Non
		Census Card No. 3059, P. O. Eufaula, Enrolled April 24, 1901										
8670	1	Mitchell, Aggie	78	F	F		Unknown	D	Cr	Unknown	D	Cr
		No. 1 died March 1, 1904										
		Census Card No. 3060, P. O. Council Hill, Enrolled April 27, 1901; No. 6 May 22, 1901										
8671	1	Brown, Zenie	31	F	¾		Wiley Vann	?	?	Mary Vann	?	?
8672	2	Brown, Ollie B.	11	F	⅜	D	Gold Brown	L	Non	No. 1	L	Cr
8673	3	Brown, Ellen	9	F	⅜	D	Gold Brown	L	Non	No. 1	L	Cr
8674	4	Brown, Neilson	7	M	⅜	S	Gold Brown	L	Non	No. 1	L	Cr
8675	5	Brown, Samuel B.	3	M	⅜	S	Gold Brown	L	Non	No. 1	L	Cr
8676	6	Brown, Mabel	1	F	⅜	D	Gold Brown	L	Non	No. 1	L	Cr
		No. 6 died March 25, 1905										
		Census Card No. 3061, P. O. Braggs, Enrolled April 24, 1901										
8677	1	Israel, Ella	2	F	⅜		John Israel	L	Cher	Louisa Israel	D	Cr
		No. 1 died November 1899										
		Census Card No. 3062, P. O. Carroll, Enrolled May 1, 1901										
8678	1	Morris, Ollie May	9	F	¼		C. D. Morris	L	Non	Susanna Morris	D	Cr
8679	2	Morris, Pearl Garland	6	F	¼	Sis	C. D. Morris	L	Non	Susanna Morris	D	Cr
		No. 2 died December 15, 1910										
		Census Card No. 3063, P. O. Hanna, Enrolled April 30, 1901										
8680	1	Peter, Joseph	19	M	F		Simon Peter	D	Cr	Nicey	D	Cr
		No. 1 died March 25, 1900										
		Census Card No. 3064, P. O. Eufaula, Enrolled April 26, 1901										
8681	1	Johnson, Robert	53	M	F		Arbeka Harjo	D	Cr	Unknown	D	Cr
8682	2	Johnson, Judy	41	F	F	Wf	Parkee	D	Cr	Amy McGilbray	L	Cr
8683	3	Johnson, Polly	17	F	F	D	No. 1	L	Cr	No. 2	L	Cr
8684	4	Johnson, Susie	15	F	F	D	No. 1	L	Cr	No. 2	L	Cr
8685	5	Johnson, Coweta	9	F	F	D	No. 1	L	Cr	No. 2	L	Cr
		Census Card No. 3065, P. O. Eufaula; No. 2 Wetumka, Enrolled May 2, 1901										
8686	1	Bear, John	35	M	F		Nargusta Amarthar	D	Cr	Feeskah	D	Cr
8687	2	Bear, Jakey	46	F	F	Wf	Tommy Harjo	D	Cr	Unknown	D	Cr
8688	3	Gibson, Elsie	12	F	F	GrS No. 2	Walter Gibson	D	Cr	Lida Gibson	D	Cr
		No. 3 died January 1902										
		Census Card No. 3066, P. O. Eufaula, Enrolled May 2, 1901										
8689	1	Deere, John	48	M	F		Unknown	D	Cr	Jovixico	D	Cr
		Census Card No. 3067, P. O. Hanna, Enrolled May 2, 1901										
8690	1	Marshall, Sam	34	M	F		Chopotkey Marshall	D	Cr	Yahoey Marshall	D	Cr
8691	2	Marshall, Aggie	37	F	F	Wf	Unknown	D	Cr	Ledifka	D	Cr
8692	3	Marshall, James	10	M	F	S	No. 1	L	Cr	No. 2	L	Cr

Roll No.	No.	NAME	Age	Sex	Blood	Rel.	NAME OF FATHER	Liv.	Cit.	NAME OF MOTHER	Liv.	Cit.
		Census Card No. 3068, P. O. Eufaula, Enrolled April 24, 1901										
8693	1	Beaver, Byer	41	M	F		Itshas Micco	D	Cr	Tikee	?	Cr
8694	2	Beaver, Mulsey	30	F	F	Wf	Klova	?	Cr	Lucy Wesley	?	Cr
8695	3	Beaver, Roman	13	M	F	S	No. 1	L	Cr	No. 2	L	Cr
8696	4	Beaver, Roley	11	M	F	S	No. 1	L	Cr	No. 2	L	Cr
8697	5	Beaver, Colbert	6	M	F	S	No. 1	L	Cr	No. 2	L	Cr
8698	6	Beaver, Turner	5	M	F	S	No. 1	L	Cr	No. 2	L	Cr
		No. 5 reported dead										
		Census Card No. 3069, P. O. Lenna, Enrolled April 29, 1901; No. 2 May 22, 1901										
8699	1	Fox, Jimmie	31	M	F		Chola Fixico	L	Cr	Tnahoha	D	Cr
8700	2	Fox, Addie	20	F	F	Wf	Garfield	D	Cr	Leider	D	Cr
		No. 2 reported dead										
		Census Card No. 3070, P. O. Lenna, Enrolled April 29, 1901										
8701	1	Salumba, Peggie	28	F	F		Nehie Yahola	?	Cr	Pufncy Yahola	D	Cr
8702	2	Salumba, Lucy	10	F	F	D	Dave Salumba	D	Cr	No. 1	L	Cr
		No. 1 died June 1907										
		Census Card No. 3071, P. O. Fame, Enrolled April 26, 1901										
8703	1	Hawkins, Lizzie	19	F	⅜		Samuel Hawkins	D	Cr	Cynthia Hawkins	?	Non
8704	2	Hawkins, Sarah	15	F	⅜	Sis	Samuel Hawkins	D	Cr	Cynthia Hawkins	?	Non
8705	3	Hawkins, Johnnie	13	F	⅜	Sis	Samuel Hawkins	D	Cr	Cynthia Hawkins	?	Non
		Census Card No. 3072, Fame, Enrolled April 26, 1901										
8706	1	Hawkins, Katie	21	F	⅜		Samuel Hawkins	D	Cr	Cynthia Hawkins	?	Non
		No. 1 died September 12, 1900										
		Census Card No. 3073, P. O. Eufaula, Enrolled April 24, 1901										
8707	1	Sarwanoke, Mitchell	33	M	F		Sarwanoke	D	Cr	Ajenny	D	Cr
8708	2	Sarwanoke, Nancy	33	F	F	Wf	Jack Lewis	D	Cr	Hannah Lewis	D	Cr
8709	3	Sarwanoke, Mary	18	F	F	D	No. 1	L	Cr	Fannie Sarwanoke	D	Cr
8710	4	Dick, Joe	13	M	F	StS	Dick	?	Cr	No. 2	L	Cr
8711	5	Dick, Lucy	11	F	F	StD	Dick	?	Cr	No. 2	L	Cr
8712	6	Dick, Junie	8	F	F	StD	Dick	?	Cr	No. 2	L	Cr
8713	7	Dick, Janatta	4	F	F	StD	Dick	?	Cr	No. 2	L	Cr
		No. 3 reported dead										
		Census Card No. 3074, P. O. Salem, Enrolled May 2, 1901										
8714	1	Riley, Chatman	41	M	F		Sumihitchka	D	Cr	Lila Riley	D	Cr
8715	2	Riley, John	6	M	½	S	No. 1	L	Cr	Amanda Riley	L	Non
8716	3	Riley, Minnie	9	F	½	D	No. 1	L	Cr	Amanda Riley	L	Non
8717	4	Riley, George	7	M	½	S	No. 1	L	Cr	Amanda Riley	L	Non
		Census Card No. 3075, P. O. Eufaula, Enrolled April 30, 1901										
8718	1	Smith, Joe	22	M	F		George Smith	L	Cr	Matilda Smith	L	Cr
		Census Card No. 3076, P. O. Holdenville, Enrolled April 24, 1901										
8719	1	Manley, David	30	M	F		Mose Manley	D	Cr	Tisey Manley	D	Cr
8720	2	Manley, Eliza	25	F	F	Wf	Wallesa	L	Cr	Unknown	D	Cr
		No. 2 died December 4, 1913										
		Census Card No. 3077, P. O. Okfuskee, Enrolled May 2, 1901										
8721	1	Blake, Simon	33	M	F		Peter Blake	D	Cr	Sarheeja	D	Cr
8722	2	Blake, Louisa	33	F	F	Wf	Tuckabatchee	D	Cr	Sally Kelley	L	Cr
8723	3	Blake, Phema	12	F	F	D	No. 1	L	Cr	No. 2	L	Cr
		Nos. 1 and 3 reported dead										
		Census Card No. 3078, P. O. Eufaula, Enrolled April 24, 1901										
8724	1	Johnson, Sam	41	M	F		Arbeka Harjo	D	Cr	Wumhola	D	Cr
8725	2	Johnson, Lydia	30	F	F	Wf	Unknown	D	Cr	Unknown	D	Cr
8726	3	Johnson, Sallie	20	F	F	D	No. 1	L	Cr	Millie Johnson	L	Cr
8727	4	Johnson, Edmond	17	M	F	S	No. 1	L	Cr	Millie Johnson	L	Cr
8728	5	Johnson, Youman	4	M	F	S	No. 1	L	Cr	No. 2	L	Cr
		No. 2 possible duplicate Enrollment No. 7917 this roll. For information, see Card No. 2711. Nos. 1 and 4 reported dead										
		Census Card No. 3079, P. O. Eufaula, Enrolled May 2, 1901										
8729	1	Johnson, Sallie	54	F	F		Arbeka Harjo	D	Cr	Wumhohla	D	Cr
		No. 1 died January 22, 1906										
		Census Card No. 3080, P. O. Vivian, Enrolled April 30, 1901										
8730	1	Bear, Taylor	35	M	F		Nargusta Emarthar	D	Cr	Feeska	D	Cr
8731	2	Bear, Kizzie	29	F	F	Wf	Coxey Hill	D	Cr	Suma Hill	L	Cr
8732	3	Bear, Caesar	10	M	F	S	No. 1	L	Cr	No. 2	L	Cr
8733	4	Bear, Sunthape	8	M	F	S	No. 1	L	Cr	No. 2	L	Cr
8734	5	Bear, Roman	6	M	F	S	No. 1	L	Cr	No. 2	L	Cr
8735	6	Bear, Jessie	3	F	F	D	No. 1	L	Cr	No. 2	L	Cr
		No. 2 died March 5, 1907. No. 6 died November 10, 1898. Nos. 4 and 5 reported dead.										
		Census Card No. 3081, P. O. Quinton, Enrolled May 2, 1901										
8736	1	Kiyer, Annie	38	F	F		Erke Haka	D	Cr	Ecke Soma	D	Cr
8737	2	Colbert, Malissa	20	F	½	D	Willis Colbert	D	Chic	No. 1	L	Cr
8738	3	Colbert, Leemon	18	M	½	S	Willis Colbert	D	Chic	No. 1	L	Cr
8739	4	Colbert, Kizzie	27	F	F	Wf.No.3	Jim Benson	L	Cr	Nancy Mitchell	L	Cr
		Census Card No. 3082, P. O. Mellette, Enrolled May 2, 1901										
8740	1	Fixico, Nocus	43	M	F		Comseh Fixico	D	Cr	Unknown	D	Cr
8741	2	Fixico, Sallie	18	F	F	D	No. 1	L	Cr	Annie Fixico	D	Cr
		Census Card No. 3083, P. O. Pierce, Enrolled May 2, 1901										
8742	1	Wolf, Roley	24	M	F		Yoha Fixico	D	Cr	Lydia Fixico	D	Cr
8743	2	Wolf, Levina	30	F	F	Wf	William Fish	D	Cr	Manday	D	Cr
8744	3	Wolf, Mandy	4mo	F	F	D	No. 1	L	Cr	No. 2	L	Cr
		No. 3 died July 24, 1900. No. 1 died 1906.										
		Census Card No. 3084, P. O. Brush Hill, Enrolled May 2, 1901										
8745	1	Wolf, Sam	15	M	F		Yaha Fixico	D	Cr	Lydia Fixico	D	Cr

Roll No.	No.	NAME	Age	Sex	Blood	Rel.	NAME OF FATHER	Liv.	Cit.	NAME OF MOTHER	Liv.	Cit.
		Census Card No. 3085, P. O. Eufaula, Enrolled May 2, 1901										
8746	1	Polokee, Tom	44	M	F		Tommy Harjo	D	Cr	Nassie Harjo	D	Cr
8747	2	Polokce, Susie	45	F	F	Wf	Joe Harjo	D	Cr	Unknown	D	Cr
8748	3	Polokee, Esal	16	M	F	S	No. 1	L	Cr	No. 2	L	Cr
		Census Card No. 3086, P. O. Eufaula, Enrolled May 2, 1901										
8749	1	Polokee, Ludie	24	F	F		Tom Polokee	L	Cr	Susie Polokee	L	Cr
		No. 1 died June 19, 1903										
		Census Card No. 3087, P. O. Sasakwa, Enrolled May 2, 1901										
8750	1	Barnett, Timothy W.	26	M	F		James Barnett	D	Cr	Anna Barnett	D	Cr
		No. 1 died May 2, 1900										
		Census Card No. 3088, P. O. Eufaula, Enrolled April 24, 1901										
8751	1	Lewis, Maxey	22	M	F		Billie Lewis	D	Cr	Bapsey Lewis	?	Cr
		Census Card No. 3089, P. O. Eufaula, Enrolled May 23, 1901										
8752	1	Billy, Simon	56	M	F		Billy Longey	D	Cr	Rina	D	Cr
8753	2	Billy, Emma	56	F	F	Wf	Kenah Harjo	D	Cr	Unknown	D	Cr
		No. 1 died November 3, 1909. No. 2 died August 18, 1909.										
		Census Card No. 3090, P. O. Eufaula, Enrolled May 2, 1901										
8754	1	Haney, Emma	53	F	F		Unknown	D	Cr	Unknown	D	Cr
8755	2	Porter, Isom	12	M	1/4	GrS	James Porter	?	Chic	Polly Hache	D	Cr
		Census Card No. 3091, P. O. Eufaula, Enrolled May 2, 1901										
8756	1	Hill, Jacob	21	M	F		Commey Hill	?	Cr	Linda Hill	D	Cr
8757	2	Hill, John	19	M	F	Bro	Commey Hill	?	Cr	Linda Hill	D	Cr
		No. 1 died February 27, 1904										
		Census Card No. 3092, P. O. Eufaula, Enrolled May 2, 1901										
8758	1	Charity, Lady	29	F	F		Tom Polokee	L	Cr	Susie Polokee	L	Cr
8759	2	Charity, Christie	4	F	F	D	Loona Charity	D	Cr	No. 1	L	Cr
		Census Card No. 3093, P. O. Okmulgee, Enrolled May 2, 1901										
8760	1	Ellis, Willie	28	M	F		Bob Ellis	D	Cr	Martha Enkona	?	Cr
		No. 1 died 1901										
		Census Card No. 3094, P. O. Eufaula, Enrolled May 2, 1901										
8761	1	Deere, Silla	30	F	F		Echo Emarthla	L	Cr	Ticarhobca	D	Cr
		No. 1 died April 2, 1899										
		Census Card No. 3095, P. O. Eufaula, Enrolled May 6, 1901										
8762	1	Thomas, Tumsey	22	M	3/4		Harley Thomas	L	Cr	Bettie Thomas	D	Cr
		Census Card No. 3096, P. O. Eufaula, Enrolled April 24, 1901										
8763	1	Welakoche	63	F	F		Unknown	D	Cr	Unknown	D	Cr
		No. 1 died September 28, 1910										
		Census Card No. 3097, P. O. Eufaula, Enrolled April 24, 1901										
8764	1	Scott, Annie	43	F	F		Unknown	D	Cr	Welakoche	L	Cr
		Census Card No. 3098, P. O. Eufaula, Enrolled April 24, 1901										
8765	1	Lewis, Johnson	40	M	F		Jackson Lewis	L	Cr	Hannah Lewis	L	Cr
8766	2	Lewis, Lucinda	34	F	F	Wf	James Watlen	D	Cr	Sallie Wotlen	L	Cr
8767	3	Lewis, Colman	5	M	F	S	No. 1	L	Cr	No. 2	L	Cr
8768	4	Lewis, Dollie	7	F	F	D	No. 1	L	Cr	No. 2	L	Cr
		No. 2 died January 15, 1906										
		Census Card No. 3099, P. O. Eufaula, Enrolled April 24, 1901										
8769	1	Cosar, George	48	M	F		Cosar Yarhola	D	Cr	Unknown	D	Cr
8770	2	Cosar, Lucinda	33	F	F	Wf	Unknown	D	Cr	Hannah Lewis	L	Cr
8771	3	Cosar, Melissa	16	F	F	D	No. 1	L	Cr	No. 2	L	Cr
8772	4	Cosar, Chester	6	M	F	S	No. 1	L	Cr	No. 2	L	Cr
		No. 1 died June 21, 1914. No. 4 died September 28, 1903.										
		Census Card No. 3100, P. O. Seminole, Enrolled April 27, 1901										
8773	1	Coker, London	68	M	1/2		Alex Coker	D	Non	Unknown	D	Cr
		Census Card No. 3101, P. O. Calvin, Enrolled April 27, 1901										
8774	1	Hawkins, James	20	M	F		Wiley Hawkins	L	Cr	Eliza Hawkins	L	Cr
		Census Card No. 3102, P. O. Wetumka, Enrolled May 1, 1901										
8775	1	Hopiye, Sam	23	M	F		Hopiye Sammie	D	Cr	Sina	D	Cr
		No. 1 died April 28, 1902										
		Census Card No. 3103, P. O. Hanna, Enrolled April 26, 1901										
8776	1	Bullett, John	23	M	F		Bailey Bullett	D	Cr	Hulley Yarba	D	Cr
		Census Card No. 3104, P. O. Eufaula, Enrolled April 26, 1901										
8777	1	Conahke	55	F	F		Foshutsee	D	Cr	Unknown	D	Cr
		No. 1 died October 5, 1899										
		Census Card No. 3105, P. O. Eufaula, Enrolled April 29, 1901										
8778	1	Fish, Jennie	33	F	F		Thlathlo Yahola	D	Cr	Yahkuppa	D	Cr
8779	2	Fish, Jimsey	20	M	1/2	S	Parnoskey	?	Sem	No. 1	L	Cr
		No. 2 died April 5, 1902. No. 1 died 1908.										
		Census Card No. 3106, P. O. Eufaula, Enrolled April 29, 1901										
8780	1	Jackson, Sallie	37	F	F		Thlathlo Yahola	D	Cr	Yahkuppa	D	Cr
		No. 1 died November 1907										
		Census Card No. 3107, P. O. Eufaula, Enrolled April 29, 1901										
8781	1	Wolke	113	F	F		Unknown	D	Cr	Unknown	D	Cr
		No. 1 died January 1904										
		Census Card No. 3108, P. O. Micawber, Enrolled April 26, 1901										
8782	1	Bluford, Fickey	20	M	F		Holucka	?	Cr	Lydia Bear	D	Cr
		Census Card No. 3109, P. O. Wewoka, Enrolled May 2, 1901										
8783	1	Asbury, Wesley	25	M	F		Jim Asbury	L	Cr	Betsey Foster	?	Cr
		Census Card No. 3110, P. O. Hanna; No. 3, Eufaula, Enrolled April 26, 1901										
8784	1	Suryokiche	43	F	F		John Riley	D	Cr	Cherokee Riley	D	Cr
8785	2	Riley, Johnson	21	M	F	S	Kernip Yahola	D	Cr	No. 1	L	Cr
8786	3	Riley, Jas.	11	M	F	Neph	Jo Riley	D	Cr	Marlilly	D	Cr
		No. 1 died March 1901										

Roll No.	No.	NAME	Age	Sex	Blood	Rel.	NAME OF FATHER	Liv.	Cit.	NAME OF MOTHER	Liv.	Cit.
		Census Card No. 3111, P. O. Hanna, Enrolled April 26, 1901										
8787	1	Riley, Parfna	31	M	F		John Riley	D	Cr	Cherokee Riley	D	Cr
		No. 1 died September 14, 1900										
		Census Card No. 3112, P. O. Little, Enrolled April 26, 1901										
8788	1	Joseph, George	48	M	½		Jos. Canard	D	Sem	Louiney	?	Cr
8789	2	Joseph, Jeannatta	25	F	¾	D	No. 1	L	Cr	Puety	?	Cr
8790	3	Tulsa, Willie	5	M	⅜	GrS	Wm. Tulsa	D	Sem	No. 2	L	Cr
		No. 3 died March 23, 1901										
		Census Card No. 3113, P. O. Seminole, Enrolled April 24, 1901										
8791	1	Thompson, Thomas	23	M	F		Thompson	D	Cr	Susie Thompson	D	Cr
		Census Card No. 3114, P. O. Carson, Enrolled April 29, 1901										
8792	1	Proctor, Lumber	22	M	F		Louis Proctor	D	Cr	Annie Proctor	D	Cr
		Census Card No. 3115, P. O. Wybark, Enrolled August 30, 1901										
8793	1	Perkins, Gus	22	M	F		John Perkins	D	Cr	Nancy Perkins	D	Cr
8794	2	Reed, Lucy	16	F	F	Sis	John Perkins	D	Cr	Nancy Perkins	D	Cr
		No. 2 died 1905. No. 1 died September 21, 1909.										
		Census Card No. 3116, P. O. Muskogee, Enrolled April 20, 1901										
8795	1	Bemo, Leon	16	M	⅜		Douglas Bemo	D	Cr	Katie Bemo	L	Non
		Census Card No. 3117, P. O. Muskogee, Enrolled April 26, 1901										
8796	1	Collins, Sunday	53	M	F		Unknown	D	Cr	Unknown	D	Cr
		No. 1 died March 16, 1900										
		Census Card No. 3118, P. O. Pecos, Tex. Enrolled April 26, 1901										
8797	1	Lipscomb, Mattie R.	13	F	1-16		J. T. H. Lipscomb	L	Non	Mattie R. Lipscomb	L	Cr
8798	2	Lipscomb, Helen V.	11	F	1-16		J. T. H. Lipscomb	L	Non	Mattie R. Lipscomb	L	Cr
8799	3	Lipscomb, Lillian L.	9	F	1-16	D	J. T. H. Lipscomb	L	Non	Mattie R. Lipscomb	L	Cr
		Census Card No. 3119, P. O. Onapa, Enrolled April 27, 1901										
8800	1	Simmons, Mary	24	F	F		Mart Simmons	D	Cr	Nafey Simmons	D	Cr
		Census Card No. 3120, P. O. Checotah, Enrolled April 22, 1901										
8801	1	Keys, Richard	28	M	1-16		Samuel H. Keys	D	Cher	Sarah Keys	?	Cr
		No. 1 reported dead										
		Census Card No. 3121, P. O. Kellyville, Enrolled May 2, 1901										
8802	1	Holder, Washington	33	M	F		Dickson	D	Cr	Annie	D	Cr
		Census Card No. 3122, P. O. Beggs, Enrolled April 25, 1901										
8803	1	Marshall, Lizzie	10	F	F		Marshall Barnett	D	Cr	Susannah Marshall	L	Cr
		No. 1 died July 1900										
		Census Card No. 3123, P. O. Kellyville, Enrolled April 25, 1901										
8804	1	Fulsom, Pantenay	43	F	F		Unknown	D	Cr	Unknown	D	Cr
		No. 1 died June 10, 1900										
		Cencus Card No. 3124, P. O. Kellyville, Enrolled April 25, 1901										
8805	1	Soccontay	16	F	F		Sahconcahney	?	Cr	Ahhalonaney	?	Cr
		No. 1 died October 1900										
		Census Card No. 3125, P. O. Kellyville, Enrolled April 25, 1901										
8806	1	Kakoconney	21	M	F		Tahcaney	L	Cr	Tarpanfah	?	Cr
		Census Card No. 3126, P. O. Tulsa, Enrolled April 29, 1901										
8807	1	Starr, Annie	19	F	F		Chesley Starr	L	Cr	Susie Starr	L	Cr
8808	2	Grayson, Wiley	20	M	F	Cous	Tom Grayson	D	Cr	Katie Starr	D	Cr
8809	3	Grayson, Amy	17	F	F	Cous	Tom Grayson	D	Cr	Katie Starr	D	Cr
		No. 3 died March 8, 1905. No. 1 reported dead.										
		Census Card No. 3127, P. O. Fisher; No. 2, Bristow, Enrolled May 2, 1901										
8810	1	Fisher, Amos	53	M	F		Timmie Fisher	D	Cr	Hepsey Fisher	D	Cr
8811	2	Fisher, Aggie	53	F	F	Wf	Taylor Postoak	D	Cr	Sallie	D	Cr
8812	3	Fisher, Cheparney	14	M	F	S	No. 1	L	Cr	No. 2	L	Cr
		Census Card No. 3128, P. O. Wetumka; No. 5, Holdenville; No. 6, McAlester, Enrolled April 26, 1901										
8813	1	Fish, Jimsey	43	M	F		Unknown	D	Cr	Unknown	D	Cr
8814		Fish, Hannah	25	F	F	Wf	Hallok Harjochee	D	Cr	Southlarpecher	L	Cr
8815		Fish, Peter	15	M	F	S	No. 1	L	Cr	Lucy Fisher	?	Cr
8816		Fish, Nicey	13	F	F	D	No. 1	L	Cr	Lucy Fisher	?	Cr
8817		Fish, Wiley	18	M	F	Neph	Hopethle	?	Cr	Southlarpecher	L	Cr
8818	6	Low, Kizzie	11	F	F	Sis-L	Jim Low	?	Cr	Southlarpecher	L	Cr
		No. 2 died February 4, 1900. No. 4 died February 14, 1908. No. 6 died. No. 5 died 1907.										
		Census Card No. 3129, P. O. Vivian, Enrolled April 26, 1901										
8819	1	Fish, Jennie	33	F	F		Siah Fish	D	Cr	Unknown	D	Cr
8820	2	McIntosh, Ella	13	F	F	D	Alex McIntosh	L	Cr	No. 1	L	Cr
8821	3	Smith, Freeman	11	M	F	Neph	Louis Smith	?	Cr	Katie Fish	L	Cr
		No. 1 died November 11, 1904. No. 3 died November 1906.										
		Census Card No. 3130, P. O. Pierce, Enrolled April 30, 1901										
8822	1	Jacobs, Cinda	15	F	F		Wotko Micco	D	Cr	Sallie Jacobs	D	
		Census Card No. 3131, P. O. Paden, Enrolled April 29, 1901										
8823	1	Caesar, Samego	30	M	F		Caesar	D	Cr	Judy Caesar	D	Cr
8824	2	Caesar, Rachael	23	F	F	Wf	Wiley Wallow	D	Cr	Sallie Wallow	L	Cr
		Census Card No. 3132, P. O. Tulsa, Enrolled May 7, 1901										
8825	1	Day, Henry	18	M	F		William Tea	D	Cr	Millie Tea	D	Cr
		Census Card No. 3133, P. O. Eufaula, Enrolled May 2, 1901										
8826	1	Kanard, Jennie	17	F	F		Cy Kanard	?	Cr	Louisa Kanard	D	Cr
8827	2	Kanard, Melissa	15	F	F	Sis	Cy Kanard	?	Cr	Louisa Kanard	D	Cr
		Census Card No. 3134, P. O. Okmulgee, Enrolled May 3, 1901										
8828	1	Derisaw, Ben	48	M	F		Joe Derisaw	D	Cr	Lizzie Derisaw	D	Cr
		No. 1 died 1900										

Roll No.	No.	NAME	Age	Sex	Blood	Rel.	NAME OF FATHER	Liv.	Cit.	NAME OF MOTHER	Liv.	Cit.

Census Card No. 3135, P. O. Eufaula, Enrolled April 26, 1901

Roll No.	No.	NAME	Age	Sex	Blood	Rel.	NAME OF FATHER	Liv.	Cit.	NAME OF MOTHER	Liv.	Cit.
8829	1	Gibson, Micco	42	M	½		John Gibson	D	Non	Eliza Gibson	D	Cr
8830	2	Gibson, Isparhecher	19	M	¼	S	No. 1	L	Cr	Lizzie Gibson	?	Non
8831	3	Gibson, Daisy	11	F	¼	D	No. 1	L	Cr	Lizzie Gibson	?	Non
8832	4	Gibson, May Della	10	F	¼	D	No. 1	L	Cr	Lizzie Gibson	?	Non
8833	5	Gibson, Pearl	9	F	¼	D	No. 1	L	Cr	Lizzie Gibson	?	Non
8834	6	Gibson, Irene	7	F	¼	D	No. 1	L	Cr	Lizzie Gibson	?	Non

No. 1 died October 1, 1904. No. 3 died April 20, 1912. No. 4 died March 13, 1908. No. 5 died November 26, 1910

Census Card No. 3136, P. O. Grayson, Enrolled May 2, 1901

Roll No.	No.	NAME	Age	Sex	Blood	Rel.	NAME OF FATHER	Liv.	Cit.	NAME OF MOTHER	Liv.	Cit.
8835	1	Barnett, Mary Ann	67	F	F		Unknown	D	Cr	Unknown	D	Cr

No. 1 died December 1900

Census Card No. 3137, P. O. Burney, Enrolled April 24, 1901

Roll No.	No.	NAME	Age	Sex	Blood	Rel.	NAME OF FATHER	Liv.	Cit.	NAME OF MOTHER	Liv.	Cit.
8836	1	Thompson, Alex	24	M	F		March Thompson	L	Cr	Nisey Thompson	L	Cr

No. 1 died August 23, 1899

Census Card No. 3138, P. O. Eufaula, Enrolled May 2, 1901

Roll No.	No.	NAME	Age	Sex	Blood	Rel.	NAME OF FATHER	Liv.	Cit.	NAME OF MOTHER	Liv.	Cit.
8837	1	Jimsey, Hannah	37	F	F		Dick Greenwood	L	Cr	Susie Greenwood	D	Cr
8838	2	Jimsey, Canoe	15	M	F	S	Unknown	?	Cr	No. 1	L	Cr
8839	3	Jimsey, Unah	11	M	F	S	Unknown	?	Cr	No. 1	L	Cr

No. 1 possible duplicate of roll No. 8493. No. 1 died 1908.

Census Card No. 3139, P. O. Eufaula, Enrolled May 2, 1901

Roll No.	No.	NAME	Age	Sex	Blood	Rel.	NAME OF FATHER	Liv.	Cit.	NAME OF MOTHER	Liv.	Cit.
8840	1	Manley, Mary	21	F	F		Jimsey	D	Cr	Hannah Jimsey	L	Cr
8841	2	Waitie Osie,	3	M	F	D	Stanwaite	L	Cr	No. 1	L	Cr

No. 2 illigitimate

Census Card No. 3140, P. O. Phillipsburg, Enrolled May 2, 1901

Roll No.	No.	NAME	Age	Sex	Blood	Rel.	NAME OF FATHER	Liv.	Cit.	NAME OF MOTHER	Liv.	Cit.
8842	1	Jack, Kernal	30	M	F		Jack Tebohee	D	Cr	Lizzie Tebohee	D	Cr
8843	2	Jack, Parney	18	M	F	Neph	Nocha Jack	D	Cr	Lizzie Jack	L	Cr

No. 1 died February 16, 1903. No. 2 died December 19, 1902.

Census Card No. 3141, P. O. Coweta, Enrolled May 7, 1901

Roll No.	No.	NAME	Age	Sex	Blood	Rel.	NAME OF FATHER	Liv.	Cit.	NAME OF MOTHER	Liv.	Cit.
8844	1	Miller, Lewis	21	M	F		Jim Miller	L	Cr	Susie Miller	D	Cr

Census Card No. 3142, P. O. Bristow, Enrolled May 6, 1901

Roll No.	No.	NAME	Age	Sex	Blood	Rel.	NAME OF FATHER	Liv.	Cit.	NAME OF MOTHER	Liv.	Cit.
8845	1	Barnett, Lydia	33	F	F		Jack Tebohee	D	Cr	Lizzie Tebohee	D	Cr

Census Card No. 3143, P. O. Okfuskee, Enrolled May 2, 1901

Roll No.	No.	NAME	Age	Sex	Blood	Rel.	NAME OF FATHER	Liv.	Cit.	NAME OF MOTHER	Liv.	Cit.
8846	1	Cloud, Stephen	25	M	F		Lasley Cloud	L	Cr	Cinna Cloud	D	Cr

Census Card No. 3144, P. O. Bristow, Enrolled April 24, 1901

Roll No.	No.	NAME	Age	Sex	Blood	Rel.	NAME OF FATHER	Liv.	Cit.	NAME OF MOTHER	Liv.	Cit.
8847	1	Ulaahcontayna	43	M	F		Kataquinnay	D	Cr	Thlaggie	D	Cr
8848	2	Kalawee	33	F	F	Wf	Tapaluwe	D	Cr	Katawe	L	Cr

No. 2 died July 1, 1901

Census Card No. 3145, P. O. Okmulgee, Enrolled April 26, 1901

Roll No.	No.	NAME	Age	Sex	Blood	Rel.	NAME OF FATHER	Liv.	Cit.	NAME OF MOTHER	Liv.	Cit.
8849	1	Grayson, Daniel	33	M	⅝		Simpson Grayson	D	Cr	Katie Grayson	D	Cr

No. 1 died August 1900

Census Card No. 3146, P. O. Mannford, Enrolled May 2, 1901

Roll No.	No.	NAME	Age	Sex	Blood	Rel.	NAME OF FATHER	Liv.	Cit.	NAME OF MOTHER	Liv.	Cit.
8850	1	Harjo, Cheparnoche	6	M	F		Tuskegee Harjo	D	Cr	Pinner Harjo	D	Cr
8851	2	Harjo, Yarma	10	M	F	½Bro	Tuskegee Harjo	D	Cr	Lydia Jack (Barnett)	L	Cr
8852	3	Harjo, Melene	8	F	F	½Sis	Tuskegee Harjo	D	Cr	Lydia Jack(Barnett)	L	Cr

No. 3 reported dead

Census Card No. 3147, P. O. Eufaula; Nos. 1 and 2, Sapulpa, Enrolled April 24, 1901

Roll No.	No.	NAME	Age	Sex	Blood	Rel.	NAME OF FATHER	Liv.	Cit.	NAME OF MOTHER	Liv.	Cit.
8853	1	Frank, Noah	34	M	¾		Dave Frank	D	Cr	Polly Frank	D	Cr
8854	2	Frank, Levina	25	F	¾	Wf	Wesley	D	Cr	Rosa Davis	?	Cr
8855	3	Frank, Jennie	6	F	¾	D	No. 1	L	Cr	No. 2	L	Cr

Census Card No. 3148, P. O. Sapulpa, Enrolled April 24, 1901

Roll No.	No.	NAME	Age	Sex	Blood	Rel.	NAME OF FATHER	Liv.	Cit.	NAME OF MOTHER	Liv.	Cit.
8856	1	Byrd, Sandy (Leader)	22	M	F		Thomas Byrd	D	Cr	Susie Byrd	?	Cr

No. 1 died January 23, 1901

Census Card No. 3149, P. O. Wewoka, Enrolled May 2, 1901

Roll No.	No.	NAME	Age	Sex	Blood	Rel.	NAME OF FATHER	Liv.	Cit.	NAME OF MOTHER	Liv.	Cit.
8857	1	Foster, Betsey	41	F	F		Tusekia Hutcogee	D	Cr	Lillie Kernel	?	Cr
8858	2	Foster, Adam	19	M	½	S	Sam Foster	?	Sem	No. 1	L	Cr
8859	3	Foster, Sukey	17	F	½	D	Sam Foster	?	Sem	No. 1	L	Cr
8860	4	Foster, Charles	14	M	½	S	Sam Foster	?	Sem	No. 1	L	Cr
8861	5	Foster, Lizzie	9	F	½	D	Sam Foster	?	Cr	No. 1	L	Cr

Census Card No. 3150, P. O. Eufaula, Enrolled April 26, 1901

Roll No.	No.	NAME	Age	Sex	Blood	Rel.	NAME OF FATHER	Liv.	Cit.	NAME OF MOTHER	Liv.	Cit.
8862	1	Stidham, Buckner Lawrence	7	M	⅛		George Stidham	L	Cr	Hallie Chastain	?	Non

Census Card No. 3151, P. O. Eram, Enrolled April 27, 1901

Roll No.	No.	NAME	Age	Sex	Blood	Rel.	NAME OF FATHER	Liv.	Cit.	NAME OF MOTHER	Liv.	Cit.
8863	1	Hill, Cinda	13	F	F		George Hill	L	Cr	Jennie King	L	Cr

Census Card No. 3152, P. O. Holdenville, Enrolled April 29, 1901

Roll No.	No.	NAME	Age	Sex	Blood	Rel.	NAME OF FATHER	Liv.	Cit.	NAME OF MOTHER	Liv.	Cit.
8864	1	Hulsa, Ross	17	M	⅛		John Hulsey	?	Non	Eliza Hulsey	D	Cr

No. 1 died January 26, 1901

Census Card No. 3153, P. O. Holdenville, Enrolled April 29, 1901

Roll No.	No.	NAME	Age	Sex	Blood	Rel.	NAME OF FATHER	Liv.	Cit.	NAME OF MOTHER	Liv.	Cit.
8865	1	Charles, Lousannah	43	F	F		Palmer	D	Cr	Unknown	D	Cr
8866	2	Charles, Sam	20	M	½	S	Little Charles	?	Sem	No. 1	L	Cr
8867	3	Charles, Louisa	16	F	½	D	Little Charles	?	Sem	No. 1	L	Cr
8868	4	Charles, Lucinda	10	F	½	D	Little Charles	?	Sem	No. 1	L	Cr

No. 2 died December 28, 1900

Census Card No. 3154, P. O. Holdenville, Enrolled April 29, 1901

Roll No.	No.	NAME	Age	Sex	Blood	Rel.	NAME OF FATHER	Liv.	Cit.	NAME OF MOTHER	Liv.	Cit.
8869	1	Charles, Thomas	23	M	½		Little Charles	?	Sem	Losewa Charles	?	Cr

No. 1 died 1901

Census Card No. 3155, P. O. Holdenville, Enrolled April 29, 1901

Roll No.	No.	NAME	Age	Sex	Blood	Rel.	NAME OF FATHER	Liv.	Cit.	NAME OF MOTHER	Liv.	Cit.
8870	1	Charles, David	29	M	½		Little Charles	?	Sem	Losewa Charles	?	Cr

No. 1 died March 22, 1899

Census Card No. 3156, P. O. Holdenville, Enrolled April 29, 1901

Roll No.	No.	NAME	Age	Sex	Blood	Rel.	NAME OF FATHER	Liv.	Cit.	NAME OF MOTHER	Liv.	Cit.
8871	1	Sewell, Thomas	25	M	¾		Washington Sewell	L	Cr	Louisa Sewell	?	Cr
8872	2	Sewell, Frank	5	M	⅜	S	No. 1	L	Cr	Ruxy Sewell	?	Non

Roll No.	No.	NAME	Age	Sex	Blood	Rel.	NAME OF FATHER	Liv.	Cit.	NAME OF MOTHER	Liv.	Cit.
		Census Card No. 3157, P. O. Wetumka, Enrolled April 26, 1901										
8873	1	Tiger, Louis	45	M	F		Abahalee	D	Cr	Chesoppey	D	Cr
8874	2	Powell, Hannah	46	F	F	Wf	Argee Yahola	D	Cr	Unknown	D	Cr
8875	3	Tiger, Hully	11	M	F	S	No. 1	L	Cr	No. 2	L	Cr
8876	4	Tiger, Joseley	7	M	F	S	No. 1	L	Cr	No. 2	L	Cr
		No. 2 died October 10, 1905. No. 1 died April 26, 1899.										
		Census Card No. 3158, P. O. Holdenville, Enrolled April 29, 1901										
8877	1	Parnoskey, Sarah	46	F	¾		Robert W. Stewart	D	Ad-Wt	Sophia Stewart	D	Cr
		No. 1 died September 6, 1899										
		Census Card No. 3159, P. O. Wetumka, Enrolled May 1, 1901										
8878	1	Harjo, Nancy	31	F	F		Unknown	D	Cr	Unknown	D	Cr
8879	2	Bear, Edward	4	M	¾	S	Robert E. Bear	D	Cr	No. 1	L	Cr
8880	3	Scott, Winey	16	F	F	D	Hogie Scott	D	Cr	No. 1	L	Cr
8881	4	Scott, James	14	M	F	S	Hogie Scott	D	Cr	No. 1	L	Cr
8882	5	Beaver, Annie	7	F	F	D	Mody Beaver	?	Cr	No. 1	L	Cr
		Census Card No. 3160, P. O. Wetumka, Enrolled May 1, 1901										
8883	1	Yahola, Dora	20	F	F		Nehi Yahola	D	Cr	Sarcoquhoka	D	Cr
8884	2	Yahola, Pollie	16	F	F	Sis	Nehi Yahola	D	Cr	Sarcoquhoka	D	Cr
		No. 1 died May 1899. No. 2 reported dead.										
		Census Card No. 3161, P. O. Sasakwa, Enrolled April 29, 1901										
8885	1	Puntka, Cinda	26	F	F		Arnogee	D	Cr	Nannie Rabbit	L	Cr
8886	2	Puntka, Eliza	9	F	½	D	Puntka	L	Sem	No. 1	L	Cr
8887	3	Puntka, Mikey	6	M	½	S	Puutka	L	Sem	No. 1	L	Cr
8888	4	Puutka, Jimsey	5	M	½	S	Puntka	L	Sem	No. 1	L	Cr
8889	5	Puntka, Lucy	2	F	½	D	Puntka	L	Sem	No. 1	L	Cr
		No. 5 died December 10, 1901										
		Census Card No. 3162, P. O. Holdenville, Enrolled April 29, 1901										
8890	1	Micco, Aktiyarchee	88	M	F		Unknown	D	Cr	Unknown	D	Cr
		No. 1 died March 1900										
		Census Card No. 3163, P. O. Holdenville, Enrolled April 29, 1901										
8891	1	Tustenuggy, Takoser	88	M	F		Unknown	D	Cr	Unknown	D	Cr
		No. 1 died September 25, 1899										
		Census Card No. 3164, P. O. Sasakwa, Enrolled April 29, 1901										
8892	1	Caesar, Sowikee	35	M	F		Ceasar	D	Cr	Judy Ceasar	D	Cr
8893	2	Caesar, George	22	M	F	Bro	Ceasar	D	Cr	Judy Ceasar	D	Cr
8894	3	Davis, Ilsey	19	F	F	Sis	Ceasar	D	Cr	Judy Ceasar	D	Cr
8895	4	Stricken from roll										
		No. 2 died July 3, 1902										
		Census Card No. 3165, P. O. Arbeka, Enrolled April 29, 1901										
8896	1	Tiger, Sophia	40	F	F		Nokpuk Harjo	D	Sem	Laskey	?	Cr
8897	2	Tiger, Noah	11	M	½	S	Bob Tiger	D	?	No. 1	L	Cr
8898	3	Tiger, Rhoda	5	F	½	D	Bob Tiger	D	?	No. 1	L	Cr
		No. 2 reported dead										
		Census Card No. 3166, P. O. Hanna, Enrolled April 29, 1901										
8899	1	Harjo, Tulsa	45	M	F		Emarthla Harjo	D	Cr	Unknown	D	Cr
		No. 1 died May 16, 1901										
		Census Card No. 3167, P. O. Holdenville, Enrolled April 29, 1901										
8900	1	Harjo, Sookey	48	F	F		Tommy Harjo	?	Cr	Kennatta	D	Cr
8901	2	Harjo, George	18	M	½	S	Mekko Harjo	?	Cr	No. 1	L	Cr
8902	3	Harjo, Jemima	10	F	½	D	Mekko Harjo	?	Cr	No. 1	L	Cr
8903	4	Harjo, Josiah	5	M	½	S	Mekko Harjo	?	Cr	No. 1	L	Cr
		No. 2 died July 13, 1899. No. 1 died June 23, 1913.										
		Census Card No. 3168, P. O. Paden, Enrolled April 29, 1901										
8904	1	McCulla, Tulmarsey	40	M	F		Sapinkahully	D	Cr	Cumsey Lockwa	D	Cr
8905	2	McCulla, Mary	40	F	F	Wf	Wollow	D	Cr	Lasley	?	Cr
8906	3	McCulla, Thomas	11	M	F	S	No. 1	L	Cr	No. 2	L	Cr
8907	4	McCulla, George	7	M	F	S	No. 1	L	Cr	No. 2	L	Cr
8908	5	McCulla, George	15	M	F	S	No. 1	L	Cr	No. 2	L	Cr
8909	6	Kernal, Cheparney	18	F	F	StD	Peter Kernal	?	Cr	No. 2	L	Cr
8910	7	McCulla, Nancy	3	F	F	D	No. 1	L	Cr	No. 2	L	Cr
		No. 3 died July 2, 1900. No. 7 died May 1901.										
		Census Card No. 3169, P. O. Paden, Enrolled April 29, 1901										
8911	1	Chardy, Susie	33	F	F		Tulwa Micco	D	Cr	Lucy Chardy	D	Cr
		Census Card No. 3170, P. O. Price, Enrolled April 29, 1901										
8912	1	Coker, Polly	23	F	F		Choahdey Chupco	D	Cr	Lizzie Coker	D	Cr
8913	2	Coker, Colbert	8	M	F	S	Charley Coker	L	Cr	No. 1	L	Cr
8914	3	Coker, Jipsey	4	M	F	S	Charley Coker	L	Cr	No. 1	L	Cr
8915	4	Coker, Lucy	3	F	F	D	Charley Coker	L	Cr	No. 1	L	Cr
		Census Card No. 3171, P. O. Carson, Enrolled April 29, 1901										
8916	1	Harjo, Noah	18	M	F		Tblo Harjo	D	Cr	Yoapka Bruner	?	Cr
8917	2	Harjo, Susie	17	F	F	Wf	Wash Kanard	L	Cr	Lizzie Kanard	L	Cr
		No. 1 died June 1913. No. 2 died November 1908.										
		Census Card No. 3172, P. O. Calvin, Enrolled April 30, 1901										
8918	1	Bruner, Lucinda	20	F	F		Siah Bruner	L	Cr	Ogeesah	?	Cr
8919	2	Frazier, Alice	10	F	F	D	Johnson Frazier	?	Choc	No. 1	L	Cr
		Census Card No. 3173, P. O. Wetumka, Enrolled April 19, 1901										
8920	1	Toothoye	47	F	F		Artus Fixico	D	Cr	Imogene	D	Cr
		No. 1 died March 11, 1901										
		Census Card No. 3174, P. O. Paden, Enrolled April 29, 1901										
8921	1	Fixeco, Cano	21	M	F		Nocos Fixico	L	Cr	Seluskey Bear	?	Cr
		No. 1 died February 14, 1904										

Roll No.	No.	NAME	Age	Sex	Blood	Rel.	NAME OF FATHER	Liv.	Cit.	NAME OF MOTHER	Liv.	Cit.
		Census Card No. 3175, P. O. Wewoka, Enrolled April 29, 1901										
8922	1	Harjo, Eliza	30	F	½		Nufky	?	Sem	Wechee Harjo	D	Cr
8923	2	Harjo, Lucinda	9	F	¼	D	Ah Harjo	?	Sem	No. 1	L	Cr
8924	3	Harjo, Thomas	7	M	¼	S	Ah Harjo	?	Sem	No. 1	L	Cr
		No. 3 died 1903										
		Census Card No. 3176, P. O. Wewoka, Enrolled April 29, 1901										
8925	1	Harjo, Lilly	27	F	F		Nufky	?	Sem	Wechee Harjo	D	Cr
		Census Card No. 3177, P. O. Weleetka, Enrolled April 19, 1901										
8926	1	Harjo, Totkis	63	M	F		Lahta Harjo	D	Cr	Timahtoe	D	Cr
8027	2	Harjo, Susie	63	F	F	Wf	Artus Hobiah	D	Cr	Satoutcha	D	Cr
8928	3	Harjo, Chotkee	17	M	StS		Alberta Harjo	L	Cr	No. 2	L	Cr
8929	4	Harjo, Rhoda	18	F	F	D	No. 1	L	Cr	Timashoey	D	Cr
		Census Card No. 3178, P. O. Wetumka, Enrolled April 19, 1901										
8930	1	Harjo, Seaver	29	M	F		Toatkis Harjo	L	Cr	Timashoey	D	Cr
		No. 1 died February 9, 1901										
		Census Card No. 3179, P. O. Wetumka, Enrolled April 19, 1901										
8931	1	Harjo, Tommoche	26	M	F		Lahta Harjo	D	Cr	Timahtoe	D	Cr
		Census Card No. 3180, P. O. Wetumka, Enrolled April 19, 1901										
8932	1	Fixeco, Parhos	68	M	F		Okchun Harjo	D	Cr	Unknown	D	Cr
		Census Card No. 3181, P. O. Wetumka, Enrolled April 19, 1901										
8933	1	Johnson, Cooper	44	M	F		Hospotok Hoye	D	Cr	Tona Hoye	D	Cr
8934	2	Johnson, Judy	35	F	F	Wf	Totkus Harjo	L	Cr	Temos Hoye	L	Cr
		No. 2 died May 24, 1913										
		Census Card No. 3182, P. O. Wetumka, Enrolled April 19, 1901										
8935	1	Hobia, Isaac	27	M	F		Cooper Johnson	L	Cr	Rosanna	D	Cr
		Census Card No. 3183, P. O. Wetumka, Enrolled April 19, 1901										
8936	1	Harjo, Thlathlo	73	M	F		Unknown	D	Cr	Unknown	D	Cr
		No. 1 died March 3, 1903										
		Census Card No. 3184, P. O. Wetumka, Enrolled May 2, 1901										
8937	1	Thompson, Little	16	M	F		Hillis Jackson	D	Cr	Unknown	D	Cr
		No. 1 died December 25, 1901										
		Census Card No. 3185, P. O. Wetumka, Enrolled May 1, 1901										
8938	1	Harjo, Stephen	23	M	F		Tulwa Harjo	D	Cr	Nannie Harjo	D	Cr
8939	2	Harjo, Kogee	20	F	F	Wf	Tuskona	D	Cr	Lungee	D	Cr
		Census Card No. 3186, P. O. Stringtown, Enrolled April 25, 1901										
8940	1	Chief, Wilburn	35	M	½		Jim Chief	?	Choc-F	Celia Chief	D	Cr
		No. 1 died August 25, 1899										
		Census Card No. 3187, P. O. Wewoka, Enrolled May 4, 1901										
8941	1	McGirt, Jim	21	M	F		George McGirt	D	Cr	Loskey	L	Cr
		No. 1 died December 1910										
		Census Card No. 3188, P. O. Earlsboro, Enrolled April 24, 1901										
8942	1	Kernel, George	19	M	F		George Kernel	D	Cr	Tahdie	D	Cr
		No. 1 reported dead										
		Census Card No. 3189, P. O. Holdenville, Enrolled May 4, 1901										
8943	1	Larney, Polly	15	F	F		Louis Larney	D	Cr	Lydia Larney	D	Cr
		No. 1 died August 6, 1899										
		Census Card No. 3190, P. O. Sasakwa, Enrolled May 1, 1901										
8944	1	Tebe, Wisey	28	F	F		Parhos Harjo	D	Cr	Unknown	D	Cr
8945	2	Tebe, Willie	10	M	½	S	Stephen	?	Sem	No. 1	L	Cr
8946	3	Tebe, Yarner	8	F	½	D	Stephen	?	Sem	No. 1	L	Cr
8947	4	Tebe, Tarbie	3	M	½	S	Stephen	?	Sem	No. 1	L	Cr
		No. 4 died May 8, 1900										
		Census Card No. 3191, P. O. Wetumka, Enrolled April 27, 1901										
8948	1	Butler, John	10	M	F		Butler	D	Cr	Mahoye Butler	D	Cr
8949	2	Butler, Emma	4	F	F	Sis	Butler	D	Cr	Mahoye Butler	D	Cr
		No. 1 died January 25, 1900. No. 2 died January 11, 1900										
		Census Card No. 3192, P. O. Spaulding, Enrolled May 6, 1901										
8950	1	Okfuskee, Leah	48	F	F		Unknown	D	Cr	Unknown	D	Cr
8951	2	Cumseh, Parnoskey	19	M	F	S	Cumseh	D	Sem	No. 1	L	Cr
8952	3	Cumseh, Manie	15	F	F	D	Cumseh	D	Sem	No. 1	L	Cr
		Census Card No. 3193, P. O. Bearden, Enrolled April 25, 1901										
8953	1	Harjo, Louisa	47	F	F		Unknown	D	Cr	Unknown	D	Cr
8954	2	Harjo, Linda	18	F	F	D	Cowe Harjo	D	Cr	No. 1	L	Cr
8955	3	Harjo, John	18	M	F	S	Cowe Harjo	D	Cr	No. 1	L	Cr
8956	4	Harjo, Hannah	13	F	F	D	Cowe Harjo	D	Cr	No. 1	L	Cr
8957	5	Harjo, Frank	9	M	F	S	Cowe Harjo	D	Cr	No. 1	L	Cr
8958	6	Harjo, Joe Tiger	3	M	F	S	Cowe Harjo	D	Cr	No. 1	L	Cr
		No. 6 died May 1900. No. 1 reported dead.										
		Census Card No. 3194, P. O. Red Fork, Enrolled April 20, 1901										
8959	1	Ishmael, Fannie	12	F	⅛		B. R. Ishmael	?	Non	Maggie Ishmael	D	Cr
8960	2	Ishmael, Maggie	9	F	⅛	Sis	B. R. Ishmael	?	Non	Maggie Ishmael	D	Cr
8961	3	Ishmael, Mary	5	F	⅛	Sis	B. R. Ishmael	?	Non	Maggie Ishmael	D	Cr
		Census Card No. 3195, P. O. Okmulgee, Enrolled May 2, 1901										
8962	1	Sizemore, William	24	M	F		Dave Sizemore	D	Cr	Illinois	D	Cr
		Census Card No. 3196, P. O. Wewoka, Enrolled May 24, 1901										
8963	1	Carter, Jim	46	M	½		Fred Carter	D	Cr	Rachel Carter	?	Cr

Roll No.	No.	NAME	Age	Sex	Blood	Rel.	NAME OF FATHER	Liv.	Cit.	NAME OF MOTHER	Liv.	Cit.
		Census Card No. 3197, P. O. Hoffman, Enrolled June 17, 1901										
8964	1	Thompson, Billy	40	M	F		Thompson	D	Cr	Semiah	D	Cr
8965	2	Thompson, Lettie	40	F	F	Wf	Wills	D	Cr	Amey	?	Cr
8966	3	Blunt, Phillip	14	M	F	StS	John Blunt	D	Cr	No. 2	L	Cr
8967	4	Davis, Charlotte	9	F	F	StD	Sam Davis	L	Cr	No. 2	L	Cr
8968	5	Thompson, Cinda	6	F	F	D	No. 1	L	Cr	No. 2	L	Cr
8969	6	Thompson, Nellie	4	F	F	D	No. 1	L	Cr	No. 2	L	Cr
		No. 1 died January 9, 1909										
		Census Card No. 3198, P. O. Hoffman, Enrolled July 3, 1901										
8970	1	Wills, Joseph	24	M	F		Wills	D	Cr	Amy	?	Cr
8971	2	Wills, Eliza	22	F	F	Wf	Dick Davis	D	Cr	Sally	D	Cr
8972	3	Wills, Thomas	4	M	F	S	No. 1	L	Cr	No. 2	L	Cr
		No. 2 died August 7, 1901. No. 3 died March 31. 1910.										
		Census Card No. 3199, P. O. Salem, Enrolled July 3, 1901										
8973	1	Davis, Dennis	24	M	F		Dick Davis	D	Cr	Sallie	?	Cr
8974	2	Davis, Hannah	30	F	F	Wf	Unknown	D	Cr	Amy Jackson	L	Cr
8975	3	Davis, Siney	7	F	F	StD	Sam Davis	L	Cr	No. 2	L	Cr
		Census Card No. 3200, P. O. Hoffman; No. 3. Salem, Enrolled July 3, 1901										
8976	1	Davis, Jeff	29	M	F		Wills	D	Cr	Amy	?	Cr
8977	2	Davis, Eli	14	M	F	S	No. 1	L	Cr	Jennie Walker	D	Cr
8978	3	Davis, Emma	13	F	F	D	No. 1	L	Cr	Jennie Walker	D	Cr
8979	4	Davis, Moody	12	M	F	S	No. 1	L	Cr	Jennie Walker	D	Cr
8980	5	Davis, Bettie	8	F	F	D	No. 1	L	Cr	Jennie Walker	D	Cr
		No. 4 died 1908										
		Census Card No. 3201, P. O. Hoffman, Enrolled July 3, 1901										
8981	1	Jackson, Billie	60	M	F		Unknown	D	Cr	Lucy	D	Cr
8982	2	Jackson. Amy	70	F	F	Wf	Unknown	D	Cr	Unknown	D	Cr
8983	3	Davis, Cathie	6	F	F	GrD	Jeff Davis	L	Cr	Jennie Davis	D	Cr
		No. 2 died April 23, 1914										
		Census Card No. 3202, P. O. Muskogee, Enrolled May 23, 1901										
8984	1	McNac, Dave	63	M	F		Tustunnocoche	D	Cr	Unknown	D	Cr
		No. 1 died January 27, 1905										
		Census Card No. 3203, P. O. Little, Enrolled May 23, 1901										
8985	1	Sarkecher	60	M	F		Heloke Harjo	D	Cr	Meley	D	Cr
		No. 1 died March 6, 1909										
		Census Card No. 3204, P. O. Eufaula, Enrolled May 24, 1901										
8986	1	Bear, Thomas	33	M	F		Bear	?	Cr	Faska Bear	?	Cr
		Census Card No. 3205, P. O. Wetumka, Enrolled May 24, 1901										
8987	1	Deere, Sinah	40	F	F		Mahtup Yahola	D	Cr	Senaka	D	Cr
8988	2	Manley, Louis	13	M	F	S	Harvey Manley	D	Cr	No. 1	L	Cr
8989	3	Manley, Mary	10	F	F	D	Harvey Manley	D	Cr	No. 1	L	Cr
8990	4	Manley, Jack	9	M	F	S	Harvey Manley	D	Cr	No. 1	L	Cr
8991	5	Mingo. John	6	M	F	S	Josie Mingo	D	Cr	No. 1	L	Cr
		No. 1 died February 10, 1902										
		Census Card No. 3206, P. O. Eufaula, Enrolled May 24, 1901										
8992	1	Deere. Ben	45	M	F		Suego	D	Cr	Yamahike	L	Cr
		No. 1 died July 20, 1913										
		Census Card No. 3207, P. O. Tuskegee, Enrolled September 28, 1901										
8993	1	Harry. Caroline	80	F	¼		Unknown	D	?	Unknown	D	?
		No. 1 died June 18, 1899										
		Census Card No. 3208 [Void]										
8994	1	Stricken from roll										
8995	2	Stricken from roll										
		Census Card No. 3209, P. O. Calvin, Enrolled September 24, 1901										
8996	1	Herrod, David	42	M	F		Harge Yoholer	D	Cr	Unknown	D	Cr
		Census Card No. 3210, P. O. Holdenville, Enrolled September 24, 1901										
8997	1	Anderson, Billie	25	M	F		Tom Anderson	D	Cr	Geley Anderson	D	Cr
		No. 1 died March 1909										
		Census Card No. 3211, P. O. Wetumka, Enrolled September 24, 1901										
8998	1	Yaffie	32	M	F		Arharlox Fixico	D	Cr	Uthlaka	D	Cr
		No. 1 died October 24, 1899										
		Census Card No. 3212, P. O. Wetumka, Enrolled September 24, 1901										
8999	1	Bruner, Nellie	49	F	F		Aktiachee	D	Cr	Yophogee	D	Cr
		No. 1 died December 24, 1899										
		Census Card No. 3213, P. O. Holdenville, Enrolled September 24, 1901										
9000	1	Homer, John	61	M	F		Homer	D	Cr	Unknown	D	Cr
		No. 1 died May 13, 1909										
		Census Card No. 3214, P. O. Heliswa, Enrolled September 24, 1901										
9001	1	Susanna	46	F	F		Cody	D	Cr	Lizzie	D	Cr
		No. 1 died August 14, 1899										
		Census Card No. 3215, P. O. Holdenville, Enrolled September 24, 1901										
9002	1	Thomas, Kate	31	F	F		Thomas Reed	D	Cr	Bulby Reed	D	Cr
		No. 1 died July 7, 1899										
		Census Card No. 3216, P. O. Okfuskee, Enrolled May 23, 1901										
9003	1	Ellis, Martha	42	F	F		Unknown	D	Cr	Unknown	D	Cr
		No. 1 died April 20, 1900										
		Census Card No. 3217, P. O. Wagoner, Enrolled October 29, 1901										
9004	1	Posey, Richard T.	50	M	¼		T. B. Posey	D	Cr	Elizabeth Posey	D	Cr
9005	2	Posey, Dennis	19	M	⅛	S	No. 1	D	Cr	Beatrice E. Posey	L	Non
9006	3	Posey, Jonathan R.	18	M	⅛	S	No. 1	D	Cr	Beatrice E. Posey	L	Non
9007	4	Posey, Beatrice	9	F	⅛	D	No. 1	D	Cr	Beatrice E. Posey	L	Non

191

Roll No.	No.	NAME	Age	Sex	Blood	Rel.	NAME OF FATHER	Liv.	Cit.	NAME OF MOTHER	Liv.	Cit.
	Census Card No. 3218, P. O. Eufaula, Enrolled May 23, 1901											
9008	1	Manley, Thomas	27	M	F		Lofa Manley	L	Cr	Lizzie Manley	L	Cr
		No. 1 died February 25, 1905										
	Census Card No. 3219, P. O. Wagoner, Enrolled Oxtober 30, 1901											
9009	1	Posey, William A.	22	M	1/8		R. T. Posey	L	Cr	Beatrice E. Posey	L	Non
	Census Card No. 3220, P. O. Holdenville, Enrolled May 22, 1901											
9010	1	Waspee	20	M	F		Parnoche	D	Cr	Lizzie	D	Cr
		No. 1 died April 5, 1899										
	Census Card No. 3221, P. O. Holdenville, Enrolled November 29, 1901											
9011	1	Holata, Susey	27	F	1/2		Ponkilley	D	Sem	Meley	D	Cr
9012	2	Holata, Willie	5	M	1/4	S	John Holata	?	Sem	No. 1	L	Cr
		No. 1 died September 29, 1906. No. 2 died September 15, 1912.										
	Census Card No. 3222, P. O. Wewoka, Enrolled May 23, 1901											
9013	1	Sampson, Vina	45	F	F		Unknown	D	Cr	Unknown	D	Cr
		No. 1 died May 13, 1989										
	Census Card No. 3223, P. O. Okfuskee, Enrolled January 31, 1902											
9014	1	Nancy	33	F	F		Enublee	D	Cr	Millie Yahola	D	Cr
		No. 1 died 1899										
	Census Card No. 3224, P. O. Burney, Enrolled December 31, 1901											
9015	1	Dixon, Jonas	42	M	F		Dixon	D	Cr	Mullie Dixon	D	Cr
		No. 1 died December 15, 1900										
	Census Card No. 3225, P. O. Holdenville, Enrolled January 21, 1902											
9016	1	Long, Matilda	1	F	F		Washington Long	L	Cr	Martha Long	L	Cr
		No. 1 died October 10, 1899										
	Census Card No. 3226, P. O. Tulsa, Enrolled March 27, 1900											
9017	1	Perryman, Louis	33	M	1/2		Lewis Perryman	D	Cr	Unknown	D	Cr
		No. 1 died April 7, 1899										
	Census Card No. 3227, P. O. Bristow, Enrolled February 7, 1902											
9018	1	Williams, Jane	2	F	1/4		Sam Williams	?	Sem	Rena Williams	L	Cr
	Census Card No. 3228, P. O. Creek, Enrolled July 10, 1902											
9019	1	Simmons, John	27	M	F		Cabecha Fixico	D	Cr	Bassochee	D	Cr
		No. 1 died April 21, 1899										
	Census Card No. 3229, P. O. Sapulpa, Enrolled March 10, 1902											
9020	1	Spocogee, Polly	42	F	F		William Eufaula	D	Cr	Unknown	D	Cr
		No. 1 died December 2, 1900										
	Census Card No. 3230, P. O. Okmulgee, Enrolled March 17, 1902											
9021	1	Riley, Willie	3	M	F		Tiger Riley	L	Cr	Nannie Broadnax	L	Cr
		No. 1 died July 17, 1899										
	Census Card No. 3231, P. O. Carson, Enrolled May 16, 1901											
9022	1	Jones, William	25	M	F		Stepney Jones	D	Cr	Hopie	D	Cr
9023	2	Jones, Mary	25	F	F	Wf	Daniel Tiger	D	Cr	Sally	D	Cr
		No. 1 died February 8, 1908										
	Census Card No. 3232, P. O. Wetumka, Enrolled May 22, 1901											
9024	1	Johnson, Jinney	23	F	F		Hulley Miller	?	Cr	Loweney	D	Cr
9025	2	Johnson, Taylor	7	M	F	D	Joe Buck	L	Cr	No. 1	L	Cr
		No. 1 died Summer 1905										
	Census Card No. 3233, P. O. Dustin; No. 8 and 9, Hanna, Enrolled May 23, 1901											
9026	1	Harjo, Nocus	45	M	F		Artus Hopaye	D	Cr	Simome	D	Cr
9027	2	Harjo, Tilla	40	F	F	Wf	Unknown	D	Cr	Chenochige	?	Cr
9028	3	Simpson, Shelby	25	M	F	S	No. 1	L	Cr	No. 2	L	Cr
9029	4	Simpson, Archie	24	M	F	S	No. 1	L	Cr	No. 2	L	Cr
9030	5	Simpson, Joe	12	M	F	S	No. 1	L	Cr	No. 2	L	Cr
9031	6	Simpson, Malinda	18	F	F	D	No. 1	L	Cr	No. 2	L	Cr
9032	7	Simpson, Susie	7	F	F	D	No. 1	L	Cr	No. 2	L	Cr
9033	8	Simpson, Tahahke	27	F	F	Niece2	Tahkosa Harjo	D	Cr	Sinthodey	?	Cr
9034	9	Harjo, Missie	6	F	F	D-8	No. 1.	L	Cr	No. 8	L	Cr
		No. 5 died September 3, 1904. No. 7 died September 13, 1904. No. 6 died August 11, 1912. No. 1 died March 1901.										
	Census Card No. 3234, P. O. Broken Arrow, Enrolled November 21, 1900											
9035	1	Boles, Jennie P.	31	F	1/8		Daniel Harmon	L	Cr	Cynthia Harmon	D	Cr
9036	2	Boles, Fred	12	M	1-16	S	Frank C Boles	L	Non	No. 1	L	Cr
9037	3	Boles, Holland	10	M	1-16	S	Frank C. Boles	L	Non	No. 1	L	Cr
9038	4	Boles, Pearl	8	F	1-16	D	Frank C. Boles	L	Non	No. 1	L	Cr
9039	5	Boles, Cherokee	6	F	1-16	D	Frank C. Boles	L	Non	No. 1	L	Cr
9040	6	Boles, Ruby	4	F	1-16	D	Frank C. Boles	L	Non	No. 1	L	Cr
9041	7	Boles, Laura H.	2	F	1-16	D	Frank C. Boles	L	Non	No. 1	L	Cr
		No. 1 reported dead										
	Census Card No. 3235, P. O. Lenna, Enrolled April 29, 1901											
9042	1	"Wa-co-che"	39	M	F		Unknown	?	Cr	Bardy	D	Cr
9043	2	Wacoche, Lotta	33	F	F	Wf	Oche Harjo	D	Cr	Unknown	?	Cr
9044	3	Wacoche, Isaac	16	M	F	S	No. 1	L	Cr	No. 2	L	Cr
9045	4	Wacoche, Benjamin	17	M	F	S	No. 1	L	Cr	No. 2	L	Cr
9046	5	Wacoche, Johnson	14	M	F	S	No. 1	L	Cr	Miley	D	Cr
9047	6	Wacoche, Jimmie	20	M	F	S	No. 1	L	Cr	Miley	D	Cr
9048	7	Wacoche, Alex	11	M	F	S	No. 1	L	Cr	No. 2	L	Cr
9049	8	Wacoche, Aggie	7	F	F	D	No. 1	L	Cr	No. 2	L	Cr
9050	9	Wacoche, Eliza	3	F	F	D	No. 1	L	Cr	No. 2	L	Cr
		No. 1 died January 1908. No. 3 died December 1910. No. 6 reported dead										
	Census Card No. 3236, P. O. Castle, Enrolled May 23, 1901											
9051	1	Fixeco, Mollie	26	F	F		Unknown	D	Cr	Fola	D	Cr

Census Card No. 3237, P. O. Leonard, Enrolled May 23, 1901

| 9052 | 1 | Spaniard, John | 35 M F | Spaniard Harjo | D Cr | Wicey | ? Cr |

Census Card No. 3238, P. O. Hanna, Enrolled April 30, 1901

| 9053 | 1 | Pigeon, Cemilane | 33 M F | John Pigeon | L Cr | Sally Pigeon | D Cr |

Census Card No. 3239, P. O. Mahussody, Enrolled April 24, 1901

| 9054 | 1 | Coker, Thomas | 40 M ½ | London Coker | L Cr | Mary Waspin | D ? |

Census Card No. 3240, P. O. Checotah, Enrolled May 2, 1901

| 9055 | 1 | Gooden, Daniel | 45 M F | Pgijepka | D Cr | Unknown | ? Cr |

No. 1 died May 15, 1900

Census Card No. 3241, P. O. Brush Hill, Enrolled April 19, 1901

| 9056 | 1 | McIntosh, Abraham | 43 M ½ | Jim McIntosh | D Slave | Wisey McIntosh | D Cr |
| 9057 | 2 | McIntosh, Martha | 38 F F | Wf | Unknown | ? Cr | Unknown | ? Cr |

No. 1 died 1908 or 1909. No. 2 died 1906

Census Card No. 3242, P. O. Bristow, Enrolled April 20, 1901; No. 6, September 22, 1902

9058	1	Biggs, George C.	29 M F	Unknown	? Cr	Unknown	? Cr
9059	2	Biggs, Jeannetta	25 F F	Wf	Unknown	? Cr	Unknown	? Cr
9060	3	Biggs, Sinda	10 F F	D	No. 1	L Cr	No. 2	L Cr
9061	4	Biggs, Susan	8 F F	D	No. 1	L Cr	No. 2	L Cr
9062	5	Biggs, Robert	6 M F	S	No. 1	L Cr	No. 2	L Cr
9063	6	Biggs, Homer	3 M F	S	No. 1	L Cr	No. 2	L Cr

Census Card No. 3243, P. O. Sapulpa, Enrolled April 24, 1901

| 9064 | 1 | Sizemore, Nicey | 63 F F | Gov. Nero | D Cr | Lucy Sizemore | D Cr |

No. 1 died April 14, 1899

Census Card No. 3244, P. O. Sapulpa, Enrolled April 24, 1901

| 9065 | 1 | Sah-ta-quan-ney | 43 F F | Unknown | ? Cr | Unknown | D Cr |

Census Card No. 3245, P. O. Sapulpa, Enrolled April 24, 1901

| 9066 | 1 | Washington, John | 10 M F | Washington Holder | L Cr | Heloy | D Cr |

No. 1 died April 15, 1901

Census Card No. 3246, P. O. Dustin, Enrolled April 24, 1901

| 9067 | 1 | Low, Cinda | 19 F F | Cannuga Low | D Cr | Lena | D Cr |

Census Card No. 3247, P. O. Wetumka, Enrolled April 19, 1901

9068	1	Yarholar, Oktayache	41 M F	Harchee Yarhola	D Cr	Ahsehe	D Cr
9069	2	Yarholar, Annie	23 F F	Wf	Woxie Harjo	D Cr	Ucey	D Cr
9070	3	Yarholar, Lena	18 F F	D	No. 1	L Cr	Eliza Yoholar	D Cr
9071	4	Yarholar, Amos	14 M F	S	No. 1	L Cr	Eliza Yoholar	D Cr

No. 1 died November 18, 1908

Census Card No. 3248, P. O. Wetumka, Enrolled April 30, 1901

| 9072 | 1 | Yarholar, Aney | 21 F F | Oktayohche Yarholar | L Cr | Eliza Yaholar | D Cr |

No. 1 died June 5, 1905

Census Card No. 3249, P. O. Arbeka, Enrolled May 23, 1901

| 9073 | 1 | "Loskey" | 90 F F | Concharty | D Cr | Unknown | D Cr |

No. 1 died November 27, 1904

Census Card No. 3250, P. O. Wewoka, Enrolled May 23, 1901

| 9074 | 1 | Richardson, Lina | 20 F ½ | Tom Anderson | L Cr | Louena Chief | ? Choc |
| 9075 | 2 | Anderson, Lottie | 15 F ½ | Sis | Tom Anderson | L Cr | Louena Chief | ? Choc |

No. 1 died January 25, 1905. No. 2 died July 6, 1901

Census Card No. 3251, P. O. Henryetta, Enrolled May 10, 1901

| 9076 | 1 | Harjo, Cheparney | 4 M F | Lewis Harjo | ? Cr | Wisey Harjo | ? Cr |

Census Card No. 3252, P. O. Wetumka, Enrolled May 23, 1901

| 9077 | 1 | Watson, John | 35 M ¾ | John Watson | D Cr | Annie Watson | D Cr |

No. 1 died February 15, 1900

Census Card No. 3253, P. O. Bristow, Enrolled May 23, 1901

| 9078 | 1 | Jack, Jackson | 24 M F | Micco Harjo | D Cr | Nannie Jack | D Cr |

No. 1 died March 28, 1901

Census Card No. 3254, P. O. Checotah, Enrolled June 27, 1900

| 9079 | 1 | Baker, Ella B. | 20 F 1-32 | Lloyd C. Freeman | ? Non | Josie Freeman | D Cr |

Census Card No. 3255, P. O. Muskogee, Enrolled November 13, 1900

| 9080 | 1 | Willison, Irene | 19 F 1-16 | James D. Willison | D Cr | Mary J. Willison | ? Cher |

Census Card No. 3256 P. O. Gibson Station, Enrolled Nov. 13, 1900

| 9081 | 1 | Willison, James M. | 17 M 1-16 | James D. Willison | D Cr | Mary J. Willison | ? Cher |
| 9082 | 2 | Willison, Helen | 9 F 1-16 | | | | | |

Census Card No. 3257, P. O. Wagoner, Enrolled Nov. 13, 1900

| 9083 | 1 | Willison, Howard D. | 21 M 1-16 | James D. Willison | D Cr | Mary J. Willison | ? Cher |

Census Card No. 3258, P. O. Sapulpa, Enrolled June 19, 1901

9084	1	Hengst, Emma J.	31 M ¼	Thomas McCann	D Cr	Mary E. Shuel	? Non
9085	2	Hengst, William H.	8 M ⅛	S	W. C. Hengst	? Non	No. 1	L Cr
9086	3	Hegst, Virginia P.	6 F ⅛	D	W. C. Hengst	? Non	No. 1	L Cr
9087	4	Hengst, Frankfort	3 M ⅛	S	W. C. Hengst	? Non	No. 1	L Cr
9088	5	Hengst, Arena Marie	2 F ⅛	D	W. C. Hengst	? Non	No. 1	L Cr

Census Card No. 3259, P. O. Muskogee, Enrolled July 1, 1901

| 9089 | 1 | McIntosh, Miley | 40 F F | John Lott | D Cr | Mary Ann | D Cr |

Census Card No. 3260, P. O. Checotah, Enrolled August 20, 1901,

| 9090 | 1 | Freeman, Lloyd C. | 25 M 1-32 | Lloyd C. Freeman | ? Non | Josephine Freeman | L Cr |

Census Card No. 3261, P. O. Checotah, Enrolled August 20, 1901,

| 9091 | 1 | Freeman, Emma J. | 23 F 1-32 | Lloyd Freeman | ? Non | Josephine Freeman | L Cr |

Census Card No. 3262, P. O. Eufaula, Enrolled April 24, 1901

| 9092 | 1 | Manley, Isaac | 25 M F | Moses Manley | D Cr | Disey Manley | D Cr |

Roll No.	No.	NAME	Age	Sex	Blood	Rel.	NAME OF FATHER	Liv.	Cit.	NAME OF MOTHER	Liv.	Cit.
		Census Card No. 3263, P. O. Checotah, Enrolled June 10, 1901										
9093	1	McIntosh, A. G.	53	M	¼		D. N. McIntosh	D	Cr	Jane E. McIntosh	D	Cr
9094	2	McIntosh, Freeland	20	M	⅛	S	No. 1	L	Cr	Mollie McIntosh	L	Cr
9095	3	McIntosh, Van A.	17	M	⅛	S	No. 1	L	Cr	Mollie McIntosh	L	Cr
9096	4	McIntosh, Daniel N.	10	M	⅛	S	No. 1	L	Cr	Mollie McIntosh	L	Cr
9097	5	McIntosh, Waldoe E.	8	M	⅛	S	No. 1	L	Cr	Mollie McIntosh	L	Cr
		Census Card No. 3264, P. O. Laredo, Texas, Enrolled August 16, 1901										
9098	1	Tarvin, Pleasant F.	42	M	⅛		Marion E. Tarvin	L	Cr	Sophia F. Tarvin	L	Non
9099	2	Tarvin, Marion	9	M	1-16	S	No. 1	L	Cr	Patient Tarvin	L	Non
9100	3	Tarvin, Randon	7	M	1-16	S	No. 1	L	Cr	Patient Tarvin	L	Non
9101	4	Tarvin, Fannie	4	F	1-16	D	No. 1	L	Cr	Patient Tarvin	L	Non
9102	5	Tarvin, Seboy M.	2	F	1-16	D	No. 1	L	Cr	Patient Tarvin	L	Non
		Census Card No. 3265, P. O. Checotah, Enrolled August 28, 1901										
9103	1	Freeman, Joseph L.	27	M	1-32		Lloyd C. Freeman	?	Non	Josephine Freeman	L	Cr
		Census Card No. 3266, P. O. Eufaula, Enrolled August 25, 1901										
9104	1	Kizzie	42	F	F		Thlathlo Yarholar	D	Cr	Yarkappee	D	Cr
		No. 1 died December 1899										
		Census Card No. 3267, P. O. Hoffman, Enrolled August 14, 1901										
9105	1	Freeman, Josephene	47	F	1-16		Dr. Howell	?	Non	M. L. Weatherford	D	Cr
9106	2	Freeman, Theodore O.	17	M	1-32	S	L. C. Freeman	?	Non	No. 1	L	Cr
9107	3	Freeman, Carlyle D.	14	M	1-32	S	L. C. Freeman	?	Non	No. 1	L	Cr
9108	4	Freeman, Lynne S.	12	M	1-32	S	L. C. Freeman	?	Non	No. 1	L	Cr
9109	5	Freeman, Estella E.	12	F	1-32	D	L. C. Freeman	?	Non	No. 1	L	Cr
		Census Card No. 3268, P. O. Wagoner, Enrolled November 15, 1899										
9110	1	Posey, James S.	43	M	¼		T. B. Posey	D	Cr	Huldy Posey	L	Non
9111	2	Posey, Andy W.	22	M	⅛	S	No. 1	L	Cr	Emily Posey	L	Non
9112	3	Posey, Thomas U.	18	M	⅛	S	No. 1	L	Cr	Emily Posey	L	Non
9113	4	Posey, Lena L.	12	F	⅛	D	No. 1	L	Cr	Emily Posey	L	Non
9114	5	Posey, Nora S.	9	F	⅛	D	No. 1	L	Cr	Emily Posey	L	Non
9115	6	Posey, Kennie	6	F	⅛	D	No. 1	L	Cr	Emily Posey	L	Non
9116	7	Posey, Boyce W.	3	M	⅛	S	No. 1	L	Cr	Emily Posey	L	Non
		Census Card No. 3269, P. O. Ridge, Enrolled June 24, 1901										
9117	1	Taylor, John W.	50	M	¼		Granderson Taylor	D	Non	Parthenia Beams	D	Cr
		No. 1 died October 30, 1909										
		Census Card No. 3270, P. O. Eufaula, Enrolled April 30, 1901										
9118	1	Beaver, Sanger	48	M	F		Itshars Micco	D	Cr	Tikee	D	Cr
9119	2	Beaver, Elsa	33	F	½	Wf	Unknown	?	?	Millie	?	?
9120	3	Beaver, Nellie	14	F	¾	D	No. 1	L	Cr	No. 2	L	Cr
9121	4	Sarnie, Annie	15	F	F	Niece	Sarnie	D	Cr	Katie Sarnie	D	Cr
9122	5	Hutton, James	20	M	F	Neph	Mulda Hutman	L	Cr	Leah Hutman	D	Cr
9123	6	Stricken from roll										
		No. 2 died December 24, 1909. No. 3 reported dead.										
		Census Card No. 3271, P. O. Tecumseh, Enrolled April 25, 1901										
9124	1	Polecat, Sapesa	60	F	F		Unknown	D	Cr	Unknown	D	Cr
9125	2	Stricken from roll										
9126	3	Polecat, Pahlatahshee-nay	8	M	F	S	Polecat	?	Shaw	No. 1	L	Cr
9127	4	Polecat, Kanochee-shunar	11	M	F	S	Polecat	?	Shaw	No. 1	L	Cr
		Census Card No. 3272, P. O. Sasakwa, Enrolled May 23, 1901										
9128	1	Powell, Cinda	36	F	½		Narkoche	?	Sem	Jonah	D	Cr
9129	2	Jonah, Louisiana	13	F	½	Sis	Narkoche	?	Sem	Jonah	D	Cr
9130	3	Johnson, Mollie	12	F	¼	D	Johnson Tallon	?	Sem	No. 1	L	Cr
9131	4	Johnson, Daniel	14	M	¼	S	Johnson Tallon	?	Sem	No. 1	L	Cr
9132	5	Powell, Hannah	4	F	¼	D	Willie Powell	?	Sem	No. 1	L	Cr
		No. 1 died February 1901. No. 5 died 1904.										
		Census Card No. 3273, P. O. Hanna, Enrolled May 22, 1901										
9133	1	Harjo, Effie	55	F	F		Tulsa Micco	D	Cr	Unknown	D	Cr
9134	2	Harjo, Houston	50	F	F	Sis	Tulsa Micco	D	Cr	Unknown	?	Cr
9135	3	Harjo, Millie	15	F	F	D	No. 1	L	Cr	Unknown	?	Cr
9136	4	Harjo, Sallie	12	F	F	D	No. 1	L	Cr	Unknown	?	Cr
9137	5	Harjo, Segar	20	F	F	Cou	Yaha Harjo	D	Cr	Waitchee	D	Cr
		No. 5 died February 20, 1908										
		Census Card No. 3274, P. O. Scipio, Enrolled May 23, 1901										
9138	1	Jackson, Louis	35	M	F		Jackson	D	Cr	Inchuskeler	D	Cr
9139	2	Betsey,	30	F	F	Niece	Nakaney	?	Sem	Jennie	D	Cr
9140	3	Polly	18	F	F	Niece	Cho Harjoche	D	Cr	Hepsey	D	Cr
9141	4	Missie	30	F	F	Niece	Pin Harjo	D	Cr	Nancy	D	Cr
9142	5	Louisiana	8	F	F	Gr-N	Unknown	?	Cr	No. 4	L	Cr
		No. 3 died July 15, 1904. No. 5 died 1904. No. 4 possible duplicate No. 1508. Int married Choctaw roll.										
		Census Card No. 3275, P. O. Brush Hill, Enrolled May 23, 1901										
9143	1	Lynch, Cora	16	F	½		Rufe Whaley	D	Non	Elizabeth Lynch	D	Cr
		No. 1 died May 1901										
		Census Card No. 3276, P. O. Okemah, Enrolled April 25, 1901										
9144	1	Holahta, Nocus	68	M	F		Chuwosta Emarthla	D	Cr	Sitkolage	D	Cr
9145	2	Holahta, Arlinda	48	F	F		Unknown	?	Cr	Sakanaka	D	Cr
9146	3	Holahta, Larnee	8	F	F	D	No. 1	L	Cr	No. 2	L	Cr
9147	4	Holahta, John	3	M	F	S	No. 1	L	Cr	No. 2	L	Cr
		No. 1 died December 30, 1910										

194

Roll No.	No.	NAME	Age	Sex	Blood	Rel.	NAME OF FATHER	Liv.	Cit.	NAME OF MOTHER	Liv.	Cit.
		Census Card No. 3277, P. O. Arbeka, Enrolled April 25, 1901										
9148	1	Billey, John	8	M	F		Nehayaholage	D	Cr	Leah	D	Cr
9149	2	Billey, Pilot	7	M	F	Bro	Nehayaholage	D	Cr	Leah	D	Cr
		No. 1 died February 13, 1910										
		Census Card No. 3278, P. O. Eufaula, Enrolled May 23, 1901										
9150	1	Kelly, John	45	M	F		Unknown	?	Cr	Jennie Kelly	D	Cr
9151	2	Kelly, Sallie	43	F	F	Wf	Unknown	?	Cr	Unknown	D	Cr
9152	3	Kelly, James	19	M	F	S	No. 1	L	Cr	Bettie Kelly	D	Cr
9153	4	Kelly, Sarah	17	F	F	D	No. 1	L	Cr	Bettie Kelly	D	Cr
9154	5	Kelly, Johnnie	5	M	F	S	No. 1	L	Cr	No. 2	L	Cr
9155	6	Deere, Lucy	17	F	F	StD	Unknown	?	Cr	No. 2	L	Cr
		No. 4 died May 12, 1899. No. 2 died June 4, 1906. No. 6 died February 26, 1910.										
		Census Card No. 3279, P. O. Arbeka, Enrolled May 2, 1901										
9156	1	Fixico, Benoche	19	M	F		Cusseta Fixico	D	Cr	Warney Fixico	D	Cr
		Census Card No. 3280, P. O. Eufaula, Enrolled April 26, 1901										
9157	1	Greenwood, Dick	53	M	F		Greenwood	D	Cr	Togee	D	
		Census Card No. 3281, P. O. Senora, Enrolled April 26, 1901										
9158	1	Sampson, David J.	39	M	½		James Sampson	D	Sem	Lucinda Sampson	D	
		Census Card No. 3282, P. O. Eufaula, Enrolled May 23, 1901										
9159	1	Cowe, Porter	35	M	F		Cowe Harjo	D	Cr	Unknown	D	Cr Cr
		No. 1 died December 1, 1905										
		Census Card No. 3283, P. O. Fort Gibson, Enrolled May 17, 1901										
9160	1	Berry, Frances	54	F	½		Spire Hagerty	D	Non	Rebecca Hagerty	D	Cr
9161	2	Berry, Adesta	19	F	¼	D	John H. Berry	L	Non	No. 1	L	Cr
9162	3	Berry, Josephine	16	F	¼	D	John H. Berry	L	Non	No. 1	L	Cr
9163	4	Berry, Spire McIntosh	14	M	¼	S	John H. Berry	L	Non	No. 1	L	Cr
9164	5	Berry, Louise	12	F	¼	D	John H. Berry	L	Non	No. 1	L	Cr
		No. 1 died October 8, 1902										
		Census Card No. 3284, P. O. Wagoner, Enrolled May 17, 1901										
9165	1	McQuarie, Ray Lee	18	M	½		J. H. McQuarie	?	Non	Alice McQuarie	D	Cr
		Census Card No. 3285, P. O. Wetumka, Enrolled April 30, 1901										
9166	1	Fixeco, Tommy	35	M	F		Fixico	?	Cr	Unknown	D	Cr
		No. 1 died February 28, 1910										
		Census Card No. 3286, P. O. Eufaula, Enrolled April 24, 1901										
9167	1	Billy, Annie	24	F	F		Lumber Billy	L	Cr	Nancy Billy	L	Cr
9168	2	Billy, Emma	3	F	F	D	Unknown	?	Cr	No. 1	L	Cr
		No. 1 died March 1910										
		Census Card No. 3287, P. O. Okemah, Enrolled April 25, 1901										
9169	1	Monarye	53	F	F		Unknown	?	Cr	Unknown	?	Cr
		No. 1 died March 1913										
		Census Card No. 3288, P. O. Okemah, Enrolled April 25, 1901										
9170	1	Simmer, Charley	31	M	F		Simmer	D	Cr	Sinda Simmer	D	Cr
9171	2	Simmer, Kizzie	27	F	F	Wf	Upna Hill	D	Cr	Lucinda Hill	D	Cr
9172	3	Simmer, Joseph	5	M	F	S	No. 1	L	Cr	No. 2	L	Cr
9173	4	Simmer, Emma	4	F	F	D	No. 1	L	Cr	No. 2	L	Cr
		Census Card No. 3289, P. O. Dustin, Enrolled May 21, 1901										
9174	1	Berryhill, Eveline	46	F	F		V. J. Wills	D	Cr	G. A. Berryhill	D	Cr
9175	2	Burns, Alvin	15	M	F	S	Ike Burns	D	Cr	No. 1	L	Cr
9176	3	Burns, Isaac	13	M	F	S	Ike Burns	D	Cr	No. 1	L	Cr
		Census Card No. 3290, P. O. Bristow, Enrolled April 25, 1901										
9177	1	Washington	31	M	F		Nocus Holokta	L	Cr	Martha	D	Cr
9178	2	Fixeco, Dicey	26	F	F	Wf	Afalokey	D	Cr	Lucinda	?	Cr
		No. 2 died November 30, 1904										
		Census Card No. 3291, P. O. Wewoka, Enrolled April 25, 1901										
9179	1	Yahola, Eliza	19	F	F		Thomas Yahola	L	Cr	Lizzie Yahola	L	Cr
		No. 1 died September 9, 1914										
		Census Card No. 3292, P. O. Bristow, Enrolled May 17, 1901										
9180	1	Scott, George Washington	6	M	½		Alex Scott	D	Cr	Dora Scott	D	Non
9181	2	Scott, Daisy	4	F	½	Sis	Alex Scott	D	Cr	Dora Scott	D	Non
		Census Card No. 3293, P. O. Pryor, Enrolled May 14, 1901										
9182	1	McIntosh, Lucile	23	F	⅛		Freeland McIntosh	L	Cr	Lou McIntosh	?	Cher
		Census Card No. 3294, P. O. Muskogee, Enrolled November 2, 1900										
9183	1	Stidham, Nellie	23	F	F		Johnson Stidham	D	Cr	Nutwoche	D	Cr
		Census Card No. 3295, P. O. Wewoka, Enrolled April 27, 1901										
9184	1	Smith, John Jr.	33	M	⅝		Tecumseh Smith	D	Cr	Bettie Smith	D	Cr
		Census Card No. 3296, P. O. Eufaula, Enrolled May 2, 1901										
9185	1	Yamahike	73	F	F		Unknown	D	Cr	Unknown	D	Cr
		No. 1 died March 23, 1904										
		Census Card No. 3297, P. O. Wagoner, Enrolled May 1901										
9186	1	Vann, James S.	42	M	¼		James Vann	D	Cher	Mary Wadsworth	D	Cr
9187	2	Vann, Sarah Heland	16	F	⅛	D	No. 1	L	Cr	Alice Vann	?	Cher
		Census Card No. 3298, P. O. Sperry, Enrolled May 24, 1901										
9188	1	Chisholm, Henry	10	M	½		Colbert Chisholm	D	Cr	Susie Skahker	?	Shaw
9189	2	Stricken from roll										
		Census Card No. 3299, P. O. Wetumka, Enrolled March 26, 1901										
9190	1	Robison, George F.	37	M	⅛		William Robison	D	Cr	Adeline Robison	D	Chick

Roll No.	No.	NAME	Age	Sex	Blood	Rel.	NAME OF FATHER	Liv.	Cit.	NAME OF MOTHER	Liv.	Cit.
		Census Card No. 3300, P. O. Wagoner, Enrolled April 27, 1900; Nos. 2 and 3, May 1, 1901										
9191	1	Brady, Foil M.	44	M	½		Sam R. Brady	D	Cher	Eliza Brady	D	Cr
9192	2	Brady, Charley	11	M	¼	S	No. 1	L	Cr	Martha Brady	D	Cr
9193	3	Brady, Sam R.	19	M	¼	S	No. 1	L	Cr	Martha Brady	D	Cr
		No. 2 died December 21, 1913										
		Census Card No. 3301, P. O. Sasakwa, Enrolled April 5, 1902										
9194	1	Wildcat, John	25	M	½		Cowokochee	?	Sem	Mapetha	D	Cr
9195	2	Wildcat, Albert	22	M	½	Bro	Cowokochee	?	Sem	Mapetha	D	Cr
		No. 1 died October 23, 1909. No. 2 died November 1903.										
		Census Card, No. 3302, P. O. Sand Springs, Enrolled August 23, 1901										
9196	1	Lannan, Jennie	35	F	⅛		G. P. Lott	?	Non	Mary E. Terrell	L	Cr
9197	2	Lannan, Mary	11	F	1-16	D	Will Lannon	?	Non	No. 1	L	Cr
9198	3	Lannan, Maggie	4	F	1-16	D	Will Lannon	?	Non	No. 1	L	Cr
		Census Card No. 3303, P. O. Newby, Enrolled May 23, 1901										
9199	1	Brown, Conpesinney	50	M	F		Cosannah	D	Cr	Tahfah	D	Cr
9200	2	Brown, Loda	27	F	F	Wf	Long Jim	D	Cr	Annie	D	Cr
9201	3	Brown, Tabsaconthle- ney	9	M	F	S	No. 1	L	Cr	No. 2	L	Cr
9202	4	Brown, Cahkaleco- conthla	7	M	F	S	No. 1	L	Cr	No. 2	L	Cr
9203	5	Brown, Tahconfah	16	F	F	D	No. 1	L	Cr	Annie	D	Cr
9204	6	Brown, Yahlane	19	M	F	S	No. 1	L	Cr	Annie	D	Cr
9205	7	Brown, Dakesahco- contaney	2	F	F	D	No. 1	L	Cr	No. 2	L	Cr
		No. 1 died January 15, 1910. No. 5 died April 27, 1910.										
		Census Card No. 3304, P. O. Eufaula, Enrolled May 18, 1901										
9206	1	Shwinogee, Winey	50	F	F		Unknown	D	Cr	Unknown	D	Cr
9207	2	Hutkey, Kizzie	25	F	F	D	Shwinogee	D	Chic	No. 1	L	Cr
		Census Card No. 3305, P. O. Okfuskee, Enrolled April 8, 1901										
9208	1	Joney, Milley	46	F	F		Tommy Harjo	D	Cr	Unknown	D	Cr
		No. 1 died April 16, 1899										
		Census Card No. 3306										
9209	1	Stricken from roll										
		Census Card No. 3307, P. O. Eufaula; No. 3, Raiford, Enrolled April 24, 1901										
9210	1	Conner, Abbie	33	F	F		George Cosar	L	Cr	Annie Cosar	D	Cr
9211	2	Conner, Nettie	10	F	F	D	Thomas Conner	L	Cr	No. 1	L	Cr
9212	3	Conner, Willie	7	M	F	S	Thomas Conner	L	Cr	No. 1	L	Cr
9213	4	Conner, John	3	M	F	S	Thomas Conner	L	Cr	No. 1	L	Cr
		Census Card No. 3308, P. O. Mounds, Enrolled April 9, 1902										
9214	1	Tiger, Sahcopochuny	31	F	F		Unknown	D	Cr	Kittie Squire	D	Cr
		No. 1 died April 10, 1899										
		Census Card No. 3309, P. O. Okemah, Enrolled April 10, 1902										
9215	1	Daniel, Thompson	16	M	F		Eli Daniel	D	Cr	Metta Daniel	D	Cr
		No. 1 died February 1900										
		Census Card No. 3310, P. O. Wetumka, Enrolled April 26, 1901										
9216	1	Bruner, John	17	M	F		Wiley Bruner	D	Cr	Haley Anderson	D	Cr
9217	2	Anderson, Norman	7	M	F	½Bro	Tom Anderson	D	Cr	Haley Anderson	D	Cr
9218	3	Anderson, Samuel	6	M	F	½Bro	Tom Anderson	D	Cr	Haley Anderson	D	Cr
		Census Card No. 3311, P. O. Lenna, Enrolled April 11, 1902										
9219	1	Turk, Benjamin	9	M	F		Frank Turk	L	Cr	Lena Fields	D	Cr
		Census Card No. 3312, P. O. Mounds, Enrolled April 27, 1901										
9220	1	Tiger, Lucinda	13	M	F		Thomas Tiger	D	Cr	Lovey Tiger	D	Cr
		Census Card No. 3313, P. O. Phillipsburg, Enrolled April 25, 1901										
9221	1	Sannah	18	M	F		Kocoquanney	L	Cr	Pothlar	D	Cr
		No. 1 died February 17, 1901										
		Census Card No. 3314, P. O. Texanna, Enrolled April 22, 1901										
9222	1	Watts, Mary	63	F	½		Wadsworth	D	Non	Levina Wadsworth	D	Cr
		Census Card No. 3315, P. O. Sapulpa, Enrolled April 16, 1902										
9223	1	Weaver, Rena	22	F	⅛		Mr. Brown	D	Non	Rosa A. Norman	L	Cr
9224	2	Weaver, Helen R.	5	F	1-16	D	Bert Weaver	?	Non	No. 1	L	Cr
		Census Card No. 3316, P. O. Checotah, Enrolled April 16, 1902										
9225	1	Norman, Rosa Alabama	54	F	¼		Esaw Kelleam	D	Non	Caroline Norman	D	Cr
		No. 1 died April 20, 1911										
		Census Card No. 3317, P. O. Sapulpa, Enrolled April 16, 1902										
9226	1	Powell, Sammie	23	F	⅛		Mr. Brown	D	Non	Rosa A. Norman	L	Cr
9227	2	Powell, Pearl	4	F	1-16	D	Robert Powell	?	Non	No. 1	L	Cr
9228	3	Powell, Park	3	M	1-16	S	Robert Powell	?	Non	No. 1	L	Cr
		Census Card No. 3318, P. O. Onapa, Enrolled April 17, 1902										
9229	1	Carr, Etta	5	F	F		Willie Carr	L	Cr	Addie Carr	L	Cr
9230	2	Carr, Mabel	4	F	F	Sis	Willie Carr	L	Cr	Addie Carr	L	Cr
		Census Card No. 3319, P. O. Wetumka, Enrolled April 18, 1902										
9231	1	Harjo, Neha Thlocco	61	M	F		Sumnubba	D	Cr	Semardaryee	D	Cr
		No. 1 died April 17, 1900										
		Census Card No. 3320, P. O. Fentress, Enrolled April 18, 1902										
9232	1	Dacon, Nannie	17	F	F		Sarty Dacon	L	Cr	Harney Dacon	L	Cr
		No. 1 died January 1, 1900										
		Census Card No. 3321, P. O. Wetumka, Enrolled April 19, 1902										
9233	1	Sarthlepoche	43	F	F		Artus Fixico	D	Cr	Quogue	D	Cr
		No. 1 died October 8, 1900										

Census Card No. 3322, P. O. Checotah, Enrolled April 22, 1902

Roll No.	No.	NAME	Age	Sex	Blood	Rel.	NAME OF FATHER	Liv.	Cit.	NAME OF MOTHER	Liv.	Cit.
9234	1	Self, James R.	26	M	⅛		John B. Self	L	Cr	Bettie Self	L	Non

Census Card No. 3323, P. O. Wagoner, Enrolled April 21, 1902

| 9235 | 1 | Childers, Daisy | 1 | F | ⅞ | | Anderson Childers | L | Cr | Lydia Childers | L | Cr |

No. 1 died June 28, 1899

Census Card No. 3324, P. O. Hanna, Enrolled May 23, 1901

| 9236 | 1 | Proctor, Jeannetta | 25 | F | F | | Tommie Fixico | D | Cr | Wisey Proctor | D | Cr |

No. 1 died November 24, 1901

Census Card No. 3325, P. O. Morse, Enrolled May 20, 1901

| 9237 | 1 | Harjo, Dave | 25 | M | F | | Unknown | D | Cr | Miatka | D | Cr |

No. 1 possible duplicate No. 4136 this roll.

Census Card No. 3326, P. O. Bearden, Enrolled April 25, 1901

| 9238 | 1 | Arfulka | 53 | F | F | | Unknown | ? | Cr | Unknown | D | Cr |
| 9239 | 2 | Fixico, Ben | 23 | M | F | S | Timmie Marthoche | D | Cr | No. 1 | L | Cr |

No. 2 died September 15, 1906

Census Card No. 3327, P. O. Okemah, Enrolled April 26, 1901

| 9240 | 1 | Miller, Annie | 18 | F | F | | Houston, Miller | D | Cr | Tewoliche | D | Cr |
| 9241 | 2 | Miller, Susie | 4 | F | F | Sis | Houston Miller | D | Cr | Tewoliche | D | Cr |

No. 2 died November 1, 1901

Census Card No. 3328, P. O. Okemah, Enrolled April 27, 1901

| 9242 | 1 | Harjo, Ginnie | 43 | F | F | | Pahos Harjo | D | Cr | Monadege | D | Cr |
| 9243 | 2 | Harjo, Huntie | 18 | M | F | ½Bro | Pahos Harjo | D | Cr | Cinda | ? | Cr |

Census Card No. 3329, P. O. Paden, Enrolled April 27, 1901

| 9244 | 1 | Thompson, Thomas | 12 | M | F | | Cardimney | D | Cr | Nunochee | D | Cr |
| 9245 | 2 | Thompson, Lucy | 10 | F | F | Sis | Cardimney | D | Cr | Nunochee | D | Cr |

Census Card No. 3330, P. O. Okmulgee, Enrolled April 30, 1902

| 9246 | 1 | Davis, Jesse | 34 | M | F | | Pin Harjo | D | Cr | Rosanna Harjo | D | Cr |

No. 1 died April 15, 1899

Census Card No. 3331, P. O. Wetumka, Enrolled May 14, 1901

| 9247 | 1 | Moffitt, Annie | 4 | F | F | | Joseph Harjo | ? | Cr | Mary Siah | L | Cr |

No. 1 died October 21, 1901

Census Card No. 3332, P. O. Tabor, Enrolled May 24, 1901

9248	1	Freeman, Rhoda	61	F	¼		Bungy	D	Cr	Molly Butler	D	Cr
9249	2	Mikey, Lizzie	23	F	⅛	D	Nickson James	D	Cr	No. 1	L	Cr
9250	3	Mikey, Magnolia	3	F	1-16	GrD	Josiah Mikey	L	F-Ch	No. 2	L	Cr
9251	4	Mikey, Robinson	1	M	1-16	GrS	Josiah Mikey	L	F-Ch	No. 2	L	Cr

No. 1 died October 7, 1907

Census Card No. 3333, P. O. Eufaula, Enrolled May 3, 1902

| 9252 | 1 | Sullivan, Lucy | 65 | F | F | | Unknown | D | Cr | Unknown | D | Cr |

No. 1 died January 1, 1900

Census Card No. 3334, P. O. Okfuskee, Enrolled May 2, 1901

| 9253 | 1 | Emarthloche, Daniel | 20 | M | F | | Tulmarsey | L | Cr | Karsalarnee | D | Cr |

Census Card No. 3335, P. O. Okfuskee, Enrolled May 2, 1901

| 9254 | 1 | Selvina | 73 | F | F | | Unknown | D | Cr | Unknown | D | Cr |

No. 1 died October 17, 1905

Census Card No. 3336, P. O. Morse, Enrolled April 19, 1901

| 9255 | 1 | Taylor, Mannie | 11 | F | F | | Sam Taylor | D | Cr | Silvey | D | Cr |

No. 1 died March 6, 1900

Census Card No. 3337, P. O. Bristow, Enrolled May 23, 1901

| 9256 | 1 | Angie | 21 | F | F | | Kacoquana | ? | Cr | Ninna | D | Cr |

Census Card No. 3338, P. O. Kellyville, Enrolled May 5, 1902

| 9257 | 1 | Tiger, Goody | 51 | M | F | | Coquan | D | Cr | Cohahda | D | Cr |
| 9258 | 2 | Goody, Jim | 13 | M | F | S | No. 1 | L | Cr | Ahcoconey | D | Cr |

No. 1 died September 8, 1899. No. 2 died August 29. 1899.

Census Card No. 3339, P. O. Eufaula, Enrolled April 24, 1901

9259	1	Manley, Adam	28	M	F		Moses Manley	D	Cr	Disey Manley	D	Cr
9260	2	Manley, Leeda	27	F	F	Wf	Dick Bear	D	Cr	Amy Bear	D	Cr
9261	3	Bear, David	16	M	F	Bro-L	Dick Bear	D	Cr	Amy Brea	D	Cr

No. 3 died December 1905

Census Card No. 3340, P. O. Mellette, Enrolled April 29, 1901

9262	1	Crow, Melissa	33	F	F		Osa Yahola	D	Cr	Konahagey	D	Cr
9263	2	Crow, Cinda	12	F	D	F	George Crow	D	Cr	No. 1	L	Cr
9264	3	Crow, Sarnie	10	F	F	D	George Crow	D	Cr	No. 1	L	Cr
9265	4	Crow, Mary	3	F	F	D	George Crow	D	Cr	No. 1	L	Cr

No. 2 died April 5, 1899. No. 4 died August 29, 1899.

Census Card No. 3341, P. O. Castle, Enrolled April 19, 1901

| 9266 | 1 | Samuel, Monie | 15 | F | F | | Lubby Samuel | ? | Cr | Lizzie Samuel | ? | Cr |

Census Card No. 3342, P. O. Hanna, Enrolled May 13, 1902

| 9267 | 1 | Chisholm, Tom | 40 | M | ½ | | John Chisholm | D | Cher | Polly Chisholm | D | Cr |

No. 1 died January 7, 1900

Census Card No. 3343, P. O. Weleetka, Enrolled April 19, 1901

9268	1	Harjo, Legus	33	M	F		Tommy Harjo	D	Cr	Nightska	D	Cr
9269	2	Imly	31	F	F	Wf	Espaney Yahola	D	Cr	Lucy Annie	D	Cr
9270	3	Navey	11	F	F	D	No. 1	L	Cr	No. 2	L	Cr
9271	4	Dewochee	18	M	F	Bro-L	Sinhelupke	D	Cr	Lucy Annie	?	Cr

No. 2 died September 1900. No. 4 reported dead. No. 3 died February 1900.

Census Card No. 3344, P. O. Holdenville, Enrolled May 29, 1902

| 9272 | 1 | Tayoposka | 60 | F | F | | Konepoche | D | Cr | Lachehche | D | Cr |

No. 1 died April 6, 1899

Census Card No. 3345, P. O. Okfuskee, Enrolled May 31, 1902

| 9273 | 1 | Hennehuchee, Harjo | 19 | M | F | | Henahochee | D | Cr | Narcissee | D | Cr |

No. 1 died 1899

Census Card No. 3346, P. O. Oktaha, Enrolled May 23, 1901

| 9274 | 1 | Setehme | 45 F F | Okchiye Emarthla | D | Cr | Singer | D | Cr |
| 9275 | 2 | Peloche | 12 M F S | Taylor | D | Cr | No. 1 | L | Cr |

No. 1 died April 16, 1901

Census Card No. 3347, P. O. Eufaula, Enrolled May 23, 1901

| 9276 | 1 | Emarthla, Echo | 65 M F | Unknown | D | Cr | Unknown | D | Cr |

No. 1 died October 21, 1899

Census Card No. 3348, P. O. Dustin, Enrolled June 3, 1902

| 9277 | 1 | Kanard, Josiah | 7 M F | George Kanard | L | Cr | Rosana Kanard | L | Cr |

Census Card No. 3349, P. O. Okmulgee, Enrolled April 24, 1901

| 9278 | 1 | Lee, David | 15 M F | Arpalah Lee | D | Cr | Lucy Lee | D | Cr |

No. 1 died February 23, 1901

Census Card No. 3350, P. O. Morse, Enrolled May 22, 1901

| 9279 | 1 | Johnson, Susie | 60 F F | Unknown | D | Cr | Unknown | D | Cr |

No. 1 died December 15, 1899

Census Card No. 3351, P. O. Eufaula, Enrolled June 19, 1902

| 9280 | 1 | Cato, Ben | 26 M F | Cato | D | Cr | Rody Cato | D | Cr |

No. 1 died March 15, 1900

Census Card No. 3352, P. O. Creek, Enrolled June 20, 1902

| 9281 | 1 | Davis, Joseph | 18M F | John Davis | L | Cr | Mehaka | D | Cr |

No. 1 died April 7, 1899

Census Card No. 3353, P. O. Kellyville, Enrolled June 21, 1902

| 9282 | 1 | Bushyhead, Cleveland | 50 M F | Gotahney | D | Cr | Unfahne | D | Cr |

No. 1 died April 15, 1899

Census Card No. 3354, P. O. Hanna, Enrolled May 22, 1901

| 9283 | 1 | Smith, Leo | 5 M F | Wattie Fish | L | Cr | Nellie Byrd | L | Cr |

No. 1 died September 15, 1899

Census Card No. 3355, P. O. Vivian, Enrolled June 24, 1902

| 9284 | 1 | Colbert, Nellie | 2 F F | Thompson Colbert | L | Cr | Ellen Colbert | L | Cr |

No. 1 died December 31, 1899

Census Card No. 3356, P. O. Keokuk Falls, Enrolled May 22, 1901

| 9285 | 1 | Fife, Minnie | 2 F ¾ | Louis Fife | ? | Sem | Jeannetta Fife | ? | Cr |

Census Card No. 3357, P. O. Beggs, Enrolled June 26, 1902

| 9286 | 1 | Blunt, Joe | 50 M F | Chotke | D | Cr | Sofie | D | Cr |

Census Card No. 3358, P. O. Bristow, Enrolled May 23, 1901

9287	1	Cloud, Laslie	60 M F	Tokis Harjo	D	Cr	Cinda	D	Cr
9288	2	Cloud, Lizize	20 F F D	No. 1	L	Cr	Sinnie Cloud	D	Cr
9289	3	Cloud, Charles	7 M F S	No. 1	L	Cr	No. 4	L	Cr
9290	4	Cloud, Mary	50 F F Wf	Leha Harjoche	D	Cr	Harjochee	D	Cr
9291	5	Cloud, Jennie	30 F F Wf	Joe Blunt	L	Cr	Annie Blunt	D	Cr
9292	6	Houston, Turner	14 M F StS	Sam Houston	D	Cr	No. 5	L	Cr
9293	7	Houston, George	9 M F StS	Sam Houston	D	Cr	No. 5	L	Cr
9294	8	Houston, Jesse	6 M F StS	Sam Houston	D	Cr	No. 5	L	Cr

No. 1 died December 8, 1905.   No. 6 died 1904.   No. 3 died October 1, 1900.   No. 4 died February 14, 1901.   No. 5 died January 1904.

Census Card No. 3359

| 9295 | 1 | Stricken from roll |

Census Card No. 3360, P. O. Checotah, Enrolled July 27, 1901

| 9296 | 1 | Stevenson, Mamie | 23 F 1-32 | L. C. Freeman | ? | Non | Josephine Freeman | L | Cr |

No. 1 died July 22, 1909

Census Card No. 3361, P. O. Tulsa, Enrolled July 1, 1902

| 9297 | 1 | Harry, Martha | 2 F ½ | John Harry | L | ? | Mary Harry | L | ? |

Census Card No. 3362, P. O. Holdenville, Enrolled July 1, 1902

| 9298 | 1 | Harjo, Ispokoke | 46 M F | Osage Harjo | D | Cr | Hannah Chupco | D | Cr |

No. 1 died November 15, 1899

Census Card No. 3363, P. O. Okemah, Enrolled July 2, 1902

| 9299 | 1 | Dunn, Noah | 2 M F | Tupper Dunn | L | Cr | Susie Dunn | L | Cr |

Census Card No. 3364, P. O. Sapulpa, Enrolled July 3, 1902

| 9300 | 1 | Mayes, James | 1 M ½ | W. A. Mayes | L | Non | Martha Mayes | L | Cr |

No. 1 died October 21, 1901

Census Card No. 3365, P. O. Checotah, Enrolled July 3, 1902

| 9301 | 1 | McIntosh, John R. | 1½ M 1-32 | Roley C. McIntosh | L | Cr | Fannie McIntosh | L | Cr |

Census Card No. 3366, P. O. Calvin, Enrolled August 29, 1902

| 9202 | 1 | Williams, Ellen | 18 F ¾ | Charles Williams | L | Cr | Cilla Williams | D | Cr |

No. 1 died July 3, 1899

Census Card No. 3367, P. O. Salem, Enrolled May 17, 1901

9303	1	Taylor, Roley	35 M F	Charley Taylor	D	Cr	Artie	?	Cr
9304	2	Taylor, Nellie	33 F F Wf	Unknown	D	Cr	Unknown	D	Cr
9305	3	Taylor, Leah	14 F F D	No. 1	L	Cr	No. 2	L	Cr
9306	4	Taylor, Loma	12 F F D	No. 1	L	Cr	No. 2	L	Cr
9307	5	Taylor, Ellis	10 M F S	No. 1	L	Cr	No. 2	L	Cr
9308	6	Taylor, Sarah	8 F F D	No. 1	L	Cr	No. 2	L	Cr
9309	7	Taylor, Albert	6 M F S	No. 1	L	Cr	No. 2	L	Cr
9310	8	Taylor, Cub	2 M F S	No. 1	L	Cr	No. 2	L	Cr

No. 1 died May 18, 1907.   No. 2 died 1906.

Roll No.	No.	NAME	Age	Sex	Blood	Rel.	NAME OF FATHER	Liv.	Cit.	NAME OF MOTHER	Liv.	Cit.
		Census Card No. 3368, P. O. Pierce, Enrolled May 21, 1901										
9311	1	Timothy, Noah	35	M	F		Timothy	D	Cr	Mustoche		Cr
9312	2	Timothy, Eliza	30	F	F	Wf	Suda Thompson	D	Cr	Nicey Thompson		Cr
9313	3	Pigeon, Misser	16	M	F	StS	Unknown	D	Cr	Lucy Timothy		Cr
9314	4	Timothy, Sandy	9	M	F	S	No. 1	L	Cr	Lucy Timothy		Cr
9315	5	Beartail, John	4	M	F	StS	Nocus Hutche	D	Cr	No. 2		Cr
9316	6	Beartail, Louisa	3	F	F	StD	Nocus Hutche	D	Cr	No. 2	D	Cr
		No. 1 died October 30, 1904. No. 2 died June 28, 1903.										
		Census Card No. 3369, P. O. Hanna, Enrolled May 22, 1901										
9317	1	Harjo, Kuncheya	32	M	F		Kapetcha Harjo	D	Cr	Missie Hutkey	L	Cr
9318	2	Harjo, Marsey	25	M	F	Bro	Kapetcha Harjo	D	Cr	Missie Hutkey	L	Cr
		No. 1 died April 10, 1901. No. 2 died June 10, 1909.										
		Census Card No. 3370, P. O. Checotah, Enrolled May 23, 1901										
9319	1	Murray, Helen	42	F	F		W. B. Self	L	Cr	Mary Self	L	Non
9320	2	Murray, John	20	M	1-16	S	W. D. Murray	?	Non	No. 1	L	Cr
9321	3	Murray, Whig	13	F	1-16	D	W. D. Murray	?	Non	No. 1	L	Cr
9322	4	Murray, Ruth	10	F	1-16	D	W. D. Murray	?	Non	No. 1	L	Cr
9323	5	Murray, William	8	M	1-16	S	W. D. Murray	?	Non	No. 1	L	Cr
		Census Card No. 3371, P. O. Hanna, Enrolled April 26, 1901										
9324	1	Riley, Lewis	28	M	F		Yohola Harjo	D	Cr	Saryokinchee	L	Cr
9325	2	Riley, Lucy	23	F	F	Wf	Unknown	?	Cr	Unknown	?	Cr
		No. 2 died October 1902										
		Census Card No. 3372, P. O. Francis, Enrolled July 11, 1902										
9326	1	Killcrease, Wade	36	M	½		Nelson Killcrease	?	Chic	Emma Hanney	L	Cr
		Census Card No. 3373, P. O. Okmulgee, Enrolled April 27, 1901										
9327	1	Green, Louisa	13	F	F		Tawee Green	D	Cr	Eliza Green	D	Cr
		Census Card No. 3374, P. O. Muskogee, Enrolled July 15, 1902										
9328	1	Coonhead, Joshua	14	M	F		Wm. Coonhead	D	Cr	Eliza Coonhegd	D	Cr
		No. 1 died April 17, 1899										
		Census Card No. 3375, P. O. Bearden, Enrolled July 25, 1902										
9329	1	Harjo, Jimmie	25	M	F		Tulmochuss Harjo	D	Cr	Kepsey Harjo	?	Cr
		No. 1 died April 12, 1899										
		Census Card No. 3376, P. O. Mounds, Enrolled July 25, 1902										
9330	1	Self, John B. Jr.	34	M	⅛		John B. Self	L	Cr	Elizabeth Self	?	Non
		Census Card No. 3377, P. O. Morris, Enrolled July 29, 1902										
9331	1	Simmer, Samuel	13	M	F		Simmer	D	Cr	Jennie Tiger	L	Cr
		Census Card No. 3378										
9332	1	Stricken from roll										
9333	2	Stricken from roll										
9334	3	Stricken from roll										
9335	4	Stricken from roll										
9336	5	Stricken from roll										
9337	6	Stricken from roll										
9338	7	Stricken from roll										
		Census Card No. 3379, P. O. Eufaula, Enrolled April 24, 1901										
9339	1	Taylor, Jennie	21	F	F		Taylor Bear	L	Cr	Rody Cato	D	Cr
		No. 1 died March 1, 1905										
		Census Card No. 3380, P. O. Wewoka, Enrolled April 25, 1901										
9340	1	Sarwoliche	43	F	F		Unknown	D	Cr	Unknown	D	Cr
		Census Card No. 3381, P. O. Hanna, Enrolled April 24, 1901										
9341	1	Williams, Thomas	24	M	F		Wilyarme	D	Cr	Rody Wilyarme	?	Cr
		Census Card No. 3382, P. O. Dustin, Enrolled May 21, 1901										
9342	1	Field, Nellie	5	F	F		Ablow Field	L	Cr	Ayumker	D	Cr
		Probably duplicate of Enrollment No. 4721. This enrollment cancelled, as to allotment or money see Department Letter No. 2155, 1913										
		Census Card No. 3383, P. O. Eufaula, Enrolled May 2, 1901										
9343	1	Henry, James	29	M	F		Bat Henry	D	Cr	Millie Henry	D	Cr
		No. 1 an idiot. Wm. Givens, Eufaula, Okla., Guardian										
		Census Card No. 3384, P. O. Eufaula, Enrolled April 26, 1901										
9344	1	Beaver, Willie	28	M	F		Unknown	?	Cr	Chamiche	D	Cr
9345	2	Beaver, Annie	25	F	F	Wf	Robert Jackson	L	Cr	Jady Johnson	L	Cr
		Census Card No. 3385, P. O. Eufaula, Enrolled May 2, 1901										
9346	1	Emarthla, Karpetcher	83	M	F		Unknown	D	Cr	Unknown	D	Cr
		No. 1 died July 15, 1903										
		Census Card No. 3386, P. O. Eufaula, Enrolled April 27, 1901										
9347	1	Peter, Locahull	73	F	F		Unknown	D	Cr	Unknown	D	Cr
		No. 1 died February 1904										
		Census Card No. 3387, P. O. Weumka, Enrolled April 19, 1901										
9348	1	Harjo, Leah	27	F	F		Totkis Harjo	L	Cr	Timashoey	D	Cr
		No. 1 died January 1906										
		Census Card No. 3388, P. O. Eufaula, Enroll d April 27, 1901										
9349	1	Harjo, Yarkinbar	53	M	F		Iyeche	D	Cr	Susanna Iyeche	D	Cr
		No. 1 died September 12, 1907										
		Census Card No. 3389, P. O. Okemah, Enrolled July 29, 1902										
9350	1	Jimboy, Thomas	17	M	F		William Jimboy	L	Cr	Mahala Jimboy	L	Cr
		No. 1 died April 30, 1899										
		Census Card No. 3390, P. O. Okmulgee, Enrolled August 1, 1901										
9351	1	Holleyman, Thomas J. 2		M	½		Thomas E. Holleyman	Non		Maggie E. Holleyman	L	Cr
		Census Card No. 3391, P. O. Raiford, Enrolled April 29, 1901										
9352	1	Field, Washington	38	M	F		Chaboof Micco	D	Cr	Unknown	D	Cr
9353	2	Field, Annie	23	F	F	Wf	Cowa Harjo	D	Cr	Lotta	?	Cr
		No. 2 died June 25, 1904. No. 1 died April 20, 1910										

Roll No.	No.	NAME	Age	Sex	Blood	Rel.	NAME OF FATHER	Liv.	Cit.	NAME OF MOTHER	Liv.	Cit.
		Census Card No. 3392, P. O. Hoffman, Enrolled April 27, 1901										
9354	1	Tiger, Jackson	43	M	F		Cotsa Fustanagee	D	Cr	Lucy Tiger	D	Cr
		Census Card No. 3393, P. O. Checotah, Enrolled August 1, 1902										
9355	1	Spaulding, George W.	1½	M	1-32		Homer R. Spaulding	L	Non	Edith Spaulding	L	Cr
		Census Card No. 3394, P. O. Wetumka, Enrolled April 19, 1901										
9356	1	Lasley, Louisa	21	F	F		Sam Lasley	D	Cr	Sally	D	Cr
		Census Card No. 3395, P. O. Hanna, Enrolled April 30, 1901										
9357	1	Catch, Willie	30	M	F		Cubbie Yahola	D	Cr	Mary Yahola	D	Cr
		Census Card No. 3396, P. O. Pierce, Enrolled April 19, 1901										
9358	1	Grayson, Rina	38	F	½		Jim McIntosh	D	Cr	Wisey McIntosh	D	Cr
		Census Card No. 3397, P. O. Okemah, Enrolled April 25, 1901										
9359	1	Deer, Romsey	23	M	F		Jofola	D	Cr	Miley	D	Cr
9360	2	Deer, Munna	23	F	F	Wf	Affaloye	D	Cr	Lucinda Hill	D	Cr
9361	3	Deer, Ellen	4	F	F	D	No. 1	L	Cr	No. 2	L	Cr
9362	4	Deer, Barney	3	M	F	S	No. 1	L	Cr	No. 2	L	Cr
9363	5	Deer, Nancy	16	F	F	Wf	Upna Hill	L	Cr	Lucinda Hill	L	Cr
		No. 2 died December 1900. No. 4 died 1904. No. 5 reported dead										
		Census Card No. 3398, P. O. Wetumka, Enrolled August 30, 1901										
9364	1	Lasley Tewe	12	M	F		Chaegey	D	Cr	Winey Lasley	L	Cr
9365	2	Lasley, Nancy	2	F	F	Sis	Colbert Lasley	L	Cr	Winey Lasley	L	Cr
		No. 1 died August 1899. No. 2 died October 1899.										
		Census Card No. 3399, P. O. Weleetka, Enrolled May 23, 1901										
9366	1	Fife, Levina	15	F	F		Turner Scott	D	Cr	Melinda Fife	L	Cr
		Census Card No. 3400, P. O. Eufaula, Enrolled April 24, 1901										
9367	1	Lewis, Thompson	20	M	F		Billie Lewis	D	Cr	Bapsey Lewis	D	Cr
		Census Card No. 3401, P. O. Okfuskee, Enrolled May 1, 1901										
9368	1	Emarthloche, Sampson	6	M	F		Cho Emarthloche	L	Cr	Polly Emarthloche	D	Cr
		No. 1 died July 13, 1900										
		Census Card No. 3402, P. O. Hitchita, Enrolled April 27, 1901										
9369	1	Field, Lydia	23	F	F		Hartupke	D	Cr	Amoche	D	Cr
		Census Card No. 3403, P. O. Pierce, Enrolled April 25, 1901										
9370	1	Smith, Hinty	23	F	F		Chuoste Fixico	D	Cr	Lucindogee	?	Cr
		No. 1 died 1908										
		Census Card No. 3404, P. O. Boley, Enrolled April 29, 1901										
9371	1	Coker, Charley	40	M	½		Chissoe Harjo	?	Sem	Seloska	?	Cr
9372	2	Coker, Leah	15	F	¾	D	No. 1	L	Cr	Lizzie Coker	D	Cr
9373	3	Coker, Ober	12	M	¾	S	No. 1	L	Cr	Lizzie Coker	D	Cr
9374	4	Coker, Gibson	7	M	¾	S	No. 1	L	Cr	Lizzie Coker	D	Cr
		Census Card No. 3405, P. O. Muskogee, Enrolled May 7, 1901										
9375	1	Hodge, Virginia	15	F	½		Johnson Hodge	D	Cr	Margaret Hodge	D	Non
		No. 1 died December 8, 1900										
		Census Card No. 3406, P. O. Castle, Enrolled April 26, 1901										
9376	1	Harjo, Kosapa	50	F	F		Ahharluk Harjo	D	Cr	Unknown	D	Cr
9377	2	Harjo, Needa	8	F	F	D	Yaha Harjo	D	Cr	No. 1	L	Cr
		Census Card No. 3407, P. O. Hanna, Enrolled May 23, 1901										
9378	1	Harjo, Maleya	25	F	F		Sawanoke Harjo	L	Cr	Unknown	D	Cr
9379	2	Harjo, Lumsey	20	M	F	Bro	Sawanoke Harjo	L	Cr	Unknown	?	Cr
		No. 2 died December 15, 1901										
		Census Card No. 3408, P. O. Hanna, Enrolled May 3, 1901										
9380	1	Hill, Jesse	28	M	F		Unknown	D	Cr	Watly Hill	D	Cr
		Census Card No. 3409, P. O. Schulter, Enrolled July 28, 1902										
9381	1	Kanard, Thomas B.	1½	M	F		Washington Kanard	L	Cr	Fannie Kanard	L	Cr
		Census Card No. 3410, P. O. Wetumka, Enrolled May 23, 1901										
9382	1	"Wilyumka"	43	M	F		Thlarthlo Harjo	D	Cr	Miheecha	D	Cr
9383	2	"Sylla"	43	F	F	Wf	Coocwooye	D	Cr	Semahee	D	Cr
9384	3	"Miley"	15	F	F	D	No. 1	L	Cr	No. 2	L	Cr
9385	4	"Melosa"	12	F	F	D	No. 1	L	Cr	No. 2	L	Cr
9386	5	"Rhoda"	11	F	F	D	No. 1	L	Cr	No. 2	L	Cr
9387	6	"Williamochee"	9	M	F	S	No. 1	L	Cr	No. 2	L	Cr
		No. 2 died November 30, 1911. No. 4 died 1906. No. 5 died 1907. No. 6 died 1906										
		Census Card No. 3411, P. O. Wetumka, Enrolled July 28, 1902										
9388	1	Robison, James Abner	2	M	⅜		J. S. Robison	L	Cr	Mattie Robison	L	Cr
		Census Card No. 3412, P. O. Okemah, Enrolled July 29, 1902										
9389	1	Harvison, Thelma B.	1½	F	1-16		George D. Harvison	L	Cr	Lula E. Harvison	L	Cr
		Census Card No. 3413, P. O. Okmulgee, Enrolled July 29, 1902										
9390	1	Bird, Hannah	1½	F	F		Moses Bird	L	Cr	Sallie Bird	L	Cr
		Census Card No. 3414, P. O. Bixby, Enrolled July 29, 1902										
9391	1	Fox, Ada	1½	F	F		Luke Fox	L	Cr	Maggie Fox	L	Cr
		Census Card No. 3415, P. O. Morse, Enrolled July 29, 1902										
9392	1	Harjochee, Sas-ho-ye	1½	F	F		Isparney Harjochee	L	Cr	Amanda Harjochee	L	Cr
		Census Card No. 3416, P. O. Salem, Enrolled July 29, 1902										
9393	1	Thompson, Russell	1½	F	F		Thomas Thompson	L	Cr	Rose Thompson	L	Cr
		Census Card No. 3417, P. O. Beardon, Enrolled July 29, 1902										
9394	1	Bunner, Addie	2	F	F		Bunner	L	Cr	Losie Bunner	L	Cr
		Census Card No. 3418, P. O. Okmulgee, Enrolled July 29, 1902										
9395	1	Brinton, Ruth	1½	F	F		Samuel Brinton	L	Cr	Sussie Brinton	L	Cr
		Census Card No. 3419, P. O. Wetumka, Enrolled July 29, 1902										
9396	1	Canard, James	1½	M	F		Jeff Canard	L	Cr	Simmer Canard	L	Cr
		Census Card No. 3420, P. O. Okmulgee, Enrolled July 28, 1902										
9397	1	Kanard, Judy	1½	F	F		Thomas J. Kanard	L	Cr	Eliza Kanard	L	C

Roll No.	No.	NAME	Age	Sex	Blood	Rel.	NAME OF FATHER	Liv.	Cit.	NAME OF MOTHER	Liv.	Cit.
		Census Card No. 3421, P. O. Okmulgee, Enrolled July 28, 1902										
9398	1	Snakeya, Tobe	1½	M	F		David Snakeya	L	Cr	Mollianna Snakeya	L	Cr
		No. 1 died December 1911										
		Census Card No. 3422, P. O. Beardon, Enrolled July 28, 1902										
9399	1	Deer, Philip	1½	M	F		Pinkey Deer	L	Cr	Linda Deer	L	Cr
		Census Card No. 3423, P. O. Okemah, Enrolled July 28, 1902										
9400	1	Fixico, Nellie	2	F	F		Oscoce Fixico	L	Cr	Semarhichkar Fixico	L	Cr
		Census Card No. 3424, P. O. Fentress, Enrolled July 28, 1902										
9401	1	Cook, Hammond	1½	M	¾		Daniel Cook	L	Cr	Leah Cook	L	Cr
		Census Card No. 3425, P. O. Fentress, Enrolled July 29, 1902										
9402	1	Deer, Eddie	1	M	F		Ben Deer	L	Cr	Katie Deer	L	Cr
		No. 1 died December 1901										
		Census Card No. 3426, P. O. Holdenville, Enrolled July 28, 1902										
9403	1	Long, Richmond	3	M	F		Sam Long	L	Cr	Kizzie Long	L	Cr
		No. 1 died 1900										
		Census Card No. 3427, P. O. Okmulgee, Enrolled August 6, 1902										
9404	1	Brown, Bertha Alice	2	F	⅜		Robert S. Brown	L	Non	Eliza Brown	L	Cr
		Census Card No. 3428, P. O. Wetumka, Enrolled August 6, 1902										
9405	1	McCoy, Ruthie May	2	F	½		Wm. A. McCoy	L	Non	Ida McCoy	L	Cr
		Census Card No. 3429, P. O. Eufaula, Enrolled September 3, 1902										
9406	1	Scott, Annie	1½	F	F		Albert Scott	L	Cr	Bettie Scott	L	Cr
		Census Card No. 3430, P. O. Broken Arrow, Enrolled August 6, 1902										
9407	1	Haikey, Maymie	1½	F	F		Ben Haikey, Jr.	L	Cr	Louisa Haikey	L	Cr
		No. 1 died January 5, 1905										
		Census Card No. 3431, P. O. Calvin, Enrolled August 6, 1902										
9408	1	Canard, Stephen	2	M	F		Felix Canard	L	Cr	Nancy Canard	L	Cr
		No. 1 died September 16, 1908										
		Census Card No. 3432, P. O. Muskogee, Enrolled August 7, 1902										
9409	1	Huckaby, Andrew	1½	M	¼		R. W. Huckaby	L	Non	Elsie Huckaby	L	Cr
		Census Card No. 3433, P. O. Okmulgee, Enrolled August 7, 1902										
9410	1	Daniel, Annie	2	F	F		Unah Daniel	L	Cr	Mary Daniel	L	Cr
		Census Card No. 3434, P. O. Wagoner, Enrolled August 7, 1902										
9411	1	Chissoe, Theodore S.	1¼	M	⅞		Sam Chissoe	L	Cr	Lena E. Chissoe	L	Cr
		No. 1 died October 6, 1901										
		Census Card No. 3435, P. O. Arbeka, Enrolled August 7, 1902										
9412	1	Tiger, William	1½	M	F		Tamer Tiger	L	Cr	Mesaley Tiger	L	Cr
		Census Card No. 3436, P. O. Laredo, Texas, Enrolled August 7, 1902										
9413	1	Tarvin, Theresa	1½	F	1-16		Pleasant F. Tarvin	L	Cr	Patience Tarvin	L	Non
		Census Card No. 3437, P. O. Lenora, Enrolled August 8, 1902										
9414	1	Johnson, Alice	2	F	½		Fred Johnson	L	Cr	Wisey Johnson	L	Cr
		No. 1 died December 24, 1905										
		Census Card No. 3438, P. O. Eufaula, Enrolled Augu t 8, 1902										
9415	1	Stover, Reuben	1½	M	F		Daniel Stover	L	Cr	Lavina Stover	L	Cr
		Census Card No. 3439, P. O. Vivian, Enrolled August 8, 1902										
9416	1	Wolfe, John	1½	M	F		William Wolf	L	Cr	Ellen Wolf	L	Cr
		No. 1 died January 1902										
		Census Card No. 3440, P. O. Brush Hill, Enrolled August 8, 1902										
9417	1	McNac, William McKinley	1½	M	½		Fred McNac	L	Cr	Annie McNac	L	Cr
		Census Card No. 3441, P. O. Coweta, Enrolled August 9, 1902										
9418	1	Orcutt, William Mc-Kinley	1½	M	⅛		A. D. Orcutt	L	Non	Adaline Orcutt	L	Cr
		No. 1 died November 1906										
		Census Card No. 3442, P. O. Tulsa, Enrolled August 9, 1902										
9419	1	Burnette, Myrtle	1⅓	F	⅛		A. T. Burnette	L	Non	Mary Jane Burnette	L	Cr
		Census Card No. 3443, P. O. Wagoner, Enrolled August 9, 1902										
9420	1	Tapp, Marie	1½	F	¼		Perry Tapp	L	Non	Laura Barr	L	Cr
		Census Card No. 3444, P. O. Morse, Enrolled July 29, 1902										
9421	1	Hopewood, Ira Homer	1½	M	1-32		Kellem F. Hopwood	L	Cr	Millie Hopwood	L	Non
		Census Card No. 3445, P. O. Wewoka, Enrolled July 29, 1902										
9422	1	Wolf, Birdie	2½	M	½		Copley Wolf	L	Sem	Annie Wolf	L	Cr
		Census Card No. 3446, P. O. Tulsa, Enrolled August 9, 1902										
9423	1	Scott, Ida	1	F	⅞		Andy Scott	L	Cr	Nora Scott	L	Cr
		No. 1 reported dead										
		Census Card No. 3447, P. O. Okfuskee, Enrolled August 11, 1902										
9424	1	Deere, Isaac	2	M	F		Mose Deere	L	Cr	Eliza Deere	L	Cr
		No. 1 died June 30, 1901										
		Census Card No. 3448, P. O. Sapulpa, Enrolled August 11, 1902										
9425	1	Clayton, Bessie	2	F	¼		Charlie Clayton	L	Non	Della Clayton	L	Cr
		Census Card No. 3449, P. O. Wekiwa, Enrolled August 11, 1902										
9426	1	Johnson, Mollie	2½	F	F		Sandy Johnson	L	Cr	Jinnie Johnson	L	Cr
		Census Card No. 3450, P. O. Wagoner, Enrolled August 11, 1902										
9427	1	Couch, Roy L.	1½	M	¼		John C. Couch	L	Non	Amanda Couch	L	Cr
		Census Card No. 3451, P. O. Tulsa, Enrolled August 11, 1902										
9428	1	Perryman, Georgia R.	5 mo	F	⅜		E. G. Perryman	L	?	Ollie Perryman	L	Cr
		No. 1 reported dead										
		Census Card No. 3452, P. O. Checotah, Enrolled August 12, 1902										
9429	1	McIntosh, Lula T.	1½	F	⅛		D. N. McIntosh, Jr.	L	Cr	Alice McIntosh	L	Non
		Census Card No. 3453, P. O. Coweta, Enrolled August 12, 1902										
9430	1	Childers, Jim	2	M	F		Wm. Childers	L	Cr	Annie Childers	L	Cr

Roll No.	No.	NAME	Age	Sex	Blood	Rel.	NAME OF FATHER	Liv.	Cit.	NAME OF MOTHER	Liv.	Cit.
		Census Card No. 3454, P. O. Vivian, Enrolled August 12, 1902										
9431	1	Colbert, Linda	11 mo	F	F		Thompson Colbert	L	Cr	Ellen Colbert	L	Cr
		No. 1 reported dead										
		Census Card No. 3455, P. O. Muskogee, Enrolled August 12, 1902										
9432	1	Davis, Roy Edgar	1¾	M	⅛		Lewis H. Davis	L	Cr	Susanna Davis	L	Non
		Census Card No. 3456, P. O. Hanna, Enrolled August 13, 1902										
9433	1	Washington, Brutus	1½	M	F		David Washington	L	Cr	Susanna Thompson	L	Cr
		Census Card No. 3457, P. O. Mounds, Enrolled August 13, 1902										
9434	1	Berryhill, Mildred E.	2	M	1-16		Andrew J. Berryhill	L	Cr	Lula Berryhill	L	Non
		Census Card No. 3458, P. O. Hitchita, Enrolled August 13, 1902										
9435	1	King, Peter	1½	M	¾		Peter King	L	Cr	Kizzie Sevier	L	Cr
		Census Card No. 3459, P. O. Okfuskee, Enrolled August 13, 1902										
9436	1	Yarhola, Martha C.	1½	F	F		Aaron Yarhola	L	Cr	Miley Yarhola	L	Cr
		No. 1 died 1902										
		Census Card No. 3460, P. O. Gonzales, Texas, Enrolled August 14, 1902										
9437	1	Grayson, Webster	1½	M	⅛		Warrior Grayson	L	Non	Ellen Grayson	L	Cr
		Census Card No. 3461, P. O. Beggs, Enrolled August 14, 1902										
9438	1	Lunsford, Winnie	1¼	F	⅜		John C. Lunsford	L	Cr	Martha Lunsford	L	Cr
9439	2	Lunsford, Charley	1¼	M	⅜	Bro	John C. Lunsford	L	Cr	Martha Lunsford	L	Cr
		Census Card No. 3462, P. O. Broken Arrow, Enrolled August 14, 1902										
9440	1	Nave, Laura	1½	F	¼		John C. Nave	L	Non	Alice Nave	L	Cr
		Census Card No. 3463, P. O. Sapulpa, Enrolled August 14, 1902										
9441	1	Fife, Bixby	1½	M	F		Timmie Fife	L	Cr	Sarah Fife	L	Cr
		Census Card No. 3464, P. O. Coweta, Enrolled August 14, 1902										
9442	1	Harman, Laura A.	1¼	F	1-16		Ben T. Harman	L	Cr	Laura Harman	L	Non
		Census Card No. 3465, P. O. Arlington, Enrolled August 14, 1902										
9443	1	Nichols, Grace Alva	1¼	F	1-16		S. F. Nichols	L	Non	Emma Nichols	L	Cr
		Census Card No. 3466, P. O. Mounds, Enrolled August 15, 1902										
9444	1	Bear, Harry	1¾	M	F		Walter Bear	L	Cr	Pollie Bear	L	Cr
		Census Card No. 3467, P. O. Kellyville, Enrolled August 15, 1902										
9445	1	Brown, Addie	1½	F	F		Jake Brown	L	Cr	Sallie Brown	L	Cr
		Census Card No. 3468, P. O. Henryetta, Enrolled August 15, 1902										
9446	1	Grayson, Clarence	2	M	3-16		Joe Grayson	L	Non	Alice Grayson	L	Cr
		Census Card No. 3469, P. O. Checotah, Enrolled August 15, 1902										
9447	1	Audd, Joseph Mc-Donald	1¼	M	1-16		R. Y. Audd	L	Non	Flora R. Audd	L	Cr
		Census Card No. 3470, P. O. Wagoner, Enrolled August 15, 1902										
9448	1	Perryman, Susie	1½	F	F		Sam Perryman	L	Cr	Mollie Perryman	L	Cr
		Census Card No. 3471, P. O. Sapulpa, Enrolled August 15, 1902										
9449	1	Island, Sunday	1½	M	F		George Island	L	Cr	Callie Island	L	Cr
		Census Card No. 3472, P. O. Catoosa, Enrolled August 16, 1902										
9450	1	Hooks, Rudie	1½	F	¼		L. P. Hooks	L	Non	Alice Hooks	L	Cr
		Census Card No. 3473, P. O. Creek, Enrolled August 16, 1902										
9451	1	Vanderslice, Mary Ann	2½	F	1-32		J. R. Vanderslice	L	Non	Roxan Vanderslice	L	Cr
		Census Card No. 3474, P. O. Broken Arrow, Enrolled August 16, 1902										
9452	1	Childers, Richard	1½	M	⅜		R. H. P. Childers	L	Cr	Daisy Childers	L	Non
		Census Card No. 3475, P. O. Checotah, Enrolled August 18, 1902										
9453	1	Collins, Dora	2½	F	F		Willie Collins	L	Cr	Kogee Collins	L	Cr
		Census Card No. 3476, P. O. Carson, Enrolled August 18, 1902										
9454	1	Wilson, Robert B.	1½	M	⅜		R. B. Wilson	L	Non	Hettie Wilson	L	Cr
		Census Card No. 3477, P. O. Wagoner, Enrolled August 18, 1902										
9455	1	Bethel, Howard R.	1½	M	⅛		D. F. Bethel	L	Non	Dora Bethel	L	Cr
		Census Card No. 3478, P. O. Stidham, Enrolled August 19, 1902										
9456	1	Pitman, Cecil	1½	M	⅛		John W. Pitman	L	Non	Rosanna Pitman	L	Cr
		Census Card No. 3479, P. O. Bixby, Enrolled August 19, 1902										
9457	1	Swingle, Levi	1⅓	M	1-16		Washington Swingle	L	Non	Cordee Swingle	L	Cr
		No. 1 died January 11, 1903										
		Census Card No. 3480, P. O. Eufaula, Enrolled August 19, 1902										
9458	1	McIntosh, Tiger	4	M	F		Louis McIntosh	L	Cr	Jennie Harley	L	Cr
		Census Card No. 3481, P. O. Keokuk Falls, Enrolled August 19, 1902										
9459	1	Cochran, Walter Lee	1½	M	½		George Cochran	?	Cher	Mary Chisholm	L	Cr
		Census Card No. 3482, P. O. Mounds, Enrolled August 19, 1902										
9460	1	Bigpond, Albert	2	M	F		Daniel Bigpond	L	Cr	Nancy Bigpond	L	Cr
		Census Card No. 3483, P. O. Carson, Enrolled August 19, 1902										
9461	1	Harper, Lizzie	3½	F	F		Shawnee Harper	L	Cr	Somaye Harper	L	Cr
9462	2	Harper, Mattie	2	F	F	Sis	Shawnee Harper	L	Cr	Somaye Harper	L	Cr
		Census Card No. 3484, P. O. Morse, Enrolled August 19, 1902										
9463	1	Knight, Jasper	8 mo	M	F		Ramsey Knight	L	Cr	Amy Knight	L	Cr
		No. 1 reported dead										
		Census Card No. 3485, P. O. Sapulpa, Enrolled August 20, 1902										
9464	1	Behen, Asa	1¼	F	F		Micco Behen	L	Cr	Jennetta Behen	L	Cr
		Census Card No. 3486, P. O. Lee, Enrolled August 20, 1902										
9465	1	Hutton, Gracie	1½	F	⅛		Henry Hutton	L	Cr	Annie Hutton	L	Cr
		Census Card No. 3487, P. O. Beggs, Enrolled August 20, 1902										
9466	1	Hance, Bessie	1½	F	⅜		J. D. Hance	L	Non	Jennie L. Hance	L	Cr
		Census Card No. 3488, P. O. Broken Arrow, Enrolled August 20, 1902										
9467	1	Boles, Charlie O.	1½	M	1-16		Charles Boles	L	Non	Mattie Boles	L	Cr
		Census Card No. 3489, P. O. Beggs, Enrolled August 20, 1902										
9468	1	Johnson, Katie	1¼	F	F		Colbert Johnson	L	Cr	Millie Johnson	L	Cr
		Census Card No. 3490, P. O. Broken Arrow, Enrolled August 20, 1902										
9469	1	Castello, Nora	1¼	F	¼		George Castello	L	Non	Nettie Castello	L	Cr

Roll No.	No.	NAME	Age	Sex	Blood	Rel.	NAME OF FATHER	Liv.	Cit.	NAME OF MOTHER	Liv.	Cit.
		Census Card No. 3491, P. O. Broken Arrow, Enrolled August 20, 1902										
9470	1	Drew, Mont	1¼	M	½		Amos Drew	L	Cr	Nettie Drew	L	Cr
		Census Card No. 3492, P. O. Wagoner, Enrolled August 21, 1902										
9471	1	Childers, Arthur	1¼	M	⅞		Anderson Childers	L	Cr	Lydia Childers	L	Cr
		Census Card No. 3493, P. O. Red Fork, Enrolled August 21, 1902										
9472	1	Atkins, Louisa C.	1½	F	½		Robert D. Atkins	L	Cr	Alice Atkins	L	Cr
		Census Card No. 3494, P. O. Broken Arrow, Enrolled August 21, 1902										
9473	1	Litka, John	1½	M	½		Dick Litka	?	Sem	Martha Litka	L	Cr
		Census Card No. 3495, P. O. Broken Arrow, Enrolled August 21, 1902										
9474	1	Chisholm, Pauline	1½	F	F		Anderson Chisholm	L	Cr	Rosa Chisholm	L	Cr
		Census Card No. 3496, P. O. Broken Arrow, Enrolled August 21, 1902										
9475	1	Johnson, Katie	1½	F	⅝		Isaac Johnson	L	Cr	Nicey Johnson	L	Cr
		Census Card No. 3497, P. O. Bristow, Enrolled August 21, 1902										
9476	1	Hamilton, Alex	1¼	M	F		Peter Hamilton	L	Cr	Ellen Hamilton	L	Non
		Census Card No. 3498, P. O. Carson, En olled August 22, 1902										
9477	1	Benham, Willie	1¼	M	½		C. A. Benham	L	Non	Malinda Behnam	L	Cr
		Census Card No. 3499, P. O. Stone Bluff, Enrolled August 22, 1902										
9478	1	Smith, Grace	1½	F	⅛		Stephen Smith	L	Cr	Emma Smith	L	Non
		Census Card No. 3500, P. O. Wagoner, Enrolled August 22, 1902										
9479	1	Posey, T. C.	1¼	M	⅛		J. S. Posey	L	Cr	Emily Posey	L	Non
		Census Card No. 3501, P. O. Olive, Enrolled August 22, 1902										
9480	1	Forty-four, Billy	1½	M	F		Codenny Forty-four	L	Cr	Hannah Forty-four	D	Cr
		Census Card No. 3502, P. O. Tuskegee, Enrolled August 22, 1902										
9481	1	Harjo, Mamie	1½	F	F		Peter Harjo	L	Cr	Annie Harjo	L	Cr
		Census Card No. 3503, P. O. Morse, Enrolled August 22, 1902										
9482	1	Smith, Willie	1½	M	F		Belcher Smith	L	Cr	Sarah Smith	L	Cr
		Census Card No. 3504, P. O. Wetumka, Enrolled August 22, 1902										
9483	1	King, Maxsey	1¼	M	F		Amos King	L	Cr	Simondy King	L	Cr
		No. 1 died January 8, 1902										
		Census Card No. 3505, P. O. Eufaula, Enrolled August 23, 1902										
9484	1	Boone, Madge	7 mo	F	⅜		Charlie Boone	L	Cr	Sallie Boone	L	Non
		No. 1 died June 1901										
		Census Card No. 3506, P. O. Okmulgee, Enrolled August 23, 1902										
9485	1	Harjo, Alice	1½	F	F		Henry M. Harjo	L	Cr	Katie M. Harjo	L	Cr
		No. 1 died April 16, 1906										
		Census Card No. 3507, P. O. Mohawk, Enrolled August 23, 1902										
9486	1	Kanard, Hully	48	M	F		Arharlock Yahola	D	Cr	Tilda Yahola	D	Cr
		No. 1 died July 22, 1899										
		Census Card No. 3508, P. O. Holdenville, Enrolled August 25, 1902										
9487	1	Noon, Alex	1½	M	F		James Noon	L	Cr	Sophia Noon	L	Cr
		Census Card No. 3509, P. O. Wewoka, Enrolled August 25, 1902										
9488	1	Factor, Kenneth J.	1½	M	½		William Factor	L	Cr	Nancy Factor	L	Cr
		Census Card No. 3510, P. O. Checotah, Enrolled August 25, 1903										
9489	1	Coon, Gracie Amber	1½	F	1-16		Fred C. Coon	L	Non	Sallie Coon	L	Cr
		Census Card No. 3511, P. O. Wagoner, Enrolled May 23, 1901										
9490	1	Fish, Thomas	15	M	F		Johnson Fish	D	Cr	Winey Fish	L	Cr
		No. 1 died February 24, 1900										
		Census Card No. 3512, P. O. Okemah, Enrolled August 26, 1902										
9491	1	Harjo, Minnie	1½	F	F		Larger Looney	L	Cr	Minda Harjo	L	Cr
		Census Card No. 3513, P. O. Haskell, Enrolled August 26, 1902										
9492	1	Smith, Clarence N.	1½	M	¼		Daniel B. Smith	L	Cr	Mary I. Smith	L	Cr
		Census Card No. 3514, P. O. Coweta, Enrolled August 26, 1902										
9493	1	McKellop, Wilson	2 mo	M	F		Peter McKellop	L	Cr	Betsey McKellop	L	Cr
		No. 1 reported dead										
		Census Card No. 3515, P. O. Coweta, Enrolled August 25, 1902										
9494	1	Childers, Thomas	11 mo	M	¾		Benjamin Childers	L	Cr	Annie Childers	L	Cr
		No. 1 died October 6, 1901										
		Census Card No. 3516, P. O. Wetumka, Enrolled August 26, 1902										
9495	1	Winters, Leether	1½	F	⅛		Ed. Winters	L	?	Clara Winters	L	?
		Census Card No. 3517, P. O. Eufaula, Enrolled August 26, 1902										
9496	1	Francis, Martha	1¼	F	F		Robert Francis	L	Cr	Millie Francis	L	Cr
		Census Card No. 3518, P. O. Holdenville, Enrolled August 26, 1902										
9497	1	McCoy, Minnie	3	F	F		Burney McCoy	L	Cr	Susan McCoy	L	Cr
9498	2	McCoy, Israel	1½	M	F	Bro	Burney McCoy	L	Cr	Susan McCoy	L	Cr
		Census Card No. 3519, P. O. Mounds, Enrolled August 26, 1902										
9499	1	Tiger, Mary	1½	F	F		Stanwaitie Tiger	L	Cr	Lizzie Tiger	L	Cr
		Census Card No. 3520, P. O. Okmulgee, Enrolled August 26, 1902										
9500	1	Sneed, William	29	M	⅜		Charley Sneed	D	Non	Martha Smith	D	Cr
		Census Card No. 3521, P. O. Holdenville, Enrolled August 26, 1902										
9501	1	Stewart, George E.	1½	M	¾		Albert P. Stewart	L	Cr	Louisa Stewart	L	Cr
		Census Card No. 3522, P. O. Wier, Enrolled August 27, 1902										
9502	1	Cox, Ludie	1	F	¾		John Cox	L	Cr	Nancy Cox	L	Cr
		No. 1 died June 2, 1902										
		Census Card No. 3523, P. O. Checotah, Enrolled August 27, 1902										
9503	1	Davis, Peter	5	M	⅜		Ben Davis	L	Cr	Sarah Baughman	L	Cr
9504	2	Baughman, Fannie	1¼	F	¼	½-Sis	Fayette Baughman	L	Non	Sarah Baughman	L	Cr
		No. 2 died 1903										
		Census Card No. 3524, P. O. Checotah, Enrolled August 27, 1902										
9505	1	McIntosh, Willie	1¼	F	1-16		Freeland B. McIntosh	L	Cr	Kate McIntosh	L	Non

Roll No.	No.	NAME	Age	Sex	Blood	Rel.	NAME OF FATHER	Liv.	Cit.	NAME OF MOTHER	Liv.	Cit.
		Census Card No. 3525, P. O. Red Fork, Enrolled May 24, 1901										
9506	1	Berryhill, Littleton	49	M	⅛		John Berryhill	D	Cr	America Berryhill	?	Non
		No. 1 died September 22, 1899										
		Census Card No. 3526										
9507	1	Stricken from roll										
9508	2	Stricken fr m roll										
9509	3	Stricken from roll										
9510	4	Stricken from roll										
9511	5	Stricken from roll										
		Census Card No. 3527, P. O. Tulsa, Enrolled August 27, 1902										
9512	1	Gillis, Taylor A.	14	M	½		C. B. Gillis	L	Non	Nancy Gillis	D	Cr
		No. 1 die December 28, 1899										
		Census Card No. 3528, P. O. Sasakwa, Enrolled August 28, 1902										
9513	1	Palmer, David	1¼	M	¼		Tom Palmer	?	Sem	Mary Palmer	L	Cr
		Census Card No. 3529, P. O. Tulsa, Enrolled August 28, 1902										
9514	1	Bruner, Esther	1¼	F	F		Wm. G. Bruner	L	Cr	Jennie Bruner	L	Cr
		Census Card No. 3530, P. O. Holdenville, Enrolled August 28, 1902										
9515	1	Anderson, Thomas	1¼	M	F		Billie Anderson	L	Cr	Ella Anderson	L	Cr
		Census Card No. 3531, P. O. McDermott, Enrolled August 28, 1902										
9516	1	McDermott, Walter	4 mo	M	½		Lewis McDermott	L	Non	Mary McDermott	L	Cr
		No. 1 died September 1901										
		Census Card No. 3532, P. O. Mounds, Enrolled August 29, 1902										
9517	1	Harry, Roy	2	M	⅝		Simon Harry	L	Cr	Rebecca Harry	L	Cr
		Census Card No. 3533, P. O. Fry, Enrolled August 29, 1902										
9518	1	Thatcher, Edmon	1½	M	⅛		Douglas Thatcher	L	Non	Nancy Thatcher	L	Cr
		Census Card No. 3534, P. O. Okemah, Enrolled August 29, 1902										
9519	1	Sullivan, George	1¾	M	F		William Sullivan	L	Cr	Kizzie Sullivan	L	Cr
		Census Card No. 3535, P. O. Oktaha, Enrolled August 29, 1902										
9520	1	Johnson, Oda Casey	1¼	F	⅛		Thomas Johnson	L	Non	Nellie C. Johnson	L	Cr
		Census Card No. 3536, P. O. Calvin, Enrolled August 30, 1902										
9521	1	Williams, Tarner	1½	F	¾		Charles Williams	L	Cr	Emma Williams	L	Cr
		No. 1 died September 3, 1902										
		Census Card No. 3537, P. O. Checotah, Enrolled September 2, 1902										
9522	1	Backbun, Duffy A.	1½	M	1-32		Cal Backburn	L	Cher	Arnecie Backburn	L	Cr
		Census Card No. 3538, P. O. Arbeka, Enrolled September 2, 1902										
9523	1	Baker, George K.	1¼	M	½		Kinkehe N. Baker	L	Sem	Rebecca J. Baker	L	Cr
		Census Card No. 3539, P. O. Wetumka, Enrolled September 2, 1902										
9524	1	Tiger, Edward B.	2 mo	M	¾		Johnson E. Tiger	L	Cr	Lena B. Tiger	L	Cr
		No. 1 died June 13, 1901										
		Census Card No. 3540, P. O. Bixby, Enrolled September 3, 1902										
9525	1	Rodgers, Mack Albert	4mo	M	⅛		Robert F. Rodgers	L	Non	Emma Rodgers	L	Cr
		No. 1 died September 30, 1901										
		Census Card No. 3541, P. O. Mounds, Enrolled September 3, 1902										
9526	1	Applegeet, Orvill B.	2	M	1-32		W. F. Applegeet	L	Non	Cora Applegeet	L	Cr
		Census Card No. 3542, P. O. Wetumka, Enrolled September 3, 1902										
9527	1	Thomas, Willie	11 mo	M	F		Waitie Thomas	L	Cr	Polly Wesley	L	Cr
		No. 1 died July 25, 1901										
		Census Card No. 3543, P. O. Gibson Station, Enrolled September 2, 1902										
9528	1	Tell, Addie	23	F	½		Ollie Davis	L	Cr	Rose Grayson	L	Cr
		No. 1 reported dead										
		Census Card No. 3544, P. O. Hitchita, Enrolled September 4, 1902										
9529	1	Foshee, Dewey Mc-Kinley	1½	M	1-16		Wm. R. Foshee	L	Cr	Lillian Foshee	L	Non
		Census Card No. 3545, P. O. Mounds, Enrolled September 4, 1902										
9530	1	Bighead, Jack	1¼	M	F		Stanwaitie Bighead	L	Cr	Millie Bighead	L	Cr
		Census Card No. 3546, P. O. Kellyville, Enrolled September 4, 1902										
9531	1	Self, Ira B.	1½	M	1-16		James A. Self	L	Cr	Mattie Self	L	Non
		Census Card No. 3547, P. O. Tulsa, Enrolled September 4, 1902										
9532	1	Bell, Aaron	1¼	M	¼		John Bell	L	Non	Clarissa Bell	L	Cr
		Census Card No. 3548, P. O. Holdenville, Enrolled September 5, 1 02										
9533	1	Harrison, Emma	1¼	F	F		Napoleon Harrison	L	Cr	Susan Harrison	L	Cr
		Census Card No. 3549, P. O. Wealaka, Enrolled September 5, 1902										
9534	1	Pumpkin, Thomas	37	M	F		Bumkin	D	Cr	Annie	D	Cr
		No. 1 died May 12, 1899										
		Census Card No. 3550, P. O. Eufaula, Enrolled September 2, 1902										
9535	1	Richard, Sallie	1½	F	F		Jasper Richard	L	Cr	Minnie Richard	L	Cr
		Census Card No. 3551, P. O. Okmulgee, Enrolled September 5, 1902										
9536	1	Tiger, Helen May	1¼	F	⅝		George W. Tiger	L	Cr	Susan H. Tiger	L	Cr
		Census Card No. 3552, P. O. Bristow, Enrolled September 5, 1902										
9537	1	Davis, Lillie	2	F	⅜		Redmond Davis	L	Cr	Millie Davis	L	Cr
		Census Card No. 3553, P. O. Sapulpa, Enrolled September 5, 1902										
9538	1	Perryman, Edith M.	1½	F	⅜		Moses Perryman	L	Cr	Lula Perryman	L	Cr
		Census Card No. 3554, P. O. Creek, Enrolled September 20, 1902										
9539	1	Harjo, Amos	5	M	F		Tuskegee Harjo	D	Cr	Pinner Harjo	D	Cr
		No. 1 died June 10, 1900										
		Census Card No. 3555, P. O. Summit, Enrolled September 6, 1902										
9540	1	Bullet, Mary Ann	9 mo	F	F		James Bullet	L	Cr	Lucy Bullet	L	Cr
		No. 1 reported dead										
		Census Card No. 3556, P. O. Henryetta, Enrolled September 6, 1902										
9541	1	Woods, Ralph M.	2	M	⅛		John W. Woods	L	Non	Eliza J. Woods	L	Cr

Roll No.	No.	NAME	Age Sex Blood Rel.	NAME OF FATHER	Liv.	Cit.	NAME OF MOTHER	Liv.	Cit.
		Census Card No. 3557, P. O. Mounds, Enrolled September 6, 1902							
9542	1	Stevens, Clarence O.	10 moM 1-16	Cicero Stevens	L	Non	Idella M. Stevens	L	Cr
		No. 1 died March 2, 1902							
		Census Card No. 3558, P. O. Eufaula, Enrolled September 6, 1902							
9543	1	Belcher, Jennie	1¼F ¾	Tobe Belcher	L	Cr	Martha Belcher	L	Cr
		Census Card No. 3559, P. O. Bristow, Enrolled September 5, 1902							
9544	1	Sorrell, Lillie	2 F ⅛	William Sorrell	L	Non	Dorothy Sorrell	L	Cr
		Census Card No. 3560, P. O. Brush Hill, Enrolled September 6, 1902							
9545	1	Jackson, Lurena	1½F ⅛	Stepney Jackson	L	Cr	Lou Jackson	L	?
		Census Card No. 3561, P. O. Bristow, Enrolled September 6, 1902							
9546	1	John, Wosey	2 F F	Sannorka	L	Cr	Malinda Sannorka	L	Cr
		Census Card No. 3562, P. O. Hitchita, Enrolled September 6, 1902							
9547	1	McGilbray, Abbie	1¼F F	Captain McGilbray	L	Cr	Lizzie McGilbray	L	Cr
		Census Card No. 3563, P. O. Morse, Enrolled September 6, 1902							
9548	1	Fields, William	1¾M F	Ponsey Fields	L	Cr	Sindy Fields	L	Cr
		No. 1 died April 11, 1904							
		Census Card No. 3564, P. O. Haskell, Enrolled September 6, 1902							
9549	1	Anderson, Augusta	1½F ½	Solomon Anderson	L	Cr	Emma Anderson	L	Cr
		Census Card No. 3565, P. O. Morse, Enrolled September 8, 1902							
9550	1	Fixico, Sampson	1¾M F	Tulmochuss Fixico	L	Cr	Sallie Fixico	L	Cr
		Census Card No. 3566, P. O. Okmulgee, Enrolled September 8, 1902							
9551	1	Shepherd, Elisha	2 M ⅛	George Shepherd	L	Non	Annie Shepherd	L	Cr
		Census Card No. 3567, P. O. Leonard, Enrolled September 8, 1902							
9552	1	Cooper, Sarah	1¼F F	Sam Cooper	L	Cr	Ella Cooper	L	Cr
		Census Card No. 3568, P. O. Walden, Ark., Enrolled September 8, 1902							
9553	1	Hall, George	1½M ⅜	Samuel Hall	L	Non	Hannah E. Hall	L	Cr
		Census Card No. 3569, P. O. Fry, Enrolled September 9, 1902							
9554	1	McKim, Fannie Maree	2 F 1-16	Robert A. McKim	L	Cr	Minnie G. McKim	L	Non
		Census Card No. 3570, P. O. Bristow, Enrolled September 9, 1902							
9555	1	Vance, William	1¾M ½	W. H. Vance	L	Non	Sarah Vance	L	Cr
		Census Card No. 3571, P. O. Arbeka, Enrolled April 26, 1901							
9556	1	Ko-chuk-ne, Nocus	55 M F	Unknown	?	Cr	Unknown	?	Cr
		No. 1 died October 1904							
		Census Card No. 3572, P. O. Okmulgee, Enrolled September 10, 1902							
9557	1	Gibson, Milder	1¼M F	Joseph Gibson	L	Cr	Hettie Gibson	L	Cr
		No. 1 reported dead							
		Census Card No. 3573, P. O. Okemah, Enrolled September 10, 1902							
9558	1	Fat, Sammy	2¾M F	Dick Fatt	L	Cr	Mollie Harjo	L	Cr
		Census Card No. 3574, P. O. Thurman, Enrolled September 11, 1902							
9559	1	Moore, James	1¼M ½	John W. Moore	L	Non	Henry Moore	L	Cr
		No. 1 died February 15, 1910							
		Census Card No. 3575, P. O. Sapulpa, Enrolled September 11, 1902							
9560	1	Berryhill, Gracie I.	1½F 1-16	Thomas J. Berryhill	L	Cr	Nellie Berryhill	L	Non
		Census Card No. 3576, P. O. Coweta, Enrolled September 11, 1902							
9561	1	Childers, Edward	1¾M ¾	N. B. Childers	L	Cr	Kizzie Davis	L	Cr
		Census Card No. 3577, P. O. Mounds, Enrolled September 11, 1902							
9562	1	Montgomery, Alfred	1½M ¼	George B. Montgomery	L	Non	Bessie Montgomery	L	Cr
9563	2	Montgomery, Henry	5 moM ¼ Bro	George B. Montgomery	L	Non	Bessie Montgomery	L	Cr
		No. 2 died July 8, 1901							
		Census Card No. 3578, P. O. Eufaula, Enrolled September 11, 1902							
9564	1	Doyle, Laura	2 F ⅛	Seaborn J. Doyle	L	Cr	Dell Doyle	L	Non
		Census Card No. 3579, P. O. Mounds, Enrolled September 11, 1902							
9565	1	Rowley, Eveline X.	1¼F ¼	Charles Rowley	L	Cr	Annie Rowley	L	Non
		Census Card No. 3580, P. O. Eufaula, Enrolled September 12, 1902							
9566	1	Lewis, David	2 M F	Daniel Lewis	L	Cr	Pollie Lewis	L	Cr
		Census Card No. 3581, P. O. Checotah, Enrolled September 13, 1902							
9567	1	Bruner, Benjamin	2¼M F	Sulda Bruner	L	Cr	Lucy Bruner	L	Cr
		No. 1 died May 28, 1901							
		Census Card No. 3582, P. O. Senora, Enrolled September 13, 1902							
9568	1	Tiger, Turner	3¾M F	Wilson Tiger	D	Cr	Eliza Tiger	D	Cr
		No. 1 died January 14, 1908							
		Census Card No. 3583, P. O. Bristow, Enrolled September 13, 1902							
9569	1	Bruner, Cassie	1¼F ½	Freeland Bruner	L	Cr	Rhoda Bruner	L	Cr
		Census Card No. 3584, P. O. Holdenville, Enrolled September 13, 1902							
9570	1	Marks, John B.	2 M ½	John N. Marks	L	?	Martha Marks	L	Cr
		Census Card No. 3585, P. O. Owl, Enrolled May 2, 1902							
9571	1	Butler, Delpha	67 F ¼	Bungy	D	Cr	Mollie Butler	D	Cr
		No. 1 died 1900							
		Census Card No. 3586, P. O. Keefton, Enrolled September 15, 1902							
9572	1	Stephens, Vadie	1¼F ¼	Green Stephens	L	Non	Millie Stephens	L	Cr
		Census Card No. 3587, P. O. Tulsa, Enrolled September 15, 1902							
9573	1	Orcutt, Lela M.	1½F ⅛	S. A. Orcutt	L	Non	Annie B. Orcutt	L	Cr
		Census Card No. 3588, P. O. Tulsa, Enrolled September 15, 1902							
9574	1	Jones, Maude Cox	1¼F ½	Thomas Jones	L	Non	Lydia C. Jones	L	Cr
		Census Card No. 3589, P. O. Tulsa, Enrolled September 16, 1902							
9575	1	Childers, Quincy	1 F F	Chisso Childers	L	Cr	Millie Childers	L	Cr
		No. 1 died August 3, 1901							
		Census Card No. 3590, P. O. Okmulgee, Enrolled September 16, 1902							
9576	1	Throckmorton, Eva B.	1¾F ⅜	James W. Throckmorton	L	Cr	Ida L. Throckmorton	L	Cr

Census Card No. 3591, P. O. Holdenville, Enrolled September 16, 1902

| 9577 | 1 | Stubblefield, Joseph S. | 1½ | M | 1-16 | | E. S. Stubblefield | L | Non | Lousanna Stubble-field | L | Cr |

Census Card No. 3592, P. O. Holdenville, Enrolled September 16, 1902

| 9578 | 1 | Cornell, Moses | 1¾ | M | ⅞ | | Willie Cornell | L | Cr | Mamie Cornell | L | Cr |

Census Card No. 3593, P. O. Okemah, Enrolled September 17, 1902

| 9579 | 1 | Tiger, Philip | 1½ | M | F | | George W. Tiger | L | Cr | Hepsie Jimboy | L | Cr |

Census Card No. 3594, P. O. Coweta, Enrolled September 17, 1902

| 9580 | 1 | Washington, Thomas | 1¾ | M | ⅛ | | Willie Washington | L | Cr | Rosanna McGilbray | L | Cr |

No. 1 died 1908

Census Card No. 3595, P. O. Calvin, Enrolled September 17, 1902

| 9581 | 1 | Bruner, Siah | 57 | M | F | | Tulwa Harjo | D | Cr | Unknown | D | Cr |

No. 1 died June 20, 1899

Census Card No. 3596, P. O. Eufauls, Enrolled September 17, 1902

| 9582 | 1 | Francis, John | 1¼ | M | F | | William Francis | L | Cr | Minkey Francis | L | Cr |

No. 1 died January 8, 1902

Census Card No. 3597, P. O. Creek, Enrolled September 18, 1902

| 9583 | 1 | Grant, Stella | 1¾ | F | F | | Niffey Grant | L | Cr | Miley Grant | L | Cr |

Census Card No. 3598, P. O. Henryetta, Enrolled September 18, 1902

| 9584 | 1 | Davis, Marshall | 1 | M | F | | Dennis Davis | L | Cr | Hannah Davis | L | Cr |

Census Card No. 3599, P. O. Holdenville, Enrolled May 1, 1901

| 9585 | 1 | Beaver, George | 13 | M | F | | Enoch Beaver | D | Cr | Tilda Beaver | D | Cr |

No. 1 died March 4, 1913

Census Card No. 3600, P. O. Stroud, Enrolled September 19, 1902

| 9586 | 1 | Hosey, Nora F. | 1½ | F | 1-32 | | John B. Hosey | L | Cr | Lillie F. Hosey | L | Non |

Census Card No. 3601, P. O. Sapulpa, Enrolled September 19, 1902

| 9587 | 1 | Hay, Johnson | 1¾ | M | F | | John Hay | L | Cr | Egie Hay | L | Cr |

Census Card No. 3602, P. O. Fry, Enrolled September 19, 1902

| 9588 | 1 | Bright, Leon DeWitt | 2 | M | 1-16 | | Luke Bright | L | Non | Mary L. Bright | L | Cr |

Census Card No. 3603, P. O. Holdenville, Enrolled May 2, 1901

| 9589 | 1 | Lowe, Sallie | 2 | F | F | | Canuky Lowe | L | Cr | Toche Lowe | L | Cr |

Census Card No. 3604, P. O. Porter, Enrolled September 23, 1902

| 9590 | 1 | Childers, Stella | 1½ | F | F | | Lewis Childers | L | Cr | Sarah Childers | L | Cr |

Census Card No. 3605, P. O. Eufaula, Enrolled Sptember 24, 1902

| 9591 | 1 | Greenwood, Alice | 1½ | F | F | | Lewis Greenwood | L | Cr | Jennie Greenwood | L | Cr |

Census Card No. 3606, P. O. Mounds, Enrolled September 24, 1902

| 9592 | 1 | Boling, Connie M. | 1¼ | F | 1-16 | | W. F. Boling | L | Non | Martha F. Boling | L | Cr |

Census Card No. 3607, P. O. Wagoner, Enrolled September 25, 1902

| 9593 | 1 | Posey, Homer H. | 1½ | M | ⅛ | | Walter Posey | L | Cr | Mary L. Posey | L | Cr |

No. 1 died January 3, 1905

Census Card No. 3608, P. O. Lenna, Enrolled September 25, 1902

| 9594 | 1 | Collins, Susanna | 1¼ | F | F | | Lewis Collins | L | Cr | Sophie Collins | L | Cr |

Census Card No. 3609, P. O. Creek, Enrolled September 25, 1902

| 9595 | 1 | Fixico, Katie | 5 | F | F | | Cussetah Fixico | L | Cr | Warney Fixico | L | Cr |

Census Card No. 3610, P. O. Beggs, Enrolled September 25, 1902

| 9596 | 1 | Grayson, Thomas | 2½ | M | ⅜ | | George Grayson | L | Cr | Annie Grayson | L | Cr |

Census Card No. 3611, P. O. Sapulpa, Enrolled September 26, 1902

| 9597 | 1 | McKellop, Alice | 1½ | F | ½ | | Almarine E.McKellop | L | Cr | Hattie McKellop | L | Non |

No. 1 died August 31, 1904

Census Card No. 3612, P. O. Kellyville, Enrolled September 26, 1902

| 9598 | 1 | Peeper, Clarence | 1½ | M | ½ | | Frank Peeper | L | Non | Mary Peeper | L | Cr |

Census Card No. 3613, P. O. Okmulgee, Enrolled September 26, 1902

| 9599 | 1 | Hardridge, Helen | 5mo | F | F | | Eli E. Hardridge | L | Cr | Millie Hardridge | L | Cr |

No. 1 died July 28, 1901

Census Card No. 3614, P. O. Wagoner, Enrolled September 26, 1902

| 9600 | 1 | Wiley, Lizzie | 1⅓ | F | ½ | | Andrew Wiley | L | Cr | Cora Wiley | L: | Non |

Census Card No. 3615, P. O. Sapulpa, Enrolled September 27, 1902

| 9601 | 1 | Cosar, Sam | 2 | M | F | | Tom Cosar | L | Cr | Jennie Cosar | L | Cr |

No. 1 died November 1902

Census Card No 3616, P. O. Kellyville, Enrolled September 29, 1902

| 9602 | 1 | Fulsom, Wicey | 2 | F | F | | Thomas Fulsom | L | Cr | Millie Fulsom | L | Cr |

Census Card No. 3617, P. O. Eufaula, Enrolled September 29, 1902

| 9603 | 1 | Nelson, Frankie L. | 1½ | M | 1-16 | | W. W. Nelson | L | Non | Mary S. Nelson | L | Cr |

Census Card No. 3618, P. O. Eufaula, Enrolled September 29, 1902

| 9604 | 1 | McIntosh, Lula | 1½ | F | F | | Louis McIntosh | L | Cr | Leah McIntosh | L | Cr |

No. 1 reported dead

Census Card No. 3619, P. O. Beggs, Enrolled September 27, 1902

| 9605 | 1 | Gooden, Frank | 1⅓ | M | ⅜ | | Jacob Gooden | L | Cr | Louisa Gooden | L | Cr |

Census Card No. 3620, P. O. Muskogee, Enrolled September 30, 1902

| 9606 | 1 | Davis, James O. | 3 | M | ¼ | | Lewis H. Davis | L | Cr | Susanna Davis | L | Non |

No. 1 died September 6, 1903

Census Card No. 3621, P. O. Eufaula, Enrolled September 30, 1902

| 9607 | 1 | White, William | 1½ | M | ¼ | | M. H. White | L | Non | Phenia White | L | Cr |

Census Card No. 3622, P. O. Sasakwa, Enrolled September 30, 1902

| 9608 | 1 | Davis, Billy | 4 | M | ¼ | | Sunday Davis | L | Sem | Ilsey Davis | L | Cr |
| 9609 | 2 | Davis, Cheparney | 1¾ | M | ½ | Bro | Sunday Davis | L | Sem | Ilsey Davis | L | Cr |

Census Card No. 3623, P. O. Hanna, Enrolled May 20, 1901; No. 4, May 21, 1901

9610	1	Grayson, Adeline	40	F	½		Henderson Grayson	D	?	Abbie Grayson	D	?
9611	2	Bruner, Willie	20	M	¾	S	Miller Bruner	D	Cr	No. 1	L	Cr
9612	3	Arbor, Henderson	11	M	¼	S	Fagley Arbor	D	Sem	No. 1	L	Cr
9613	4	Arbor, Caney	10	M	¼	S	John Arbor	D	Sem	No. 1	L	Cr

No. 4 died November 1912

Roll No.	No.	NAME	Age	Sex	Blood	Rel.	NAME OF FATHER	Liv.	Cit.	NAME OF MOTHER	Liv.	Cit.
		Census Card No. 3624, P. O. Muskogee, Enrolled October 2, 1902										
9614	1	Evans, Lela	1½	F	⅛		Alex Evans	L	Non	Laura Evans	L	Cr
		Census Card No. 3625, P. O. Arbeka, Enrolled October 2, 1902										
9615	1	Jackson, Martha	1⅓	F	F		Saber Jackson	L	Cr	Annie Jackson	L	Cr
		Census Card No. 3626, P. O. Mounds, Enrolled October 3, 1902										
9616	1	Withers, Joseph A.	1¾	M	⅛		Robert Withers	L	Non	Lydia Withers	L	Cr
		Census Card No. 3627, P. O. Eufaula, Enrolled April 24, 1901										
9617	1	Thomas, Harley	55	M	½		Sampson Thomas	?	Cher	Lucy Thomas	D	Cr
9618	2	Thomas, Lydia	25	F	F	Wf	Little Tiger	D	Cr	Sissa Tiger	D	Cr
9619	3	Thomas, Lena	17	F	¾	D	No. 1	L	Cr	Bettie Thomas	D	Cr
9620	4	Thomas, Eliza	12	F	¾	D	No. 1	L	Cr	Bettie Thomas	D	Cr
9621	5	Sulphur, Alex	6	M	F	StS	Jim Sulphur	L	Cr	No. 2	L	Cr
		No. 4 died February 15, 1903. No. 3 died April 10, 1904.										
		Census Card No. 3628, P. O. Stone Bluff, Enrolled October 8, 1902										
9622	1	Berryhill, Andrew J.	6mo	M	1-64		Geo. F. Berryhill	L	Cr	Clementine Berryhill	L	Non
		No. 1 died November 1901										
		Census Card No. 3629, P. O. Fentress, Enrolled July 28, 1902										
9623	1	Deer, John	1⅓	M	F		Moses Deer	L	Cr	Ellen Deer	L	Cr
		Census Card No. 3630, P. O. Hoffman, Enrolled October 8, 1902										
9624	1	Jenkins, Buna E. M.	2	F	⅛		G. R. Jenkins	L	Non	Henrietta Jenkins	L	Cr
		Census Card No. 3631, P. O. Sasakwa, Enrolled December 18, 1902										
9625	1	Charlesey, Jennie	1½	F	½		Charlesey	L	Sem	Ellen Charlesey	L	Cr
9626	2	Charlesey, Lizzie	4mo	F	½	Sis	Charlesey	L	Sem	Ellen Charlesey	L	Cr
		No. 2 died May 28, 1901										
		Census Card No. 3632, P. O. Okmulgee, Enrolled October 19, 1902										
9627	1	Sugar, James Jr.	2mo	M	F		James Sugar, Sr.	L	Cr	Helen Sugar	L	Cr
		No. 1 died June 11, 1901										
		Census Card No. 3633, P. O. Eufaula, Enrolled June 27, 1903										
9628	1	Cox, Jennie	23	F	F		Nocus Fixeco	D	Cr	Chowina	D	Cr
		No. 1 died August 15, 1901										
		Census Card No. 3634, P. O. Checotah, Enrolled October 9, 1902										
9629	1	Hood, Joe	1mo	M	⅛		Sterling P. Hood	L	Non	Sarah Hood	L	Cr
		No. 1 died June 6, 1901										
		Census Card No. 3635, P. O. Bristow, Enrolled October 10, 1902										
9630	1	Wright, Clida Owen	1½	M	1-16		W. C. Wright	L	Non	Lula T. Wright	L	Cr
		Census Card No. 3636, P. O. Eufaula, Enrolled October 11, 1902										
9631	1	Riddle, Rufus	1¾	M	⅛		Stewart Riddle	L	Choc	Tokee Riddle	L	Cr
		No. 1 died December 1907										
		Census Card No. 3637, P. O. Okmulgee, Enrolled October 15, 1902										
9632	1	Miller, Polly	1½	F	⅞		Seborn Miller	L	Cr	Effa Miller	L	Cr
		Census Card No. 3638, P. O. Holdenville, Enrolled October 15, 1902										
9633	1	Yargee, Alexander	36	M	F		Dave Yargee	D	Cr	Sarwarnechee	D	Cr
		No. 1 died June 29, 1899										
		Census Card No. 3639, P. O. Eufaula, Enrolled October 15, 1902										
9634	1	Manley, Bunnie	1½	M	F		Thomas Manley	L	Cr	Mary Manley	L	Cr
		Census Card No. 3640, P. O. Henryetta, Enrolled October 17, 1902										
9635	1	Hall, Louis S.	1⅓	M	½		Harrison Hall	L	Non	Lena A. Hall	L	Cr
		Census Card No. 3641, P. O. Beggs, Enrolled October 18, 1902										
9636	1	Bruner, Dewey	2	M	¾		Thomas Bruner	L	Cr	Julia Bruner	L	Cr
		Census Card No. 3642, P. O. Eufaula, Enrolled October 20, 1902										
9637	1	Polk, Winey	6	F	F		Daniel W. Polk	L	Cr	Silla Polk	L	Cr
		Census Card No. 3643, P. O. Wetumka, Enrolled October 21, 1902										
9638	1	Tiger, Louisa	43	F	F		Unknown	D	Cr	Unknown	D	Cr
		No. 1 died August 4, 1899										
		Census Card No. 3644, P. O. Quinton, Enrolled October 22, 1902										
9639	1	Carney, Wallace Jr.	6	M	½		Wallace Carney Sr.	?	Non	Amey Carney	L	Cr
		Census Card No. 3645, P. O. Henryetta, Enrolled October 23, 1902										
9640	1	Sloan, Jemima	6	F	⅛		Peter Sloan	?	Sem	Watsey Sloan	D	Cr
		Census Card No. 3646, P. O. Okmulgee, Enrolled October 24, 1902										
9641	1	Larney, Daniel	1¾	M	F		Thompson Larney	L	Cr	Betsy Larney	L	Cr
		Census Card No. 3647, P. O. Henryetta, Enrolled October 24, 1902										
9642	1	Colbert, Bettie	1½	F	F		Daniel Colbert	L	Cr	Lucy Colbert	L	Cr
		No. 1 died June 14, 1901										
		Census Card No. 3648, P. O. Sapulpa, Enrolled October 27, 1902										
9643	1	Gregory, Clemmie R.	1¾	F	½		Noah G. Gregory	L	Cr	Carrie E. Gregory	L	Cr
		Census Card No. 3649, P. O. Lenna, Enrolled October 27, 1902										
9644	1	Loney, Leah	1½	F	F		Sam Loney	L	Cr	Rachael Loney	L	Cr
		No. 1 died June 12, 1905										
		Census Card No. 3650, P. O. Lenna, Enrolled October 27, 1902										
9645	1	Turk, Jerry	2	M	F		Frank Turk	L	Cr	Peggie Turk	L	Cr
		Census Card No. 3651, P. O. Wagoner, Enrolled October 27, 1902										
9646	1	Williams, Walter E.	1½	M	1-16		John H. Williams	L	Non	Sarah E. Williams	L	Cr
		Census Card No. 3652, P. O. Bristow, Enrolled October 27, 1902										
9647	1	Tiger, Tahperscoyka	3½	M	F		Jim Tiger	L	Cr	Nonpechee Polecat	L	Cr
		Census Card No. 3653, P. O. Krebs, Enrolled October 28, 1902										
9648	1	Brown, Lorena M.	2	F	⅛		Jackson Brown	L	Cr	Laura Brown	L	Non
		Census Card No. 3654, P. O. Lenna, Enrolled October 29, 1902										
9649	1	Morrison, Lily	1⅓	F	¼		Hence Morrison	L	Cr	Nancy Morrison	L	Non
		Census Card No. 3655, P. O. Checotah, Enrolled October 30, 1902										
9650	1	Sampson, Burleigh R.	1½	M	⅛		George P. Sampson	L	Non	Mary Sampson	L	Cr

Roll No.	No.	NAME	Age	Sex	Blood	Rel.	NAME OF FATHER	Liv.	Cit.	NAME OF MOTHER	Liv.	Cit.
Census Card No. 3656, P. O. Wetumka, Enrolled October 30, 1902												
9651	1	Gaddis, Eliza	25	F	F		Jesse Chummty	D	Cr	Mary Chummty	L	Cr
		No. 1 reported dead										
Census Card No. 3657, P. O. Kellyville, Enrolled October 31, 1902												
9652	1	Littlehead, Hannah	1½	F	F		Willie Littlehead	L	Cr	Nannie Littlehead	L	Cr
		No. 1 died June 30, 1902										
Census Card No. 3658, P. O. Pierce, Enrolled October 31, 1902												
9653	1	Wolf, Lee	1⅓	M	F		Roley Wolf	L	Cr	Levina Wolf	L	Cr
Census Card No. 3659, P. O. Krebs, Enrolled October 31, 1902												
9654	1	Hendrickson, Thomas	2	M	1-16		James Hendrickson	L	Non	Eliza Hendrickson	L	Cr
Census Card No. 3660, P. O. Henryetta, Enrolled November 1, 1902												
9655	1	Summers, Fannie	7	M	1-16		Clinton P. Summers	L	Cr	M. J. Summers	L	Non
		No. 1 died July 26, 1899										
Census Card No .3661, P. O. Muskogee, Enrolled November 1, 1902												
9656	1	Herrick, Willie J.	2	M	1-16		L. Herrick	L	Non	Mary Herrick	L	Cr
Census Card No. 3662, P. O. Stidham ,Enrolled November 1, 1902												
9657	1	Walker, Mineola	1½	F	⅜		Ed. Walker	L	Cr	Eula Walker	L	Cr
Census Card No. 3663, P. O. Okemah, Enrolled November 1, 1902												
9658	1	Brook, Frederick H.	1½	M	¼		John H. Brook	L	Non	Jennetta A. Brook	L	Cr
Census Card No. 3664, P. O. Mounds, Enrolled November 3, 1902												
9659	1	Leath, Thomas F.	1¾	M	1-32		Thomas J. Leath	L	Cr	Ida J. Leath	L	Non
Census Card No. 3665, P. O. Sapulpa, Enrolled November 3, 1902												
9660	1	Aubrey, Samuel	1½	M	⅜		C. B. Aubrey	L	Non	Millie Aubrey	L	Cr
Census Card No. 3666, P. O. Mounds, Enrolled November 6, 1902												
9661	1	Maxwell, Joseph L.	5mo	M	1-16		John C. Maxwell	L	Cr	Laura J. Maxwell	L	Non
		No. 1 died June 17, 1901										
Census Card No. 3667, P. O. Kellyville, Enrolled November 6, 1902												
9662	1	Wildcat, Maxey	3½	M	F		James Wildcat	L	Cr	Liza Wildcat	L	Cr
Census Card No. 3668, P. O. Fame, Enrolled November 6, 1902												
9663	1	Gray, Moses	1½	M	F		Siah Gray	L	Cr	Mary Gray	L	Cr
Census Card No. 3669, P. O. Bristow, Enrolled November 6, 1902												
9664	1	Allen, Jesse Will	2	M	⅝		Jesse Allen	L	Cr	Lizzie Allen	L	Cr
Census Card No. 3670, P. O. Eufaula, Enrolled November 6, 1902												
9665	1	Ansiel, Jennie M.	1½	F	1-32		Robert L. Ansiel	L	Cr	Sadie A. Andiel	L	?
Census Card No. 3671, P. O. Bixby, Enrolled November 7, 1902												
9666	1	Morrison, Felix G.	1¾	M	¾		J. C. Morrison	L	Cr	Mary Morrison	L	Cr
Census Card No. 3672, P. O. Weleetka, Enroled November 8, 1902												
9667	1	Barnett, Lonie	1½	M	¼		Dick Barnett	L	Cr	Annie Barnett	L	Cr
Census Card No. 3673, P. O. Okmulgee, Enrolled November 8, 1902												
9668	1	Carter, Minnie Lou	1½	F	1-16		Joseph B. Carter	L	Non	Annie Carter	L	Cr
Census Card No. 3674, P. O. Checotah, Enrolled November 8, 1902												
9669	1	Murray,Nettie Belle	1½	F	1-32		Charles E. Murray	L	Cr	Delphie A. Murray	L	Non
Census Card No. 3675, P. O. Okmulgee, Enrolled November 8, 1902												
9670	1	Berryhill, Peggie	2	F	¾		Alex Berryhill	L	Cr	Annie Berryhill	L	Cr
Census Card No. 3676, P. O. Okmulgee, Enrolled November 8, 1902												
9671	1	Berryhill, Martha	1½	F	F		Harrison Berryhill	L	Cr	Bettie Berryhill	L	Cr
Census Card No. 3677, P. O. Keokuk Falls, Enrolled April 29, 1901												
9672	1	Micco, Kapitche	88	M	F		Unknown	D	Cr	Unknown	D	Cr
		No. 1 died September 25, 1901										
Census Card No. 3678, P. O. Eufaula, Enrolled November 10, 1902												
9673	1	Isbell, Catherine C.	1½	F	¼		J. G. Isbell	L	Non	Mary E. Isbell	L	Cr
Census Card No. 3679, P. O. Okemah, Enrolled November 10, 1902												
9674	1	Fippo, Vernie	2	M	1-16		Samuel M. Fipps	L	Non	Alice M. Fipps	L	Cr
Census Card No. 3680, P. O. Eufaula, Enrolled November 10, 1902												
9675	1	Doyle, Mable	2	F	⅛		Sam H. Doyle Jr.	L	Cr	Bedie Doyle	L	Non
		No. 1 died April 26, 1903										
Census Card No. 3681, P. O. Weleetka, Enrolled November 10, 1902												
9676	1	Robison, Ida	2	F	¾		Amos R. Robison	L	Cr	Louisa Robison	L	Cr
Census Card No. 3682, P. O. Okmulgee, Enrolled November 11, 1902												
9677	1	Sanger, Claude	1½	M	⅛		Stephen Sanger	L	Cr	Viola Sanger	L	Non
Census Card No. 3683, P. O. Checotah, Enrolled November 11, 1902												
9678	1	Storm, Gladys	1½	F	⅛		John Storm	L	Non	Lou Storm	L	Cr
Census Card No. 3684, P. O. Hanna, Enrolled April 24, 1902												
9679	1	Fixeco, Chippie	22	F	F		Tommie Fixico	D	Cr	Wisey	D	Cr
9680	2	Harjo, Kina	20	F	F	Sis	Tommie Fixico	D	Cr	Wisey	D	Cr
		No. 2 died July 3, 1899										
Census Card No. 3685, P. O. Fentress, Enrolled November 13, 1902												
9681	1	Foster, Malinda	1½	F	¼		G. C. Foster	L	Non	Lonie Foster	L	Cr
Census Card No. 3686, P. O. Mounds, Enrolled November 15, 1902												
9682	1	Wills, Buck H.	2	M	1-16		Henry F. Wills	L	Cr	Mary A. Wills	L	Non
Census Card No. 3687, P. O. Sapulpa, Enrolled November 18, 1902												
9683	1	Weaver, Etta May	3	F	1-16		Bert W. Weaver	L	Non	Rena Weaver	L	Cr
Census Card No. 3688, P. O. Kellyville, Enrolled November 18, 1902												
9684	1	Self, Duffie LeRoy	1½	M	1-16		John Robbins	L	Non	Blanche C. Self	L	Cr
Census Card No. 3689, P. O. Bristow, Enrolled November 18, 1902												
9685	1	Big Mosquito, Agnes	2	F	F		Big Mosquito	L	Cr	Jensey Big Mosquito	L	Cr
Census Card No. 3690, P. O. Kiefer, Enrolled November 18, 1902												
9686	1	Kiefer, Stella F.	1½	F	1-16		Smith H. Kiefer	L	Non	Martha Lee Kiefer	L	Cr
Census Card No. 3691, P. O Mounds, Enrolled November 19, 1902												
9687	1	Lannan, Jennie	1½	F	1-16		William Lannan	L	Non	Jennie Lannan	L	Cr
Census Card No. 3692, P. O. Weleetka, Enrolled November 19, 1902												
9688	1	Robison, Sekice	2½	M	⅞		Amos R. Robison	L	Cr	Maggie Robison	L	Cr

Roll No.	No.	NAME	Age	Sex	Blood	Rel.	NAME OF FATHER	Liv.	Cit.	NAME OF MOTHER	Liv.	Cit.
		Census Card No. 3693, P. O. Oktaha, Enrolled November 19, 1902										
9689	1	Evans, Myrtle G.	1½	F	7-16		James H. Evans	L	Cr	Stella A. Evans	L	Non
		Census Card No. 3694, P. O. Mounds, Enrolled November 19, 1902										
9690	1	Stewart, Edna	1½	F	⅛		William H Stewart	L	Non	America Stewart	D	Cr
		Census Card No. 3695, P. O. Okemah, Enrolled November 20, 1902										
9691	1	Wind, Job	1½	M	¾		George Wind	L	Cr	Milly Wind	L	Cr
		Census Card No. 3696, P. O. Weleetka, Enrolled November 21, 1902										
9692	1	Buckley, Emma	2	F	F		Ceasar Buckley	L	Cr	Betsey Buckley	L	Cr
		No. 1 died November 1, 1901										
		Census Card No. 3697, P. O. Creek, Enrolled November 22, 1902										
9693	1	Foster, Martha	1½	F	F		David Foster	L	Cr	Mcleny Foster	L	Cr
		Census Card No. 3698, P. O. Beggs, Enrolled November 25, 1902										
9694	1	Mukes, Jospeh	1½	M	⅜		Thomas Mukes	L	Non	Alice Mukes	L	Cr
		Census Card No. 3699, P. O. Brush Hill, Enrolled November 28, 1902										
9695	1	Lewallen, Lillie	1½	F	⅛		John Lewallen	L	Non	Louisa Lewallen	L	Cr
		Census Card No. 3700, P. O. Checotah, Enrolled April 8, 1901; No. 2, November 29, 1902										
9696	1	Lerblance, Lillian	5	F	½		E. H. Lerblance	D	Cr	Minnie B. Shay	?	Cher
9697	2	Lerblance, Pearl	2	F	½	Sis	E. H. Lerblance	D	Cr	Minnie B. Shay	?	Cher
		No. 2 died November 1, 1900										
		Census Card No. 3701, P. O. Henryetta, Enrolled July 23, 1902										
9698	1	Wilson, Annie	3	F	½		Jesse Wilson	L	Cr	Ida Wilson	L	Non
		Census Card No. 3702, P. O. Mounds, Enrolled December 2, 1902										
9699	1	Vowell, Jospeh LeRoy	2	M	⅛		Sam Vowell	L	Cr	Rosa Vowell	L	Non
		Census Card No. 3703, P. O. Kellyville, Enrolled December 2, 1902										
9700	1	Self, Elsie Ray	1½	M	1-16		John H. Self	L	Cr	Dollie Self	L	Non
		Census Card No. 3704, P. O. Bristow, Enrolled December 2, 1902										
9701	1	Cahtahwon, Lucinda	2	F	F		Cahtahwon	L	Cr	Soconthlaney	L	Cr
		No. 1 reported dead										
		Census Card No. 3705, P. O. Henryetta, Enrolled December 2, 1902										
9702	1	King, Lillian Beatrice	2	F	½		William King	L	Non	Elizabeth King	L	Cr
		Census Card No. 3706, P. O. Shafer, Enrolled December 5, 1902										
9703	1	Dale, Mabel	1¾	F	1-16		Oliver C. Dale	L	Non	Izora E. Dale	L	Cr
		Census Card No. 3707, P. O. Checotah, Enrolled December 8, 1902										
9704	1	Dyer, William McKinley	2	M	1-32		Fred S. Dyer	L	Non	Eliza Dyer	L	Cr
		Census Card No. 3708, P. O. Catoosa, Enrolled December 9. 1902										
9705	1	Chamberlain, Ruth Hazel	2	F	⅛		J. C Chamberlain	L	Non	Susie Chamberlain	L	Cr
		Census Card No. 3709, P. O. Checotah, Enrolled December 10, 1902										
9706	1	Escoe, Johnnie	4	M	⅛		Charlie J. Escoe	L	Cr	Dora Escoe	L	Cher-F
9707	2	Escoe, Luther	2	M	⅛	Bro	Charlie J. Escoe	L	Cr	Dora Escoe	L	Cher-F
		Census Card No. 3710, P. O. Coweta, Enrolled December 12, 1902										
9708	1	Murphy, Richard L.	5	M	1-16		Gomy Myrphy	L	Cr	Sarah Murphy	L	Cher
9709	2	Murphy, Catherine	3	F	1-16	Sis	Gomy Murphy	L	Cr	Sarah Murphy	L	Cher
		Census Card No. 3711, P. O. Foyil, Enrolled December 12, 1902										
9710	1	Foreman, George E.	37	M	¼		Jeremiah E. Foreman	D	Cr	Selestine Stidham	D	Cher
9711	2	Foreman, Maggie Belle	12	F	⅛	D	No. 1	L	Cr	Isabelle Foreman	?	Cher
9712	3	Foreman, Jeremiah E.	11	M	⅛	S	No. 1	L	Cr	Isabelle Foreman	?	Cher
9713	4	Foreman, Sarah C.	10	F	⅛	D	No. 1	L	Cr	Isabelle Foreman	?	Cher
9714	5	Foreman, Minnie E.	8	F	⅛	D	No. 1	L	Cr	Isabelle Foreman	?	Cher
9715	6	Foreman, Annie	6	F	⅛	D	No. 1	L	Cr	Isabelle Foreman	?	Cher
9716	7	Foreman, Stephen S.	4	M	⅛	S	No. 1	L	Cr	Isabelle Foreman	?	Cher
		Census Card No. 3712, P. O. Eufaula, Enrolled December 12, 1902										
9717	1	Stidham, Ben	1¾	M	⅝		Theo. E. Stidham	L	Cr	Hattie Bush	L	Cr
		No. 1 illegitimate										
		Census Card No. 3713, P. O. Stidham, Enrolled December 13, 1902										
9718	1	Franklin, William Penn	1¾	M	¼		William Franklin	L	Non	Lena Franklin	L	Cr
		Census Card No. 3714, P. O. Tullahassee, Enrolled December 15, 1902										
9719	1	Bowers, Edith	3	F	¼		Fred Bowers	L	Cr	Ida Bowers	L	Cher
9720	2	Bowers, Frederick	2	M	¼	Bro	Fred Bowers	L	Cr	Ida Bowers	L	Cher
		No. 1 died June 11, 1901. No. 2 died June 11, 1899.										
		Census Card No. 3715, P. O. Wewoka, Enrolled December 16, 1902										
9721	1	Long, Wewoka John	4	M	⅜		Daniel A Long	L	Cr	Kate Long	L	Sem
		Census Card No. 3716, P. O. Sasakwa, Enrolled December 16, 1902										
9722	1	Miller, Charles L.	2	M	⅜		Samuel H. Miller	L	Cr	Nora F. Miller	L	Sem
		Census Card No. 3717, P. O. Stroud, Enrolled December 16, 1902										
9723	1	McIntosh, Vera Thelma	2	F	⅜		Charles McIntosh	L	Cr	Bertha McIntosh	L	Non
		Census Card No. 3718, P. O. Pierce, Enrolled December 17, 1902										
9724	1	Beartail, Lydia	8mo	F	F		Louis Beartail	D	Cr	Eliza Timothy	L	Cr
9725	2	Timothy, Wesley	1⅓	M	F	½Bro	Noah Timothy	L	Cr	Eliza Timothy	L	Cr
		No. 1 died August 19, 1899. No. 2 died August 19, 1902.										
		Census Card No. 3719, P. O. Mellette, Enrolled December 18, 1902										
9726	1	Givens, Charley	1¾	M	F		William Givens	L	Cr	Annie Givens	L	Cr
		Census Card No. 3720, P. O. Mellette, Enrolled December 18, 1902										
9727	1	Francis, Louis	1⅓	M	F		Robert Francis	L	Cr	Annie Givens	L	Cr
		No. 1 died August 8, 1901										
		Census Card No. 3721, P. O. Bearden, Enrolled May 7, 1901										
9728	1	Little, John	6mo	M	F		Thomas Little	L	Cr	Sallie Little	L	Cr
		No. 1 died June 16, 1900										

Roll No.	No.	NAME	Age	Sex	Blood	Rel.	NAME OF FATHER	Liv.	Cit.	NAME OF MOTHER	Liv.	Cit.
		Census Card No. 3722, P. O. Holdenville, Enrolled December 18, 1902										
9729	1	Tiger, John	5	M	F		Tom Tiger	L	Cr	Rose Tiger	L	Cr
9730	2	Tiger, Louisa	3	F	F	Sis	Tom Tiger	L	Cr	Rose Tiger	L	Cr
		Census Card No. 3723, P. O. Eufaula, Enrolled December 18, 1902										
9731	1	Givens, Hepsey	24	F	F		Choctaw Givens	L	Cr	Silla	D	Cr
		No. 1 died April 15, 1899										
		Census Card No. 3724, P. O. Holdenville, Enrolled December 20, 1902										
9732	1	Harper, Simon	3	M	F		Shawnee Harper	L	Cr	Somaye Harper	L	Cr
		No. 1 died May 21, 1899										
		Census Card No. 3725, P. O. Owyhee, Nev. Enrolled December 22, 1902										
9733	1	Callahan, Mary Alice	4	F	1-32		Walter K. Callahan	L	Cr	Alice Callahan	L	Cher
		Census Card No. 3726, P. O. Checotah, Enrolled December 22, 1902										
9734	1	Wolf, Amy	3	F	F		George Wolf	L	Cr	Nannie Wolf	L	Cr
		No. 1 died June 20, 1899										
		Census Card No. 3727, P. O. Muskogee, Enrolled December 23, 1902										
9735	1	Davis, Cherokee	4	F	1-16		John Davis	L	Cr	Martha Davis	L	Cher
9736	2	Davis, Gooty	2	F	1-16	Sis	John Davis	L	Cr	Martha Davis	L	Cher
		No. 2 died 1901										
		Census Card No. 3728, P. O. Haskell, Enrolled December 23, 1901										
9737	1	Ingley, Columbus F.	26	M	⅛		John Ingley	D	Non	Liza McIntosh	D	Cr
		Census Card No. 3729, P. O. Tulsa, Enrolled November 17, 1899; No. 5, June 2, 1900; No. 6, March 23,190										
9738	1	Owens, Martha	39	F	¼		Unknown	D	Non	Jane Wolf	D	Cr
9739	2	Owens, Elva	13	F	⅛	D	C. A. Owens	?	Non	No. 1	L	Cr
9740	3	Owens, Addie	5	F	⅛	D	C. A. Owens	?	Non	No. 1	L	Cr
9741	4	Owens, Ollie M.	7	F	⅛	GrD	John Wolf	?	Non	Dora Pendleton	D	Cr
9742	5	Owens, Albert Poage	10	M	⅛	S	C. A. Owens	?	Non	No. 1	L	Cr
9743	6	Feeley, Charles	16	M	⅛	S	Henry Feeley	D	Non	No. 1	L	Cr
		No. 1 died January 8, 1902										
		Census Card No. 3730, P. O. Wetumka, Enrolled December 30, 1902										
9744	1	Yahola, Bettie	31	F	F		Sam Buckler	D	Cr	Mahala	D	Cr
		No. 1 died January 6, 1900										
		Census Card No. 3731, P. O. Citra, Enrolled December 30, 1902										
9745	1	Chief, Reuben	29	M	½		Jim Chief	L	Chic	Celia hCief	D	Cr
		Census Card No. 3732, P. O. Coweta, Enrolled January 3, 1902										
9746	1	Childers, Tilda	8mo	F	F		Grafield Childers	L	Cr	Ida Childers	L	Cr
		No. 1 died July 27, 1901										
		Census Card No. 3733, P. O. Creek, Enrolled January 3, 1902										
9747	1	Halley, Taylor	13	M	F		Joe Haley	D	Cr	Nancy Halley	D	Cr
		No. 1 died April 1899										
		Census Card No. 3734, P. O. Eufaula, Enrolled January 7, 1902										
9748	1	Billy, Lumber	54	M	F		Langley Billy	D	Cr	Rina Billy	D	Cr
9749	2	Billy, Nancy	44	F	F	Wf	Kenah Harjo	D	Cr	Unknown	D	Cr
9750	3	Billy, William	16	M	F	S	No. 1	L	Cr	No. 2	L	Cr
9751	4	Billy, David	12	M	F	S	No. 1	L	Cr	No. 2	L	Cr
9752	5	Billy, Susan	8	F	F	D	No. 1	L	Cr	No. 2	L	Cr
9753	6	Billy, Tookah	6	F	F	D	No. 1	L	Cr	No. 2	L	Cr
		No. 2 died December 28, 1909. No. 5 died May 13, 1914. No. 1 reported dead.										
		Census Card No. 3735, P. O. Broken Arrow, Enrolled January 9, 1904										
9754	1	Trusler, Lucile Frances	1½	F	¼		Frank Trusler	L	Non	Phoebe B. Trusler	L	Cr
		Census Card No. 3736, P. O. Morse, Enrolled January 9, 1903										
9755	1	Knight, Annie	6mo	F	F		London Knight	L	Cr	Susan Knight	L	Cr
		No. 1 died December 7, 1901										
		Census Card No. 3737, P. O. Wewoka, Enrolled March 26, 1901										
9756	1	Brown, William J.	1	M	¼		Clarence Brown	L	Cr	Rebecca Brown	L	Sem
		No. 1 died June 6, 1901										
		Census Card No. 3738, P. O. Okmulgee, Enrolled January 11, 1903										
9757	1	Myers, Willie Frances	1½	F	¼		William F. Myers	L	Non	Betsey Myers	L	Cr
		Census Card No. 3739, P. O. Burney, Enrolled January 13, 1903										
9758	1	Stand, Thomas	2	M	⅞		Philip Stand	L	Cr	Lizzie Stand	L	Cr
		Census Card No. 3740, P. O. Eufaula, Enrolled January 14, 1903										
9759	1	Jones, Ella	5	F	F		Haikey Jones	L	Cr	Levina Jones	L	Cr
		Census Card No. 3741, P. O. Eufaula, Enrolled January 16, 1903										
9760	1	Mitchell, Hannah	10	F	F		Sarwenoge Mitchell	L	Cr	Eliza Mitchell	L	Cr
		Census Card No. 3742, P. O. Wewoka, Enrolled January 16, 1903										
9761	1	Starr, Adam	45	M	F		Unknown	D	Cr	Unknown	D	Cr
		No. 1 died April 26, 1899										
		Census Card No. 3743, P. O. Hanna, Enrolled January 17, 1903										
9762	1	Bullett, Jennie	6	F	F		Halak Yarholer	D	Cr	Kizzie Bullett	D	Cr
		No. 1 died January 31, 1914										
		Census Card No. 3744, P. O. Goode, Enrolled January 19, 1903										
9763	1	Collins, Nancy D.	3	F	⅛		Jacob N. Collins	L	Cr	Nancy D. Collins	L	Cr
		Census Card No. 3745, P. O. Barnard, Enrolled January 19, 1903										
9764	1	Tebe, Jennie	2½	F	½		Tebe	L	Sem	Wisey Tebe	L	Cr
		Census Card No. 3746, P. O. Eufaula, Enrolled January 20, 1902										
9765	1	Bean, Sabena	5	F	F		Monday Bean	L	Cr	Lena Bean	L	Cr
9766	2	Bean, Okfuske	4	M	F	Bro	Monday Bean	L	Cr	Lena Bean	L	Cr
		Census Card No. 3747, P. O. Hanna, Enrolled January 21, 1903										
9767	1	Hill, Jefferson	3	M	F		James Hill	L	Cr	Polly Hill	L	Cr
		Census Card No. 3748, P. O. Stroud, Enrolled January 21, 1903										
9768	1	Rogers, Annie	11mo	F	½		Sam Rogers	L	Cher	Hannah Rogers	L	Cr
		No. 1 died November 1901										

Census Card No. 3749, P. O. Okmulgee, Enrolled January 22, 1903

Roll No.	No.	NAME	Age	Sex	Blood	Rel.	Name of Father	Liv.	Cit.	Name of Mother	Liv.	Cit.
9769	1	Kanard, Eliza	2	F	F		James Kanard	L	Cr	Nellie Kanard	L	Cr

Census Card No. 3750, P. O. Bristow, Enrolled January 22, 1903

| 9770 | 1 | Barnett, Nancy | 1½ | F | ½ | | Wm. Bowleg | L | Sem | Lydia Barnett | L | Cr |

No. 1 died July 15, 1899

Census Card No. 3751, P. O. Wewoka, Enrolled January 22, 1903

| 9771 | 1 | Abaisse, Fremus | 1½ | M | ½ | | Abaisse | L | Sem | Sissie Ahaisse | L | Cr |

Census Card No. 3752, P. O. Okemah, Enrolled January 22, 1903

| 9772 | 1 | Barnett, George | 2 | M | F | | Daniel Barnett | L | Cr | Eliza Barnett | L | Cr |

Census Card No. 3753, P. O. Dustin, Enrolled January 28, 1903

| 9773 | 1 | Wesley, Nettie | 1½ | F | F | | Keeper Wesley | L | Cr | Leah Wesley | L | Cr |

No. 1 died March 9, 1902

Census Card No. 3754, P. O. Holdenville, Enrolled January 16, 1903

| 9774 | 1 | Fish, Sam | 3moM | F | | | Wattie Fish | L | Cr | Annie Fish | L | Cr |

No. 1 died May 14, 1899

Census Card No. 3755, P. O. Barnard, Enrolled February 4, 1903

| 9775 | 1 | Lott, Losie | 2 | F | F | | Thomas Lott | L | Cr | Lena Lott | L | Cr |

Census Card No. 3756, P. O. Sapulpa, Enrolled February 6, 1901

| 9776 | 1 | Glenn, Elmer | 2 | M | 1-16 | | Robert J. Glenn | L | Non | Ida E. Glenn | L | Cr |

Census Card No. 3757, P. O. Mounds, Enrolled February 11, 1903

| 9777 | 1 | Self, John B. | 76 | M | ¼ | | Baxter Self | D | Non | Susan Self | D | Cr |

No. 1 died February 14, 1905

Census Card No. 3758, P. O. Cushing, Enrolled February 21, 1903

| 9778 | 1 | McIntosh, Lewis | 14moM | ⅜ | | | Wm. R. McIntosh | L | Cr | Thodocia McIntosh | L | Cr |

No. 1 died October 15, 1899

Census Card No. 3759, P. O. Carson, Enrolled February 10, 1903

| 9779 | 1 | Proctor, Sampson | 3 | M | F | | Hully Proctor | L | Cr | Jennetta Proctor | L | Cr |

No. 1 died November 15, 1904

Census Card No. 3760, P. O. Eufaula, Enrolled February 12, 1903

| 9780 | 1 | Holuby, Hattie | 40 | F | F | | Unknown | D | Cr | Muskogee | D | Cr |

No. 1 died January 4, 1900

Census Card No. 3761, P. O. Sax and Fox Agency, Enrolled August 29, 1902

9781	1	Narwallepese	50	F	½		Hopawae	?	Shaw	Sommahuhte	D	Cr
9782	2	Washington, Mary	11	F	¼		Tom Washington	?	Shaw	No. 1	L	Cr
9783	3	Washington, Walter	8	M	¼		Tom Washington	?	Shaw	No. 1	L	Cr
9784	4	Washington, Willie	6	M	¼		Tom Washington	?	Shaw	No. 1	L	Cr

Census Card No. 3762, P. O. Depew, Enrolled May 23, 1901

| 9785 | 1 | Chequawa | 36 | F | F | | Unknown | ? | Cr | Kaahsee | ? | Cr |

Census Card No. 3763, P. O. Eufaula, Enrolled February 27, 1903

| 9786 | 1 | Harley, Alex | 2 | M | F | | Samson Harley | L | Cr | Jennie Harley | L | Cr |

Census Card No. 3764, P. O. Holdenville, Enrolled February 28, 1903

| 9787 | 1 | Tiger, Martha | 2 | F | ¼ | | John Tiger | L | Sem | Cinda Tiger | L | Cr |

Census Card No. 3765, P. O. Wekiwa, Enrolled March 4, 1903

| 9788 | 1 | Johnson, Unah | 1½ | M | F | | Sandy Johnson | L | Cr | Jinnie Johnson | L | Cr |

No. 1 died September 3, 1899

Census Card No. 3766, P. O. Yeager, Enrolled March 6, 1903

| 9789 | 1 | Bruner, Dick | 1¾ | M | F | | Miller Bruner | L | Cr | Liza Bruner | L | Cr |

Census Card No. 3767, P. O. Mounds, Enrolled March 7, 1903

| 9790 | 1 | Simms, Louisa | 17 | F | F | | John Simms | L | Cr | Betche | | Cr |

Census Card No. 3768, P. O. Calvin, Enrolled March 13, 1903

| 9791 | 1 | Walter, Isaac | 18 | M | F | | Partese Walter | D | Cr | Unknown | ? | Cr |

Census Card No. 3769, P. O. Oktaha, Enrolled March 14, 1903

| 9792 | 1 | Coffee, Lucy | 2 | F | F | | Micco Coffee | L | Cr | Polly Coffee | L | Cr |

Census Card No. 3770, P. O. Morse, Enrolled March 16, 1903

| 9793 | 1 | Davis, Susan | 2½ | F | ½ | | Louis Davis | L | Sem | Kanneyah Davis | L | Cr |

Census Card No. 3771, P. O. Wetumka, Enrolled March 17, 1903

| 9794 | 1 | Jacob, George | 28 | M | F | | Pahos Yahola | D | Cr | Jennie Yahola | L | Cr |

No. 1 died December 16, 1900

Census Card No. 3772, P. O. Sapulpa, Enrolled March 17, 1903

| 9795 | 1 | Holden, Sarah | 22 | F | F | | George Talladega | D | Cr | Mary Tulladega | L | Cr |

No. 1 died February 2, 1900

Census Card No. 3773, P. O. Kellyville, Enrolled March 19, 1903

| 9796 | 1 | Wildcat, Jesse | 3 | M | F | | Jim Wildcat | D | Cr | Farloconweney | L | Cr |

No. 1 died August 4, 1900

Census Card No. 3774, P. O. Holdenville, Enrolled March 24, 1903

| 9797 | 1 | Manley, Dicey | 5 | F | F | | David Manley | L | Cr | Eliza Manley | L | Cr |

Census Card No. 3775, P. O. Paden, Enrolled April 1, 1903

| 9798 | 1 | Sands, Albert | 2 | M | F | | Taylor Sands | L | Cr | Annie Sands | L | Cr |

Census Card No. 3776, P. O. Okemah, Enrolled April 25, 1901

| 9799 | 1 | Chupko, Betsey | 53 | F | F | | Unknown | D | Cr | Unknown | ? | Cr |

No. 1 died February 28, 1901

Census Card No. 3777, P. O. Holdenville, Enrolled May 7, 1903

| 9800 | 1 | Proctor, Mahala | 9 | F | F | | Tulsa Harjo | D | Cr | Mandy Proctor | L | Cr |

No. 1 died July 10, 1899

Census Card No. 3778, P. O. Arbeka, Enrolled May 12, 1903

| 9801 | 1 | Harjoche, Lena | 2½ | F | F | | Nokos Harjoche | L | Cr | Melosey Harjoche | L | Cr |

Census Card No. 3779, P. O. Clearview, Enrolled May 13, 1903

| 9802 | 1 | McCoy, Lina | 2 | F | ¼ | | Tecumseh McCoy | D | Ch-F | Delphie McCoy | L | Cr |

Roll No.	No.	NAME	Age	Sex	Blood	Rel.	NAME OF FATHER	Liv.	Cit.	NAME OF MOTHER	Liv.	Cit.
		Census Card No. 3780, P. O. Weleetka, Enrolled June 1, 1903										
9803	1	Fields, Jobe	6	M	F		Taylor Fields	L	Cr	Melinda Fife	L	Cr
9804	2	Fields, Solomonlb	3	M	F	Bro	Taylor Fields	L	Cr	Melinda Fife	L	Cr
		Census Card No. 3781, P. O. Wagoner, Enrolled August 26, 1899										
9805	1	Parks, Margaret Atkins	28	F	1/8		Richard Atkins	D	Adp	Sarah Atkins	L	Non
9806	2	Atkins, John H.	26	M	1/8	Bro	Richard Atkins	D	Adp	Sarah Atkins	L	Non
9807	3	Atkins, James A.	21	M	1/8	Bro	Richard Atkins	D	Adp	Sarah Atkins	L	Non
9808	4	Atkins, Nathaniel	19	M	1/8	Bro	Richard Atkins	D	Adp	Sarah Atkins	L	Non
9809	5	Atkins, Annanias A.	18	M	1/8	Bro	Richard Atkins	D	Adp	Sarah Atkins	L	Non
9810	6	Atkins, Naoma	15	F	1/8	Sis	Richard Atkins	D	Adp	Sarah Atkins	L	Non
9811	7	Atkins, Leola	11	F	1/8	Sis	Richard Atkins	D	Adp	Sarah Atkins	L	Non
9812	8	Atkins, Bertie	6	F	1/8	Sis	Richard Atkins	D	Adp	Sarah Atkins	L	Non
		No. 3 died January 3, 1912										
		Census Card No. 3782, P. O. Senora, Enrolled July 1, 1903										
9813	1	Fife, Una	2	M	F		Jimmie Fife	L	Cr	Lucinda Fife	L	Cr
		Census Card No. 3783, P. O. Okemah, Enrolled July 10, 1903										
9814	1	Foster, Summer	3	M	F		Henry Foster	L	Cr	Janie Foster	L	Cr
		No. 1 died February 1905										
		Census Card No. 3784, P. O. Dustin, Enrolled July 27, 1903										
9815	1	Kanard, Albert	1	M	F		George Kanard	L	Cr	Rosana Kanard	L	Cr
		No. 1 died September 25, 1900										
		Census Card No. 3785, P. O. Bristow, Enrolled May 23, 1901										
9816	1	Zonkeoteetay	20	M	F		Sammy	D	Cr	Chequawa	?	Cr
		Census Card No. 3786, P. O. Henryetta, Enrolled September 12, 1903										
9817	1	Burgess, James Jr.	3	M	3/4		James Burgess	L	Cr	Susanna Burgess	L	Cr
		Census Card No. 3787, P. O. Braggs, Enrolled May 22, 1901										
9818	1	Yahola, Polly	67	F	F		Conheler Harjo	D	Cr	Unknown	?	Cr
9819	2	Foloppa, Sam	25	M	F	S	Unknown	?	Cr	No. 1	L	Cr
		No. 1 probable duplicate of Cherokee Enrollment No. 29108.										
		No. 2 probable duplicate of Cherokee Enrollment No. 28501.										
		Census Card No. 3788, P. O. Wetumka, Enrolled September 22, 1903										
9820	1	Thompson, Mussie	1	M	F		Tumasochee (Tomsogee Harjo)	D	Cr	Leah Harjo	L	Cr
		No. 1 died January 1902										
		Census Card No. 3789, P. O. Bristow, Enrolled October 3, 1905										
9821	1	Big Mosquito, Careconcothlana	3mo	F	F		Big Mosqiuto	L	Cr	Jensey Big Mosquito	L	Cr
		No. 1 died June 1899										
		Census Card No. 3790, P. O. Sapulpa, Enrolled October 10, 1903										
9822	1	Grayson, Lealah	12	F	F		James Grayson	L	Cr	Mollie Grayson	D	Cr
		No. 1 died										
		Census Card No. 3791, P. O. Mekesukey, Enrolled October 20, 1903										
9823	1	Coker, Richmond	3¾	M	1/4		David Coker	L	Cr	Hettie Coker	L	Sem
		Census Card No. 3792, P. O. Shawnee, Enrolled May 23, 1901										
9824	1	Norbe	29	M	F		Arbebeeasic	D	Cr	Thalwequa	D	Cr
		Census Card No. 3793, P. O. Okmulgee, Enrolled November 12, 1903										
9825	1	Sneed, George	29	M	3/8		Charles Sneed	D	Non	Martha Sneed	D	Cr
9826	2	Sneed, George Everett	8	M	3-16	S	No. 1	L	Cr	Hannah Sneed	L	Non
9827	3	Sneed, Maron	6	M	3-16	S	No. 1	L	Cr	Hannah Sneed	L	Non
9828	4	Sneed, Leonard	4	M	3-16	S	No. 1	L	Cr	Hannah Sneed	L	Non
		Census Card No. 3794, P. O. Eufaula, Enrolled November 12, 1903										
9829	1	Roberts, Annie	5	F	F		Noah Roberts	L	Cr	Miller Roberts	D	Cr
		No. 1 died December 27, 1900										
		Census Card No. 3795, P. O. Wagoner, Enrolled November 12, 1903										
9830	1	Brady, Martha	49	F	Cher		Sam Hensley	D	Non	Jane Hensley	D	Cher
		No. 1 died March 1900										
		Census Card No. 3796, P. O. Calvin, Enrolled Nov. 12, 1903.										
9831	1	Leno, Robert	60	M	Span		Unknown	?	?	Unknown	?	?
		No. 1 died April 16, 1899.										
		Census Card N.o 3797, P. O. Holdenville, Enrolled Nov. 12, 1903.										
9832	1	Duckworth, Cecil	3M	F	1/4		Robert Duckworth	L	Non	Ruth E. Duckworth	L	Cr
		No. 1 died July 9, 1901.										
		Census Card No. 3798, P. O. Muskogee, Enrolled Nov. 14, 1903.										
9833	1	Steele, Mary	24	F	1/8		Robert Steele	?	Cher	Catherine C. Steele	D	Cr
		Census Card No. 3799, P. O. Bristow, Enrolled Nov. 14, 1903.										
9834	1	Williams, Willie	1	M	1/8		Sam Williams	?	Sem	Rena Williams	L	Cr
		No. 1 died October 22, 1899.										
		Census Card No. 3800, P. O. Eufaula, Enrolled Mov. 14, 1903.										
9835	1	Billy, Eliza	8	F	F		Lumber Billy	L	Cr	Nancy Billy	L	Cr
		No. 1 died December 10, 1900.										
		Census Card No. 3801, P. O. Paden, Enrolled Nov 14, 1903.										
9836	1	Gray, Henry	3	M	1/2		Geo. C. Gray	L	Non	Mesulta Gray	L	Cr
		Census Card No. 3802, P. O. Coweta, Enrolled Nov. 14, 1903.										
9837	1	Flowers, Mintie	47	F	1/8		Edley Adair	D	Cr	Martha Adair	D	Cr
		No. 1 died May 17, 1900.										
		Census Card No. 3803, P. O. Braggs, Enrolled Nov. 20, 1903.										
9838	1	Henehochee, Hopoeth	67	M	F		Unknown	?	Cr	Unknown	?	Cr
		No. 1 died March 20, 1908.										

Roll No.	No.	NAME	Age	Sex	Blood	Rel.	NAME OF FATHER	Liv.	Cit.	NAME OF MOTHER	Liv.	Cit.
		Census Card No. 3804, P. O. Hanna, Enrolled, May 23, 1901; No. 2, Dec. 8, 1903.										
9839	1	Heneha, Mary,	20	F	F		Cho Harjoche	D	Cr	Hepsey	D	Cr
9840	2	Heneha Lussie	5	F	F	D	Chukchat Heneka	D	Cr	No. 1	L	Cr
		No. 1 reported dead.										
		Census Card No. 3805, P. O. Dustin, Enrolled Dec. 9, 1903.										
9841	1	Long, Mattie	2	F	F		Jesse Long	L	Cr	Wiggie Long	D	Cr
9842	2	Long, Peter	1	M	F	Bro.	Jesse Long	L	Cr	Wiggie Long	D	Cr
		No. 1 died July 13, 1900. No. 2 died November 13, 1899.										
		Census Card No. 3806, P. O. Eufaula, Enrolled Feb. 28, 1903.										
9843	1	Ansill, Josh Lee	2	M	1-16		Samuel E. Ansill	L	Cr	Roxie Ansill	L	Non
		Census Card No. 3807, P. O. McDermott, Enrolled Feb. 17, 1904.										
9844	1	Foster, Willie Frances	8	F	1-16		Geo. W. Foster	L	Non	Mary E. Foster	L	Cr
		Census Card No. 3808, P. O. Mounds, Enrolled May 20, 1903.										
9845	1	Harwell, Walter B.	19	M	1-16		A. B. Harwell	L	Non	Mary L. Harwell	L	Cr
9846	2	Harwell, Lilla M.	17	F	1-16	Sis	A. B. Harwell	L	Non	Mary L. Harwell	L	Cr
9847	3	Harwell, Lena M.	15	F	1-16	Sis	A. B. Harwell	L	Non	Mary L. Harwell	L	Cr
9848	4	Harwell, Nina P.	12	F	1-16	Sis	A. B. Harwell	L	Non	Mary L. Harwell	L	Cr
		Census Card No. 3809, P. O. Holdenville, Enrolled Feb. 27, 1904.										
9849	1	Kernels, Johnson	1	M	½		George Kernel	L	Cr	Retta Kernel	L	Sem
		No. 1 died June 14, 1901.										
		Census Card No. 3810, P. O. Okmulgee, Enrolled March 3, 1904.										
9850	1	Sneed, John	36	M	⅜		Charlie Sneed	D	Non	Martha Sneed	L	Cr
		Census Card No. 3811, P. O. Wetumka, Enrolled March 8, 1904.										
9851	1	Alexander, Nancy	3	F	¼		Robert L. Alexander	L	Cr	Martha Alexander	?	Sem
		Census Card No. 3812, P. O. Bristow, Enrolled March 9, 1904.										
9852	1	Tiger, Cotala	6	M	F		Phillip Tiger	D	Cr	Lodie Tiger	D	Cr
9853	2	Tiger, Elba	3	M	F	Bro.	Phillip Tiger	D	Cr	Lodie Yiger	D	Cr
		Census Card Mo.3813, P. O. Eufaula, Enrolled Jan. 8, 1904.										
9854	1	Davis, Billie	8	M	F		Unknown	?	Cr	Sarah Smith	D	Cr
		Census Card No. 3814, P. O. Okemah, Enrolled Feb. 5, 1904.										
9855	1	Fixico, Cinda	28	F	F		Tulmochus Harjo	L	Cr	Monaye	D	Cr
9856	1	Fixico, Annie	5	F	F	D	Gotcha Fixico	L	Cr	No. 1	L	Cr
		No. 2 died 1904.										
		Census Card No. 3815, P. O. Jenks, Enrolled March 30, 1904.										
9857	1	Donaldson, Bernie	15	F	1-16		Jim Donaldson	?	Non	Margaret Atkins Parks	L	Cr
9858	2	Donaldson, Sallie	12	F	1-16	Sis	Jim Donaldson	?	Non	Margaret Atkins Parks	L	Cr
9859	3	Parks, Fronie	10	F	1-16	Sis	William Parks	L	Non	Margaret Atkins Parks	L	Cr
9860	4	Parks, Fannie	8	F	1-16	Sis	William Parks	L	Non	Margaret Atkins Parks	L	Cr
9861	5	Parks, Julius	6	M	1-16	Bro	William Parks	L	Non	Margaret Atkins Parks	L	Cr
9862	6	Parks, Chaney	8moF		1-16	Bro	William Parks	L	Non	Margaret Atkins Parks	L	Cr
		No. 6 died February 6, 1901.										
		Census Card No. 3816, P. O. Checotah, Enrolled March 30, 1899.										
9863	1	Escoe, Bessie	2W	F	⅛		Charlie J. Escoe	L	Cr	Dora Escoe	L	Cher
		No. 1 died April 15, 1899.										
		Census Card No. 3817, P. O. Keokuk Falls, Enrolled March 30, 1904.										
9864	1	Kernal, Loske	5	F	½		Jimmey Leader	?	Sem	Lucy Kernal	L	Cr
		Census Card No. 3818, P. O. Henryetta, Enrolled March 31, 1904.										
9865	1	Robinson, Willie	4	M	3-16		Dave Robinson	?	?	Annie Robinson	L	Cr
		No. 1 died March, 1903.										
		Census Card No. 3819, P. O. Carson, Enrolled March 31, 1904:										
9866	1	Chissoe, Sarah	1	F	⅛		Willie Chissoe	L	Cr	Melinda Benham	L	?
		Census Card No. 3820, P. O. Yeager, Enrolled March 31, 1904										
9867	1	Bruner, Millie	1	F	¾		Miller Bruner	L	Cr	Wynie Harjo	L	Cr
		No. 1 died June 6, 1901										
		Census Card No. 3821, P. O. Henry, Enrolled March 31, 1904										
9868	1	Starr, Emma	9	F	F		Chesley Starr	L	Cr	Mollie Starr	L	Cr
		No. 1 reported dead										
		Census Card No. 3822, P. O. Okemah, Enrolled March 31, 1904										
9869	1	Simmer, Louinie	4	F	F		Charley Simmer	L	Cr	Kizzie Simmer	L	Cr
		Census Card No. 3823, P. O. Beggs, Enrolled April 4, 1904										
9870	1	Bruner, David	44	M	½		Richard R. Bruner	L	Cr	Polly	D	Cr
		No. 1 died November 13, 1899										
		Census Card No. 3824, P. O. Okemah, Enrolled April 4, 1904										
9871	1	Barnett, Minnie	4	F	F		William Barnett	L	Cr	Annie Miller	L	Cr
		Census Card No. 3825, P. O. Sapulpa, Enrolled April 5, 1904										
9872	1	Tate, Mary	38	F	¼		Barnett	D	?	Tehoksie	?	Cr
9873	2	Barnett, Johnny	13	F	⅛	D	Unknown	?	?	No. 1	L	Cr
9874	3	Barnett, Tom	15	M	⅛	S	Unknown	?	?	No. 1	L	Cr
9875	4	Tate, Twintilla	7	F	⅛	D	John Wash Tate	?	?	No. 1	L	Cr
9876	5	Tate, Maty	5	F	⅛	D	Jhon Wash Tate	?	?	No. 1	L	Cr

Roll No.	No.	NAME	Age	Sex	Blood	Rel.	NAME OF FATHER	Liv.	Cit.	NAME OF MOTHER	Liv.	Cit.
Census Card No. 3826, P. O. Henryetta, Enrolled December 29, 1902												
9877	1	Thornsberry, Annie	34	F	¼		James Smith	D	?	Eliza Smith	D	Cr
9878	2	Thornsberry, John	15	M	⅛	S	Wm. M. Thornberry	L	Non	No. 1	L	Cr
9879	3	Thornsberry, Lena	13	F	⅛	D	Wm M. Thornsberry	L	Non	No. 1	L	Cr
9880	4	Thornsberry, Rachael	10	F	⅛	D	Wm M. Thornsberry	L	Non	No. 1	L	Cr
9881	5	Thornsberry, Willie	9	F	⅛	D	Wm M. Thornsberry	L	Non	No. 1	L	Cr
9882	6	Thornsberry, Wynema	5	F	⅛	D	Wm. M. Thornberry	L	Non	No. 1	L	Cr
No. 1 died October 17, 1899. No. 6 died September 3, 1899. No. 2 died November 19, 1909. No. 3 died April 20, 1905.												
Census Card No. 3827, P. O. Eufaula, Enrolled April 6, 1904												
9883	1	Derrisaw, Jimmie	3	M	F		Cooper, Derrisaw	L	Cr	Katy Downing	L	Cr
Census Card No. 3828, P. O. Coweta, Enrolled April 6, 1904												
9884	1	Thomas, Leaster	6mo	F	¾		Sam Thomas	L	Cr	Sophia Thomas	L	Cr
No. 1 died April 6, 1899												
Census Card No. 3829, P. O. Sapulpa, Enrolled April 6, 1904												
9885	1	Hohlahta, Martha	2	F	F		Cheparn Hohlahta	L	Cr	Lucy Hohlahta	L	Cr
No. 1 died May 1899												
Census Card No. 3830, P. O. Weleetka, Enrolled May 19, 1904												
9886	1	Ben, Robert	1	M	F		Big Ben	L	Cr	Martha Ben	L	Cr
No. 1 died October 15, 1900												
Census Card No. 3831, P. O. Bristow, Enrolled May 19, 1904												
9887	1	Cloud, Dave	1½	M	F		Laslie Cloud	L	Cr	Mary Cloud	L	Cr
9888	2	Cloud, Miley	1	F	F	Niece	Dave Foster	L	Cr	Lizzie Cloud	L	Cr
No. 1 died September 10, 1899. No. 2 died July 10, 1900												
Census Card No. 3832, P. O. Bristow, Enrolled June 4, 1904												
9889	1	Tiger, Jessley	2	M	F		Daniel Tiger	L	Cr	Sarah Tiger	L	Cr
No. 1 died June 5, 1900												
Census Card No. 3833, P. O. Salem, Enrolled June 4, 1904												
9890	1	Beaver, Joe	3	M	F		Unknown	?	Cr	Rosa Beaver	L	Cr
Census Card No. 3834, P. O. Morse, Enrolled June 9, 1904												
9891	1	West, Nellie	3	F	F		Robert West	L	Cr	Parsinder West	L	Cr
No. 1 died October 1903												
Census Card No. 3835, P. O. Beggs, Enrolled June 9, 1904												
9892	1	Tiger, John	2½	M	⅞		Jacob Tiger	L	Cr	Mary Gooden	L	Cr
Census Card No. 3836, P. O. Dustin, Enrolled June 9, 1904												
9893	1	Nubbie, Wilson	23	M	F		Unknown	?	Cr	Unknown	?	Cr
9894	2	Nubbie, Malissa	6	F	F	D	No. 1	L	Cr	Louisa Scott	D	Cr
No. 1 died July 1, 1899												
Census Card No. 3837, P. O. Okmulgee, Enrolled June 9, 1904												
9895	1	Proctor, Myrtle	1	F	¾		Toney E. Proctor	L	Cr	Susan Proctor	L	Cr
No. 1 died June 10, 1899												
Census Card No. 3838, P. O. Henryetta, Enrolled June 9, 1904												
9896	1	Beams, Lilly	2	F	½		Charley Beams	L	Choc	Annie Beams	L	Cr
No. 1 died October 13, 1899												
Census Card No. 3839, P. O. Morse, Enrolled June 9, 1904												
9897	1	Narchechar	18	F	F		Unknown	?	Cr	Unknown		Cr
No. 1 died July 17, 1900												
Census Card No. 3840, P. O. Tulsa, Enrolled June 9, 1904												
9898	1	Steen, Robert	3	M	½		Walter Steen	L	Non	Katie Steen	L	Cr
No. 1 died February 28, 1907												
Census Card No. 3841, P. O. Henryetta, Enrolled June 9, 1904												
9899	1	Barnett, Lucy	19	F	F		Dave Fisher	L	Cr	Larney Fisher	L	Cr
No. 1 died September 12, 1899												
Census Card No. 3842, P. O. Sapulpa, Enrolled June 9, 1904												
9900	1	Washington, Thomas	3	M	¾		Isaac Washington	L	Cr	Mollie Like	L	Cr
Census Card No. 3843, P. O. Wetumka, Enrolled February 27, 1903												
9901	1	Siah, John	2	M	F		Soloman Siah	L	Cr	Mary Siah	L	Cr
No. 1 died												
Census Card No. 3844, P. O. Mounds, Enrolled June 9, 1904												
9902	1	Boling, John R.	8	M	1-16		W. F. Boling	L	Non	Martha F. Boling	L	Cr
Census Card No. 3845, P. O. Wetumka, Enrolled June 9, 1904												
9903	1	Fisher, Timmie	25	M	F		Unknown	?	Cr	Unknown	?	Cr
No. 1 died May 1899												
Census Card No. 3846, P. O. Weir, Enrolled June 10, 1904												
9904	1	Icheney	80	F	F		Unknown	?	Cr	Unknown	?	Cr
No. 1 died April 1899												
Census Card No. 3847, P. O. Morse, Enrolled June 10, 1904												
9905	1	West, Johnnie	1	M	F		Waddie West	L	Cr	Sissy West	L	Cr
No. 1 died 1900												
Census Card No. 3848, P. O. Okmulgee, Enrolled June 30, 1904												
9906	1	Fife, William	1	M	F		Judy Fife	L	Cr	Sissie Fife	L	Cr
No. 1 died July 1, 1899												
Census Card No. 3849, P. O. Eufaula, Enroleed Julne 30, 1904												
9907	1	Fisher, Elsie	8	F	F		Barney Fisher	L	Cr	Nancy Tiger	L	Cr
No. 1 died March 31, 1899												
Census Card No. 3850, P. O. Sapulpa, Enrolled July 28, 1904												
9908	1	Helton, Jesse Newman	3	M	½		W. B. Helton	L	Non	Nellie Helton	L	Cr
Census Card No. 3851, P. O. Holdenville, Enrolled July 28, 1904												
9909	1	Martha	60	F	F		Unknown	?	Cr	Unknown	?	Cr
No. 1 died October 22, 1899												
Census Card No. 3852, P. O. Checotah, Enrolled July 28, 1904												
9910	1	Carr, Harley	4	M	⅛		Thomas Carr	L	Cr	Mary McCuen	L	Non

Roll No.	No.	NAME	Age	Sex	Blood	Rel.	NAME OF FATHER	Liv.	Cit.	NAME OF MOTHER	Liv.	Cit.
		Census Card No. 3853, P. O. Eufaula, Enrolled July 23, 1904.										
9911	1	Sullivan, Sulphur	31	M	F		Jimmy Sullivan	D	Cr	Sally Sullivan	L	Cr
		No. 1 died January 1900										
		Census Card No. 3854, P. O. Broken Arrow, Enrolled July 28, 1904										
9912	1	Cooper, Stella	3	F	½		Elbert Cooper	L	Non	Annie Cooper	L	Cr
		Census Card No. 3855, P. O. Hanna, Enrolled August 19, 1904										
9913	1	Smith, Sam	3	M	F		Mickey Smith	L	Cr	Aggie Smith	L	Cr
		Census Card No. 3856, P. O. Eufaula, Enrolled November 7, 1904										
9914	1	Long, Selena	8	F	F		John Long	L	Cr	Eliza Long	L	Cr
		Census Card No. 3857, P. O. Okmulgee, Enrolled November 7, 1904										
9915	1	Webster, Bunner	½	M	F		Jefferson Webster	L	Cr	Mattie Webster	L	Cr
		No. 1 died September 30, 1900										
		Census Card No. 3858, P. O. Wagoner, Enrolled October 18, 1900										
9916	1	Trent, Chaney	41	F	⅛		Richard Atkins	D	Ad-W	Lettie Shannon	D	Non
9917	2	Trent, Frank	24	M	⅛	S	Jim Trent	L	Non	No. 1	L	Cr
9918	3	Trent, Mary	22	F	⅛	D	Jim Trent	L	Non	No. 1	L	Cr
9919	4	Trent, Will	20	M	⅛	S	Jim Trent	L	Non	No. 1	L	Cr
9920	5	Trent, Susie	12	F	⅛	D	Jim Trent	L	Non	No. 1	L	Cr
9921	6	Trent, Lee Drew	10	M	⅛	S	Jim Trent	L	Non	No. 1	L	Cr
9922	7	Trent, Bennie	8	M	⅛	S	Jim Trent	L	Non	No. 1	L	Cr
9923	8	Trent, Fannie C.	6	F	⅛	D	Jim Trent	L	Non	No. 1	L	Cr
		No. 5 died 1905										
		Census Card No. 3859, P. O. Indianola, Enrolled January 5, 1905										
9924	1	Fish, Elsie	1	F	F		Jimsey Fish	L	Cr	Hunny Fish	D	Cr
		No. 1 died May 16, 1901										
		Census Card No. 3860, P. O. Mellette, Enrolled January 21, 1905										
9925	1	Roberts, Millie	41	F	F		Sam Brown	D	Cr	Lucy Brown	D	Cr
		No. 1 died October 6, 1900										
		Census Card No. 3861, P. O. Wetumka, Enrolled January 21, 1905										
9926	1	Walker, Liza	22	F	F		Geo. W. Walker	L	Cr	Mollie Walker	L	Cr
		No. 1 died December 1899										
		Census Card No. 3862, P. O. Lenna, Enrolled January 21, 1905										
9927	1	Coker, Cheparney	4	M	¼		Lewis Coker	L	Cr	Litchie Coker	L	Sem
		Census Card No. 3863, P. O. Coweta, Enrolled January 21, 1905										
9928	1	Flowers, Johnny	1½	M	⅜		John Flowers	L	Cr	Mentie Flowers	L	Cr
		No. 1 died August 1899										
		Census Card No. 3864, P. O. Wetumka, Enrolled January 23, 1905										
9929	1	Harjo, Jessie	4	F	F		Tommoche	L	Cr	Millie	L	Cr
		Census Card No. 3865, P. O. Morse, Enrolled January 21, 1905										
9930	1	Taryolie, Turner	1	M	F		Taryole	L	Cr	Marfey Mikey	L	Cr
		No. 1 died September 1901										
		Census Card No. 3866, P. O. Coweta, Enrolled January 21, 1905										
9931	1	Frank, Lizzie	30	F	F		Unknown	?	Cr	Unknown		Cr
		No. 1 died January 6, 1900										
		Census Card No. 3867, P. O. Holdenville, Enrolled January 23, 1905										
9932	1	Buckner, Nannie	3	F	F		Wiley Buckner	L	Cr	Susie Buckner	L	Cr
		No. 1 reported dead										
		Census Card No. 3868, P. O. Dustin, Enrolled January 23, 1905										
9933	1	Fisher, Willie	35	M	½		William Fisher	L	Cr	Betty Fisher	D	Cr
		Census Card No. 3869, P. O. Sapulpa, Enrolled January 23, 1905										
9934	1	Wanakee, Lizzie	17	F	F		Wanakee	?	Cr	Unknown	?	Cr
		No. 1 died September 1899										
		Census Card No. 3870, P. O. Mounds, Enrolled January 23, 1905										
9935	1	Newton, Samantha E.	49	F	⅛		John B. Self	L	Cr	Elizabeth Self	L	Non
9936	2	Newton, Connie O.	22	F	1-16	D	Sir Isaac Newton	D	Non	No. 1	L	Cr
9937	3	Newton, Ollin	18	M	1-16	S	Sir Isaac Newton	D	Non	No. 1	L	Cr
9938	4	Newton, Vera S.	16	F	1-16	D	Sir Isaac Newton	D	Non	No. 1	L	Cr
9939	5	Newton, John P.	14	M	1-16	S	Sir Isaac Newton	D	Non	No. 1	L	Cr
		Census Card No. 3871, P. O. Dustin, Enrolled January 23, 1905										
9940	1	Fife, Willie	8	M	F		Sunday Fife	L	Cr	Louisa Fife	L	Cr
9941	2	Fife, Mammie	4	F	F	Sis	Sunday Fife	L	Cr	Louisa Fife	L	Cr
		Census Card No. 3872, P. O. Hasson, Enrolled January 23, 1905										
9942	1	Haikey, Kono	64	F	F		Artaryiche Yahola	D	Cr	Patokike	D	Cr
9943	2	Hulma	16	M	F	GrS	Katchee Homahte	L	Cr	Marlesa	D	Cr
		No. 1 reported dead. No. 2 died November 12, 1899.										
		Census Card No. 3873, P. O. Weleetka, Enrolled January 23, 1905										
9944	1	Johnson, Yuna	5	F	F		Cooper Johnson	L	Cr	Sukey Johnson	L	Cr
		Census Card No. 3874, P. O. Kellyville, Enrolled January 23, 1905										
9945	1	Fulsom, Emma	1	F	F		Thomas Fulsom	L	Cr	Millie Fulsom	L	C
		No. 1 died April 20, 1899										
		Census Card No. 3875, P. O. McAlester, Enrolled January 23, 1905										
9946	1	Wadsworth, Thomas	2½	M	⅝		Caddo Wadsworth	L	Cr	Louisa Wadsworth	L	Cr
		No. 1 died October 1903										
		Census Card No. 3876, P. O. Eufaula, Enrolled January 23, 1905										
9947	1	Blake, Peter	60	M	F		Unknown	?	Cr	Unknown	?	Cr
		No. 1 died March 29, 1901										
		Census Card No. 3877, P. O. Eufaula, Enrolled January 23, 1905										
9948	1	Frank, Louis	6	M	⅜		Noah Frank	L	Cr	Louina Frank	L	Cr
		Census Card No. 3878, P. O. Eufaula, Enrolled January 23, 1905										
9949	1	Washington, Walter	5	M	F		George Washington	D	Cr	Peggie Salumba	D	Cr

Roll No.	No.	NAME	Age	Sex	Blood	Rel.	NAME OF FATHER	Liv.	Cit.	NAME OF MOTHER	Liv.	Cit.
		Census Card No. 3879, P. O. Holdenville, Enrolled January 21, 1905										
9950	1	Campbell, Frank	24	M	1/8		Bill Campbell	?	Non	Mary Alex	L	Non
		Census Card No. 3880, P. O. Muskogee, Enrolled February 23, 1905										
9951	1	Callahan, Ruby	4	F	1-32		Walter K. Callahan	L	Cr	Alice Callahan	?	Cher
		Census Card No. 3881, P. O. Eufaula, Enrolled February 33, 1905										
9952	1	Field, Mattie	2	F	F		Washington Field	L	Cr	Annie Field	L	Cr
		No. 1 died 1902										
		Census Card No. 3882, P. O. Hasson, Enrolled February 23, 1905										
9953	1	Smith, Betsy	38	F	F		Unknown	?	Cr	Unknown	?	Cr
		No. 1 died February 17, 1901. Pencil notation on this Census Card shows Sam Hawkins, Father; Sohema, Mother.										
		Census Card No. 3883, P. O. Hanna, Enrolled June 27, 1904										
9954	1	Emarthla, Hotulke	55	M	F		Unknown	?	Cr	Unknown	?	Cr
		No. 1 died November 19, 1899										
		Census Card No. 3884, P. O. Dustin, Enrolled February 23, 1905										
9955	1	Whitlow, Edward	4	M	F		Wm. Whitlow	L	Sem	Simhoye	L	Cr
		Census Card No. 3885, P. O. Sapulpa, Enrolled February 23, 1905										
9956	1	Soffeeney	56	M	F		Unknown	?	Cr	Unknown	?	Cr
9957	2	Hetahcocotan	12	M	F	GrS	Yohtargokotha	?	Cr	Kakothlar	D	Cr
9958	3	Youcotahlarney	9	M	F	GrS	Yohtargokotha	?	Cr	Kakothlar	D	Cr
		No. 1 died September 7, 1900. No. 2 died June 1900. No. 3 died August 1900.										
		Census Card No. 3886, P. O. Tulsa, Enrolled February 23, 1905										
9959	1	Thlocco, Fus	50	M	F		Unknown	?	Cr	Unknown	?	Cr
		No. 1 died October 25, 1899										
		Census Card No. 3887, P. O. Beggs, Enrolled February 23, 1905										
9960	1	Adams, Felix	4	M	1/4		George W. Adams	L	Cr	Sarah Adams	L	Cr
		Census Card No. 3888, P. O. Calvin, Enrolled February 23, 1905										
9961	1	Leader, Thomas	1	M	3/4		Barney Leader	L	Cr	Tilda Leader	L	Cr
		No. 1 died November 1900										
		Census Card No. 3889, P. O. Eufaula, Enrolled February 23, 1905										
9962	1	Stidham, William	3	M	F		George Stidham	L	Cr	Mary Asbury	L	Cr
		No. 1 died August 12, 1901										
		Census Card No. 3890, P. O. Sapulpa, Enrolled February 23, 1905										
9963	1	Peter, John	29	M	F		Unknown	?	Cr	Harkowathlany	L	Cr
		No. 1 died June 29, 1900										
		Census Card No. 3891, P. O. Hanna, Enrolled March 6, 1905										
9964	1	Gano, Harriet	45	F	F		Unknown	?	Cr	Unknown	?	Cr
		No. 1 died April 17, 1899										
		Census Card No. 3892.										
9965	1	Stricken from roll										
9966	2	Stricke nfrom roll										
9967	3	Stricken from roll										
9968	4	Stricken from roll										
9969	5	Stricken from roll										
9970	6	Stricken from roll										
9971	7	Stricken from roll										
9972	8	Stricken from roll										
		Census Card No. 3893, P. O. Fry, Enrolled NMarch 9, 1905										
9973	1	Ayers, Walter	6mo	M	1/4		Wm. Ayers	L	Non	Gussie Ayers	L	Cr
		No. 1 died June 16, 1899										
		Census Card No. 3894, P. O. Calvin, Enrolled March 9, 1905										
9974	1	Alexander, Robert	5	M	F		David Alexander	L	Cr	Lizzie Alexander	L	Cr
		No. 1 died August 22, 1899										
		Census Card No. 3895										
9975	1	Stricken from roll										
		Census Card No. 3896, P. O. Eufaula, Enrolled March 9, 1905										
9976	1	Morrison, Louisa	2	F	3/8		Waity Morrison ?	L	?	Emma Smith	L	Cr
		No. 1 died June 1899										
		Census Card No. 3897, P. O. Dustin, Enrolled March 9, 1905										
9977	1	Casey, Joseph	26	M	1/2		Unknown	?	?	Peggie Solomon	L	Cr
		No. 1 died 1899										
		Census Card No. 3898, P. O. Yeager, Enrolled March 9, 1899										
9978	1	McKane, William	4	M	7/8		John McKane	L	Cr	Hepsey McKane	L	Cr
		Census Card No. 3899, P. O. Wetumka, Enrolled April 10, 1905										
9979	1	Penn, Mary	1	F	F		William Penn	L	Cr	Miley Penn	L	Cr
		No. 1 died August 31, 1900										
		Census Card No. 3900, P. O. Okmulgee, Enrolled April 10, 1905										
9980	1	Harjo, Aholak	35	M	F		Unknown	?	Cr	Unknown	?	Cr
		No. 1 died after April 1, 1899										
		Census Card No. 3901, P. O. Morse, Enrolled April 10, 1905										
9981	1	Micco, Willie Tulwar	41	M	F		Tulwar Micco	D	Cr	Unknown	D	Cr
		No. 1 died November 5, 1904										
		Cen;us Card No. 3902, P. O. Holdenville, Enrolled April 10, 1905										
9982	1	Alex, Mary	41	F	1/4		Allen Lucas	D	?	Mary Smith	D	?
		Census Card No. 3903, P. O. McAlester, Enrolled April 10, 1905										
9983	1	Cohn, Joe	12	M	1/2		Rhod Cohn	?	Non	Oklosey Cohn	D	Cr
		Census Card No. 3904, P. O. Hanna, Enrolled April 10, 1905										
9984	1	Given, George	15	M	F		Jack Givens	D	Cr	Wutsy Givens	D	Cr
		No. 1 died Spring 1900										
		Census Card No. 3905, P. O. Bristow, Enrolled September 1, 1904										
9985	1	Tiger, Nancy	3	F	F		Thomas Tiger	L	Cr	Mollie Tiger	L	Cr
		No. 1 died September 10, 1899										

Roll No.	No.	NAME	Age	Sex	Blood	Rel.	NAME OF FATHER	Liv.	Cit.	NAME OF MOTHER	Liv.	Cit.
		Census Card No. 3906, P. O. Holdenville, Enrolled April 10, 1905										
9986	1	Holata, Wileya	6	M	½		John Holata	D	Sem	Susey Holata	L	Cr
		Census Card No. 3907, P. O. Henryetta, Enrolled April 10, 1905										
9987	1	Sloane, Sallie	9	F	½		Peter Sloane	?	Sem	Watsey	L	Cr
9988	2	Sloane, Sampson	3	M	½	Bro	Peter Sloane	?	Sem	Watsey	L	Cr
		No. 1 died September 5, 1900. No. 2 died January 15, 1901										
		Census Card No. 3908, P. O. Eufaula, Enrolled April 10, 1905										
9989	1	Deerhead, Jennie	17	F	F		Deerhead	D	Cr	Matilda Deerhead	D	Cr
		No. 1 reported dead										
		Census Card No. 3909, P. O. Sasakwa, Enrolled April 10, 1905										
9990	1	Barnett, Salina	7	F	½		Jim Barnett	L	Sem	Mahala Barnett	L	Cr
		Census Card No. 3910, P. O. Oktaha, Enrolled April 10, 1905										
9991	1	Hutchee, Nocus	65	M	F		Unknown	D	Cr	Unknown	D	Cr
		No. 1 died Spring of 1904										
		Census Card No. 3911, P. O. Hanna, Enrolled April 10, 1905										
9992	1	Fish, Eliza	3	F	F		Lewis Fish	L	Cr	Meleya Fish	L	Cr
		No. 1 died March 19, 1904										
		Census Card No. 3912, P. O. Red Fork, Enrolled June 16, 1905										
9993	1	Berryhill, Rosa Lee	2	F	1-16		Thomas H. Berryhill	L	Cr	Sarah Berryhill	L	Non
		No. 1 died April 13, 1899										
		Census Card No. 3913, P. O. Okmulgee, Enrolled June 16, 1905										
9994	1	Hamby, Dora	24	F	1-32		Henry Baker	?	Non	Susan Baker	D	Cr
9995	2	Hamby, Myrtle	6	F	1-64	D	A. H. Hamby	L	Non	Dora Hamby	L	Cr
9996	3	Hamby, Archie	1	M	1-64	S	A. H. Hamby	L	Non	Dora Hamby	L	Cr
9997	4	Baker, John	21	M	1-32	Bro	Henry Baker	?	Non	Suasan Baker	D	Cr
		No. 3 died died August 1901										
		Census Card No. 3914, P. O. Eufaula, Enrolled June 16, 1905										
9998	1	Gibson, Lizzie	45	F	Wht		Unknown	?	?	Unknown	?	?
		Census Card No. 3915, P. O. Boley, Enrolled June 16, 1905										
9999	1	Chisholm, John	4	M	F		Joe Chisholm	L	Cr	Monnie Chisholm	L	Cr
		No. 1 died August 26, 1903										
		Census Card No. 3916, P. O. Henryetta, Enrolled June 16, 1905										
10000	1	Tiger, John	4	M	F		Leetka Tiger	L	Cr	Jinalee Tiger	L	Cr
10001	2	Tiger, Johnson	4	M	F	Bro	Leetka Tiger	L	Cr	Jinalee Tiger	L	Cr
		Census Card No. 3917, P. O. Boley, Enrolled June 16, 1905										
10002	1	Fixseko, Cusseta	60	M	F		Unknown	?	Cr	Unknown	?	Cr
		No. 1 died January 6, 1900										
		Census Card No. 3918, P. O. Hanna, Enrolled June 16, 1905										
10003	1	Proctor, Sarah	13	F	F		Hopioche	L	Cr	Slumker	L	Cr
		Census Card No. 3919, P. O. Yeager, Enrolled June 16, 1905										
10004	1	Davis, Lizzie	1	F	F		John Davis	L	Cr	Polly Da.vs	D	Cr
		No. 1 died July 25, 1899										
		Census Card No. 3920, P. O. Wetumka, Enrolled June 16, 1905										
10005	1	Barnett, Millie	1	F	⅞		Tucker K. Barnett	L	Cr	Cilla Barnett	D	Cr
		No. 1 died December 19, 1900										
		Census Card No. 3921, P. O. Mellette, Enrolled June 16, 1905										
10006	1	Barnett, David	23	M	F		Unknownlb	?	Cr	Unknown		Cr
		No. 1 died April 5, 1899										
		Census Card No. 3922, P. O. Sapulpa, Enrolled June 16, 1905										
10007	1	Warnaskee, Winnie	12	F	F		Unknown	?	Cr	Unknown	.	Fr
		No. 1 died April 15, 1899										
		Census Card No. 3923, P. O. Weleetka, Enrolled June 16, 1905										
10008	1	West, Hettie	5	F	F		Billy West	L	Cr	Louisa West	L	Cr
		Census Card No. 3924, P. O. Holdenville, Enrolled June 16, 1905										
10009	1	Goat, Sallie	2	F	F		Wardley Goat	L	Cr	Susie Goat	L	Cr
		No. 1 died December 16, 1899										
		Census Card No. 3925, P. O. Weleetka, Enrolled June 16, 1905										
10010	1	Simmer, Jesse	4	M	F		John Simmer	L	Cr	Lena Simmer	L	Cr
		Census Card No. 3926										
10011	1	Stricken from roll										
		Census Card No. 3927, P. O. Wewoka, Enrolled June 30, 1905										
10012	1	Mitchell, Sissie	4	F	½		Waitie Mitchell	L	Sem	Mandy Mitchell	L	Cr
10013	2	Mitchell, Cheparney	3	M	½	Bro	Waitie Mitchell	L	Sem	Mandy Mitchell	L	Cr
		No. 2 died September 27, 1899										
		Census Card No. 3928, P. O. Hallett, Enrolled June 30, 1905										
10014	1	Harris, Lula	21	F	¼		Dan David Voorhees	L	Non	Ellen Harrid	D	Cr
		Census Card No. 3929, P. O. Burney, Enrolled June 30, 1905										
10015	1	Johnson, Lucy	1	F	F		Peter Johnson	L	Non	Chotkey Kinha	L	Cr
		No. 1 died May 1899										
		Census Card No. 3930, P. O. Hanna, Enrolled July 12, 1905										
10016	1	Deo, Kogee	2	F	F		Thomas Deo	L	Cr	Alice Dorsey	L	Cr
		No. 1 died Spring 1901										
		Census Card No. 3931, P. O. Muskogee, Enrolled June 30, 1905										
10017	1	Harris, Red Bird	63	M	Cher		Unknown	?	?	Unknown	:	:
		No. 1 died June 20, 1902										
		Census Card No. 3932, P. O. Sapulpa, Enrolled June 30, 1905										
10018	1	Tarvin, Mary B.	68	F	White		Jacob Cates	?	Non	Catherine Cates	?	Non
		No. 1 died May 13, 1910										
		Census Card No. 3933, P. O. Kellyville, Enrolled June 30, 1905										
10019	1	Yellowhead, Saloma	8	F	F		Folsom Yellowhead	L	Cr	Lizzie Deere	D	Cr
		No. 1 died April 1899										

Roll No.	No.	NAME	Age	Sex	Blood	Rel.	NAME OF FATHER	Liv.	Cit.	NAME OF MOTHER	Liv.	Cit.
		Census Card No. 3934, P. O. Kellyville, Enrolled June 30, 1905										
10020	1	Littlehead, Leslie	1	M	F		Willie Littlehead	L	Cr	Nannie Littlehead	L	Cr
		No. 1 died June 20, 1899										
		Census Card No. 3935, P. O. Bearden, Enrolled June 30, 1905										
10021	1	Harjo, Sallie	4	F	F		Jonas Harjo	L	Cr	Nancy	L	Cr
10022	2	Harjo, Thlucpolikey	2	M	F	Bro	Jonas Harjo	L	Cr	Nancy	L	Cr
		Nos. 1 and 2 reported dead										
		Census Card No. 3936, P. O. Wetumka, Enrolled May 24, 1901										
10023	1	Cowee, Ella	4	F	F		Major Cowee	D	Cr	Nancy Cowee	L	Cr
		No. 1 died September 20, 1899										
		Census Card No. 3937, P. O. Wetumka, Enrolled June 30, 1905										
10024	1	Suder, Choatkey	2	M	F		Robert Sutor	L	Cr	Warlesee	L	Cr
		No. 1 died April 1899										
		Census Card No. 3938, P. O. Hanna, Enrolled June 30, 1905										
10025	1	Jackson, Simon	18	M	F		Helis Jackson	D	Cr	Jane Jackson	D	Cr
		Census Card No. 3939, P. O. Bristow, Enrolled June 30, 1905										
10026	1	Crow, Sina	20	F	F		Hokoletche	D	Cr	Fannie Crow(Ahlaco-honney)	L	Cr
10027	2	Crow, Susie	1	F	F	D	Kernal Jack	L	Cr	Fannie Crow	L	Cr
		No. 1 died August 15, 1899. No. 2 died September 19, 1899.										
		Census Card No. 3940, P. O. Carson, Enrolled June 30, 1905										
10028	1	Gooden, Hoplin	50	M	F		Kamamee	D	Cr	Hannah Jones	L	Cr
		No. 1 died December 18, 1900										
		Census Card No. 3941, P. O. McAlester, Enrolled June 30, 1905										
10029	1	Owen, Clarence	1	M	1/8		Chauncey A. Owen	L	Non	Martha Owen	L	Cr
		No. 1 died August 24, 1899										
		Census Card No. 3942, P. O. Welty, Enrolled March 27, 1901										
10030	1	Fixico, Susan		F	F		Sohsuka or Sudcharkey	D	Cr	Amoge or Millie	D	Cr
10031	2	Foster, George	50	M	F	Cou	Sarfarsody Foster	D	Cr	Nancy	D	Cr
10032	3	Fixico, Hully	25	M	F	S	Neha Fixico	L	Cr	No. 1	L	Cr
10033	4	Fixico, Cheparney	20	M	F	S	Neha Fixico	L	Cr	No. 1	L	Cr
10034	5	Fixico, Jenatte	16	F	F		Neha Fixico	L	Cr	No. 1	L	Cr
10035	6	Fixico, Sarna	12	M	F	S	Neha Fixico	L	Cr	No. 1	L	Cr
10036	7	Fixico, Henehoche	9	M	F	S	Neha Fixico	L	Cr	No. 1	L	Cr
10037	8	Fixico, Mina	14	F	F		Neha Fixico	L	Cr	No. 1	L	Cr
10038	9	Sudcharkey, Sampson		M	F	Bro	Sohsuka Sudcharkey	D	Cr	Kidey	D	Cr
		No. 4 died 1903. No. 2 died November 27, 1904. No. 1 died November 24, 1904. No. 5 died December 1899. No. 8 died July 1903. No. 9, September 1905.										
		Census Card No. 3943, P. O. Dustin, Enrolled August 21, 1905										
10039	1	McQueen, Nancy	1	F	F		Willie McQueen	L	Cr	Muna Whitlow	L	Sem
		No. 1 died September 15, 1901										
		Census Card No. 3944, P. O. Eufaula, Enrolled August 21, 1905										
10040	1	Sulphur, Hattie	4	F	F		James Sulphur	L	Cr	Kizzie Sulphur	L	Cr
		Census Card No. 3945, P. O. Okemah, Enrolled August 21, 1905										
10041	1	Thluppa or Thloppie	15	M	F		Cho. Fixico	D	Cr	Checowee (Sukie)	D	Cr
		No. 1 died October 1899										
		Census Card No. 3946, P. O. Jenks, Enrolled July 9, 1903										
10042	1	Adkins, Richard	52	M	1/2		Thomas Adkins	D	Cr	Nellie Marshall	D	Cr
10043	2	Adkins, Nat	11	M	1/4		No. 1	L	Cr	Sallie Adkins	L	Non
		Census Card No. 3947, P. O. Boley, Enrolled August 21, 1905										
10044	1	Stevens, Sarah	38	F	1/2		Wiley McGilbra	D	Cr	Susie McGilbra	D	Cr
10045	2	Stevens, Wiley	7	M	1/4		William Stevens	?	Non	No. 1	L	Cr
10046	3	Stevens, Mose	5	M	1/4		William Stevens	?	Non	No. 1	L	Cr
		Census Card No. 3948, P. O. Eufaula, Enrolled November 2, 1905										
10047	1	Hutton, Essie	4	F	1-16		Walter Hutton	D	Cr	Nancy Hutton	L	Non
		Census Card No. 3949, P. O. Bristow, Enrolled November 2, 1905										
10048	1	Long, Ella	1	F	F		Henry Long	L	Cr	Lizzie Long	L	Cr
		No. 1 died October 8, 1899										
		Gen;us Card No. 3950, P. O. Lenora, Enrolled November 2, 1905										
10049	1	Sands, Lena	3	F	F		Phillip Sands	L	Cr	Martha Sands	L	Cr
		No. 1 died December 4, 1904										
		Census Card No. 3951, P. O. Dustin, Enrolled November 2, 1905										
10050	1	Temunthlahpe, Tiger	10	M	F		George Temunthlahpe	L	Cr	Nellie Temunthlahpe	L	Cr
10051	2	Temunthlahpe, Dollie	2	F	F	Sis	George Temunthlahpe	L	Cr	Nellie Temunthlahpe	L	Cr
10052	3	Temunthlahpe, Prince	4	M	F	Bro	George Temunthlahpe	L	Cr	Nellie Temunthlahpe	L	Cr
		No. 2 died about 1901. No. 1 died November 1907. No. 3 died May 1906										
		Census Card No. 3952, P. O. Salt Lake City, Utah, Enrolled December 11, 1905										
10053	1	March, Willie H.	34	M	1-16		A. K. March	D	Non	S. M. Self	D	Cr
10054	2	March, Nicholas	12	M	1-32	Sis	No. 1	L	Cr	Capitola Goosbeck	?	Non
10055	3	March, Gracie	9	F	1-32	D	No. 1	L	Cr	Stella March	?	Non
10056	4	March, Lloyd	6	M	1-32	S	No. 1	L	Cr	Stella March	?	Non
		Census Card No. 3953, P. O. Stidham, Enrolled December 11, 1905										
10057	1	Fox, Jennetty	5	F	F		Jimmie Fox	L	Cr	Addie Fox	L	Cr
		Census Card No. 3954, P. O. Pierce, Enrolled December 11, 1905										
10058	1	Deere, Mindy	8	F	1/2		John Deere	?	Sem	Lizzie Deere	L	Cr
10059	2	Deere, Mary	5	F	1/2	Sis	John Deere	?	Sem	Lizzie Deere	L	Cr

Roll No.	No.	NAME	Age	Sex	Blood	Rel.	NAME OF FATHER	Liv.	Cit.	NAME OF MOTHER	Liv.	Cit.
		Census Card No. 3955, P. O. Crawson, Enrolled December 11, 1905										
10060	1	Francis, Elizabeth	6	F	F		William Francis	L	Cr	Annie Francis	L	Cr
10061	2	Francis, Amos	8	M	F	Bro	William Francis	L	Cr	Annie Francis	L	Cr
		Census Card No. 3956, P. O. Weleetka, Enrolled December 11, 1905										
10062	1	Barnett, Annanias	9	F	⅛		Scipio Barnett	L	Cr	Patsy Barnett	L	Non
		No. 1 died July 26, 1913										
		Census Card No. 3957, P. O. Brush Hill, Enrolled December 11, 1905										
10063	1	Grayson, Johnsgn	1	M	⅝		Robert Grayson	L	Cr	Louisa Grayson	L	Cr
10064	2	Grayson, Annie	1	F	⅝	Sis	Robert Grayson	L	Cr	Louisa Grayson	L	Cr
		No. 1 died February 13, 1899. No. 2 died February 1901										
		Cen;us Card No. 3958, P. O. Henryetta, Enrolled January 29, 1906										
10065	1	Whetstone, Nancy C.	60	F	¼		Unknown	?	?	Unknown	?	?
		No. 1 died January 15, 1900										
		Cen;us Card No. 3959, P. O. Wetumka, Enrolled January 29, 1906										
10066	1	Hill, Nancy	2	F	F		Jesse Hill	L	Cr	Louisa Hill	L	Cr
10067	2	Hill, Amy	1	F	F	Sis	Jesse Hill	L	Cr	Louisa Hill	L	Cr
		No. 1 died September 10, 1899. No. 2 died November 1, 1899										
		Cen;us Card No. 3960, P. O. Henryetta, Enrolled January 29, 1906										
10068	1	Wesley, Cogee	2	F	F		Keeper Wesley	L	Cr	Louisana	L	Cr
		No. 1 died October 26, 1902										
		Census Card No. 3961, P. O. Econtuckka, Enrolled January 29, 1906										
10069	1	Wilson, Nora	22	F	½		Muntloope	D	Cr	Sequannie	D	Shaw
		Census Card No. 3962, P. O. Haskell, Enrolled January 29, 1906										
10070	1	Beams, Jacob	52	M	¼		Mitchell Beams	D	Cr	Becky	D	Cr
		Census Card No. 3963, P. O. Oktaha, Enrolled January 29, 1906										
10071	1	Lewis, Nellie	14	F	F		Louie	D	Cr	Seyahe	D	Cr
		No. 1 died April 25, 1899										
		Census Card No. 3964, P. O. Wewoka, Enrolled January 29, 1906										
10072	1	Wolf, Kimbo	1	F	½		Wallace Wolf	?	Sem	Nancy Wolf	L	Cr
		No. 1 died July 1, 1901										
		Census Card No. 3965, P. O. Hanna, Enrolled January 29, 1906										
10073	1	Red, Leah	2	F	¾		Thomas Red	L	Cr	Martha Red	L	Cr
		No. 1 died August 23										
		Cen;us Card No. 3966, P. O. Okemah, Enrolled January 29, 1906										
10074	1	Chupco, Johnson Taylor	1	M	F		Mistaley Chupco	L	Cr	Nicey Ahfonoke	L	Cr
		No. 1 died about 1901										
		Census Card No. 3967, P. O. Wagoner, Enrolled January 29, 1906										
10075	1	Atkins, William Sherman	38	M	¼		Richard Atkins	D	Cr	Victoria Atkins	D	Non
		No. 1 died January 15, 1904										
		Census Card No. 3968, P. O. Trenton, Enrolled January 29, 1906										
10076	1	Harjo, Mitchell	9	M	F		Marsey Harjo	L	Cr	Kina Harjo	D	Cr
		Census Card No. 3969,										
10077	1	Stricken from roll										
		Census Card No. 3970, P. O. Eufaula, Enrolled January 29, 1906										
10078	1	Sartie	16	M	F		John Chupco	D	Cr	Sallie Jackson	D	Cr
		No. 1 died about 1900										
		Census Card No. 3971, P. O. Okmulgee, Enrolled January 29, 1906										
10079	1	Sneed, John	18	M	3-16		Charley Sneed	L	Cr	Pamina Sneed	L	Non
10080	2	Sneed, Sue Willie	15	F	3-16	Sis	Charley Sneed	L	Cr	Pamina Sneed	L	Non
10081	3	Sneed, Charles, Jr.	13	M	3-16	Bro	Charley Sneed	L	Cr	Pamina Sneed	L	Non
10082	4	Sneed, Ernest	10	M	3-16	Bro	Charley Sneed	L	Cr	Pamina Sneed	L	Non
		Census Card No. 3972, P. O. Wagoner; No. 2 Depew, Enrolled March 29, 1906										
10083	1	Wilson, Mary E.	35	F	⅛		Richard Atkins	?	?	Sallie Atkins	?	Non
10084	2	Winn, Geneva Atkins	31	F	⅛	Sis	Richard Atkins	?	?	Sarah Atkins	?	Non
10085	3	Taborn, Nancy Atkins	29	F	⅛	Sis	Richard Atkins	?	?	Sarah Atkins	?	Non
10086	4	Taborn, Susie Atkins	10	F	1-16	Niece	Calvin Taborn	L	Non	No. 3	L	Cr
		Census Card No. 3973, P. O. Checotah, Enrolled November 22, 1906										
10087	1	Wolf, Bertha	1	F	¼		Oscar Woodley	L	Non	Lucy Snowden	L	Cr
		Illegitimate. No. 1 died October 17, 1900										
		Census Card No. 3974, P. O. Holdenville, Enrolled November 22, 1906										
10088	1	Marshall, Mollie	18	F	F		Ispohoke Harjo	L	Cr	Aggie Marshall	L	Cr
		No. 1 died about 1900										
		Census Card No. 3975, P. O. Arbeka, Enrolled November 22, 1906										
10089	1	Heneha, Osa	25	M	F		Sinlupke	D	Cr	Miley	D	Cr
		Census Card No. 3976, P. O. Little, Enrolled November 22, 1906										
10090	1	Joseph, Jemima	6	F	¾		George Joseph	D	Cr	Cindy Joseph	L	Sem
		Census Card No. 3977, P. O. Wetumka, Enrolled November 22, 1906										
10091	1	Lakey, Jimmie	1	M	F		Thomas Lakey	D	Cr	Mollie Lakey	D	Cr
		No. 1 died February 1900										
		Census Card No. 3978, P. O. Kellyville, Enrolled November 22, 1906										
10092	1	Sewell, Robert	46	M	⅜		Ben Sewell	D	Cr	Buffnee (or)Parthenia	D	Cr
		Census Card No. 3979, P. O. Yeager, Enrolled December 14, 1906										
10093	1	Harjo, Mona	5	F	F		Lumka Harjo	L	Cr	Kissie Harjo	L	Cr
		Census Card No. 3980, P. O. Dustin, Enrolled January 8, 1907										
10094	1	Riley, Unus	5	M	⅝		William Riley	L	Sem	Annie Riley	L	Cr
		No. 1 died October 15, 1906										
		Census Card No. 3981, P. O. Senora, Enrolled March 11, 1903										
10095	1	Arbuckle, Salinee	10	F	F		Shawnee Jacob	L	Cr	Hepsey Arbuckle	L	Cr

Roll No.	No.	NAME	Age	Sex	Blood	Rel.	NAME OF FATHER	Liv.	Cit.	NAME OF MOTHER	Liv.	Cit.
		Census Card No. 3982, P. O. Eufaula, Enrolled January 15, 1907										
10096	1	Thomas, Emily	6	F	¾		Hardy Thomas	L	Cr	Lydia Thomas	L	Cr
		Census Card No. 3983, P. O. Eufaula, Enrolled January 16, 1907										
10097	1	Canawa, Missie	50	F	F		Unknown	?	Cr	Unknown	?	Cr
10098	2	Tiger, Louisa	25	F	F	D	Robert Canawa	D	Cr	No. 1	L	Cr
10099	3	Tiger, Anna	23	F	F	D	Robert Canawa	D	Cr	No. 1	L	Cr
		No. 1 died November 10, 1906										
		Census Card No. 3984, P. O. Shawnee, Enrolled January 18, 1907										
10100	1	Starr, Cora Ellis	40	F	¼		Coblar	?	Shaw	Jannie Ellis	D	Cr
10101	2	Starr, Henry	17	M	⅛	S	Charley Star	?	Shaw	No. 1	L	Cr
10102	3	Starr, Annie	12	F	⅛	D	Charley Star	?	Shaw	No. 1	L	Cr
10103	4	Starr, Gertrude	9	F	⅛	D	Charley Star	?	Shaw	No. 1	L	Cr
		Census Card No. 3985, P. O. Oktaha, Enrolled January 25, 1907										
10104	1	Bullet, Sam	3	M	F		James Bullet	L	Cr	Lucy Bullet	L	Cr
		No. 1 died April 1901										
		Census Card No. 3986, P. O. Earlsboro, Enrolled January 25, 1907										
10105	1	Harjo, Lizzie	55	F	F		Unknown	?	Cr	Unknown	?	Cr
		No. 1 died qbout 1900										
		Census Card No. 3987, P. O. Bearden, Enrolled January 28, 1907										
10106	1	Anderson, Thomas	39	M	F		Tom Anderson	D	Cr	Louena Chief	?	Chic
		No. 1 died about 1900										
		Census Card No. 3988, P. O. Braggs, Enrolled January 29, 1907										
10107	1	Micco, Mullie	38	M	F		Hobeth Harjo	D	Cr	Unknown	D	Cr
		No. 1 died about 1900										
		Census Card No. 3989, P. O. Henryetta, Enrolled January 29, 1907										
10108	1	Harjo, Maria	31	F	F		Unknown	D	Cr	Unknown	D	Cr
10109	2	Harjo, Jessie	11	M	F	S	Nathan Harjo	D	Sem	No. 1	L	Cr
		No. 1 died December 26, 1911										
		Census Card No. 3990, P. O. Mellette, Enrolled February 1, 1907										
10110	1	Harjo, Rina	30	F	F		George Holupe	L	Cr	Katie	D	Cr
10111	2	Harjo, Chuckaleesa	8	M	F	S	Jack Harjo	L	Cr	No. 1	L	Cr
		No. 1 died January 5, 1911										
		Census Card No. 3991, P. O. Bristow, Enrolled February 1, 1907										
10112	1	Tiger, He-con-con-thla	13	M	F		Jim Tiger	L	Cr	Yahsahcocontany	D	Cr
		Census Card No. 3992, P. O. Wealaka, Enrolled February 5, 1907										
10113	1	Deere, Ruth	5 mo	F	⅞		Tecumseh Deere	L	Cr	Nancy Deere	L	Cr
		No. 1 died April 23, 1899										
		Census Card No. 3993, P. O. Sapulpa, Enrolled February 4, 1907										
10114	1	Dickson, Anna	44	F	F		Unknown	?	Cr	Unknown	?	Cr
		No. 1 died about 1900										
		Census Card No. 3994, P. O. Bixby, Enrolled February 5, 1907										
10115	1	Rolland, Rufus	1	M	F		Master Rolland	L	Cr	Annie Rolland	L	Cr
		No. 1 died about 1900										
		Census Card No. 3995, P. O. Hanna, Enrolled February 8, 1907										
10116	1	Bullett, Jemima	10	F	½		John Bullett	L	Cr	Zoye Pullett	?	Non
		Census Card No. 3996, P. O. Hoffman, Enrolled February 21, 1907										
10117	1	Litia	50	F	F		Unknown	?	Cr	Unknown	?	Cr
		Above No. 1 also appears on Card No. 4013 under same number. In published Government Index Card No. 3996 does not appear. No. 1 died October 1901										
		Census Card No. 3997, P. O. Bryant, Enrolled February 15, 1907										
10141	1	Hill, Jesse	6	M	⅞		Charley Hill	L	Cr	Herlerthoye King	L	Cr
		Illegitimate. No. 1 died November 1906										
		Census Card No. 3998, P. O. Little, Enrolled February 15, 1907										
10142	1	Bearhead, Yanah	11	F	F		Moser Bearhead	?	Sem	Nancy Bearhead	L	Cr
10143	2	Bearhead, Mollie	9	F	F		Moser Bearhead	?	Sem	Nancy Bearhead	L	Cr
		No. 2 died August 15, 1907. No. 1 possible duplicate of No. 8117										
		Census Card No. 3999, P. O. Eufaula, Enrolled February 15, 1907										
10144	1	Cato, Rhoda	8	F	F		Ben Cato	L	Cr	Lydia Bear	L	Cr
		Census Card No. 4000, P. O. Mellette, Enrolled February 15, 1907										
10145	1	Roberts, Millie	6	F	F		Josie Roberts	L	Cr	Mahala Roberts	L	Cr
		Census Card No. 4001, P. O. Morse, Enrolled February 15, 1907										
10146	1	Harjoche, Lottie	7	F	F		Yarteka Harjoche	L	Cr	Losana Harjoche	L	Cr
		Census Card No. 4002, P. O. Eufaula, Enrolled February 15, 1907										
10147	1	Scott, Setepakee	6	F	F		Edward Scott	L	Cr	Tena Scott.	L	Cr
		Census Card No. 4003, P. O. Mellette, Enrolled February 18, 1907										
10148	1	Benton, Daniel	6	M	¾		Robert Benton	L	Cr	Jennie Benton	L	Cr
		Census Card No. 4004, P. O. Kellyville, Enrolled February 20, 1907										
10149	1	Ralston, Nancy	70	F	½		Unknown	?	Non	Unknown	?	Cr
10150	2	Ralston, Allen W.	52	M	¼	S	Joseph Ralston	?	Non	No. 1	L	Cr
10151	3	Ralston, Charles C.	26	M	¼	S	Joseph Ralston	?	Non	No. 1	L	Cr
		No. 1 died December 17, 1908										
		Census Card No. 4005, P. O. Sapulpa, Enrolled February 20, 1907										
10152	1	Ralston, Benjamin F.	49	M	¼		Joseph Ralston	?	Non	Nancy Ralston	L	Cr
10153	2	Ralston, Joseph W.	24	M	⅛	S	No. 1	L	Cr	Sarah Emarthla	?	Non
10154	3	Ralston, Benjamin F. Jr.	18	M	⅛	S	No. 1	L	Cr	Sarah Emarthla	?	Non
10155	4	Ralston, Roy P.	16	M	⅛	S	No. 1	L	Cr	Sarah Emarthla	?	Non
10156	5	Ralston, Mary B.	12	F	1-16	D	No. 1	L	Cr	Sarah Emarthla	?	Non
10157	6	Ralston, John F.	9	M	⅛	S	No. 1	L	Cr	Sarah Emarthla	?	Non
10158	7	Ralston, Ella E.	7	F	⅛	D	No. 1	L	Cr	Sarah Emarthla	?	Non
		No. 5 died June 22, 1901										

Rol No.	No.	NAME	Age	Sex	Blood	Rel.	NAME OF FATHER	Liv.	Cit.	NAME OF MOTHER	Liv.	Cit.
		Census Card No. 4006, P. O. Sapulpa, Enrolled February 20, 1907										
10159	1	Stanley, Mattie E.	36	F	¼		Joseph Ralston	?	Non	Nancy Ralston	L	Cr
10160	2	Stanley, Earl A.	15	M	⅛	S	Charles Stanley	?	Non	No. 1	L	Cr
10161	3	Stanley, Pearl A.	13	F	⅛	D	Charles Stanley	?	Non	No. 1	L	Cr
10162	4	Stanley, Joseph C.	12	M	⅛	S	Charles Stanley	?	Non	No. 1	L	Cr
10163	5	Stanley, Pleasant	6	F	⅛	D	Charles Stanley	?	Non	No. 1	L	Cr
		Census Card No. 4007, P. O. Sapulpa, Enrolled February 20, 1907										
10164	1	Ralston, John F.	28	M	¼		Joseph Ralston	?	Non	Nancy Ralston	L	
10165	2	Ralston, Sadie Pearl	7	F	⅛		No. 1	L	Cr	Florence Ralston	?	Non
10166	3	Ralston, Nancy Jane	3mo	F	⅛		No. 1	L	Cr	Florence Ralston	?	Non
		No. 3 died August 1, 1900										
		Census Card No. 4008, P. O. Sapulpa, Enrolled Febraury 20, 1907										
10167	1	Shreffner, Mary E.	44	F	¼		Joseph Ralston	?	Non	Nancy Ralston	L	Cr
10168	2	Shreffner, Joseph W.	26	M	⅛		David Shreffner	?	Non	No. 1	L	Cr
10169	3	Shreffner, David W.	20	M	⅛		David Shreffner	?	Non	No. 1	L	Cr
		Census Card No. 4009, P. O. Glenco; Nos. 1, 2, 3 and 4, Sapulpa, Enrolled February 20, 1907										
10170	1	Harriott, Nettie	45	F	¼		Joseph Ralston	?	Non	Nancy Ralston	L	Cr
10171	2	Harriott, Amos W.	22	M	⅛	S	John F. Harriott	?	Non	No. 1	L	Cr
10172	3	Harriott, Louisa M.	16	F	⅛	D	John F. Harriott	?	Non	No. 1	L	Cr
10173	4	Harriott, Joseph F.	14	M	⅛	S	John F. Harriott	?	Non	No. 1	L	Cr
10174	5	Terry, Annettie Josephine	25	F	⅛	D	John F. Harriott	?	Non	No. 1	L	Cr
		Census Card No. 4010, P. O. Sapulpa, Enrolled February 20, 1907										
10175	1	Allen, Myrtle May	26	F	⅛		David Shreffner	?	Non	Mary E. Shreffner	L	Cr
10176	2	Allen, Rosette	8	F	1-16	D	Unknown	?	Non	No. 1	L	Cr
		Census Card No. 4011, P. O. Bearden, Enrolled February 20, 1907										
10177	1	Cain, Legey	2	F	F		Daniel Cain	L	Cr	Nicey Cain	L	Cr
10178	2	Cain, Marsey	1	M	F	Sis	Daniel Cain	L	Cr	Nicey Cain	L	Cr
		No. 1 died 1899. No. 2 died 1899										
		Census Card No. 4012, P. O. Hanna, Enrolled April 24, 1905										
10179	1	Lindsey Tosa	8	F	F		Phillip Lindsey	L	Cr	Silla Lindsey	L	Cr
		Census Card No. 4013, P. O. Sapulpa, Enrolled February 14, 1907										
10180	1	Tom, Louanna	6	F	F		Euchee Tom	L	Cr	Lucy Tom	L	Cr
10117	2	Litia	50	F	F	None	Unknown	?	Cr	Unknown	?	Cr
		Census Card No. 4014, P. O. Bunch, Enrolled February 21, 1907										
10181	1	Alexander	34	M	F		Isaac	D	Cr	Unknown	D	Cr
		No. 1 died about 1903										
		Census Card No. 4015, P. O. Holdenville, Enrolled February 25, 1907										
10118	1	Harjo, Pen	8	M	F		Billy Harjo	?	Sem	Docher Harjo	L	Cr
		Census Card No. 4016, P. O. Muskogee, Enrolled February 25, 1907										
10119	1	Davis, Ollie	1	M	¼		Eli Davis	L	Cr	Lucy Thomas	L	Non
		No. 1 died June 6, 1903										
		Census Card No. 4017, P. O. Morse, Enrolled February 25, 1907										
10120	1	Deer, Thomas	2	M	F		Joe Deer	L	Cr	Yarnar Deer	L	Cr
		No. 1 died Januafy 8, 1903										
		Census Card No. 4018, P. O. Holdenville, Enrolled February 25, 1907										
10121	1	Nelson, William	3	M	F		Amos Nelson	L	Cr	Sollie Nelson	L	Cr
		No. 1 died June 1, 1902										
		Census Card No. 4019, P. O. Beggs, Enrolled May 29, 1902										
10122	1	Parker, Martha	70	F	F		Isaac Guess	D	Cr	Millie Guess	?	Cr
		No. 1 died October 18, 1905										
		Census Card No. 4020, P. O. Russelville, Enrolled February 25, 1907										
10123	1	Henry, Edmond	24	M	¼		Pat Henry	D	Cr	Martha Henry	D	Cr
		No. 1 died December 22, 1900										
		Census Card No. 4021, P. O. Holdenville, Enrolled February 27, 1907										
10124	1	Fish, John	8	M	F		Wiley Fish	L	Cr	Hettie Fish	L	Cr
		Census Card No. 4022, P. O. Oktaha, Enrolled February 27, 1907										
10125	1	Longbread, Nannie	22	F	F		James Bullet	?	Cr	Tagee	?	Cr
10126	2	Logbread, Lyddie	20	F	F	Sis	James Bullet	?	Cr	Tagee	?	Cr
		Census Card No. 4023, P. O. Bunch, Enrolled February 27, 1907										
10127	1	Honechike	65	F	F		Unknown	?	Cr	Unknown	?	Cr
10128	2	Marley	25	F	F	D	Unknown	?	Cr	Unknown	?	Cr
10129	3	Tahkee	23	F	F	D	Unknown	?	Cr	Unknown	?	Cr
10130	4	Thomas	18	M	F	D	Unknown	?	Cr	Unknown	?	Cr
		No. 3 probably duplicate of Cherokee Indian Enrollment No. 18654 as Lizzie Kingfisher										
		Census Card No. 4024, P. O. Braggs; No. 1, Okemah, Enrolled February 27, 1907										
10131	1	Arch, Sarwike	30	M	F		Heneha Chupco	D	Cr	Seneche	D	Cr
10132	2	Arch, John	65	M	F	F	Unknown	?	Cr	Unknown	?	Cr
10133	3	Arch, Dick	27	M	F	Bro	No. 2	L	Cr	Susie	D	Cr
10134	4	Arch, Hokte	25	F	F	Sis	No. 2	L	Cr	Seneche	D	Cr
10135	5	Rabbit, Jack	28	M	F	Cou	Sleeping Rabbit	?	Cher	Sallie Rabbit	?	Cr
10136	6	Rabbit, Sissie	26	F	F	Cou	Sleeping Rabbit	?	Cher	Sallie Rabbit	?	Cr
		No. 6 died 1910. No. 5 died March 1905. No. 2 died November 16, 1909. No. 4 died April 1, 1906										
		Information regarding parentage of above enrolled, does not appear on Census Card, but was secured by examination of testimony taken at application for enrollment.										
		Census Card No. 4025, P. O. Bristow, Enrolled February 27, 1907										
10137	1	Looma	6	M	F		Narpiyecher	L	Cr	Lucy	L	Sem

221

Roll No.	No.	NAME	Age	Sex	Blood	Rel.	NAME OF FATHER	Liv.	Cit.	NAME OF MOTHER	Liv.	Cit.
		Census Card No. 4026, P. O. Bunch, Enrolled February 28, 1907										
10138	1	Simmons, John (or Tissie)	19	M	F							
10139	2	Simmons, George (or Hothkoper or Hoe Kapo)	28	M	F							
10140	3	Lydia	60	F	F							
		Note.—Further testimony regarding parentage of above enrolled does not show, and upon research none can be found.										
		Census Card No. 4015, P. O. Sapulpa, Enrolled August 1, 1914										
10182	1	Allen, Wootsey	8	F	1-16		Jess Allen	L	Non	Myrtle May Allen	L	Cr
		Census Card No. 4016, P. O. Bacone, Enrolled August 1, 1914										
10183	1	Archibald or Narchubby Smedlon	13	M	½		Allen Archiblad or Narchubby or Chubby	D	Cher	Sallie Archibald or Narchubby	D	Cr
10184	2	Archibald or Narchubby, Cain	11	M	½	Bro	Allen Archibald	D	Cher	Sallie Archibald	D	Cr
10185	3	Archibald or Narchubby, Abel	11	M	½	Bro	Allen Archibald	D	Cher	Sallie Archibald	D	Cr
10186	4	Archibald or Narchubby, Adda	10	F	½	Sis	Whiteman	?	Non	Szallie Archibald	D	C r
		Census Card No. 4017, P. O. Eufaula, Enrolled August 1, 1914										
10187	1	Ashbury, Coweescoowee	12	M	F		Thomas Ashbury	L	Cr	Sallie Johnson	L	Cr
		Census Card No. 4018, P. O. Wetumka, Enrolled August 1, 1914										
10188	1	Barnett, Peggy	60	F	F		Unknown	?	Cr	Unknown	?	Cr
		No. 1 died July 3, 1899										
		Census Card No. 4019, P. O. Tuskegee, Enrolled August 1, 1914										
10189	1	Bear, Lucinda	8	F	F		Marche Bear	L	Cr	Nitty Marshall	L	Cr
		Census Card No. 4020, P. O. Eufaula, Enrolled August 1, 1914										
10190	1	Billy, Chotkey	10	F	F		Lumber Billy	L	Cr	Nancy Billy	D	Cr
		No. 1 died January 17, 1910										
		Census Card No. 4021, P. O. Wwleetka, Enrolled August 1, 1914										
10191	1	Birdcreek, Lewis	13	M	⅞		Jesse Birdcreek	L	Cr	Mandy Birdcreek	L	Cr
		Census Card No. 4022, Enrolled August 1, 1914										
10192	1	Brown, Hannah	9	F	F		Cotenney Brown	D	Cr	Yacancothla Brown	D	Cr
		Census Card No. 4023, P. O. Mellette, Enrolled August 1, 1914										
10193	1	Brown, Sam	8	M	F		Wilson Brown	L	Cr	Sallie Tiger	L	Cr
		Census Card No. 4024, P. O. Weleetka, Enrolled August 1, 1914										
10194	1	Chupco, Mollie	14	F	⅝		Johnny Chupco	D	Sem	Louisa Jack	L	Cr
		Census Card No. 4025, P. O. Eufaula, Enrolled August 1, 1914										
10195	1	Cosar, Susie	16	F	F		George Cosar	L	Cr	Lucinda Cosar	L	Cr
		Census Card No. 4026, P. O. Lenna, Enrolled August 1, 1914										
10196	1	Downing, Ambrose	24	M	⅛		Barney Downing	D	Cr	Early Downing	D	Non
		Census Card No. 4027, P. O. Wetumka, Enrolled August 1, 1914										
10197	1	Fish, Eli	18	M	F		Wilyumka	L	Cr	Sylla	L	Cr
		Census Card No. 4028, P. O. Dustin, Enrolled August 1, 1914										
10198	1	Fish, Willie	9	M	⅞		Elmer Fish	L	Cr	Millie Harper	L	Cr
		Census Card No. 4029, P. O. Preston, Enrolled August 1, 1914										
10199	1	Foster, Sallie	2	F	F		Noah Foster	L	Cr	Jennette Foster	L	Cr
		Census Card No. 4030, P. O. Mellette, Enrolled August 1, 1914										
10200	1	Givens, Luther	5	M	F		Choctaw Givens	L	Cr	Kizzie Givens	L	Cr
		No. 1 died September 1, 1910										
		Census Card No. 4031, P. O. Hanna, Enrolled August 1, 1914										
10201	1	Green, Jeanetta	21	F	F		Bennie Green	D	Cr	Lucy	?	Cr
10202	2	Green, Siah	18	M	F	Bro	Bennie Green	D	Cr	Lucy	?	Cr
		Census Card No. 4032, P. O. Okemah, Enrolled August 1, 1914										
10203	1	Johnson, Addie	11	F	F		Colberson W. Johnson	L	Cr	Millie Johnson	L	Cr
		No. 1 died October 1910										
		Census Card No. 4033, P. O. Henryetta, Enrolled August 1, 1914										
10204	1	Jones, Martha	9	F	F		Sulloly Jones	?	Cr	Leah Jones	?	Cr
		Census Card No. 4034, P. O. Wetumka, Enrolled August 1, 1914										
10205	1	Lasley, Sulphur	14	M	F		Colbert Lasley	D	Cr	Winey Lasley	L	Cr
		Census Card No. 4035, P. O. Wetumka, Enrolled August 1, 1914										
10206	1	Lasley, Tobe	31	M	F		Wiley Lasley	D	Cr	Linoche	D	Cr
		Census Card No. 4036, P. O. Eufaula, Enrolled August 1, 1914										
10207	1	Lasley, Tustunnuga	16	M	F		Alex Lasley	D	Cr	Jeanetta Hill	L	Cr
		Census Card No. 4037, P. O. Eufaula, Enrolled August 1, 1914										
10208	1	Lewis, Sampson	24	M	F		Seaborn Lewis	D	Cr	Kashockle	D	Cr
		Census Card No. 4038, P. O. Bristow, Enrolled August 1, 1914										
10209	1	Long, Lucy	11	F	F		George Long	L	Cr	Ekoconney	D	Cr
		Census Card No. 4039, P. O. Gore, Enrolled August 1, 1914										
10210	1	Mully, Jennie	63	F	F		Watho Harjo	D	Cr	Unknown	?	Cr
10211	2	Mully, Mitchell	30	M	F	S	Mullie Micco	D	Cr	No. 1	L	Cr
10212	3	Mully, Barney	32	M	F	S	Mullie Micco	D	Cr	No. 1	L	Cr
10213	4	Mully, Simon	23	M	F	S	Mullie Micco	D	Cr	No. 1	L	Cr
10214	5	Mully, Katie	9	F	½	GrD	No. 3	L	Cr	Fannie Mully	?	Cher
		No. 2 died 1909. No. 4 died 1909.										
		Census Card No. 4040, P. O. Eufaula, Enrolled August 1, 1914										
10215	1	Perry, James	38	M	½		Gibson Perry	D	Chic	Cunnussa	D	Cr
10216	2	Perry, Susie	9	F	¾		Gibson Perry	D	Chic	Peggy Henry	D	Cr

Census Card No. 4041, P. O. Eufaula, Enrolled August 1, 1914

Roll No.	No.	NAME	Age	Sex	Blood	Rel.	NAME OF FATHER	Liv.	Cit.	NAME OF MOTHER	Liv.	Cit.
10217	1	Polk, Siah	15	M	F		Daniel W. Polk	L	Cr	Annie Billy	L	Cr

Census Card No. 4042, P. O. Hanna, Enrolled August 1, 1914

10218	1	Proctor, Freeman	8	M	F		Lumber Proctor	L	Cr	Lena Proctor	L	Cr

Census Card No. 4043, P. O. Dustin, Enrolled August 1, 1914

10219	1	Proctor, Maxie	6	M	F		Hopiyoche	L	Cr	Slumber	L	Cr
		No. 1 died 1901										

Census Card No. 4044, P. O. Eufaula, Enrolled August 1, 1914

10220	1	Raiford, Washington	3	M	3/8		Ossie Raiford	L	Cr	Selina Raiford	D	Sem
		No. 1 died December 25, 1908										

Census Card No. 4045, P. O. Sapulpa, Enrolled August 1, 1914

10221	1	Ralston, Elva Leona	15	F	1/8		Benjamin F. Ralston	L	Cr	Maggie Ralston	D	Non

Census Card No. 4046, P. O. Kellyville, Enrolled August 1, 1914

10222	1	Ralston, Fred E.	11	M	1/8		John F. Ralston	L	Cr	F. M. Ralston	L	Non
10223	2	Ralston, Jeannetta Louise	8	F	1/8	Sis	John F. Ralston	L	Cr	F. M. Falston	L	Non

Census Card No. 4047, P. O. Henryetta, Enrolled August 1, 1914

10224	1	Riley, Washie	13	M	F		Cheesie Riley	D	Cr	Maley Riley	D	Cr

Census Card No. 4048, P. O. Henryetta, Enrolled August 1, 1914

10225	1	Scott, Mary	18	F	F		Haney Scott	L	Cr	Narchker Haney	L	Cr

Census Card No. 4049, P. O. Braggs, Enrolled August 1, 1914

10226	1	Screechowl, Annie	39	F	F		Tumker	?	Cr	Annie	?	Cr
10227	2	Screechowl, Concharty Micco	10	M	F	S	Thompson Screechowl	D	Cher	No. 1	L	Cr
		No. 1 died August 28, 1913										

Census Card No. 4050, P. O. Hanna, Enrolled August 1, 1914

10228	1	Simmons, Samuel	15	M	F		Charley Simmons	L	Cr	Dochee Simmons	L	Cr
10229	2	Simmons, Della	12	F	F	Sis	Charley Simmons	L	Cr	Dochee Simmons	L	Cr
10230	3	Simmons, Mandy	11	F	F	Sis	Charley Simmons	L	Cr	Dochee Simmons	L	Cr

Census Card No. 4051, P. O. Hanna, Enrolled August 1, 1914

10231	1	Simpson, George	13	M	F		Shelby Simpson	L	Cr	Lucy Simpson	?	Cr
10232	2	Simpson, Nettie	12	F	F	Sis	Shelby Simpson	L	Cr	Lucy Simpson	?	Cr
10233	3	Simpson, Mallie	10	F	F	Sis	Shelby Simpson	L	Cr	Lucy Simpson	?	Cr
10234	4	Simpson, Melissa	1	F	F	Sis	Shelby Simposn	L	Cr	Lucy Simpson	?	Cr
		No. 4 died April 9, 1907										

Census Card No. 4052, P. O. Kellyville, Enrolled August 1, 1914

10235	1	Stanley, Wootsey	9	F	1/8		Chas. A. Stanley	?	Non	Mattie E. Stanley	L	Cr

Census Card No. 4053, P. O. Salem, Enrolled August 1, 1914

10236	1	Starr, Mollie	25	F	F		Robert Starr	D	Cr	Sarne Starr	D	Cr
		No. 1 died December 30, 1906										

Census Card No. 4054, P. O. Sapulpa, Enrolled August 1, 1914

10237	1	Terry, Alpha Omega	11	M	1-16		William Terry	?	Non	A. J. Terry	L	Cr
10238	2	Terry, Albert	10	M	1-16	Ero	William Terry	?	Non	A. J. Terry	L	Cr

Census Card No. 4055, P. O. Dustin, Enrolled August 1, 1914

10239	1	Wattie, Albert Willie	13	M	F		Thomas Wattie	D	Cr	Polly	D	Cr

Census Card No. 4056, P. O. Okemah, Enrolled August 1, 1914

10240	1	Wesley, Ada	13	F	F		Victor Wesley	D	Cr	Elsie Wesley	L	Cr

Census Card No. 4057, P. O. Henryetta, Enrolled August 1, 1914

10241	1	West, Nellie	13	F	F		Lumsey West	L	Cr	Emma Hill	L	Cr

Census Card No. 4058, P. O. Hanna, Enrolled August 1, 1914

10242	1	White, Edmund	17	M	F		George White	L	Cr	Katie White	?	Cr

Census Card No. 4059, P. O. Hanna, Enrolled August 1, 1914

10243	1	Byrd, Mattie	15	F	F		Thomas Byrd	D	Cr	Dudie Byrd	L	Cr

ABSTRACT

OF

NEW BORN CREEK CENSUS CARDS

Enrolled under Act of March 3, 1905

In the preparation of these New Born and Minor Creek rolls the Dawes Commission used a card somewhat different from the card used in making the original roll, and in this Abstract I have omitted three of the column headings which I used in the Abstract of the original cards, to-wit:—I have omitted the column under the heading "Relationship to No. 1." This because of the fact that all of the citizens enrolled on these two rolls are children born since April 1st, 1899, and their parents and older brothers and sisters would not appear on this roll.

I have omitted also the column under the heading "Living" after the name of the father. Also the column under the heading "Living" after the name of the mother. In place of these two columns I have added two others. Under the column heading in each case "Roll No." This means that in these columns will be given the "Roll No." of the father, or of the mother, in case either be an enrolled citizen of the Creek Nation of Indians.

It is possibly true that some who are enrolled as Creek citizens have not a roll number in these columns, if so, we have been unable to so identify them, and the records in the office of the Superintendent does not enlighten us.

You will also note another change in these cards, in this, where the date of enrollment is given on the preceeding cards the date of birth of the citizen is given on the following New Born and Minor Creek Cards.

In other particulars the explanations given preceeding the Abstract of the original cards are applicable to these cards.

The New Borns and Minors which are enrolled on the two following rolls do not participate in the Creek Equalization payment, therefor, no proofs of death are now being taken of those dead, and as a result we note only those shown to be dead by the Census Cards.

NEW BORN CREEK CENSUS CARDS

Enrolled under Act of March 3, 1905

Roll No.	No.	NAME	Age	Sex	Blood	NAME OF FATHER	Roll No.	Cit.	NAME OF MOTHER	Roll No.	Cit.
	New Born Census Card No. 1, P. O. Muskogee, Date of Birth June 22, 1904										
1	1	McDermott, Helen	1	F	½	Jesse McDermott	1263	Cr	Alice McDermott		Non
		Died June 19, 1906									
	New Born Census Card No. 2, P. O. Checotah, Date of Birth No. 1, March 25, 1904; No. 2, August 26, 1902										
2	1	Stidham, Thomas Edward	1	M	⅛	G. W. Stidham, Sr.	2259	Cr	Jennie Stidham		Non
3	2	Stidham, Cleo	3	F	⅛	G. W. Stidham, Sr.	2259	Cr	Jennie Stidham		Non
	New Born Census Card No. 3, P. O. Muskogee, Date of Birth February 6, 1902										
4	1	Posey, Wynema Torrans	3	F	¼	Alexander S. Posey	3671	Cr	Minnie Posey		Non
	New Born Census Card No. 6, P. O. Muskogee, Date of Birth July 6, 1903										
5	1	Farmer, Natalie	3	F	¼	Nathan K. Farmer		Non	Liza Farmer	1885	Cr
	New Born Census Card No. 7, P. O. Muskogee, Date of Birth October 2, 1902										
6	1	Harris, Charlie	2	M	1-16	William R. Harris	4480	Cr	Lela Harris		Non
	New Born Census Card No. 8, P. O. Muskogee, Date of Birth July 17, 1902										
7	1	Porter, Mildred	3	F	¼	William A. Porter	1527	Cr	Mildred M. Porter		Non
	New Born Census Card No. 9, P. O. Natura, Date of Birth October 13, 1902										
8	1	Bell, Agnes	3	F	⅞	James Bell	2894	Cr	Emma Bell	1229	Cr
	New Born Census Card No. 10, P. O. Natura, Date of Birth No. 1, May 21, 1902; No. 2, March 13, 1905										
9	1	Roberts, Tura E.	3	F	⅛	William J. Roberts	1708	Cr	Annie A. Roberts		Non
10	2	Roberts, Walter H.	1	M	⅛	William J. Roberts	1708	Cr	Annie A. Roberts		Non
		No. 2 died February 22, 1904									
	New Born Census Card No. 12, P. O. Coweta, Date of Birth July 26, 1903										
11	1	Orcutt, Guy B.	2	M	⅛	A. D. Orcutt		Non	Adaline Ocrutt	1808	Cr
	New Born Census Card No. 15, P. O. Sapulpa, Date of Birth August 7, 1901										
12	1	Bruner, J. Esther	4	F	½	Joseph Bruner	3142	Cr	Margaret Bruner		Non
	New Born Census Card No. 17, P. O. Checotah, Date of Birth No. 1, May 2, 1902; No. 2, December 8, 1903; No. 3, February 11, 1905										
13	1	Baughman, Jefferson Enel	3	M	⅛	Bert Baughman		Non	M. L. Baughman	515	Cr
14	2	Baughman, Gay L.	1	M	⅛	Bert Baughman		Non	M. L. Baughman	515	Cr
15	3	Baughman, Ella May	1	F	⅛	Bert Baughman		Non	M. L. Baughman	515	Cr
	New Born Census Card No. 24, P. O. Eufaula, Date of Birth December 9, 1904										
16	1	Saltsman, Gordon P.	1	M	1-64	E. F. Saltsman		Non	Mary U. Saltsman	6313	Cr
	New Born Census Card No. 28, P. O. Eufaula, Date of Birth December 15, 1904										
17	1	McCombs, Nathaniel N.	1	M	⅝	W. McCombs, Jr.	5634	Cr	Alice L. McCombs	1651	Cr
	New Born Census Card No. 29, P. O. Fry, Date of Birth April 29, 1904										
18	1	Haikey, Bertha	1	F	F	Ben Haikey, Jr.	947	Cr	Louisa Haikey	956	Cr
	New Born Census Card No. 31, P. O. Broken Arrow, Date of Birth October 2, 1904										
19	1	Haikey, Sissie	1	F	F	Ben Haikey	950	Cr	Louisa Haikey	2197	Cr
		Died in January 1903									
	New Born Census Card No. 32, P. O. Eufaula, Date of Birth January 3, 1903										
20	1	Phillips, Lydia	2	F	F	Johnson Phillips	6304	Cr	Hettie Phillips	6305	Cr
	New Born Census Card No. 34, P. O. Checotah, Date of Birth February 19, 1904										
21	1	Arnett, Abbie Lee	1	F	¼	Albert W. Arnett		Non	Maggie Arnett	2609	Cr
	New Born Census Card No. 35, P. O. Clarksville, Date of Birth No. 1, August 29, 1902; No. 2, September 1, 1904										
22	1	Marshall, Benjamin Jr.	3	M	5-16	Benjamin Marshall	1942	Cr	Lizzie B. Marshall		Non
23	2	Marshall, George Freeman	1	M	5-16	Benjamin Marshall	1942	Cr	Lizzie B. Marshall		Non
	New Born Census Card No. 38, P. O. Muskogee, Date of Birth August 11, 1904										
24	1	Harris, Mary J.	1	F	1-16	William R. Harris	4480	Cr	Lela Harris		Non
	New Born Census Card No. 39, P. O. Muskogee, Date of Birth June 20, 1902										
25	1	Ross, Lena M.	3	F	¼	J. Ewing Ross	1402	Cr	Nellie Ross		Non
	New Born Census Card No. 40, P. O. Checotah, Date of Birth No. 1, June 20, 1902; No. 2, October 3, 1904										
26	1	Howard, Myrtle May	3	F	⅛	George Howard	D	Non	Abbie L. Johnson	521	Cr
27	2	Johnson, Viola	1	F	⅛	Charlie Johnson		Non	Abbie L. Johnson	521	Cr
	New Born Census Card No. 42, P. O. Bixby, Date of Birth July 30, 1902										
28	1	Coppedge, Velma G.	3	F	1-16	C. E. Coppedge		Non	Emma Coppedge	1555	Cr
	New Born Census Card No. 13, P. O. Hanna, Date of Birth May 20, 1902										
29	1	Cummings, Susie	3	F	½	David Cummings	6818	Cr	Louisa Cummings	6819	Cr
	New Born Census Card No. 48, P. O. Paden, Date of Birth March 23, 1903										
30	1	Nichols, Leo Carlton	2	M	1-32	Steve F. Nichols		Non	Emma Nichols	8608	Cr
	New Born Census Card No. 49, P. O. Mounds, Date of Birth July 23, 1904										
31	1	Skeeter, Fred	1	M	F	Willie Skeeter	6111	Cr	Susanna Skeeter	1807	Cr
	New Born Census Card No. 50, P. O. Paden, Date of Birth March 5, 1904										
32	1	Gray, Johnson	1	M	½	George C. Gray		Non	Mesulta Gray	6348	Cr
	New Born Census Card No. 53, P. O. Mounds, Date of Birth August 15, 1902										
33	1	Bigpond, Wilson	3	M	F	Daniel Bigpond	1838	Cr	Nancy Bigpond	1839	Cr
	New Born Census Card No. 54, P. O. Muskogee, Date of Birth June 18, 1901										
34	1	Harris, Winnie Davis	4	F	1-16	Cheasquah Harris	2180	Cr	Nellie Harris		Non
	New Born Census Card No. 55, P. O. Eufaula, Date of Birth September 17, 1903										
35	1	Richard, Albert	1	M	½	Sam Richard	6088	Cr	Lula Richard		Non

Roll No.	No.	NAME	Age	Sex	Blood	NAME OF FATHER	Roll No.	Cit.	NAME OF MOTHER	Roll No.	Cit.
		New Born Census Card No. 56, P. O. Gibson Station, Date of Birth September 27, 1902									
36	1	Hays, Sallie Willison	2	F	1-16	W. Pierce Hays		Non	Sallie H. Hays	6801	Cr
		New Born Census Card No. 57, P. O. Muskogee, Date of Birth December 28, 1901									
37	1	Wilcox, John	3	M	1-32	H. H. Wilcox		Non	Ella Wilcox	6040	m
		New Born Census Card, No. 58, P. O. Muskogee, Date of Birth No. 1, August 15, 1903; No. 2, 17, 1905									
38	1	Webb, Ethel Samantha	2	F	3-16	George W. Webb		Non	Myrtle L. Webb	3932	Cr
39	2	Webb, Ettie Jane	1	F	3-16	George W. Webb		Non	Myrtle L. Webb	3932	Cr
		New Born Census Card No. 60, P. O. Checotah, Date of Birth August 9, 1903									
40	1	McGuire, Marcus Wilson	2	M	1-32	George W. McGuire		Non	Sophia McGuire	977	Cr
		New Born Census Card No. 62, P. O. Bald Hill, Date of Birth August 25, 1904									
41	1	Hart, Florence E.	1	F	¼	Edward Hart		Non	Florence A. Hart	2121	Cr
		New Born Census Card No. 63, P. O. Sanderson, Texas, Date of Birth No. 1, January 1, 1902; No. 2, February 13, 1905									
42	1	Wilson, Ida	3	F	½	Jason Wilson		Non	Martha Wilson	2942	Cr
43	2	Wilson, Otto	1	M	½	Jason Wilson		Non	Martha Wilson	2942	Cr
		New Born Census Card No. 65, P. O. Okmulgee, Date of Birth November 10, 1903									
44	1	Daniel, Unah Jr.	1	M	F	Unah Daniel	353	Cr	Mary Daniel	354	Cr
		New Born Census Card No. 66, P. O. Eufaula, Date of Birth September 30, 1901									
45	1	Smock, Anna Louise	3	F	¼	John C. Smock		Non	Eloise Grayson Smock	6137	Cr
		New Born Census Card No. 67, P. O. Sapulpa, Date of Birth June 6, 1903									
46	1	Aubrey, Alice Hiawatha	2	F	⅜	Charles Aubrey		Non	Millie Aubrey	4170	Cr
		New Born Census Card No. 71, P. O. Bixby, Date of Birth October 18, 1903									
47	1	Sherrill, Gracie	1	F	⅛	William Sherrill		Non	Mattie M. Sherrill	1764	Cr
		New Born Census Card No. 76, P. O. Oktaha, Date of Birth No. 1, September 22, 1904; No. 2, August 14, 1902									
48	1	Carter, Susie	1	F	⅝	Henry Carter	3650	Cr	Annie Carter	3651	Cr
49	2	Carter, Jennie	3	F	⅝	Henry Carter	3650	Cr	Annie Carter	3651	Cr
		New Born Census Card No. 77, P. O. Muskogee, Date of Birth October 3, 1904									
50	1	Murphy, Eva Dorcas	1	F	1-32	William S. Murphy	2461	Cr	Nettie Murphy		Non
		New Born Census Card No. 81, P. O. Okemah, Date of Birth November 23, 1902									
51	1	Fixico, Icey	2	F	½	Unknown		Fr	Pefeny Fixico	4123	Cr
		New Born Census Card No. 82, P. O. Weer, Date of Bitth August 15, 1902									
52	1	Williams, Charley	3	M	⅛	Nat Williams		Non	Mary M. Williams	1309	Cr
		New Born Census Card No. 85, P. O. Broken Arrow, Date of Birth November 1, 1903									
53	1	Drew, Clarence	1	M	½	Amos Drew	2495	Cr	Nettie Drew	2496	Cr
		New Born Census Card No. 86, P. O. Elam, Date of Birth March 9, 1904									
54	1	Haikey, Jessie Illegitimate	1	M	F	Unknown		Cr	Susanna Haikey	718	Cr
		New Born Census Card No. 87, P. O. Broken Arrow, Date of Birth No. 1, October 6, 1903; No. 2, February 2, 1905									
55	1	Cooper, Wheeler	1	M	½	Grant Cooper		Non	Eliza Cooper	717	Cr
56	2	Cooper, Effie	1	F	½	Grant Cooper		Non	Eliza Cooper	717	Cr
		New Born Census Card No. 90, P. O. Braggs, Date of Birth September 10, 1904									
57	1	Yahola, Jennetta	1	F	½	Happy Yahola		Cher	Winey Yahola	384	Cr
		New Born Census Card No. 92, P. O. Tulsa, Date of Birth No. 1, November 12, 1902; No. 2, August 8, 1904									
58	1	Strouvelle, Charles Edward Jr.	2	M	⅜	C. E. Strouvelle		Non	Susanna Barnett Strouvelle	1	Cr
59	2	Strouvelle, Alice Kendall	1	F	⅜	C. E. Strouvelle		Non	Susanna Barnett Strouvelle	1	Cr
		New Born Census Card No. 94, P. O. Mounds, Date of Birth February 8, 1904									
60	1	Bighead, Lizzie	1	F	F	Stanwaite Bighead	1855	Cr	Millie Bighead	1856	Cr
		New Born Census Card No. 97, P. O. Muskogee, Date of Birth December 11, 1903									
61	1	Grayson, Pearl	1	F	⅛	James L. Grayson	870	Cr	Matilda Grayson		Non
		New Born Census Card No. 98, P. O. Natura, Date of Birth January 8, 1904									
62	1	Bruner, Richard Douglas	1	M	¾	Billy Bruner	2086	Cr	Adaline Bruner	2087	Cr
		New Born Census Card No. 100, P. O. Morris, Date of Birth No. 1, July 31, 1903; No. 2, February 14, 1905									
63	1	Brian, John William	2	M	⅛	Charley Brian		Non	Hettie E. Brian	203	Cr
64	2	Brian, Mary Ellen	1	F	⅛	Charley Brian		Non	Hettie E. Brian	203	Cr
		New Born Census Card No. 101, P. O. Oktaha, Date of Birth January 3, 1904									
65	1	Escoe, William Albert	1	M	5-16	Walter J. Escoe	3953	Cr	Sarah M. Escoe	3514	Cr
		New Born Census Card No. 103, P. O. Wetumka, Date of Birth June 30, 1903									
66	1	Tiger, Ethan Allen H.	2	M	⅝	Johnson E. Tiger	224	Cr	Lena Tiger	64	Cr
		New Born Census Card No. 104, P. O. Canadian, Date of Birth No. 1, June 29, 1902; No. 2, April 17, 1904									
67	1	Burton, Ethel V.	3	F	1-16	Robert O. Burton	5460	Cr	Mollie E. Burton		Non
68	2	Burton, Wynema Owen	1	F	1-16	Robert O. Burton	5460	Cr	Mollie E. Burton		Non
		New Born Census Card No. 105, P. O. Canadian, Date of Birth August 3, 1902									
69	1	Wilson, Oleta	3	F	⅛	C. H. Wilson		Non	Lydia Wilson	8597	
		New Born Census Card No. 106, P. O. Haskell, Date of Birth October 27, 1903									
70	1	Smith, Terry Steven	1	M	⅛	Stephen Smith	2246	Cr	Emma Smith		Non
		New Born Census Card No. 108, P. O. Muskogee, Date of Birth No. 1, February 8, 1902; No. 2, April 23, 1904									
71	1	Callahan, Mary Elizabeth	3	F	1-16	James O. Callahan	1425	Cr	Mary E. Callahan		Non
72	2	Callahan, Etta Sibyl	1	F	1-16	James O. Callahan	1425	Cr	Mary E. Callahan		Non
		New Born Census Card No. 109, P. O. Haskell Date of Birth March 25, 1904									
73	1	Bruner, Mineffie	1	F	F	Miller Bruner	2154	Cr	Lucy Bruner	2155	Cr
		New Born Census Card No. 113, P. O. Weer, Date of Birth March 13, 1902									
74	1	Martin, Loney	3	F	F	Johnson Martin	649	Cr	Susanna Martin	1453	Cr

Roll No.	No.	NAME	Age	Sex	Blood	NAME OF FATHER	Roll No.	Cit.	NAME OF MOTHER	Roll No.	Cit.
	New Born Census Card No. 114, P. O. Morse, Date of Birth October 21, 1902										
75	1	Callahan, Sam	2	M	1-32	Benton Callahan	1746	Cr	Cecilia Callahan		Non
	New Born Census Card No. 116, P. O. Haskell, Date of Birth December 23, 1902										
76	1	Smith, Ruth	2	F	⅛	Daniel B. Smith	135	Cr	Mary I. Smith	136	Cr
	New Born Census Card No. 117, P. O. Morris, Date of Birth November 26, 1904										
77	1	Cable, Virgie Plimmer	1	F	1-16	Adam M. Cable		Non	Mary I. Cable	1133	Cr
	New Born Census Card No. 118, P. O. Wetumka, Date of Birth February 11, 1903										
78	1	Cowe, Effa	2	F	F	Sarty Cowe	4891	Cr	Melinda Cowe	4889	Cr
	New Born Census Card No. 121, P. O. Coweta, Date of Birth July 2, 1902										
79	1	Sarty, Mamie	3	F	F	Ned Sarty	436	Cr	Eliza Sarty	712	Cr
	New Born Census Card No. 125, P. O. Tulsa, Date of Birth May 12, 1903										
80	1	Burnette, Moses	2	M	⅛	A. T. Burnette		Non	Mary Jane Burnette	2227	Cr
	New Born Census Card No. 127, P. O. Muskogee, Date of Birth April 2, 1902										
81	1	Jobe, Leo J.	3	M	⅛	Louis N. B. Jobe	1205	Cr	Mollie G. Jobe		Non
	New Born Census Card No. 130, P. O. Henryetta, Date of Birth No. 1. August 8, 1902; No. 2 March 20, 1904										
82	1	McNac, Charley	3	M	F	Peter McNac	1268	Cr	Lousanna McNac	1269	Cr
83	2	McNac, Marcy	1	M	F	Peter McNac	1268	Cr	Lousanna McNac	1269	Cr
	New Born Census Card No. 131, P. O. Wealaka, Date of Birth No. 1 and 2 (twins) April 1, 1903; No. 3 July 2, 1904										
84	1	Gilcrease, Elmer Lee	2	M	⅛	William L. Gilcrease		Non	Lizzie Gilcrease	1504	Cr
85	2	Gilcrease, Mabel	2	F	⅛	William L. Gilcrease		Non	Lizzie Gilcrease	1504	Cr
86	3	Gilcrease, Bessie	1	F	⅛	William L. Gilcrease		Non	Lizzie Gilcrease	1504	Cr
	New Born Census Card No. 133, P. O. Mounds, Date of Birth October 1, 1904										
87	1	Withers, Oliver Lee	1	M	⅛	Robert O. Withers		Non	Lydia Withers	2602	Cr
	New Born Census Card No. 135, P. O. Tulsa, Date of Birth April 10, 1904										
88	1	Bell, Lelia May	1	F	¼	Jack Bell		Non	Clarissa Bell	2219	Cr
	New Born Census Card No. 139, P. O. Yale, Date of Birth August 17, 1903										
89	1	Dale, Charles Henry	2	M	1-16	Oliver Bell		Non	Izora E. Dale	3188	Cr
	New Born Census Card No. 143, P. O. Weer, Date of Birth No. 1 November 11, 1902; No. 2 October 24, 1904										
90	1	McHenry, Abbie	2	F	½	Lewis McHenry	634	Cr	Silla McHenry	635	Cr
91	2	McHenry, Bettie	1	F	½	Lewis McHenry	634	Cr	Silla McHenry	635	Cr
	New Born Census Card No. 144, P. O. Checotah, Date of Birth No. 1 March 12, 1902; No. 2 September 6, 1904										
92	1	McIntosh, Edith Edna	3	F	½	Thomas F. McIntosh	3199	Cr	Kate McIntosh	3193	Cr
93	2	McIntosh, Vivian	1	F	½	Thomas F. McIntosh	3199	Cr	Kate McIntosh	3193	Cr
	New Born Census Card No. 147, P. O. Okmulgee, Date of Birth October 1, 1902										
94	1	Webster, Seeley	2	F	F	Jefferson Webster	4688	Cr	Mattie Webster	4689	Cr
	New Born Census Card No. 149, P. O. Wagoner, Date of Birth No. 1 February 27, 1905; No. 2 April 30, 1903										
95	1	Damet, Susan	1	F	⅛	John P. Damet		Non	Eliza Damet	6901	Cr
96	2	Damet, William F.	2	M	⅛	John P. Damet		Non	Eliza Damet	6901	Cr
	New Born Census Card No. 150, P. O. Muskogee, Date of Birth January 2, 1904										
97	1	Minter, Thelma Agnes	1	F	1-16	Mark Minter	215	Cr	Bertie Minter		Non
	New Born Census Card No. 151, P. O. Coweta, Date of Birth May 31, 1902										
98	1	McKellop, Louisa	3	F	F	Peter McKellop	800	Cr	Betsey McKellop	7757	Cr
	New Born Census Card No. 152, P. O. Wagoner, Date of Birth No. 1 May 26, 1902; No. 2 September 11, 1904										
99	1	Couch, Gertie May	3	F	¼	J. C. Couch		Non	Amanda Couch	2565	Cr
100	2	Couch, Allie B.	1	F	¼	J. C. Couch		Non	Amanda Couch	2565	Cr
	New Born Census Card No. 154, P. O. Fry, Date of Birth October 25, 1903										
101	1	Williford, Joe Brown	1	M	5-16	M. M. Williford		Non	Lou Williford	6181	Cr
	New Born Census Card No. 155, P. O. Porter, Date of Birth No. 1 February 21, 1902; No. 2 October 26, 1904										
102	1	Porter, Pleasant	3	M	¾	Lewis Porter	417	Cr	Elsie Porter	416	Cr
103	2	Porter, McKinley	1	M	¾	Lewis Porter	417	Cr	Elsie Porter	416	Cr
	New Born Census Card No. 159, P. O. Coweta, Date of Birth August 8, 1904										
104	1	Howard, Maxie	1	F	½	H. B. Howard		Non	Mattie Howard	269	Cr
	New Born Census Card No. 162, P. O. Redfork, Date of Birth July 8, 1901										
105	1	Russell, Clemmie	4	F	1-32	James W. Russell		Non	Mary A. Russell	1221	Cr
	New Born Census Card No. 164, P. O. Checotah, Date of Birth January 11, 1904										
106	1	Hughes, Lena Ethel	1	F	⅛	Robert Hughes	1581	Cr	Lizzie Hughes		Non
	New Born Census Card No. 165, P. O. Checotah, Date of Birth November 29, 1904										
107	1	McIntosh, Edith Louise	1	F	1-16	Freeland B. McIntosh	2877	Cr	Kate McIntosh		Non
	New Born Census Card No. 166, P. O. Okfuskee, Date of Birth January 23, 1903										
108	1	Martin, Leona	2	F	⅛	Thomas Martin		Non	Annie Martin	180	Cr
	New Born Census Card No. 70, P. O. Bixby, Date of Birth December 7, 1904										
109	1	Allen, Millard E.	1	M	⅛	John W. Allen	1760	Cr	Cora Lou Allen		Non
	New Born Census Card No. 167, P. O. Wetumka, Date of Birth November 21, 1904										
110	1	Atkins, Robert Meagher	1	M	⅛	James P. Atkins		Non	Isabelle M. Atkins	2	Cr
	New Born Census Card No. 168, P. O. Weer, Date of Birth No. 1 August 30, 1904; No. 2 August 23, 1901										
111	1	Kerr, Commodore, Jr.	1	M	¼	Henry Kerr		Non	Arcenoe Kerr	2548	Cr
695	2	Kerr, Ethel	4	F	¼	Henry Kerr		Non	Arcenoe Kerr	2548	Cr
	New Born Census Card No. 169, P. O. Sasakwa, Date of Birth October 7, 1904										
112	1	Miller, Eugene	1	M	⅜	Samuel H. Miller	5585	Cr	Nora F. Miller		Sem

Roll No.	No.	NAME	Age	Sex	Blood	NAME OF FATHER	Roll No.	Cit.	NAME OF MOTHER	Roll No.	Cit.
		New Born Census Card No. 170, P. O. Muskogee, Date of Birth November 11, 1903									
113	1	Campbell, Tine Winburn	1	M	1/8	Tom Campbell		Non	Jessie Campbell	5812	Cr
		New Born Census Card No. 171, P. O. Checotah, Date of Birth October 27, 1903									
114	1	Minton, Ada	1	F	1-32	Chaine Minton		Non	Aurelia Minton	1022	Cr
		New Born Census Card No. 174, P. O. Morse, Date of Birth July 28, 1903									
115	1	Hopwood, Ora Pearle	2	F	1-32	rinam F. Hopwood	3182	Cr	Mollie Hopwood		Non
		New Born Census Card No. 176, P. O. Big Springs, Date of Birth No. 1 September 19, 1901; No. 2 October 25, 1903									
116	1	Miles, Jennie Murrell	3	F	1/4	W. S. Miles		Non	Rosalie Miles	906	Cr
117	2	Miles, Vivian	1	F	1/4	W. S. Miles		Non	Rosalie Miles	905	Cr
		New Born Census Card No. 177, P. O. Bixby, Date of Birth October 14, 1902									
118	1	Applegeet, Zelma Fay	2	F	1-32	W. F. Applegeet		Non	Cora F. Applegeet	2585	Cr
		New Born Census Card No. 178, P. O. Wealaka, Date of Birth No. 1 September 25, 1904; No. 2 January 16, 1903									
119	1	Maxey, Eugene Willie	1	M	1/4	Eugene Maxey		Non	Neosho P. Maxey	2964	Cr
120	2	Maxey, Simeon C.	2	M	1/4	Eugene Maxey		Non	Neosho P. Maxey	2964	Cr
		New Born Census Card No. 180, P. O. Wetumka, Date of Birth No. 1 April 7, 1902; No. 2 October 1, 1903									
121	1	Robison, Adeline Belle	3	F	3/8	Joe S. Robison	6008	Cr	Mattie Robison	6003	Cr
122	2	Robison, Newman Joseph	1	M	3/8	Joe S. Robison	6008	Cr	Mattie Robison	6003	Cr
		New Born Census Card No. 181, P. O. Bristow, Date of Birth April 23, 1903									
123	1	Mikey, Lewis	2	M	1/2	Josiah Mikey		Chic-Fr	Lizzie Mikey	4153	Cr
		New Born Census Card No. 185, P. O. Checotah, Date of Birth October 22, 1902									
124	1	Dawson, Dessie Lee Illegitimate	2	F	1/8	Cooper Dawson		Non	Martha Wells	2365	Cr
		New Born Census Card No. 188, P. O. Checotah, Date of Birth May 20, 1903									
125	1	Pressgrove, Joseph	2	M	1/8	Aaron Pressgrove		Non	Lizzie Pressgrove	2367	Cr
		New Born Census Card No. 190, P. O. Redfork, Date of Birth June 13, 1904									
126	1	Naharkey, Millie	1	F	3/4	Moses Naharkey	4363	Cr	Martha Naharkey	8138	Cr
		New Born Census Card No. 191, P. O. Checotah, Date of Birth January 24, 1903									
127	1	McIntosh, Annie Lila	2	F	1/4	D.N.McIntosh,Jr.	2711	Cr	Alice McIntosh		Non
		New Born Census Card No. 193, P. O. Eufaula, Date of Birth February 7, 1904									
128	1	Highland, Patrick, Jr.	1	M	1-16	Pat Highland		Cher	Lula N. Highland	1775	Cr
		New Born Census Card No. 194, P. O. Okmulgee, Date of Birth, No. 1 June 17, 1902; No. 2 September 21, 1904									
129	1	Dillsaver, Orvel Dean	3	M	3-16	Mode Dillsaver		Non	Missouri Dillsaver	2348	Cr
130	2	Dillsaver, Robert Lowe	1	M	3-16	Mode Dillsaver		Non	Missouri Dillsaver	2348	Cr
		New Born Census Card No. 196, P. O. Eufaula, Date of Birth January 23, 1903									
131	1	Wallace, Tully Mae	2	F	1-16	W. A. Wallace		Non	Ella Wallace	3114	Cr
		New Born Census Card No. 197, P. O. Holdenville, Date of Birth August 4, 1904									
132	1	Jacobs, William R.	1	M	3/4	Newman F. Jacobs	275	Cr	Ella L. Jacobs	6250	Cr
		New Born Census Card No. 198, P. O. Holdenville, Date of Birth September 26, 1902									
133	1	Miller, Samuel H., Jr.	2	M	13-16	Louis M. Miller	5040	Cr	Lillie Miller	5041	Cr
		New Born Census Card No. 200, P. O. Olive, Date of Birth No. 1 October 20, 1901; No. 2 June 4, 1905									
134	1	Raabe, Stella	3	F	1/8	Chris Raabe		Non	Ida May Raabe	3454	Cr
135	2	Raabe, Celia	1	F	1/8	Chris Raabe		Non	Ida May Raabe	3454	Cr
		New Born Census Card No. 201, P. O. Checotah, Date of Birth No. 1 November 29, 1903; No. 2 January 11, 1905									
136	1	Rogers, Woods Cooper	1	M	7-16	Wm. P. Rogers	89	Cr	Augusta Rogers		Non
137	2	Rogers, John	1	M	7-16	Wm. P. Rogers	89	Cr	Augusta Rogers		Non
		New Born Census Card No. 202, P. O. Bristow, Date of Birth November 20, 1904									
138	1	Barney, Albert Emmet	1	M	1/8	Albert Barney		Non	Bessie Barney	3456	Cr
		New Born Census Card No. 204, P. O. Council Hill, Date of Birth July 11, 1902									
139	1	Brown, Daniel W.	3	M	3/8	Gold C. Brown		Non	Zenie Brown	8671	Cr
		New Born Census Card No. 205, P. O. Bristow, Date of Birth February 23, 1904									
140	1	Bruce, Browder F.	1	M	3/8	Moten Bruce		Non	Pheba Bruce	1483	Cr
		New Born Census Card No. 207, P. O. Weer, Date of Birth March 3, 1904									
141	1	Sarty, Manuel	1	M	F	Rollie Sarty	3285	Cr	Hepsy Sarty	}8019 1399	Cr
		New Born Census Card No. 208, P. O. Oktaha, Date of Birth No. 1 June 28, 1903; No. 2 February 19, 1905									
142	1	Evans, Phidelta Lee	2	F	1-16	James Evans	3626	Cr	Stella Evans		Non
143	2	Evans, James, Jr.	1	M	1-16	James Evans	3626	Cr	Stella Evans		Non
		New Born Census Card No. 209, P. O. Checotah, Date of Birth November 13, 1904									
144	1	Coon, Oda M.	1	F	1-16	Fred C. Coon		Non	Sallie Coon	2373	Cr
		New Born Census Card No. 210, P. O. Mounds, Date of Birth February 1, 1903									
145	1	Goode, Rowena	2	F	1-16	George Goode		Non	Myrtle M. Goode	2784	Cr
		New Born Census Card No. 211, P. O. Mounds, Date of Birth September 27, 1904									
146	1	Puryear, William H.	1	M	1-16	Frank M. Puryear		Non	Emma H. Puryear	2783	Cr
		New Born Census Card No. 213, P. O. Coweta, Date of Birth November 26, 1903									
147	1	Canard, Lena	1	F	7/8	Martin Canard	695	Cr	Annie Lovett	253	Cr
		New Born Census Card No. 214, P. O. Wetumka, Date of Birth July 13, 1903									
148	1	Tiger, Ewnah J.	2	M	7/8	Barney Tiger	5183	Cr	Katie Tiger	5184	Cr
		New Born Census Card No. 215, P. O. Tulsa, Date of Birth May 16, 1904									
149	1	Perryman, Okema	1	F	3/8	George Perryman	2629	Cr	Ophia Perryman		Non
		New Born Census Card No. 217, P. O. Broken Arrow, Date of Birth May 8, 1904									
150	1	Johnson, Miley	1	F	5/8	Issac Johnson	709	Cr	Nicey Johnson	710	Cr
		New Born Census Card No. 218, P. O. Tulsa, Date of Birth June 10, 1904									
151	1	Parker, Charles Edward	1	M	7-16	William E. Parker		Non	Jessie Parker	7625	Cr

Roll No.	No.	NAME	Age	Sex	Blood	NAME OF FATHER	Roll No.	Cit.	NAME OF MOTHER	Roll No.	Cit.
New Born Census Card No. 219, P. O. Tulsa, Date of Birth November 9, 1904											
152	1	Bruner, Flora	1	F	F	William G. Bruner	5813	Cr	Jennie Bruner	5314	Cr
New Born Census Card No. 220, P. O. Wagoner, Date of Birth March 9, 1903											
153	1	Posey, Terry O.	2	M	1/8	Walter Posey	1742	Cr	Mary L. Posey		Non
New Born Census Card No. 221, P. O. Okmulgee, Date of Birth February 24, 1903											
154	1	Alexander, Mary	2	F	F	Arty Alexander	357	Cr	Nancy Alexander	358	Cr
New Born Census Card No. 222, P. O. Dustin, Date of Birth July 11, 1904											
155	1	Pike, Fay	1	F	7-16	Vester Pike		Non	Edna Pike	1992	Cr
New Born Census Card No. 223, P. O. Wagoner, Date of Birth May 20, 1903											
156	1	Posey, Hugh F.	2	M	1/8	John M. Posey	2639	Cr	Laura E. Posey		Non
New Born Census Card No. 227, P. O. Sapulpa, Date of Birth August 10, 1903											
157	1	Fife, Dawes	2	M	F	Timmie Fife	4653	Cr	Sarah Fife	4654	Cr
New Born Census Card No. 228, P. O. Broken Arrow, Date of Birth October 22, 1903											
158	1	Cooper, Florence	1	F	1/2	E. E. Cooper		Non	Annie Cooper	931	Cr
New Born Census Card No. 229, P. O. Checotah, Date of Birth No. 1 February 26, 1903; No. 2 September 26, 1904											
159	1	Turnbow, James Henry	2	M	1/8	Aaron Turnbow		Non	Katie Turnbow	96	Cr
160	2	Turnbow, Charlie	1	M	1/8	Aaron Turnbow		Non	Katie Turnbow	96	Cr
New Born Census No. 230, P. O. Sapulpa, Dtae of Birth April 8, 1902											
161	1	Burgess, Ruby	3	F	1/2	Ed Burgess	6327	Cr	May Burgess	6328	Cr
New Born Census Card No. 232, P. O. Coweta, Date of Birth No. 1, August 7, 1902; No. 2, February 20, 1905											
162	1	Tiger, Edward	3	M	3/4	Dave Tiger	1136	Cr	Neosho Tiger	1137	Cr
163	2	Tiger, George No. 2 died May 20, 1905	1	M	3/4	Dave Tiger	1136	Cr	Neosho Tiger	1137	Cr
New Born Census Card No. 239, P. O. Broken Arrow, Date of Birth December 20, 1903											
164	1	Johnson, George	1	M	1/4	Joe Johnson		Non	Ruth Johnson	1499	Cr
New Born Census Card No. 240, P. O. Wagoner, Date of Birth December 24, 1902											
165	1	Trent, Jesse	2	M	1/8	Jim Trent		Non	Chaney Trent	9916	Cr
New Born Census Card No. 243, P. O. Henryetta, Date of Birth May 19, 1904											
166	1	Freeman, Theodore R.	1	M	1/2	John W. Freeman		Non	Lena Freeman	5601	Cr
New Born Census Card No. 247, P. O. Owyhee, Nev. Date of Birth March 15, 1903											
167	1	Callahan, Josephine Nevada	2	F	1-32	Walter K. Callahan	1538	Cr	Alice A. Callahan		Non
New Born Census Card No. 255, P. O. Catoosa, Date of Birth February 1, 1902											
168	1	Tiger, Mary	3	F	7/8	Thomas Tiger	693	Cr	Nicey Tiger	1104	Cr
New Born Census Card No. 226, P. O. Fry, Date of Birth December 12, 1903											
169	1	Bright, Thelma Beatrice	1	F	1-16	Luke O. Bright		Non	Mary Bright	2144	Cr
New Born Census Card No. 284, P. O. Muskogee, Date of Birth October 10, 1902											
170	1	Du Bois, Elizabeth Gladys	2	F	1-32	B. R. Du Bois	6753	Cr	Elizabeth C. Du Bois		Non
New Born Census Card No. 287, P. O. Bixby, Date of Birth February 15, 1903											
171	1	McCoy, Ollie	2	F	F	Henry McCoy	1982	Cr	Sallie Clinton McCoy	1874	Cr
New Born Census Card No. 288, P. O. Muskogee, Date of Birth No. 1, December 8, 1903; No. 2, May 11, 9102											
172	1	Burton, Charles Checotah	1	M	1/4	Jesse Burton		Non	Mary Burton	6809	Cr
173	2	Burton, Rufus Cheestell	3	M	1/4	Jesse Burton		Non	Mary Burton	6809	Cr
New Born Census Card No. 290, P. O. Weleetka, Date of Birth November 1, 1901											
174	1	Asbury, Joseph	3	M	3/4	Joshua Asbury	4442	Cr	Nancy Asbury	4449	Cr
New Born Census Card No. 297, P. O. Fentress, Date of Birth August 26, 1903											
175	1	Davis, Lizzie	2	F	F	Barney Davis	4936	Cr	Susan Davis	4937	Cr
New Born Census Card No. 4, P. O. Checotah, Date of Birth No. 1, January 10, 1905; No. 2, October 4, 1902											
176	1	McIntosh, Cheesie	1	M	9-32	Roley C. McIntosh	1766	Cr	Fannie McIntosh	1767	Cr
177	2	McIntosh, Sequoah	2	M	9-32	Roley C. McIntosh	1766	Cr	Fannie McIntosh	1767	Cr
New Born Census Card No. 5, P. O. Checotah, Date of Birth March 6, 1902											
178	1	Baker, Eula Blanche	3	F	1-64	Sam Baker		Non	Ella Blanche Baker	9079	Cr
New Born Census Card No. 11, P. O. Eufaula, Date of Birth August 31, 1904											
179	1	Brook, Annetta May	1	F	1/4	John Brook		Non	Jennetta A. Brook	6138	Cr
New Born Census Card No. 16, P. O. Natura, Date of Birth June 12, 1902											
180	1	Throckmorton, William D.	3	M	3/8	James W. Thockmorton	2059	Cr	Ida L. Thockmorton	2060	Cr
New Born Census Card No. 19, P. O. Eufaula, Date of Birth No. 1, October 5, 1901; No. 2, March 28, 1903											
181	1	Gibson, Verna Marie	3	F	5-16	Chester Gibson	6902	Cr	Modenia M.Gibson	2734	Cr
182	2	Gibson, Charles Counterman	2	M	5-16	Chester Gibson	6902	Cr	Modenia M.Gibson	2734	Cr
New Born Census Card No. 22, P. O. Sapulpa, Date of Birth No. 1, January 12, 1902; No. 2, December 20, 1903											
183	1	Tiger, Aby	3	F	F	Conzie Tiger	3100	Cr	Fancy Tiger	3101	Cr
184	2	Tiger, Waxin	1	M	F	Conzie Tiger	3100	Cr	Fancy Tiger	3101	Cr
New Born Census Card No. 27, P. O. Eufaula, Date of Birth November 7, 1902											
185	1	King, Jessie	2	M	F	Johnson King	1388	Cr	Millie King	1389	Cr
New Born Census Card No. 41, P. O. Okmulgee, Date of Birth June 9, 1904											
186	1	Gaither, Maggie Emily	1	F	3-16	W. J. Gaither		Non	Alice M. Gaither	177	Cr
New Born Census Card No. 43, P. O. Paden, Date of Birth July 13, 1903											
187	1	Harjo, Johnnie	2	M	1/2	Jimmie Harjo		Non	Susie Harjo	8911	Cr
New Born Census Card No. 44, P. O. Broken Arrow, Date of Birth June 25, 1904											
188	1	Haikey, Burney	1	M	F	Dave Haikey	952	Cr	Nicey Haikey	6424	Cr
New Born Census Card No. 61, P. O. Coweta, Date of Birth May 23, 1903											
189	1	Murphy, Blanch	2	F	1-16	Conny Murphy	217	Cr	Sarah R. Murphy		Che

Roll No.	No.	NAME	Age	Sex	Blood	NAME OF FATHER	Roll No.	Cit.	NAME OF MOTHER	Roll No.	Cit.
	New Born Census Card No. 68, P. O. Coweta, Date of Birth July 13, 1904										
190	1	Marshall, Lena May	1	F	5-16	Thomas J. Marshall	5855	Cr	Belle Marshall		Non
	New Born Census Card No. 72, P. O. Wagoner, Date of Birth No. 1, April 3, 1902; No. 2, February 23, 1904										
191	1	Renfro, Elza Tillman	3	M	1/8	William D. Renfro		Non	Bettie Renfro	5878	Cr
192	2	Renfro, Alef Adelaide	1	F	1/8	William D. Renfro		Non	Bettie Renfro	5878	Cr
	New Born Census Card No. 74, P. O. Oktaha, Date of Birth September 14, 1903										
193	1	Chenubia Martha Illegitimate	1	F	3/4	David Hall	3622	Cr	Susie Chenubia	576	Cr
	New Born Census Card No. 75, P. O. Oktaha, Date of Birth December 17, 1904										
194	1	Hall, Mollie	1	F	1/4	Sandy Hall	3621	Cr	Martha Hall		Non
	New Born Census Card No. 78, P. O. Sharpe, Date of Birth No. 1, October 17, 1901, No. 2 September 8, 1904										
195	1	Palmer, James W.	3	M	1/4	John W. Palmer		Non	Eliza Palmer	80	Cr
196	2	Palmer, Daniel B.	1	M	1/4	John W. Palmer		Non	Eliza Palmer	80	Cr
	New Born Census Card No. 79, P. O. Sapulpa, Date of Birth November 4, 1902										
197	1	Land, Helen	2	F	3/4	Joseph H. Land	1695	Cr	Salina Land	1696	Cr
	New Born Census Card No. 80, P. O. Tulsa, Date of Birth No. 1, September 11, 1902; No. 2, August 23, 1904										
198	1	Drew, Earl E.	2	M	1/4	Ernest Drew		Non	Alice Drew	2635	Cr
199	2	Drew, Roy W.	1	M	1/4	Ernest Drew		Non	Alice Drew	2635	Cr
	New Born Census Card No. 83, P. O. Coweta, Date of Birth September 1904										
200	1	Simon, George	1	M	F	Caesar Simon	2080	Cr	Mary Byrd	5229	Cr
	New Born Census Card No. 84, P. O. Broken Arrow, Date of Birth October 9, 1903										
201	1	Bough, Willie E.	1	M	1/2	John Bough		Non	Rachel Bough	3833	Cr
	New Born Census Card No. 88, P. O. Weleetka, Date of Birth September 8, 1902										
202	1	Looney, Sullivan	2	M	F	Josiah Looney	1681	Cr	Fanny Looney	1682	Cr
	New Born Census Card No. 99, P. O. Broken Arrow, Date of Birth September 23, 1903										
203	1	Castillo, Mabel	1	F	1/2	Geo. C. Castillo		Non	Nettie Castillo	610	Cr
	New Born Census Card No. 102, P. O. Bixby, Date of Birth May 13, 1903										
204	1	Barnett, Jensey	2	F	F	Joe Barnett	3267	Cr	Wanney Barnett	3268	Cr
	New Born Census Card No. 110, P. O. Haskell, Date of Birth October 16, 1903										
205	1	Anderson, Lydia C.	1	F	1/2	Solomon Anderson	3151	Cr	Emma Anderson	3152	Cr
	New Born Census Card No. 111, P. O. Redfork, Date of Birth January 21, 1904										
206	1	Smith, Oliver Russell	1	M	1-16	Enoch O. Smith		Non	Janie Smith	2560	Cr
	New Born Census Card No. 112, P. O. Jenks, Date of Birth No. 1, September 19, 1904; No. 2, January 2, 1903										
207	1	Ishmael, James L.	1	M	1-16	James M. Ishmael	2558	Cr	Maude Ishmael		Non
208	2	Ishmael, Eva J.	2	F	1-16	James M. Ishmael	2558	Cr	Maude Ishmael		Non
	New Born Census Card No. 115, P. O. Morse, Date of Birth July 25, 1901										
209	1	McKinnon, Lila Belle	4	F	1/8	R. W. McKinnon		Non	Amanda S. McKinnon	202	Cr
	New Born Census Card No. 119, P. O. Naudeck, Date of Birth No. 1, August 5, 1903; No. 2, October 20, 1901										
210	1	Porter, L. Ray	2	M	1/8	Sam Porter		Non	Susan Porter	167	Cr
211	2	Porter, Edith P.	3	F	1/8	Sam Porter		Non	Susan Porter	167	Cr
	New Born Census Card No. 120, P. O. Holdenville, Date of Birth September 3, 1904										
212	1	Jacobs, Elsie B.	1	F	1/4	John A. Jacobs	5093	Cr	Mary Jacobs		Non
	New Born Census Card No. 123, P. O. Tulsa, Date of Birth August 21, 1902										
213	1	Hodge, Gusta A.	3	F	1/4	John N. Hodge	5978	Cr	Minnie L. Hodge		Non
	New Born Census Card No. 129, P. O. Bald Hill, Date of Birth May 31, 1902										
214	1	Morton, Roy Ray	3	M	1-16	Thomas Morton		Non	Joanna Morton	3663	Cr
	New Born Census Card No. 132, P. O. Wetumka, Date of Birth April 13, 1903										
215	1	Canard, Lizzie	2	F	F	Sam Canard	4668	Cr	Nancy Canard	4671	Cr
	New Born Census Card No. 134, P. O. Coweta, Date of Birth April 9, 1904										
216	1	Oliver, Louis	1	M	1/2	Frank Oliver		Non	Hattie Sarty Oliver	839	Cr
	New Born Census Card No. 136, P. O. Okfuskee, Date of Birth August 28, 1904										
217	1	Hinneha, John	1	F	F	Jonas Hinneha	4201	Cr	Annie Hinneha	567	Cr
	New Born Census Card No. 138, P. O. Okmulgee, Date of Birth No. 1, August 11, 1902; No. 2, February 7, 1904										
218	1	Dice, Freddie James	3	M	1-16	Jim Dice		Non	Dove Dice	5361	Cr
219	2	Dice, Liza Jane	1	F	1-16	Jim Dice		Non	Dove Dice	5361	Cr
	New Born Census Card No. 140, P. O. Okmulgee, Date of Birth March 15, 1904										
220	1	Tiger, Hettie	1	F	3/8	Amos Tiger	81	Cr	Deovocha Tiger		Non
	New Born Census Card No. 141, P. O. Carson, Date of Birth July 20, 1903										
221	1	Harjo, Nettie	2	F	F	Willie Harjo	1279	Cr	Sukey Harjo	5105	Cr
	New Born Census Card No. 142, P. O. Edna, Date of Birth No. 1, December 25, 1903; No. 2, March 25, 1902										
222	1	Scott, Christie Annie	1	F	F	Scott, Sam	3918	Cr	Nancy Scott	3919	Cr
223	2	Scott, John	3	M	F	Scott, Sam	3918	Cr	Nancy Scott	3919	Cr
	New Born Census Card No. 145, P. O. Coweta, Date of Birth February 18, 1903										
224	1	Boudinot, Mitchel	2	M	F	Cornelius Boudinot	643	Cr	Susanna Boudinot	644	Cr
	New Born Census Card No. 153, P. O. Okemah, Date of Birth June 14, 1904										
225	1	Jimboy, Peggy Illegitimate	1	F	F	Wiley Jimboy	1714	Cr	Sissie Tiger	6497	Cr
	New Born Census Card No. 156, P. O. Inola, Date of Birth August 10, 1903										
226	1	Gregory, Frank Lee	2	M	5-16	Archie A. Gregory	458	Cr	Florence L. Gregory		Non
	New Born Census Card No. 157, P. O. Wagoner, Date of Birth No. 1, February 4, 1904; No. 2, August 5, 1902										
227	1	Cane, Robert Carl	1	M	1-16	Charlie R. Cane	39	Cr	Mollie B. Cane		Non
228	2	Cane, William R.	3	M	1-16	Charlie R. Cane	39	Cr	Mollie B. Cane		Non

Roll No.	No.	NAME	Age	Sex	Blood	NAME OF FATHER	Roll No.	Cit.	NAME OF MOTHER	Roll No.	Cit.
		New Born Census Card No. 160, P. O. Hanna, Date of Birth No. 1, May 31, 1901; No. 2, August 9, 1904									
229	1	Hill, Lucy	4	F	F	James Hill	6373	Cr	Polly Hill	6374	Cr
347	2	Hill, Mandy	1	F	F	James Hill	6373	Cr	Polly Hill	6374	Cr
		New Born Census Card No. 163, P. O. Checotah, Date of Birth No. 1, October 3, 1902 (?); No. 2, March 3, 1905 (?)									
230	1	Combs, Pearl	2	F	1/8	John W. Combs		Non	Katie Combs	1617	Cr
694	2	Combs, John Boyd	1	M	1/8	John W. Combs		Non	Katie Combs	1617	Cr
		New Born Census Card No. 166, P. O. Okfuskee, Date of Birth October 5, 1901									
231	1	Martin, Jesse	3	M	1-16	Thomas Martin	L	Non	Anna Martin	180	Cr
		New Born Census Card No. 172, P. O. Hanna, Date of Birth No. 1, January 18, 1903; No. 2, September 24, 1904									
232	1	Aultman, Claud L.	2	M	1-16	Frank B. Aultman	678	Cr	Millie Aultman		Non
233	2	Aultman, Franklin C.	1	M	1-16	Frank B. Aultman	678	Cr	Millie Aultman		Non
		New Born Census Card No. 182, P. O. Tulsa, Date of Birth No. 1, December 24, 1902; No. 2, November 28, 1904									
234	1	Doyle, Eva	2	F	1-16	Burris Doyle	3055	Cr	Ada Doyle		Non
235	2	Doyle, Walter	1	M	1-16	Burris Doyle	3055	Cr	Ada Doyle		Non
		New Born Census Card No. 184, P. O. Inola, Date of Birth January 17, 1904									
236	1	Gregory, Rose Ida	1	F	5-16	Gilbert R. Gregory	456	Cr	Iva Gregory		Non
		New Born Census Card No. 186, P. O. Checotah, Date of Birth July 20, 1901									
237	1	Arnett, Iola	4	F	1/4	A. W. Arnett		Non	Maggie Arnett	2609	Cr
		New Born Census Card No. 187, P. O. Checotah, Date of Birth September 21, 1904									
238	1	Reynolds, Oscar Lee	1	M	1-64	Clarence Reynolds		Non	Leila Reynolds	971	Cr
		New Born Census Card No. 189, P. O. Wagoner, Date of Birth No. 1, June 15, 1902; No. 2, August 17, 1904									
239	1	Williams, John F.	3	M	1-16	John H. Williams		Non	Sarah E. Hackett	2775	Cr
351	2	Williams, Henryetta	1	F	1-16	John H. Williams		Non	Sarah E. Hackett	2775	Cr
		New Born Census Card No. 195, P. O. Bristow, Date of Birth No. 1, July 24, 1901; No. 2, March 22, 1904									
240	1	Bigpond, Susie	4	F	F	John Bigpond	3432	Cr	Nancy Bigpond	3428	Cr
241	2	Bigpond, Anderson	1	M	F	John Bigpond	3432	Cr	Nancy Bigpond	3428	Cr
		New Born Census Card No. 199, P. O. Checotah, Date of Birth No. 1, December 19, 1901; No. 2, January 15, 1904									
242	1	Bard, Daniel Lee	3	M	1/8	Daniel N. Bard	2131	Cr	Emma Bard		Non
243	2	Bard, Oda May	1	F	1/8	Daniel N. Bard	2131	Cr	Emma Bard		Non
		New Born Census Card No. 203, P. O. Hitchita, Date of Birth No. 1, December 4, 1902; No. 2, January 21, 1905									
244	1	Baughman, Malvin W.	2	M	1/4	G. G. Baughman		Non	Sarah Baughman	1130	Cr
245	2	Baughman, Gold C. Jr.	1	M	1/4	G. G. Baughman		Non	Sarah Baughman	1130	Cr
		New Born Census Card No. 206, P. O. Broken Arrow, Date of Birth No. 1, October 8, 1902; No. 2, October 27, 1904									
246	1	Bough, Henry	2	M	1/2	Arthur Bough		Non	Emma Bough	720	Cr
247	2	Bough, Ethel	1	F	1/2	Arthur Bough		Non	Emma Bough	720	Cr
		New Born Census Card No. 212, P. O. Henryetta, Date of Birth No. 1, March 18, 1903; No. 2, January 1, 1904									
248	1	Henry, Howard H.	3	M	1-16	James P. Henry	4430	Cr	Carrie Henry		Non
249	2	Henry, Edith Clair	1	F	1-16	James P. Henry	4430	Cr	Carrie Henry		Non
		New Born Census Card No. 224, P. O. Stroud, Date of Birth February 1, 1903									
250	1	Foster, John W.	2	M	1-16	Edward Foster	5215	Cr	Grace M. Foster		
		New Born Census Card No. 225, P. O. Eufaula, Date of Birth No. 1, March 15, 1903; No. 2, May 30, 1904									
251	1	Francis, Bettie	2	F	F	Robert Francis	6202	Cr	Millie Francis	6203	Cr
252	2	Francis, Jeff	1	M	F	Robert Francis	6202	Cr	Millie Francis	6203	Cr
		New Born Census Card No. 231, P. O. Broken Arrow, No. 1, July 4, 1902; No. 2, July 16, 1904									
253	1	Bible, William McHenry	3	M	3/4	Lewis Bible	942	Cr	Mulsie Bible	943	Cr
254	2	Bible, David	1	M	3/4	Lewis Bible	942	Cr	Mulsie Bible	943	Cr
		New Born Census Card No. 233, P. O. Bristow, Date of Birth December 14, 1904									
255	1	Beaver, Earnest	1	M	1/2	John Beaver	5924	Cr	Ella Beaver		Non
		New Born Census Card No. 235, P. O. Weleetka, Date of Birth No. 1, June 12, 1901; No. 2, May 12, 1904									
256	1	Berryhill, Alice	4	F	F	Joe Berryhill	4820	Cr	Sallie Berryhill	4821	Cr
257	2	Berryhill, Reno	1	M	F	Joe Berryhill	4820	Cr	Hepsie Berryhill	1606	Cr
		New Born Census Card No. 237, P. O. Broken Arrow, Date of Birth January 8, 1902									
258	1	Trusler, Fred	3	M	1/4	Frank Trusler		Non	Phoebe B. Trusler	5415	Cr
		New Born Census Card No. 238, P. O. Muskogee, Date of Birth October 21, 1901									
259	1	Daily, Margaret Willison	3	F	1-16	Dr. C. E. Daily		Non	Lucy S. Daily	5775	Cr
		New Born Census Card No. 242, P. O. Coweta, Date of Birth February 13, 1903									
260	1	Wadsworth, Mary	2	F	1/2	Mitchell Wadsworth	6195	Cr	Emma Wadsworth	2444	Cr
		New Born Census Card No. 244, P. O. Wetumka, Date of Birth No. 1, January 31, 1902; No. 2, February 2, 1904									
261	1	Wesley, Peter	1	M	F	John Wesley	6224	Cr	Polly Wesley	6448	Cr
353	2	Wesley, Tiger	3	M	F	John Wesley	6224	Cr	Polly Wesley	6448	Cr
		New Born Census Card No. 246, P. O. Wetumka, Date of Birth August 30, 1903									
262	1	King, Lucy	2	F	F	Amos King	6479	Cr	Simondy King	6480	Cr
		New Born Census Card No. 248, P. O. Bristow, Date of Birth August 24, 1901									
263	1	Clinton, Nexie	4	M	F	George Clinton	7010	Cr	Sallie Clinton	7011	Cr
		New Born Census Card No. 249, P. O. Fame, Date of Birth September 3, 1904									
264	1	Gray, Addie	1	F	F	Siah Gray	6530	Cr	Mary Gray	6531	Cr
		New Born Census Card No. 250, P. O. Coweta, Date of Birth April 15, 1904									
265	1	Wofford, Jackson	1	M	1/2	Sherly Wofford		Non	Lizzie Wofford	1008	Cr
		New Born Census Card No. 254, P. O. Coweta, Date of Birth No. 1, February 12, 1902; No. 3, March 11, 1904									
266	1	Tiger, Phillip	3	M	F	James Tiger	1122	Cr	Nancy Tiger	1123	Cr
1228	2	Tiger, Joanna	1	F	F	James Tiger	1122	Cr	Nancy Tiger	1123	Cr

Roll No.	No.	NAME	Age	Sex	Blood	NAME OF FATHER	Roll No.	Cit.	NAME OF MOTHER	Roll No.	Cit.
New Born Census Card No. 256, P. O. Okemah, Date of Birth No. 1, June 15, 1903; No. 2, October 1, 1904											
267	1	Harjo, Lizzie	2	F	F	Tulsa Harjo	6720	Cr	Mollie Harjo	7738	Cr
268	2	Harjo, Melissa	1	F	F	Tulsa Harjo	6720	Cr	Mollie Harjo	7738	Cr
New Born Census Card No. 257, P. O. Broken Arrow, Date of Birth No. 1, April 14, 1902; No. 2, October 3, 1903											
269	1	Bemore, Dora	3	F	¼	Charlie Bemore		Non	Maggie Bemore	7556	Cr
270	2	Bemore, Lewis	1	M	¼	Charlie Bemore		Non	Maggie Bemore	7556	Cr
New Born Census Card No. 260, P. O. Tulsa, Date of Birth November 28, 1902											
271	1	McBirney, Dorothy Vera	2	F	1-16	James H. McBirney		Non	Vera McBirney	3083	Cr
New Born Census Card No. 261, P. O. Sapulpa Date of Birth No. 1, August 15, 1903; No. 2, January 27, 1905											
272	1	Miller, George Thomas	2	M	1-16	Benjamin F. Miller		Non	Margaret A. Miller	2440	Cr
273	2	Miller, James Franklin	1	M	1-16	Benjamin F. Miller		Non	Margaret A. Miller	2440	Cr
New Born Census Card No. 263, P. O. Eufaula, Date of Birth No. 1, June 7, 1902; No. 2, May 1, 1904											
274	1	Francis, Roley	3	M	F	William Francis	399	Cr	Minkey Francis	400	Cr
275	2	Francis, Samuel	1	M	F	William Francis	399	Cr	Minkey Francis	400	Cr
New Born Census Card No. 264, P. O. Tulsa, Date of Birth December 27, 1903											
276	1	Enrigues, William	1	M	½	Jesus Enrigues		Non	Lizzie Enrigues	7111	Cr
New Born Census Card No. 270, P. O. Bixby, Date of Birth August 1, 1902											
277	1	Berryhill, Charles Percy	3	M	1-16	Andrew J. Berryhill	1734	Cr	Lula Berryhill		Non
New Born Census Card No. 271, P. O. Sapulpa, Date of Birth No. 1, June 28, 1902; No. 2, January 2, 1904											
278	1	Ricketts, Clarence Francis	3	M	1-16	Robert J. Ricketts	2438	Cr	Ethel J. Ricketts		Non
279	2	Ricketts, Goldie Ardell	1	F	1-16	Robert J. Ricketts	2438	Cr	Ethel J. Ricketts		Non
New Born Census Card No. 273, P. O. Sapulpa, Date of Birth No. 1, September 20, 1901; No. 2, November 12, 1903											
280	1	Weaver, Lois Alleen	3	F	1-16	Bert W. Weaver		Non	Rena Weaver	9223	Cr
281	2	Weaver, Bert Leo	1	F	1-16	Bert W. Weaver		Non	Rena Weaver	9223	Cr
New Born Census Card No. 274, P. O. Brush Hill, Date of Birth November 1, 1904											
282	1	Grayson, Samson	1	M	⅝	Robert Grayson	4023	Cr	Louiza Grayson	4024	Cr
New Born Census Card No. 277, P. O. Coweta, Date of Birth August 17, 1904											
283	1	McDonald, Edward Ray	1	M	1-16	Martin J. McDonald		Non	MattieB.McDonald	2001	Cr
New Born Census Card No. 278, P. O. Calvin, Date of Birth May 29, 1903											
284	1	Wiseman, Harry	2	M	¼	Charley Wiseman		Non	Hepsie Wiseman	7397	Cr
New Born Census Card No. 281, P. O. Boynton, Date of Birth No. 1, September 14, 1901; No. 2, July 14, 1903; No. 3, October 21, 1904											
285	1	Weaver, May	4	F	¼	Edward Weaver	490	Cr	Lizzie Weaver		Non
286	2	Weaver, Billie	2	M	¼	Edward Weaver	490	Cr	Lizzie Weaver		Non
287	3	Weaver, Amos	1	M	¼	Edward Weaver	490	Cr	Lizzie Weaver		Non
New Born Census Card No. 282, P. O. Bixby, Date of Birth December 29, 1902											
288	1	Squire, Sarah	2	F	F	John Squire	1930	Cr	Annie Squire	1915	Cr
New Born Census Card No. 283, P. O. Stonebluff, Date of Birth August 6, 1901											
289	1	Rothammer, Ernest Ralph	4.	M	⅛	Joseph Rothhammer		Non	LouisaJ.Rothhammer	148	Cr
New Born Census Card No. 289, P. O. Wagoner, Date of Birth August 12, 1902											
290	1	Parks, Dora Ellen	3	F	1-16	Wm. Parks		Non	Margaret Atkins Parks	9805	Cr
New Born Census Card No. 298, P. O. Arbeka, Date of Birth, No. 1 March 30, 1902; Zo. 2, December 29, 1903											
291	1	Harjo, Roman	3	M	½	A. E. Harjo		Non	Amey Harjo	6446	Cr
292	2	Harjo, Mord	1	F	½	A. E. Harjo		Non	Amey Harjo	6446	Cr
New Born Census Card No. 300, P. O. Fentress, Date of Birth January 26, 1904											
293	1	Berryhill, Charlie	1	M	⅞	Sam Berryhill	3837	Cr	Sophia Berryhill	3838	Cr
New Born Census Card No. 301, P. O. Arbeka, Date of Birth July 3, 1903											
294	1	Frank, Leah	2	F	F	Barney Frank	32	Cr	Lidda Frank	33	Cr
New Born Census Card No. 302, P. O. Paden, Date of Birth June 2, 1902											
295	1	Fixico, California	3	M	F	Cano Fixeco	8921	Cr	Lucy Fixeco	8909	Cr
New Born Census Card No. 303, P. O. Paden, Date of Birth December 13, 1904											
296	1	Musgrove, Herold D.	1	M	1-32	George Musgrove		Non	Myrta May Musgrove	1518	Cr
New Born Census Card No. 304, P. O. Okemah, Date of Birth October 19, 1902											
297	1	Fipps, Eva	2	F	1-16	Sam Fipps		Non	Alice M. Fipps	1517	Cr
New Born Census Card No. 306, P. O. Keokuk Falls, Date of Birth July 5, 1902											
298	1	Wolf, Seaner	3	F	½	Wallace Wolf		Non	Nancy Wolf	6234	Cr
New Born Census Card No. 307, P. O. Paden, Date of Birth No. 1, February 14, 1905; No. 2, December 24, 1902											
299	1	Foster, Oceola	1	M	F	Dzvid Foster	6637	Cr	Melanie Foster	6638	Cr
300	2	Foster, Jimmie	2	M	F	David Foster	6637	Cr	Melanie Foster	6638	Cr
New Born Census Card No. 308, P. O. Haskell, Date of Birth No. 1, January 12, 1905; No. 2, March 14, 1903											
301	1	Kelly, Elizabeth	1	F	⅝	Ferdinand Kelly	905	Cr	Lizzie Moore Kelly	1089	Cr
302	2	Kelly, Roland E.	2	M	⅝	Ferdinand Kelly	905	Cr	Lizzie Moore Kelly	1089	Cr
New Born Census Card No. 310, P. O. Irene, Date of Birth No. 1, September 14, 1902; No. 2, February 3, 1904											
303	1	Baker, Luther I.	2	M	½	Kinkehee N. Baker		Non	Rebecca J. Baker	5833	Cr
304	2	Baker, Everett M.	1	M	½	Kinkehee N. Baker		Non	Rebecca J. Baker	5833	Cr
New Born Census Card No. 312, P. O. Schulter, Date of Birth No. 1, July 16, 1904; No. 2, September 5, 1902											
305	1	Baker, Inez W.	2	F	½	Billy Baker		Non	Susie Baker	6642	Cr
1023	2	Baker, Pauline E.	1	F	½	Billy Baker		Non	Susie Baker	6642	Cr

Roll No.	No.	NAME	Age	Sex	Blood	NAME OF FATHER	Roll No.	Cit.	NAME OF MOTHER	Roll No.	Cit.
		New Born Census Card No. 313, P. O. Wagoner, Date of Birth January 9, 1904									
306	1	Childers, Stella	1	F	⅞	Anderson J Childers	3970	Cr	Lydia Childers	3971	Cr
		New Born Census Card No. 315, P. O. Boynton, Date of Birth February 28, 1903									
307	1	Hutton, Iola	2	F	⅛	Henry Hutton	427	Cr F	Annie Hutton	885	Cr
		New Born Census Card No. 316, P. O. Boley, Date of Birth No. 1, May 20, 1902; No. 2, March 8, 1904									
308	1	Johnson, Leora	3	F	⅛	Paro Johnson	673	Cr-F	Hannah Johnson	5265	Cr
309	2	Johnson, Ella	1	F	⅛	Paro Johnson	673	Cr-F	Hannah Johnson	5265	Cr
		New Born Census Card No. 317, P. O. Tullahassee, Date of Birth April 13, 1903									
310	1	Murrell, Wiley	2	M	½	Calhoun Murrell	3460	Cr-F	Lucy Murrell	1607	Cr
		New Born Census Card No. 318, P. O. Henryetta, Date of Birth September 4, 1904									
311	1	Tiger, Jefferson	1	M	F	Lilly Tiger	7944	Cr	Lucinda Tiger	5067	Cr
		New Born Census Card No. 319, P. O. Dustin, Date of Birth October 10, 1903									
312	1	John, Albert	1	M	¾	Short John	7189	Cr	Winey John	7190	Cr
		New Born Census Card No. 320, P. O. Dustin, Date of Birth No. 1, February 17, 1902; No. 2, May 8, 1904									
313	1	Brown, Ada	3	F	½	Joe Brown	7680		Lizzie Brown	7681	Cr
314	2	Brown, Sandy	2	M	½	Joe Brown	7680		Lizzie Brown	7681	Cr
		New Born Census Card No. 321, P. O. Hanna, Date of Birth March 12, 1904									
315	1	Brooks, Thomas Clifford	1	M	⅜	John Brooks		Non	Bettie Brooks	6146	Cr
		New Born Census Card No. 323, P. O. Wetumka, Date of Birth May 15, 1904									
316	1	Sandy, Stella	1	F	F	Jacob Sandy	5125	Cr	Sophia Sandy	5126	Cr
		New Born Census Card No. 324, P. O. Henryetta, Date of Birth January 29, 1904									
317	1	Key, Hugh Benjamin	1	M	1-16	John E. Key		Non	Luella Key	3642	Cr
		New Born Census Card No. 325, P. O. Henryetta, Date of Birth February 4, 1902									
318	1	Henry, Hillibe Micco	3	M	⅛	Hugh Henry	3641	Cr	Mintie Henry		Non
		New Born Census Card No. 328, P. O. Arbeka, Date of Birth No. 1, May 18, 1903; No. 2, June 7, 1904									
319	1	Davis, Ross	2	M	⅜	Jess Davis		Non	Ella Davis	5875	Cr
320	2	Davis, Eugene	1	M	⅜	Jess Davis		Non	Ella Davis	5875	Cr
		New Born Census Card No. 330, P. O. Oktaha, Date of Birth April 5, 1902									
321	1	Newberry, Buford	3	M	¼	John Newberry		Non	Jeannetta Newberry	2714	Cr
		New Born Census Card No. 331, P. O. Boley, Date of Birth June 16, 1904									
322	1	Cobb, Johnnie	1	M	½	John Cobb	4900	Cr-F	Addie Cobb	4407	Cr
		New Born Census Card No. 332, P. O. Coweta, Date of Birth No. 1, July 13, 1902; No. 2, June 6, 1904									
323	1	Childers, Ruthie	3	F	¾	Ben Childers	650	Cr	Annie B. Childers	651	Cr
324	2	Childers, Mose	1	M	¾	Ben Childers	650	Cr	Annie B. Childers	651	Cr
		New Born Census Card No. 333, P. O. Clarksville, Date of Birth November 28, 1902									
325	1	Perryman, Montie	2	M	½	Benjamin Perryman	5102	Cr	Mary Perryman		Non
		New Born Census Card No. 338, P. O. Hanna, Date of Birth No. 1, June 9, 1902; No. 2, March 3, 1905									
326	1	Reynolds, Arthur Leroy	3	M	¼	John R. Reynolds		Non	Eva Edna Reynolds	7461	Cr
327	2	Reynolds, Lizzie	1	F	¼	John R. Reynolds		Non	Eva Edna Reynolds	7461	Cr
		New Born Census Card No. 342, P. O. Henryetta, Date of Birth December 5, 1902									
328	1	Deere, Raymond	2	M	F	Thompson Deere	7626	Cr	Lucy Deere	7789	Cr
		New Born Census Card No. 344, P. O. Castle, Date of Birth No. 1, October 7, 1902; No. 2, September 13, 1904									
329	1	Anderson, Bessie	2	F	½	Bennie Anderson		Non	Winey Anderson	5381	Cr
330	2	Anderson, Wisey	1	F	½	Bennie Anderson		Non	Winey Anderson	5381	Cr
		New Born Census Card No. 345, P. O. Dustin, Date of Birth No. 1, September 7, 1902; No. 2, December 23, 1904									
331	1	Henry, Eugene Rolley	3	M	1-16	W. A. Henry		Non	Lula Henry	3548	Cr
332	2	Henry, Willie Jackson	1	M	1-16	W. A. Henry		Non	Lula Henry	3548	Cr
		New Born Census Card No. 347, P. O. Sapulpa, Date of Birth No. 1, September 11, 1903; No. 2, September 11, 1904									
333	1	Helton, Ruthia Ellen	1	F	½	William B. Helton		Non	Nellie Helton	663	Cr
334	2	Helton, Romie Robert	1	M	½	William B. Helton		Non	Nellie Helton	663	Cr
		New Born Census Card No. 349, P. O. Henryetta, Date of Birth February 17, 1905									
335	1	Henry, Tebinina	1	F	⅛	Hugh Henry	3641	Cr	Mintie Henry		Non
		New Born Census Card No. 89, P. O. Quinton, Date of Birth No. 1, July 1, 1902; No. 2, September 12, 1904									
336	1	Leath, Jessie May	3	F	1-64	Thomas Jefferson Leath	1999	Cr	Ida Jane Leath		Non
337	2	Leath, James Henry	1	M	1-64	Thomas Jefferson Leath	1999	Cr	Ida Jane Leath		Non
		New Born Census Card No. 45, P. O. Paden, Date of Birth March 9, 1904									
338	1	Grant, Lena	1	F	F	Niffie Grant	5661	Cr	Mary Grant	5662	Cr
		New Born Census Card No. 51, P. O. Tullahassee, Date of Birth No. 1, March 12, 1902; No. 2, September 25, 1904									
339	1	Futrell, Jimmie	3	M	¼	Frank Futrell		Non	Alice Futrell	780	Cr
340	2	Futrell, Pearlic	1	F	¼	Frank Futrell		Non	Alice Futrell	780	Cr
		New Born Census Card No. 64, P. O. Eufaula, Date of Birth January 20, 1903									
341	1	McCalvey, Joseph Hiram	2	M	1-16	Joseph McCalvey	4438	Cr	Ella McCalvey		Non
		New Born Census Card No. 73, P. O. Oktaha, Date of Birth No. 1, April 17, 1903; No. 2, December 12, 1904									
342	1	Stephens, Willie	2	M	¼	Green Stephens		Non	Millie Stephens	3661	Cr
343	2	Stephens, Johnnie	1	M	¼	Green Stephens		Non	Millie Stephens	3661	Cr
		New Born Census Card No. 96, P. O. Krebs, Date of Birth No. 1, May 6, 1904; No. 2, May 2, 1902									
344	1	Hendrickson, Elijah	1	M	1-16	Joseph Hendrickson		Non	Mary Hendrickson	3397	Cr
692	2	Hendrickson, Peter	3	M	1-16	Joseph Hendrickson		Non	Mary Hendrickson	3397	Cr
		New Born Census Card No. 128, P. O. Haskell, Date of Birth July 7, 1902									
345	1	Davis, Elizabeth E.	3	F	½	J. R. Davis		Non	Nancy Pigeon	5345	Cr
		New Born Census Card No. 137, P. O. Wetumka, Date of Birth April 12, 1904									
346	1	Dunzy, Velma	1	F	¾	Jackson Dunzy	3201	Cr	Lucinda Dunzy	3202	Cr

Roll No.	No.	NAME	Age	Sex	Blood	NAME OF FATHER	Roll No.	Cit.	NAME OF MOTHER	Roll No.	Cit
	New Born Census Card No. 160										
347	1	Hill, Mandy	1	F	F	For data, see same card as enrollment No. 229.					
	New Born Census Card No. 173, P. O. Holdenville, Date of Birth No. 1, February 28, 1902; No. 2, March 22, 1904										
348	1	Yahola, Roman	3	M	F	Jackson Yahola	5293	Cr	Celia Yahola	5294	Cr
349	2	Yahola, Houston	1	M	F	Jackson, Yahola	5293	Cr	Celia Yahola	5294	Cr
	New Born Census Card No. 175, P. O. Holdenville, Date of Birth January 29, 1902										
350	1	Anderson, Charley Illegitimate	3	M	F	Newman Jacobs	275	Cr	Martha Anderson	6520	Cr
	New Born Census Card No. 189										
351	1	Williams, Henryetta	1	F	1-16	For date, see same card as Enrollment No. 239					
	New Born Census Card No. 241, P. O. Beggs, Date of Birth July 6, 1902										
352	1	Stake, Missie	3	F	F	Albert Stake	1414	Cr	Sallie Stake	1415	Cr
	New Born Census Card No. 244, P. O. Wetumka, Date of Birth January 31, 1902										
353	1	Wesley, Tiger	3	M	F	John Wesley	6224	Cr	Polly Wesley	6448	Cr
	New Born Census Card No. 259, P. O. Beggs, Date of Birth No. 1, March 22, 1903; No. 2, January 12, 1905										
354	1	Washington, George	2	M	11-16	Dixon Washington	6385	Cr	Aggie Washington	3876	Cr
355	2	Washington, Sadie	1	F	11-16	Dixon, Washington	6385	Cr	Aggie Washington	3876	Cr
	New Born Census Card No. 265, P. O. Haskell, Date of Birth September 16, 1901										
356	1	Deer, Ellen Both parents dead	3	F	F	Silas Deer	2207	Cr	Nancy Deer	3595	Cr
	New Born Census Card No. 267, P. O. Checotah, Date of Birth May 31, 1903										
357	1	Carr, Verna Vinita	2	F	⅛	Thomas Carr	2378	Cr	Ada Carr		Non
	New Born Census Card No. 272, P. O. Stidham, Date of Birth June 18, 1903										
358	1	Moore, Susie	2	F	½	Albert Moore	1867	Cr	Leah Moore	1868	Cr
	New Born Census Card No. 276, P. O. Coweta, Date of Birth July 8, 1902										
359	1	Haynie, Felix Jr.	3	M	F	Felix Haynie	726	Cr	Mary Haynie	5731	Cr
	New Born Census Card No. 286, P. O. Yeager, Date of Birth October 14, 1904										
360	1	Scott, Lillian	1	F	½	James Scott	4864	Cr	Lucy Scott		Semi
	New Born Census Card No. 291, P. O. Weleetka, Date of Birth February 24, 1905										
361	1	Asbury, Eliza	1	F	⅞	George T. Asbury	4445	Cr	Sarah Asbury	4740	Cr
	New Born Census Card No. 292, P. O. Weleetka, Date of Birth March 13, 1902										
362	1	Simmons, Samuel	3	M	F	John Simmons	4739	Cr	Sarah Asbury	4740	Cr
	New Born Census Card No. 299, P. O. Morse, Date of Birth No. 1, October 25, 1903; No. 2, September 22, 1904										
363	1	Cherry, Colona Blanche	1	F	⅜	Joe Cherry		Non	Jennie Cherry	6587	Cr
364	2	Cherry, Francis Doyle	1	M	⅜	Joe Cherry		Non	Jennie Cherry	6587	Cr
	New Born Census Card No. 311, P. O. Catoosa, Date of Birth March 10, 1904										
365	1	Asbury, Sippie	1	M	⅞	Francis Asbury	1142	Cr	Jennetta Asbury	1143	Cr
	New Born Census Card No. 326, P. O. Hanna, Date of Birth January 20, 1904										
366	1	Gatlin, Helen	1	F	½	C. C. Gatlin		Non	Lucy Ann Gatlin	7054	Cr
	New Born Census Card No. 327, P. O. Weleetka, Date of Birth January 12, 1905										
367	1	Ditzler, James Albert	1	M	½	Will Ditzler		Non	Melvina Ditzler	4953	Cr
	New Born Census Card No. 343, P. O. Morse, Date of Birth February 26, 1905										
368	1	Unussee, Mardie	1	M	F	Barnossee Unussee	7935	Cr	Nicey Unussee	4037	Cr
	New Born Census Card No. 346, P. O. Wewoka, Date of Birth May 20, 1903										
369	1	Bell, Nellie	2	F	½	Josie Bell		Non	Lizzie Marshall Bell	22	Cr
	New Born Census Card No. 353, P. O. Arbeka, Date of Birth March 12, 1904										
370	1	Frank, William	1	M	⅞	Tingo Frank	34	Cr	Amanda J. Frank	35	Cr
	New Born Census Card No. 354, P. O. Dustin, Date of Birth March 23, 1904										
371	1	Fife, James	1	M	F	Sandy Fife	7971	Cr	Louisa Fife	8031	Cr
	New Born Census Card No. 356, P. O. Newby, Date of Birth January 1, 1903 (Twins)										
372	1	Mayes, Martha Jr.	2	F	½	Wyatt Mayes		Non	Martha Mayes	3322	Cr
373	2	Mayes, Marry	2	F	½	Wyatt Mayes		Non	Martha Mayes	3322	Cr
	New Born Census Card No. 357, P. O. Dustin, Date of Birth No. 1, September 18, 1904; No. 2, October 20, 1901										
374	1	Whitlow, Sissie	1	F	½	William Whitlow		Non	Simhoye Whitlow	8014	Cr
	New Born Census Card No. 358, P. O. Checotah, Date of Birth No. 1, June 23, 1901; No. 2, March 18, 1904										
375	1	Lewis, Frank Turner	4	M	⅛	Osker Lewis		Non	Ellen Lewis	2364	Cr
376	2	Lewis, John David	1	M	⅛	Osker Lewis		Non	Ellen Lewis	2364	Cr
	New Born Census Card No. 360, P. O. Checotah, Date of Birth April 1, 1903										
377	1	Hood, Reid Lee	2	M	⅛	Sterling P. Hood		Non	Sarah Malinda Hood	2357	Cr
	New Born Census Card No. 361, P. O. Checotah, Date of Birth March 16, 1902										
378	1	Wright, Olive A.	3	F	1-16	C. J. Wright		Non	Jane P. Wright	4081	Cr
	New Born Census Card No. 362, P. O. Slumker, Date of Birth March 24, 1903										
379	1	Moore, John	2	M	½	John Moore		Non	Haney Moore	6314	Cr
	New Born Census Card No. 364, P. O. Carson, Date of Birth No. 1, February 6, 1905; No. 2, February 1, 1903										
389	1	Benham, Lucy Etta	1	F	½	Claude Benham		Non	Melinda Benham	4607	Cr
381	2	Benham, James Albert	2	M	½	Claude Benham		Non	Melinda Benham	4607	Cr
	New Born Census Card No. 365, P. O. Bristow, Date of Birth March 15, 1904										
382	1	Mosquito, Kattie	1	F	F	Albert Mosquito	1906	Cr	Polly Mosquito	1967	Cr
	New Born Census Card No. 366, P. O. Broken Arrow, Date of Birth February 17, 1904										
383	1	Hewlett, Myrtle Illegitimate	1	F	⅛	Will Hewlett		Non	Katie Cowans	1320	Cr
	New Born Census Card No. 367, P. O. Okemah, Date of Birth March 14, 1903										
384	1	Tarvin, Marie Louisa	2	F	1-16	Pleasant F. Tarvin	9098	Cr	Patience F. Tarvin		Non
	New Born Census Card No. 368, P. O. Dustin, Date of Birth No. 1, June 29, 1902; No. 2, October 28, 1904										
385	1	Henry, Viola Velmer	3	F	1-16	James S. Henry		Non	Lucy Henry	3545	Cr
386	2	Henry, James Pier	1	M	1-16	James S. Henry		Non	Lucy Henry	3545	Cr

Roll No.	No.	NAME	Age	Sex	Blood	NAME OF FATHER	Roll No.	Cit.	NAME OF MOTHER	Roll No.	Cit.
		New Born Census Card No. 370, P. O. Broken Arrow, Date of Birth April 23, 1902									
387	1	Childers, Ruby Mildred	3	F	7/8	Daniel Childers	2708	Cr	Mildred Childers	2709	Cr
		New Born Census Card No. 372, P. O. Dustin, Date of Birth December 26, 1901									
388	1	Looney, Forest Leonard	3	M	7-16	N. W. Looney		Non	Ella Looney	1991	Cr
		New Born Census Card No. 373, P. O. Morse, Date of Birth January 22, 1904									
389	1	Knight, Leaster	1	F	F	Ramsey Knight	532	Cr	Amy Knight	533	Cr
		New Born Census Card No. 374, P. O. Morse, Date of Birth July 1, 1903									
390	1	Tiger, Ada	1	F	F	Jumbo Tiger	6663	Cr	Soconthlaney Tiger	6705	Cr
		New Born Census Card No. 375, P. O. Okemah, Date of Birth December 27, 1902									
391	1	Hill, Arney	2	F	F	Elmer Hill	6524	Cr	Lottie Hill	6921	Cr
		New Born Census Card No. 376, P. O. Bixby, Date of Birth July 4, 1903									
392	1	Fox, Katie	2	F	F	Luke Fox	1816	Cr	Maggie Fox	1817	Cr
		New Born Census Card No. 379, P. O. Summit, Date of Birth January 7, 1905									
393	1	Smith, Gladdis G.	1	F	1-64	J. M. Smith		Non	Rachel Smith	2502	Cr
		New Born Census Card No. 380, P. O. Tullahassee, Date of Birth November 25, 1901									
394	1	Davis, Annie	3	F	1-16	John Davis	60	Cr	Martha Napier		Non
		New Born Census Card No. 381, P. O. Henryetta, Date of Birth November 30, 1904									
395	1	Powell, John	1	M	1/2	Charles Powell		Non	Martha Powell	5334	Cr
		New Born Census Card No. 382, P. O. Weleetka, Date of Birth July 20, 1902									
396	1	Stephenson, Siney	3	F	1/2	A. P. Stephenson		Non	Polly Stephenson	5103	Cr
		New Born Census Card No. 383, P. O. Wetumka, Date of Birth No. 1, September 10, 1901; No. 2, March 1, 1903; No. 3, November 29, 1904									
397	1	Lucas, Rufus	3	M	1/2	Thomas Lucas		Non	Mary Lucas	6582	Cr
398	2	Lucas, Frank	2	M	1/2	Thomas Lucas		Non	Mary Lucas	6582	Cr
399	3	Lucas, Josephine	1	F	1/2	Thomas Lucas		Non	Mary Lucas	6582	Cr
		New Born Census Card No. 385, P. O. Morse; Date of Birth February 27, 1902									
400	1	Knight, Jenetta	3	F	F	London Knight	538	Cr	Susan Knight	539	Cr
		New Born Census Card No. 386, P. O. Okfuskee, Date of Birth March 31, 1903									
401	1	Porter, Benjamin	3	M	F	James Porter	4193	Cr	Nancy Porter	4194	Cr
		New Born Census Card No. 387, P. O. Dustin, Date of Birth December 2, 1903									
402	1	Looney, Della May	1	F	7-16	N. W. Looney		Non	Ella Looney	1991	C
		New Born Census Card No. 388, P. O. Leonard, Date of Birth No. 1, September 22, 1902; No. 2, May 3, 1904									
403	1	Bell, Thompson	2	M	F	Eli Bell	2311	Cr	Silby Bell	2312	Cr
404	2	Bell, Suthie	1	M	F	Eli Bell	2311	Cr	Silby Bell	2312	Cr
		New Born Census Card No. 390, P. O. Okemah, Date of Birth July 30, 1901									
405	1	Morton, Claude S.	4	M	1/8	Mossie Morton	4261	Cr	Josie A. Morton		Non
		New Born Census Card No. 392 or 3, P. O. Weleetka, Date of Birth March 2, 1904									
406	1	Harris, Cora	1	F	1/8	Charley Harris		Non	Polly Harris	3127	Cr
		New Born Census Card No. 394, P. O. Brush Hill, Date of Birth August 23, 1902									
407	1	McNac, Flossie	3	F	1/2	Fred McNac	4811	Cr-F	Annie McNac	494	Cr
		New Born Census Card No. 395, P. O. Dustin, Date of Birth July 11, 1901									
408	1	Wills, William H.	4	M	1/8	John J. Wills	1539	Cr	Ollie Ann Wills		Non
		New Born Census Card No. 398, P. O. Broken Arrow, Date of Birth, November 10, 1902									
409	1	Litka, Newman	2	M	1/2	Richard Litka		Non	Martha Litka	1448	Cr
		New Born Census Card No. 399, P. O. Carson, Date of Birth May 16, 1902									
410	1	Wilson, Bennie	3	M	F	Charley Wilson	8479	Cr	Lizzie Wilson	8018	Cr
		New Born Census Card No. 400, P. O. Mounds, Date of Birth No. 1 December 1901; No. 2 September 1903									
411	1	Frank, Neddie	3	M	F	Short Frank	1830	Cr	Betty Frank	1831	Cr
412	2	Frank, Mahala	2	F	F	Short Frank	1830	Cr	Betty Frank	1831	Cr
		New Born Census Card No. 402, P. O. Okemah, Date of Birth July 28, 1904									
413	1	Morrow, Elva	1	M	1/2	Alfred Morrow		Non	Marsey Morrow	1234	Cr
		New Born Census Card No. 403, P. O. Weleetka, Date of Birth December 10, 1903									
414	1	Baker, George	1	M	F	Lasley Baker	5065	Cr	Anna Baker	5366	Cr
		New Born Census Card No. 404, P. O. Grayson, Date of Birth No. 1 December 2, 1903; No. 2 February 16, 1902									
415	1	Smith, Albert K.	1	M	1/8	Thomas M. Smith	3104	Cr	Adeline Smith		Non
416	2	Smith, Steve J.	3	M	1/8	Thomas M. Smith	3104	Cr	Adeline Smith		Non
		New Born Census Card No. 409, P. O. Okfuskee, Date of Birth March 22, 1904									
417	1	Davis, Alice	1	F	F	Joe Davis	3767	Cr	Coger Davis	3768	Cr
		New Born Census Card No. 410, P. O. Okemah, Date of Birth July 6, 1903									
418	1	Fixico, Willie	2	M	F	Katcher Fixico	7234	Cr	Cinda Fixico	9855	Cr
		New Born Census Card No. 411, P. O. Checotah, Date of Birth No. 1 January 14, 1903; No. 2 December 19, 1904									
419	1	Storm, Bertha	2	F	1/8	John Storm		Non	Lou Storm	2353	Cr
420	2	Storm, Pocahontas	1	F	1/8	John Storm		Non	Lou Storm	2353	Cr
		New Born Census Card No. 413, P. O. Oktaha, Date of Birth December 31, 1903									
421	1	Evans, Nettie	1	F	1-16	Richard Evans	3627	Cr	Della A. Evans		Non
		New Born Census Card No. 414, P. O. Dustin, Date of Birth, No. 1 October 16, 1903; No. 2 February 15, 1902									
422	1	Wilson, Raymond	1	M	3/8	R. B. Wilson		Non	Hettie Wilson	2656	Cr
423	2	Wilson, Sarah Jane	3	F	3/8	R. B. Wilson		Non	Hettie Wilson	2656	Cr
		New Born Census Card No. 415, P. O. Coweta, Date of Birth No. 1 Devember 20, 1904; No. 2 August 8, 1902									
424	1	Charles, Sophia	1	F	1/4	Nero Charles	C.F.3355	Cr-F	Ellen Charles	1052	Cr
425	2	Charles, Ellis Buffington	3	M	1/4	Nero Charles	C.F.3355	Cr-F	Ellen Charles	1052	Cr
		New Born Census Card No. 416, P. O. Creek, Date of Birth June 22, 1904									
426	1	Micco, Lucy	1	F	F	Henry Micco	4011	Cr	Dochee Micco	6257	Cr

Roll No.	No.	NAME	Age	Sex	Blood	NAME OF FATHER	Roll No.	Cit.	NAME OF MOTHER	Roll No.	Cit
		New Born Census Card No. 417, P. O. Henryetta, Date of Birth No. 1 March 22, 1902; No. 2 August 1, 1904									
427	1	Kelly, Roman	3	M	F	Wadly Kelly	1275	Cr	Mahala Kelly	1276	Cr
428	2	Kelly, Alabama	1	F	F	Wadly Kelly	1275	Cr	Mahala Kelly	1276	Cr
		New Born Census Card No. 418, P. O. Morris, Date of Birth No. 1 June 28, 1902; No. 2 November 21, 1904									
429	1	Yardy, Hettie	3	F	¾	Thomas Yardy	683	Cr	Armer Yardy	1649	Cr
430	2	Yardy, Dock	1	M	¾	Thomas Yardy	683	Cr	Armer Yardy	1649	Cr
		New Born Census Card No. 419, P. O. Coweta, Date of Birth February 16, 1903									
431	1	Childers, Maria	2	F	F	William Childers	1055	Cr	Annie Childers	1056	Cr
		New Born Census Card No. 420, P. O. Sapulpa, Date of Birth July 8, 1902									
432	1	McKim, Willie Byno	3	M	1-16	Robert A. McKim	3060	Cr	Minnie G. McKim		Non
		New Born Census Card No. 421, P. O. Coweta, Date of Birth May 7, 1902									
433	1	Childers, Emmet	3	M	F	Garfield Childers	1004	Cr	Ida Childers	1042	Cr
		New Born Census Card No. 422, P. O. Eufaula, Date of Birth January 4, 1905									
434	1	Simpson, Mary Elizabeth	1	F	1-64	Robert L. Simpson	1188	Cr	Agnes Simpson		Non
		New Born Census Card No. 423, P. O. Castle, Date of Birth November 5, 1903									
435	1	Fixico, Robert	1	M	F	Tulmochus Fixico	6692	Cr	Sally Fixico	6693	Cr
		New Born Census Card No. 424, P. O. Tullahassee, Date of Birth August 30, 1904									
436	1	Woodward, Edith	1	F	¼	Herbert E. Woodward		Non	Nellie E. Woodward	2213	Cr
		New Born Census Card No. 425, P. O. Wagoner, Date of Birth August 2, 1902									
437	1	Cunningham, William Leo	2	M	¼	C. N. Cunningham		Non	Laura Cunningham	2445	Cr
		New Born Census Card No. 426, P. O. Checotah, Date of Birth January 31, 1904									
438	1	Richard, Annie	1	F	F	Jasper Richard	2671	Cr	Minnie Richard	2672	Cr
		New Born Census Card No. 427, P. O. Kellyville, Date of Birth No. 1 March 20, 1903; No. 2 February 6, 1905									
439	1	Self, Ivory Bell	2	F	1-16	James A. Self	3023	Cr	Mattie Self		Non
440	2	Self, Nellie E.	1	F	1-16	James A. Self	3023	Cr	Mattie Self		Non
		New Born Census Card No. 428, P. O. Kellyville, Date of Birth No. 1 October 25, 1902; No. 2 September 15, 1904									
441	1	Self, William K.	2	M	1-16	John H. Self	3032	Cr	Dollie Self		Non
442	2	Self, Edward N.	1	M	1-16	John H. Self	3032	Cr	Dollie Self		Non
		New Born Census Card No. 429, P. O. Fry, Date of Birth May 17, 1903									
443	1	Chisholm, Minnie	2	F	F	Anderson Chisholm	844	Cr	Rosa Chisholm	845	Cr
		New Born Census Card No. 430, P. O. Fry, Date of Birth April 9, 1904									
444	1	Larney, Almarine	1	M	¾	Dave Larney	72	Cr	Nancy Larney Alexander	7557	Cr
		New Born Census Card No. 431, P. O. Bixby, Date of Birth December 10, 1902									
445	1	Swingle, Hattie	2	F	1-16	Willoughby Swingle		Non	Corda Swingle	1561	Cr
		New Born Census Card No. 433, P. O. Morse, March 9, 1904									
446	1	Deer, Sealy	1	F	F	Joe Deer	4042	Cr	Yarner Deer	4043	Cr
		New Born Census Card No. 434, P. O. Oktaha, Date of Birth February 26, 1905									
447	1	Eubanks, William Albert	1	M	1-16	William Eubanks		Non	Minnie Eubanks	3614	Cr
		New Born Census Card No. 436, P. O. Weleetka, Date of Birth No. 1 March 4, 1904; No. 2 February 7, 1905									
448	1	Robison, Christie	1	F	¾	Amos Robison	4665	Cr	Louisa Robison	4612	Cr
449	2	Robison, Richard Chisholm	1	M	⅝	Amos Robison	4665	Cr	Lizzie Robison	6025	Cr
		New Born Census Card No. 438, P. O. Sapulpa, Date of Birth November 21, 1903									
450	1	Beaver, Mary Capitola	1	F	½	Samuel Beaver	3551	Cr	Ollie Beaver		Non
		New Born Census Card No. 442, P. O. Edna, Date of Birth July 28, 1904									
451	1	Bruner, Iva M.	1	F	½	Freeland Bruner	2821	Cr	Rhoda Bruner	2822	Cr
		New Born Census Card No. 445, P. O. Fentress, Date of Birth No. 1 July 31, 1902; No. 2 May 18, 1904									
452	1	McDermott, Lizzie	3	F	½	L. H. McDermott		Non	Mary McDermott	4692	Cr
453	2	McDermott, Charlie	1	M	½	L. H. McDermott		Non	Mary McDermott	4692	Cr
		New Born Census Card No. 447, P. O. Okemah, Date of Birth July 21, 1903									
454	1	Hall, Alta	2	F	⅜	Samuel Hall		Non	Hannah E. Hall	4112	Cr
		New Born Census Card No. 448, P. O. Quinton (Trenton), Date of Birth November 16, 1902									
455	1	Proctor, Lillie	2	F	F	Dave Proctor	7841	Cr	Katie Proctor	8199	Cr
		New Born Census Card No. 449, P. O. Edna, Date of Birth April 5, 1904									
456	1	Gooden, Carrie	1	F	¾	Henderson Gooden	3345	Cr	Dora Gooden	6999	Cr
		New Born Census Card No. 453, P. O. Carson, Date of Birth March 23, 1902									
457	1	Gown, Sarah Illegitimate.	3	F	½	Bud Gown		Non	Peggie Harper	8130	Cr
		New Born Census Card No. 454, P. O. Jennings, Date of Birth No. 1 January 23, 1903; No. 2 January 28, 1905									
458	1	Harris, Lulu May	2	F	⅛	Walter Harris	3636	Cr	Myrtle Harris		Non
459	2	Harris, Theodore Quincy	1	M	⅛	Walter Harris	3636	Cr	Myrtle Harris		Non
		New Born Census Card No. 455, P. O. Morse, Date of Birth July 1, 1903									
460	1	Stoddard, Joseph	2	M	F	William Stoddard	2858	Cr	Lousanna Stoddard	2859	Cr
		New Born Census Card No. 456, P. O. Morris, Date of Birth May 27, 1903									
461	1	Yahola, Abraham	2	M	F	Billy Yahola	524	Cr	Winey Yahola	525	Cr
		New Born Census Card No. 458, P. O. Oktaha, Date of Birth No. 1 July 30, 1902; No. 2 February 1, 1904									
462	1	Newton, Ewell Durant	4	M	1-32	Eugene Newton		Non	Sarah E. Newton	2572	Cr
463	2	Newton, Guy Jackson	1	M	1-32	Eugene Newton		Non	Sarah E. Newton	2572	Cr

Roll No.	No.	NAME	Age	Sex	Blood	NAME OF FATHER	Roll No.	Cit.	NAME OF MOTHER	Roll No.	Cit.
		New Born Census Card No. 461, P. O. Okemah, Date of Birth No. 1 June 14, 1903; No. 2 January 25, 1905									
464	1	Barnett, James	2	M	F	Daniel Barnett	4593	Cr	Cookie Barnett	4680	Cr
465	2	Barnett, Jesse	1	M	F	Daniel Barnett	4593	Cr	Cookie Barnett	4680	Cr
		New Born Census Card No. 463, P. O. Choska, Date of Birth January 19, 1902 (Twins)									
466	1	Gooch, Maudie	3	F	¼	Ed Gooch	7773	Cr	Adella Gooch		Non
467	2	Gooch, Claudie	3	M	¼	Ed Gooch	7773	Cr	Adella Gooch		Non
		New Born Census Card No. 465, P. O. Oktaha, Date of Birth July 27, 1904									
468	1	White, Romie Loundine	1	F	1-16	J. T. White		Non	Mary White	3613	Cr
		New Born Census Card No. 466, P. O. Brush Hill, Date of Birth August 8, 1903									
469	1	Fox, Elzie	2	M	F	John Fox	4265	Cr	Lena Fox	4266	Cr
		New Born Census Card No. 467, P. O. Wagoner, Date of Birth May 12, 1903									
470	1	Posey, Thomas Owen	2	M	1-16	Andy W. Posey	9111	Cr	Minnie Posey		Non
		New Born Census Card No. 468, P. O. Oktaha, Date of Birth August 8, 1903									
471	1	Lewis, Jimmy Illegitimate	2	M	F	Thomas Lewis	8422	Cr	Lucy Baker	588	Cr
		New Born Census Card No. 469, P. O. Sapulpa, Date of Birth No. 1 July 25, 1903; No. 2 February 28, 1905									
472	1	Island, Luvena	1	F	F	George Island	3157	Cr	Callie Island	3158	Cr
1041	2	Island, Louisa	1	F	F	George Island	3157	Cr	Callie Island	3158	Cr
		New Born Census Card No. 471, P. O. Broken Arrow, Date of Birth December 25, 1904									
473	1	Hooks, Richard Roy	1	M	¼	Lem P. Hooks		Non	Alice Hooks	3990	Cr
		New Born Census Card No. 472, P. O. Morse, Date of Birth No. 1 March 11, 1904; No. 2 November 1, 1901									
474	1	Benson, Edward	1	M	¾	William Benson	65	Cr	Katie Benson	4518	Cr
475	2	Benson, Billie	3	M	¾	William Benson	65	Cr	Katie Benson	4518	Cr
		New Born Census Card No. 473, P. O. Bixby, Date of Birth February 3, 1903									
476	1	Cooper, Nellie	2	F	F	Sam Cooper	1955	Cr	Nancy Cooper	1950	Cr
		New Born Census Card No. 474, P. O. Brush Hill, Date of Birth No. 1 September 2, 1903; No. 2 September 26, 1904									
477	1	Watson, Lela	2	F	7-16	Santa Watson	7659	Cr	Annie Watson	2744	Cr
935	2	Watson, Dave	1	M	7-16	Santa Watson	7659	Cr	Annie Watson	2744	Cr
		New Born Census Card No. 475, P. O. Wagoner, Date of Birth December 19, 1903									
478	1	Wiley, Haley	1	M	½	Andy Wiley	1473	Cr	Cora Wiley		Non
		New Born Census Card No. 476, P. O. Fentress, Date of Birth August 1, 1903									
479	1	Foster, Lula B.	2	F	¼	G. C. Foster		Non	Lonie Foster	3175	Cr
		New Born Census Card No. 478, P. O. Coweta, Date of Birth December 19, 1903									
480	1	Wiley, Charlie Illegitimate	1	M	F	Unknown			Susie Wiley	1475	Cr
		New Born Census Card No. 479, P. O. Fentress, Date of Birth No. 1 December 19, 1901; No. 2 May 16, 1903									
481	1	Proctor, Stella	3	F	¾	Wash Proctor	6096	Cr	Leah Proctor	5273	Cr
482	2	Proctor, Sam	2	M	F	Wash Proctor	6096	Cr	Katie Proctor	5281	Cr
		New Born Census Card No. 480, P. O. Tehuscana, Date of Birth April 27, 1904									
483	1	Posey, Lola Colesta	1	F	1-16	William A. Posey	9009	Cr	Nellie H. Posey		Non
		New Born Census Card No. 483, P. O. Wetumka, Date of Birth October 21, 1902									
484	1	Winters, Elijah	2	M	⅛	Ed Winters	2923	Cr	Clara Winters		Non
		New Born Census Card No. 484, P. O. Sapulpa, Date of Birth March 17, 1904									
485	1	Coser, Lena	1	F	F	Nuttetsa Coser	3685	Cr	Lizzie Coser	3686	Cr
		New Born Census Card No. 485, P. O. Okemah, Date of Birth May 11, 1902									
486	1	Deer, Minnie	3	F	F	Lemsey Deer	9359	Cr	Nancy Deer	9363	Cr
		New Born Census Card No. 486, P. O. Kellyville, Date of Birth No. 1 July 17, 1902; No. 2 June 27, 1904									
487	1	Tiger, Robert	3	M	F	David Tiger	6840	Cr	Mollie Crow Tiger	8523	Cr
488	2	Tiger, Josie	1	F	F	David Tiger	6840	Cr	Mollie Crow Tiger	8523	Cr
		New Born Census Card No. 487, P. O. Wetumka, Date of Birth June 12, 1904									
489	1	Gray, Roley Illegitimate	1	M	½	Unknown			Annie Gray	6415	Cr
		New Born Census Card No. 489, P. O. Brush Hill, Date of Birth July 11, 1902									
490	1	Washington, Claud	3	M	¾	David Washington	6849	Cr	Millie Washington	3209	Cr
		New Born Census Card No. 491, P. O. Bristow, Date of Birth No. 1 June 17, 1901; No. 2 March 11, 1904									
491	1	Williams, Davis	3	M	¼	Sam Williams		Non	Rena Williams	3910	Cr
492	2	Williams, Viola	1	F	¼	Sam Williams		Non	Rena Williams	3910	Cr
		New Born Census Card No. 492, P. O. Mantel, Date of Birth No. 1 February 24, 1902; No. 2 March 15, 1904									
493	1	Simon, Peyton	3	M	⅛	Joe Simon	3374	Cr	Emma Simon		Non
494	2	Simon, Levada	1	F	⅛	Joe Simon	3374	Cr	Emma Simon		Non
		New Born Census Card No. 493, P. O. Wewoka, Date of Birth March 1, 1905?									
495	1	Brown, Thomas Jefferson	1	M	⅛	Thomas J. Brown		Non	Julia Brown	1180	Cr
		New Born Census Card No. 494, P. O. Dustin, Date of Birth November 8, 1904									
496	1	Riley, Martha	1	F	½	William Riley		Non	Annie Riley	4547	Cr
		New Born Census Card No. 495, P. O. Yeager, Date of Birth June 14, 1902 (Twins)									
497	1	Hallford, Nathan	3	M	1-16	M. A. Hallford		Non	Euraline Hallford	3162	Cr
498	2	Hallford, Lynn	3	M	1-16	M. A. Hallford		Non	Euraline Hallford	3162	Cr
		New Born Census Card No. 496, P. O. Hitchita, Date of Birth May 14, 1902									
499	1	Morton, Okland	3	M	1-16	J. C. Morton		Non	Mattie Morton	313	Cr
		New Born Census Card No. 498, P. O. Weleetka, Date of Birth March 10, 1904									
500	1	Barnett, Leola	1	F	⅛	Scipio Barnett	3124	Cr	Lucy Barnett		Non
		New Born Census Card No. 499, P. O. Weleetka, Date of Birth December 15, 1902									
501	1	Ditzler, Fannie Ann	2	F	½	Will Ditzler		Non	Melvina Ditzler	4953	Cr

Roll No.	No.	NAME	Age	Sex	Blood	NAME OF FATHER	Roll No.	Cit.	NAME OF MOTHER	Roll No.	Cit.
		New Born Census Card No. 501, P. O. Red Fork, Date of Birth September 21, 1903									
502	1	Atkins, Mildred	1	F	½	Robert D. Atkins	3569	Cr	Alice Atkins	3566	Cr
		New Born Census Card No. 503, P. O. Wetumka, Date of Birth July 27, 1903									
503	1	Alexander, Bettie	2	F	¼	Robert L. Alexander	6010	Cr	Martha Alexander		Non
		New Born Census Card No. 504, P. O. Wetumka, Date of Birth No. 1, April 26, 1902; No. 2, August 16, 1904									
504	1	Alexander, Jacob	2	M	13-16	John L. Alexander	5999	Cr	Hettie Alexander	6000	Cr
505	2	Alexander, Christie	1	F	13-16	John L. Alexander	5999	Cr	Hettie Alexander	6000	Cr
		New Born Census Card No. 505, P. O. Mekusuky, Date of Birth November 20, 1904									
506	1	Coker, London	1	M	¼	Dave Coker	5096	Cr	Hettie Coker		Non
		New Born Census Card No. 507, P. O. Earlsboro, Date of Birth January 29, 1903									
507	1	Lowry, Amos	2	M	½	John Lowry		Non	Lucy Lowry	6969	Cr
		New Born Census Card No. 508, P. O. Holdenville, Date of Birth August 11, 1902									
508	1	Marks, George	3	M	½	John Marks		Non	Martha Marks	5037	Cr
		New Born Census Card No. 510, P. O. Fort Gibson, Date of Birth January 25, 1902									
509	1	Anderson, Viola	3	F	¼	Amos Anderson		Non	Jennie Anderson	2779	Cr
		New Born Census Card No. 514, P. O. Holdenville, Date of Birth No. 1, March 16, 1903; No. 2, March 1, 1905									
510	1	Adelhelm, Chester	2	M	¼	William Adelhelm		Non	Jennie Adelhelm	3515	Cr
511	2	Adelhelm, Charlie Antion	1	M	¼	William Adelhelm		Non	Jennie Adelhelm	3515	Cr
		New Born Census Card No. 515, P. O. Wagoner, Date of Birth February 22, 1903									
512	1	Posey, William Edward	2	M	1-16	Henry A. Posey	2494	Cr	Mary E. Posey		Non
		New Born Census Card No. 516, P. O. Red Fork, Date of Birth January 11, 1904									
513	1	Bewley, Eugene L.	1	M	⅛	Lawrence W. Bewley		Non	Elizabeth Bewley	2789	Cr
		New Born Census Card No. 519, P. O. Red Fork, Date of Birth February 13, 1904									
514	1	Barber, Mary E.	1	F	1-16	Robert T. Barber	881	Cr	Carrie Barber		Non
		New Born Census Card No. 520, P. O. Broken Arrow, Date of Birth November 16, 1902									
515	1	Childers, Virgie	2	F	⅜	Pratt Childers	2615	Cr	Daisy Childers Miller		Non
		New Born Censss Card No. 526, P. O. Wewoka, Date of Birth No. 1, January 28, 1905; No. 2, April 11, 1903									
516	1	Factor, Cogee	1	F	½	William Factor		Non	Nancy Factor	5412	Cr
517	2	Factor, George	2	M	½	William Factor		Non	Nancy Factor	5412	Cr
		New Born Census Card No. 529, P. O. Holdenville, Date of Birth January 18, 1903									
518	1	Jackson, Diamond	2	M	½	Anton Jackson		Non	Sallie Jackson	6087	Cr
		New Born Census Card No. 530. P. O. Wetumka, Date of Birth No. 1, May 17, 1903; No. 2, October 3, 1901									
519	1	Leader, Lizzie	2	F	F	Dave Leader	7470	Cr	Nancy Leader	5550	Cr
520	2	Leader, Allice	3	F	F	Dave Leader	7470	Cr	Nancy Leader	5550	Cr
		New Born Census Card No. 531, P. O. Barnard, Date of Birth August 24, 1904									
521	1	Bear, Lillie	1	F	F	Polar Bear	7393	Cr	Kizzie Bear	1315	Cr
		New Born Census Card No. 532, P. O. Mounds, Date of Birth August 31, 1901									
522	1	Wills, Hazel Irene	4	F	1-16	Henry F. Wills	2191	Cr	Mary A. Wills		Non
		New Born Census Card No. 533, P. O. Sasakwa, Date of Birth March 10, 1903									
523	1	Barnett, Cheparney	2	M	½	Jimmie Barnett		Non	Mahaley Barnett	8405	Cr
		New Born Census Card No. 535, P. O. Sasakwa, Date of Birth June 29, 1904									
524	1	Fleet, John J.	1	M	⅛	James H. Fleet		Non	Alice J. Fleet	6264	Cr
		New Born Census Card No. 536, P. O. Senora, Date of Birth February 10, 1903									
525	1	Fife, Josey	2	M	F	James Fife	6437	Cr	Lucinda Fife	6438	Cr
		New Born Census Card No. 541, P. O. Yeager, Date of Birth August 9, 1904									
526	1	Hill, George	1	M	F	Mitchell Hill	5789	Cr	Hilly Hill	5443	Cr
		New Born Census Card No. 543, P. O. Wetumka, Date of Birth No. 1, April 27, 1902; No. 2, January 3, 1905									
527	1	McCoy, Nettie	3	F	½	William A. McCoy		Non	Ida McCoy	235	Cr
528	2	McCoy, Robert Elihu	1	M	½	William A. McCoy		Non	Ida McCoy	235	Cr
		New Born Census Card No. 545, P. O. Burney, Date of Birth February 27, 1904									
529	1	Wills, Lilly	1	F	½	Joseph Wills	8970	Cr	Nancy Wills		Non
		New Born Census Card No. 548, P. O. Hoffman, Date of Birth March 12, 1904									
530	1	Easley, John Pickard	1	M	⅛	E. C. Easley		Non	H. Tookah Easley	7042	Cr
		New Born Census Card No. 549, P. O. Fame, Date of Birth December 28, 1901									
531	1	McIntosh, Isaiah J.	3	M	⅝	John McIntosh	6300	Cr	Mary McIntosh	6301	Cr
		New Born Census Card No. 550, P. O. Wewoka, Date of Birth February 10, 1902									
532	1	Harjo, Wilson Illegitimate	3	M	½	Cheparney Harjo		Non	Judy Bruner	6226	Cr
		New Born Census Card No. 551, P. O. Wetumka, Date of Birth March 5, 1902									
533	1	Bruner, Lewis	3	M	F	Taylor Bruner	7640	Cr	Nancy Bruner	7641	Cr
		New Born Census Card No. 552, P. O. Haskell, Date of Birth October 17, 1902									
534	1	Gibson, Joseph B.	2	M	1-32	William S. Gibson	3571	Cr	Ethel Gibson		Non
		New Born Census Card No. 553, P. O. Kellyville, Date of Birth March 24, 1904									
535	1	Watashe, Joe	1	M	F	Watashe	6884	Cr	Rosa Watashe	6885	Cr
		New Born Census Card No. 555, P. O. Mounds, Date of Birth March 4, 1904									
536	1	John, Lena	1	F	F	McCully John	5992	Cr	Alice John	1640	Cr
		New Born Census Card No. 556, P. O. Wewoka, Date of Birth June 19, 1903									
537	1	Simmer, Hinney	2	F	F	John Simmer	4234	Cr	Jemima Simmer	5551	Cr
		New Born Census Card No. 559, P. O. Holdenville, Date of Birth February 1, 1904									
538	1	Narcomay, Alice	1	F	F	Thomas Narcomey	6581	Cr	Kizzie Narcomey	5921	Cr
		New Born Census Card No. 560, P. O. Wetumka, Date of Birth September 12, 1904									
539	1	Dunson, Millie	1	F	F	Thos. H. Dunson	1547	Cr	Ellen Dunson	4695	Cr

Roll No.	No.	NAME	Age	Sex	Blood	NAME OF FATHER	Roll No.	Cit.	NAME OF MOTHER	Roll No.	Cit.
New Born Census Card No. 627, P. O. Nerotown, Date of Birth April 12, 1902											
540	1	McIntosh, Ida	3	F	F	Dick McIntosh	7253	Cr	Susanna McIntosh	7614	Cr
New Born Census Card No. 562, P. O. Mannford, Date of Birth No. 1, October 6, 1902; No. 2, October 6, 1904											
541	1	Nave, Nara	2	F	¼	John Calvin Nave		Non	Alice Nave	2477	Cr
542	2	Nave, Otha	1	M	¼	John Calvin Nave		Non	Alice Nave	2477	Cr
New Born Census Card No. 564, P. O. Holdenville, Date of Birth June 26, 1903											
543	1	Tate, Joseph	2	M	¼	Deck Tate		Non	Mary Tate	5255	Cr
New Born Census Card No. 566, P. O. Holdenville, Date of Birth No. 1, March 15, 1902; No. 2, October 14, 1903											
544	1	Todd, Bertha	3	F	¼	James Todd		Non	Katy Todd	5206	Cr
545	2	Todd, Arthur Lee	1	M	¼	James Todd		Non	Katy Todd	5206	Cr
New Born Census Card No. 567, P. O. Spaulding, Date of Birth November 12, 1901											
546	1	Birdhead, Yanah	3	F	½	Tuseke (or Birdhead)		Non	Cinda Birdhead	7430	Cr
New Born Census Card No. 570, P. O. Calvin, Date of Birth November 5, 1901											
547	1	Leader, Jennie	3	F	¾	Barney Leader	6802	Cr	Tilda Leader	6803	Cr
New Born Census Card No. 571, P. O. Morse, Date of Birth No. 1, December 23, 1901; No. 2, May 3, 1903; No. 3, January 29, 1905											
548	1	Harjo, Amos	3	M	F	Chofolup Harjo	4181	Cr	Amy Harjo	4152	Cr
549	2	Harjo, Unasee	2	M	F	Chofolup Harjo	4181	Cr	Amy Harjo	4152	Cr
946	3	Harjo, Fanny	1	F	F	Chofolup Harjo	4181	Cr	Amy Harjo	4152	Cr
New Born Census Card No. 572, P. O. Holdenville, Date of Birth No. 1, August 12, 1903; No. 2, June 10, 1901											
550	1	Caesar, Hannah	2	F	F	Samego Caesar	8823	Cr	Rachael Caesar	8824	Cr
551	2	Caesar, Moser	4	M	F	Samego Caesar	8823	Cr	Rachael Caesar	8824	Cr
New Born Census Card No. 573, P. O. Weleetka, Date of Birth November 15, 1902											
552	1	Barnett, Hulley	2	M	F	Daniel Barnett	4593	Cr	Linda Barnett	4677	Cr
New Born Census Card No. 575, P. O. Morse, Date of Birth November 25, 1902											
553	1	Taryole, Frank	2	M	F	Taryole	4188	Cr	Marfy Taryole	4189	Cr
New Born Census Card No. 575, P. O. Holdenville, Date of Birth No. 1, August 31, 1902; No. 2, May 29, 1904											
554	1	McPerryman, Lewis	3	M	F	Alex Perryman	7489	Cr	Sophia McPerryman	7257	Cr
555	2	McPerryman, Eli	1	M	F	Alex Perryman	7489	Cr	Sophia McPerryman	7257	Cr
New Born Census Card No. 557, P. O. Wewoka, Date of Birth September 30, 1901											
556	1	Alex Jacob	3	M	¾	Freeland Alex	6101	Cr	Elizabeth Alex	6102	Cr
New Born Census Card No. 578, P. O. Yeager, Date of Birth No. 1, November 20, 1904; No. 2, May 11, 1902											
557	1	McNevins, Willie Clay	1	M	⅝	Lee McNevins	4648	Cr	Nancy McNevins	4649	Cr
558	2	McNevins, Flora	3	F	⅝	Lee McNevins	4648	Cr	Nancy McNevins	4649	Cr
New Born Census Card No. 579, P. O. Holdenville, Date of Birth January 5, 1905											
559	1	Stubblefield, McAffee	1	M	1-16	Ed Stubblefield		Non	Lousanna Subblefield	5360	Cr
New Born Census Card No. 581, P. O. Emahaka, Date of Birth August 16, 1904											
560	1	Harjo, Alice	1	F	½	Cheparney Harjo		Non	Lizzie Harjo	6225	Cr
New Born Census Card No. 585, P. O. Holdenville, Date of Birth No. 1, December 10, 1911; No. 2, March 17, 1903; No... 3, February 23, 1905											
561	1	King, Claudy J.	3	M	¼	Charlie King		Non	Mattie King	5203	Cr
562	2	King, Berry W.	2	M	¼	Charlie King		Non	Mattie King	5203	Cr
563	3	King, Luther Lewis	1	M	¼	Charlie King		Non	Mattie King	5203	Cr
New Born Census Card No. 590, P. O. Sasakwa, Date of Birth April 2, 1903											
564	1	Palmer, Ella	2	F	¼	Jim Palmer		Non	Mary Palmer	6898	Cr
New Born Census Card No. 591, P. O. Coweta, Date of Birth August 22, 1902											
565	1	Flowers, Willie Eva	3	F	⅛	Joseph Flowers	6296	Cr	Alice Flowers		Non
New Born Census Card No. 592, P. O. Leonard, Date of Birth May 2, 1903											
566	1	Pense, Alice	2	F	½	J. H. Pense		Non	Malissa Pense	790	Cr
New Born Census Card No. 593, P. O. Krebs, Date of Birth December 17, 1902											
567	1	Hendrickson, Sarrah Jane	2	F	1-16	James Hendrickson		Non	Eliza Hendrickson	3399	Cr
New Born Census Card No. 594, P. O. Henryetta, Date of Birth No. 1, June 28, 1904; No. 2, July 2, 1902; No. 3, July 7, 1901											
568	1	Lewis, Mosey	1	M	F	John Lewis	4762	Cr	Manna Lewis	4763	Cr
569	2	Lewis, Lillie	3	F	F	John Lewis	4762	Cr	Manna Lewis	4763	Cr
570	3	Lewis, Eddie	4	M	F	John Lewis	4762	Cr	Manna Lewis	4763	Cr
New Born Census Card No. 595, P. O. Red Fork, Date of Birth January 31, 1904											
571	1	Vance, William Mellette	1	M	1-16	Joseph Vance	2341	Cr	Ora Myrtle Vance		Non
New Born Census Card No. 597, P. O. Holdenville, Date of Birth February 28, 1903											
572	1	Cornell, David	2	M	⅞	Willie Cornell	5454	Cr	Manie Cornell	5455	Cr
New Born Census Card No. 598, P. O. Mounds, Date of Birth No. 1, January 12, 1902; No. 2, January 20, 1904											
573	1	Colmon, Nettie Alice	3	F	1-16	W. E. Colman		Non	Nettie G. Colman	6746	Cr
574	2	Colmon, Gladdys Leuna	1	F	1-16	W. E. Colman		Non	Nettie G. Colman	6746	Cr
New Born Census Card No. 599, P. O. Bristow, Date of Birth No. 1, August 2, 1901; No. 2, September 15,1904											
575	1	Roberson, Leo	4	M	½	Philip Roberson	4846	Cr	Mary Roberson	6231	Cr
576	2	Roberson, Ellen	1	F	½	Philip Roberson	4846	Cr	Mary Roberson	6231	Cr
New Born Census Card No. 600, P. O. Morse, Date of Birth No. 1, September 8, 1901; No. 2, February 17, 1904											
577	1	Self, Maggie Ophelia	3	F	⅛	William J. Self	3579	Cr	Delila Self		Non
578	2	Self, Golie Ray	1	F	⅛	William J. Self	3579	Cr	Delila Self		Non
New Born Census Card No. 601, P. O. Beggs, Date of Birth September 17, 1903											
579	1	Lunsford, Hattie	1	F	⅜	John C. Lunsford	3383	Cr	Martha Lunsford	3384	Cr

Roll No.	No.	NAME	Age	Sex	Blood	NAME OF FATHER	Roll No.	Cit.	NAME OF MOTHER	Roll No.	Cit.
		New Born Census Card No. 604, P. O. Senora, Date of Birth December 13, 1904									
580	1	Sands, Nettie	1	F	F	Phillip H. Sands	5674	Cr	Martha Sands	5675	Cr
		New Born Census Card No. 605, P. O. Hanna, Date fo Birth August 10, 1902									
581	1	Reed, John	3	M	F	Porter Reed	5048	Cr	Jennie Reed	5049	Cr
		New Born Census Card No. 606, P. O. Mellette, Date of Birth No. 1, August 11, 1903; No. 2, December 4, 1901									
582	1	Davis, Fanny	2	F	F	Sampson Davis	1384	Cr	Bettie Davis	1385	Cr
583	2	Davis, Minnie	3	F	F	Sampson Davis	1384	Cr	Bettie Davis	1385	Cr
		New Born Census Card No. 607, P. O. Holdenville, Date of Birth No. 1, February 24, 1902; No. 2, September 7, 1903									
584	1	Stubblefield, Minnie	3	F	1-16	John Stubblefield		Non	Ida Stubblefield	6518	Cr
585	2	Stubblefield, Johnnie	1	M	1-16	John Stubblefield		Non	Ida Stubblefield	6518	Cr
		New Born Census Card No. 613, P. O. Eufaula, Date of Birth No. 2, June 6, 1902; No. 1, February 7, 1905									
586	1	Beaver, Lecus	1	M	F	Poyer Beaver	8693	Cr	Mulsie Beaver	8694	Cr
1055	2	Beaver, Walter	3	M	F	Poyer Beaver	8693	Cr	Mulsie Beaver	8694	Cr
		New Born Census Card No. 614, P. O. Stidham, Date of Birth No. 1, September 1, 1902; No. 2, February 6, 1904									
587	1	Hawkins, Kate	3	F	¾	Daniel Hawkins	3841	Cr	Rhoda Hawkins	671	Cr
588	2	Hawkins, Melissa	1	F	¾	Daniel Hawkins	3841	Cr	Rhoda Hawkins	671	Cr
		New Born Census Card No. 615, P. O. Mounds, Date of Birth August 31, 1903									
589	1	Stewart, Floyd Lee	2	M	⅛	William H. Stewart		Non	America Stewart	3589	Cr
		New Born Census Card No. 616, P. O. Okemah, Date of Birth No. 2, May 1, 1902; No. 1, February 5, 1904									
590	1	Johnson, Bessie	1	F	F	Cully Johnson	4098	Cr	Mahala Johnson	4099	Cr
949	2	Johnson, Ulter	3	M	F	Cully Johnson	4098	Cr	Mahala Johnson	4099	Cr
		New Born Census Card No. 620, P. O. Eufaula, Date of Birth September 12, 1902									
591	1	Ansiel, Albert Robert	2	M	1-32	Robert Lee Ansiel	6335	Cr	Statie Ann Ansiel		Non
		New Born Census Card No. 621, P. O. Eufaula, Date of Birth May 8, 1903									
592	1	Smith, Edna	2	F	1-16	Wade Smith		Non	Martha Smith	5395	Cr
		New Born Census Card No. 639, P. O. Eufaula, Date of Birth March 19, 1902									
593	1	McIntosh, Jeannetta	3	F	¾	Bunnie McIntosh	6258	Cr	Leah McIntosh	6259	Cr
		New Born Census Card No. 624, P. O. Eufaula, Date of Birth April 1902									
594	1	Francis, Susie	3	F	F	Mitchell Francis	443	Cr	Menaffee Francis	444	Cr
		New Born Census Card No. 437, P. O. Wealaka, Date of Birth July 15, 1903									
595	1	Lewis, Ella Died September 29, 1905	2	F	F	Jack Lewis	4014	Cr	Delila Lewis	4015	Cr
		New Born Census Card No. 628, P. O. Bixby, Date of Birth No. 1, December 27, 1901; No. 2, February 21, 1904									
596	1	Crosby, Berry Martin	3	M	½	Charles E. Crosby	1112	Cr	Elizabeth A. Crosby	1113	Cr
597	2	Crosby, Ferdinand Wilber	1	M	¼	Charles E. Crosby	1112	Cr	Elizabeth A. Crosby	1113	Cr
		New Born Census Card No. 629, P. O. Eufaula, Date of Birth December 27, 1903									
598	1	McGilbray, Melissa	1	F	F	Jackson McGilbra	1397	Cr	Cinda McGilbra	9220	Cr
		New Born Census Card No. 630, P. O. Red Fork, Date of Birth No. 1, October 25, 1901; No. 2, October 7, 1903									
599	1	Postoak, Arthur E.	3	M	F	Lincoln Postoak	2324	Cr	Lillie Postoak	2325	Cr
600	2	Postoak, Hattie L.	1	F	F	Lincoln Postoak	2324	Cr	Lillie Postoak	2325	Cr
		New Born Census Card No. 631, P. O. Red Fork, Date of Birth June 12, 1902									
601	1	Clarkston, Raymond	3	M	⅛	Alex Clarkston		Non	Maggie J. Clarkston	1569	Cr
		New Born Census Card No. 633, P. O. Okfuskee, Date of Birth February 18, 1905									
602	1	Morton, Leo Britt	1	M	⅛	Osborn A. Morton	1741	Cr	Mittie B. Morton		Non
		New Born Census Card No. 634, P. O. Okemah, Date of Birth March 26, 1903									
603	1	Wind, Jesse	2	M	¾	George Wind	4768	Cr	Millie Wind	4769	Cr
		New Born Census Card No. 635, P. O. Wewoka, Date of Birth No. 1, March 17, 1902; No. 2, June 5, 1904									
604	1	Brown, Ruth	3	F	¼	Clarence W. Brown	6451	Cr	Rebecca Brown		Non
605	2	Brown, John William	1	M	¼	Clarence W. Brown	6451	Cr	Rebecca Brown		Non
		New Born Census Card No. 637, P. O. Eufaula, Date of Birth No. 1, July 24, 1901; No. 2, December 15, 1903									
606	1	Dixon, Ethel Lulee	4	F	1-16	Sam Dixon		Non	Della Dixon	1846	Cr
607	2	Dixon, Henry Jefferson	1	M	1-16	Sam Dixon		Non	Della Dixon	1846	Cr
		New Born Census Card No. 640, P. O. Stidham, Date of Birth July 10, 1903									
608	1	Pitman, Vonnie	2	M	1-16	Lewis Pitman	3730	Cr	Florence Pitman		Non
		New Born Census Card No. 641, P. O. Eufaula, Date of Birth May 21, 1902									
609	1	Kite, Lucy May	3	F	⅜	A. L. Kite		Non	Jemima Kite	3891	Cr
		New Born Census Card No. 644, P. O. Stidham, Date of Birth September 7, 1903; No. 2, July 3, 1901									
610	1	Island, Lizzie	2	F	¼	Napoleon B. Island	5565	Cr	Maggie Island		Non
611	2	Island, Leggues	4	M	¼	Napoleon B. Island	5535	Cr	Maggie Island		Non
		New Born Census Card No. 645, P. O. Eufaula, Date of Birth July 7, 1901									
612	1	McIntosh, Ida M.	4	F	½	L. G. McIntosh	5743	Cr	Leonie McIntosh	5744	Cr
		New Born Census Card No. 646, P. O. Brush Hill, Date of Birth February 16, 1902									
613	1	Maloney, Lena	3	F	⅛	Jim Maloney		Non	Annie Maloney	7159	Cr
		New Born Census Card No. 647, P. O. Stidham, Date of Birth No. 1, July 31, 1902; No. 2, December 10, 1904									
614	1	Walker, George Washington	3	M	⅜	Edward H. Walker	3407	Cr	Eula Walker	3408	Cr
615	2	Walker, Edith	1	F	⅜	Edward H. Walker	3407	Cr	Eula Walker	3408	Cr
		New Born Census Card No. 652, P. O. Eufaula, Date of Birth April 3, 1902									
616	1	Brown, Eva May	3	F	5-16	A. W. Brown		Non	Ada J. Brown	5232	Cr

Roll No.	No.	NAME	Age	Sex	Blood	NAME OF FATHER	Roll No.	Cit.	NAME OF MOTHER	Roll No.	Cit.

New Born Census Card No. 653, P. O. Brush Hill, Date of Birth No. 1, February 16, 1902; No. 2, April 13, 04

| 617 | 1 | Shepherd, May | 3 | F | 1-16 | K. H. Shepherd | | Non | Addie M. Shepherd | 6810 | Cr |
| 618 | 2 | Shepherd, Maggie | 1 | F | 1-16 | K. H. Shepherd | | Non | Addie M. Shepherd | 6810 | Cr |

New Born Census Card No. 654, P. O. Eufaula, Date of Birth March 8, 1904

| 619 | 1 | Nelson, David Jefferson | 1 | M | 1-16 | William W. Nelson | | Non | Mary S. Nelson | 4308 | Cr |

New Born Census Card No. 655, P. O. Eufaula, Date of Birth No. 1, October 14, 1901; No. 2, May 10, 1903

| 620 | 1 | Post, Samantha | 3 | F | 1-16 | Thomas Post | 2755 | Cr | Laura Post | | Non |
| 621 | 2 | Post, El Louisa | 2 | F | 1-16 | Thomas Post | 2755 | Cr | Laura Post | | Non |

New Born Census Card No. 659, P. O. Eufaula, Date of Birth November 16, 1902

| 622 | 1 | Scott, Hepsey | 2 | F | F | Sam Scott | 1779 | Cr | Nancy Scott | 1780 | Cr |

New Born Census Card No. 663, P. O. Eufaula, Date of Birth No. 1, January 7, 1902; No. 2, June 25, 1904

| 623 | 1 | Givens, Minnie | 3 | F | F | Choctaw Givens | 6797 | Cr | Kizzie Givens | 6798 | Cr |
| 624 | 2 | Givens, Lonie | 1 | F | F | Choctaw Givens | 6797 | Cr | Kizzie Givens | 6798 | Cr |

New Born Census Card No. 664, P. O. Cheotah, Date of Birth May 26, 1904

| 625 | 1 | Murray, Helen M. | 1 | F | 3-32 | John Murray | 9330 | Cr | Lucy Murray | 4439 | Cr |

New Born Census Card No. 666, P. O. Okmulgee, Date of Birth July 26, 1902

| 626 | 1 | Meyers, Herbert | 3 | M | 1/4 | Charles E. Meyers | | Non | Martha Meyers | 3288 | Cr |

New Born Census Card No. 669, P. O. Tullahassee, Date of Birth July 31, 1903

| 627 | 1 | Jefferson, Senora | 2 | F | F | Walter Jefferson | 738 | Cr | Annie Jefferson | 8807 | Cr |

New Born Census Card No. 670, P. O. Checotah, Date of Birth August 31, 1903

| 628 | 1 | Wadsworth, James | 2 | M | 1/2 | John Wadsworth | | Non | Eliza Wadsworth | 8628 | Cr |

New Born Census Card No. 671, P. O. Kellyville, Date of Birth August 13, 1903

| 629 | 1 | Tiger, Nancy | 2 | F | F | Cooper Tiger | 6839 | Cr | Salina Tiger | 6105 | Cr |

New Born Census Card No. 672, P. O. Dawson, Date of Birth No. 1, July 4, 1901; No. 2, September 11, 1904

630	1	Woods, Lillie Rosell	4	F	1/8	Willis Woods		Non	Cora Woods	6047	Cr
1057	2	Woods, Argethel	1	F	1/8	Willis Woods		Non	Cora Woods	6047	Cr
		No. 1 died August 24, 1905									

New Born Census Card No. 673, P. O. Tullahassee, Date of Birth June 14, 1902

| 631 | 1 | Davis, Nora | 3 | F | 1/2 | J. W. Davis | | Non | Nancy W. Davis | 2125 | Cr |

New Born Census Card No. 675, P. O. Tullahassee, Date of Birth July 23, 1901

| 632 | 1 | Drew, Moses Warrner | 4 | M | 1/4 | Clifton C. Drew | | Non | Emma Drew | 2173 | Cr |

New Born Census Card No. 676, P. O. Eufaula, Date of Birth No. 1, August 28, 1904; No. 2, April 20, 1902

| 633 | 1 | Byrd, Yahdeka | 1 | M | 3/8 | Sunny Byrd | 565 | Sem | Tamisa Byrd | 8762 | Cr |
| 634 | 2 | Byrd, Jemima | 3 | F | 3/8 | Sunny Byrd | 565 | Sem | Tamisa Byrd | 8762 | Cr |

New Born Census Card No. 677, P. O. Eufaula, Date of Birth November 6, 1903

| 635 | 1 | Sanger, Wahnabka | 1 | F | 1-16 | Joseph C. Sanger | 6912 | Cr | Gertrude L. Sanger | 3669 | Cr |

New Born Census Card No. 678, P. O. Beggs, Date of Birth January 11, 1904

| 636 | 1 | Adams, Theodore | 1 | M | 1/2 | George W. Adams | 3780 | Cr | Sarah Adams | 3781 | Cr |

New Born Census Card No. 679, P. O. Mellette, Date of Birth December 30, 1903

| 637 | 1 | Crow, Tommy | 1 | M | 1/2 | George Osawah | | Non | Melissa Osawah (or Crow) | 9262 | Cr |

New Born Census Card No. 680, P. O. Tullahassee, Date of Birth March 8, 1902

| 638 | 1 | Jack, Mandy Amy | 3 | F | 1/8 | John Jack | | Non | Alice Jack | 2788 | Cr |

New Born Census Card No. 682, P. O. Oktaha, Date of Birth No. 1, December 7, 1901; No. 2, March 29, 1903; No. 3, October 1, 1904

639	1	Casey, Vera Irene	3	F	3-16	John Casey	2212	Cr	Savanah Casey	3629	Cr
640	2	Casey, Alvro Edgar	2	M	3-16	John Casey	2212	Cr	Savanah Casey	3629	Cr
641	3	Casey, Eli	1	M	3-16	John Casey	2212	Cr	Savanah Casey	3629	Cr

New Born Census Card No. 683, P. O. Eufaula, Date of Birth April 19, 1903

| 642 | 1 | Clark, Alex | 2 | M | 1/2 | George Clark | | Non | Louisa Clark | 6714 | Cr |

New Born Census Card No. 686, P. O. Wetumka, Date of Birth No. 1, March 11, 1903; No. 2, January 20, 1905

| 643 | 1 | Morrison, Ernest | 2 | M | 1/4 | Hence Morrison | 3068 | Cr | Nancy Morrison | | Non |
| 644 | 2 | Morrison, Hettie Jane | 1 | F | 1/4 | Hence Morrison | 3068 | Cr | Nancy Morrison | | Non |

New Born Census Card No. 687, P. O. Eufaula, Date of Birth October 4, 1902

| 645 | 1 | Ansiel, Samuel E. O. | 2 | M | 1-16 | John G. Ansiel | 4277 | Cr | Lula Ansiel | | Non |

New Born Census Card No. 691, P. O. Wewoka, Date of Birth No. 1, January 2, 1902; No. 2, February 4, 1904

| 646 | 1 | Walker, Johnson | 3 | M | 1/4 | Jeff Walker | | Non | Mabel Walker | 8588 | Cr |
| 647 | 2 | Walker, Annie | 1 | F | 1/4 | Jeff Walker | | Non | Mabel Walker | 8588 | Cr |

New Born Census Card No. 693, P. O. Hitchita, Date of Birth September 11, 1902

| 648 | 1 | Watts, William T. Jr. | 2 | M | 1/4 | William T. Watts | | Non | Anna H. Watts | 5348 | Cr |

New Born Census Card No. 694, P. O. Mellette, Date of Birth August 18, 1903

| 649 | 1 | Givens, Harper | 2 | M | F | William Givens | 8055 | Cr | Annie Givens | 7908 | Cr |

New Born Census Card No. 695, P. O. Tidmore, Date of Birth August 29, 1902

| 650 | 1 | Wolf, Timmie Barnett | 3 | M | 1/4 | Jackson Wolf | | Non | Sukey Wolf | 8859 | Cr |

New Born Census Card No. 696, P. O. Holdenville, Date of Birth February 3, 1904

| 651 | 1 | Goat, Eddieline | 1 | F | F | Wadley Goat | 5473 | Cr | Minnie Goat | 4897 | Cr |

New Born Census Card No. 697, P. O. Lenna, Date of Birth November 13, 1902

| 652 | 1 | Loney, James | 2 | M | F | Sam Loney | 8564 | Cr | Lizzie Willingham | 1359 | Cr |

New Born Census Card No. 698, P. O. Lenna, Date of Birth August 23, 1901

| 653 | 1 | Watson, Minnie | 4 | F | 9-16 | Sandy Watson | 7659 | Cr | Lena Morrison | 5625 | Cr |
| | | Illegitimate | | | | | | | | | |

New Born Census Card No. 699, P. O. Eufaula, Date of Birth November 5, 1903

| 654 | 1 | Simpson, Catherine Elizabeth | 1 | F | 1-64 | James H. Simpson | 4142 | Cr | Alice M. Simpson | | Non |

242

Roll No.	No.	NAME	Age	Sex	Blood	NAME OF FATHER	Roll No.	Cit.	NAME OF MOTHER	Roll No.	Cit.
New Born Census Card No. 700, P. O. Tullahassee, Date of Birth May 15, 1903											
655	1	Hickory, Louina	2	F	F	Thomas Hickory	3963	Cr	Jennie Hickory	3964	Cr
New Born Census Card No. 701, P. O. Holdenville Date of Birth March 11, 1903											
656	1	Duckworth, Vera Oma	2	F	¼	Robert D. Duckworth		Non	Ruth E. Duckworth	5170	Cr
New Born Census Card No. 720, P. O. Eufaula, Date of Birth September 23, 1903											
657	1	Coodey, Walter Lee	1	M	1-16	William S. Coody	2422	Cr	Levena Coody		Non
New Born Census Card No. 705, P. O. Brush Hill, Date of Birth October 3, 1902											
658	1	Lewallen, Lucy	2	F	¼	John Lewallen		Non	Louisa Lewallen	6281	Cr
New Born Census Card No. 706, P. O. Holdenville, Date of Birth No. 1, July 19, 1902; No. 2, November 7, 1904											
659	1	Goat, Angeline	3	F	F	Alfred Goat	5487	Cr	Rachael Goat	5488	Cr
660	2	Goat, Alice Sukey	1	F	F	Alfred Goat	5487	Cr	Rachael Goat	5488	Cr
New Born Census Card No. 20, P. O. Weleetka, Date of Birth November 14, 1901											
661	1	Baker, Martha	3	F	F	Lasley Baker	5065	Cr	Anna Baker	5366	Cr
New Born Census Card No. 709, P. O. Catoosa, Date of Birth November 10, 1904											
662	1	Robinson, Myrtice A.	1	F	1-32	Will R. Robison		Non	Maysie A. Robison	1550	Cr
New Born Census Card No. 711, P. O. Yeager, Date of Birth No. 1, July 10, 1901; No. 2, March 22, 1903; No. 3, March 2, 1905											
663	1	Harjo, Alfred	4	M	F	Lily Harjo	5918	Cr	Rhoda Harjo	5919	Cr
664	2	Harjo, Nancy	2	F	F	Lily Harjo	5918	Cr	Rhoda Harjo	5919	Cr
1060	3	Harjo, Winey	1	F	F	Lily Harjo	5918	Cr	Rhoda Harjo	5919	Cr
New Born Census Card No. 712, P. O. Sasakwa, Date of Birth October 5, 1904 (Twins)											
665	1	Charlesey, Flora	1	F	½	Charlesey	169	Sem	Ellen Charlesey	7059	Cr
666	2	Charlesey, Martha	1	F	½	Charlesey	169	Sem	Ellen Charlesey	7059	Cr
		Nos. 1 and 2 illegitimate									
New Born Census Card No. 713, P. O. Wagoner, Date of Birth No. 1, March 21, 1903; No. 2, November 5, 1904											
667	1	Pitts, Drannan	2	F	1-16	Frank Fields Pitts		Non	Emma Pitts	2278	Cr
668	2	Pitts, Burrell H.	1	M	1-16	Frank Fields Pitts		Non	Emma Pitts	2278	Cr
New Born Census Card No. 714, P. O. Checotah, Date of Birth September 8, 1903											
669	1	Grayson, Mamie	1	F	3-16	Joseph Grayson		Non	Alice Grayson	3844	Cr
New Born Census Card No. 716, P. O. Sasakwa, Date of Birth No. 1, August 31, 1902; No. 2, August 2, 1904											
670	1	Tebe, Arthur	3	M	½	Stebbin Martin		Non	Wisey Stebbin	8944	Cr
671	2	Tebe, Nellie	1	F	½	Stebbin Martin		Non	Wisey Stebbin	8944	Cr
New Born Census Card No. 719, P. O. Huttonville, Date of Birth November 12, 1903											
672	1	Brown, Alex	1	M	½	Dave Brown		Non	Maria Brown	8558	Cr
New Born Census Card No. 721, P. O. Wagoner, Date of Birth No. 1, March 29, 1902; No. 2, August 3, 1903											
673	1	Chissoe, Please S.	3	M	⅞	Sam Chissoe	449	Cr	Lena E. Chissoe	450	Cr
744	2	Chissoe, Sam Jr.	2	M	⅞	Sam Chissoe	449	Cr	Lena E. Chissoe	450	Cr
New Born Census Card No. 725, P. O. Eufaula, Date of Birth March 25, 1903											
674	1	McGilbra Sanford .	2	M	F	Lewis McGilbra	5398	Cr	Leah Green	6060	Cr
		Illegitimate									
New Born Census Card No. 726, P. O. Coyle, Date of Birth January 27, 1903											
675	1	Burnett, Joseph L.	2	M	⅛	E. H. Burnett		Non	Vinita Burnett	1322	Cr
New Born Census Card No. 728, P. O. Checotah, Date of Birth February 27, 1905											
676	1	Hancock, Lizzie	1	F	3-16	C. A. Hancock		Non	Hattie L. Hancock	1671	Cr
New Born Census Card No. 729, P. O. Beggs, Date of Birth July 19, 1901											
677	1	Foster, Mary Josephine	3	F	1-16	George W. Foster		Non	Mary E. Foster	3297	Cr
New Born Census Card No. 731, P. O. Checotah, Date of Birth December 13, 1903											
678	1	McGilbry, George L.	1	M	⅜	George McGilbry	1524	Cr	Laura McGilbry		Non
New Born Census Card No. 732, P. O. Eufaula, Date of Birth July 16, 1904											
679	1	Brightman, Lyeman	1	M	1-16	Earl Brightman		Non	Fannie Brightman	6913	Cr
New Born Census Card No. 738, P. O. Cathay, Date of Birth February 23, 1902											
680	1	Wadsworth, Jessie Eulalie	3	F	⅜	P. J. Wadsworth		Non	Mattie Wadsworth	1869	Cr
New Born Census Card No. 744, P. O. Dustin, Date of Birth August 22, 1904											
681	1	Robertson, Andrew Jackson	2	M	¼	I. W. Robertson		Non	Lilly Robertson	66	Cr
New Born Census Card No. 750, P. O. Checotah, Date of Birth September 14, 1904											
682	1	Churchill, Ethel May	1	F	⅛	Amry Churchill		Non	Maude M. Churchill	1878	Cr
New Born Census Card No. 770, P. O. Hitchita, Date of Birth September 7, 1902											
683	1	Doyle, Cecil Lee	2	M	⅛	Sebron J. Doyle	989	Cr	Dill Doyle		Non
New Born Census Card No. 812, P. O. Beggs, Date of Birth No. 1, March 10, 1902; No. 2, August 19, 1904											
684	1	Harry, Wilson,	3	M	9-16	Jackson Harry	3867	Cr	Rosanna Harry	3802	Cr
685	2	Harry, Jessie	1	M	9-16	Jackson Harry	3867	Cr	Rosanna Harry	3802	Cr
New Born Census Card No. 902, P. O. Coweta, Date of Birth June 28, 1904											
686	1	Posey, Eloise	1	F	⅝	Frank Posey	2199	Cr	Carrie Posey	2701	Cr
New Born Census Card No. 1063, P. O. Holdenville, Date of Birth October 5, 1902											
687	1	Brown, Edward S.	2	M	¼	Stanton Brown		Non	Julia Brown	4425	Cr
New Born Census Card No. 561, P. O. Holdenville, Date of Birth October 9, 1902											
688	1	McCosar, Arthur	2	M	F	Bunnie McCosar	7115	Cr	Nellie McCosar	7700	Cr
New Born Census Card No. 18, P. O. Gibson Station, Date of Birth January 19, 1903											
689	1	Sookey, Josephine	2	F	½	Boney Sookey	2134	Cr	Mamie Sookey		Non
New Born Census Card No. 47, P. O. Paden, Date of Birth July 10, 1902											
690	1	Johnson, Winey	3	F	½	Gilbert Johnson		Non	Betsey Johnson	3607	Cr
New Born Census Card No. 91, P. O. Beggs, Date of Birth August 7, 1904											
691	1	Gooden, Charley	1	M	⅜	Jacob Gooden	6992	Cr	Louisa Gooden	6993	Cr

Roll No.	No.	NAME	Age	Sex	Blood	NAME OF FATHER	Roll No.	Cit.	NAME OF MOTHER	Roll No.	Cit.
		New Born Census Card No. 96									
692	1	Hendrickson, Peter	For data see card at Roll No 344								
		New Born Census Card No. 146, P. O. Beggs, Date Iof Birth January 11, 1902									
693	1	Asbury, Joseph	3	M	F	Thomas Asbury	3436	Cr	Eliza Asbury	1477	Cr
		New Born Census Card No. 163									
694	1	Combs, John Boyd	1	M	⅛	For data see card at Roll No. 230					
		New Born Census Card No. 168									
695	1	Kerr, Ethel	4	F	¼	For data see card at Roll No. 111					
		New Born Census Card No. 268, P. O. Okemah, Date of Birth September 1, 1904									
696	1	Morton, Ellis M	1	M	⅛	Mossie Morton	4261	Cr	Josie A. Morton		Non
		New Born Census Card No. 285, P. O. Wewoka, Date of Birth June 15, 1904									
697	1	Noon, Lucinda	1	F	F	Wiley Noon	5282	Cr	Louisa Noon	5416	Cr
		New Born Census Card No. 335, P. O. Dustin, Date of Birth February 26, 1905									
698	1	Smith, Ester	1	F	3-16	John F. Smith	1988	Cr	Eurania Smith	1989	Cr
		New Born Census Card No. 481, P. O. Hot Springs, Ark., Date of Birth January 9, 1904									
699	1	Crowell, Otis Buel	1	M	1-16	Ben F. Crowell	47	Cr	Neta E. Crowell		Non
		New Born Census Card No. 512, P. O. Hitchita, Date of Birth No. 1, January 23, 1905; No. 2, April 5, 1903; No. 3, July 17, 1901									
700	1	Doyle, Susie Lee	1	F	⅜	Wallace Doyle	5971	Cr	Maud S. Doyle		Non
701	2	Doyle, Minnie May	2	F	⅜	Wallace Doyle	5971	Cr	Maud S. Doyle		Non
702	3	Doyle, Clarinda	4	F	⅜	Wallace Doyle	5971	Cr	Maud S. Doyle		Non
		New Born Census Card No. 517, P. O. Coweta, Date of Birth August 7, 1904									
703	1	Wilson, Robert Henry	1	M	1-16	H. C. Wilson		Non	Lucy Wilson	2002	Cr
		New Born Census Card No. 539, P. O. Yeager, Date of Birth No. 1, June 28, 1902; No. 2, June 15, 1904									
704	1	Riley, Claud	3	M	⅛	Horace Riley	3090	Cr	Mattie Riley		Non
705	2	Riley, Henry Earl	1	M	⅛	Horace Riley	3090	Cr	Mattie Riley		Non
		New Born Census Card No. 563, P. O. Yeager, Date of Birth July 29, 1904									
706	1	Long, Newman	1	M	F	Noah Long	4882	Cr	Eliza Long	3207	Cr
		New Born Census Card No. 568, P. O. Wewoka, Date of Birth April 17, 1902									
707	1	Buck, Sarah	3	F	⅛	Simpson Buck	5690	Cr	Rhoda Buck		Non
		New Born Census Card No. 569, P. O. Yeager, Date of Birth July 6, 1904									
708	1	Long, Anna	1	F	F	Henry Long	5318	Cr	Losanna Long	8427	Cr
		New Born Census Card No. 574, P. O. Spaulding Date of Birth No. 1, February 23, 1903; No. 2, January 23, 1902									
709	1	Tiger, Emma	2	F	F	Panosky Tiger		Non	Kizzie Tiger	7422	Cr
1053	2	Tiger, Nina	3	M?	F	Panosky Tiger		Non	Kizzie Tiger	7422	Cr
		New Born Census Card No. 583, P. O. Bristow, Date of Birth June 19, 1904									
710	1	Freeman, Hovah Monroe	1	M	1-16	Ezra Freeman		Non	Cordelia Freeman	3031	Cr
		New Born Census Card No. 584, P. O. Wetumka, Date of Birth May 28, 1903									
711	1	Mingo, Bessie	2	F	F	Joseph Mingo	5717	Cr	Aggie Mingo	5718	Cr
		New Born Census Card No. 589, P. O Brush Hill, Date of Birth August 6, 1904									
712	1	Thompson, Ollie	1	F	F	Legus Thompson	6287	Cr	Lina Thompson	6288	Cr
		New Born Census Card No. 596, P. O. Krebs, Date of Birth June 22, 1904									
713	1	Brown, Cleller	1	F	⅛	Jackson Brown	6286	Cr	Laura Brown		Non
		New Born Census Card No. 602, P. O. Red Fork, Date of Birth December 14, 1904									
714	1	Kelly, Perry	1	M	F	Reuben Kelly	2606	Cr	Nancy Kelly	3080	Cr
		New Born Census Card No. 603, P. O. Holdenville, Date of Birth June 1, 1901									
715	1	Watson, Nora	4	F	F	Homer Watson	1324	Cr	Emma McGirt	8086	Cr
		New Born Census Card No. 610, P. O. Cathay, Date of Birth September 11, 1903									
716	1	Reynolds, Clarence Andrew	1	M	1-32	Charley Reynolds		Non	Ada Reynolds	2541	Cr
		New Born Census Card No. 611, P. O. Lenna, Date of Birth January 2, 1905									
717	1	Morrison, Hettie Ola	1	F	5-16	Major Morrison	2653	Cr	Carrie Morrison		Non
		New Born Census Card No. 612, P. O. Sapulpa, Date of Birth February 6, 1905									
718	1	Collins, Noah	1	M	F	Lewis Collins	1365	Cr	Sophia Collins	1366	Cr
		New Born Census Card No. 617, P. O. Holdenville, Date of Birth March 18, 1904									
719	1	McGirtt, George	1	M	F	Billy McGirt	5045	Cr	Emma McGirt	8086	Cr
			Died September 16, 1905								
		New Born Census Card No. 618, P. O. Mellette, Date of Birth No. 1, March 3, 1902; No. 2, December 28, 1903									
720	1	Bright, Reubin	3	M	F	John Bright	6560	Cr	Rhoda Bright	6564	Cr
721	2	Bright, Lafa	1	M	F	John Bright	6560	Cr	Rhoda Bright	6564	Cr
		New Born Census Card No. 619, P. O. Eufaula, Date of Birth No. 1, August 26, 1902; No. 2, January 25, 1905									
722	1	Ansiel, William F.	3	M	1-32	Charlie Ansiel	6337	Cr	Mary Ansiel		Non
723	2	Ansiel, Robert Leroy	1	M	1-32	Charlie Ansiel	6337	Cr	Mary Ansiel		Non
		New Born Census Card No. 632, P. O. Eufaula, Date of Birth No. 1, June 12, 1901; No. 2, June 13, 1904									
724	1	Barnett, Edmund	4	M	½	Austin Barnett	8320	Cr	Liza Barnett		Non
725	2	Barnett, Hammer	1	M	½	Austin Barnett	8320	Cr	Liza Barnett		Non
		New Born Census Card No. 638, P. O. Eufaula, Date of Birth May 21, 1903									
726	1	Lewis, Lulu	2	F	F	Johnson Lewis	8765	Cr	Lucinda Lewis	8766	Cr
		New Born Census Card No. 643, P. O. Eufaula, Date of Birth No. 1, January 16, 1903; No. 2, December 4 1904									
727	1	Manley, Lindy Isaac	2	F	½	Isaac Manley	9092	Cr	Martha Manley		Non
728	2	Manley, Melah	1	F	½	Isaac Manley	9092	Cr	Martha Manley		Non
		New Born Census Card No. 648, P. O. Eufaula, Date of Birth March 1, 1903									
729	1	Depriest, Luther	2	M	9-16	James Depriest	2452	Cr	Emily Depriest	2453	Cr

Roll No.	No.	NAME	Age	Sex	Blood	NAME OF FATHER	Roll No.	Cit.	NAME OF MOTHER	Roll No.	Cit.

New Born Census Card No. 660, P. O. Eufaula, Date of Birth No. 1, December 5, 1902; No. 2, October 29, 1901

730	1	Ewing, Eulelia	2	F	⅝	Peter R. Ewing	3218	Cr	Susie A. Ewing	3219	Cr
731	2	Ewing, Ethel	3	F	⅝	Peter R. Ewing	3218	Cr	Susie A. Ewing	3219	Cr

New Born Census Card No. 661, P. O. Eufaula, Date of Birth April 6, 1904

| 732 | 1 | Young, Lucius | 1 | M | ⅛ | Harry Young | 3680 | Cr | Elizabeth Young | | Non |

New Born Census Card No. 662, P. O. Eufaula, Date of Birth July 6, 1904

| 733 | 1 | Watts, Minnie | 1 | F | ½ | Nobe Watts | | Non | Susan Watts | 1395 | Cr |

New Born Census Card No. 667, P.O. Eufaula;Date of Birth No. 1, July 18, 1904, No. 2;May 18, 1902

| 734 | 1 | Washington, Melah | 1 | F | ¾ | Watson Washington | 6349 | Cr | Lucy Washington | 6350 | Cr |
| 735 | 2 | Washington, Mandy | 3 | F | ¾ | .Watson Washington | 6349 | Cr | Lucy Washington | 6350 | Cr |

New Born Census Card No. 668, P. O. Lenna, Date of Birth December 16, 1903

| 736 | 1 | Derrisaw, Carrie | 1 | F | F | William Derrisaw | 7245 | Cr | Polly Derrisaw | 1341 | Cr |

New Born Census Card No. 674, P. O. Bristow, Date of Birth February 21, 1905

| 737 | 1 | Big Mosquito, Jennie | 1 | F | F | Big Mosquito | 1904 | Cr | Jensey Big Mosquito | 1905 | Cr |

New Born Census Card No. 685, P. O. Boynton, Date of Birth December 22, 1904

| 738 | 1 | Ansill, Henry F. | 1 | M | 1-16 | Samuel E. Ansill | 1406 | Cr | Roxie Ansill | | Non |

New Born Census Card No. 707, P. O. Eufaula, Date of Birth July 27, 1903

| 739 | 1 | Greenwood, Effie Belle | 2 | F | F | Lewis Greenwood | 8634 | Cr | Jennie Greenwood | 7618 | Cr |

New Born Census Card No. 708, P. O. Muskogee, Date of Birth August 25, 1902

| 740 | 1 | Minugh, Jesse L. | 3 | M | 1-16 | C: E. Minugh | | Non | Alice V. Minugh | 6252 | Cr |

New Born Census Card No. 715, P. O. Sasakwa, Date of Birth No. 1, June 25, 1901; No. 2, March 13. 1903

| 741 | 1 | Fixico, Winey | 4 | F | ¼ | Watty Fixico | | Non | Fanny Fixico | 7713 | Cr |
| 742 | 2 | Fixico, Jeffy | 2 | M | ¼ | Watty Fixico | | Non | Fanny Fixico | 7713 | Cr |

New Born Census Card No. 720, P. O. Eufaula Date of Birth October 28, 1903

| 743 | 1 | McCalvey, Emmit | 1 | M | 1-16 | Everett McCalvey | 4437 | Cr | Nora McCalvey | | Non |

New Born Census Card No. 721

| 744 | 1 | Chissoe, Sam Jr. | 2 | M | ⅞ | For data see card at Roll No. 673 | | | | | |

New Born Census Card No. 724, P. O. Eufaula, Date of Birth No. 1, December 25, 1904; No. 2, September 24, 1903

| 745 | 1 | Corey, Cordelia | 1 | F | ⅛ | Frank Corey | | Non | Josee Corey | 3358 | Cr |
| 1061 | 2 | Corey, Tom | 1 | M | ⅛ | Frank Corey | | Non | Josee Corey | 3358 | Cr |

New Born Census Card No. 727, P. O. Mounds, Date of Birth June 5, 1904

| 746 | 1 | Wills, Arthur Rex | 1 | M | 1-16 | John S. Wills | 3951 | Cr | Eunice May Wills | | Non |

New Born Census Card No. 730, P. O. Eufaula, Date of Birth February 28, 1905

| 747 | 1 | Polk, Ethel | 1 | F | ¾ | Daniel Polk | 6846 | Cr | Katie Polk | 6847 | Cr |

New Born Census Card No. 733, P. O. Sapulpa, Date of Birth July 28, 1903

| 748 | 1 | Fulsom, Ladee | 2 | M | F | Robert Fulsom | 7286 | Cr | Lucy Fulsom | 2869 | Cr |

New Born Census Card No. 736, P. O. Newby, Date of Birth February 3, 1904

| 749 | 1 | Davis, Mack | 1 | M | ⅜ | Redmond C. Davis | 4842 | Cr-F | Millie C. Davis | 4553 | Cr |

New Born Census Card No. 739, P. O. Kellyville, Date of Birth March 1, 1905

| 750 | 1 | Brink, Lizzie | 1 | F | F | Willie Brink | 8806 | Cr | Lusanna D. Brink | 3433 | Cr |

New Born Census Card No. 740, P. O. Lenna, Date of Birth September 18, 1902

| 751 | 1 | Leverett, Bessie | 2 | F | 5-16 | Walter Leverett | | Non | Kogee Leverett | 2655 | Cr |

New Born Census Card No. 741, P. O. Clearview, Date of Birth July 12, 1903

| 752 | 1 | Reynolds, Ernest | 2 | M | ¼ | Joseph Reynolds | | Non | Delphie Reynolds | 3009 | Cr |

New Born Census Card No. 754, P. O. Brush Hill, Date of Birth June 16, 1903

| 753 | 1 | Howell, Samuel Webster | 2 | M | 3-16 | Tallie H. Howell | | Non | Lizzie Howell | 8703 | Cr |

New Born Census Card No. 756, P. O. Oktaha, Date of Birth September 7, 1904

| 754 | 1 | Lewis, Emma | 1 | F | F | Harley Lewis | 3655 | Cr | Effie Lewis | 3656 | Cr |

New Born Census Card No. 758, P. O. Checotah, Date of Birth November 16, 1904

| 755 | 1 | Carr, Cecil Raymond | 1 | M | ⅛ | William M. Carr | 2686 | Cr | Vida Carr | | Non |

New Born Census Card No. 762, P. O. Bryant, Date of Birth No. 1, January 11, 1902; No. 2, January 23, 1904

| 756 | 1 | Fisher, Lizzie | 3 | F | ⅞ | Joe Fisher | 1726 | Cr | Nancy Fisher | 1727 | Cr |
| 757 | 2 | Fisher, Bertha | 1 | F | ⅞ | Joe Fisher | 1726 | Cr | Nancy Fisher | 1727 | Cr |

New Born Census Card No. 763, P. O. Cathay, Date of Birth October 2, 1903

| 758 | 1 | Fisher, Aubrey | 1 | M | ¼ | Sam Fisher | 2449 | Cr | Carrie Fisher | | Non |

New Born Census Card No. 769,P.O.Haskell,Date of Birth No. 1,January 29, 1902; No. 2, May 19, 1904

| 759 | 1 | Bruner, Bertha | 3 | F | F | Daniel Bruner | 2462 | Cr | Betty Bruner | 2463 | Cr |
| 760 | 2 | Bruner, Maggie | 1 | F | F | Daniel Bruner | 2462 | Cr | Betty Bruner | 2463 | Cr |

New Biorn Census Card No. 771, P. O. Stone Bluff, Date of Birth August 11, 1904

| 761 | 1 | Brown, Henry | 1 | M | F | Thomas Brown | 1815 | Cr | Annie Brown | 1898 | Cr |

New Born Census Card No. 774, P. O. Morse, Date of Birth No. 1, February 10, 1905; No. 2, January 18. 1903

| 762 | 1 | Roberts, Gainey | 1 | M | F | Kendall Roberts | 4295 | Cr | Mary Roberts | 4296 | Cr |
| 1065 | 2 | Roberts, Indie | 2 | F | F | Kendall Roberts | 4295 | Cr | Mary Roberts | 4296 | Cr |

New Born Census Card No. 777, P. O. Bristow, Date of Birth March 11, 1904

| 763 | 1 | Tiger, Martha | 1 | F | F | Daniel Tiger | 3935 | Cr | Sarah Tiger | 2062 | Cr |

New Born Census Card No. 779, P. O. Bixby, Date of Birth September 25, 1901

| 764 | 1 | Call, Charles | 3 | M | 1-16 | John M. Call | | Non | Pearl Call | 1557 | Cr |

New Born Census Card No. 781, P. O. Summit, Date of Birth June 5, 1904

| 765 | 1 | Berryhill, Ione | 1 | F | 1-64 | James Berryhill | 2501 | Cr | Elnora Berryhill | | Non |

New Born Census Card No. 783, P. O. Texana, Date of Birth April 17, 1903

| 766 | 1 | Johnson, Floyd Ila | 2 | M | ⅛ | Elijah T. Johnson | | Non | Lorena Johnson | 3678 | Cr |

New Born Census Card No. 787, P. O. Checotah, Date of Birth August 22, 1902

| 767 | 1 | Mackey, Bessie Adella | 3 | F | ¼ | George Mackey | | Non | Cherokee Mackey | 1875 | Cr |

Roll No.	No.	NAME	Age	Sex	Blood	NAME OF FATHER	Roll No.	Cit.	NAME OF MOTHER	Roll No.	Cit.
		New Born Census Card No. 790, P. O. Henryetta, Date of Birth No. 1, December 28, 1901; No. 2, August 19, 1903									
768	1	King, Henry Lee	3	M	½	W. L. King		Non	Elizabeth King	5998	Cr
769	2	King, John B.	2	M	½	W. L. King		Non	Elizabeth King	5998	Cr
		New Born Census Card No. 792, P. O. Eufaula, Date of Birth No. 1, January 6, 1902; No. 2, February 15, 1903									
770	1	Day, Beatrice	3	F	⅛	Robert Day		Non	Vinita Day	3850	Cr
771	2	Day, Robert Jr.	2	M	⅛	Robert Day		Non	Vinita Day	3850	Cr
		New Born Census Card No. 794, P. O. Bristow, Date of Birth November 5, 1904									
772	1	White, Clara	1	F	5-32	Craft White		Non	Emma White	4279	Cr
		New Born Census Card No. 795, P. O. Senora, Date of Birth No. 1, December 27, 1901; No. 2, March 13, 1904									
773	1	McIntosh, Mandy Van	3	F	¾	Amos McIntosh	2183	Cr	Louina McIntosh	2184	Cr
774	2	McIntosh, Malissa Christa	1	F	¾	Amos McIntosh	2183	Cr	Louina McIntosh	2184	Cr
		New Born Census Card No. 796, P. O. Bristow, Date of Birth November 15, 1902									
775	1	Ellis, James	2	M	5-16	James Ellis		Non	Hannah Mann	4278	Cr
		New Born Census Card No. 797, P. O. Eufaula, Date of Birth April 10, 1903									
776	1	Washington, Sue	2	F	1-64	E. M. Washington		Non	Catherine Washington	6298	Cr
		New Born Census Card No. 798, P. O. Depew, Date of Birth No. 1, December 29, 1903; No. 2, January 19, 1905									
777	1	Mukes, Hattie	1	F	⅜	Thomas Mukes		Non	Alice Mukes	1018	Cr
778	2	Mukes, Ada	1	F	⅜	Thomas Mukes		Non	Alice Mukes	1018	Cr
		New Born Census Card No. 799, P. O. Tuskegee, Date of Birth September 3, 1904									
779	1	Knight, Wiley	1	M	F	David Knight	4136	Cr	Hannah Knight	3926	Cr
		New Born Census Card No. 802, P. O. Bristow, Date of Birth March 2, 1904									
780	1	Grayson, Gertrude	1	F	9-16	Pete Grayson	1078	Cr	Hattie Grayson	1482	Cr
		New Born Census Card No. 804, P. O. Bristow, Date of Birth July 25, 1903									
781	1	Foster, Susie Mills	2	F	⅞	Abraham Foster	2292	Cr	Lucy Foster	6238	Cr
		New Born Census Card No. 806, P. O. Mounds, Date of Birth August 14, 1901									
782	1	Self, Jackson C.	4	M	⅛	John R. Self	3405	Cr	Sarah E. Self		Non
		New Born Census Card No. 807, P. O. Mounds, Date of Birth August 24, 1902									
783	1	Robins, Thomas	3	M	½	Mack Robins	4056	Cr-F	Sefarye (Short)	3038	Cr
		Sefarye identified as Chefargee Behen No. 3 on Card No. 937									
		New Born Census Card No. 811, P. O. Sapulpa, Date of Birth No. 1, March 21, 1902; No. 2, July 18, 1904									
784	1	Leader, Absalom	3	M	F	Joshua Leader	2934	Cr	Mahala Leader	5246	Cr
785	2	Leader, Edward	1	M	F	Joshua Leader	2934	Cr	Mahala Leader	5246	Cr
		New Born Census Card No. 816, P. O. Beggs, Date of Birth No. 1, January 12, 1903; No. 2, February 28, 1905									
786	1	Adams, Andrew	2	M	¼	Lewis Adams	3790	Cr	Annie Adams		Non
787	2	Adams, Ethel	1	F	¼	Lewis Adams	3790	Cr	Annie Adams		Non
		New Born Census Card No. 820, P. O. Henryetta, Date of Birth August 21, 1901									
788	1	Selvidge, Clarence	4	M	¼	R. B. Selvidge		Non	Susie Selvidge	143	Cr
		New Born Census Card No. 822, P. O. Mounds, Date of Birth No. 1, February 6, 1905; No. 2, November 4, 1902									
789	1	Staley, Nellie	2	F	F	John Staley	1909	Cr	Sakcota Staley	1910	Cr
1071	2	Staley, Kissie	1	F	F	John Staley	1909	Cr	Sakcota Staley	1910	Cr
		New Born Census Card No. 823, P. O. Sapulpa, Date of Birth No. 1, December 6, 1901; No. 2, September 23, 1904									
790	1	Hengst, Joseph A.	3	M	⅛	William C. Hengst		Non	Emma J. Hengst	9084	Cr
791	2	Hengst, Charles Augustus	1	M	⅛	William C. Hengst		Non	Emma J. Hengst	9084	Cr
		New Born Census Card No. 824, P. O. Mounds, Date of Birth August 21, 1902									
792	1	Tiger, Porter	3	M	F	Standwaity Tiger	1935	Cr	Lizzie Thomas Tiger	1938	Cr
		New Born Census Card No. 825, P. O. Sapulpa, Date of Birth July 22, 1903									
793	1	Gregory, Fletcher Raymond	2	M	½	Noah Gregory	2333	Cr	Carrie Gregory	2334	Cr
		New Born Census Card No. 828, P. O. Sapulpa, Date of Birth August 8, 1902									
794	1	Pitman, Robert Jr.	3	M	½	Robert Pitman		Non	Lucinda Pitman	1833	Cr
		New Born Census Card No. 831, P. O. Coweta, Date of Birth July 29, 1902									
795	1	Mantooth, Isabella	3	F	½	James H. Mantooth		Non	Annie Mantooth	1029	Cr
		New Born Census Card									
796	1	Stricken from roll									
		New Born Census Card No. 833, P. O. Sapulpa, Date of Birth September 9, 1903									
797	1	Frank, Vera	1	F	⅜	Noah Frank	8853	Cr	Hannah Frank		Non
		New Born Census Card No. 837, P. O. Kellyville, Date of Birth March 2, 1904									
798	1	Fulsom, Rhoda	1	F	F	Thomas Fulsom	7277	Cr	Millie Fulsom	7278	Cr
		New Born Census Card No. 838, P. O. Sapulpa, Date of Birth No. 1, September 9, 1901; No. 2, July 26, 1903									
799	1	Tate, Annie May	4	F	⅛	J. W. Tate		Non	Mary Tate	9872	Cr
800	2	Tate, Flora Ada	2	F	⅛	J. W. Tate		Non	Mary Tate	9872	Cr
		New Born Census Card No. 839, P. O. Kellyville, Date of Birth December 23, 1904									
801	1	Peeper, Viney May	1	F	½	Frank Peeper		Non	Many Peeper	6880	Cr
		New Born Census Card No. 840, P. O. Red Fork, Date of Birth No. 1, March 1, 1903; No. 2, September 20, 1901									
802	1	Bland, Davis M.	1	M	¼	John C. W. Bland		Non	Sue A. Bland	3559	Cr
803	2	Bland, Arlie S.	3	F	¼	John C. W. Bland		Non	Sue A. Bland	3559	Cr

Roll No.	No.	NAME	Age	Sex	Blood	NAME OF FATHER	Roll No.	Cit.	NAME OF MOTHER	Roll No.	Cit.
		New Born Census Card No. 841, P. O. Kellyville, Date of Birth May 27, 1903									
804	1	Littlehead, Ada	2	F	F	Willie Littlehead	7958	Cr	Nannie Littlehead	7959	Cr
		New Born Census Card No. 843, P. O. Keystone, Date of Birth Nos. 1 and 2, March 5, 1902 (Twins); No. 3, July 12, 1904									
805	1	Harry, Liza	3	F	½	John Harry	2883	Cr	Mary Harry	2884	Cr
806	2	Harry, Susie	3	F	½	John Harry	2883	Cr	Mary Harry	2884	Cr-
807	3	Harry, Bunch	1	F	½	John Harry	2883	Cr	Mary Harry	2884	Cr
		New Born Census Card No. 845, P. O. Mounds Date of Birth June 19, 1904									
808	1	Glenn, Elma	1	F	1-16	R. J. Glenn		Non	Ida Estella Glenn	2968	Cr
		New Born Census Card No. 192, P. O. Yeager, Date of Birth August 15, 1903									
809	1	Lowe, Joe	2	M	F	Canuky Lowe	4092	Cr	Toche Lowe	4903	Cr
		New Born Census Card No. 846, P. O. Coweta, Date of Birth February 1, 1902									
810	1	Bruner, Lady Beatrice	3	F	F	Richard Bruner	5571	Cr	Sarah Bruner	5572	Cr
		New Born Census Card No. 848, P. O. Beggs, Date of Birth March 16, 1903 (twins)									
811	1	Boon, Ikey	2	M	½	Peter Boon	C.F.4848	Cr-F	Martha Boon	2147	Cr
812	2	Boon, Isaac	2	M	½	Peter Boon	C.F.4848	Cr-F	Martha Boon	2147	Cr
		New Born Census Card No. 849, P. O. Braggs, Date of Birth June 2, 1901									
813	1	Dansby, Lucinda	4	F	⅛	Walter Dansby		Non	Vick Dansby	1967	Cr
		New Born Census Card No. 850, P. O. Okmulgee, Date of Birth May 24, 1904									
814	1	Berryhill, Leola May	1	F	9-16	Pleasant Berryhill	117	Cr	Jeanetta Berryhill	7144	Cr
		New Born Census Card No. 851, P. O. Fry, Date of Birth No. 1 June 14, 1902; No. 2 February 8, 1904									
815	1	Grayson, Ollie	3	F	F	Buck Grayson	7145	Cr	Manewe Grayson	7301	Cr
816	2	Grayson, Lillie	1	F	F	Buck Grayson	7145	Cr	Menewe Grayson	7301	Cr
		New Born Census Card No. 853, P. O. Huttonville, Date of Birth No. 1 December 24, 1904; No. 2 June 17, 1902									
817	1	Crabtree, Rebecca	1	F	3-16	George Crabtree	2805	Cr	Tooka Hutton	3476	Cr
818	2	Crabtree, Hattie	3	F	3-16	George Crabtree	2805	Cr	Tooka Hutton	3476	Cr
		New Born Census Card No. 854, P. O. Okmulgee, Date of Birth March 5, 1903									
819	1	Berryhill, Katie	2	F	⅞	Aleck Berryhill	130	Cr	Annie Berryhill	131	Cr
		New Born Census Card No. 857, P. O. Okmulgee, Date of Birth February 5, 1903									
820	1	Carter, William Thomas	2	M	1-16	Joe Carter		Non	Anna Carter	3582	Cr
		New Born Census Card No. 862, P. O. Mounds, Date of Birth October 1, 1903									
821	1	Huston, Thomas Adison	1	M	1-16	J. M. Huston		Non	Lula F. Huston	3415	Cr
		New Born Census Card No. 865, P. O. Wagoner, Date of Birth July 30, 1902									
822	1	Turnham, Lillie May	3	F	⅛	Joe Turnham		Non	Curley Turnham	1788	Cr
		New Born Census Card No. 866, P. O. Morse, Date of Birth February 7, 1904									
823	1	Douglas, Duard C.	1	M	½	Harry Douglas		Non	Louie Mikey Douglas	8667	Cr
		New Born Census Card No. 873, P. O. Boynton, Date of Birth December 25, 1903									
824	1	Haley, George Elmer	1	M	¼	W. D. Haley		Non	Lena Haley	482	Cr
		New Born Census Card No. 875, P. O. Mounds, Date of Birth February 11, 1904									
825	1	Kiefer, Clarence Ebert	1	M	1-16	Smith Kiefer		Non	Martha Lee Keifer	2514	Cr
		New Born Census Card No. 876, P. O. Schulter, Date of Birth No. 1 May 8, 1903; No. 2 January 1, 1905									
826	1	Burgess, Daniel	2	M	⅞	James Burgess	5638	Cr	Susanna Burgess	5639	Cr
827	2	Burgess, Bird	1	M	⅞	James Burgess	5638	Cr	Susanna Burgess	5639	Cr
		New Born Census Card No. 877, P. O. Muskogee, Date of Birth May 13, 1904									
828	1	Boone, Ladossa Fredre	1	F	¼	Imy R. Boone	3356	Cr	Mrs. Imy R. Boone		Non
		New Born Census Card No. 878, P. O. Coweta, Date of Birth February 24, 1905									
829	1	Taylor, Lucile	1	F	½	William Taylor		Non	Rosa Taylor	1013	Cr
		New Born Census Card No. 883, P. O. Sapulpa, Date of Birth No. 1 March 2, 1905; No. 2 December, 1902									
830	1	Clayton, Ernest	1	M	¼	Charlie Clayton		Non	Della Jacobs Clayton	3362	Cr
831	2	Clayton, William McKinley	2	M	¼	Charlie Clayton		Non	Della Jacobs Clayton	3362	Cr
		New Born Census Card No. 886, P. O. Mounds, Date of Birth No. 1 October 10, 1901; No. 2 January 24, 1904									
832	1	Berryhill, Lum	3	M	1-16	William Berryhill	2511	Cr	Alice Berryhill		?
833	2	Berryhill, Archie	1	M	1-16	William Berryhill	2511	Cr	Alice Berryhill		
		New Born Census Card No. 891, P. O. Okmulgee, Date of Birth September 28, 1902									
834	1	Grayson, Sarah Illegitimate	3	F	½	George Grayson	446	Cr-F	Bettie Adams	3003	Cr
		New Born Census Card No. 892, P. O. Henryetta, Date of Birth No. 1 September 15, 1901; No. 2 March 15, 1904									
835	1	Gray, Fannie	4	F	⅞	Willie Gray	7225	Cr	Millie Gray	1093	Cr
836	2	Gray, Susie	1	F	⅞	Willie Gray	7225	Cr	Millie Gray	1093	Cr
		New Born Census Card No. 893, P. O. Stone Bluff, Date of Birth No. 1 April 21, 1902; No. 2 September 24, 1904									
837	1	Berryhill, Charlie S.	3	M	⅛	Columbus Berryhill	2101	Cr	Emma Berryhill	2102	Cr
838	2	Berryhill, Emma C.	1	F	48	Columbus Berryhill	2101	Cr	Emma Berryhill	2102	Cr
		New Born Census Card No. 895, P. O. Lenna, Date of Birth September 24, 1903									
839	1	Morrison, Mary	1	F	⅝	Waitie Morrison	4324	Cr	Eliza Morrison	4325	Cr
		New Born Census Card No. 896, P. O. Bristow, Date of Birth July 10, 1901									
840	1	Mikey, Enos Vey	4	M	1-16	Josiah Mikey		Non	Lizzie Mikey	9249	Cr
		New Born Census Card No. 897, P. O. Bixby, Date of Birth December 21, 1903									
841	1	Tiger, Susannah	1	F	F	John Tiger	3224	Cr	Millie Tiger	3225	Cr
		New Born Census Card No. 900, P. O. Checotah, Date of Birth No. 2 May 20, 1902; No. 1 February 8, 1904									
842	1	Dyer, Lotta	1	F	1-32	Fred S. Dyer		Non	Eliza Dyer	3981	Cr
1082	2	Dyer, Emmett	3	M	1-32	Fred S. Dyer		Non	Eliza Dyer	3981	Cr

Roll No.	No.	NAME	Age	Sex	Blood	NAME OF FATHER	Roll No.	Cit.	NAME OF MOTHER	Roll No.	Cit.
		New Born Census Card No. 901, P. O. Okmulgee, Date of Birth August 17, 1903									
843	1	Johnson, Amandy	2	F	F	Weley Johnson	1072	Cr	Kizzie Johnson	7592	Cr
		New Born Census Card No. 907, P. O. Okmulgee, Date of Birth November 18, 1904									
844	1	Miller, Sarah	1	F	7/8	Seborn Miller	1738	Cr	Effa Miller	1739	Cr
		New Born Census Card No. 910, P. O. Stone Bluff, Date of Birth October 21, 1902									
845	1	Barnett, Linda	2	F	F	Daniel Barnett	2128	Cr	Samara Barnett	2129	Cr
		New Born Census Card No. 912, P. O. Red Fork, Date of Birth No. 1 November 21, 1902; No. 1 January 21, 1905									
846	1	Davis, Clarence B.	2	M	1/8	Lewis H. Davis	1571	Cr	Susanna Davis		Non
847	2	Davis, Harvie L.	1	M	1/8	Lewis H. Davis	1571	Cr	Susanna Davis		Non
		New Born Census Card No. 913, P. O. Broken Arrow, Date of Birth August 8, 1902									
848	1	Pitman, Moses	3	M	1-16	Edward Pitman	3731	Cr	Susie Pitman		Non
		New Born Census Card No. 914, P. O. Beggs, Date of Birth September 28, 1902									
849	1	Shepherd, Sammie	2	M	1/8	George Shepherd		Non	Annie Shepherd	3835	Cr
		New Born Census Card No. 918, P. O. Henryetta, Date of Birth December 17, 1901									
850	1	Brown, Lula	3	F	1/2	Jimsy Brown		Non	Rosanna Brown	3148	Cr
		New Born Census Card No. 924, P. O. Oktaha, Date of Birth July 29, 1903									
851	1	Fife, Exie	2	F	F	Elijah Fife	393	Cr	Millie Fife	394	Cr
		New Born Census Card No. 928, P. O. Kellyville, Date of Birth March 1903									
852	1	Bucktrot, Sagie	2	F	F	Con-Char-Cher Bucktrot	7860	Cr	Mattie Bucktrot	7861	Cr
		New Born Census Card No. 940, P. O. Kellyville, Date of Birth December 3, 1903									
853	1	Hay, Modie	1	M	F	John Hay	6895	Cr	Eggie Hay	6896	Cr
		New Born Census Card No. 943, P. O. Sapulpa, Date of Birth August 13, 1902									
854	1	Ispocogee, Noah	3	M	F	Belcher Ispokogee	6149	Cr	Jennie Ispogee	6150	Cr
		New Born Census Card No. 964, P. O. Okmulgee, Date of Birth May 1, 1903									
855	1	Sanger, Jaunitta	2	F	1/8	Stephen Sanger	3391	Cr	Viola Sanger		Non
		New Born Census Card No. 977, P. O. Okmulgee, Date of Birth September 20, 1901									
856	1	McFarland, Ned Illegitimate	4	M	1/2	James McFarland		Non	Melissa Wiley	1097	Cr
		New Born Census Card No. 983, P. O. Broken Arrow, Date of Birth December 23, 1902									
857	1	Boles, Pearl Amy	2	F	1-16	C. A. Boles		Non	Mattie Boles	1332	Cr
		New Born Census Card No. 987, P. O. Eufaula, Date of Birth December 22, 1904									
858	1	Manley, Peepsie	1	F	F	Tom Manley	6347	Cr	Katy Manley	8537	Cr
		New Born Census Card No. 989, P. O. Eufaula, Date of Birth January 14, 1904									
859	1	Mitchell, Morris	1	M	F	Lewis Mitchell	8481	Cr	Bettie Mitchell	8482	Cr
		New Born Census Card No. 996, P. O. Boynton, Date of Birth December 13, 1903									
860	1	Granberry, Alma Dee	1	F	1/2	James Granberry		Non	Mattie Granberry	1612	Cr
		New Born Census Card No. 1008, P. O. Hitchita, Date of Birth February 7, 1902									
861	1	King, Caesar	3	M	F	Jackson King	1465	Cr	Jennie King	1466	Cr
		New Born Census Card No. 1009, P. O. Hanna, Date of Birth No Date Given.									
862	1	Simmons, Emma	1	F	F	Walter Simmons	2873	Cr	Chippie Simmons	9679	Cr
		New Born Census Card No. 1016, P. O. Hanna, Date of Birth December 17, 1904									
863	1	Buckner, Jack	1	M	F	Wiley Buckner	8541	Cr	Susie Buckner	8542	Cr
		New Born Census Card No. 1018, P. O. Henryetta, Date of Birth September 9, 1901									
864	1	Ryal, Willie B.	4	M	1/2	L. B. Ryal		Non	Annie Ryal	6542	Cr
		New Born Census Card No. 1020, P. O. Carson, Date of Birth August 7, 1902									
865	1	Johnson, Hotulke	3	M	F	Ceasar Johnson	7340	Cr	Eliza Johnson	7341	Cr
		New Born Census Card No. 1022, P. O. Henryetta, Date of Borth November 9, 1903									
866	1	Rentie, Lucreesey	1	F	3-16	Lewis Rentie	479	Cr-F	Peggie Rentie	3862	Cr
		New Born Census Card No. 1025, P. O. Carson, Date of Birth No. 1 March 2, 1902; No. 2 September 12, 1904									
867	1	Stidham, Mattie	3	F	F	Timmy Stidham	7352	Cr	Eliza Stidham	7353	Cr
1197	2	Stidham, Johnny	1	M	F	Timmy Stidham	7352	Cr	Eliza Stidham	7353	Cr
		New Born Census Card No. 1028, P. O. Naudack, Date of Birth August 13, 1904									
868	1	Sampson, Wiley	1	M	F	Wash Sampson	1329	Cr	Cindy Sampson	8863	Cr
		New Born Census Card No. 1036, P. O. Morris, Date of Birth September 21, 1903									
869	1	Thompson, Nora	2	F	F	Manuel Thompson	3279	Cr	Cogee Thompson	1471	Cr
		New Born Census Card No. 1041, P. O. Carson, Date of Birth June, 1903									
870	1	Jones, Caddo	2	F	F	Willie Jones	9022	Cr	Sallie Casey	7385	Cr
		New Born Census Card No. 1053, P. O. Bristow, Date of Birth No. 1 December 10, 1902; No. 2 August 22, 1904									
871	1	Wadsworth, Leo E.	2	M	1-16	Ben W. Wadsworth	1192	Cr	Martha F. Wadsworth		Non
872	2	Wadsworth, Elle E.	1	F	1-16	Ben W. Wadsworth	1192	Cr	Martha F. Wadsworth		Non
		New Born Census Card No. 1057, P. O. Henryetta, Date of Birth August 23, 1903									
873	1	Watson, Ellen	2	F	1/4	Garland Grayson		Non	Katie Watson	4518	Cr
		New Born Census Card No. 1058, P. O. Mellette, Date of Birth April 29, 1902									
874	1	Roberts, Joseph	3	M	F	Noah Roberts	7753	Cr	Hannah Roberts	7754	Cr
		New Born Census Card No. 1060, P. O. Wagoner, Date of Birth August 9, 1904									
875	1	Ware, Ima	1	F	1/8	Henderson Ware		Non	Lula Ware	1791	Cr
		New Born Census Card No. 1075, P. O. North Fork, Date of Birth No. 1 January 1903; No. 2 Pebruary, 1904									
876	1	Lewis, Albert	2	M	F	Sahala Lewis	4942	Cr	Annie Lewis	4943	Cr
877	2	Lewis, John	1	M	F	Sahala Lewis	4942	Cr	Annie Lewis	4943	Cr
		New Born Census Card No. 1081, P. O. Wagoner, Date of Birth September 26, 1902									
878	1	Letts, Oscar Lovick	2	M	1-16	Frank B. Letts		Non	Susan L. Letts	882	Cr
		New Born Census Card No. 1083, P. O. Eufaula, Date of Birth December, 1901									
879	1	Bear, Lena	3	F	F	Thomas Bear	8986	Cr	Lydia Bear	8749	Cr
		New Born Census Card No. 1086, P. O. Broken Arrow, Date of Birth May 25, 1904									
880	1	Gillis, Elmer	1	M	1/4	Ed Gillis		Non	Anna Perryman	1501	Cr

Roll No.	No.	NAME	Age	Sex	Blood	NAME OF FATHER	Roll No.	Cit.	NAME OF MOTHER	Roll No.	Cit.
	New Born Census Card No. 1088, P. O. Bryant, Date of Birth No. 1 June 29, 1903; No. 2 September 24, 1904; No. 3 January 31, 1902										
881	1	Barnett, John	2	M	7/8	Tom Barnett	4502	Cr	Sukey Barnett	7858	Cr
882	2	Barnett, Charlie	1	M	7/8	Tom Barnett	4502	Cr	Sukey Barnett	7858	Cr
883	3	Barnett, Alice	3	F	7/8	Tom Barnett	4502	Cr	Sukey Barnett	7858	Cr
	New Born Census Card No. 1094, P. O. Sapulpa, Date of Birth February 2, 1903										
884	1	Marshall, Henry	2	M	F	Charlie Marshall	3229	Cr	Martha Marshall	6109	Cr
	New Born Census Card No. 1098, P. O. Eufaula, Date of Birth February 20, 1903										
885	1	Raiford, Jaunetta	2	F	1/2	Arthur E. Raiford	5691	Cr	Tookah Raiford	5631	Cr
	New Born Census Card No. 1101, P. O. Wagoner, Date of Birth June 10, 1903										
886	1	Bethel, Julia Lavinia	2	F	1/8	David F. Bethel		Non	Dora Bethel	1794	Cr
	New Born Census Card No. 1105, P. O. Okmulgee, Date of Birth No. 1 February 10, 1902; No. 2 July 27, 1903										
887	1	Wisener, Bessie	3	F	5/8	Ben J. Wisener	2294	Cr	Susan Wisener	6657	Cr
1117	2	Wisener, Minnie	2	F	5/8	Ben J. Wisener	2294	Cr	Susan Wisener	6657	Cr
	New Born Census Card No. 1106, P. O. Senora, Date of Birth September 15, 1903										
888	1	Colbert, William	1	M	F	Daniel Colbert	7843	Cr	Jemima Colbert	7598	Cr
	New Born Census Card No. 844, P. O. Sapulpa, Date of Birth July 2, 1904										
889	1	Ispocogee, Sam	1	M	F	Belcher Ispokgee	6149	Cr	Jennie Ispokogee	6150	Cr
	New Born Census Card No. 1108, P. O. Okmulgee, Date of Birth No. 1 June 23, 1903; No. 2 January 27, 1905										
890	1	Myers, Oscar D.	2	M	F	Wm. F. Myers		Non	Betsey Myers	2995	Cr
891	2	Myers, Laura M.	1	F	F	Wm. F. Myers		Non	Betsey Myers	2995	Cr
	New Born Census Card No. 1110, P. O. Hitchita, Date of Birth No. 1 September 24, 1902; No. 2 December 9, 1904; No. 3 July 10, 1901										
892	1	Patton, Lora	2	F	1/2	J. P. Patton		Non	Emma Patton	5567	Cr
893	2	Patton, Dora	1	F	1/2	J. P. Patton		Non	Emma Patton	5567	Cr
894	3	Patton, Leo Ora	4	F	1/2	J. P. Patton		Non	Emma Patton	5567	Cr
	New Born Census Card No. 1114, P. O. Henryetta, Date of Birth No. 1 May 20, 1902; No. 2 April 27, 1904										
895	1	Beams, Tishie M.	3	F	1/2	Charles Beams		Non	Annie Beams	4504	Cr
896	2	Beams, Rhoda	1	F	1/2	Charles Beams		Non	Annie Beams	4504	Cr
	New Born Census Card No. 1127, P. O. Okmulgee, Date of Birth May 29, 1903										
897	1	Harjo, Ella Ruth	2	F	F	H. M. Harjo	1795	Cr	Katie M. Harjo	1796	Cr
	New Born Census Card No. 1129, P. O. Broken Arrow, Date of Birth February 7, 1905										
898	1	Drew, Madella E.	1	F	9-32	Legus C. Drew	6548	Cr	Leila Drew	1551	Cr
	New Born Census Card No. 1131, P. O. Broken Arrow, Date of Birth February 27, 1903										
899	1	Thatcher, Charley Dee L.	2	M	1/8	S. D. Thatcher		Non	Nancy Thatcher	872	Cr
	New Born Census Card No. 1132, P. O. Beggs, Date of Birth No. 1 July 5, 1902; No. 2 March 3, 1905										
900	1	Postoak, Julia	3	F	1/8	Charley Postoak	707	CrF	Rachel Postoak	2231	Cr
901	2	Postoak, Jennie	1	F	1/8	Charley Postoak	707	CrF	Rachel Postoak	2231	Cr
	New Born Census Card No. 1133, P. O. Boynton, Date of Birth March 16, 1903										
902	1	McNac, Bettie	2	F	1/4	Robinson McNac	4577	Cr-F	Emma McNac	486	Cr
	New Born Census Card No. 1135, P. O. Mounds, Date of Birth No. 1 June 2, 1903; No. 2 October 30, 1904										
903	1	Boling, Walter Gilmore	2	M	1-16	W. F. Boling		Non	Martha F. Boling	5916	Cr
1128	2	Boling, Dixie Self	1	F	1-16	W. F. Boling		Non	Martha F. Boling	5916	Cr
	New Born Census Card No. 1136, P. O. Okmulgee, Date of Birth January 1, 1902										
904	1	Bruner, Pearl	3	F	1/4	Nathan Bruner	3185	Cr	Lou Bruner		Non
	New Born Census Card No. 1137, P. O. Okmulgee, Date of Birth September 12, 1902										
905	1	Proctor, Dennis Flinn	2	M	3/4	Toney E. Proctor	2575	Cr	Susan Proctor	2576	Cr
	New Born Census Card No. 1150, P. O. Hanna, Date of Birth January 30, 1905										
906	1	Fish, Posey	1	F	F	Lewis Fish	8337	Cr	Melega Fish	9378	Cr
	New Born Census Card No. 1169, P. O. Eufaula, Date of Birth September 4, 1902										
907	1	Lewis, Billy	3	M	F	Maxey Lewis	8751	Cr	Jennie Lewis	8826	Cr
	New Born Census Card No. 874, P. O. Mounds, Date of Birth No. 1 January 15, 1904; No. 2 February 24, 1905										
908	1	Berryhill, Flora Edna	1	F	1-16	Thos. J. Berryhill	3329	Cr	Nellie Berryhill		Non
909	2	Berryhill, May Belle	1	F	1-16	Thos. J. Berryhill	3329	Cr	Nellie Berryhill		Non
	New Born Census Card No. 14, P. O. Checotah, Date of Birth October 13, 1903										
910	1	Aultman, Agnes	1	F	1-16	Benjamin Aultman	431	Cr	Louisa Aultman		Non
	New Born Census Card No. 33, P. O. Irene, Date of Birth March 16, 1902										
911	1	Fields, Legus	3	M	F	Mitchell Fields	8426	Cr	Indy Fields	9370	Cr
	New Born Census Card No. 46, P. O. Dustin, Date of Birth November 9, 1904										
912	1	Moffer, Wilson	1	M	F	Waitie Moffer	8124	Cr	Eliza Moffer	4571	Cr
	New Born Census Card No. 59, P. O. Muskogee, Date of Birth July 24, 1904										
913	1	Jones, Clarence	1	M	1/4	Harrison Jones		Non	Lela Jones	6360	Cr
	New Born Census Card No. 148, P. O. Weleetka, Date of Birth July 10, 1904										
914	1	Yaholar, Jimmie	1	M	F	Josey Yaholar	5120	Cr	Betsey Yaholar	5121	Cr
	New Born Census Card No. 183, P. O. Wetumka, Date of Birth February 5, 1903										
915	1	Yarholar, Clarence	2	M	F	Chapley Yarholar	4851	Cr	Wisey Yarholar	4852	Cr
	New Born Census Card No. 236, P. O. Checotah, Date of Birth No. 1 November 14, 1904; No. 2 September 14, 1901										
916	1	Horn, Jessie	1	F	1/4	Sam Horn	1580	Cr	Lillie Horn		Non
917	2	Horn, Fannie Lee	4	F	1/4	Sam Horn	1580	Cr	Lillie Horn		Non
	New Born Census Card No. 266, P. O. Mounds, Date of Birth November 27, 1904										
918	1	Brown, Thomas	1	M	F	Co-den-ny	5593	Cr	You-con-co-con-thla-nay	5594	Cr
	New Born Census Card No. 279, P. O. Coweta, Date of Birth November 8, 1904										
919	1	Harmon, Lonie	1	F	1-16	Ben T. Harmon	2498	Cr	Mary J. Harmon		Non
		No. 1 died July 2, 1905									

New Born Census Card No. 309, P. O. Okemah, Date of Birth January 14, 1903

Roll No.	No.	NAME	Age	Sex	Blood	NAME OF FATHER	Roll No.	Cit.	NAME OF MOTHER	Roll No.	Cit.
920	1	Smith, Estella	2	F	F	Belcher Smith	6762	Cr	Sarah Harjo	6763	Cr

New Born Census Card No. 363, P. O. Weleetka, Date of Birth No. 2, September 20, 1901; No. 1, February 2, 1904

| 921 | 1 | Canard, Millie | 1 | F | F | Billy Canard | 4964 | Cr | Kizzie Canard | 4997 | Cr |
| 1105 | 2 | Canard, Louisa | 3 | F | F | Billy Canard | 4964 | Cr | Kizzie Canard | 4997 | Cr |

New Born Census Card No. 371, P. O. Fentress, Date of Birth September 17, 1901

| 922 | 1 | Foster, George Cameron | 3 | M | 1/8 | William C. Foster | 5286 | Cr | Jennie May Foster | | Non |

New Born Census Card No. 378, P. O. Hanna, Date of Birth August 23, 1903

| 923 | 1 | Simmons, William | 2 | M | F | George Simmons | 8340 | Cr | Martha Simmons | 8341 | Cr |

New Born Census Card No. 389, P. O. Wetumka, Date of Birth April 22, 1903

| 924 | 1 | Lucas, Tony | 2 | M | 1/2 | Nevie Lucas | | Non | Lucy Lucas | 6573 | Cr |

New Born Census Card No. 391, P. O. Weleetka, Date of Birth No. 1, February 23, 1902; No. 2, March 27, 1904

| 925 | 1 | Robinson, Nelson | 3 | M | 3-16 | Dave Robinson | 368 | Cr | Annie Robinson | 6125 | Cr |
| 926 | 2 | Robinson, Louisa | 1 | F | 3-16 | Dave Robinson | 368 | Cr | Annie Robinson | 6125 | Cr |

New Born Census Card No. 396, P. O. Carson, Date of Birth June 12, 1903

| 927 | 1 | Washington, Lillie | 3 | F | F | Colbert Washington | 7292 | Cr | Polly Washington | 7551 | Cr |

New Born Census Card No. 406, P. O. Okemah, Date of Birth January 9, 1902

| 928 | 1 | Berryhill, Clent | 3 | M | 7/8 | Sam Berryhill | 3837 | Cr | Sophie Berryhill | 3838 | Cr |

New Born Census Card No. 440, P. O. Dustin, Date of Birth May 16, 1902

| 929 | 1 | Haynes, Roley | 3 | M | F | James Haynes | 5925 | Cr | Martha Haynes | 5926 | Cr |

New Born Census Card No. 441, P. O. Holdenville, Date of Birth No. 1, February 12, 1903; No. 2, July 2, 1904

| 930 | 1 | Sewell, Ellen | 2 | F | 15-16 | Ben Sewell | 3811 | Cr | Emma Sewell | 6017 | Cr |
| 931 | 2 | Sewell, Elliott | 1 | M | 15-16 | Ben Sewell | 3811 | Cr | Emma Sewell | 6017 | Cr |

New Born Census Card No. 452, P. O. Bristow, Date of Birth No. 1, July 10, 1902; No. 2, January 15, 1904

| 932 | 1 | Wright, Ynema B. | 3 | F | 1-16 | Walter C. Wright | | Non | Lula T. Wright | 3029 | Cr |
| 933 | 2 | Wright, Ava E. | 1 | F | 1-16 | Walter C. Wright | | Non | Lula T. Wright | 3029 | Cr |

New Born Census Card No. 457, P. O. Tulsa, Date of Birth April 2, 1904

| 934 | 1 | Grayson, Panzie May | 1 | F | 1/8 | Joe Grayson | 3747 | Cr | Dora Grayson | | Non |

New Born Census Card No. 474

| 935 | 1 | Watson, Dave | 1 | M | 7-16 | For data see card at Roll No. 477 | | | | | |

New Born Census Card No. 488, P. O. Carson, Date of Birth No. 1, June 8, 1902; No. 2, February 8, 1905

| 936 | 1 | Bruner, Bunnie | 3 | M | F | John Bruner | 7403 | Cr | Sallie Bruner | 7404 | Cr |
| 937 | 2 | Bruner, Thomas | 1 | M | F | John Bruner | 7403 | Cr | Sallie Bruner | 7404 | Cr |

New Born Census Card No. 490, P. O. Depew, Date of Birth March 10, 1903

| 938 | 1 | Cloud, Hattie | 2 | F | F | Stephen Cloud | 8864 | Cr | Absey Cloud | 8532 | Cr |

New Born Census Card No. 502, P. O. Bristow, Date of Birth March 2, 1905

| 939 | 1 | Bigpond, Louis | 1 | M | F | James Bigpond | 7016 | Cr | Selah Bigpond | 6484 | Cr |

New Born Census Card No. 509, P. O. Yeager, Date of Birth August 23, 1903

| 940 | 1 | Yargee, Amos | 2 | M | 7/8 | Cully Yargee | 5394 | Cr | Katie Yargee | 4986 | Cr |

New Born Census Card No. 525, P. O. Holdenville, Date of Birth April 6, 1902

| 941 | 1 | McGirt, John | 3 | M | F | Buckner McGirt | 5325 | Cr | Linda McGirt | 5326 | Cr |

New Born Census Card No. 537, P. O. Calvin, Date of Birth December 8, 1903

| 942 | 1 | Williams, John Randolph | 1 | M | 3/4 | Charley Williams | 5465 | Cr | Emma Williams | 5466 | Cr |
| 943 | 2 | For data see card at Roll No. 1160 | | | | | | | | | |

New Born Census Card No. 558, P. O. Wewoka, Date of Birth No. 1, July 13, 1902; No. 2, November 30, 1904

| 944 | 1 | Benden, Ida | 3 | F | F | Louis Benden | 5194 | Cr | Dicey Benden | 5195 | Cr |
| 945 | 2 | Benden, Louisa | 1 | F | F | Louis Benden | 5194 | Cr | Dicey Benden | 5195 | Cr |

New Born Census Card No. 571

| 946 | 1 | Harjo, Fanny | 1 | F | F | For data see card at Roll No. 548 | | | | | |

New Born Census Card No. 580, P. O. Wetumka, Date of Birth March 28, 1904

| 947 | 1 | Buck, Sappho | 1 | F | F | William Buck | 5956 | Cr | Haney Buck | 5538 | Cr |

New Born Census Card No. 608, P. O. Lenna, Date of Birth June 18, 1901

| 948 | 1 | Carr, Washington | 4 | M | F | Limbo Carr | 5826 | Cr | Millie Carr | 5827 | Cr |

New Born Census Card No. 616

| 949 | 1 | Johnson, Ulter | 3 | M | F | For data, see card at Roll No. 590 | | | | | |

New Born Census Card No. 623, P. O. Lenna, Date of Birth No. 1, April 24, 1902; No. 2, February 19, 1905

| 950 | 1 | Riley, Tootie | 3 | F | F | Thomas Riley | 1371 | Cr | Emma Willingham | 7246 | Cr |
| 951 | 2 | Riley, Leah | 1 | F | F | Thomas Riley | 1371 | Cr | Emma Willingham | 7246 | Cr |

New Born Census Card No. 636, P. O. Coweta, Date of Birth December 18, 1903

| 952 | 1 | Vann, Lydia | 1 | F | F | Watlie Vann | 3200 | Cr | Emma Vann | 1062 | Cr |

New Born Census Card No. 651, P. O. Catoosa, Date of Birth January 12, 1903

| 953 | 1 | Frank, Austin | 2 | M | F | Austin Frank | 7155 | Cr | Lizzie Frank | 1083 | Cr |

New Born Census Card No. 665, P. O. Eufaula, No. 1, January 5, 1903; No. 2, November 3, 1904

| 954 | 1 | Bean, Supsie | 2 | F | 7/8 | Monday Bean | 8250 | Cr | Lean Bean | 9619 | Cr |
| 955 | 2 | Bean, John | 1 | M | 7/8 | Monday Bean | 8250 | Cr | Lena Bean | 9619 | Cr |

New Born Census Card No. 692, P. O. Eufaula, Date of Birth June 26, 1904

| 956 | 1 | Manley, Arthur Died March 15, 1905 | 1 | M | F | Thomas Manley | 9008 | Cr | Millie Manley | 8840 | Cr |

New Born Census Card No. 717, P. O. Stidham, Date of Birth No. 1, December 9, 1904; No. 2, November 10, 1901

| 957 | 1 | Nubbie, Robert | 1 | M | F | George W. Nubbie | 4354 | Cr | Harley Nubbie | 5725 | Cr |
| 1235 | 2 | Nubbie George | 3 | M | 1/2 | George W. Nubbie | 4354 | Cr | Sophia Nubble | | Non |

Roll No.	No.	NAME	Age	Sex	Blood	NAME OF FATHER	Roll No.	Cit.	NAME OF MOTHER	Roll No.	Cit.
New Born Census Card No. 752, P. O. Eufaula, Date of Birth July 20, 1902											
958	1	Lewis, Mattie	3	F	F	Daniel Lewis	8485	Cr	Polly Lewis	8486	Cr
New Born Census Card No. 757, P. O. Bristow, Date of Birth February 20, 1903											
959	1	Hamilton, Mary	2	F	5-16	Peter Hamilton	2748	Cr	Ellen Hamilton		Non
New Born Census Card No. 764, P. O. Eufaula, Date of Birth September 9, 1902											
960	1	McFarland, Yancy	2	M	½	James McFarlaad		Non	Mary Smith	7602	Cr
New Born Census Card No. 765, P. O. Eufaula, Date of Birth March 3, 1903											
961	1	Doyle, Leo	2	M	⅛	Sam H. Doyle Jr.	6784	Cr	Bedia Doyle		Non
New Born Census Card No. 767, P. O. Wealaka, Date of Birth February 3, 1904											
962	1	Tecumseh, Mary	1	F	⅞	Austin Tecumseh	2473	Cr	Rosa Tecumseh	2075	Cr
New Born Census Card No. 775, P. O. Wealaka, Date of Birth May 14, 1904											
963	1	Kelley, Rosella	1	F	F	Wesley Kelley	1060	Cr	Susanna Kelley	3597	Cr
New Born Census Card No. 789, P. O. Stidham, Date of Birth February 11, 1904											
964	1	Ingram, Sudie	1	F	⅞	Thomas J. Ingram	6187	Cr	Jannatte Ingram	6188	Cr
New Born Census Card No. 808, P. O. Fentress, Date of Birth September 16, 1902											
965	1	Dunson, Raymond	2	M	F	Luna E. Dunson	2036	Cr	Lucy Dunson	4839	Cr
New Born Census Card No. 809, P. O. Leonard, Date of Birth February 27, 1904											
966	1	Clinton, Rachel	1	F	F	Willis E. Clinton	4085	Cr	Ella Clinton	792	Cr
New Born Census Card No. 815, P. O. Okmulgee, Date of Birth No. 1, September 25, 1902; No. 2, March 2, 1905											
967	1	Derisaw, Lila	3	F	½	David Derisaw	3180	Cr	Maggie Derisaw		Non
968	2	Derisaw, Willie	1	M	½	David Derisaw	3180	Cr	Maggie Derisaw		Non
New Born Census Card No. 817, P. O. Checotah, Date of Birth October 6, 1902											
969	1	Pemberton, Reacy Adeline	2	F	1-16	William T. Pemberton	2017	Cr	Naoma Pemberton		Non
New Born Census Card No. 818, P. O. Checotah, Date of Birth October 1, 1902											
970	1	Escoe, Leo Bennett	2	M	⅛	Charlie J. Escoe	908	Cr	Dora Escoe		Non
New Born Census Card No. 827, P. O. Olive, Date of Birth February 13, 1903											
971	1	Brown, Georgia	2	F	F	Larry Brown	1983	Cr	Hardin Brown	1984	Cr
New Born Census Card No. 829, P. O. Lenna, Date of Birth No. 1, August 17, 1902; No. 2, November 24, 1904											
972	1	Morrison, Lula Mildred	3	F	5-16	Manny Morrison	2651	Cr	Julia Morrison		Non
973	2	Morrison, Stan Waitie	1	M	5-16	Manny Morrison	2651	Cr	Julia Morrison		Non
New Born Census Card No. 835, P. O. Morris, Date of Birth February 17, 1905											
974	1	Scott, Billie	1	M	½	James Scott	1239	Cr	Malesky Scott	1615	Cr
		Died July 2, 1905.	Identification of parents questionable								
New Born Census Card No. 836, P. O. Beggs, Date of Birth December 27, 1904											
975	1	Simms, Lucinda	1	F	F	Maxey Simms	266	Cr	Louisa Simms	6650	Cr
New Born Census Card No. 847, P. O. Basin Idaho,, Date of Birth May 12, 1904											
976	1	Posey, Mina E.	1	F	⅛	Albert W. Posey	6813	Cr	Mary A. Posey		Non
New Born Census Card No. 852, P. O. Sapulpa, Date of Birth November 4, 1902											
977	1	Cosar, Galvos	2	M	F	Tom Cosar	5210	Cr	Jennie Cosar	5211	Cr
New Born Census Card No. 856, P. O. Okmulgee, Date of Birth December 26, 1901											
978	1	Bosen, Pearlie Illegitimate	3	F	⅞	George Bosen	6100	Cr	Josephine Asbury	4446	Cr
New Born Census Card No. 859, P. O. Mannford, Date of Birth September 7, 1903											
979	1	Postoak, Eli	1	M	F	Lincoln Poastoak	2324	Cr	Patty Bruner Bridges	2330	Cr
New Born Census Card No. 860, P. O. Sapulpa, Date of Birth No. 1, January 4, 1905; No. 2, January 24, 1902											
980	1	Johnson, Martin	1	M	F	Sandy Johnson	8120	Cr	Jinnie Johnson	8121	Cr
981	2	Johnson, Emma	3	F	F	Sandy Johnson	8120	Cr	Jinnie Johnson	8121	Cr
New Born Census Card No. 861, P. O. Broken Arrow, Date of Birth No. 1, September 30, 1902; No. 2, December 10, 1904											
982	1	Chamberlain, Dewey	3	M	⅛	John C. Chamberlain		Non	Susie Chamberlain	1307	Cr
983	2	Chamberlain, Ruby	1	F	⅛	John C. Chamberlain		Non	Susie Chamberlain	1307	Cr
New Born Census Card No. 864, P. O. Coweta, Date of Berth April 2, 1904											
984	1	Davis, Hattie Johnson Illegitimate	1	F	½	Isaac Johnson	709	Cr	Kizzie Davis	613	Cr
New Born Census Card No. 868, P. O. Wagoner, Date of Birth January 5, 1902											
985	1	Mingo, Joseph	3	M	¾	Robert J. Mingo	2704	Cr	Irene Mingo	2705	Cr
New Born Census Card No. 870, P. O. Stone Bluff, Date of Birth September 23, 1902											
986	1	Berryhill, Sam Bob	2	M	1-64	Geo. Franklin Berryhill	7912	Cr	Clemantine Berryhill		Non
New Born Census Card No. 880, P. O. Sapulpa, Date of Birth No. 1, July 23, 1901; No. 2, April 8, 1903											
987	1	Berryhill, Ves	4	M	1-16	Theodore Berryhill	2519	Cr	Rilla Berryhill		Non
988	2	Berryhill, Earl	2	M	1-16	Theodore Berryhill	2519	Cr	Rilla Berryhill		Non
New Born Census Card No. 885, P. O. Strand, Date of Birth May 29, 1902											
989	1	Doyle, Beulah Illegitimate	3	F	1-16	John N. Doyle	3609	Cr	Rhoda Doyle		Non
New Born Census Card No. 888, P. O. Okmulgee, Date of Birth December 3, 1904											
990	1	Bird, Kizzie	1	F	F	Moses Bird	259	Cr	Sallie Bird	260	Cr
New Born Census Card No. 889, P. O. Okmulgee, Date of Birth July 26, 1904											
991	1	Gibson, Martha	1	F	F	Jospeh Gibson	106	Cr	Hettie Gibson	1488	Cr
New Born Census Card No. 894, P. O. Okmulgee, Date of Birth March 29, 1903											
992	1	Huckaby, Ora	2	F	¼	R. W. Huckaby		Non	Elsie Huckaby	1195	Cr

Roll No.	No.	NAME	Age	Sex	Blood	NAME OF FATHER	Roll No.	Cit.	NAME OF MOTHER	Roll No.	Cit.
		New Born Census Card No. 898, P. O. Schulter, Date of Birth January 13, 1903 (Twins)									
993	1	Holleyman, Marcellus	2	M	1/8	T. E. Holleyman		Non	Maggie G. Holleyman	2847	Cr
994	2	Holleyman, Marcella	2	F	1/8	T. E. Holleyman		Non	Maggie G. Holleyman	2847	Cr
		New Born Census Card No. 899, P. O. Checotah, Date of Birth August 15, 1901									
995	1	Keys, James	4	M	1-32	Sam R. Keys	5791	Cr	Martha Keys		Non
		New Born Census Card No. 904, P. O. Okmulgee, Date of Birth November 15, 1903									
996	1	Kannard, Melissa	1	F	1/2	Martin Kannard	4388	Cr	Minah Kannard		Non
		New Born Census Card No. 905, P. O. Holdenville, Date of Birth January 5, 1903									
997	1	Lindsey, Addie	2	F	1/2	Walter Lindsey	6460	Cr	Hettie Lindsey		Non
		New Born Census Card No. 911, P. O. Okmulgee, Date of Birth March 20, 1904									
998	1	Snakeya, Heness	1	F	F	David Snakeya	1254	Cr	Molleanna Snakeya	1255	Cr
		New Born Census Card No. 917, P. O. Bixby, Date of Birth No. 2, December 7, 1901; No. 1, February 6, 1904									
999	1	Bruner, Archie	1	M	F	John Bruner	55	Cr	Pamela Bruner	56	Cr
1085	2	Bruner, Minnie	3	F	F	John Bruner	55	Cr	Pamela Bruner	56	Cr
		New Born Census Card No. 920, P. O. Edna, Date of Birth No. 1, July 10, 1903; No. 2, January 15, 1905									
1000	1	Bruner, Bettie	2	F	1/4	Henry Bruner	2013	Cr	Leoner Bruner		Non
1001	2	Bruner, Jessie	1	F	1/4	Henry Bruner	2013	Cr	Leoner Bruner		Non
1002	3	Bruner, Bessie	1	F	1/4	Henry Bruner	2013	Cr	Leoner Bruner		Non
		New Born Census Card No. 923, P. O. Bearden, Date of Birth November 30, 1903									
1003	1	Graham, Sissie	1	F	1/4	Lewis Graham		Non	Millie Graham	5721	Cr
		New Born Census Card No. 926, P. O. Okemah, Date of Birth July 28, 1901									
1004	1	Connie, Larley	4	F	F	Thomas Connie	6570	Cr	Martha Connie	6473	Cr
		New Born Census Card No. 937, P. O. Bristow, Date of Birth July 19, 1903									
1005	1	Cates, Governor	2	M	F	Joseph Cates	6366	Cr	Lydia Cates	8845	Cr
		New Born Census Card No. 942, P. O. Sapulpa, Date of Birth May 20, 1904									
1006	1	Rogers, Lucy	1	F	F	Chepon Rogers	3118	Cr	Jemima Rogers	2994	Cr
		Died January 10, 1906									
		New Born Census Card No. 944, P. O. Beggs, Date of Birth January 27, 1905									
1007	1	Hogan, Willie D.	1	F	1/8	Robert Hogan		Non	Julia Hogan	3541	Cr
		New Born Census Card No. 948, P. O. Kellyville, Date of Birth November 3, 1903									
1008	1	Snap, Andy	1	M	F	James Snap	1300	Cr	Mabele Snap	5993	Cr
		New Born Census Card No. 961, P. O. Wagoner, Date of Birth August 22, 1901									
1009	1	Price, Minnie May	4	F	1-16	M. B. Price		Non	Sallie Price	2331	Cr
		New Born Census Card No. 967, P. O. Okmulgee, Date of Birth No. 1, April 27, 1902; No. 2, May 15, 1904									
1010	1	Sneed, Susie Rose	3	F	3-16	George Sneed	9825	Cr	Hannah Sneed		Non
1011	2	Sneed, Larzar	1	M	3-16	George Sneed	9825	Cr	Hannah Sneed		Non
		New Born Census Card No. 991, P. O. Eufaula, Date of Birth July 4, 1904									
1012	1	Williams, John	1	M	F	Thomas Williams	9341	Cr	Annie Williams	9167	Cr
		New Born Census Card No. 997, P. O. Henryetta, Date of Birth August 16, 1903									
1013	1	Gilbert, Jeniry	2	F	1-16	Louis W. Gilbert		Non	Jude Gilbert	3522	Cr
		New Born Census Card No. 1082, P. O. Wagoner, Date of Birth July 15, 1901									
1014	1	Pitts, Major Barbee	4	M	1-16	Frank Fields Pitts		Non	Emma Pitts	2278	Cr
		New Born Census Card No. 1095, P. O. Stroud, Date of Birth June 2, 1902									
1015	1	McIntosh, Charles Curtis	3	M	3/8	Charles McIntosh	3470	Cr	Bertha A. McIntosh		Non
		New Born Census Card No. 863, P. O. Mounds, Date of Birth April 30, 1903									
1016	1	Barber, John Thomas	2	M	1-16	John W. Barber	3414	Cr	Cora Barber		Non
		New Born Census Card No. 973, P. O. Okmulgee, Date of Birth April 12, 1903									
1017	1	Tobler, Pleasant Illegitimate	2	M	1/2	Fred Tobler	390	Cr-F	Mary Tobler	2148	Cr
		New Born Census Card No. 205, P. O. Okemah, Date of Birth No. 1, October 5, 1902; No. 2, February 24, 1905									
1018	1	Hencha, Roy	2	M	F	Mitchell Heneha	26	Cr	Lucy Heneha	7446	Cr
1019	2	Heneha, Ralph	1	M	F	Mitchell Heneha	26	Cr	Lucy Heneha	7446	Cr
		New Born Census Card No. 296, P. O. Weleetka, Date of Birth August 16, 1904									
1020	1	Harjo, Lilley	1	F	F	Joseph Harjo	4698	Cr	Mehaley Harjo	4858	Cr
		New Born Census Card No. 305, P. O. Keokuk Falls, Date of Birth No. 1, July 18, 1901; No. 2, May 12, 1904									
1021	1	Spencer, Lanah	4	F	1/2	Ramsey Spencer		Non	Ludie Spencer	500	Cr
1022	2	Spencer, Loma	1	M	1/2	Ramsey Spencer		Non	Ludie Spencer	500	Cr
		New Born Census Card No. 312									
1023	1	Baker, Pauline E.	1	F	1/2	For data, see card at Roll No. 305					
		New Born Census Card No. 329, P. O. Wetumka, Date of Birth October 1, 1903									
1024	1	Harjo, Sallie	1	F	F	Yahola Harjo	7803	Cr	Lucy Harjo	7804	Cr
		Died September 30, 1906									
		New Born Census Card No. 334, P. O. Wetumka, Date of Birth May 5, 1904									
1025	1	Harjo, Susie	1	F	F	Tom Harjo	8931	Cr	Millie Harjo	8128	Cr
		Died September 9, 1905									
		New Born Census Card No. 337, P. O. Wetumka, Date of Birth September 12, 1903									
1026	1	Josie, Jennie	1	F	3/4	Soffley Josie		Non	Lena Josie	7130	Cr
		New Born Census Card No. 348, P. O. Okemah, Date of Birth July 30, 1904									
1027	1	Tiger, Lousanna	1	F	F	Thomas Tiger	8297	Cr	Louisa Tiger	5986	Cr
		New Born Census Card No. 350, P. O. Morse, Date of Birth July 4, 1902									
1028	1	Butcher, Lela	3	F	F	Norfer Butcher	4312	Cr	Munsey Butcher	4313	Cr
		New Born Census Card No. 369, P. O. Wewoka, Date of Birth September 20, 1901									
1029	1	Brown, McKinley	4	M	1/8	Jeff Brown		Non	Julia Brown	1180	Cr

252

Roll No.	No.	NAME	Age	Sex	Blood	NAME OF FATHER	Roll No.	Cit.	NAME OF MOTHER	Roll No.	Cit.
		New Born Census Card No. 377, P. O. Henryetta, Date of Birth May 12, 1902									
1030	1	Brown, Hettie	3	F	⅝	Joe Brown	7680	Cr	Betsey Manawee	4493	Cr
		New Born Census Card No. 393, P. O. Weleetka, Date of Birth February 4, 1905									
1031	1	Watson, Dave	1	M	9-16	Sandy Watson	7659	Cr	Mina Scott	4576	Cr
		New Born Census Card No. 397, P. O. Carson, Date of Birth No. 1, March 27, 1902; No. 2, November 1093									
1032	1	Wilson, Wisey	3	F	F	Thomas Wilson	8478	Cr	Bettie Wilson	7904	Cr
1033	2	Wilson, Minnie	2	F	F	Thomas Wilson	8478	Cr	Bettie Wilson	7904	Cr
		New Born Census Card No. 401, P. O. Carson, Date of Birth July 2, 1904									
1034	1	Bruner, Willie	1	M	F	David Bruner	7185	Cr	Isley Bruner	7186	Cr
		Reported dead									
		New Born Census Card No. 405, P. O. Weleetka, Date of Birth January 19, 1904									
1035	1	Barnett, Rosanna	1	F	⅞	Tucker Barnett	4797	Cr	Katie Barnett	4965	Cr
		New Born Census Card No. 407, P. O. Castle, Date of Birth May 29, 1904									
1036	1	Harjo, Roller	1	F	F	Frank Harjo	8090	Cr	Daley Harjo	6695	Cr
		New Born Census Card No. 412, P. O. Oktaha, Date of Birth No. 1, January 3, 1903; No. 2, June 4, 1904									
1037	1	Miller, Malvin H.	2	M	¼	Quint H. Miller		Non	Rose Etta Miller	3513	Cr
1038	2	Miller, Cecil	1	M	¼	Quint H. Miller		Non	Rose Etta Miller	3513	Cr
		New Born Census Card No. 459, P. O. Okemah, Date of Birth No. 1, January 24, 1902; No. 2, March 10, 1904									
1039	1	Foster, Henry	3	M	F	Chotka Foster	4583	Cr.	Many Foster	5590	Cr
1040	2	Foster, Lula	1	F	F	Chotka Foster	4583	Cr	Many Foster	5590	Cr
		New Born Census Card No. 469									
1041	1	Island, Louisa	1	F	F	For data, see card at Roll No. 472					
		New Born Census Card No. 470, P. O. Muskogee, Date of Birth April 15, 1903									
1042	1	Sudduth, Rosetta	2	F	½	Bob Sudduth		Non	Phoebe Sudduth	776	Cr
		New Born Census Card No. 497, P. O. Hitchita, Date of Birth December 27, 1902									
1043	1	Foshee, Henry C.	2	M	1-16	William R. Foshee	309		Lillian Foshee		Non
		New Born Census Card No. 511, P. O. Yeager, Date of Birth February 27, 1904									
1044	1	Culler, Leah	1	F	F	Thomas Culler	4786	Cr	Mary Culler	4787	Cr
		New Born Census Card No. 513, P. O. Holdenville, Date of Birth June 22, 1903									
1045	1	McKan, George	2	M	⅞	John McKan	5238	Cr	Hepsey McKan	5239	Cr
		New Born Census Card No. 778, P. O. Bristow, Date of Birth March 8, 1904									
1046	1	Hawkins, Louis	1	M	53-64	Eddie Jack	2733	Cr	Fannie Hawkins	2063	Cr
		New Born Census Card No. 523, P. O. Henryetta, Date of Birth January 22, 1904									
1047	1	Taylor, Eli	1	M	F	Sarpsey Taylor	7597	Cr	Liza Taylor	3725	Cr
		New Born Census Card No. 524, P. O. Spaulding, Date of Birth April 20, 1903									
1048	1	Tiger, Selanie	2	F	¾	John Tiger		Non	Cinda Tiger	7711	Cr
		New Born Census Card No. 527, P. O. Holdenville, Date of Birth February 10, 1905									
1049	1	Harrison, Bettie	1	F	F	Peter Harrison	5499	Cr	Rhoda Harrison	6115	Cr
		New Born Census Card oN. 534, P. O. Barney, Date of Birth February 21, 1904									
1050	1	Downing, Jesse	1	M	½	Ambrose Downing		Non	Katie Downing	6742	Cr
		New Born Census Card No. 538, P. O. Emahaka, Date of Birth February 11, 1904									
1051	1	Frank, Johnson	1	M	½	Alfred Frank		Non	Sissy Frank	7708	Cr
		New Born Census Card No. 546, P. O. Earlsboro, Date of Birth No. 2, October 27, 1902; No. 1, February 28, 1905									
1052	1	Kernel, Freeman	1	M	½	George Kernel	8942	Cr	Anetta Kernel		Non
1157	2	Kernel, Harry	2	M	½	George Kernel	8942	Cr	Anetta Kernel		Non
		New Born Census Card No. 574									
1053	1	Tiger, Nina	3	M	F	For data, see card at Roll No. 709					
		New Born Census Card No. 586, P. O. Yeager, Date of Birth August 25, 1902									
1054	1	Chupco, Cilla	3	F	F	Toney Chupco	4918	Cr	Loday Long	5512	Cr
1055	1	Beaver, Walter	3	M	F	For data, see card at Roll No. 586					
		New Born Census Card No. 622, P. O. Eufaula, Date of Birth October 16, 1903									
1056	1	Gambler, Martin	1	M	F	John Gambler	8595	Cr	Hepsey McGilbray	1399	Cr
		New Born Census Card No. 672									
1057	1	Woods, Argethel	1	F	⅛	For data, see card at Roll No. 630					
		New Born Census Card No. 684, P. O. Weleetka, Date of Birth February 1, 1905									
1058	1	Fixico, Roley	1	M	F	Bassta Fixico	4597	Cr	Jemima Fixico	4690	Cr
		New Born Census Card No. 704, P. O. Vivian, Date of Birth December 14, 1903									
1059	1	Colbert, Kizzie	1	F	F	Thompson Colbert	8546	Cr	Ellen Colbert	8547	Cr
		New Born Census Card No. 711									
1060	1	Harjo, Winey	1	F	F	For data, see card at Roll No. 663					
		New Born Census Card No. 724									
1061	1	Corey, Tom	1	M	⅛	For data, see card at Roll No. 745					
		New Born Census Card No. 766, P. O. Wealaka, Date of Birth No. 1, February 19, 1903; No. 2, January 1, 1905									
1062	1	Tecumseh, Effie	2	F	⅞	Nero Tecumseh	2474	Cr	Nancy Tecumseh	3599	Cr
1063	2	Tecumseh, Edward	1	M	⅞	Nero Tecumseh	2474	Cr	Nancy Tecumseh	2599	Cr
		New Born Census Card No. 768, P. O. Eufaula, Date of Birth March 3, 1905									
1064	1	White, Laura	1	F	¼	Mac White		Non	Phenia White	3674	Cr
		New Born Census Card No. 774									
1065	1	Roberts, Indie	1	F	F	For data, see card at Roll No. 762					

Roll No.	No.	NAME	Age	Sex	Blood	NAME OF FATHER	Roll No.	Cit.	NAME OF MOTHER	Roll No.	Cit.
		New Born Census Card No. 784, P. O. Pierce, Date of Birth October 30, 1903									
1066	1	Deere, Willey	1	M	½	John Deere		Non	Lizzie Deere	8239	Cr
		New Born Census Card No. 788, P. O. Senora, Date of Birth March 19, 1902									
1067	1	Hope, Beaden	3	M	F	Robert Hope	6728	Cr	Emma Hope	8978	Cr
		New Born Census Card No. 793, P. O. Eufaula, Date of Birth August 11, 1904									
1068	1	Harley, Joseph	1	M	F	Sampson Harley	7406	Cr	Jenⅼiɔ Harley	7407	Cr
		New Born Census Card No. 805, P. O. Olive, Date of Birth July 20, 1902									
1069	1	McIntosh, John Granville	3	M	⅝	William R. McIntosh	2554	Cr	Ellen McIntosh	7633	Cr
		New Born Census Card No. 819, P. O. Crawson, Date of Birth April 30, 1903									
1070	1	Francis, Freeland Died June 22, 1905	2	M	¾	William Francis	460	Cr	Annie Francis	8304	Cr
		New Born Census Card No. 822									
1071	1	Staley, Kissie	1	F	F	For data, see card at Roll No. 789					
		New Born Census Card No. 830, P. O. Mounds, Date of Birth No. 1, April 23, 1902; No. 2, May 2, 1904									
1072	1	Cumsey, Lena	3	F	F	Lewis Cumsey	3167	Cr	Casey Cumsey	3226	Cr
1073	2	Cumsey, Annie	1	F	F	Lewis Cumsey	3167	Cr	Casey Cumsey	3226	Cr
		New Born Census Card No. 855, P. O. Morse, Date of Birth March 25, 1904									
1074	1	West, Elsie	1	F	F	Robert West	4254	Cr	Parsinder West	4589	Cr
		New Born Census Card No. 858, P. O. Schulter, Date of Birth May 19, 1904									
1075	1	Burgess, Roman	1	M	¾	William Burgess		Non	Fannie Burgess	6526	Cr
		New Born Census Card No. 879, P. O. Salem, Date of Birth March 14, 1904									
1076	1	McNac, Tullie	1	M	⅝	Phillip McNac	7123	Cr	Wisey McNac	511	Cr
		New Born Census Card No. 881, P. O. Okmulgee, Date of Birth December 27, 1902									
1077	1	Beaver, Wilson	2	M	F	Harry Beaver	6384	Cr	Louisa Beaver	4157	Cr
		New Born Census Card No. 882, P. O. Okmulgee, Date of Birth November 12, 1904									
1078	1	Kanard, Cilla	1	F	F	James Kanard	1230	Cr	Nellie Kanard	1233	Cr
		New Born Census Card No. 884, P. O. Okmulgee, Date of Birth December 10, 1903									
1079	1	Davis, Nicey	1	F	F	Alex Davis	90	Cr	Lucy Davis	110	Cr
		New Born Census Card No. 890, P. O. Hitchita, Date of Birth No. 1, June 24, 1902; No. 2, January 27, 1904									
1080	1	Sevier, Tom	3	M	F	Lewis Sevier	5689	Cr	Amanda Sevier	6734	Cr
1081	2	Sevier, Lena	1	F	F	Lewis Sevier	5689	Cr	Amanda Sevier	6734	Cr
		New Born Census Card No. 900									
1082	1	Dyer, Emmett	3	M	1-32	For data, see card at Roll No. 842					
		New Born Census Card No. 915, P. O. Okmulgee, Date of Birth February 25, 1905									
1083	1	Daniel, Robert	1	M	F	Unah Daniel	353	Cr	Miley Daniel	359	Cr
		New Born Census Card No. 916, P. O. Kellyville, Date of Birth March 12, 1904									
1084	1	Snow, Ada	1	F	F	Capahny Snow	6648	Cr	Farloconweney	8103	Cr
		New Born Census Card No. 917									
1085	1	Bruner, Minnie	3	F	F	For data, see card at No. Roll 999					
		New Born Census Card No. 927, P. O. Bristow, Date of Birth April 21, 1903									
1086	1	Long, Sake	2	F	F	Lewis Long	8109	Cr	Lannie Long	8110	Cr
		New Born Census Card No. 934, P. O. Bristow, Date of Birth No. 1, April 21, 1902; No. 2, March 12, 1904									
1087	1	Brown, Willie	3	M	F	Jim Brown	9199	Cr	Loda Brown	9200	Cr
1088	2	Brown, John	1	M	F	Jim Brown	9199	Cr	Loda Brown	9200	Cr
		New Born Census Card No. 946, P. O. Haskell, Date of Birth July 10, 1903									
1089	1	Davis, Tom	2	M	F	Addie Davis	7909	Cr	Nancy Davis	7910	Cr
		New Born Census Card No. 949, P. O. Holdenville, Date of Birth May 2, 1904									
1090	1	Johnson, Nora Illegitimate	1	F	¼	John Johnson	1573	Cr	Delila Sango		Non
		New Born Census Card No. 954, P. O. Bristow, Date of Birth January 6, 1902									
1091	1	Beaver, Joseph Charles	4	M	½	John Beaver	3924	Cr	Ella Beaver		Non
		New Born Census Card No. 957, P. O. Beggs, Date of Birth October 1, 1901									
1092	1	Friday, Willie	3	M	¾	Berry Friday	1189	Cr-F	Jennie Nash	5582	Cr
		New Born Census Card No. 960, P. O. Burney, Date of Birth November 1, 1903									
1093	1	Perryman, Leah	1	F	F	Ed. Perryman	1077	Cr	Sarah Perryman	5934	Cr
		New Born Census Card No. 963, P. O. Henryetta, Date of Birth May 10, 1902									
1094	1	Whetstone, Eula Pearl	3	F	1-16	James Whet tone	2318	Cr	Theodosia Whetstone		Non
		New Born Census Card No. 981, P. O. Wetumka, Date of Birth June 1902									
1095	1	Hopiye, Lucindy	2	F	F	Span Hopiye	5900	Cr	Jennie Hopiye	5901	Cr
		New Born Census Card No. 990, P. O. Eufaula, Date of Birth March 10, 1904									
1096	1	Hill, Nettic	1	F	F	John Hill	8765	Cr	Sarah Deere	7627	Cr
		New Born Census Card No. 995, P. O. Hanna, Date of Birth No. 1, July 4, 1902; No. 2, November 9, 1904									
1097	1	Hawkins, Pink	3	M	F	Conner Hawkins	8274	Cr	Subʒlla Hawkins	7085	Cr
1098	2	Hawkins, Nellie	1	F	F	Conner Hawkins	8274	Cr	Subella Hawkins	7085	Cr
		New Born Census Card No. 998, P. O. Trenton, Date of Birth July 2, 1902									
1099	1	Fisher, Bettie	3	F	¾	Willie Fisher	9933	Cr	Lucy Fisher	8227	Cr
		New Born Census Card No. 1015, P. O. Henryetta, Date of Birth November 17, 1904									
1100	1	Randall, Roman	1	M	F	Sam Randall	4742	Cr	Dicy Randall	4743	Cr
		New Born Census Card No. 1019, P. O. Carson, Date of Birth No. 1, December 10, 1901; No. 2, March 1, 1903									
1101	1	Lott, Lucy	3	F	F	Tommie Lott	7379	Cr	Lena Lott	7380	Cr
1102	2	Lott, Jennie	2	F	F	Tommie Lott	7379	Cr	Lena Lott	7380	Cr

Roll No.	No.	NAME	Age	Sex	Blood	NAME OF FATHER	Roll No.	Cit.	NAME OF MOTHER	Roll No.	Cit.
	New Born Census Card No. 1029, P. O. Wetumka, Date of Birth No. 1, September 5, 1901; No. 2, February 7, 1904										
1103	1	Parnosky, Cindy	4	F	F	Willie Parnosky	7479	Cr	Salina Parnosky	7480	Cr
1104	2	Parnosky, Cheparney	1	M	F	Willie Parnosky	7479	Cr	Salina Parnosky	7480	Cr
	New Born Census Card No. 363										
1105	1	Canard, Louisa	3	F	For data, see card at Roll No. 921						
	New Born Census Card No. 1034, P. O. Bearden, Date of Birth No. 1, February 12, 1902; No. 2, March 13, 1904										
1106	1	Deer, Minnie	2	F	F	Sparney Deer	8042	Cr	Sophia Deer	8043	Cr
1200	2	Deer, Edmund	1	M	F	Sparney Deer	8042	Cr	Sophia Deer	8043	Cr
	New Born Census Card No. 1038, P. O. Sharpe, Date of Birth June 7, 1904										
1107	1	Tiger, Bryan	1	M	5/8	George W. Tiger	6034	Cr	Susan H. Tiger	6035	Cr
	New Born Census Card No. 1039, P. O. Morse, Date of Birth January 1, 1902										
1108	1	Harjo, Lesta	3	F	F	Dickey Harjo	4149	Cr	Hunter Harjo	4150	Cr
	New Born Census Card No. 1043, P. O. Weleetka, Date of Birth May 28, 1902										
1109	1	Harjo, Emma	3	F	F	Legusie[Legus]Harjo	9268	Cr	Louisa Harjo	7654	Cr
	New Born Census Card No. 1045, P. O. Wetumka, Date of Birth No. 1, September 1902; No. 2, February 1905										
1110	1	Fish, George	3	M	F	Willeya Fish	7742	Cr	Nellie Fish	7743	Cr
1111	2	Fish, Nache	1	F	F	Willeya Fish	7742	Cr	Nellie Fish	7743	Cr
	New Born Census Card No. 1087, P. O. Briartown, Date of Bith September 6, 1903										
1112	1	Collins, Roy	1	M	1/8	Jacob M. Collins	2411	Cr	Nancy D. Collins		Non
	New Born Census Card No. 1089, P. O. Bryant, Date of Birth December 24, 1901										
1113	1	Barnett, Mary	3	F	F	Dave Barnett	4951	Cr	Nancy Barnett	4496	Cr
	New Born Census Card No 1090, P. O. Edna, Date of Birth August 15, 1904										
1114	1	Harjo, Ethel	1	F	F	Sulphur Harjo	3900	Cr	Liza Harjo	3901	Cr
	New Born Census Card No. 1099, P. O. Brush Hill, Date of Birth April 13, 1904										
1115	1	Doyle, Clarrance William	1	M	1-16	Arthur Doyle	3054	Cr	Lava Doyle		Non
	New Born Census Card No. 1100, P. O. Stidham, Date of Birth July 29, 1902										
1116	1	Doyle, Mose	3	M	3/8	Thomas E. Doyle	3578	Cr	Roseter E. Doyle		Non
	New Born Census Card No. 1105										
1117	1	Wisener, Minnie	2	F	5/8	For data, see card at Roll No. 887					
	New Born Census Card No. 1107, P. O. Beggs, Date of Birth February 4, 1903										
1118	1	Bighead, Sam	2	M	F	Sampson Bighead	3371	Cr	Salina Bighead	3372	Cr
	New Born Census Card No. 1109, P. O. Schulter, Date of Birth May 23, 1904										
1119	1	Pakoska, Winford	1	M	F	Lewis Pakoska	5702	Cr	Jennie Pakoska	1622	Cr
	New Born Census Card No. 1112, P. O½ Okmulgee, Date of Birth August 21, 1904										
1120	1	Kelly, Marshall	1	M	F	Newman Kelly	2150	Cr	Susan Kelly	3108	Cr
	New Born Census Card No. 1113, P. O. Price, Date of Birth October 15, 1904										
1121	1	Tiger, Nancy	1	F	F	Litka Tiger	4725	Cr.	Jinalee Tiger	4726	Cr
	New Born Census Card Bo. 1119, P. O. Tulsa, Date of Birth December 6, 1904										
1122	1	Childers, Effie	1	F	F	Chisso Childers	783	Cr	Millie Childers	784	Cr
	New Born Census Card No. 1122, P. O. Wetumka, Date of Birth January 1, 1904										
1123	1	Artusse, Mose	1	M	F	John Artussee	3739	Cr	Annie Artussee	2049	Cr
	New Born Census Card No. 1124, P. O. Stroud, Date of Birth No. 1 August 15, 1902; No. 2 January 28, 1904.										
1124	1	Tilley, Frank	3	M	1/2	James Tilley		Non	Ennah Tilley	4080	Cr
1125	2	Tilley, Laura May	1	F	1/2	James Tilley		Non	Ennah Tilley	4080	Cr
	New Born Census Card No. 1128, P. O. Salem, Date of Birth March, 1902										
1126	1	Harjo, Bennie	3	M	F	Lewis Harjo	8254	Cr	Wisey Harjo	6828	Cr
	New Born Census Card No. 1130, P. P. Senora, Date of Birth December 1, 1903										
1127	1	Jacob, John	1	M	F	Shawnee Jacob	8149	Cr	Jeannetta Jacob	8450	Cr
	New Born Census Card No. 1135, P. O.										
1128	1	Boling, Dixie Self	1	F	1-16	For data see card at Roll No. 903.					
	New Born Census Card No. 1059, P. O. Henryetta, Date of Birth January 27, 1903										
1129	1	Toney, Foley	2	M	F	Lijah Toney	8435	Cr	Losanna Lowe	7813	Cr
	New Born Census Card No. 36, P. O. Paden, Date of Birth December 28, 1902										
1130	1	Caesar, Panuggee	2	M	1/2	London Harjo		Non	Sissie Caesar	8895	Cr
	New Born Census Card No. 69, P. O. Lenna, Date of Birth August 28, 1904										
1131	1	McIntosh, Nathaniel	1	M	F	Cick McIntosh	7253	Cr	Rosa McIntosh	1493	Cr
	New Born Census Card No. 314, P. O. Boley, Date of Birth October 7, 1903										
1132	1	Mitchell, Albert	1	M	1/4	Willie Mitchell		Non	Peggie Mitchell	6961	Cr
	New Born Census Card No. 322, P. O. Holdenville, Date of Birth February 22, 1905										
1133	1	Mitchell, Joseph	1	M	1/2	Sam Mitchell	7741	Cr	Nellie Mitchell		Non
	New Born Census Card No. 336, P. O. Dustin, Date of Birth August 19, 1901.										
1134	1	Long, Roley	4	M	F	Jesse Long	8004	Cr	Wiggie Long	7795	Cr
	New Born Census Card N. 340, P. O. Hanna, Date of Birth July 12, 1901										
1135	1	Scott, Bessie	4	F	7/8	Turner Scott	4722	Cr	Lucinda Scott	4723	Cr
	New Born Census Card No. 351, P. O. Paden, Date of Birth March 15, 1904										
1136	1	Johnson, Carr Raymond	1	M	1/2	Sam Warrior	9824	Cr	Minnie Johnson		Non
		Illegitimate. Sam Warrior identified as Norbe No. 1 on Card No. 3792.									
	New Born Census Card No. 352, P. O. Paden, Date of Birth December 10, 1902										
1137	1	Wilson, Bessie	2	F	1/2	Clark Wilson	7919	Cr	Minnie Johnson		Non
		Clark Wilson No. 7919 identified as Cahcokethlon No. 1 on Card No. 2713.									
	New Born Census Card No. 357, P. O.										
1138	1	Whitlow, John	3	M	1/2	For data see card at Roll No. 374.					
	New Born Census Card No. 359, P. O. Castle, Date of Birth February 23, 1904										
1139	1	Wesley, Ida	1	F	F	Thomas Wesley	6673	Cr	Toche Wesley	5841	Cr

Roll No.	No.	NAME	Age	Sex	Blood	NAME OF FATHER	Roll No.	Cit.	NAME OF MOTHER	Roll No.	Cit.
		New Born Census Card No. 432, P. O. Wetumka, Date of Birth August 8, 1903									
1140	1	Bullet, Chitto Harjo	1	M	½	John Bullet	8776	Cr	Zoye Bullet		Non
		New Born Census Card No. 439, P. O. Henryetta, Date of Birth No. 1 October, 1904; No. 2 October, 1901									
1141	1	West, Robert	1	M	F	Lumsey West	4944	Cr	Emma West	4731	Cr
1142	2	West, William	3	M	F	Lumsey West	4944	Cr	Emma West	4731	Cr
		New Born Census Card No. 443, P. O. Weleetka, Date of Birth May 22, 1902									
1143	1	Wildcat, Peter	3	M	F	Sandy Wildcat	5072	Cr	Losanna Wildcat	5073	Cr
		New Born Census Card No. 444, P. O. Hanna, Date of Birth No. 1 June 17, 1902; No. 2, January 4, 1905									
1144	1	Deo, Amos	2	M	F	Thomas Deo	8202	Cr	Nancy Deo	7695	Cr
1145	2	Deo, Susie	1	F	F	Thomas Deo	8202	Cr	Nancy Deo	7695	Cr
		New Born Census Card No. 446, P. O. Holdenville, Date of Birth June 16, 1904									
1146	1	Tiger, Eli	1	M	F	Thomas Tiger	7948	Cr	Rose Tiger	8336	Cr
		New Born Census Card No. 450, P. O. Hanna, Date of Birth September 30, 1904									
1147	1	Salt, Edward	1	M	F	Melicha Salt	8156	Cr	Annie Salt	8152	Cr
		New Born Census Card No. 451, P. O. Okemah, Date of Birth December 26, 1903									
1148	1	Field, Ida	2	F	F	William Field	6709	Cr	Louina Fields	4133	Cr
		New Born Census Card No. 460, P. O. Morse, Date of Birth February 21, 1905									
1149	1	Long, Wallace	1	M	F	Simmer Ahfonoke	4038	Cr	Yusie Long	862	Cr
		Illegitimate									
		New Born Census Card No. 462, P. O. Morse, Date of Birth September 17, 1904									
1150	1	Foster, Lowiney	1	F	F	Sayochee Ahfonoke	4039	Cr	Janie Foster	5976	Cr
		Illegitimate									
		New Born Census Card No. 464, P. O. Senora, Date of Birth April 26, 1904									
1151	1	King, Sallie	1	F	F	Peter King	7979	Cr	Mollie King	4761	Cr
		New Born Census Card No. 477, P. O. Okemah, Date of Birth December 15, 1902									
1152	1	Simmer, Andy	2	M	F	Charley Simmer	9170	Cr	Kizzie Simmer	9171	Cr
		New Born Census Card No. 482, P. O. Dustin, Date of Birth February 24, 1904									
1153	1	Watson, Johnny	1	M	F	Daniel Wa'son	4539	Cr	Louisa Watson	5084	Cr
		New Born Census Card No. 518, P. O. Mellette, Date of Birth October 13, 1904									
1154	1	Fish, Lizzie	1	F	F	Jimsey Fish	8813	Cr	Sucky Fish	7733	Cr
		No. 2 died spring 1906									
		New Born Census Card No. 528, P. O. Barnard, Date of Birth September 22, 1901									
1155	1	Lowe, Jennie	3	F	F	Tobeler Lowe	5545	Cr	Sallie Lowe	5546	Cr
		New Born Census Card No. 542, P. O. Emahaka, Date of Virth May 19, 1903									
1156	1	Tiger, Roman	2	M	F	Chepamey Simon		Non	Manie Cumseh	8952	Cr
		New Born Census Card No. 546, P. O.									
1157	1	Kernel, Harry	2	M	½	For data see card at Roll No. 1052					
		New Born Census Card No. 554, P. O. Sasakwa, Date of Birth No. 1 February 2, 1902; No. 2 January 18, 1905									
1158	1	Puntka, Josie	3	M	F	Puntka		Non	Cinda Puntka	8885	Cr
1159	2	Puntka, Winey	1	F	F	Puntka		Non	Cinda Puntka	8885	Cr
		New Born Census Card No. 557, P. O. Tidmore, Date of Birth No. 1 Fall of 1902; No. 2 December 25, 1903									
1160	1	Harjo, Ida	3	F	¼	Ah Harjo		Non	Eliza Harjo	8922	Cr
943	2	Harjo, Sunday	1	M	¼	Ah Harjo		Non	Eliza Harjo	8922	Cr
		New Born Census Card No. 582, P. O. Calvin, Date of Birth March 10, 1903									
1161	1	Beaver, Polly	2	F	F	Pahte Beaver	7538	Cr	Lucy Beaver	7539	Cr
		New Born Census Card No. 587, P. O. Yeager, Date of Birth March 15, 1903									
1162	1	Compier, Willie	2	M	F	Mitchell Compier	5240	Cr	Millie Goat	4898	Cr
		New Born Census Card No. 689, P. O. Hanna, Date of Birth June 21, 1904									
1163	1	Bullett, Bailey	1	M	F	Solomon Bullett	8663	Cr	Millie Bullett	8658	Cr
		New Born Census Card No. 718, P. O. Checotah, Date of Birth March 1, 1905									
1164	1	Backbun, Etta May	1	F	1-32	Cal Backbun		Non	Arnecie Backbun	2633	Cr
		New Born Census Card No. 723, P. O. Lenna, Date of Birth September 9, 1904									
1165	1	Bear, Turner	1	M	F	Lewis Bear	7720	Cr	Annie Bear	7820	Cr
		New Born Census Card No. 734, P. O. Okmulgee, Date of Birth November 1, 1901									
1166	1	Monahwee, Ella	3	F	⅞	John Manahwee	6736	Cr	Cinda Manahwee	6737	Cr
		No. 1 died August 15, 1905									
		New Born Census Card No. 745, P. O. Eufaula, Date of Birth July 16, 1901									
1167	1	Matoy, Annie	4	F	⅛	Charles Matoy	5889	Cr	Maud Matoy		Non
		New Born Census Card No. 760, P. O. Raiford, Date of Birth March 23, 1903									
1168	1	Tar-lo-shaw, Louisa	2	F	F	Tahlosa (Tar-lo-shaw)	7952	Cr	Sally Tar-lo-shaw	8741	Cr
		New Born Census Card No. 772, P. O. Muskogee, Date of Birth No. 1 November 22, 1902; No. 2 February 24, 1905									
1169	1	Davis, Mattie	2	F	17-32	Benjamin Davis	61	Cr	Melindy Davis	4358	Cr
1286	2	Davis, Samuel	1	M	17-32	Benjamin Davis	61	Cr	Melindy Davis	4358	Cr
		New Born Census Card No. 782, P. O. Mellette, Date of Birth April 11, 1902									
1170	1	Yarhola, Jefferson	3	M	F	Sampson Yahola	7311	Cr	Sarah White	7312	Cr
		New Born Census Card No. 791, P. O. Eufaula, Date of Birth April 7, 1903									
1171	1	Chotky, William	2	M	F	Chotky		Non	Lucy Deere	9155	Cr
		New Born Census Card No. 800, P. O. Newby, Date of Birth, August 21, 1903									
1172	1	Bear, Roley	2	M	F	March Bear	3924	Cr	Nettie Bear	4001	Cr
		New Born Census Card No. 821, P. O. Haskell, Date of Birth October 25, 1902									
1173	1	Barnett, Clifford Marion	2	M	¼	George Barnett	6129	Cr	Hattie Barnett		Non
		New Born Census Card No. 834, P. O. Eufaula, Date of Birth July 8, 1902									
1174	1	Nero, Fannie	3	F	17-32	Governer Nero	7026	Cr	Mary Nero	8709	Cr
		New Born Census Card No. 903, P. O. Tuskegee, Date of Birth July 12, 1903									
1175	1	Arpoika, William	3	M	F	George Arpoika	7416	Cr	Sissie Arpoika	7417	Cr

Roll No.	No.	NAME	Age	Sex	Blood	NAME OF FATHER	Roll No.	Cit.	NAME OF MOTHER	Roll No.	Cit.
		New Born Census Card No. 908, P. O. Dustin, Date of Birth September 13, 1902									
1176	1	Wildcat, Bessie	3	F	F	Willie Wildcat	4730	Cr	Matilda Wesley	8029	Cr
		New Born Census Card No. 919, P. O. Senora, Date of Birth April 8, 1903									
1177	1	Thompson, Isreal	2	M	F	George Thompson	3280	Cr	Chotkey Kinha	7726	Cr
		Illegitinate									
		New Born Census Card No. 921, P. O. Paden, Date of Birth No. 1 February 28, 1902; No. 2 December 9, 1903									
1178	1	Coker, Sallo	3	F	½	Charley Coker	9371	Cr	Hetty Coker	4634	Cr
1179	2	Coker, Ella	1	F	½	Charley Coker	9371	Cr	Hetty Coker	4634	Cr
		New Born Census Card No. 925, P. O. Carson, Date of Birth January 1903									
1180	1	Anderson, Martha	2	F	F	Willie Anderson	5529	Cr	Sissy Jim	7303	Cr
		New Born Census Card No. 941, P. O. Kellyville, Date of Birth May 5, 1904									
1181	1	Char-co-te-ten-na, Ella	1	F	F	He-ca-tah	1837	Cr	Katie Char-co-te-ten-na	6893	Cr
		Illegitimate									
		New Born Census Card No. 947, P. O. Carson, Date of Birth February 15, 1904									
1182	1	Lindsey, Columbia	1	F	F	Freeland Lindsey	8059	Cr	Nancy Proctor	3714	Cr
		New Born Census Card No. 952, P. O. Coweta, Date of Birth Februsry 10, 1905									
1183	1	Crowell, Francis Williard	1	F	1-16	Edward L. Crowell, Jr.	43	Cr	Ida May Crowell		Non
		New Born Census Card No. 978, P. O. Bristow, Date of Birth, Spring of 1903									
1184	1	Beaver, Wisey	2	F	F	Wattie Beaver	2026	Cr	Nancy Beaver		Non
		New Born Census Card Nol 980, P. O. Bristow, Date of Birth 1904									
1185	1	Pinehill, Mary	1	F	F	Lasley Pinehill	2907	Cr	Sallie Pinehill	2908	Cr
		New Born Census Card No. 984, P. O. Dustin, Date of Birth June 15, 1901									
1186	1	Butler, Eddie	3	M	½	Myron Butler		Non	Lydia Field	7690	Cr
		New Born Census Card No. 993, P. O. Hanna, Date of Birth No. 1 December 9, 1901; No. 2 October 10, 1902									
1187	1	Proctor, Sam	3	M	F	Chaeller Proctor	7868	Cr	Sucky Proctor	7833	Cr
1188	2	Proctor, Lydia	2	F	F	Chaeller Proctor	7868	Cr	Sucky Proctor	7833	Cr
		New Born Census Card No. 1005, P. O. Hanna, Date of Birth No. 1 1902 or 1903; No. 2 February 1905									
1189	1	Williams, Bettie	3	F	F	Big William	7795	Cr	Cinda Williams	7796	Cr
1190	2	Williams, Baby	1	M	F	Big William	7795	Cr	Cinda Williams	7796	Cr
		New Born Census Card No. 1006, P. O. Wetumka, Date of Birth August 24, 1902									
1191	1	Lindsey, Sarah	3	F	F	Freeland Lindsey	8059	Cr	Louina Deo	7084	Cr
		New Born Census Card No. 1011, P. O. Hanna, Date of Birth January 31, 1905									
1192	1	Hill, Lumsey	1	M	F	John Hill	8319	Cr	Millie Hill	9135	Cr
		New Born Census Card No. 1012, P. O. Hanna, Date of Borth November 21, 1904									
1193	1	Pigeon, Nache	1	F	F	Jim Pigeon	9053	Cr	Jennie Pigeon	8204	Cr
		New Born Census Card No. 1013, P. O. Eufaula, Date of Birth No. 1 January 6, 1903; No. 2 March 8, 1904									
1194	1	Raiford, Pearl	2	F	⅛	Ossie Raiford	5696	Cr	Selina Raiford		Non
1195	2	Raiford, Lena	1	F	⅛	Ossie Raiford	5696	Cr	Selina Raiford		Non
		New Born Census Card No. 1023, P. O. Calvin, Date of Birth December 1901									
1196	1	Herrod, Tarpie	3	M	F	David Herrod	8996	Cr	Eliza Herrod	7767	Cr
		New Born Census Card No. 1025,									
1197	1	Stidham, Johnny	1	M	F	For data, see card at Roll No. 867					
		New Born Census Card No. 1026, P. O. Calvin, Date of Birth September 22, 1904									
1198	1	Hellet, Adam	1	M	F	Samey Hellet	8326	Cr	Sarah Hellet	6857	Cr
		New Born Census Card No. 1033, P. O. Bearden, Date of Birth November 4, 1904									
1199	1	Hale, Billy	1	M	F	Jasper Hale	8635	Cr	Maggie Hale	6166	Cr
		New Born Census Card No. 1034, P. O.									
1200	1	Deer, Ednubd	1	M	F	For data, see card at Roll No. 1106					
		New Born Census Card No. 1042, P. O. Wetumka, Date of Birth September 15, 1904									
1201	1	Johnson, Emma	1	F	F	Cooper Johnson	8933	Cr	Judy Johnson	8934	Cr
		New Born Census Card No. 1046, P. O. Weleetka, Date of Birth No. 1 October 1901; No. 2 October 1903									
1202	1	Cubbie, Liza	4	F	¾	Jacob Cubbie	4989	Cr	Rhoda Cubbie	4990	Cr
1203	2	Cubbie, Daniel	1	M	¾	Jacob Cubbie	4989	Cr	Rhoda Cubbie	4990	Cr
		New Born Census Card No. 1065, P. O. Senora, Date of Birth December 25, 1904									
1204	1	Tiger, Melah	1	F	F	George Tiger	7239	Cr	Annie Tiger	8451	Cr
		New Born Census Card No. 1070, P. O. Senora, Date of Birth May 20, 1904									
1205	1	Taylor, Judy	1	F	F	Roley Taylor	9303	Cr	Nellie Taylor	9304	Cr
		New Born Census Card No. 1072, P. O. Dustin, Date of Birth No. 1 February 25, 1903; No. 2 December 17, 1904									
1206	1	Scott, Lumber	2	M	⅜	Turner Scott	4722	Cr	Pollie Scott		Non
1207	2	Scott, Rufus	1	M	⅜	Turner Scott	4722	Cr	Pollie Scott		Non
		New Born Census Card No. 1079, P. O. Eufaula, Date of Birth No. 1 September 1901; No. 2 1904									
1208	1	Beaver, Kaska	4	F	F	Willie Beaver	9344	Cr	Annie Beaver	9345	Cr
1209	2	Beaver, Heliswa	2	M	F	Willie Beaver	9344	Cr	Annie Beaver	9345	Cr
		New Born Census Card No. 1080, P. O. Eufaula, Date of Birth May 1903									
1210	1	Kelly, Amy	2	F	F	Jim Kelly	9152	Cr	Susie Johnson	8684	Cr
		New Born Census Card No. 1091, P. O. Pierce, Date of BirtF January 29, 1902									
1211	1	Richard, Minnie	3	F	F	Eastman Richard	7664	Cr	Yarna Richard	7665	Cr
		New Born Census Card No. 1093, P. O. Schulter, Date of Birth No. 1 September 2, 1902; No. 2 December 13, 1903									
1212	1	Monday, Edna	3	F	¼	March Monday	2874	Cr	Lizzie Monday	1648	Sem
1213	2	Monday, Annie	1	F	¼	March Monday	2874	Cr	Lizzie Monday	1648	Sem
		New Born Census Card No. 1102, P. O. Yeager, Date of Birth No. 1 February 9, 1902; No. 2 November 12, 1904									
1214	1	Harjo, Hannah	4	F	F	Peter Harjo	5303	Cr	Susie Harjo	5302	Cr
1215	2	Harjo, Robert	1	M	F	Peter Harjo	5303	Cr	Susic Harjo	5302	Cr

Roll No.	No.	NAME	Age	Sex	Blood	NAME OF FATHER	Roll No.	Cit.	NAME OF MOTHER	Roll No.	Cit.
		New Born Census Card No. 1104, P. O. Edna, Date of Birth March 6, 1902									
1216	1	Johnson, Harpley	3	M	F	Keeper Johnson	3906	Cr	Jeanetta Johnson	3907	Cr
		New Born Census Card No. 1117, P. O. Bristow, Date of Birth December 6, 1903									
1217	1	Seber, Jimmie	1	M	F	Sampson Seber	3962	Cr	Lizzie Seber	9288	Cr
		New Born Census Card No. 1121, P. O. Bixby, Date of Birth No. 1 May 16, 1902; Mo. 2 May 8, 1904									
1218	1	Wilson, Enus	3	M	F	Thomas Wilson	2193	Cr	Grace Wilson	2196	Cr
1219	2	Wilson, Annie	1	F	F	Thomas Wilson	2193	Cr	Grace Wilson	2196	Cr
		New Born Census Card No. 1123, P. O. Senora, Date of Birth June 1902									
1220	1	Toney, Wiley	3	M	F	Lodger Toney	8435	Cr	Milea Toney	7583	Cr
		New Born Census Card No. 1125, P. O. Okmulgee, Date of Birth August 19, 1902									
1221	1	Williams, John	3	M	1/2	Eli Williams	2911	Cr	Mary Williams		Non
		New Born Census Card No. 1134, P. O. Tulsa, Date of Birth January 8, 1904									
1222	1	Burgess, Raymond B.	1	M	1/4	Ben Burgess	1220	Cr	Lyddia C. Burgess		Non
		New Born Census Card No. 1153, P. O. Fentress, Date of Birth No. 1 March 7, 1903; No. 2 January 20, 1905									
1223	1	Sawyer, Almon	2	M	F	Wesley Sawyer	4836	Cr	Eliza Sawyer	4705	Cr
1224	2	Sawyer, Samuel	1	M	F	Wesley Sawyer	4836	Cr	Eliza Sawyer	4705	Cr
		New Born Census Card No. 1170, P. O. Weleetka, Date of Birth June 2, 1904									
1225	1	Field, Sonnie Illegitimate	1	M	F	Walter Field	7691	Cr	Eliza Harjo	5001	Cr
		New Born Census Card No. 93, P. O. Beggs, Date of Birth April 29, 1904									
1226	1	Friday, Clarence	5-16	M	Berry Friday		1189	Cr-F	Susan Gooden	3854	Cr
		New Born Census Card No. 161, P. O. Weer, Date of Birth March 15, 1902									
1227	1	Johnson, Rena	3	F	1/8	Robert F. Johnson	722	Cr	Annie Johnson		Non
		New Born Census Card No. 254, P. O.									
1228	1	Tiger, Joanna	1	F	F	For data, see card at Roll No. 266					
		New Born Census Card No. 280, P. O. Oktaha, Date of Birth December 7, 1904									
1229	1	Washington, Lizzie Died April 29, 1905	1	F	1/2	Peter Washington	390	Cr	Lizzie Washington		Non
		New Born Census Card No. 522, P. O. Holdenville, Date of Birth February 18, 1904									
1230	1	Bighead, Pa-thlim-ka	1	M	1/4	George Bighead		Non	Jennie Bighead	7514	Cr
		New Born Census Card No. 649, P. O. Lima, Date of Birth April 10, 1904									
1231	1	Moore, Jessie Susan	1	F	1-16	Bob Moore	4239	Cr	Mary Moore		Non
		New Born Census Card No. 650, P. O. Fame, Date of Birth January 18, 1904									
1232	1	Wolf, Jennie	1	F	F	William Wolf	7410	Cr	Ellen Wolfe	7486	Cr
		New Born Census Card No. 657, P. O. Fame, Date of Birth December 27, 1904									
1233	1	Roberson, Clarence Died in August 1905	1	M	1/2	Henry Roberson		Non	Nancy Roberson	7023	Cr
		New Born Census Card No. 681, P. O. Indianola, Date of Birth August 2, 1904									
1234	1	McGilbray, George	1	M	F	Jackson McGilbray	1397	Cr	Nicey McGilbray	8816	Cr
		New Born Census Card No. 717, P. O.									
1235	1	Nubbie, George	3	M	1/2	For data, see card at Roll No. 957					
		New Born Census Card No. 780, P. O. Mellette, Date of Birth, December 17, 1904									
1236	1	White, Lizzie	1	F	F	George White	8359	Cr	Sarah White	7312	Cr
		New Born Census Card No. 931, P. O. Tulsa, Date of Birth No. 1 July 19, 1902; No. 2 August 31, 1904									
1237	1	Frick, Jay	3	M	3/8	J. L. Frick		Non	Mamie Frick	2628	Cr
1238	2	Frick, William	1	M	3/8	J. L. Frick		Non	Mamie Frick	2628	Cr
		New Born Census Card No. 933, P. O. Bristow, Date of Birth Spring of 1903									
1239	1	Biggs, Martha	2	F	F	George C. Biggs	9058	Cr	Jeannetta Biggs	9059	Cr
		New Born Census Card No. 994, P. O. Hanna, Date of Birth March 16, 1902									
1240	1	Bullett, Jacob	3	M	F	Maxey Bullett		Non	Hanna Bullett	8429	Cr
		New Born Census Card No. 1000, P. O. Wetumka, Date of Birth No. 1 1902; No. 2 September 1904									
1241	1	Lasley, Lizzie	3	F	F	Sam Lasley	8221	Cr	Wisey Lasley	8222	Cr
1242	2	Lasley, Sam	1	M	F	Sam Lasley	8221	Cr	Wisey Lasley	8222	Cr
		New Born Census Card No. 1002, P. P. Hanna, Date of Birth November 30, 1903									
1243	1	Fixeco, Joseph	3	M	F	Yarhola Fixeco	8209	Cr	Foluthoker Fixeco	7881	Cr
		New Born Census Card No. 1003, P. O. Hanna, Date of Birth July 9, 1902									
1244	1	Foley, Arney	3	F	F	Taylor Foley	7836	Cr	Melindy Foley	8210	Cr
		New Born Census Card No. 1030, P. O. Wetumka, Date of Birth April 27, 1904									
1245	1	Yaholar, Della	1	F	F	Roman Yahola	6370	Cr	Nellie Fife	4701	Cr
		New Born Census Card No. 1031, P. O. Bearden, Date of Birth April 9. 1902									
1246	1	King, Janelly	3	F	F	Haney King	6565	Cr	Sallie King	6928	Cr
		New Born Census Card No. 1032, P. O. Bearden, Date of Birth August 18, 1904									
1247	1	Bunner, Susie	1	F	F	Mosey Bunner	18	Cr	Ollie Bunner	8048	Cr
		New Born Census Card No. 1037, P. O. Morse, Date of Birth No. 1 September 1902; No. 2 April 4, 1904									
1248	1	Harjoche, Martha	2	F	F	Yahdehka Harjoche	4343	Cr	Losana Harjoche	4220	Cr
1249	2	Harjoche, Adam	1	M	F	Yahdehka Harjoche	4343	Cr	Losana Harjoche	4220	Cr
		New Born Census Card No. 1050, P. O. Mellette, Date of Birth November 27, 1902									
1250	1	Roberts, Sister	2	F	F	Joe Roberts	8257	Cr	Mary Roberts	7752	Cr
		New Born Census Card No. 1051, P. O. Hanna, Date of Birth October 1904									
1251	1	Stepney, Lizzie	1	F	F	Thompson Stepney	8331	Cr	Susie Stepney	8358	Cr
		New Born Census Card No. 1055, P. O. Indianola, Date of Birth February 12, 1903									
1252	1	Emarthla, Walter	2	M	F	Micco Emarthla	7760	Cr	Sallie Emarthla	7761	Cr
		New Born Census Card No. 1066, P. O. Eufaula, Date of Birth No. 1 July 1903; No. 2 December 1901									
1253	1	Kano, Nicey	2	F	F	George Kano	8389	Cr	Louisa Kano	8391	Cr
1254	2	Kano, Katy	4	F	F	George Kano	8389	Cr	Louisa Kano	8391	Cr
		New Born Census Card No. 1067, P. O. Eufaula, Date of Birth No. 1 1901; No. 2 December 24, 1902									
1255	1	Johnson, Susanna	5	F	F	Sam Johnson	8724	Cr	Leda Johnson	8725	Cr
1256	2	Johnson, Onate	3	F	F	Sam Johnson	8724	Cr	Leda Johnson	8725	Cr
		New Born Census Card No. 1068, P. O. Senora, Date of Birth 1902									
1257	1	Harjo, George	3	F	F	Hillis Harjo	7650	Cr	Mary Harjo	7651	Cr

258

Roll No.	No.	NAME	Age Sex Blood	NAME OF FATHER	Roll No.	Cit.	NAME OF MOTHER	Roll No.	Cit.
		New Born Census Card No. 1069, P. O. Salem, Date of Birth No. 1 May 1902; No. 2 1903 or 1904							
1258	1	Fry, Sandy	3 M F	Sam Fry	8488	Cr	Leechie Fry	8442	Cr
1259	2	Fry, Sarty	1 M F	Sam Fry	8488	Cr	Leechie Fry	8442	Cr
		New Born Census Card No. 1071, P. O. Senora, Date of Birth No. 1 March 10, 1902; No. 2 February 25, 1904							
1260	1	Kelly, Sallie	3 F ½	Sam Kelly	4549	Cr	Maria Kelly		Non
1261	2	Kelly, David	1 M ½	Sam Kelly	4549	Cr	Maria Kelly		Non
		New Born Census Card No. 1076, P. O. Senora, Date of Birth March 14, 1900							
1262	1	King, Luila	2 F F	Peter King	7979	Cr	Mucly King	4761	Cr
		New Born Census Card No. 1118, P. O. Stidham, Date of Birth March 16, 1903							
1263	1	Fox, Sandy	2 M F	Jim Fox	8699	Cr	Ada Fox	8700	Cr
		New Born Census Card No. 1130, P. O. Senora, Date of Birth February 22, 1900;							
1264	1	Jacob, Nicey	5 F F	Shawnee Jacob	8449	Cr	Jeanetta Jacob	8450	Cr
		New Born Census Card No. 1138, P. O. Depew, Date of Birth October 19, 1904							
1265	1	Sladen, Sam	1 M I-16	John Sladen		Non	Nora Rogers	2234	Cr
		New Born Census Card No. 1159, P. O. Wetumka, Date of Birth October 3, 1904							
1266	1	Harjo, Philliby	1 M F	Sango Harjo	6398	Cr	Rosey Harjo		Non
		New Born Census Card No. 1167, P. O. Eufaula, Date of Birth July 10, 1902							
1267	1	Deere, Annie	3 F ½	Esal Deere	8748	Cr	Louina Deere		Non
		New Born Census Card No. 1171, Wetumka, Date of Birth April 14, 1904							
1268	1	Yahola, Minnie	1 F F	Wiley Yahola	7847	Cr	Addie Yahola	7848	Cr
		Died January 12, 1906							
		New Born Census Card No. 506, P. O. Cheyarko, Date of Birth No. 1 June 5, 1903; No. 2 September 18, 1901							
1269	1	Bearhead, Jesse	2 M F	Moses Bearhead		Non	Nancy Bearhead	499	Cr
1270	2	Bearhead, Wylie	3 M F	Moses Bearhead		Non	Nancy Bearhead	499	Cr
		One of these children died March 18, 1905							
		New Born Census Card No. 786, P. O. Shawnee, Date of Birth July 22, 1901							
1271	1	Starr, Jesse J.	4 M ¼	Charles Starr		Non	Cora Ellis Starr	10100	Cr
		New Born Census Card No. 801, P. O. Eufaula, Date of Birth March 25, 1903							
1272	1	Sarwanokee, Fannie	2 F F	Mitchell Sarwanokee	8707	Cr	Nancy Sarwanokee	8708	Cr
		New Born Census Card No. 803, P. O. Eufaula, Date of Birth January 4, 1904							
1273	1	Pahoseyahola, Bennie	1 M F	Josie Pahoseyahola	7399	Cr	Soatka Pahoseyahola	7400	Cr
		New Born Census Card No. 1040, P. O. Bearden, Date of Birth May 9, 1904							
1274	1	Deer, Jessie	1 M F	Pinkey Deer	6178	Cr	Linda Deer	8954	Cr
		New Born Census Card No. 1044, P. O. Weleetka, Date of Birth 1904							
1275	1	Harjo, Jimmie	1 M F	Jonas Fish?	5130	?	Polly Harjo	5116	Cr
		Illegitimate							
		New Born Census Card No. 1047, P. O. Weleetka, Date of Birth February 20, 1905							
1276	1	Buckley, Cora	1 F F	Ceasar Buckley	5112	Cr	Betsey Buckley	5113	Cr
		New Born Census Card No. 1049, P. O. Mellette, Date of Birth March 9, 1902							
1277	1	Benton, Thomas	3 M ¾	Robert Benton	8070	Cr	Jennie Benton	8367	Cr
		New Born Census Card No. 1096, P. O. Eufaula, Date of Birth No. 1 June 1901; No. 2 April 15, 1903							
1278	1	Deere, Lumsey	4 M F	Noah Deere	8553	Cr	Maley Deere	8554	Cr
1279	2	Deere, Charlie	2 M F	Noah Deere	8553	Cr	Maley Deere	8554	Cr
		New Born Census Card No. 1097, P. O. Lenna, Date of Birth June 4, 1902							
1280	1	Derrisaw, Tuxey	3 F F	Barney Derrisaw	7243	Cr	Toche Derrisaw	7244	Cr
		New Born Census Card No. 1103, P. O. Pierce, Date of Birth July 27, 1903							
1281	1	Timothy, Eliza	2 F F	John Timothy	7685	Cr	Ella Timothy	7686	Cr
		New Born Census Card No. 1154, P. O. Barnard, Date of Birth November 10, 1903							
1282	1	Deer, Lula	2 F F	Joe Deer	7358	Cr	Miley Deer	7359	Cr
		New Born Census Card No. 1158, P. O. Wetumka, Date of Birth February 28, 1903							
1283	1	Harjo, Fred	2 M F	Stephen Harjo	8938	Cr	Kogee Harjo	8939	Cr
		New Born Census Card No. 339, P. O. Checotah, Date of Birth April 8, 1903							
1284	1	Coonhead, John	2 M F	Willie Coonhead	7985	Cr	Susan Coonhead	381	Cr
		New Born Census Card No. 521, P. O. Oktaha, Date of Birth June 27, 1904							
1285	1	Washington, Ralph	1 M ⅛	Alfred Washington		Non	Maria Herrod	1412	Cr
		New Born Census Card No. 772, P. O.							
1286	1	Davis, Samuel	1 M 17-32	For data, see Card at Roll No. 1169					
		New Born Census Card No. 1010, P. O. Hanna, Date of Birth 1904							
1287	1	Larney, Cheparney	1 M F	Jacob Larney	8291	Cr	Bittie Larney	8292	Cr
		New Born Cenaua Card No. 1017, P. O. Hanna, Date of Birth No. 1 April 2, 1902; No. 2 June 15, 1904							
1288	1	Gray, Johnnie	3 M F	Jimmy Gray (Nocus Elle)	8243	Cr	Nancy Gray	6552	Cr
1289	2	Gray, Mandy	1 F F	Jimmy Gray (Nocus Elle)	8243	Cr	Nancy Gray	6552	Cr
		New Born Census Card No. 1035, P. O. Bearden, Date of Birth July 30, 1903							
1290	1	Wolf, Matilda	3 F ½	Cobley Wolf		Non	Annie Yahola	8352	Cr
		New Born Census Card No. 1056, P. O. Mellette, Date of Birth December 1, 1904							
1291	1	Fish, George	1 M F	Wiley Fish	8817	Cr	Hettie Fish	7734	Cr

MINOR CREEK CENSUS CARDS

Enrolled under Act of March 3, 1905

Roll No.	No.	NAME	Age	Sex	Blood	NAME OF FATHER	Roll No.	Cit.	NAME OF MOTHER	Roll No.	Cit.
		Minor Creek Census Card No. 1, P. O. Weir, Date of Birth February 2, 1906									
1	1	Martin, March	1	M	F	Johnson Martin	649	Cr	Susanna Martin	1453	Cr
		Minor Creek Census Card No. 4, P. O. Muskogee, Date of Birth November 11, 1905									
2	1	Callahan, Lillian Alice	1	F	1-16	Jas. O. Callahan	1425	Cr	Mary E. Callahan		Non
		Minor Creek Census Card No. 5, P. O. Muskogee, Date of Birth October 8, 1903									
3	3	Adair, Edwin Brewer	1	M	1-32	L. A. Adair		Non	Gipsie Adair	1537	Cr
		Minor Creek Census Card No. 7, P. O. Muskogee, Date of Birth December 13, 1905									
4	1	Wayman, Claud Mc-Causland	1	M	5-32	E. T. Wayman		Non	Bessie Wayman	1179	Cr
		Minor Creek Census Card No. 8, P. O. Muskogee, August 1, 1905									
5	1	Lieber, Albert Leon	1	M	1-16	John G. Lieber		Non	Dora Lieber	2188	Cr
		Minor Creek Census Card No. 10, P. O. Morse, Date of Birth February 17, 1906									
6	1	Deer, Mary	1	F	F	Joe Deer	4042	Cr	Yarner Deer	4043	Cr
		Minor Creek Census Card No. 11, P. O. Muskogee, Date of Birth March 17, 1905									
7	1	Porter, James Summer-field	1	M	¼	William A. Porter	1527	Cr	Mildred M. Porter		Non
		Minor Creek Census Card No. 14, P. O. Gibson Station, Date of Birth December 31, 1905									
8	1	Hays, Mary Shannon	1	F	1-16	Williard P. Hays		Non	Sally H. Hays	6801	Cr
		Minor Creek Census Card No. 15, P. O. Wagoner, Date of Birth April 24, 1905									
9	1	Betts, Kathryn W.	1	F	1-32	C. L. Betts		Non	Sue Hettie Betts	134	Cr
		Minor Creek Census Card No. 16, P. O. Oktaha, Date of Birth September 11, 1905									
10	1	Escoe, Leona G.	1	F	5-16	Walter J. Escoe	3953	Cr	Sarah Escoe	3514	Cr
		Minor Creek Census Card No. 17, P. O. Muskogee, Date of Birth August 1, 1905									
11	1	Martin, Joe Ross	1	M	¼	Joe Martin		Non	Susie Martin	1401	Cr
		Minor Creek Census Card No. 18, P. O. Choteau, Date of Birth January 23, 1906									
12	1	Ross, J. E., Jr.	1	M	¼	J. Ewing Ross	1402	Cr	Nellie E. Ross		Non
		Minor Creek Census Card No. 19, P. O. Bixby, Dtae of Birth March 18, 1905									
13	1	McGuire, Oscar H.	1	M	⅛	Louis P. McGuire		Non	Eliza McGuire	1756	Cr
		Minot Creek Census Card No. 20, P. O. Muskogee, Date of Birth October 1, 1905									
14	1	Bradley, Calvin Durant	1	M	1-32	Cass M. Bradley		Non	Belle Bradley	1604	Cr
		Minor Creek Census Card No. 21, P. O. Eufaula, Date of Birth August 7, 1905									
15	1	Tolleson, Alfred Washington	1	M	⅛	William A. Tolleson		Non	George Ella Tolleson	2645	Cr
		Minor Creek Census Card No. 22, P. O. Checotah, Date of Birth December 18, 1905									
16	1	Richard, Velva	1	F	½	Sam Richard	6088	Cr	Lula Richard		Non
		Minor Creek Census Card No. 23, P. O. Sapulpa, Date of Birth August 10, 1905									
17	1	Behen, Noah	1	M	F	Micco Behen	3037	Cr	Jennetta Behen	2111	Cr
		Minor Creek Census Card No. 24, P. O. Sapulpa, Date of Birth May 14, 1905									
18	1	Fulsom, Henry	1	M	F	Robert Fulsom	7286	Cr	Couthlany Fulsom	2869	Cr
		Minor Creek Census Card No. 25, P. O. Yale, Date of Birth February 21, 1906									
19	1	Dale, Georgie	1	F	1-16	Oliver C. Dale		Non	Izora E. Dale	3188	Cr
		Minor Creek Census Card No. 26, P. O. Carson, Date of Birth August 29, 1905									
20	1	Robison, Samuel	1	M	½	Barney C. Robison	5256	Cr	Ida B. Robison	5257	Cr
		Minor Creek Census Card No. 28, P. O. Morse, Date of Birth April 22, 1905									
21	1	Doyle, John Henry	1	M	1-16	Albert Doyle	3053	Cr	Amanda Doyle		Non
		Minor Creek Census Card No. 29, P. O. Wagoner, Date of Birth January 19, 1906									
22	1	Posey, Ruth Lucile	1	F	⅛	Walter Posey	1742	Cr	Mary L. Posey		Non
		Minor Creek Census Card No. 30. P. O. Okemah, Date of Birth May 22, 1905									
23	1	Harvison, Hazel Vivian	1	F	1-16	George D. Harvison	561	Cr	Lula E. Harvison	562	Cr
		Minor Creek Census Card No. 31, P. O. Wetumka, Date of Birth November 6, 1905									
24	1	Winters, Grace	1	F	⅛	Ed Winters	2923	Cr	Clara Winters		Non
		Minor Creek Census Card No. 33, P. O. Eufaula, Date of Birth November 5, 1905									
25	1	Kite, Edna Bettie	1	F	⅜	A. L. Kite		Non	Jemima Kite	3891	Cr
		Minor Creek Census Card No. 34, P. O. Eufaula, Date of Birth August 24, 1905									
26	1	Lewis, Micco	1	M	F	Ellis J. Lewis	8440	Cr	Halley Manley	6845	Cr
		Minor Creek Census Card No. 35, P. O. Checotah, Date of Birth March 25, 1905									
27	1	Sampson, Jessie D.	1	F	⅛	G. P. Sampson		Non	Mary Sampson	2391	Cr
		Minor Creek Census Card No. 36, P. O. Eufaula, Date of Birth September 21, 1905									
28	1	Post, Thomas Jr.	1	M	1-16	Thomas Post	2755	Cr	Laura Post		Non
		Minor Creek Census Card No. 37, P. O. Lenna, Date of Birth April 24, 1905									
29	1	Leverett, Fanny	1	F	5-16	Walter Leverett		Non	Kogee Leverett	2655	Cr
		Minor Creek Census Card No. 38, P. O. Lenna, Date of Birth May 16, 1905									
30	1	Morrison, Tully	1	M	1-16	John Morrison Jr.	2645	Cr	Lena Morrison	5625	Cr
		Minor Creek Census Card No. 39, P. O. Tulsa, Date of Birth November 24, 1905									
31	1	McGee, Princess Aline	1	F	9-128	John W. McGee	2771	Cr	Eulala McGee	2878	Cr
		Minor Creek Census Card No. 40, P. O. Lenna, Date of Birth September 20, 1905									
32	1	Morrison, Andrew Jackson	1	M	⅝	Waitie Morrison	4324	Cr	Eliza Morrison	4325	Cr
		Minor Creek Census Card No. 41, P. O. Eufaula, Date of Birth April 3, 1905									
33	1	McIntosh, Kitty	1	F	¾	Bennie McIntosh	6258	Cr	Leah McIntosh	6259	Cr
		Minor Creek Census Card No. 42, P. O. Eufaula, Date of Birth April 27, 1905									
34	1	Lewis, Washie	1	M	F	Daniel Lewis	8485	Cr	Polly Lewis	8486	Cr

Roll No.	No.	NAME	Age	Sex	Blood	NAME OF FATHER	Roll No.	Cit.	NAME OF MOTHER	Roll No.	Cit.
		Minor Creek Census Card No. 43, P. O. Eufaula, Date of Birth May 20, 1905									
35	1	Ernest, Anna Lee	1	F	⅛	H. B. Ernest		Non	Leola May Ernest	5653	Cɪ
		Minor Creek Census Card No. 44, P. O. Huttonville, Date of Birth August 25, 1905									
36	1	Brown, Delilah	1	F	½	Charles Brown		Non	Maria Brown	8558	Cr
		Minor Creek Census Card No. 45, P. O. Mellette, Date of Birth February 16, 1906									
37	1	Bright, Lizzie	1	F	F	John Bright	6560	Cr	Rhoda Bright	6564	Cr
		Minor Creek Census Card No. 46, P. O. Eufaula, Date of Birth May 1, 1905									
38	1	Boone, Stella May	1	F	⅝	Newman Boone	3357	Cr	Polly Boone	6562	Cr
		Minor Creek Census Card No. 47, P. O. Okmulgee, Date of Birth February 22, 1906									
39	1	Gaither, Myrtle Washington	1	F	3-16	W. J. Gaither		Non	Alice M. Gaither	177	Cr
		Minor Creek Census Card No. 48, P. O. Bixby, Date of Birth January 4, 1906									
40	1	Posey, Charles Kenneth	1		1-16	Andy W. Posey	9111	Cr	Minnie Posey		Non
		Minor Creek Census Card No. 49, P. O. Wagoner, Date of Birth December 20, 1905									
41	1	Cane, Cecil	1	F	1-16	Charlie R. Cane	39	Cr	Mollie B. Cane		Non
		Minor Creek Census Card No. 52, P. O. Redfork, Date of Birth August 16, 1905									
42	1	Bewley, George Henry	1	M	⅛	Lawrence W. Bewley		Non	Elizabeth Yargee Bewley	2789	Cr
		Minor Creek Census Card No. 55, P. O. Bristow, Date of Birth December 16, 1905									
43	1	Clinton, Ida	1	F	F	George Clinton	7010	Cr	Sallie Clinton	7011	Cr
		Minor Creek Census Card No. 59, P. O. Henryetta, Date of Birth June 1, 1905									
44	1	Whetstone, Verna C.	1	F	1-16	Presley Whetstone	2673	Cr	Mammie M. Whetstone		Non
		Minor Creek Census Card No. 62, P. O. Wetumka, Date of Birth May 22, 1905									
45	1	Cowe, Maydella	1	F	F	Sarty Cowe	4891	Cr	Malinda McGirt Cowe	4889	Cr
		Minor Creek Census Card No. 63, P. O. Coweta, Date of Birth January 2, 1906									
46	1	Harmon, Benjamin T.	1	M	1-16	Ben T. Harmon	2498	Cr	Mary J. Harmon		Non
		Minor Creek Census Card No. 66, P. O. Okmulgee, Date of Birth November 1, 1905									
47	1	Hardridge, Clarence	1	M	⅞	Eli E. Hardridge	3507	Cr	Amanda Hardridge	51	Cr
		Minor Creek Census Card No. 67, P. O. Sapulpa, Date of Birth October 31, 1905									
48	1	Aubrey, Herbert F.	1	M	¾	C. B. Aubrey		Non	Millie Aubrey	4170	Cr
		Minor Creek Census Card No. 69, P. O. Cathay, Date of Birth April 15, 1905									
49	1	Depriest, Theodore R.	1	M	3-16	Thompson Depriest	2257	Cr	Pearl Depriest	990	Cr
		Minor Creek Census Card No. 70, P. O. Eufaula, Date of Birth September 23, 1905									
50	1	Phillips, Nancy	1	F	F	Johnson Phillips	6304	Cr	Hettie Phillips	6305	Cr
		Minor Creek Census Card No. 71, P. O. Eufaula, Date of Birth September 12, 1905									
51	1	Day, John Raymond	1	M	⅛	Robert Day		Non	Vinita Day	3850	Cr
		Minor Creek Census Card No. 72, P. O. Cathay, Date of Birth July 7, 1905									
52	1	Fisher, Fillisee Norene	1	F	¼	Sam Fisher	2449	Cr	Carrie Fisher		Non
		Minor Creek Census Card No. 73, P. O. Eufaula, Date of Birth March 1, 1905									
53	1	Hardridge, Jasper	1	M	F	Solomon Hardridge	5772	Cr	Lillie Hardridge	5751	Cr
		Minor Creek Census Card No. 74, P. O. Cathay, Date of Birth July 18, 1905									
54	1	Doyle, Blanche	1	F	⅛	Sam H. Doyle Jr.	6784	Cr	Bedia Doyle		Non
		Minor Creek Census Card No. 75, P. O. Eufaula, Date of Birth No. 1, December 27, 1901; No. 2, July 9, 1905									
55	1	Washington, Frank	•5	M	⅝	Isaac Washington	5635	Cr	Lizzie Colbert	5616	Cr
56	2	Washington, Alice	1	F	⅝	Isaac Washington	5635	Cr	Lizzie Colbert	5616	Cr
		Nos. 1 and 2 illegitimate									
		Minor Creek Census Card No. 76, P. O. Eufaula, Date of Birth May 10, 1905									
57	1	Sulphur, Andrew	1	M	F	James Sulphur	2863	Cr	Jennie Sulphur	903	Cr
		Minor Creek Census Card No. 77, P. O. Raiford, Date of Birth April 2, 1905									
58	1	Cosar, Peter	1	M	F	Willie Cosar	7362	Cr	Abbie Conner	9210	Cr
		Illegitimate									
		Minor Creek Census Card No. 78, P. O. Huttonville, Date of Birth October 7, 1905									
59	1	Hutton, Sally	1	F	1-16	Walter Hutton	4172	Cr-F	Nancy Hutton	3016	Cr
		Minor Creek Census Card No. 79, P. O. Raiford, Date of Birth September 13, 1905									
60	1	McIntosh, Wanda Wynona	1	F	¼	Lucius G. McIntosh	5745	Cr	Laura Bonnie McIntosh		Non
		Minor Creek Census Card No. 80, P. O. Fame, Date of Birth December 25, 1905									
61	1	Highland, Leroy	1	M	1-16	Patrick Highland		Non	Lula H. Highland	1775	Cr
		Minor Creek Census Card No. 81, P. O. Weleetka, Date of Birth November 21, 1905									
62	1	Stephenson, Eddie	1	M	½	A. P. Stephenson		Non	Polly Stephenson	5103	Cr
		Minor Creek Census Card No. 82, P. O. Hoffman, Date of Birth April 24, 1905									
63	1	Bennefield, John Franklin	1	M	1-16	William Bennefield		Non	Mollie Bennefield	5579	Cr
		Minor Creek Census Card No. 83, P. O. Council Hill Date of Birth April 23, 1905									
64	1	Chastain, Roland	1	M	1-16	Fritz Chastain		Non	Ottie Chastain	2260	Cr
		Minor Creek Census Card No. 84, P. O. Haskell, Date of Birth December 8, 1905									
65	1	Gibson, Frankie	1	F	1-32	John E. Gibson	3572	Cr	Maud Gibson		Non
		Minor Creek Census Card No. 85, P. O. Weer, Date of Birth February 22, 1906									
66	1	Williams, Monroe	1	M	⅛	Matt Williams		Non	Mary M. Williams	1309	Cr
		Minor Creek Census Card No. 87, P. O. Mellette, Date of Birth January 1, 1906									
67	1	Jones, Lizzie	1	F	¾	Thomas Jones	1583	Cr	Cindy Jones		Non
		Minor Creek Census Card No. 88, P. O. Hitchita, Date of Birth September 27, 1905									
68	1	Island, Lawrence	1	M	¼	Boney Island	5565	Cr	Maggie Island		Non
		Minor Creek Census Card No. 89, P. O. Stidham, Date of Birth December 27, 1905									
69	1	Derrisaw, Lydia	1	F	F	William Derrisaw	7245	Cr	Polly Derrisaw	1341	Cr
		Minor Creek Censu Card No. 90, P. O. Stidham, Date of Birth April 6, 1905									
70	1	Pitman, Clarence	1	M	⅛	J. W. Pitman		Non	Rosanna Pitman	3729	Cr

Roll No.	No.	NAME	Age	Sex	Blood	NAME OF FATHER	Roll No.	Cit.	NAME OF MOTHER	Roll No.	Cit.
	Minor Creek Census Card No. 91, P. O. Cathay, Date of Birth January 3, 1906										
71	1	Reynolds, Addie Lee	1	F	1-32	Charles Reynolds		Non	Ada Reynolds	2541	Cr
	Minor Creek Census Card No. 92, P. O. Stidham, Date of Birth November 8, 1905										
72	1	Stover, Daniel Jr.	1M		F	Daniel Stover	3261	Cr	Lavina Stover	3262	Cr
	Minor Creek Census Card No. 94, P. O. Eufaula, Date of Birth September 18, 1905										
73	1	Matoy, Gertrude	1	F	⅛	Charles Matoy	5889	Cr	Maude Matoy		Non
	Minor Creek Census Card No. 95, P. O. Wetumka, Date of Birth October 8, 1905										
74	1	Cooper, Ada Illegitimate	1	F	⅝	Willie Cooper		Non	Martha Jones	1586	Cr
	Minor Creek Census Card No. 96, P. O. Yeager, Date of Birth March 2, 1905										
75	1	Wesley, Rose Etta	1	F	9-16	Roley Wesley	2301	Cr	Mary Ann Wesley	2296	Cr
	Minor Creek Census Card No. 97, P. O. Broken Arrow, Date of Birth November 3, 1905										
76	1	Jones, Adzel	1	F	¼	V. T. Jones		Non	Maggie Jones	2549	Cr
	Minor Creek Census Card No. 98, P. O. Raiford, Date of Birth November 16, 1905										
77	1	Fellows, Leona	1	F	3-32	Claude Fellows		Non	Callie M. Fellows	5760	Cr
	Minor Creek Census Card No. 99, P. O. Mounds, Date of Birth November 5, 1905										
78	1	Vowell, Earl Lafayette	1	M	⅛	Sam Vowell	2588	Cr	Rosa C. Vowell		Non
	Minor Creek Census Card No. 100, P. O. Stidham, Date of Birth June 6, 1905										
79	1	Gray, Carl	1	M	⅜	James Gray	8622	Cr	Mary Gray		Non
	Minor Creek Census Card No. 102, P. O. Bixby, Date of Birth November 11, 1905										
80	1	Call, Voisy	1	F	1-16	John M. Call		Non	Pearl Call	1557	Cr
	Minor Creek Census Card No. 104, P. O. Okemah, Date of Birth July 9, 1905										
81	1	Fixico, Sulter	1	M	F	Unknown			Pefeny Fixico	4123	Cr
	Minor Creek Census Card No. 105, P. O. Checotah, Date of Birth July 3, 1905										
82	1	Murray, Margaret Mary	1	F	1-16	John Murray	9320	Cr?	Lucy Murray	4439	Cr
	Minor Creek Census Card No. 108, P. O. Coweta, Date of Birth December 6, 1905										
83	1	Orcutt, Pearlie	1	F	⅛	Adolphus D. Orcutt		Non	Adaline Ocrutt	1808	Cr
	Minor Creek Census Card No. 109, P. O. Stroud, Date of Birth October 26, 1905										
84	1	Foster, Lewis E.	1	M	1-16	Edward Foster	5215	Cr	Grace M. Foster		Non
	Minor Creek Census Card No. 111, P. O. Checotah, Date of Birth August 23, 1905										
85	1	Watson, Chancy Lee	1	M	⅛	Robert Watson	2250	Cr	Annie Watson		Non
	Minor Creek Census Card No. 112, P. O. Eufaula, Date of Birth February 26, 1906										
86	1	Francis, May Della	1	F	F	Robert Francis	6202	Cr	Millie Francis	6203	Cr
	Minor Creek Census Card No. 113, P. O. Mounds, Date of Birth September 3, 1905										
87	1	Bigpond, Eliza	1	F	F	Daniel Bigpond	1838	Cr	Nancy Bigpond	1839	Cr
	Minor Creek Census Card No. 114, P. O. Wagoner, Date of Birth July 17, 1905 (Twins)										
88	1	Letts, Vernon Milford	1	M	1-16	F. B. Letts		Non	Susan L. Letts	882	Cr
89	2	Letts, Vera May	1	F	1-16	F. B. Letts		Non	Susan L. Letts	882	Cr
	Minor Creek Census Card No. 116, P. O. Tulsa, Date of Birth August 4, 1905										
90	1	Enrigues, Winnie	1	F	½	Jesus Enrigues		Non	Lizzie Enrigues	7111	Cr
	Minor Creek Census Card No. 117, P. O. Muskogee, Date of Birth February 20, 1906										
91	1	Campbell, Bertha	1	F	⅛	Tom Campbell		Non	Jessie Campbell	5812	Cr
	Minor Creek Census Card No. 118, P. O. Broken Arrow, Date of Birth January 7, 1906										
92	1	Haikey, Masey	1	F	F	Dave Haikey	952	Cr	Nicey Haikey	6424	Cr
	Minor Creek Census Card No. 120, P. O. Coweta, Date of Birth August 11, 1905										
93	1	Bruner, Lottie	1	F	F	Richard Bruner	5571	.Cr	Sarah Bruner	5572	Cr
	Minor Creek Census Card No. 123, P. O. Brush Hill, Date of Birth November 24, 1905										
94	1	Jackson, Birtha	1	F	⅛	Stepney Jackson	4881	Cr-F	Lou Jackson	2678	Cr
	Minor Creek Census Card No. 124, P. O. Okmulgee, Date of Birth October 14, 1905										
95	1	Moore, Carl Orlando	1	M	¼	Mark R. Moore		Non	Lydia A. Moore	1033	Cr
	Minor Creek Census Card No. 126, P. O. Coweta, Date of Birth February 24, 1906										
96	1	Sarty, Joe	1	M	F	Ned Sarty	436	Cr	Eliza Sarty	712	Cr
	Minor Creek Census Card No. 127, P. O. Stillwater, Date of Birth June 15, 1905										
97	1	Burnett, Richard Stanrord	1	M	⅛	E. H. Burnett		Non	Vinita Gordon Burnett	1322	Cr
	Minor Creek Census Card No. 130, P. O. Sapulpa, Date of Birth January 29, 1906										
98	1	Berryhill, Oleta Pearl	1	F	1-64	Geo. Franklin Berryhill	7912	Cr	Clementine Berry-hill		Non
	Minor Creek Census Card No. 131, P. O. Okmulgee, Date of Birth July 4, 1905										
99	1	Sanger, Pauline	1	F	⅛	Stephen Sanger	3391	Cr	Viola Sanger		Non
	Minor Creek Census Card No. 133, P. O. Checotah, Date of Birth August 19, 1904										
100	1	Davis, Malissie	1	F	¼	Sam Davis		Non	Janey Davis	8363	Cr
	Minor Creek Census Card No. 134, P. O. Okmulgee, Date of Birth January 21, 1906										
101	1	Williams, Haddie	1	F	F	Eli Williams	2911	Cr	Mary Williams		Non
	Minor Creek Census Card No. 135, P. O. Morris, Date of Birth November 7, 1905										
102	1	Ackley, Morris	1	M	1-16	Bart Ackley		Non	Goldie Ackley	461	Cr
	Minor Creek Census Card No. 137, P. O. Okmulgee, Date of Birth February 28, 1906										
103	1	Huckaby, Mary Alice	1	F	¼	R. W. Huckaby		Non	Elcy Huckaby	1195	Cr
	Minor Creek Census Card No. 139, P. O. Wagoner, Date of Birth April 13, 1905										
104	1	Price, Nora Nellie Marie	1	F	1-16	Moses B. Price		Non	Sallie Price	2331	Cr
	Minor Creek Census Card No. 140, P. O. Checotah, Date of Birth July 11, 1905										
105	1	Carr, Homer Lee	1	M	⅛	Thomas Carr	2378	Cr	Ada Bell Carr		Non
	Minor Creek Census Card No. 143, P. O. Senora, Date of Birth March 20, 1905										
106	1	Fife, Hannah	1	F	F	Jimmie Fife	6437	Cr	Lucinda Fife	6438	Cr
	Minor Creek Census Card No. 144, P. O. Henryetta, Date of Birth October 7, 1905										
107	1	Grayson, Lela Illigitimate	1	F	½	Garland Grayson		Non	Katie Watson	4518	Cr
	Minor Creek Census Card No. 145, P. O. Hanna, Date of Birth October 10, 1905										
108	1	Cummings, Alice	1	F	½	David Cummings	6818	Cr	Louisa Cummings	6819	Cr
	Minor Creek Census Card No. 146, P. O. Okemah, Date of Birth April 24, 1905										
109	1	Fipps, Ellie	1	F	1-16	Samuel Fipps		Non	Alice M. Fipps	1517	Cr

No.	NAME	Age	Sex	Blood	NAME OF FATHER	Roll No.	Cit.	NAME OF MOTHER	Roll No.	Cit.

Minor Creek Census Card No. 147, P. O. Dustin, Date of Birth April 11, 1905
| 1 | Wilson, Jack Elton | 1 | M | 3/8 | R. B. Wilson | | Non | Hettie Wilson | 2656 | Cr |

Minor Creek Census Card No. 148, P. O. Dustin, Date of Birth November 7, 1905
| 1 | Brooks, Rufus Claude | 1 | M | 3/8 | John Brooks | | Non | Bettie Brooks | 6146 | Cr |

Minor Creek Census Card No. 149, P. O. Carson, Date of Birth September 18, 1905
| 1 | Bruner, Alice | 1 | F | F | Taylor Bruner | 7640 | Cr | Nancy Bruner | 7641 | Cr |

Minor Creek Census Card No. 150, P. O. Okfuskee, Date of Birth August 7, 1905
| 1 | Martin, Henry | 1 | M | 1/8 | Thomas Martin | | Non | Anna Martin | 180 | Cr |

Minor Creek Census Card No. 151, P. O. Coweta, Date of Birth July 18, 1905
| 1 | Boudinot, Cornelius Jr. | 1 | M | F | Cornelius Boudinot | 634 | Cr | Susanna Boudinot | 644 | Cr |

Minor Creek Census Card No. 154, P. O. Olive, Date of Birth March 1, 1906 (Twins)
| 1 | Brown, Melvin A. | 1 | M | F | Larry Brown | 1983 | Cr | Hardin Brown | 1984 | Cr |
| 2 | Brown, Sherman | 1 | M | F | Larry Brown | 1983 | Cr | Hardin Brown | 1984 | Cr |

Minor Creek Census Card No. 160, P. O. Jenks, Date of Birth September 4, 1905
| 1 | Gregory, Mina Crete | 1 | F | 1/2 | Noah Gregory | 2333 | Cr | Carrie E. Gregory | 2334 | Cr |

Minor Creek Census Card No. 161, P. O. Okemah, Date of Birth August 31, 1905
| 1 | Wind, Charlie | 1 | M | 3/4 | George Wind | 4768 | Cr | Milly Wind | 4769 | Cr |

Minor Creek Census Card No. 162, P. O. Hitchita, Date of Birth December 18, 1905
| 1 | Hamilton, James M. | 1 | M | 1-32 | S. H. Hamilton | | Non | Cassie Hamilton | 4630 | Cr |

Minor Creek Census Card No. 163, P. O. Broken Arrow, Date of Birth No. 1, September 14, 1905; No. 2, May 24, 1902
| 1 | Tiger, John Washington | 1 | M | F | Ben Tiger | 1118 | Cr | Mary Tiger | 1119 | Cr |
| 2 | Tiger, Annie | 4 | F | F | Ben Tiger | 1118 | Cr | Mary Tiger | 1119 | Cr |

Minor Creek Census Card No. 165, P. O. Bristow, Date of Birth May 30, 1905
| 1 | Bruce, Lena Ester | 1 | F | 3/8 | Moten Bruce | | Non | Phoebe Bruce | 1483 | Cr |

Minor Creek Census Card No. 168, P. O. Okemah, Date of Birth July 11, 1905
| 1 | Harjo, Joe | 1 | M | F | Huntie Harjo | 9243 | Cr | Sarah Harjo | 6763 | Cr |

Minor Creek Census Card No. 169, P. O. Okemah, Date of Birth October 24, 1905
| 1 | Douglas, Raymond R. | 1 | M | 1/2 | Harry Douglas | | Non | Louie Douglas | 8667 | Cr |

Minor Creek Census Card No. 170, P. O. Mounds, Date of Birth September 16, 1905
| 1 | Wills, Jack Harbert | 1 | M | 1-16 | Henry F. Wills | 2191 | Cr | Mary A. Wills | | Non |

Minor Creek Census Card No. 171, P. O. Bixby, Date of Birth November 1, 1905
| 1 | Cooper, Rosa | 1 | F | F | Sam Cooper | 1955 | Cr | Nancy Cooper | 1950 | Cr |

Minor Creek Census Card No. 173, P. O. Dustin, Date of Birth December 23, 1905
| 1 | Fife, Lena | 1 | F | F | Sandy Fife | 7971 | Cr | Louisa Fife | 8031 | Cr |

Minor Creek Census Card No. 174, P. O. Dustin, Date of Birth February 15, 1905
| 1 | Thomas, Susie | 1 | F | 1/2 | David S. Thomas | | Non | Aggie Thomas | 6132 | Cr |

Minor Creek Census Card No. 175, P. O. Henryetta, Date of Birth April 22, 1905
| 1 | Field, Frank | 1 | M | F | David Field | 1364 | Cr | Mary Field | 4421 | Cr |

Minor Creek Census Card No. 176, P. O. Henryetta, Date of Birth December 6, 1905
| 1 | Hickman, Alva | 1 | M | 1/2 | Mac Hickman | | Non | Mebaley Hickman | 4749 | Cr |

Minor Creek Census Card No. 178, P. O. Yeager, Date of Birth July 26, 1905
| 1 | Wesley, Lillie | 1 | F | F | Joe Wesley | 5922 | Cr | Cherokee Wesley | 4932 | Cr |

Minor Creek Census Card No. 179, P. O. Clearview, Date of Birth June 23, 1905
| 1 | Reynolds, Napoleon | 1 | M | 1/4 | Joe Reynolds | | Non | Delphie Reynolds | 3009 | Cr |

Minor Creek Census Card No. 180, P. O. Weleetka, Date of Birth May 10, 1905
| 1 | Jones, Wesley | 1 | M | F | Sulloly Jones | 7819 | Cr | Melinda Jones | 8041 | Cr |

Minor Creek Census Card No. 181, P. O. Bryant, Date of Birth July 26, 1905
| 1 | Looney, Beckie Lena | 1 | F | F | Josiah Looney | 1681 | Cr | Fannie Looney | 1682 | Cr |

Minor Creek Census Card No. 182, P. O. Wetumka, Date of Birth April 30, 1905
| 1 | Dunson, Hettie | 1 | F | F | Lewis Dunson | 2037 | Cr | Kizzie Dunson | 1689 | Cr |

Minor Creek Census Card No. 183, P. O. Weleetka, Date of Birth May 30, 1905
| 1 | Jimboy, Mannie | 1 | F | F | Wiley Jimboy | 1714 | Cr | Louisa Jimboy | 4836 | Cr |

Minor Creek Census Card No. 184, P. O. Bryant, Date of Birth March 3, 1906
| 1 | Fisher, Ben | 1 | M | 7/8 | Joe Fisher | 1726 | Cr | Nancy Fisher | 1727 | Cr |
| 2 | Fisher, Eddie | 1 | M | 7/8 | Joe Fisher | 1726 | Cr | Nancy Fisher | 1727 | Cr |

Minor Creek Census Card No. 189, P. O. Okfuskee, Date of Birth January 25, 1906
| 1 | Davis, Barney, | 1 | M | F | Joe Davis | 3767 | Cr | Kogee Davis | 3768 | Cr |

Minor Creek Census Card No. 192, P. O. Henryetta, Date of Birth November 22, 1905
| 1 | Rentie, Gracie | 1 | F | 3-16 | Lewis Rentie | 479 | Cr-F | Peggie Rentie | 3862 | Cr |

Minor Creek Census Card No. 193, P. O. Weleetka, Date of Birth April 3, 1905
| 1 | Simmer, Peter | 1 | M | F | John Simmer | 3212 | Cr | Lena Simmer | 3213 | Cr |

Minor Creek Census Card No. 194, P. O. Wetumka, Date of Birth December 28, 1905
| 1 | Wesley, Bettie | 1 | F | F | John Wesley | 62224 | Cr | Polly Wesley | 6448 | Cr |

Minor Creek Census Card No. 197, P. O. Weleetka, Date of Birth February 25, 1906
| 1 | Watson, Mehaley | 1 | F | 11-16 | Santy Watson | 7659 | Cr | Hannah Canard | 4574 | Cr |

Minor Creek Census Card No. 199, P. O. Weleetka, Date of Birth June 3, 1905
| 1 | Harjo, Samuel | 1 | M | 13-16 | Sunday Harjo | 4907 | Cr | Maggie Harjo | 4983 | Cr |

Minor Creek Census Card No. 200, P. O. Wetumka, Date of Birth No. 1, June 10, 1905; No. 2, March 21, 1903
| 1 | Deer, Lizzie | 1 | F | F | Moses Deer | 5007 | Cr | Ellen Deer | 5008 | Cr |
| 2 | Deer, Lizzie | 3 | F | F | Moses Deer | 5007 | Cr | Ellen Deer | 5008 | Cr |

Minor Creek Census Card No. 201, P. O. Wetumka, Date of Birth December 20, 1905
| 1 | Buck, Susanna | 1 | F | 13-16 | William Buck | 5956 | Cr | Annie Benson | 7672 | Cr |

Minor Creek Census Card No. 204, P. O. Weleetka, Date of Birth October 17, 1905
| 1 | Barnett, Elizabeth | 1 | F | 3/8 | Dick Barnett | 397 | Cr-F | Annie Barnett | 3130 | Cr |

Minor Creek Census Card No. 205, P. O. Okemah, Date of Birth November 1, 1905
| 1 | Berryhill, Willie | 1 | M | F | Joseph Berryhill | 4820 | Cr | Hepsie Berryhill | 1606 | Cr |

Minor Creek Census Card No. 207, P. O. Beggs, Date of Birth July 8, 1905
| 1 | Boon, Robert | 1 | M | 1/2 | Peter Boon | 4848 | Cr-F | Martha Boon | 2147 | Cr |

Minor Creek Census Card No. 211, P. O. Hitchita, Date of Birth September 13, 1905
| 1 | Foshee, Ernest | 1 | M | 1-16 | Sinnon Lee Foshee | 303 | Cr | Emily Foshee | | Non |

263

Roll No.	No.	NAME	Age	Sex	Blood	NAME OF FATHER	Roll No.	Cit.	NAME OF MOTHER	Roll No.	Cit.
		Minor Creek Census Card No. 215, P. O. Wetumka, Date of Birth August 7, 1905									
152	1	Fish, Johnson	1	M	F	Jonas Fish	5130	Cr	Morleyar Fish	5131	Cr
		Minor Creek Census Card No. 216, P. O. Wetumka, Date of Birth February 3, 1902									
153	1	Dacon, Susanna	4	F	F	Sardy Dacon	5017	Cr	Harney Dacon	5018	Cr
		Minor Creek Census Card No. 217, P. O. Wetumka, Date of Birth July 7, 1905									
154	1	Deere, Gilbert	1	M	½	Paro Deere		Non	Wunche Deere	7181	Cr
		Minor Creek Census Card No. 218, P. O. Coweta, Date of Birth March 29, 1905									
155	1	Tiger, Edna	1	F	⅞	Thomas Tiger	693	Cr	Nicey Tiger	1104	Cr
		Minor Creek Census Card No. 220, P. O. Wetumka, Date of Birth May 6, 1905									
156	1	Tiger, Louise	1	F	⅝	Johnson E. Tiger	224	Cr	Lena Benson Tiger	64	Cr
		Minor Creek Census Card No. 223, P. O. Holdenville, Date of Birth May 22, 1905									
157	1	Sewell, Willie Illegitimate	1	M	15-16	Ben Sewell	3811	Cr	Kizzie Taylor	6018	Cr
		Minor Creek Census Card No. 224, P. O. Holdenville, Date of Birth February 7, 1906									
158	1	McCosar Alice Illegitimate	1	F	F	Bunnie McCosar	7115	Cr	Martha Anderson	6520	Cr
		Minor Creek Census Card No. 225, P. O. Butner, Date of Birth September 11, 1905									
159	1	Simmer, Lillie	1	F	F	John Simmer	4234	Cr	Jemima Simmer	5551	Cr
		Minor Creek Census Card No. 226, P. O. Holdenville, Date of Birth September 4, 1905									
160	1	Ellis, Fred	1	M	⅝	Amos Ellis	6494	Cr	Stella Shawnego	6247	Cr
		Minor Creek Census Card No. 228, P. O. Holdenville, Date of Birth September 10, 1905									
161	1	Stout, Ethel	1	F	⅛	James C. Stout		Non	Lou Ellen Stout	3099	Cr
		Minor Creek Census Card No. 229, P. O. Holdenville, Date of Birth February 18, 1906									
162	1	Narcomay, Lizzie	1	F	F	Thomas Narcomay	6581	Cr	Kizey Narcomay	5921	Cr
		Minor Creek Census Card No. 230, P. O. Wewoka, Date of Birth December 16, 1905									
163	1	Walker, Joseph	1	M	F	Hardy Walker		Non	Bettie Walker	7207	Cr
		Minor Creek Census Card No. 231, P. O. Holdenville, Date of Birth August 25, 1905									
164	1	Hasley, Josephine Illegitimate	1	F	¼	Noah Hasley		Non	Lucinda Brooks	5164	Cr
		Minor Creek Census Card No. 232, P. O. Bearden, Date of Birth No. 1, April 9, 1902; No. 2, July 4, 1905									
165	1	Cain, Bettie	3	F	F	Daniel Cain	5726	Cr	Nisey Cain	5727	Cr
166	2	Cain, Thomas	1	M	F	Daniel Cain	5726	Cr	Nisey Cain	5727	Cr
		Minor Creek Census Card No. 233, P. O. Sasakwa, Date of Birth February 4, 1906									
167	1	Palmer, Jack Frost	1	M	½	James Palmer		Non	Mary Palmer	6898	Cr
		Minor Creek Census Card No. 234, P. O. Calvin, Date of Birth September 18, 1905									
168	1	Bruner, Minnie	1	F	F	James Bruner	7475	Cr	Togy Bruner	7476	Cr
		Minor Creek Census Card No. 235, P. O. Wewoka, Date of Birth May 22, 1905									
169	1	Buck, Nathan	1	M	⅜	Simpson Buck	5690	Cr	Rhoda Buck		Non
		Minor Creek Census Card No. 236, P. O. Sasakwa, Date of Birth July 10, 1905									
170	1	Fixico, Yano	1	F	¾	Watty Fixico		Non	Fannie Fixico	7713	Cr
		Minor Creek Census Card No. 237, P. O. Holdenville, Date of Birth April 29, 1905									
171	1	Colvin, Charley Illegitimate, died September 2, 1906	1	M	⅜	Lewis Colvin		Non	Abbie Williams	5467	Cr
		Minor Creek Census Card No. 238, P. O. Holdenville, Date of Birth April 5, 1905									
172	1	Hulsey, John Henry	1	M	1-16	George Hulsey	6614	Cr	Carline Hulsey		Non
		Mine Creek Census Card No. 239, P. O. Holdenville, Date of Birth April 26, 1905									
173	1	Tate, Elmer	1	M	¼	Deck Tate		Non	Mary Tate	5255	Cr
		Mine Creek Census Card No. 241, P. O. Holdenville, Date of Birth December 21, 1905									
174	1	Stubblefield, Ross Marion	1	M	1-16	John Stubblefield		Non	Ida Stubblefield	6518	Cr
		Minor Creek Census Card No. 242, P. O. Holdenville, Date of Birth October 2, 1905									
175	1	Lowe, William	1	M	F	Conuky Lowe	4902	Cr	Toche Lowe	4903	Cr
		Minor Creek Census Card No. 243, P. O. Wewoka, Date of Birth December 30, 1905									
176	1	Miller, James A.	1	M	13-16	Louis Miller	5040	Cr	Lillie Miller	5041	Cr
		Minor Creek Census Card No. 345, P. O. Wewoka, Date of Birth March 31, 1905									
177	1	Buck, Alex	1	M	½	Joe Buck	4904	Cr	Lily Buck		Non
		Minor Creek Census Card No. 301, P. O. Okmulgee, Date of Birth April 3, 1905									
178	1	Wisener, Oyama	1	M	⅝	Ben J. Wisener	2294	Cr	Susan Wisener	6657	Cr
		Minor Creek Census Card No. 247, P. O. Okemah, Date of Birth September 2, 1905									
179	1	Harjo, Mollie	1	F	F	Alex Harjo	6469	Cr	Nancy Harjo	6470	Cr
		Minor Creek Census Card No. 248, P. O. Yeager, Date of Birth July 11, 1905									
180	1	Long, Bettie	1	F	F	Washington Long	5340	Cr	Martha Long	5341	Cr
		Minor Creek Census Card No. 249, P. O. Yeager, Date of Birth February 6, 1906									
181	1	Hill, Jacob	1	M	F	Mitchell Hill	5789	Cr	Hilley Hill	5443	Cr
		Minor Creek Census Card No. 250, P. O. Wagoner, Date of Birth September 20, 1905									
182	1	Chissoe, Quinton	1	M	⅞	Sam Chissoe	449	Cr	Lena E. Chissoe	450	Cr
		Minor Creek Census Card No. 251, P. O. Tulsa, Date of Birth February 9, 1906									
183	1	Andrews, Minor	1	M	½	Minor Andrews		Non	Annie Andrews	7113	Cr
		Minor Creek Census Card No. 258, P. O. Spaulding, Date of Birth May 28, 1905									
184	1	Tiger, Lapsey Died September 18, 1906	1	M	F	Parnosky Tiger		Non	Kizzie Tiger	7422	Cr
		Minor Creek Census Card No. 260, P. O. Okfuskee, Date of Birth October 7, 1905									
185	1	Yahola, Martha	1	F	F	Billy Yahola	524	Cr	Winey Yahola	525	Cr
		Minor Creek Census Card No. 262, P. O. Checotah, Date of Birth February 17, 1906									
186	1	Lewis, Eula Velma	1	F	⅛	Oscar Lewis		Non	Ellen Lewis	2364	Cr
		Minor Creek Census Card No. 264, P. O. Stone Bluff, Date of Birth July 26, 1905									
187	1	Sullins, Gladys May	1	F	½	James N. Sullins		Non	Muskogee Essie Sullins	8568	Cr
		Minor Creek Census Card No. 267, P. O. Earlsboro, Date of Birth September 24, 1905									
188	1	Lowry, Ama C. Died April 7, 1906. Father may be Seminole	1	F	F	James Lowry	1267	Cr	Lucy Lowry	6969	Cr

Minor Creek Census Card No. 268, P. O. Holdenville, Date of Birth February 14, 1906
1 McGirt, Bessie 1 F ⅛ William McGirt 6423 Cr Emma Smith 8086 Cr
Illegitimate
Minor Creek Census Card No. 269, P. O. Holdenville, Date of Birth May 7, 1905
1 McCosar, Solomon 1 M F Bunnie McCosar 7115 Cr Nellie McCosar 7700 Cr
Minor Creek Census Card No. 270, P. O. Paden, Date of Birth December 16. 1905
1 Sumka, Henry 1 M F Sumka 5615 Cr Nellie 1299 Cr
Minor Creek Census Card No. 271, P. O. Paden, Date of Birth October 17, 1905
1 Kalaney, Chepon 1 M F Kalaney 8267 Cr Sissie Kalaney 8895 Cr
Minor Creek Census Card No. 272, P. O. Okemah, Date of Birth September 1, 1905
1 Dunn, Ralph 1 M F Tupper Dunn 8 Cr Susie Dunn 9 Cr
Minor Creek Census Card No. 273, P. O. Irene. Date of Birth September 3, 1905
1 Baker, Josephine 1 F F K. N. Baker 1549 Sem Rebecca J. Baker 5833 Cr
Minor Creek Census Card No. 276, P. O. Castle, Date of Birth December 26, 1905
1 Wesley, Lizzie 1 F F Thomas Wesley 6673 Cr Tochee Wesley 5841 Cr
Minor Creek Census Card No. 278, P. O. Paden, Date of Birth February 20, 1906
1 Caesar, Toche 1 F F Samego Caesar 8823 Cr Rachael Caesar 8824 Cr
Minor Creek Census Card No. 279, P. O. Boynton, Date of Birth June 22, 1905
1 Haley, Kizzie 1 F ¼ W. D. Haley Non Lena Haley 482 Cr
Minor Creek Census Card No. 283, P. O. Hitchita, Date of Birth May 16, 1905
1 Foshee, Homer L. 1 M 1-16 William R. Foshee 309 Cr Lillian F. Foshee Non
Minor Creek Census Card No. 284, P. O. Natura, Date of Birth November 5, 1905
1 Brown, Edith 1 F ⅜ Sherman Brown Non Eliza Brown 2053 Cr
Minor Creek Census Card No. 285, P. O. Okmulgee, Date of Birth January 19, 1906
1 Grayson, Hellen 1 F ⅝ Dave Grayson 3497 Cr Fannie Grayson 5688 Cr
Minor Creek Census Card No. 286, P. O. Okmulgee, Date of Birth September 25, 1905
1 Adams, Mary 1 F ¾ Richard Adams 512 Cr Salina Harjo 2164 Cr
Illegitimate
Minor Creek Census Card No. 287, P. O. Okmulgee, Date of Birth January 15, 1906
1 Tobler, Benjamin 1 M ½ Sandy Tobler 389 Cr-F Hepsey Adams 3305 Cr
Illegitimate
Minor Creek Census Card No. 288, P. O. Okmulgee, Date of Birth February 27, 1906
1 Roberts, Liley 1 F F George Roberts 3223 Cr Lizzie Roberts Non
Minor Creek Census Card No. 293, P. O. Okmulgee, Date of Birth August 4, 1905
1 Dice, Elmer 1 M 1-16 Jim Dice Non Dove Dice 5361 Cr
Minor Creek Census Card No. 294, P. O. Newby, Date of Birth January 8, 1906
1 Mayes, Minnie 1 F ½ Wiatt Mayes Non Martha Mayes 3322 Cr
Minor Creek Census Card No. 296, P. O. Bristow, Date of Birth March 30, 1905
1 Mikey, Helen 1 F 1-16 Josiah Mikey 543 Cr-F Lizzie Mikey 9249 Cr
Minor Creek Census Card No. 298, P. O. Henryetta, Date of Birth October 21, 1905
1 Whetstone, Dorothea Theodocia Whet-
Cleo 1 F 1-16 James R.Whetstone 2318 Cr stone Non
Minor Creek Census Card No. 300, P. O. Okmulgee, Date of Birth August 17, 1905
1 Atkins, Elza 1 M 1-16 Annanias A. Atkins 9809 Cr-F Hettie Atkins Non
Minor Creek Census Card No. 2, P. O. Braggs, Date of Birth January 4, 1900
1 Sarnie, Joe 6 M F Sarnie Non Sallie 8260 Cr
Mine Creek Census Card No. 3, P. O. Broken Arrow, Date of Birth July 3, 1905
1 Jefferson, McDora 1 F F Moses Jefferson 736 Cr Nancy W. Jefferson 2125 Cr
Minor Creek Census Card No. 6, P. O. Wagoner.. Date of Birth September 3, 1905
1 Trent, Ned Richard 1 M ⅛ Jim Trent Non Chaney Trent 9916 Cr
Minor Creek Census Card No. 56, P. O. Bristow, Date of Birth October 23, 1905
1 Mann, Hazel May 1 F 5-16 J. F. Mann Non Hannah Mann 4278 Cr
Minor Creek Census Card No. 12, P. O. Muskogee, Date of Birth April 12, 1905
1 Escoe, Myrtle Josephine 1 F 1-16 Charlie J. Escoe 3945 Cr Octavia Escoe Non
Minor Creek Census Card No. 13, P. O. Fry, Date of Birth February 5, 1906
1 Beaver, Beatrice 1 F F Harry Beaver 741 Cr Jennetta Beaver 951 Cr
Minor Creek Census Card No. 27, P. O. Sapulpa, Date of Birth June 10, 1905
1 Frank, Stella 1 F ⅜ Noah Frank 8853 Cr Hannah Frank Non
Minor Creek Census Card No. 50, P. O. Tulsa, Date of Birth September 20, 1905
1 Burnette, Violet 1 F ¼ Thomas Burnette Non Mary J. Burnette 2227 Cr
Minor Creek Census Card No. 51, P. O. Elam, Date of Birth August 6, 1905
1 Hodge, Nathaniel 1 M 1-16 Elum B. Hodge 1216 Cr Annie Dobson Hodge Non
Minor Creek Census Card No. 53, P. O. Henryetta, Date of Birth January 11, 1906
1 Henry, James Harvey 1 M 1-16 James P. Henry 4430 Cr Carie Henry Non
Minor Creek Census Card No. 54, P. O. Inola, Date of Birth October 10, 1905
1 Gregory, Delila May 1 F 5-16 Archie A. Gregory 458 Cr Florence L. Gregory Non
Minor Creek Census Card No. 57, P. O. Oktaha, Date of Birth September 10, 1905
1 Evans, Savannah 1 F 1-16 Richard Evans 3627 Cr Della A. Evans Non
Minor Creek Census Card No. 58, P. O. Checotah, Date of Birth, September 3, 1905
1 Price, Mary Lucile 1 F 1-64 Owen Price 973 Cr Belle Price Non
Minor Creek Census Card No. 60, P. O. Wetumka, Date of Birth September 27, 1904
1 Penn, Emoney 1 M F William Penn 646 Cr Miley Penn 6462 Cr
Minor Creek Census Card No. 61, P. O. Henryetta, Date of Birth April 5, 1905
1 Furr, Albert Clinton 1 M 1-32 Benjamin C. Furr 3524 Cr Stella Furr Non
Minor Creek Census Card No. 64, P. O. Sapulpa, Date of Birth June 17, 1905
1 Land, Knaustaway 1 M ¾ Joseph Henry Land 1695 Cr Salina Land 1696 Cr
Minor Creek Census Card No. 65, P. O. Coweta, Date of Birth August 9, 1905
1 Crowell, Constantine
Edward 1 M 1-16 Thos. J. Crowell 54 Cr Ollie May Crowell Non
Minor Creek Census Card No. 68, P. O. Mellette, Date of Birth May 1, 1900
1 Conner, Thomas Jr. 6 M F Thomas Conner 8593 Cr Abbie Conner 9210 Cr

Roll No.	No.	NAME	Age	Sex	Blood	NAME OF FATHER	Roll No.	Cit.	NAME OF MOTHER	Roll No.	Cit

Minor Creek Census Card No. 86, P. O. Muskogee, Date of Birth June 23, 1905

| 227 | 1 | Statham, Elizabeth | 1 | F | 1-32 | W. H. Statham | | Non | Gertrude Bennett Statham | 7921 | Cr |

Minor Creek Census Card No. 93, P. O. Lenna, Date of Birth August 31, 1905

| 228 | 1 | Price, Mamie | 1 | F | ½ | J. M. Price | | Non | Susan Price | 2854 | Cr |

Minor Creek Census Card No. 101, P. O. Bald Hill, Date of Birth March 24, 1905

| 229 | 1 | Morton, Thomas Allen | 1 | M | 1-16 | Thomas Morton | | Non | Joan Morton | 3663 | Cr |

Minor Creek Census Card No. 103, P. O. Bicley, Date of Birth July 29, 1905

| 230 | 1 | Coppedge, Bernice | 1 | F | 1-16 | C. E. Coppedge | | Non | Emma Coppedge | 1555 | Cr |

Minor Creek Census Card No. 106, P. O. Olive, Date of Birth June 22, 1905

| 231 | 1 | Swingle, Alice | 1 | F | 1-16 | Willoughby Swingle | | Non | Corda Swingle | 1561 | Cr |

Minor Creek Census Card No. 107, P. O. Checotah, Date of Birth January 26, 1906

| 232 | 1 | Reynolds, Miles C. | 1 | M | 1-64 | C. D. Reynolds | | Non | Leila Reynolds | 971 | Cr |

Minor Creek Census Card No. 121, P. O. Oktaha, Date of Birth January 13, 1906

| 233 | 1 | Grissom, John Edward Franklin | 1 | M | 3-16 | John F. Grissom | 171 | Cr | Minnie Grissom | | Non |

Minor Creek Census Card No. 125, P. O. Coweta, Date of Birth May 8, 1905

| 234 | 1 | McKellop, Lydia | 1 | F | F | Peter McKellop | 800 | Cr | Betsey McKellop | 7757 | Cr |

Minor Creek Census Card No. 132, P. O. Bristow, Date of Birth No. 1, March 4, 1905; No. 2, January 27, 1906

| 235 | 1 | Littlehead, Lasawee | 1 | M | F | Whiteman, Little-head | 7961 | Cr | Yahlawe Little-head | 289 | Cr |
| 236 | 2 | Littlehead, Maggie | 1 | F | F | Whiteman, Little-head | 7961 | Cr | Yahlawe Little-head | 289 | Cr |

Minor Creek Census Card No. 142, P. O. Broken Arrow, Date of Birth December 19, 1905

| 237 | 1 | Bemore, Annie | 1 | F | ½ | Chartey Bemore | | Non | Maggie Bemore | 7556 | Cr |

Minor Creek Census Card No. 153, P. O. Wagoner, Date of Birth January 7, 1906

| 238 | 1 | Hockett, Agnes Diana | 1 | F | 1-16 | F. J. Hockett | | Non | Sarah E. Hockett | 2775 | Cr |

Minor Creek Census Card No. 155, P. O. Boley, Date of Birth No. 1, June 22, 1902; No. 2, March 20, 1905

| 239 | 1 | Stevens, Ida Bell | 4 | F | ¼ | Wm. A. Stevens | | Non | Sarah Stevens | 10044 | Cr |
| 240 | 2 | Stevens, Lenon | 1 | M | ¼ | Wm. A. Stevens | | Non | Sarah Stevens | 10044 | Cr |

Minor Creek Census Card No. 157, P. O. Bristow, Date of Birth January 12, 1906

| 241 | 1 | Hendrickson, Joe | 1 | M | 1-16 | Joe Hendrickson | | Non | Mary Hendrickson | 3397 | Cr |

Minor Creek Census Card No. 166, P. O. Inola, Date of Birth February 2, 1902

| 242 | 1 | Thomas, Nora | 4 | F | ⅝ | Mack Thomas | 1921 | Cr | Sarah Thomas | 1922 | Cr |

Minor Creek Census Card No. 167, P. O. Hollow, Date of Birth October 4, 1905

| 243 | 1 | McCann, William C. | 1 | M | 1-32 | W. H. McCann | | Non | Josiee C. McCann | 6325 | Cr |

Minor Creek Census Card No. 177, P. O. Henryetta, Date of Birth July 22, 1905

| 244 | 1 | Randall, Sandy Illegitimate | 1 | M | F | Timmie Randall | 4321 | Cr | Winey Fish | 4748 | Cr |

Minor Creek Census Card No. 186, P. O. Wetumka, Date of Birth August 1, 1905

| 245 | 1 | Harjo, Lucy | 1 | F | F | Joseph Harjo | 4698 | Cr | Mahaley Harjo | 4858 | Cr |

Minor Creek Census Card No. 187, P. O. Tulsa, Date of Birth January 12, 1906

| 246 | 1 | Steen, John Howard | 1 | M | ½ | Walter H. Steen | | Non | Katie Steen | 1193 | Cr |

Minor Creek Census Card No. 190, P. O. Haskell, Date of Birth June 28, 1905

| 247 | 1 | Anderson, Stella Terrasa | 1 | F | ½ | Solomon Anderson | 3151 | Cr | Emma Anderson | 3152 | Cr |

Minor Creek Census Card No. 191, P. O. Neodosha, Date of Birth November 26, 1905

| 248 | 1 | Cunningham, Charles Newton R. | 1 | M | ¼ | Wm. J. Cunningham | | Non | Laura Cunningham | 2445 | Cr |

Minor Creek Census Card No. 195, P. O. Weleetka, Date of Birth January 8, 1906

| 249 | 1 | Barnett, Polly | 1 | F | ⅞ | Tucker Barnett | 4979 | Cr | Katie Barnett | 4965 | Cr |

Minor Creek Census Card No. 196, P. O. Weleetka, Date of Birth February 15, 1906

| 250 | 1 | Canard, Tilda | 1 | F | F | Billy Canard | 4964 | Cr | Kizzie Canard | 4997 | Cr |

Minor Creek Census Card No. 202, P. O. Weleetka, Date of Birth March 4, 1905

| 251 | 1 | Barnett, Dick | 1 | M | ⅞ | Jackson Barnett | 4617 | Cr | Nancy Barnett | 4449 | Cr |

Minor Creek Census Card No. 206, P. O. Stidham, Date of Birth September 4, 1905

| 252 | 1 | Hawkins, Jennie | 1 | F | ¾ | Daniel Hawkins | 3841 | Cr | Rhoda Hawkins | 671 | Cr |

Minor Creek Census Card No. 214, P. O. Wetumka, Date of Birth March 8, 1903

| 253 | 1 | Buck, Lonnie | 3 | M | 15-16 | William Buck | 5956 | Cr | Sallie Buck | 6071 | Cr |

Minor Creek Census Card No. 219, P. O. Mounds, Date of Birth August 1, 1905

| 254 | 1 | Goode, Annie Elderrein | 1 | F | 1-16 | George C. Goode | | Non | Myrtle M. Goode | 2784 | Cr |

Minor Creek Census Card No. 448, P. O. Eufaula, Date of Birth January 16, 1905

| 255 | 1 | Lewis, Nut-te-che | 1 | M | F | Maxey Lewis | 8751 | Cr | Jennie Lewis | 8826 | Cr |

Minor Creek Census Card No. 227, P. O. Holdenville, Date of Birth December 12, 1905

| 256 | 1 | Goodwin, Reese | 1 | M | ¼ | Van H. Goodwin | | Non | Mabel Goodwin | | Cr |

Minor Creek Census Card No. 240, P. O. Yeager, Date of Birth June 1, 1905

| 257 | 1 | Jimboy, Mary | 1 | F | F | Fuller Jimboy | 5262 | Cr | Mollie Jimboy | 5263 | Cr |

Minor Creek Census Card No. 246, P. O. Wewoka, Date of Birth December 22, 1905

| 258 | 1 | Coker, Eliza | 1 | F | ¾ | Lewis Coker | 4783 | Cr | Litsey Coker | 295 | Cr |

Minor Creek Census Card No. 253, P. O. Mounds, Date of Birth November 27, 1905

| 259 | 1 | Lannon, Ora | 1 | F | 1-16 | William J. Lannon | | Non | Jennie Lannon | 9196 | Cr |
| 260 | 2 | Lannon, Nora | 1 | F | 1-16 | William J. Lannon | | Non | Jennie Lannon | 9196 | Cr |

Minor Creek Census Card No. 254, P. O. Coweta, Date of Birth June 30, 1905

| 261 | 1 | Thomas, Grant | 1 | M | ⅝ | Sam Thomas | 1924 | Cr | Sophia Thomas | 1925 | Cr |

Minor Creek Census Card No. 255, P. O. Bixby, Date of Birth October 3, 1905

| 262 | 1 | Barnett, Amos | 1 | M | F | Joe Barnett | 3267 | Cr | Wannie Barnett | 3268 | Cr |

Minor Creek Census Card No. 256, P. O. Allen, Date of Birth June 10, 1905

| 263 | 1 | Baccus, Mattie Belle | 1 | F | 1-16 | Willie Baccus | | Non | Rebella Baccus | 3477 | Cr |

Roll No.	No.	NAME	Age	Sex	Blood	NAME OF FATHER	Roll No.	Cit.	NAME OF MOTHER	Roll No.	Cit.
Minor Creek Census Card No. 261, P. O. Holdenville, Date of Birth No. 1 June 27, 1903; No. 2 October 28, 1905											
264	1	Green, Nancy	2	F	F	Hagie Green	7727	Cr	Sallie Green	3382	Cr
265	2	Green, Kizzie	1	F	F	Hagie Green	7727	Cr	Sallie Green	3382	Cr
Minor Creek Census Card No. 263, P. O. Tulsa, Date of Birth May 24, 1905											
266	1	Orcutt, Winnie M.	1	F	1/8	S. A. Orcutt		Non	Annie B. Orcutt	4174	Cr
Minor Creek Census Card No. 266, P. O. Emahaka, Date of Birth November 13, 1905											
267	1	Frank, George	1	M	F	Alfred Frank		Non	Sissie Frank	7708	Cr
Minor Creek Census Card No. 275, P. O. Holdenville, Date of Birth June 26, 1905											
268	1	Herrod, Robert Andrew	1	M	F	Andy Herrod	5467	Cr	Rhoda Herrod	6674	Cr
Minor Creek Census Card No. 282, P. O. Stone Bluff, Date of Birth August 20, 1905											
269	1	Berryhill, Faith	1	F	1/8	Columbus Berryhill	2101	Cr	Emma Berryhill	2102	Cr
Minor Creek Census Card No. 289, P. O. Edmonton, Canada, Date of Birth August 4, 1905											
270	1	Hooks, Virgie	1	F	1-16	Sam Hooks		Non	Naoma Hooks	9810	Cr
Minor Creek Census Card No. 290, P. O. Cobb, Date of Birth October 6, 1905											
271	1	Hodge, Major Benjamin	1	M	1/4	Horace Hodge	2523	Cr	Lidia Hodge		Non
Minor Creek Census Card No. 291, P. O. Tulsa, Date of Birth January 9, 1906											
272	1	Burgess, India Illegitimate. Died March 4, 1906	1	F	3/4	Noah Frank	8853	Cr	Nora Burgess	3967	Cr
Minor Creek Census Card No. 297, P. O. Tulsa, Date of Birth April 27, 1905											
273	1	Grayson, Ella	1	F	9-16	Pete Grayson	1078	Cr	Hattie Grayson	1482	Cr
Minor Creek Census Card No. 302, P. O. Okmulgee, Date of Birth March 2, 1906											
274	1	Snakeya, Amos	1	M	F	David Snakeya	1254	Cr	Molleanna Snakeya	1255	Cr
Minor Creek Census Card No. 303, P. O. Okmulgee, Date of Birth January 29, 1906											
275	1	Snakeya, Nora Illegitimate	1	F	F	Abram Snakeya	1257	Cr	Louisa Berryhill	9327	Cr
Minor Creek Census Card No. 304, P. O. Okmulgee, Date of Birth August 2, 1905											
276	1	Briley, Paul W.	1	M	1/8	Winfree Briley		Non	Ella Briley	1012	Cr
Minor Creek Census Card No. 305, P. O. Okmulgee, Date of Birth June 14, 1905											
277	1	Nelson, Lizzie	1	F	F	Eli Wilson	156	Cr	Rhoda Nelson	2177	Cr
Minor Creek Census Card No. 306, P. O. Beggs, Date of Birth June 9, 1905											
278	1	Lunsford, Ida	1	F	3/8	John C. Lunsford	3383	Cr	Martha Lunsford	3384	Cr
Minor Creek Census Card No. 307, P. O. Okmulgee, Date of Birth February 25, 1906											
279	1	Miller, Samuel	1	M	7/8	Sebron Miller	1738	Cr	Effa Miller	1739	Cr
Minor Creek Census Card No. 308, P. O. Okmulgee, Date of Birth June 26, 1905											
280	1	Checote, Jefferson Davis	1	M	5/8	Samuel J. Checote	245	Cr	Annie Checote	246	Cr
Minor Creek Census Card No. 310, P. O. Okfusky, Date of Birth December 29, 1905											
281	1	Porter, Jemima	1	F	F	James Porter	4193	Cr	Nancy Porter	4194	Cr
Minor Creek Census Card No. 313, P. O. Bixby, Date of Birth August 27 1905											
282	1	Tiger, Melissa	1	F	F	John Tiger	3224	Cr	Millie Tiger	3225	Cr
Minor Creek Census Card No. 314, P. O. Arbeka, Date of Birth February 12, 1906											
283	1	Davis, Earl	1	M	5-16	Jesse E. Davis		Non	Ella S. Davis	5875	Cr
Minor Creek Census Card No. 315, P. O. Sapulpa, Date of Birth January 20, 1906											
284	1	Helton, George Thomas	1	M	1/2	William Helton		Non	Nellie Helton	663	Cr
Minor Creek Census Card No. 316, P. O. Bristow, Date of Birth February 16, 1906											
285	1	Williams, Ada	1	F	1/4	Samuel B. Williams		Non	Rena Williams	3910	Cr
Minor Creek Census Card No. 317, P. O. Kellyville, Date of Birth September 20, 1905											
286	1	Barnett, Jackson	1	M	F	Pompey Barnett	288	Cr	Babie Barnett	1298	Cr
Minor Creek Census Card No. 319, P. O. Bristow, Date of Birth February 17, 1906											
287	1	Mosquito, Ira	1	M	F	Albert Mosquito	1906	Cr	Polly Mosquito	1967	Cr
Minor Creek Census Card No. 320, P. O. Wetumka, Date of Birth July 31, 1904											
288	1	Harjo, Freeda	1	F	F	Stephen Harjo	8939	Cr	Kogee Harjo	8939	Cr
Minor Creek Census Card No. 321, P. O. Tulsa, Date of Birth February 22, 1906											
289	1	Woodward, James H.	1	M	1/4	H. E. Woodward		Non	Nellie E. Woodward	2213	Cr
Minor Creek Census Card No. 322, P. O. Burney, Date of Birth September 1, 1905											
290	1	Broadnax, Bessie	1	F	3/4	James Broadnax		Non	Nannie Broadnax	3426	Cr
Minor Creek Census Card No. 323, P. O. Okmulgee, Date of Birth December 2, 1905											
291	1	Berryhill, George	1	M	7/8	Alec Berryhill	130	Cr	Annie Berryhill	131	Cr
Minor Creek Census Card No. 324, P. O. Olive, Date of Birth November 23, 1905											
292	1	Tiger, Oda	1	M	F	Jumbo Tiger	6663	Cr	So-con-tha-ny Tiger	6705	Cr
Minor Creek Census Card No. 325, P. O. Jenks, Date of Birth September 14, 1905											
293	1	Parks, Rosetta	1	F	1-16	William Parks		No	Margaret Atkins Parks	9805	Cr
Minor Census Card No. 326, P. O. Kellyville, Date of Birth August 14, 1905											
294	1	Littlehead, Joe	1	M	F	Willie Littlehead	7985	Cr	Nannie Littlehead	7959	Cr
Minor Creek Census Card No. 327, P. O. Kellyville, Date of Birth January 2, 1905											
295	1	Yellowhead, Samuel	1	M	F	Fulsom Yellowhead	3272	Cr	Tahcowee Yellowhead	3273	Cr
Minor Creek Census Card No. 328, P. O. Sapulpa, Date of Birth January 24, 1906											
296	1	Weaver, Thelma	1	F	1-16	Bert W. Weaver		Non	Rena Weaver	9223	Cr
Minor Creek Census Card No. 329, P. O. Sapulpa, Date of Birth February 23, 1906											
297	1	Lee, Robert E.	1	M	F	Gano Lee	1701	Cr	Sissie Lee	5389	Cr
Minor Creek Census Card No. 330, P. O. Sapulpa, Date of Birth September 28, 1905											
298	1	Tate, Jesse	1	M	1/8	J. W. Tate		Non	Mary Tate	9872	Cr
Minor Creek Census Card No. 331, P. O. Wybark, Date of Birth February 11, 1902											
299	1	Rogers, Legus	4	M	1/4	John Rogers		Non	Melvina Rogers	5947	Cr
Minor Creek Census Card No. 333, P. O. Beggs, Date of Birth November 25, 1905											
300	1	Stake, Louisa	1	F	F	Albert Stake	1414	Cr	Sallie Stake	1415	Cr
Minor Creek Census Card No. 334, P. O. Okmulgee, Date of Birth March 1, 1906											
301	1	Davis, Addie	1	F	F	Alex Davis	90	Cr	Lucy Davis	110	Cr

Roll No.	No.	NAME	Age	Sex	Blood	NAME OF FATHER	Roll No.	Cit.	NAME OF MOTHER	Roll No.	Cit.
		Minor Creek Census Card No. 335, P. O. Cathay, Date of Birth October 31, 1905									
302	1	Doyle, Seabron	1	M	1/8	Seaborn J. Doyle	989	Cr	Dell Doyle		Non
		Minor Creek Census Card No. 337, P. O. Redfork, Date of Birth June 1, 1905									
303	1	Perryman, Sarah Ann	1	F	1/4	Cornelius B.-Perryman	2245	Cr	Rosalie Perryman		Non
		Minor Creek Census Card No. 338, P. O. Lawton, Date of Birth January 8, 1906									
304	1	Tilley, John Willis	1	M	1/2	James Tilley	Non		Annie Tilley	4080	Cr
		Minor Creek Census Card No. 339, P. O. Okfuskee, Date of Birth December 15, 1905									
305	1	Yarhola, Nellie	1	F	F	Elon Yarhola	4225	Cr	Millie Yarhola	4223	Cr
		Miner Creek Census Card No. 340, P. O. Little, Date of Birth April 4, 1905									
306	1	Fife, Dixon	1	M	5/8	Louis M. Fife	Non		Jeanetta Fife	8789	Cr
		Minor Creek Census Card No. 347, P. O. Wetumka, Date of Birth April 30, 1901									
307	1	Lucas, Delphine	4	F	1/2	John F. Lucas	Non		Sallie Lucas	6567	Cr
		Minor Creek Census Card No. 351, P. O. Wagoner, Date of Birth January 8, 1906									
308	1	Brady, William Penn	1	M	1/4	Sam R. Brady	9193	Cr	Jullah Brady	1768	Cr
		Minor Creek Census Card No. 354, P. O. Mounds, Date of Birth April 17, 1905									
309	1	Bittle, Mary Marina	1	F	1-16	Jacob Bittle	3146	Cr	Arminda Bittle		Non
		Minor Creek Census Card No. 356, P. O. Kellyville, Date of Birth February 15, 1906									
310	1	Snow, John	1	M	F	Ca-pah-ny Snow	6648	Cr	FarloconweneySnow	8103	Cr
		Minor Creek Census Card No. 357, P. O. Bixby, Date of Birth March 20, 1905									
311	1	Bruner, Reuben	1	M	1/4	Pinkey Bruner	2009	Cr	Georgia Bruner		Non
		Minor Creek Census Card No. 358, P. O. Bristow, Date of Birth March 11, 1905									
312	1	Hamilton, Mahala	1	F	5-16	Peter Hamilton	2748	Cr	Ellen Hamilton		Non
		Minor Creek Census Card No. 360, P. O. Mounds, Date of Birth October 26, 1905									
313	1	Barber, Gertie May	1	F	1-16	John W. Barber	3414	Cr	Cora Barber		Non
		Minor Creek Census Card No. 361, P. O. Tulsa, Date of Birth February 16, 1906									
314	1	Harris, Naoma	1	F	1-16	Cleveland Harris	Non		Elva Harris	9739	Cr
		Minor Creek Census Card No. 362, P. O. Okfuskee, Date of Birth February 1, 1906									
315	1	Knight, Jessie	1	M	F	London Knight	538	Cr	Susan Knight	539	Cr
		Minor Creek Census Card No. 363, P. O. Kellyville, Date of Birth December 15, 1905									
316	1	Watashe, James	1	M	F	Wa-ta-she	6884	Cr	Rosa Wa-ta-she	6885	Cr
		Minor Creek Census Card No. 364, P. O. Morse, Date of Borth November 26, 1905									
317	1	Stoddard, Stella	1	F	F	William Stoddard	2858	Cr	Lousanna Stoddard	2859	Cr
		Minor Creek Census Card No. 365, P. O. Kellyville, Date of Birth December 24, 1905									
318	1	Fulsom, Wiley	1	M	F	Willie Fulsom	7287	Cr	Sallie Fulsom	1964	Cr
						Died August 1, 1906					
		Minor Creek Census Card No. 366, P. O. Red Fork, Date of Birth January 25, 1906									
319	1	Smith, Violet Elizabeth	1	F	1-16	Enoch O. Smith	Non		Janie Smith	2560	Cr
		Minor Creek Census Card No. 371, P. O. Castle, Date of Birth No. 1 March 30, 1902; No.2 December 15, 1905									
320	1	Bear, Washbarney	1	M	F	Washington Bear	9177	Cr	Monny Bear	6768	Cr
321	2	Bear, Josie	1	M	F	Washington Bear	9177	Cr	Monny Bear	6768	Cr
		Minor Creek Census Card No. 376, P. O. Welty, Date of Birth January 19, 1906									
322	1	West, Nora	1	F	F	Siker West	4116	Cr	Annie West	4103	Cr
		Minor Creek Census Card No. 377, P. O. Henryetta, Date of Birth July 18, 1905									
323	1	King, Pearl Leverh	1	F	1/2	Wm. King	Non		Elizabeth King	5998	Cr
		Minor Creek Census Card No. 379, P. O. Wetumka, Date of Birth April 15, 1904									
324	1	Scott, Lola	1	F	F	William Scott	6387	Cr	Mahoye Scott	6388	Cr
		Minor Creek Census Card No. 381, P. O. Broken Arrow, Date of Birth December 24, 1905									
325	1	Boles, Wilmer Burns	1	M	1-16	Charles Boles	Non		Mattie Boles	1332	Cr
		Minor Creek Census Card No. 385, P. O. Mounds, Date of Birth February 8, 1906									
326	1	Colmon, Georgia Evelean	1	F	1-16	William E. Colman	Non		Nettie G. Colman	6746	Cr
		Minor Creek Census Card No. 390, P. O. Broken Arrow, Date of Birth February 22, 1906									
327	1	Cooper, Pleasant Porter	1	M	1/2	Ezra E. Cooper	Non		Annie Cooper	931	Cr
		Minor Creek Census Card No. 392, P. O. Checotah, Date of Birth April 7, 1903									
328	1	Collins, Mattie	2	F	F	Willie Collins	6395	Cr	Addie Collins	6346	Cr
		Minor Creek Census Card No. 393, P. O. Hitchita, Date of Birth October 13, 1905									
329	1	Kernells, Minnie	1	F	F	Temiye Kernells	331	Cr	Sissie Kernells	332	Cr
		Minor Creek Census Card No. 396, P. O. Tuscon, Ariz. (Muskogee), Date of Birth May 18, 1905									
330	1	Meagher, Katherine Frances	1	F	1/8	Thomas F. Meagher, Jr.	7	Cr	Francis Mitchell Meagher		Non
		Minor Creek Census Card No. 397, P. O. Holdenville, Date of Birth March 4, 1905									
331	1	Sewel, Louisa	1	F	F	Thomas Sewel	3812	Cr	Lena Sewel	5500	Cr
		Minor Creek Census Card No. 398, P. O. Porter, Date of Birth February 7, 1906									
332	1	Marshall, Mamie	1	F	3/8	Lewis Marshall	415	Cr	Amanda Marshall		Non
		Minor Creek Census Card No. 399, P. O. Oktaha, Date of Birth December 8, 1905									
333	1	Simmons, Lena	1	F	9-16	Charley Simmons	382	Cr	Dora Simmons	3630	Cr
		Minor Creek Census Card No. 403, P. O. Carson, Date of Birth September 20, 1905									
334	1	Bruner, Lucinda	1	F	7/8	Robertson Bruner	7371	Cr	Louisa Bruner	5260	Cr
		Minor Creek Census Card No. 410, P. O. Las Animas, Cal., Date of Birth October 6, 1905									
335	1	Wallace, Laura C.	1	F	1/4	William A. Wallace	Non		Ella Wallace	3114	Cr
		Minor Creek Census Card No. 411, P. O. Okemah, Date of Birth January 4, 1906									
336	1	Hall, Cleo C.	1	M	3/4	Samuel Hall	Non		Hannah E. Hall	4112	Cr
		Minor Creek Census Card No. 417, P. O. Wagoner, Date of Birth January 14, 1906									
337	1	White, Raymond	1	M	F	Sam Perryman	2793	Cr	Millisa White	1154	Cr
						Illegitimate					
		Minor Creek Census Card No. 432, P. O. Sharp, Date of Birth March 4, 1905									
338	1	Pinky, Lizzie	1	F	4/5	Willie Pinkey	3724	Cr	Lilia Pinkey	3709	Cr
		Minor Creek Census Card No. 446, P. O. Raiford, Date of Birth December 12, 1905									
339	1	Tarloshaw, Mista	1	M	F	Tarloshaw	7952	Cr	Sally Tarloshaw	8741	Cr

Roll No.	No.	NAME	Age	Sex	Blood	NAME OF FATHER	Roll No.	Cit.	NAME OF MOTHER	Roll No.	Cit.
		Minor Creek Census Card No. 461, P. O. Salem, Date of Birth February 7, 1906									
340	1	Scott, Adam	1	M	F	George Scott	8472	Cr	Mannie Scott	1272	Cr
		Minor Creek Census Card No. 467, P. O. Mellette, Date of Birth December 24, 1905									
341	1	Hall, Sunnie	1	M	⅜	Unknown			Nora Hall	8369	Cr
		Illegitimate									
		Minor Creek Census Card No· 471, P· O· Mellette, Date of Birth No. 1 July 28, 1897; No. 2 April 2, 1905									
342	1	Starr, Walter	8	M	F	Chipley Starr	6551	Cr	Hannah Roberts	7754	Cr
343	2	Roberts, Annie	1	F	F	Noah Roberts	7753	Cr	Hannah Roberts	7754	Cr
		Chipley Starr died in 1902									
		Minor Creek Census Card No. 472, P. O. Lenna, Date of Birth December 20, 1905									
344	1	Wa-co-che, Jane	1	F	F	Johnson Wa-co-che	9046	Cr	Lizzie Wa-co-che	1359	Cr
		Minor Creek Census Card No. 473, P. O. Stidham, Date of Birth June 13, 1905									
345	1	Loney, Ellen	1	F	F	Sam Loney	8564	Cr	Rachael Long	1338	Cr
		Minor Creek Census Card No. 485, P. O. Calvin, Date of Birth January 8, 1906									
346	1	Hellet, Aman	1	M	F	Sam Hellet	8326	Cr	Sarah Herrod	6857	Cr
		Minor Creek Census Card No. 489, P. O. Eufaula, Date of Birth No. 1 March 15, 1899; No. 2 February 22, 1901									
347	1	Sarwanoke, Turner	7	M	F	Mitchell Sarwanoke	8707	Cr	Nancy Sarwanoke	8708	Cr
348	2	Sarwanoke, Bessie	5	M?	F	Mitchell Sarwanoke	8707	Cr	Nancy Sarwanoke	8708	Cr
		Minor Creek Census Card No. 490, P. O. Eufaula, Date of Birth No. 1 February 19, 1906; No. 2 March 3, 1898; No. 3 May 3, 1901									
349	1	Mitchell, Hettie	10	F	F	Lewis Mitchell	8481	Cr	Bittle Mitchell	8482	Cr
350	2	Mitchell, Firsey	2	F	F	Lewis Mitchell	8481	Cr	Bittle Mitchell	8482	Cr
351	3	Mitchell, Selanie	5	F	F	Lewis Mitchell	8481	Cr	Bittie Mitchell	8482	Cr
		Minor Creek Census Card No. 491, P. O. Hanna, Date of Birth November 17, 1901									
352	1	Hill, Sallie	4	F	F	John Hill	8319	Cr	Melindy Hill	8749	Cr
		Minor Creek Census Card No. 9, P. O. Checotah, Date of Birth June 27, 1905									
353	1	Escoe, Lindsey	1	M	⅛	Charlie J. Escoe	908	Cr	Dora Escoe		Non
		Minor Creek Census Card No. 110, P. O. Broken Arrow, Date of Birth February 26, 1906									
354	1	Childers, Eloise	1	F	⅞	Daniel Childers	2708	Cr	Mildred Childers	2709	Cr
		Minor Creek Census Card No. 119, P. O. Dustin, Date of Birth August 14, 1905									
355	1	Evans, Alva Arizona	1	F	1-16	Charlie Evans	3628	Cr	Mary J. Evans		Non
		Minor Creek Census Card No. 156, Oktaha, Date of Birth January 20, 1906									
356	1	Hall, Manima	1	F	¼	Sandy Hall	3601	Cr	Martha Hall		Non
		Minor Creek Census Card No. 158, P. O. Henryetta, Date of Birth January 25, 1906									
357	1	Deere, John	1	M	F	Thompson Deere	7626	Cr	Lucy Deere	7789	Cr
		Minor Creek Census Card No. 188, P. O. Sapulpa, Date of Birth March 2, 1906									
358	1	Bridges, Monte Robert	1	M	½	Wade Elmer Bridges		Non	Patty Bruner Bridges	2330	Cr
		Minor Creek Census Card No. 203, P. O. Okemah, Date of Birth January 11, 1906 (Twins)									
359	1	Morrow, Jesse	1	M	½	Alfred Morrow		Non	Marsey Morrow	1264	Cr
360	2	Morrow, Lester	1	M	½	Alfred Morrow		Non	Marsey Morrow	1264	Cr
		Minor Creek Census Card No. 208, P. O. Coweta, Date of Birth July 3, 1905									
361	1	Reed, Robert	1	M	⅞	Jim Reed	2085	Cr	Mary Reed	617	Cr
		Minor Creek Census Card No. 209, P. O. Okmulgee, Date of Birth January 21, 1906									
362	1	Ingley, Gladys G.	1	F	1-16	Columbus F. Ingley	9737	Cr	Grace Ingley		Non
		Minor Creek Census Card No. 210, P. O. Beggs, Date of Birth March 1, 1906									
363	1	Adams, David	1	M	½	George W. Adams	3780	Cr	Sarah Adams	3781	Cr
		Minor Creek Census Card No. 213, P. O. Sapulpa, Date of Birth February 16, 1906									
364	1	Beaver, Sammie B.	1	F	½	Samuel C. Beaver	3551	Cr	Ollie V. Beaver		Non
		Minor Creek Census Card No. 221, P. O. Eufaula, Date of Birth October 15, 1905									
365	1	Deere, Sumsie	1	M	F	Israel Deere	8748	Cr	Lou Annie Deere		Non
		Minor Creek Census Card No. 244, P. O. Holdenville, Date of Birth September 26, 1905									
366	1	Lindsey, Noah	1	M	¾	Walter Lindsey	6460	Cr	Hettie Lindsey		Non
		Minor Creek Census Card No. 257, P. O. Broken Arrow, Date of Birth April 4, 1905									
367	1	Wright, Eugene M.	1	M	1-32	Charles F. Wright	1549	Cr	Sarah A. Wright		Non
		Minor Creek Census Card No. 265, P. O. Tulsa, Date of Birth September 17, 1905									
368	1	Beaver, George Milton	1	M	½	David Beaver	2632	Cr	Buna Beaver		Non
		Minor Creek Census Card No. 274, P. O. Checotah, Date of Birth December 18, 1905									
369	1	Roberson, Joe T.	1	M	½	Henry Roberson		Non	Nancy Roberson	7023	Cr
		Minor Creek Census Card No. 277, P. O. Boley, Date of Birth March 2, 1906									
370	1	Franklin, Polly	1	F	1-16	Frank Franklin	6338	Cr	Annie Franklin		Non
		Minor Creek Census Card No. 299, P. O. Okfuskee, Date of Birth September 4, 1905									
371	1	Yarhola, Mary	1	F	F	Nocus Yarhola	4213	Cr	Helen Yarhola		Non
		Minor Creek Census Card No. 309, P. O. Wetumka, Date of Birth No. 1, January 5, 1902; No. 2, May 3, 1905									
372	1	Scott, Lizzie	4	F	F	Wiley Scott	6454	Cr	Rosanna Scott	6455	Cr
373	2	Scott, Lelia	1	F	F	Wiley Scott	6454	Cr	Rosanna Scott	6455	Cr
		Minor Creek Census Card No. 312, P. O. Catoosa, Date of Birth No. 1, Decmeber 19, 1901; No. 2, February 22, 1905									
374	1	Taborn, Albert	4	M	1-16	Calvin Taborn		Non	Nancy Atkins Taborn	10085	Cr
375	2	Taborn, Gertrude	1	F	1-16	Calvin Taborn		Non	Nancy Atkins Taborn	10085	Cr
		Minor Creek Census Card No. 343,, P. O. Wentworth, Mo. Date of Birth February 15, 1906									
376	1	Inman, Naomi	1	F	½	Clifton Inman		Non	Cora Inman	1291	Cr
		Minor Creek Census Card No. 352, P. O. Newby, Date of Birth February 19, 1906									
377	1	Long, Ahlacoganay	1	M	F	Lewis Long	8109	Cr	Lannie Long	8110	Cr
		Minor Creek Census Card No. 353, P. O. Eufaula, Date of Birth September 28, 1905									
378	1	Nero, Samuel	1	M	17-32	Governor Nero	7026	Cr	Mary Nero	8709	Cr

269

Roll No.	No.	NAME	Age	Sex	Blood	NAME OF FATHER	Roll No.	Cit.	NAME OF MOTHER	Roll No.	Cit.

Minor Creek Census Card No. 359, P. O. Ft. Smith. Ark., Date of Birth March 4, 1905

| 379 | 1 | Rowley, Henry Stevens | 1 | M | ¼ | Charles Rowley | 980 | Cr | Anna Rowley | | No. |

Minor Creek Census Card No. 372, P. O. Bryant, Date of Birth February 24, 1906

| 380 | 1 | Fisher, Elsie | 1 | F | ½ | Seaborn Fisher | 4517 | Cr | Rosie Fisher | | (|

Minor Creek Census Card No. 375, P. O. Depew, Date of Birth September 9, 1905

| 381 | 1 | Grayson, Roosevelt | 1 | F | ⅛ | Willie Grayson | 1190 | Cr | Nancie Grayson | | No. |

Minor Creek Census Card No. 380, P. O. Weer, Date of Birth March 18, 1905

| 382 | 1 | Simmons, Sadie | 1 | F | F | Charley Simmons | 5564 | Cr | Nancy Simmons | 1457 | C |

Minor Creek Census Card No. 382, P. O. Senora, Date of Birth May 27, 1905

| 383 | 1 | Smith, Ruth | 1 | F | 5-16 | John Smith | 5990 | Cr | Tillie May Smith | | No. |

Minor Creek Census Card No. 383,

384	1	Stricken from roll									
385	2	Stricken from roll									
386	3	Stricken from roll									

Minor Creek Census Card No. 384, P. O. Sapulpa, Date of Birth February 27, 1906

| 387 | 1 | Partridge, Jonas | 1 | M | F | Toby Partridge | 6416 | Cr | Mary Partridge | 6417 | C: |

Minor Creek Census Card No. 374, P. O. Grayson, Date of Birth March 2, 1906

| 388 | 1 | Smith, Margaret Ellen | 1 | F | ⅛ | Thomas M. Smith | 3104 | Cr | Adeline Smith | | Nor |

Minor Creek Census Card No. 391, P. O. Stidham, Date of Birth March 4, 1906

| 389 | 1 | Moore, Elizza | 1 | F | ½ | Albert Moore | 1867 | Cr | Leah Moore | 1868 | C: |

Minor Creek Census Card No. 394, P. O. Holdenville, Date of Birth September 10, 1904

| 390 | 1 | King, George | 1 | M | F | Peter King | 5280 | Cr | Lizzie King | 5449 | Cr |

Minor Creek Census Card No. 395, P. O. Okemah, Date of Birth April 14, 1905

| 391 | 1 | Knight, Iola | 1 | F | F | Fuller Knight | 5991 | Cr | Lucy Knight | 6761 | Cr |

Minor Creek Census Card No. 400, P. O. Quitman, Texas, Date of Birth May 5, 1905

| 392 | 1 | Leath, Muskogee | 1 | F | 1-64 | John Henry Leath | 1998 | Cr | Daisy Leath | | Non |

Minor Creek Census Card No. 401, P. O. Weleetka, Date of Birth May 20, 1901

| 393 | 1 | Thompson, Martha | 4 | F | F | Little Thompson | 8937 | Cr | Leah Thompson | 9348 | Cr |

Minor Creek Census Card No. 404, P. O. Haskell, Date of Birth January 18, 1906

| 394 | 1 | Isaac John | 1 | F | ½ | Leland Davis | Non | | Lena Isaac | 2420 | Cr |
| | | Illegitimate | | | | | | | | | |

Minor Creek Census Card No. 413, P. O. Morse, Date of Birth March 18, 1905

| 395 | 1 | Chupco, Maxey | 1 | M | F | Bamoche Chupco | 730 | Cr | Lucy Chupco | 4044 | Cr |

Minor Creek Census Card No. 415, P. O. Stidham, Date of Birth August 8, 1905

| 396 | 1 | Moore, Winnie Mary | 1 | F | 1-16 | Thomas J. Moore | 4245 | Cr | Matilda Moore | | Non |

Minor Creek Census Card No. 416, P. O. Senora, Date of Birth July 13, 1905

| 397 | 1 | McNac, Katie | 1 | F | ⅝ | Phillip McNac | 7123 | Cr | Wisey McNac | 511 | Cr |

Minor Creek Census Card No. 418, P. O. Beggs, Date of Birth March 2, 1906

| 398 | 1 | Nash, Ora | 1 | M | ¼ | Frank Nash | Non | | Jennie Nash | 5582 | Cr |

Minor Creek Census Card No. 424, P. O. Wetumka, Date of Birth October 29, 1905

| 399 | 1 | Johnson, Sissie | 1 | F | F | Cooper Johnson | 8933 | Cr | Judy Johnson | 8934 | Cr |

Minor Creek Census Card No. 425, P. O. Eufaula, Date of Birth July 1905

| 400 | 1 | Tiger, Lindy | 1 | F | F | Chotky Tiger | 1547 | Sem | Lucy Deere | 9155 | Cr |

Minor Creek Census Card No. 426, P. O. Okmulgee, Date of Birth August 16, 1902

| 401 | 1 | Atkins, John | 3 | M | 1-16 | Nathaniel Atkins | 9808 | Cr | Callie Atkins | | Non |
| | | Died September 16, 1906 | | | | | | | | | |

Minor Creek Census Card No. 427, P. O. Muskogee, Date of Birth April 13, 1905

| 402 | 1 | Wiley, Virginia Dorothy | 1 | F | ½ | Walter Wiley | 904 | Cr | Hattie Wiley | | Non |

Minor Creek Census Card No. 434, P. O. Weleetka, Date of Birth June 1905

| 403 | 1 | West, Eliza | 1 | F | F | Billy West | 4525 | Cr | Louisa West | 4526 | Cr |

Minor Creek Census Card No. 439, P. O. Carson, Date of Birth October 10, 1905

| 404 | 1 | Lott, Addie | 1 | F | F | Thomas Lott | 7379 | Cr | Lena Lott | 7380 | Cr |

Minor Creek Census Card No. 441, P. O. Dustin, Date of Birth December 6, 1905

| 405 | 1 | Field, Butler | 1 | M | F | Harper Field | 7067 | Cr | Marfe Field | 8129 | Cr |

Minor Creek Census Card No. 442, P. O. Hanna, Date of Birth June 9, 1905

| 406 | 1 | Simmons, Ida | 1 | F | F | Sandy Simmons | 8174 | Cr | Sallie Simmons | 7878 | Cr |

Minor Creek Census Card No. 445, P. O. Raiford, Date of Birth February 26, 1906

| 407 | 1 | Field, Sunday | 1 | M | F | Washington Field | 9352 | Cr | Lydia Field | 8079 | Cr |

Minor Creek Census Card No. 449, P. O. Trenton, Date of Birth June 6, 1905

| 408 | 1 | Smith, Martin | 1 | M | F | Mickey Smith | 7526 | Cr | Millie Smith | 8414 | Cr |
| | | Died October 17, 1906 | | | | | | | | | |

Minor Creek Census Card No. 453, P. O. Trenton, Date of Birth September 17, 1905

| 409 | 1 | Tiger, Toche | 1 | F | F | Amos Tiger | 7945 | Cr | Lena Tiger | 7262 | Cr |
| | | Died September 11, 1906 | | | | | | | | | |

Minor Creek Census Card No. 454, P. O. Weleetka, Date of Birth No. 1, July 3, 1905; No. 2, August 17, 1902

| 410 | 1 | Lasley, Sallie | 1 | F | F | Colbert Lasley | 5133 | Cr | Winey Lasley | 5134 | Cr |
| 411 | 2 | Lasley, Jackson | 3 | M | F | Colbert Lasley | 5133 | Cr | Winey Lasley | 5134 | Cr |

Minor Creek Census Card No. 460, P. O. Senora, Date of Birth January 18, 1900

| 412 | 1 | Talomase, Emma | 6 | F | F | Dickey Talomase | 7811 | Cr | Eliza Talomase | 7812 | Cr |

Minor Creek Census Card No. 481, P. O. Okmulgee, Date of Birth November 16, 1905

| 413 | 1 | Lowe, Albert Chastain | 1 | M | ⅜ | Martin Chastain | Non | | Susie Lowe | 1196 | Cr |
| | | Illegitimate | | | | | | | | | |

Minor Creek Census Card No. 484, P. O. Calvin, Date of Birth July 3, 1902

| 414 | 1 | Bruner, Susie | 3 | F | F | Willie Bruner | 7530 | Cr | Addie Bruner | 7531 | Cr |

Minor Creek Census Card No. 488, P. O. Hoffman, Date of Birth November 17, 1905

| 415 | 1 | Lovett, Loran Alfred | 1 | M | ⅞ | John J. Lovett | Non | | Matilda Lovett | 1472 | Cr |

Minor Creek Census Card No. 493, P. O. Wetumka, Date of Birth November 2, 1901

| 416 | 1 | Brooks, Nola | 2 | F | F | Joe Brooks | 7770 | Cr | Annie Brooks | 7771 | Cr |

270

Roll No.	No.	NAME	Age	Sex	Blood	NAME OF FATHER	Roll No.	Cit.	NAME OF MOTHER	Roll No.	Cit

Minor Creek Census Card No. 495, P. O. Holdenville, Date of Birth No. 1, June 30, 1905; No. 2, March 11, 1904

Roll No.	No.	NAME	Age	Sex	Blood	NAME OF FATHER	Roll No.	Cit.	NAME OF MOTHER	Roll No.	Cit
417	1	Harjo, Alva	6	M	F	Jimsey Harjo	5553	Cr	Mikey Tiger	5556	Cr
418	2	Harjo, Minnie	2	F	F	Jimsey Harjo	5553	Cr	Mikey Tiger	5556	Cr

Nos. 1 and 2 Illegitimate

Minor Creek Census Card No. 496, P. O. Hazel, Date of Birth July, 1905

419	1	Church, Bettie	1	F	F	Sam Church		Non	Sallie Church	8601	Cr

Minor Creek Census Card No. 499, P. O. Trenton, Date of Birth February 1899

420	1	Tuffer, Hettie	7	F	F	Tuffer	8169	Cr	Sena Tuffer	8170	Cr

Minor Creek Census Card No. 500, P. O. Bryant, Date of Birth February 1901

421	1	Wildcat, Rhoda	5	F	F	Sandy Wildcat	5072	Cr	Losanna Wildcat	5073	Cr

Minor Creek Census Card No. 501, P. O. Holdenville, Date of Birth February 9, 1901

422	1	Byrd, Billie	5	M	F	Thomas Byrd	7876	Cr	Sallie Simmons	7878	Cr

Minor Creek Census Card No. 502, P. O. Weleetka, Date of Birth February 1901

423	1	Baker, John	5	M	F	Sandy Baker	5064	Cr	Sanie (or Billy)		

Minor Creek Census Card No. 503, P. O. Mellette, Date of Birth No. 1, November 26, 1898; No. 2, June 5, 1902

424	1	Sullivan, Emma	7	F	3/4	William Sullivan	7622	Cr	Hagey Sullivan		Non
425	2	Sullivan, John	3	M	3/4	William Sullivan	7622	Cr	Hagey Sullivan		Non

Minor Creek Census Card No. 129, P. O. Okemah, Date of Birth February 27, 1906

426	1	Thompson, Simon Pearcy	1	M	1/8	Simon Thompson		Non	Virona Thompson	5737	Cr

Minor Creek Census Card No. 136, P. O. Senora, Date of Birth May 4, 1905

427	1	Davis, Leona	1	F	1/2	Ely Davis	8977	Cr	Bessie Davis		Non

Minor Creek Census Card No. 159, P. O. Boynton, Date of Birth March 2, 1906

428	1	McNac, Hallie	1	F	1/4	Robinson McNac	4577	Cr-F	Emma McNac	486	Cr

Minor Creek Census Card No. 212, P. O. Coweta, Date of Birth May 14, 1905

429	1	Sarty, Lena	1	F	3/4	Jasper Sarty	831	Cr	Retta Sarty	640	Cr

Minor Creek Census Card No. 281, P. O. Wewoka, Date of Birth March 22, 1905

430	1	Bell, Jimmie	1	M	F	Josie Bell		Non	Lizzie Bell	22	Cr

Minor Creek Census Card No. 311, P. O. Checotah, Date of Birth June 1905

431	1	Richard, Lesslie	1	M	F	Jasper Richard	2671	Cr	Minnie Richard	2672	Cr

Minor Creek Census Card No. 318, P. O. Sapulpa, Date of Birth June 22, 1905

432	1	Pitman, Edith Lucinda	1	F	1/2	Robert Pitman		Non	Lucinda Pitman	1833	Cr

Minor Creek Census Card No. 336, P. O. Yeager, Date of Birth September 14, 1905

433	1	Hallford, Esther	1	F	1-16	M A.. Hallford		Non	Emaline Hallford	3162	Cr

Minor Creek Census Card No. 349, P. O. Tulsa, Date of Birth November 15, 1903

434	1	Owens, Nellie	2	F	1-16	Unknown			Elva Owens	9739	Cr

Illegitimate

Minor Creek Census Card No. 350, P. O. Okmulgee, Date of Birth No. 1, October 14, 1984; No. 2, March 22, 1986; No. 3, March 13, 1898; No. 4, December 13, 1899; No. 5, March 14, 1902; No. 6, April 14, 1904

435	1	Winn, Richard E.	11	M	1-16	Oscar Winn		Non	Geneva Atkins Winn	10084	Cr
436	2	Winn, Henry O.	9	M	1-16	Oscar Winn		Non	Geneva Atkins Winn	10084	Cr
437	3	Winn, Tabbie	7	F	1-16	Oscar Winn		Non	Geneva Atkins Winn	10084	Cr
438	4	Winn, Prebble	6	F	1-16	Oscar Winn		Non	Geneva Atkins Winn	10084	Cr
439	5	Winn, Valley	3	F	1-16	Oscar Winn		Non	Geneva Atkins Winn	10084	Cr
440	6	Winn, Urceil	1	F	1-16	Oscar Winn		Non	Geneva Atkins Winn	10084	Cr

Minor Creek Census Card No. 402, P. O. Henryetta, Date of Birth April 1, 1905

441	1	Crawford, Edna	1	F	1/8	Henry Crawford	5888	Cr	Ida Crawford		Non

Minor Creek Census Card No. 433, P. O. Wetumka, Date of Birth April 1, 1904

442	1	Kernal, Lilly	2	F	F	Lewis Kernal	4877	Cr	Lizzie Hill	7168	Cr

Minor Creek Census Card No. 435, P. O. Henryetta, Date of Birth February 20, 1902

443	1	Johnson, Weetsie	4	F	F	Little Tom Johnson	5372	Cr	Ellie Johnson	5373	Cr

Minor Creek Census Card No. 455, P. O. Weleetka, Date of Birth September 18, 1905

444	1	Harjo, Martha	1	F	F	Tarsee Harjo	5024	Cr	Lody Harjo	9386	Cr

Minor Creek Census Card No. 456, P. O. Morse, Date of Birth April 10, 1905

445	1	Taryole, Tupper	1	M	F	Taryole	4188	Cr	Marfy Taryole	4189	Cr

Died August 15, 1906

Minor Creek Census Card No. 457, P. O. Morse, Date of Birth December 14, 1905

446	1	Dan, Consey	1	M	F	Somecher Dan	4248	Cr	Lizzie Dan	4153	Cr

Minor Creek Census Card No. 462, P. O. Senora, Date of Birth February 28, 1906

447	1	McNac, Joseph	1	M	F	Peter McNac	1268	Cr	Lousanna McNac	1269	Cr

Minor Creek Census Card No. 464, P. O. Senora, Date of Birth August 15, 1905

448	1	Starr, Lena	1	F	F	Lewis Starr	7939	Cr	Mahala Starr	8437	Cr

Minor Creek Census Card No. 468, P. O. Okemah, Date of Birth March 2, 1906

449	1	Simmer, Aggie	1	F	F	Charley Simmer	9170	Cr	Kizzie Simmer	9171	Cr

Minor Creek Census Card No. 469, P. O. Castle, Date of Birth No. 1, March 31, 1902; No. 2, April 1, 1903

450	1	Panoske, Lydia	1	F	F	Daniel Panoske	6764	Cr	Melsey Panoske	6765	Cr
451	2	Panoske, Penie	3	M	F	Daniel Panoske	6764	Cr	Melsey Panoske	6765	Cr

No. 1 died September 8, 1906

Minor Creek Census Card No. 470, P. O. Morse, Date of Birth July 10, 1905

452	1	Bullet, Sarne	1	F	F	Solomon Bullet	8663	Cr	Munner Coon	544	Cr

Illegitaimte

Minor Creek Census Card No. 497, P. O. Hazel, Date of Birth June 1901

453	1	Chupco, Tingka	5	M		Echoille Chupco		Non	Mullie Chupco	8598	Cr

Minor Creek Census Card No. 506, P. O. Weleetka, Date of Birth May 25, 1901

454	1	Jacobs, Emma	4	F	F	Charles Jacobs	4585	Cr	Nancy Jacobs	4586	Cr

Minor Creek Census Card No. 507, P. O. Wetumka, Date of Birth August 19, 1901

455	1	Green, Barney	5	M	F	Hagie Green	7727	Cr	Sallie Green	3382	Cr

271

Roll No.	No.	NAME	Age	Sex	Blood	NAME OF FATHER	Roll No.	Cit	NAME OF MOTHER	No.	Cit
	Minor Creek Census Card No. 141, P. O. Oktaha, Date of Birth October 21, 1905										
456	1	Colbert, Albertha	1	F	1/2	George Colbert	3049	Cr-F	C. Bell Colbert		Non
	Minor Creek Census Card No. 164, P. O. Wetumka, Date of Birth December 31, 1905										
457	1	Tiger, William Henry	1	M	1/2	Roley Tiger	6591	Cr	Zoye Tiger		Non
	Minor Creek Census Card No. 259, P. O. Claremore, Date of Birth December 1, 1901										
458	1	Sewell, Willie	4	M	3/8	Thomas Sewell	8871	Cr	Roxie Messing		Non
	Minor Creek Census Card No. 332, P. O. Okmulgee, Date of Birth No. 1, April 15, 1902; No. 2, September 25, 1904										
459	1	March, Edith	4	F	1-32	Willie H. March	10053	Cr	Stella March		Non
460	2	March, William K.	1	M	1-32	Willie H. March	10053	Cr	Stella March		Non
	Minor Creek Census Card No. 341, P. O. Porter, Date of Birth April 25, 1905										
461	1	Clarkston, Jauneta Murrel	1	F	1/8	Alex Clarkston		Non	Maggie J. Clarkston	1569	Cr
	Minor Creek Census Card No. 344, P. O. Wagoner, Date of Birth No. 1, May 1, 1889; No. 2, March 18, 1893; No. 3, February 19, 1896; No. 3, April 7, 1889; No. 5, September 9, 1904										
462	1	Wilson, John Wesley	16	M	1-16	Julius Wilson		Non	Mary E. Wilson	10083	Cr
463	2	Wilson, Hubbard	13	M	1-16	Julius Wilson		Non	Mary E. Wilson	10083	Cr
464	3	Wilson, Howard	10	M	1-16	Julius Wilson		Non	Mary E. Wilson	10083	Cr
465	4	Wilson, Zana	6	F	1-16	Julius Wilson		Non	Mary E. Wilson	10083	Cr
466	5	Wilson, Stephen	1	M	1-16	Julius Wilson		Non	Mary E. Wilson	10083	Cr
	Minor Creek Census Card No. 367, P. O. Okemah, Date of Birth March 17, 1905										
467	1	Tarvin, B. C. Jr.	1	M	1-16	P. F. Tarvin	9098	Cr	Patience Tarvin		Non
	Minor Creek Census Card No. 386, P. O. Okmulgee, Date of Birth September 7, 1905										
468	1	Fife, Andrew	1	M	F	Samuel Fife	1462	Cr	Sarah Fife		Non
	Minor Creek Census Card No. 436, P. O. Bearden, Date of Birth 1905										
469	1	Yahola, Mary	1	F	F	Willie Yahola	8641	Cr	Annie Smith	8352	Cr
	Minor Creek Census Card No. 437, P. O. Paden, Date of Birth 1905										
470	1	Coker, Annie	1	F	1/2	Charley Coker	9371	Cr	Sissie Coker	4634	Cr
	Minor Creek Census Card No. 447, P. O. Hanna, Date of Birth May 10, 1905 (?)										
471	1	Mitchell, Amy	1	F	F	Waitie Mitchell		Non	Mandy Mitchell	7984	Cr
	Minor Creek Census Card No. 458, P. O. Pierce, Date of Birth March 1, 1906										
472	1	Richard, Rina	1	F	1	Eastman Richard	7664	Cr	Yarna Richard	7665	Cr
	Minor Creek Census Card No. 463, P. O. Salem. Date of Birth Prior to March 4, 1906										
473	1	Bird, Lonie	1	F	F	Dick Bird	3740	Cr	Minnie Bird	2051	Cr
	Minor Creek Census Card No. 466, P. O. Senora, Date of Birth Prior to March 4, 1906										
474	1	Emarthla, Jospeh	1	M	F	Sam Emarthla	8488	Cr	Leechie Emarthla	8442	Cr
	Minor Creek Census Card No. 474, P. O. Burney, Date of Bitrh Supposed prior to March 4, 1906										
475	1	Jacobs, Johnny	2	M	F	Sampson Jacobs	7982	Cr	Salina Jones	8025	Cr
		Salina Jones is daughter of Crazy Snake									
	Minor Creek Census Card No. 475, P. O. Lenna, Date of Birth Prior to March 4, 1906										
476	1	Coffee, Winey	1	F	3/4	John Coffee	7763	Cr	Susie Coffee		Non
	Minor Creek Census Card No. 476, P. O. Hanna, Date of Birth Prior to March 4, 1906										
477	1	Okchunpulla	1	M	F	Big Jack	8291	Cr	Bettie	8292	Cr
	Minor Creek Census Card No. 477, P. O. Hanna, Date of Birth Prior to March 4, 1906										
478	1	Gouge, Chunna	1	F	F	Jack Gouge	8498	Cr	Lucinda Gouge	8294	Cr
	Minor Creek Census Card No. 505, P. O. Eufaula, Date of Birth November 20, 1901										
479	1	McFarland, Leah	4	F	1/2	James McFarland		Non	Louisa Tiger	10098	Cr
	Minor Creek Census Card No. 412, P. O. Bearden, Date of Birth June 5, 1905										
480	1	McGertt, Nathan	1	M	F	John McGertt	4888	Cr	India McGertt	17	Cr
	Minor Creek Census Card No. 429, P. O. Brush Hill, Date of Birth February 27, 1906										
481	1	McNac, Lizzie	1	F	1/2	Fred McNac	4811	Cr-F	Annie McNac	494	Cr
	Minor Creek Census Card No. 443, P. O. Morse, Date of Birth February 1905										
482	1	Harjo, Macel	1	F	F	Chenosky	4180	Cr	Nity Harjoche	4346	Cr
		Died in October 1906									
	Minor Creek Census Card No. 450, P. O. Trenton Date of Birth March 4, 1905										
483	1	Barnett, David	1	M	F	William Barnett	7888	Cr	Hallie Barnett	4094	Cr
	Minor Census Card No. 465, P. O. Senora, Date of Birth July 1903										
484	1	Harjo, Lillie	2	F	F	Hillis Harjo	7650	Cr	Mary Harjo	7651	Cr
	Minor CrCensus Cad No. 509, P. O. Henryetta, Date of Birth No. 1, January 5, 1900; No. 2, September 6, 1903; No. 3, July 29, 1904										
485	1	Sloan, Albert	6	M	F	Willie		Non	Maria Harjo	10108	Cr
486	2	Sloan, Lillie	3	F	F	Peter Sloan		Non	Maria Harjo	10108	Cr
487	3	Sloan, Loney	1	M	F	Peter Sloan		Non	Maria Harjo	10108	Cr
	Minor Creek Census Card No. 510, P. O. Barnard, Date of Birth April 5,1 905										
488	1	Deer, Mattie	1	F	F	Barney Deer		Non	Miley Deer	7359	Cr
	Minor Creek Census Card No. 478, P. O. Hanna, Date of Birth No. 1, 1898; No. 2, 1900; No. 3, After May 25, 1901; No. 4, Prior to April 19, 1905										
489	1	Gouge, Pewter	8	M	F	Earnest Gouge	8497	Cr	Nicey Gouge	8293	Cr
490	2	Gouge, Sam	6	M	F	Earnest Gouge	8497	Cr	Nicey Gouge	8293	Cr
491	3	Gouge, Suckcho	4	M	F	Earnest Gouge	8497	Cr	Nicey Gouge	8293	Cr
492	4	Gouge, Casawka	2	M	F	Earnest Gouge	8497	Cr	Nicey Gouge	8293	Cr
	Minor Creek Census Card No. 115, P. O. Tulsa, Date of Birth March 4, 1904										
493	1	Grayson, Nochey	2	M	F	Wiley Grayson	8808	Cr	Toche Grayson		Non
	Minor Creek Census Card No. 428, P. O. Okfuskee, Date of Birth January 6, 1906										
494	1	Micco, Iseral	1	M	F	Henry Micco	4011	Cr	Amanda Micco	4050	Cr
	Minor Creek Census Card No. 688, P. O. Eufaula, Date of Birth March 21, 1905										
495	1	Thomas, Minnie Harris	1	F	3/4	Harley Thomas	9617	Cr	Lydia Thomas	9618	Cr

KEY TO INDEX

The following index includes the names of the father and mother, as well as the name of the enrolled citizen. It is arranged alphabetically, both as to the sir and christian names. We have been very careful in its preparation and have spent months in an effort to make it as complete and useful as possible. We do not expect that it, in connection with the Abstract, will answer all questions in every case. It will however be a very great help to those who will make a proper use of it, and use it in difficult cases in connection with information received outside the record.

Many of the Indians have more than one name. They have their family name, sometimes a school name, which is different and also a bust name. We have knowledge only of the names written on the Census Cards, and such names we have used in our Index, however when we could determine that different spelling of a name stood for the same person we have cross indexed.

In the preparation of the enrollment records different clerks, in the office of the Dawes Commission, took testimony for the record. As the Indian names were pronounced to these clerks, the clerks on hearing the names, and hearing different pronunciations, spelled the names differently, and this different spelling is carried on the cards, in fact, it is common for the same name to appear on the same card twice, and both times under a different spelling. Again, the same name may appear on several cards and the spelling in each case be different. We remember one case where the name of a father was on five cards, and no two instances was the spelling similar, yet we have attempted to overcome this and by our system of cross indexing refer you to all cards where the name of the party you are looking up appears. We realize that we have not been enabled to do this in every case. This would be an impossibility, but we do know that in thousands of cases we have been able to make these citations which will be of great help to you.

In making your investigation of the record you will undoubtedly find many "leads." If you will take these "leads" with the information secured outside of the record, and turn to the index and run them down you will undoubtedly secure that which will make the relationship clear to you. This Abstract and Index is a help and not a cure-all.

We note the following instructions and aids in using the index.

(1) All numbers not prefixed are citations to card numbers and the card numbers are those first following a name, and shows the name on the census card prepared under the Original Creek Agreement. The prefix **NB** refers you to New Born Creek **Roll** Number. The prefix **M** refers you to Minor Creek **Roll** Number. **C. E.** refers you to Congressional Enrollment Creek Census card numbers. Note that the citations to the original cards and to the Congressional Enrollment cards are to **card** numbers, and the New Born and Minor Creek citations are to **roll** numbers. This was necessary because of the fact that the New Born and Minor Creek card numbers were not in order.

(2) If you are cited to a card and on turning to that card do not find the name, do not conclude that the citation is an error. It is not. Why we made the citation we have not stated, but, we have made no citations unless there was some reason for it, or we believed that there was some reason for it. If in such cases you will run down the different names on the card referred to you will undoubtedly see our reason.

(3) Examine the Index under every conceivable spelling that the name may have. It may be indexed under " K " or it may be under " C ". Not only is this true of the first letter but of the entire spelling of the name.

(4) In case of an odd Indian name examine a few names just preceeding the place where you think the name ought to be, and also look at a few of the succeeding names. The name may not be just what you think it is, but you will undoubtedly recognize it if you see it and on turning to the card the information there given will undoubtedly show whether or not you have found the name of the party, or parties, desired.

(5) In making an investigation as to the members of any particular family you have more or less information to start with. Use this information with your Abstract and Index. Make this Abstract and Index valuable to you. It will be so in proportion to your intelligent use of it.

INDEX

Ah fono'ːe, Sayochee, 1260, NB1150.
Ahfonoke, Simmer, 1260, NB1149.
Ahgogethlon, 1898.
Ahgokela, 1935.
Ahgokela, Waittie, 1935.
Ahgothany, 2161.
Ahhalonaney, 3124.
Ah Harjo, 3175.
Ahjola, 2620.
Ahkacofah, 1000.
Ahkate, 417.
Ahkohkee, 2418.
Ahkona, 43, 563.
Ahkonah, Nellie, 43.
Ahkotaney, 400.
Ahlaahcotaney, 2708.
Ahlacohonney, 400, 3939.
Ahlacontay, 2705.
Ahlaconthlaney, 2982.
Ahlaquan, 2252.
Ahlejetchchee, 37.
Ahlikouncona, 566.
Ahpoke, 2800.
Ahmana, 1318.
Ahochtey, 604.
Ahquntha, 233.
Ahrens, A. J. W., 597.
Ahrens, Henry Shaw, 597.
Ahrens, Juliette, 597.
Ahrens, Kate E., 597.
Ahsechage, 1260.
Ahsehe, 3247.
Ahseke, 2351.
Absey, 2984, NB938.
Abtah, 1899.
Ahtaqueney, 2717.
Ahtata, 1057.
Ahtushahola, 1587.
Ahwe, 1004, 1006.
Ahweththla, 1384.
Ajenny, 3073.
Ajubee, 567.
Akans, James, 865.
Akans, Noah, 865.
Aknutana, 569.
Akotaney, 2416.
Aktiachee, 3212.
Akuonko, 563.
Alacuuncona, 571.
Albert, 1670.
Albert, David, 2376.
Albert, Hesahar, 2376.
Albert, Jackson, 2376.
Albert, Prince, 2376.
Albert, Sallie, 2376.
Albert, Watty, 2376.
Albutta, 2824.
Alecher, 2874.
Aleck, 328.
Alex, Elizabeth, 1946, NB556.
Alex, F. G., 1946, NB556.
Alex, Freeland, 1946, NB556.
Alex, H., 1946
Alex, Jacob, NB556.
Alex, Mary, 3879, 3902.
Alex, Susan, 1946.
Alexander, 94, 97, 808, 4014.
Alexander, Alex, 97, 1837, 2237.
Alexander, Arty, 97, 100, NB154.
Alexander, Bettie, NB503.
Alexander, Christie, NB505.

Alexander, Cora, 2012.
Alexander, David, 2237, 3894.
Alexander, G. A., 1602, 1630, 1902, 1903, 1
    2011, 2241.
Alexander, George, 97.
Alexander, George, A., 1602. 1630, 1902, 19
    1904. 2011. 2241.
Alexander, Hannah M., 2241.
Alexander, Hettie, 1902, NB504, NB505.
Alexander, Jacob, NB504.
Alexander, James, 1602. 1837.
Alexander, James H., 2241.
Alexander, John L., 1902, NB504, NB505.
Alexander, Leah, 2012.
Alexander, Lewis, 1602.
Alexander, Lity, 94.
Alexander, Liza, 97.
Alexander, Lizzie, 2237, 2747, 3894, NB410.
Alexander, Loley, 256.
Alexander, Louis, 2012.
Alexander, Lucy, 2012.
Alexander, Martha, 2237, 3811, NB503.
Alexander, Mary, 94, NB154.
Alexander, Mattie G., 1902.
Alexander, Miley, 97, NB1083.
Alexander, Nancy, 97, 100, 1602, 1630, 183
    1902, 1903, 1904, 2011, 224.
    3811, NB154.
Alexander, Nancy Larney, NB444.
Alexander, Nathan, 1902.
Alexander, Reuben, 97.
Alexander, Robert, 3894, 1904, 3811, NB503.
Alexander, Robert L., 1904, 3811, 3894, NB503
Alexander, Roly, 100.
Alexander, Sallie, 2237, 1837.
Alexander, Sally, 1837, 2237.
Alexander, Sealy, 97.
Alexander, Tecumseh, 97.
Alexander, Tisey, 100.
Alexander, Willie, 256.
Algogehney, 1208.
Allen, Abraham, 1062.
Allen, Ada, 1062.
Allen, Annie, 1062.
Allen, Benjamin, T., 541.
Allen, Bill, 1062.
Allen, Cora, 540.
Allen, Cora Lou, NB109.
Allen, Eliza H., 538, 539, 540, 541, 542, 595.
Allen, Ella, 1062.
Allen, Ivey M., 540.
Allen, James, 1062.
Allen, Jess, 92, 1062, 3669, CE4015.
Allen, Jesse, 92, 1062. 3669, CE4015.
Allen, Jesse Will, 3669.
Allen, Joe, 538, 539, 540, 541, 542.
Allen, John W., 540, NB109.
Allen, Joseph, 1062.
Allen, Joseph W., 540.
Allen, Lizzie, 1062, 3669.
Allen, Louina, 1772.
Allen, Louisa, 1062.
Allen, Louvina, 1237.
Allen, Lovnia, 1771.
Allen, Lucinda, 1062, 1062.
Allen, Lular, 92.
Allen, Millard E., NB109.
Allen, Myrtle May, 4010, CE4015.
Allen, Rosette, 4010.
Allen, Roy, 1062.
Allen, Wootsey, CE4015.

Allicky, 1250.
Allinda, 2202.
Allummee, 1820.
Allyah, 2059.
Alpatochee, 2238.
Alwir, Lucy, 7.
Amarthar. Nargusta, 3065, 3080.
Amey, 336, 343, 435, 2205, 2206, 2468, 2696,
    3197, 3198, 3200.
Amoche, 3402.
Amochee, 1792.
Amoge, 3942.
Amos, 1588.
Amster, Susana, 2880.
Amy, 336, 343, 435, 2205, 2206, 2468, 2696, 3197,
    3198, 3200.
Ancil, William, 2244.
Anderson, Alma, 2115.
Anderson, Amos, 1469, NB509.
Anderson, Amy, 229
Anderson, Andrew, 871.
Anderson, Annie, 1469, 2115.
Anderson, Augusta, 3564.
Anderson, Austin, 961.
Anderson, Beatrice, 976.
Anderson, Bennie, NB329, NB330.
Anderson, Bessie, NB329.
Anderson, Betsey, 976, 1225.
Anderson, Billie, 3210, 3530.
Anderson, Geley, 2115, 3210.
Anderson, Charles, 2694, NB350.
Anderson, Charley, 2694, NB350.
Anderson, Cilla, 871.
Anderson, David, 976, 1225.
Anderson, David V., 1225, 976.
Anderson, Earnest, 976.
Anderson, Eliza, 2574, 871, 2878.
Anderson, Ella, 2149, 3530.
Anderson, Emma, 976, 2149, 3564, NB205,
    M247.
Anderson, Emmett A., 976.
Anderson, Geo., 352, 581, 640, 871, 961, 1225.
Anderson, George W., 1225, 352, 581, 961, 640,
    871.
Anderson, Green, 2574.
Anderson, Haley, 1705, 3310.
Anderson, Hannah, 1062.
Anderson, James, 1062, 1059.
Anderson, Jennie, NB509.
Anderson, Jim, 1059, 1062.
Anderson, Leah, 1643.
Anderson, Liza, 871, 2574, 2878.
Anderson, Lizzie, M., 1225.
Anderson, Lottie, 3250.
Anderson, Lucy, 961, 2488.
Anderson, Lydia C., NB205.
Anderson, Martha, 2115, M158, NB350,
    NB1180, M158.
Anderson, Mille, 1797, NB1003.
Anderson, Minnie, 1705.
Anderson, Mose, 2488.
Anderson, Nancy, 352, 581, 961, 1225.
Anderson, Nannie, 640.
Anderson, Narto, 1469.
Anderson, Nellie, 1225.
Anderson, Norman, 3310.
Anderson, Phoebe, 229, 1797, NB1042.
Anderson, Richmond, 2149.
Anderson, Robert, 1225.
Anderson, Ruth, 961.

Anderson, Sam, 1716, 1717, 3310.
Anderson, Sam Clarence, 976.
Anderson, Sampson, 1716.
Anderson, Samuel, 3310, 1716, 1717.
Anderson, Simon, 1469.
Anderson, Soloman, 976, 3564, NB205, M247.
Anderson, Solomon, 976, 3564, NB205, M247
Anderson, Stella Terrasa, M. 247.
Anderson, Susan, 960, 1059, 1062, NB1120.
Anderson, Thomas, 1705, 2878, 3530, 3987,
    1797, 2115, 3210, 3250, 3310.
Anderson, Tifney, 1469.
Anderson, Timmie, 2591.
Anderson, Tom, 1705, 1797, 2115, 3210, 3250,
    3310, 3987, 2878, 3530.
Anderson, Viola, 1716.
Anderson, Viola, NB509.
Anderson, Walter, 871.
Anderson, Wiley, 1643.
Anderson, William, 871, 2149, 2591.
Anderson, Willie, 1717, NB1180.
Anderson, Winey, NB329, NB330.
Anderson, Wisey, NB330.
Andrews, Annie, M183.
Andrews, Minor, M183.
Andy, Cornelius, 1877.
Andy, Lee, 1877.
"Angie," 3337.
Anna, 1403.
Anna, Mollie, 1800.
Anneha, 1328.
Annie, 149, 176, 445, 565, 1247, 1469, 1536,
    2356, 2397, 2495, 2667, 2784, 2947,
    3054, 3303, 3121, 3549, CE4049,
    NB1204.
Annie, Lucy, 3343.
Annie, Millie, 884.
Anoche, 1696, 2598.
Anochee, 1696, 2598.
Ansiel, Albert Robert, NB591.
Ansiel, Arnecie, 807, NB1164.
Ansiel, Charles A., 2041, NB722, NB723.
Ansiel, Charley D., 807.
Ansiel, Charlie, 2041, NB722, NB723.
Ansiel, James F., 648.
Ansiel, Jennie M., 3670.
Ansiel, John G., 1335, NB645.
Ansiel, Lula, NB645.
Ansiel, Mary, NB722, NB723.
Ansiel, Robert L., 2040, 3670, NB591.
Ansiel, Robert Lee, 2040, 3670, NB591.
Ansiel, Robert Leroy, NB723.
Ansiel, Sadie A., 2040, 3670.
Ansiel, Samuel E. O., NB645.
Ansiel, Statie Ann, NB591.
Ansiel, William, 2040, 2041.
Ansiel, William F., NB722.
Ansiel, William W., 2040.
Ansil, Stephen, 428, 648.
Ansil, Will, 807.
Ansill, Daisy, 428.
Ansill, Henry F., NB738.
Ansill, John Lee, 3806.
Ansill, Kate, 428.
Ansill, Roxie, 3806, NB738.
Ansill, Sallie, 428.
Ansill, Samuel E., 428, 3806, NB738.
Ansill, Stephen, 428, 648.
Ansill, Wm. Oscar, 428.
Ansill, Wm. Stephen, 1335.

Anteline, 1462.
Antige, 2769.
A pe cor ney, 2428.
Applegeet, Cora, 3541, NB118.
Applegeet, Cora F., 3541, NB118.
Applegeet, Orvill B., 3541.
Applegeet, W. F., 3541, NB118.
Applegeet. Zelma Fay, NB118.
Appo gey, 3000.
Apueka, Jemima, 62.
Apueka, Micco, 1409, 1423, 1425.
Apueka, Nancy, 62.
Apueka, Nathaniel, 62.
Apueka, Setty, 62.
Apueka, Tooka, 62.
Apueka, William, 62.
Apueka, Willie, 62.
Aquanay, 2428, 400.
Aquanay, Lucy, 2428, 400.
Arabella, 23.
Arbebeeasic, 3792.
Arbeka, Jim, 1992.
Arber, 1503.
Arbifhoge, 2778.
Arbor, Caney, 3623.
Arbor, Fagley, 3623.
Arbor, Henderson, 3623.
Arbor, John, 3623.
Arbuckle, 2950.
Arbuckle, Battle, 2950.
Arbuckle, Betsey, 2950.
Arbuckle, Fanny, 2950.
Arbuckle, Hepsey, 3981.
Arbuckle, Louisa, 2950.
Arbuckle, Millie, 2950.
Arbuckle, Napsey, 2950.
Arbuckle, Salinee, 3981.
Arbuckle, Tommy, 2950.
Arch, Dick, 4024.
Arch, Hokte, 4024.
Arch, John, 4024.
Arch, Sarwike, 4024.
Archibald, Abel, CE4016.
Archibald, Adda, CE4016.
Archibald, Allen, CE4016.
Archibald, Cain, CE4016.
Archibald, Sallie, CE4016.
Archibald, Smedlow, CE4016.
Archola, 1573, 2758.
Archopa, 1174.
Ardodey, 1269.
"Arfulka," 3326.
Arhalokoche, 1970.
Arhalokoche, George, 1970.
Arhalokoche, Lewis, 1970.
Arkalokoche, Maggie, 1970, NB1199.
Arhalokoche, Maxey, 1970.
Arhalokoche, Rosanna, 1970.
Arhalokoche, Sofa, 1970.
Arhalokoche, Winey, 1970.
Arkahneche, 220.
Arkie, 1124.
Arlaquinnay, 957.
Arlie, 1674.
Arlike, 2947.
Arlinda, 2642.
Armarner, 2399.
Arnakke, 2688.
Arnay, 6.
Arnett, Abbie Lee, NB21.

Arnett, Albert W., 803, NB21, NB237.
Arnett, A. W., 803, NB21, NB237.
Arnett, Fred, 803.
Arnett, Iola, NB237.
Arnett, Iona, 803.
Arnett, Maggie, 803, NB21, NB237.
Arnicha, 1355.
Arnie, 2368.
Arnogee, 3161.
Arpincinlike, 2630.
Arpinculikee, 2125.
Arpoika, George, 2470, NB1175.
Arpoika, Meka, 2470.
Arpoika, Sissie, 2470, NB1175.
Arpoika, William, NB1175.
Arpueka, Louisa, 62.
Arpueka, Una, 62.
Arsamarhe, 1249.
Arsehme, 1569.
Arshotopehe, 2568.
Arsluthlecha, 441.
Arsoyakee, Lovina, 2338, NB1191.
Arssee, 2892.
Arssee, Albert, 2892.
Arstohartar, 1550.
Artarkinnay, 2713.
Artie, 3367.
Artochee, 144.
Artus, Hopaye, 3233.
Artusbahe, 2337.
Artusse, Annie, 626, NB1123.
Artusse, John, 1155, NB1123.
Artusse, Mose, NB1123.
Artussee, Mary, 2233.
Arwolichee, 1592.
Ary, Ann, 2706, 637, 770, 771, 772, 844, 1129.
Asbell, Art, 1338.
Asbell, Emma, 1338.
Asbell, Glen, 1338.
Asbell, Sarah, 1338, 2055, 1749, 1748.
Asbell, S. C., 2055.
Asbell, Wallace, 1338.
Asbill, Brina, 1748.
Asbill, Edna, 1748.
Asbill, Samuel, 1748.
Asbill, Sarah, 1749, 1338, 2055, 1748.
Asbill, Sarah A., 1748, 1749, 1338, 2055.
Asbury, Anderson, 448.
Asbury, Coody, 635.
Asbury, Cooty, 343.
Asbury, Cooweescoowee, CE4017.
Asbury, Daniel, 343.
Asbury, Eliza, 343, NB361, NB693.
Asbury, Francis, 343, NB365.
Asbury, George, 1397, NB361.
Asbury, George T., 1397, NB361.
Asbury, Jack, 1987.
Asbury, James, 1397.
Asbury, Jennetta, 343, NB365.
Asbury, Jim, 1987, 2544, 2546, 2547, 3109.
Asbury, John, 2546.
Asbury, Joseph, NB174, NB693.
Asbury, Josephine, 1397, NB978.
Asbury, Josiah, 1397, 1450.
Asbury, Joshua, 1397, NB174.
Asbury, Katie, 343.
Asbury, Lizzie, 1397.
Asbury, Louina, 32.
Asbury, Lucy, 32, NB1079, M301.
Asbury, Mary, 1397, 2546, 2544, 3889, NB960.

278

Asbury, Miley, 1397.
Asbury, Moses, 32, 1061.
Asbury, Nancy, 2547, NB174.
Asbury, Nicey, 32, 1061.
Asbury, Polly, 1987.
Asbury, Rhoda, 32.
Asbury, Rosie, 1397.
Asbury, Sarah, NB361, NB362.
Asbury, Siah E., 1397.
Asbury, Sippie, NB365.
Asbury, Thomas, 448, 1061, 2547, CE4017, NB693.
Asbury, Vicey, 2544.
Asbury, Wesley, 3109.
Asbury, Wisey, 1987.
Ashley, Adolphus K., 54.
Ashley, Amanda S., 54, NB209.
Ashley, Daniel, 54.
Askley, Emma, 51.
Ashley, George S., 54.
Ashley, Hettie E., 54, NB63, NB64.
Ashley, Isabel Jane, 54, 341.
Ashley, J. R., 54, 341.
Ashley, James T., 54.
Ashley, John R., 54, 341.
Ashutebgee, 2702.
Asoyaleer, Lovina, 2338. NB1191.
Atarthle, 1675.
Atkin, Thomas, 585.
Atkins, Alice, 1101, 3493, NB502.
Atkins, Anderson, 248.
Atkins, Annanias A., 3781, M208.
Atkins, Annie, 174.
Atkins, Bertie, 3781.
Atkins, Billy, 74, 174, 248.
Atkins, Callie, M401.
Atkins, Charles, 1101.
Atkins, Daniel, 174.
Atkins, Elmira, 174.
Atkins, Elza, M. 208.
Atkins, Hellen C., 1101.
Atkins, Hettie, M208.
Atkins, Isabelle M., NB110.
Atkins, James, 952, 1101, 1134, 3781.
Atkins, James A., 3781, 952, 1101, 1134.
Atkins, James P., NB110.
Atkins, Jane, 291.
Atkins, Janie, 174.
Atkins, John, 2905, M401.
Atkins, John H., 3781.
Atkins, Katie, 1602.
Atkins, Lee, 1602.
Atkins, Leola, 3781.
Atkins, Louisa C., 3493.
Atkins, Mary, 174, 1134, 1602, M361.
Atkins, Mary Jane, 952, 2022.
Atkins, May, 1101.
Atkins, Mildred, NB502.
Atkins, Minnie, 2707.
Atkins, Missena, 174.
Atkins, Nancy, 2022.
Atkins, Naoma, 3781, M270.
Atkins, Nathaniel, 3781, M401.
Atkins, Richard, 3781, 3858, 3967, 3972.
Atkins, Rina, 14, 2905.
Atkins, Robert D., 1101, 3493, NB502.
Atkins, Robert Meagher, NB110.
Atkins, Salina, 248.
Atkins, Sallie, 3972.
Atkins, Sarah, 3781, 3972.

Atkins, Susan, 173, 174
Atkins, Thomas, 14, 174, 248, 585, 2022, 2707, 2905.
Atkins, Tom, 291.
Atkins, Tommy, 14.
Atkins, Victoria, 3967.
Atkins, Wiley, 174.
Atkins, William Sherman, 3967.
Aubrey, Alice Hiawatha, NB46.
Aubrey, C. B., 1304, 3665, M48.
Aubrey, Charles, NB46.
Aubrey, Herbert F., M48.
Aubrey, Millie, 1304, 3665, NB46, M48.
Aubrey, Olla, 1304.
Aubrey, Samuel, 3665.
Audd, Clarence Y., 737.
Audd, Clyde B., 737.
Audd, Coodey I., 737.
Audd, Ellen M., 737.
Audd, Flora R., 737, 3469.
Audd, Joseph McDonald, 3469.
Audd, Leonard G., 737.
Audd, Oma M., 737.
Audd, R. Y., 737, 3469.
Aultman, Agnes, NB910.
Aultman, Benjamin, 119, NB910.
Aultman, Claud L., NB232.
Aultman, Frank B., 193, NB232, NB233.
Aultman, Franklin C., NB233.
Aultman, Georgia A., 193.
Aultman, Henry, 119, 193, 194, 783, 843.
Aultman, Henry E., 119, 193, 194, 783, 843.
Aultman, H. E., 843, 119, 193, 783, 194.
Aultman, James, 194.
Aultman, Jessie M., 193.
Aultman, Louisa, NB910.
Aultman, Melvina, 119, 843.
Aultman, Millie, NB232, NB233.
Auquanay, 400, 2428.
Austin, Daniel, 692.
Austin, Hannah, 2149.
Austin, Oldman, 2355.
Austin, Susan, 692.
Austin, Taylor, 2149, 2355.
Ayah, 1270, 1375.
Ayamka, 1480.
Ayechiche, John, 126.
Ayers, Gussie, 436, 3893.
Ayers, Lester, 436.
Ayers, Walter, 3893.
Ayers, William, 436, 3893.
Ayumker, 2585, 3382.
Azulie, Chepan, 964.
Baccus, Mattie Belle, M263.
Baccus, Rebella, 1074, M263.
Baccus, Willie, M263.
Backburn, Arnecie, 807, 3537, NB1164.
Backburn, Cal 3537, NB1164.
Backbun, Duffy A., 3537.
Backbun, Etta May, NB1164.
Bailey, Charles, 398, 780.
Bailey, Elizabeth, 780.
Bailey, George Ella, 814, M15.
Bailey, Georgie Ella, 814.
Bailey, Howard L., 814.
Bailey, Joe A., 22.

Bailey, Joseph Martin, 22.
Bailey, Lonie Lee, 814.
Bailey, Mattie, 22.
Bailey, W. H., 814.
Baily, Moses, 398.
Baker, Anna, 1668, NB661, NB414.
Baker. Annie, 160, 163.
Baker, Benjamin W., 1838.
Baker. Billy, NB305, NB1023.
Baker, Butler, 1838.
Baker, Clara Belle, 1838.
Baker, Eldo, 1838.
Baker, Ella B., 3254, NB178.
Baker. Ella Blanche, 3254, NB178.
Baker, Emma, 1570.
Baker, Eula Blanche, NB178.
Baker, Everett M., NB304.
Baker, George, NB414.
Baker, George K., 3538.
Baker, Henry, 160, 163, 3913.
Baker, Inez W., NB305.
Baker, John, 1558, 1570, 3913, M423.
Baker, Josephine, M194.
Baker, K. N., 1838, 2158, 3538, NB303, NB304, M194.
Baker, Kinkehee, N., 1838, 2158, 3538, NB 303, NB304, M194.
Baker, Kinkehe N., 1838, 2158, 3538, NB303, NB304, M194.
Baker, Lasley, 1570, NB414, NB661.
Baker, Lucy, 163, NB471.
Baker, Luther I., NB303.
Baker, Martha, NB661.
Baker, Maud Anna, 1838.
Baker, Mentie, 1558.
Baker, Pauline E., NB1023.
Baker, Rebecca J., 1838, 3538, NB303, NB-304, M194.
Baker, Sam, NB178.
Baker, Sandy, 1570, M423.
Baker, Sanie (or Billy), 1568, M423.
Baker, Sunday, 1570, M423.
Baker, Susan, 3913.
Baker, Susie, 2158, NB305, NB1023.
Baker, Tarsey, 1558, M444.
Baker, Wiley, 1558.
Barbee, Sarah M., 580.
Barber, Alice A., 1055, 2198.
Barber, Alice Ann, 1055, 2198.
Barber, Carrie, N. B. 514.
Barber, Cora, N. B. 1016, M313.
Barber, Dovie E., 1055.
Barber, Gertie May, M '13·
Barber, John C., 267, 268, 2035.
Barber, John Thomas, NB1016.
Barber, John W., 1055, NB1016, M313.
Barber, Josephine C., 268.
Barber, Lula F., 1055, NB821.
Barber, Mary E., NB514.
Barber, Minnie P., 1055.
Bar'.er, Mollie, 267.
Barber, Robert T., 267, 1055, 2198, NB514.
Barber, Sarah A., 267, 1055.
Barber, Sarah Ann, 267, 1055.
Barber, Shellie L., 1055.
Barber, Silas H., 267, 1055.
Barber, Walter C., 1055.
Bard, Daniel Lee, NB242.
Bard, Daniel N., 643, NB242, NB243.
Bard, Emma, 643, NB242., NB243.

Bard, Lucy, 643.
Bard, Oda May, NB243.
Bard, Richard, 643.
Bard, William J. B., 643.
Bardy, 3235.
Barefoot, 1837.
Barbeche, 67 .
Barkinson, Jonathan, 1019.
Barnett, 1056, 1240, 3825.
Barnett, Ada P., 1957.
Barnett, Albert, 1933.
Barnett, Aldine, 1433.
Barnett, Alice, NB883.
Barnett, Amos, 1540, M262.
Barnett, Anna, 3087.
Barnett, Annie, 88, 966, 1012, 3672, M148.
Barnett, Annanias, 3956.
Barnett, Austin, 966, 1433, 1654, 2880, NB·724, NB725.
Barnett, Babie, 400, M286.
Barnett, Benache, 75.
Barnett, Bennie, 1933.
Barnett, Billy, 556.
Barnett, Charles, 1812.
Barnett, Charlie, 2761, NB882.
Barnett, Cheparney, NB523.
Barnett, Chillie, 966.
Barnett, Cilla, 1546, 3920.
Barnett, Cita, 51.
Barnett, Clifford Marion, NB1173.
Barnett, Columbus R., 1957.
Barnett, Cookie, 1468, NB464, NB465.
Barnett, Daniel, 61, 642, 822, 1433, 1443, 1547, 1566, 1594, 1720, 3752, NB-464, NB465, NB552, NB-845.
Barnett, Daniel W., 1929.
Barnett, Dave, 642, 1929, 1930, 1540, 2863, NB1113.
Barnett, David, 1411, 1412, 1413, 1540, 3921, NB1113, M483.
Barnett, David C., 1851.
Barnett, Dennis, 1933.
Barnett, Dock, 966.
Barnett, Dick, 966, 1445, 3672, M251.
Barnett, Dick, Creek Frd., 397, M148.
Barnett, Edmond, 2761.
Barnett, Edmund, NB724.
Barnett, Eliza, 1443, 3752.
Barnett, Elizabeth, 966, M148.
Barnett, Ella, 1812.
Barnett, Ellen, 1240.
Barnett, Ellie, 1573.
Barnett, Frank, 233.
Barnett, George, 51, 1407, 1411, 1812, 1957, 3752, NB1173.
Barnett, Hallie, 1278, M483.
Barnett, Hammer, NB725.
Barnett, Hannah, 1056, 1387, 1546, 1808.
Barnett, Harley, 1800, NB957, NB1235.
Barnett, Hattie, 1957, NB1173.
Barnett, Helie, 1407.
Barnett, Hettie, 1540.
Barnett, Himer, 1412.
Barnett, Hothlochee, 2313.
Barnett, Hulley, NB552.
Barnett, Ida, 1411.
Barnett, Jackson, 51, 75, 76, 233, 1397, 1419, 1448, 1701, M251, M286.
Barnett, Jacob, 2313, 2502.

Barnett, Sally, 61, 233, 232, 235, 1720.
Barnett, Samara, 642, NB845.
Barnett, Samochee, 1566.
Barnett, Sampson, 1445.
Barnett, Samuel, 1812, 2761.
Barnett, Sandy, 966.
Barnett, Sarah, 642, 1547, 1553.
Barnett, Satney, 232, 233, 235.
Barnett, Scipio, 966, 1432, 3956, NB500.
Barnett, Siah, 1415, 1419, 1488, 1540.
Barnett, Soocer, 1432.
Barnett, Stephen, 2201.
Barnett, Sukey, 2685, NB881, NB882, NB-
        883.
Barnett, Susannah, 76.
Barnett, Susie, 2201.
Barnett, Sussanna, 1, NB58, NB59.
Barnett, Tarhinner, 1932.
Barnett, Thomas, 232, 1387, 1575, 1745, 1808,
        1933, 2761.
Barnett, Tim, 1932.
Barnett, Timothy, 1929, 1932.
Barnett, Timothy W., 3087.
Barnett, Tochee, 1443, 1445, 1466.
Barnett, Tom, 1412, 2454, 3825, NB881, NB-
        882, NB883.
Barnett, Toney, 1928.
Barnett, Tony, 1546.
Barnett, Tucker, 1546, 1553, 3920, NB1035,
        M. 249.
Barnett, Tucker, K. 1546, 1553, 3920, NB-
        1035, M249.
Barnett, Wanney, 1012, NB204, M262.
Barnett, Wannie, 1012, NB204, M262.
Barnett, Wash, 1933.
Barnett, Wealache, 2502.
Barnett, Wesley, 88, 1540, 2358.
Barnett, William, 75, 1575, 1928, 2233, 2694,
        3824, M483.
Barnett, William A., Jr., 75.
Barnett, Winey, 1388, 1546.
Barnett, Yahlawe, 77, M235.
Barnett, Yarda, 1798, 1799.
Barnette, Alex, 412.
Barnette, Benjamin, 413.
Barnette, James, 413.
Barnette, John, 413.
Barnette, Judie; 412, 413.
Barnette, Lizzie, 412.
Barnette, Lucy, 413.
Barnette, Martha, 413.
Barnette, Polly, 412, NB736, M69.
Barnette, Susie, 412.
Barnette, Tilsey, 412.
Barnette, Wesley, 413.
Barnette, Wm., 412.
Barnette, Yarda, 412, 413.
Barney, 2233.
Barney, Albert, NB138.
Barney, Albert Emmet, NB138.
Barney, Bessie, 1066, NB138.
Barney, Lee, 338.
Barnogee, 1444.
Barnwell, David, 486.
Barnwell, Jane, 1226.
Barnwell, Joe, 1737.
Barnwell, John, 486, 1226.
Barnwell, Katie, 386, 486.
Barnwell, Robinson, 1737.
Barnwell, Sissy, 1737.

281

Barnwell, Vicey, 486.
Barnwell, Wisey, 1226.
Barr, Emma, 741, NB260.
Barr, J. C., 740, 741, 753.
Barr, Laura, 741, 3443, NB437, M248.
Barrett, Billy, 556.
Bartley, Leah, 1147.
Bassochee, 3228.
Baughman, Bert, NB13, NB14, NB15.
Baughman, Ella May, NB15.
Baughman, Fannie, 3523.
Baughman, Fayetta, 3523.
Baughman, Gay L., NB14.
Baughman, G. G., NB244, NB245.
Baughman, Gold C., Jr., NB245.
Baughman, Jefferson Euel, NB13.
Baughman, Malvin W., NB244.
Baughman, Mary Lula, 140, NB13, NB14, NB15.
Baughman, Sarah, 339, 3523, NB244, NB-245.
Baysinger, Columbus, 539.
Baysinger, Eliza, 539, M13.
Baysinger, Nellie, 539.
Baysinger, Perry, 539.
Baysinger, William, 539.
Beams, Annie, 1413, 3838, NB895, NB896.
Beams, Becky, 3962.
Beams, Charles, 1413, 3838, NB895, NB896.
Beams, Charley, 1413, 3838, NB895, NB896
Beams, Isom, 1413.
Beams, Jacob, 1222, 3962.
Beams, Jake, 1222.
Beams, Lilly, 3838.
Beams, Mitchell, 1074, 1222, 3962.
Beams, Parthenia, 3269.
Beams, Rhoda, NB896.
Beams, Tishie M., NB895.
Beams, Tooka, 1074.
Bean, Gideon, 1414.
Bean, Jacob, 190.
Bean, John, 2849, NB955.
Bean, Lena, 3627, 3746, NB954, NB955.
Bean, Monday, 2849, 3746, NB954, NB955.
Bean, Money, 2874.
Bean, Nancy, 1414.
Bean, Okfuske, 3746.
Bean, Parthena, 239.
Bean, Rhoda, 190, NB587, NB588, M252
Bean, Sabena, 3746.
Bean, Supsie, NB954.
Bear, 3204.
Bear, Albert, 1674.
Bear, Alexander, 2388.
Bear, Amy, 3339.
Bear, Annie, 889, 2663, NB1165.
Bear, Bamma, 2915.
Bear, Bennie, 2388.
Bear, Ceasar, 3080.
Bear, Cinda, 1354.
Bear, David, 3339.
Bear, Dick, 3339.
Bear, Edward, 3159.
Bear, Fannie, 2898.
Bear, Faska, 3204.
Bear, Haney, 2915, 2995.
Bear, Hannah, 1218.
Bear, Harry, 3466.
Bear, Harty, 2915.
Bear, Hepsey, 2930, 2931.

Bear, Hilly, 2294.
Bear, Jakey, 3065.
Bear, Jessie, 3080.
Bear, John, 3065.
Bear, Johnson, 1356.
Bear, Jolly, 606.
Bear, Joseph, 2388.
Bear, Josie, M321.
Bear, Juda, 1218.
Bear, Katie, 1218.
Bear, Kizzie, 2430, 3080, NB521.
Bear, Lena, N. B. 879.
Bear, Lewis, 2599, NB1165.
Bear, Lillie, NB521.
Bear, Little, 1356, 2039.
Bear, Lonie, 1356
Bear, Lottie, 2925.
Bear, Louis, 2995.
Bear, Louisa, 2632.
Bear, Lowina, 1257, 1258, 1259, 1319.
Bear, Lucinda, 2388, CE4019.
Bear, Lucy, 1607.
Bear, Lydia, 3086, 3108, 3999, NB879, M352.
Bear, Mahala, 2915.
Bear, Mannie, 2461.
Bear, March, 1218, CE4019, NB1172.
Bear, Marche, 1218, CE4019, BN1172.
Bear, Monny, 2206, M321, M320.
Bear, Munnie, 1299.
Bear, Nancy, 2929, 2930.
Bear, Nettie, 1243, NB1172.
Bear, Nocos Elle, 2388.
Bear, Paro, 1218.
Bear, Pinar, 1356.
Bear, Polar, 2461, NB521.
Bear, Pollie, 3466.
Bear, Polly, 606, NB382, M287.
Bear, Rhina, 2277.
Bear, Robert E., 3159.
Bear, Roley, NB1172.
Bear, Roman, 3080.
Bear, Ryder, 2929.
Bear, Sammie, 1356.
Bear, Sampson, 1356.
Bear, Samuel, 2388.
Bear, Sarah, 2248, NB1198, M346.
Bear, Sarley, 1356.
Bear, Seluskey, 2278, 3174.
Bear, Senie, 1356.
Bear, Sine, 2632.
Bear, Sunthape, 3080.
Bear, Susanna, 2841.
Bear, Taylor, 3080, 3379.
Bear, Thomas, 3204, NB879.
Bear, Tinor, 2841.
Bear, Turner, NB1165.
Bear, Ulsar, 2388.
Bear, Walter, 606, 3466.
Bear, Washbarney, M320.
Bear, Washington, 3290, M320, M321.
Bear, Wilson, 2843.
Bear, Yarner, 2787.
Bearhead, Barney, 2742.
Bearhead, Betsey, 2742.
Bearhead, Cooper, 2210.
Bearhead, Jake, 2175.
Bearhead, Jesse, NB1269.
Bearhead, Louisa, 2210.
Bearhead, Lucinda, 2210, 2991.
Bearhead, Mollie, 3998.

Bearhead, Moser, 3998.
Bearhead, Moses, NB1269, NB1270.
Bearhead, Nancy, 136, 3998, NB1269, NB-1270.
Bearhead, Polly, 2742.
Bearhead, Robinson, 2210.
Bearhead, Wylie, NB1270.
Bearhead, Yanah, 3998.
Beartail, John, 3368.
Beartail, Louis, 3718.
Beartail, Louisa, 3368.
Beartail, Lydia, 3718.
Beartail, Mary, 1275.
Beaty, 1159.
Beaver, 1101, 1870, 2380.
Beaver, Alex, 2380.
Beaver, Annie, 3159, 3384, NB1208, NB-1209.
Beavrr, Babie, 1695.
Beaver, Barney, 2665.
Beaver, Beatrice, M214.
Beaver, Beckey, 218.
Beaver, Buck, 399.
Beaver, Buna, M368.
Beaver, Byer, 3068, NB586, NB1055.
Beaver, Colbert, 3068.
Beaver, Cora, 399, M376.
Beaver, Daniel, 537, 2473.
Beaver, David, 809, M368.
Beaver, Earnest, NB255.
Beaver, Ella, NB255, NB1091.
Beaver, Elsa, 3270.
Beaver, Emma, 152.
Beavèr, Enoch 3599.
Beaver, Fanny, 1296.
Beaver, Frank, 399.
Beaver, Fred, 1176.
Beaver, George, 243, 3599.
Beaver, George Milton, M368.
Beaver, Halleyamson, 218, 2063, NB1077, M214.
Beaver, Harry, 218, 2063, NB1077, M214.
Beaver, Heliswa, NB1209.
Beaver, Jennetta, 288, M214.
Beaver, Jennie, 1029, 2009, 2380.
Beaver, Jimsey, 1577, 1585, 1586.
Beaver, Joe, 1296, 3833.
Beaver, John, 1176, 1296, 1870, NB255, NB-1091
Beaver, Joseph Charles, NB1091.
Beaver, Kaska, NB1208.
Beaver, Katie, 218.
Beaver, Lecus, NB586.
Beaver, Lela, 1296.
Beaver, Levina, 2473.
Beaver, Lizzie, 2380.
Beaver, Lou Ella, 2380.
Beaver, Louisa, 1300, NB1077.
Beaver, Lousanna, 2933, NB708.
Beaver, Lucy, 399, 2515, NB1161.
Beaver, Lydia, 809, 1095, 1101.
Beaver, Martain, 2009.
Beaver, Martha, 537.
Beaver, Martin, 537.
Beaver, Marty, 2380.
Beaver, Mary Capitola. NB450.
Beaver, Milton, 809, 1095.
Beaver, Mody, 3159.
Beaver, Mollie, 1727, 2462.
Beaver, Monte, 1029.

Beaver, Motey, 1727, 2462.
Beaver, Moty, 1727, 2462.
Beaver, Mulsey, 3068, NB586, NB1055.
Beaver, Mulsie, 3068, NB586, NB1055.
Beaver, Nancy, NB1184.
Beaver, Nansoche, 2473.
Beaver, Nellie, 3270.
Beaver, Nicey, 2516.
Beaver, Oklow, 2462.
Beaver, Ollie, 1095, NB450, M364.
Beaver, Ollie V., 1095, NB450, M364.
Beaver, Pahte, 2515, NB1161.
Beaver, Party, 2515, NB1161.
Beaver, Peter, 1095.
Beaver, Polly, NB1161.
Beaver, Poyer, 3068, N. B. 586, N. B. 1055.
Beaver, Riley, 1577.
Beaver, Roley, 3068.
Beaver, Roman, 3068.
Beaver, Rosa, 453, 3833, NB1131.
Beaver, Sam, 1586.
Beaver, Sammie B. M364.
Beaver, Samuel, 1095, NB450, M364.
Beaver, Samuel C., 1095, NB450, M364.
Beaver, Sandy, 453.
Beaver, Sanger, 3270.
Beaver, Simmer, 1695.
Beaver, Sophie, 243.
Beaver, Thomas, 1577.
Beaver, Tilda, 3599.
Beaver, Tillar, 218, 312.
Beaver, Tiller, 218, 312.
Beaver, Tiner, 1577.
Beaver, Turner, 3068.
Beaver, Viola, 1095.
Beaver, Walter, NB1055.
Beaver, Wattie, 621, NB1184.
Beaver, Willie, 3384, NB1208, NB1209.
Beaver, Williamsee, 2473.
Beaver, Wilson, 152, 1296, 2473, NB1077.
Beaver, Wisey, NB1184.
Beck, Fannie, 2292.
Beck, Gerty, 2292.
Beck, Leonard, 2292.
Beck, Odus, 2292.
Beck, Otto, 2292.
Beckett, Mariah, 854.
Becky, 3962.
Beddoe, Hettie, R., 1805.
Beddoe, Lonzo, 1805.
Beddoe, Lonzo A., 1805.
Beddoe, Malvina P., 1805.
Beddoe, Martha A., 1805.
Beddoe, Morellis R., 1805.
Beddoe, Virona, 1805, M428.
Beef, Fanny, 898.
Beef, Jim, 898.
Beef, John, 898.
Beef, Kizzie, 898.
Behaye, 2061.
Behen, 882, 937.
Behen, Asa, 3485.
Behen, Chefargee, 937, NB783.
Behen, Helay, 937.
Behen, Jennetta, 638, 3485, M17.
Behen, Judy, 882.
Behen, July, 937.
Behen, Micco, 937, 3485, M17.
Behen, Noah, M17.
Behen, Walie, 937.

Belcher, Alen, 29.
Belcher, Bessie, 2423.
Belcher, Christopher C., 1085.
Belcher, Eliza, 1085.
Belcher, Emma, 2423.
Belcher, Geo. W., 1085.
Belcher, Jennie, 3558.
Belcher, John, 2423.
Belcher, Martha, 2423, 3558.
Belcher, Sila, 29.
Belcher, Simon, 237.
Belcher, Sunny, 2423.
Belcher, Tobe, 2423, 3558.
Bell, Aaron, 3547.
Bell, Agnes, NB8.
Bell, Clarissa, 677, 3547, NB88.
Bell, Cornelius, 706.
Bell, Eli, 706, NB403, NB404.
Bell, Emma, 378, NB8.
Bell, George, 627, 890, 945, 960.
Bell, Georgiana, 627.
Bell, Jack, NB88.
Bell, James, 890, NB8.
Bell, Jasper, 945.
Bell, Jim, 960.
Bell, Jimmie, M430.
Bell, John, 3547.
Bell, Josie, NB369, M430.
Bell, Lelia May, NB88.
Bell, Lizzie, 6, NB369, M430.
Bell, Lizzie Marshall, 6, NB369,¹M430.
Bell, Losmar, 706.
Bell, Martha, 706:
Bell, Nellie, NB369.
Bell, Oliver, NB89.
Bell, Silby, 706, NB403, NB404.
Bell, Silla, 706.
Bell, Suthie, NB404.
Bell, Thompson, NB403.
Bell, Willie, 706.
Bell, Yarnah, 890, 945.
Bellen, Nellie, 2910.
Bellsted, Chas., 498.
Bellsted, Myrtle, 498.
Bellsted, Tookah, 498.
Bellstedt, Catharine, 1399.
Bellstedt, George, 1399.
Bellstedt, Lula, 1399.
Bemar, Lizzie, 2430.
Bemar, Siah, 2430.
Bemo, Alexander, 3038.
Bemo, Douglas, 3116.
Bemo, John, 3038.
Bemo, Katie, 3116.
Bemo, Leon, 3116.
Bemo, Myrtle L., 1221, NB38, NB39.
Bemore, Alice, 1221.
Bemore, Annie, M237.
Bemore, Charlie, NB269, NB270.
Bemore, Chartey, M237.
Bemore, Dora, NB269.
Bemore, John, 1221.
Bemore, Lewis, NB270.
Bemore, Maggie, 2523, M237, NB269, NB-
    270.
Ben, 159.
Ben, Big, 1423, 1425, 1435, 1436, 1584, 3830.
Ben, John, 1436.
Ben, Martha, 1436, 3830.
Ben, Mary, 1423, 1425, 1435, 1436, 1584.

Ben, Robert, 3830.
Ben, Samuel, 3031.
Ben, Wicey, 1436.
Ben, Willie, 1436.
Benden, Anna, 1609.
Benden, Dicey, 1609, NB944, NB945.
Benden, George, 1609.
Benden, Ida, NB944.
Beuden, Jeff, 1609.
Benden, Jonas, 1721.
Benden, Joseph, 1721.
Benden, Louis, 1609, NB944,[NB945.
Benden, Louisa, NB945.
Benden, Thomas, 1609, 1721, 1724.
Benham, C. A., 3498, NB380, NB381
Benham, Claude, 3498, NB380, NB381.
Benham, James Albert, NB381.
Benham, Lucy Etta, NB380.
Benham, Malinda, 1446, 3498, 3819,[NB380,
    NB381.
Benham, Willie, 3498.
Benjamin, Mulsey, 2435.
Benjamin, Timmie, 2435.
Bennefield, John Franklin, M63.
Bennefield, Mollie, 1736, M63.
Bennefield, William, M63.
Bennett, Anna C., 2715.
Bennett, Gertrude, 2714, M227.
Bennett, Leo E., 2714.
Bennett, Lonie, 2714.
Bennett, Lou Ellen, 956, M161.
Benny, 1593.
Benson, Annie, 2577, M147.
Benson, Billie, NB475.
Benson, David M., 20.
Benson, Edward, NB474.
Benson, Haney, 1424.
Benson, Hattie, 20.
Benson, Jack, 20, 1931.
Benson, James, 2577.
Benson, Jim, 1424, 2754, 3081.
Behson, Johnson, 2876.
Benson, Josiah, 2577.
Benson, Katie, 1417, 2577, NB474, NB475.
Benson, Kokey, 2754.
Benson, Lena E., 20, NB66, M156.
Benson, Lillie M., 20, NB681.
Beuson, Louisa, 20.
Benson, Lydia, 1931.
Benson, Mary. 2754.
Benson, Matilda, 2754, NB1176.
Benson, Rhoda, 20.
Benson, Sallie, 2577.
Benson, Silpie, 2577.
Benson, Waley, 2577.
Benson, William, 20, NB474, NB475.
Benton, Bob, 2903.
Benton, Daniel, 4003.
Benton, Jennie, 2903, 4003, NB1277.
Benton, Lewis, 2563.
Benton, Louisa, 1685, NB697.
Benton, Mary, 290?.
Benton, Robert, 2771, 4003, NB1277.
Benton, Thomas, 1683, 1685, NB1277.
Benton, Washington, 2563.
Berry, Adesta, 3283.
Berry, Anna Marie, 1890.
Berry, Frances, 3283.
Berry, John H., 3283.
Berry, Josephine, 3283.

Berry, Louisa, 392
Berry, Louise, 3283.
Berry, Louise A., 1890.
Berry, Spire McIntosh, 3283.
Berry, W. D., 1890.
Berryhill, 1289.
Berryhill, Airy Ann, 637, 770, 771, 772, 844, 1129, 2706.
Berryhill, A. J., 532, 854.
Berryhill, Albert, 25, 637, 1443.
Berryhill, Alec, 37, 3675, NB819, M291.
Berryhill, Aleck, 37, 3675, NB819, M291.
Berryhill, Alex., 37, 3675, NB819, M291.
Berryhill, Alice, 770, 916, NB256, NB832, NB833.
Berryhill, Altie, May, 532,
Berryhill, America, 797, 3525.
Berryhill, Anderson, 1360, 1508.
Berryhill, Andrew J., 532, 3457, 3628, NB277.
Berryhill, Annie, 37, 1508, 2675, NB819, M291
Berryhill, Ara Ann, 637, 770, 771, 772, 844, 1129, 2706.
Berryhill, Archie, NB833.
Berryhill, Arie A., 637, 770, 771, 772, 844, 1129, 2706.
Berryhill, Ary Ann, 637, 770, 771, 772, 844, 1129, 2706.
Berryhill, Benjamin F., 39, 916.
Berryhill, Benjamin Franklin, 39, 916.
Berryhill, Bessie, 765.
Berryhill, Bettie, 351, 3676.
Berryhill, Bluford W., 844.
Berryhill, Buford O., 532.
Berryhill, Carl C., 844.
Berryhill, Charles Lawson, 844.
Berryhill, Charles Percy, NB277.
Berryhill, Charlie, 1499, NB293.
Berryhill, Charles S., NB837.
Berryhill, Clarence, 35.
Berryhill, Clementine, 3628, NB986, M98.
Berryhill, Clent, NB928.
Berryhill, Columbus, 637, NB837, NB838, M269.
Berryhill, Columbus D. 637.
Berryhill, Cora F., 797, NB118.
Berryhill, Daniel B., 637.
Berryhill, David, 637.
Berryhill, David L., 30, 37, 370.
Berryhill, Della I., 797.
Berryhill, Earl, NB988.
Berryhill, Effie, L. 35.
Berryhill, Eli, 467.
Berryhill, Eliza, 370.
Berryhill, Elizabeth, 351.
Berryhill, Ellander, 467.
Berryhill, Elnora, NB765
Berryhill, Elsie, 351, 537.
Berryhill, Emma, 637, 1508, 2843, NB837, NB838, M269.
Berryhill, Emma C., NB838.
Berryhill, Evaline, 467, 3028, 3289.
Berryhill, Eveline, 467, 3028, 3289.
Berryhill, Faith, M269.
Berryhill, Fannie, 1226.
Beeryhill, F. B., 334.
Berryhill, Fickhumker, 623.
Berryhill, Flora Edna, NB908.
Berryhill, George, M291.
Berryhill, George F., 844, 3628.
Berryhill, Geo. Franklin, 2706, NB986, M98.

Berryhill, Geo. W., 637, 770, 771, 772, 844, 1129, 2703.
Berryhill, Georgia Ann, 3289.
Berryhill, Gertrude, 765.
Berryhill, Gracie I., 3575.
Berryhill, G. W., 637, 770, 771, 772, 844, 1129, 2706.
Berryhill, Hare, 637, 770, 771, 772, 844, 1129, 2706.
Berryhill, Harris, 1030, 1032.
Berryhill, Harrison, 351, 3676.
Berryhill, Harvis, 1030, 1032.
Berryhill, Henrietta, 178
Berryhill, Hepsie, 488, M149, NB256, NB-257.
Berryhill, Hepsey, 2843.
Berryhill, Hokosy, 622, 623.
Berryhill, Houston, 623.
Berryhill, Huelda, 1030, 1032.
Berryhill, Hulda, 1030, 1032.
Berryhill, Ida Belle, 467.
Berryhill, Ione, NB765.
Berryhill, Isabenda, 83.
Berryhill, Jackson, G. 772.
Berryhill, Jake (A. J.) 765.
Berryhill, James, 184, 765, NB765.
Berryhill, Jane, 82, 765, 1102.
Berryhill, Jeannetta, 2366, NB814.
Berryhill, Jeff, 35, 37, 533, 765, 924.
Berryhill, Jefferson, 35, 37, 533, 765, 924
Berryhill, Jennie, 237, 2623.
Berryhill, Jessie L., 844.
Berryhill, Jim, 237.
Berryhill, Joe, 23, 1508, NB256, NB257, M149.
Berryhill, John, 23, 325, 623, 797, 982, 1508, 3525.
Berryhill, John H., 637.
Berryhill, John P., 797.
Berryhill, Joseph, 23, 1508, NB256, NB-257, M149.
Berryhill, Joseph F., 770.
Berryhill, Josephine, 35, 1772.
Berryhill, Katie, NB819.
Berryhill, Konsie, 325.
Berryhill, Lee, 765.
Berryhill, Leola May, NB814.
Berryhill, Little Deer, 1360.
Berryhill, Littleton, 3525.
Berryhill, Lizzie, 2843, NB1066.
Berryhill, Lony Love, 772.
Berryhill, Louisa, 1193, 1499, 1508, 3373, M136, M275.
Berryhill, Lucinda, 623.
Berryhill, Lucy, 237, 351.
Berryhill, Lula, 532, 3457, NB277.
Berryhill, Lum, NB832.
Berryhill, Maria, 532.
Berryhill, Martha, 623, 755, 1508, 3676.
Berryhill, Maudie, 1193.
Berryhill, May Belle, NB909.
Berryhill, Mildred E., 3457.
Berryhill, Millie, 23.
Berryhill, Minda, 2843.
Berryhill, Nancy, 35, 765, 844.
Berryhill, Nellie, 3575, NB908, NB909.
Berryhill, Nevada, 770.
Berryhill, Newman, 30.
Berryhill, Nicey, 325.

285

Berryhill, Oleta Pearl, M98.
Berryhill, Oliver P., 854.
Berryhill, Ollie, 772.
Berryhill, Oscar, 35.
Berryhill, P. D., 83.
Berryhill, Peggie, 3675.
Berryhill, Peggy, 30, 37, 533, 924.
Berryhill, Pleasant, 30, 35, NB814.
Berryhill, Peter, 2843.
Berryhill, Rachel, 765, 1802, NB393.
Berryhill, Reno, NB257.
Berryhill, Richard, 1772.
Berryhill, Rilla, 772, NB987, NB988.
Berryhill, Robert, 351, 537.
Berryhill, Roby B., 916.
Berryhill, Rosa Lee, 3912.
Berryhill, Sallie, 1508, NB256.
Berryhill, Sally, 1193, 1360.
Berryhill, Sam, 1193, 1226, 1443, 1772, 2076,
    NB293, NB928.
Berryhill, Sam Bob, NB986.
Berryhill, Samuel, 1289, 1499.
Berryhill, Sanford, 844.
Berryhill, Sarah, 797, 3912.
Berryhill, Sarah H. 375.
Berryhill, Sarah Lee, 35.
Berryhill, Simon, 623, 1193, 1508.
Berryhill, Sophia, 1193, NB293, NB928.
Berryhill, Sophie, 1193, NB293, NB928.
Berryhill, Susanna, 1499.
Berryhill, Susannah, C., 83.
Berryhill, Susie, 25.
Berryhill, Theodore, 772, NB987, NB988.
Berryhill, Theodore F., 797.
Berryhill, Thomas J., 1032, 3575, NB908,
    NB909.
Berryhill, Thos. H., 375, 797, 3912.
Berryhill, Tobe, 2843.
Berryhill, Ves, NB987.
Berryhill, Walter Ray, 532.
Berryhill, William, 82, 237, 351, 637, 770, 1102,
    1802, NB832, NB833.
Berryhill, William T., 755, 797.
Berryhill, Willie, 2076, M149.
Berryhille, Winnie, 30.
Berryhill, Zachariah T., 467, 755.
Berryhill, Zena, 916.
Berryhill, Z. T., 467, 755.
Bethrolf, Alice K., 861.
Bertholf, Amanda J., 861.
Bertholf, Bettie L., 861.
Bertholf, Dewitt T., 861.
Bertholf, Emma H., 861, NB146.
Bertholf, Myrtle M., 861, M254, NB145.
Bertholf, Rubie Cherokee, 861.
Bertholf, W. H., 861.
Besey, 126.
Beshers, Mary, 1303.
Bessie, 353, 2330.
Betche, 3767.
Bethel, D. F., 3477, NB886.
Bethel, David, F., 3477, NB886.
Bethel, Dora, 554, 3477, NB886.
Bethel, Howard R., 3477.
Bethel, Julia Lavinia, NB886.
Betsey, 600, 605, 612, 1366, 1745, 1892, 2770,
    3274.
Betsey, Lizzie, 1571, 2542, 2959.
Betsie, 1899.
Betsy, 889, 2021.

Betsy, Lizzie, 1571, 2542, 2959.
Bettie, 1001, 2158, 2867, NB1287, M477.
Betts, C. L., M9.
Betts, Kathryn W., M9.
Betts, Sue Hettie, 38, M9.
Betty, 1590.
Bety, 1578.
Bewley, Elizabeth, 862, M42, NB513.
Bewley, Elizabeth Yargee, 862, M42, NB513
Bewley, Eugene L., NB513.
Bewley, George Henry, M42.
Bewley, Lawrence W., NB513, M42.
Bible, David, NB254.
Bible, Emmet, 284.
Bible, Lewis, 284, 2345, NB253, NB254.
Bible, Lewis Jr., 284.
Bible, Mulsie, 284, NB253, NB254.
Bible, Tigo, 284.
Bible, William McHenry, NB253.
Big, Ben, 1423, 1425, 1435, 1584, 3830.
Big, Jack, 2867, NB1287, M477.
Big, John, 1646.
Big, Sam, 751.
Biggs, George, 1627.
Biggs, George C., 3242, NB1239.
Biggs, Homer, 3242.
Biggs, Jeannetta, 3242, NB1239.
Biggs, Martha, NB1239.
Biggs, Pompey, 747.
Biggs, Robert, 3242.
Biggs, Sinda, 3242.
Biggs, Susan, 3242.
Biggs, Susanna, 747.
Biggs, William, 1627.
Biggs, Yarnah, 747.
Bighead, Addie, 573.
Bighead, George, 980, 2505, NB1230.
Bighead, Jack, 3545.
Bighead, Jennie, 2505, NB1230.
Bighead, Jimmie, 2505.
Bighead, John, 1042.
Bighead, Konzie, 573.
Bighead, Lizzie, 2505, NB60.
Bighead, Lottie, 2505.
Bighead, Millie, 373, 3545, NB60.
Bighead, Nancy, 573, 2505.
Bighead, Pathlumka, NB1230.
Bighead, Sakcofahny, 1206.
Bighead, Salina, 1042, NB1118.
Bighead, Sallie, 573.
Bighead, Sam, NB1118.
Bighead, Sampsey, 1042, NB1118.
Bighead, Sampson, 1042, NB1118.
Bighead, Stanwaite, 573, 3545, NB60.
Bighead, Stanwaitie, 573, 3545, NB60.
Big Mosquito, 587, 1949, 3689, 3789, N B737.
Big Mosquito, Agnes, 3689.
Big Mosquito, Albert, 587, NB382, M287.
Big Mosquito, Carecoconthlana, 3789.
Big Mosquito, Coyoufolany, 587.
Big Mosquito, Jennie, NB737.
Big Mosquito, Jensey, 587, 3689, 3789, NB73 7
Big Mosquito, Lizzie, 587, 1949.
Big Mosquito, Tacoconwee, 587.
Bigpond, Albert, 1187, 3482.
Bigpond, Anderson, NB241.
Bigpond, Billie, 1878, 3031.
Bigpond, Billy, 1059, 2312.
Bigpond, Charles, 557.
Bigpond, Charley, 2313.

Bigpond, Coneah, 999, 1008.
Bigpond, Daniel, 567, 3482, NB33, M87.
Bigpond, Eliza, M87.
Bigpond, Ella, 1676.
Bigpond, Gosse, 2104, 2107.
Bigpond, Jackson, 1206.
Bigpond, James, 2104, 2312, NB939.
Bigpond, James Jr., 2104.
Bigpond, Joe, 1187.
Bigpond, John, 567, 1059, 1206, 1676, 2103, 2104, NB240, NB241.
Bigpond, Johnson, 1008.
Bigpond, Joseph, 567.
Bigpond, Kalakony, 1187.
Bigpond, Kizzie, 1059, 2312.
Bigpond, Lallie, 1206.
Bigpond, Lallo, 1206.
Bigpond, Louis, NB939.
Bigpond, Louisa, 2313.
Bigpond, Lucy, 1008.
Bigpond, Martha, 3031.
Bigpond, Nancy, 567, 1059, 3482, M87, NB-33, NB240, NB241.
Bigpond, Ninnie, 1008.
Bigpond, Odie, 2104.
Bigpond, Rachel, 1206.
Bigpond, Sam, 1206.
Bigpond, Sarah, 2312.
Bigpond, Selah, 2103, NB939.
Bigpond, Shackleford, 567.
Bigpond, Sissie, 1676.
Bigpond, Sophia, 3031.
Bigpond, Sophie, 1878.
Bigpond, Susanna, 557, NB31.
Bigpond, Susie, NB240.
Bigpond, Uconthla, 2104.
Bigpond, William, 2104.
Bigpond, Wilson, NB33.
Big William, 2893, 2935, NB1189, NB1190.
Big William, Hannah, 2935, NB1240.
Bigwood, 2380.
Bigwood, Linda, 2380.
Billey, John, 3277.
Billey, Pilot, 3277.
Billie, 2460.
Billie, Emma, 1878.
Billie, Jonas, 1878.
Billie, Lina, 1878.
Billiy, Billiy, 1567.
Billy, 175, 1568.
Billy, Annie, 3286, CE4041, NB1012
Billy, Billy, 1567
Billy, Captain, 2839.
Billy, Chotkey, CE4020.
Billy, David, 3734.
Billy, Eliza, 3800.
Billy, Emma, 3089, 3286.
Billy, Euchee, 2308.
Billy, Hannah, 1568.
Billy, Langley, 3734.
Billy, Lumber, 3286, 3734, 3800, CE4020.
Billy, Millisey, 1568.
Billy, Minnechar, 1568.
Billy, Nancy, 3286, 3734, 3800, CE4020.
Billy, Rina, 3734.
Billy, Simon, 3089.
Billy, Sinnie, 1568, M423.
Billy, Sophia, 2839.
Billy, Susan, 3734.
Billy, Tookah, 3734.

Billy, William, 1567, 1568, 3734.
Binney, 1951.
Bird, Ada, 2691.
Bird, Albert, 1824.
Bird, Amanda, 68.
Bird, Annie, 175, 1553.
Bird, Billie, 2691
Bird, Charlie, 175, 1824.
Bird, Dick, 1155, M473.
Bird, Dudie, 2672.
Bird, Edmund, 1824.
Bird, Eliza, 175.
Bird, Ellis, 68.
Bird, Eva, 175.
Bird, Felix, 2120.
Bird, Hannah, 3413.
Bird, Hughey Elmer, 406.
Bird, Hullie, 1824.
Bird, Hames, 2100.
Bird, Jim, 2672.
Bird, Jimmie, 1553.
Bird, Joanna, 175.
Bird, Katie, 1824.
Bird, Kizzie, NB990.
Bird, Lewis, 241, 1621.
Bird, Lonie, M473.
Bird, Louisa, 68.
Bird, Malinda, 2100.
Bird, Margaret, 175.
Bird, Melissa, 2129.
Bird, Minnie, 626, M473.
Bird, Moses, 68, 3413, NB990.
Bird, Nancy, 175, 2061.
Bird, Nannie, 68.
Bird, Nellie, 2387.
Bird, Nelsie, 2100.
Bird, Polly, 2396.
Bird, Sallie, 68, 3413, NB990.
Bird, Sandy, 406.
Bird, Sarah Ann, 241.
Bird, Sissie, 2791.
Bird, Stella, 2120.
Bird, Susie, 1080.
Bird, Thomas, 2061.
Bird, Uplee, 175, 241.
Bird, Upler, 175, 241.
Bird, Walter, 241.
Bird, Willie, 1824, 2100.
Bird, Yanah, 241.
Birdcreek, Belcher, 1450.
Birdcreek, Jesse, 1450, CE4021.
Birdcreek, Lewis, CE4021.
Birdcreek, Mandy, 1450, CE4021.
Birdcreek, Moses, 1450.
Birdcreek, Peggie, 1450.
Birdcreek, Stanley, 1450.
Birdcreek, Timmie, 1450.
Birdhead, 2471, 2472, 2474, 2500, NB546.
Birdhead, Cinda, 2474, NB546.
Birdhead, Lucy, 2471.
Birdhead, Meloche, 2474.
Birdhead, Mollie, 2472, 2474.
Birdhead, Robison, 2474.
Birdhead, Sinda, 2474, NB546.
Birdhead, Willochee, 2474.
Birdhead, Yanah, NB546.
Bittle, Arminda, M309.
Bittle, George, 1915, 3004.
Bittle, Jacob, 746, 973, M309.
Bittle, Mary M., 746, 973.

Bittle, Mary Marina, M309.
Bittle, Muskogee Essie, 3004, M187.
Bittle, William, 1915.
Blackbird, 829.
Blackgrass, 2406, 2412.
Blackgrass, Wisey, 2608.
Blackston, Albert, 485.
Blackstone, Patsy, 485.
Blackstone, Tom, 485.
Blackwell, Henry, 462, 463.
Blackwell, Lucy, 2060.
Blackwell, Tecumseh, 462.
Blackwell, Thomas, 462.
Blake, Louisa, 3077.
Blake, Peter, 3077, 3876.
Blake, Phema, 3077.
Blake, Simon, 3077.
Bland, Arlie, S., NB803.
Bland, Davis M., NB802.
Bland, Era, 1099.
Bland, Hazel M., 1099.
Bland, J. C. W., 1099, NB802, NB803
Bland, John C., 1099.
Bland, John C. W., 1099, NB802, NB803.
Bland, Owen W., 1099.
Bland, Sue A., 1099, NB802,ᶦNB803.
Bland, Vera, 1099.
Blend, Joe, 1765.
Blend, Lucy, 1765.
Blend, Roley, 1765.
Blue, Sampson, 26.
Bluford, Fickey, 3108.
Blunt, Annie, 3358.
Blunt, Joe, 3357, 3358.
Blunt, John, 3197.
Blunt, Phillip, 3197.
Boatmun, Laura, 2236.
Boles, C. A., NB857.
Boles, Charles, 410, 3488, M325.
Boles, Charlie O., 3488.
Boles, Cherokee, 3234.
Boles, Frank C., 3234.
Boles, Fred, 3234.
Boles, Holland, 3234.
Boles, James, 410.
Boles, Jennie P., 3234.
Boles, Laura H., 3234.
Boles, Mattie, 410, 3488, NB857, M325.
Boles, Pearl, 3234.
Boles, Pearl Amy, NB857.
Boles, Ruby, 3234.
Boles, Wilmer Burns, M325.
Boling, Connie M., 3606.
Boling, Dixie Self, NB1128.
Boling, John R., 3844.
Boling, Martha, 1865, 3606, 3844, NB903, NB1128.
Boling, Martha F., 1865, 3606, 3844, NB903, NB1128.
Boling, Sophia O., 1865.
Boling, W. F., 1865, 3606, 3844, NB903, NB-1128.
Boling, Walter Gilmore, NB903.
Bolling, 3035.
Bonbee, 2717.
Bone, Tiger, 398.
Bones, Eliza, 617.
Bones, Joe, 617.
Boney, 2800.
Boney, James, 2800.

Boon, Dock, 1038.
Boon, Ikey, NB811.
Boon, Isaac, NB812.
Boon, Martha, 651, NB811, NB812, M150
Boon, Peter, Creek Frd., 4848, NB811, NB-812, M150.
Boon, Robert, M150.
Boone, Belle, 3030.
Boone, Blanche, 3030.
Boone, Charley, 474, 3505.
Boone, Charlie, 474, 3505.
Boone, Daniel, 1038.
Boone, Dock, 1038.
Boone, Imy, 1038, NB828.
Boone, Imy, R. 1038, NB828.
Boone, Mrs. Imy R., NB828.
Boone, Josephine, 1038, NB745, NB1061.
Boone, Ladossa Fredre, NB828.
Boone, Madge, 3505.
Boone, Millie, 1038.
Boone, Newman, 1038, M38.
Boone, Otto, 3030.
Boone, Polly, 2127, M38.
Boone, Priscilla, 474.
Boone, Sallie, 474, 3505.
Boone, Stella May, M38.
Boone, Thomas, 474, 1038.
Boone, Ural, 474.
Boone, Zenus, 474.
Bosen, Amos, 2083
Bosen, Elsie, 454.
Bosen, George, 1945, NB978.
Bosen, John, 1457, 1945.
Bosen, Lousanna, 1945.
Bosen, Mary, 2083.
Bosen, Pearlie, NB978.
Bosen, Peggy, 2083.
Bosen, Sam, 1457.
Boudinot, Belfoure, 180.
Boudinot, Cornelius, 180, NB224, M114.
Boudinot, Cornelius Jr., M114.
Boudinot, Jessie, 180.
Boudinot, Mitchell, NB224.
Boudinot, Susanna, 180, NB224, M114.
Bough, Arthur, NB246, NB247.
Bough, Emma, 210, NB246, NB247.
Bough, Ethel, NB247.
Bough, Henry, NB246.
Bough, John, NB201.
Bough, Rachel, 1191, NB201.
Bough, Willie E., NB201.
Boulton, Etta C., 1091.
Boulton, Etta Marie, 1091.
Boulton, Geo. H., 1091.
Boulton, Howard H., 1091.
Boulton, Noco C., 1091.
Bowers, Edith, 3714.
Bowers, Fred, 107, 3714.
Bowers, Frederick, 3714.
Bowers, Harold, 107.
Bowers, Ida, 107, 3714.
Bowers, Lewis, 107.
Bowers, Rebecca, 107.
Bowleg, Wm., 3750.
Bowlegs, Ethel, 2486.
Bowlegs, Florence, 2486.
Bowlegs, Lulu, 2486.
Bowlegs, Lulu Winnie, 2486.
Bowlegs, Robert, 2486.

288

Bowling, 3034.
Bowman, Dolly, 471, 472.
Bradley, Adaline, 2756.
Bradley, Belle, 487, M14.
Bradley, Calvin Durant, M14.
Bradley, Cass M., M14.
Bradley, Lewis, 319.
Bradley, Sam, 35, 319.
Brady, Albert, 503, 1701.
Brady, Charley, 3300.
Brady, Dora, 1701.
Brady, Eliza, 3300.
Brady, Fall M., 2265, 3300.
Brady, Foil M., 2265, 3300.
Brady, Jallah-Cherokee, 1708, M308.
Brady, Lucinda, 503.
Brady, Martha, 2265, 3300, 3795.
Brady, Mary, 1701.
Brady, Sam R., 3300, M308.
Brady, Saucer, 608.
Brady, William Penn, M308.
Brammir, 2539, 2640.
Bray, Mary, 158.
Bray, Vicey, 158.
Bray, William, 158.
Breeding, Dick Bland, 1500.
Breeding, Eliza, 1500.
Breeding, Henry, 1500.
Brewer, Jessie, 1877.
Brewer, Nick, 1877.
Brian, Charley, NB63, NB64.
Brian, Hettie E., 54, NB63, NB64.
Brian, John William, NB63.
Brian, Mary Ellen, NB64.
Bridges, Elizabeth, 926, 1020.
Bridges, Ellis, 926, 1020.
Bridges, Ellison, 926, 1020.
Bridges, Montie Robert, M358.
Bridges, Patty Bruner, 710, NB979, M358.
Bridges, Wade Elmer, M358.
Bright, John, 2127, NB720, NB 21, M37
Bright, Lafa, NB721.
Bright, Leon De Witt, 3602.
Bright, Lizzie, M37.
Bright, Luke, 3602, NB169.
Bright, Luke O., 3602, NB169.
Bright, Lumber, 2349.
Bright, Mary, 650, NB169.
Bright, Mary L., 3602.
Bright, Nannie, 423.
Bright, Reubin, NB720.
Bright, Rhoda, 2127, NB720, NB721, M37
Bright, Thelma Beatrice, NB169.
Bright, Watty, 423.
Brightman, Earl, NB679.
Brightman, Fannie, 2271, NB679.
Brightman, Lyeman, NB679.
Briley, Ella, 303, M276.
Briley, Paul W., M276.
Briley, Winfree, M276.
Brimer, George, 2539, 2640.
Brimer, Wilbert, 2640.
Brink, Lizzie, NB750.
Brink, Lusanna D., 1060, NB750.
Brink, Willie, 3125, NB750.
Brinton, Carrie, 911.
Brinton, Edith, 911.
Brinton, George, 1907.
Brinton, Ruth, 3418.
Brinton, Samuel, 911, 2505, 3418.

Brinton, Sarney, 911.
Brinton, Sussie, 911, 3418.
Brinton, Tilda, 2505.
Brister, 511, 512.
Bristor, 511, 512.
Bristor, Sudom, 512.
Bristow, 1822.
Broadnax, Ben, 523.
Broadnax, Bessie, M290.
Broadnax, James, M290.
Broadnax, Nannie, 1058, 3230, M290.
Brock, Jennetta, A., 1961, 3663, NB179.
Brock, Jennetta L., 1961.
Brock, John, 1961.
Brock, Lillie, 1961.
Brock, Lucile E., 1961.
Brockman, Mary E., 333, 887.
Brook, Annetta May, NB179.
Brook, Eck E., 3005.
Brook, Frederick H., 3663.
Brook, Jennetta A., 1961, 3663, NB179.
Brook, J. H., 1961, 3663, NB179.
Brook, John, 1961, 3663, NB179.
Brook, John H., 1961, 3663, NB179.
Brook, Nina, 3005.
Brook, Nina T., 3005.
Brooks, 1603.
Brooks, Annie, 2632, M416.
Brooks, Bettie, 1963, NB315, M111.
Brooks, Eddie, 1603.
Brooks, Emma, 2632.
Brooks, George, 1603, 2632.
Brooks, Joe, 2632, M416.
Brooks, John, NB315, M111.
Brooks, Louisa, 2632.
Brooks, Lucinda, 1603, M164.
Brooks, Mona, 1603.
Brooks, Nola, M416.
Brooks, Rufus Claude, M111.
Brooks, Thomas Clifford, NB315.
Brooks, Widey, 1603.
Brown, Ada, NB313.
Brown, Ada J., 1632, NB616.
Brown, Addie, 3467.
Brown, A. J., 1906, 2091.
Brown, Albert, 2335.
Brown, Alec, 2376.
Brown, Alex, 1446, 2582, NB672.
Brown, Alice, 915, 2011, NB524.
Brown, Annie, 586, 2258, 2582, NB761.
Brown, Athalene, 1622.
Brown, A. W., 1622, NB616.
Brown, Banner, 1643.
Brown, Bernard, 1609.
Brown, Bertha, 1391.
Brown, Bertha Alice, 3427.
Brown, Bessie, 612, 915.
Brown, Bettie, 1906.
Brown, Billy, 223.
Brown, Buster, 612.
Brown, Cahkalecoconthla, 3303.
Brown, Carrie C., 460.
Brown, Chailey, 1686.
Brown, Charity, 356.
Brown, Charlie, 1048.
Brown, Charles, 356, 2258, M36.
Brown, Charley, 248, 1224, 1236, 2335, 2983.
Brown, Cilla, 1038, 1277.
Brown, Clarence, 2091, 3737, NB604, NB605.

Brown, Clarence W., 2091, 3737, NB604, NB-
    605.
Brown, Claud W., 1622.
Brown, Cleller, NB713.
Brown, Conpesinney, 2785, 3303, NB1087,
    NB1088..
Brown, Conthlany, 882, NB748, M18.
Brown, Cosaye, 2878.
Brown, Cotenney, CE4022.
Brown, Dakesahcocontaney, 3303.
Brown, Daniel W., NB139.
Brown, Dave, NB672.
Brown, Delilah, M36.
Brown, Dewey, 190.
Brown, Dick, 252.
Brown, Echoluste, 975.
Brown, Edith, M199.
Brown, Edward S., NB687.
Brown, Elijah, 1048, 1049, 1050, 2018.
Brown, Eliza, 617, 627, 3427, M199.
Brown, Elizabeth, 1304, 1974.
Brown, Elizabeth A., 2011.
Brown, Ella, 234, NB966.
Brown, Ellen, 3060.
Brown, Elmer Wesley, 795.
Brown, Elwood, 356.
Brown, Esther M., 1277.
Brown, Eva May, NB616.
Brown, Flora, 627.
Brown, Flora A., 1500.
Brown, Frances, 1048, 1049, 1050, 1391, 2018.
Brown, Francis, 1048, 1049, 1050, 1391, 2018.
Brown, George, 559, 1184.
Brown, George A., 627.
Brown, Georgia, NB971.
Brown, Geraldine, 795.
Brown, Gold, 3060.
Brown, Gold C., NB139.
Brown, Hannah, CE4022.
Brown, Hardin, 612, NB971, M. 115, M. 116.
Brown, Hardy, 1686.
Brown, Henry, N. B. 761.
Brown, Hettie, N. B. 1030.
Brown, Jackson, 2011, 2018, 3653, NB713.
Brown, Jake, 605, 3467.
Brown, James, 460, 882, 2011.
Brown, James C., 1391.
Brown, Jeff, NB1029.
Brown, J. F., 2011.
Brown, Jennette, 605.
Brown, Jennie, 915, 2013.
Brown, Jennie E., 915.
Brown, Jerry, 1643.
Brown, Jim, 3303, NB1087, NB1088.
Brown, Jimsey, 975, 1407, 2878.
Brown, Jimsy, NB850.
Brown, Joanna, 855.
Brown, Joe, 1048, 2582, NB313, NB314,
    NB1030.
Brown, John, 115, 190, 356, 855, 1877, 197 ,
    2115, NB1088.
Brown, John William, NB605.
Brown, Joseph, 2258.
Brown, Joseph Wm., 795.
Brown, Josephine, 2011.
Brown, Josiah, 1048, 2582, NB313, NB314,
    NB1030.
Brown, Julia, 356, 1092, 1391, NB495, NB-
    687, NB1007, NB1029.
Brown, J. W., 795.

Brown, Katie, 560, 567, 606, 612, 2582.
Brown, Kichee, 882.
Brown, Kiger, 233, 234.
Brown, Lalley, 1236.
Brown, Larry, 612, NB971, M115, M116.
Brown, Laura, 3653, NB713.
Brown, Legus, 1184.
Brown, Lilly, 1500.
Brown, Lisha, 1609.
Brown, Lizzie, 115, 55⁰, 1184, 1382, 2582, NB-
    313, NB314.
Brown, Loda, 3303, NB1087, NB1088.
Brown, Lorena M., 3653.
Brown, Lou, 1974, 2091, 2537, NB101.
Brown, Louis, 2011.
Brown, Louisa, 2335.
Brown, Lucinda, 1048.
Brown, Lucy, 1236, 2225, 3860.
Brown, Lula, NB850.
Brown, Lydia, 2774, M407.
Brown, Mabel, 3060.
Brown, Madison, 356.
Brown, Madison H., 1277.
Brown, Maria, 2996, NB672, M36.
Brown, Martha, 252, 1943.
Brown, McKinley, NB1029.
Brown, Melia, 1391.
Brown, Melinda, 1446, NB380, NB381.
Brown, Melvin A., M115.
Brown, Minnie, 356.
Brown, Mollie, 1643.
Brown, Mr., 3315, 3317.
Brown, Myrtle, 627.
Brown, Nancy, 795, 2013.
Brown, Nannie, 1664, 1877.
Brown, Nathaniel, 682.
Brown, Neosho, 915.
Brown, Neosho P., 915, 1277, NB119, NB-
    120.
Brown, Neilson, 3060.
Brown, Nellie, 1236.
Brown, Nettie, 1277.
Brown, Nick, 2013.
Brown, Nora, 223.
Brown, Oliver, 627.
Brown, Ollie B., 3060.
Brown, Peter, 1048.
Brown, Pilot, 252.
Brown, Polly, 2785.
Brown, Ralph, 627.
Brown, Rebecca, 3737, NB604, NB605
Brown, Robert, 560, 567, 606, 612, 1500.
Brown, Robert S., 627, 3427.
Brown, Roland, 1382.
Brown, Rosanna, 975, NB850.
Brown, Rosannah, 975, NB850.
Brown, Rose, 356.
Brown, Ruth, NB604.
Brown, Sallie, 605, 3467, M318.
Brown, Sam, 2225, 3860, CE4023.
Brown, Sammie, 1277.
Brown, Samuel, 115.
Brown, Samuel B., 3060.
Brown, Samuel W., 915, 1277, 1304.
Brown, Samuel W. Jr., 915.
Brown, Sandy, NB314.
Brown, S. E., 1391.
Brown, Sealy, 252.
Brown, Sherman, M116, M119.
Brown, Simon, 1092, 1192.

290

Brown, Simpsey, 1686.
Brown, Sinnie, 759.
Brown, Sparhechar, 758.
Brown, Stanton, NB687.
Brown, Susan, 915.
Brown, S. W., 915, 1277, 1304.
Brown, Tahconfah, 3303.
Brown, Tussekiehutkie, 460.
Brown, Tahsaconthleney, 3303.
Brown, Taylor, 248.
Brown, Thomas, 559, NB761, NB918.
Brown, Thomas J., 356, NB495.
Brown, Thomas Jefferson, NB495.
Brown, Timmie, 600.
Brown, T. J., 356, NB495.
Brown, William C., 49.
Brown, W. F., 49, 682.
Brown, William F., 49, 682.
Brown, William J., 3737.
Brown, Willie, 855, 1092, 1446, NB1087.
Brown, Wilson, 2225, 2774, CE4023.
Brown, Yacancothla, CE4022.
Brown, Yahlane, 3303.
Brown, Younger, 252.
Brown, Zenie, 3060, NB139.
Brown, Zora, 2011.
Broyles, Ida B., 1887.
Bruce, Browder F., NB140.
Bruce, Lena Ester, M122.
Bruce, Moten, NB140, M122.
Bruce, Pheba, 449, NB140, M122.
Bruce, Phoebe, 449, NB140, M122.
Brummet, Annie, 1121, 1134.
Brummett, Annie, 1121, 1134.
Brummett, Texanna, 618, 650.
Brunell, Texanna, 944.
Bruner, Abney, 1566.
Bruner, Adaline, 635, NB62.
Bruner, Addie, 2510, M414.
Bruner, Alec, 2609
Bruner, Aley, 750.
Bruner, Alice, M112.
Bruner, Amanda. 989.
Bruner, Anna, 1499, 2076.
Bruner, Annie, 923, 1499, 1601, 2567.
Bruner, Archie, 922, NB999.
Bruner, Arlie, 655.
Bruner, Arlinger, 710.
Bruner, Arthur, 2489.
Bruner, Barney, 2329.
Bruner, Benj., 18, 3581.
Bruner, Berry, 1610, 1611, 1612.
Bruner, Bertha, NB759.
Bruner, Bessie, 635, NB1002.
Bruner, Bettie, 725, NB1000.
Bruner, Betty, 750, NB759, NB760.
Bruner, Biker, 2666.
Bruner, Billy, 635, NB62.
Bruner, Bunnie, NB936.
Bruner, Cassie, 3583.
Bruner, Cessie, 922.
Bruner, Charles Eberle, 655.
Bruner, Charley, 1067, 1404.
Bruner, Cumsey, 2042.
Bruner, Daniel, 665, 750, 986, NB759, NB-760.
Bruner, Dave, 899, 1611.
Bruner, David, 1639, 2385, 2938, 3823, NB-1034.
Bruner, Dewey, 2479, 3641.

Bruner, Dick, 3766.
Bruner, Drefus, 1731.
Bruner, Eddie, 1610, 1694.
Bruner, Edward, 655.
Bruner, Eli, 103, 710, 899.
Bruner, Eliza, 725, 1956.
Bruner, Eliza Jane, 617.
Bruner, Emanuel, 1831.
Bruner, Emma, 655, 1301.
Bruner, Emmett, 1802.
Bruner, Esther, 3529.
Bruner, Fannie, 655.
Bruner, Flora, NB152.
Bruner, Freeland, 591, 872, 3583, NB451.
Bruner, George, 1499, 1831, 2076.
Bruner, George E., 1802.
Bruner, Georgia, 1802, M311.
Bruner, Grace, 665, NB1218, NB1219.
Bruner, Haley, 2970.
Bruner, Hannah, 1983, 2592.
Bruner, Harriet, 617, 679, 872.
Bruner, Henry, 617, NB1000, NB1001, NB1002.
Bruner, Hyman, 2390.
Bruner, Ida, 2510, M414.
Bruner, Ilsey, 2385, NB1034.
Bruner, Iona, 635.
Bruner, Iva M., NB451.
Bruner, Jackson, 1601, 2293, 2348, 2970.
Bruner, Jacob, 617.
Bruner, James, 2489, M168.
Bruner, Jane, 989.
Bruner, Jarey, 1521.
Bruner, J. Esther, NB12.
Bruner, Jemime, 2385.
Bruner, Jennetta, 1454.
Bruner, Jennie, 1648, 1831, 3529, NB152.
Bruner, Jensy, 591.
Bruner, Jerry, 1694, 1933, 1983.
Bruner, Jesse, 1426, 1994, 2413, 2479.
Bruner, Jessie, NB1001.
Bruner, Jim, 1998.
Bruner, Jimboy, 1631.
Bruner, Joe, 888, 1610, 2567, 2588.
Bruner, John, 18, 888, 970, 1454, 2235, 2465, 2666, 3310, NB936, NB 937, NB999, NB1085.
Bruner, Joseph, 970, NB12.
Bruner, Josie, 899.
Bruner, Judy, 1994, NB532.
Bruner, Julia, 3641.
Bruner, Katie, 989.
Bruner, Kissie, 1738
Bruner, Kizzie, 909.
Bruner, Kogee, 2567.
Bruner, Lady Beatrice, NB810.
Bruner, Ledeger, 2413.
Bruner, Lee, 655.
Bruner, Lena, 1694.
Bruner, Lente, 2938.
Bruner, Leoner, NB1000, NB1001, NB-1002.
Bruner, Lewis, 18, 922, 989, 1831, NB533.
Bruner, Lillie, 2385.
Bruner, Lilly, 635.
Bruner, Linda, 2453.
Bruner, Link, 750.
Bruner, Liza, 1521, 3766.
Bruner, Lizzie, 1694, 2465.
Bruner, Loney, 635.

291

Bruner, Losanna, 2111.
Bruner, Lottie, M93.
Bruner, Lou, NB904
Bruner, Loucinda, 2453.
Bruner, Louis, 734, 750, 2592.
Bruner, Louisa, 1630. M334.
Bruner, Lowina, 2666.
Bruner, Lucinda, 1426, 1610, 1639, 3172, M334.
Bruner, Lucy, 655, 970, 1301, 2489, 3581, NB73.
Bruner, Luna, 1734.
Bruner, Luney, 655, 2374.
Bruner, Luny, 655, 2374.
Bruner, Lyman, 635.
Bruner, Mack, 1140, 1142.
Bruner, Maggie, 922, 2248, NB760.
Bruner, Mahala, 750.
Bruner, Mamie, 103.
Bruner, Margaret, 2235, NB12.
Bruner, Mary, 922, 1140, 1142, 1802, 2383, 2385, 2390, 2592, NB359.
Bruner, Mattie, 750.
Bruner, Mattie L., 1610.
Bruner, May Belle, 18.
Bruner, Meculla, 103.
Bruner, Megually, 103.
Bruner, Mekey, 2111.
Bruner, Miller, 655, 1521, 3623, 3766, 3820, NB73.
Bruner, Millie, 2453, 3820.
Bruner, Mindie H., 1610.
Bruner, Mineffie, NB73.
Bruner, Minnie, 2453, NB1085, M168.
Bruner, Mitchell, 872
Bruner, Nan, 18, 922.
Bruner, Nancy, 635, 680, 734, 750, 2374, 2567, NB533, M112.
Bruner, Nannie, 18, 922.
Bruner, Nathan, 986, NB904.
Bruner, Nellie, 635, 3212.
Bruner, Nicey, 655, 235.
Bruner, Nola, 2453.
Bruner, Overton, 750.
Bruner, Pamela, 18, NB999, NB1085.
Bruner, Parmela, 18, NB999, NB1085.
Bruner, Paro, 725, 1956.
Bruner, Patty, 710, NB979, M358.
Bruner, Pearl, NB904.
Bruner, Pinkey, 617, M311.
Bruner, Polly, 1610, 1611, 1612, 3823.
Bruner, Rachel, 1734.
Bruner, Rentie, 2451, 2465.
Bruner, Reuben, M311.
Bruner, Rhoda, 872, 922, 3583, NB451.
Bruner, Richard, 1734, 1802, NB810, M93.
Bruner, Richard Douglas, NB62.
Bruner, Richard R., 617, 679, 872, 3823.
Bruner, Richmond, 725.
Bruner, Rider, 1067.
Bruner, Rider F., 989.
Bruner, Robert, 1994, 2383, 2413, 2592.
Bruner, Robertson, 2453, M334.
Bruner, Roman, 2453.
Bruner, Salina, 103, 710.
Bruner, Sallie, 2293, 2465, 2466, NB936, NB-937.
Bruner, Sam, 1142.
Bruner, Sampson, 845.
Bruner, Sarah, 899, 1734, NB810, M93.
Bruner, Senie, 2453.

Bruner, Siah, 1454, 2383, 2385, 2390, 2392, 2567, 3172, 3595.
Bruner, Silla, 2609.
Bruner, Sindoche, 1142.
Bruner, Sopsey, 2384, 2510.
Bruner, Sorbse, 2012, 2329.
Bruner, Sorbsey, 2012, 2329.
Bruner, Sulda, 1301, 3581.
Bruner, Susie, 2451, M414.
Bruner, Susy, 1998.
Bruner, Suther, 1994.
Bruner, Taylor, 2489, 2567, NB533, M112.
Bruner, Tecumseh, 1632.
Bruner, Tena, 1632.
Bruner, Thomas, 679, 2111, 3641, NB937.
Bruner, Thompson, 1064.
Bruner, Togy, 2489, M168.
Bruner, Toley, 2012, 2329, 2384, 2510.
Bruner, Tom, 1956.
Bruner, Wash, 1983.
Bruner, Wego, 2517.
Bruner, Wiley, 2970, 3310.
Bruner, William, 635, 1404, 2510, M414.
Bruner, William G., 1831, 3529, NB152.
Bruner, Willie, 103, 2293, 2510, 3623, NB1034, M414.
Bruner, Wilson, 2517.
Bruner, Winfield, 1734.
Bruner, Yoapka, 2692, 3171.
Buck, 584.
Buck, Alex, M177.
Buck, Annie, 590, 1817, NB288.
Buck, Daniel, 1817, 1881, 1883.
Buck, Haney, 1720, NB947.
Buck, Hepsey, 1525.
Buck, Joe, 1525, 3232, M177.
Buck, John, 5 4, 586, 589, 591.
Buck, Josa, 1525.
Buck, Joseph, 1817.
Buck, Lily, M177.
Buck, Lonnie, M253.
Buck, Lottie, 2273, NB391.
Buck, Marse, 584.
Buck, Mary, 1817, 1881, 1883.
Buck, Nathan, M169.
Buck, Perryman, 590.
Buck, Reuben, 584.
Buck, Rhoda, NB707, M169.
Buck, Roley, 1881.
Buck, Roman, 1817.
Buck, Rosa, 584, 589, 591.
Buck, Rufus, 590.
Buck, Sallie, 1930, M253.
Buck, Sappho, NB947.
Buck, Sarah, NB707.
Buck, Sillibee, 584
Buck, Simpson, 1780, NB707, M169.
Buck, Susanna, M147.
Buck, Toney, 1881.
Buck, Walter, 1780.
Buck, Warrior, 584.
Buck, William, 1883, NB947, M147, M253.
Buckler, Mahala, 3730.
Buckler, Sam, 3730.
Buckley, Betsey, 1588, 3696, NB1276.
Buckley, Ceasar, 1588, 3696, NB1276.
Buckley, Cora, NB1276.
Buckley, Eli:a, 1588.
Buckley, Emma, 3696.
Buckley, George, 1479.

Buckley, Henry, 1479.
Buckley, James, 1479.
Buckley, Liza, 1478, 1479.
Buckley, Lucinda, 1479.
Buckley, Polly, 1478.
Buckley, Rufus, 1479.
Buckley, Sallie, 1479.
Buckley, Sam, 1478, 1479, 1588.
Buckley, Solomon, 1479.
Buckner, Jack, NB863.
Buckner, Lizzie, 2889, 2890, 2891.
Buckner, Nancy, 2988.
Buckner, Nannie, 3867.
Buckner, Samuel, 2699.
Buckner, Scott, 2988.
Buckner, Susie, 2988, 3867, NB863.
Buckner, Wiley, 2699, 2988, 3867, NB863.
Bucktrot, 2687, 2730, NB852.
Bucktrot, Angee, 2687.
Bucktrot, Concharcher, 2687, NB852.
Bucktrot, Conzey, 2687.
Bucktrot, Lucy, 2687.
Bucktrot, Madie (Wydie), 2687, NB852.
Bucktrot, Mattie, 2687, NB852.
Bucktrot, Sagie, NB852.
Bucktrot, Sam Green, 2687.
Bucktrot, Wydie, 2687.
Bucktrot, Wysena, 2687.
Buffalo, George, 377.
Buffalo, Meley, 1058.
Buffalo, Yana, 377.
Buffnee, 3978.
Buflow, Miley, 379.
Buflow, Peter, 379.
Bullet, Annie, 164.
Bullet, Arthur, 164.
Bullet, Ben, 164.
Bullet, James, 164, 3555, 3985, 4022.
Bullet, John, NB1140.
Bullet, Johnnie, 164.
Bullet, Lucy, 164, 3555, 3985.
Bullet, Mary Ann, 3555.
Bullet, Nellie, 164.
Bullet, Sam, 3285.
Bullet, Sarne, M452.
Bullet, Solomon, 3053, M452, NB1163.
Bullet, Tagee, 4022.
Bullet, Zoye, 3995, NB1140.
Bullett, Bailey, 3103, NB1163.
Bullett, Bill, 3053.
Bullett, Chitto Harjo, NB1140.
Bullett, Edward, 2988.
Bullett, Hanna, 2935, NB1240.
Bullett, Jacob, NB1240.
Bullett, Jemima, 3995.
Bullett, Jennie, 3743.
Bullett, John, 3103, 3995.
Bullett, Kizzie, 3743.
Bullett, Maxey, NB1240.
Bullett, Millie, 3053, NB1163.
Bullett, Soloman, 3053, NB1163, M452.
Bullett, Solomon, 3053, NB1163, M452.
Bullett, Zoye, 3995, NB1140.
Bullette, Disey, 2045.
Bumkin, 3549.
Bumkin, Annie, 3549.
Bundy, 2540.
Bungee, Annie, 824.
Bungee, John, 824.
Bunger, 1235.

Bunger, Annie, 824, 1235.
Bunger, Beckie, 1235.
Bunger, Enoch, 1235.
Bunger, John, 824, 1235.
Bunger, William, 824.
Bungy, 3332, 3585.
Bunner, 6, 3417.
Bunner, Addie, 3417.
Bunner, Barney, 6.
Bunner, Fenie, 6.
Bunner, Indie, 6. M480
Bunner, Losie, 6. 3417.
Bunner, Masaner, 6.
Bunner, Martha, 6.
Bunner, Miley, 6.
Bunner, Mosey, 6, NB1247.
Bunner, Nancy, 6.
Bunner, Ollie, 2760, NB1247.
Bunner, Susie, NB1247.
Bunney, Ahohulch, 2877.
Bunney, Martha, 2877.
Bunny, George, 2734.
Bunny, Jeannetta, 2734.
Burdett, Sudie M., 1640.
Burgess, Albert, 1761.
Burgess, Alice, 256.
Burgess, Barney, 1761.
Burgess, Bean, 2037.
Burgess, Ben, 374, NB1222.
Burgess, Benjamin E., 2037, NB161.
Burgess, Bird, NB827.
Burgess, Caesar, 950, 1653.
Burgess, Ceasar, 950, 1653.
Burgess, Cumseh, 243.
Burgess, Daniel, 256, 332, 1320, 2038, NB826.
Burgess, Dave, 332, 1760, 1761.
Burgess, Dick, 243.
Burgess, Ed., 2037, NB161.
Burgess, Edmond, 1770.
Burgess, Edmund, 312.
Burgess, Edward, 1761.
Burgess, Ellen, 312, 332.
Burgess, Ellis, 1760.
Burgess, Emma, 1760.
Burgess, Ethel, 2037.
Burgess, Fain, 372, 374.
Burgess, Fannie, 2117, NB1075.
Burgess, Gussie, 2038.
Burgess, Hettie, 265.
Burgess, Ida, 312, NB433.
Burgess, India, M272.
Burgess, James, 1760, 3786, NB826, NB827
Burgess, James, Jr., 3786.
Burgess, Jane, 373.
Burgess, John, 678.
Burgess, John B., 265.
Burgess, Katie, 1770.
Burgess, Lee, 243, 950.
Burgess, Louisa, 442.
Burgess, Lowisa, 1320, 2038.
Burgess, Lyddia E., NB1222.
Burgess, Malissa, 264, 265.
Burgess, Martha, 2037.
Burgess, Mary E., 1761
Burgess, Mattie, 265.
Burgess, May, 2037, NB161.
Burgess, Nora, 1232, M272.
Burgess, Raymond B., NB1222.
Burgess, Riley, 1761.
Burgess, Roman, NB1075.

293

Burgess, Ruby, NB161.
Burgess, Sampson, 1770.
Burgess, Sarah, 265, 678.
Burgess, Senora, 1760.
Burgess, Susanna, 1760, 3786, NB826, NB-827.
Burgess, Tina, 1760, 1761.
Burgess, Tyler, 1320.
Burgess, Walter, 2037.
Burgess, William, NB1075.
Burgess, Yarna, 1761.
Burke, John, 475.
Burke, John Thomas, 475.
Burke, Maggie J., 475, NB601, M461.
Burnett, E. H., M97, NB675.
Burnett, Joseph L., NB675.
Burnett, Richard Stanford, M97.
Burnett, Vinita, 406, M97, NB675.
Burnett, Vinita Gordon, 406, NB675, M97
Burnette, A. T., 3442, NB80.
Burnette, Mary J., 678, 3442, NB80, M216
Burnette, Mary Jane, 678, 3442, NB80, M21
Burnette, Moses, NB80.
Burnette, Myrtle, 3442.
Burnette, Thomas, M216.
Burnette, Violet, M216.
Burns, 3028.
Burns, Alvin, 3289.
Burns, Ike, 3289.
Burns, Isaac, 3289.
Burrow, John D., 777.
Burrow, Thomas R., 777.
Burrow, Wiley, 777.
Burrows, Isaac, 1495.
Burt, Eliza 993, NB706.
Burton, Abi L., 1698.
Burton, Charles Checotah, NB172.
Burton, Eliza N., 1698.
Burton, Ethel V., NB67.
Burton, Jesse, NB172, NB173.
Burton, Lucinda, 3024.
Burton, Lydia, 3024, NB69.
Burton, Mack, 3024.
Burton, Mary, 2227, NB172, NB173.
Burton, Mary E., 1698.
Burton, Minnie Ola, 1698.
Burton, Mollie E., NB67, NB68
Burton, Robert, 3924.
Burton, Robert O., 1698, NB67, NB68.
Burton, Rober· P., 1698.
Burton, Rufus Cheestell, NB173.
Burton, Samuel, 1698.
Burton, Wynema Owen, NB68.
Bush, Hattie, 2931, 3712.
Bush, Jessie, 2931.
Bush, Jonas, 2931.
Bushyhead, Cleveland, 3353.
Buslar, James, 209.
Buster, Betsey, 710.
Buster, John, 710.
Butcher, 1348, 1376.
Butcher, Edmond, 1376.
Butcher, Lela, NB1028.
Butcher, Mussy, 1348, NB1028.
Butcher, Norfer, 1348, NB1028.
Butler, 3191.
Butler, Anna, 1989·
Butler, Delpha, 3585.
Butler, Dinah, 909, 1731.
Butler, Eddie, NB1186.

Butler, Edward, 315, 729, 1989.
Butler, Elizabeth, 315, 729, 1989.
Butler, Emma, 3191.
Butler, Fount G., 1989.
Butler, Henderson, 1040.
Butler, James, 909, 1731, 2319.
Butler, Jennie, 195.
Butler, Jim, 195, 446.
Butler, John, 2066, 3191.
Butler, Legus, 2319.
Butler, Mahoye, 3191.
Butler, Manny G., 1989.
Butler, Mollie, 1040, 3585.
Butler, Molly, 3332.
Butler, Myron, NB1186.
Butler, Pusler, 2066.
Butler, Sam, 195, 446.
Butler, Sammie, 1989.
Butler, Susan Ann, 9.
Buzzard, 2587.
Byrd, Ada, 2691.
Byrd, Annie C., 1085.
Byrd, Betsey, 1085.
Bryd, Billie, M422.
Byrd, Chiska, 1590.
Byrd, Coleman, 2691.
Byrd, Dudie, 2691, CE4059, M406, M422.
Byrd, Eda, 2328.
Byrd, Felix, 2691.
Byrd, James, 1591, 2061.
Byrd, Jemima, NB634.
Byrd, Jennetta, 2061.
Byrd, Judy, 2061.
Byrd, Leader, 3148.
Byrd, Leah, 1575.
Byrd, Louisa, 1576.
Byrd, Lucinda, 1590.
Byrd, Lucy Ann, 2328, NB366.
Byrd, Mary, 1621, NB200.
Byrd, Mattie, CE4059.
Byrd, Melissee, 1621.
Byrd, Nellie, 2672, 3354.
Byrd, Sandy (Leader), 3148.
Byrd, Seborn, 1576.
Byrd, Sunny-Sem, 565, NB633, NB634.
Byrd, Susie, 3148.
Byrd, Tamisa, 3095, NB633, NB634.
Byrd, Thomas, 2691, 3148, CE4059, M422
Byrd, William, 1085, 2328.
Byrd, Yakdeka, NB633.
Caahthlenna, 586.
Cabecha, 1751, 2047.
Cabecha, Nannie, 2047.
Cable, Adam M, 341, NB77.
Cable, Cora E., 341.
Cable, John Henry, 341.
Cable, Mary I., 341, NB77.
Cable, Mary Isabel, 341, NB77.
Cable, Virgie Plimmer, NB77.
Caddie, 2534.
Caesar, 3131.
Caesar, Annie, 443.
Caesar, George, 3164.
Caesar, Hannah, NB550.
Caesar, Judy, 3131.
Caesar, Moser, NB551.
Caesar, Panuggee, NB1130.
Caesar, Rachael, 3131, NB550, NB551, M196.

Caesar, Samego, 5131, NB550, NB551, M196.
Caesar, Sissie, 2598, NB1130.
Caesar, Sowikee, 3164.
Caesar, Toche, M196.
Cagee, 1286.
Cahcokethlon, 2713, NB1137.
Cahkokethlon, 940.
Cahkokothlon, Agie, 940.
Cahlowe, 2730.
Cahlowee, 578.
Cahtahwon, 2180, 2626, 3704.
Cahtahwon, Lucinda, 3704.
Cahtahwon, Maggie, 2180.
Cahtahwon, Minnie, 2180.
Cahtahwon, Willie, 2180.
Cahtutah, 1275.
Cahwee, 601, 946, 1334.
Cahwee, Betsey, 601, 946, 1334.
Cahwee, Ekalarney, 946.
Cahwee, Peter, 601.
Cain, Allie, 1801.
Cain, Bettie, M165.
Cain, Daniel, 1801, 4011, M165, M166.
Cain, Legey, 4011.
Cain, Marsey, 4011.
Cain, Mary J., 2482.
Cain, Nisey, 1801, 4011, M165, M166.
Cain, Ottawa, 2482.
Cain, Polly, 1801
Cain, Roman, 1801.
Cain, Sildy, 2482.
Cain, Thomas, M166.
Calachoney, 571.
Call, Archibald, 471.
Call, Charles, NB764.
Call, Gracie, 471.
Call, John, 471, NB764, M80.
Call, John M., 471, NB764, M80.
Call, Nellie, 471.
Call, Pearl, 471, NB764, M80.
Call, Voisy, M80.
Callahan, Alice, 3725, 3880.
Callahan, Alice A., NB167.
Callahan, Benton, 536, NB75.
Callahan, Cecilia, 536, NB75.
Callahan, Celia M., 536, NB75.
Callahan, Etta Sibyl, NB72.
Callahan, Eula, 433.
Callahan, Evelyn, 464.
Callahan, Gipsie, 464, M3.
Callahan, Homer Bryan, 536.
Callahan, James O., 433, 464, M2, NB71,
    NB72.
Callahan, James W., 536.
Callahan, Josie E., 433.
Callahan, Josephine Nevada, NB167.
Callahan, Lillian Alice, M2.
Callahan, Mary Alice, 3725.
Callahan, Mary E., NB71, NB72, M2.
Callahan, Mary Elizabeth, NB71, NB72,
    M2.
Callahan, Muskogee, J., 536.
Callahan, Ruby, 3880.
Callahan, Sam, 1092, NB75.
Callahan, Samuel B., 433, 440, 464, 465, 536.
Callahan, Sarah, 433, 440, 464, 465, 536.
Callahan, Sarah E., 433, 440, 464, 465, 536.
Callahan, S. B., 433, 440, 464, 465, 536.
Callahan, Walter K., 465, 3725, 3880, NB167.
Campbell, Albert, 929.

Campbell, Bertha, M91.
Campbell, Bill, 3879.
Campbell, Fannie, 929.
Campbell, Frank, 3879.
Campbell, Jessie, 1830, NB113, M91.
Campbell, Susan, 929.
Campbell, Tine Winburn, NB113.
Campbell, Tom, NB113, M91.
Campbell, William, 929.
Campbell, Willie, 1334.
Canard, 1771.
Canard, Billy, 1543, NB921, NB1105, M250
Canard, Cogee, 1925, 1926.
Canard, David, 1437.
Canard, Felix, 1513, 1520, 3431.
Canard, George, 2372.
Canard, Hannah, 1437, M143.
Canard, Harris, 1926.
Canard, Hully, 1437.
Canard, James, 2163, 3419.
Canard, Jeff, 1514, 3419.
Canard, Jennie, 1812.
Canard, Jim, 2195.
Canard, Joseph, 1543, 3112.
Canard, Judy, 1464.
Canard, Katie, 1543, 2195, NB1050, M24 .
Canard, Kizzie, 1552, NB921, NB1105, M250.
Canard, Lena, NB147.
Canard, Lizzie, 2340, NB215.
Canard, Louiney, 3112.
Canard, Louisa, 2407, NB1105.
Canard, Lucy, 1543.
Canard, Lusaryar, 1543.
Canard, Maggie, 1464.
Canard, Malinda, 2163.
Canard, Martha, 2372.
Canard, Martin, 202, NB147.
Canard, Millie, NB921.
Canard, Nancy, 1464, 3431, NB215.
Canard, Narburg, 1543.
Canard, Pitchie, 2163.
Canard, Pusley, 1520.
Canard, Rachel, 1514.
Canard, Roly, 1514
Canard, Rosanna, 1543.
Canard, Sallie, 1437, 1438.
Canard, Sam, 1464, NB215.
Canard, Samuel, 1464, NB215.
Canard, Siah, 1789.
Canard, Simmer, 1514, 3419.
Canard, Sophia, 1464.
Canard, Susan, 2163, 2195, NB887, NB1117,
    M178.
Canard, Susanna, 2195, 2163, NB887, NB1117,
    M178.
Canard, Stephen, 3431.
Canard, Tampa, 1620.
Canard, Tilda, M250.
Canard, Thomas, 1464, 1512, 1513, 1514, 1515,
    1739.
Canard, Tom, 1464, 1512, 1513, 1514, 1515, 1739.
Canard, Wash, 1812, 2340.
Canard, Yarner, 1512, 1513, 1514.
Canawa, Missie, 3983.
Canawa, Robert, 3983.
Cane, Cecil, M41.
Cane, Charles, 1276, 12, 711.
Cane, Charlie, 12, 711, 1276.

Cane, Charlie R.,12 NB227, NB 228, M41
Cane, Hattie N., 12.
Cane, Minnie, P. 12.
Cane, Mollie B., 12, NB227, NB228, M41.
Cane, Robert Carl, NB227.
Cane, Priscilla, 12.
Cane, William R., NB228.
Caney, 1635.
Ganie, 2482.
Canpethlela, 940.
Capeconey, 2307.
Capitcher, 2475.
Caponey, 587, 638.
Carbage, John, 1076.
Carbage, Monky, 1076.
Cardimney, 3329.
Carey, Jessie, 2557, NB151.
Carey, Tuxie, 2557.
Carhokee, 2823.
Carlile, Bessie, 1066, NB138.
Carlile, Ora, 1066.
Carlile, Sylvia, 1065, 1066.
Carlile, Thos., 1065, 1066.
Carna, 1895.
Garnard, Annie, 546.
Carnard, Harry, 546.
Carnard, Samuel, 546.
Carney, Amey, 3644.
Carney, Fulsom, 2879.
Carney, Robert, 2879.
Carney, Wallace Jr., 3644.
Carney, Wallace Sr., 3644.
Carnie, Chitto, 117.
Carr, 509.
Carr, Ada, NB357. M105.
Carr, Ada Bell, NB357, M105.
Carr, Addie, 61, 2044, 3318, M328.
Carr, Albert, 722, 825.
Carr, Alex, 443.
Carr, Annie, 443.
Carr, Annis, 61.
Carr, Archie, 2963.
Carr, Bessie, 1836.
Carr, Bettie, 61, 2101.
Carr, Billy, 491.
Carr, Caroline, 309, 976.
Carr, Cecil Raymond, NB755.
Carr, Chipley, 509.
Carr, Cornelius, 244.
Carr, David, 309, 976.
Carr, Eliza, 491.
Carr, Ellen, 1836.
Carr, Etta, 3318.
Carr, Eunice, 1417.
Carr, Frank, 722.
Carr, George, 2370, 2959.
Carr, Harley, 3852.
Carr, Hepsey, 453.
Carr, Homer Lee, M105.
Carr, Ida, 61, NB527, NB528.
Carr, John, 282, 443.
Carr, Leaster, 1360.
Carr, Limbo, 1836, NB948.
Carr, Lucy, 244.
Carr, Lulu, 61.
Carr, Mabel, 3318.
Carr, Millie, 1836, NB948.
Carr, Nancy, 282, 722.
Carr, Nellie, 1914.
Carr, Nicey, 453.

Carr, Paddy, 722.
Carr, Rachael, 1914, 2370.
Carr, Rachel, 1914, 2370.
Carr, Richard, 244.
Carr, Robért, 61, 2101.
Carr, Salina, 1836.
Carr, Sallie, 443, 721, 722, 2561, 2963.
Carr, Severs, 722.
Carr, Siah, 919.
Carr, Susan E., 825.
Carr, Susanna, 443, NB74, M1.
Carr, Thomas, 722, 1914, 2370, 3852, NB357 ,
    M105.
Carr, Timbo, 2561.
Carr, Tom, 1914, 2370, 2666, 2963.
Carr, Topley, 1789.
Carr, Verna Vinita, NB357.
Carr, Vida, NB755.
Carr, Washington, NB948.
Carr, Will, 807.
Carr, Willie, 919, 1417, 2561, 3318.
Carr, William, 825, NB755.
Carr, William H., 807.
Carr, William M., 825, NB755.
Carruth, Dicey, 386.
Carruth, Katie, 386.
Carruth, Lewis, 386.
Carter, Anna, 1105, 551, 697, 1124, 3673, NB-
    48, NB49, NB820.
Carter, Annie, 551, 697, 1105, 1124, 3673, NB-
    48, NB49, NBS20.
Carter, Berry, 432.
Carter, Ethel Lee, 1105.
Carter, Fred, 1124, 3196.
Carter, George, 551, 655.
Carter, Henry, 1124, NB48, NB49.
Carter, Jennie, NB49.
Carter, Jim, 3196.
Carter, Joe, NB820.
C rter, John Calvin, 432.
Carter, John W., 697.
Carter, Joseph, 1105, 3673.
Carter, Joseph B., 3673, 1105.
Carter, Minnie Lou, 3673.
Carter, Millie C., 697.
Carter, Rachel, 1124, 3196.
Carter, Rosa, 697.
Carter, Rufus M., 432.
Carter, Sallie, 697.
Carter, Sarah, 432.
Carter, Susie, NB48.
Carter, William Thomas, NB820.
Carthlony, 571, 582.
Carthlony, Tahsalay, 571.
Carthonnay, 560.
Carvy, John, 913.
Carvy, Lewis, 913.
Casekayamikko, 2385.
Casey, Alvro Edgar, NB640.
Casey, Eli, NB641.
Casey, John, 673, 990, NB639, NB640
    NB641.
Casey, John Jr., 673.
Casey, Joseph, 3897.
Casey, Julia, 673, 990.
Casey, Nellie, 673.
Casey, Sallie, 2456, NB870.
Casey, Savannah, NB639, NB640, NB641.
Casey, Vera Irene, NB639.

Casteel, Hose, 1143, 1147, 1170.
Casteel, Hosey, 1143, 1147, 1170.
Casteel, Lizzie, 1143, 1147.
Casteel, Sammie, 1143.
Castello, George, 3490.
Castello, Ettie, 3490.
Castello, Nora, 3490.
Castile, Hose, 936.
Castile, Lizzie, 936.
Castillo, Geo. C., NB203.
Castillo, Mabel, NB203.
Castillo, Nettie, 172, NB203.
Cat, Annie, 1333.
Cat, John, 1333.
Cat, Lou, 1333.
Cat, Matildia, 1333.
Cat, Monday, 1333.
Cat, Tilda, 888.
Catah, 600, 605, 612.
Catch, Willie, 3395.
Catchoche, 2140.
Cates, Catherine, 3932.
Cates, Governor, NB1005.
Cates, Jacob, 3932.
Cates, Harriet, 2054.
Cates, Jeff, 2054.
Cates, Joseph, 2054, NB1005.
Cates, Lydia, 3142, NB1005.
Cathumka, 2613, 2615.
Cato, 3351.
Cato, Ben, 3351, 3999.
Cato, Rhoda, 3999.
Cato, Rody, 3351, 3379.
Cayado, 2799.
Cayponney, 587, 638.
Ceasar, 2598, 3164.
Ceasar, Judy, 3164.
Cedar, Susan, 2255.
Celey, 2115, 2364.
Celie, 2115, 2364.
Ceyado, 2555.
Chacogee, 2145.
Chaegey, 3398.
Chahoya, 1470.
Chakie, 1428.
Chalakee, Daniel, 331.
Chalakee, Jimsey, 331.
Chalakee, Jimmy, 331.
Chalakee, Johnny, 331.
Chalakee, Louvina, 331.
Chalakee, Mary, 331.
Chalakee, Nicey, 331, NB168, M155
Chalakee, Thomas, 331.
Chalega, 1261, 1262, 1263.
Chaleka, 1965.
Chaluggee, 105.
Chamberlain, Charlie Leroy, 402.
Chamberlain, Dewey, NB982.
Chamberlain, John C., 402, 3708, NB982, NB983.
Chamberlain, Ruby, NB983.
Chamberlain, Ruth Hazel, 3708.
Chamberlain, Susie, 402, 3708, NB982, NB983.
Chambers, Dick 805.
Chambers, Lewis, 805.
Chamela, 1560.
Chapana, 561.
Chapman, Frank, 140, 143.

Chapman, Mary Lu, 140, NB13, NB14 NB15.
Charcotetenna, 2261, 2262.
Charcotetenna, Elder, 2261.
Charcotetenna, Ella, NB1181.
Charcotetenna, Katie, 2261, NB1181.
Charcotetenna, Polly, 2261, 2262.
Chardy, Lucy, 3169.
Chardy, Susie, 3169, NB187.
Charity, Christie, 3092.
Charity, Lady, 3092.
Charity, Loona, 3092.
Charkoche, 174.
Charlage, 1843.
Charles, David, 3155.
Charles, Ellen, 316, 2956, NB424, NB425.
Charles, Ellis Buffington, NB425.
Charles, Gustavus A., 316.
Charles, James, 2956.
Charles, Little, 3153, 3154, 3155.
Charles, Losewa, 3153, 3154, 3155.
Charles, Louisa, 3153.
Charles, Lousannah, 3153, 3154, 3155.
Charles, Lucinda, 3155.
Charles, Nero, 316.
Charles, Nero, Creek Frd., 3355, NB424 NB425.
Charles, Reuben, 316.
Charles, Sam, 3153.
Charles, Sammie, 2956.
Charles, Sophia, NB424.
Charles, Sukey, 2956.
Charles, Thomas, 3154.
Charles, William, 2582.
Charlesey, 3631, NB65, NB666.
Charlesey, Ellen, 2330, 3631, NB665, NB666.
Charlesey, Flora, NB665.
Charlesey, Jennie, 3631.
Charlesey, Lizzie, 3631.
Charlesey, Martha, NB666.
Charley, Stella, 2115.
Charley, Thomas, 2115.
Charlie, Lucy, 2112.
Charlie, Micco, 431.
Charlochee, 2146, 2471.
Charlochie, 2510.
Charmosey, 2651.
Charnoche, 1240.
Charta, 2887.
Charte, Micco, 1864.
Chartie, Washington, 367.
Chartla, 957.
Charty, Chak, 1035.
Charty, Chok, 531.
Charty, Micco, 1144, 1438.
Charty, Nero, 1084.
Chasmiche, 3384.
Chastain, Fritz, M64.
Chastain, Hallie, 3150.
Chastain, Martin, M413.
Chastain, Ottie, 689, M64.
Chastain, Roland, M64.
Chastine, Hallie, 689.
Chastieskey, 105.
Chatete, 588.
Chatma, 1328.
Chatotey, 598.
Chawazte, 3046.
Chawee, 2432.

Chebe, 2479.
Chebonagie, 2554.
Checotah, Cilla, 28, 31, 451. 1704.
Checotah, Lizzie, 378.
Checotah, Louisianna, '28·
Checotah, Martin, 28.
Checotah, Millie, 329, NB835, NB836.
Checotah, Priscella, 28, 31, 451, 1704.
Checotah, Sam, 28, 31, 451, 1704.
Checotah, Samuel, 28, 31, 378, 1704.
Checotah, Silla, 28, 31, 451, 1704.
Checote, Annie, 63, M280.
Checote, Eliza J., 63.
Checote, Emma, 378, NB8.
Checote, George W., 63.
Checote, Jefferson, 63.
Checote, Jefferson Davis, M280.
Checote, Lizzie, 66.
Checote, Martin L., 63.
Checote, Samuel, 63, 66, M280.
Checote, Samuel J., 63, 66, M280.
Checote, Samuel J., Jr., 63.
Checowee, 3945.
Cheek, Levia, 1677.
Cheesupka, 65.
Chehegee, 2910.
Chelaha, 2857.
Chelokkee, 277.
Chemarye, 1359.
Chemehaka, 1397.
Chemonah, 1329, 1340.
Chenashe, 1482.
Chenewee, 185.
Chenewee, Ella, 185. ˋ
Chenewee, Joe, 185.
Chenewee, Rider, 185.
Cheniwee, 277.
Chenochige, 3233.
Chenoska, 2386.
Chenosky, 1306, M482.
Chenubia, Martha, NB193.
Chenubia, Susie, 159, NB193.
Chenupy, Jennie, 1067.
Chenupy, Tom, 1067.
Cheparney, 235, 2918, 2947.
Cheponaka, 1003.
Chequawa, 2716, 3762, 3785.
Cherry, Colona Blanche, NB363.
Cherry, Francis Doyle, NB364.
Cherry, Jennie, 213, NB363, NB364.
Cherry, Joe, NB8363, NB364.
Chesopka, 450.
Chesoppey, 3157.
Cheyanny, 148.
Chief, Celia, 928, 1502, 1797, 3186, 3731.
Chief, Jim, 928, 1502, 1797, 3186, 3731.
Chief, Louena, 3250, 3987.
Chief, Reuben, 3731.
Chief, Wilburn, 3186.
Chicka, 1155.
Childers, Alice, 183.
Childers, Amos, 245.
Childers, Anderson, 1234, 3323, 3492, NB306.
Childers, Anderson J., 1234, 3323, 3492, NB.
    306.
Childers, Annie, 183, 317, 3453, 3515, NB323,
    NB324, NB431.
Childers, Annie B., 183, 317, 3453, 3515, NB-
    323, NB324. NB431.
Childers, Arthur, 3492.

Childers, Ben, NB323, NB324.
Childers, Benjamin, 183, 3515.
Childers, Bill, 245.
Childers, Bob, 291.
Childers, Bowman, 291.
Childers, Chisso, 231, 3589, NB1122.
Childers, Clarence Wm., 835.
Childers, Cooie, 779.
Childers, Daisy, 3323, 3474, NB515.
Childers, Daniel, 183, 266, 804, 835, NB387
    M354.
Childers, Edward, 291, 3576.
Childers, Effie, 740, NB1122.
Childers, Eliza, 291.
Childers, Ellis, 291.
Childers, Ellis B., 1156.
Childers, Eloise, M354.
Childers, Emma, 210, 779, NB246, NB. 247.
Childers, Emmet, 231, NB433.
Childers, Fannie, 1156.
Childers, Garfield, 302, 3732, NB433.
Childers, Googee, 242.
Childers, Hattie, 171, 740.
Childers, Henry, 210, 1191.
Childers, Hubert, 779.
Childers, Ida, 231, 312, 3732, NB433.
Childers, Irene, 1156.
Childers, James, 302, 317, 804.
Childers, James E., 1975.
Childers, Jane, 317.
Childers, Jennie, 317.
Childers, Jim, 3453.
Childers, Joe, 804, 1885.
Childers, John, 291.
Childers, Lena, 231.
Childers, Lewis, 292, 3604.
Childers, Lewis C., 245.
Childers, Lizzie, 183.
Childers, Louis, 242, 1885.
Childers, Lucy, 210, 230.
Childers, Lydia, 266, 804, 835, 1234, 3323, 3492,
    NB306.
Childers, Lyddie, 183.
Childers, Maggie, 1191.
Childers, Mahaley, 245.
Childers, Mandy, 335.
Childers, Maria, 302, 245, 863, 2067, NB431.
Childers, Mariah, 245, 302, 863, 2067, NB431.
Childers, Mary, 19, 210, 291, 292, 317, 1191·
Childers, Matilda, 302, 317.
Childers, Mattie, 1975.
Childers, Mildred, 835, NB387, M354.
Childers, Millie, 231, 3589, NB1122.
Childers, Mose, NB324.
Childers, NB316, 779, 863, 1156, 1234, 1975,
    3576.
Childers, Paul, 804.
Childers, Pearlie, 302.
Childers, Pratt, 804, NB515.
Childers, Quincey, 3589.
Childers, Rachel, 171, 231, 1191, 2255, 2298,
    2977, NB201.
Childers, Rachael, 171, 231, 1191, 2255, 2298,
    2977, NB201.
Childers, Red Eagle, 183.
Childers, R. H. P., 3474.
Childers, Richard, 3474.
Childers, Robert, 171, 210, 230, 231, 266, 616,
    2255, 2298, 2977.
Childers, Robert, Jr., 616.

Chisholm, Sophia, 408.
Chisholm, Tilda, 408.
Chisholm, Tom, 1963, 3342.
Chisholm, William, 1661, 1912.
Chism, Finney, 1623.
Chism, Kate, 1623.
Chisse, Rhoda, 2787.
Chisso, 78.
Chissoe, 122, 179, 1982.
Chissoe, Annie B., 91.
Chissoe, Austin, 89.
Chissoe, Dora, 89.
Chissoe, Elnora, 89.
Chissoe, Hazel, 91.
Chissoe, Lena E., 124, 3434, NB673, NB711
      M182.
Chissoe, Mahaley, 179, 1982.
Chissoe, Mary, 179.
Chissoe, Newton B., 91.
Chissoe, Oldman, 89, 91.
Chissoe, Please S., NB673.
Chissoe, Quinton, M182.
Chissoe, Sadie, 91.
Chissoe, Sally, 89.
Chissoe, Sam, 124, 3434, NB673, BN744
      M182.
Chissoe, Sam, Jr., NB744.
Chissoe, Sarah, 3819.
Chissoe, Taylor, 89, 91, 124.
Chissoe, Theodore S., 3434.
Chissoe, William, 91, 124.
Chissoe, Willie, 179, 3819.
Chiye, 2190.
Chlechuchee, 1290
Cho Hachoche, 2819.
Chocawaptah, 2726.
Chocfolecha, 1210.
Chockley, 204.
Chockley, Billie, 204.
Chockley, Inlooker, 204.
Chockley, Mary, 209.
Chockley, Mollie, 204.
Chockley, Pusler, 204, 209.
Chockley, Sebon, 204.
Choctiger, 2075.
Choelle, 2825.
Chofochaye, 1549.
Chofoloche, 2911.
Chogee, 2822.
Chogottey, 1024.
Chohoba, 2841.
Choka, 2142.
Chokcharty, 1080.
Chokfalitchee, 1716, 1717.
Chokiapy, 2529.
Chokussahola, 114.
Chormiller, 1560.
Chotka, 2402.
Chotke, 3357.
Chotke, Barney, 2498.
Chotke, Sophie, 3357.
Chotkey, Addie, 2940.
Chotkey, Billy, CE4020.
Chotkey, Mahala, 2940, M448.
Chotkey, Nancy, 2940.
Chotky, NB1171.
Chotky, William, NB1171.
Chotlar, 1014.
Choty, Fish, 1214.
Chowa, 2512.

Cobb, Johnnie, NB322.
Coblar, 3984.
Cocan, 400.
Co cath la ney, 596, 604.
Cocheryah, 1977.
Cocheryah, Lucy, 1977.
Cohn, Joe, 3903.
Cohn, Oklosey, 3903.
Cohn, Rhod, 3903.
Coch nek ny, 3050.
Cochran, George, 3481.
Cochran, Jesse, 704.
Cochran, Rockey F., 704.
Cochran, Walter Lee, 3401.
Co con wee, 1010, 1012.
Coco se, 2729. 2730.
Co co tah la ney, 2308.
Co den ny, 1745, NB918.
Codeny , 2945.
Cody, 3214.
Cody, Lizzie, 3214.
Coffee, Effie, 1125, NB754.
Coffee, Jimmy, 1130.
Coffee, John, 207, 2627, 2681, M476.
Coffee, Lucy, 3769.
Coffee, Micco, 1126, 3769.
Coffee, Polly, 1126, 3769.
Coffee, Susie, 2681, M476.
Coffee, Willie, 1125.
Coffee, Winey, M476. `
Cogee, 2385.
Cogegee, 1404.
Cohahda, 3338.
Coker, Alex., 3100.
Coker, Annie, 2952, M470.
Coker, Charley, 3170, 3404, NB1178, NB-
          1179, M470.
Coker, Cheparney, 3862.
Coker, Colbert, 3170.
Coker, Dave, 1581, 3791, NB506.
Coker, David, 1581, 3791, NB506.
Coker, Ella, NB1179.
Coker, Eliza, 80, M258.
Coker, Emma, 2974.
Coker, Gibson, 3404.
Coker, Henry, 80.
Coker, Hettie, 1452, 3791, NB506, NB1178,
          NB1179, M470.
Coker, Hetty, 1452, 3791, NB506, NB1178
          NB1179, M470.
Coker, Jipsey, 3170.
Coker, Kogie, 2271.
Coker, Leah, 3404.
Coker, Lewis, 1501, 3862, M258.
Coker, Litchee-Seminole, 295, M258.
Coker, Litchie, 3862.
Coker, Litsey-Seminole, 295, M258.
Coker, Lizzie, 3170, 3404.
Coker, London, 73, 1500, 1501, 1509, 1581, 1626,
          1629, 2271, 2952, 3100, 3239, N-
          B506.
Coker, Lucy, 3170.
Coker, Mary, 73, 1581, 1626, 1629.
Coker, Ober, 3404.
Coker, Polly, 3170.
Coker, Richmond, 3791.
Coker, Sallo, NB1178.
Coker, Sissie, 1452, 3791, NB506, NB1178,
          NB1179, M470.
Coker, Thomas, 3239.

301

Coker, William, 1626.
Coker, Wisey, 2952.
Cokey, 1683, 1685.
Colbert, Albertha, M456.
Colbert, Benjamin, 1070.
Colbert, Bettie, 3647.
Colbert, C. Bell., M456.
Colbert, Charley, 2014.
Colbert, Daniel, 2676, 3647, NB888.
Colbert, Dick, 2676, 2945.
Colbert, Ella, 1070.
Colbert, Ellen, 2990, 3355, 3454, NB1059.
Colbert, George, 1070, Fr. 3649, M456.
Colbert, Jackson, 2014.
Colbert, James, 1753.
Colbert, Jemima, 2543, NB888.
Colbert, Joe, 1752, 2014.
Colbert, Kizzie, 3081, NB1059.
Colbert, Leemon, 3081.
Colbert, Linda, 3454.
Colbert, Lizzie, 1752, M55, M56.
Colbert, Louis, 3027.
Colbert, Louvina, 1070.
Colbert, Lucy, 2676, 3647.
Colbert, Mahala, 2210, 2990.
Colbert, Mahale, 2210, 2990.
Colbert, Malissa, 3081.
Colbert, Mary, 661, 1752.
Colbert, Matilda, 3026.
Colbert, Nellie, 3355.
Colbert, Peggy, 3027.
Colbert, Robert, 1752.
Colbert, Sam, 2999, 3027.
Colbert, Sarah, 2014.
Colbert, Semondy, 2014.
Colbert, Thompson, 2990, 3355, 3454, NB-
    1059.
Colbert, Walter, 3027.
Colbert, William, 2210, NB888.
Colbert, Willie, 1752.
Colbert, Willis, 3081.
Collins, Addie, 2044, 2068, M328.
Collins, Annie, 730.
Collins, Arcelia, 723.
Collins, Aurora, 1386.
Collins, Austin, 420.
Collins, Bryan S., 1386.
Collins, Cora L., 1386.
Collins, Dina, 169.
Collins, Dora, 3475.
Collins, Emma L., 1386.
Collins, Henry, 1386.
Collins, Howard R., 1386.
Collins, Jacob M., 731, 3744, NB1112.
Collins, Jennie, 420, 2068.
Collins, Jinnie, 161.
Collins, John, 723, 731.
Collins, Kogee, 3475.
Collins, Lewis, 420, 3608, NB718.
Collins, Lila, 161.
Collins, Linda, 161, 723, 724, 2068.
Collins, Lucy, 420.
Collins, Mattie, M328.
Collins, Nancy D., 3744, NB1112.
Collins, Ned, 169.
Collins, Nicey, 577, 2068.
Collins, Noah, NB718.
Collins, Norma, 1386.
Collins, Orvid L., 1386.
Collins, Parsey, 838.

Collins, Peter, 730.
Collins, Roman, 420.
Collins, Roy, NB1112.
Collins, Sandy, 161, 169.
Collins, Shannon R., 1386.
Collins, Shawnee, 723, 724, 2068.
Collins, Sophie, 420, 3608, NB718.
Collins, Sunday, 3117.
Collins, Susana, 3608.
Collins, Wash, 577, 2068.
Collins, Wash Jr., 2068.
Collins, Willie, 2068. 3475, M328.
Collins, Wynema, 1386.
Colman, Nettie G., M326, NB573, NB-
    574.
Colman, W. E., NB573, NB 574, M326.
Colman, William E., NB573, NB574, M
    326.
Colmon, Dollie C., 2198.
Colmon, Georgia Evelean, M326.
Colmon, Gladdys Leuna, NB574.
Colmon, Nettie Alice, NB573.
Colmon, Nettie G., 2198.
Colmon, William E., 2198.
Colonel, Agnes, 1516.
Colonel, George, 1516.
Colvin, Charley, M171.
Colvin, Lewis, M171.
Combs, Birl, 494.
Combs, John Boyd, NB694.
Combs, John W., 494, NB694, NB230.
Combs, Joseph, 494.
Combs, J. W., 494, NB230, NB694.
Combs, Katie, 494, NB230, NB694.
Combs, Pearl, NB230.
Combs, Rena, 494.
Comie, Larley, NB1004.
Comie, Martha, 2099, NB1004.
Comie, Thomas, 2131, NB1004.
Commesee, 2717.
Company, 136.
Company, Daniel, 2757.
Company, Garrett, 2757.
Company, Lizzie, 339, 514.
Company, Sam, 2757.
Compeer, Harper, 399.
Compier, Albert, 2812.
Compier, Mary, 1455.
Compier, Mitchell, 1624, NB1162.
Compier, Willie, NB1162.
Conahigee, 105.
Conahke, 3104.
Conarhohay, 1839.
Conchartoge, 201.
Concharty, 206, 481, 1387, 2195, 3249.
Coneisenney, 2982.
Coney, Liza, 1510.
Coney, Moses, 1510.
Coney, Tom, 1510.
Coneyoh, 2982.
Confahny, 2162.
Conhegee, 2461.
Conley, Oscar, 2463.
Conley, William, 2463.
Connahcha, 2511.
Conner, 2164, 2643.
Conner, Abbie, 3307, M58, M226.
Conner, Adam, 2643.
Conner, Amey, 2740.
Conner, John, 3307.

Conner, Lucy, 2098, 2099, 2643.
Conner, Nettie, 3307.
Conner, Thomas, 3022, 3307, M226.
Conner, Thomas Jr., M226.
Conner, Willie, 3307.
Conner, Lizzie, 197.
Conpethlela, 1935.
Conpethloney, 2103.
Conseney, 1224.
Conthenny, 2166.
Conwe, 235.
Coocwooye, 3410.
Coodey, Amanda, 735.
Coodey, Joseph, 735, 737, 1053.
Coodey, Mary, 1053.
Coodey, Minnie, 735.
Coodey, Sarah J., 2371.
Coodey, Walter Lee, NB657.
Coodey, William S., 735, NB657.
Coody, Joseph M., 2371
Coody, Levena, NB657.
Coody, Thornberry, 2371.
Coody, Takey, 2522.
Coody, William S., 735, NB657.
Cook, Chily, 696.
Cook, Daniel, 696, 3423.
Cook, Hammond, 3424.
Cook, Hannah, 696, 1748.
Cook, Hannah L., 696, 1748.
Cook, Jesse, 696.
Cook, Joseph, 696.
Cook, Leah, 2057, 3424.
Cook, Louisa, 696.
Cook, Rueben, 696, 1748.
Cook, Wallace, 696.
Cooks, Zachariah, 696, 1634.
Coon, Albert, 721.
Coon, Charles, 721.
Coon, Cumpsy, 1267.
Coon, Fred, 721, 3510, NB144.
Coon, Fred C., 721, 3510, NB144.
Coon, Freddie Carr, 721.
Coon, Gracie Amber 3510.
Coon, Jackson, 2504.
Coon, Kaney, 1267.
Coon, Lader, 2504.
Coon, Lizzie, 148.
Coon, Lumsey, 2864.
Coon, Munner, 148, M452.
Coon, Narlie, 148.
Coon, Oda M., NB144.
Coon, Roy, 721.
Coon, Sallie, 721, 3510, NB144.
Coon, Sam, 148.
Coon, Sealey, 1267.
Coon, Simer, 148.
Coon, Suckie, 1783.
Coon, Taylor, 148.
Coon, Tobler, 1267.
Coon, William, 1267.
Coon, Watka, 148.
Coonhead, 2739.
Coonhead, Eliza, 370, 633, 3374.
Coonhead, Hannah, 633.
Coonhead, John, NB1284.
Coonhead, Joshua, 3374.
Coonhead, Nessie, 2739.
Coonhead, Nicey, 633.
Coonhead, Susan, 105, NB1284.
Coonhead, Willie, 2739, NB1284.

Coonhead, Wm., 633, 3374.
Cooper, 603.
Cooper, Ada, M74.
Cooper, Albert, 603.
Cooper, Annie, 213, 281, 3854, NB158, M327.
Cooper, E. E., 281, NB158, M327.
Cooper, Effie, NB56.
Cooper, Elbert, 3854.
Cooper, Eliza, 210, NB55, NB56.
Cooper, Ella, 3567.
Cooper, Emma, 287.
Cooper, Ezra E., 281, M327, NB158.
Cooper, Florence, N. B. 158.
Cooper, Grant, NB55, NB56.
Cooper, John, 603.
Cooper, Nancy, 602, NB476, M126.
Cooper, Nellie, NB476.
Cooper, Pleasant Porter, M327.
Cooper, Rosa, M126.
Cooper, Sam, 603, 3567, NB476, M126.
Cooper, Sarah, 3567.
Cooper, Stella, 3854.
Cooper, Wheeler, NB55.
Cooper, Willie, M74.
Cooty, 224.
Copahtanney, 2982.
Copathanney, 1224.
Coppedge, Bernice, M230.
Coppedge, C. E., M230, NB28.
Coppedge, Charles E., NB28, M230.
Coppedge, Emma, 470, NB28, M230.
Coppedge, Velma G., NB28.
Coquan ,3338.
Coquay, 2117
Cordry, Charlotte, 860.
Cordry, Earl, 860.
Corey, Cordelia, NB745.
Corey, Frank, NB745, NB1061.
Corey, Josee, 1038, NB745, NB1061.
Corey, Tom, NB1061.
Cornelius, Elias, 8.
Cornelius, George, 1842.
Cornelius, Millie, 1839, 1842, 1846.
Cornell, Annie, 1696.
Cornell, Benjamin, 1696.
Cornell, Cinda, 1696.
Cornell, David, 1696, NB572.
Cornell, Emily, 1696.
Cornell, Mamie, 3592, NB572.
Cornell, Manie, 1696, NB572.
Corbell, Moses, 3592.
Cornell, Robert, 1516.
Cornell, Timmye, 326.
Cornell, Willie, 1696, 3592, NB572.
Cornells, Absalom, 1692.
Cornells, Emma, 1516.
Cornells, Lucy, 1692.
Cornells, Melissey, 1516.
Coronel, Temish, 1699.
Cosannah, 3303.
Cosar, Annie, 3307.
Cosar, Beeker, 1614.
Cosar, Chester, 3099.
Cosar, Galvos, NB977.
Cosar, George, 3099, 3307, CE4025.
Cosar, Jennie, 1614, 3615, NB977.
Cosar, Lillie, 1705.
Cosar, Lucinda, 3099, CE4025.
Cosar, Lydia, 1614.
Cosar, Mack, 1705.

Cosar, Melissa, 3099.
Cosar, Peter, M58.
Cosar, Sam, 3615.
Cosar, Sissie, 1705.
Cosar, Susie, CE4025.
Cosar, Tom, 1614, 1615, NB977.
Cosar, Willie, 2449, M58.
Coser, 444.
Coser, Annie, 444, 2965.
Coser, Lena, NB485.
Coser, Lizzie, 1137, NB485.
Coser, Mattie, 2965.
Coser, Nancy, 444, 1137, M382.
Coser, Nuttetsa, 1137, NB485.
Cosoe, 61.
Cossunger. 1366.
Cotah, 1745.
Cotahganey, 2716.
Cotahsowena. 562.
Cotanny, 1188.
Cotcher, 2442.
Cotcherthlepaya, 1721.
Cotchute, 1707.
Cotenney, CE4022.
Cotesa, 1014.
Cotetan, 2103.
Cotimmy, 2240.
Cotimmy, Lucy, 2240.
Cotoesee, 236, 2188, 2731.
Cotoney, 2260.
Couch, Allie B., NB100.
Couch, Amanda, 3450, 791, NB99, NB100.
Couch, Gertie May, NB99.
Couch, J. C., 3450, NB99, NB100.
Couch, John C., 3450, NB99, NB100.
Couch, Roy L., 3450.
Cousin, Thompson, 182.
Cousins, Mattie, 71, NB104.
Cousins, Willie, 71.
Covey, Byron, 538.
Covey, Byron L., 538.
Covey, John, 538.
Covey, Marcus William, 538.
Covey, Mary K., 538.
Cowans, Austin, 404.
Cowans, Hugh, 402, 404, 406.
Cowans, Katie, 404, NB383.
Cowans, Thompson, 404.
Cowasta, 1114, 1841.
Cowe, Annie, 2567.
Cowe, Effa, NB78.
Cowe, Major, 2567.
Cowe, Malinda McGirt, 1520, NB78, M45.
Cowe, Maydella, M45.
Cowe, Melinda, 1520, NB78, M45.
Cowe, Porter, 3282.
Cowe, Samuel, 2567.
Cowe, Sarde, 2847, 2849.
Cowe, Satre, 2849, 2847.
Cowe, Sarty, 1520, NB78, M45.
Cowe, Wisey, 2849.
Cowee, Ella, 3936.
Cowee, Major, 3936.
Cowee, Nancy, 3936.
Coweny, 2294.
Coweny, Jude, 1060.
Cowesee, 2424.
Cowesee, Losey, 2424.
Coweta, 2080.
Cowetachee, 2568, 2702.

Cowetoche, 2568, 2702.
Cowokochee, 3301.
Cox, Annie, 2523.
Cox, Burrel, 230.
Cox, Cheparnie, 2774.
Cox, Cooty, 841.
Cox, Culla, 2774.
Cox, Daniel, 841.
Cox, D. C., 1849.
Cox, Isparhecher, 230.
Cox, Jennie, 3633.
Cox, John, 841, 3522.
Cox, Kullar, 2774.
Cox, Lewis, 841 .
Cox, Louis, 2523.
Cox, Lucy, 1849, 1850.
Cox, Ludie, 3522.
Cox, Lydia, 230.
Cox, Maggie, 2523, NB269, NB270, M237.
Cox, Nancy, 2523, 3522, NB444.
Cox, Sarah, 2774.
Cox, Wm. McKinley, 230.
Coyarkah, 2716.
Crabtree, Amelia, 1096.
Crabtree, Bessie, 1364.
Crabtree, Braxton B., 1364.
Crabtree, Dollie, 1074.
Crabtree, Elizabeth, 868.
Crabtree, Gabriel B., 1364.
Crabtree, Gabriel M., 1364, 1828.
Crabtree, George, 866, 1074, NB817, NB-
    818.
Crabtree, Gertie, 724.
Crabtree, G. N., 1640.
Crabtree, Hattie, 868, NB818.
Crabtree, Hattie H., 868.
Crabtree, James, 866.
Crabtree, James C., 1828.
Crabtree, James H., 724, 1096.
Crabtree, James Walrond, 1096.
Crabtree, Janie, 1828.
Crabtree, Leotia, 1096.
Crabtree, Lurline B., 1828.
Crabtree, Lynn, 1364.
Crabtree, Malinda, 1364, NB1169, NB1286.
Crabtree, Priscilla, 868, 1294.
Crabtree, Rebecca, NB817.
Crabtree, Sallie, 1364, 1828.
Crabtree, Sarah, 1640.
Crabtree, Shelton B., 1828.
Crabtree, Sue Anna, 868.
Crabtree, William B., 1364.
Crabtree, William F. Sr., 868.
Crabtree, William F. Jr., 868.
Crabtree, W. D., 868, 1294.
Craig, John, 434, 436.
Craig, Phoebe, 434, 436.
Crawford, Edna, M441.
Crawford, Henry, 1854, M441.
Crawford, Ida, M441.
Crawford, Victoria, 1854.
Crawford, Virgil, 1854.
Creeksahni, 2856.
Criswell, Mary J., 663.
Crosby, Berry Martin, NB596.
Crosby, B. M., 334, 887.
Crosby, Charles E., 334, NB596, NB-
    597.
Crosby, Elizabeth A., 334, NB596, NB597.
Crosby, Ellis Charles, 334.

Crosby, Ferdinand Wilber, NB597.
Crosby, Mary A., 333, 334, 887.
Crosby, Mary Elizabeth, 334.
Cross, Moses, 2272.
Cross, Sammy, 2272.
Crosslin. Martha, 492, NB974.
Crow, 946, 2017.
Crow, Ahlacohonny, 400, 3939.
Crow, Babie, 400, M286.
Crow, Cinda, 3340.
Crow, Fannie, 400, 3939.
Crow, George, 2806, 3340.
Crow, James, 2017.
Crow, Mary, 3340.
Crow, Melissa, 3340, NB637.
Crow, Mollie, 400.
Crow, Sarnie, 3340.
Crow, Sina, 3939.
Crow, Susie, 3939.
Crow, Tommy, NB637.
Crowell, Ben F., 15, NB699.
Crowell, Benjamin F., 15, NB699.
Crowell, Constantine Edward, M225.
Crowell, Edw., 13, 15, 17.
Crowell, Edward L. Jr., 13, NB1183.
Crowell, Francis Willard, NB1183.
Crowell, Ida May, NB1183.
Crowell, J. E., 13, 639.
Crowell, Joseph, 13, 639.
Crowell, Martha, 13, 15, 17, 639.
Crowell, Neta E., NB699.
Crowell, Ollie May, M225.
Crowell, Otis Buel, NB699.
Crowell, Robert A., 13.
Crowell, Thos. J., 17, M225.
Crowels, Annie, 2806, NB1147.
Crowels, Cilla, 2806.
Crowels, Freeman, 2806.
Crowels, Jonah, 2806.
Crowels, Katie, 2806.
Cruel, John, 89.
Cruel, Sally, 89.
Cubbie, Daniel, NB1203.
Cubbie, Jacob, 1549, NB1202, NB1203.
Cubbie, John J., 1549.
Cubbie, Liza, NB1202.
Cubbie, Rhoda, 1549, NB1202, NB1203.
Cubbitcha, 2027, 2243.
Cubbitcha, Lucy, 2027.
Cuffee, Bunnie, 2681.
Cuffy, Jim, 492.
Cuffy, Vicey, 492.
Culbert, 1816.
Culler, Annie, 1503.
Culler, David, 1503.
Culler, Jimmie, 1503.
Culler, Johnny, 1503.
Culler, Leah, NB1044.
Culler, Major, 1503.
Culler, Mary, 1503, NB1044.
Culler, Susie, 1503.
Culler, Thomas, 1503, NB1044.
Culler, Winnie, 1503.
Culler, Yarner, 1503.
Culley, 2469.
Culley, Albert, 2469.
Culley, Lucy, 2469.
Cummings, Alice, M108.
Cummings, Benjamin, 2232.
Cummings, Boyd, 232.

Cummings, David, 628, 833, 1396, 2232, NB-29, M108.
Cummings, Howard, 2232.
Cummings, Lonie, 1396.
Cummings, Louisa, 2232, NB29, M108.
Cummings, Mildred, 628, 1396.
Cummings, Millie, 833.
Cummings, Rufus, 2232.
Cummings, Susie, NB29.
Cummings, Thomas R , 2232.
Cumseh, 1670, 3192.
Cumseh, Annie, 220.
Cumseh, Charley, 220.
Cumseh. Fannie, 220.
Cumseh, John, 220.
Cumseh, Lucy, 220.
Cumseh, Manie, 3192, NB1156.
Cumseh, Moses, 220.
Cumseh, Myer, 220.
Cumseh, Parnoskey, 3192.
Cumseh, Sissie, 220.
Cumseh, Thomas, 220.
Cumsey, Annie, NB1073.
Cumsey, Casey, 999, NB1072, NB1073.
Cumsey, Charley, 979.
Cumsey, Emma, 979.
Cumsey, Lena, NB1072.
Cumsey, Lewis, 979, NB1072, NB1073.
Cumsey, Vinita, 2175.
Cundarlee, 2273.
Cunke, Charley, 1510.
Cunningham, Charles N., NB437, M248.
Cunningham, Charles Newton R., M248.
Cunningham, C. N., N. B. 437, M248.
Cunningham, Laura, 741, NB437, M248.
Cunningham, William Leo, NB437.
Cunnussa, CE4040.
Cuntullie, Willie, 2582.
Curtain, Becky, 632, 1563.
Curtain, Dick, 632, 1563.
Curtain, Lewis, 1563.
Curtain, Rebecca, 632, 1563.
Curtain, Richard, 632, 1563.
Custanugge, Cosar, 706.
Cuthenay, 605.
Cynda, 665, 2154.
Cyntoxgee, 1479.
Dacon, Chilly, 1557.
Dacon, Harney, 1557, 3320, M153.
Dacon, Lina, 1557.
Dacon, Nannie, 3320.
Dacon, Sandy, 1557.
Dacon, Sardy, 1557, 3320, M153.
Dacon, Sarty, 1557, 3320, M153
Dacon, Susanna, M153.
Daily, Dr. C. E., NB259.
Daily, Lucy S., 1815, NB259.
Daily, Margaret Willison, NB259.
Dale, Charles Henry, NB89.
Dale, Georgie, M19.
Dale, Izora E., 3706, 988, NB89, M19.
Dale, Mabel, 3706.
Dale, Oliver C., 3706, M19.
Damet, Eliza, 2265, NB95, NB96.
Damet, John P., NB95, NB96.
Damet, Susan, NB95.
Damet, William F., NB96.
Dan, Amy, 511.
Dan, Benjamin, 511.
Dan, Billy, 511.

Dan, Consey, M446.
Dan, Hobie, 493.
Dan, Lizzie, 1298, M446.
Dan, Sampson, 511.
Dan, Sandy, 493.
Dan, Siah, 493.
Dan, Somecher, 1328, M446.
Dan, Tena, 511.
Danbow, 2680,
Daniel, 100, 1060, 2474.
Daniel, Annie, 97, 3433.
Daniel, Eli, 3309.
Daniel, John, 95.
Daniel, Kano, 1300.
Daniel, Lizzie, 2194.
Daniel, Lusanna, 1060, NB750.
Daniel, Martin, 2194.
Daniel, Mary, 95, 3433, NB44.
Daniel, Metta, 3309.
Daniel, Miley, 97, NB1083.
Daniel, Robert, NB1083.
Daniel, Sallie, 1300.
Daniel, Thompson, 3309.
Daniel, Unah, 95, 97, 3433, NB44, NB1083.
Daniel, Unah Jr., NB44.
Daniel, Wm., 2194.
Daniels, 392.
Daniels, Bob, 589, 608.
Daniels, Jasper, 589.
Daniels, Josiah, 1480.
Daniels, Lemus, 608.
Daniels, Mollie, 608.
Daniels, Saloma, 589.
Daniels, Sanford, 608.
Danley, Hettie, 1443, 1444, 1508.
Danly, Hittie, 1465.
Dannar, 1848.
Dansby, Andy, 607.
Dansby, Bertha, 607.
Dansby, Ella, 607.
Dansby, Lucinda, NB813.
Dansby, Martha, 607.
Dansby, Vick, 607, NB813.
Dansby, Vicy, 607, NB813.
Dansby, Walter, 607, NB813.
Dasacowee, 601.
Dasher, Annie, Zora 2072.
Dasher, Frank, 1209, 2072.
Dasher, Ida Belle, 2072, 1214.
Dasher, Jane, 888, 1209, 1214, 2072.
Dasher, Louisa, 2072.
Daugherty, James, 1131.
Davey, 1324.
Davis, 319, 692.
Davis, Addie, NB1089, M301.
Davis, Alex, 25, NB1079, M301.
Davis, Alice, NB417.
Davis, Allie, 1280.
Davis, Amanda S., 439, 464.
Davis, Amos, 641.
Davis, Annie, 184, 1553, NB394.
Davis, Annie C. 44.
Davis, Arabella, 19.
Davis, Arlie, 856, 1099, 1197.
Davis, Barney, 1533, NB175, M139.
Davis, Ben, 423, 3523.
Davis, Benjamin, 19, 1414, NB1169, NB-
          1286.
Davis, Bessie, M427.
Davis, Bettie, 423, 3200, NB582, NB583.

Davis, Betty, 423, 3200, NB582, NB583.
Davis, Bill, 720.
Davis, Billie, 3813.
Davis, Billy, 3622.
Davis, Cally, 2509.
Davis, Carrie Ethel 856.
Davis, Cathie, 3201.
Davis, Celina, 319.
Davis, Charlotte, 3197.
Davis, Cheparnee, 184.
Davis, Cheparney, 3622.
Davis, Chepon, 184.
Davis, Cherokee, 3727.
Davis, Cinda, 1166.
Davis, Clarance B., NB846.
Davis, Cogee, 1166, NB417, M139.
Davis, Cokey, 1939.
Davis, Dennis, 3199, 3598.
Davis, Dick, 3198, 3199.
Davis, Dochee, 2641.
Davis, Earl, M. 283.
Davis, Ella, 1850, NB319, NB320, M283.
Davis, Ella S., 1850, NB319, NB320, M 283
Davis, Eli, 1922, 3200, 4016, M427.
Davis, Eliza, 1532, 1541.
Davis, Elizabeth E., NB345.
Davis, Ellen, 734.
Davis, Ely, 1922, 3200, 4016, M427.
Davis, Emma, 1999, 3200, NB1067.
Davis, Esther, 1541·
Davis, Ethel Irene, 856.
Davis, Eugene, NB320.
Davis, Fanny, NB582.
Davis, Florence M., 476.
Davis, George, 25, 1506, 2174, 2289.
Davis, Gooty, 3727.
Davis, Hannah, 25, 946, 1069, 3199, 3598.
Davis, Harvie L., NB847.
Davis, Hattie, 944.
Davis, Hattie Johnson, NB984.
Davis, Hilly, 184.
Davis, Ilsey, 3164, 3622.
Davis, J. R., NB345.
Davis, J. W., NB631.
Davis, Jack, 1507.
Davis, James, 1541, 2289.
Davis, James O., 3620.
Davis, Janey, 2902, M100.
Davis, Jeff, 3200, 3201.
Davis, Jennie, 3201.
Davis, Jenny, 1193, 1533, 1541.
Davis, Jess, NB319, NB320.
Davis, Jesse, 1212, 1850, 1939, 3330.
Davis, Jesse E., M283.
Davis, Jim, 1999.
Davis, Jimmie, 2509.
Davis, Job, 19.
Davis, Joe, 1166, NB417, M139.
Davis, John, 19, 115, 225, 319, 379, 610, 641,
          972, 1069, 1414, 1441, 1506, 1507,
          1533, 2174, 3352, 3727, 3919, N-
          B175, NB394.
Davis, Joseph, 946, 3352.
Davis, Josiah, 25.
Davis, Joslin, 1193, 1533, 1541.
Davis, Kanneyah, 1321, 3770.
Davis, Karneyoh, 1321, 3770.
Davis, Katie, 1506, 2289.
Davis, Kizzie, 173, 3576, NB984.
Davis, Kogee, 1166, NB417, M139.

Davis, Leland, M394.
Davis, Lena, 641, 1506.
Davis, Leona, M427.
Davis, Lewis H., 476, 3455, 3620, NB846, NB847.
Davis, Lillie, 3552.
Davis, Lizzie, 3919, NB175.
Davis, Louis, 3770.
Davis, Lucy, 25, 184, NB1079, M301.
Davis, Mack, NB749.
Davis, Malissie, M. 100.
Davis, March, 1166.
Davis, Mariah, 115.
Davis, Marshall, 3598.
Davis, Martha, 184, 3727.
Davis, Martin, 946.
Davis, Mattie, NB1169.
Davis, Mehaka, 972.
Davis, Melindy, 1364, NB1169, NB1286.
Davis, Milley, 1433, NB749.
Davis, Millie, 2289, 3552.
Davis, Millie C., 1433, NB749.
Davis, Minnah, 186, 946.
Davis, Minnie, NB583.
Davis, Moody, 3200.
Davis, Munna, 1166.
Davis, Nancy, 19, 692, NB1089.
Davis, Nancy W., 641, NB631, M210.
Davis, Nellie, 225.
Davis, Nettie, 641.
Davis, Nicey, NB1079.
Davis, Noah, 66.
Davis, Nocos, 1506.
Davis, Nora, NB631.
Davis, Oliver, 808.
Davis, Ollie, 1879, 1922, 3542, 4016.
Davis, Peggie, 1507.
Davis, Peter, 3523.
Davis, Phoebe, 1324.
Davis, Polly, 1506, 1507, 3919.
Davis, Rebecca, 19.
Davis, Redmond, 3552.
Davis, Redmond C., 1352, Creek Frd. NB-749.
Davis, Rosa, 3147.
Davis, Ross, NB319.
Davis, Roy Edgar, 3455.
Davis, Sallie, 1185, 3199.
Davis, Sally, 319, 3199.
Davis, Sam, 476, 808, 1441, 1900, 3197, 3199, M100.
Davis, Sam B., 2682.
Davis, Samuel, NB1286.
Davis, Samuel C. 856.
Davis, Sampson, 423, NB582, NB583.
Davis, Sarah, 720.
Davis, Sartie, 1166.
Davis, Selina, 1900, 2288, 2289.
Davis, Siney, 3199.
Davis, Sissie, 1506.
Davis, Sissy, 1414.
Davis, Sunda, 3622.
Davis, Susan, 1533, 3770, NB175.
Davis, Susanna, 476, 3455, 3620, NB846, NB847.
Davis, Tommie, 225.
Davis, Tom, 25, 946, NB1089.
Davis, Turner, 1507.
Davis, W. T., 856, 1099, 1197.
Davis, William, 1166.

Davis, Willie, 1850.
Davis, Wisey, 1939.
Davis, Yoman, 423.
Davison, David, 381.
Davison, Dicey, 331.
Davison, John, 331.
Davy, 2972.
Davy, Wantay, 2972.
Dawson, 116.
Dawson, Alice, 1832.
Dawson, Cooper, NB124.
Dawson, Dessie Lee, NB124.
Dawson, Martha, 1832.
Dawson, Willie, 1832.
Day, Beatrice, NB770.
Day, Henry, 3132.
Day, John Raymond, M51.
Day, Lena, 1401.
Day, Millie, 1401.
Day, R. L., 1198.
Day, Robert, NB770, NB771, M51.
Day, Robert Jr., NB771.
Day, Roy L., 1198.
Day, Vinita, 1198, NB770, NB 771, M51.
Day, Vinita, 1198, NB770, NB771, M51.
Day, Wm, 1401.
Daycha, 562.
Deconsac, 2705.
Deconthla, 602.
Deer, Alfred, 2759.
Deer, Alice, 3008.
Deer, Amos, 1403.
Deer, Anna, 1403.
Deer, Barney, 670, 671, 2780, 3397, M48S.
Deer, Ben, 1466, 1534, 3425.
Deer, Bettie, 1242.
Deer, Butler, 1403.
Deer, Challie, 2447.
Deer, Charles, 574.
Deer, Cinda, 2221.
Deer, Daniel, 1242, 1261, 1519, 2835.
Deer, Dicey, 670, 671.
Deer, Eddie, 3425.
Deer, Edmond, 2331, NB1200.
Deer, Edmund, 2331, NB1200.
Deer, Elizabeth, 574.
Deer, Ella, 2759.
Deer, Ellen, 1555, 3397, 3629, NB356, M145. M146.
Deer, Enos, 1555.
Deer, George, 1242.
Deer, Hepsey, 1403.
Deer, Huldy, 1242.
Deer, Isaac, 829, 1439.
Deer, Isreal, 2426.
Deer, Jackson, 2835.
Deer, James, 2331.
Deer, Jessie, NB1274.
Deer, Jim, 2828.
Deer, Jimsey, 1638.
Deer, Joe, 1261, 1262, 1263, 2447, 4017, NB446, NB1282, M6.
Deer, John, 3629.
Deer, Jonas, 283, 2015, 2016, 2331, 2704.
Deer, Katie, 3425.
Deer, Lawyer, 1403, 1638.
Deer, Lemsey, 3397, NB486.
Deer, Lillie, M146.
Deer, Linda, 3193, 3422, NB1274.
Deer, Lizzie, 1165, 3008, M145.

307

Deer, Louis, 1242, 1516.
Deer, Louisa, 796.
Deer, Lucy, 1261, 2331, 2835, 2958, 3008, M395
Deer, Lula, NB1282.
Deer, Lydia, 2835.
Deer, Mabel, 1516.
Deer, Mary, 1242, 2059, 2447, NB1282, M6, M488.
Deer, Mary A., 2331.
Deer, Mattie, M488.
Deer, Miley, 1242, 2059, 2447, NB1282, M-488.
Deer, Minnie, NB486, NB1106.
Deer, Moses, 1555, 3629, M145, M146.
Deer, Munna, 3397.
Deer, Nancy, 1109, 3397, NB356, NB486.
Deer, Nellie, 2331.
Deer, Nora, 2015.
Deer, Philip, 3422.
Deer, Pinky, 1972.
Deer, Pinkey, 3422, NB1274.
Deer, Pollie, 150.
Deer, Romsey, 3397, NB486.
Deer, Sarforcher, 1439.
Deer, Sealy, NB446.
Deer, Silas, 670, NB356.
Deer, Sinah, 2828.
Deer, Sophia, 2759, NB1106, NB1200.
Deer, Sparny, 2759, NB1106, NB1200.
Deer, Thomas, 1242, 4017.
Deer, Tom, 796.
Deer, Walter, 1403.
Deer, Wash, 1165, 2426, 2702.
Deer, Wesley, 150, 671, 3008.
Deer, William, 1403.
Deer, Willie, 1403, 1466.
Deer, Wisey, 1519, 1520.
Deer, Yarnar, 1261, 4017, NB446, M6.
Deer, Yarner, 1261, 4017, NB446, M6.
Deere, Albert, 1007, 2400.
Deere, Annie, 2514, NB1267.
Deere, August, 574.
Deere, Ben, 2558, 2559, 2560, 3206.
Deere, Bessie, 2498.
Deere, Betty, 2286, 2287.
Deere, Charlie, NB1279.
Deere, Cinda, 2521.
Deere, Eliza, 1312, 1313, 3447.
Deere, Esal, 3085, NB1267.
Deere, Gilbert, M154.
Deere, Hannah, 1007.
Deere, Hence, 2995.
Deere, Henry, 2560.
Deere, Hullie, 1312.
Deere, Hunter, 2742.
Deere, Isaac, 829, 3447.
Deere, Israel, M365.
Deere, Jacob, 2521.
Deere, Jennie, 1007.
Deere, Joe, 2995.
Deere, John, 2400, 2498, 2519, 3066, 3954, M-357, NB1066.
Deere, Joseph, 2560.
Deere, Katie, 2498.
Deere, Lawyer, 1403, 1638.
Deere, Levina, 2734.
Deere, Lewis, 2560.
Deere, Lizzie, 2843, 3933, 3954, NB1066.
Deere, Lou Annie, M365.
Deere, Louina, NB1267.

Deere, Louis, 1007.
Deere, Lucy, 2243, 2645, 3278, NB328, N-B1171, M400. M357
Deere, Lumsey, NB1278.
Deere, Mahala, 2995.
Deere, Maley, 2995, 3954, NB1278, NB1279
Deere, Mary, 2995, 3954, NB1278, NB1279.
Deere, Melanie, 150.
Deere, Millie, 2995.
Deere, Mindy, 3954.
Deere, Mose, 1312.
Deere, Moses, 3447.
Deere, Nancy, 1111, 3992, NB1062, NB-1063.
Deere, Nellie, 2400.
Deere, Newman, 2559.
Deere, Noah, 1111, 2995, NB1278, NB1279.
Deere, Orey, 2558, 2559, 2560.
Deere, Paro, M154.
Deere, Peter, 2286.
Deere, Raymond, NB328.
Deere, Ruth, 3992.
Deere, Sallie, 398.
Deere, Sarah, 2559, NB1096.
Deere, Silla, 3094.
Deere, Sinah, 3205.
Deere, Sumsie, M365.
Deere, Tecumseh, 1111, 3992.
Deere, Thomas, 1007.
Deere, Thompson, 2558, M35 , NB328.
Deere, Wesley, 1355.
Deere, Willey, NB1066.
Deere, Wisey, 1520.
Deere, Wunche, 2382, M154.
Deere, Wysie, 1619.
Deerhead, 3908.
Deerhead, Jennie, 3908.
Deerhead, Matilda, 3908.
Deerisaw, Chepon, 418, 1023.
Deerisaw, Polly, 418, 1023.
Dejamon, 2315.
Dejamon, Hollie, 2315.
Denton, John, 113.
Denton, Susan, 113.
Deo, Amos, NB1144.
Deo, Jennie, 2830, NB1193.
Deo, John, 2830.
Deo, Kogee, 3930.
Deo, Louina, 2338, NB1191.
Deo, Nancy, 2587, NB1144, NB1145.
Deo, Nasa, 2830.
Deo, Sakiye, 2830.
Deo, Susie, NB1145.
Deo, Thomas, 3930, 2830, NB1144, NB1145
Deo, Thompson, 2830.
Depriest, Alex, 470, 727, 774, 902.
Depriest, Bettie, 745.
Depriest, Cordie, 471, NB445, M231.
Depriest, Eliz, 687.
Depriest, Eliza, 745, 775.
Depriest, Emily, 745, NB729.
Depriest, Franklin, 775.
Depriest, James, 745, NB729.
Depriest, Jeff, 472.
Depriest, John, 687, 745, 775.
Depriest, Luther, NB729.
Depriest, Nicey, 471.
Depriest, Patience, 470, 727, 774, 902, 906.
Depriest, Pearl, 298, M49.

309

Doyle, Jackson, 298, 1604.
Doyle, John Henry, M21.
Doyle, John N., 1115, NB989.
Doyle, Laura, 3578.
Doyle, Lava, NB1115.
Doyle, Lee, 943.
Doyle, Leo, NB961.
Doyle, Lydia, 943.
Doyle, Mable, 3680.
Doyle, Mary, 298, 439.
Doyle, Maud S., NB700, NB701, NB702.
Doyle, Minnie May, NB701.
Doyle, Mose, NB1116.
Doyle, Myrtle, 943.
Doyle, Nancy, 192, 943.
Doyle, N. C., 2290.
Doyle, Nimrod, 439.
Doyle, Nimrod N., 943.
Doyle, Nimrod P., 1115.
Doyle, Pearl, 298, M49.
Doyle, Precilla, 196, 1283, 2138.
Doyle, Priscilla, 2138, 196, 1283.
Doyle, Rachel, 2212.
Doyle, Rachel A., 298.
Doyle, Rhoda, NB989.
Doyle, Roseter E., NB1116.
Doyle, Roy, 943.
Doyle, Sam H., Jr., 2212, 3680, M54, NB961.
Doyle, Sam H., Sr., 298, 2212.
Doyle, Samuel, 1728.
Doyle, Sarah, 298, 1604.
Doyle, Sarah A., 1103.
Doyle, Scilla, 1889, 2109.
Doyle, Seabron J., 298, 3578, NB683, M302.
Doyle, Seabron. M302.
Doyle, Sissie, 2757.
Doyle, Susie Lee, NB700.
Doyle, Thomas E., 1103, NB1116.
Doyle, Tyler, 2109.
Doyle, Wallace, 1889, NB700, NB701, NB702.
Doyle, Walter, NB235.
Doyle, William, 943.
Doyle, Winchester, 192, 943.
Drake, Benjamin H., 2297.
Drake, Nancy, 2297.
Drake, Richard, 2297.
Drake, Susan, 482.
Drew, Alice, 208, 811, NB198, NB199.
Drew, Amos, 203, 763, 3491, NB53.
Drew, Charley, 530.
Drew, Clarence, NB53.
Drew, Clifton, 658.
Drew, Clifton C., NB632.
Drew, Daniel, 208, 518, 530, 658, 763, 2123.
Drew, Dave, 658.
Drew, Delilah, 165, 2557.
Drew, Earl E., NB198.
Drew, Earnest, NB198, NB199.
Drew, Ella, 518.
Drew, Emma, 658, NB632.
Drew, Emmet, 203.
Drew, Ernest, NB198, NB199.
Drew, Legus C., 2123, NB898.
Drew, Leila, 469, NB898.
Drew, Madella E., NB898.
Drew, Maggie, 208, 518, 530, 658, 763, 2123.
Drew, Martha, 761.
Drew, Mont, 3491.
Drew, Moses Warrner, NB632.
Drew, Nancy, 2969.

Drew, Nettie, 763, 3491, NB53.
Drew, Rachel F., 658.
Drew, Roy W., NB199.
Drew, William, 165, 2557.
Dryden, Henry R., 615.
Dryden, Leona, 615.
Dryden, Lucy, 615, NB703.
Dryden, Mary E., 615.
Dryden, Mattie B., 615, NB283.
Dryden, Rosella, 615.
Dryden, William, 615.
DuBois, Barney, 2200, 2379.
DuBois, B. R., 2200, NB170.
DuBois, Elizabeth C., NB170.
DuBois, Elizabeth Gladys, NB170.
DuBois, Lizzie, 2200, 2379.
DuBois, Mildred, 2379.
Duckworth, Cecil, 3797.
Duckworth, Robert, 3797.
Duckworth, Robert D., NB656.
Duckworth, Ruth E., 1604, 3797, NB65
Duckworth, Vera Oma, NB656.
Dufney, 2531.
Dunison, Joseph, 1902.
Dunn, Beaver, 5.
Dunn, Beulah, 80.
Dunn, Harry, 5.
Dunn, Jennie, 1400.
Dunn, Joseph, 80.
Dunn, Nannie, 5.
Dunn, Noah, 3363.
Dunn, Ralph, M193.
Dunn, Reubon, 5.
Dunn, Susie, 5, 3363, M193.
Dunn, Thomas, 80.
Dunn, Tupper, 5, 3363, M193.
Dunnase, 3025.
Dunson, Alice, 623.
Dunson, Andy, 622.
Dunson, David, 713.
Dunson, Edmond, 622.
Dunson, Ellen, 1473, NB539.
Dunson, Hettie, M135.
Dunson, Hokosey, 468.
Dunson, Kokty, 622.
Dunson, Jemima, 623.
Dunson, Joseph, 468, 623.
Dunson, Kizzie, 521, M135.
Dunson, Lewis, 623, M135.
Dunson, Lucy, 623, 1512, NB965.
Dunson, Luna A., 623.
Dunson, Luna E., 623, NB965.
Dunson, Mattie, 623.
Dunson, Millie, NB539.
Dunson, Raymand, NB965.
Dunson, Thomas, 468.
Dunson, Thos. H., NB539.
Dunzy, Dallas, 992.
Dunzy, Henry, 992.
Dunzy, Joseph, 992.
Dunzy, Jackson, 992, 1464, NB346.
Dunzy, Kogee, 992.
Dunzy, Louis, 992.
Dunzy, Lucinda, 992, NB346.
Dunzy, Nathan, 992.
Dunzy, Philip, 1464.
Dunzy, Sahweheche, 3019.
Dunzy, Velma, NB346.
Durant, Adam, 2496.
Durant, A. J., 487.

Ellis, Nocos, 2154.
Ellis, Willie, 3093.
Elowatahge, 2458.
Emartha, Fixico, 2728.
Emartha, Isparne, 659.
Emartha, Sodedon, 2132.
Emarthar, Micke, 2172.
Emarthar, Mik, 2186.
Emarthar, Nargusta, 3065, 3080.
Emarthar, Nellie, 2172.
Emarthla, 898, 2254, 2571, 2961.
Emarthla, Ahala, 1262, 1541.
Emarthla, Aharle, 1541, 1262, 2578.
Emarthla, Aholle, 2578, 1262, 1541.
Emarthla, Carchee, 2570, 1005.
Emarthla, Catche, 1005, 2570.
Emarthla, Cho, 1789.
Emarthla, Chokotte, 486.
Emarthla, Chuwosta, 3276.
Emarthla, Conchart, 1213.
Emarthla, Cooweescoowee, 2619, 2620.
Emarthla, Cotser, 633.
Emarthla, Echo, 1007, 2221, 2565,[3094, 3347.
Emarthla, Efi, 758, 1251.
Emarthla, Eli, 1251, 758.
Emarthla, Fa, 1775.
Emarthla, Fus, 381.
Emarthla, Fushutch, 2093, 2095, 2100.
Emarthla, Fushutcha, 2100, 2093, 2095.
Emarthla, Gabriel, 2254.
Emarthla, Hattie, 2254.
Emarthla, Hillabee, 2462, 1894.
Emarthla, Hillubbe, 1894, 2462.
Emarthla, Hotulke, 3883.
Emarthla, Isparne, 659.
Emarthla, Joseph, M474.
Emarthla, Jimhoker, 2254.
Emarthla, Karpetcher, 3385.
Emarthla, Konip, 2817.
Emarthla, Leechie, 2942, NB1258,♥ NB1259.
   M474.
Emarthla, Lidda, 2566, 1894.
Emarthla, Linda, 1894, 2566.
Emarthla, Lizzie, 2053, 2732.
Emarthla, Martha, 1465, 2073.
Emarthla, Melissa, 2093, 2095, 2100.
Emarthla, Micco, 2625, NB1252.
Emarthla, Mickie, 2001.
Emarthla, Millie, 2001, 1345.
Emarthla, Milly, 1345, 2001.
Emarthla, Nocus, 2732, 1299.
Emarthla, Nohos, 1299, 2732.
Emarthla, Osachee, 1556, 1465, 2073.
Emarthla, Osoche, 2073, 1465, 1556.
Emarthla, Okchiye, 3346.
Emarthla, Okchum, 2524, 2696.
Emarthla, Osegee, 1465, 1556, 2073.
Emarthla, Pahos, 149, 2695, 2299, 2701.
Emarthla, Parhos, 2299, 2701, 149, 2695.
Emarthla, Parthos, 2701, 2299, 149, 2695.
Emarthla, Pena, 397.
Emarthla, Pin, 2053.
Emarthla, Sallie, 2625, NB1252.
Emarthla, Sam, 2961, NB1258, NB1259, M474.
Emarthla, Sarah, 4005.
Emarthla, Selina, 2524.
Emarthla, Singer, 3346.
Emarthla, Tom, 2615, 2825, 1286.
Emarthla, Tulmarscy, 1322, 1345, 1375.
Emarthla, Tulmarsy, 1345, 1375, 1322.

Fipps, William B., 458.
Firlina, 1295.
Fish, 680.
Fish, Annie, 2384, 3754.
Fish, Arnikee, 2513.
Fish, Bessie, 2384.
Fish, Billy, 1488.
Fish, Choty,. 1214.
Fish, Daniel, 2614.
Fish, Eli, 2649, 2889, 2890, CE4027.
Fish, Eliza, 1488, 3911.
Fish, Elmer, 1480, CE4028.
Fish, Elsie, 3859
Fish. Elson, 2882.
Fish, Frazier, 1488.
Fish, George, 1480, 2127, NB1110. NB1291.
Fish, Hannah, 3128.
Fish, Hattie, 2607, 4021, NB1291.
Fish, Hunny, 3859.
Fish, Jack, 151.
Fish, Jackson, 2614.
Fish, Janie, 1271.
Fish, Jennie, 3105, 3129.
Fish, Jimsey, 3105, 3128, 3859, NB1154.
Fish, John, 4021.
Fish, Johnson, 3511, M152.
Fish, Jonas, 1593, NB1275, M152.
Fish, Joseph, 680.
Fish, Josiah, 1245.
Fish, Katie, 1488, 3129.
Fish, Lewis, 2890, 3911, NB906.
Fish, Little, 1488.
Fish, Lizzie, NB1154.
Fish, Long, 900.
Fish, Lucinda, 2424.
Fish, Mandy, 2513, 3083.
Fish, Mehaley, 1488, M130.
Fish, Meleya, 3911, NB906.
Fish, Milley, 1488.
Fish, Morleyar, 1593, M152.
Fish, Nache, NB1111.
Fish, Nancy, 680.
Fish, Nellie, 2614, NB1110, NB1111.
Fish, Nicey, 3128, NB1234.
Fish, Okchie, 2621.
Fish, Posey, NB906.
Fish, Peter, 2424, 3128.
Fish, Robert, 2513.
Fish, Rose, 2889, NB1146.
Fish, Salina, 838.
Fish, Sam, 3754.
Fish, Sampson. 838.
Fish, Siah, 3129.
Fish. Sotka, 680.
Fish, Sucky, 2607, NB1154.
Fish, Thomas, 3511.
Fish, Tom, 900.
Fish, Toochie, 1989.
Fish, Wattie, 2649, 3354, 3754.
Fish, Watty, 2384.
Fish, Weleya, 2614, NB1110, NB1111.
Fish, Wiley, 3128, 4021, NB1291.
Fish, Willeya, 2614, NB1110, NB1111.
Fish, William, 2513, 3083.
Fish, Willie, 1271, 2614, CE4028.
Fish, Winey, 1488, 3511, M244.
Fish, Wisey, 2877.
Fish, Wothlarsha 400.
Fisher, 2219.
Fisher, Aggie, 977, 3127.

Fisher, Albert, 1389.
Fisher, Alice, 529.
Fisher, Amos, 977, 1389, 3127.
Fisher, Aubrey, NB758.
Fisher, Barney, 3849, 2230.
Fisher, Becky, 732, 3868.
Fisher, Ben, M137.
Fisher, Bertha, NB757.
Fisher, Bettie, NB1099.
Fisher, Betty, 732, 3868.
Fisher, Billie, 2839.
Fisher, Carrie, 301, M52, NB758
Fisher, Cheparney, 3127.
Fisher, Daniel, 2809.
Fisher, Dave, 529,3840.
Fisher, Dinah, 63.
Fisher, Eddie, M138.
Fisher, Elijah, 1445, 1466.
Fisher, Eliza, 1420.
Fisher, Eloise B., 301.
Fisher, Elsie, 3849, M380.
Fisher, Fillisee, Norene, M52.
Fisher, Folothoke, 2975.
Fisher, Freida Chena, 744.
Fisher, George, 63, 2230, 2231, 2975.
Fisher, Hannah, 1415, 1416, 2809.
Fisher, Henry C., 301.
Fisher, Hepsey, 917, 3127.
Fisher, James, 1415, 1416.
Fisher, Joe, 529, 872, 1389, M137, M138, NB756, NB757.
Fisher, Larney, 529, 3840.
Fisher, Lena, 744.
Fisher, Lewis, 1415.
Fisher, Lizzie, NB756.
Fisher, Lewis Henry, 744.
Fisher, Lucy, 1201, 1412, 2839, 3128, NB1099.
Fisher, Lucy B., 301.
Fisher, Mariah, 1415.
Fisher, Mary, 865.
Fisher, Mikey, 2975.
Fisher, Nancy, 312, 529, NB756, NB757, M137, M138.
Fisher, Ollie C. 301.
Fisher, Rosie, M380.
Fisher, Sally, 653.
Fisher, Sam, 744, 872. M52, NB758
Fisher, Samuel, 653, 865.
Fisher, Sarah, 301, 624, 653, 744, 1662.
Fisher, Sarah A., 1777.
Fisher, Seaborn, 1416, M380.
Fisher, Timmie,1598, 3127, 3845, 1415, 917.
Fisher, Timmy, 917, 1415, 1598, 3127, 3845.
Fisher, William, 301, 624, 653, 732, 744. 1415. 1662, 3868.
Fisher, Willie, 2839, 3868, NB1099.
Fisher, Yarner, 529.
Fittadega, 2451.
Fittadega, Selina, 2451.
Fixeco, Arhaloc, 2700.
Fixeco, Artus, 2441.
Fixeco, Ben, 2248.
Fixeco, Betsey. 2615.
Fixeco, Cano, 3174, NB295.
Fixeco, Chippie, 3684, NB862.
Fixeco, Chula, 2911.
Fixeco, Coser, 2965.
Fixeco, Cusseta, 1081, 3279.
Fixeco, Dicey, 3290.
Fixeco, Edward, 1477.

315

Fixeco, Espana, 2398.
Fixeco, Fannie, 2965.
Fixeco, Foluthoker, 2692, NB1243.
Fixeco, Fushutche, 2838.
Fixeco, Helus, 2735, 2736, 2737.
Fixeco, Heneha, 2834
Fixeco, Itshar, 2527.
Fixeco, Joseph, NB1243.
Fixeco, Karwassat, 2765.
Fixeco, Katcha, 2674, 2794.
Fixeco, Kisse, 1477.
Fixeco, Lucy, 3168, NB295.
Fixeco, Mollie, 3236.
Fixeco, Nocus,2887, 3633.
Fixeco, Okchiye, 2467.
Fixeco, Okchum, 2806.
Fixeco, Pahose, 1477.
Fixeco, Parhos,3180.
Fixeco, Polly, 2907.
Fixeco, Salina, 2794.
Fixeco, Sparney, 2242, 2907.
Fixeco, Sumka, 2441.
Fixeco Thlethlo. 2424.
Fixeco, Tommy, 3285.
Fixeco, Tulsa, 3002.
Fixeco, Willie, 3016.
Fixeco, Yahola, 2828.
Fixeco, Yarhola, 2832, NB1243.
Fixecoche, Nocos,2031.
Fixico, 1881, 1882, 3285.
Fixico, Adaline, 1631.
Fixicio, Anderson, 2278.
Fixico, Angie, 1323.
Fixico, Annie, 3082, 3814.
Fixico, Arbeka, 2378, 2388.
Fixico, Arharlock, 2279.
Fixico, Arharlox, 3211.
Fixico, Arholoc, 397.
Fixico, Arholox, 1069.
Fixico, Arkleyarchee, 1715, 1715.
Fixico, Artus, 1366, 3173, 3321.
Fixico, Barney, 2176.
Fixico, Bassta, 1439, NB1058.
Fixico, Bastie, 1439, NB1058.
Fixico, Ben, 2248, 3326.
Fixico, Benjamin, 1358.
Fixico, Benoche, 3279.
Fixico, Betsie, 1267.
Fixico, Cano, 3174, NB295.
Fixico, Cabeche, 3228.
Fixico, Caesar, 1705.
Fixico, California, NB295.
Fixico, Capecha, 2081.
Fixico, Carpitcha. 2069.
Fixico, Catus, 2186.
Fixico, Char, 1651.
Fixico, Cheyamy, 1341.
Fixico, Cheparney, 1358, 3942.
Fixico, Chluhart, 1644.
Fixico, Cho, 2754, 3945.
Fixico, Cho Emarthla, 2797.
Fixico, Chocla, 2987.
Fixico, Choela, 2911.
Fixico, Chola, 3069.
Fixico, Cholar, 561, 562, 1217.
Fixico, Chowastiye, 2419.
Fixico, Chular, 1369,
Fixico, Chuoste, 3403.
Fixico, Cinda, 2402, 3814, NB418.
Fixico, Conchart, 2818.

Fixico, Conip, 2480.
Fixico, Conup 1886.
Fixico, Conseh, 3082.
Fixico, Cosa, 2353.
Fixico, Cosar, 1507, 1616.
Fixico, Cotcha, 148, 1287, 2402, 3814, NB418.
Fixico, Cotso, 1125.
Fixico, Cusseta, 1081, 3279.
Fixico, Cussetah, 3609.
Fixico, Daley, 2176, NB1036.
Fixico, Elizabeth, 2948.
Fixico, Emma, 1616.
Fixico, Fannie, 2595, M170, NB741, NB742.
Fixico, Fanny, 2595, NB741, NB742, M170.
Fixico, Fologa, 1217.
Fixico, Fushutche, 1574.
Fixico, Fuskatcha, 2690.
Fixico, Harney, 2480.
Fixico, Hebsey, 1282, 1295.
Fixico, Heles 2735, 2736, 2737.
Fixico, Heneha, 2238, 2274, 2404, 2405.
Fixico, Henehoche, 3942.
Fixico, Hillis, 1682, 2695.
Fixico, Hinny, 1244.
Fixico, Hodulga, 2169.
Fixico, Holata, 693.
Fixico, Hotulka, 1223.
Fixico, Hotulke, 1295, 2646.
Fixico, Hulberta, 1322.
Fixico, Hulbutta, 1669.
Fixico, Hully, 3942.
Fixico, Hutchcutte, 1571, 1572.
Fixico, Hutchecutte, 1571, 1572.
Fixico Icey, NB51.
Fixico, Ilba, 1444.
Fixico, Itchar, 1695.
Fixico, Itsus, 2933.
Fixico, Jeffy, NB742.
Fixico, Jenatte, 3942.
Fixico, Jemima, 1470, NB1058.
Fixico, John. 995.
Fixico, Jowastagee, 2422.
Fixico, Katie, 2353, 2378, 3609.
Fixico, Katy, 1705.
Fixico, Kanip, 1859.
Fixico, Kapecha, 2958.
Fixico, Karsha, 2721.
Fixico, Katcha, 1627.
Fixico, Katcher, 148, 1287, 2402, 3814, NB418.
Fixico, Lahta, 3009.
Fixico, Leah, 2204.
Fixico, Lettif, 1244.
Fixico, Linda, 1125, 1467, NB552.
Fixico, Liddie, 1371.
Fixico, Lindy, 2401.
Fixico, Liza, 975.
Fixico, Lizzie, 2415.
Fixico, Locher, 1291.
Fixico, Lousoche, 1322.
Fixico, Lucy, 3168, NB295.
Fixico, Lydia, 2190, 3083, 3084.
Fixico, Maley, 1616.
Fixico, Mapetta, 1618.
Fixico, Martha, 2176.
Fixico, Mary, 693.
Fixico, Mickey, 3009.
Fixico, Mina, 3942.
Fixico, Minta, 2176.
Fixico, Nagusche, 1249.
Fixico, Nanny, 1245.

316

Fixico, Neha, 2173, 3942.
Fixico, Nellie, 3423.
Fixico, Nocos, 3174.
Fixico, Nocus, 1218, 1710, 2218, 2277, 2278,
    2524, 2778, 3053, 3082.
Fixico, Nokus, 1319.
Fixico, Nupsey, 237, 707, 1616.
Fixico, Okchema, 6.
Fixico, Okchiye, 1269.
Fixico, Okchon, 2388.
Fixico, Oktaiche, 1323, 1381.
Fixico, Oktiarchee, 1323, 1381.
Fixico, Osab, 1212, 1884.
Fixico, Osach, 2827, 2829.
Fixico, Oscoce, 1444, 3423.
Fixico, Osoche, 2827, 2829.
Fixico, Osuch, 2061.
Fixico, Pahos, 280, 995, 2759.
Fixico, Pahose, 280, 995, 2759.
Fixico, Parhos, 1862, 2415.
Fixico, Pefeny, 1287, NB51, M81.
Fixico, Pickcarty, 1577.
Fixico, Pin, 2204, 2442.
Fixico, Polly, 1254.
Fixico, Quasada, 2401.
Fixico, Robert, NB435.
Fixico, Roley, NB1058.
Fixico, Roman, 2176.
Fixico, Sallie, 1369, 2176, 3082, 3565, NB435,
    NB1168, M339.
Fixico, Sally, 1369, 2176, 3082, 3565, NB435,
    NB1168, M339.
Fixico, Sampson, 3565.
Fixico, Samson, 2402.
Fixico, Sarfarchar, 1467.
Fixico, Sarna, 3942.
Fixico, Semarhichkar, 1444, 3423.
Fixico, Sewika, 1371.
Fixico, Simhejeschee, 1358.
Fixico, Siney, 2442.
Fixico, Sparney, 2242, 2850.
Fixico, Spoko, 2768.
Fixico, Sulter, M81.
Fixico, Sunderler, 1254.
Fixico, Sunduller, 2415.
Fixico, Sunny, 1439.
Fixico, Susan, 3942.
Fixico, Tagie, 1439.
Fixico, Taho, 2190.
Fixico, Thlechimy, 1681.
Fixico, Thlotho, 1371.
Fixico, Thomas, 1371.
Fixico, Thorthlo, 1245, 1371, 1482, 1486, 1487
Fixico, Tommie, 2818, 3324, 3684.
Fixico, Tulmars, 2056.
Fixico, Tulmóchus, 1631, 3565, NB435.
Fixico, Tulmochuss, 2176, 3565, NB435.
Fixico, Tulsa, 23, 1559, 1560, 2688.
Fixico, Tulwa, 1267, 2086.
Fixico, Tummie, 2518.
Fixico, Warney, 3279, 3609.
Fixico, Watka, 2823.
Fixico, Watty, NB741, NB742, M170.
Fixico, Wegus, 1223.
Fixico, Willie, 1414, NB418.
Fixico, Winey, NB741.
Fixico, Wisely, 1381.
Fixico, Wisey, 1507, 2818, 2933
Fixico, Wizo, 1345.
Fixico, Wotka, 1358.

Fixico, Woxie, 1881, 1882.
Fixico, Yaha, 1295, 1298, 1299, 2832, 3083, 3084.
Fixico, Yahola, 975, 1571, 2542, 2692, 2918,
    2959.
Fixico, Yana, M170.
Fixico, Yarhar, 216.
Fixico, Yohola, 2959.
Fixoco, Cho, 2745, 3945.
Fixseko, Cusseta, 3917.
Flack, Cornelia, 490.
Flack, Enoch, 490.
Flack, John, 490.
Flack, Mattie, 490, NB860.
Flanders, Edward, 635.
Flanley, Edward, 224.
Flanley, William, 224.
Fleet, Alice J., 2011, NB524.
Fleet, James H., NB524.
Fleet, John J., NB524.
Flint, Brown, 828.
Flint, Lizzie, 828.
Flint, Morris, 828.
Flint, Thomas, 828.
Flippin, Jerome, 372.
Flippin, Mary Jane, 372.
Flippin, Walter, 372.
Flowers, Alice, NB565.
Flowers, Arminta, 20.3, 2024, 2264.
Flowers, Joe, 2023.
Flowers, John, 2023, 2024, 2264, 3863.
Flowers, Johnny, 3863.
Flowers, Joseph, 2024, NB565.
Flowers, Lewis, 2264.
Flowers, Mattie, 2023.
Flowers, Mentie, 3863.
Flowers, Mintie, 3802.
Flowers, Susan, 2023.
Flowers, Willie Eva, NB565.
Fo bits co yee, 1596.
Foh lok he, 72.
Fo ko lo da ga, 2655, 2656, 2657
Fola, 1493, 1536, 3236.
Fo le che che, 2826.
Foley, Arney, 1951, NB1244.
Foley, Eliza, 2233, 2670.
Foley, John, 1951.
Foley, Kissie, 1951.
Foley, Kizzie, 2670.
Foley, Lonie, 1951.
Foley, Melindy, 2832, NB1244.
Foley, Minnie, 1951.
Foley, Taylor, 2670, NB1244.
Foley, William, 1951.
Fo lis cha, 1070.
Follker, 2649.
Foloppa, Sam, 3787.
Fo lot ho ge, 2857.
Fo lot ho ka, 122.
Fo lot ho kee, 2219, 2230.
Fo lot hok ko che, 89, 91.
Fo lot ka, 362.
Fo lot ker, 1485.
Folsom, Rufus, 89.
Foluthoker, 2692, NB1213.
Fo lut ti ke, 2701.
Fol wa tus ta no ga, 1836.
Foreman, Annie, 3711.
Foreman, George E., 3711.
Foreman, Isabelle, 3711.
Foreman, Jeremiah E., 3711.

Freeman, Lucy, 120.
Freeman, Lynne S., 3267.
Freeman, Mary, 223.
Freeman, Major, 707.
Freeman, Mitchell, 503.
Freeman, Peter, 1613.
Freeman, Pikey, 2747.
Freeman, Rhoda, 3332.
Freeman, Rueben, 120.
Freeman, Sudie, 1753.
Freeman, Theodore, O., 3267.
Freeman, Theodore R., NB166.
Freeman, William, 120.
Frick, Jay, NB1237.
Frick, J. L., NB1237, NB1238.
Frick, Mamie, 808, NB1237, NB1238.
Frick, William, NB1238.
Friday, Jennie, 2485.
Friday, Berry-Creek Frd., 198, NB1092, NB-1226.
Friday, Clarence, NB1226.
Friday, Jennie, 1738, NB1092, M398.
Friday, Lewis, 2485.
Friday, Willie, NB1092.
Fronges, John, 1418.
Fry, Dema, 434.
Fry, Lawrence, 434.
Fry, Leechie, 2942, NB1258, NB1259, M474.
Fry, Leona, 434.
Fry, Lottie, 434.
Fry, Milly, 434.
Fry, Robert, 434.
Fry, Sam, 2961, NB1258, NB1259, M474.
Fry, Sandy, NB1258.
Fry, Sarty, NB1259.
Fry, Susie, 346.
Fulga, 2508.
Fulhoge, 2419.
Fulley, 2492.
Fullhoogee, 1999.
Fulotka, 310.
Fulotka, Nellie, 310.
Fulotka, Oscar, 310.
Fulotka, Susan, 310.
Fulsom, Conthlany, 882, M18.
Fulsom, Emma, 3874.
Fulsom, George, 400.
Fulsom, Henry, M18.
Fulsom, Joe, 2416.
Fulsom, Kosa, 2420.
Fulsom, Ladee, NB748.
Fulsom, Louisa, 1216.
Fulsom, Lucy, 882, NB748.
Fulsom, Millie, 2416, 3616, 3874, NB798.
Fulsom, Pantenay, 3123.
Fulsom, Rhoda, NB798.
Fulsom, Robert, 2420, NB748, M18.
Fulsom, Sallie, 605, M318.
Fulsom, Salo, 2421.
Fulsom, Sam, 2421.
Fulsom, Sarah, 2421.
Fulsom, Thomas, 1216, 2416, 2420, 2421, 3616, 3874, NB798.
Fulsom, Wicey, 3616.
Fulsom, Wiley, M318.
Fulsom, William, 89.
Fulsom, Willie, 2421, M318.
Fulsome, 1042.
Fulton, 1878.
Fulton, Friday, 1878.

Funnaske, 2689.
Furr, Albert Clinton, M223.
Furr, Archie D., 1089.
Furr, Arthur, 1089. .
Furr, Arthur B., 1089.
Furr, Benjamin C., 1089, M223.
Furr, Jude, 1089, NB1013.
Furr, Mamie, 1089.
Furr, Perry, 1089.
Furr, Samuel, 1089.
Furr, Stella, M223.
Furr, William G., 1089.
Furvaga, 1906.
Fuseke, NB546.
Fuseke, Cinda, NB546.
Fustanagee, Cotsa, 3392.
Fustinnokochee, 1574.
Fuswa, Mary, 3007.
Futchahokke, 252.
Futloka, 254.
Futrell, Alice, 230, NB339, NB340.
Futrell, Frank, NB339, NB340.
Futrell, Jimmie, NB339.
Futrell, Pearlie, NB340.
Gaber, 2894.
Gaddis, Eliza, 3656.
Gaines, 211.
Gaines, Willie, 211.
Gaino, Aggie, 2201.
Gaino, Amanda, 2201.
Gaino, Harriet, 2201.
Gaino, Sallie, 2201.
Gaino, Yabe, 2201.
Gaither, Alice M., 48, NB186, M3 ᐟ
Gaither, Maggie Emily, NB186.
Gaither, Myrtle Washington, M39.
Gaither, W. J., 48, NB186, M39.
Gaither, Woolery L. F., 48.
Gamble, Billy, 94, 3023.
Gamble, Howard Lee, 1018.
Gamble, Polly, 2043.
Gamble, Robert Lee, 1018.
Gamble, Sukey, 3023.
Gamble, Willie S., 1018.
Gambler, 1042.
Gambler, Billie, 94, 3023.
Gambler, John, 3023, NB1056.
Gambler, Lizzie, 94.
Gambler, Martin, NB1056.
Gambler, Miley, 94.
Gambler, Rhoda, 94.
Gambler, Tommie, 94.
Gambler, Wallace, 3023.
Gano, Harriet, 3891.
Gano, Oscar, 2915.
Gano, Winnie, 2742.
Gant, Cordelia, 394.
Garfield, 3069.
Garland, David M., 1582.
Garland, Floyd H, 1582.
Garland, Libbie M., 1582.
Garland, Louis, 1582.
Garland, S. F., 1582.
Garland, Tookah, 1582.
Garner, Gus, 1055.
Garner, John L, 268.

Garner, Robert T., 1055.
Garner, Susan L., 268, M88, M89, NB878.
Garner, Virginia Ann, 1055.
Garner, Willie B., 268.
Garner, Wm., 268.
Garrett, Mary, 715.
Gathlocco. Fun, 2435.
Gatlin, C. C., NB366.
Gatlin, Helen, NB366.
Gatlin, Lucy Ann, 2328, NB366.
Gatts, Henry, 870.
Geneva, Joe, 1621.
Geneva, Sallie, 1621.
Gentry, Abbie, 572.
Gentry, Bluford M., 509.
Gentry, Boyd D., 509.
Gentry, Caroline, 504, 509, 572, 834.
Gentry, Etta, 504.
Gentry, James, 504, 509, 572, 834.
Gentry, Lizzie, 504.
Gentry, Mary E., 509.
Gentry, Pearl, 504.
Gentry, Rachel J., 509.
Gentry, R. J., 504.
Gentry, Robert J., Jr., 504.
Gentry, Robert L., 509.
Gentry, Sallie D., 509.
Gentry, Sallie P., 509.
Gentry, Scott, 572.
Gentry, William E., 509.
George, 2151.
George, Alexander, 2308.
George, Bessie, 2020.
George, Dave, 2966.
George, Jeffrey, 353, 2020.
George, Jeffry, 2020, 353.
George, Jensie, 235.
George, John, 2308.
George, Lizzie, 2308.
George, Long, 235, 1521.
George, Willie, 2308.
Gibson, 2894.
Gibson, Charles, 2266, NB181, NB182.
Gibson, Charles Counterman, NB182.
Gibson, Cheparney, 31.
Gibson, Chester, 2266, NB181, NB182.
Gibson, Daisy, 3135.
Gibson, Dicey, 229, 1809.
Gibson, Eliza, 3135.
Gibson, Elsie, 3065.
Gibson, Ethel, NB534.
Gibson, Frankie, M65.
Gibson, Gilbert, 31.
Gibson, Hettie, 451, 3572, NB991.
Gibson, Irene, 3135.
Gibson, Isparhecher, 3135.
Gibson, James T., 1102.
Gibson, Jerusha, 1102.
Gibson, John, 1713, 2266, 2831, 2807, 3135.
Gibson, John C., 1713, 2266, 2807, 2831, 3135.
Gibson, John E., 1102, M65.
Gibson, Joseph, 31, 1102, 3572, NB991.
Gibson, Joseph A., 1102.
Gibson, Joseph B., NB534.
Gibson, Josephine, 838.
Gibson, Leonard, 183, 1809.
Gibson, Lida, 3065.
Gibson, Lizzie, 183, 3135, 3914.
Gibson, Martha, 31, NB991.
Gibson, Mary, 31.

Gibson, Mary E., 1102.
Gibson, Maud, M65.
Gibson, May Della, 3135.
Gibson, Micco, 3135.
Gibson, Milder, 3572.
Gibson, Modenia M., 843, NB181, NB182
Gibson, Montie, 1116.
Gibson, Pearl, 3135.
Gibson, Polly, 2266.
Gibson, Rose, 1116.
Gibson, Silas B., 1102.
Gibson, Toge, 2831.
Gibson, Verna Marie, NB181.
Gibson, Walter, 1116, 3065.
Gibson, Wilson, 2831.
Gibson, William S., 1102, NB534.
Gilbert, Jeniry, NB1013.
Gilbert, Jude, 1089, NB1013.
Gilbert, Louis W., NB1013.
Gilcrease, Ben, 456.
Gilcrease, Bessie, NB86.
Gilcrease, Eddie, 456.
Gilcrease, Elmer Lee, NB84.
Gilcrease, Florence, 456.
Gilcrease, Lena, 456.
Gilcrease, Lizzie, 456, NB84, NB85, NB86.
Gilcrease, Mabel, NB85.
Gilcrease, Thomas, 456.
Gilcrease, William L., 456, NB84, NB85, NB86.
Gilhoa, Muchie, 2922.
Gillis, C. B., 3527.
Gillis, Ed., NB880.
Gillis, Elmer, NB880.
Gillis, Nancy, 3527.
Gillis, Taylor A., 3527.
Given, George, 3904.
Givens, Annie, 3719, 3720, 2704, NB649.
Givens, Charley, 3719.
Givens, Charte, 2766, 2767, 2774, 2219, 2429,
      3723, CE 4030, NB623, NB624.
Givens, Chocta, 2219, 2429, 2766, 2767, 2774,
      3723, CE4030, NB623, NB624.
Givens, Choctaw, 2219, 2429, 2774, 2766, 2767,
      3723, CE-4030, NB623, NB624.
Givens, Eddie, 2766.
Givens, Harper, NB649.
Givens, Hepsey, 3723.
Givens, Jack, 3904.
Givens, Kizzie, 2219, CE4030, NB623, NB624.
Givens, Lawyer, 2219.
Givens, Lonie, NB624.
Givens, Luther, CE4030.
Givens, Minnie, NB623.
Givens, Robert, 2219.
Givens, Sam, 2219.
Givens, Silla, 2219, 3723.
Givens, Sillier, 2429.
Givens, William, 2766, 3719, NB649.
Givens, Wutsy, 3904.
Glass, Neller, 1860.
Glenn, Elma, NB808.
Glenn, Elmer, 3756.
Glenn, Gracie, 916.
Glenn, Ida E., 916, 3756, NB808.
Glenn, Ida Estella, 916, 3756, NB808.
Glenn, Mabel C., 916.
Glenn, R. J., NB808.
Glenn, Robert J., 916, 3756.
Goat, Alfred, 1704, NB659, NB660.
Goat, Alice Sukey, NB660.

321

Goat, Angeline, 1702, 1703, 1704, NB659.
Goat, Eddiehnie, NB651.
Goat, John R., 1702, 1703, 1704.
Goat, Katie, 1702.
Goat, Martin. 1702.
Goat, Millie, 1523, NB1162.
Goat, Minnie, 1523, NB651.
Goat, Peggy, 1702.
Goat, Rachael, 1704, NB659, NB660.
Goat, Roman, 1702.
Goat, Sallie, 3924.
Goat, Susie, 1703, 3924.
Goat, Wadley, 1703, 3924, NB651.
Goat, Wardley, 1703, 3924, NB651.
Goat, Wisey, 1703. '
Gobler, Emma, 654, 668.
Gobler, Jack, 654, 668
Goliah, 3019.
Goober, John, 1424.
Goober, Nicey, 1424.
Gooch, Adella, 2633, NB466, NB467.
Gooch, Arthur, 2634.
Gooch, Claudie, NB467.
Gooch, Dollie, 2633.
Gooch, Ed., 2633, NB466, NB467.
Gooch, George, 1988.
Gooch, Henry, 1988.
Gooch, Jesse, 1988, 2633, 2634.
Gooch, Maudie, NB466.
Gooch, Tochey, 1989.
Gooch, Tochie, 2633, 2634.
Goode, Annie Elderrein, M254.
Goode, George, NB145.
Goode, George C., M254.
Goode, Myrtle M., 861, NB145, M254.
Goode, Rowena, NB145.
Goodee, Charity, 2925.
Goodee, John, 2925.
Gooden, 2352.
Gooden, Annie, 2352, M183.
Gooden, Bessie, 1158.
Gooden, Carrie, NB456.
Gooden, Charley, 967, 2301, NB691.
Gooden, Charlie, 2789.
Gooden, Chauker, 2683.
Gooden, Chotie, 646.
Gooden, Daniel, 137, 659, 2352, 3240.
Gooden, David, 2488, 2495, 2683.
Gooden, Dora, 2306, NB456.
Gooden, Edward, 1199.
Gooden, Eliza, 1546.
Gooden, Elsie, 2317.
Gooden, Frank, 3619.
Gooden, George, 2488.
Gooden, Henderson, 1035, NB456.
Gooden, Hoplin, 3940.
Gooden, Jacob, 2301, 3619, NB691.
Gooden, Jim, 1140, 1157, 1158.
Gooden, Joe, 2317.
Gooden, John, 967.
Gooden, Leah, 2301.
Gooden, Lizzie, 2352.
Gooden, Louisa, 1046, 1158, 2301, 3619, NB691.
Gooden, Mary, 1140, 3836.
Gooden, Nancy, 1157.
Gooden, Nellie, 2301, 2651.
Gooden, Sam, 872, 1035.
Gooden, Sagone. 967.
Gooden, Sordie, 2352.
Gooden, Sukey, 2789.

Gooden, Susan, 1199, NB1226.
Gooden, Susanna, 2495.
Gooden, Toney, 137.
Gooden, Tontah, 2306, NB456.
Gooden, William, 1046, 1199, 2352.
Goodey, Jadie, 1301.
Goodey, John, 1301.
Goodin, George, 141.
Goodin, Lizzie, 141.
Goodman, Ahhaconanny, 2162.
Goodman, Dave, 3035.
Goodman, Sahconcahny, 2162.
Goodman, Tatahlacoconthla, 2162.
Goodwin, Mabel, 1604, M256.
Goodwin, Reese, M256.
Goodwin, Van H., M256.
Goody, Jim, 3338.
Goosbeck, Capitol, 3952.
Gordon, Vinita, 406, NB675, M97.
Gotahney, 3353.
Gotts, Harry, 870.
Gotts, Lucy R., 870.
Gouge, Amanda, 845.
Gouge, Casawka, M492.
Gouge, Chunna, M478.
Gouge, Daisy, 1783.
Gouge, Dave, 1783.
Gouge, Earnest, 2966, M489, M490, M491, M492.
Gouge, Jack, 2966, M478.
Gouge, Lucinda, 2867, M477.
Gouge, Nicey, 2867, M489, M490, M491, M492.
Gouge, Pewter, M489.
Gouge, Sam, M490.
Gouge, Suckcjo, M491.
Gown, Bud, NB457.
Gown, Sarah, NB457.
Grace, George, 783.
Grace, John, 486.
Grace. Peter, 486.
Graham, Lewis, NB1003.
Graham, Millie, 1797, NB1003.
Graham, Sissie, NB1003.
Grammar, Charles, 2525.
Granberry, Alma Dee, NB860.
Granberry, James, NB860.
Granberry, Mattie, 490, NB860.
Grant, Assie, 563.
Grant, Billie, 1767.
Grant, Billy, 1767.
Grant, Frank, 563.
Grant, Lena, NB338.
Grant, Lucy, 563.
Grant, Mary, 1767, NB338.
Grant, Meley, 1767, NB338.
Grant, Miley, 3597.
Grant, Minnie, 1767.
Grant, Niffie, 1767, 3597, NB338.
Grant, Niffey, 1767, 3597, NB338.
Grant, Sam Miller ,563.
Grant, Stella, 3597.
Grant, Timmie, 563.
Grant, U. S., 563.
Graves, Bonnie Gertrude, 783.
Graves, Leona, 783.
Gray, Absey, 3003.
Gray, Addie, NB264.
Gray, Amos, 886.
Gray, Amy, 88, 2398.
Gray, Annie, 2075, 2083, NB489.

Gray, Barney, 3035.
Gray, Belle, 2907.
Gray, Ben, 2864.
Gray, Carl, M79.
Gray, Cemme, 2504.
Gray, Cumsey, 3003.
Gray, Daniel, 2504.
Gray, Dickson, 3035.
Gray, Dorsey, 2504.
Gray, Dosey, 2504.
Gray, Edmond, 2119.
Gray, Elijah, 2075.
Gray, Eliza, 2498.
Gray, Emma, 2119.
Gray, Fannie, NB835.
Gray, George C., 3801, NB32.
Gray, Henry, 3801.
Gray, Isaac, 849.
Gray, Jackson, 1664.
Gray, James, 305, 726, 1664, 3035, M79.
Gray, James L., 2907.
Gray, Jim, 2122.
Gray, Jimmy (Nocus Elle), 2733, 2845, NB1288,
    NB1289.
Gray, Jobie, 2119.
Gray, Johnnie, NB1288.
Gray, Johnson, NB32.
Gray, Josiah, 2845.
Gray, Lee, 1664.
Gray, Lena, 3035.
Gray, Lewis, 2083.
Gray, Lizzie, 329, 726.
Gray, Louie, 2425.
Gray, Louina, 88, 886.
Gray, Louis, 726.
Gray, Louisa, 305, 726, 822, 1664, 2075, 2122.
    3035.
Gray, Lucinda, 2119.
Gray, Mandy, NB1289.
Gray, Maria, 2907.
Gray, Mary, 1380, 2119, 3668, M79, NB264.
Gray, Mesulta, 2046, 3801, NB32.
Gray, Mildred, 2907.
Gray, Miley, 726.
Gray, Millie, 329, NB835, NB836.
Gray, Moses, 3668.
Gray, Motey, 2350.
Gray, Nancy, 726, 2119, 2125, NB1288, NB1289
Gray, Neteche, 2504.
Gray, Nettie, 2119.
Gray, Roley, NB489.
Gray, Sandy, 88.
Gray, Siah, 2119, 3668, NB264
Gray, Silanie, 2425.
Gray, Susan, 849, 1098.
Gray, Susie, NB836.
Gray, Thomas, 2119.
Gray, Walter, 2075, 3035.
Gray, Will, 329.
Gray, Willie, 2398, NB835, NB836.
Gray, Winey, 2350.
Grayson, Abbey, 1145, 3623.
Grayson, Abbie, 3623, 1145.
Grayson, Addie, 1943.
Grayson, Adeline, 3623.
Grayson, Agnes P., 760.
Grayson, Alice, 1196, 3468, NB669.
Grayson, Amy, 608, 3126.
Grayson, Annie, 908, 1078, 1079, 1160, 1498,
    1608, 1960, 3610, 3957.

Grayson, Austin, 636
Grayson, Ben, 80, 283, 908.
Grayson, Betsey, 651.
Grayson, Bill, 439, 1256.
Grayson, Billy, 1256.
Grayson, Buck, 2337, NB815, NB816.
Grayson, Cecil W., 3058.
Grayson, Charles C., 1697.
Grayson, Charley, 760, 1877.
Grayson, Chimker, 2740.
Grayson, Chloe, 1877.
Grayson, Christina, 80.
Grayson, Clarence, 3468.
Grayson, Claude R., 1920.
Grayson, Cleveland, 1697.
Grayson, Colbert, 64, 1697.
Grayson, Cora, 883.
Grayson, Daniel, 3145.
Grayson, Dave, 1079, M200.
Grayson, David, 636.
Grayson, Della E., 1690.
Grayson, Dick, 646.
Grayson, Dickie, 2367.
Grayson, Doc., 262, 263, 358, 359, 508, 1146,
    1793.
Grayson, Dock, 1200.
Grayson, Dora, NB934.
Grayson, Edmond, 668.
Grayson, Eli, 668, 883.
Grayson, Elijah, 760.
Grayson, Elizabeth, 1697.
Grayson, Ella, M273.
Grayson, Ellen, 883, 1835, 3460.
Grayson, Elliott, 2686.
Grayson, Ellis, 2686.
Grayson, Emma, 636, 1123, 1256.
Grayson, Enoch, 3610.
Grayson, Fannie, 1778, M200.
Grayson, Foster, 2250, 2800.
Grayson, Garland, M107, NB873.
Grayson, George, 908, 927, 3610.
Grayson, George-Creek Frd., 446, NB834.
Grayson, George W., 1498, 1608, 1960.
Grayson, Gertrude, NB780.
Grayson, Gibson, 64, 2366.
Grayson, G. W., 1498, 1608, 1960.
Grayson, Hattie, 449, M273, NB780.
Grayson, Hellen, M200.
Grayson, Henderson, 1145, 3623.
Grayson, Henry, 80, 304, 320, 324, 583, 668,
    1168, 1940.
Grayson, Hepsey, 405.
Grayson, Hillabee, 45.
Grayson, Hope, 1352.
Grayson, Isaac, 508.
Grayson, James, 636, 1401, 1 08, 1835, 1920.
    2363, 3790.
Grayson, James L., 262, NB61.
Grayson, Jane, 1920.
Grayson, Janie, 2367.
Grayson, Jeannetta, 2366, NB814.
Grayson, Jeff, 2363.
Grayson, Jenetta, 654.
Grayson, Jennetta, 669.
Grayson, Jennie, 270, 1401, 1402, 1608, 2740.
    M57.
Grayson, Jennie May, 1920.
Grayson, Jim, 525, 583, 646, 2068.
Grayson, Jimson, 528, 2136.
Grayson, Joe, 1079, 1146, 3468, NB934.

Hagen, Sukey, 763.
Hagerty, Rebecca, 3283.
Hagerty, Spire, 3283.
Hagie, Ben, 1010.
Hah kee, Simer, 2694.
Haikey, 256, 288.
Haikey, Ben, 285. 288, NB19.
Haikey, Ben Jr., 285, 444, 3430, NB18.
Haikey, Bertha, NB18.
Haikey, Burney, NB188.
Haikey, Dave, 288, NB188, M92.
Haikey, Edward, 288.
Haikey, Eliza, 210, NB55, NB56.
Haikey, Ella, 210.
Haikey, Ellis, 288.
Haikey, Frank, 203.
Haikey, Jennetta, 288, M214.
Haikey, Jessie, NB54.
Haikey, John, 203, 210, 281, 288.
Haikey, Kono, 3872.
Haikey, Louisa, 289, 666, 3430, NB18, NB19.
Haikey, Macey, 285, 288.
Haike , Nancy, 203.
Haikey, Nicev, 2079, M92, NB188.
Haikey, Malissa, 444.
Haikey, Masey, M92.
Haikey, Maymie, 3430.
Haikey, Sissie, NB19.
Haikey, Sookey, 281.
Haikey, Sukey, 203, 210.
Haikey, Susanna, 210, NB54.
Hailey, John, 1442.
Hailey, Lony, 1442.
Hailey, Melissa, 1442.
Haines, David W., 2997.
Haines, Keziah, 2997.
Haines, Newton, 2997.
Hair, Jess, 2874.
Haka, Erke, 3081.
Ha ke pah ny, 2162.
Hala hoc key, 1280.
Halat a hee, 1345.
Hale, Billy, NB1199
Hale, Go poat ker, 3041
Hale, Jacob, 2895.
Hale, Jasper, 3041, NB1199
Hale, Lucy, 1512, NB965.
Hale, Mabel, 1512.
Hale, Maggie, 1970, NB1199.
Hale, Ollie, 2760, NB1247.
Hale, Sumner, 1512.
Haley, 2970.
Haley, George Elmer, NBS24.
Haley, Joe, 1383, 3733.
Haley, Kizzie, M197.
Haley, Lena, 133, M197, NBS24
Haley, Nancy, 1383.
Haley, W. D., NBS24, M197.
Hall, Alta, NB454
Hall, A vie, 1283.
Hall, Cleo C., M336.
Hall, David, 1118, NB193.
Hall, George, 1118, 3568.
Hall, Hannah E., 1283, 3568, NB454, M336.
Hall, Harrison, 3640.
Hall, James, 1118.
Hall, Joe, 2903.
Hall, Joseph, 1118, 1128.
Hall, Lena, 2082.
Hall, Lena A , 3640.

Hall, Louis, S., 3640.
Hall, Manima, M356.
Hall, Martha, M356, NB194.
Hall, Melburn, 1283.
Hall, Mollie, NB194.
Hall, Nora, 2903, M341.
Hall, Samuel, 1283, 3568, NB454, M336.
Hall, Sandy, 1118, NB194, M356.
Hall, Sunnie, M341.
Hall, Wynie, 1118, 1128.
Hallada, 2464, 2466.
Halley, Hosa, 1383.
Halley, Joe, 3733.
Halley, Nancy, 3733.
Halley, Taylor, 3733.
Hallford, Annie Bell, 978.
Hallford, Anoma, 978.
Hallford, Emaline, 978, NB497, NB498, M433.
Hallford, Esther, M433.
Hallford, Euraline, 978, NB497, NB498.
Hallford, Lynn, NB498.
Hallford, M. A., 978. NB497, NB498, M433.
Hallford, Nathan, NB497.
Hallford, Ross, 978.
Hal lo ga, 1848.
Halthmia, 2571.
Hamby, A. H., 3913.
Hamby, Archie, 3913.
Hamby, Dora, 3913.
Hamby, Myrtle, 3913.
Hamilton, Alec, 848.
Hamilton, Alex, 1336, 3497.
Hamilton, Cassie, 1451, M119.
Hamilton, Ellen, 3497, NB959, M312.
Hamilton, James M., M119.
Hamilton, Mahala, M312.
Hamilton, Mary, NB959.
Hamilton, Pearly, 805.
Hamilton, Peter, 848, 3497, NB959, M312.
Hamilton, Price, 805.
Hamilton, Rose, 848.
Hamilton, Sallie, 848.
Hamilton, S. H., M119.
Hammer, Louis, 2939.
Hammond, Betsey, 1393.
Hammond, John, 1393.
Hammonds, Embry, 1393.
Hammonds, Jennie, 1393.
Hampton, 1916.
Hampton, Amanda, 647.
Hampton, John, 1916.
Hampton, John M., 647.
Hance, Bessie, 3487.
Hance, Elzonie, 874.
Hance, Jennie, 874.
Hance, Jennie L., 3487.
Hance, J. D., 3487.
Hance, John, 874.
Hance, William W., 874.
Hancock, C. A., NB676.
Hancock, Hattie L., 513, NB676.
Hancock, Lizzie, NB676.
Haney, 2948.
Haney, Emma, 3090, 3372.
Haney, Leah, 2948.
Haney, Lena, 2948.
Haney, Narchker, 2948, CE4048.
Haney, Philip, 173.
Haney, Waley, 207.
Haney, William, 173.

Hannah, 808, 889, 1555, 1641, 1643, 1653, 2192, 2448, 2465.
Hanson, Dollie, 657.
Hanson, Jim, 657.
Harchoche, Dicey, 1344.
Harchoche, Finar, 1344.
Harchoche, Lydia, 1344.
Harchoche, Tulwar, 1344.
Hardage, David, 1967.
Hardage, Hannah, 1604.
Hardage, Joseph H., 1604.
Hardage, Lewis, 1604.
Hardage, Lucy, 1967.
Hardage, May, 1604, M256.
Hardage, Rebecca, 1604.
Hardage, Ruth E., 1604, NB656.
Harday, 2541, 2542, 2543, 2548, 2942.
Hardridge, Adam, 636, 1433.
Hardridge, Amanda, 16, M47.
Hardridge, Billy, 522, 893.
Hardridge, Clarence, M47.
Hardridge, David D., 303.
Hardridge, Edmond, 1433.
Hardridge, Eli E., 1083, 3613, M47.
Hardridge, Ella, 303, M276.
Hardridge, Goldie, 128, M102.
Hardridge, Helen, 3613.
Hardridge, Jasper, M53.
Hardridge, Joe, 128.
Hardridge, Julia, 29.
Hardridge, Lillie, 1808, M53.
Hardridge, Lizzie, 636, 1654.
Hardridge, Lona, 29.
Hardridge, Lucy, 1083, 1088.
Hardridge, Millie, 1083, 3613.
Hardridge, Moche, 636.
Hardridge, Nancy, 636.
Hardridge, Shawnee, 29.
Hardridge, Siah, 889.
Hardridge, Solomon, 1812, M53.
Hardridge, Taylor, 128, 893, 1812.
Hardridge, Young, 1083.
Harge, 3048.
Harge, George, 3048.
Harger, Hannah, 1377.
Harjo, 1006, 1881, 2279, 2922, 3007.
Harjo, Abbie, 1491.
Harjo, Addie, 1505, 2399.
Harjo, A. E., NB291, NB292.
Harjo, Aggie, 2627.
Harjo, Ah, 3175, NB943, NB1160.
Harjo, Ahate, 2855.
Harjo, A har lock, 2718.
Harjo, Aharlok, 1024.
Harjo, Aharluck, 2108.
Harjo, Ah har luk, 3406.
Harjo, Ah hor lock, 1279.
Harjo, Ah le pah te, 10.
Harjo, Ah lip ah te, 2089.
Harjo, Aholak, 3900.
Harjo, Ailsey, 2287.
Harjo, Albata, 1568, 2721.
Harjo, Albert, 2099.
Harjo, Alberta, 3177.
Harjo, Albutter, 1568, 2721.
Harjo, Alec Little, 2397.
Harjo, Alex, 2098, 2528, M179.
Harjo, Alfred, NB663.
Harjo, Alice, 3506, NB560.
Harjo, Alleah, 2881.

326

Harjo, Concharty, 1081, 1212.
Harjo, Con he ler, 3787.
Harjo, Conip, 1503, 2722.
Harjo, Connuggy, 1589.
Harjo, Cono, 1881, 2652.
Harjo, Contah, 2886.
Harjo, Coosie, 270.
Harjo, Cosar, 923, 1137, 1614, 2149, 2726
Harjo, Cossa, 1361.
Harjo, Cotcha, 2524.
Harjo, Cotsey, 2235.
Harjo, Cowa, 3391.
Harjo, Cowe, 1160, 1545, 2087, 2111, 2538, 3193,
        3282.
Harjo, Cussetah, 733.
Harjo, Cynda, 2154.
Harjo, Daley, 2176, NB1036.
Harjo, Daniel, 2368.
Harjo, Dave, 3325.
Harjo, Dello, 2286.
Harjo, Dickey, 1297, NB1108.
Harjo, Dinah, 2130.
Harjo, Docher, 4015.
Harjo, Ebner, 2187.
Harjo, Echo, 2218.
Harjo, Edmond, 1605.
Harjo, Edmund, 1527.
Harjo, Efer, 1939.
Harjo, Effie, 2648, 3273.
Harjo, Eliza, 1554, 2001, 2187, 3175, NB943,
        NB1160, NB1225.
Harjo, Eliza Fosh, 1390.
Harjo, Ella Ruth, NB897.
Harjo, Ema, 1845.
Harjo, Emma, NB1109.
Harjo, Emarthla, 794, 1742, 1941, 3166.
Harjo, Emarthler, 1911.
Harjo, Emarthley, 1839.
Harjo, Enath, 215.
Harjo, En sa che, 1001.
Harjo, Esparne, 1558, 2436.
Harjo, Esparney, 2436.
Harjo, Espotoke, 2976.
Harjo, Estonahe, 2824.
Harjo, Ethel, NB1114.
Harjo, Eufaula, 1284, 2126, 2855.
Harjo, Fal loppo, 2627.
Harjo, Fannie, 2599, 2600.
Harjo, Fanny, NB946.
Harjo, Farcosa, 1740.
Harjo, Finchee, 2816.
Harjo, Fit te da, 2322.
Harjo, Fixico, 283.
Harjo, Fok co hesty, 1645.
Harjo, Fola, 1493.
Harjo, Folohkec, 2134.
Harjo, Fos, 1824.
Harjo, Fosh, 1390.
Harjo, Foshutche, 1542, 2092.
Harjo, Frank, 3193, 2778, NB1036.
Harjo, Fred, NB1283.
Harjo, Freeda, M288.
Harjo, Fres, 3056.
Harjo, Fuchus, 2778.
Harjo, Fus, 68, 1041, 2401, 2833.
Harjo, Fushatchi, 2697.
Harjo, Fushutche, 1554, 2092.
Harjo, Fushutja, 2814.
Harjo, Fuswa, 2119.
Harjo, George, 2571, 3167, NB1257.

327

Harjo, H. M., 555, 3506, NB897.
Harjo, Habeche, 1125, 1126, 1130.
Harjo, Hagee, 1160.
Harjo, Hagie, 1635.
Harjo, Haleya, 2866.
Harjo, Hannah, 1323, 3193, NB1214.
Harjo, Harthun, 1479.
Harjo, Hathlen, 2073.
Harjo, Haton, 1202.
Harjo, Heloke, 3203.
Harjo, Henry, 2126.
Harjo, Henry M., 555, 3506, NB897.
Harjo, Hepsey, 1041.
Harjo, Hezekiah, 2333.
Harjo, Hillabee, 1540, 2674.
Harjo, Hillis, 323, 2571, 2862, 2857, 2864, NB-
    1257, M484.
Harjo, Hobeth, 3988.
Harjo, Hobuth, 319, 383.
Harjo, Ho buth ke, 319, 383.
Harjo, Hodalga, 1846.
Harjo, Holleputa, 1321.
Harjo, Hoputh, 1323.
Harjo, Ho tel ko chee, 1495.
Harjo, Hotulke, 1323, 2828.
Harjo, Houston, 2665, 3273.
Harjo, Hulberta, 2653.
Harjo, Hulleputa, 1344, 1669.
Harjo, Hulleputta, 1344. 1669.
Harjo, Hunter, 1297, NB1108.
Harjo, Huntie, 3328, M123.
Harjo, Hutchenubbe, 1280, 1266.
Harjo, Huthlan, 1886.
Harjo, Ida, NB1160.
Harjo, Inechuppo, 149.
Harjo, Intermish, 1542.
Harjo, Ipohoke, 1527, 3362, 3974.
Harjo, Is pa hoke, 1504.
Harjo, Isparney, 1719.
Harjo, Isperney, 88.
Harjo, Ispokoke, 1527, 3362, 3974.
Harjo, Isponney, 2443.
Harjo, Israel, 2126.
Harjo, Itshars, 2443.
Harjo, Itshas, 2380, 2665, 2895.
Harjo, Ithus, 1936.
Harjo, Jack, 1727, 3990.
Harjo, Jackson, 1006.
Harjo, James, 1554, 2132.
Harjo, James Larney, 2653.
Harjo, Jane, 1076, 1289, 1900.
Harjo, Janie, 2320.
Harjo, Jannetta, 1024.
Harjo, Jeannetta, 2780.
Harjo, Jenna, 1527.
Harjo, Jennetta, 383.
Harjo, Jennie, 1545, 2399, 2780, 2986, 3051.
Harjo, Jemima, 3167.
Harjo, Jessie, 3864, 3994.
Harjo, Jim, 2368.
Harjo, Jimmie, 3375 NB187. NB1275.
Harjo, Jimsey, 1725, 2368, M417, M418.
Harjo, Jo, 1403.
Harjo, Joastare, 94.
Harjo, Jockey, 1024.
Harjo, Joe, 1041, 3085, M123.
Harjo, Joe Tiger, 3193.
Harjo, John, 2399, 3193.
Harjo, Johnnie, NB187.
Harjo, Johnson, 1081, 1289, 1592.

Harjo,
Harjo,
Harjo,
Harjo,

Harjo,
Harjo,
Harjo,
Harjo,
Harjo,
Harjo,
Harjo,
Harjo,
Harjo,
Harjo,
Harjo,
Harjo,
Harjo,
Harjo,
Harjo,
Harjo,
Harjo,
Harjo,
Harjo,
Harjo,
Harjo,
Harjo,
Harjo,
Harjo,
Harjo,
Harjo,
Harjo,
Harjo,
Harjo,
Harjo,
Harjo,
Harjo,
Harjo,
Harjo,
Harjo,
Harjo,
Harjo,
Harjo,
Harjo,
Harjo,
Harjo,
Harjo,
Harjo,
Harjo,
Harjo,
Harjo,
Harjo,
Harjo,
Harjo,
Harjo,
Harjo,
Harjo,
Harjo,
Harjo,

Louisa, 446, 1001, 1212, 1941, 1971, 2571, 3193, NB1109.
Louvina, 1041, 1289, NB1148.
Lowina, 1041, 1289, NB1148.
Lowiney, 2139.
Lucinda, 1171, 1307, 1994, 2119, 3175.
Lucy, 1212, 1307, 1505, 1515, 2132, 2612, 2653, NB924, NB1024, M245.
Luffie, 2066.
Lumka, 1509, 3979.
Lumpka, 2841.
Lumsey, 1289, 1839, 3407.
Lydia, 626, 2548.
Macel, M482.
Macheska, 2349.
Madowa, 2648.
Maggie, 1547, 1742, M144.
Magillis, 1635, 1801.
Mahaley, 1171, M245.
Maleya, 3407, NB906.
Malinda, 2571.
Mamie, 3302.
Marchie, 1726.
Marge, 1725.
Maria, 3989, M485, M486, M487.
Marsey, 555, 1527, 2134, 2898, 3368, 3969.
Martha, 2099, 2349, M444, NB1004.
Martin, 3051.
Mary, 656, 2145, 2571, 2827, NB1257, M484.
Mattie, 626, 2089.
Maudie, 2069.
Mecheska, 2273.
Mechiska, 2127.
Mechusco, 778.
Meglus, 1635, 1801.
Mehilley, 1515, NB1020.
Mejeaka, 2397.
Mekks, 3167.
Melene, 3146.
Meley, 3203.
Melina, 319, 383.
Melinhoda, 1265.
Melissa, NB268.
Melosia, 1558.
Micco, 446, 2968, 3253.
Mikko, 2319.
Milley, 2827.
Millie, 1505, 1506, 1999, 2185, 2443, 2795, 2881, 3273, NB1025,NB1192
Millyanna, 1265.
Minar, 1589.
Minda, 626, 3512, M473.
Minnie, 3512, M418.
Miloche, 2397.
Minte, 2069.
Missey, 1280.
Missie, 2616, 3233.
Mitchell, 3968.
Mitchie, 1347.
Mockta, 2127.
Moleyar, 2285.
Mollea, 159.
Mollie, 1727, 2073, 2423, 2611, 3573, NB267, NB268, M179.
Mona, 3979.
Mord, NB292.
Moser, 1171.
Mulley, 1266.

Harjo, Munna, 1727.
Harjo, Muscogee, 1041.
Harjo, Muska, 2448.
Harjo, Mussey, 1589.
Harjo, Mutta, 2152.
Harjo, Nancy, 1266, 1332, 1503, 1505, 1572, 1625, 2098, 2126, 2550, 2852, 2968 3159, 3274, 3935, NB664, M179.
Harjo, Nannie, 1288, 2792, 3185.
Harjo, Naomi, 555.
Harjo, Narbuchay, 90.
Harjo, Narbuchchee, 2187.
Harjo, Narbutche, 1270.
Harjo, Nargie, 1509.
Harjo, Narne, 2663.
Harjo, Nassie, 3085.
Harjo, Nathan, 1041, 3989.
Harjo, Nechthlocco, 1589, 1592.
Harjo, Neckthlocco, 1589, 1592.
Harjo, Needa, 3406.
Harjo, Neha, 1323, 1436, 1437, 2434, 2528.
Harjo, Neha Thlocco, 3319.
Harjo, Nekie, 1266.
Harjo, Nellie, 2338, 2339.
Harjo, Nettie, NB221.
Harjo, Newman, 1605.
Harjo, Nicey, 2528.
Harjo, Ninna Chubba, 3053.
Harjo, Ninnechupco, 321.
Harjo, Ninnechuppo, 291
Harjo, Noah, 2399, 2866, 3171.
Harjo, Nocos, 626.
Harjo, Nocossille, 2478.
Harjo, Nocus, 1015, 1126, 1151, 1625, 1815, 2285, 2434, 2550, 2551, 2740, 2898, 2965, 3233.
Harjo, Nocus Ille, 2248.
Harjo, Nokaf, 1368.
Harjo, Nokas, 1261.
Harjo, Nokos, 2192.
Harjo, Nokosela, 2461.
Harjo, Nokpuk, 3165.
Harjo, Nokus, 1288, 2744.
Harjo, Norcus, 2548.
Harjo, Nosey, 1932.
Harjo, Obie, 1041.
Harjo, Oche, 217, 384, 2069, 2143, 2478, 3235.
Harjo, Ochee, 1505, 2143, 2478.
Harjo, Ochees, 1347.
Harjo, Oches, 346, 516, 2207.
Harjo, Ochess, 396.
Harjo, Ogee, 2567.
Harjo, Okchun, 1408, 1539, 2399, 3180.
Harjo, Okfuska, 528, 2661.
Harjo, Okfuske, 528, 2661.
Harjo, Okdasus, 1846.
Harjo, Oklossie, 1266.
Harjo, Okoche, 2864.
Harjo, Okolabisha, 949.
Harjo, Oktayarchee, 1271.
Harjo, Osache, 1148.
Harjo, Osage, 1505, 2399, 3362.
Harjo, Osagee, 1504.
Harjo, Osar, 2671.
Harjo, Oscar, 1151.
Harjo, Oshee, 1824, 1825.
Harjo, Osoch, 2001, 2660, 3013.
Harjo, Osoche, 2001, 3013, 2660.
Harjo, Osotock, 1542.
Harjo, Ospatock, 1551.

329

Harjo, Ospotoch, 1554.
Harjo, Pahos, 1727, 2126, 3328.
Harjo, Pahose, 1555.
Harjo, Pakalee, 2497.
Harjo, Parhos, 892, 2019, 2056, 3190.
Harjo, Parhose, 2098, 2154, 2577.
Harjo, Peecher, 2814.
Harjo, Pefotka, 1539.
Harjo, Peggy, 2087.
Harjo, Pen, 1463, 1572, 2397, 2615, 3274, 3330, 2822, 4015.
Harjo, Pena, 414.
Harjo, Peney, 2155.
Harjo, Peter, 1041, 1645, 2397, 3502, NB1214, NB1215.
Harjo, Philliby, NB1266.
Harjo, Pin, 1463, 1572, 2397, 2615, 2822, 3274, 3330, 4015.
Harjo, Pinner, 3146, 3554.
Harjo, Poley, 2571.
Harjo, Polly, 131, 1589, 2187, 2397, 3051, 3053, NB1275.
Harjo, Posuk, 62.
Harjo, Quesko, 1667.
Harjo, Rhoda, 1137, 1866, 3177, NB663, NB664, NB1060.
Harjo, Rina, 3990.
Harjo, Robert, NB1215.
Harjo, Roller, NB1036.
Harjo, Roman, NB291.
Harjo, Rosanna, 1041, 1993, 3330.
Harjo, Rosey, NB1266.
Harjo, Sallie, 1669, 3273, 3935, NB1024.
Harjo, Salina, 656, 2322, M201.
Harjo, Sampson, 1554.
Harjo, Samson, 1266.
Harjo, Samuel, M144.
Harjo, Sandy, 2069.
Harjo, Saney, 2679.
Harjo, Sango, 2069, NB1266.
Harjo, Sarah, 656, 2204, NB920, M123.
Harjo, Sartupe, 159.
Harjo, Sarwakhoche, 2132.
Harjo, Sarwanoke, 3407.
Harjo, Seaver, 3178.
Harjo, Segar, 3273.
Harjo, Selina, 2285.
Harjo, Seyada, 1509.
Harjo, Shanco, 2069, NB1266.
Harjo, Shawnee, 2886.
Harjo, Silbie, 1266.
Harjo, Silla, 2399.
Harjo, Simon, 2881.
Harjo, Sinna, 713.
Harjo, Sofa, 2019.
Harjo, Sookey, 3167.
Harjo, Sophia, 2504, 3018.
Harjo, Sophie, 2504.
Harjo, Sothee, 2721.
Harjo, Sowanoke, 2613, 2827, 2881.
Harjo, Spaniard, 3237.
Harjo, Spanney, 3020.
Harjo, Stephen, 3185, NB1283, M288.
Harjo, Sukey, 1585, NB221.
Harjo, Sulka, 1726.
Harjo, Sulphur, 1212, NB1114.
Harjo, Sulsey, 2126.
Harjo, Sunday, 1527, 1554, NB943, M144.
Harjo, Sunduller, 1645.
Harjo, Suntilla, 2473.

Harjo, Susan, 159, 1125, 1130, NB193.
Harjo, Susie, 62, 733, 1645, 2369, 2653, 3169, 3171, 3177, NB187, NB1028, NB1214, NB1215.
Harjo, Suwerneryeche, 1489.
Harjo, Tabus, 2066.
Harjo, Tabkosa, 3233.
Harjo, Takosa, 2235.
Harjo, Talof, 2500.
Harjo, Talop, 2663.
Harjo, Talup, 2483.
Harjo, Talwa, 1653.
Harjo, Tarkosar, 2291, 2764.
Harjo, Tarsee, 1558, 2824, M444.
Harjo, Tasikia, 2720.
Harjo, Taskeeg, 1161.
Harjo, Taskeek, 1358.
Harjo, Taye, 2897.
Harjo, Taylor, 3051.
Harjo, Thaneda, 1265.
Harjo, Tharlip, 1439, 1467.
Harjo, Tharthlo, 1593, 3410.
Harjo, Thlathlo, 3183.
Harjo, Thlechuma, 2945.
Harjo, Thlechumme, 1422, 1535, 1537.
Harjo, Thlegummie, 1420.
Harjo, Thlejummy, 1180.
Harjo, Thlo, 3171.
Harjo, Thlocco, 2610, 2612, 2614.
Harjo, Thlucpolikey, 3935.
Harjo, Thomas, 3175.
Harjo, Thompson, 1527.
Harjo, Tiah, 870.
Harjo, Tibbie, 2610.
Harjo, Tiger, 1616.
Harjo, Tilda, 1635.
Harjo, Tilla, 3233.
Harjo, Tina, 2449, 2511, 2860.
Harjo, Toatkis, 3177, 3178, 3181, 3387.
Harjo, Tokis, 3358.
Harjo, Tokus, 2872.
Harjo, Tolaf, 889.
Harjo, Tom, 3179, NB1025.
Harjo, Tommie, 381, 2108.
Harjo, Tommoche, 3179, NB1025.
Harjo, Tommy, 531, 626, 949, 1314, 1688, 1932, 2134, 2359, 2593, 2979, 3065, 3085, 3167, 3305, 3343.
Harjo, Tomsogee, 3788.
Harjo, Toney, 1265, 1718.
Harjo, Totkie, 1598.
Harjo, Totkis, 3177, 3178, 3181, 3587.
Harjo, Totkus, 3177, 3178, 3181, 3387.
Harjo, Tuckabatchee, 2145, 2816.
Harjo, Tuhnar, 1474.
Harjo, Tulnochus, 1329, 1340, 1534, 1556, 2897, 3020, 3375, 3814.
Harjo, Tulsa, 2187, 2337, 2675, 3166, 3777, NB267, NB268.
Harjo, Tulwa, 870, 1266, 1627, 2073, 2631, 2792, 3185, 3595.
Harjo, Tulwar, 2514.
Harjo, Tumme, 1362, 1372.
Harjo, Tunnie, 1362, 1372.
Harjo, Tupios, 2130, 2132, 2133.
Harjo, Turpus, 2130, 3132, 2133.
Harjo, Tusekia, 2191, 2585, 2587.
Harjo, Tusekiah, 2585, 2587, 2191.
Harjo, Tusica, 1605.
Harjo, Tuska, 1592.

Harjoche, Martha, NB1248.
Harjoche, Melosey, 2202, 3778.
Harjoche, Nity, 1359, M482.
Harjoche, Nokos, 2202, 3778.
Harjoche, Thotho, 2621.
Harjoche, Yahdehka, 1359, 4001, NB1248, NB1249.
Harjoche, Yarteka, 1359, 4001, NB1248, NB-1249.
Harjochee, 3358.
Harjochee, Alberta, 278.
Harjochee. Amanda, 1263, 3415, M494.
Harjochee, Amos, 1263.
Harjochee, Chular, 1602.
Harjochee, Clothlo, 1296.
Harjochee, Conchart, 1310.
Harjochee, Conip, 1264, 1293.
Harjochee, Conup, 1264, 1293.
Harjochee, Hallok, 3128.
Harjochee, Harper, 1318.
Harjochee, Isparney, 1263, 3415.
Harjochee, Ithas, 2860
2571,   Harjochee, Jimmie, 1318.
Harjochee, Joseph, 1310.
Harjochee, Leah, 1296.
Harjochee, Losana, 1318.
Harjochee, Lucy, 1310.
Harjochee, Oktaryarchee, 1286, 1287.
Harjochee, Sashoye, 3415.
Harjochee, Wiley, 1264.
Harjochee, Yahtika, 1318.
Harjoge, Chagee, 2778.
2896,   Harjoge, Cho, 1972.
Harjoge, Frank, 2778, 3193, NB1036.
Harjoge, Hulputta, 2778.
Harjoge, Marfey, 2778.
Harjogee, Chular, 2155.
Harjogee, Parhose, 2362.
Harjogee, Sophia, 2155.
Harkaconthlaney, 2252.
Harkawathlany, 1000, 3890.
Harkowathlany, 1000, 3890.
Harlarchar, 2252.
Harley, Alex, 3763.
Harley, Jennie, 2466, 3480, 3763, NB1068.
Harley, Joseph, NB1068.
Harley, Sampson, NB1068
Harley, Samson, 2466, 3763.
Harman, Ben T., 3464, 764, NB919, M46.
Harman, Laura, 410, 411, 764, 3464.
Harman, Laura A., 3464.
Harmon, Ben T., 764, 3464, NB919, M46.
Harmon, Benj., 410, 411, 764.
Harmon, Benjamin T., 746, 3464, NB919, M46.
Harmon, Cynthia, 3234.
Harmon, Dan A., 411.
Harmon, Daniel, 3234.
Harmon, Laura, 410, 411, 764, 3464.
Harmon, Laura A., 3464.
Harmon, Lonie, NB919.
Harmon, Mary J., NB919, M46.
Harmon, Will S., 764.
Harner, Ella, 810.
Harner, Leo George, 810.
Harner, W. M., 810.
Harney, 1617, 2445, 2446, 2458, 2719.
Harnie, 2394.
Harnogee, 1681.
Harper, 2949.
Harper, Albert, 399, 1624, 2189.

Harper, Alfred, 399.
Harper, Betsey, 2924.
Harper, Fannie, 2949.
Harper, Ida, 2189.
Harper, Jennie, 399.
Harper, Jim, 2797.
Harper, John, 2949.
Harper, Koke, 2797.
Harper, Lizzie, 3483.
Harper, Marfe, 2796, M405.
Harper, Mary, 2924, M408.
Harper, Mattie, 3483.
Harper, Millie, CE4028.
Harper, Peggie, 2796, 2797, NB457.
Harper, Pettie, 2796.
Harper, Shawnee, 2924, 3483, 3724.
Harper, Simon, 3724.
Harper, Somaye, 2797, 3483, 3724.
Harpogee, 2728.
Harrid, Ellen, 3928.
Harriet, 49, 2484.
Harrington, Allie, 791.
Harrington, Amanda, 791, NB99, NB100.
Harrington, Isaac, 791.
Harrington, Lucy, 791.
Harriott, Amos W., 4009.
Harriott, John F., 4009.
Harriott, Joseph F., 4009.
Harriott, Louisa N., 4009.
Harriott, Nettie, 4009.
Harris, 1655.
Harris, Bird, 660, 1405.
Harris, Buena Vista, 660.
Harris, Charles, 1394.
Harris, Charley, NB406.
Harris, Charlie, NB6.
Harris, Cheasquah, 660, NB34.
Harris, Cleveland, M314.
Harris, Cora, NB406.
Harris, D. W., 1120.
Harris, Elva, 3729, M314.
Harris, Ellen, 660, 1120, 1394, 1405.
Harris, Henry, 1899.
Harris, Isparhecher, 1405.
Harris, Johnson E., 1405.
Harris, Lela, 1405, NB6, NB24.
Harris, Lula, 3928.
Harris, Lulu May, NB458.
Harris, Mabel Anna, 660.
Harris, Mabele, 1899, NB1008.
Harris, Mary J., NB24.
Harris, Minnie, 1655.
Harris, Myrtle, NB458, NB459.
Harris, Naoma, M314.
Harris, Nellie, 660, NB34.
Harris, Polly, 966, NB406.
Harris, R. B, 1394, 1405, 3031.
Harris, Red Bird, 1394, 1405, 3931.
Harris, Su Anna, 1405.
Harris, Theodore Quincy, NB459.
Harris, Thomas, 155.
Harris, Walter, 1120, NB458, NB459.
Harris, William R., 1405, NB6, NB24.
Harris, Willie, 1899.
Harris, Winnie Davis, NB34.
Harrison, Adaline, 911.
Harrison, Benjamin, 326.
Harrison, Bettie, NB1049.
Harrison, Charles, 1655.
Harrison, Eli, 326.

Harrison, Elizabeth, 1016.
Harrison, Ellen, 326.
Harrison, Emma, 3548.
Harrison, Hannah, 1013.
Harrison, Harvey, 1655.
Harrison, Hepsey, 963.
Harrison, Jimmy, 326.
Harrison, John, 1706.
Harrison, Keltie, 963.
Harrison, Keyulta, 911.
Harrison, Lena, 1706, M331.
Harrison, Lizzie, 326, NB953.
Harrison, Lucy, 1706.
Harrison, Malinda, 1702, 1706.
Harrison, Mamie, 586.
Harrison, Napoleon, 1706, 3548.
Harrison, Nero, 326.
Harrison, Peter, 963, 1013, 1702, 1706, NB1049.
Harrison, Rhoda, 1951, NB1049.
Harrison, Susan, 1706, 2699, 3548.
Harrison, William, 1068.
Harrison, Wilson, 586.
Harrod, Sarah, 2748 .
Harry, 1035, 1200.
Harry, Aggie, 1201, NB354, NB355.
Harry, Albert, 1189, 1190, 2305.
Harry, August, 1201.
Harry, Bess, 1189.
Harry, Bessie, 1040, 1204.
Harry, Bunch, NB807.
Harry, Caroline, 1034, 1035, 1189, 1200, 1201, 3207.
Harry, Cornelius, 1190.
Harry, David, 501, 1181, 1200, 1955.
Harry, Dick, 1189.
Harry, Eddie, 1201.
Harry, Edmond, 1034.
Harry, Eliza, 1190, 2980.
Harry, Ella, 1034.
Harry, Grace, 501, 1181, 1200.
Harry, Harry, 1034, 1189, 1201.
Harry, Henry, 888, 1201.
Harry, Jackson, 1201, NB684, NB685.
Harry, Jessie, NB685.
Harry, John, 888, 3361, NB805, NB806, NB807.
Harry, Legus, 1200.
Harry, Liza, 2305, NB805.
Harry, Luke, 1200.
Harry, Martha, 1200, 3361.
Harry, Mary, 888, 1333, 3361, NB805, NB806, NB807.
Harry, Micey, 1201.
Harry, Nellie, 1201.
Harry, Nora, 1200.
Harry, Peggie, 1200, M140, NB866.
Harry, Rebecca, 501, 3532.
Harry, Robert, 1181, 1201.
Harry, Rosanna, 1178, NB684, NB685.
Harry, Roy, 3532.
Harry, Rufus, 1201.
Harry, Sally, 1181.
Harry, Sartarpeka, 1034.
Harry, Shawnee, 1034.
Harry, Simon, 501, 3532.
Harry, Susie, NB806.
Harry, Tony, 1201.
Harry, Wheaton, 2305.
Harry, Willie, 888, 1034.
Harry, Wilson, NB684.
Hart, Edward, NB41.

Hawkins, Joseph. 680.
Hawkins, Kate, NB587.
Hawkins, Katie, 2247, 3072.
Hawkins, Lewe, 2879.
Hawkins, Littie, 2417.
Hawkins, Lizzie, 3071, NB753.
Hawkins, Louis, NB1046.
Hawkins, Louisa, 2387.
Hawkins, Lucinda, 1026, 2767.
Hawkins, Lucy, 629.
Hawkins, Lydia, 2407, 2408, 2861.
Hawkins, Mack, 2580.
Hawkins, Martha, 226.
Hawkins, Mary, 1761, 1791.
Hawkins, Melissa, NB588.
Hawkins, Millie, 1820.
Hawkins, Nellie, NB1098.
Hawkins, Nicey, 2444.
Hawkins, Okla Hosta, 2249.
Hawkins, Farney, 1791.
Hawkins, Pink, 2407, 2408, 2417, 2418, 2861,
          NB1097.
Hawkins, Rebecca, 56.
Hawkins, Rhoda, 190, NB587, NB588, M252.
Hawkins, Sallie, 2012, 2329.
Hawkins, Sam, 135, 452, 1026, 1028, 1036, 1194,
          2418, 3071, 3882.
Hawkins, Samuel, 135, 452, 1026, 1028, 1036,
          1194, 2418, 3071.
Hawkins, Sarah, 629, 3071, NB763.
Hawkins, Sepile, 2339, NB1097, NB1098.
Hawkins, Simpson, 2012.
Hawkins, Subella, 2339, NB1097, NB1098.
Hawkins, Sunday, 629.
Hawkins, Susan, 2861.
Hawkins, Susie, 2967.
Hawkins, Tom, 1820.
Hawkins, Turner, 2579.
Hawkins, Wiley, 1703, 2209, 2247, 2249. 2387,
          2431, 3101.
Hawkins, Winey, 629.
Hawkins, Wizey, 2209.
Hay, Deshalecoweney, 2262.
Hay, Eggie, 2262, 3601, NB853.
Hay, Egie, 2262, 3601, NB853.
Hay, John, 2262, 3601, NB853.
Hay, Johnson, 3601.
Hay, Modie, NB853.
Haye, Halok, 2752.
Haye, Hotkle, 2752.
Hayes, Marchie, 2165.
Hayes, Parhie, 2165.
Hayes, Shawnee, 1457.
Hayne, Annie, 2871.
Hayne, Mollie, 2871.
Haynes, Dicey, 1794.
Haynes, Elijah, 1778.
Haynes, James, 1871, NB929.
Haynes, John, 213, 1778, 1794, 1871.
Haynes, Joseph, 1794.
Haynes, Lasley, 213, 281.
Haynes, Laslie, 971.
Haynes, Liddie, 281.
Haynes, Lizzie, 213.
Haynes, Lucy, 377.
Haynes, Martha, 1871, NB929.
Haynes, Roley, NB929.
Haynes, Samuel J., 1778.
Haynes, Sarah, 1778.
Haynes, Sinta, 1871.

Haynes, Stella J., 1778.
Haynes, Thomas, 280, 377, 2815.
Haynes, Thomas, Jr., 280.
Haynes, Toche, 2815.
Haynes, Tochee, 280.
Haynie, 71, 93.
Haynie, Andy, 93.
Haynie, Edward, 93.
Haynie, Fannie, 93.
Haynie, Felix, 214, NB359.
Haynie, Felix, Jr., NB359.
Haynie, Jeff, 71.
Haynie, March, 93.
Haynie, Mariah, 93.
Haynie, Mary, 1802, NB359.
Haynie, Minnie May, 93.
Haynie, Mofah, 93.
Haynie, Susanna, 214.
Haynie, Thomas, 214.
Hays, Carpetha, 2165.
Hays, Henry, 1457.
Hays, Martha, 2165.
Hays, Mary Shannon, M8.
Hays, Sallie H., 2220, NB36, M8.
Hays, Sallie Willison, NB36.
Hays, Sally H., 2220, M8, NB36.
Hays, W. Pierce, NB36, M8.
Hays, Williard P., M8, NB36.
Haywood, Nancy M., 261.
Healey, 1630.
Heatchonay, 609.
Heber, John, 1659.
Hecahlothany, 1206.
Hecatah, 566, NB1181.
Heehjoya, 831.
Hekaconthla, 958.
Hekawahthlaney, 958.
Helay, 979.
Hellet, Adam, NB1198.
Hellet, Aman, M346.
Hellet, Sam, 2883, NB1198, M346.
Hellet, Samey, 2883, NB1198, M346.
Hellett, Sarah, 2248, NB1198, M346.
Heloy, 3245.
Helton, George Thomas, M284.
Helton, Jesse Newman, 3850.
Helton, Lonie, 186.
Helton, Nellie, 186, 3850, NB333, NB334, M284.
Helton, Romie Robert, NB334.
Helton, Ruthia Ellen, NB333.
Helton, W. B., 3850, NB333, NB334.
Helton, Will, 186.
Helton, William, M284.
Helton, William B., 3850, NB333, NB334.
Hemer, Louie, 2815.
Hen, Betsey, 1408, NB1030.
Hen, Eblow, 1408.
Hen, Thomas, 1436.
Hen, Willie, 1436.
Henahochee, 3345.
Hendrickson, Eliza, 1050, 3659, NB567.
Hendrickson, Elijah, NB344.
Hendrickson, Frank, 1050.
Hendrickson, James, 3659, NB567.
Hendrickson, Jim, 1050.
Hendrickson, Joe, M241.
Hen lrickson, Joseph, NB344, NB692.
Hendrickson, Mary, 1049, NB344, NB692, M241
Hendrickson, Peter, NB692.
Hendrickson, Sarah Jane, NB567.

Hendrickson, Thomas, 3659.
Henechochee, 1317.
Henegochee, 30.
Heneha, 1508.
Heneha, Artus, 2325.
Heneha, Artussee, 2460.
Heneha, Chochat, 2692.
Heneha, Chukchat, 2831.
Heneha, Eannah, 1273, M304, NB1124, NB112
Heneha, Hopoethla, 2549.
Heneha, Janie, 2549.
Heneha, Jonas, 157.
Heneha, Lena, 157.
Heneha, Lucy, 2480, NB1018, NB1019.
Heneha, Lussie, 3804.
Heneha, Mary, 3804.
Heneha, Matup, 2832.
Heneha, Mitchell, 7, NB1018, NB1019.
Heneha, Nancy, 452.
Heneha, Osa, 3975.
Heneha, Ralph, NB1019.
Heneha, Roy, NB1018.
Heneha, Tulmarsee, 2325.
Heneha, Tulmas, 452.
Heneha, Tuske, 2242.
Henehar, Artus, 7.
Henehochee, Beenie, 1349.
Henehochee, Engie, 1349.
Henehochee, Hopoeth, 3803.
Henehochee, Lena, 1349.
Henehochee, Miny, 1349.
Henehochee, Quechus, 2854.
Henehochee, Will, 1349.
Henehutche, Quakus, 1309.
Heneka, Chukchat, 3804.
Hengst, Arena Marie, 3258.
Hengst, Charles Augustus, NB791.
Henget, Emma J., 3258, NB790, NB791.
Hengst, Frankfort, 3258.
Hengst, Joseph A., NB790.
Hengst, Virginia P., 3258.
Hengst, W. C., 3258, NB790, NB791.
Hengst, William C., NB790, NB791.
Hengst, William H., 3258.
Henneha, 1443, 1444, 2202.
Henneha, Artus, 1155.
Henneha, Hobe, 1273.
Henneha, Thlokchat, 1577.
Hennehah, Eli, 150.
Hennehah, Hokalis, 276.
Hennehah, Lucinda, 150.
Hennehah, Susan, 276.
Hennehuchee, Hardy, 3345.
Hennehughee, Hene, 1317.
Hennehughee, Roney, 1317.
Hennehughee, Watley, 1317.
Henry, Ann, 1392.
Henry, Annie May, 1122.
Henry, Bat, 3383.
Henry, Beulah, 1094.
Henry, Carrie, M218, NB248, NB249
Henry, Edith Clair, NB249.
Henry, Edmond, 4020.
Henry, Estella May, 1093.
Henry, Eugene Rolley, NB331.
Henry, Francis, 1862.
Henry, Frank, 1204.
Henry, Grace, 1955.
Henry, Hettie, 1122.
Henry, Hillibe Micco, NB318.

Henry, Howard H., NB248.
Henry, Hugh, 1122, 1392, NB335, NB318.
Henry, Hugh Jr., 1122.
Henry, James, 1392, 3383, M218, NB24S, NB-249.
Henry, James Harvey, M218.
Henry, James P.,1392, 3383, M218, NB248,NB-249.
Henry, James Pier, NB386.
Henry, James S., 1093, NB385, NB386.
Henry, Jane, 1222.
Henry, Jessie, 1094.
Henry, Joe, 3039.
Henry, Louise, 1093.
Henry, Lucy, 1093, NB385, NB386.
Henry, Luella, 1122.
Henry, Lula, 1094, NB331, NB332.
Henry, Mack, 1122.
Henry, Martha, 4020.
Henry, Mary, 1862.
Henry, Massey, 3039.
Henry, Millie, 3383.
Henry, Mintie, 1122, NB318, NB335.
Henry, Pat, 4020.
Henry, Patrick, 1122.
Henry, Peggy, 3039, CE4040.
Henry, Suepee, 1204.
Henry, Tchinina, NB335.
Henry, Thomas, 1862.
Henry, Vicey, 1122.
Henry, Viola Velmer, NB385.
Henry, Walter, 1862.
Henry, W. A. NB331, NB332.
Henry, Willie, A., 1094.
Henry, Willie Jackson, NB332.
Henry, Wood, 1122.
Henry, Woodson, 1122.
Henshaw, Lou. 1514.
Henshaw, Malinda, 1514.
Henshaw, Thomas, 1514.
Hensley, Jane, 3795.
Hensley, Sam, 3795.
Hepsey, 286, 1415, 1525, 1526, 1609, 1635, 3094, 3804.
Hepsy, 3274.
Hermante, Katcher, 2826.
Herrick, Juanita, 365.
Herrick, L., 3661.
Herrick, Leo, 365.
Herrick, Leo Jr., 365.
Herrick, Mary, 365, 3661.
Herrick, Willie J., 3661.
Herrod, 429.
Herrod, Andy, 1699, M268.
Herrod, Cilla, 430.
Herrod, Cyrus, 430.
Herrod, Dave, 1699.
Herrod, David, 2631, 2883, 3209, NB1196.
Herrod, Eliza, 2631, NB1196.
Herrod, Hotachee, 994, 2007.
Herrod, Hotochee, 994, 2007.
Herrod, John, 2553.
Herrod, Lena, 2631.
Herrod, Liza, 2631, NB1196.
Herrod, Maria, 430, NB1285.
Herrod, Mary, 430, 994, 2007.
Herrod, Mary L., 645.
Herrod, Nettie, 2631.
Herrod, Rhoda, 2168, M268.
Herrod, Robert Andrew, M268.

Herrod, Rosanna, 2408, 2409, 2553, NB540
Herrod, Samuel, 429.
Herrod, Sarah, 2248, NB1198, M346.
Herrod, Sophia, 1003, 2553.
Herrod, Tarpie, NB1196.
Herrod, Widey, 2883.
He tah co co tan, 3885.
Hetahcoweney, 2103.
He tak owe, 573.
Hethlucky, 2209, 2249.
Hettie, 2338, 2576, 2607, NB1291.
Hewlett, Myrtle, NB383.
Hewlett, Will, NB383.
Hickman, Alva, M130.
Hickman, Eliza, 1880.
Hickman, Jack, 1880.
Hickman, Mac, M130.
Hickman, Mehaley, 1488, M130.
Hickman, Nellie, 1880.
Hickory, Addie, 2329.
Hickory, Amos, 2329.
Hickory, Dick, 2329.
Hickory, Jennie, 1231, NB655.
Hickory, Joe, 516.
Hickory, Louina, NB655.
Hickory, Lucinda, 1231.
Hickory, Sallie, 2329.
Hickory, Thomas, 1231, NB655.
Hicks, Bunner, 277.
Hicks, Bunny, 1004.
Hicks, Dicey, 1004, 1005, 1009.
Hicks, Elsie, 144, 277, 879.
Hicks, George, 144, 277, 879, 1004, 1005, 1009, 1285.
Hicks, Henry, 1005.
Hicks, Joe, 1005.
Hicks, Johnson, 277.
Hicks, Louana, 1005.
Hicks, Mary E., 620.
Hicks, Robert, 277.
Hicks, Wesley, 1285.
Hiepa, 2480.
Higgins, Josephine, 1830.
Highland, Leroy, M61.
Highland, Lula H., 547, NB128, M61.
Highland, Lula N., 547, NB128, M61.
Highland, Pat, NB128, M61.
Highland, Patrick, M61, NB128.
Highland, Patrick Jr., NB128.
Hightower, Lydia A., 309, M195.
Hightower, Tom, 309.
Hightower, William S., 309.
Hill, Ada, 333.
Hill, Amanda, 16, M47.
Hill, Amos, 2089, 2759, 2760.
Hill, Amy, 3959.
Hill, Annie, 2378.
Hill, Arlington, 2378, 2382.
Hill, Arney, 2089, NB291, NB292, NB391.
Hill, Belcher, 1484.
Hill, Charley, 1460.
Hill, Cilla, 1459.
Hill, Cinda, 3151, NB868.
Hill, Conney, 3091.
Hill, Coxey, 3080, 2774.
Hill, Coxie, 2774, 308).
Hill, Dave, 2151.
Hill, David, 1063, 2000.
Hill, Elmer, 2116, NB391.
Hill, Emma, 1484, NB1141, NB1142, CE4057.

335

Hodge, Virginia, 3405.
Hodges, Green F., 1966.
Hodulge, 752.
Hoe, Kapo, 4026.
Hoɔ koh, 6.
Hoethle, 2920.
Hoey, Homa, 1795.
Hoey, Ista, 8.
Hogan, Berry, 3030.
Hogan, Julia, 1092, NB1007.
Hogan, Malissa, 3030.
Hogan, Robert, NB1007.
Hogan, Willie D., NB1007.
Hoge, Hene, 2576.
Hoge, Hettie, 2576.
Hoge, Shoktas, 94, 97.
Hohke, George, 2914.
Hohlahta, Cheparn, 3829.
Hohlahta, Lucy, 3829.
Hohlahta, Martha, 3829.
Hojahda, 87.
Hokar, Satim, 1439.
Hokey, Sakhatup, 527.
Hoko, 2841.
Hokoletche, 400, 3939.
Hoksetahsque, 2717.
Hokte, 426, 2069, 2275, 2325.
Hoktee, 187, 188, 189, 191.
Hoktekarney, 151, 2683.
Hoktethlocco, 1593.
Hoktoche, Ahfonoke, 1348, 1376.
Hoktochee, Ahfonoke, 1348, 1376.
Hokussey, 135.
Hola, Hosiah, 1812.
Holahta, Arlinda, 3276.
Holahta, Cheparn, 1138.
Holahta, Hettie, 2272.
Holahta, John, 3276.
Holahta, Larnee, 3276.
Holahta, Lucy, 1138.
Holahta, Nocus, 2202, 3276.
Holahta, Seborn, 2272.
Holata, John, 3221, 3906.
Holata, Susey, 3221, 3906.
Holata, Wileye, 3906.
Holata, Willie, 3221.
Holatka, Woxie, 3041.
Holatoche, Noxie, 2701.
Holatte, Woxie, 1489.
Holden, 585.
Holden, Becky, 585.
Holden, Kate, 585, 1981.
Holden, Sarah, 3772.
Holden, Thomas, 585.
Holder, 2260.
Holder, John, 2310.
Holder, Washington, 3121, 3245.
Holen, 2844.
Holen, David, 2844.
Hollada, 2464, 2466.
Hollada, Kizzie, 2464, 2466.
Hollea, 397.
Holleddey, Kizzie, 2464, 2466.
Holleyman, Delila, 876.
Holleyman, Herman O., 876.
Holleyman, Homer A., 876.
Holleyman, Maggie E., 3390.
Holleyman, Maggie G., 876, NB993, NB994.
Holleyman, Marcella, NB994.
Holleyman, Marcellus, NB993.
Holleyman, Myrtle V., 876.

Holleyman, T. E., NB993, NB994.
Holleyman, Thomas E., 3390, 876
Holleyman, Thomas J., 3390.
Hollie, 2315.
Holloddey, 2464, 2466.
Holman, Dora, 554, NB886
Holmes, Hully, 1593.
Holohta, Woxey, 1512.
Holokta, Martha, 3290.
Holokta, Nocus, 3290
Holome, 938.
Holotachee, 1138.
Holotka, Arlinda, 2642.
Holotka, Nocus, 2642,
Holotka, Woxie, 1999, 2000.
Holotta, 26.
Holt, Abbie, 866.
Holt, Emanuel, 866.
Hoit, Henry, 866.
Holt, Littleton, 866.
Holt, Mattie, 866.
Holt, Sarah Jane, 866.
Holuby, Cooper, 2772.
Holuby, George, 2772.
Holuby, Hattie, 2772, 3760.
Holuby, Mollie, 2772.
Holuby, Nettie, 2772.
Holuby, Nora, 2772.
Holuby, Sally, 2772.
Holuby, Turner, 2772.
Holucka, 3108.
Holupe, George, 2904, 3990.
Holupe, Katie, 3990.
Homahhoey, 1441.
Homahite, 2817.
Homahoey, 1795.
Homahta, Hane, 2826.
Homahta, Mesela, 2826.
Homahta, Thomas, 2826,
Homahte, Gotcha, 2403.
Homahte, Harnoche, 2403.
Homahte, Katchee, 3872.
Homahte, Lena, 2829.
Homahte, Nochiheche, 2829.
Homahte, Watko, 2829.
Homarhoywee, 1515.
Homarta, Cotcha, 2538, 2939.
Homarte, Watko, 1282.
Homathe, Katcha, 2160.
Homatie, Wotko, 2821.
Homer, 3213.
Homer, Alex, 1127, 2081, 2082
Homer, Henry, 1127.
Homer, John, 3213.
Homer, Lolie, 1593.
Homer, Mary, 1127.
Homoletke, 756.
Homota, Kotsar, 2764.
Honade, Artus, 385, 2233.
Honechike, 4023.
Honeel, 2894.
Honley, Rosa, 2197.
Honuhbe, Artus, 385, 2233.
Honyjagee, 2742.
Hood, Henry, 719.
Hood, Jackson, 719.
Hood, James, 719.
Hood, Joe, 3634.
Hood, John, 719.
Hood, Reid Lee, NB377.

Hood, Sarah, 719, 3634.
Hood, Sarah Malinda, NB377.
Hood, Sterling, 719.
Hood, Sterling P., 3634, NB377.
Hood, William, 719.
Hooks, Alice, 1241, 3472, NB473.
Hooks, Lem P., 1241, 3472, NB473.
Hooks, L. P., 1241, 3472.
Hooks, Naoma, 3781, M270.
Hooks, Richard Roy, NB473.
Hooks, Ruby Mildred, 1241.
Hooks, Rudie, 3472.
Hooks, Ruth, 1241.
Hooks, Sam, M270.
Hooks, Virgie, M270.
Hopawae, 3761.
Hopaye, Ahalek, 2097.
Hopaye, Artus, 3233.
Hope, 1073, 2191, 2756.
Hope, Beaden. NB1067.
Hope, Emma, 3200, NB1067.
Hope, Fannie, 1352, 2191, 2756.
Hope, Dannie, 1073.
Hope, Henry, 138, 2190, 2191.
Hope, Millie, 2191.
Hope, Mollie, 138, 2840.
Hope, Nellie, 135, 136, 2757.
Hope, Rebecca, 2756.
Hope, Robert, 2190, NB1067.
Hope, Sanford, 2840.
Hope, Sharper, 1352.
Hope, Sunnyboy, 2840
Hope, Willie, 2840.
Hopethle, 3128.
Hopie, 3231.
Hopie, Abalak, 1951.
Hopioche, 2701, 3918, CE4043.
Hopiye, Edmond, 1859.
Hopiye, Isparnee, 142.
Hopiye, Isparney, 1859, NB1095.
Hopiye, Jennie, 1859, NB1095.
Hopiye, Lucindy, NB1095.
Hopiye, Sam, 3102.
Hopiye, Span, 1859, NB1095.
Hopiye, 1493.
Hopiye, Artus, 105.
"Hopiyoche," 2701, 3918, CE4043.
Hopper, Samuel, 748.
Hopper, Sarah, 748.
Hopsey, 2651.
Hopwood, Alfred, 431.
Hopwood, Edgar Denton, 985.
Hopwood, Elizabeth, 985.
Hopwood, George W., 983.
Hopwood, Ira Homer, 3444.
Hopwood, Jennie, 983.
Hopwood, John L., 985.
Hopwood, Kellam F., 985, 3444, NB115.
Hopwood, Kellem F., 985, 3444, NB115.
Hopwood, Len, 983, 985.
Hopwood, Leonard, 983, 985.
Hopwood, Mary E., 983.
Hopwood, Mary L , 983.
Hopwood, Millie, 3444.
Hopwood, Mollie, 985, NB115.
Hopwood, Ora Pearle, NB115.
Horche, Yulke, 2279.
Horn, Fannie Lee, NB917.
Horn, Jessie, NB916.
Horn, John, 410.

Horn, Lillie, NB916, NB917.
Horn, Mattie E., 410.
Horn, Minnie E., 410.
Horn, Nellie W., 410.
Horn, Sam, 479, NB916, NB917.
Hoscussee, 2757.
Hosea, Harriet, 840.
Hosea, Isaac, 840.
Hosey, Harriet, 631, 774, 776, 1274.
Hosey, Isaac, 631, 776, 1274.
Hosey, John B., 776, 3600.
Hosey, Lee, 774.
Hosey, Lillie F., 3600.
Hosey, Maggie, 776.
Hosey, Nora F., 3600.
Hosey, Orlando, 776.
Hosmer, Fannie, 838.
Hosmer, Frank, 838.
Hosmer, Solomon, 838.
Hosmer, Susie, 838.
Hotala, 1726.
Hotapulfkee, 1217.
Hothkoper, 4026.
Hotka, 584, 2905.
Hotke, 1773.
Hotke, Arne, 2812.
Hotke, Tusekiah, 1773.
Hotopka, 1577, 1585.
Hotulchoche, 1162.
Hotulge, 1163.
Hotulkoce, 1485.
Hounbee, Idas, 2670.
House, Lottie, 2270.
Houston, 2665, 2668.
Houston, Carrie, 754.
Houston, Eva C., 754.
Houston, George, 754, 3358.
Houston, Jesse, 3358.
Houston, Lucien A., 754.
Houston, Sam, 3358.
Houston, Turner, 3358.
Howard, Abbie Lee, 143, NB26, NB27.
Howard, Benjamin F., 143.
Howard, George, 143, NB26.
Howard, H. B., NB104.
Howard, Mattie, 71, NB104.
Howard, Maxie, NB104.
Howard, Myrtle May, NB26.
Howard, Polly Lue, 143.
Howell, Annie, 846, NB477, NB935.
Howell, Dr., 3267.
Howell, Lee, 846.
Howell, Lizzie, 3071, NB753.
Howell, Samuel Webster, NB753.
Howell, Scott, 846.
Howell, Tallie H., NB753.
Howie, Cochart, 1577.
Hoye, 555, 938.
Hoye, Hospotok, 3181.
Hoye, Semich, 2273.
Hoye, Temos, 3181.
Hoye, Tona, 3181.
Hoyebar, 1224.
Hoyecha, 1345.
Hoyee, Halob, 2378.
Hoyihche, 2696.
Hoyka, Sema, 3042.
Hoyoker, 1979.
Hoyoper, 2690.
Huckaby, Aaron, 363.

Hutchee, Nokus, 1359.
Hutchenubbe, 2830.
Hutcogee, Tusekia, 3149.
Huthlucky, 2209, 2249.
Hutka, Charley, 2899.
Hutka, George, 1360.
Hutka, Lieka, 422.
Hutka, Mekko, 2591.
Hutka, Sally, 2899.
Hutka, Tusekiah, 109, 425.
Hutke, Jennie, 1994.
Hutke, Mary, 2150.
Hutke, Micco, 1994.
Hutke, Polly, 2427.
Hutke, Tussekiah, 109, 425.
Hutkey, 2962.
Hutkey, Kizzie, 3304.
Hutkey, Missie, 2673, 2674, 3369.
Hutkoye, Temo, 2987.
Hutman, Leah, 3270.
Hutman, Mulda, 3270.
Hutton, Alex, 269.
Hutton, Annie, 269, 3486, NB307.
Hutton, Ben, 1074.
Hutton, Bessie, 269.
Hutton, Billy, 269.
Hutton, Essie, 3948.
Hutton, Fannie, 1074.
Hutton, Gracie, 3486.
Hutton, Henry, 269, 3486, NB307.
Hutton, Henry-Creek Frd., 427, NB307.
Hutton, Houston, 269.
Hutton, Iola, NB307.
Hutton, James, 3270.
Hutton, Jeff, 1074.
Hutton, Joe, 1679.
Hutton, Joe, Jr., 1074, 1075.
Hutton, Lizzie, 1074.
Hutton, Lou, 1679.
Hutton, Louisa, 1074, 1075.
Hutton, Lucy, 1074.
Hutton, Nancy, 930, 3948, M59.
Hutton, Rebella, 1074, M263.
Hutton, Robert, 269.
Hutton, Salina, 269.
Hutton, Sally, M59.
Hutton, Sarah, 1074.
Hutton, Sedalia, 269.
Hutton, Tooka, 1074, NB817, NB818.
Hutton, Walter, 3948, M59.
Hutton, Walter-Creek Frd., 4172, M59.
Iamakka, 229.
Icheney, 3846.
Ieka, 1295.
Ijenny, 208.
Iksossoche, 621.
Ille, Nocus, 2235.
Illinois, 3195.
"Imly", 3343.
Imogene, 3173.
Inche, 409, 1744.
Inchuskeler, 3274.
Ingersoka, 2525.
Ingley, Columbus F., 3728, M362.
Ingley, Gladys G., M362.
Ingley, Grace, M362.
Ingley, John, 3728.
Ingram, David C., 1776, 1977, 1978.
Ingram, David P., 1978.
Ingram, Elizabeth, 1984.

Ingram, Eliza J., 1978.
Ingram, Janetta, 1978, NB964.
Ingram, Jannatte, 1978, NB964.
Ingram, John F., 1976, 1984.
Ingram, Lotta C., 1978.
Ingram, Louisa, 1777, 1976, 1977.
Ingram, Mary, 1776.
Ingram, Mary A., 1977, 1978.
Ingram, Maty Ella, 1978.
Ingram, Sudie, NB964.
Ingram, Thomas J., 1978, NB964.
Ingram, Wiley, 1777, 1976, 1977.
Inkaney, 2416.
Inledegho, 2967.
Inman, Clifton, M376.
Inman, Cora, 399, M376.
Inman, Naomi, M376.
Innaney, 228.
Inscho, Charles, 1121.
Inscho, Claburn, 1121.
Inscho, Hattie, 1121.
Inscho, Ruth, 1121.
Inscho, Willie, 1121.
Insucka, 412, 413.
Iny, 149.
Iogee, 1766.
Iokee, 2488.
Iokee, Mary, 2488.
Ipsey, 1598.
Ireland, John, 994.
Ireland, Mildred, 994, NB490.
Ireland, Susan, 994, 1053, 1054.
Isaac, 4014.
Isaac, Dick, 2121.
Isaac, Jacob, 137.
Isaac, John, M394.
Isaac, Lena, 734, M394.
Isaac, Louis, 734.
Isaac, Lydia, 734.
Isaac, Richard, 734.
Isbell, Catherine C., 3678.
Isbell, J. G., 3678.
Isbell, Mary E., 3678.
Ishmael, Ben R., 787, 789, 3194.
Ishmael, B. R., 3194, 787, 789.
Ishmael, Eva J., NB208.
Ishmael, Fannie, 3194.
Ishmael, James L., NB207.
Ishmael, James M., 787, NB207, NB208.
Ishmael, Maggie, 787, 789, 3194.
Ishmael, Mary, 3194.
Ishmael, Maude, NB207, NB208.
shodoche, 2524.
Ishueka, 622.
Iskawapee, 154.
Iskochuckney, 2214.
Island, Ben, 229, 1746, 1809.
Island, Bessie M., 1730.
Island, Billy, 390.
Island, Boney, 1730, NB610, NB611, M68.
Island, Callie, 977, 3471, NB1041, NB472.
Island, Easy, 222.
Island, Eliza, 977, 1986.
Island, George, 977, 3471, NB472, NB1041.
Island, Haymen, 1809.
Island, Henry, 942, 994, 1730, 2197.
Island, Hettie, 1809.
Island, Jim, 977.
Island, Joe, 222.
Island, John, 977.

Island, Laurence, M68.
Island, Leggues, NB611.
Island, Lizzie, 390, NB610.
Island, Louisa, NB1041.
Island, Luvena, NB472.
Island, Madison, 1746.
Island, Maggie, 1730, M60 NB610, NB611.
Island, Mamie, 229.
Island, Milloche, 390.
Island, Napoleon B., 1730, NB610, NB611,M68.
Island, Sallie, 222.
Island, Sunday, 3471.
Island, Susan, 942, 1730.
Island, William, 2197.
Isnahaley, 527.
Isparcher, 376, 1149.
Isparhecher, 376, 1149.
Isparhecher, Cindochee, 376.
Ispocogee, 2531.
Ispocogee, Belcher, 1964, NB854, NB889.
Ispocogee, Jennie, 1964, NB854, NB889.
Ispocogee, Noah, NB854.
Ispocogee, Polly, 1964.
Ispocogee, Sam, NB889.
Ispocogee, Topley, 1964, 2538.
Ispocogee, Yadie, 1964.
Ispogee, Jennie, 1964, NB854, NB889.
Ispogoche, Linda, 2535.
Ispogoche, Topley, 2535.
Ispokee, Belcher, 1964, NB889, NB854.
Ispokogee, 1138.
Ispokogee, Belcher, 1964, NB854, NB889.
Ispokogee, Jennie, 1964, NB889, NB854.
Israel, Ella, 3061.
Israel, John, 3061.
Israel, Louisa, 3061.
Istahiye, 1996.
Istohoye, 1842.
Iswihhohke, 2325.
Itchke, 2621.
Itcolache, 1820.
Ithlococeha, 2519.
Iuquena, 75.
Iyan, 1263.
Iyechache, 2065.
Iyeche, 3388.
Iyeche, Susanna, 3388.
Iyogee, 1839.
Iyoka, 337.
Iyoke, 2191.
Iyokhogee 108.
Jache, Luddy, 2645.
Jack, 1034, 2104.
Jack, Alice, 862, NB638.
Jack, Alice Luvina, 862.
Jack, Bettie, 2867, NB1287, M477.
Jack, Big, 2867, N477, NB1287.
Jack, Caesar, 842.
Jack, Chapley, 2358.
Jack, Colonel, 1060.
Jack, Eddie, 842, NB1046.
Jack, Elizabeth, 682, 950.
Jack, Fannie, 884.
Jack, Jackson, 3253.
Jack, Jennie, 2267.
Jack, John, 862, NB638.
Jack, Katie, 2267.
Jack, Kernal, 3140, 3939.
Jack, Lena, 2358, NB1026.
Jack, Lizzie, 1034, 1201, 3140.

Jacob, Nancy, 1441.
Jacob, Nicey, NB1264.
Jacob, Pilot, 1217.
Jacob, Sam, 1441, 2803, NB1127, NB1264.
Jacob, Shawnee, 5981, NB1127, NB1264.
Jacobs, S73, 1939, 2803.
Jacobs, Ben, 874.
Jacobs, Bessie, 874.
Jacobs, Betsey, 73.
Jacobs, Charles, M454.
Jacobs, Cinda, 3130.
Jacobs, Della, 1040, NBS30, NBS31.
Jacobs, Eli, 73, 1040, 1133, 1758.
Jacobs, Ella L., 2004, NB132.
Jacobs, Elsie B., NB212.
Jacobs, Emma, M454.
Jacobs, Frank, 1580, 2010, 2537, 73, 743, 1946
Jacobs, Frank D., 73, 743, 1946, 1580, 2010,
        2537.
Jacobs, Jennie, 2211.
Jacobs, Jennie C., 73, 743.
Jacobs, John A., 1580, NB212.
Jacobs, Johnny, M475.
Jacobs, Joseph, 2211.
Jacobs, Josie, 73.
Jacobs, Lizzie, 1580.
Jacobs, Louis, 73.
Jacobs, Lucinda, 2537.
Jacobs, Lucy, 1754, 1755.
Jacobs, Mary, 1580, NB212.
Jacobs, Nancy, M454.
Jacobs, Newman, 73, NB132, NB350.
Jacobs, Newman F., 73, NB132, NB350.
Jacobs, Rebecca, 1580, 1946, 2010.
Jacobs, Sallie, 2738, 3130.
Jacobs, Sampson, 2738, M475.
Jacobs, Sarah, 73.
Jacobs, Stephen, 2211.
Jacobs, William R., NB132.
Jacobs, Willie, 73.
Jacobs, Thomas, 2746.
James, 2967.
James, Betsey, 2315.
James, Billie, 1150, 1167, 2967.
James, Billy, 1150, 1167, 2967.
James, Chotkey, 2315.
James, Edward, 1360.
James, Geo., 2699.
James, Gibson, 2967.
James, John, 1360.
James, Martha, 2967.
James, Millie, 2315.
James, Morris, 1992.
James, Nancy, 2315, M369.
James, Nickson, 3332.
James, Sophia, 1150, 1167.
Jameson, Hepsey, 1384, 2588.
Jamison, Hebsey, 2588, 1384.
Jamon, D. E., 2315.
Jane, 1251.
Janie, 2320, 2652, 2653.
Janoleezie, 2108.
Jarney, Taletsa, 1051.
Jatahkoconcahney, 2705.
Jefferson, Annie, 3126, NB627.
Jefferson, Davis, 1399.
Jefferson, Jane, 353.
Jefferson, John, 441.
Jefferson, Lena, 217.
Jefferson, Manuel, 353, 1400.

Jefferson, McDora, M210.
Jefferson, Mollie, 1333.
Jefferson, Moses, 217, M210.
Jefferson, Nancy W., 641, M210.
Jefferson, Polly, 1399.
Jefferson, Prince, 2976.
Jefferson, Senora, NB627.
Jefferson, Silas, 1141, 1333, 1400.
Jefferson, Thomas, 217.
Jefferson, Walter, 217, NB627.
Jefley, Cogee, 1468, NB464, NB465.
Jefley, John, 1468.
Jefley, Satie, 1468, 1469.
Jefley, Tewee, 1468.
Jefley, Thomas, 1468, 1469.
Jefley, Willie, 1468.
Jemima, 385.
Jenkins, Buna E. M., 3630.
Jenkins, G. R., 2321, 3630.
Jenkins, Gibson R., 2321, 3630.
Jenkins, Henrietta, 2321, 3630.
Jenkins, Thomas DeWitt, 2321.
Jennetta, 28, 1149, 1453, 2459, 2947, NB1127,
    NB1264.
Jennie, 367, 1300, 1441, 1545, 1566, 2279, 2315,
    2780, 3274.
Jennie, Fiddler John, 2315.
Jerry, Louis, 235.
Jesse, Bunnie, 2415.
Jesse, Eliza, 2415.
Jesse, Jennetta, 2415.
Jesse, Massie, 2415.
Jesse, Timmie, 2415.
Jesse, Willie, 2415.
Jessie, Billy, 425.
Jessie, Emma, 425.
Jessie, Katie, 2033.
Jessie, Lika, 425.
Jessie, Lillie, 1827.
Jessie, Mary, 423, 425.
Jessie, Sampson, 2033.
Jessie, Susan, 425, NB733.
Jicoche, 2921.
Jicoche, Mulleanna, 2921.
Jim, Annie, 2784, 3303.
Jim, Arbeka, 1992.
Jim, Fort, 286.
Jim, Long, 2784, 2785, 2981, 3303.
Jim, Louisianna, 2971.
Jim, Lucy, 2785.
Jim, Sissy, 2426, NB1180.
Jim, Tom, 2971.
Jimalee, 2833.
Jimboy, Addie, 1631.
Jimboy, Alex, 527.
Jimboy, Amanda, 527.
Jimboy, Amos, 527.
Jimboy, Bruner, 1631.
Jimboy, Fannie, 527.
Jimboy, Fuller, 1631, M257.
Jimboy, Hopsie, 488, 3593, NB256, NB257,
    M149.
Jimboy, J. S. Lamar, 527.
Jimboy, Lizzie, 527.
Jimboy, Louisa, 1508, M136.
Jimboy, Lucy, 527.
Jimboy, Mahala, 488, 527, 3389.
Jimboy, Mary, M257.
Jimboy, Mollie, 1631, M257.
Jimboy, Nannie, M136.

Jimboy, Newton, 527.
Jimboy, Peggy, NB225.
Jimboy, Reuben, 527.
Jimboy, Thomas, 3389.
Jimboy, Wiley, 527, M136, NB225.
Jimboy, William, 488, 527, 3389.
Jimboy, Willie, 527.
Jimka, 2498.
Jlmkee, 2445.
Jimkee, Nettie, 2445.
Jimmie, 2351.
Jims, Holee, 1359.
Jimsey, 2856. 3139.
Jimsey, Canoe, 3138.
Jimsey, Culla, 2790.
Jimsey, Hannah, 3138, 3139.
Jimsey, Jeannetta, 2790.
Jimsey, Soshaye, 2790.
Jimsey, Unah, 3138.
Jinney, 1471, 2540.
Jinnie, 1471, 2540.
Jobe, Cherokee, 366, 749.
Jobe, Cherokee Mary, 366.
Jobe, Eliza M., 366.
Jobe, Florence, 366.
Jobe, Gertrude, 366.
Jobe, L. P., 366.
Jobe, Leo J., 749, NB81.
Jobe, Leroy, 749, NB81.
Jobe, Louis N. B., 366, NB81.
Jobe, Mary, 366, NB81.
Jobe, Mary G., 366, NB81.
Jobé, Mollie G., 366, NB81.
Jobelafahny, 610.
Jobelafahny, Mary, 610.
Jobelafahny, Sarah, 610.
Jobelafahny, Wesley, 610.
Jocoche, 18.
Joconfah, 2729
Joconfah, Melissa, 2729.
Joconfah, Poconweney, 2729.
Joe, 1488.
Jofola, 3397.
John, 1318, 2856.
John, Albert, NB312.
John, Alicè, 503, NB536.
John, Big, 1646.
John, Fiddler, 2315.
John, Johny, 2386.
John, Katie, 2386.
John, Lena, NB526.
John, Little, 308.
John, Louisa, 2386.
John, McCully, 1898, NB536.
John, Short, 2386, NB312.
John, Whooping, 2179.
John, Winey, 2386, NB312.
John, Wosey, 3561.
Johnche, 1566.
Johnogee, 1641.
Johnson, 104, 2494, 2789.
Johnson, Abbie Lee, 143, NB26, NB27.
Johnson, Ada, 1632.
Johnson, Adam, 1319.
Johnson, Addie, CE4032.
Johnson, Albert, 1669.
Johnson, Alex, 2223.
Johnson, Alice, 3437.
Johnson, Amandy, NB843.
Johnson, Anderson, 566, NB1181.

Johnson, Lucy, 3929.
Johnson, Lydia, 2085, 3078.
Johnson, Maggie, 1278.
Johnson, Mahala, 1279, 2085, NB590, NB949.
Johnson, Mahaley, 1279, 2085, NB590, NB949.
Johnson, Martin, NB980.
Johnson, Melissa, 321.
Johnson, Miley, 574, 1319, NB150, M305.
Johnson, Miller, 1278, 1279.
Johnson, Millie, 1258, 3078,3489,CE4032,M305.
Johnson, Minnie, NB1136, NB1137.
Johnson, Missaley, 1279.
Johnson, Mollie, 3272, 3449.
Johnson, Moses, 145.
Johnson, Nannie, 1257.
Johnson, Nathan, 1632.
Johnson, Nellie C., 3535.
Johnson, Nicey, 3496, 208, NB150.
Johnson, Noah, 145.
Johnson, Nora, NB1090.
Johnson, Oda Casey, 3535.
Johnson, Onate, NB1256.
Johnson, Paro, 1632, Creek Frd. 182, NB308.
                NB309.
Johnson, Patsy, 1689.
Johnson, Peter, 2085, 145, 473, 3929.
Johnson, Polly, 477, 1632, 3064.
Johnson, Rena, NB1227.
Johnson, Robert, 3384, 2222, 3064.
Johnson, Robert F., 212, NB1227.
Johnson, Rosanna; 3182.
Johnson, Ruth, 455, NB164.
Johnson, Sallie, 3078, 3079, CE4017.
Johnson, Sam, 3078, NB1255, NB1256.
Johnson, Samuel, 380, 1290.
Johnson, Sandy, 2789, 3449, 3765, NB980,NB-
                981.
Johnson, Sango, 1366.
Johnson, Sissie M., 399.
Johnson, Sophia, 294, NB40.
Johnson, Sukey, 3873.
Johnson, Sunny, 1279.
Johnson, Susan, 2930.
Johnson, Susanna, NB1255.
Johnson, Susie, 1213, 3064, 3350, NB1210.
Johnson, Taylor, 3232.
Johnson, Tenner, 1279.
Johnson, Thomas, 3535.
Johnson, Todd, 294.
Johnson, Tom, 1377, 1966.
Johnson, Ulter, NB949.
Johnson, Unah, 3765.
Johnson, Viola, NB27. .
Johnson, Walter, 2347.
Johnson, Weetsie, M443.
Johnson, Weley, 321, NB843.
Johnson, Wesley, 2442.
Johnson, Wiley, 321.
Johnson, Willie, 1278.
Johnson, Winey, NB690.
Johnson, Wisey, 138, 3437, M397, NB1076
Johnson, W. L., 294.
Johnson, Yarner, 1257.
Johnson, Youman, 3078.
Johnson, Yuna, 3873.
Joilla, 1993, 3042.
Joilly, Ochee, 1970.
Joker, 1544.
Jonah, 3272.
Jonah, Louisiana, 3272.

Jonasee, Parcilla, 1342.
Jonasie, 2781.
Jones, 1714.
Jones, Adzel, M76.
Jones, Albert, 2750.
Jones, Annie, 2663, NB1165.
Jones, Benjamin, 1440.
Jones, Betsey, 829.
Jones, Caddo, NB870.
Jones, Charlie, 102, 2512, 2836.
Jones, Cindy, M67.
Jones, Clarance, NB913
Jones, David, 2564.
Jones, Eliza, 1769.
Jones, Ella, 3740.
Jones, Emma, 1849.
Jones, George, 2663.
Jones, Goliah, 1714.
Jones, Haikey, 2916, 3740.
Jones, Hannah, 2521, 2703, 3940.
Jones, Harrison, NB913.
Jones, Hattie, 2521.
Jones, Hogie, 2663.
Jones, Hopie, 3231.
Jones, Jemima, 1470, NB1058.
Jones, John, 1849.
Jones, Kawee, 940.
Jones, Leah, CE4033.
Jones, Legus, 2751.
Jones, Lela, 2051, NB913.
Jones, Levina, 2663, 3740.
Jones, Lila, 481.
Jones, Lillie, 1849.
Jones, Lizzie, 2599, M67.
Jones, Loney, 2836.
Jones, Louiney, 481.
Jones, Louisa, 2512.
Jones, Lucinda, 11, 1849.
Jones, Lucy, 1715.
Jones, Lydia C., 3588.
Jones, Maggie, 785, M76.
Jones, Martha, 481, CE4033, M74.
Jones, Martin, 2521.
Jones, Mary, 3231.
Jones, Maude Cox, 3588.
Jones, Maxey, 2752.
Jones, Malinda, 2758, M133.
Jones, Mikey, 1715.
Jones, Milea, 829.
Jones, Mollie, 2600, 2836.
Jones, N. B., 451, 1849, 1850.
Jones, Nancy, 481, 2564.
Jones, Napoleon, 451, 1849, 1850.
Jones, Nellie, 2663.
Jones, Nero, 1769.
Jones, Pearl D., 166.
Jones, Pollie, 2521, NB927.
Jones, Rabbit, 829.
Jones, Rose, 114.
Jones, Salina, 2751, M475.
Jones, Sallie, 1470, 2521.
Jones, Stepney, 3231.
Jones, Su loly, 2663, CE4033, M133.
Jones, Taylor, 829.
Jones, Thomas, 481, 2752, 3588, M67.
Jones, V. T., M76.
Jones, Washington, 1470.
Jones, Wesley, M133.
Jones, William, 451, 1440, 1715, 1830, 2663, 3231.

Jones, Willie, 1769, NB870.
Joney, 389.
Joney, Milley, 3305.
Jonutua, 2922.
Jordan, Emma, 936.
Joseph, 1675.   •
Joseph, Cindy, 3976.
Joseph, George, 3112, 3976.
Joseph, Jeannatta, 3112.
Joseph, Jemina, 3976.
Joseph, Kittie, 2565.
Josie, 385.
Josie, Jennie, NB1026.
Josie, Lena, 2358, NB1026.
Josie, Sofley, NB1026.
Jourdan, Arlie, 9.
Jourdan, John C., 9.
Jourdan, Mason F., 9.
Jovixico, 3066.
Judy, 1575, 1576, 2320, 2436.
Julie, 2545.
July, Louisa, 87, 820.
July, Sam, 87, 820.
July, Turner, 87.
Jutkie, 1936.
Kaahsee, 3762.
Kaalay, 569.
Kacoquana, 3337.
Kacoquanney, 77, 2786, 3313.
Kakoconney, 3125, NB750.
Kakothlar, 3885.
Kalaney, 2857, M192.
Kalaney, Chepon, M192.
Kalaney, Sissie, M192.
Kalawee, 3144.
Kaley, 2472.
Kamamee, 3940.
Kanard, Albert, 3784.
Kanard, Annie, 60, 379, 2394.
Kanard, Bettie, 2117.
Kanard, Cilla, NB1078.
Kanard, Cy., 3133.
Kanard, Eliza, 60, 3420, 3749.
Kanard, Fannie, 2117, 3409, NB1075.
Kanard, George, 2394, 3348, 3784.
Kanard, Hully, 3507.
Kanard, James, 379, 3749, NB1078.
Kanard, Jennie, 3133, NB907, M255.
Kanard, Jim, 60.
Kanard, Josiah, 3348.
Kanard, Judy, 3420.
Kanard, Louis, 60.
Kanard, Louisa, 60, 3133.
Kanard, Lumber, 2394.
Kanard, Lizzie, 2341, 3171.
Kanard, Melissa, 3133, NB996.
Kanard, Nellie, 379, 3749, NB1078.
Kanard, Peter, 661, 2117.
Kanard, Polly, 60.
Kanard, Puttie, 2117.
Kanard, Roman, 817.
Kanard, Rosana, 2394, 3348, 3784.
Kanard, Simeno, 60.
Kanard, Susan, 2394.
Kanard, Thomas B., 3409.
Kanard, Thomas J., 3420, 60.
Kanard, Thomas, Jr., 60, 3420.
Kanard, Tilda, 2394.
Kanard, Wash, 3171.
Kanard, Washington, 817, 2117, 3409

344

Kelleam. Esaw, 3316.
Keller, Dan. 2664.
Kelley, 1067.
Kelley, Annie, 170.
Kelley, Edna, 960.
Kelley, Eliza, 318.
Kelley, Emma, 318, NB952.
Kelley, Ferdinand, 272, NB301. NB302.
Kelley, Hulley, 1067.
Kelley, Ida, 170.
Kelley, Louie, 1067.
Kelley, Lucy, 170.
Kelley, Mary, 1067, 690, 802, 855.
Kelley, Marsey, 170.
Kelley, Minnie, 170.
Kelley, Mose, 318.
Kelley, Robert 981.
Kelley, Rosella. NB968.
Kelley, Sally, 3077, 3278, NB1260.
Kelley, Sukey, 318, 2008.
Kelley, Susanna, 1110, NB963.
Kelley, Tobey, 310, 318.
Kelley, Tilsie, 318, 310.
Kelley, Wesley, 318, NB963.
Kelley, Wiley, 2326, 2323, 2324.
Kelley, Wilson, 1067.
Kelly, A. B., 272.
Kelly, Alabama, NB428.
Kelly, Albert, 2323.
Kelly, Amy, NB1210.
Kelly, Bettie, 3278.
Kelly, David, 395, NB1261.
Kelly, Elizabeth, NB301.
Kelly, Ferdinand, 272, NB301, NB302.
Kelly, Jackson, 395.
Kelly, James, 802, 855, 3278, NB1210.
Kelly, Jennie, 3278.
Kelly, Jim, 802, 855, 3278, NB1210.
Kelly, John, 1171, 2324, 3278.
Kelly, Johnnie, 3278.
Kelly, Joseph, 170.
Kelly, Jurie, 652.
Kelly, Levina, 2735.
Kelly, Louina, 802.
Kelly, Lucinda, 981, 2326.
Kelly, Lownie, 395.
087, 2112,   Kelly, Lizzie, Moore, 327, NB301, NB302.
3990, NB-   Kelly, Mahaha, 395, NB427, NB428.
Kelly, Mahaley, 395, NB427, NB428.
Kelly, Maria, NB1260, NB1261.
Kelly, Mary, 690, 802, 855, 1067.
Kelly, Marshall, 625, NB1120.
Kelly, Nancy, 951, NB714.
Kelly, Newman, 652, 960, 1171, NB1120.
Kelly, Perry, NB714.
Kelly, Reuben, 802, NB714.
Kelly, Roland E., NB302.
Kelly, Roman. NB427.
Kelly, Sallie, 3077, 3278, NB1260.
Kelly, Sam, 1430, NB1260), NB1261.
Kelly, Sarah, 272, 3278.
Kelly, Sukey, 2008, 318.
Kelly, Susan, 960, NB1120.
Kelly, Susanna, 185.
Kelly, Tecumseh, 981, 2326.
Kelly, Thomas, 802.
Kelly, Tilsie, 310, 318.
Kelly, Wadley, 395, NB427, NB428.
Kelly. Wadly, 395, NB427, NB428.
Kelly, Watty, 185.

345

Kelly, Wiley, 2323, 2324, 2326.
Kemarye, 1381.
Kenard, Bettie, 203, 178, 246.
Kenard, Mary, 379.
Kenard, Major, 379.
Kenard, Mitchell, 202, 180.
Kenard, Nicey, 280.
Kenard, Parthena, 202.
Kenda, 2279.
Keneha, Fus, 1864.
Ke ne hah ho payh, 1403.
Kenerd, Martin, 202, NB147.
Kennard, Bettie, 178, 203, 246.
Kennard, Fannie, 839.
Kennard, George, 839.
Kennard, James, 1373.
Kennard, Johnson, 839.
Kennard, Lizzie, 1372.
Kennard, Louisa, 1372.
Kennard, Mary, 839.
Kennard, Mitchell, 180, 202.
Kennard, Fitchee, 1373.
Kennard, Sisey, 1372.
Kennard, Smith, 1372.
Kennard, William, 839.
Ken nat ta, 3167.
Kenny, George, 2847.
Kernal, Aggie, 1337, 2515.
Kernal, Amey, 1337.
Kernal, Charlie, 1337.
Kernal, Chotka, 1518.
Kernal, David, 1518.
Kernal, Isaac, 1337.
Kernal, Joe, 2523.
Kernal, Johnson, 1337.
Kernal, Lewis, M442.
Kernal, Lilly, M442.
Kernal, Louis, 1337, 1518.
Kernal, Louisa, 1518.
Kernal, Loske, 3817.
Kernal, Lucy, 3168, 3817, NB295.
Kernal, Mary, 1518.
Kernal, Nancy, 2523.
Kernal, Nellie, 1518.
Kernal, Peter, 3168.
Kernal, Sam, 1337.
Kernal, Winey, 1518.
Kernall, Cheparney, 1368.
Kernall, Mose, 1368.
Kernall, Sallie, 1368.
Kernall, Sophia, 1368.
Kernel, Arretta, NB1052, NB1157.
Kernel, Freeman, NB1052.
Kernel, George, 3188, 3809, NB1052, NB1157.
Kernel, Harry, NB1157.
Kernel, Lillie, 3149.
Kernel, Retta, 3809.
Kernell, Dixon, 1900.
Kernell, Ida, 1900.
Kernell, Joe, 1900, 1964.
Kernell, Lucinda, 1084.
Kernell, Lucy, 1900, 219, 1368.
Kernell, Nancy, 2113.
Kernell, Poppy, 2113.
Kernell, Sam, 2113.
Kernells, Amanda, 90.
Kernells, Annie, 90.
Kernells, Lucy, 219, 1368, 1900.
Kernells, Martha, 219.
Kernells, Minnie, M329.

Kernells, Nettie, 90.
Kernells, Sissie, 90, M329.
Kernells, Te mah ye, 1368.
Kernells, Timiye, 219, 90, M329.
Kernels, Johnson, 3809.
Kernels, Lucinda, 349.
Kerr, Arcenoe, 785, NB111, NB695.
Kerr, Commodore Jr., NB111.
Kerr, Ethel, NB695.
Kerr, Henry, NB111, NB695.
Ker se la hne, 2275.
Kerwarphoka, 2218.
Keselar, 2668, 2669.
Kessella, 2957.
Key, Charley, 3047, 1262.
Key, Ety, 1282.
Key, Hugh Benjamin, NB317.
Key, John E., NB317.
Key, Katy, 3047.
Key, Luella, 1122, NB317.
Key, Naggy, 3047.
Key, Simma hitchka, 3047.
Key, Thomas, 146.
Keys, Ada, 1986.
Keys, Charley, 1262, 3047.
Keys, Edward, 766.
Keys, Ella, 1986.
Keys, James, 767, NB995.
Keys, Jesse, 1823.
Keys, Lee, 1255.
Keys, Lesta, 1262.
Keys, Martha, 1823, NB995.
Keys, Pearl, 1823.
Keys, Richard, 3120.
Keys, Sam, 766, 767, 1239, 1255, 1823, 1986.
Keys, Sam R., 1823, NB995.
Keys, Samuel H., 3120.
Keys, Sarah, 766, 767, 1239, 1255, 1823, 198
   3120.
Keys, Semarhetchkar, 1262.
Kiamiame, 2703.
Kidey, 3942.
Kiefer, Annie E., 771.
Kiefer, Clarence Ebert, NB825.
Kiefer, George, D., 771.
Kiefer, John D., 771.
Kiefer, Leroy R., 771.
Kiefer, Martha Lee, 771, 3690, NB825.
Kiefer, Smith H., 771, 3690, NB825.
Kiefer, Stella F., 3690.
Ki he tar, 1317.
Killcrease, Nelson, 3372.
Killcrease, Wade, 3372.
Killer, Adam, 2213.
Killer, Ceasar, 2213.
Killer, Lowina, 1430.
Kimohiwa, 2386.
King, 136, 510.
King, Albert, 136.
King, Amos, 2102, 3504, NB262.
King, Annie, 1372, 1971, 2737.
King, Berry W., NB562.
King, Billy, 2336.
King, Caesar, NB861.
King, Charlie, NB561, NB562, NB563.
King, Chotkey, 1971.
King, Claudy J., NB561.
King, Cogee, 446, NB869.
King, Dick, 2001.
King, Edmond, 2737.

Lee, Albert, 525.
Lee, Arpalah, 3349.
Lee, Barney, 338.
Lee, Cinda, 525.
Lee, David, 1025, 3349.
Lee, Gano, 525, M297.
Lee, Lucy, 338, 525· 2079· 3349.
Lee, Nicey, 2079, NB188, M92.
Lee, Robert, 338, M297.
Lee, Robert E., 338, M297.
Lee, Sallie, 525.
Lee, Sally, 525.
Lee, Sissie, 1676, M297.
Lee, Timmy, 525.
Lee, Willie, 525.
Leecher, 2693.
Leecher, Mutter, 1345.
Leetka, Martha, 2345.
Legus, 1566.
Leider, 2728, 3069.
Lena, 588, 598, 1000, 1452, 1506, 3246.
Lena, Bessie, 1849.
Lena, Betsey, 1849.
Lena, Hettie, 1452, 3791, NB1178, NB1179, M470.
Lena, John, 1849.
Lena, Loda, 1849.
Lena, Low, 2755.
Lena, Peter, 1849.
Lena, Willie, 1849.
Leno, Robert, 3796.
Lerblance, Addie L., 1888.
Lerblance, Alice, 507, NB17.
Lerblance, Andrew, 1934.
Lerblance, E. H., 1888, 3700.
Lerblance, Eliza, 507, 1934.
Lerblance, Ellen, 1858.
Lerblance, Frank H., 1888.
Lerblance, Harriet, 1858.
Lerblance, Howard P., 1888.
Lerblance, Jeannetta, 1858.
Lerblance, Jennie, 1858.
Lerblance, Lillian, 3700.
Lerblance, Lizzie, 1888.
Lerblance, Nettie, 1888.
Lerblance, Nora, 1934.
Lerblance, Pearl, 3700.
Lerblance, Willie, 1934.
Lerblance, W. P., 507, 1858, 1934.
Letkah, 1011.
Letts, F. B., M88, M89, NB878.
Letts, Frank B., M88, M89, NB878.
Letts, Oscar Lovick, NB878.
Letts, Susan L., 268, M88, M89, NB878.
Letts, Vera May, M89.
Letts, Vernon Milford, M88.
Leverett, Bessie, NB751.
Leverett, Fanny, M29.
Leverett, Kogee, 816, M29, NB751.
Leverett, Walter, M29, NB751.
Lewallen, John, 3699, NB658.
Lewallen, Lillie, 3699.
Lewallen, Louisa, 2015, 3699, NB658.
Lewallen, Lucy, NB658.
Lewestey, 1721.
Lewis, 1124, 1125, 1867.
Lewis, Albert, NB876.
Lewis, Annie, 1536, NB876, NB677.
Lewis, Babe, 1913.
Lewis, Bapsey, 3088, 3400.

5.

6,

349

Lewis, Benjamin, 2960.
Lewis, Billie, 3088, 3400, NB907.
Lewis, Billy, 3088, 3400, NB907.
Lewis, Colman, 3098.
Lewis, Daniel, 2930, 2941, 2960, 3580, M34, NB958.
Lewis, David, 3580.
Lewis, Delila, 1251, NB595.
Lewis, Delilah, 1251, NB595.
Lewis, Dobe, 1705.
Lewis, Dollie, 3098.
Lewis, Eddie, NB570.
Lewis, Edmond, 1493.
Lewis, Effie, 1125, NB754.
Lewis, Ella, NB595.
Lewis, Ellen, 720, NB375, NB376, M186.
Lewis, Ellis J., 2941, M26.
Lewis, Emma, NB754.
Lewis, Eula Velma, M186.
Lewis, Fannie, 1493.
Lewis, Francis, 1913.
Lewis, Frank Turner, NB375.
Lewis, Frazier, 2941.
Lewis, Hannah, 2960, 3073, 3098, 3099.
Lewis, Harriet, 3038.
Lewis, Harley, 1125, NB754.
Lewis, Holly, 1125, NB754.
Lewis, Jack, 1251, 3073, NB595.
Lewis, Jackson, 1561, 2359, 2499, 2960, 3098.
Lewis, Jane, 1913, 1664.
Lewis, Jennie, 3133, M255, NB907.
Lewis, Jimmy, NB471.
Lewis, John, 1251, 1493, 1700, NB568, NB569, NB570, NB877.
Lewis, John David, NB376.
Lewis, John E., 645.
Lewis, Johnson, 3098, NB726.
Lewis, Kizey, 1867, M162, NB538.
Lewis, Lillie, NB569.
Lewis, Lizzie, 865, 1135.
Lewis, Louis, 1700.
Lewis, Louisa, 645.
Lewis, Lucinda, 3098, NB726.
Lewis, Lucy, 1328.
Lewis, Lulu, NB726.
Lewis, Manna, 1493, NB568, NB569, NB570.
Lewis, Mary, 969, 1863, 1929.
Lewis, Mattie, NB958.
Lewis, Maxey, 3088, M255, NB907.
Lewis, Micco, M26.
Lewis, Mose, 1328.
Lewis, Mosey, NB568.
Lewis, Nancy, 1561, 2359.
Lewis, Nellie, 3063.
Lewis, Nutteche, M255.
Lewis, Oscar, M186.
Lewis, Osker, NB375, NB376.
Lewis, Pollie, 3580, 2960, M34, NB958.
Lewis, Polly, 2960, 3580, M34, NB958.
Lewis, Ruth Oneita, 865.
Lewis, Sahala, 1536, NB876, NB877.
Lewis, Sarah, 1941.
Lewis, Sarhilla, 1536, NB876, NB877.
Lewis, Sampson, CE4037.
Lewis, Seaborn, CE4037.
Lewis, Thomas, 758, 2930, NB471.
Lewis, Thompson, 3400.
Lewis, Washie, M34.
Lewis, Wm., 865.
Libbie, 1256.

Lidda, 2556.
Liddie, 2092, 2612.
Liddy, 1512, 2092.
Lieber, Albert Leon, M5.
Lieber, Dora, 662, M5.
Lieber, James Howard, 662.
Lieber, John G., 662, M5.
Lihtiffee, 218.
Lika, Jessie, 425.
Like, Mollie, 3842.
Likowski, Frank, 2110.
Likowski, Frank, Jr., 2110.
Likowski, Herman A., 1776.
Likowski, James B., 2110.
Likowski, John W., 1776.
Likowski, Joseph, 2110.
Likowski, Lydia Lucile, 2110.
Likowski, Sarah A., 1776.
Likowski, Senora E., 2110.
Likowski, William H., 1776.
Lina, 2847.
Linda, 1070, 1321, 1484, 1894, 2145, 2277, 2380 2477, 2505, 2507, 2509, 2535, 2782 2789.
Lindaneha, 2334.
Lindsey, 1526, 2094, 2096.
Lindsey, Addie, NB997.
Lindsey, Amos, 1526.
Lindsey, Columbia, NB1182.
Lindsey, Dorsey, 2914.
Lindsey, Freeland, 2768, NB1182, NB1191.
Lindsey, Hepsey, 1526.
Linsdey, Hettie, M366, NB997.
Lindsey, Kizzie, 2768.
Lindsey, Lewis, 2768.
Lindsey, Lila D., 113.
Lindsey, Lydia, 2768.
Lindsey, Minnie, 2096.
Lindsey, Mulka, 2096.
Lindsey, Nancy, 2768.
Lindsey, Noah, M366.
Lindsey, Phillip, 4012, 2768.
Lindsey, Roley, 2914.
Lindsey, Samantha, 1724.
Lindsey, Sarah, NB1191.
Lindsey, Silla, 4012, 2914.
Lindsey, Tosa, 4012.
Lindsey, Walter, 1724, 2094, M366, NB997.
Lino, Robert, 3796.
Linoche, CE4035.
Linton, Pauline B., 1367.
Linton, Pauline E., 1367.
Linton, Shannon R., 1367.
Linton, Wm. E., 1367.
Lipscomb, Helen V., 3118.
Lipscomb, J. T. H., 3118.
Lipscomb, Lillian L., 3118.
Lipscomb, Mattie R., 3118.
Lisochee, 1285, 1359.
Lissar, 2552.
Listka, Eliza, 1542.
Litia, 3996, 4013.
Litka, Arma, 506, NB429, NB430.
Litka, Charley, 2539.
Litka, Dick, 442, 3494.
Litka, Joe, 506.
Litka, John, 3494.
Litka, Lucy, 442.
Litka, Martha, 442, 3494, NB409.
Litka, Newman, NB409.

Loler, Wilson, 256.
London, Betsey, 1768, 2156.
London, Dosha, 2562.
London, Ellen, 2562, NB1069.
London, Olhe, 2562.
Loney, 118, 575, 3000.
Loney, Annie, 966.
Loney, Ellen, M345.
Loney, James, NB652.
Loney, Leah, 3649.
Loney, Lucy, 118, 575.
Loney, Major, 118.
Loney, Rachael, 3649.
Loney, Sam, 3649, 3000, NB652, M345.
Long, Adeline, 1650.
Long, Ahlacoganay, M377.
Long, Anna, NB708.
Long, Annie, 1521, 1650.
Long, Ben, 1603.
Long, Bettie, M180.
Long, Betsy, 1519.
Long, Bessie, 1625.
Long, Bob, 2784.
Long, Bunny, 1528.
Long, Carcharty, 1625.
Long, Coley, 1709.
Long, Daniel A., 1803, 3715.
Long, David, 1519.
Long, Eliza, 993, 3856, NB706.
Long, Ella, 3949.
Long, Fish, 900.
Long, George, 992, 1521, 1528, 1638, 1656,
        CE4038.
Long, Hannah, 1555, 1709.
Long, Harry, 2785.
Long, Henry, 1650, 2784, 3949, NB708.
Long, Isreal, 259.
Long, Jacob, 1452, 1803.
Long, Jesse, 1650, 3805, NB1134.
Long, Jessie, 2743.
Long, Jim, 2981, 2784, 2785, 3303.
Long, Jimmie, 2784, 2785, 2981, 3303.
Long, John, 2403, 2743, 3856.
Long, Joshway, 1709.
Long, Judy, 2502.
Long, Kate, 3715.
Long, Kizzie, 1709, 2743, 3426.
Long, Lannie, 2785, M377, NB1086.
Long, Lewis, 2785, M377, NB1086.
Long, Lizzie, 2784, 3949.
Long, Lody, 1709, NB1054.
Long, Loday, 1709, NB1054.
Long, Losanna, 2933, NB708.
Long, Lucy, 1803, 1804, 2743, CE4038.
Long, Lucy B., 1803, 1804, 2743, CE4038.
Long, Mahala, 1709.
Long, Martha, 1650, 1656, 3225, M180.
Long, Matilda, 1656, 3225.
Long, Mattie, 3805.
Long, Mesulta, 2046, NB32.
Long, Milton, 1650.
Long, Newman, NB706.
Long, Noah, 1519, NB706.
Long, Peter, 3805.
Long, Rachael, 415, M345.
Long, Richmond, 3426.
Long, Roley, NB1134.
Long, Sake, NB1086'
Long, Sakquanny, 2981.
Long, Sallie, 2773.

Long, Sam, 441, 1555, 1709, 3426.
Long, Sawena, 2785.
Long, Selena, 3856.
Long, Selver, 1638.
Long, Sindy, 1519.
Long, Sukey, 2403.
Long, Susanna, 1528.
Long, Susie, 1519.
Long, Taylor, 1519.
Long, Thomas, 1519, 1709, 2502.
Long, Tilda, 992.
Long, Tom, 2502, 1519, 1709.
Long, Wallace, NB1149.
Long, Wash, 1625, 1656, 3225, M180.
Long, Washington; 1625, 1656, 3225, M180.
Long, Wewoka John, 3715.
Long, Wiggie, 2741, 3805, NB1134.
Long, Yusie, 259, NB1149.
Longbread, Lyddie, 4022.
Longbread, Nannie, 4022.
Longey, Billy, 3089.
Longey, Rina, 3089.
Lonie, 2714.
Looma, 4025.
Looney, 520.
Looney, Beckie Lena, M134.
Looney, Conger, 966.
Looney, Charles William, 520.
Looney, Della May, NB402.
Looney, Ella, NB388, NB402.
Looney, Fannie, 520, M134, NB202.
Looney, Fanny, 520, NB202, M134.
Looney, Forest Leonard, NB388.
Looney, George Barney, 520.
Looney, Josiah, 520, M134, NB202.
Looney, Larger, 3512.
Looney, N. W., NB388, NB402.
Looney, Raney, 520.
Looney, Sullivan, NB202.
Loparklartchchee, 1299.
Losana, 1817.
Losay, 2530.
Loschokee, 2377.
Losenney, 2981.
Losey, 2424, 2606, 2608, 1939.
Losie, 2606, 2608, 1939, 2424.
Loska, 184, 1875, 2124.
Loskey, 2974, 3187, 3249.
Loskochee, 1452.
Losochee, 108, 1450.
Losogegee, 1368.
Lossie, 1939, 2606, 2608, 2424.
Losutchey, 1944.
Lothokkee, 160.
Lotka, 2238, 2747.
Lotka, Supsie, 2238.
Lott, Addie, M404.
Lott, Amy, 1604.
Lott, Annie, 2455.
Lott, G. P., 3302.
Lott, Jennie, NB1102.
Lott, John, 3259.
Lott, Lena, 2455, 3755, NB1101, NB1102,
        M404.
Lott, Losie, 3755.
Lott, Lucy, NB1101.
Lott, Mary Ann, 3259.
Lott, Millie, 2455.
Lott, Nancy, 208, 212, 2455.
Lott, Nannie, 2455.

Lott, Thomas, 2455, 3755, M404, MN
        NB1102.
Lott, Tommie, 2455, 3755, M404, NE
        NB1102.
Lott, William, 2455.
Lott, Willie, 2455.
Lotta, 3391.
Lottie, 2805.
Louanna, 481.
Loucinda, 94, 220, 326, 431, 523, 1307,
        1323, 1481, 1676, 1774, 1775,
        1864, 2295, 2296, 2326, 2493,
        2636, 2867, 3024, 3046,
        M478.
Louie, 3963.
Louina, 266, 964, 2033, 2567.
Louiney, 2351, 3112.
Louis, 23.
Louisa, 23, 201, 206, 251, 389, 712, 794,
        1720, 1721, 1722, 1723, 1862,
        1867, 1941, 2499, 2675, 2782
Louisana, 3960, 2658, 3274.
Louisanah, 2510.
Louisiana, 2658, 3274, 3960.
Lousally, 525.
Louviney, 1847.
Louzanna, 3010.
Love, Jonas, 401.
Love, Robert, 401.
Love, Willie, 401.
Lovell, Docia, 543.
Lovett, Annie, 66, NB147.
Lovett, Austin, 903.
Lovett, George, 66, 205, 903.
Lovett, John J., M415.
Lovett, Kizzie, 71, 74.
Lovett, Lawrence, 205.
Lovett, Loran Alfred, M415.
Lovett, Liza, 205.
Lovett, Lizzie, 66.
Lovett, Lucy, 66.
Lovett, Matilda, 446, M415.
Lovett, Philie, 66, 71.
Lovett, Phillip, 832.
Lovett, Pilot, 205.
Lovett, Sallie, 66, 205, 903.
Lovett; Wisey, 66, 71.
Low, Annie, 2755.
Low, Cannuga, 3246.
Low, Canuka, 2755.
Low, Cinda, 3246.
Low, Jim, 2897, 2898, 3128.
Low, Kizzie, 3128.
Low, Lena, 2755, 3246.
Low, Louisa, 2755, NB371, M127.
Low, Susie, 2898, NB1251.
Low, Taylor, 2755.
Lowakoche, 2277.
Lowe, Abbie, 140, 141, 222, 1963.
Lowe, A. D., 1657.
Lowe, Albert Chastain, M413.
Lowe, Alex, 363, 1545.
Lowe, Amos, 2143.
Lowe, Canuky, 1524, 3606, M175, NB809
Lowe, Columbus, 2478.
Lowe, Comma, 1504.
Lowe, Eliza, 1436, NB912.
Lowe, Gertrude, 715.
Lowe, Jackson, 1825.
Lowe, Jennie, 2894, NB1155.

9.
23,
64,
36,

353

Maco, Tomathle, 1520.
Madison, Alice, 230, NB339, NB340.
Madison, John, 230.
Madison, William, 230.
Maeche, Heneha, 2732.
Mafolage, 201.
Mafolika, 130.
Mageeley, 1617.
Magethhoge, 2087.
Magethloke, 2299.
Maggie, 142.
Magilbe, Mistohale, 90, 1510.
Mahahchee, 1341.
Mahala, 1548, 1836, 2279, 2685, 2915, 3730.
Mahaley, 1621.
Mahonihche, 1862.
Mahta, 1215.
Mahtar, 2218.
Mahte, 2797.
Mahtee, 2139, 2153.
Majole, 1898.
Major, 2347.
Major, Ida, 2347.
Major, Loby, 2347.
Major, Maley, 2347.
Major, Nellie, 2347.
Major, Sallie, 2347.
Major, Sally, 2563.
Maka, 2416.
Makakpoyah, 62.
Makannocke, 67.
Makithle, 85.
Malarher, 1488.
Maley, 2347.
Malinda, 1794.
Malone, Hepsey, 756.
Maloney, Annie, 2375, NB613.
Maloney, Annie C., 869.
Maloney, Dave, 869.
Maloney, Jim, NB613.
Maloney, Lena, NB613.
Maloney, Ruby, 869.
Mamie, 1487.
Manac, Betsey, 1141.
Manac, Jeffrey, 1141.
Managee, 2765.
Manahwee, Cinda, 2194, NB1166.
Manahwee, John, 1704, 2194, NB1166.
Manawa, Bunnie, 2300.
Manawa, George, 2300.
Manawa, Leah, 2300.
Manawa, Lydia, 2300.
Manawee, Betsey, 1408, NB1030.
Mandy, 2513, 3083.
Manechee, 1246.
Manhosena, 1742, 1743.
Manka, 2262.
Manley, Adam, 3339.
Manley. Arthur, NB956.
Manley, Bunnie, 3639.
Manley, David, 3076, 3774.
Manley, Dicey, 3774.
Manley, Disey, 3262, 3339.
Manley, Eliza, 3076, 3774.
Manley, Fannie, 1706, 2967.
Manley, Halley, 2242, M26.
Manley, Hallie, 2242, M26.
Manley, Harvey, 3205.
Manley, Isaac, 3262, NB727, NB728.
Manley, Jack, 3205.

Manley, Jonas, 20.
Manley, Joseph, 1864.
Manley, Katy, 2986, NB858.
Manley, Leeda, 3339.
Manley, Lena, 2334.
Manley, Linda, 2242, 2334
Manley, Lindy Isaac, NB727.
Manley, Lizzie, 2127, 2242, 3218.
Manley, Lofa, 2127, 2242, 3218.
Manley, Louis, 3205.
Manley, Martha, 2334, NB727, NB728.
Manley, Mary, 3139, 3205, 3639, NB956.
Manley, Melah, NB728.
Manley, Millie, 3139, NB956.
Manley, Mose, 3076.
Manley, Moses, 2045, 3262, 3339.
Manley, Peepsie, NB858.
Manley, Pompey, 2334.
Manley, Samuel, 1864.
Manley, Sarah, 1864.
Manley, Siah, 20.
Manley, Sunny, 1864.
Manley, Tarby, 20.
Manley, Thomas, 3218, 3639, NB956.
Manley, Tisey, 3076.
Manley, Tom, 2045, NB858.
Manly, Fannie, 2689, 2691.
Manly, Lawyer, 2501, 2503.
Manly, Levi, 1931.
Manly, Lydia, 2501, 2503.
Manly, Sina, 1931.
Manly, Tobe, 1931.
Mann, Addie B., 639.
Mann, Hannah, 1336, NB775. M212.
Mann, Hazel, 639.
Mann, Hazel May, M212.
Mann, J. F., M212.
Mann, Manila, 639.
Mann, Sarah E., 639.
Mann, Thomas E., 639.
Mann, William, 639.
Mann, Wm. J., 639.
Mannie, 2522.
Mantooth, Annie, 308, NB795.
Mantooth, Isabella, NB795.
Mantooth, James H., NB795.
Mantooth, Jim, 308.
Mantooth, Laura, 308.
Manuel, Lucy, 1033.
Manuel, Mary, 239, 2848.
Manuel, Robert, 1170.
Manuel, Sam, 1092.
Manuel, Thomas, 1170.
Manuel, Tom, 1092.
Manwarring, Melita, 921.
Manwarring, Melita Grace, 921.
Manwarring, Silver, 921.
Manwarring, T. A., 921.
Mapetha, 3301.
Marbeah, 1329.
Marcey, 979.
March, A. K., 3952.
March, Edith, M459.
March, Gracie, 3952.
March, Lloyd, 3952.
March, Nicholas, 3952.
March, Stella, 3952, M459, M460.
March, William K., M460.
March, Willie H., 3952, M459, M460.
Marcum, Doc, 1086.

Marshall, Choatkey. 417.
Marshall, Chopotkey. 3067.
Marshall, Cordelia. 303.
Marshall, David. 703, 1081.
Marshall, Delaphine, 1196.
Marshall, Delphine, 803.
Marshall, Dinah, 644.
Marshall, Eliza. 1081, 1990.
Marshall, Elizabeth. 599, 1810, 1844, 2025.
Marshall, Ellen, 303.
Marshall, Elsie, 114, NB102, NB103.
Marshall, Elvina, 1954.
Marshall, Freeland, 303.
Marshall, George, 599, 1810, 1844, 2025.
Marshall, George Freeman, NB23.
Marshall, Gertrude Belle, 599.
Marshall, Henry, NB884.
Marshall, Hepsey, 1243.
Marshall, Hildred, 703.
Marshall, Ida, 122.
Marshall, Jacob, 1311.
Marshall, James, 122, 3067.
Marshall, Jeff, 1139, 1159.
Marshall, Jim, 1159.
Marshall, Joe, 969.
Marshall, John, 851, 1139.
Marshall, Johnny, 1504.
Marshsll, Judy, 1159.
Marshall, Lafayette, 303.
Marshall, Laura, 703.
Marshall, Lena May, NB190.
Marshall, Leonidas. 2070.
Marshall, Lewis, 114, M332.
Marshall, Liley, 1159.
Marshall, Lizzie, 6, 1023, 3122, NB369, M430.
Marshall, Lizzie B., 599, NB22, NB23.
Marshall, Londo, 1159.
Marshall, Louisa, 1953.
Marshall, Mamie, M332.
Marshall, Martha, 1948, NB884.
Marshall, Mary, 1168.
Marshall, Mattie, 122, 303.
Marshall, Millie, 494, 1504.
Marshall, Mitchell, 114, 292.
Marshall, Mollie, 3974.
Marshall, Molsie, 1504.
Marshall, Nancy, 1746.
Marshall, Nellie, 3946.
Marshall, Nettie, 851, 1810.
Marshall, Nicholson, 1990.
Marshall, Nitty, 1243, CE4019, NB1172.
Marshall, Nora, 851, 2025.
Marshall, Parney, 1243.
Marshall, Philip, 1081, 1504.
Marshall, Phillip, 1834.
Marshall, Phillips, 1380.
Marshall, Polly, 815.
Marshall, Rachel, 112, 122.
Marshall, Rufus, 111.
Marshall, Sallie, 716.
Marshall, Sally, 1380.
Marshall, Sam, 3067.
Marshall, Susanah, 1185.
Marshall, Susannah, 3122.
Marshall, Susie, 1504.
Marshall, Thomas, 122.
Marshall, Thomas J., 1844, NB190.
Marshall, Timmie, 1081.
Marshall, Tip, 851, 1196.
Marshall, Tucker, 2127.

Marshall, Violet, 1810
Marshall, Waitie, 122.
Marshall, Walter, 1834.
Marshall, Warrior, 703.
Marshall, Watie, 1504.
Marshall, Willie, 644.
Marshall, Wm., 815.
Marshall, Winey, 111, 703, 1953, 1954.
Marshall, Wor, 111, 703, 1953, 1954.
Marshall, Yahoey, 3067.
Marshall, Yarner, 1081.
Marston, John 705.
Marston, Mary S., 705.
Marston, May Malinda, 705.
Marston, Nannie, 705.
Marston, Thos., W., 705.
Marte, 2894.
Martha, 237, 256, 288, 995, 1090, 1465, 1497,
  1556, 2380, 2393, 2456, 2468, 2741,
  2920, 2982, 3290, 3851.
Martha noc kee, 1839.
Marthla, Ak tar yar che, 1350.
Marthla, Nocose, 1137, 1299, 2732.
Marthla, Oktyche, 1341.
Marthlar, Cobarse, 155.
Marthoche, Timmie, 3326.
Martie, 2814.
Martin, Anna, 50, M113.
Martin, Annie, NB108, NB231.
Martin, Betsy, 1466.
Martin, Dave, 1614.
Martin, Etta Elmory, 50.
Martin, Evaline, 1083.
Martin, Henry, 1083, 1445, 1466, M113.
Martin, Ida May, 50.
Martin, Jackson, 182.
Martin, James, 50.
Martin, Jesse, NB231.
Martin, Joe, M11.
Martin, Joe Ross, M11.
Martin, Johnson, 182, NB74, M1.
Martin, Leona, NB108.
Martin, Lewis, 1912.
Martin, Liley, 182.
Martin, Loney, NB74.
Martin, March, M1.
Martin, Nancy, 1217.
Martin, Polly, 1912.
Martin, Samuel, 2505.
Martin, Stebbin, NB670, NB671.
Martin, Susanna, 443, NB74, M1.
Martin, Susie, 427, M11.
Martin, Thomas, 50, NB108, NB231, M113.
Marts, Daisy, 1153.
Marty, 2505.
Martyr, Tommy, 2310.
Marwakike, 2202.
Marwcoly, 1162.
"Marwole,' 2788.
Mary, 346, 516, 556, 819, 939, 1016, 1581, 1626,
  1629, 2488.
Mary, Ann, 3259.
Marye, Hothle, 2572.
Maryticka, 1288, 1292.
Maschya, 2666.
Mason, 1372.
Mason, Polly, 1372.
Mastin, Wm. J., 705.
Mat a lo ke, 443.
Matalokee, 2056.

Mat a luk ke, 995.
Ma ta tah ke, 246.
Mathewson, F. M., 1684, 2332.
Mathewson, Hettie Ann, 1684, 2332
Mathewson, Phoebe B., 1684, NB258.
Matilda, 2175.
Mat i ye cher, 2014.
Matoy, Annie, NB1167.
Matoy, Charles, 1855, NB1167, M73.
Matoy, Gertrude, M73.
Matoy, John, 1198, 1855.
Matoy, Lydia, 2581.
Matoy, Martha, 1198.
Matoy, Maud, NB1167, M73.
Matoy, Maude, NB1167, M73.
Mattie, 10, 2089.
Mauda, 2520.
Ma wo ki gee, 2525.
Ma wo ki ke, 2274.
Mawsy, 1444.
Maxey, 2962.
Maxey, Eugene, NB119, NB120.
Maxey, Eugene Willie, NB119.
Maxey, Fannie, 2962.
Maxey, Neosho P., 915, NB119, NB120.
Maxey, Simeon C., NB120.
Maxwell, Colbert J., 799.
Maxwell, Jessie, L., 799.
Maxwell, John B., 799.
Maxwell, John C., 799, 3666.
Maxwell, Joseph L., 3666.
Maxwell, Laura E., 799.
Maxwell, Laura J., 799, 3666.
Maxwell, Leona V., 799.
Maxwell, Maude P., 799.
Maxwell, Rollie C., 799.
Maxwell, Sarophy, 799.
Maxwell, Thomas, 799.
Mayatka, 1646.
Mayes, James, 3364.
Mayes, Marry, NB373.
Mayes, Martha, 1029, 3364, NB372, NB373,
  M205.
Mayes, Martha, Jr., NB372.
Mayes, Minnie, M205.
Mayes, Thomas, 1029.
Mayes, W. A., 1029, 3364.
Mayes, Wiatt, NB372, NB373, M205.
Mayes, Wyatt, NB373, NB372, M205.
Meagher, Edward, 2.
Meagher, Frances Mitchell, M330.
Meagher, Isabelle, 2, NB110.
Meagher, John S., 3.
Meagher, Katherine Frances, M330.
Meagher, Mary, 2, 3, 4.
Meagher, Sarah, 2.
Meagher, T. F., 2, 3, 4.
Meagher, Thos. F., Jr., 4, M330.
Meagher, Walter, 2.
Mechiskoche, 2831, 2864.
Mechussey, 2763.
Medutwikey, 2811.
Meeks, Martha, 3004.
Mehaka, 379, 3352.
Mehakee, 2774.
Mehakey, 1895.
Mehale, 967.
Mehate, 2908.
Mehie, 1997.
Mehiti, 2827.

Micco, Hully, 2065.
Micco, Hulpatta, 566, 2590.
Micco, Iege, 1257.
Micco, Immeha, 1220.
Micco, Iseral, M494.
Micco, Itshars, 3068, 3270.
Micco, Itshas, 3068, 3270.
Micco, Jogarty Yahola, 1505.
Micco, John, 1300, 1792.
Micco, Johnson, 1328.
Micco, Kapitche, 3677.
Micco, Katcha, 2691, 2967·
Micco, Katie, 1288, 1637, NB482.
Micco, Kintar, 1349, 1350, 1354, 1670.
Micco, Kochus, 2102·
Micco, Lahta, 1328.
Micco, Lahtar, 1288.
Micco, Lizzie, 1680.
Micco, Lucy, 328, 329, 330, 2131, 2518, NB426.
Micco, Lydia, 863, 1633.
Micco, Mannie, 393, M340.
Micco, Marsey, 1300, 1792.
Micco, Mary, 1743, NB1039, NB1040
Micco, Mullie, 3988, CE4039.
Micco, Nahkup, 1845.
Micco, Neha, 2999.
Micco, Nuscup, 1633.
Micco, Okchiye, 2342.
Micco, Okfuskee, 1243, 1244, 1249.
Micco, Okfusky, 1243, 1244, 1249.
Micco, Parfena, 322.
Micco, Peter, 259.
Micco, Polly, 2736.
Micco, Rhoda, 1505.
Micco, Robert, 259.
Micco, Saena, 566.
Micco, Sarkinnarne, 1288.
Micco, Sartelo, 108.
Micco, Seber, 2777.
Micco, Soma, 2999.
Micco, Susanna, 2128.
Micco, Tahnarthe, 1516, 1518, 1519.
Micco, Tamarthlee, 1516, 1518, 1519.
Micco, Tasekia, 2603.
Micco, Thompson, 1249.
Micco, Tikee, 3270.
Micco, Tuckabatchee, 1618.
Micco, Tulmachus, 322, 1166, 1310.
Micco, Tulmarthla, 1516, 1518, 1519.
Micco, Tulmochus, 322, 1166, 1310.
Micco, Tulsa, 3273.
Micco, Tulwa, 313, 634, 2951, 3169.
Micco, Tulwar, 3901.
Micco, Tusekiah, 422.
Micco, Tuskeego, 3022.
Micco, Tuskegee, 1680, 2019.
Micco, Willie Tulwar, 3901.
Micco, Wotka, 2738, 3130.
Micco, Wotko, 2738, 3130.
Micco, Yahola, 2515, 2516, 2654, 2737
Micco, Yarkinka, 2436.
Miccoche, 1372, 1375.
Miccochee, Nokus, 1372, 1375.
Mickens, G. W., 1398.
Mickens, Margie, 1398.
Mickens, Nettie, 1398.
Mickens, Oscar, 1398.
Mickens, Walter, 1398.
Mickey, 2762, 3009.
Mickey, Mollie, 3009.

Mickey, Palmer, 3009.
Mickey, Sandy. 3009.
Mickiley, 7, NB1018, NB1019.
Mickogee, 2947, 2950.
Miheecha, 3410.
Mihege, 2614.
Mikay, Silvah, 3057.
Mikey, 1298, 1308, 1309.
Mikey, Amy, 1298, NB548, NB549, NB946.
Mikey, Bessie. 3057.
Mikey, Enos Vey, NB840.
Mikey, Helen, M206.
Mikey, Josiah-Chick. Frd., 543, 3332, NB123, NB840, M206.
Mikey, Lewis, NB123.
Mikey, Lizzie, 1298, 3332, NB123, NB840, M206, M446.
Mikey, Loley, 1359.
Mikey, Louie, 3057, NB823, M124.
Mikey, Magnolia, 3332.
Mikey, Marfy, 1309, 3865, NB553, M445.
Mikey, Ollie, 1359.
Mikey, Robinson, 3332.
Mikey, Silwar, 1298, 1309.
Mikey, Simon, 1308.
Mikko, Casekaya, 2385.
Mikko, Harjo, 2319.
Mikko, Mekko Harjo. 1253.
Mikko, Tulmarthla, 1709.
Milam, A. M., 1728.
Milam, Arthelus M., 1728.
Milam, Kate W., 1728.
Milam, Laura T., 1728.
Miles, Jennie Murrell, NB116.
Miles, Louise, 273.
Miles, Rosalie, 273, NB117, NB116.
Miles, Vivian, NB117.
Miles, W. S., 273, NB116, NB117.
Miley, 1847, 2779, 3235, 3397, 3410, 3975.
Milford, Kizzie, 372, 374.
"Milker", 2739.
Milker, Lucy, 37.
Millaka, 388.
Miller, 910, 2276.
Miller, Ambrose, 987.
Miller, Annie, 3327, 3824.
Miller, Benjamin F., NB272, NB273.
Miller, Bluford, 640.
Miller, Bluford W., 640.
Miller, Betty, 1209.
Miller, Betsey, 1910.
Miller, Catherine, 1980.
Miller, Cecil, NB1038.
Miller, Charles H., 987, 988.
Miller, Charles L., 3716.
Miller, Covilla, 987, 988.
Miller, Daisy Childers, NB515.
Miller, Daniel, 177, 1562, 1564.
Miller, David, 1980.
Miller, Effa, 533, 3637, NB844, M279.
Miller, Emma, 1500.
Miller, Eugene, NB112.
Miller, Florence A., 640, NB41.
Miller, George Thomas, NB272.
Miller, Houston, 3327.
Miller, Hulley, 3232.
Miller, Ida T., 640.
Miller, Jacob, 640, 788, 987.
Miller, James A., M176.
Miller, James Franklin, NB273.

Miller, Jennie, 860, 1895, NB509.
Miller, Jim, 1210, 2036, 2276, 3141.
Miller, John, 37, 2276.
Miller, Johnson, 132, 969, 2536.
Miller, Joney, 1895.
Miller, Katie, 136.
Miller, Kissie, 1607.
Miller, Lewis, 3141.
Miller, Lillie, 1562, NB133, M176.
Miller, Lizzie, 1562, 1895.
Miller, Lizzie A., 640.
Miller, Lizzie M., 2292.
Miller, Louis, 1562, NB133, M176.
Miller, Louis M., 1562, NB133, M176.
Miller, Louisa, 1895, NB1027.
Miller, Malvin H., NB1037.
Miller, Margaret A., 739, NB272, NB273.
Miller, Mary M., 640.
Miller, Mollie, 1740.
Miller, Nancy, 969.
Miller, Nessey, 1895.
Miller, Nick, 1910.
Miller, Nora F., 3716, NB112.
Miller, Okaska, 2787.
Miller, Okosko, 136.
Miller, Otto, 1562.
Miller, Polly, 533, 2536, 3637.
Miller, Quint H., NB1037, NB1038.
Miller, Reuben J., 1980.
Miller, Robert, 132, 860.
Miller, Rose Etta, 1086, NB1037, NB1038.
Miller, Sam, 533, 1895, 2536.
Miller, Samuel, 1500, 1740, M279.
Miller, Samuel H., 1740, 3716, NB112.
Miller, Samuel H., Jr., NB133.
Miller, Sarah, NB844.
Miller, Sarah Field, 640, 788.
Miller, Seborn, 533, 3637, NB844, M279.
Miller, Sophia, 1562, 1564, 1740.
Miller, Susan, 1210, 2036, 2276.
Miller, Susie, 3141, 3327.
Miller, Taylor, 1209.
Miller, Thomas, 2036.
Miller, Tobias, 533.
Miller, Wilson, 177.
Miller, Zula, 860.
Milley, 1546, 2136.
Millie, 351, 1316, 1319, 1337, 1504, 1895, 2140, 2357, 2436, 2443, 2521, 2795, 2856, 3046, 3270, 3864, 3942, NB1025.
Millie, Annie, 884.
Milloche, 2806, NB1147.
Milter, 1306.
Minda, 2843.
Mingo, 832, 920, 2145.
Mingo, Aggie, 1795, NB711.
Mingo, Bessie, NB711.
Mingo, Bettie, 832.
Mingo, Billy, 1795.
Mingo, Carrie, 832, NB686.
Mingo, Goulay 564.
Mingo, Irene, 833, NB985.
Mingo, Joe, 667.
Mingo, John, 3205.
Mingo, Joseph, 408, 832, 833, 1795, NB711, NB985.
Mingo, Josie, 3205.
Mingo, Louisana, 832, 408.
Mingo, Louisanna, 408, 832.
Mingo, Lousana, 833, 667.

358

Mingo, Lousanna, 667, 833.
Mingo, Louella, 831.
Mingo, Monroe, 1795.
Mingo, Narbe, 920.
Mingo, R. J., 833.
Mingo, Robert J., 833, NB985.
Mingo, Warner, 831.
Mingo, Youpehake, 833.
Minna, 77, 3337.
Minnechar, 100, 1566, 1594.
Minter, Bertie, NB97
Minter, Coachman, 55.
Minter, Douglas, 55.
Minter, Harry, 55.
Minter, John, 55.
Minter, Marcus S., 55.
Minter, Mark, 55, NB97.
Minter, Millie, 55.
Minter, Rupert, 55.
Minter, Thelma Agnes, NB97.
Minton, Ada, NB114.
Minton, Aurelia, 306, NB114.
Minton, Chaine, NB114.
Minton, Chaney, 306.
Minton, Ida Amelia, 306, NB114.
Minton, Jarritt O , 306.
Minton, Malven, 306.
Minton, Nona, 306.
Minugh, Alice V., 2006, NB740.
Minugh, C. E., 2006, NB740.
Minugh, Clarence E., 2006, NB740.
Minugh, Daisy Lee, 2006.
Minugh, Jesse L., NB740.
Minus, John, 162.
Minus, Vicey, 162.
Miska, 2403.
Missah, 384.
Misseb, 1524.
"Missie", 3274.
Missouri, Davis, 997.
Missouri, Fox, 997.
Missouri, Nellie, 997.
Misteothle, 318.
Mitchell, Addie, 1385, NB322.
Mitchell, Aggie, 3059.
Mitchell, Albert, 1220, NB1132.
Mitchell, Amy, M471.
Mitchell, Anna, 1624.
Mitchell, Ben, 2865.
Mitchell, Bettie, 2959, NB859, M349, M350, M351.
Mitchell, Billie, 2959, NB859, M349, M350, M351.
Mitchell, Bittie, 2959, NB859,M349,M350,M351
Mitchell, Bunnie, 2865.
Mitchell, Cheparney, 3927.
Mitchell, Dan, 2354.
Mitchell, Eliza, 3741.
Mitchell, Emma, 2739.
Mitchell, Enoch, 1370.
Mitchell, Firsey, M350.
Mitchell, Francis, 2043.
Mitchell, Hannah, 407, 1370, 1417, 1421, 2117, 3741.
Mitchell, Hettie, M349.
Mitchell, Joseph, NB1133.
Mitchell, Levi, 1220.
Mitchell, Lewis, 1301, 2959, NB859, M349, M350, M351.
Mitchell, Louvina, 2865.

Mitchell, Mack, 1385.
Mitchell, Mandy, 2739, 3927, M471.
Mitchell, Melesie, 1220.
Mitchell, Mintie, 1421.
Mitchell, Monroe, 1385.
Mitchell, Morris, NB859.
Mitchell, Moses, 2959.
Mitchell, Nancy, 2354, 2865, 3081.
Mitchell, Nellie, NB1133.
Mitchell, Peggie, 2286, NB1132.
Mitchell, Rachel, 1421.
Mitchell, Sam, 1370, 1417, 1421, 2611, 2613, NB1133.
Mitchell, Sally, 1220.
Mitchell, Sarwenoge, 3741.
Mitchell, Selanie, M351.
Mitchell, Selina, 2739.
Mitchell, Severs, 1301.
Mitchell, Sissie, 2354, 3927.
Mitchell, Soloman, 2959.
Mitchell, Waitie, 2739, 3927, M471.
Mitchell, Wattie, 2739, 3927, M471.
Mitchell, Willie, NB1132.
Mitchelly, 2812.
Mitchey, 42.
Mitiagne, 1045, 1795, 2093.
Mitiague, 1045, 1795, 2093.
Mittewaky, 622.
Mittilahke, 1809.
Mocknarlee, 21.
Mockta, 2127.
Moffer, Eliza, 1436, NB912.
Moffer, Waitie, 2792, NB912.
Moffer, Wilson, NB912.
Moffitt, Annie, 3331.
Moka, Tom, 2736.
Molitche, 1534.
Mollesy, 2926.
Mollie, 18, 102, 159, 733, 1568, 2472, 2474, 2543, 2727, 2866, 2968.
Mollieanna, 1800.
Mollier, 1309.
Molloche, 1927, 2637.
Molone, Billy, 666.
Molone, Louisa, 666, NB10.
Molone, Sissie, 666.
Molone, Wattie, 666.
Monack, Mary, 1818.
Monadege, 3328.
Monadezie, 2108.
Monah, 187.
Monahwee, Cynda, 2194, NB1166.
Monahwee, David, 2004, 2194, 2241.
Monahwee, Ella, 2004, NB1166.
Monahwee, John, 1701, 2194, NB1166.
Monahwee, Miley, 2004, 2241.
Monahwee, Millie, 2194.
Monahwee, Minnie, 1704.
Monahwee, Sambo, 2194.
"Monarye", 3287.
Monaye, 3814.
Monday, 884, 1708, 2526.
Monday, Annie, NB1213.
Monday, Edna, NB1212.
Monday, Haga, 2526.
Monday, Jackson Louis, 329.
Monday, Jennetta, 884.
Monday, Lizzie, Seminole 1648, NB1212, NB1213.
Monday, March, 329, 884, NB1212, NB1213.

Monday, Martin, 884.
Monday, McKinley, 329.
Monday, Teakah, 1708.
Monday, Tookah, 2526.
Monecha, 2636.
Monie, 2498.
Monk, George, 849.
Monk, Nancy, 849.
Monkey, 1011.
Monnawee, David, 555.
Monnetta, 2842.
Monni, 103.
Monochagee, 1359.
Montarly, 1440.
Montgall, Lizzie E., 788.
Montgomery, Alfred, 3577.
Montgomery, Bessie, 296, 3577.
Montgomery, Eliza, 296.
Montgomery, George, 296.
Montgomery, George B., 3577.
Montgomery, Hattie, 296.
Montgomery, Henry, 3577.
Montgomery, Josie Belle, 296.
Montgomery, Thomson, 296.
Moody, 342.
Moon, Johnnie, 1312, 1313.
Moonie, Sallie, 1180, 1186.
Moore, 2494.
Moore, Ada V., 1327.
Moore, Albert, 576, NB358, M389.
Moore, Annie, 1432.
Moore, Bessie, 2031.
Moore, Bob, 1327, NB1231.
Moore, Carr Orlando, M95.
Moore, Carrie, 576.
Moore, Elizza, M389.
Moore, Georgiana, 1327.
Moore, Haney, 2031, 3574, NB379.
Moore, Heney, 2031, NB379.
Moore, James, 3574.
Moore, Jessie Susan, NB1231.
Moore, Jim, 576.
Moore, John, NB379.
Moore, John R., 327.
Moore, John W., 2031, 3574.
Moore, Julie, 478.
Moore, Leah, 576, M389, NB358.
Moore, Limon, 478.
Moore, Linney, 478.
Moore, Lizzie, 327, 450, 478, 1303, 1327.
Moore, Lola, 218.
Moore, Lucy, 59.
Moore, Lydia A., 309, M95.
Moore, Mamie, 463.
Moore, Mark, 450.
Moore, Mark R., M95.
Moore, Martha, 327.
Moore, Mary, NB1231.
Moore, Matilda, M396.
Moore, Mattie, 478.
Moore, Moses, 478, 1303, 1327.
Moore, Napoleon B., 59.
Moore, Noah, 218.
Moore, Oliver Lee, 1327.
Moore, Phillip, 2031.
Moore, Robert, 1327, NB1231.
Moore, Robert Lee, 1327.
Moore, Rosa, 478.
Moore, Saltie, 2244.
Moore, Susan, 327, 576.

Moore, Susie, NB358.
Moore, Thomas, 478.
Moore, Thomas J., 1327, M396.
Moore, Verna Ellen, 1327.
Moore, Winnie, 1327.
Moore, Winnie Mary, M396.
Moore, Wm., 59.
Moore, Wm. N., 327.
Moore, Wright, 327.
Morey, 181
Morey, Anson, 681.
Morey, Calley D., 681, 1018, 121
Morey, George W., 681.
Morey, Jacob, 181.
Morey, Samuel, 681.
Morey, Tally D., 681.
Morey, Wm., 681, 1018, 1021.
Morgan, Chilly W., 227.
Morgan, Edith M., 227.
Morgan, Edwin L., 227.
Morgan, Fannie, 1984.
Morgan, Florence, 227.
Morgan, Frank, 1984.
Morgan, Lawrence, 227.
Morgan, Leona P., 1984.
Morgan, Lizzie, 227.
Morgan, Luther F., 1984.
Morgan, Milly, 227.
Morgan, Ranny M., 227.
Morris, C. D., 3062.
Morris, Cheparney, 336.
Morris, Emma, 336.
Morris, Henry, 79, 129.
Morris, Ollie May, 3062.
Morris, Pearl Garland, 3062.
Morris, Peggy, 79, 129.
Morris, Susan, 336.
Morris, Susanna, 3062.
Morrison, A., 255.
Morrison, Addie, 1876.
Morrison, Ananias, 265.
Morrison, Anannias R., 257.
Morrison, Andrew Jackson, M32.
Morrison, Bessie, 255.
Morrison, Bluford, 255.
Morrison, Carrie, NB717.
Morrison, Duffey, 258.
Morrison, Eliza, 1352, NB839, M32.
Morrison, Ellen, 1353.
Morrison, Ennis, 258.
Morrison, Ernest, NB643.
Morrison, Felix G., 3671.
Morrison, Hence, 947, 3654, NB643, NB644.
Morrison, Henry, 255, 257, 258.
Morrison, Hettie Jane, NB644.
Morrison, Hettie Ola, NB717.
Morrison, J. C., 3671.
Morrison, Jeremiah C., 255.
Morrison, Jerry, 258.
Morrison, John, 815, 947, 1353, 2879.
Morrison, John, Jr., 815, M30.
Morrison, John, Sr., 815, 816, 817.
Morrison, Julia, NB972, NB973.
Morrison, Lena, 1754, NB653, M30.
Morrison, Lily, 3654.
Morrison, Louisa, 815, 816, 817, 947, 1353, 3896.
Morrison, Luke, 947.
Morrison, Lula Mildred, NB972.
Morrison, Major, 815, NB717.
Morrison, Manny, 815, NB972, NB973.

Morrison, Martha, 255, 258.
Morrison, Mary, 255, 815, 3671, NB839.
Morrison, Nancy, 947, 3654, NB643, NB644.
Morrison, Nicotia, 815.
Morrison, Sallie, 258.
Morrison, Sally, 257.
Morrison, Stan Watie, NB973.
Morrison, Tully, M30.
Morrison, Waitie, 1353, NB839, M32.
Morrison, Waity, 3896.
Morrison, Watie, 1876.
Morrow, Alfred M., 359, M360, NB413.
Morrow, Elva, NB413.
Morrow, Jesse, M359.
Morrow, Lester, M360.
Morrow, Marsey, 392, M359, M360, NB413.
Morton, Airy Ethel, 1129.
Morton, Annie, 1601.
Morton, Austin A., 86.
Morton, Benjamin H., 86.
Morton, Clarence, 1377.
Morton, Claude S., NB405.
Morton, Delilah, 499, 534, 1219, 1330, 1377, 1378, 1379, 1601.
Morton, Ellis, 1377.
Morton, Ellis M., NB696.
Morton, George F., 1129.
Morton, Irene, 1601.
Morton, J. C., NB499.
Morton, Joan, 1129, NB214, M229.
Morton, Joanna, 1129, NB214, M229.
Morton, Joseph, 86.
Morton, Joseph L., 86.
Morton, Josie A., NB405, NB696.
Morton, Felora, 1378.
Morton, Leo Britt, NB602.
Morton, Martha L., 499.
Morton, Mattie, 86, NB499.
Morton, Minnie May, 86.
Morton, Mittie B., NB602.
Morton, Mossie, 1330, NB305, NB696.
Morton, Okland, NB499.
Morton, Osborn A., 534, NB602.
Morton, Oscar M., 499.
Morton, Perry K., 1601.
Morton, Richard L., 499.
Morton, Roy H., 499.
Morton, Roy Ray, NB214.
Morton, Stanton R., 499.
Morton, Thomas, 1129, NB214, M229.
Morton, Thomas Allen, M229.
Morton, Tucker W., 499.
Morton, Walter W., 1379.
Morton, William, 499, 534, 1219, 1330, 1377, 1378, 1379, 1601.
Morton, William Arthur, 86.
Morton, William P., 1219.
Morton, William V., 499.
Moses, Willie, 2862, 3001.
Mosey, 1314, 1492, 2995.
Mosquito, Albert, 587, NB382, M287.
Mosquito, Big, 1949, 3689.
Mosquito, Ira, M287.
Mosquito, Jensey Big, 3689.
Mosquito, Katie, NB382.
Mosquito, Polly, 606, NB382, M287.
Motahle, 2181.
Mothlachee, 1556.
Mothliche, 1962.
Mothoye, 1598.

Mothyoyetchee, 2378.
Motley, Chewey, 2059.
Motlie, 222.
Moulton, Mose, 1109.
Mowelagee, 2648.
Mowelahke, 248.
Muckey, Sarah, 1092.
Muckner, 1536.
Mukes, Ada, NB778.
Mukes, Alex., 1179.
Mukes, Alice, 1179, 3698, NB777, NB778.
Mukes, Hattie, NB777.
Mukes, Joseph, 3698.
Mukes, Maggie, 1178.
Mukes, Thomas, 3698, NB777, NB778.
Mukes, Tom, 1178, 1179.
Mulga, 2747.
Mulgussie, 2203.
Mulgussie, Cinda, 2203.
Mulgussie, Lucy, 2203.
Mulkersy, 2174.
Mulkusee, Sente, 3050.
Mulleana, 397.
Mulleanna, 2921.
Mullen, Celestie, 796.
Mulley, 2195.
Mullie, 751, 1528, 3025, M453.
Mullie, Phenie, 3025.
Mullie, Sallie, 3025, M419.
Mullie, Sam, 3025.
Mullie, Siah, 3025.
Mullie, Willie, 3025.
Mully, Barney, CE4039.
Mully, Fannie, CE4039.
Mully, Jennie, CE4039.
Mully, Katie, CE4039.
Mully, Mitchell, CE4039.
Mully, Simon, CE4039.
Mulsey, 2894.
Munihoche, 2202.
Munna, 1715, 1718, 1727.
Muntloope, 3961.
Munzey, 213.
Murphy, Augustus, 57.
Murphy, Blanch, NB189.
Murphy, Catherine, 3710.
Murphy, C. M., 22, 749, 1959.
Murphy, Conny, 57, 2270, 3710, NB189.
Murphy, Conny, Jr., 57.
Murphy, C. W., 22, 749, 1959.
Murphy, Eliza, 22, 749, 1959.
Murphy, Eliza J., 57, 749.
Murphy, Eliza Jane, 57.
Murphy, Eva Dorcas, NB50.
Murphy, Mattie, 57.
Murphy, Nettie, NB50.
Murphy, N. P., 1959.
Murphy, Richard L., 3710.
Murphy, Robert, 57.
Murphy, Sallie, 57.
Murphy, Sarah, 57, 2270, 3710.
Murphy, Sarah R., NB189.
Murphy, William S., 49, NB50.
Murray, Ada, 782, NB716, M71.
Murray, A. J., 723, 782, 806, 807.
Murray, Charles E., 806, 3674.
Murray, Clarence Lee, 782.
Murray, Delphie A., 806, 3674.
Murray, Delphine, 806, 3674.
Murray, Gerti May, 806.

361

Murray, Helen, 3370.
Murray, Helen M., NB625.
Murray, Jesse, 782.
Murray, John, ? 370, NB625, M82.
Murray, Lucy, 1395, NB625, M82.
Mutray, Margaret Mary, M82.
Murray, Martha, 723, 782, 806, 807.
Murray, Nettie Belle, 3674.
Murray, Ruth, 3370.
Murray, W. B., 3370.
Murray, Whig, 3370.
Murray, William, 3370.
Murray, William A., 806.
Murrell, Calhoun, Cr. Frd., 3460, NB310.
Murrell, Crawford, 489.
Murrell, Louisa, 489.
Murrell, Lucy, 489, NB310.
Murrell, Sambo, 489.
Murrell, Wiley, NB310.
Muscogee, 1041, 52, 858, 3760.
Musgrove, George, NB296.
Musgrove, Herold D., NB296.
Musgrove, Myrta May, 458, NB296.
Muska, 1868, 2470.
Musker, 2426.
Muskogee, 52, 858, 3760, 1041.
Mustoche, 3368.
Mutalocha, 1555.
Muteloka, 2470.
Mutleloke, 2306.
Mutta, 2152.
Muttellokee, 434.
MutteLoke, 2311.
Mutte Loke, Willie, 2311.
Myers, Betsey, 924, 3738, NB890, NB891.
Myers, Dave, 1654.
Myers, Caroline, 1654.
Myers, Jefferson M., 924.
Myers, Laura M., NB891.
Myers, Lizzie, 1654.
Myers, Minnie L., 924.
Myers, Oscar D., NB890.
Myers, Sallie, 2588..
Myers, William F., 924, 3738, NB890, NB891.
Myers, Willie Frances, 3738.
Mylie, 1892.
McBirney, Dorothy Vera, NB271.
McBirney, James H., NB271.
McBirney, Vera, 952, NB271.
McCalvey, Cornelius, 1395.
McCalvey, Edward, 1395.
McCalvey, Ella, NB341.
McCalvey, Emmit, NB743.
McCalvey, Everett, 1395, NB743.
McValvey, Joseph, 1395, NB341.
McCalvey, Joseph Hiram, NB341.
McCalvey, Lucy, 1395, NB625, M82.
McCalvey, Margaret, 1395.
McCalvey, Nora, NB743.
McGann, Elizabeth, 333, 1039.
McCann, Josie C., 2035, M243.
McCann, Michael, 333, 1039.
McCann, Thomas, 3258.
McCann, W. H., M243.
McCann, William C., M243.
McCaslin, Jennie, 1087, NB510, NB511.
McCaslin, Jessie, 1087.
McCaslin, John, 1087.
McCaslin, May, 1087.
McCaslin, Myrtle, 1087.

McCaslin, Nettie, 1087.
McCaughan, L. Elizabeth, 926.
McCaughan, John, 926.
McCaughan, Nellie, 926.
McCaughan, Minon, 926.
McCaughan, Thomas, 926.
McClosky, Mami M., 1390.
McCombs, Joaeph, 2088.
McCombs, Alice L., 507, NB17.
McCombs, Bessie, 1754.
McCombs, Bettie, 1755.
McCombs, David, 1754, 1759.
McCombs, George W., 1755.
McCombs, James, 1759.
McCombs, Joseph, 1758, 2088.
McCombs, Leah, 1754.
McCombs, Lena, 1754, M30.
McCombs, Marcellus, 2088.
McCombs, Marshall, 409.
McCombs, Millie, 1754, 1759.
McCombs, Mollie, 409.
McCombs, Nathaniel H., NB17.
McCombs, Pollie, 1754.
McCombs, Sally, 1752, 1755, 996, 1756.
McCombs, Sam'l, 1754, 1755, 1758.
McCombs, Sarah, 2775.
McCombs, Susan, 1754, 1755, 1758.
McCombs, Susie, 1755.
McCombs, Tom, 1754.
McCombs, Tooker, 1755, NB885.
McCombs, William, 996, 1755, 1752, 1753, 1756.
McCombs, Wm., Jr., NB17.
McCombs, William P., 1756.
McCombs, Yarna, 409.
McCombs, Yarner, 2088.
McCosar, Alice, M158.
McCosar, Arthur, NB688.
McCosar, Bessie, 2353.
McCosar, Bettie, 1602, 2353.
McCosar, Bunnie, 2353, M258, M190, NB688.
McCosar, Bunny, 1602.
McCosar, Eliza, 2353.
McCosar, Elliott, 2353.
McCosar, Ida, 2353.
McCosar, Katie, 1602.
McCosar, Nellie, 2591, M190, NB688.
McCosar, Solomon, M190.
McCoy, 611, 894, 1277, 2160.
McCoy, Barney, 2160.
McCoy, Burney, 3518.
McCoy, David T., 929.
McCoy, Delphie, 928, 3779, NB752, M132.
McCoy, Henry, 611, NB171.
McCoy, Ida, 61, 3428, NB527, NB528.
McCoy, Israel, 3518.
McCoy, Joe, 1020.
McCoy, Lemuel, 928.
McCoy, Lina, 3779.
McCoy, Liza, 611.
McCoy, Mary, 894.
McCoy, Minnie, 3518.
McCoy, Nettit, NB527.
McCoy, Ollie, NB171.
McCoy, Robert, 1020.
McCoy, Robert Elihu, NB528.
McCoy, Ruthie May, 3428.
McCoy, Sallie Clinton, 578, NB171.
McCoy, Susan, 2160, 3518.
McCoy, Tecumseh, 928, 3779.
McCoy, William A., 3428, NB527, NB528.

McCray, Otto, 1666.
McCray, Tommy, 1666.
McCuen, Mary, 3852.
McCulla, Cheparney, 3168.
McCulla, George, 3168.
McCulla, Mary, 3168.
McCulla, Nancy, 3168.
McCulla, Thomas, 3168.
McCulla, Tulmarsey, 3168.
McCully, John, 1898.
McDermit, Ella Grace, 769.
McDermit, Ella May, 769.
McDermit, Henry, 769.
McDermit, Leona, 769.
McDermit, William, 769.
McDermite, William, 27.
McDermite, Winnie, 27.
McDermott, Allie, NB1.
McDermott, Charlie, NB453.
McDermott, Helen, NB1.
McDermott, Jesse, 392, NB1.
McDermott, Lewis, 3531.
McDermott, L. H., NB452, NB453.
McDermott, Lizzie, NB452.
McDermott, Mary, 1472, 3531, NB452, NB453.
McDermott, Walter, 3531.
McDonald, Edward Ray, NB283.
McDonald, Martin J., NB283.
McDonald, Mattie B., 615, NB283.
McDuff, A. J., 754.
McDuff, Rachel, 834.
McDuff, Sally, 754.
McElroy, Clarence, 1952.
McElroy, Emmett, 1952.
McElroy, Geo. H., 1952.
McElroy, Hattie, 1281.
McElroy, Jennie H., 1281.
McElroy, Joanna, 1952.
McElroy, Oma G., 1281.
McElroy, W. A., 1281.
McFarland, David, 2433.
McFarland, James, 2433, M479, NB856, NB960.
McFarland, Leah, M479.
McFarland, Lena, 2433.
McFarland, Lilly, 2433.
McFarland, Ned, NB856.
McFarland, Sam, 1890.
McFarland, Sarah, 2433.
McFarland, Yancy, NB960.
McFields, Joe, 2159.
McGee, Clarence, 930.
McGee, Cornelia, 930.
McGee, Elizabeth, 857.
McGee, Eulala, 885, M31.
McGee, Frank, 930.
McGee, John W., 857, M31.
McGee, Mary, 930.
McGee, Nancy, 930, M59.
McGee, Princess Aline, M31.
McGee, R. C., 857.
McGee, Richmond, 930.
McGee, Sudie, 930.
McGee, Tamar Belle, 857.
McGee, Walter, 930.
McGeeley, 1681.
McGeeley, Timmie, 1681.
McGertt, Inda, 6, M480.
McGertt, John, 1519, M480.
McGertt, Linda, 1520, NB78, M45.
McGertt, Nathan, M480.

McGilbra, 2948.
McGilbra, Amie, 1680, 2021, 2123.
McGilbra, Amy, 1680, 2021, 2123.
McGilbra, Annie, 2704, NB649.
McGilbra, Barney, 2951.
McGilbra, Capt., 2747.
McGilbra, Cinda, 1680, NB598.
McGilbra, Hailey, 1663.
McGilbra, Hepsey, 2747.
McGilbra, Jackson, NB598.
McGilbra, Jennie, 2331, 2704.
McGilbra, John, 818.
McGilbra, Johny, 818.
McGilbra, Joseph, 1680.
McGilbra, Lettie, 2704.
McGilbra, Lewis, 1680, NB674.
McGilbra, Lizzie, 2033, 2704.
McGilbra, Miley, 1663.
McGilbra, Mistahala, 90.
McGilbra, Sanford, NB674.
McGilbra, Silla, 2948.
McGilbra, Solomon, 1680.
McGilbra, Susie, 3947.
McGilbra, Wiley, 3947.
McGilbra, Winey, 818.
McGilbray, 500, 1961.
McGilbray, Abbie, 3562.
McGilbray, Amy, 1961, 3064.
McGilbray, Captain, 282, 3562.
McGilbray, Daniel, 426, 2466, 2704.
McGilbray, Farsey, 187.
McGilbray, George, 459, NB1234.
McGilbray, Haley, 198.
McGilbray, Hepsey, 426, NB1056.
McGilbray, Jackson, 426, NB1234.
McGilbray, Jennie, 189, 190.
McGilbray, John, 191.
McGilbray, Kattie, 282.
McGilbray, Linda, 188.
McGilbray, Lipscomb, 459.
McGilbray, Lizzie, 282, 426, 2466, 3562.
McGilbray, Louisa, 282.
McGilbray, Lucy, 282.
McGilbray, Melissa, NB598.
McGilbray, Minnie, 282.
McGilbray, Nicey, 3128, NB1234.
McGilpray, Polly, 818.
McGilbray, Rosanna, 1663, 3594.
McGilbray, Rose, 191.
McGilbray, Susie, 459.
McGilbray, Walter, 818.
McGilbray, Wisey, 426, 500.
McGilbry, George, 459, NB678.
McGilbry, George L., 459, NB678.
McGilbry, Laura, NB678.
McGillwary, Daniel, 123.
McGillwary, Lizzie, 123.
McGirt, 1517.
McGirt, Aaron, 3010.
McGirt, Alex, 1434, 1564, 1647, 1651.
McGirt, Bessie, M189.
McGirt, Billy, 1578, 1564, NB719.
McGirt, Buckner, 1651, NB941.
McGirt, Daniel, 1503, 1514, 1520, 1923, 2078, 2096, 3015.
McGirt, Dick, 3015.
McGirt, Emma, 2776, NB719, NB715.
McGirt, George, 3187.
McGirt, Hattie, 2419.
McGirt, Hepsey, 3017.

McGirt, Hepsie, 2096.
McGirt, Isaac, 1923.
McGirt, Jackson, 1646.
McGirt, Jennie, 1923, 3015.
McGirt, Jim, 3187.
McGirt, Jimmie, 2419.
McGirt, John, 1722, 3010, NB941.
McGirt, Lincoln, 1647.
McGirt, Linda, 1651, NB941.
McGirt, Louie, 2419.
McGirt, Loskey, 3187.
McGirt, Lusana, 1646.
McGirt, Mongy, 1722.
McGirt, Robert, 1651.
McGirt, Sodes, 1434.
McGirt, Sodes, 1434.
McGirt, Solomon, 2419.
McGirt, Susie, 1503, 2078.
McGirt, William, 2078, M189.
McGirt, Wisey, 1514, 2096.
McGirth, Houston, 1903.
McGirth, John, 1903.
McGirth, Pollie, 1903.
McGirtt, Billy, 1564, 1578, NB719.
McGirtt, Dora, 1564.
McGirtt, George, NB719.
McGirtt, Sophia, 1564.
McGuire, Eliza, 539, M13.
McGuire, George W., NB40.
McGuire, Louis P., M13.
McGuire, Marcus Wilson, NB40.
McGuire, Oscar H., M13.
McGuire, Sophia, 293, NB40.
McHenry, Abbie, NB90.
McHenry, Bettie, NB91.
McHenry, David, 178.
McHenry, Greely, 178.
McHenry, James, 178, 2978.
McHenry, Jesse, 178.
McHenry, Lewis, 178, NB90, NB91.
McHenry, Lewis, Jr., 178.
McHenry, Rachel, 178.
McHenry, Silla, 178, NB90, NB91.
McIntosh, Abraham, 3241.
McIntosh, A. G., 3263.
McIntosh, Al, 2409.
McIntosh, Alex, 226, 3129.
McIntosh, Alice, 836, NB127.
McIntosh, Allie, 3452.
McIntosh, Annie, 124, 786, 885.
McIntosh, Annie Lila, NB127.
McIntosh, Amos, 661, NB773, NB774.
McIntosh, Annetta, 116.
McIntosh, Arsyno, 785.
McIntosh, August, 936.
McIntosh, Ben, 873.
McIntosh, Ben Dave, 1972.
McIntosh, Bennie, M33.
McIntosh, Ben R., 873.
McIntosh, Bertha, 873, 3717.
McIntosh, Bertha A., NB1015.
McIntosh, Bessie, 835, 2010.
McIntosh, Bessie Lee, 1807.
McIntosh, Bettie, 990.
McIntosh, Bunnie, 2010, NB593.
McIntosh, Catherine, 33.
McIntosh, Charles, 1072, 3717, NB1015.
McIntosh, Charles Curtis, NB1015.
McIntosh, Charles Lee, 1072.
McIntosh, Chessie, NB176.

McIntosh, Chillie, 1807.
McIntosh, Chilly, 2027.
McIntosh, Commodore, 785.
McIntosh, Cora, 226.
McIntosh, Cuffey, 2077.
McIntosh, Daniel, 547, 548.
McIntosh, Daniel M., 547, 548.
McIntosh, Daniel N., 3263.
McIntosh, David, 2554.
McIntosh, David H., 873.
McIntosh, Del, 873.
McIntosh, Delilah, 2893.
McIntosh, Della, 785.
McIntosh, Dick, 2553, NB540, NB1131.
McIntosh, D. N., 544, 836, 885, 1072, 1090, 3263.
McIntosh, D. N., Jr., 836, 3452, NB127.
McIntosh, E. B., 1091.
McIntosh, Edna, 785.
McIntosh, Edith Edna, NB92.
McIntosh, Edith Louise, NB107.
McIntosh, Ella, 3129.
McIntosh, Ellen, 2562, 2295, NB1069.
McIntosh, Emma B., 547, 548.
McIntosh, Etta, 116.
McIntosh, Fannie, 544, 3365, NB176, NB177.
McIntosh, Eulala, 885, M31.
McIntosh, Freeland, 885, 3263, 3293, 3524, NB107
McIntosh, Freeland B., 885, 3263, 3293, 3524, NB107.
McIntosh, George, 1097.
McIntosh, Grace, 873.
McIntosh, Greely, 2409.
McIntosh, Hannah Vera, 836.
McIntosh, Hannie, 661.
McIntosh, Hector, 544.
McIntosh, Henry, 2554.
McIntosh, Hepsey, 1965, 2554.
McIntosh, Ida, NB540.
McIntosh, Ida M., NB612.
McIntosh, Iona, 785.
McIntosh, Isaiah J., NB531.
McIntosh, Jane, 544, 885.
McIntosh, Jane E., 836, 3263.
McIntosh, Jemima, 785.
McIntosh, Jennette, 140, 1807, NB593.
McIntosh, Jewel, 990.
McIntosh, Jim, 805, 3241, 3396.
McIntosh, Job, 2027.
McIntosh, John, 115, 116, 140, 226, 661, 785, 990, 1901, 2027, 2110, 2196, 2296, 2553, 2602, NB531.
McIntosh, John D., 873.
McIntosh, John Granville, NB1069.
McIntosh, John R., 3365.
McIntosh, Julia, 990.
McIntosh, Kate, 885, 990, 3524, NB92, NB93, NB107.
McIntosh, Katie, 673, 1072.
McIntosh, Kitty, M33.
McIntosh, Kogee, 2196.
McIntosh, Laura Bonnie, M60.
McIntosh, Leah, 1807, 2010, 2183, 2554, 3618, M33, NB593.
McIntosh, Leona, 1807, NB612.
McIntosh, Leonie, 1807, NB612.
McIntosh, Lewis, 3758.
McIntosh, L. G., 1807, NB612.
McIntosh, Liza, 3728.
McIntosh, Lizzie, 785, 873, 2554, NB739.

McIntosh, Waldoe E., 3263.
McIntosh, Walley, 661.
McIntosh, Walter, 2902.
McIntosh, Wanda Wynona, M60.
McIntosh, William, 226, 673, 1077, 3524.
McIntosh, William C., 873.
McIntosh, William Yancey, 547.
McIntosh, Willie, 3524, 226, 673, 1077.
McIntosh, Wm. R., 786, 3758, NB1069.
McIntosh, W. F., 124, 990, 1986.
McIntosh, Winnie, 873, 877, 1046, 1072, 1620.
McIntosh, Wisey, 2077, 3241, 3396.
McIntosh, Zolena Kaniah, 547.
McIntosh, Xenophon, 548.
McKan, George, NB1045.
McKan, Hepsey, 1624, NB1045.
McKan, James, 1624.
McKan, John, 1624, NB1045.
McKan, Sukey, 1624.
McKane, Hepsey, 3898.
McKane, John, 3898.
McKane, William, 3898.
McKellop, 1452.
McKellop, Albert P., 110.
McKellop, Alena, 110, 259, 1531.
McKellop, Alice, 3611.
McKellop, Almarine E., 1302, 3611.
McKellop, Annie, 110, 1302, 1531.
McKellop, Arthur A., 110.
McKellop, Barney, 110.
McKellop, Betsey, 2623, 3514, M234, NB98.
McKellop, Cherokee, 1531, M131.
McKellop, Effie, 1531.
McKellop, Eliza, 208, NB79, M96.
McKellop, Grace, 1302.
McKellop, Hattie, 3611.
McKellop, Hattie S., 1302.
McKellop, James, 1302, 1531.
McKellop, James E., 1302.
McKellop, James M., 110.
McKellop, Joseph, 259.
McKellop, Joseph M., 110, 1531.
McKellop, Louisa, NB98.
McKellop, Lucinda, 1452.
McKellop, Lydia, M234.
McKellop, Minnie, 259.
McKellop, Peter, 237, 3514, M234, NB98.
McKellop, Robert, 398.
McKellop, Ruth A., 1302.
McKellop, Sallie, 1531.
McKellop, Thomas, 1531.
McKellop, Wilson, 208, 237, 3514.
McKellop, Yarnah, 237.
McKim, Fannie Maree, 3569.
McKim, Hattie, 618.
McKim, Maggie, 618.
McKim, Minnie G., 3569, NB432.
McKim, Robert A., 944, 3569, NB432.
McKim, Robert M., 944.
McKim, W. A., 618, 650, 944, 1121.
McKim, William, 1121, 618, 650, 944.
McKim, William A., 618.
McKim, Willie Byno, NB432.
McKinney, Albert, 1711.
McKinney, Anna B., 1712.
McKinney, Hepsey, 1598.
McKinney, John A., 1712.
McKinney, Roley, 1598.
McKinney, Russell, 1112, 1711, 1712.
McKinney, Sadie C., 1712.

5.
77.

B92,

365

McKinney, Sam, 1598, 1599.
McKinney, Susan, 1112, 1711,·1712.
McKinney, Susie, 1598.
McKinney, Unah, 1599.
McKinnon, Amanda S., 54, NB209.
McKinnon, Lila Belle, NB209.
McKinnon, R. W., NB209.
McLemore, Charlotte, 861.
McLemore, James, 861.
McLish, Sallie, 1077.
McMinn, Annie, 694.
McNac, Albert, 305.
McNac, Alex, 305.
McNac, Alice, 305, NB777, NB778.
McNac, Annie, 136, 3440, M481, NB407.
McNac, Bettie, NB902.
McNac, Cully, 1829, 2215.
McNac, Dave, 392, 393, 3202.
McNac, Dicey, 305, 392, 393.
McNac, Dick, 725.
McNac, Elic, 1806.
McNac, Ellen, 133.
McNac, Emma, 134, M428, NB902.
McNac, Flossie, NB407.
McNac, Fred, 136, 3440, NB407, M481.
McNac, Hallie, M428.
McNac, John, 2490.
McNac, Johnny, 2356.
McNac, Joseph, M447.
McNac, Julia, 134.
McNac, Katie, M397.
McNac, Leah, 1829, 2215.
McNac, Lena, 1829.
McNac, Lizzie, M481.
McNac, Louie, 426.
McNac, Lousanna, 393, M447, NB82, NB83.
McNac, Martha, 393.
McNac, Marcy, NB83.
McNac, Mary, 305.
McNac, Mollie, 725.
McNac, Mulsey, 2272.
McNac, Myrtie, 305.
McNac, Nannie, 2356.
McNac, Parney, 393.
McNac, Peter, 393, 2272, M447, NBS2, NB83.
McNac, Phillip, 2356, M397, NB1076.
McNac, Robert, 136.
McNac, Robinson, 134, Creek Frd., 1242, M428, NB902.
McNac, Sam, 133, 2490.
McNac, Sandy, 2327.
McNac, Susie, 2215.
McNac, Tommie, 393.
McNac, Tullie, NB1076.
McNac, Vicey, 1806.
McNac, Wallace, 305.
McNac, Wallace C., 1806.
McNac, William McKinley, 3440.
McNac, Wisey, 138, M397, NB1076.
McNack, Aaron, 1183.
McNack, Aleck, 1177, 1183.
McNack, Alex, 1178, 1179, 1183.
McNack, Berry, 1177.
McNack, Caroline, 1177, 1178, 1179, 1183.
McNack, Charley, 1178, 2327.
McNack, Dicey, 818.
McNack, Dick, 1178.
McNack, Mollie, 1178.
McNack, Rosana, 1178, NB684, NB685.
McNack, Shawnee, 1178.

McNack, Stella, 1178.
McNally, Belle, 1451.
McNally, Cassie, 1451, M119.
McNally, Mack, 1451.
McNally, N. N., 1451.
McNally, Samuel, 1451.
McNally, Susan, 1451, 2228.
McNally, V. N., 2228.
McNevins, 1455·
McNevins, Andrew S., 1455.
McNevins, Flora, NB558.
McNevins, George Dewey, 1455.
McNevins, Lee, 1455, NB557, NB558.
McNevins, Nancy, 1455, NB557, NB558.
McNevins, Willie Clay, NB557.
McNulty, Annie, 579.
McNulty, Beulah, 579.
McNulty, Cherokee, 579.
McNulty, George W., 579.
McNulty, Jeff, 579.
McNulty, John, 579.
McNulty, Lena, 579.
McNulty, Maude M., 579.
McNulty, Thomas J., 579.
McNulty, Wanney, 579.
McPerryman, 2495, NB554, NB555.
McPerryman, Celia, 2495.
McPerryman, Eli, NB555.
McPerryman, Lewis, NB554.
McPerryman, Sophia, NB554, NB555.
McQuarie, Alice, 3284.
McQuarie, John Harold, 3284.
McQuarie, Ray Lee, 3284.
McQueen, Dave, 778, 2394, 2639.
McQueen, David, 2639, 778, 2394.
McQueen, Harnie, 2394.
McQueen, James, 778.
McQueen, Keno, 2042.
McQueen, Nancy, 3943.
McQueen, Sarah, 778.
McQueen, Sophia, 1404.
McQueen, Tena, 1648.
McQueen, Willie, 2639, 3943.
McRay, Belizora, 1087.
McRay, Frank, 1087.
McWilliams, Hannah, 2157.
McWilliams, Miley, 1818.
McWilliams, Thomas, 1818, 2157.
Nachakee, 1248.
Nadahee, 2276.
Nafage, 2828.
Nagee, 1042.
Naguftache, 2882.
Naharkey, 1365.
Naharkey, Martha, NB126.
Naharkey, Millie, 1365, NB126.
Naharkey, Moses, 1365, NB126.
Naharkey, Sammie, 1365.
Naharkey, Wehiley, 1365.
Nail, 290, 728.
Nail, Adam, 975.
Nail, Cornelius, 975.
Nail, James, 728.
Nail, Joe, 1174.
Nail, Sally, 290.
Nakaney, 3274.
Nakaney, Jennie, 3274.

367

Newton, Samantha E., 3780.
Newton, Sarah E., 793, NB462, NB463.
Newton, Sarah Elizabeth, 793, NB462, NB463.
Newton, Sir Isaac, 3870.
Newton, Valley Ruth, 793.
Newton, Vera S., 3870.
Niccatoya, 2879.
Nicey, 65, 450, 980, 2705, 2867, 3052, 3063.
Nichols, Emma, 3028, 3465, NB30.
Nichols, Grace Alva, 3465.
Nichols, Leo Carlton, NB30.
Nichols, S. F., 3465, NB30.
Nichols, Steve F., 3465, NB30.
Nichols, William B., 3028.
Nidy, 2857.
Niggie, 2285.
Nightska, 3343.
Nimhoktee, 1631.
Ninnee, 999, 1008.
Nitketa, 1041.
Nivins, Jessie, 1830, NB113, M91.
Nivins, Willie, 1830.
Noble, Annie V. 1662.
Noble, J. H., 1662.
Noble, Lucile, 1662.
Noble, Mariah, 2020.
Noble, Minnie, 1982.
Noble, Myrtle, 1662.
Noble, Susan, 2853.
Noble, Wesley, 2853.
Nocha, Jack, 884.
Nocihe, 2744.
Nocoseloche, 2471.
Nocosemarthla, 1137.
Nocoska, 3013.
Nocosse, 2599.
Nocuseka, 2742.
Nocusille, 2235,
Nogaska, 1504.
Nokeche, 2846.
Nokehche, 1687.
Nokose, 1328, 2929, 2930.
Nokosee, 2929, 2930, 1328.
Nokoseka, 326, 1068, 159.
Nokoseke, 159, 326, 1068.
Nolan, Henry,162.
Nolan, Isaac. 162.
Nolan, James, 162.
Nolan, Martha Ann Eliz., 162.
Nolan, Sarah Jane, 162.
Nolan, Thomas Jefferson, 162.
Nolen, Jesse, 1020.
Nolen, Lee, 1020.
Nolen, Lucy, 929, 1020.
Nolen, Samuel, 1020.
Nolen, William, 1020.
Noon, Alex, 3508.
Noon, Annie, 1339, 1617.
Noon, Billy, 1339, 1403, 1617, 1638, 1656, 1933.
Noon, Fisher, 1617.
Noon, Hepsey, 1656.
Noon, James, 3508.
Noon, Jim, 1339.
Noon, Louisa, NB697.
Noon, Lucinda, NB697.
Noon, Martha, 1617.
Noon, Nathan, 1339.
Noon, Palmer, 1617.
Noon, Sophia, 3508, 1339.
Noon, Sophie, 1339, 3508.

Noon, Wiley, 1638, NB697.
Norbe, 2984, 3792, NB1136.
Norman, Caroline, 3316.
Norman, Navelle, 784.
Norman, Novella, 712.
Norman, Rosa A., 3315, 3317, 3316.
Norman, Rosa Alabama, 3316, 3315, 3317.
Norman, W. G , 712, 784.
Norman, Wesley G., 784, 712.
Nosey, 1362, 1372, 1442, 1932.
Notchee, 6.
Nothohye, 1833.
Nuba, Micco, 2795.
Nubba, Micco, 1149.
Nubbe, Hutche, 2830.
Nubbie, George, 1361, NB1235, NB957.
Nubbie, George W., 1361, NB957, NB1235.
Nubbie, Harley, NB957, NB1235.
Nubbie, Malissa, 3836.
Nubbie, Robert, NB957.
Nubbie, Sophia, NB957, NB1235.
Nubbie, Wilson, 3836.
Nuchaka, 1262.
Nufky, 3175, 3176.
Nukmellee, 1051.
Nukmellee, Meshaney, 1051.
Nukmellee, Rosa, 1051.
Nukmellee, Willie, 1051.
Numpsey, 3040.
Nunochee, 2156, 3329.
Nuppa, Micco, 2419.
Nupper, Micco, 2357.
Nupper, Millie, 2357.
Nutwoche, 3294.
Oatkey, Alice, 741.
O'Brien, Albert Victor, 261.
O'Brien, Thomas, 261.
Oche, Joilly, 1970.
Oclayache, 1524.
Ocloosie, 2697.
Oclossie, 2464, 2796.
Ocolekcke, 2982.
Odache, 2185.
Offutt, Bessie, 1197.
Offutt, J. W., 1197.
Offutt, Minnie, 1197.
Offutt, Raymond, 1197.
Ogee, 1301.
Ogeeleesawa, 146.
Ogeeseh, 3172.
Ogeisie, 2235.
Ohcunda, 1544.
Ohhahoye, 2695.
Ohlepasa, 1439.
Ohme, 211.
Ohme, Sabse, 2325.
Okautina, 75.
Okchunobiyee, 1359.
Okchunpulla, M477.
Okfuskee, 3192.
Okhuskochee, 2986.
Okkumo, 881.
Oklabesar, 1468.
Oklarney, 182.
Oklosachupco, 2516.
Oklossie, 2796.
Okowelahgee, 1840.
Okpethlonay, 606.
Oktootche, 2692.
Okunda, 2845.

Olageskee, 2333.
Old Sands, 1840.
Oliver, Frank, NB216.
Oliver, Hattie Sarty, 253, NB216.
Oliver, Louis, NB216.
Ollieseja, 2465.
Oneka, 414.
Onuffer, 2289.
Orcutt, A. D., 3441, NB11.
Orcutt, Adaline, 558, 3441, NB11, M83.
Orcutt, Adolphus D., M83.
Orcutt, Alvin, 558.
Orcutt, Annie, 558.
Orcutt, Annie B., 1305, 3587, M266.
Orcutt, Archibald M., 1305.
Orcutt, Christina, 558.
Orcutt, David, 558.
Orcutt, Dolph, 558.
Orcutt, Elam, 558.
Orcutt, Guy R., NB11.
Orcutt, Homer A., 1305.
Orcutt, Lela M., 3587.
Orcutt, Ollie, 558.
Orcutt, Pearlie, M83.
Orcutt, Pleasant E., 1305.
Orcutt, S. A., 1305, 3587, M266.
Orcutt, William A., 1305.
Orcutt, William McKinley, 3441.
Orcutt, Winnie M., M266.
Orey, 2558, 2559, 2560.
Osah, Solomon, 1884.
Osawah, 2833.
Osawah, George, NB637.
Osawah, Melissa (or Crow), 3340, NB637.
Oscahola, 14.
Osier, Estes, 1026.
Ossetame, 1575.
Oswalt, C. D., 738.
Oswalt, Marion W., 738.
Oswalt, Mary E., 738.
Oswalt, Nancy, 738.
Oswalt, William M., 738.
Otokka, 2342.
Ottawa, 2884.
Owen, Chauncey A., 3729, 3941.
Owen, Clarence, 3941.
Owen, Martha, 1153, 3729, 3941.
Owen, Mary, 438, 454, 1687.
Owen, Mary Severs, 827.
Owen, Myrtle, 1687.
Owen, Pearl, 1687.
Owen, Samuel, 1687.
Owens, Addie, 3729.
Owens, Albert Poage, 3729.
Owens, C. A., 1687, 3729, 3941.
Owens, Elva, 3729, M314, M434.
Owens, Ollie M., 3729.
Owens, Martha, 1153, 3729, 3941.
Owens, Mary, 438, 454, 1687.
Owens, Nellie, M434.
Oyekitche, 2585, 2587.
Pacananney, 51.
Pachaney, 2421, 2985.
Paconthla, 2261.
Pacoweney, 2784.
Pahcahney, 2421, 2985.
Pahcoquah, 2308.
Pahhe, 252.
Pahose, Chake, 2399.
Pahoseyahola, Bennie, NB1273.

Pahoseyahola, John, 2464.
Pahoseyahola, Josie, 2464, NB1273.
Pahoseyahola, Lodie, 2464.
Pahoseyahola, Soutka, 2464, NB1273.
Paine, Eliza, 2684.
Painkiller, Peter, 2259.
Pakoska, Jennie, 495, NB1119.
Pakoska, Lewis, 1788, NB1117.
Pakoska, Liza, 1788.
Pakoska, Lucy, 1788.
Pakoska, Noah, 1788.
Pakoska, Winford, NB119.
Palmer, 1605, 2601, 3153.
Palmer, Daniel, NB196.
Palmer, David, 3528.
Palmer, Eliza, 23, NB195, NB196.
Palmer, Ella, NB564.
Palmer, Jack Frost, M167.
Palmer, James, M167.
Palmer, James W., NB195.
Palmer, Jennie, 2263.
Palmer, Jim, NB564.
Palmer, John W., NB195, NB196.
Palmer, Lucy, 1605, 2601.
Palmer, Malinda, 2601.
Palmer, Mary, 2263, 3528, NB564, M167.
Palmer, Tom, 2263, 3528.
Palmer, Watty A., 1605.
Panoska, 105.
Panoska, Allie, 106.
Panoske, 2205.
Panoske, Andy, 2205.
Panoske, Daniel, 2205, M450, M451.
Panoske, Lydia, M450.
Panoske, Melsey, 2205, M450, M451.
Panoske, Penie, M451.
Panoske, Susan, 2205.
Panoske, Wagey, 2205.
Panoskey, 2482.
Panoskey, Lydia, 2482.
Panoskey, Tom, 3052.
Pantany, 2262, 2416.
Panter, Jemima, 1724, NB537, M159.
Pantoney, 400.
Paquain, 2783.
Parcheneya, 2459.
Parcinda, 2599.
Parheche, 1224.
Parhose, 1440, 1441, 2181.
Parhose, Jennie, 1441.
Parhosey, 1280.
Parhosey, Jemima, 1280.
Parkany, 605.
Parkee, 3064.
Parker, Catherine, 748.
Parker, Charles Edward, NB151.
Parker, Jessie, 2557, NB151.
Parker, Martha, 4019.
Parker, William E., NB151.
Parkinson, Jennie, 1019.
Parkinson, Jim, 598.
Parkinson, Jonathan, 1019.
Parks, Chaney, 3815.
Parks, Dora Ellen, NB190.
Parks, Fannie, 3815.
Parks, Fronie, 3815.
Parks, Julius, 3815.
Parks, Margaret Atkins, 3781, 3815, NB290, M293.
Parks, Rosetta, M293.

Parks, William, 3815, NB290, M293.
Parlie, 1674.
Farney, 1315, 1407.
Parnoche, 3220.
Parnockey, Sarah, 3158.
Parnoche, Lizzie, 3220.
Parnosk, Rosanna, 2491.
Parnoskey, 3105.
Parnoskie, Barnoge, 3052.
Parnosky, 938, 2491, 2492.
Parnosky, Cheparney, NB1104.
Parnosky, Cindy, NB1103.
Parnosky, Minnie, 2491.
Parnosky, Noah, 2491.
Parnosky, Salina, 2491, NB1103, NB1104.
Parnosky, Sarah, 1780.
Parnosky, Willie, 2491, NB1103, NB1104.
Parsachkee, 1542.
Parskover, 1307, 2566, 2581.
Partahkazolee, 2984.
Partaka, Dickey, 1418.
Partaka, Liza, 1418.
Partarke, Lucy, 2976.
Parthena, 180.
Parthenia, 3978.
Parthla, 957,
Partridge, Alice, 2076.
Partridge, Amos, 2076.
Partridge, Anna, 1831.
Partridge, Beeker, 2076.
Partridge, Bessie, 103.
Partridge, Clara, 1169.
Partridge, Gibson, 103, 314.
Partridge, Jemima, 923, NB1006.
Partridge, Jonas, M387.
Partridge, Kazzie, 910.
Partridge, Leonard C., 1169.
Partridge, Louisa, 808.
Partridge, Lucinda, 103.
Partridge, Mary, 2076, M387.
Partridge, Noah, 923, 2076.
Partridge, Ollie, 2076.
Partridge, Reuben L., 1169.
Partridge, Ruby M., 1169.
Partridge, Sam, 314.
Partridge, Thahepne, 2076.
Partridge, Toby, 2076, M387.
Pascover, 1307, 2566, 2581.
Patake, John, 2272.
Patarkey, John, 85.
Patcheshe, 1382.
Pathla, 1010, 1012.
Patokike, 3872.
Patterson, Wm., 454.
Patton, Dora, NB893.
Patton, Emma, 1731, NB892, NB893, NB894.
Patton, J. O., NB892, NB893, NB894.
Patton, Leo Ora, NB894.
Patton, Lora, NB892.
Paygee, 1616.
Payne, Charley, 308.
Payne, Heaster, 1241.
Payne, Richard, 308.
Peck, 2458.
Peconweny, 236.
Peeche , 2814.
Peep r, Clarence, 3612.
Peeper, Ev rett, 2257.
Peeper, Frank, 2257, 3612, NB801.
Peeper, Mary, 2257, 3612, NBS01.

Peeper, Viney May, NB801.
Peester, 85.
Pefatka, 1408, 1539.
Pefotka, 1408, 1539.
Peggy, 170, 174, 1469, 2111, 2153.
Pehoye, 2827, 2829.
Pelah, 2103, NB939.
"Peloche,"3346.
Pemberton, Charity R., 619, 1346.
Pemberton, Ida L., 619.
Pemberton, James A., 619.
Pemberton, John C., 619.
Pemberton, Naoma, NB969.
Pemberton, Reacy Adeline, NB969.
Pemberton, Viola C., 619.
Pemberton, Washington L., 619.
Pemberton, Wm. J., 619, 1346.
Pemberton, William T., 619, NB969.
Pemberton, Wilton, 619.
Penaka, 858.
Pendelton, Dora, 3729.
Pendelton, Enoch, 1153.
Penn, 1517.
Penn, Annie, 2095.
Penn, Emoney, M222.
Penn, Mary, 3899.
Penn, Miley, 2095, 3899, M222.
Penn, Sharpsey, 2095.
Penn, William, 2095, 3899, M222.
Pense, Alice, NB566.
Pense, J. H., NB566.
Pense, Malissa, 233, NB566.
Perkins, Gus, 3115.
Perkins, John, 3115.
Perkins, Nancy, 3115.
Perry, Charles Owen, 843.
Perry, Cunnussa, CE4040.
Perry, Ed., 843.
Perry, Gibson, CE4040.
Perry, James, CE4040.
Perry, Maud, 843, NB181, NB182.
Perry, Susie, CE4040.
Perryman, Ab, 808.
Perryman, Adam, 1400.
Perryman, Addie, 677.
Perryman, Alex, NB554, NB555.
Perryman, Andrew, 910.
Perryman, Anna, 455, 864, 2495, NB880.
Perryman, Annie, 455, 864, 2495, NB880.
Perryman, Arparye, 910.
Perryman, Aurthur R., 2199.
Perryman, Ben, 1238, 1583, NB325.
Perryman, Benjamin, 1238, 1583, NB325.
Perryman, Celie, 2364.
Perryman, Cinda, 594.
Perryman, Clarissa, 677.
Perryman, Cornelius B., 683, M303.
Perryman, Cosetta, 812.
Perryman, Daniel, 229, 432, 1583
Perryman, Dicey, 1583
Perryman, Dora, 229
Perryman, Ed, 323, NB1003.
Perryman, Eddie, 323, NB1093.
Perryman, Edith M., 3553.
Perryman, Ebmond, 1861.
Perryman, E. G., 3451.
Perryman, Eliza, 792, 1016.
Perryman, Ella, 2199.
Perryman, Ellen, 158, 910, 1887, 1990.
Perryman, Ellen B., 158, 910, 1887, 1990.

Perryman, Rosalie. M303.
Perryman, Rose, 402, 404, 406.
Perryman, Ruth, 455, 475.
Perryman, Sallie, 323, 581, 802.
Perryman, Sam, 310, 449, 683, 864, 3470, M337.
Perryman, Samuel, 340, 449, 683, 864, 3470, M337.
Perryman, Sanford, 312, 688.
Perryman, Sarah, 1876, NB1093.
Perryman, Sarah Ann, M303.
Perryman, Silla, 1653.
Perryman, Sophia, 1238, 2410, NB554, NB555.
Perryman, Susanna, 449.
Perryman, Susie, 895, 3470.
Perryman, Tecumseh, 2147.
Perryman, Thomas L., 2199.
Perryman, Thomas W., 1887, 2199.
Perryman, Thompson, 594, 804.
Perryman, Trona, 340.
Perryman, Walter L., 2199.
Perryman, Wash, 681.
Perryman, Washington L., 681.
Perryman, William, 323, 340, 681, 1653.
Perryman, Willie, 299, 681.
Perryman, Wright, 158, 2364.
Pesogee, 2857
Petelle, 2724.
Peter, 1867.
Peter, Jennie, 2505, NB1230.
Peter, John, 3890.
Peter, Joseph, 3063.
Peter, Linda, 2505, 2507, 2509.
Peter, Little, 2505, 2507
Peter, Lizzie, 2127.
Peter, Locahull, 3386.
Peter, Louisa, 2505.
Peter, Millie, 2507.
Peter, Nicey, 2127, 2256, 3063.
Peter, Sallie, 2509.
Peter, Simon, 2127, 2256, 3063.
Peters, 907.
Peters, Ben, 1002.
Peters, Betsey, 1002.
Peters, Cilla, 1002.
Peters, Ellen, 1002, 2374.
Peters, Isom, 1707.
Peters, Jesse, 1707.
Peters, Kizzie, 1002.
Peters, Louisa, 1707, 2034.
Peters, Lula, 1707.
Peters, Sampson, 1002.
Peters, Simon, 907.
Petha, 2825.
Petochey, 2720.
Pettit, Frank, 685.
Pgifepka, 3240.
Phelama, 2846.
Phillip, Jane, 1853.
Phillip, Tiger, 1853.
Phillips, Abbie, 2184.
Phillips, B. H., 2028.
Phillips, Ben, 2028, 2775.
Phillips, Bettie, 270.
Phillips, Betsey, 2183, 2184.
Phillips, Betsie, 2028.
Phillips, Billy, 2775.
Phillips, Coosie, 270.
Phillips, Daniel, 2028.
Phillips, Eliza, 270, 496, 2028.

Phillips, Hannah, 2028.
Phillips, Hattie, 270.
Phillips, Hettie,'2028, NB20, M50.
Phillips, Jennetta, 270.
Phillips, Jennie, 2775.
Phillips, Joe, 270.
Phillips, John, 275.
Phillips, Johnson, 2028, NB20, M50.
Phillips, Kate, 905.
Phillips, Lewis E., 496.
Phillips, Louisa, 2184, NB642.
Phillips, Lydia, NB20.
Phillips, Mattie, 2775.
Phillips, Nancy, M50.
Phillips, P. H., 270, 496, 2184.
Phillips, Pahos Harjo, 270, 496, 2184.
Phillips, Parhose Harjo, 2184, 270, 493.
Phillips, Sarah, 270.
Phillips, Taylor, 2184.
Phillips, Tecumseh, 270, 275, 1364.
Phillips, Thomas, 270.
Phillips, Wallace, 2028.
Phillips, Walter, 270.
Phillips, Wicey, 1364.
Phillips, Wysie, 275.
Pholothoka, 78.
Pickett, Ada, 556.
Pickett, Albert, 638.
Pickett, Arlaquinny, 939.
Pickett, Daniel, 556.
Pickett, Ella, 556.
Pickett, Jennetta, 556, 638.
Pickett, Jennie, 556.
Pickett, Johnson, 939.
Pickett, Lucy, 556.
Pickett, Louisa, 556.
Pickett, Malinda, 556, 557.
Pickett, Marshie, 578.
Pidgeon, Jesse, 448.
Pidgeon, Dave, 448.
Pidgie, 2618.
Piegon, Leetchee, 1882.
Pierce, Jacob, 949.
Pierce, Jennetta, 949.
Pierce, Sallie, 949.
Pierce, Silla, 949.
Pigeon, Cemelane, 3238, NB1193.
Pigeon, Dave, 1658.
Pigeon, Jakeman, 2411.
Pigeon, Jennie, 2830, NB1193.
Pigeon, Jesse, 35.
Pigeon, Jim, 3238, NB1193.
Pigeon, Jimmy, 2154.
Pigeon, Joe, 1658, 2411.
Pigeon, John, 2139, 2153, 2411, 3238
Pigeon, Jonas, 2411.
Pigeon, Joseph, 2411.
Pigeon, Lena, 2411, M409.
Pigeon, Lesbee, 2154.
Pigeon, Lizzie, 35.
Pigeon, Mahtee, 2153.
Pigeon, Mate, 2411.
Pigeon, Misser, 3368.
Pigeon, Nache, NB1193.
Pigeon, Nancy, 1658, NB345.
Pigeon, Peggy, 1658.
Pigeon, Robert, 35.
Pigeon, Sallie, 35, 3238.
Pigeon, Sally, 35, 3238.
Pigeon, Tiger, 1658.

Pike, Albert, 206.
Pike, Edna,'613' NB155.
Pike, Fay, NB155.
Pike, George, 206.
Pike, Joseph, 206.
Pike, Pamelia, 206.
Pike, Wester, NB155.
Pinehill, Abner, 665.
Pinehill, Lasley, 895, NB1185.
Pinehill, Leo, 895.
Pinehill, Mary, NB1185.
Pinehill, Robert, 311.
Pinehill, Sallie, 895, NB1185.
Pinehill, Sally, 895, NB1185.
Pinehill, Sarah, 344.
Pinehill, Wm., 895.
Pingolichchee, 886.
Pinkey, Lilia, 1147, M338.
Pinkey, Willie, 1150, M338.
Pinky, 1150.
Pinky, Lizzie, M338.
Pinky, Willie, 1150, M338.
Pinnege, 389.
Pinyer, 1827.
Fitchee, 621.
Pitcher, Seco, 1587.
Pitman, Arthur 1154.
Pitman, Bob, 5˚5.
Pitman, Cecil, 3478.
Pitman, Clarence, M70.
Pitman, Edith Lucinda, M432.
Pitman, Edward, 1154, NB848.
Pitman, Florence, NB608.
Pitman, Homer, 1154.
Pitman, J. W., M70.
Pitman, John W., 1154, 3478.
Pitman, Laurel, 1154.
Pitman, Lewis, 1154, NB608.
Pitman, Lucinda, 565, NB794, M432.
Pitman, Mary, 1154.
Pitman, Moses, NB848.
Pitman, Robert, NB794, M432.
Pitman, Robert, Jr., NB794.
Pitman, Rosanna, 1154, 3478, M70.
Pitman, Rosella, 1154.
Pitman, Rowie Elizabeth, 565.
Pitman, Sammie, 1154.
Pitman, Susie, NB848.
Pitman, Vonnie, NB608.
Pitman, Walter, 1154, 2375.
Pittman, Celia, 2138.
Pittman, Edwin, 2138.
Pittman, Jennie, 2138, NB363, NB364.
Pitts, Burrell H., NB668.
Pitts, Drannan, NB667.
Pitts, Emma, 695, NB667, NB668, NB1014.
Pitts, Frank, 695.
Pitts, David Franklin, 695.
Pitts, Frank Fields, NB667, NB668, NB1014.
Pitts, Major Barbee, NB1014.
Pitts, Pearlie, 695.
Pitts, William R., 695.
Prisa, 2482.
Pocananney, 77.
Pocco, Hokte, 2304.
Pocharney, 3032.
Pocofah, 2729, 2730.
Poconweny, 236, 2188, 2731.
Poeca, Micco, 1218.
Pofner, 1558.

372

Pokoconweney, 2705.
Pokoska, Joe, 1788.
Polakaconthla, 2252.
Polecat, 3271.
Polecat, Kanocheeshumar, 3271.
Polecat, Nonpechee, 3652.
Polecat, Pahlatahsheeney, 3271.
Polecat, Sapesa, 3271.
Polk, Benjamin, 2050.
Polk, Billy, 2393.
Polk, Cinda, 2243.
Polk, Comfort, 2050.
Polk, Delilah, 2050.
Polk, Daniel, 2243, 3642, CE4041, NB747.
Polk, Daniel W., 2243, 3642, CE4041, NB747.
Polk, Ethel, NB747.
Polk, Katie, 2243, NB747.
Polk, Lucinda, 1985, 2029.
Polk, Martha, 2393.
Polk, Mose, 2393.
Polk, Sarshoye, 2029.
Polk, Siah, CE4041.
Polk, Silla, 2671, 3642.
Polk, Thomas, 1985, 2029, 2243.
Polk, Thomas H., 1985, 2243, 2029.
Polk, Thomas K., 1985, 2029, 2243.
Polk, Walter, 2050.
Polk, Walter R., 2050.
Polk, Winey, 3642.
Polledagee, 215.
Pollie, 604, 149, 283, 672, 818, 969, 1206, 1215,
        1293, 1562, 1587, 1905, 2029, 2187.
        2532, 2785, 2907, 3053, 3274, 3823,
        CF4055.
Pologe, 2739.
Polly, 149, 283, 604, 672, 818, 969, 1206, 1215,
        1293, 1562, 1587, 1905, 2029, 2187,
        2532, 2785, 2907, 3053, 3274, 3823,
        CE4055.
Poloke, Lucy, 2530.
Poloke, Sam, 2530.
Polokee, Esal, 3085, NB1267.
Polokee, Ludie, 3086, NB879, M352.
Polokee, Susie, 3085, 3086, 3092.
Polokee, Tom, 3085, 3086, 3092.
Ponkilley, 3221.
Ponkilley, Melely, 3221.
Pootka, 1482.
Poquin, Mattie, 2309.
Porchee, 2368.
"Porter," 1816.
Porter, Annetta Mary, 1991.
Porter, Ben, 1517, 1739.
Porter, Ben E., 729, 3005.
Porter, Benjamin, 1991, NB401.
Porter, Betsey, 683.
Porter, Edith P., NB211.
Porter, Edward B., 729.
Porter, Elizabeth, 13.
Porter, Elsie, 114, NB102, NB103.
Porter, Hager, 1374.
Porter, Isom, 3090.
Porter, Jack, 1311.
Porter, James, 1311, 3090, NB401, M281.
Porter, James Summerfield, M7.
Porter, Jemima, M281.
Porter, John, 114, 1058, 1271, 1374, 2163.
Porter, John S., 1739.
Porter, Katie May, 46.
Porter, L. Ray, NB210.

Porter, Lena, 1739.
Porter, Leonora E., 1991.
Porter, Lewis, 114, NB102, NB103.
Porter, March, 1374.
Porter, Martha, 265.
Porter, Mary E., 461.
Porter, Mary, 1739.
Porter, Mary Ellen, 1991.
Porter, Mattie L., 1991.
Porter, McKinley, NB103.
Porter, Mildred M., M7, NB7.
Porter, Milly M., 461.
Porter, Misey, 1271.
Porter, Nancy, 1311, NB401, M281.
Porter, Nellie, 2466.
Porter, Ochee, 1272.
Porter, Pen, 2466.
Porter, Phoebe, 1517, 1991.
Porter, Pleasant, 461, 1991, NB102.
Porter, Pleasant, Jr., 461.
Porter, Sallie, 1271.
Porter, Sam, 46, NB210, NB211.
Porter, Sarah, 3005.
Porter, Stockton, 461.
Porter, Susan, 46, NB210, NB211.
Porter, Tildy, 444.
Porter, Tobie, 2529.
Porter, Topsy, 1271, 1272.
Porter, Will, 461.
Porter, William A., 461, NB7, M7.
Posey, Albert W., 2229, NB976.
Posey, Alexander L., 1132, NB4.
Posey, Andy W., 3268, NB470, M40.
Posey, Annie L., 813.
Posey, Beat ice, 3217.
Posey, Beatrice E., 3217, 3219.
Posey, Benjamin, 595.
Posey, Bettie, 736.
Posey, Bill, 762.
Posey, Boyce W., 3268.
Posey, Carrie, 832, NB686.
Posey, Charles Kenneth, M40.
Posey, Canny, 892.
Posey, Darwin, 892.
Posey, Dennis, 3217.
Posey, Dora M., 535.
Posey, Edith, 978.
Posey, Edward U., 620.
Posey, Eli, 714.
Posey, Eliza, 595.
Posey, Elizabeth, 2224, 2229, 3217.
Posey, Ella, 892.
Posey, Elmer Carl, 2229.
Posey, Emily, 3268, 3500.
Posey, Eloise, NB686.
Posey, Emma, 667.
Posey, Frank, 667, NB686.
Posey, Flora, 736.
Posey, George A., 620.
Posey, Gertrude, 667.
Posey, Harriet, 892.
Posey, Henry, 762, NB512.
Posey, Henry A., 762, NB512.
Posey, Homer H., 3607.
Posey, Horace, 892.
Posey, Hugh F., NB156.
Posey, Hulda E., 535, 813, 3268.
Posey, Huldy, 535, 813, 3268.
Posey, Hurley E., 535, 813, 3268.
Posey, Irving, 1132.

Posey, J. S., 3268, 3500.
Posey, James S., 3268, 3500.
Posey, Jim H., 813.
Posey, Johann, 859.
Posey, John, 892.
Posey, John M., 813, M156.
Posey, John W., 813.
Posey, Jonathan R., 3217.
Posey, Kennie, 3268.
Posey, Kipling, 1132.
Posey, L. H., 847, 892, 896, 1132.
Posey, L. Hena, 667.
Posey, Laura E., 813, NB156.
Posey, Laura S., 535.
Posey, Lee A., 736.
Posey, Lena L., 3268.
Posey, Leonard Earle, 2229.
Posey, Lewis H., 847, 892, 896, 1132.
Posey, Lola Colesta, NB483.
Posey, M. A., 2224.
Posey, Mary A., NB976.
Posey, Mary Ann, 2229.
Posey, Mary E., 714, 736, NB512.
Posey, Mary L., 535, 3607, NB153, M22.
Posey, Mary V., 620.
Posey, Mattie, 892.
Posey, Mendum, 892.
Posey, Minnie, 1132, NB4, NB470, M40.
Posey, Nancy, 667, 847, 892, 896, 1132.
Posey, Nellie H., NB483.
Posey, Nina E., NB976.
Posey, Nora S., 3268.
Posey, Ola B., 535.
Posey, R. T., 3219.
Posey, Richard T., 3217, 3219.
Posey, Robert A., 736.
Posey, Ruby, 813.
Posey, Ruth Lucile, M22.
Posey, Susan, 762.
Posey, T. C., 3500.
Posey, Terry O., NB153.
Posey, Thos. B., 535, 813, 3217, 3268.
Posey, Thomas Owen, NB470.
Posey, Thomas U., 3268.
Posey, Uriah, 620.
Posey, W. A., 2224, 2229.
Posey, Walter, 535, 859, 3607, NB153, M22.
Posey, Walter A., 813.
Posey, Will, 978.
Posey, William, 736, 892, 896.
Posey, William A., 736, 3219. NB483.
Posey, William Edward, NB512.
Posey, Wynema Torrans, NB4.
Post, Cornelius, 850.
Post, El Louisa, NB621.
Post, Homer, 1856.
Post, John, 850, 1856, 1860, 1968.
Post, Laura, 850, NB620, NB621, M28.
Post, Samantha, NB620.
Post, Thomas, 850, NB620, NB621, M28.
Post, Thomas, Jr., M28.
Post, William, 1968.
Postoak, Arthur E., NB599.
Postoak, Bettie, 680.
Postoak, Charley, 680.
Postoak, Charley, NB900, NB901, Creek Frd.
    707.
Postoak, Eli, NB979.
Postoak, George, 680.
Postoak, Gracie, 710.

Postoak, Hattie L., NB600.
Postoak, Jennie, NB901.
Postoak, Julia, NB900.
Postoak, Lillie, 710, NB599, NB600.
Postoak, Lilly, 710, NB599, NB600.
Postoak, Lincoln, 710, NB599, NB600, NB979.
Postoak, Mollie, 2727.
Postoak, Nannie, 710.
Postoak, Rachael, 680, NB900, NB901.
Postoak, Rachel, 680, NB900, NB901.
Postoak, Sallie, 3127.
Postoak, Taylor, 710, 2727, 3127.
Postoak, Tecumseh, 710.
Potato, Mollie, 2500.
Pothka, 1680.
Pothla, 1010, 1012, 1208.
Pothlar, 3313.
Pothoigee, 2661, 2692.
Potogigee, 2661, 2692.
Potoka, 2988.
Potolige, 2343.
Powell, Carline, 2395.
Powell, Charles, NB395.
Powell, Cinda, 3272.
Powell, Elizabeth, 2744.
Powell, Hannah, 3157, 3272.
Powell, John, 2395, 2744, NB395.
Powell, Martha, 1653, NB395.
Powell, Park, 3317.
Powell, Pearl, 3317.
Powell, Pesaka, 2744.
Powell, Robert, 3317.
Powell, Sammie, 3317.
Powell, Willie, 3272.
Presley, Arthur, 403.
Presley, Farilla, 403.
Presley, Harrison, 403.
Presley, Harrison E., 403.
Presley, Lillie, 403.
Presley, Louisa, 403.
Presley, Mary M., 403, NB52, M66.
Presley, Rosetta, 403.
Presley, Smith, 403.
Presley, Thomas Jefferson, 403.
Pressgrove, Aaron, NB125.
Pressgrove, Joseph, NB125.
Pressgrove, Lizzie, 720, NB125.
Price, Belle, M221.
Price, Benny, 293.
Price, James, 878.
Price, James, Jr., 878.
Price, James Lawrence, 711.
Price, J. M., M228.
Price, Lelia, 293, M232, NB238.
Price, Louina, 2375.
Price, Louvina, 1154, 2007.
Price, Lucy, 878.
Price, M. B., NB1009, M104.
Price, Mamie, M228.
Price, Mary Lucile, M221.
Price, Minnie May, NB1009.
Price, Mose B., 711.
Price, Moses B., M104, NB1009.
Price, Nora Nellie Marie, M104.
Price, Oscar, 293.
Price, Owen, 293, M221.
Price, Pleasant Porter, 878.
Price, Priscilla, 711.
Price, Sallie, 711, NB1009, M104.
Price, Susan, 878, M228.

Puntka, Lucy. 3161.
Puntka, Mikey, 3161.
Puntka, Winey, NB1159.
Puryear, Emma H., 861, NB146.
Puryear, Frank M., NB146.
Puryear, William H., NB146.
Pussey, Sarah, 1314.
Puttie, 2117.
Quasarty, 2358.
Quasarty, Nannie, 2358.
Quassarty, 2851.
Qussarte, 2402.
Quogue, 3321.
Quosoday, 322.
Raabe, Celia, NB135.
Raabe, Chris, 1065, NB134, NB135.
Raabe, Ida May, 1065, NB134, NB135.
Raabe, Rosa Pearl, 1065.
Raabe, Stella, NB134.
Rabbit, 2483.
Rabbit, Amos, 2483.
Rabbit, Edmond, 2483.
Rabbit, Jack, 4024.
Rabbit, James, 2483.
Rabbit, Lundey, 2483.
Rabbit, Nannie, 2598, 3161.
Rabbit, Oldman, 980.
Rabbit, Sakoyike, 2483.
Rabbit, Sallie, 4024.
Rabbit, Sissie, 4024.
Rabbit, Sleeping, 4024.
Rachael, 1914, 2370.
Raiford, Arthur E., 1781, NBS85.
Raiford, Ferdinand, 1782.
Raiford, Jannetta, 1782, NB885.
Raiford, Jennetta, 1781, 1784, 1807.
Raiford, Lena, NB1195.
Raiford, Ossie, 1784, CE4044, NB1194, NB1195.
Raiford, Pearl, NB1194.
Raiford, P. H., 1807.
Raiford, Philip, 1781, 1782, 1784.
Raiford, Selina, CE4044, NB1194, NB1195.
Raiford, Tookah, 1755, NB885.
Raiford, Washington, CE4044.
Ralston, Allen W., 4004.
Ralston, Benjamin F., 4005, CE4045.
Ralston, Benjamin F., Jr., 4005.
Ralston, Charles C., 4004.
Ralston, Electa J., 891.
Ralston, Ella E., 4005.
Ralston, Elva Leona, CE4045.
Ralston, Florence, 4007.
Ralston, Florence May, CE4046.
Ralston, Fred E., CE4046.
Ralston, Jeanetta Louise, CE4046.
Ralston, John F., 4005, 4007, CE4046.
Ralston, Joseph, 4004, 4005, 4006, 4007, 4008, 4009.
Ralston, Joseph W., 4005.
Ralston, Maggie, CE4045.
Ralston, May B., 4005.
Ralston, Nancy, 4004, 4005, 4006, 4007, 4008, 4009.
Ralston, Nancy Jane, 4007.
Ralston, Roy P., 4005.
Ralston, Sadie Pearl, 4007.
Randall, Amy, 1487.
Randall, Anna, 1760.
Randall, Boney, 1487.
Randall, Bony, 1351.

Randall, Dicy, 1487, NB1100.
Randall, Elsie, 1786.
Randall, Emma, 1487.
Randall, Ida, 1487.
Randall, James, 1763.
Randall, Jemima, 1351.
Randall, Jim, 1787, 1788.
Randall, John, 95.
Randall, Lizzie, 1351.
Randall, Loska, 95.
Randall, Mamie, 1487.
Randall, Matulka, 1351, 1382.
Randall, Mollie, 1787.
Randall, Noksa, 1760.
Randall, Peter, 1787.
Randall, Roman, NB1100.
Randall, Sallie, 1351.
Randall, Sally, 1382.
Randall, Sam, 1487, NB1100.
Randall, Sandy, M244.
Randall, Thomas, 1763.
Randall, Timmie, 1351, M244.
Randall, Ulsa, 1760.
Rawson, Susan, 1445, 1471.
Red, Foxie, 2798.
Red, Leah, 3965.
Red, Martha, 2798, 3965, NB126.
Red, Thomas, 2798, 2966, 3965.
Red, Wash, 2966.
Reddy, Kizziah, 130.
Reddy, Maggie, 130.
Reddy, Mededahka, 130.
Redmouth, 1610.
Reed, Andrew, 2389.
Reed, Benjamin J., 2482.
Reed, Bulby, 3215.
Reed, Charley, 1578.
Reed, David, 2189.
Reed, Ella, 1565.
Reed, Jennie, 1565, NB581.
Reed, Jim, 634, M361.
Reed, Jimson, 1550.
Reed, John, 1523, 1565, 1578, 1693, 2389,   NB-
    581.
Reed, Johnson, 1867.
Reed, Judie, 1578.
Reed, Leah, 1404, 1605, 2389.
Reed, Lecha, 1523.
Reed, Leister, 1565.
Reed, Liester, 1921.
Reed, Lister, 1565.
Reed, Lucy, 3115.
Reed, Martha, 1605, 2389.
Reed, Mary, 353, 174, M361.
Reed, Miss, 1458.
Reed, Phe, 353.
Reed, Porter, 1565, NB581.
Reed, Rachel, 1565, 1578, 1693.
Reed, Robert, 634, 2482, M361.
Reed, Stephen, 1550.
Reed, Thomas, 3215.
Reed, Toney, 1921.
Reed, Walter, 2389.
Reilly, Nancy, 1978.
Renfro, Alef Adelaide, NB192.
Renfro, Bettie, 1852, NB191, NB192.
Renfro, Elza Tillman, NB191.
Renfro, Roy Tillman, 1852.
Renfro, William, 1852.
Renfro, William D., NB191, NB192.

Renfro, Willie, 1852.
Reno, Robert, 2489.
Rentie, Gracie, M140.
Rentie, Lewis, NB866, M140.
Rentie, Lucreesey, NB866.
Rentie, Peggie, 1200, NB866, M140.
Rentie, Susan, 260.
Renty, 1565.
Reynolds, Ada, 782, NB716, M71.
Reynolds, Addie Lee, M71.
Reynolds, Annie, 2484.
Reynolds, Anty, 849.
Reynolds, Ariadne, 2484.
Reynolds, Arthur Leroy, NB326.
Reynolds, C. D., M232.
Reynolds, Charles, M71.
Reynolds, Charley, NB716.
Reynolds, Clarence, NB238.
Reynolds, Clarence Andrew, NB716.
Reynolds, Dave, 2217.
Reynolds, Delphie, 928, NB752, M132.
Reynolds, Eliza, 2217.
Reynolds, Ellis, 849.
Reynolds, Elsey, 1098.
Reynolds, Ernest, NB752.
Reynolds, Eva Edna, NB326, NB327.
Reynolds, G. W., 849, 1098.
Reynolds, Jerry, 2217.
Reynolds, Joe, M132.
Reynolds, J. R., 2484, NB326, NB327.
Reynolds, John R., 2484, NB326, NB327.
Reynolds, Joseph, NB752.
Reynolds, Laura, 2484.
Reynolds, Leila, 293, M232, NB238.
Reynolds, Leona, 849.
Reynolds, Lewis, 2217.
Reynolds, Lizzie, NB327.
Reynolds, Lucy, 1098.
Reynolds, Miles C., M232.
Reynolds, Napoleon, M132.
Reynolds, Oscar Lee, NB238.
Reynolds, Richard, 2217.
Reynolds, Silas, 1098.
Reynolds, Susie, 2217.
Reynolds, William E., 2484.
Rhoda, 1137, 1505, 3410, M444.
Rhodes, Annie May, 918.
Rhodes, John P., 918.
Rhodes, Leona Dee, 918.
Rhodes, Martha Ella, 918.
Rhodes, Taylor, 918.
Rhyne, Altus, 1131.
Rhyne, Elizabeth, 1131.
Rhyne, J. S., 1131.
Richard, Albert, NB35.
Richard, Annie, NB438.
Richard, Dick, 1271.
Richard, Eastman, 2575, NB1211, M472.
Richard, Jasper, 820, 3550, NB438, M431.
Richard, Jennetta, 2575.
Richard, Jemima, 2575.
Richard, Kizzie, 819, 820, 2062.
Richard, Kogee, 2062.
Richard, Lesslie, M431.
Richard, Lula, NB35, M16.
Richard, Mary, 650, NB169.
Richard, Minnie, 820, 3550, NB438, NB1211,
    M431.
Richard, Polly, 1937.
Richard, Rina, M472.

376

Riley, Martha, NB496.
Riley, Mary, 954, 955, 956.
Riley, Mary Elizabeth, 954.
Riley, Marzell, 954.
Riley, Mattie, NB704, NB705.
Riley, Micco, 954, 955, 956.
Riley, Minnie, 3074.
Riley, Moese, 2048.
Riley, Moses, 421.
Riley, Nancy, 421, 946, 974, 2028.
Riley, Parfna, 3111.
Riley, Peter, 421.
Riley, Sookey, 3055.
Riley, Sophie, 1048.
Riley, Suter, 421.
Riley, Thomas, 421, NB950, NB951.
Riley, Tiger, 2954, 3230.
Riley, Tootie, NB950.
Riley, Tulsa, 674.
Riley, Unus, 3980.
Riley, Warnie, 1425.
Riley, Washie, CE4047.
Riley, Washington, 1428.
Riley, William, 3980, NB496.
Riley, Willie, 3230.
Riley, Wilyumka, 1425, 1429.
Rina, 3089.
Robbins, John, 3688.
Roberson, Amos, 1995.
Roberson, Clarence, NB1233.
Roberson, Ellen, NB576.
Roberson, Hannah, 1178.
Roberson, Henry, NB1233, M369.
Roberson, Joe T., M36`.
Roberson, Leo, NB575.
Roberson, Mary, 1995, NB575, NB576.
Roberson, Nancy, 2315, NB1233, M369.
Roberson, Philip, 1995, NB575, NB576, Creek
          Frd., 4846.
Robert, Daniel, 2334.
Robert, Osliddy, 2334.
Roberts, Annie, 526, 2256, 3794, M343.
Roberts, Annie A., NB9, NB10.
Roberts, Arnie, 1315.
Roberts, Cainey, NB762.
Roberts, Cholichar, 1315.
Roberts, Church, 526.
Roberts, Daniel, 415, 996, 1925.
Roberts, Edward L., 526.
Roberts, Ethel, 526.
Roberts, George, 998, M203.
Roberts, Hannah, 2620, NB874, M342, M343.
Roberts, Hannah Tyler, 2620, NB874, M342,
          M343.
Roberts, Indie, NB1065.
Roberts, James, 2452.
Roberts, Joe, 1315, 2854, NB1250.
Roberts, Johnson, 1340.
Roberts, Joseph, NB874.
Roberts, Josie, 2854, 4000.
Roberts, Kendall, 1340, NB762, NB1065.
Roberts, Liley, M203.
Roberts, Lizzie, M203.
Roberts, Louisa, 1315.
Roberts, Lydia, 996, 1925.
Roberts, Mahala, 2619, 4000, NB1250.
Roberts, Mary, 1340, 2619, NB762, NB1065,
          NB1250.
Roberts, Maud, 526.
Roberts, Miller, 3794.

Roberts, Millie, 3860, 4000.
Roberts, Mitchell, 1315.
Roberts, Noah, 2620, 3794, NBS74, M343.
Roberts, Sister, NB1250.
Roberts, Tura E., NB9.
Roberts, Walter H., NB10.
Roberts, Warley, 1315.
Roberts, Weleyar, 1315.
Roberts, William J., 526, NB9, NB10.
Roberts, Wisey, 1315.
Robertson, Andrew Jackson, NB681.
Robertson, I. W., NB681.
Robertson, Lilly, 20, NB681.
Robertson, Myer, 1496.
Robertson, Sophia, 1521.
Robin, Charley, 1179.
Robin, Lulu, 1179.
Robin, Will, 1201.
Robins, John, 401.
Robins, Johnson, 1201.
Robins, Mack, NB783, Creek Frd., 4056.
Robins, Thomas, NB783.
Robinson, 1000.
Robinson, Addie, 1000.
Robinson, Annie, 1955, 3818, NB925, NB926.
Robinson, Dave, 1955, 3818, NB925, NB926,
    Creek Frd., 368.
Robinson, George, 401, 1955.
Robinson, Henry, 1955.
Robinson, Lena, 1000.
Robinson, Louisa, NB926.
Robinson, Myrtice A., NB662.
Robinson, Nelson, NB925.
Robinson, Robert, 401.
Robinson, Willie, 3818.
Robinson, Adeline, 1903, 1973, 3299.
Robison, Adeline Belle, NB121.
Robison, Alex, 692.
Robison, Alexander W., 1630.
Robison, Amos, 1447, 1459, 1462, 3681, 3692,
    NB448, NB449.
Robison, Amos R., 1459, 1462, 1447, 3681, 3692,
    NB448, NB449.
Robison, Annie, 1693.
Robison, Anteline, 1462.
Robison, Arline, 1459.
Robison, Augusta, 1973.
Robison, Barney C., 1630, M20.
Robison, Benjamin, 1447.
Robison, Celia, 1693.
Robison, Cherokee, 692, 1630.
Robison, Christie, NB448.
Robison, Clem, 1634.
Robison, Daniel, 1693.
Robison, David, 1433.
Robison, Eddie, 1634.
Robison, Eddie A., 1447.
Robison, Elizabeth, 692.
Robison, Fannie, 1630.
Robison, Frazier, 1630.
Robison, George E., 1630.
Robison, George F., 3299.
Robison, Geo. Frazier, 692.
Robison, George H., 1903.
Robison, Hannah, 1446.
Robison, Hilley, 1693, NB526, M181.
Robison, Holmes, 1447.
Robison, Ida, 3681.
Robison, Ida B., 1630, M20.
Robison, Jack, 1607, 1693.

Robison, James Abner, 3411.
Robison, Jane, 692, 1630, 1973.
Robison, Joe S., 1903, 3411, NB121, NB122.
Robison, Josephus, 1447.
Robison, J. S., 3411, 1903, NB121, NB122.
Robison, Leah, 1634, NB481, NB482.
Robison, Lizzie, 1459, 1903, NB449.
Robison, Lona, 1693.
Robison, Louisa, 1447, 3681, NB448.
Robison, Lucy, 1607.
Robison, Maggie, 1547, 3692, M144.
Robison, Mariah, 1459.
Robison, Mattie, 1903, 3411, NB121, NB122.
Robison, Maysie A., NB662.
Robison, Monkey, 1693.
Robison, Newman Joseph, NB122.
Robison, Richard Chisholm, NB449.
Robison, Rufus M., 1903.
Robison, Samuel, M20.
Robison, Sekice, 3692.
Robison, Soma, 1496.
Robison, Sophia, 1693.
Robison, Susie, 1634.
Robison, Thomas, 1433.
Robison, Will R., 692, 1462, 1903, 1973, 1446
    3299, 1630, NB662.
Robison, William, 692, 1446, 1462, 1903, 1973
    3299, 1630, NB662.
Robison, William R., 1903, 1973, 1462, 692,
    1446, 3299, 1630. NB662,
Robison, York, 1496.
Rochokne, Henehar, 1306.
Roda, 2635.
Rodgers, Emma, 3540.
Rodgers, Mack Albert, 3540.
Rodgers, Robert F., 3540.
Rogers, Annie, 3748.
Rogers, Atoney, 572.
Rogers, Augusta, 2292, NB136, NB137.
Rogers, Caesar, 831.
Rogers, Chepon, 964, NB1006.
Rogers, Hannah, 3748.
Rogers, Jemima, 923, NB1006.
Rogers, John, 1879, NB137, M299.
Rogers, Johnnie, 964.
Rogers, Kate D., 24, 165, 166, 167.
Rogers, Legus, M299.
Rogers, Louvina, 572.
Rogers, Lucy, NB1006.
Rogers, Mary Ann, 1394.
Rogers, Mary R., 165.
Rogers, Melvina, 1879, M299.
Rogers, Mollie, 831.
Rogers, Nora, 680, NB1265.
Rogers, Robert, 964, 1394.
Rogers, Sam, 3748.
Rogers, Sarney, 964.
Rogers, Susan M., 2557.
Rogers, Viola, 1879.
Rogers, Wm. P., 24, NB136, NB137.
Rogers, W. B., 24, 165, 166, 167.
Rogers, Wood B., 24, 165, 166, 167.
Rogers, Woods Cooper, NB136.
Roland, Joseph, 586.
Rolland, Amos, 52.
Rolland, Annie, 586, 3994, NB761.
Rolland, Honnie, 586.
Rolland, Jacob, 52.
Rolland, Joseph, 586.
Rolland, Master, 586, 3994.

Rolland, Peter, 52.
Rolland, Rufus, 3994.
Rolland, Susie, 586.
Rolland, Temarye, 586.
Rolland, Wilson. 586.
Rollins, Patsy, 1241.
Root, 741.
Root, Jennie, 914.
Root, Martha Mary, 914.
Root, Thomas, 914.
Rosana, 1279, 1638, 3182.
Rose, Mary, 185.
Roseanna, 2106.
Ross, Frank Leslie, 427.
Ross, J. E., Jr., M12.
Ross, Jennie, 2490.
Ross, Jennie P., 427.
Ross, J. Ewing, 427, NB25, M12.
Ross, John Y., 427.
Ross, Joshua, 273, 427.
Ross, Lena M., NB25.
Ross, Muskogee, 273, 427.
Ross, Nellie, 427, NB25.
Ross, Nellie E., M12.
Ross, Susie, 427, M11.
Rothhammer, Ernest Ralph, NB289.
Rothhammer, J. H., 41.
Rothhammer, Joseph, NB289.
Rothhammer, Joseph H. Jr., 41.
Rothhammer, Lillie E., 41.
Rothhammer, Louisa J., 41, NB289.
Rothhammer, Willie A., 41.
Rowland, Low, 52.
Rowlands, Joe, 52.
Rowley, Anna, M379.
Rowley, Annie, 3579.
Rowley, Charles, 295, 3579, M379.
Rowley, Eveline X., 3579.
Rowley, Henry, 295, 296, 297, 394, 460, 462.
Rowley, Henry Stevens, M379.
Rowley, Josie, 297.
Rowley, Mrs. Thompson, 295, 296, 297, 394, 460, 462.
Rucker, Mary M., 647.
Rulison, Edgar R., 9.
Rulison, Edgar R., Jr., 9.
Rulison, Irving M., 9.
Rulison, Ruth L., 9.
Rumsey, Alonzo, 1036.
Rumsey, Daniel, 1036.
Rumsey, Della, 1036.
Rumsey, Edmond, 1036.
Rumsey, Elisha P., 1028.
Rumsey, Frank M., 1036.
Rumsey, Jennie, 1028.
Rumsey, Louisa, 1028.
Rumsey, Mitchell, 1028.
Rumsey, Napoleon, 1028.
Rumsey, Pink, 1028.
Rumsey, Sam J., 1036.
Runner, Bunnie, 1226.
Runner, Dave, 1226.
Runner, Louisa, 429, 1226.
Rurner, Susan, 1226.
Russell, Clemmie, NB105.
Russell, Earl C., 375.
Russell, Estle I., 375.
Russell, James W., 375, NB105.
Russell, Leva, 375.
Russell, Mary A., 375, NB105.

Ryal, Annie, 2122. NB864.
Ryal, Emma, 2122.
Ryal, Grover. 2122.
Ryal, Hallie. 2122.
Ryal, John B., 2122.
Ryal, L. B., 2122, NB864.
Ryal, Lewis J., 2122.
Ryal, Willie B., NB864.
Ryan, 23.
Ryan, Eliza, 23, NB195, NB196.
Sabieche, 231.
Saboke, 381.
Sachpa, 2295.
Sachpa, Katie, 2295.
Sacohokey, 2679.
Sacopocheney, 598.
Sadeloke, 385, 2070.
Sadie, 879, 1833.
Safixchumba, 1161.
Sagetha, 1518, 1519.
Sagodaney, 2785.
Sahahgee, 1510.
Sahalhoga, 2795.
Sahcahjabthla, 2786.
Sahconcabney, 1185, 2626, 3124.
Sahconcahny, 1185, 2626, 3124.
Sahcontany, 2162.
Sahconthlanny, 1188.
Sahecher, 2219.
Sahepahke, 423, 2624, 2625.
Sahkonokke, 240.
Sahlahoga, 2795, 2828, 2829.
Sahni Creek, 2856.
Sahobiye, 905.
Sahpahieche, 449.
Sahtah, 2107.
Sahtaquanney, 3244.
Sahtehikee, 1967.
Sahwahoke, 2797.
Sahyekehe, 2208.
Saidahkahhe, 1064.
Sakaahtheny, 2166.
Sakanaka, 3276.
Sakhalegee, 2755.
Sakkasenny, 2268.
Sakkoyege, 2518
Sakomah, 132.
Sakquenay, 610.
Saktolumba, 2327.
Sakuntanay, 587.
Sakyothlike, 2793.
Salarhogee, 2853.
Salb, Annie, 2806, NB1147.
Salconcahney. 2705.
Salihohkee, 1783.
Salina, 344, 1566, 2322, 2935.
Salker, 2447.
Salle, 889.
Sallie, 259, 310, 1504, 1527, 1616, 1669, 1866, 2351, 2451, 2501, 2741, 2856, 3127, 3199, M209.
Salmer, 3007.
Salothoga, 1859.
Sally, 1344, 1429, 1545, 3199, 3231, 3394
Salt, Edward. NB1147.
Salt, Melicha, 2806, NB1147.
Saltsman, Eugene F., NB16.
Saltsman, Gordon P., NB16.
Saltsman, Mary C., 2030, NB16,
Salumba, Dave, 3070.

Salumba, Louisa, 2725.
Salumba, Lucy, 3070.
Salumba, Martha, 2722.
Salumba, Peggie, 3070, 3878.
Sam, Big, 751.
Sam, Kizzie, 2565.
Sam Long, 441.
Sammie, Hopiye, 3102.
Sammoche, 1345, 1792, 2565, 2679.
Sammy, 2716, 3785.
Sammy, Jim, 1514.
Sammy, Lizzie, 1514.
Sammy, Lucinda, 1514.
Samoche, 1345, 1792, 2565, 2679.
Samochee, 1345, 1792, 2565, 2679.
Samogee, 2876.
Sampson, 659, 668, 672, 1318, 2336.
Sampson, Bonnie A., 727.
Sampson, Burleigh R., 3655.
Sampson, Cindy, 3151, NB868.
Sampson, Dan, 511.
Sampson, David J., 3281.
Sampson, Elsie, 1318.
Sampson, George, 727, 3655, M27.
Sampson, George P., 727, 3655, M27.
Sampson, G. P., 727, 3655, M27.
Sampson, James, 3281.
Sampson, Jessie D., M27.
Sampson, Jim, 1426.
Sampson, John, 659, 1744.
Sampson, Johnson, 1318.
Sampson, Joseph, 727.
Sampson, Lee, 727.
Sampson, Lucinda, 3281.
Sampson, Lucy, 659, 668.
Sampson, Martha, 409.
Sampson, Mary, 727, 3655, M27.
Sampson, Obelia, 727.
Sampson, Pat, 727.
Sampson, Rhoda, 659, M277.
Sampson, Thomas, 409.
Sampson, Vina, 3222.
Sampson, Vinnie, 409.
Sampson, Walter, 659.
Sampson, Wash, 409, NB868.
Sampson, Washington, 409, NB868.
Sampson, Wiley, NB868.
Samsoche, 1554, 1744.
Samsochee, 1554, 1744.
Samuel, Ab-aham Pin, 977.
Samuel, Ben, 977, 1676, 3031.
Samuel, Jennie, 1878, 3031.
Samuel, Lizzie, 3341.
Samuel, Lubby, 3341.
Samuel, Montie, 3341.
Sana, 3016.
Sand, Dinah, 1767.
Sand, Hully, 1530.
Sand, Isaac, 1530.
Sand, Lotto Harjo, 1767.
Sand, Solomon, 1592, 1710.
Sand, Wisey, 1591.
Sanders, Edna, 729.
Sanders, Elizabeth, 729.
Sanders, John W., 729.
Sanders, Maud, 729.
Sanders, Millard, 729.
Sanders, Sarah E., 729.
Sands, Albert, 3775.
Sands, Amous, 1846.

Sands, Annie, 1848, 3775.
Sands, Carlano, 1848.
Sands, Daniel, 1839, 1840.
Sands, Ella, 1848.
Sands, Emma, 1846.
Sands, John, 1846.
Sands, Lena, 3950.
Sands, Louisa, 1846.
Sands, Martha, 1774, 3950, NB580.
Sands, Moley, 1846.
Sands, Miley, 1839, 1840.
Sands, Nettie, NB580.
Sands, Old, 1840.
Sands, Phillip, 1774, 3950, NB580.
Sands, Phillip H., 1774, 3950 NB580.
Sands, Roberts, 1840.
Sands, Roley, 1839.
Sands, Stella, 1774.
Sands, Taylor, 1848, 3775.
Sandy, 1592.
Sandy, Jacob, 1591, NB316.
Sandy, Lida, 1591.
Sandy, Malinda 1591.
Sandy, Sophia, 1591, NB316.
Sandy, Stella, NB316.
Sangana, 2729.
Sanger, Amanda, 794, 1047, 2271.
Sanger, Claude, 3682.
Sanger, Clemmie H., 784.
Sanger, Ed E., 1047 2271.
Sanger, E. E., 1047, 2271.
Sanger, Fannie E., 2271, NB679.
Sanger, F. M., 2037.
Sanger, George H., 1628.
Sanger, George N., 784.
Sanger, George P., 784.
Sanger, Ge:trude L., 1131, NB635.
Sanger, Hannah, 1517, 2037.
Sanger, Jannitta, NB855.
Sanger, Joseph C., 2271, NB635.
Sanger, Lena, 1517, 1628.
Sanger, Mabel M., 1628.
Sanger, Paul ne M., 99.
Sanger, (Alies Tiger) Stella, 1608.
Sanger, Stephen, 1037, 3682, NB855, M99.
Sanger, Viola, 3682, NB855, M99.
Sanger, Wah nah ka, NB635.
Sanger, Walter G., 2271.
Sanger, Ward W., 1628.
Sango, Bertha, 1092.
Sango, Delila, NB1090.
Sango, Edward, 1092.
Sango, Millie, 1092, 1170, 1192.
Sango, Morris, 1092, 2749.
Sango, Thomas, 2749.
Sankothla, 582.
Sanlanhohkey, 1625.
Sannah, 3313.
Sannorka, 2716, 3561.
Sannorka, Malinda, 3561.
Sanogay, 1111.
Sansoche, 409.
Sapaxta, 2529.
Sapinkahully, 3168.
Sapiye, 344.
Sapulpa, 1016, 1457, 2088.
Sapulpa, Eliza, 2088.
Sapulpa, Elizabeth, 522.
Sapulpa, Esther, 186.
Sapulpa, George A., 1016.

381

382

383

Sicogee, 1862
Siejasse, 2527.
Sigolo, Thomas, 2990.
Silbey, 2749.
5, 2220. Silby, 1972.
Silda, 1337.
Siley, 36.
815,2220 Silla, 109, 2609, 2766, 2767, 2723.
Siller, 1696.
Sillibbee, 2180.
Sillubbee, 400.
Silpee, 1149.
Silvey, 3336.
Silwy, 1343.
Simapoka, 2909.
Simbalily, 2652, 3653.
Simenchatkey, 1653.
Simer, Millie, 1792.
Simer, Moonie, 1792.
Simetah, 1675.
Simbok, 1400.
Simhoye, 2647, 2745, 3884, NB374, NB1138.
Simma, 2092.
Sommabihye, 1551.
Simmahta, 1003.
Simmer, 94, 1969, 2647, 3288, 3377.
Simmer, Aggie, M449.
Simmer, Alex, 995.
Simmer, Andy, NB1152.
Simmer, Annie, 1486.
Simmer, Arch, 1969.
Simmer, Charley, 1406, 3288, 3822. NB1152.
          M449.
Simmer, Emma, 3288.
Simmer, Hattie, 994.
Simmer, Hinney, NB537.
618. Simmer, Jemima, 1724, NB587, M159.
Simmer, Jennie, 1406.
Simmer, Jessi , 3925.
Simmer, John, 995, 1323, 1486, 3925, NB362,
          M141, M159,
Simmer, Joseph, 3288
Simmer, Kizzie, 3288, 3822, NB1152, M449.
Simmer, Kogee, 1486.
Simmer, Lena, 995, 3925, M141.
Simmer, Lillie, M159.
Simmer, Louinie, 3822.
Simmer, Lucinda, 995.
Simmer, Peter, M141.
Simmer, Sallie, 1969.
Simmer, Sam, 1486, 2690.
Simmer, Sammy, 94.
Simmer, Samuel, 3377.
Simmer, Sarls, 1311, 1323.
Simmer, Selie, 1486, NB361.·
Simmer, Sinda, 3288.
Simmesee, 1944.
Simmissee, 1729.
Simmoyhe, 2459.
Simmons, 105.
Simmons, Alex, 483.
Simmons, Annie, 2506, 2647, 2820.
Simmons, Benhakka, 1287.
Simmons, Bettie, 1286.
Simmons, Clara, 746.
Simmons, Charley, 105, 1729, 2647, 2668,
          CE4050, M382, M333.
Simmons, Chippie, 3684, NB862
Simmons, Chowestas, 2032.
Simmons, Della, CE4050.

385

Siwoke, 2698.
Sizemore, Cumseh, 511.
Sizemore, Dave, 3195.
Sixemore, David, 837.
Sizemore, Ellen, 837.
Sizemore, Illinois, 3195.
Sizemore, Lucy, 3243.
Sizemore, Nicey, 3243.
Sizemore, Sam, 838.
Sizemore, Sindy, 114.
Sizemore, Stephen, 511.
Sizemore, William, 3195.
Skahker, Susie, 3298.
Skeen, James R., 552, 553.
Skeen, Julia, 551, 552, 553, 554.
Skeeter, Fred, NB31.
Skeeter, Susanna, 557, NB31.
Skeeter, Willie, 1949, NB31.
Skull, 1232.
Sladen, John, NB1265.
Sladew, Sam, NB1265.
Slabuggay, 2862.
Slafiche, 158.
Sleep, Saheche, 1710.
Sleep, Tom, 1710.
Sleeping Rabbit, 4024.
Sloan, Albert, M485.
Sloan, Jemima, 3645.
Sloan, Lillie, M486.
Sloan, Loney, M487.
Sloan, Peter, 3645, M485, M486, M487.
Sloan, Watsey, 3645.
Sloane, Peter, 3907.
Sloane, Sallie, 3907.
Sloane, Sampson, 3907.
Sloane, Watsey, 3907.
Slumber, 2701, 3918, CE4043.
Slunche, 2625.
Smiley, Allen, 2269.
Smiley, Earnest, 2269.
Smiley, Lottie, 2269.
Smith, Matilda, 2344.
Smiley, Nora, 2269.
Smiley, T. E , 2269.
Smith, Adeline, 959, NB415, NB416, M388.
Smith, Aggie, 45, 2506, 3855.
Smith, Albert K., NB415.
Smith, Albert L., 39.
Smith, Alfred C. 39.
Smith, Allen, 941.
Smith, Anna A., 684.
Smith, Anna Eliza, 2032.
Smith, Annie, 1918, 2896, 3445, NB1290, M36?.
Smith, Annie Belle, 1679.
Smith, Arthur Ray, 684.
Smith, Belcher, 2204, 3503, NB920.
Smith, Betsey, 2912, 3882.
Smith, Betsy, 2912, 3882.
Smith, Betsy, 2912, 3882.
Smith, Bettie, 3295.
Smith, Bill, 424.
Smith, Charity, 1835.
Smith, Charles S., 1401, 1622.
Smith, Chatman, 2183, 2941.
Smith, Chella, 2508.
Smith, Cinda, 2508.
Smith, Clarence N., 3513.
Smith, Daniel B., 39, 3513, NB76.
Smith, Daniel B., No. 2, 334.
Smith, Dinah, 2527.

Smith, Edna, 613, NB455, NB592.
Smith, Eliza, 700, 2463, 2489, 2776, 382?.
Smith, Ella, 613, 2169, 2912.
Smith, Emily, 2847.
Smith, Emma, 392, C84, 2776, 3499, 3896, NB-
 70, NB715, NB719, M189.
Smith, Enoch O., NB206, M319.
Smith, Estella, NB920.
Smith, Ester, NB698.
Smith, Eurania, 613, NB698.
Smith, Freeman, 3129.
Smith, Frank, 1851.
Smith, Franklin M., 39.
Smith, George, 1918, 2527, 2698, 2941, 3075.
Smith, George W., 700, 701, 912, 941, 978.
Smith, Gladdis G., NB393.
Smith, Grace, 1785, 3499.
Smith, Guy, 613.
Smith, Hattie, 462, 463.
Smith, Hinty, 3403, NB911.
Smith, Hodge, 2452.
Smith, Horace Greeley, 1401.
Smith, Ida, 1736.
Smith, Isaac, 1736.
Smith, James, 24 2, 2527, 3826.
Smith, James M.C. 47.
Smith, James, Ross, 912.
Smith, Janie, 789, NB206, M319.
Smith, Jay G., 1401.
Smith, Jeffrey, 3014.
Smith, Jemima, 701, 941, 978.
Smith, Jim, 803, 830, 959, 2250.
Smith, Joe, 1918, 2527, 3075.
Smith, John, 1258, 1896, 2186, 2204, 2776, M-
 383.
Smith, John F., 613, 1896, NB698.
Smith, John G., 613, 1131, 1401, 1402.
Smith, John Jr., 3295.
Smith, John T., 1785, 2006.
Smith, J. M., NB393.
Smith, Joseph, 830.
Smith, Katie, 1918.
Smith, Kogee, 1918.
Smith, Lawa, 993.
Smith, Lawrence, 613.
Smith, Lee Anderson, 1835.
Smith, Lena, 2250.
Smith, Loe, 3354.
Smith, Lewis, 292, 613.
Smith, Lina, 2847.
Smith, Liza, 1735.
Smith, Lizzie, 114, 292, 424, 2250, 2452, 2941.
Smith, Louina, 993, 2032.
Smith, Louis, 3129.
Smith, Louis N., 1402.
Smith, Louisa, 1679, 1851, 1896, 2776.
Smith, Louisa B., 1401, 1622.
Smith, Lucile, 1401.
Smith, Lucinda, 39, 41, 613, 637, 684, 748, 1131,
 1401, 1402.
Smith, Lumsey, 392, 2847.
Smith, Lydia, 2217, 2218, 2508.
Smith, Margaret Ellen, M388.
Smith, Maria E., 1039.
Smith, Marsey, 392, M359, M360.
Smith, Martha, 101, 307, 912, 1012, 1022, 1679
 3520, NB592.
Smith, Martin, 1735, 1736, 2941, M408.
Smith, Martin W., 959.

Smith, Mary, 830, 959, 1258, 2169, 2186, 2204, 2544, 3035, 3902, NB960.
Smith, Mary I., 39, 3513, NB76.
Smith, Matilda, 446, 1918, 2344, 3075.
Smith, Mickey, 2108, 3855, M408.
Smith, Micky, 2508, 3855, M408.
Smith, Miley, 3014.
Smith, Millie, 1736, M408.
Smith, Mollie, 1736, 2452, M63.
Smith, Mose, 114.
Smith, Nannie Lou, 1402.
Smith, Napka, 1826.
Smith, Neeley, 1736.
Smith, Nellie, 2183, 2941.
Smith, Nina, 334.
Smith, Oliver Russell, NB206.
Smith, Orrey, 2169.
Smith, Pearl, 39, 613.
Smith, Peggy, 47.
Smith, Phatimma, 959.
Smith, Rachel, 765, 1785, 2006, NB393.
Smith, Rannie, 613, NB698.
Smith, Rashie C., 1402.
Smith, Rhoda, 2250.
Smith, Rosa, 2381.
Smith, Rose, 1918.
Smith, Ruth, NB76, M383.
Smith, Sallie, 114, 2250, 3946.
Smith, Sally, 392.
Smith, Sam, 446, 700, 959, 1735, 2756, 3855.
Smith, Samuel, 334.
Smith, Samuel C., 959.
Smith, Sarah, 446, 2204, 3503, 3813, NB920 M123.
Smith, Sarney, 2869.
Smith, Sarty, 2912.
Smith, Segomaha, 2912.
Smith, Seper, 1826.
Smith, Sheldon, 41.
Smith, Shelton, 637, 684, 748.
Smith, Stephen, 684, 748, 3499, NB70.
Smith, Steve J., NB416.
Smith, Susan, 1736.
Smith, Susie, 2452.
Smith, Tecumseh, 3295.
Smith, Terry Steven, NB70.
Smith, Thomas M., 959, NB415, NB416, M388.
Smith, Tilda, 1918, 2527.
Smith, Tildy, 1918, 2527.
Smith, Tillie May, M383.
Smith, Violet Elizabeth, M319.
Smith, Wade, 1679, NB592.
Smith, Walter C., 1401.
Smith, Washington, 2247, 2248.
Smith, Wesley, 2032.
Smith, Wiley, 1918, 2250.
Smith, Wililam, 2169, 2527.
Smith, William S., 39.
Smith, Willie, 3503.
Smith, Willie G., 1835.
Smith, Willis, 613.
Smith, Winey, 2169.
Smith, Zular M., 1402.
Smock, Anna Louise, NB45.
Smock, Eloise Grayson, 1960, NB45.
Smock, John C., NB45.
Smoermeryeche, 1449.
Smudayee, 980.
Snake, Cotahyar, 175.
Snakeya, Abram, 389, M275

Snakeya, Amos, M274.
Snakeya, David, 389, 3421, NB998, M274.
Snakeya, Gabriel, 389.
Snakaya, Heness, NB998.
Snakeya, Mary, 389.
Snakeya, Molleanna, 389, 3421, NB998, M274
Snakeya, Mollianna, 3421, 389, NB998, M274.
Snakeya, Nora, M275.
Snakeya, Onie, 389.
Snakeya, Tobe, 3421.
Snap, Andy, NB1008.
Snap, Dickson, 2486.
Snap, James, 400, NB1008.
Snap, Mabele, 1899, NB1008.
Snap, Mary, 2486.
Snapp, Amanda, 1333.
Snapp, Dick, 1333.
Sneed, Almorence, 307.
Sneed, Artra, 101.
Sneed, Charles, 1033, 3793, 101, 307, 1013, 1022, 3520, 3971.
Sneed, Charles, Jr., 3971.
Sneed, Charley, 101, 307, 1013, 1022, 1033, 3520, 3793, 3971.
Sneed, Charlie, 3810.
Sneed, Ernest, 3971.
Sneed, Frank, 1013.
Sneed, George, 3793, NB1010, NB1011.
Sneed, George Everett, 3793.
Sneed, Hannah, 3793, NB1010, NB1011.
Sneed, John, 3810, 3971.
Sneed, Larzar, NB1011.
Sneed, Leonard, 3793.
Sneed, Maron, 3793.
Sneed, Martha, 307, 101, 1033, 3793, 3810.
Sneed, Pamima, 3971.
Sneed, Panina, 307.
Sneed, Peoria, 307.
Sneed, Sue Willie, 3971.
Sneed, Susie Rose, NB1010.
Sneed, William, 3520.
Snow, Ada, NB1084.
Snow, Ca-pah-ny, 2161, 2257, NB1084, M310.
Snow, Cheparney, 2257.
Snow, Far-lo-con-we-ney, 2783, M310.
Snow, Harthlee, 2161.
Snow, Jessie, 1948.
Snow, John, M310.
Snow, Louisa, 2161, NB975.
Snow, Martha, 1948, NB884.
Snow, Tecumseh, 1948, 2161.
Snow, Wesley, 2161.
Snow, Yar-la-co-we-ney, 2161.
Snowden, Lucy, 3973.
Soapey, 1071.
Sobige, Artus, 2459.
Soc-con-tay, 3124.
Socer, 1962.
Sochalage, 1483, 1572, 1484.
Sochalagee, 1483, 1484, 1572.
Sochee, Nancy, 1558.
Sochee, Tom, 1558.
Sochker, 1554.
Sochonagee, 1716, 2480.
So-con-thla-ney, 2180, 3704, NB390, M292.
Soc you thlikee, 2773, 2801.
Soda, 2618.
Sofa, 446, 1645, 1695.
Sofallah, Hannah, 2308.
Sofalley, 2982.

Sophia, 2119, 2553, 3011.
Sophie, 282, 2504.
Sophoyee, 2530.
Sopsey, 2384, 2510.
Sorbe, Anna Belle, 1700.
Sorbe, Mary E., 1700.
Sorbe, Susan, 1700.
Sorbe, Wm., 1700.
Sorrell, Dorothy, 1209, 3559.
Sorrell, Julia, 1209.
Sorrell, Lillie, 3559.
Sorrell, William, 1209, 3559.
Sosah, 2771.
Sosar, 2145.
Sosaye, 2720.
Soska, 1709.
Sosolee, 146.
Sotanhley, 2231.
Sothar, 1265, 1266.
Sounah, 1195.
Southlarpecher, 3128.
Southlope, Louisa, 2311.
Sowa, 693.
Sowanhoke, 81.
Sowarley, 1454.
Soweka, 1452.
Soweka, Lewis, 1452.
Sowite, 2090.
Sowwihe, 659.
Soxlopinkala, 14.
Spaniard, Alice, 2443.
Spaniard, Annie, 2443.
Spaniard, Chiler, 2497.
Spaniard, Chotie, 2497.
Spaniard, Henry, 2497.
Spaniard, James, 2443, 2454, 2457.
Spaniard, Jemima, 2443.
Spaniard, Joe, 2443.
Spaniard, John, 3237.
Spaniard, Louisa, 2497.
Spaniard, Malinda, 2443.
Spaniard, Martha, 2497.
Spaniard, Misselda, 2443.
Spaniard, Simon, 2443.
Spaulding, Edith, 2055, 3393.
Spaulding, Etta, 440.
Spaulding, George W., 3393.
Spaulding, Grace B., 440.
Spaulding, H. B., 440.
Spaulding, Homer, O., 440.
Spaulding, Homer R., 3393.
Spaulding, James S., 440.
Spaulding, Josephine, 440.
Spaulding, Lelia A., 440.
Spaulding, Samuel B., 440.
Spaulding, Sophia, 974.
Spaulding, Thomas L., 440.
Speeny, 1162.
Spencer, Lonah, NB1021.
Spencer, Loma, NB1022.
Spencer, Ludie, 136, NB1021, 1022.
Spencer, Ramsey, NB1021, NB1022.
Speeney, 1162.
Spocogee, Polly, 3229.
Spogeyhula, 2769.
Spoka, 1691.
Spuncher, 173.
Squire, 233.
Squire, Alashoconconay, 596.
Squire, Annie, 590, NB288.

389

Squire, Beckie, 604.
Squire, Candy, 604.
Squire, Delia, 604.
Squire, Hannah, 604.
Squire, Hepsey, 604.
Squire, John, 596, 604, NB288.
Squire, Kittie, 3308.
Squire, Noah, 604.
Squire, Sarah, NB288.
Squire, Sukey, 596.
Squire, Tekecoconay, 604. '
Squire, Tom, 604.
Stake, Albert, 431, NB352, M300.
Stake, David, 131.
Stake, Eliza, 448, NB693.
Stake, Ellen, 431.
Stake, Lizzie, 131.
Stake, Louisa, M300.
Stake, James, 1313.
Stake, Jeffie, 431.
Stake, Jennie, 431.
Stake, Jonas, 431, 448, 1792.
Stake, Joseph, 131.
Stake, Missie, NB352.
Stake, Salina, 131.
Stake, Sallie, 431, NB352, M300.
Stake, Winey, 1792.
Staley, Enconcoconthla, 588.
Staley, John, 588, NB789, NB1071.
Staley, Kissie, NB1071.
Staley, Nellie, NB789.
Staley, Sakcota, 588, NB789, NB1071.
Staley, Tar-so-con-thla, 588.
Stalla, Miste, 1458.
Stand, Lizzie, 3739.
Stand, Phillip, 2920, 3739.
Stand, Thomas, 3739.
Standwaitie, 1675.
Standwaitie, Joseph, 1675.
Standwaitie, Toady, 1675.
Standwaitie, Wilson, 1675.
Stanley, Chas. A., CE4052.
Stanley, Charles, 4006.
Stanley, Earl A., 4006.
Stanley, Joseph C., 4006.
Stanley, Mattie, E., 4006, CE4052.
Stanley, Pearl A., 4006.
Stanley, Pleasonit, 4006.
Stanley, Wootsey, CE4052.
Stanwaite, 3139.
Star, Charley, 3984, NB1271.
Star, Robert, 1539.
Star, Sina, 1539.
Starfey, 2843.
Starr, Adam, 3742.
Starr, Annie, 2720, 3126, 3984, NB627.
Starr, Charles, 3984, NB1271.
Starr, Chesley, 2052, 3126, 3821.
Starr, Chipley, 2125, M342.
Starr, Cora Ellis, 3984, NB1271.
Starr, Daniel, 1773.
Starr, Edward, 2720.
Starr, Ella, 1747.
Starr, Emma, 3821.
Starr, Gertrude, 3984.
Starr, Hebsey, 1539.
Starr, Henry, 3984.
Starr, James, 2720.
Starr, Jesse J., NB1271.
Starr, Katie, 2052, 3126.

Starr, Lena, 1747, NB166, M448.
Starr, Lewis, 2720, M448.
Starr, Lillie, 1747.
Starr, Lizzie, 2720.
Starr, Lona, 1747.
Starr, Louisa, 1773.
Starr, Lucinda, 2365.
Starr, Lydia, 1747.
Starr, Mahala, 2940, M448.
Starr, Martin, 2125, 2630.
Starr, Martha, 2052.
Starr, Melissa, 2720.
Starr, Miley, 522, 893.
Starr, Minnie, 1539.
Starr, Mollie, 3821, CE4053.
Starr, Moses, 1539.
Starr, Nancy, 2125, NB1288, NB1289.
Starr, Nellie, 2720.
Starr, Nina, 1539.
Starr, Pulhokey, 2720.
Starr, Reuben, 2125.
Starr, Robert, 1492, 1747, CE4053.
Starr, Sallie, 2630.
Starr, Sarne, CE4053.
Starr, Susie, 1539, 3126.
Starr, Thomas, 1747.
Starr, Walter, M342.
Statham, Elizabeth, M227.
Statham, Gertrude Bennett, 2714, M227.
Statham, W. H., M227.
Stebbin, Martin, NB670, NB671.
Stebbin, Wisey, 3190, NB670, NB671
Steel, Mary, 676.
Steele, Alex W., 915.
Steele, Catherine C., 1399, 3798.
Steele, Dave, 617.
Steele, Edward, 287.
Steele, Lena N., 915.
Steele, Louisa, 287.
Steele, Mamie, 2733.
Steele, Mary, 3798.
Steele, Rachel, 915.
Steele, Robert, 3798.
Steele, Samuel Edward, 915.
Steele, Simon, 2733.
Steele, Susan, 2733.
Steele, Tula, 617.
Steele, Wyley, 287.
Steen, John Howard, M246.
Steen, Katie, 362, 3840, M246.
Steen, Robert, 3840.
Steen, Walter, 3840, M246.
Steen, Walter H., 3840, M246
· Steinmachee, John, 886.
Stephen, 2678, 3190.
Stephens, Green, 3586, NB342, NB343.
Stephens, Johnnie, NB343.
Stephens, Millie, 1128, NB342, NB343.
Stephens, Mollie, 3586.
Stephens, Vadie, 3586.
Stephens, Willie, NB342.
Stephenson, A. P., 1584, NB396, M62.
Stephenson, Augusta, 1584.
Stephenson, Eddie, M62.
Stephenson, Nancy, 2587, NB1144, NB1145.
Stephenson, Polly, 1584, NB396, M62.
Stephenson, Siney, NB396.
Stepney, 2750, 2885.
Stepney, Liley, 2885.
Stepney, Lizzie, NB1251.

Stepney, Sissie, 2885.
Stepney, Susie, 2898, NB1251.
Stepney, Thompson, 2885, NB1251.
Sterbargee, 2864.
Stevens, Bryan, 1049.
Stevens, Cicero, 1030, 3557.
Stevens, Clarence O., 3557.
Stevens, Ida Bell, M239.
Stevens, Idella, 3557, M1030.
Stevens, Lenow, M240.
Stevens, Mary, 1049, NB344, NB692, M241.
Stevens, Mose, 3947.
Stevens, Myrtle M., 1030.
Stevens, Pearl V., 1030.
Stevens, Sarah, 3947, M239, M240.
Stevens, Stella I., 1030.
Stevens, Wiley, 3947.
Stevens, William, 1049, 3947, M239, M240.
Stevens, Wm. A., 1049, 3947, M239, M240.
Stevenson, Mamie, 3360.
Stewart, Albert P., 1691, 3521.
Stewart, Alice, 1108.
Stewart, America, 1108, 3694, NB589.
Stewart, Ammie, 1108.
Stewart, Annie, 1692.
Stewart, Clyde, 1691.
Stewart, Edna, 3694.
Stewart, Effie, 1108.
Stewart, Floyd Lee, NB589.
Stewart, George E , 3521.
Stewart, John, 586.
Stewart, Louisa, 1691, 3521.
Stewart, Lucy, 1404.
Stewart, Noah, 1404.
Stewart, Rhoda, 2517.
Stewart, Robert, 586, 1804.
Stewart, Robert W., 1404, 1691, 1692, 3158.
Stewart, Ruthie Pearl, 1108.
Stewart, Sofa, 1804.
Stewart, Sophia, 1691, 1692, 3158.
Stewart, Thomas A., 1692.
Stewart, William H., 1108, 3694, NB589.
Stewart, Wm., 1076.
Stick, Jennie, 132.
Stidham, Albert L., 689.
Stidham, Albert P., 2715.
Stidham, Ara A., 1764.
Stidham, Ariada, 1608.
Stidham, Ben, 3712.
Stidham, Buckner Lawrence, 3150.
Stidham, Cleo, NB3.
Stidham, Clifford, 2715.
Stidham, Edward, 2445.
Stidham, Eliza, 2445, NB867, NB1197, NB1200.
Stidham, Eloita, 1764.
Stidham, George, 2445, 3150, 3889.
Stidham, Geo. W., 360, 689, 814, 1608, 1764, 2715.
Stidham, Geo. W. Jr., 689.
Stidham, George W. Sr., 689, NB2, NB3.
Stidham, Georgiana, 1764.
Stidham, G. W., 360, 6 9, 814, 1608, 1764, 2715
Stidham, Harney, 2445, 2446.
Stidham, Harriet, 2484.
Stidham, Jack, 81.
Stidham, Jennie, 689, NB2, NB3.
Stidham, John, 1939, 2446.
Stidham, Johnny, NB1197.
Stidham, Johnson, 2445, 2446, 3294.
Stidham, Kittie, 689.

Stidham, Leah, 1939.
Stidham, Lee, 2484.
Stidham, Lela, 689.
Stidham, Leola May, 1764.
Stidham, Leonidas G., 1764.
Stidham, Lura M., 1764.
Stidham, Marie Oleta, 689.
Stidham, Mattie, NB867.
Stidham, Millie, 1939.
Stidham, Nellie, 3294.
Stidham, Nutwoche, 3294.
Stidham, Ottie, 689, M64.
Stidham, Polly, 2445.
Stidham, Rose, 2159.
Stidham, Sarah, 360, 689, 814, 2715.
Stidham, Sarah C., 360, 689, 814, 2715.
Stidham, Selestine, 3711.
Stidham, Thomas Edward, NB2.
Stidham, Theodore E., 360, 3712.
Stidham, Theo E., 3712, 360.
Stidham, Timmie, 2445, NB867, NB1197, NB-
   1200.
Stidham, Timmy, 2445, NB867, NB1197, NB-
   1200.
Stidham, William, 3889.
Stidham, Wilson, 81.
Stinson, Charley, 2292.
Stoddard, Jesse, 879.
Stoddard, Joseph, NB460.
Stoddard, Lousanna, 879, NB460, M317.
Stoddard, Mamie, 879.
Stoddard, Stella, M317.
Stoddard, William, 879, NB460, M317.
Storm, Annie, 718.
Storm, Bertha, NB419.
Storm, Eliza ,718.
Storm, Gladys, 3683.
Storm, John, 718, 3683, NB419, NB420.
Storm, Lou, 718, 3683, NB419, NB420.
Storm, Parelee, 718.
Storm, Pocahontas, NB420.
Stout, Ethel, M161.
Stout, James C., M161.
Stout, Lou Ellen, 956, M161.
Stover, Daniel, 1011, 3438, M72.
Stover, Daniel Jr., M72.
Stover, Eli, 1011.
Stover, Lavina, 1011, 3438, M72.
Stover, Lillie, 1011.
Stover, Reuben, 3438.
Stover, Wasa, 1011.
Stover, Willie, 1011.
Stratton, Louisa, 880.
Strickland, Jennie, 906.
Strickland, Sam, 906.
Strouvelle, Alice Kendall, NB58
Strouvelle, C. E., NB58, NB59.
Strouvelle, Charles Edward Jr., NB58.
Strouvelle, Susanna Barnett, 1, NB58, NB59.
Stubblefield, Ed, NB559.
Stubblefield, Ella M., 2114.
Stubblefield, E. S., 3591.
Stubblefield, Ida, 2114, NB584, NB585, M174.
Stubblefield, J. M., 2114.
Stubblefield, John, NB584, NB585, NB174.
Stubblefield, Johnnie, NB585.
Stubblefield, Joseph S., 3591.
Stubblefield, Lousanna, 1665, 3591, NB559.
Stubblefield, McAfee, NB559.
Stubblefield, Minnie, NB584.

Stubblefield, Ross Marion, M174.
Suattala, 2614.
Subbioye, 2497.
Suche, 1509.
Suchemerica, 2359.
Suckhecha, 1463.
Suckie, 2745.
Sucky, 2607, NB1154.
Sudcharkey, 3942.
Sudcharkey, Kidney, 3942.
Sudcharkey, Sampson, 3942.
Sudcharkey, Sohsuka, 3942.
Sudduth, Bob, NB1042.
Sudduth, Phoebe, 229, NB1042.
Sudduth, Rosetta, NB1042.
Sudeka, 2859.
Suder, Choatkey, 3937.
Suder, Lobla, 2170.
Suder, Bunny, 2170.
Suego, 3206.
Suequegah, 2176.
Suffanefka, 2830.
Suffekah, 381.
Suffochechee, 1463.
Sugar, Adaline, 36, 117, 200.
Sugar, Adeline, 36, 117, 200.
Sugar, Armster, 117.
Sugar, Eddie, 1734.
Sugar, Ellen, 1171.
Sugar, Helen, 657, 904, 1734, 3632.
Sugar, James, 657, 904, 1171, 1734.
Sugar, James, Jr., 3632.
Sugar, James, Sr., 3632.
Sugar, Jennie, 897.
Sugar, Joseph, 904.
Sugar, Kizzie, 657.
Sugar, Nancy, 117, 657, 1927.
Sugar, Pilot, 657.
Sugar, Sam, 1734.
Sugar, Thomas, 117, 200, 657, 1927.
Sugar, Togy, 117, 938.
Sugar, Tom, 117, 200, 657, 1927.
Sugar, Wesley, 36, 117, 200.
Sugar, Yarner, 657.
Suhkene, 2914.
Sukanatah, 2207.
Sukey, 181, 1524, 1573, 1624, 1625, 1691, 1786,
        2459, 2758, 2789, 2886, 2947, 3014.
Sukie, 3945.
Sukkahke, 399, 704.
Sula, Kogee, 1051.
Sulka, 1325, 1724, 2100.
Sulkoyeste, 2847.
Sullen, Tom, 425.
Sullins, Gladys May, M187.
Sullins, James N., M187.
Sullins, Muskogee Essie, 3004, M187.
Sullivan, 1142.
Sullivan, Addie, 521.
Sullivan, Annie, 23.
Sullivan, Becky, 520.
Sullivan, Charlie, 423, 2625.
Sullivan, Eliza, 1242.
Sullivan, Ellen, 520.
Sullivan, Emma, M424.
Sullivan, George, 520, 1242, 1420, 1609, 3534.
Sullivan, Hagey, M424, M425.
Sullivan, Hattie, 5.
Sullivan, Helen, 23.
Sullivan, Jim, 1523.

Sullivan, Jimmie, 1523.
Sullivan, Jimmy, 3853.
Sullivan, James, 5, 23.
Sullivan, Jinney, 1471.
Sullivan, John, M425.
Sullivan, Lizzie, 521, 3534, M135
Sullivan, Louina, 388.
Sullivan, Louisa, 23.
Sullivan, Lucy, 3333.
Sullivan, Mary Ann, 1242.
Sullivan, Minnie, 1523, NB651.
Sullivan, Obey, 23.
Sullivan, Peggy, 520, 1242.
Sullivan, Sallie, 388, 2555, 2799.
Sullivan, Sally, 3853.
Sullivan, Sam, 388.
Sullivan, Stephen, 1471.
Sullivan, Sulphur, 3853.
Sullivan, Sunday, 521.
Sullivan, Thomas, 2799.
Sullivan, William, 388, 521, 2555, 3534, M424,
        M425.
Sullivan, Willie, 2799.
Sulma, 2465.
Sulphur, Alex, 3627.
Sulphur, Andrew, M57.
Sulphur, Chepon, 880, 881.
Sulphur, Edmond, 881.
Sulphur, George, 881.
Sulphur, Hattie, 3944.
Sulphur, James, 881, 3944, M57.
Sulphur, Jennie, 270, M57.
Sulphur, Jim, 3627.
Sulphur, Kizzie, 881, 3944.
Sumaga, 1743.
Sumehcha, 1328, M446.
Sumeyischee, 1535, 1536.
Sumhohka, 1230.
Sumihahye, 1242.
Sumihitchka, 3074.
Sumka, 1452, 1751, 2441, M191.
Sumka, Henry, M191.
Sumka, Willie, 1452.
Summers, Ada, 875.
Summers, Clinton B., 3660.
Summers, Clinton P., 875.
Summers, Cordia, 875.
Summers, Dee, 875.
Summers, Fannie, 3660.
Summers, Frank, 875.
Summers, James, 875.
Summers, Mary, 875.
Summers, M. J., 875, 3660.
Summers, Pet, 875.
Summers, Thos., 777, 875.
Sumnubba, 3319.
Sumsey, 1820.
Sumsey, Sissie, 1820.
Sunday, 1567, 1568.
Sunday, Alex, 300.
Sunday, Anderson, 300.
Sunday, Edmund, 115.
Sunday, Ellen, 300.
Sunday, Ellis, 115, 1918, 2662.
Sunday, Ellis B., 115, 1918, 2662.
Sunday, Kizzie, 300.
Sunday, Mattie, 2662.
Sunday, Miley, 115.
Sunday, Mollie, 1918, 2662.
Sunday, Tilda, 1918.

Tarvin, Marie Louisa, NB384.
Tarvin, Marion, 3264.
Tarvin, Marion E., 345, 347, 3264.
Tarvin, Mary B., 3932.
Tarvin, Patience, 345, 3436, M467.
Tarvin, Patience F., NB384.
Tarvin, Patient, 3264.
Tarvin, P. F., 345, 3264, 3436, NB384, M467.
Tarvin, Pleasant F., 345, 3264, 3436, NB384, M467.
Tarvin, Random, 3264.
Tarvin, Rita, 345.
Tarvin, Sehoy M., 3264.
Tarvin, Sophia F., 347, 3264.
Tarvin, Theresa, 345, 3436.
Tarwoligee, 1278. .
Taryoboska, 1688.
Taryole, 1309, 3865, NB553, M445.
Taryole, Frank, NB553.
Taryole, Marfy, 1309, M445, NB553.
Taryole, Tupper, M445.
Taryolie, Turner, 3865.
Tasathla, 603.
Tasehoke, 1114.
Tasheteapathla, 604.
Taskegee, 2356, 2915.
Taskegee, Annie, 2356.
Taskegee, Wicey, 2915.
Tasonkaynay, 2705.
Tate, Annie May, NB799.
Tate, Deck, NB543, M173.
Tate, Elmer, M173.
Tate, Flora Ada, NB800.
Tate, Jesse, M298.
Tate, John Wash, 3825.
Tate, Joseph, NB543.
Tate, J. W., NB799, NB800, M298.
Tate, Mary, 1629, 3825, NB543, NB799, NB-800, M173, M298.
Tate, Maty, 3825.
Tate, Twintilla, 3825.
Tathlatakee, 2740.
Taye, 2897.
Taylor, 629, 1147, 1366, 1908, 1909, 2428, 2948, 3346.
Taylor, Ab, 1031.
Taylor, Abraham, 1147.
Taylor, Ad, 828, 1678.
Taylor, Ada, 2428.
Taylor, Albert, 3367.
Taylor, Artie, 3367.
Taylor, Barney, 1109.
Taylor, Charles, 2541, 2542, 2543, 2548, 2942, 3367.
Taylor, Charley, 2541, 2542, 2543, 2548, 2942, 3367.
Taylor, Cub, 1167, 3367.
Taylor, Dick, 961, 1109.
Taylor, Dumsey, 2548.
Taylor, Eli, NB1047.
Taylor, Eliza, 2428, 2543, 2948.
Taylor, Ellen, 1109.
Taylor, Ellis, 3367.
Taylor, Emma, 1909, 2540, NB930, NB931.
Taylor, Frank, 1031, 1907.
Taylor, Fred, 545.
Taylor, Granderson, 3269.
Taylor, Grandison, 545.
Taylor, Grayson, 239.
Taylor, Hardy, 2541, 2542, 2543, 2548, 2942.

Taylor, Harry C., 304.
Taylor, Isaac, 2540.
Taylor, Jacob, 2543.
Taylor, James, 192.
Taylor, Jemima, 2543, NB888.
Taylor, Jennie, 3379.
Taylor, John W., 3269.
Taylor, Jololonfah, 2428.
Taylor, Jonas, 2206.
Taylor, Judy, NB1205.
Taylor, Kizzie, 1909, M157.
Taylor, Leah, 3367.
Taylor, Leechie, 2942, NB1258, NB1259, M474
Taylor, Lewis, 1908.
Taylor, Lila, 1072.
Taylor, Lilia, 1147, M338.
Taylor, Liza, 1151, NB1047.
Taylor, Lizzi , 2548.
Taylor, Lucile, NB829.
Taylor, Lucinda, 2540.
Taylor, Lucy, 2291, NB507, M188.
Taylor, Major, 698.
Taylor, Mannie, 3336.
Taylor, Marchie, 2548.
Taylor, Maria, 1907, 1908, 1909.
Taylor, Mary, 2727.
Taylor, Melvina L., 192, 193, 194, 783.
Taylor, Milea, 2540, NB1220.
Taylor, Mitchell, 1326.
Taylor, Mollie, 2206.
Taylor, Monny, 2206, M320, M321.
Taylor, Nancy, 1109, NB356.
Taylor, Nellie, 545, 2301, 3367, NB1205.
Taylor, Parthenia, 545.
Taylor, Pearl, 304.
Taylor, Peggy, 828, 1031.
Taylor, Roley, 3367, NB1205.
Taylor, Rosa, 304, NB829.
Taylor, Royal B., 192.
Taylor, Sam, 1343, 2206, 3336.
Taylor, Sammy, 1147.
Taylor, Sarah, 3367.
Taylor, Sarpsey, 2543, NB1047.
Taylor, Silla, 2206.
Taylor, Silvey, 3336.
Taylor, Silwey, 2206.
Taylor, Sissie, 1150.
Taylor, Sol, 2301.
Taylor, Solomon, 545.
Taylor, Soma, 3367.
Taylor, Sinda, 1343,
Taylor, Susana, 1326.
Taylor, Susie, 2543.
Taylor, Taylor, 2540, 2548.
Taylor, Teperke, 282.
Taylor, Timmie, 2428.
Taylor, Tom, 1326.
Taylor, Turne· F., 1150.
Taylor, Will, 304.
Taylor, William, 192, NB829.
Tayoposka, 3344.
Tea, Amos, 1688.
Tea, Anna, 1688.
Tea, Ellen, 1688.
Tea, Emma. 1688.
Tea, Judy, 1688.
Tea, Lucy, 1688.
Tea, Millie, 3132.
Tea, Mollie, 2210.
Tea, Nancy, 1688.

Thlocco, Toger, 886.
Thlocco, Yahar, 1485.
Thloccochee, Nehar, 1695.
Thloccogee, Neho, 1645.
Thloskogee, 2238.
Thlssacoweney, 2710.
Thlucco, Pote, 1939.
Thluppa (or Thloppie), 3945.
Throckmorton, Ida, 628, NB180.
Throckmorton, James W., 628, NB180.
Thomas, 61, 1522, 1523, 1562, 4023.
Thomas, Adam, 1328.
Thomas, Aggie, 1958, M128.
Thomas, Albert, 2943.
Thomas, Amos, 1522.
Thomas, Bepsey, 1522, 1523.
Thomas, Bettie, 1328, 1523, 2655, 3095, 3627.
Thomas, Boxy, 412, 413.
Thomas, Crawford, 792.
Thomas, David S., M128.
Thomas, Dick, 2811.
Thomas, Douglass, 948.
Thomas, Eliza, 3627.
Thomas, Emily, 3982.
Thomas, Emma, 592, 593, 594. 1523.
Thomas, George W., 948.
Thomas, Grant, M261.
Thomas, Hardy, 3982.
.Thomas, Harley, 3095, 3627, M495.
Thomas, James A., 1958.
Thomas, James C., 1958.
Thomas, John, 948, 1328, 1782, 2362.
Thomas, Johnson, 594.
Thomas, Kaley, 1328.
Thomas, Kate, 3215.
Thomas, Katie, 2541.
Thomas, Leaster, 3828.
Thomas, Lena, 3627, NB954, NB955.
Thomas, Linda, 2541.
Thomas, Lizzie, 598, 1915, NB792.
Thomas, Lizzie Lou, 1958.
Thomas, Louisa, 2541.
Thomas, Lucy, 3627, 4016.
Thomas, Lydia, 3627, 3982, M495.
Thomas, Mack, 592, M242.
Thomas, Mary Ellen, 948.
Thomas, Melesse, 724.
Thomas, Melissi, 792.
Thomas, Millie, 2541.
Thomas, Milly, 1523, NB1162.
Thomas, Minnie Harris, M495.
Thomas, Mollie E., 948.
Thomas, Nora, M242.
Thomas, Parnosky, 1328.
Thomas, Philip, 592.
Thomas, Polly, 393.
Thomas, Sam, 593, 3828, M261.
Thomas, Sampson, 3627.
Thomas, Sarah, 592, M242.
Thomas, Sophia, 593, 3828, M261.
Thomas, Susie, M128.
Thomas, Tumsey, 3095, NB633, NB634.
Thomas, Waitie, 2362, 3542.
Thomas, William, 594.
Thomas, Willie, 2804, 3542.
Thomas, Wm. R., 592, 593, 594.
Thomasey, 2541.
Thomasoche, 2471.
Thompson, 911, 2946, 3113, 3197.
Thompson, Alex, 65, 3137.

Thompson.
Thompson,
Thompson,
Thompson,
Thompson,
Thompson,
Thompson,
Thompson,
Thompson,
Thompson,
Thompson,
Thompson,
Thompson,
Thompson,
Thompson,
Thompson,
Thompson,
Thompson,
Thompson,
Thompson,
Thompson,
Thompson,
Thompson,
Thompson,
Thompson,
Thompson,
Thompson,
Thompson,
Thompson,
Thompson,
Thompson,
Thompson,
Thompson,
Thompson,
Thompson,

Thompson,

Thompson,
Thompson,
Thompson,
Thompson,
Thompson,
Thompson,
Thompson,
Thompson,
Thompson,
Thompson,
Thompson,
Thompson,
Thompson,
Thompson,

Thompson,

Thompson,
Thompson,
Thompson,
Thompson,
Thompson,

Tiger, Anna, 3983.
Tiger, Annie, 157, 1003, 2120, 2319, 2472, M121, NB1204, NB217.
Tiger, Archie, 2033, 2944.
Tiger, Arnie, 2368.
Tiger, Barney, 1607, NB148.
Tiger, Ben, 246, 335, M120, M121.
Tiger, Benny, 2472.
Tiger, Bermose, 2472.
Tiger, Bessie, 1224, 2944.
Tiger, Betsey, 958.
Tiger, Billy, 201, 336, 1265, 1559, 1871.
Tiger, Bob, 3165.
Tiger, Bryan, NB1107.
Tiger, Candy, 1720, 1721, 1722, 1723.
Tiger, Cartogee, 2571.
Tiger, Casey, 999, NB1072, NB1073.
Tiger, Catchochee, 1571.
Tiger, Chapley, 1723.
Tiger, Charkocharney, 3033.
Tiger, Charley, 1607.
Tiger, Choc, 2075.
Tiger, Chotke, (1547 Seminole), M400.
Tiger, Chotky, (Seminole 1547), M400.
Tiger, Cinda, 392, 2594, 3764, NB1048.
Tiger, Cochar, 1144.
Tiger, Coge, 1721.
Tiger, Coketharney, 3033.
Tiger, Consana, 1948, 1600, 1947.
Tiger, Consanna, 1600, 1947, 1948.
Tiger, Conzie, 957, NB183, NB184.
Tiger, Coody, 2163.
Tiger, Cooper, 2240, NB629.
Tiger, Cotala, 3812.
Tiger, Cotchar, 1202.
Tiger, Cotsar, 342.
Tiger, Daniel, 1202, 1224, 2868, 3231, 3832, NB 763.
Tiger, Dave, 342, 1600, 1721, NB162, NB163.
Tiger, David, 1224, 2240, NB487, NB488.
Tiger, Deovocha, NB220.
Tiger, Dewitt T., 1916.
Tiger, Dollie, 598.
Tiger, Dosie, 2112.
Tiger, Edna, M155.
Tiger, Edward, NB162.
Tiger, Edward, B., 3539.
Tiger, Elba, 3812.
Tiger, Eli, NB1146.
Tiger, Eliza, 201, 215, 395, 398, 2174, 2403, 2732, 3582.
Tiger, Elsie, 253.
Tiger, Emma, 2868, NB709.
Tiger, Ethan Allen H., NB66.
Tiger, Eugene M., 1916.
Tiger, Ewnah J., NB148.
Tiger, Fancy, 957, NB183, NB184.
Tiger, Fannie, 1516, 1607, 1608.
Tiger, Farney, 969.
Tiger, George, 1003, 1607, 1743, 2106, 2235, 2403, 2725, 2817, NB163, NB1204.
Tiger, George W., 40, 3551, 1916, NB1107.
Tiger, Geo. W., 3593.
Tiger, Goody, 3034, 3338.
Tiger, Hannah, 2629.
Tiger, Hapsey, 2319.
Tiger, Heconconthla, 3991.
Tiger, Helen May, 3551.
Tiger, Hettie, 23, 58, 1571, 1916, NB220
Tiger, Homat, 1559.

Tiger, Hully, 3157.
Tiger, Ida R., 1916.
Tiger, Isaac, 633.
Tiger, Jack, 186, 398, 2107, 3033.
Tiger, Jackson, 3392.
Tiger, Jacob, 969, 1559, 2074, 2733, 3835.
Tiger, James, 1947, 1948, 2944, NB266, NB1228
Tiger, Jane, 428, 648, 2040, 2041, 2244.
Tiger, Jeanetta, 1571.
Tiger, Jeannetta, 2721.
Tiger, Jeff, 1720.
Tiger, Jefferson, NB311.
Tiger, Jennetta, 398.
Tiger, Jennie, 422, 3033, 3377.
Tiger, Jesse, 598, 1571.
Tiger, Jessley, 3832.
Tiger, Jim, 247, 336, 392, 1600, 2166, 3033, 3652,
         3991.
Tiger, Jinalee, 1482, 3916, NB1121.
Tiger, Joanna, NB1228.
Tiger, Joe, 2234.
Tiger, John Mrs., 1335.
Tiger, John, 40, 336, 519, 889, 969, 999, 1163,
         1173, 1181, 1608, 2166, 2233, 2240,
         2246, 2304, 2594, 2764, 3722, 3764,
         3835, 3916, NB1048, NB629, NB-
         841, M282.
Tiger, John Washington, M120.
Tiger, Johnson, 818, 3916.
Tiger, Johnson, E., 58, 3539, NB66.
Tiger, Joseley, 3157.
Tiger, Joseph, 1633, 2112.
Tiger, Josie, 1649, 2145, 2302, NB488.
Tiger, Judy, 937, 968.
Tiger, Jumbo, 2166, M292, NB390.
Tiger, Kakaney, 2166.
Tiger, Katie, 592, 593, 1607, 2112, 3029, NB148
Tiger, Keecokaney, 3034.
Tiger, Kissie, 23, 597.
Tiger, Kizzie, 2472, M184, NB1053, NB709.
Tiger, Kogee, 1720, NB947.
Tiger, Lapsy, M184.
Tiger, Leah, 2160, 2442, 2538, 2939.
Tiger, Leaster, 246.
Tiger, Leetka, 3916.
Tiger, Lena, 20, 422, 2411, NB66, M409, M156.
Tiger, Lena B., 3539.
Tiger, Lena Benson, 20, 422, 2411, M409, M-
         156.
Tiger, Leona, 1607.
Tiger, Lewis, 1743.
Tiger, Lietka, 1482, NB1121.
Tiger, Lilah, 201.
Tiger, Liley, 336.
Tiger, Lillie, 2112.
Tiger, Lilly, 2721, NB311.
Tiger, Linda, 2535.
Tiger, Lindy, M400.
Tiger, Lissa, 3627.
Tiger, Litka, 1482, NB1121.
Tiger, Little, 3627.
Tiger, Lizzie, 1202, 2401, 3519.
Tiger, Lizzie Thomas, 598, NB792.
Tiger, Lodie, 247, 598, 2107, 3812.
Tiger, Lonie, 1221.
Tiger, Louina, 2033.
Tiger, Louis, 1633, 2120, 2538, 2594, 3157.

Tiger, Louisa, 215, 311, 313, 1720, 1721, 1
         1723, 1886, 1895, 1906, 3643, 37
         3983, M479, NB1027.
Tiger, Louise, M156.
Tiger, Lousanna, NB1027.
Tiger, Lovey, 422, 3312.
Tiger, Lucinda, 1181, 1571, 3312, NB311.
Tiger, Lucy, 3392, 392, 398, 1003, 1947.
Tiger, Lumyer, 1 60.
Tiger, Luther, 40.
Tiger, Lydia, 311, 497.
Tiger, Lyman, 201.
Tiger, Malinda, 1202, 2981.
Tiger, Manday, 335.
Tiger, Marchie, 313.
Tiger, Marcy, 215.
Tiger, Marsey, 2368.
Tiger, Marshe, 999.
Tiger, Martha, 246, 311, 3764, NB763.
Tiger, Mary, 335, 633, 1110, 1111, 1202, 3519,
         NB168, M120, M121.
Tiger, Matilda, 36, 1944.
Tiger, Mattie, 1482.
Tiger, Medelia, 1224.
Tiger, Melah, NB1204.
Tiger, Melissa, M282.
Tiger, Mesaley, 2368, 3435.
Tiger, Mickey, 1726, M417, M418.
Tiger, Mikey, 1726, M417, M418.
Tiger, Miller, 1571.
Tiger, Millie, 889, 999, M282, NB841.
Tiger, Minerva, 2535.
Tiger, Minnie, 40, 598.
Tiger, Mollie, 585, 2981, 3905, NB487, NB488.
Tiger, Mollie Crow, 585, 2981, 3905, NB487,
         NB488.
Tiger, Motey, 23, 58, 1916, 2163.
Tiger, Nancy, 40, 336, 1723, 2033, 2043, 2732,
         3849, 3905, NB1228, NB266, NB-
         629, NB1121.
Tiger, Nellie, 186, NB333, NB334, M284.
Tiger, Neosho, 342, NB162, NB163.
Tiger, Nettie, 1633.
Tiger, Nicey, 331, 2233, 2246, 2689, NB168, M-
         151.
Tiger, Niloge, 215.
Tiger, Nina, NB1053.
Tiger, Noah, 1947, 3165.
Tiger, Oda, M292.
Tiger, Oscar, 40.
Tiger, Palmer, 1224.
Tiger, Panosky, M184, NB709, NB1053.
Tiger, Parnosky, NB709, NB1053, M184.
Tiger, Pasakta, 3034.
Tiger, Philip, 2107, 3593.
Tiger, Phillip, 1853, 3812, NB266.
Tiger, Pinar, 2106.
Tiger, Piner, 1511.
Tiger, Polly, 2304.
Tiger, Porter, NB792.
Tiger, Pufney, 1202.
Tiger, Rebecca W., 40.
Tiger, Rhoda, 1633, 3165.
Tiger, Robert, 2226, NB487.
Tiger, Roley, 2140, 2944, M457.
Tiger, Roman, 1202, NB1156.
Tiger, Rose, 1916, 2889, 3722, NB1146.
Tiger, Roseanna, 2106.
Tiger, Rosie, 335.
Tiger, Sahcopochuny, 3308.

Tiger, Salina 1947 2721, NB629.
Tiger, Sallie, 422, 960, 1741, CE4023.
Tiger, Sally, 3231.
Tiger, Saloma, 1947.
Tiger, Sam, 311, 2174.
Tiger, Sampson, 1741.
Tiger, Samuel, 969.
Tiger, Sandy, 2106, 2319.
Tiger, Sarah, 336, 629, 1224, 1633, 3832, NB-763.
Tiger, Selanie, NB1048.
Tiger, Selina, 215.
Tiger, Semima, 2868.
Tiger, Senna, 1224.
Tiger, Siller, 398.
Tiger, Silvia, 2944.
Tiger, Simpson, 422.
Tiger, Sissie, 2106, NB225.
Tiger, Sissy, 2106, NB225.
Tiger, Soconthany, 2180, M292, NB390.
Tiger, Soconthlaney, 2180, NB390, M292.
Tiger, Sophia, 2319, 3165.
Tiger, Stand Waity, 598, 3519, NB792.
Tiger, Stanwaitie, 598, 3519, NB792.
Tiger, Stella, 1608.
Tiger, Sukey, 2319.
Tiger, Sunday, 1511.
Tiger, Susan, 40, 446, 1649, NB788.
Tiger, Susan H., 1916, 3551, NB1107.
Tiger, Susannah, NB841.
Tiger, Susie, 1202.
Tiger, Tahperscoyka, 3652.
Tiger, Tamer, 2368, 3435.
Tiger, Tasharlacoconthla, 2107.
Tiger, Taylor, 2319.
Tiger, Tecumseh, 967.
Tiger, Ten, 1160.
Tiger, Thloppie, 2074.
Tiger, Thomas, 178, 201, 203, 246, 422, 1003, 2629, 2722, 2868, 3312, 3905, NB-168, NB1027, NB1146, M155.
Tiger, Timmie, 889, 1947.
Tiger, Tobe, 446, 1649.
Tiger, Toche, M409.
Tiger, Tom, 2722, 3722, NB1146.
Tiger, Tommie, 2319.
Tiger, Tommy, 2174.
Tiger, Turner, 2106, 3582.
Tiger, Walter, 398.
Tiger, Wattie, 2868.
Tiger, Waxin, NB184.
Tiger, Wesley, 593, 592, 2732, 3029.
Tiger, Wicey, 1202, 1144.
Tiger, Wiley, 592, 593.
Tiger, Wiliam, 311, 313, 2033, 3435.
Tiger, William Henry, M457.
Tiger, Willie, 157, 201, 253, 342, 1003, 2166 2227, 2226, 2403.
Tiger, Wilson, 395, 1809, 1987, 2732, 3582.
Tiger, Winey, 1559, 969, 1202.
Tiger, Wisey, 969, 1144.
Tiger, Zoye, M457.
Tigochie, 2093.
Tibad ahkey, 2183.
Tikee, 3068, 3270.
Tinkoche, 1996, 1997.
Tikticihti, 154.
Tilda, 1519, 1543, 2394.
Tiller, John, 2092.
Tiller, Loodie, 2092.

Tiller, Noah, 2151.
Tilley, Annie, 1273, M304.
Tilley, Eannah, 1273, NB1124, NB1125, M304.
Tilley, Frank, NB1124.
Tilley, James, NB1124, NB1125, M304.
Tilley, John Willis, M304.
Tilley, Laura May, NB1125.
Tilly, Anna, 1606.
Tilly, Christie, 1606.
Tilly, Ina, 1606.
Tilly, J. S., 1606.
Tilly, Myrtle, 1606.
Tilly, Nannie E., 1606.
Tilsey, 1002.
Tilsie, 1342.
Timahtoe, 3177, 3179.
Timarlarchy, 1644.
Timashoey, 3177, 3178, 3387.
Timchehe, 995.
Timmunchee, Mollie, 118, 575.
Timmunichee, 575.
Timmunichee, Mollie, 575, 118.
Timmunichee, Mary, 575.
Timmunichee, Taylor, 575.
Timobusche, 1595.
Timochocte, 3018.
Timothy, 2575, 2583, 2584, 3368.
Timothy, Eliza, 3368, 3718, NB1281.
Timothy, Ella, 2584, NB1281.
Timothy, John, 2584, NB1281.
Timothy, Lucy, 3368.
Timothy, Mollie, 2584.
Timothy, Noah, 3368, 3718.
Timothy, Sandy, 3368.
Timothy, Taylor, 2583.
Timothy, Turner, 2584.
Timothy, Warsey, 2584.
Timothy, Wesley, 3718.
Timshonney, 1012.
Tina, 1453, 2449, 2511, 2860, 2876.
Tina, David, 1453.
Tina, Jennetta, 1453.
Tiner, Dave, 1950.
Tiner, John, 523.
Tiner, Katie, 523, 529.
Tiner, Katy, 1389, 1950.
Tiner, Martha, 1950.
Tiner, Tecumseh, 523, 529.
Tinfolagee, 1357.
Tiplow, Lizzie, 1514.
Tiplow, John, 1514.
Tiplow, Saw, 1514.
Tiplow, Susan, 1514.
Tissie, 4026.
Titanecha, 1774, 1775.
Tnahoha, 3069.
Tobce, 1374.
Tobe, 1427.
Tobler, Adeline, 2996.
Tobler, Alvan, 2996.
Tobler, Benjamin, M202.
Tobler, Fred, Cr. Fr , 390, NB1017.
Tobler, Jack, 2996.
Tobler, Maria, 2996, NB672, M36.
Tobler, Mary, 651, NB1017.
Tobler, Paulina, 2996.
Tobler, Pleasant, NB1017.
Tobler, Sandy, Cr. Fr., 389, M202.
Tobosky, 1168.
Toche, 2815.

Tocokqney, 2982.
Todd, Arthur Lee, NB545.
Todd, Bertha, NB544.
Todd, James, NB544, NB545.
Todd, Jesse J., 1612.
Todd, J. W., 1612.
Todd, Katie, 1612, NB544, NB545.
Todd, Katy, 1612, NB544, NB545.
Todd, Lela E., 1612.
Toffeka, 42.
Toge, 2831.
Togee, 3280.
Tohkullikee, 2031.
Tokhahke, 2694.
Tokkieheste, 1709.
Tokogee, 2967.
Tokothee, 2821.
Toladey, 895.
Tolahte, 245.
Tolleson, Alfred Washington, M15.
Tolleson, George Ella, 814, M15.
Tolleson, William A:, M15.
Tom, 1216.
Tom, Euchee, 2084, 4013.
Tom, Louanna, 4013.
Tom, Lucy, 4013.
Tomechichee, 1541.
Tommie, Hulpata, 2164.
Tommoche, 3864.
Tommy, 818, 1090.
Tomosey, 1328.
Tomsey, 2921.
Toney, 1565, 2043.
Toney, Barney, 1404.
Toney, Foley, NB1129.
Toney, Jim, 2158, 2940.
Toney, Jimmy, 2158, 2940.
Toney, Lijah, 2940, NB1129.
Toney, Lizzie, 2987.
Toney, Lodger, 2940, NB1220.
Toney, Lucy, 1900.
Toney, Milea, 2540, NB1220.
Toney, Rogers, 2940, NB1220.
Toney, Wiley, NB1220.
Tonoke, 2411.
Tony, 1489.
Tootchee, 2947.
Toothoye, 3173.
Topartheche, 1064.
Tophosie, 2458.
Toskey, 1789, 1790, 2357.
Toskey, Annie, 1789, 1790.
Toskey, Cinda, 1789.
Toskey, Eli, 1790.
Toskey, Lucy, 1789.
Toskey, Ned, 1789.
Toskey, Susana, 1789.
Totee, 2032.
Tothohyee, 1816.
Totothlike, 900.
Totulkah, 1559.
Tovey, Annie M., 2035.
Town, Emma, 889.
Town, James, 889.
Town, James Jr., 889.
Town, Sallie, 889.
Toyeh, 2151.
Toyoposka, 1951.
Trent, Bennie, 3858.
Trent, Chaney, 3858, NB165, M211.

Trent, Fannie C., 3858.
Trant, Frank, 3858.
Trant, Jesse, NB165.
Trent, Jim, 3858, NB165, M211.
Trent, Lee Drew, 3858.
Trent, Mary, 3858.
Trent, Ned Richard, M211.
Trent, Susie, 3858.
Trent, Will, 3858.
Trusler, Frank, 3735, NB258.
Trusler, Fred, NB258.
Trusler, Lucile Frances, 3735.
Trusler, Phoebe B., 3735, NB258.
Tuckabache, 2870.
Tuckabatchee, 1999, 2346, 3077.
Tuckabatchee, Davis, 1999.
Tuckabatchee, Ned, 2346.
Tucker, Hettie, 845.
Tuckharkee, 2648.
Tuffer, 2818, M420.
Tuffer, Hettie, M420.
Tuffer, Lizzie, 2818.
Tuffer, Mary, 2818.
Tuffer, Sene, 2818, M420.
Tukwelala, 198.
Tulla, 2611.
Tullahasse, 2436.
Tullahasse, Millie, 2436.
Tullamassie, 2655, 2656, 2657.
Tulladega, Mary, 3772.
Tullega, 2740.
Tulmarsey, 2127, 2254, 3334.
Tulmarsey, Bettie, 2127.
Tulmarsey, Tom, 122.
Tulmuchesse, 1098, 2468.
Tulmuchesse, Martha, 1098, 2468.
Tulmochusse, 1098, 2468.
Tulmochusse, Martha, 1098, 2468.
Tulsa, Emma, 444.
Tulsa, Joe, 444, 3002.
Tulsa, Mary, 444.
Tulsa, Willie, 3112.
Tulsa, Wm., 3112.
Tulwomicco, 3018.
Tumasochee, 3788.
Tumfumahke, 1809.
Tumker, CE4049.
Tumker, Annie, CE4049.
Tunupsee, 665.
Tuparliche, 2273.
Turk, Benjamin, 3311.
Turk, Frank, 118, 414, 3311, 3650.
Turk, George, 118.
Turk, Jerry, 3650.
Turk, Lucinda, 414.
Turk, Peggie, 414, 3650.
Turk, Nepsey, 118.
Turkey, Colbert, 1987.
Turkey, Frank, 1987.
Turnbow, Aaron, NB159, NB160.
Turnbow, Charlie, NB160.
Turnbow, James Henry, NB159.
Turnbow, Katie, 27, NB159, NB160.
Turner, Annie, 53.
Turner, Clarence W. Jr., 315.
Turner, C. W., 315.
Turner, Fannie X, 53.
Turner, George P M., 53.
Turner, Hammer, 53.
Turner, Hamner G. Jr., 53.

Vowell, Rena, 457.
Vowell, Rosa, 798, 3702.
Vowell, Rosa C., M78.
Vowell, Sam, 798, 3702, M78.
Vowell, Tom, 457.
Wacoche, 3235.
Wacoche, Aggie, 3235.
Wacoche, Alex, 3235.
Wacoche, Benjamin, 3235.
Wacoche, Eliza, 3235.
Wacoche, Isaac, 3235.
Wacoche, Jane, M344.
Wacoche, Jimmie, 3235.
Wacoche, Johnson, 3235, M344.
Wacoche, Lizzie, 415, M344.
Wacoche, Lotta, 3235.
Waddie, 2289.
Wadey, 2842.
Wadsworth, 1772, 3314.
Wadsworth, Annie, 3037.
Wadsworth, Ben, 361, NB871, NB872.
Wadsworth, Ben W., 361, NB871, NB872.
Wadsworth, Cad, 361, 1237, 3875.
Wadsworth, Caddo, 1237, 3875, 361.
Wadsworth, Daniel, 3037.
Wadsworth, Eliza, 3037, NB628.
Wadsworth, Elle E., NB872.
Wadsworth, Emma, 741, NB260.
Wadsworth, Irene, 577.
Wadsworth, James, NB628.
Wadsworth, Jessie Eulalie, NB680.
Wadsworth, John, 577, 3037, NB628.
Wadsworth, Joshua, 1237.
Wadsworth, Leo E., NB871.
Wadsworth, Levina, 3314.
Wadsworth, Louisa, 3875.
Wadsworth, Lussie, 2628.
Wadsworth, Malinda, 361.
Wadsworth, Martha F., NB871, NB872.
Wadsworth, Mary, 3297, 260.
Wadsworth, Mattie, 577, NB680.
Wadsworth, Mitchell, 1981, NB260.
Wadsworth, Newman, 577.
Wadsworth, P. J., 577, NB680.
Wadsworth, Pude J., 577, NB680.
Wadsworth, Richard, 3037.
Wadsworth, Thomas, 3875.
Wadsworth, William, 577.
Wagey, 2205.
Wagie, Two, 1607.
Wahhiley, 1365.
Wahnahuche, 2826.
Wahnahye, 444.
Wahouto, 939.
Waitchee, 3273.
Waitie, Osie, 3139.
Waitte, 2319.
Wakige, 2494.
Waley, 1293, 2549, 2550, 2551.
Walker, Annie, NB647.
Walker, Benjamin, 1926.
Walker, Bettie, 2392, M163.
Walker, Billie, 320.
Walker, Cinda, 715.
Walker, Daniel, 308.
Walker, Dick, 1155, M473.
Walker, Ed, 3662.
Walker, Eddie, 134, 1472, 1926.
Walker, Edith, NB615.
Walker, Edward H., 1053, NB614, NB615.

Walker, Ellen, 1473, NB539.
Walker, Eula, 1053, 3662, NB614, NB615.
Walker, Florence, 742.
Walker, George, 1414.
Walker, Geo. H., 1472.
Walker, Geo. W., 521, 1053, 1054, 1473, 3861.
Walker, George Washingtoon, NB614.
Walker, Hardy, 2392, M163.
Walker, Henry, 54.
Walker, Isaac, 2392.
Walker, Izora E., 988, NB89.
Walker, Jeff, NB646, NB647.
Walker, Jennie, 3200.
Walker, Jim, 163.
Walker, Joel, 261.
Walker, John, 1414.
Walker, Johnson, NB646.
Walker, Joseph, M163.
Walker, Josephine, 308.
Walker, Minnie, 320.
Walker, Knightley, 259, 1839.
Walker, Knighty, 259, 1839.
Walker, Louis, 2392.
Walker, Liza, 3861.
Walker, Lucy, 163, NB471.
Walker, Mabel, 3017, NB646, NB647.
Walker, Martha J., 1713, 1855.
Walker, Martha Jane, 1713, 1855.
Walker, Mary, 134, 1053, 1472, NB452, NB453.
Walker, Mineola, 3662.
Walker, Mollie, 521, 1472, 1473, 3861.
Walker, Nancy, 54.
Walker, Nettie, 320.
Walker, Susan, 1473.
Walker, William, 449, 1473.
Walker, William Walter, 261.
Walker, Wisey, 2392.
Wallace, Albert, 962.
Wallace, Ella, 962, NB131, M335.
Wallace, Jamison, 2003.
Wallace, Laura, C., M335.
Wallace, Tula, 962.
Wallace, Tully Mae, NB131.
Wallace, William A., 962, NB131, M335.
Wallesa, 3076.
Wallie, 1293, 2549, 2550, 2551.
Wallow, 3168.
Wallow, Lasley, 3168.
Wallow, Lizzie, 822.
Wallow, Lucy, 822.
Wallow, Nellie, 2591, NB688, M190.
Wallow, Peter, 2591.
Wallow, Salla, 3009.
Wallow, Sallie, 2591, 3131.
Wallow, Simmer, 2591.
Wallow, Wiley, 2591, 3131.
Wallow, Wilson, 822.
Walter, Isaac, 3768.
Walter, Partese, 3768.
Walters, John, 554.
Walufhogee, Tema, 2607.
Wanakee, 3869.
Wanakee, Lizzie, 3869.
Warcheeman, 1509.
Warcheenar, 1625.
Warcoche, 2607.
Ward, 1411.
Ward, Charlie, 853.
Ward, Ed, 853.
Ward, Effie, 853.

Washington, Peter, 106, NB1229.
Washington, Polly, 2521, NB927.
Washington, Ralph, NB1285.
Washington, Rhoda, 106.
Washington, Roda, 2635.
Washington, Sadie, NB355.
Washington, Sallie, 2245.
Washington, Sarah, 1757.
Washington, Sue, NB776.
Washington, Sukey, 2422.
Washington, Thomas, 2805, 3594, 3842.
Washington, Tom, 3761.
Washington, Waitie, 1705, 2494.
Washington, Walter, 2251, 3761, 3878.
Washington, Watson, 2047, NB734, NB735.
Washington, Wesley, 106.
Washington, William, 651.
Washington, Willie, 279, 1705, 3594, 3761.
Washington, Winey, 106, NB57.
Waspee, 3220.
Waspin, Mary, 3239.
Wasse, 2403.
Wata, 1424.
Watashe, 2259, 2260, NB535, M316
Watashe, Barney, 2260.
Watashe, Celia, 2260.
Watashe, Eliza, 2260.
Watashe, James, M316.
Watashe, Joe, NB535.
Watashe, Lofahye, 2260.
Watashe, R sa, 2260, NB535, M316.
Watashe, Wiley, 2260.
Watkins, U. S., 1304.
Watkins, U. S. Grant, 1304.
Watkoche, 1267.
Watkogee, 3051.
Watlen, James, 3098.
Watsey, 2658, 2659, 2677, 3907.
Watson, Aggie, 2433.
Watson, Amos, 2117.
Watson, Annie, 685, 3252, 846, NB477, NB935
          M85.
Watson, Annie L., 238.
Watson, Bella, 2453.
Watson, Bessie, 1417.
Watson, Chancy Lee, M85.
Watson, Chammy, 2405.
Watson, Daniel, 238, 1420, 1124, 2879 NB1153
Wat on, Daniel G., 1434, 2574.
Watson, Dave, NB935, NB1031.
Watson, David C., 2433, 2573, 2574.
Watson, Eddie, 1585.
Watson, Ellen, 685, NB873.
Watson, Fannie, 1434, 2391, 2404, 2405, 2574.
Watson, Fanny Anna, 543.
Watson, George, 685, 1417.
Watson, Hannah, 60, M143.
Watson, Hettie, 1434.
Watson, Homer, 407, 1576, 1585, NB715.
Watson, Ida, 1575.
Watson, Jane, 238, 1434.
Watson, Joe, 407, 1575, 2117.
Watson, John, 685, 2453, 3252.
Watson, Johnny, NB1153.
Watson, Josiah, 60, 1417, 1434.
Watson, Kate, 238.
Watson, Katie, 1417, NB474 NB475, NB873
          M107.
Watson, Lela, NB477.
Watson, Louisa, 685, 1576, NB1153

403

Watson, Mahala, 476.
Watson, Mahala A., 75.
Watson, Mehaley, M143.
Watson, Milburn L., 238.
Watson, Minnie, NB653.
Watson, Nellie, 685, 1434.
Watson, Nora, NB715.
Watson, Parnoska, 2404.
Watson, Pollie, 2582.
Watson, Polly, 3001.
Watson, Robert, 543, 685, M85.
Watson, Sallie, 1480, 2573, 2574, 2577.
Watson, Sandy, 2573, NB653, NB1031, NB477,
    NB935, M143.
Watson, Santa, 2573, NB774, NB653, NB935,
    NB1031, M143.
Watson, Santy, 2573, NB477, NB653, NB935,
    NB1031, M143.
Watson, Thos., 685.
Watson, Webster, 1434.
Watson, Yarner, 1434.
Watson, Young, 238.
Wattie, 1114, 1271, 2103.
Wattie, Albert Willie, CE4055.
Wattie, Parnie, 2822.
Wattie, Polly, CE4055.
Wattie, Thomas, 2822, CE4055.
Watts, Anna H., 1659, NB648.
Watts, Mary, 579, 2321, 3314.
Watts, Mary Etta, 1659.
Watts, Minnie, NB733.
Watts, Nobe, NB733.
Watts, Robert L., 1659.
Watts, Susan, 425, NB733.
Watts, Thomas, 579, 2321.
Watts, William T., 1659, NB648.
Watts, William T., Jr., NB648.
Wayman, Bessie, 355, M4.
Wayman, Clyde McCausland, M4.
Wayman, E. T., M4.
Watty, 2353.
Way, Thos., 988.
Way, Vida M., 988.
Wealey, 187, 188, 189, 191.
Weatherford, 153.
Weatherford, Mary Levitia, 3267.
Weatherspoon, Vicey, 717.
Weaver, Amos, NB287.
Weaver, Bert, 3315.
Weaver, Bert Leo, NB281.
Weaver, Bert W., 3687, NB280, NB281, M296
Weaver, Billie, NB286.
Weaver, Edward, 135, NB285, NB286, NB287.
Weaver, Emma, 134, NB902, M428.
Weaver, Etta May, 3687.
Weaver, Georgia, 135.
Weaver, Helen R., 3315.
Weaver, Lizzie, NB285, NB286, NB287.
Weaver, Lois Alleen, NB280.
Weaver, Mary, 135.
Weaver, May, NB285.
Weaver, Mollie, 134.
Weaver, Paul, 134, 135.
Weaver, Rena, 3315, 3687, NB280, NB281, M-
    296.
Weaver, Thelma, M296.
Webb, Ethel Samantha, NB38.
Webb, Ettie Jane, NB39.
Webb, George W., NB38, NB39.
Webb, Myrtle L., 1221, NB38, NB39.

Webber, Louis, 175.
Webster, Albert, 23.
Webster, Betsey, 23.
Webster, Bunner, 3857.
Webster, Daniel, 23, 1470.
Webster, Edward, 23.
Webster, Jefferson, 1470, 3857, NB94.
Webster, Mattie, 1470, 3857, NB94.
Webster, Seeley, NB94.
Webster, Sookey, 23.
Webster, Winey, 1470.
Welakacochee, 2132.
Welakoche, 3096, 3097.
Weldon, A. E., 33.
Weldon, Mrs. Ruby D., 33, 34, 38.
Weldon, Robert Lee, 33.
Weldon, Ruby D., 34, 38.
Weldon, Viola, 33.
Welorkee, 1911.
Wells, Ellen, 720, M186, NB375, NB376.
Wells, Frank, 718, 720.
Wells, Joseph, 720.
Wells, Lee, 720.
Wells, Lizzie, 720, NB125.
Wells, Loyal, 720.
Wells, Lydia, 718, 719, 720.
Wells, Martha, 720, NB124.
Wells, Viola, 720.
Wells, Walter, 720.
Wells, Watie, 720.
Welorkee, 1911.
Wesley, 3147.
Wesley, Ada, CE4056.
Wesley, Bella, 822.
Wesley, Bessie, 2167.
Wesley, Bettie, M142.
Wesley, Bettie May, 701.
Wesley, Charley, 1410.
Wesley, Cherokee, 1531, M131.
Wesley, Cogee, 3960.
Wesley, Daniel, 822.
Wesley, Eddie, 2782.
Wesley, Elsie, 2167, CE4056.
Wesley, Hulka, 1869.
Wesley, Ida, NB1139.
Wesley, Jimsey, 45.
Wesley, Joe, 1868, M131.
Wesley, John, 1993, 2167, 2168, NB261, N
    353, M142.
Wesley, John Lowe, 701.
Wesley, Keeper, 2782, 3753, 3960.
Wesley, Kentucky, 1869.
Wesley, Leah, 2782, 3753.
Wesley, Lillie, M131.
Wesley, Linda, 2167, 2168.
Wesley, Lizzie, 2168, M195.
Wesley, Louis, 2167.
Wesley, Louisa, 702, 2782.
Wesley, Louisana, 3960.
Wesley, Lucy, 3068.
Wesley, Major, 2958.
Wesley, Mary Ann, 701, M75.
Wesley, Mitilda, 2754, NB1176.
Wesley, Nettie, 3753.
Wesley, Nutka, 702, 822, 2075.
Wesley, Nutta, 702, 822, 2075.
Wesley, Peter, NB261.
Wesley, Polly, 2090, 3542, NB261, NB353,
    142.
Wesley, Rhoda, 2168, M268.

Wesley, Roley, 701, 702, M75.
Wesley, Rose Etta, M75.
Wesley, Sikey, 2835.
Wesley, Thomas, 2168, NB1139, M195.
Wesley, Tiger, NB353.
Wesley, Toche, 1839, NB1139, M195.
Wesley, Victor, 2167, CE4056.
Wesley, Washington, 45.
West, Annie, 1279, M322.
West, Arabella W., 34.
West, Bessie, 2330.
West, Billy, 1414, 1420, 3923, M403.
West, Cogee, 1140.
West, Daniel, 1420.
West, Eliza, 1157, M403.
West, Ella, 1329.
West, Elsie, NB1074.
West, Emma, 1484, NB1141, NB1142.
West, Feny, 1442.
West, George, 1140, 1157, 1158, 1284, 1293.
West, Hettie, 3923.
West, John, 168.
West, Johnnie, 3847.
West, Katie, 1329.
West, Kizzie, 1157.
West, Ledie, 1284.
West, Lizzie, 520.
West, Losanna, 1449.
West, Louisa, 1140, 1157, 1158, 1420, 3923, M-403.
West, Lucy, 1158.
West, Lumsey, 520, 1537, CE4057, NB1141, NB1142.
West, Milochee, 1293.
West, Nafey, 168.
West, Nellie, 3834, CE4057.
West, Nora, M322.
West, Parsinder, 1442, 3834, NB1074.
West, Polly, 140, 143.
West, Pompey, 1414.
West, Robert, 1329, 1442, 3834, NB1074, NB-1141.
West, Rosie, 520.
West, Sally, 1157.
West, Sarnie, 1329.
West, Siker, 1284, M322.
West, Sissy, 1293, 3847.
West, Sue Hettie, 38, M9.
West, Susan, 1420.
West, Thomas, 168, 1158, 1422, 1449, 2330.
West, Waddie, 1293, 3847.
West, William, NB1142.
West, Williamsee, 1293.
West, W. R., 34, 38.
Westerna, 2884.
Wethla, 629.
Whaley, Elizabeth, D., 1331.
Whaley, Fannie, 1331.
Whaley, Rebecca, 1331.
Whaley, Rufe, 3275.
Whaley, Rufus M. Jr., 1331.
Whaley, Rufus M. Sr., 1331.
Wheeley, 149.
Whetstone, Alvin, 709.
Whetstone, Anderson, 709, 821, 918, 1089.
Whetstone, Carrie, 709.
Whetstone, Charlie, 709.
Whetstone, Dorcia, 709.
Whetstone, Dorethea Cleo, M207.
Whetstone, Edward, 709.

Whetstone, Eula Pearl, NB1094.
Whetstone, James, 709, NB1094.
Whetstone, James R., M207.
Whetstone, Mannie M., M44.
Whetstone, Mary Ella, 709.
Whetstone, N. C., 709, 777, 875, 918, 821, 1089, 3958.
Whetstone, Nancy C., 709, 777, 821, 875, 918, 1089, 3958.
Whetstone, Presley, 821, M44.
Whetstone, Theodocia, NB1094, M207.
Whetstone, Theodosia, NB1094, M207.
Whetstone, Verna C., M44.
Whisler, John, 2980.
White, Ada, 349.
White, Barney, 2436.
White, Ben, 2014.
White, Cella, 2872.
White, Clara, NB772.
White, Craft, NB772.
White, Edmund, CE1058.
White, Emma, 1336, NB772.
White, Everett B., 826.
White, Florence, 110.
White, George, 2014, 2596, 2899, CE1058, NB-1236.
White, James, 1532.
White, John, 349, 1532.
White, J. T., NB468.
White, Katie, CE1058.
White, Laura, NB1064.
White, Lizzie, NB1236.
White, Lucy, 1533.
White, Mac, 1133, NB1064.
White, Mack, 1133, NB1064.
White, Malissa, 349, M337.
White, Mary, 1117, NB468.
White, Maud Annie, 1133.
White, M. H., 3621.
White, Millisa, 349, M337.
White, Mose, 337.
White, Nancy, 1360, 2014.
White, Phenia, 1133, 3621, NB1064.
White, Peter, 2436.
White, Polly, 2081.
White, Raymond, M337.
White, Robert, 1154.
White, Romie Loundine, NB468.
White, Rosella, 1133.
White, Sally, 2175.
White, Sandy, 3009.
White, Sarah, 2429, NB1170, NB1236.
White, Sheldon, 39.
White, Susie, 1360.
White, Tellie, 349.
White, Tennessee, 826.
White, W. E., 826.
White, William, 3621.
Whiteman, 2707, 4016.
Whitfield, Millie, 1128, NB342, NB343.
Whitfield, Rachel, 1128.
Whitfield, Wm., 1128.
Whitlow, 2715.
Whitlow, Cleveland, 517.
Whitlow, D. B., 649, 1650, 364.
Whitlow, David, 364.
Whitlow, David B., 364, 517, 649.
Whitlow, Edmond, 2715.
Whitlow, Edward, 3884.
Whitlow, Elizabeth, 517.

Whitlow, John, NB1138.
Whitlow, Joseph, 517.
Whitlow, Leo, 649.
Whitlow, Mary, 517, 735, 737.
Whitlow, Millie, 364, 649.
Whitlow, Muna, 3943.
Whitlow, Ralph, 649.
Whitlow, Rosa, 649.
Whitlow, Simhoye, 2745, NB374, NB1138.
Whitlow, Sissie, NB374.
Whitlow, William, 649, 3884, NB374, NB1138.
Whitten, John, 715.
Whitten, Willie, 715.
Whooping, John, 2179.
Wicey, 757, 2847, 2915, 3237.
Wichie, 1261.
Widey, 2487, 2883.
Widy, 2918.
Wigey, 259.
Wigget, 1024.
Wiggie, 2741, NB1134.
Wika, Mosey, 2995.
Wika, Yahola, 2995.
Wike, Yarhola, 1444.
Wiker, Annie, 2922.
Wiker, Belloche, 2922.
Wiker, Marley, 2922.
Wiker, Yarhola, 2922.
Wikey, 2801.
Wikke, 486.
Wilcox, Ella, 1917, NB37.
Wilcox, H. H., NB37.
Wilcox, John, NB37.
Wildcat, 386.
Wildcat, Aleck, 1572.
Wildcat, Albert, 3301.
Wildcat, Annie, 1572.
Wildcat, Bessie, NB1176.
Wildcat, George, 1572.
Wildcat, James, 3667.
Wildcat, Jesse, 3773.
Wildcat, Jim, 2783, 3773.
Wildcat, John, 3301.
Wildcat, Liza, 3667.
Wildcat, Losanna, 1572, NB1143, M421.
Wildcat, Maxey, 3667.
Wildcat, Peter, NB1143.
Wildcat, Rhoda, M421.
Wildcat, Sandy, 1483, 1484, 1572, NB1143, M-
    421.
Wildcat, Willie, 1483, NB1176.
Wiley, 170, 447, 1630.
Wiley, Adam, 3001.
Wiley, Andrew, 447, 3614, NB478.
Wiley, Andy, 447, 3614, NB478.
Wiley, Angie, 172.
Wiley, Annie, 447.
Wiley, Benny, 172.
Wiley, Betsey, 271.
Wiley, Charlie, NB480.
Wiley, Cinda, 330.
Wiley, Cora, 3614, NB478.
Wiley, Dickson, 1208.
Wiley, George, 271.
Wiley, Haley, 171, 172, NB478.
Wiley, Hattie, M402.
Wiley, Jackson, 302, 2937.
Wiley, James, 730.
Wiley, Jennie, 2937.
Wiley, Jersey, 330

Wiley, Leah, 98, 99.
Wiley, Lizzie, 302, 3614, NB265.
Wiley, Louisa, 302.
Wiley, Lucy, 171, 172.
Wiley, Major, 330.
Wiley, Malissa, 330, NB856.
Wiley, Maria, 302, 2937.
Wiley, Martha, 330.
Wiley, Mary, 447.
Wiley, Melissa, 330, NB856.
Wiley, Milley, 447.
Wiley, Moses, 2582.
Wiley, Nettie, 172, NB203.
Wiley, Peggie, 447.
Wiley, Susie, 447, NB480.
Wiley, Virginia Dorothy, M402.
Wiley, Walter, 271, M402.
William, 2570.
William, Big, 2648, 2893, 2935, NB1189, NB-
    1190.
William, Doctor, 2151.
William, Selina, 2893.
Williamochee, 3410.
Williams, 2157.
Williams, Abbie, 1699, M171.
Williams, Ada, M285.
Williams, Alex, 348, 470.
Williams, Annie, 2423, 2427, 3286, NB1012.
Williams, Baby, NB1190.
Williams, Ben, 680.
Williams, Bettie, NB1189.
Williams, Bill, 391.
Williams, Charles, 1699, 3366, 3536, NB52, NB-
    942.
Williams, Charley, 1699, 3366, 3536, NB52, NB-
    942.
Williams, Cilla, 3366.
Williams, Cinda, 2648, NB1189, NB1190.
Williams, Clara May, 1699.
Williams, Daniel, 348.
Williams, Davis, NB491.
Williams, Eddie, 370.
Williams, Eli, 897, NB1221, M101.
Williams, Elizabeth, 1145.
Williams, Ellen, 3366.
Williams, Elmer, 370.
Williams, Emma, 470, 1699, 3536, NB942, NB-
    28, M230.
Williams, George, 348.
Williams, Haddie, M101.
Williams, Hannah, 2158.
Williams, Henryetta, NB351.
Williams, Jane, 348, 3227.
Williams, Jennie, 2158.
Williams, John, 859, NB1012, NB1221.
Williams, John F., NB239.
Williams, John H., 3651, NB239, NB351.
Williams, John Randolph, NB942.
Williams, Kepsey, 2157.
Williams, Kissie, 1699.
Williams, Lillie D., 2157.
Williams, Loster, 1007, 1207, 2475.
Williams, Louisa, 391.
Williams, Lucy, 2475, 2648.
Williams, Lusta, 1007, 1207, 2475.
Williams, Luster, 1007, 1207, 2475.
Williams, Martha, 2158.
Williams, Mary, NB1221, M101.
Williams, Mary Ann, 1699.
Williams, Mary M., 403, NB52, M66.

406

Wills, Bluford, 466.
Wills, Bonnie, 800.
Wills, Buck H., 3686.
Wills, Buford, 466.
Wills, Dottie Ruth, 664.
Wills, Eliza, 3198.
Wills, Eunice May, NB746.
Wills, Georgia Ann, 466, 484, 613, 1677.
Wills, Georgiana, 466, 484, 613, 1677.
Wills, Georgianna, 466, 484, 613, 1677.
Wills, Hazel Irene, NB522.
Wills, Henry F., 664, 3686, NB522, M125.
Wills, Jack Harbert, M125.
Wills, Joe B., 800.
Wills, John J., 466, NB408.
Wills, John S., 1227, NB746
Wills, Joseph, 3198, NB529.
Wills, Lilly, NB529.
Wills, Louis Leroy, 466.
Wills, M. J., 1227.
Wills, Mary, 663.
Wills, Mary A., 664, 3686, NB522, M125.
Wills, Mary E., 800.
Wills, Mollie L., 466.
Wills, N. J., 664. 800.
Wills, Nancy, NB529.
Wills, Narcissa, 826.
Wills, Ollie Ann, 466, NB408.
Wills, Polly Ann, 466, NB408.
Wills, Theodore Dewey, 466.
Wills, Thomas, 3198.
Wills, Vard, 466, 484, 613, 1677, 3289.
Wills, Vardy J., 466, 484, 613, 1677, 3289
Wills, V. J., 466, 613, 1677, 484, 3289.
Wills, Wm., 663, 664, 800, 826, 1227, NB408.
Wills, Wm. H., 663, 664, 800, 826, 1227, NB408.
Wilsey, 1185.
Wilson, 112.
Wilson, Abbey, 1627.
Wilson, Annie, 3701, NB1219.
Wilson, Bennie, NB410.
Wilson, Bessie, NB1137.
Wilson, Bettie, 2521, 2703, NB1032, NB1033.
Wilson, C. H., NB69.
Wilson, Charley, 2957, NB410.
Wilson, Cheparncy, 730.
Wilson, Clark, 2713, NB1137.
Wilson, Cora D., 513.
Wilson, Della, 1304.
Wilson, Earnest C., 513.
Wilson, Emily, 1075.
Wilson, Enus, NB1218.
Wilson, Frank, 1075.
Wilson, George, 2521.
Wilson, Geo. H., 1304.
Wilson, Grace, 665, NB1218, NB1219.
Wilson, Harvey, 1075.
Wilson, H. C., NB703.
Wilson, Hattie L., 513, NB676.
Wilson, Hettie, 817, 3176, NB122, NB123, M
  110.
Wilson, Howard, M161.
Wilson, Hubbard, M163.
Wilson, Ida, 3701, NB12.
Wilson, Jack Elton, M110.
Wilson, Jason, NB12, NB13.
Wilson, Jasper, 2703.
Wilson, Jesse, 342, 3701.
Wilson, John, 2957.
Wilson, John Emmet, 513.

Wilson, John W., 513.
Wilson, John Wesley, M462.
Wilson, Julius, M462, M463, M464, M465, M-466.
Wilson, Kate, 1075.
Wilson, Kessella, 2454, 2457.
Wilson, Lillie, 1075.
Wilson, Lizzie, 342, 2747, NB410.
Wilson, Lola, 442.
Wilson, Louisa, 513.
Wilson, Lucy, 615, NB703.
Wilson, Lydia, 3024, NB69.
Wilson, Mahala, 1627.
Wilson, Manana, 665.
Wilson, Margaret A., 513.
Wilson, Martha, 909, NB42, NB43.
Wilson, Mary E., 3972, M462, M463, M464, M-465, M466.
Wilson, Minnie, 986, NB1033.
Wilson, Noonley, 1627.
Wilson, Nora, 3961.
Wilson, Oleta, NB69.
Wilson, Otto, NB43.
Wilson, Raymond, NB422.
Wilson, R. B., 817, 3476, NB422, NB423, M110.
Wilson, Robert B., 3476.
Wilson, Robert Henry, NB703.
Wilson, Sarah Jane, NB423.
Wilson, Simon J., 1627.
Wilson, Solomon, 1627.
Wilson, Stephen, M466.
Wilson, Taylor, 342.
Wilson, Thomas, 665, 2521, 2703, 2957, NB1032, NB1033, NB1218, NB1219.
Wilson, Toney, 2703.
Wilson, Verbena, 817.
Wilson, William, 1075.
Wilson, Wisey, NB1032.
Wilson, Zane, M465.
Wilumpka, 2648, NB1189, NB1190.
Wilyarme, 3381.
Wilyarme, Rody, 3381.
Wilyumka, 2781, 3410, CE4027.
Winchester, Doyle, 192.
Wind, Charlie, M118.
Wind, David, 1485.
Wind, Fanny, 1485, 1495.
Wind, George, 1495, 3695, NB603, M118.
Wind, James, 1485.
Wind, Jesse, NB603.
Wind, Job, 3695.
Wind, Millie, 1495, 3695, NB603, M118.
Wind, Milly, 1495, 3695, NB603, M118.
Wind, Susie, 1495.
Wineblood, Eva, 293.
Wineblood, F. A., 293.
Wineblood, Laura, 293.
Wineblood, Mary E , 293, 294, 306.
Winey, 90, 907, 1138, 1470, 1674, 2350, NB329, NB330.
Wingo, Will, 1112.
Winie, 1138, 2380.
Winn, Geneva Atkins, 3972, M435, M436, M-437, M438, M439, M440.
Winn, Henry O., M436.
Winn, Oscar, M435, M436, M437, M438, M439, M440.
Winn, Prebble, M438.
Winn, Richard E., M435.
Winn, Tabbie, M437.

Winn, Urceil, M440.
Winn, Valley, M439.
Winnie, 1138, 1503, 2380.
Winoyahcah, 2708, 2709.
Winters, Ada, 901.
Winters, Clara, 3516, NB484, M24.
Winters, Ed, 901, 3516, M24, NB484.
Winters, Elijah, NB484.
Winters, Ellen, 2159.
Winters, Grace, M24.
Winters, Henry, 901.
Winters, Leether, 3516.
Winters, Mary, 901.
Winters, Matilda, 901.
Winters, Nelson, 901.
Winters, Rosa, 901.
Winters, Williams, 901.
Wisely, 1323, 1381.
Wiseman, Charley, NB284.
Wiseman, Harry, NB284.
Wiseman, Hepsie, 2463, NB284.
Wisener, Annie, 848.
Wisener, Ben, 1059.
Wisener, Ben J., 699, NB887, NB1117, M178.
Wisener, Bessie, NB887.
Wisener, Douglas, 699.
Wisener, Joe, 1059.
Wisener, Katie, 1059.
Wisener, Minnie, NB1117.
Wisener, Oyama, M178.
Wisener, Susan, 2163, NB1117, NB887, M178
Wisey, 1144, 1541, 1591, 1641, 1695, 1710, 172
2214, 2303, 2818, 2841, 2849, 291
3684.
Wisner, Annie D., 92.
Wisner, Douglas, 92.
Wistoche, 2575, 2583, 2584.
Wistochee, 2566.
Withers, Joseph A., 3626.
Withers, Loney Ethel, 801.
Withers, Lydia, 801, 3626, NB87.
Withers, Maggie, 781.
Withers, Oliver Lee, NB87.
Withers, Robert, 3626, 801, NB87.
Withers, Robert O., 801, 3626, NB87.
Withers, Roberts, 801, 3626, NB87.
Witochee, 150.
Wity, 858.
Woddie, 1528.
Wofford, Jackson, NB265.
Wofford, Lizzie, 302, NB265.
Wofford, Sherly, NB265.
Wolf, Amy, 3726.
Wolf, Annie, 3056, 3445.
Wolf, Bertha, 3973.
Wolf, Bettie, 2468.
Wolf, Birdie, 3445.
Wolf, Buck, 901.
Wolf, Cobley, 3445, NB1290.
Wolf, Copley, 3445, NB1290.
Wolf, Elba, 1215.
Wolf, Ella, 1997.
Wolf, Ellen, 3439.
Wolf, Enoch, 2468.
Wolf, Francis, 2902.
Wolf, Freeland, 1997.
Wolf, George, 819, 1215, 2248, 3726.
Wolf, Hannah, 1838.
Wolf, Isla, 1215.
Wolf, Jackson, NB650.

408

Wray, Lee, 790.
Wray, Lillie, 790.
Wray, Sarah E., 780.
Wright, Annie E , 469.
Wright, Annie F., 1274.
Wright, Ava E., NB933.
Wright, C. J., 1274, NB378.
Wright, Charles F., 469, M367.
Wright, Clida Owen, 3635.
Wright, Cora Adeline, 1274.
Wright, E. A., 469.
Wright, Eugene M., M367.
Wright, Jane P., 1274, NB378.
Wright, Judge William, 1274.
Wright, Lela L., 469, NB898.
Wright, Lula T., 934, 3635, NB932, NB933.
Wright, Mary E., 469.
Wright, Maysie, A., 469.
Wright, Olive A., NB378.
Wright, Sarah A., M367.
Wright, W· C., 3625.
Wright, Walter C., NB932, NB933.
Wright, Walter D., 469.
Wright, Ynema B., NB932.
Wumhohla, 3078, 3079.
Wumhola, 3078, 3079.
Wydie, 2687.
Wynn, Earl, 1480.
Wynn, Lizzie, 1480.
Wynn, Pearl L., 1480.
Wynne, 2488.
Wysa, 1651.
Wyyahka, 2313.
Yaconney, 2103, 2104.
Yacopahnay, 562.
Yaffie, 3211.
Yahkuppa, 3105, 3106.
Yahofke, 2830.
Yahola, 2748.
Yahola, Abraham, NB461.
Yahola, Addie, 144. 2679, NB1268.
Yahola, Ahaloe, 2697.
Yahola, Ahalok, 2173.
Yahola, Aharloc, 1397.
Yahola, Aharlok, 1826, 2529, 197.
Yahola, Aharloke, 197, 1826, 2529.
Yahola, Ahharlox, 733.
Yahola, Aholoe, 2464.
Yahola, Ahse, 2488.
Yahola, Aktayihchu, 2146.
Yahola, Amey, 2205, 2206.
Yahola, Annie, 2896, NB1290.
Yahola, Arbeka, 397.
Yahola, Arche, 2748, 1895.
Yahola, Archie, 1895, 2748.
Yahola, Argee, 1519, 3157
Yahola, Arharlock, 2394, 3507.
Yahola, Arharlox, 215.
Yahola, Artaryichee, 3872.
Yahola, Artus. 69, 2571.
Yahola, Barney, 1833, 1838
Yahola, Bessey, 3012·
Yahola, Bettie, 3730.
Yahola, Billey, 141, M185, NB461.
Yahola, Billy, 141, M185, NB461
Yahola, Carbecher, 1962.
Yahola, Carpeche, 2427.
Yahola, Catcha, 2990.
Yahola, Celia, 1611, NB348 NB349
Yahola, Cha, 726.

409

Yahola, Charfukner, 733.
Yahola, Checotah, 329, 330.
Yahola, Chofolup, 1312.
Yahola, Chokate, 2770.
Yahola, Chokota, 1786.
Yahola, Chola, 1215, 1260.
Yahola, Cinda, 1215.
Yahola, Cona, 2338.
Yahola, Conip, 1215.
Yahola, Cono, 2953.
Yahola, Conup, 1642.
Yahola, Conchart, 1595, 68.
Yahola, Concharty, 68, 1595.
Yahola, Cosar, 2912.
Yahola, Gotcha, 2210, 2504, 2516.
Yahola, Cowake, 335.
Yahola, Cubbie, 1958, 3395.
Yahola, Cussehta, 1369.
Yahola, Dora, 3160.
Yahola, Echas, 2063.
Yahola. Echu 818.
Yahola, Efar, 1951.
Yahola, Efer, 1650.
Yahola, Elder, 2441.
Yahola, Eliza, 3291.
Yahola, Emala, 2924.
Yahola, Emarthla, 2797.
Yahola, Emmie, 2167.
Yahola, Espaney, 3343.
Yahola, Fus, 2918, 2940.
Yahola, Fushutche, 1650.
Yahola, Haffy, NB57.
Yahola, Hardy, 2841.
Yahola, Heluck, 2205, 2206.
Yahola, Henry, 1650.
Yahola, Hillis, 237, 995.
Yahola, Holuck, 2205, 2206.
Yahola, Holuk, 2167.
Yahola, Hotulke, 2359.
Yahola, Houston, NB349.
Yahola, Hullok, 2176.
Yahola, Ida, 2441.
Yahola, Ishpok, 2176.
Yahola, Itseharse, 2473.
Yahola, Jackson, 1641, NB348, NB349.
Yahola, James, 3042.
Yahola, Jennetta, NB57.
Yahola, Jennie, 3771.
Yahola, Joe, 3054.
Yahola, Karpitcher, 2437, 2438, 2439, 2440, 2441.
Yahola, Katch, 2645.
Yahola, Katie, 144, 1441.
Yahola, Kawockkockie, 1270.
Yahola, Kernip, 3110.
Yahola, Kizzie, 1833.
Yahola, Lahta, 1371, 2477, 2481, 2479.
Yahola, Larney, 69.
Yahola, Lata, 2481, 2762, 2477, 2479, 1371.
Yahola, Latah, 2479, 2481, 2477, 1371.
Yahola, Lena, 2618.
Yahola, Lila, 2273.
Yahola, Linda, 1270.
Yahola, Lizzie, 2274, 2357, 3042, 3043, 3044, 3291.
Yahola, Lochar, 481.
Yahola, Loda, 2441.
Yahola, Loper, 144.
Yahola, Lottie, 2805.
Yahola, Lowe, 2273.

Yahola, Lucinda, 3043.
Yahola, Lucy, 2201.
Yahola, Mahtup, 3205.
Yahola, Mannie, 2441.
Yahola, Martha, M185.
Yahola, Mary, 144, 1958, 3395, M469.
Yahola, Mawokike, 2273.
Yahola, Mctesha, 2834.
Yahola, Micco, 388, 2654.
Yahola, Millie, 1895, 3223.
Yahola, Minnie, NB1268.
Yahola, Mollie, 144, 2611, NB267, NB268
Yahola, Nancy, 733, 2351.
Yahola, Neha, 1716, 2467, 2632, 2679.
Yahola, Nehei, 152.
Yahola, Nchi, 3160.
Yahola, Nehie, 3070.
Yahola, Nellie, 2274, 2656, 2657.
Yahola, Nelly, 1270.
Yahola, Nettie, 2632.
Yahola, Nocha, 1833.
Yahola, Nocus, 1404, 1455, 1516, 1607, 2841, 2956.
Yahola, Nokos, 1801.
Yahola, Ocer, 1248.
Yahola, Oche, 377, 2693.
Yahola, Okfuska, 23 2.
Yahola, Osa, 3340.
Yahola, Osee, 2656, 2657.
Yahola, Osoche, 2351.
Yahola, Pahos, 3771.
Yahola, Parhose, 2111, 2273, 2274.
Yahola, Parnogee, 1641.
Yahola, Peggy, 2111.
Yahola, Pettie, 1312.
Yahola, Pollie, 3160.
Yahola, Polly, 3787.
Yahola, Pulth, 2700.
Yahola, Pufney, 3070.
Yahola, Rhoda, 397, 1951, 2274, 2437, 2439, 2440, NB1049.
Yahola, Roman, NB348, NB1245.
Yahola, Ruth, 2673.
Yahola, Sadie, 144.
Yahola, Salizy, 68.
Yahola, Sallie, 1045.
Yahola, Sampson, NB1170.
Yahola, Sissy, 1801.
Yahola, Sokugker, 2207.
Yahola, Spokoke, 2805.
Yahola, Sunday, 1270.
Yahola, Tarcos, 2087.
Yahola, Tilda, 1519, 2394, 3507.
Yahola, Thlathlo, 3105, 3106.
Yahola, Thlotko, 151.
Yahola, Thomas, 1045, 1795, 3042, 3044,
Yahola, Tom, 693.
Yahola, Tommy, 32, 2453.
Yahola, Tuskabatchee, 2095.
Yahola, Tulmarsey, 2357, 2830.
Yahola, Tulmas, 2646.
Yahola, Tulsa, 1037, 1529, 1859.
Yahola, Tulwa, 2745, 2859.
Yahola, Ussee, 2210.
Yahola, Wanchee, 1270.
Yahola, Wattey, 733.
Yahola, Watup, 2507.
Yahola, Wegus, 2201.
Yahola, Wewoka, 2694.
Yahola, Wiley, 2679, NB1268.

Yahola, Willie, 397, 3044, M469.
Yahola, Winey, 144, NB57, M185, NB461.
Yahola, Woatko, 1369.
Yahola, Wotka, 1270, 2838.
Yahola, Wotko, 1269.
Yahola, Woxie, 21, 67, 1248, 2284.
Yahola, Wynne, 2488.
Yaholar, 1590.
Yaholar, Artus, 1670.
Yaholar, Betsey, 1590, NB914.
Yaholar, Conup, 1520.
Yaholar, Cosar, 2250.
Yaholar, Della, NB1245.
Yaholar, Eliza, 3247, 3248.
Yaholar, Ispokok, 1625.
Yaholar, Jimmie, NB914.
Yaholar, Josey, 1590, NB914.
Yaholar, Louis, 2058.
Yaholar, Lucy, 1590.
Yaholar, Martha, 1688.
Yaholar, Mary, 2056, 2057, 2058.
Yaholar, Millie, 1557.
Yaholar, Neha, 1527, 1616, 1866, 2132, 1504.
Yaholar, Nehar, 1504, 1527, 1616, 1866, 2132.
Yaholar, Roman, 2056.
Yaholar, Sallie, 1504, 1527, 1616, 1045, 2693,
        M264, M265, M455.
Yaholar, Thomas, 1557, 2056, 2057, 2058.
Yaholar, Ussy, 1688.
Yahologee, 1866.
Yahponna, 398.
Yahsahcocontany, 3991.
Yahtahwe, 939.
Yahtalevy, 591.
Yahtalonwe, 602.
Yahweho, 1184.
Yamahike, 3206, 3296.
Yanfohcoconthla, 2084.
Yanha, Louisa, 2499.
Yanba, Tusko, 2499.
Yarba, Hulley, 3103.
Yarbrough, Betsey, 1114.
Yarbrough, James, 1841.
Yarbrough, John, 1114.
Yarbrough, Thomas, 1114.
Yarcharney, 2783.
Yardy, Armer, 506, NB429, NB430.
Yardy, Dock, NB430.
Yardy, Hettie, NB429.
Yardy, Joseph, 197.
Yardy, Thomas, 197, 506, NB429, NB430.
Yardy, Thomas Jr., 197.
Yardy, Willie, 506.
Yardy, Wisey, 197, 506.
Yargee, Alex, 1555, 1720, 2071, 2145.
Yargee, Alexander, 3638.
Yargee, Alvey, 1720.
Yargee, Amos, NB940.
Yargee, Annie, 1579, 1678.
Yargee, Bunny, 2034.
Yargee, Capt., 1762.
Yargee, Charley, 1517.
Yargee, Cordelia, 1144.
Yargee, Culley, 1678, NB940.
Yargee, Cullie, 2145.
Yargee, Cully, 1678, NB940.
Yargee, Dave, 1555, 3638.
Yargee, David, 1338, 1749.
Yargee, Elizabeth, 862, NB513, M42.
Yargee, George, 1579.

Yargee, Hannah, 1642.
Yargee, Hattie, 1720.
Yargee, Hattie L., 1517.
Yargee, James, 1144, 2520.
Yargee, Jeff, 1497.
Yargee, Jennie, 1497.
Yargee, John, 913, 915, 1044, 1144 2034 2 is
Yargee, John I., 1517.
Yargee, Katie, 1548, NB940
Yargee, Lizzie, 1144.
Yargee, Mandy, 1144.
Yargee, Mariah, 1762.
Yargee, Martha, 1497.
Yargee, Millie, 1082, 2520
Yargee, Mitchell, 1762.
Yargee, Monday, 2678.
Yargee, Nancy, 1517, 1762
Yargee, Nathaniel V., 1517.
Yargee, Peter, 1517.
Yargee, Pheasant, 1517.
Yargee, Rhody, 1144.
Yargee, Sam, 2071.
Yargee, Susan, 913, 915, 1044.
Yargee, Susie, 2678.
Yargee, Walter 1144.
Yargee, William, 1749.
Yargee, Willie, 3025.
Yargee, Wynie, 1678.
Yarger, 427.
Yarger, Bunny, 2034.
Yarger, Jennie, 427.
Yarger, John, 913.
Yarger, Millie, 1082.
Yarger, Susan, 1044.
Yarharlargee, 1641.
Yarhogee, 1568.
Yarhogee, Marfos, 3020.
Yarhola, Aaron, 1319, 3459, M305
Yarhola, Arche, 1318.
Yarhola, Arharlok, 1543.
Yarhola, Arsfolechar, 1315.
Yarhola, Artarjiche, 3872.
Yarhola, Artaryochee, 2661.
Yarhola, Billy, 1544.
Yarhola, Cona, 1316, 1319, 2129
Yarhola, Cosar, 3099.
Yarhola, Cussehta, 1544.
Yarhola, Elon, 1319, M305.
Yarhola, Fushutche, 1551, 1552, 1553.
Yarhola, George, 1595.
Yarhola, Harchee, 3247.
Yarhola, Helen, M371.
Yarhola, Jefferson, NB1170.
Yarhola, Jemima, 2129.
Yarhola, Joe, 1667.
Yarhola, Judy, 1316.
Yarhola, Karpitchar, 118.
Yarhola, Karpitcher, 2155.
Yarhola, Kizzie, 1552, NB921, NB1105 M250
Yarhola, Lessey, 1544.
Yarhola, Linda, 1544.
Yarhola, Loda, 2155.
Yarhola, Luley, 1321.
Yarhola, Magie, 1490.
Yarhola, Maley, 1544.
Yarhola, Malinda, 1551.
Yarhola, Martha C., 3459
Yarhola, Mary, 1551, 1552, 1553 M371
Yarhola, Miley, 3459.
Yarhola, Millie, 1319, M305.

411

412

APPENDIX A
THE DAWES COMMISSION RECORDS

Comparatively few people have any idea of the magnitude of the records of the Dawes Commission. Beginning at an early date after its creation the Dawes Commission began the work of securing data relative to the status of claimants for membership as citizens of the Five Civilized Tribes, together with the value of the land and the improvements thereon. The census cards, a enrollment, and the patents to the individual members was the sequel of their work.

The Commission first began to enroll members of the Creek Tribe of Indians, and its procedure was not systematized to the extent adopted when the work of enrollment of the other Tribes began. As a result in a very large percentage of the Creek enrollment cases we find no record or transcript of the testimony adduced before the Commission, as a basis for enrollment. Testimony was taken, before the Commission, in every case, but this testimony was not transcribed and kept in the files, and as a result there is now no record of it. However, in a large number of cases, and in all contested enrollment cases the testimony was transcribed, and a copy of the same may now be found in the enrollment jackets.

Persons seeking to buy, or lease, allotted lands in any of the Five Nations should see to it that there is presented to them with the abstract of title a certified copy of the census card, a certified allottment plat, and, in case there be any doubt as to the age of the allottee, a certified copy of the enrollment record, or so much thereof as tends to show the age of the allottee. You will note that in this last statement we suggest that you secure "So much of the enrollment record as tends to show the age of the allottee." We say this for the reason that in many instances the enrollment records cover hundreds of pages of testimony, possibly only three or four pages of which or three or four lines of which show anything tending to fix the age. It would be useless for you to secure the entire record, and it would work a great hardship on you, not only in original cost, but in having it inserted in any court record, and paying for copies thereof thereafter in a case-made on appeal. In a very large percentage of cases you had best get the entire record, but there are cases in which you should make your order specific and request only such parts of this record as tends to show the age of the citizen whose age you are seeking to know. In such cases as these last referred to the office of the Superintendent will undoubtedly charge an additional fee for making the investigation and culling out from the record and evidence in the office such portions as will tend to show the age of the particular allottee. This matter, however, should first be taken up with the Superintendent. Remember this, always, that the ages given on the census cards are not to be taken as a verity. The law says that the "enrollment record" is the evidence of the age and you must get this from the office of the Superintendent to the Five Civilized Tribes. You can get it no where else.

It is interesting to know that in the making of these enrollments and allotment records the Dawes Commission went over Indian Territory with a fine-tooth comb and gradually gathered in all letters, bills of sale, notes, mortgages, birth affidavits, death affidavits, marriage licenses, marriage certificates, and other such data, and these are now on file in the office of the Commission, and are attached as Exhibits to the record, in enrollment and allotment contest cases. The purpose of this was to show the status of the citizen or land he was seeking to allot. In certain cases it may be necessary for you to search back through these old records, but such cases will be rare. This search must be made by some one of the office force and on proper request and proper showing of reasons for wanting the search made, the Superintendent will detail some one familiar with the files to make the search and you can then purchase such certified copies as you desire.

An idea of the cost of certified copies may be seen from the following:

Deeds, Census Cards	$1.00	each
Birth and death affidavits	1.00	"
Application for allotment	1.00	"
Miscellaneous records, per hundred words	.10	"
(Minimum charge 50c)		
Copy of Approved Roll (For each name)	.25	
Plats, (showing one allottee's land in one setion)	.25	"
Tribal Rolls, (1866, 1888, 1896, one name)	.50	"
Plats unallotted land, (per tract)	.25	
Schedules unallotted land per tract,(Name and address-purchaser)	.25	"
Allotment certificate stubs	.50	"
Lease, (Printed form)	1.25	
Lease (typewritten)	2.50	"
Stipulation	.50	
Assignment	.50	
Ledger Sheet (full page)	2.50	
Ledger Sheet (½ page or less)	1.50	
Proof of Heirship	1.00	
Removal of Restrictions Certificate	.25	
Order of Removal of Restrictions	1.00	
Lease Certificate	.25	
Miscellaneous records, per hundred words	.10	
(Minimum charge 25c)		
Town Lot Plats	1.00	"

With your remittance for each certified copy, for the present, send 10c additional for documentary stamp, under the recent Internal Revenue Law. This will avoid delay.

Send all communications at present to Gabe E. Parker, Superintendent to the Five Civilized Tribes, Muskogee, Oklahoma, and make your remittances by bank draft, or money order, payable to W. M. Baker, Cashier.

APPENDIX B

LAWS OF DESCENT AND DISTRIBUTION

Sec. 31.   That certain general laws of the state of Arkansas in force at the close of the session of the general assembly of that state of eighteen hundred and eighty-three, as published in eighteen hundred and eighty-four in the volume known as Mansfield's Digest of the Statutes of Arkansas, which are not locally inapplicable or in conflict with this act or with any law of congress, relating to the subjects specially mentioned in this section, are hereby extended over and put in force in the Indian Territory until congress shall otherwise provide, that is to say the provisions of the said general statues of Arkansas relating.. to descents and distributions, chapter forty-nine."

Act of Congress May 2, 1890, (26 Stat. L. C. 182, P. 81)

"That on and after January first, eighteen hundred and ninety-eight, the United States courts in said Territory shall have original and exclusive

jurisdiction and authority to try and determine all civil cases in law and equity thereafter instituted and all criminal causes for the punishment of any offense committed after January first, eighteen hundred and ninety-eight, by any person in said Territory, and the United States Commissioners in said Territory shall have and exercise the powers and jurisdiction already conferred upon them by existing laws of the United States as respects all persons and property in said Territory; and the laws of the United States and the State of Arkansas in force in the Territory shall apply to all persons therein, irrespective of race, said courts exercising jurisdiction thereof as now conferred upon them in the trial of like causes; and any citizen of any one of said tribes otherwise qualified who can speak and understand the English language may serve as a juror in any of said courts."

Act of Congress June 7, 1897 (30 Stat. L. 83)

Sec. 7.   "   *   *   *   *   *   *   The homestead of each citizen shall remain, after the death of the allottee, for the use and support of children born to him after the ratification of this agreement, but if he have no such issue, then he may dispose of his homestead by will, free from limitation herein imposed, and if this be not done, the land shall descend to his heirs according to the laws of descend and distribution of the Creek Nation, free from limitation ...."

Original Creek Agreement (31 Stat. L. 861)

Sec. 28.   "No person, except as herein provided, shall be added to the rolls of citizenship of said tribe after the date of this agreement, and no person whomsoever shall be added to said rolls after the ratification of this agreement.

All citizens who were living on the first day of April, eighteen hundred and ninety-nine, entitled to be enrolled under section twenty-one of the Act of Congress approved June twenty-eight, eighteen hundred and ninety-eight, entitled "An Act for the protection of the people of Indian Territory, and for other purposes," shall be placed upon the rolls to be made by said commission under said Act of Congress, and if any such citizen has died since that time, or may hereafter die, before receiving his allotment of lands and distributive share of all the funds of the tribe, the lands and money to which he would be entitled, if living, shall descend to his heirs, according to the law of descent and distribution of the Creek Nation, and be allotted and distributed to them accordingly.

All children born to citizens so entitled to enrollment, up to and including the first day of July, nineteen hundred, and then living, shall be placed on the rolls made by said commission; and if any such child die after said date, the lands and moneys to which it would be entitled, if living shall descend to its heirs according to the laws of descent and distribution of the Creek Nation, and be allotted and distributed to them accordingly.

The rolls so made by said commission, when approved by the Secretary of the Interior, shall be the final rolls of citizenship of said tribe, upon which the allotment of all lands and the distribution of all moneys and other property of the tribe shall be made, and to no other persons."

Original Creek Agreement (31 Stat. L. 861)

Sec. 6. "Be it further enacted, that if any person die without a will, having property and children, the property shall be equally divided among the children by disinterested persons; and in all cases where there are no children, the nearest relation shall inherit the property."

Laws of Muskogee Nation, 1880, p. 132.

Sec. 8. "The lawful or acknowledged wife of a deceased husband shall be entitled to one half of the estate, if there are no other heirs, and an heir's part, if there should be other heirs, in all cases where there is no will. The husband surviving shall inherit of a deceased wife in like manner."

Laws of Muskogee Nation, 1880, p. 60.

Sec. 1. "All non-citizens, not previously adopted, and being married to citizens of this Nation, or having children entitled to citizenship, shall have a right to live in this Nation, and enjoy all the privileges enjoyed by other citizens, except participation in the annuities and final participation in the lands."

Laws of Muskogee Nation, 1880, p. 60.

"That the act entitled "An act to ratify and confirm an agreement with the Muscogee or Creek tribe of Indians, and for other purposes," approved March first, nineteen hundred and one, in so far as it provides for descent and distribution according to the laws of the Creek Nation, is hereby repealed and the descent and distribution of lands and moneys provided for in said act shall be in accordance with the provisions of chapter forty-nine of Mansfield's Digest of the Statutes of Arkansas in force in Indian Territory."

Act of Congress May 27, 1902, (32 Stat. L. 258)
The above provision not effective until June 30, 1902 or July 1, 1902.

416

Sec. 6. "The provisions of the act of Congress approved March 1, 1901 (31 Stat. L. 861), in so far as they provide for descent and distribution ac. cording to the laws of the Creek Nation, are hereby repealed and the descent and distribution of land and money provided for by said act shall be in accord. ance with chapter 49 of Mansfield's Digest of the Statutes of Arkansas now in force in Indian Territory: Provided, That only citizens of the Creek Nation, male and female, and their Creek descendants shall inherit lands of the Creek Nation: And provided further, That if there be no person of Creek citizenship to take the descent and distribution of said estate, then the inheritance shall go to noncitizen heirs in the order named in said chapter 49."

Sec. 7. "All children born to those citizens who are entitled to enroll- ment as provided by the Act of Congress approved March 1, 1901 (31 Stat. L., 861), subsequent to July 1, 1900, and up to and including May 25, 1901, and living upon the latter date, shall be placed on the rolls made by said commission. And if any such child has died since May 25, 1901, or may here- after die before receiving his allotment of lands and distributive share of the funds of the tribe, the lands and moneys to which he would be entitled if living shall descend to his heirs as herein provided and be allotted and distributed to them accordingly."

Sec. 8. "All children who have not heretofore been listed for enrollment living May 25, 1901, born to citizens whose names appear upon the authenti- cated rolls of 1890 or upon the authenticated rolls of 1895 and entitled to en- rollment as provided by the Act of Congress approved March 1, 1901 (31 Stat. L. 861), shall be placed on the rolls made by said commission. And if any such child has died since May 25, 1901, or may hereafter die, before receiving his allotment of lands and distributive share of the funds of the tribe, the lands and moneys to which he would be entitled if living shall descend to his heirs as herein provided and be allotted and distributed to them accordingly."

Sec. 16 * * * * * * * "The homestead of each citizen shall remain, after the death of the allottee, for the use and support of children born to him after May 25, 1901, but if he have no such issue then he may dispose of his homestead by will, free from limitation herein imposed, and if this be not done the land embraced in his homestead shall descend to his heirs, free from such limitation, according to the laws of descent herein otherwise prescribed."
* * * * * * * * * ."

Supplemental Creek Treaty (32 Stat. L. 500)

"All the laws of Arkansas heretofore put in force in the Indian Territory are hereby continued and extended in their operation, so as to embrace all persons and estates in said Territory, whether Indian, freedmen, or otherwise, and full and complete jurisdiction is hereby conferred upon the district courts in said Territory in the settlements of all estates of decedents, the guardian. ships of minors and incompetents, whether Indians freedmen or other wise."

Act of Congress April 28, 1904 (33 Stat. L. 573)

(6) Mansfield's Digest of Statues of Arkansas for the year 1884.

1. Sec. 2522—When any person shall die, having title to any real estate of inheritance, or personal estate, (b), not disposed of, nor otherwise limited by marriage settlement, and shall be intestate as to such estate, it shall

417

descend and be distributed, in parcency, to his kindred, male and female, subject to the payment of his debts and the widow's dower, in the following manner:

First—To children, or their descendents, in equal parts.

Second—If there be no children, then to the father, then to the mother; if no mother, then to brothers and sisters, or their descendant, in equal parts.

Third—If there be no children, nor their descendants, father, mother, brothers or sisters, nor their descendants, then to the grandfather, grandmother, uncles and aunts, and their descendants, in equal parts, and so in other cases, without end, passing to the nearest lineal ancestor and their children and their descendants, in equal parts.

2. Sec. 2523—Posthumous children of the intestate shall inherit in like manner as if born in the life-time of the intestate, but no right of inheritance shall accrue to any person other than the children of the intestate, unless they be born at the time of the intestate's death.

3. Sec. 2524—Illegitimate children shall be capable of inheriting and transmitting an inheritance, on the part of their mother, in like manner as if they had been legitimate of their mother (c).

4. Sec. 2525—If a man have by a woman a child, or children, and afterward shall intermarry with her and shall recognize such children to be his, they shall be deemed and considered as legitimate.

5. Sec. 2526—The issue of all marriages deemed null in law, or dissolved by divorce, shall be deemed and considered as legitimate.

6. Sec. 2527—In making title by descent, it shall be no bar to a demandant that any ancestor through whom he derives his descent from the intestate is, or has been, an alien.

7. Sec. 2528.—If there be no children, or their descendants, father, mother not their descendants, or any paternal or maternal kindred capable of inheritance, the share shall go to the wife or husband of the intestate. If there be no such wife or husband, then the estate shall go to the state.

8. Sec. 2529—If any of the children of an intestate be living, and some be dead, the inheritance shall descend to the children who are living, and to the descendants of such children as shall have died, so that each child who shall be living shall inherit such share as would have descended to him if all the children of the intestate who shall have died leaving issue had been living, so that the descendants of each child who shall be dead shall inherit the same their parent would have received if living.

9. Sec. 2530—The rule of descent prescribed in the last preceding section shall apply in every case where the descendants of the intestate, entitled to share in the inheritance, shall be in equal degree of consanguinity to the intestate, so that those who are in the nearest degree of consanguinity shall take the shares which would have descended to them had all the decendants in the same degree who shall have died leaving issue been living, so that the issue of the descendants who shall have died shall respectively take the shares which their parents, if living, would have received.

10. Sec. 2531—In cases where the intestate shall die without descendants, if the estate come by the father, then it shall ascend to the father and his heirs; if by the mother, the estate, or so much thereof as came by the mother, shall ascend to the mother and her heirs; but if the estate be a new acquisition it shall ascend to the father for his life-time, and then descend, in remainder, to the collateral kindred of the intestate in the manner provided in this act; and, in default of a father, then to the mother, for her life-time then descend to the collateral heirs as before provided (d).

418

11. Sec. 2532—The estate of an intestate, in default of a father and mother shall go, first, to the brothers and sisters, and their descendants, of the father; next, to the brothers and sisters, and their descendants, of the mother. This provision applies only where there are no kindred, either lineal or collateral, who stand in a nearer relation.

12. Sec. 2533—Relations of the half-blood shall inherit equally with those of the whole blood in the same degree; and the descendants of such relatives shall inherit in the same manner as the descendants of the whole blood, unless the inheritance come to the intestate by descent, devise, or gift, of some one of his ancestors, in which case all those who are not of the blood of such ancestor shall be excluded from such inheritance.

13. Sec. 2534—In all cases not provided for by this act, the inheritance shall descend according to the course of the common law.

14. Sec. 2535—Whenever an inheritance, or a share of an inheritance, shall descend to several persons, under the provisions of this act, they shall inherit as tenants in common, in proportion to their respective shares or rights.

ADVANCEMENT

15. Sec. 2536—If any child of an intestate shall have been advanced by him in his life-time, by settlement or portion of real or personal estate, or both of them, the value thereof shall be reckoned, for the purpose of this section, only as a part of the real and personal estate of such intestate descendible to the heirs and to be distributed to his next kin, according to law; and, if such advancement be equal or superior to the amount of the share which such child would be entitled to receive of the real and personal estate of the deceased, as herein reckoned, then such child and his descendants shall be excluded from any share of the real and personal estate of the intestate.

16. Sec. 2537—In cases where such advancement is not equal to the share that such child or relative, and his descendants, shall be entitled to receive, they shall be entitled to receive so much of the real and personal estate as shall be sufficient to make all the shares of the heirs in such real and personal estate and advancement be as nearly equal as possible.

17. Sec. 2538—The value of any real or personal estate so advanced shall be deemed to be that, if any, which was acknowledged by the person receiving the same by any receipt, in writing, specifying the value; if no such written evidence exists, then such value shall be estimated according to its value at the time of advancing such money or property.

18. Sec. 2539—The maintaining, educating or giving money to a child or heir, without a view to a portion or settlement in life, shall not be an advancement within the meaning of this act.

CONSTRUCTIONS

19. Sec. 2540—The term "real estate," as used in this act, shall be construed to include every estate, interest and right, legal and equitable, in lands, tenements and hereditaments, except such as are determined o, extinguished by the death of the intestate, seized or possessed thereof in any manner, other than by lease for years and estate for the life of another person.

20. Sec. 2541—The term "inheritance" as used in this act, shall be understood to mean real estate, as herein defined, descended according to the provisions of this act.

21. Sec. 2542—Whenever, in any part of this act, any person is described as living, it shall be understood that he was living at the time of the death

419

of the intestate from whom the descent came; and, when any person is described as having died, it shall be understood that he died before the intestate.

22. Sec. 2543—The expression used in this act, "where the estate shall have come to the intestate on the part of the father," or "mother," as the case may be, shall be construed to include every case where the inheritance shall have come to the intestate by gift, devise or descent from the parent referred, to or from any relative of the blood of such parent. Rev. Stat. Chap. 49."

You will note that I have added numbers 1 to 22 in front of the sections of the Arkansas Law set forth above. I have done so in order to make clear that which follows. The Arkansas law of descent and distribution was construed as a whole by the Supreme Court of the State of Arkansas, in the case of Kelly vs. McGuire, 15 Ark. 555. The holdings of the court in the case of Kelly vs. McGuire had become rules of property before the Arkansas law was extended over and put in force in the Indian Territory. The writer of the opinion in this case was an eminent lawyer of Arkansas and was called in and made a special Justice of the Supreme Court and took a great deal of time in research and investigation before writing the opinion, and that part of his opinion that deals with real property is as follows:

"Whatever may have been the original foundation of the right of property, it admits of no question that its protection, in some shape, is engrafted into the jurisprudence of every civilized nation. In most of them, it constitutes an important feature of their organic law. No government ,however, powerful, and whether free or despotic, could long command the affections and allegiance of its members, or preserve the order and tranquility of civil society, without respecting and securing this right, and affording adequate redress for its violation.

The transmission of property, whether, by descent succession, or purchase, depends upon the municipal regulations of each State, and no duty more delicate can be imposed on courts of justice, than to pass upon and enforce regulations. It is for the judiciary to construe, not legislate; and when the real intention of the law maker is ascertained, it must be declared, regardless of consequences. If cases are omitted, which ought to have been included, or hardships arise not foreseen, the remedy for the evil rests in the wisdom and discretion of another department. For us, it is sufficient to know, ita lex scripta.

This voluminous, and really difficult case, involves the construction of our statute of Descents—presenting questions not hitherto decided in our courts, and we can safely affirme, that they have been examined with care, diligence and patience. We have to thank the respective counsel for this very able argument in the case.

The facts, as far as they have a bearing on the present branch of the subject, are, that, about the year 1810, Charles Kelly emigrated to what is now Arkansas; and, in 1815, married Mrs. Craig, a widow, who had two daughters by a former marriage, named Elizabeth and Emeline. Charles Kelly, an enterprising, shrewd business man, aided by the prudence, skill and good management of his wife, accumulated in Arkansas, where he lived, a large estate, consisting of real and personal property. He died intestate in 1834, and, by the law in force, his real estate, descended, and his personal property was distributed to James DeWitt Clinton Kelly, who was the only surviving issue of the marriage with Mrs. Craig. She died in 1836, and the son above mentioned called, for brevity, Clinton Kelly, died intestate in Arkansas, the place of his domicil, in 1844, at the age of seventeen years, without having married and without issue, leaving as claimants for his property, his paternal grandfather, Greenberry Kelly, the descendants of Mary Eikelburner, his paternal aunt, and his two sisters of the half-blood, Elizabeth and Emeline, the first of whom is the present Mrs. Marsh, and the second Mrs. McGuire. The half-blood claim the entire estate of Clinton Kelly, real and personal, as his next of kin, and to the exclusion of all other persons.

We shall say nothing, at present, of Greenberry Kelly, or the Eikelburner heirs; because, if the pretentions of the half-blood to the whole, realty and personalty, should prove to be well founded, it would be an useless enquiry.

To form a new system of descents, will always be found a work of difficulty. Human wisdom is inadequate to making out and establishing a perfect one at once. It is quite impossible to foresee all the consequences of an attempt so important, extensive and ramified. Omissions and imperfections, however, as they are discovered, must be supplied and remedied by subsequent laws.

Excepting the first section, and some minor provisions, our statute of descents was borrowed from one in New York, but with additions not calcu- lated to improve, and with attempts at brevity and perspicuity, neither happy or successful. The original was, what it purported, and was intended to be. a pure statute of descents, using appropriate technical terms, regularing the inheritance of real estate, and not looking to the distribution of personal pro- perty at all. 2 Rev. Statutes New York, 750; Digest 436.

The first section of ours was extracted from some other statute of des- cents, amended by the revisors, by the interpolation of so much as relates to the distribution of personal estate; thus blending two subjects of a totally different nature, and governed by totally different rules. And it is this, which produces no small degree of difficulty in our system. We must, however, apply to it that universal rule of construction, that a statute should be so con- sidered as that every clause, sentence, or part, shall stand, if possible; or, in other words, such construction as will best answer the intention of the mak- ers. 9 Bac. Abr., Statute J. 2, J. 5. General words or clauses in a statute, may be restrained by particular words, or clauses in the same statute. And when one section in a statute may be both general and particular, or where there are different provisions for different purposes, and penned in different words, in the same chapter, they ought to be so construed as to avoid inconsistency. Id. Campbell's case, 2 Bland. 209. The application of these rules to the case in hand, will be readily perceived.

The 1st section is general and comprehensive, embracing all lands, whether ancestral or newly acquired, subject to certain exceptions and qualifications hereafter more particularly noticed, and these exceptions refer to real estate alone. This section also constitutes the table, by which real estate is to des- cend and personal property distributed. As, by its express language, it relates to both real and personal property, it was manifestly the design of the Legis- lature, when there were descendants of the intestate, to send down both to them per capita, if in equal degree, and per stirpes, if in unequal degree, with- out any regard to the fact as to how the property had been acquired. And as to personal property, where there are no descendants of the intestate to distribute it to, collaterals will take in the same way as descendants, if there had been any; that is to say without any inquiry as to how it was acquired, and, per capita, if in equal degree, and per stirpes, if in unequal degree. This was manifestly the design of the Legislature. The sections of the statute which have reference to both real and personal property, and expressly name or allude to both, or embrace them in their spirit, are the 1st, 4th, 5th, 15th, 16th, 17th, and 18th. The 15th, 16th, 17th, and 18th, touch to subject of advancement. And, to attain the object in view, it was necessary to blend real and personal property together; because the amount received is the inquiry; and whether in land or personal property, produces the same result.

421

It may not be unworthy of remark, that neither is the 1st, 4th, 5th, nor in these sections, is the technical term "inheritance," used at all.

The 1st, 4th, 5th, 15th, 16th, 17th and 18th sections, are the only ones designed, in our opinion to apply to both real and personal estate. All the rest embrace real estate alone.

The effect of the 1st section is, to constitute the persons, who take the personal property, whether per capita, or per stirpes, and whether the whole or half-blood, the absolute owners. Nor is it material whether those persons are of the paternal or maternal or the lineal or collateral line. By that section, as already remarked, real and personal estate goes in the same channel, and if no subsequent provisions had been introduced, touching real estate, the precise bearing of which, it is probable the rivers did not perceive, our labors would have been comparatively easy. At present, nothing further need be said as to personal property, as we shall find it necessary to allude to that hereafter, and shall now speak in reference to real estate.

The effect of the first section, subject to the exceptions and qualifications alluded to, is to vest an absolute estate of inheritance in lands in the person who takes. And every estate, interest and right, legal and equitable, in lands and tenements and hereditaments, excepting only leases for years, and estate for the life of another person, are thus inheritable and descendable; or, as the first section expresses it, "having title to any real estate of inheritance" constitutes an inheritable estate, thus abolishing the common law doctrine, derived from feudal times, of actual seizin in the ancestor. Whoever claimed by descent, was bound to show that he was heir to the first purchaser; and the seizin in the last possessor, from whom he claimed as heir, was considered as presumptive evidence of his being of the blood of the first purchaser. It supplied the difficulty of investigating a descent from a distant stock, through a line of succession become dim by the lapse of ages. 4 Kent 386.

But, with us ownership, or title to property, is substituted for seizin; and maxim seisina facit stipitem, of such controlling consequence in the English scheme of descents, is entirely superseded. By descent or hereditary succession, it is understood the title whereby a person, upon the death of his ancestor, acquires the estate of the latter as his heir at law. 3 Bac. Abr. Descent 104.

We pass now to the more particular consideration of the 10th section.

The manifest intention of the first part of this section, was to preserve ancestral estate in the line of the blood from whence they came. It was a partial adoption of recognition of the common law principle, which invariably followed the line of the blood, If the estate comes to the intestate by the father, or as it may be differently, and as well expressed, on the part of the father, then it must ascend to the father and his heirs, and thus overturning the inflexible rule of the common law, that an estate could never ascend; but should rather escheat to the lord. And so, if it comes by or on the part of the mother, it goes to the mother and her heirs, in exclusion of the heirs of the father. In other words, it remains in the paternal or maternal line, from whence it was derived.

The expressions, "come by the father," or "mother" or on "the part of the father" or "mother" mean the same thing. Maffit v. Clark, 6 Watts & Serg, 260. They are familiar to, and derived from the common law, having an appropriate, technical meaning, which we must suppose the Legislature intended to adopt. They embrace not only the father, but all of the ancestors of the father, both paternal and maternal. Co. Litt. 12 a. Whenever, says Lord Coke, lands do descend from the part of the mother, the heirs of the part of the father shall never inherit. And, likewise, when lands descend from the part of the father, the heirs of the part of the mother shall never inherit. Co. Litt. 13a.

The 10th and 22nd sections must be construed together, although the exact expressions used in the latter, are not contained in any part of t e statute. But words of equivalent signification, are employed, and they are embraced within the spirit of the 22nd section. Any other exposition would render the section entirely nugatory; and we must so construe statutes as that every part may h its proper effect, if possible.

The expression, then, "come by the father, or mother, ' is is not limited to an estate acquired by descent merely, but includes an estate which comes to the intestate by gift, devise or descent from the parent referred to, or from an relation of the blood of such parent. Such is the letter and spirit of the sta tute. In other words, there are two classes of cases provided for: One, where the blood of the person, from who the estate came, whether it be by descent, devise or gift, is regarded; and the mther, where the blood of the intestate forms the stirps, or stock of descent, without respect to ancestral blood.

Chancellor Kent says there is a difference in the laws of the several states, between the succession to estates, which the intestate had acquired in the course of descent, or by purchase. "If the inheritance," says he, "was ancestral, and came to th intestate by gift, devise or descent, it passes to the kindred, who are of the blood of the ancestor from whom it came, whether in the paternal or maternal lime." 4 Kent 404.

The portion of the 10th section, as to new acquisitions, gives the father and mother a life estate only, with remainder to the colateral heirs of the intestate: such as brothers and sisters, and their descendants, and so on. A new acquisition, or newly acquired estate, does not afford of itself, an exact idea if the mode of acquisition. By the common law, there were two mo$_{de}$s of acquir ng an estate, distinguished by the general appellations of descent and purchase. In the first, it was by operation of law; and in the second, by act or agreement of parties. Devises and gifts fall in the latter class. An estate by purchase there became inheritable to the heirs general of the purchaser, first of the paternal, and then of the maternal line. 2 Bl. Com. 243.

· It must be understood, however, that a new acquisition, in the sense intended by the statute, is one which the intestate has acquired by his exertions and industry. (Brewster v. Benedict, 14 Ohio 385), or by will or deed from a stranger. In other words, it is an estate derived from any source other than descent, devise or gift, from father or mother, or any relative in the paternal or maternal line. Butler v. King. 2 Yerg. 116.

If the son should purchase land from the father or mother, for a valuable consideration, it would be a new acquisition, and descend as such; because nothing is received by way of bounty at the hands of ancestors, which is the case as to lands descended from, or devised, or given by them to the intestate, and it was thought reasonable that they should remain in the blood from which they came.

Land is to be consid$_{ered}$ as having come from, or by, or on the part of the father or mother, when it comes by gift, devise or descent, either mediately or immediateiy from them, or from any person in their respective lines. Shippen v. Isard, 1 Serg. & Rawle, 223.

The 12th section provides that, "relations of the half-blood shall inherit equally with those of the whole-blood, in the same degree, and the descendants of such relatives shall inherit in the same manner as descendants of the whole-blood, unless the inheritance come to the intestate by descent, devise or gift of some one of his ancestors, in which case, all those who are not of the blood of such ancestor, shall be excluded from such inheritance.

It has been contended, with much ability and inguenity, that the restriction in the latter clause of the section applies to the descendants of the half-blood only, and that in such is the grammatical and logical construction.

But w unable to subscribe to this argument. It would be unsafe to construe a statute according to mere grammatical rules, or to rely on punctuation as any material aid in ascertaining the true meaning. Neither bad grammer nor bad English,will vitiate a statute any more than a deed. It is well known that ancient statutes were without sections or punctuation, and hence the reasonable and universal rule that the sense must be collected from the whole set.

It is the clear that the meaning and intention of this section was to prohibit the half-blood, and their descendants alike, from sharing in the inheritance of an estate which might come to the intestate by descent, devise or gift from an ancestor, in all cases where they were not of the blood of such ancestor. The reason for excluding the half blood is just as strong as for excluding their descendants, and it is impossible to conceive any well founded distinction between the two. And whatever opinion we might entertain as to the hardships of such a rule in any given case, or as to the impolicy of establishing lines of blood at all, in a new country, where almost every man is the architect of his own fortune and the stock of descent; yet the Legislature has spoken its will; the language is too plain to be doubted, and addresses a prohibition to the courts not to be disregarded or evaded.

The half-blood are excluded from inheritances, and they and their descendants may inherit even an ancestral estate, provided they can show they are of the blood of the ancestor from whom it was transmitted to the intestate. Gardner v. Collins, 2 Peters 58. In newly acquired estates they inherit equally with the whole-blood in the same degree.

Hilliard, in his Treatise on Real Property (vol. 5,207) says; "In Arkansas, if there are no descendants, and the estate came from the father, it passes to him and his heirs. The haif-blood and descendants inherit unless the estate is ancestral, in which case, none inherit but those of the ancestral blood."

The word "blood," in its technical and natural sense, includes the half-blood. Baker v. Chalfant, 5 Wharton 477. In a note in the last edition of his commentaries, Kent says: "The words in the laws of the several States, regulating the descent of ancestral inheritances, require that the heir should be of the blood of the ancestor. This would, in the ordinary sense of the words, admit the half-blood for they may be of the blood of the ancestor, though only half-blood to the intestate." The 12th section of our statute is an exact transcript of the 15th section of the New York Revised Statutes, and, in considering that section, he further said that, not being of the blood of the ancestor, was the only ground on which the half-blood was excluded from ancestral inheritances. 4 Kent 404, note b., and authorities there cited.

In Torrey vs. Shaw, 3 Edw. Ch. R. 362, the Vice Chancellor, in commenting on a similar provision, observed that here is an exclusion as well where property comes by devise or gift-each of which is a species of purchase-as where it comes by descent, unless the parties claiming be of the blood of the donor. This proceeds, said he, upon the principle that the blood of the ancestor is necessary to enable collateral relations to take, where the property came from an ancestor by either of the modes of transmission spoken of.

In Dew v. Jones, 3 Halstead 340, the half-blood of the person dying seized, was held entitled to inherit an ancestral estate, because he was of the half-blood to the person dying seized, as well as of the blood of the ancestor from whom the lands came.

Our statute provides for ancestral and newly-acquired inheritances. The half-blood may inherit both, and will be excluded from the first only when lacking ancestral blood. With that exception, the half-blood and descendants, stand upon the same footing with the whole-blood and descendants.

After carefully considering each of the provisions of the statute, and all together as a whole, we have come to the following conclusions:

1st. That, as to both real and personal property, it was the design of the Legislature, when there were descendants of the intestate, to send down both

424

to them, per capita, if in equal degree, and per stirpes, if in unequal degree. without any regard to the fact as to how the estate was acquired.

2d. That, as to personal property, it was the design where there were no descendants, that it should go to collaterals in the same way it would have gone to descendants, if there had been any; that is to say, per capita, if in equal degree, and per stirpes, if in unequal degree, and without inquiry as to how the property was acquired by the intestate.

3d. That, as to real estate, it was the design of the Legislature, where there were o descendants, to point out the lines of the succession, and that this is to depend on the fact, whether the inheritance is ancestral or new; and if ancestral, hen whether it come from the paternal or maternal line.

4th. If the inheritance was ancestral, and come from the father's sice, then it will go to the line on the part of the father, from whence it came, not in postponement but in exclusion, of the mother's line; and so on the other hand, if it come from the mother's side, then to the line on the part of the mother, from whence it came, to the exclusion of the father's line.

5th. If the inheritance be not ancestral, but a new acquisition, then, after a life estate, reserved in succession to the father and mother, if alive, it will go in remainder, first to the line of the intestate's paternal uncle and aunts, and their descendants, in post ponement of the mother's line, until the former becomes extinc ; and then to the line of the intestate's maternal uncle and au ts, and their descendants; unless there should be kindred, lineal or collateral, who, either in right of propinquity, or by right of representation, stand in a nearer relation to the intestate than the uncles and aunts; in which case, such kindred would take the inheritance to the exclusion of both of these collateral lines; and, in their hands, it would become an ancestral estate, and always go in the blood of the relative from whence it came, in the ordinar course of descent prescribed for ancestral inheritances Digest, secs. 10, and 11, p. 437.

6th. That, when the inheritance is fixed, by these facts, in any given line, it will pursue that line until it becomes extinct, and the objects of bounty, and the order in which they succeed one another, and the proportion they take, are to be ascertained by the 1st section, which is to be considered as the general table of descent. The father, mother, brothers ,sisters, and so on, mentioned in that section, are those who are to be considered when counting from any propositus, whether the propositus of a single line only, or the concurrent propositus of both lines, as the intestate is, as to personal property.

7th. In all cases where the inheritance is in any one line, if it goes in succession, per capita, if in equal degree, and per stirpes, if in an unequal degree, precisely as if the other line was extinct, and precisely as the inheritance of a bastard would take a course in his mother's line, he having no father's line at all.

8th. The half-blood and their descendants, take personalty, as well as realty, equally with the whole-blood, except that they are excluded from real estate when ancestral, if they lack the blood of the transmitting ancestor."

S c. 23. "Every person of lawful age and sound mind may by last will and testament devise and bequeath all of his estate, real and personal, a d all interest therein; Provided, That no will of a full-blood Indian devising real estate shall be valid, if such last will and testament disinherits the parent, wife, spouse, or children of such full-blood Indian, unless acknowledged before and approved by a judge of the United States court for the Indian Territory, or a United States Commissioner."

Act of Congress April 26, 1906, (34 Stat. L. 137)

" * * * * * * * * Provided, That nothing contained in the said Constitution shall be construed to limit or impair the rights of person or property pertaining to the Indians of said Territory (so long as such rights shall remain unextinguished) or to limit or affect the authority of the Government of the United States to make any law or regulation respecting such Indians, their lands, property, or other rights by treaties, agreement, law, or otherwise, which it would have been competent to make if this Act had never been passed."

Oklahoma Enabling Act June 16, 1906. (Sec. 1)

Sec. 21. * * * * * * * * * * * All laws in force in the Territory of Oklahoma at the time of the admission of said state into the Union shall be in force throughout said State, except as modified or changed by this Act or by the constitution of the State, and the laws of the United States not locally inapplicable shall have the same force and effect within said State as elsewhere within the United States."

Enabling Act June 16, 1906.

Sec. 2. "All law in force in the Territory of Oklahoma at the time of the admission of the state into the Union, which are not repugnant to this Constitution, and which are not locally inapplicable, shall be extended to and remain in force in the State of Oklahoma until they expire by their own limitation or are altered or repealed by a law."

Schedule to Constitution of Oklahoma.

Wilson's Revised and Annotated Statutes of Oiklahoma.

(6893) Succession is the coming in of another to take the property of one who dies without disposing of it by will.
(6894) The property, both real and personal, of one who dies without disposing of it by will, passes to the heirs of the intestate, subject to the control of the probate court, and to the possession of any administrator appointed by that court for the purpose of administration.
(6895) When any person having title to any estate not otherwise limited by marriage contract, dies without disposing of the estate by will, it is succeeded to and must be distributed, unless otherwise expressly provided in this code and the chapter on probate court, subject to the payment of his debts, in the following manner:
First. If the decedent leave a surviving husband or wife, and only one child, or the lawful issue of one child, in equal shares to the surviving husband, or wife, and child, or issue of such child. 'If the decedent leave a surviving husband or wife, and more than one child living, or one child living, and the lawful issue of one or more deceased children, one-third to the surviving husband or wife, and the remainder in equal shares to his children, and to the lawful issue of any deceased child, by right of representation; but if there be no child of the decedent living at his death, the remainder goes to all his lineal descendants; and if all the descendants are in the same degree of kindred to the decedent they share equally, otherwise they take according to the right of representation. If the decedent leave no surviving husband or wife, but leaves issue, the whole estate goes to such issue, and if such issue consists of more than one child living, or one child living and the lawful issue of one or more deceased children, then the estate goes in equal shares to the children living, or to the child living, and the issue of the deceased child or children by right of representation.
Second. If the decedent leave no issue, the estate goes in equal shares

to the surviving husband or wife, and to the decedent's father. If there be no father, then one-half goes in equal shares to the brothers and sisters of the decedent, and to the children of any deceased brother or sister, by right of representation; if he leave a mother also, she takes an equal share with the b others and sisters. If decedent leave no issue, nor husband nor wi e, the estate must go to the father.

Third. If there be no issue, nor husband, nor wife, nor father, nor mother, then in equal shares to the brothers and sisters of the decedent, and to the children of any deceased brother or sister, by right of representation; if a mother survive, she takes an equal share with the brothers and sisters.

Fourth. If the decedent leave no issue, nor husband, nor wife, nor father, and no brother or sister is living at the time of his death, the estate goes to his mother to the exclusion of the issue, if any, of deceased brothers or sisters.

Fifth. If the decedent leave a surviving husband or wife, and no issue, and no father, nor mother, nor brother, nor sister, the whole estate goes to the surviving husband or wife.

Sixth. If the decedent leave no issue, nor husband, nor wife, and no father nor mother, nor brother nor sister, the estate must go to the next of kin, in equal degree, excepting that when there are two or more collateral kindred, in equal degree, but claiming through different ancestors, those who claimed through the nearest ancestors must be preferred to those claiming through an ancestor more remote. However:

Seventh. If the decedent leave several children, or one child and the issue of one or more children, and any such surviving child dies under age, and not having been married, all the estate that came to the deceased child by inheritance from such decedent descends in equal shares to the other children of the same parent, and to the issue of any such other children who are dead, by right of representation.

Eighth. If, at the death of such child who dies under age, not having been married, all the other children of his parents are also dead, and any of them have left issue, the estate that came to such child by inheritance from his parent descends to the issue of all other children of the same parent; and if all the issue are in the same degree of kindred to the child, they share the estate equally, otherwise they take according to the right of representation.

Ninth. If the decedent leave no husband, wife, or kindred, the estate escheats to the Territory for the support of common schools.

(6896) Dower and courtesy are abolished.

(6897) Every illegitimate child is an heir of the person who in writing, signed in the presence of a competent witness, acknowledges himself to be the father of such child; and in all cases is an heir of his mother; and inherits his or her estate, in whole or in part, as the case may be, in the same manner as if he had been born in lawful wedlock; but he does not represent his father or mother by inheriting any part of the estate of his or her kindred, either lineal or collateral, unless before his death his parents shall have intermarried, and his father, after such marriage, acknowledges him as his child, or adopts him into his family; in which case such child and all the legitimate children are considered brothers and sisters, and on the death of either of them, intestate, and without issue, the others inherit his estate, and are heirs as hereinbefore provided, in like manner as if all the children had been legitimate; saving to the father and mother respectively, their rights in the estate of all the children in like manner as if all had been legitimate. The issue of all marriages null in law or dissolved by divorce, are legitimate.

(6898) If an illegitimate child, who has not been acknowledged, or adopted by his father, dies intestate, without lawful issue, his estate goes to his mother, or, in case of her decease, to her heirs at law.

427

(6899) The degree of kindred is established by the number of generations, and each generation is called a degree.

(6900) The series of degrees from the line; the series of degrees between persons who descend from one another, is called direct or lineal consanguinity; and the series of degrees between persons who did not descend from one another, but spring from a common ancestor, is called the collateral line or collateral consanguinity.

(6901) The direct line is divided into a direct line descending and the direct line ascending. The first is that which connects the ancestor with those who descend from him. The second is that which connects a person with thosef rom whom he descends.

(6902) In the direct line there are as many degrees as there are generations. Thus the son is, with regard to the father, in the first degree; the grandson in the second; and vice versa with regard to the father and grandfather toward the sons and grandsons.

(6903) In the collateral line the degrees are counted by generations, from one of the relations up to the common ancestor, and from the common ancestor to the other relations. In such computation the decedent is excluded, the relative included, and the ancestor counted but once. Thus brothers are related in the second degree, uncle and nephew in the third degree, cousins german in the fourth degree, and so on.

(6904) Kindred of the half blood inherit equally with those of the whole blood in the same degree, unless the inheritance come to the intestate by descent devise or gift of some one of his ancestors, in which case all those who are not of the blood of such ancestors must be excluded from such inheritance.

(6905) Any estate, real or personal, given by the decedent in his life time, as an advancement to any child or other lineal descendant, is a part of the estate of the decedent for the purposes of division and distribution thereof among his issue, and must be taken by such child, or other lineal descendant, toward his share of the estate of the decedent.

(6906) If the amount of such advancement exceeds the share of the heir receiving the same, he must be excluded from any further protion in the division and distribution of the estate, but he must not be required to refund any part of such advancement; and if the amount so received is less than his share, he is entitled to so much more as will give him his full share of the estate of the decedent.

(6907) All gifts and grants are made as advancements, if expressed in the gift or grant to be so made, or if charged in writing by the decedent as an advancement, or acknowledged in writing as such by the child or other successor or heir.

(6908) If the value of the estate so advanced is expressed in the conveyance, or in the charge thereof made by the decedent, or in the acknowledgement of the party receiving it, it must be held as of that value in the division and distribution of the estate; otherwise it must be estimated according to its value when given as nearly as the same can be ascertained.

(6909) If any child or other lineal descendant receiving advancement, dies before the decedent, leaving issue, the advancement must be taken into consideration in the division and distribution of the estate, and the amount thereof must be allowed accordingly by the representatives of the heirs receiving the advancement, in like manner as if the advancement had been made directly to them.

(6910) Inheritance or succession by right of representation takes place when the descendants of any deceased heir take the same share or right in the estate of another person that their parents would have taken if living. Posthumous children are considered as living at the death of their parents.

(6911) Aliens may take in all cases, by succession, as well as citizens;

and no person, capable of succeeding under the provisions of this title, is precluded from such succession by reason of the alienage of any relative.

(6912) If there is no one capable of succeeding under the preceding sections, and the title fails from a defect of heirs, the property of a decedent devolves and escheats to the Territory; and an action for the recovery of such property, and to reduce it into the possession of the Territory, or for its sale and conveyances may be brought by the district attorney in the district court of the county or judicial subdivision in which the property is situated.

(6913) Real property passing to the Territory under the preceding section, whether held by the Territory or its grantees, is subject to the same charges and trusts to which it would have been subject if it had passed by succession.

(6914) Those who succeed to the property of a decedent are liable for his obligations in the cases and to the extent prescribed by chapter 18."

Sec. 9. " * * * * * * Provided, further, That if any member of the Five Civilized Tribes of one-half or more Indian blood shall die leaving issue surviving, born since March fourth, nineteen hundred and six, the homestead of such deceased allottee shall remain inalienable, unless restrictions against the alienation are removed therefrom by the Secretary of the Interior in the manner provided in section one hereof, for the use and support of such issue, during their life or lives, until April twenty-sixth, nineteen hundred and thirty-one; but if no such issue survive, then such allottee, if an adult, may dispose of his homestead by will free from all restrictions; if this be not done, or in the event the issue hereinbefore provided for die before April twenty-sixth, nineteen hundred and thirty-one, the land shall descend to the heirs, according to the laws of descent and distribution of the State of Oklahoma, free from all restrictions:

Provided further, That the provisions of section twenty-three of the act of April twenty-sixth, nineteen hundred and six, as amended by this act, are hereby made applicable to all wills executed under this section."

Act of Congress May 27, 1908 (35 Stat. L. 312)

An Act entitled an act to amend section 626, of the Statutes of Oklahoma of 1893 entitled: "Succession."

"Sec. 1. That section 6261 of the Statutes of Oklahoma of 1893 be amended so as to read as follows:

Section 6261. When any person having title to any estate not otherwise limited by marriage contract dies, without disposing of the estate by will, it descends and must be distributed in the following manner:

First. If the decedent leave a surviving husband or wife, and only one child, or the lawful issue of one child, in equal shares to the surviving husband, or wife and child, or issue of such child. If the decedent leave a surviving husband or wife and more than one child living and the lawful issue of one or more deceased children, onethird to the surviving husband or wife, and the remained in equal shares to his children, and to the lawful issue of any deceased child, by right of representation; but if there be no child of the decedent living at his death, the remainder goes to all of his lineal descendants; and if all the descendants are in the same degree of kindred to the decedent they share equally, otherwise they take according to the right of representation; Provided, if decedent shall have married more than once, the spouse at the time of death shall inherit of the property not acquired during coverture with such spouse only an equal part with each of the living children of decedent, and the lawful issue of any deceased child by right of representation. If the decedent leave no surviving husband or wife, but leaves issue the whole estate goes

429

CPSIA information can be obtained
at www.ICGtesting.com
Printed in the USA
BVOW10s0314291117
501449BV00010B/265/P